SEMINARY LEADERS

"All good theology is practical. Proper theology is for the church, not just for academics. Biblical systematic theology impacts the way we think, the way we live, and the way we feel about God, ourselves, the world, and others. John Frame always does 'good' theology. It will change your life."

—**Robert C. (Ric) Cannada Jr.**, Chancellor Emeritus, Reformed Theological Seminary

"Many times in the past I have grown in my understanding of Scripture and benefited in my practice of ministry as a consequence of John Frame's written reflections on God's Word. Now the opportunity to draw upon that thought from a work that expands and systematizes his reflections from a lifetime of study and devotion is a great treasure for the church and a great gift to all in ministry."

—**Bryan Chapell**, President Emeritus, Covenant Theological Seminary

"Theology reflects our study of God's general and special revelation and our attempt to express that theology in the language of those to whom we seek to communicate our conclusions. Theology must be faithful to the authority of the Word of God, and must be written in an understandable style. For those reasons, John Frame has once again used his gifts to give us a systematic theology that is consistently biblical and written within the framework of Reformed theology. Familiarity with the author's writings makes the reader aware of his ability to express himself clearly and to the point. He does not waste words or the reader's time. You will find an immediate appreciation of and benefit from his definitions and expressions of our Reformed doctrine. While a number of outstanding systematics reside within the family of biblically Reformed theology, Frame's will complement and deepen one's understanding and appreciation of the 'faith once delivered to the saints,' yesterday and today. Without question this work will be taught and studied in a way that will enable the reader, teacher, and student to see and understand the sovereignty of God, the kingdom of God, the lordship of Christ, and salvation with fresh minds and day-to-day application. You will find Frame, as usual, demonstrating his well-known mantra, 'theology is life and life is theology.' Each page is a constant reminder that the truth will make us free."

—**Charles Dunahoo**, Chairman of the Board, Westminster Theological Seminary; Coordinator for Christian Education and Publications, Presbyterian Church in America; pastor and teacher

"John Frame is an esteemed colleague and one of the most important contemporary Reformed systematic theologians in the English-speaking world. His *Systematic Theology: An Introduction to Christian Belief* reflects a half-century of distinguished teaching, prolific writing, and serious study. For that reason alone, especially in a day and age in which many evangelicals question the legitimacy of systematic theology, this volume commends itself to our attention. Frame (thankfully) encourages a Bible-centered approach to doing theology and (rightly) asserts that even 'practical theology' is a department of systematic theology. Here you will find the Professor Frame you have come to expect: clear, readable, restrained, and conversational in his presentation, and thoughtful, biblical, consistent, and careful in his views. Many years ago, Carl F. H. Henry suggested that we need a 'recovery of Christian belief.' May your engagement with this book serve to introduce you to and ground you in genuinely Christian belief."

> —**Ligon Duncan**, Chancellor and CEO, Reformed Theological Seminary

"John Frame is one of my favorite theologians, and his *Systematic Theology* is filled with the deep learning and warranted wisdom of a lifetime. I commend it warmly to the Lord's people everywhere."

> —**Timothy George**, Founding Dean, Beeson Divinity School of Samford University; General Editor, Reformation Commentary on Scripture

"It is always a joyous occasion when one of God's faithful servants of his Word produces the fruit of his many years of labor into a full-fledged systematic theology. This is no small undertaking, but in the grace of God, we in our generation are the happy recipients of just such a work from Professor John Frame. He is, by all odds, one of the best known and most respected Reformed theologians in our day. It is a special joy to see this, the quintessence of a lifetime of his study of God's Word, and now to commend it to all the body of Christ with thanksgiving to God for his gift of Dr. John Frame to the church."

> —**Walter C. Kaiser Jr.**, President Emeritus, Gordon-Conwell Theological Seminary

"When one thinks of modern Reformed theologians, John Frame is at the top of the list. He has the rare ability to explain complex theological truths in a manner that is simple enough for the layman and deep enough for the scholar. Moreover, his theological guidance is always wise, steady, and, more than anything else, biblical. And now we finally have the book that so many have waited for him to write—a systematic theology. This volume is a wonderful gift for the church. I cannot recommend it highly enough."

> —**Michael J. Kruger**, President, Professor of New Testament, Reformed Theological Seminary, Charlotte

"John M. Frame's *Systematic Theology: An Introduction to Christian Belief* is a remarkable achievement. It is simultaneously scholarly yet accessible, sweeping in scope but penetrating in insight, steeped in historic orthodoxy yet fresh in reflection. Frame herein develops and advances his Westminster perspective on theology and ethics, culminating in what is simply Reformed theology at its best."

> —**Peter A. Lillback**, President, Westminster Theological Seminary

"It may be said that there are levels of theologians. Most of us teach what others have written. A few will actually add creatively to others' material. And then there are the theologians of the first class. They think at a deeper level and produce the living, vital 'starter' or leavening agent that the other theological artisans will 'bake' with. Few have been starter theologians. Certainly Karl Barth was one from the last century. But the leavening was incomplete in the opinion of the most charitable confessional Christians and tainted with deadly error in the opinion of others. John Frame is a theologian of the first class in our day. His *Systematic Theology* is not a reworking of others' leavening, but is indeed a starter that, unlike Barth, produces a biblically faithful, untainted, deeply satisfying, and expectant Christian theology. This theology is capable of being dispatched for use as the central ingredient in a robust course of study to produce pastors—and believers of all vocations—who are tethered to the inerrant and infallible Word of God, who have a personal love for Christ Jesus our Lord, and who lead the flock of Christ to sunlit uplands where the triune God's promises appear to reveal not only an abundant life and the assurance of life with God after death and salvation from hell, but also the golden beams of a new heaven and a new earth. John Frame's *Systematic Theology* is thus the release of an untainted and thoroughly faithful leavening agent that will produce a starter to strengthen other theologians, train future shepherds of the church, and nourish the body of Christ for years to come. It is my honor to commend *Systematic Theology* to the church. I thank God that in this rather young new century, the first-class, original, starter theologian of our time, John Frame, is not a mere theologian of the Word, but a theologian of the propositional Word as well as the Word made flesh. We owe a debt of gratitude to Dr. Frame and to P&R Publishing for the production and release of this magisterial work."

—**Michael A. Milton**, Fourth President/Chancellor, Reformed Theological Seminary; Presbyterian (PCA) minister; author; columnist; theologian; Army Reserve chaplain; composer

"This new systematic theology comes from one of the great theological minds of our age. John Frame's contributions to theology are already massive and many, but now he has given the church a systematic theology. This is a very important book, and it represents a lifetime of consecrated theological reflection. This new volume promises to be an enduring contribution to evangelical theology."

—**R. Albert Mohler Jr.**, President, The Southern Baptist Theological Seminary

"As one who has long admired—and learned so much from—John Frame's contributions to Reformed life and thought, I am so pleased that we now have this fine volume that gathers together the insights of a half-century of serious theological scholarship. The biblical and practical nature of his perspective makes this a refreshing and much-needed resource for all of us who care about a vital Reformed theology."

—**Richard J. Mouw**, President, Professor of Christian Philosophy, Fuller Theological Seminary

"Biblical, clear, and cogent, John Frame moves through the loci of theology with ease and without 'looking to the right or to the left.' This new book is not just a cut-and-paste job from past publications. While his volume is less historical than some systematic theologies, Frame avoids bogging down in episodic intellectual controversies, without denying the importance of every 'jot and tittle.'"

—**Andrew J. Peterson**, President, Global Education, Reformed Theological Seminary

"Few in our day champion such a vision of God as massive, magnificent, and biblical as does John Frame. For decades, he has given himself to the church, to his students, and to meticulous thinking and the rigorous study of the Bible. He has winsomely, patiently, and persuasively contended for the gospel in the secular philosophical arena, as well as in the thick of the church worship wars and wrestlings with feminism and open theism. He brings together a rare blend of big-picture thinking, levelheaded reflection, biblical fidelity, a love for the gospel and the church, and the ability to write with care and clarity."

—**John Piper**, Chancellor, Bethlehem College and Seminary; Founder and Teacher, www.desiringGod.org

"Clear, thorough, intelligent, and fair to opposing views, John Frame's work will now be the standard within traditional Reformed theology."

—**Cornelius Plantinga Jr.**, President Emeritus, Calvin Theological Seminary; Senior Research Fellow, Calvin Institute of Christian Worship, Grand Rapids

"We can count on John Frame to speak of the profound complexities of biblical theology with a precision, perspicuity, and humility that represent the best tendencies of the Reformed tradition. In this work, Professor Frame gives expression to a system of belief that will serve and satisfy a variety of audiences, including the curious layperson, the young seminarian, and the experienced pastor. Never one to shy away from the difficult, thorny issues of his discipline, he explains and upholds the teaching of Scripture, even when that teaching offends modern sensibilities. I would recommend this systematic treatment to all my students."

—**John Scott Redd Jr.**, President, Associate Professor of Old Testament, Reformed Theological Seminary, Washington, D.C.

"For decades, Professor Frame has purposefully driven scholars and students, colleagues and critics, leaders and laity to the Lord Jesus Christ and to the Scriptures. That laudable objective will be magnified for generations yet to come with the release of this, the author's most provocative and mature theological expression. 'Everyone else serves his best first . . . but you have reserved your best for now.'"

—**John T. Sowell**, President, Reformed Theological Seminary, Atlanta

"Any theologian who says that 'the Bible is the most important thing' is worth listening to. But one whose life commends his theology, as John's does, is doubly worth listening to. This book is a gift to the church written by one who has a brilliant, discerning mind and a servant's heart. I was blessed by reading it."

—**Don Sweeting**, President, James Woodrow Hassell Professor of Church History, Reformed Theological Seminary, Orlando

"*Systematic Theology* is the culmination of John Frame's life's work in teaching young men who are preparing for the ministry. It is a masterful study that expresses the dogmatic method and thought of a modern Reformer. Frame's approach to systematics articulates a refined synthesis of the theological and philosophical thought of early Westminster Theological Seminary with an emphasis on contemporary religious issues. No student of theology can ignore Frame's magnum opus, which represents a modern commentary on the Reformed perspective for the third millennium. Scholars, pastors, students, and laymen who want to be well informed in modern Reformation thought must drink from the wellspring of wisdom and insight offered by this humble theologian, whose one great desire is the glory and honor of his God and teaching theology that is adaptable to the church pew."

—**Kenneth Gary Talbot**, President, Whitefield Theological Seminary

"With a half-century of teaching experience, Dr. Frame writes with an irenic lucidity that speaks clearly to students while engaging questions that animate theologians and divide denominations. Presenting theology as the application of Scripture to every area of life, Dr. Frame intends the reader to live the truth that he confesses in love. While Dr. Frame's creativity will provoke discussion among readers seeking settled conclusions, the charity of his conversation models a Christlike confession. I commend Dr. Frame's *Systematic Theology* for offering insight with humility to readers and for bringing ongoing reformation to the Reformed tradition."

—**Steven T. Vanderhill**, President, Redeemer Theological Seminary

"John Frame has added significant value to the long line of systematic theologies in print. That value emanates from his profound understanding of the Bible, steeped in personal piety. He is a theologian of the heart. The personal, transparent nature of this magnum opus distinguishes it from other systematic theologies, enabling the reader to understand and apply Scripture. A quick scan of the contents dispels any doubt about Frame's broad acquaintance with the literature of the field, but his single-minded pursuit of explaining the great message of the Bible is equally clear. Seldom does a contemporary theologian engage as he does, enriching intellectually, theologically, and spiritually."

—**Luder G. Whitlock Jr.**, Interim President, Knox Theological Seminary, Fort Lauderdale, Florida; President, Excelsis, Orlando

"Even those not as rigorously Reformed in their theology as John Frame will find great benefit in these pages. With a clear commitment to the primacy of Scripture, lucid argumentation, cogent articulation, a love for God's people, and a passion for God's glory throughout all the earth, Frame has produced what should become required reading in seminary classrooms and pastors' studies for years to come."

—**Mark Young**, President, Denver Seminary, Littleton, Colorado

PASTORS

"Trends in contemporary theology are generally split between essential and constructive approaches. The older essentialists were committed to doing theology only according to what the Bible says, most of which has been carefully summarized in numerous historic creeds and confessions. Their contemporary standard-bearers have done their best to protect the positions of the forefathers. That cultural trends helped to provide a reactionary climate for much of what essentialists codified and continue to protect as orthodox theology is clear. But no essentialist need admit that cultural trends supplied the *raison d'être* for his theological positions. That valued role is reserved for Scripture. Against this, constructive theology presents a case for doing original theology according to the present need of each generation and of the church. But it does so by drawing heavily from the norms and values of the contiguous culture. Consequently, constructive theology will always remain open-ended. Frame's *Systematic Theology* is unique in that it brings together both essential and constructive emphases in contemporary theology. Specifically, it represents vastly original work in theology, while at the same time it remains true to the finished Word of God and to the historic and orthodox confessional documents of Christianity. Frame is not the least bit interested in reconstructing theology. His is an effort to reconceptualize the *task* of theology along practical and pastoral lines. *Sola Scriptura* maintains the logic and coherence of his new exposition of theology, while 'perspectivalism' gives it its remarkable ability to explain and to apply God's Word afresh."

—**John Barber**, Pastor, Cornerstone PCA, Jupiter, Florida

"John Frame is one of the most seminal Reformed theologians of our age, and this is his most significant work."

—**Mark Driscoll**, Founder, Mars Hill Church and Resurgence; Cofounder, Acts 29

"John Frame is noted for his ability to articulate clearly and with an economy of words the contours of our Christian faith. He does that in this work with particular skill. Here is a systematic theology that clearly flows from biblical exegesis, follows the biblical story line, and is faithful to the confessional convictions of the author. It is a significant work that will bless the individual believer and serve the church well."

—**Liam Goligher**, Senior Minister, Tenth Presbyterian Church, Philadelphia

"John Frame says that he is 'immensely thankful to God' for the opportunity to produce this systematic theology. He is not alone: I am immensely thankful that God gave him this opportunity as well. Frame is a deep thinker and a clear communicator—a rare combination among theologians of his stature. Here is a man who knows his church history, his philosophy, his theological systems; but he does not allow these to sidetrack him from pointing—again and again—back to the majesty of Christ in Scripture. Frame shows that theology is not an end in itself. Loving God is the goal. And Frame's volume hits this mark."

—**J. D. Greear**, Lead Pastor, The Summit Church, Raleigh-Durham, North Carolina

"This book is as brilliant as it is personable. Dr. Frame's panoramic comprehension of the Bible and of various theologians' understandings of its content is matched only by the practical, applicable style of his writing."

—**Joel C. Hunter**, Senior Pastor, Northland—A Church Distributed, Orlando

"John Frame the author has in *Systematic Theology* captured comprehensively and with clarity what many of us have benefited from in the classroom through John Frame the professor and teacher. His biblical precision and personal passion are spread on every page, which you will quickly desire to turn in order to get to the next page as he allows and propels us to see the singular glory of the triune God revealed in his Word as Creator, Redeemer, and Sustainer."

—**Harry L. Reeder**, Pastor/Teacher, Briarwood Presbyterian Church, Birmingham

"Dr. Frame does it again! He's gifted the church with another wonderful tome of applied theology. This systematic theology—an elaborate exposition of the teaching of Scripture as he understands it—brings together a lifetime of study. It reflects the emphases of his teaching and writing, revealing interaction with theologians old and new, biblically orthodox and otherwise.

"Connoisseurs of systems of theology will note the distinctive features of Dr. Frame's method: the umbrella theme of God's lordship, both a high view and a high use of Scripture, with application to the reader's heart and life. Wedded to the supremacy of Scripture and recognizing both its divineness and its humanness, Dr. Frame sets his doctrinal discussion in redemptive-historical context, returns to his triperspectivalism, and models for us the much-needed counterbalancing of historic orthodoxy and biblical creativity. The result is a fresh, stimulating, courageous, yet winsome study. While disarmingly accessible, the volume succeeds both in teaching the theology of Scripture and in furthering discussion of how that theology is to be systematized. While the methodological discussion unfolds, we may fully expect Dr. Frame's *Systematic Theology* to draw in earnest students of Scripture at all stages of learning. It is a rich treasure trove of biblical analysis, useful for personal or group study. It will prove to be a legacy that keeps on giving. I plan to return to it time and again."

—**Tim J. R. Trumper**, Senior Minister, Seventh Reformed Church, Grand Rapids

"John Frame writes theology for those who want to use, and be used by, the Word of God. He has done his professional theologizing for many years in the context of the preparation of young men for ministry in seminary. But more to the point, his theology's practicality springs from his understanding of the nature of theological reflection itself. When I was his student over forty years ago, he told us, 'Theology is application.' His discussions of the various loci of systematic theology always have an eye on the Holy Scriptures' power and purpose to transform the lives of the people who study them—intellectually and ethically. Anyone who reads this volume will be blessed with a more comprehensive and systematic appreciation for the teachings of the Word of God and at the same time will grow in renewing the mind and life by the Holy Spirit's speaking through the Word."

—**Roger Wagner**, Pastor, Bayview Orthodox Presbyterian Church, Chula Vista, California

MINISTRIES

"Hurray for John Frame! At a time when systematics has been shoved into a corner by biblical theology in many seminaries, John has published what I can only hope will be an alternative to that imbalance. Not since A. A. Hodge's *Outlines*, Buswell, Reymond, and Grudem has a truly substantive systematic theology appeared. I expect *Systematic Theology* to become a classic, and I look forward to its publication with the greatest anticipation."

—**Jay E. Adams**, Founder, Institute for Nouthetic Studies (INS), National Association of Nouthetic Counselors (NANC), and Christian Counseling and Educational Foundation (CCEF); Author, *Competent to Counsel*

"Systematic theology is notoriously challenging to read but even more challenging to write. I tell students that too many modern theologians have given us 'cookbooks' that feed neither the mind nor the soul. John Frame is a great evangelical exception. He has mastered the historical method, and more importantly, his readers have come to expect that biblical theology will guide his systematic theology. As he says, 'The Bible is the most important thing.' I welcome this important volume and encourage all readers of theology, especially students, to have Frame's valuable work at their side."

—**John H. Armstrong**, President, ACT3 Network; Adjunct Professor, Wheaton College Graduate School

"John Frame has written a very big book—another one. Frame's strengths are once again on display: vast scope, unshakable confidence in Scripture, carefulness and generosity, a deceptively casual style. What most stands out, though, is the open-mindedness of his project. Big as it is, Frame's work raises questions even as it answers them, and as a result it opens ever-new threads in the ongoing conversation that is the Reformed tradition."

—**Peter J. Leithart**, President, Trinity House, Birmingham, Alabama

"John Frame has given the church a superb new resource in this volume. Taking as his theme the lordship of God, Frame seeks to do what he says the good theologian always does: he states the truth not for its own sake but to build up people in the Christian faith. He incorporates much of the best of modern Reformed theologians (Van Til, Murray, etc.) and addresses the hottest topics of the day, such as the length and nature of the days of Genesis 1 and whether Scripture is inerrant. Many will take issue with one or more of Frame's points, but all will be edified by a careful reading of this work."

—**Samuel T. Logan Jr.**, International Director, The World Reformed Fellowship; Special Counsel to the President, Biblical Seminary

"On my bookshelf sit numerous systematics by Charles Hodge, Louis Berkhof, Robert Reymond, and Wayne Grudem. I enjoy them all. They inform, educate, and bring clarity to different issues within Scripture. While systematics are full of precious knowledge to assist any student to better understand God and his holy Word, the reader will find none so well written, with a meekness and tenderness of heart, as Frame's. The breadth and length and height and depth of God's amazing love graces this volume of theology. If Edwards's 'Sinners in the Hands of an Angry God' can be said to have drawn sinners to Christ, Frame's work will be said to draw Christians even closer to understanding their Creator, God, and Lord more fully. This work is a necessity for every layman, pastor, and scholar alike.

"This systematic theology is written from and faithful to a Reformed perspective—glorifying God and his Word. As expected, Frame makes extensive reference to Scripture and the Westminster Confession of Faith, but he makes good use of other confessions, too. While Frame is careful to address numerous contemporary issues, his work directs the reader to Christ—to his salvation alone. This personalizes the text. Though it draws on 'yesterday,' it makes it applicable to the reader 'today and forever' (Heb. 13:8)."

—**Joseph R. Nally**, Theological Editor, Third Millennium Ministries

"No theologian in modern times combines (1) a simple, childlike faith in the Bible, (2) a razor-sharp analytical intellect, (3) a gift for conceptual and linguistic clarity, and (4) a love for Christ's church and everyday Christian people more successfully than John M. Frame. All factors considered, no theologian in recent memory—not Barth, not Brunner, not Pannenberg, not Tillich, nor even the conservatives: Millard Erickson, Carl Henry, the Hodges, Francis Pieper, Joseph Ratzinger (Pope Benedict)—measures up to Frame. He is God's unparalleled gift to the church, and his *Systematic Theology* is a wellspring of truth in a theologically parched age."

—**P. Andrew Sandlin**, President, Center for Cultural Leadership; Senior Pastor, Cornerstone Bible Church, Santa Cruz

"Does the world need one more systematic theology? That depends. It doesn't necessarily, if what you mean is another doorstop describing the contentious history of doctrines.

But it does if what you mean is systematic theology that has finally come full circle through centuries of drift from the Bible itself and from practical application, back to the early evangelists' heart for teaching God's Word for edification. When the apostle Paul was wrapping up his ministry in Ephesians, he summarized what he had done among them this way: 'You yourselves know . . . how I did not shrink from declaring to you anything that was profitable' (Acts 20:18, 20). What was good enough for Paul is evidently good enough for John Frame."
—**Andrée Seu Peterson**, Senior Writer, *WORLD* magazine

"Here, at last, is John Frame's magnum opus—the fruit of fifty years of teaching theology and training ministers of the gospel. Few other contemporary theologians have influenced me as much as Dr. Frame, and I am eager to see this culmination of his theological labors under the lordship of the triune God make its way into the heads, hands, and hearts of Christians around the world."
—**Justin Taylor**, Blogger, "Between Two Worlds"

"This fresh, lucid, and doxological work illustrates the very core of John Frame's project: theology as application. Frame understands the role and place of theology in general and of systematic theology in particular—showcasing one perspective of Christ's dynamic lordship. He avoids the ditches that frequently crisscross today's paths of theological undertaking—either pining for some prior supposed golden utopian theological era (merely quoting select Reformers), on the one hand, or, on the other hand, limiting the theological exercise to a mere propositional alchemy of privatized preparatory salve for heaven alone (life here in this yucky world consists only of a transitory pilgrimage for which the triune God lacks any true concern or effect other than 'soul-winning'). No, and decidedly no. Frame understands that we have been redeemed by the One who is Lord. We have been saved body and soul *from* something *for* something. Therefore, the 'stuff in the middle'—that is, life under the Lord between the cross and the consummation—matters to the Lord here and now and thus should matter to us in all its facets, not just the spiritual ones. Theology in this sense is earthy, and marvelously so. This work is robust, yet accessible; timely, yet evergreen; and innovative, yet orthodox (notice the triad)! Accordingly, theological endeavors hereafter will never be the same because Frame has in this work passionately demonstrated truth—all to Christ's glory and the church's edification. Don't just read this book; apply it!"
—**Jeffery J. Ventrella**, Senior Counsel, Senior Vice-President, Alliance Defending Freedom

PROFESSORS

"John Frame is one of the most important evangelical theologians of our time, a deeply biblical thinker whose work has epitomized the Reformation principles of *sola Scrip-*

tura and *soli Deo gloria*. His writings have proved that Christian scholars don't have to choose between orthodoxy and originality or between profundity and perspicuity. I've long hoped that the Lord would grant Dr. Frame the opportunity and motivation to write a full-length systematic theology, and I'm delighted to see that hope now realized. This exposition of Christian doctrine is the culmination of a lifetime of careful and submissive reflection on the whole counsel of God revealed in Scripture. It will nourish both mind and heart."

>   —**James N. Anderson**, Associate Professor of Theology and Philosophy, Reformed Theological Seminary, Charlotte

"Few scholars of our generation have done as much as John Frame to combine philosophical, biblical, and confessional concerns in an overarching theological synthesis. Here at last he offers us the fruit of his lifetime's labor as a service to the church of our day and to future generations. This is a work that will edify those who read it, and they in turn will use its message to build up the church of Christ. The wealth of teaching and insight that it contains will be a blessing to many, and we can be sure that it will be mightily used of God in the days ahead."

>   —**Gerald L. Bray**, Research Professor of Divinity, Beeson Divinity School, Samford University

"Sometimes there is a book that is so complete, so true, so instructive, and so clear that it assumes a prominent place in one's library and stays there for years. John Frame's *Systematic Theology* is that kind of book. It is a gift to the church . . . and a gift to me. This book will be an anchor to my soul and a source for my theology and faith for the rest of my life. Get it, give it, and rejoice that John Frame wrote it!"

>   —**Stephen W. Brown**, Professor of Practical Theology Emeritus, Reformed Theological Seminary, Orlando

"How do we grow in Christ? By listening intently to God's plan and promises for us in the Bible—that's the answer. But the Bible has so many different things in it, almost all of them problematic. What do they mean, all together? For you? Even better, for us? Many helpful books out there will assist you with pieces of the puzzle, but Frame assembles everything together for you. Really, try his systematic theology and see; you will come to know your God so well, in all his love and mercy and kindness."

>   —**D. Clair Davis**, Professor of Church History Emeritus, Westminster Theological Seminary

"Near the end of his long and fruitful career, John Frame has given us his *chef d'oeuvre*. His *Systematic Theology* is the distillation of a life's work in reflecting on how God's Word relates to the Christian life of the simple believer. As his readers have come to expect, his chief emphasis is on the glory of God, the God who saves, the God who loves us. It would be nearly impossible to read this volume without being drawn into fellowship and conversation with the God who is at its center. Full of quotes from poetry, traditional theology, and even hymns, this is perhaps one of the most practical systematic theologies ever penned. It belongs alongside Turretin, Hodge, Bavinck, and the other hall-of-famers in the discipline. All we can say is: thank you, John Frame!"

—**William Edgar**, Professor of Apologetics, Westminster Theological Seminary

"Our world has become one of theological confusion. Dr. Frame's *Systematic Theology* has emerged as a refreshing and practical tool for the serious student of God's Word. Frame brings systematic theology to life, and allows for easy integration with apologetics and other expressions of theology. By clarifying the biblical worldview, *Systematic Theology* equips us to communicate God's Word and engage the culture with biblical truth.

"Dr. Frame's triperspectival approach to theology is one of the greatest contributions in empowering students to understand the Bible. It allows for theological inclusiveness without compromising a high view of Scripture, and opens exciting possibilities for doing solid theology in both Western and non-Western contexts. No theological library would be complete without *Systematic Theology: An Introduction to Christian Belief.*"

—**Carl F. Ellis Jr.**, Assistant Professor of Practical Theology, Redeemer Seminary

"John Frame has faced classrooms of bright and talented students for decades. He has shared with them a biblically based theology that faithfully addresses difficult questions and problems. This text is the sweet fruit of that classroom labor. Reading it makes those who never had the opportunity to attend see a little of what we missed and those who were his students glad that they were. *Systematic Theology* reads extremely well and always points the reader to the glorious Lord who is the text's subject. Frame is to be congratulated for a job well done!"

—**Richard C. Gamble**, Professor of Systematic Theology, Reformed Presbyterian Theological Seminary

"Professor Frame's *Systematic Theology* is a long-anticipated and richly rewarding treasure. The very best of what we have valued in his decades of faithful labor are represented here in this culminating and crowning achievement. It is neither exhaustive nor thin, and readers will likely wish it accounted more for this or that question or development. But as a survey of theology that seeks to be relentlessly biblical—a most refreshing conviction!—it is a clear and fine example of the judicious, humble, and joyful spirit of theological inquiry of which Professor Frame has long been a superb example. As the author has undoubtedly hoped we would, I submit that we cannot help but come away from a patient reading of this tome with greater confidence in the truth of Holy Scripture, with zeal to submit to the wise and loving lordship of Jesus Christ, and with a longing to make him known."

—**Mark A. Garcia**, Adjunct Professor of Systematic Theology, Westminster Theological Seminary; Adjunct Professor of Church History, Reformed Presbyterian Theological Seminary; Pastor, Immanuel Presbyterian Church, Pittsburgh

"Not content merely to give us Berkhof in a different wrapper, John Frame has produced a new *Systematic Theology* that maintains continuity with the best of the Reformed tradition while breaking important new ground. Employing the same multiperspectival approach worked out in his Theology of Lordship series, Dr. Frame addresses the various loci of theology in a fresh way. He grounds his theological work in exegesis and engages widely with theologians across the theological spectrum—and across the centuries. He faithfully teaches as a Reformed theologian, always remembering that the confessional standards of the church are subordinate to Scripture. His approach is balanced and his irenic spirit commendable, though certain to displease some of a more dogmatic stripe. I believe, however, that in our fragmented and needlessly argumentative Reformed circles, we need this theology—'for such a time as this.' Years ago in a personal conversation, Dr. Frame described his approach as being 'Reformed but not angry about it.' His *Systematic Theology* is 'Reformed but not angry about it,' and the church will be greatly blessed by this contribution from our foremost theologian."

—**R. J. Gore Jr.**, Professor of Systematic Theology, Erskine Theological Seminary

"Though it is more compact on each subject, *Systematic Theology* is not an abridgment of John Frame's earlier books. His already-clear thoughts have continued to develop and crystallize. The section on covenant history that precedes the material on the doctrine of God is especially helpful. I look forward to teaching theology with this book."

—**Howard Griffith**, Associate Professor of Systematic Theology and Academic Dean, Reformed Theological Seminary, Washington, D.C.

"This is a remarkable volume—a wonderfully clear, refreshingly insightful, profoundly biblical treatment of systematic theology. While reading this book, I felt as though I once again had the privilege of being a student in John Frame's theology classes, the classes that so deeply influenced my thinking as a Westminster Seminary student forty years ago. But now the material has been enriched by a lifetime of further research and teaching. An outstanding achievement!"

—**Wayne Grudem**, Research Professor of Theology and Biblical Studies, Phoenix Seminary, Phoenix, Arizona

"Vintage Frame—the old, old story, but with new slants and new emphases to make the reader sit up and think. John 'Rabbi' Duncan remarked of Jonathan Edwards that his doctrine is all application, and his application doctrine. Frame aspires to be of Edwards's school, but he's also a teacher who sets homework for his readers. Also like Edwards, sometimes his words are spiced with a polemical hot sauce. A systematic theology to ponder and to profit from."

—**Paul Helm**, Teaching Fellow, Philosophical Theology, John Calvin, Regent College

"When Charles Hodge emerged as Presbyterianism's premier theologian in the nineteenth century, students and pastors alike awaited the completion of his three-volume

Systematic Theology. When the final volume appeared, all found what they had hoped for—a magisterial work. It was not merely a rehash of Hodge's classroom lectures but a careful reworking of material that he had successfully taught at Princeton for many decades. The fact that Hodge's volumes are still reprinted today testifies to their staying power. With the appearance of John Frame's *Systematic Theology*, one now finds a work that will likewise serve Reformed Christians for a similar length of time. Frame is well known for his perspectival theological method, his clarity and comprehensiveness in exposition of the many-sidedness of the biblical text, his apt illustrations that capture profound theological and biblical truth, and his ability to pose stimulating questions that enable students to probe even beyond his reflections. Perhaps the highest praise that can be given to theologians, besides the affirmation that their theology leads to doxology, is that their treatment sustains and further stimulates their readers' interest. I have never opened the pages of John's many works to ascertain his treatment of a given theological point or biblical text without being enlightened. More than that, however, after finding what I originally sought, I realized that I was still reading an hour later. Students of Reformed theology will find themselves similarly enthralled."

—**W. Andrew Hoffecker**, Emeritus Professor of Church History, Reformed Theological Seminary, Jackson

"If you want a philosophy and theology drenched in the Bible with literally thousands of biblical references, this book is for you—and for me! Dr. Frame deals with so many topics with the skills of both a generalist and a specialist that reading him on virtually any subject is greatly beneficial. May this magnum opus of biblical theology be widely read in the church for years to come."

—**Peter R. Jones**, Scholar in Residence, Adjunct Professor of Practical Theology, Westminster Seminary California

"Reading John Frame's *Systematic Theology* often encourages, occasionally puzzles, but almost always stimulates. Growing out of a lifetime of reflection and wrestling with biblical texts, these pages contain much that we can learn from as we all try to understand better how God glorifies his lordship in our salvation. I, for one, am thankful that we now have this one-volume synthesis of Frame's thinking."

—**Kelly M. Kapic**, Professor of Theological Studies, Covenant College

"This *Systematic Theology* is by any measure a crowning achievement in a fruitful theological career of teaching, preaching, and writing by Professor John Frame. It is the outpouring of many jars of fragrant and well-aged 'wine on the lees': the rich vintage that has been matured in a bright Christian mind that has been immersed in meditation on (and obedience to) the Word of God in the fellowship of the Reformed church for more than threescore years and ten.

"Like Frame's other works that I have read, this book is written with enthusiastic faith in God and in the Scriptures that the Holy Spirit inspired, and in fellowship with the risen Christ. It is written clearly; Frame is never ashamed of his position (traditional Calvinism), and is humble enough to say about some difficulties, 'I do not know.' His writing exhibits humility and unwavering submission before both the clear truths and the mysteries of God. He is always charitable toward those whose position he thinks is wrong and presents it fairly, and yet he does take a stand, which he knows will not suit everyone. You might not agree with all that he says, but at least you will grasp precisely what he is saying.

"Someone described C. S. Lewis as 'A Mind Awake,' and that is how I see John Frame. This volume shows how alert he is to moral, philosophical, and societal issues raised by Christian truth claims over the last three centuries in a secular culture.

"One of the great contributions of Frame's theology is that it shows the inescapable necessity of starting with—and remaining with—the presupposition of the truth of Holy Scripture, for theology and for everything else that we wish to make sense of. Along this line, not only in this book but in others that he has written, I have found very helpful his explanation of why a certain circularity of reasoning is always necessary when arguing for any ultimate authority (e.g., whether Holy Scripture, human reason, empiricism, or, perhaps, evolutionism). Rationalists have long accused Christians of circular reasoning (as concerns the Bible), but what they do not tell you is that they, too, must use the assumption of a final authority themselves, in order to prove their point.

"Frame's section on the providence of God is one of the most beautiful that I have ever read. At times I was less than comfortable with his account of the rather direct relationship of God to evil, yet I am not sure that I could treat the subject any better, if as well. But I must keep thinking about it. His discussion of how God brings about free decisions of humans—which both avoids short-circuiting our responsibility and avoids the false theory of libertarian free will (i.e., that our will is free from the control of our fallen personality, and is ultimately free from the control of the Sovereign God)—is one of the best I have seen.

"In sum, Frame's *Systematic Theology* cogently and succinctly presents the most crucial thought and practice of the long Christian tradition (especially in its Reformed branch, which has been concerned above all to be faithful to the entirety of Holy Scripture), in terms that can be understood in this twenty-first century, where we are called to live. Frame's English is lucid; his learning is great, but he does not overwhelm you with it. His doctrine is in accordance with the Westminster tradition of the seventeenth century (and behind that, Calvin of the sixteenth century, and Augustine of the fifth), always looking at these Augustinian traditions in light of God's written Word (and under it), and he helps the reader to deal with the problems of speaking and living out that tradition in an aggressively secular age. This volume is eminently suitable for a seminary or college textbook. It will also give inspiration to many a preacher (as it has to this one!). I perceive that it was written in an atmosphere of quiet joy, and I will be surprised if it does not convey something of that joy to those who read it."

—**Douglas F. Kelly**, Richard Jordan Professor of Theology, Reformed Theological
    Seminary, Charlotte

"This book by John Frame on systematic theology provides students of God's Word with a tool designed to clearly understand and effectively explain the Scriptures. It is indeed a sterling treasure that is sure to stand the test of time."
    —**Simon J. Kistemaker**, Professor of New Testament, Reformed Theological Seminary, Orlando

"Those who have appreciated Frame's contributions to theology in previous works, such as his *Doctrine of God*, will not be disappointed with his *Systematic Theology*. Adopting a strongly biblical perspective, Frame succeeds in presenting a comprehensive treatment of the various theological loci that also is highly accessible. This book will be of value for the specialist, student, and general reader alike. It marks a major milestone in Frame's distinguished career."
    —**Robert Letham**, Senior Tutor, Systematic and Historical Theology, Wales Evangelical School of Theology

"John Frame sets out to be biblical, clear, and cogent, and succeeds splendidly. Steeped in the tradition of Geerhardus Vos and John Murray, he offers a work that is firmly rooted in exegesis, comprehensive in scope, and rigorous in methodology, yet easily accessible to all serious lovers of Scripture."
    —**Donald Macleod**, Professor of Systematic Theology (Retired), Free Church College, Edinburgh

"As someone who taught systematic theology and Christian doctrine in seminary for nine years, I find John Frame's *Systematic Theology* a significant contribution to historic, orthodox, biblical theological thinking. I especially appreciate Frame's conversational style of writing—as if he were talking on a personal level with his reader. If theology is the making of distinctions, Frame does an exceptional job of bringing fresh and illuminating meaning to traditional theological terms; for example, in chapter 3, 'God's Lordship as a Unique Worldview,' he says of God's immanence that it is *'the deepest sense in which God is present in Jesus.'* A telling description, that. I also think Frame's pedagogical focus on the question 'Why does this matter?' is pointedly necessary in today's evangelical climate, and illustrates his view that 'meaning is application.' He is definitely a 'so what' theologian, yet skillfully combines both the fully worked-out objective content and the subjective dimension needed in a proper theological education. Frame's *Systematic Theology* is admirably accessible without compromising the depth and complexity of biblical theological thought.

"One of the most important elements of Frame's *Systematic Theology* is what I can best describe as its devotional dimension. Even in the discussion of complex metaphysical attributes of God, Frame presents God as an intimately personal being and not simply a philosophical abstraction. His discussion of God's lordship has deepened my own spiritual experience. (Indeed, I found myself reading chapters of *Systematic Theology* as parts of my daily devotions.)

"Were I still teaching systematic theology, Frame's thorough, illuminating, comprehensive, and spiritually powerful treatment of the classical topics of systematic theology would definitely be my primary course text."
—**Reginald F. McLelland**, Professor of Philosophy Emeritus, Covenant College

"John M. Frame, occupant of the J. D. Trimble Chair of Systematic Theology and Philosophy at Reformed Theological Seminary in Orlando, is a household name not only in Reformed circles but across a broad swath of ecclesiastical and denominational traditions. His published works in the fields of his expertise are widely respected for their adherence to biblical fidelity and the tightness of their argumentation. This major work on systematic theology maintains Frame's reputation for impeccable scholarship on the one hand and eminent practicality on the other. It is a theology that not only educates but works in everyday life."
—**Eugene H. Merrill**, Distinguished Professor of Old Testament Studies, Dallas Theological Seminary

" 'Count your blessings, name them one by one,' and I count the writings of John Frame to be *one* of my greatest blessings. He's a guide for many of us in the twenty-first century, especially in this volume—*Systematic Theology*. His treatment of all the standard theological topics is the gold standard. And as a theologically informed philosopher, I was especially interested in Frame's discussion of epistemology. Amen and Amen!"
—**David K. Naugle**, Distinguished University Professor, Dallas Baptist University

"Readers of this comprehensive work will rejoice to see a biblically saturated exposition of the great truths of the Christian faith. John Frame has now given his unique and fascinating insights to the church in one volume. This work will be invaluable for anyone who wants to see the biblical roots of Christian doctrine, and is a clear testimony against any who think that systematic theology can arise from any source other than Scripture."
—**K. Scott Oliphint**, Professor of Apologetics and Systematic Theology, Westminster Theological Seminary

"*Systematic Theology* brings together, slims down, sums up, and augments all the wisdom contained in Frame's four-volume Lordship series. It is a worthy climax to the life's work of one who has only ever sought to be a faithful servant of Christ, teaching in his church. It is a privilege to celebrate its appearing and to commend it for serious study. I guarantee that the dividends of such study will be uniformly high. Thank you, John Frame, for this superb gift."
—**J. I. Packer**, Board of Governors' Professor of Theology, Regent College, Vancouver, British Columbia

"I highly recommend this book as a solid, profound, and readable summary of theology, and at the same time a suitable introduction to John Frame's more specialized writings. It is valuable also for those who are already familiar with Frame's works. He sometimes approaches old subjects in new ways, and he includes thoughts and arguments that have not appeared elsewhere or that have appeared in print but have up till now not been integrated into his major works. The result is brilliant, practical, and edifying."

—**Vern S. Poythress**, Professor of New Testament Interpretation, Editor of the *Westminster Theological Journal*, Westminster Theological Seminary

"Many years ago, John Frame signaled his desire to show in some measure the richness of the theological resources available to Reformed orthodoxy and thereby to make that position more attractive. Today, Frame's many volumes are themselves vital resources that simultaneously fortify and adorn the Reformed theological tradition that he has expounded over many decades. In this his newest volume—Bible-centered, multiperspectival systematic theology, nurtured in the soil of Warfield, Bavinck, Murray, and Van Til—Frame demonstrates once again why he has become a teacher to this generation of Reformed pastors and theologians. Students familiar with Frame's work know what to expect and will enjoy his application of multiperspectivalism to several new loci. Those new to Frame will find his system accessible, his reflections on doctrine judicious, and his modeling of theology as essentially a study of Scripture a refreshing tonic that can be shared with all of God's people. Thank you, Professor Frame!"

—**Mark P. Ryan**, Adjunct Professor of Religion and Cultures, Covenant Theological Seminary; Director, Francis A. Schaeffer Institute

"When it comes to the field of systematic theology, anything that John M. Frame writes is certainly worth reading. This is so because Frame understands the difference between the primary standard and secondary standards. The primary source and standard for systematic theology is the written Word of God in Holy Scripture, and the secondary standards are the creeds and confessions formulated by the church across the centuries. Frame does not manipulate the text of Scripture to make it supportive of received doctrinal formulations, but subscribes to the Reformed creeds and confessions because they embody the truth that the Lord has given us in his Word. The creeds and confessions do not stand on a level with the only infallible rule of faith and practice, but are planted deep under Scripture and are subject to revision as the Holy Spirit leads the church of Christ on its way to ultimate victory when the knowledge of the Lord will fill the earth as the waters cover the sea.

"In this systematic theology, Frame has not overwhelmed us with the scholarly apparatus characteristic of so much theological literature, and as he certainly is capable of doing. Instead, he has chosen to enter into conversation with his reader, showing how he has come to understand the teaching of God's Word. He takes us with himself into a deeper and fuller exploration of God's creative and redemptive purpose in the world. Frame's work will well serve the needs and interests of the informed layman and theological student as well as the more advanced scholar."

—**Norman Shepherd**, Former Pastor; Former Professor of Systematic Theology, Holland

"For those already introduced to Frame, here is the same sober emphasis on a scripturally rooted theology combined with rigorous thinking that you can recall from live lectures or addresses. For those unfamiliar with Frame, here is a wonderful entry to his engaging and nuanced thought, which breathes a commendable evangelical catholicity."

—**Kenneth J. Stewart**, Professor of Theological Studies, Covenant College

"In his *Systematic Theology*, once again John Frame has wonderfully served the church and glorified God through his writing. Frame writes with unusual clarity, humility, and joy, which fosters a deeper love for Christ. His theological method is profoundly biblical, so the reader learns how to do evangelical theology, along with learning evangelical doctrine. Among Frame's other stellar works, his *Systematic Theology* may prove to be his most significant contribution. The beginning chapters on the story line of the Bible and the closing ones on the Christian life set this work apart from others like it. They ensure that the systematic study of doctrine is considered within the overarching story of the Bible and that God's truth informs our lives. I'm deeply grateful that this wise, seasoned, godly saint has given us this treasure trove of distilled biblical truth, and hope it has the wide, edifying influence it should."

—**Erik Thoennes**, Professor of Theology, Chair, Undergraduate Theology, Biola University/Talbot School of Theology; Pastor, Grace Evangelical Free Church, La Mirada

"John Frame's *Systematic Theology* is an important landmark in one-volume treatments of the major loci of doctrine. Frame's signature is readily apparent on every page: commitment to Scripture for everything he writes, accessible philosophical analysis of difficult questions, and, yes, triperspectivalism. This volume ranks as the most recommendable single-volume systematic theology of our time."

—**Derek W. H. Thomas**, John E. Richards Professor of Systematic and Practical Theology, Reformed Theological Seminary, Jackson; Minister of Teaching, First Presbyterian Church, Jackson

"What a gift the gracious Lord of all has given us in the person and work of John Frame. Of the many qualities that commend John Frame's *Systematic Theology*, three stand out: (1) It is eminently biblical. As Frame indicates at the outset, his main concern (rightly) is to reflect, as best he can, the wisdom and wonder of the Word of God, which shows forth the glory of God in all he is and does. (2) It is richly orthodox. John Frame knows the gospel and what doctrines and positions are necessary to sustain, support, and spread that gospel. He holds the line at every point where this is needed, in a day when many have yielded slack to, or have thrown down, that doctrinal lifeline. (3) It is deeply insightful. Frame demonstrates where theological innovation is best applied—in endeavoring to rethink and restate age-old truths with an eye both to biblical fidelity and to contemporary expression. May God be pleased to magnify his name through the broad reading and study of this great work."

—**Bruce A. Ware**, Professor of Christian Theology, The Southern Baptist Theological Seminary

SYSTEMATIC THEOLOGY

SYSTEMATIC THEOLOGY

AN INTRODUCTION TO CHRISTIAN BELIEF

JOHN M. FRAME

P&R PUBLISHING
P.O. BOX 817 • PHILLIPSBURG • NEW JERSEY 08865-0817

Printed in the United States of America

ISBN: 978-1-59638-217-6 (cloth)
ISBN: 978-1-59638-821-5 (ePub)
ISBN: 978-1-59638-822-2 (Mobi)

Library of Congress Cataloging-in-Publication Data

Frame, John M., 1939-
  Systematic theology : an introduction to Christian belief / John M. Frame.
     pages cm
  Includes bibliographical references and index.
   ISBN 978-1-59638-217-6 (cloth)
  1. Theology, Doctrinal. I. Title.
   BT75.3.F73 2013
   230'.42--dc23
                          2013023759

To the Next Generation

Adam
Amanda
Gavin
Kristina
Malena
Olivia
Rebecca
And those yet unborn

And to Carol
NKwagala nnyo!

CONTENTS

PART FOUR: THE DOCTRINE OF THE WORD OF GOD

PART FIVE: THE DOCTRINE OF THE KNOWLEDGE OF GOD

PART SIX: THE DOCTRINE OF ANGELS AND DEMONS

PART SEVEN: THE DOCTRINE OF MAN

PART EIGHT: THE DOCTRINE OF CHRIST

PART NINE: THE DOCTRINE OF THE HOLY SPIRIT

PART TEN: THE DOCTRINE OF THE CHURCH

PART ELEVEN: THE DOCTRINE OF THE LAST THINGS

PART TWELVE: THE DOCTRINE OF THE CHRISTIAN LIFE

ANALYTICAL OUTLINE

FOREWORD

REFORMED THEOLOGY PRESENTS itself (as Roman Catholic theology also does) as a comprehensive, thoroughgoing embodiment of universal Christian truth. The taproot for all versions of it has been John Calvin's catechetical treatise for preachers and adult believers, the fifth and final edition of his *Institutes*, where the wealth of truth uncovered by Martin Luther's biblical minings is consolidated for all time. Since then, three parts of the world have made major contributions to the Reformed heritage, each engendering its own conflicts and loyalties. England saw the sixteenth- and seventeenth-century Puritan development, from William Perkins to John Owen, exploring life in Christ in and through the Holy Spirit; nineteenth-century Holland produced the Kuyperian theology of human and Christian culture within a Reformed frame; and the twentieth century witnessed, within the conservative Presbyterian world, the ongoing quest for Reformed methodological authenticity, in which B. B. Warfield, Geerhardus Vos, J. Gresham Machen, and Cornelius Van Til are, by common consent, the leading names. I'd like to think that tomorrow's Reformed leaders will add John Frame's name to that list; I believe they should.

The church must ever seek in its theological life to verbalize biblically affirmed realities and biblically approved attitudes—to make clear to itself what is and will be involved in holding fast to these things and living in their light and power, and to detect and reject inauthentic alternatives. That, of course, involves interacting both with the words and ways of the surrounding world and with the heritage of the Christian past. In the nature of the case, theology is a cumulative enterprise in which each generation of thinkers stands on the shoulders of those who went before, and reflects on its intellectual legacy in the spirit of a grateful, though critical, trustee. This requires discernment and may call for challenges to what is customary, for the church's heritage contains, along with truth and wisdom, limitations and mistakes and anachronisms, so that it can not only inspire but also mislead our minds and put damaging blinders on them. That is why wise men say that the Reformed church must always be reforming (*ecclesia reformata semper reformanda*; actually, the Latin is passive: "needs always to be reformed" is the precise translation). To the church's head, our living Lord Jesus Christ, the church's well-being is a matter of abiding concern, so those who theologize in his name should always see active service in and to the church as part of their vocation.

Concern for a clear theological method and concern for the church's well-being are evident as two driving forces in John Frame's theological work, all of which anchors itself within the territory mapped out by the Westminster Standards. In the world of separatist American Presbyterianism, he has sometimes come under fire as a left-wing reformist; in the wider world of mainstream conservative Protestantism, which has the Reformed heritage at its center, he is not as well known as he should be; but where his work is noticed, he is recognized as one of the most clearheaded and best disciplined biblical systematists of our time. His status here will become apparent to anyone who takes time to study this, his magnum opus, and it is a matter for thanksgiving that he has been able to crown his career as teacher and writer by composing it. He seems to have feared lest it be unwittingly uneven, because he had not taught in the seminary classroom all the topics he covers here—but he need not have worried. At every point his probing, lucid, patient, thoroughly resourced reflections display mastery, and the easy friendliness of his style becomes the spoonful of sugar that makes the mixture go down into mind and heart in the pleasantest way possible, every time.

Clearly, the ideal reader whom Frame has in mind is the seminary or Bible college student who will one day be teaching in the church, and his aim throughout is to render that person a humble, faithful, Bible-soaked, Christ-loving, reverent communicator of the revealed truth of God. The thoroughness with which he searches the Scriptures, the firmness of his insistence that on all matters canonical Scripture must be allowed to speak the last word, and his quickness to discern where this is not being done, or not done well enough, give his discussions hermeneutical significance that his academic peers will appreciate. Also, his presentations reveal something yet more precious in a teacher of theology, namely, an awareness that it is natural for the children of God to want to know all they can learn about their heavenly Father. Over and above his primary audience, Frame writes for all who have this instinct and are willing to think about divine things at some length.

The goal of theology, as Frame understands it (and there is nothing out of the ordinary here), is the organized knowledge of God and ourselves together, in the context of our past, present, and future lives. This knowledge, which is both cognitive and relational, must be drawn, first to last, as we have already observed, from the written Word of God—the Bible. Frame sees, and stresses, that since God is infinite and we are finite, our knowledge of him and of our relationship to him cannot be other than, and so at best will be, perspectival, that is, made up of a set of distinct but correlated perspectives, each providing a thematic focus complementary to what other perspectives yield. Anyone who has driven, or can imagine driving, the sixty miles or so around the foot of Washington State's mighty Mount Rainier, stopping every few miles to view the mountain from a new angle, will appreciate what this means. Within this carefully constructed commitment to perspectivalism as the scaffolding, Frame opts for a regular procedure of what may be called heuristic triadic analysis, which opens up each point of theological substance by subdividing it into three. The procedure seems to grow out of the demonstrable advance in understanding that Frame first achieved by his archetypal analysis of God's lordship (that is, his sovereignty) in terms of control, authority, and presence. While not categorically claiming a connection between triperspectivalism and the truth of the Trinity, Frame habitually practices it as an unfailing didactic technique (in his own words, "a good pedagogical device, a set of hooks on which to hang the doctrines of the faith"). He is a master at it, and presents us with no fewer than 110 cogent triadic analyses in the course of this work, all neatly listed at the back as Appendix A. The proof of the pudding, they say, is in the eating, and there is no doubt that Frame's triads, all achieved by separating out situational/normative/existential factors in the reality, or phenomenon, under analysis, do again and again bring into his discourse a degree of clarity that is quite stunning. Familiar, faded doctrines become fresh; fuzzy doctrines become precise; dull doctrines become stimulating and exciting. History will perhaps see this technique as John Frame's major contribution to the conceptual toolkit with which systematic theology works.

Briefly, now: *Systematic Theology* brings together, slims down, sums up, and augments all the wisdom contained in Frame's four-volume Lordship series. It is a worthy climax to the life's work of one who has only ever sought to be a faithful servant of Christ, teaching in his church. It is a privilege to celebrate its appearing and to commend it for serious study. I guarantee that the dividends of such study will be uniformly high. Thank you, John Frame, for this superb gift.

J. I. Packer
Board of Governors' Professor of Theology
Regent College
Vancouver, British Columbia

PREFACE

SOME VERY GREAT systematic theologians never wrote systematic theologies, among them B. B. Warfield. Warfield never desired to write one. He thought the *Systematic Theology* of his predecessor Charles Hodge was quite adequate, and for himself he preferred to write scholarly and popular works on specific doctrinal subjects. His stature as a theologian is no less for this decision. Nevertheless, I would not be surprised to hear that most teachers in the field would dearly love to have the opportunity to summarize their thoughts in a full-scale systematics. I belong to the latter group, so I am immensely thankful to God for the opportunity to write this book, an elaborate exposition of the teaching of Scripture as I understand it.

When my friend and editor John J. Hughes suggested this project, I did not resist, but he sought to motivate me nonetheless. He pointed out that in my case the task might be easier than for others, because I have already written big systematic theology books in some areas,[1] and I have written an introductory summary of theology, including topics not covered in the larger books.[2] Certainly these earlier books have been a great help to me in writing this one, and readers of those books will see here a basic continuity of thought and approach. They might even suspect (rightly) that in many places some text has been cut and pasted from those past books. But I have tried to do more than to summarize the big books and to expand chapters of the smaller one. Rather, I have tried to rethink everything to make it more biblical, clear, and cogent.

For me, *biblical* is always the operative word. Systematic theologies, to be sure, are often full of historical lore about the theological battles of the past and present, and that is needed up to a point. Readers will misunderstand the doctrine of the Trinity, for example, if they don't see how the technical terms *substance* and *person* emerged from controversy over Sabellianism and Arianism. And I want also to include enough historical discussion to express proper gratefulness to those teachers whom God has raised up in past generations. Neither my theology nor anyone else's gets its content exclusively from an individual encounter with the Bible. And I don't want my readers to think I am claiming anything like that for my own work.

Yet the Bible is the most important thing. Only the Bible is the written Word of God made available to us. It must have the final word in all historical and contemporary

---

1. *DKG; DG; DCL; DWG.*
2. *SBL.*

controversies. So the most important aspect of theological work is to present to readers what the Bible says. And if some choice is to be made (as it must) of what to include and exclude, that choice must be on the basis of what is best suited to express the Bible's teaching to contemporary readers.

My use of this criterion has led to a systematic theology that is somewhat less historical in focus than other volumes. I have also written less than they about controversies among contemporary academic theologians, because frankly I do not think many of these controversies are helpful in bringing the Bible's teaching to Christian believers. I will have more to say on these subjects in chapter 1 of this book.

I am thankful to all who have helped to make this work possible. First among these is my dear wife, Mary, and our children, Debbie, Doreen, Skip, Justin, and Johnny. Thanks also go to the administration, faculty, and student body of Reformed Theological Seminary, who have given me constant and gracious support. P&R Publishing, which has given me many opportunities over the years to expound biblical doctrine, has now allowed me the privilege of publishing this volume. I am especially thankful to John J. Hughes, my longtime friend, who shepherded this volume through the publishing process and who has helped me much on my past writing projects. In this book he has worked together with Karen Magnuson, an outstanding copyeditor who has also done excellent work on my past projects. Thanks also to my RTS colleague John Muether, who has produced the Index of Scripture and the Index of Subjects and Names.

I have prayed that this book will also show that the hand of God, in the Spirit of Jesus, has been in it. Apart from him I can do nothing. For his work in and through me I am uniquely grateful.

ABBREVIATIONS

AGG	John M. Frame, *Apologetics to the Glory of God* (Phillipsburg, NJ: P&R Publishing, 1994)
ASV	American Standard Version
BRD	Herman Bavinck, *Reformed Dogmatics*, 4 vols. (Grand Rapids: Baker, 2003–8)
CD	Karl Barth, *Church Dogmatics*, 4 vols. (Edinburgh: T. and T. Clark, 1936–62)
CTJ	*Calvin Theological Journal*
CVT	John M. Frame, *Cornelius Van Til: An Analysis of His Thought* (Phillipsburg, NJ: P&R Publishing, 1995)
CWM	John M. Frame, *Contemporary Worship Music: A Biblical Defense* (Phillipsburg, NJ: P&R Publishing, 1997)
DCL	John M. Frame, *The Doctrine of the Christian Life* (Phillipsburg, NJ: P&R Publishing, 2008)
DG	John M. Frame, *The Doctrine of God* (Phillipsburg, NJ: P&R Publishing, 2002)
DKG	John M. Frame, *The Doctrine of the Knowledge of God* (Phillipsburg, NJ: P&R Publishing, 1987)
DWG	John M. Frame, *The Doctrine of the Word of God* (Phillipsburg, NJ: P&R Publishing, 2010)
ER	John M. Frame, *Evangelical Reunion: Denominations and the One Body of Christ* (Grand Rapids: Baker, 1991); available at http://www.frame-poythress.org; http://www.evangelicalreunion.org
ESV	English Standard Version
GST	Wayne Grudem, *Systematic Theology* (Grand Rapids: Zondervan, 1994)
HC	Heidelberg Catechism
Institutes	John Calvin, *Institutes of the Christian Religion*

IRF	John M. Frame, "Introduction to the Reformed Faith," available at http://www.frame-poythress.org
JETS	*Journal of the Evangelical Theological Society*
KJV	King James Version
LXX	The Septuagint, early Greek translation of the OT, sometimes quoted in the NT
MCW	*Collected Writings of John Murray*, 4 vols. (Edinburgh: Banner of Truth, 1977)
NASB	New American Standard Bible
NEB	New English Bible
NIV	New International Version
NKJV	New King James Version
NOG	John M. Frame, *No Other God* (Phillipsburg, NJ: P&R Publishing, 2001)
NT	New Testament
OT	Old Testament
PP	John M. Frame, "A Primer on Perspectivalism," available at http://www.frame-poythress.org
PWG	John M. Frame, *Perspectives on the Word of God* (Eugene, OR: Wipf and Stock, 2000)
RD	Heinrich Heppe, *Reformed Dogmatics* (Grand Rapids: Baker, 1950, 1978)
RSV	Revised Standard Version
SBL	John M. Frame, *Salvation Belongs to the Lord: An Introduction to Systematic Theology* (Phillipsburg, NJ: P&R Publishing, 2006)
SCG	Thomas Aquinas, *Summa contra Gentiles*
ST	Thomas Aquinas, *Summa Theologiae*
WCF	Westminster Confession of Faith (Atlanta: Committee for Christian Education and Publications, Presbyterian Church in America, 1986); published together with the Westminster Larger Catechism (WLC), the Westminster Shorter Catechism (WSC), and proof texts
WST	John M. Frame, *Worship in Spirit and Truth* (Phillipsburg, NJ: P&R Publishing, 1996)
WTJ	*Westminster Theological Journal*

PART 1

INTRODUCTION TO SYSTEMATIC THEOLOGY

CHAPTER 1

WHAT IS THEOLOGY?

THEOLOGY IS FULL of definitions of things. One of the useful features of a systematic theology is that you can turn there and get quick definitions of terms such as *justification*, *glorification*, or *hypostatic union*. Definitions are useful, but we should be warned that they are rarely, if ever, found in Scripture itself.[1] Such definitions are themselves theology in that they are the work of human beings trying to understand Scripture. This work is fallible, and theological definitions are almost never adequate in themselves to describe the complex ways in which language is used in the Bible. For example, when John speaks of those who "believed" in Jesus in John 8:31, he is not using the term in any of the classical theological definitions of *belief* or *faith*. You can tell, because in verse 44 Jesus tells them, "You are of your father the devil, and your will is to do your father's desires."

This reminder is especially appropriate when we are defining terms that are not explicitly found in Scripture itself. *Theology* itself is one of these. Theologians have developed a number of terms and concepts that are absent from Scripture itself, such as *Trinity*, *substance*, *person*, *nature*, *aseity*, *inerrancy*, *effectual calling*. There is nothing wrong with inventing new terms in order to better communicate biblical teaching. Indeed, this happens on a grand scale whenever the Bible is translated into a new language. When people first translated the Bible into French, German, English, and other languages, each time they had to come up with a whole set of new terms for everything in the Bible. From this fact, we can see that the line between translation and theology is not sharp.

Theologians came up with the term *effectual calling* to distinguish one biblical use of the term *calling* from others. Effectual calling is God's sovereign summons that actually draws a person into union with Christ. But this is not the only kind of calling mentioned in Scripture. *Calling* can also refer to a name-giving, or an invitation, or a request for someone's attention. So the term *effectual calling* isolates a particular

---

1. A few Bible passages come close to defining something, such as 1 John 3:4 (sin); 1 John 4:10 (God's love). But are these definitions, or only contextually significant descriptions? Of course, the precise distinction between definition and description is not always clear.

biblical concept, distinguishing it from others. We see again, then, how making a definition is itself a theological task. It can help us to understand something of the teaching of Scripture.

Definitions, then, can be helpful teaching tools. But we should not look at them to find what something "really is," as though a definition gave us unique insight into the nature of something beyond what we could find in the Bible itself. A theological definition of *omniscience* doesn't tell you what omniscience really is, as if the biblical descriptions of God's knowledge were somehow inadequate, even misleading or untrue. Even though there are none to few definitions in the Bible, Scripture, not any theological definition, is our ultimate authority. Theological definitions must measure up to Scripture, not the other way around.

Nor should we assume that there is only one possible definition of something. *Sin* can be defined as (1) transgression of God's law or as (2) rebellion against God's lordship. Other definitions, too, may be possible, but let's just consider these. Of course, if you define sin as transgression of God's law, you may well need to make it clear that such transgression constitutes rebellion. And if you define it as rebellion, eventually you will probably need to say that the rebellion in question is a rejection of a divine law. You may use either definition as long as you understand that each implies the other. You may choose either one as your definition, as long as you recognize the other as a description.

So of course, definitions are not something to live or die for. We should seek to understand the definitions of various writers, recognizing that someone who uses a different definition from ours might not differ with us at all on the substantive doctrine.

Long and Short Definitions

Theologians often prefer very long definitions. One of Karl Barth's definitions of *theology* is an example:

> Theology is science seeking the knowledge of the Word of God spoken in God's work—science learning in the school of the Holy Scripture, which witnesses to the Word of God; science labouring in the quest for truth, which is inescapably required of the community that is called by the Word of God.[2]

Here Barth tries to bring a large amount of theological content into his definition. This attempt is understandable, since every theologian wants his concept of theology to be governed by the content of theology. So he tries to show how the very definition of theology reflects the nature of the gospel, the content of Scripture, the preeminence of Christ, the nature of redemption, and so on.

---

2. Karl Barth, *Evangelical Theology: An Introduction* (Grand Rapids: Eerdmans, 1963), 49–50. He uses a somewhat shorter definition in *CD* for the related concept *dogmatics*: "As a theological discipline dogmatics is the scientific self-examination of the Christian Church with respect to the content of its distinctive talk about God." *CD*, 1.1:4.

I think this is a mistake. In his *Semantics of Biblical Language*,[3] James Barr warned biblical scholars of the fallacy of supposing that the meanings of biblical terms were loaded with theological content. The meaning of Scripture comes not from its individual terms, but from its sentences, paragraphs, books, and larger units. For example, the word *created*, just by itself, out of all context, teaches us nothing. But "In the beginning, God created the heavens and the earth" (Gen. 1:1) teaches us a great deal. "By him all things were created" (Col. 1:16) teaches us even more.

The same warning is appropriate for theologians. Certainly our theological methods and conclusions must be derived from God's revelation. But our definition of the word *theology* need not recapitulate those conclusions, though it must certainly be consistent with its conclusions. That is, the definition of *theology* cannot be a condensation of all the content of the Scriptures. Yet it must describe an activity that the Scriptures warrant.

Theology as Application

Let us then attempt to develop a concept or definition of theology.[4] The basic idea of theology is evident in the etymology of the term: a study of God. But we should seek a more precise definition.

As I will argue in chapters 23–28, in Christianity the study of God is a study of God's revelation of himself. Natural revelation and word revelation illumine one another. Scripture (our currently available form of word revelation) is crucial to the task of theology because as a source of divine words it is sufficient for human life (2 Tim. 3:16–17), and it has a kind of clarity not found in natural revelation. But natural revelation is a necessary means of interpreting Scripture. To properly understand Scripture, we need to know something about ancient languages and culture, and that information is not always available in Scripture alone. Nevertheless, once we have reached a settled interpretation as to what Scripture says, that knowledge takes precedence over any ideas supposedly derived from natural revelation.

So theology must be essentially a study of Scripture. It should not be defined as an analysis of human religious consciousness or feelings, as in the view of Friedrich Schleiermacher.[5] But we need to ask *how* theology is to study Scripture. Theology is not interested in finding the middle word in the Hebrew text of Ecclesiastes, for example.

Charles Hodge saw theology as a science that dealt with the facts of Scripture, as an astronomer deals with facts about the heavenly bodies or a geologist deals with facts about rocks. He said that theology "is the exhibition of the facts of Scripture in their proper order and relation, with the principles or general truths involved in the facts themselves, and which pervade and harmonize the whole."[6] If Schleiermacher's concept of theology is *subjectivist*, Hodge's might be called *objectivist*. Schleiermacher

---

3. James Barr, *Semantics of Biblical Language* (London: Oxford University Press, 1961), 129–40, 246–96.

4. In all the discussion below, it should be evident that the term *theology* refers both to the activity of seeking knowledge and to the texts in which that knowledge is recorded.

5. Friedrich Schleiermacher, *The Christian Faith* (New York: Harper, 1963).

6. Charles Hodge, *Systematic Theology* (Grand Rapids: Eerdmans, 1952), 1:19.

looked inward, Hodge outward. Schleiermacher looked primarily at subjective feelings, Hodge at objective facts. To Hodge, theology seeks the objective truth about God through Scripture. He wants the "facts" and the "truths."

Certainly Hodge's definition of theology is better than Schleiermacher's, because Hodge's is Bible-centered. But Hodge, like many orthodox evangelical theologians, leaves us confused about an important question: why do we need theology when we have Scripture?

Scripture itself, given Hodge's own view of Scripture, tells us objective truth about God. We don't need a theological science to give us that truth. So what is the role of theology?

In the statement quoted above, Hodge says that theology is an "exhibition of the facts of Scripture." But aren't the facts of Scripture already exhibited in the biblical text itself?

He further says that theology exhibits these facts "in their proper order and relation." This sounds a bit as though the order and relation of the facts in Scripture itself are somehow improper, and that theology has to put them back where they belong. People sometimes talk about the theological "system" of biblical doctrine as if that system stated the truth in a better way than Scripture itself, or even as if that system were the real meaning of Scripture hidden beneath all the stories, psalms, wisdom sayings, and so on. I don't think Hodge had anything like this in mind; such ideas are inconsistent with Hodge's high view of Scripture. But his phrase "proper order and relation" doesn't guard well against such notions. And in any case, it leaves unclear the relation between theology and Scripture.

He continues by saying that theology, together with its work of putting the facts of Scripture into proper order and relation, seeks to state "the principles or general truths involved in the facts themselves, and which pervade and harmonize the whole." Certainly this is one of the things that theologians do, and ought to do. But again we ask: hasn't Scripture done this already? And if it has, then what is left for theology to do?

In seeking a definition of theology, we need to emphasize not only its continuity with Scripture, but its discontinuity, too. The former is not difficult for orthodox Protestants: theology must be in accord with Scripture. But the latter is more difficult to formulate. Obviously, theology is something different from Scripture. It doesn't just repeat the words of Scripture. So the main question about theology is this: what is the *difference* between theology and Scripture, and how can that difference be justified?

Evidently the theologian *re*states the facts and general truths of Scripture, for some purpose. But for what purpose? Hodge does not tell us.

In my view, the only possible answer is this: the theologian states the facts and truths of Scripture for the purpose of *edification*. Those truths are stated not for their own sake, but to build up people in Christian faith.

In this way, we align the concept of theology with the concepts of teaching and preaching in the NT. The terms for *teaching*—*didasko, didache,* and *didaskalia*[7]—refer not to the stating of objective truth for its own sake, but to the exposition of God's truth in order to build up God's people. Consider Acts 2:42; 1 Cor. 14:6; 1 Tim. 1:10; 2:7; 4:6, 16; 6:3–4; 2 Tim. 4:2; Titus 1:9; 2 John 9. These passages contain words of the *didasko* group, translated "teacher," "teaching," "doctrine." Notice the frequent emphasis in these passages that teaching has the purpose of building people up in faith and obedience to God. Notice also the phrase *sound doctrine,* in which *sound* is *hygiainos,* "health-giving." The purpose of teaching is not merely to state the objective truth, but to bring the people to a state of spiritual health.

In defining theology, it is not strictly necessary to align it with a single biblical term, but it is certainly an advantage when we can do this. I propose that we define theology as synonymous with the biblical concept of teaching, with all its emphasis on edification.

So theology is not subjective in Schleiermacher's sense, but it has a subjective thrust. We need theology in addition to Scripture because God has authorized teaching in the church, and because we need that teaching to mature in the faith. Why did Hodge not state this as the reason we need theology? Perhaps he wanted to encourage respect for academic theological work, so he stressed its objective scientific character. Perhaps he was worried that reference to our subjective edification would encourage the disciples of Schleiermacher. But such considerations are inadequate to justify a definition of theology. Scripture must be decisive even here, and Scripture commends to us a kind of teaching that has people's needs in mind.

Theology, on this basis, responds to the needs of people. It helps those who have questions about, doubts about, or problems with the Bible. Normally we associate theology with questions of a fairly abstract or academic sort: How can God be one in three? How can Christ be both divine and human? Does regeneration precede faith? But of course, there are other kinds of questions as well. One might be confronted with a Hebrew word, say *dabar,* and ask what it means. Or he might ask the meaning of a Bible verse, say Genesis 1:1. A child might ask whether God can see what we are doing when Mom isn't watching. I see no reason to doubt that all these sorts of questions are proper subject matter for theology.

Nor would it be wrong to say that theology occurs in the *lives* of people, in their behavior, as well as in their speech. Behavior consists of a series of human decisions, and in those decisions believers seek to follow Scripture. Behavior, too, as well as speech, can be edifying or unedifying. Example is an important form of teaching. Imitating godly people is an important form of Christian learning, and the behavior of these people is often a revelation to us of God's intentions for us (1 Cor. 11:1). Their application of the Word in their behavior may be called theology. So theology is not merely a means of teaching people how to live; it is life itself.[8]

---

7. *Didaskalia* is translated "doctrine" in 1 Timothy 1:10; 4:6; Titus 1:9; 2:1. Of course, we today often use *doctrine* as a synonym for *theology.*

8. Another way of bringing out the practicality of theology is to note that the term has often been used (by Abraham Kuyper, for example) to denote the *knowledge* of God that believers receive by saving grace, as in John

There really is no justification for restricting theology only to academic or technical questions. (*How* academic? *How* technical?) If theology is edifying teaching, theologians need to listen to everybody's questions. My point, however, is not to divert theology from theoretical to practical questions, or to disparage in any way the theoretical work of academic theologians. But I do think that academic and technical theology should not be valued over other kinds. The professor of theology at a university or seminary is no more or less a theologian than the youth minister who seeks to deal with the doubts of college students, or the Sunday school teacher who tells OT stories to children, or the father who leads family devotions, or the person who does not teach in any obvious way but simply tries to obey Scripture. Theoretical and practical questions are equally grist for the theologian's mill.

The only term I know that is broad enough to cover all forms of biblical teaching and all the decisions that people make in their lives is the term *application*. To apply Scripture is to use Scripture to meet a human need, to answer a human question, to make a human decision. Questions about the text of Scripture, translations, interpretation, ethics, Christian growth—all these are fair game for theology. To show (by word or deed) how Scripture resolves all these kinds of questions is to *apply* it. So I offer my definition of theology: theology is *the application of Scripture, by persons, to every area of life.*[9]

Why, then, do we need theology in addition to Scripture? The only answer, I believe, is "because we need to apply Scripture to life."

Kinds of Theology

Traditionally, theology has been divided into different types. *Exegetical*[10] theology is interpreting the Bible verse by verse. That is application, because it aims to help people understand particular passages in Scripture. *Biblical* theology expounds Scripture as a history of God's dealings with us. It therefore focuses on Scripture as historical narrative. But if it is theology, it cannot be pure narrative. It must be application, dealing with the meaning[11] that narrative has for its hearers and readers.

17:3. The early pages of John Calvin's *Institutes* discuss this saving knowledge of God in Christ. On the first page Calvin says that we cannot rightly know ourselves without knowing God, and vice versa. On this concept of theology, see *SBL*, 73–78.

9. Later, I will indicate three perspectives that we can bring to bear on many theological questions. In my definition of theology, those three perspectives are Scripture (normative), persons (existential), areas of life (situational). So my definition of theology contains these three elements.

10. *Exegetical*, *biblical*, and *systematic* theology are all misnomers. Exegetical theology is not more exegetical than the others, nor is biblical theology more biblical, nor is systematic theology necessarily more systematic.

11. *Meaning* is not something different from application. See my discussion in *DKG*, 83–84, 97–98. When someone asks, "What is the meaning of this passage?" he may be asking for a number of things, including (1) a translation into his language, (2) an explanation of its function in its immediate context or in the whole Bible, and (3) help in the personal appropriation of its teaching (what does it mean *to me*?). These forms of meaning are also forms of application, so the two terms cover the same ground. It is therefore misleading for someone to claim that items 1 and 2 represent meaning, but 3 is merely application. All of these are questions about meaning and also about application. All questions about meaning are questions about application, and vice versa.

Systematic theology seeks to apply Scripture by asking what the *whole* Bible teaches about any subject. For example, it examines what David said about the forgiveness of sins, and Jesus, and Paul, and John, and tries to understand what it all adds up to. Another way of putting it is to say that systematic theology seeks to determine what *we today* should believe about forgiveness (or any other scriptural teaching). Seen that way, systematic theology is a highly practical discipline, not abstract and arcane as it is often presented.

Sometimes systematic theologians have produced systems of theology—comprehensive attempts to summarize, analyze, and defend biblical teaching as a whole. When a writer calls his book a systematic theology, a dogmatics, a body of divinity, or a *summa*, we can expect to find in that book such a system. The present volume is that sort of book. But: (1) We should not imagine that any such system is the true meaning of Scripture, lurking, as it were, beneath the text. At best, the system is a summary of Scripture, but Scripture itself (in all its narratives, wisdom deliverances, songs, parables, letters, visions) is our true authority, the true Word of God. (2) This kind of comprehensive system-making is not the only legitimate form of systematic theology. Systematics is equally interested in studies of individual doctrines and answers to individual questions.

Historical theology is the analysis of past theological work. It is truly theology when it does this study in order to better apply biblical teaching to the church of the present day. Without this goal, it is something less than theology, a mere academic discipline among others. I define historical theology as a study of the church's past theology, for the sake of its present and future.

Practical theology is, in my understanding, a department of systematic theology. It asks a particular question of Scripture, among the other questions of systematics. That question is: how should we *communicate* the Word of God? Thus, it deals with preaching, teaching, evangelism, church-planting, missions, media communications, and so on.

Theological Method

In *DKG* I discussed many aspects of theological method. Here I want to make only a single point, that theology should be Bible-centered. That is obvious, given the defi-nition of theology that I have presented. If we are to apply the Bible, we must be in constant conversation with the Bible. If we are to argue adequately for a theological view, we must be able to show the biblical basis of that view.

There are, of course, many auxiliary disciplines that aid the work of theology. God's revelation in creation illumines Scripture, as well as the reverse. So to do theology well, we need to have some knowledge from extrabiblical sources: knowledge of ancient languages and culture, knowledge of how past theologians have dealt with issues. The creeds and confessions of the church are especially important theological sources because they reflect important official agreements on doctrinal issues. It is also useful for a theologian to know the various alternatives available in the theological litera-ture of the present and for us to have some knowledge of secular disciplines, such as psychology, sociology, politics, economics, philosophy, literary criticism, and the natural sciences. Some of these aid us directly in the interpretation of Scripture. Others help us to understand the contemporary situations to which we intend to apply Scripture.

I think, however, that theology today has become preoccupied with these auxiliary disciplines to the extent of neglecting its primary responsibility: to apply Scripture itself. Theological literature today is focused, especially, on history of doctrine and contemporary thought. Often this literature deals with theological questions by comparing various thinkers from the past and from the present, with a very minimal interaction with Scripture itself.

I cannot help but mention my conviction that this problem is partly the result of our present system for training theologians. To qualify for college or seminary positions, a theologian must earn a Ph.D., ideally from a prestigious liberal university.[12] But at such schools, there is no training in the kind of systematic theology that I describe here. Liberal university theologians do not view Scripture as God's Word, and so they cannot encourage theology as I have defined it, the application of God's infallible Word. For them, one cannot be a respectable scholar unless he thinks autonomously, that is, rejecting the supreme authority of Scripture.

When I studied at Yale in the mid-1960s, *systematic theology* was defined as a historical study of theology since Schleiermacher. (Theology before Schleiermacher was called *history of doctrine*.) In such a school, systematics was a descriptive, not a normative, discipline. It set forth what people have thought about God, not what we *ought* to think about God. Of course, some normative content seeped through: not the normative content of Scripture, but normative content that emerged from the modern mind, from an autonomous rejection of the supreme authority of Scripture.

Students are welcome at such schools to study historical and contemporary theology, and to relate these to auxiliary disciplines such as philosophy and literary criticism. But they are not taught to seek ways of applying Scripture for the edification of God's people. Rather, professors encourage each student to be "up to date" with the current academic discussion and to make "original contributions" to that discussion, out of his autonomous reasoning. So when the theologian finishes his graduate work and moves to a teaching position, even if he is personally evangelical in his convictions, he often writes and teaches as he was encouraged to do in graduate school: academic comparisons and contrasts between this thinker and that, minimal interaction with Scripture itself. In my judgment, this is entirely inadequate for the needs of the church. It is one source of the doctrinal declension of evangelical churches, colleges, and seminaries in our day. Evangelical denominations and schools need to seek new methods of training people to teach theology, educational models that will force theologian candidates to mine Scripture for edifying content. To do this, they may need to cut themselves off, in

12. Full disclosure: I do not have an earned doctorate. I completed all requirements for the Ph.D. at Yale University except for the dissertation. In 2003 I received an honorary D.D. degree from Belhaven College. So critics are welcome to dismiss my comments here as sour grapes if they prefer. I trust that other readers will respond in a less ad hominem fashion.

some degree, from the present-day academic establishment. And to do that, they may have to cut themselves off from the present-day accreditation system, which seeks to make theological seminaries conform more and more to the standards of the secular academic establishment.

It is good for readers of theology to know what Augustine thought about a particular issue, or Martin Luther, John Calvin, Jonathan Edwards, Karl Barth, Rudolf Bultmann, Jürgen Moltmann, Wolfhart Pannenberg, or someone else. And it is often interesting to see how a theologian "triangulates" among these, going beyond Barth here, avoiding the extreme of Pannenberg there.

But no theological proposal fully makes its case until it shows itself to be biblical. This means that any theologian worth his salt must interact in depth with the Bible. Such interaction is not only the work of biblical scholars or of exegetical theologians. It is the work of systematic theologians as well. In fact, the systematic theologian, since he aspires to synthesize the teaching of the *whole* Bible, must spend more time with Scripture than anybody else.[13]

The application of Scripture is a very distinctive discipline. Although it depends to some extent on the auxiliary disciplines that I have listed, none of them has the distinct purpose of applying Scripture to the edification of people. To carry out that purpose requires not only academic excellence, but a heart-knowledge of Jesus, a prayerful spirit, and an understanding of the needs of people.

This present volume of systematic theology will be focused on Scripture, not on history of doctrine or contemporary theology. Of course, nobody should suppose that the ideas in this book appeared out of nowhere, with no historical context. My own confession is Reformed, and this book will certainly reflect that orientation, though I hope herein to reach out to members of other doctrinal traditions. And from time to time I will refer to secular and liberal thinkers of the past and present. But my chief interest is to state what the Bible says, that is, what it says to us.

I have no objection to theologians who want to include in their work a larger component of historical and contemporary discussion. As I said before, that is historical theology, and that discipline is often a great help to systematics. I do object to theologies in which the historical emphasis detracts from an adequate biblical focus. I question whether it is possible to do an excellent job of combining a systematic theology with a history of doctrine, though many have tried to do it. Certainly I am not competent to do it. So although I will rely on past and contemporary thinkers at many points, I will not devote much time here to expounding their views.

To say that this book is exegetical is not to say that it focuses on new exegetical ideas. For the most part, I am sticking to interpretations of Scripture that are fairly obvious and commonplace. Reformed *doctrine* has traditionally been based on the main principles of Scripture, not individual verses alone. Although new interpretations of

13. John Murray's lectures in systematic theology consist almost entirely of the exegesis of biblical passages that establish Reformed doctrines. He explains his method in his important article "Systematic Theology," in *MCW*, 4:1–21.

verses appear from time to time, this process of change in exegetical theology generally does not lead to change in the church's doctrines. Further, I think the church's problems today are not usually problems that can be solved by novel interpretations of this or that passage. Our theological problems usually arise from our failure to note what is obvious.

Key Terms

Note: Key terms are listed in the approximate order in which they are treated in the text of each chapter.

Definition
Theology (Barth)
Theology (Schleiermacher)
Theology (Hodge)
Theology (Frame)
Edification
Application
Exegetical theology
Biblical theology
Systematic theology
Historical theology
Practical theology
Meaning

Study Questions

1. "Definitions are themselves theology." Explain; evaluate.
2. Is it wrong to develop theological terminology not found in Scripture itself? Why or why not?
3. "Nor should we assume that there is only one possible definition of something." Why shouldn't we assume this? Give an example of a term that may be defined in more than one way.
4. "The definition of *theology* cannot be a condensation of all the content of the Scriptures." Explain; evaluate.
5. "But Hodge, like many orthodox evangelical theologians, leaves us confused about an important question." What question? How does Frame answer it? How do you think we should answer that question?
6. What are the advantages in defining theology by reference to the *didasko* word-group of the NT? Do you see any disadvantages?
7. Frame believes that "theology today has become preoccupied by these auxiliary disciplines to the extent of neglecting its primary responsibility." What is that primary responsibility? What have recent theologians substituted for that primary

responsibility? How is this problem related to the current methods of training theologians? How is it related to the nature of seminary accreditation?

Memory Verses

Ps. 34:11: Come, O children, listen to me;
I will teach you the fear of the Lord.

1 Cor. 11:1: Be imitators of me, as I am of Christ.

1 Tim. 4:6: If you put these things before the brothers, you will be a good servant of Christ Jesus, being trained in the words of the faith and of the good doctrine that you have followed.

2 Tim. 2:1–2: You then, my child, be strengthened by the grace that is in Christ Jesus, and what you have heard from me in the presence of many witnesses entrust to faithful men who will be able to teach others also.

Resources for Further Study

In addition to the specific suggestions that I make at the end of each chapter, it will be valuable for the student to compare the discussions here with those of other systematic theologies, such as those of Charles Hodge, Herman Bavinck, Louis Berkhof, Wayne Grudem, Robert Reymond, Douglas Kelly, and Richard Gamble.

Ames, William. *The Marrow of Theology*. Grand Rapids: Baker, 1997. Influential Puritan work on the basics of theology. He defines theology as "the science of living before God."

Calvin, John. *Institutes*. This is the most influential theological text of the Reformed tradition, and an admirable example of *theology as application*. Calvin referred to this volume as his *Summa Pietatis*, "summary of piety." Cf. Aquinas's *ST* and *SCG*.

Frame, John M. *DKG*, 76–85, 206–14.

Murray, John. "Systematic Theology," in *MCW*, 4:1–21.

CHAPTER 2

THE LORD

IN THE PREVIOUS CHAPTER, I indicated that the work of theology is not to repeat the words of Scripture, but to *teach* those words, using biblical words, but also different words from those in Scripture. The goal of that teaching is to edify people, to help them understand the gospel and its implications.

A time-honored way of teaching a complicated text such as the Bible is to choose one or more major themes from that text and expound those themes. This method communicates much (but of course not all) content from the text and also gives the reader a sense of what is most important within the text, at least in the opinion of the theologian.

Many theological writers, indeed, have chosen *one* theme around which to structure their discussions. For Martin Luther, the theme was justification by faith alone.[1] For Immanuel Kant, it was ethics; for Friedrich Schleiermacher, feeling. Others include the holy (Rudolf Otto), the fatherhood of God (Adolf von Harnack), crisis (Karl Barth), Word of God (also Barth), personal encounter (Emil Brunner), self-understanding (Rudolf Bultmann), dialectical self-negation (Paul Tillich), acts of God (G. Ernest Wright), language event (Gerhard Ebeling), hope (Jürgen Moltmann), liberation (Gustavo Gutierrez), secularity (Harvey Cox), resurrection (Wolfhart Pannenberg).

Much can be learned from studying the Bible according to such themes. Each theme, if it is really a central theme, constitutes a perspective[2] on the whole of Scripture. For example, as with Brunner, we can learn much from considering the personal encounters

---

1. It is sometimes said that for John Calvin, the sovereignty of God was his major theme. But though this concept was more central for Calvin than for many other writers, it doesn't seem to be a theme that Calvin returned to over and over again in the way that Luther kept returning to the doctrine of justification. Calvin, like Augustine and Aquinas, may have been one of those theologians who did not try to write his theology around a central theme. Though his mind was highly systematic and consistent, he tended to write whatever he thought was needed in each situation. That was true even of his *Institutes*, which began as a short summary of the faith and grew larger as Calvin found more and more issues that he thought needed to be addressed. In this respect Calvin's theology was occasional in character; indeed, it was *application* par excellence.

2. *Perspective* will turn out to be an important concept in this book, which I will expound toward the end of this chapter.

between God and human beings throughout the Bible and how those illuminate the personal relationship between God and ourselves. A full account of the types, conditions, nature, and results of personal encounters will include all the theology of the Bible. The same is true of many of the other themes mentioned in the previous paragraph.

We should keep in mind, however, that: (1) There is a difference between these themes and the Bible itself. Discussion of a biblical theme may be a good way of teaching the Bible, but it is not the Bible. Only the Bible itself may serve as our ultimate authority. (2) Certainly we should not choose a theme and use it to oppose other legitimate themes. (Some, of course, are illegitimate or unhelpful.) (3) Having chosen a theme, we should expound it according to its biblical meaning, not according to what we imagine it to imply from usage outside the Bible.

The Centrality of Divine Lordship

Having read many theologies based on themes mentioned above, I started wondering why nobody had employed God's lordship as a central theological theme.[3] Certainly God himself is central to the biblical story, and he indicates in many contexts that he wants to be known as the Lord.

In Exodus 3, he met with Moses in the burning bush. And when Moses impertinently asked his name,

> God said to Moses, "I AM WHO I AM." And he said, "Say this to the people of Israel, 'I AM has sent me to you.'" God also said to Moses, "Say this to the people of Israel, 'The LORD, the God of your fathers, the God of Abraham, the God of Isaac, and the God of Jacob, has sent me to you.' This is my name forever, and thus I am to be remembered throughout all generations." (Ex. 3:14–15)

Here, God gives Moses his mysterious name in three forms: long (I AM WHO I AM), medium (I AM), and short (Heb. *Yahweh*, translated "LORD"). These are all related to the name *Yahweh*, which in turn has some relation to the verb *to be* (*ehyeh*). In the ESV the term *Lord* (representing both *Yahweh* and *'adon* in Hebrew and *kyrios* in Greek) is found 7,776 times, in 6,603 out of 31,086 verses of the Bible.[4] Most of these refer to God, or (significantly) to Christ. Clearly, this is a term to be reckoned with.

In the passage above, God tells Moses that *Yahweh* is the name by which he wishes to be remembered forever. And throughout Scripture, the term takes on important theological meaning. Over and over, we are told that God performs his mighty deeds, so that people "shall know that I am the LORD" (Ex. 14:4; cf. 6:7; 7:5, 17; 8:22; 10:2; 14:18; 16:6, 12; 29:46; 31:13; Deut. 4:35; 29:6; 1 Kings 8:43, 60; 18:37; 20:13, 28; 2 Kings 19:19;

---

3. It might be argued that Karl Barth does this. In speaking of revelation, he repeats over and over again that "God reveals himself as the Lord." But his concept of divine lordship is very different from mine.

4. Count performed with BibleWorks 8. The term *name*, which often stands in for *Yahweh* (see below), is found 913 times, but I have not tried to discover how many of these references are specifically to the name of the Lord.

Ps. 83:18; Isa. 37:20;[5] Jer. 16:21; 24:7; Ezek. 6:7, 10, 13, 14; 7:4, 9, 27; 11:10; etc.), or so that "my name may be proclaimed in all the earth" (Ex. 9:16; see also Rom. 9:17). We find *name* and *Lord* throughout the Scriptures, in contexts central to God's nature, uniqueness, dignity, actions, and relation to his people.

The name *Lord* is as central to the message of the NT as it is to the OT. Remarkably, in the NT, the word *kyrios*, "Lord," which translates *Yahweh* in the Greek translation of the OT, is regularly applied to Jesus. If the *shema* (Deut. 6:4–5) summarizes the message of the OT by teaching that Yahweh is Lord over all, so the confession "Jesus is Lord" (Rom. 10:9; 1 Cor. 12:3; Phil. 2:11; cf. John 20:28; Acts 2:36) summarizes the message of the NT.[6]

Opponents of Lordship Theology

Unbelievably, despite the centrality of divine lordship in Scripture, a number of theologians today criticize the concept. Moltmann, for example, thinks that lordship necessarily means "power and possession," including "power of disposal over his property."[7] These concepts, in his view, should be rejected today. Part of the problem is that Moltmann misinterprets biblical lordship, understanding it according to a medieval feudal model. But for the most part, Moltmann understands lordship all too well. Scripture does indeed teach that God has power of disposal over his people. That is not all of the biblical meaning of *Lord*, but it is an important part of it, and Moltmann rejects it.

Similarly with Elizabeth Johnson, feminist theologian, who inveighs against the ideas of *power over*, dominance, and the like being ascribed to God. These are patriarchal and hierarchical, she says, and as such they have no place in her doctrine of a female god. What this means, however, is that Johnson simply does not like the biblical concept of divine lordship.[8]

Clark Pinnock, from a more evangelical tradition, does not criticize God's lordship explicitly, but he objects to the idea of God as a *monarch* (or, as he says gratuitously, an "aloof monarch"). He contrasts this picture with God as a "caring person with qualities of love and responsiveness."[9] But is biblical lordship, including its connotation of monarchy, really incompatible with the idea of God as caring, loving, and responsive?

5. See also the "I am he" passages, in which the name *Yahweh* is prominent. God will act so that Israel and the nations will know that "I am he" (Deut. 32:39; Isa. 41:4; 43:10, 13; etc.). In John, the words translated "I am he" are simply "I am" (John 8:24, 28, 58; 9:9; 18:5, 6, 8), identifying Jesus as Yahweh.

6. In Paul's writings, *Lord* (*kyrios*) regularly refers to Jesus rather than to God the Father.

7. Jürgen Moltmann, *The Trinity and the Kingdom* (San Francisco: HarperCollins, 1981), 56.

8. Elizabeth Johnson, *She Who Is* (New York: Crossroad Publishing, 1996), 20. She, like many other theologians today, develops her doctrine of God by consulting her own likes and dislikes and those of her constituency.

9. Clark Pinnock, "Systematic Theology," in *The Openness of God*, ed. Clark Pinnock et al. (Downers Grove, IL: InterVarsity Press, 1994), 103.

I confess also to being rather perplexed about the recent controversy in evangelical circles over *lordship salvation*.[10] The question concerns whether confessing the lordship of Christ is necessary at the beginning of the Christian life, or whether it can be postponed until a later time. But the lordship of Jesus is absolutely fundamental to the preaching of the gospel in the NT. It is inconceivable that anyone could respond appropriately to that gospel without confessing from the heart that Jesus is Lord (Rom. 10:9–10). To acknowledge the lordship of Christ is not, of course, to be sinlessly perfect or flawless in one's discipleship. Scripture teaches plainly that sincere believers do sin (1 John 1:8, 10); they act inconsistently with their profession. But if that profession is genuine, it will motivate them more and more to turn from sin and to seek Jesus' righteousness.

Even in Reformed circles, not all theologians encourage an emphasis on divine lordship. In Darryl Hart's *A Secular Faith*,[11] the author opposes Abraham Kuyper's appeal to "the lordship of Christ over all temporal affairs." In the interest of his Two Kingdoms distinction between church and state, Hart says that Kuyper's appeal "fails to do justice to the reduced character of Christ's sovereignty in the Christian era."[12] *Reduced* is certainly not a term appropriately attached to the sovereignty of Christ, in any period of time. To say that Christ's lordship is "reduced" is certainly incompatible with a profession of Reformed theology. Indeed, Hart has nothing positive to say about the lordship of Christ. He refers to it only as a slogan of social-gospel liberals.[13]

So despite the 7,776 references to divine lordship and the obviously central role it plays in the biblical story, a theologian should not expect to appeal to this concept without being criticized. The main problem is that we live in a world obsessed by autonomy. As with Adam and Eve in the garden, people today do not want to bow the knee to someone other than themselves. God's lordship confronts and opposes autonomy from the outset. It demands our recognition that all things belong to him and are subject to his control and authority. That demand is unacceptable to people who are outside of Christ, and to some extent even believers chafe when the demand is clearly made.

The Covenant

The most central meaning of *Lord* is to designate God's role in a relationship with his creatures, called *covenant*. Sometimes covenants are agreements between equals, "parity" covenants (as in the eternal covenant between God the Father and God the Son). But most often in Scripture, they are agreements between a great king and a

---

10. For the arguments, see John MacArthur, *The Gospel according to Jesus* (Grand Rapids: Zondervan, 1988), favoring lordship salvation. On the other side, Zane C. Hodges, *Absolutely Free! A Biblical Reply to Lordship Salvation* (Grand Rapids: Zondervan, 1989). Hodges thinks that to make the lordship of Christ fundamental to salvation is to make salvation dependent on human works. It is certainly true that God justifies us, declares us righteous, apart from works, and therefore apart from our service to Christ as Lord. But salvation is not only justification, but sanctification as well. The same grace of God that justifies also motivates the justified person to do good works (Eph. 2:8–10). So we embrace Christ as Savior and as Lord in the same act of faith.

11. Chicago: Ivan R. Dee, 2006.

12. Ibid., 230.

13. Ibid., 113, 189, 228–30.

lesser king. The terms of the agreement are not from mutual negotiation. They are unilaterally prescribed by the great king, the suzerain.

In Scripture, God makes many covenants with his creatures (not only with human beings—see Gen. 9:9–10).[14] The covenant most often mentioned in Scripture is the covenant between God and the people of Israel, made after God had delivered them from Egypt and had gathered them to worship him on Mount Sinai.[15] This is often called the *Mosaic covenant*, because Moses serves as the mediator of the covenant. Here, the Lord selects one people from among all the nations of the earth to be his own (see Deut. 4:37–38; 7:6–8; 10:15; etc.). He is the Lord, and they are his servants. He redeems them from their bondage in Egypt and demands their obedience to his law, so the covenant includes both grace and law. In the fearsome holiness of the Mount Sinai meeting, God says to them through Moses:

> Now if you obey me fully and keep my covenant, then out of all the nations you will be my treasured possession. Although the whole earth is mine, you will be for me a kingdom of priests and a holy nation. (Ex. 19:5–6)

In Exodus 20:1–17, God speaks to Israel the words that we usually call the Ten Commandments or the Decalogue. Meredith G. Kline has analyzed this passage as a "suzerainty treaty" between God and Israel.[16]

The suzerainty treaty was a type of document of which examples have been found from the ancient Hittite culture. In this literary form, a great king (a suzerain) formulates a treaty with a lesser king (a vassal). The great king is the author. He sets the terms of the relationship. The document form regularly includes certain elements: (1) The name of the great king, identifying him as the author of the document: "I am King So-and-So." (2) The "historical prologue," in which the great king tells the vassal what benefits he has brought the vassal in the past. (3) The "stipulations," laws that the vassal is expected to obey in gratefulness for the great king's past beneficence. These were often divided into general and particular commands. The general command was "love" or exclusive loyalty to the suzerain. The particular commands indicated the ways in which this exclusive suzerain expected his vassal people to behave. (4) The "sanctions," blessings for obedience and curses for disobedience. (5) "Continuity," provisions for public reading of the treaty, royal succession, adjudication of disputes, and so on.

Kline finds that the Decalogue follows this treaty pattern fairly closely. (1) God gives his name, "I am the LORD your God." Again, the mysterious name *Yahweh*, "LORD," appears. (2) Then the Lord proclaims his past blessing on Israel, identifying himself

---

14. As we will see, theologians have even spoken of a *pactum salutis*, a kind of covenant within the Trinity, a covenant by which the Father and the Son mutually pledge different roles in accomplishing salvation. This arrangement is never called *covenant* in Scripture, but I would not deny the appropriateness of that term.

15. For more on this covenant and other biblical covenants, see chapter 4.

16. Meredith G. Kline, *The Structure of Biblical Authority* (Grand Rapids: Eerdmans, 1972).

as the One "who brought you out of the land of Egypt, out of the house of slavery." (3) After this, God utters the commandments themselves. The first commandment (perhaps the first four) requires exclusive loyalty to the one God and repudiation of all other would-be gods. The other commandments spell out the implications of this commitment. (4) There are sanctions embedded in the commands (rather than relegated to a specific section, as often in the secular treaties), as in Exodus 20:5–6, 7b, 12b. (5) There is no specific continuity section in the Decalogue, but at the end of Deuteronomy there are provisions for public teaching of God's law (Deut. 31:9–13), the persistence of the covenant after Moses' death, and dealing with rebellion (vv. 14–29). Kline also analyzes the book of Deuteronomy to be a suzerainty treaty in form.

The written treaty is crucial to the relationship, both in the extrabiblical treaties and in the biblical covenants. To violate the treaty is to violate the covenant. Copies of the treaty were to be placed in the sanctuaries of the gods of the suzerain and vassal and brought out for regular public reading. This is the root of the Bible's doctrine of Scripture, which we will consider in chapters 23–28.

So Yahweh is the covenant head of Israel. But in various ways, the model of the Mosaic covenant illumines God's relationship to all his creatures, not only to Israel. In the creation narrative of Genesis 1, God defeats darkness and divides waters, as he did in Egypt.[17] His powerful word commands new creatures to come into being, and they obey. At the end of his creative labor, he makes a holy place for himself and mankind. He treats all the creatures, including man, as his covenant servants. When he says, in Isaiah 66:1, that "heaven is my throne, and the earth is my footstool," he declares himself to be the covenant Lord of the whole creation. Compared to his heavenly throne, the Israelite temple is as nothing:

> What is the house that you would build for me,
>   and what is the place of my rest?
> All these things my hand has made,
>   and so all these things came to be,
>   declares the LORD. (Isa. 66:1–2)

God rules over all things as Lord of a covenant before his covenant with Israel, even before his covenant with Adam and Eve. So God's sovereignty over everything he has made is a covenantal lordship.

Scripture describes the relationship between God and ourselves in other important ways. One is the marriage figure: he is the groom, we the bride (Ezek. 16:1–63; Hos. 1:2–11; 3:1–5; Eph. 5:25–33; Rev. 19:7–9). But marriage is a kind of covenant in Scripture (Ezek. 16:8, 59–62; Mal. 2:14). Another is the figure of sonship (see chapters 6 and 42): God is Father; we are his adopted sons and daughters (Matt. 12:50; Rom. 8:14–17; Gal. 4:6; Eph. 1:5). But we are sons and daughters of God because Christ is our Lord. Since we belong to the Son, we are in God's family. God has given us to his Son (John 17:2,

---

17. Cf. Meredith G. Kline, *Images of the Spirit* (Grand Rapids: Baker, 1980).

6), and it is the Spirit of the Son in us who enables us to cry, "Abba! Father!" (Rom. 8:15; Gal. 4:6). So our sonship presupposes Jesus' lordship.[18]

Of course, even our relation to Christ is not merely that of covenant servants. He calls us his friends (John 15:13–15). And Paul at one point speaks of servanthood as the status of OT believers, something less than fully mature sonship (Gal. 4:1–7). Yet Jesus says that even on the last day God will address us as servants (Matt. 25:21), and Paul, too, continues to refer to himself as *doulos*, "bondslave" (Rom. 1:1; cf. Rom. 14:4; Gal. 1:10; 2 Tim. 2:24; Titus 1:1). James and Jude, most likely literal brothers of Christ, also call themselves servants of Christ (James 1:1; Jude 1), as do Peter and John, two of the disciples closest to Jesus (2 Peter 1:1; Rev. 1:1).

Paul does use the slave-son contrast as a metaphor to indicate the new maturity and freedom we have in Christ, but it would be wrong to import the negative connotations of servanthood in Galatians 4 into every other biblical context where the term is found. In many other passages, as we have seen, Paul does not deny but rather affirms that we are now servants of Christ. And a servant of God is one who is in covenant with him.[19] So servanthood does not end when sonship begins. Both are legitimate biblical ways of referring to believers, and servanthood is biblically the more pervasive of the two.

So the fundamental point I wish to make in this section is this: that *Lord* names the head of a covenant. His essential relation to us is that of a great King who has delivered us from death and calls us to serve him by obeying his written Word.

But within this covenant relationship, how should we understand the nature and role of the Lord? A number of passages in Scripture focus on the nature of God's lordship, and in these passages are three recurring themes: *control, authority, and presence.* I will call these the *lordship attributes.*

We see these in the main body of the suzerainty treaty form: the historical prologue, the stipulations (commands), and the sanctions (blessings and curses). In the historical prologue, the Lord declares that he has exercised his great power in rescuing the vassal: "who brought you out of the land of Egypt, out of the house of slavery" (Ex. 20:2). His power controlled the situation for the vassal's benefit. In the stipulations, he indicates his authority to command: "You shall have no other gods before me" (v. 3). In the sanctions (blessings and curses), he indicates that he will be aware of what the vassal is doing and will be present to bless or judge: "I the LORD your God am a jealous God, visiting the iniquity of the fathers upon the children . . . , but showing steadfast love to thousands of those who love me" (vv. 5–6). Let us look at each of these lordship attributes more closely.

---

18. Some think it preferable to call God *Father* rather than *Lord*, head of a family rather than head of a covenant. The former seems to yield a kinder, gentler image of God. But covenant lordship is a far more pervasive concept in Scripture than divine fatherhood, the latter limited to the NT for the most part. And as we have seen, the family image presupposes the covenantal image. Nevertheless, I have no objection to theologies that regard God's fatherhood as a "central concept," and I will show how this can best be done in chapter 6.

19. Sonship, too, is by covenant, since (1) our redemptive sonship is an *adoption*, and (2) it exists because of our covenant relation to Christ as Lord.

Control

When God meets Moses in the burning bush and identifies himself as Lord, he comes as the mighty Deliverer. On behalf of his enslaved people, Yahweh deals a crushing defeat to the most powerful totalitarian government of the day. Not only does he defeat Pharaoh and his army, but he invokes all the forces of nature to bring plagues on the Egyptians and to deliver his own people. He defeats Egypt and its gods, and so shows himself to be Lord of heaven and earth.

God knows that

> the king of Egypt will not let you go unless compelled by a mighty hand. So I will stretch out my hand and strike Egypt with all the wonders that I will do in it; after that he will let you go. (Ex. 3:19–20)

So God's "hand," "wonders," and "great acts" are a repeated emphasis of the Exodus narrative (as in Ex. 4:21; 6:1, 6; 7:3–5; etc.). In Exodus 6:2–5, God relates the giving of the name *Yahweh* to his powerful deliverance. After this deliverance, says the Lord,

> you shall know that I am the LORD [*Yahweh*] your God, who has brought you out from under the burdens of the Egyptians. I will bring you into the land that I swore to give to Abraham, to Isaac, and to Jacob. I will give it to you for a possession. I am the LORD [*Yahweh*]. (Ex. 6:7b–8)

So the Lord is the One who controls all the forces of nature and history to deliver his people and thus to fulfill his covenant promise.

I believe that this emphasis on the Lord's sovereign rule may also be found in the mysterious terms of Exodus 3:14. However we choose to translate "I AM WHO I AM," the phrase certainly reflects God's sovereignty. There are various possible interpretations: "I am what I am," "I am who I am," "I will be what I will be," "I am because I am," and so forth. But all of them stress God's sovereignty. They indicate that Yahweh is very different from us, One who determines his own nature, or choices, or even being, without any dependence on us.

The *ani hu* passages of Deuteronomy and Isaiah also stress God's sovereignty in redemption (see Deut. 32:39; Isa. 41:4; 43:11–13). In these passages the pronoun *I* is prominent, bringing a message of divine monergism in salvation and judgment. *He* puts to death and makes alive; *he* brings judgment and mercy. Rulers and warriors are but tools in his hand. From that hand no one else can deliver, nor can anybody reverse his actions.

So *Yahweh* controls the entire course of nature and history for his own glory and to accomplish his own purposes.

The same conclusion follows from the biblical affirmation that Yahweh is King. As we have seen, Yahweh is head of his covenant, indeed of various covenants that ultimately include all his creatures. In those covenants, he is the great King; everyone and everything else is his vassal, his servant. So he sovereignly issues commands in Genesis 1, and even things that do not exist obey him, by springing into being. So the Psalms bring praise:

> The LORD [*Yahweh*] reigns; he is robed in majesty;
>   the LORD is robed; he has put on strength as his belt. (Ps. 93:1)

Cf. Pss. 97:1; 99:1; see also Pss. 2; 47; 96:10–13. Notice that the kingship of Yahweh is not only over Israel, but over all the nations of the earth.

Yahweh, then, is the sovereign, the Lord over all his creatures. Because he is the Lord, the King, he controls all things.

Authority

The relation between control and authority is between might and right. Control means that God has the power to direct the whole course of nature and history as he pleases. Authority means that he has the right to do that. From our standpoint as creatures, God's authority is his right to command, his right to tell us what we ought to do. When he issues commands, he is supremely *right* in doing so; thus his word creates for us an obligation to obey. When he makes promises, we can trust them without question, for they are infallibly right and true.

And when he tells us to believe in the truth of his word, we must do so, both because his word can never prove false and because we have a moral obligation to believe it.[20] Therefore, God is the supreme interpreter of both himself and the universe he has made. The world is what he says it is. His Word can never prove false (John 17:17) because (1) he is omniscient (Heb. 4:12–13), (2) he never lies (Titus 1:2), (3) his Word governs all creation, and—what particularly concerns us here—(4) he has the *authority* to declare what is the case.

Control and *authority* are not synonyms, but they imply each other. Since God created and governs all things, he is the original interpreter of creation, the One who understands the world in all its depths—not only its material nature, but also its ultimate meaning and purpose.[21] God, therefore, has the ultimate viewpoint on the world, the broadest, deepest understanding of it. His word, therefore, about himself or about the world, is more credible than any other word, any other means of knowing. It obligates belief, trust, and obedience.

Because God is the supreme controller of the world, he is its supreme evaluator. When God creates the world, he evaluates it: After "let there be light" (Gen. 1:3), we read that he "saw that the light was good" (v. 4), and so on through the creation week. He has established the purpose of everything, and he therefore knows whether and to what degree each created thing measures up to its purpose. God judges rightly what is

---

20. Thus my emphasis in *DKG* that epistemology is part of ethics, that human knowledge, like everything else in human life, is governed by God's commands. See chapter 24 and chapters 29–32 of this volume.

21. I will offer more argument to this effect in our discussion of God's omniscience, chapter 15.

good or bad about it, right or wrong. Ultimately, his judgments, like all his purposes, will prevail. So control implies authority.

God distinguishes between himself and the false gods in that he is able to tell the future (Isa. 41:21–29). He has authority to foretell the future because he is in control of everything in heaven and earth (40:1–41:20; cf. also 43:8–13).

Control implies authority also, because the Lord's creation and government establish him as the *owner* of all things (Deut. 10:14; 1 Chron. 29:11; Job 41:11; Pss. 24:1–2; 82:8; 89:11; Rom. 11:35). The owner of all, then, sets forth the standards of human conduct (Ps. 24:3–4). If God sets the standards, we may not argue with him. For us to debate with God is as ridiculous as for clay to debate with its potter (Isa. 45:9–11).

God made us and therefore owns us; we may not quarrel with him. When the landowner in Jesus' parable hires servants at different times of the day to work in his vineyard, he will not submit to the workers' complaints of unfairness. He keeps his promises, but beyond that he maintains the right to do as he wants with his own money (Matt. 20:1–16). He sets the standards and will not be subject to the standards of others.[22]

So God's ownership of the world, his right to do as he wants with his own (recall the potter-clay analogy), serves as a logical link between God's control and his authority.[23]

God's authority also implies his control. For God's authority to command his creatures extends through the whole universe. He has the right to tell every creature what to do, even the inanimate ones. So he controls the storms by his command (Ps. 147:15–18), and by his word he commands all things to exist (Gen. 1; Ps. 33:6–9; John 1:3; Heb. 11:3). God exercises control by his authoritative word.

Now, God's sovereign authority is an aspect of his lordship. The passages that we noted earlier, which focus on the concept of lordship, all seem to suggest not only God's control over who he is, but also his right to define himself authoritatively. He alone will reveal his nature. He will not submit to any merely human judgments as to who he is. Moses has asked for his name, a revelation of his nature. God replies mysteriously but informatively, as we have seen, in a way that maintains his sovereignty over his self-revelation. He alone will name himself, and through his mighty acts in history, he will illumine the meaning of his name. He retains full authority to reveal himself as he is.

Together with the name, God gives to Moses a message, proclaiming in advance, both to Israel and to Pharaoh, that Pharaoh must let Israel go, or he, the Lord, will

---

22. Compare the longer discussion in *AGG*, 171–79, and chapter 14 of this book. These texts give us an important perspective on the problem of evil.

23. Does this relationship between control and authority imply that might makes right, at least for God? I trust the reader will see that the argument in this section for a link between control and authority is more subtle than the bare statement that "might makes right." Nevertheless, there is a sense in which this slogan is true at the divine level, though not at the human. For God's "might" amounts to sovereignty over every aspect of reality, including the conceptual, the intellectual, the interpretative, and the ethical. No human being has that kind of might, either in degree or in universal extent. God's kind of might actually *embraces* right. God's might includes authority over interpretation. But his right also embraces his might, since it includes his right to command the natural world. So within God, might and right coalesce. Neither exists without the other. They are mutually perspectival.

bring judgment. Moses is to bring God's message to Pharaoh, a message that sharply contradicts the Egyptians' image of their own invincibility, a message that they will hate and resist, but one that comes with authority far transcending that of Pharaoh. God's power vindicates that authority, and he defeats Egypt. Yahweh is the One who gives an authoritative message, backed up by all his power.

When Yahweh appears before Israel at Mount Sinai to initiate his covenant (and therefore to expound his covenant lordship), he presents himself as Israel's Lawgiver, Israel's supreme authority:

> I am the LORD your God, who brought you out of the land of Egypt, out of the house of slavery.
>   You shall have no other gods before me. (Ex. 20:2–3)

As in the suzerainty treaty form, the Lord announces his name, describes his mighty deliverance, and then lays down the law. So he declares his name, proclaims his control, and then asserts his authority.

Throughout the Pentateuch, Yahweh is the Lawgiver. Because he has redeemed the people of Israel, he calls them again and again to obedience.[24] In Leviticus 18, for example, God tells Israel not to imitate the practices of the wicked Canaanites. Rather:

> You shall follow my rules and keep my statutes and walk in them. I am the LORD your God. You shall therefore keep my statutes and my rules; if a person does them, he shall live by them: I am the LORD. (Lev. 18:4–5)

God is Lord, Yahweh, and therefore his people must obey. If God is Yahweh, he is the supreme authority. Through Leviticus 18 and 19, "I am the LORD" appears as a refrain, motivating Israel to keep God's laws (see Lev. 18:6, 21, 30; 19:3, 4, 10, 12, 14, 16, 30, 31, 32, 34, 37).

In Deuteronomy 6, the *shema*, Israel's fundamental confession of God's lordship, is followed by a powerful admonition to keep God's commands. The connection is unmistakable:

> Hear, O Israel: The LORD our God, the LORD is one. You shall love the LORD your God with all your heart and with all your soul and with all your might. And these words that I command you today shall be on your heart. You shall teach them diligently to your children, and shall talk of them when you sit in your house, and when you walk by the way, and when you lie down, and when you rise. You shall bind them as a sign on your hand, and they shall be as frontlets between your eyes. You shall write them on the doorposts of your house and on your gates. (Deut. 6:4–9)

---

24. Notice that in the covenant, grace precedes law, and grace provides the motivation for obedience.

Note here the fundamental confession of Yahweh as Lord followed by a command to love him.[25] Then there is an extended appeal to Israel to keep all of God's commandments. That appeal is found not only here, but often in Deuteronomy; it is one of the book's major themes. Yahweh is the One who commands and deserves complete obedience.

Note also Isaiah 43:11–12, which defines God's lordship in terms of authoritative revelation. God reveals himself, he saves his people, and then he reveals himself again to proclaim his mighty deeds.

So Jesus identifies himself as the Lord not only by the power of his miracles, but also by the authority with which he speaks. To him, lordship is meaningless unless it conveys authority:

> Why do you call me "Lord, Lord," and not do what I tell you? (Luke 6:46; cf. Matt. 7:21–29)

The twofold repetition of "Lord" adds to our impression that to Jesus, authority is a defining feature of lordship. We may confirm this impression by noting the large number of passages connecting love for Jesus with obedience.[26] This relationship between obedience and love reminds us of the suzerainty treaty form in which the general law of the covenant (love = exclusive covenant loyalty) is spelled out in specific areas of response (the commandments). So again Jesus stands in the place of Yahweh as the great King, the head of his covenant people. As Lord, he commands and expects obedience.

His teaching also comes with an authority far transcending (and sometimes contradicting) that of the scribes (Matt. 7:29). Even more remarkably, he commands the evil spirits (Luke 4:36). A Roman centurion compares the authority of Jesus to heal at a distance with his own military authority: as the commander tells his troops what to do, so Jesus, even from a distance, can tell diseases to leave a person (Matt. 8:5–13).[27] Even the wind and sea obey Jesus' word, eliciting amazement (Mark 4:35–41), for in the OT, only Yahweh had control of the winds and waves. But what brings most amazement, and opposition, is Jesus' claim that he also has the authority to forgive sins. His authoritative word to the paralytic, "Rise, pick up your bed, and go home" (Matt. 9:6), vindicates his authority to say, "Take heart, my son; your sins are forgiven" (v. 2). "Who can forgive sins but God alone?" (Mark 2:7) ask his detractors, not knowing that

---

25. In the suzerainty treaty form, the commandments were first general (exclusive obedience or "love") and then particular (the specific ways in which the vassal was to show love). Here, too, *love* refers to exclusive covenant loyalty.

26. See John 14:21, 23; 15:10, 14; 1 John 2:3–6; 3:22, 24; 5:3; 2 John 6. In Revelation 12:17 and 14:12, Jesus' disciples are those who "keep the commandments of God."

27. Jesus commends the faith of the Roman centurion as greater than any he has seen in Israel (Matt. 8:10–12), and as a sign of the Gentiles' election and Israel's rejection. The centurion's faith is special because it is faith in the divine authority of Jesus' *word*. His request to Jesus can be literally translated "speak by a word," a redundant expression emphasizing that Jesus' word is the instrument of healing. The irony is that Israel, God's own people, is not willing to listen obediently to that wonderful word.

they are implicitly confessing Jesus' very nature. The crowd observing these events responded with less irony but appropriately: "they were afraid and they glorified God, who had given such authority to men" (Matt. 9:8).

We have seen that God's authority is beyond that of any creature. We may describe it as *absolute* in three ways. First, it *cannot be questioned*. God will not be tested by any authority higher than himself. His word is not subject to evaluation by human standards. It is not doubtful or disputable. As we have seen, the clay may not dispute the intentions of the potter.

We may, to be sure, ask for evidence to verify that a word is truly God's. Deuteronomy 18:20–22 subjects would-be prophets to two tests: they are false prophets if they speak in the name of other gods, or if their prophecies turn out to be false. Acts 17:11 commends the noble Bereans for testing Paul's words against the Scriptures.[28]

It is also true that God permits his prophets to argue with him in one sense: they sometimes ask him to turn back from his announced intentions. Abraham pleads with God not to destroy Sodom, the city in which his nephew Lot had chosen to live (Gen. 18:22–33). Moses intercedes for disobedient Israel, and God "relents" from his announced plan of rejecting Israel (Ex. 32:9–14). We will discuss in chapter 17 what it means for God to relent. For now, let me simply observe that neither Abraham nor Moses finds any fault with God's standards or God's assessment of the situation. Neither questions God's authority; indeed, that authority is the presupposition of these conversations. Abraham says:

> Far be it from you to do such a thing—to put the righteous to death with the wicked, so that the righteous fare as the wicked! Far be that from you! Shall not the Judge of all the earth do what is just? (Gen. 18:26)

God is the Judge of all the earth, the supreme authority; so he cannot do wrong. So Abraham and Moses appeal to God's own justice and mercy. The dialogue actually reveals those standards in a fuller way and enables us to marvel at the rightness of God's dealings with us. And for both Abraham and Moses, God has the last word; at that point the discussion ends.

Having made these qualifications, we can state the principle thus: when we know that God has truly spoken and that he has announced his ultimate intentions, we have no right to question him. When he tells us something, we have no right to demand evidence over and above God's own word. Paul commends Abraham because Abraham believed in God's promise even though other evidence seemed to contradict that promise:

> That is why it depends on faith, in order that the promise may rest on grace and be guaranteed to all his offspring—not only to the adherent of the law but also to the one who shares the faith of Abraham, who is the father of us all, as it is written, "I

28. On the testing of the prophets, see our discussion in chapter 24.

have made you the father of many nations"—in the presence of the God in whom he believed, who gives life to the dead and calls into existence the things that do not exist. In hope he believed against hope, that he should become the father of many nations, as he had been told, "So shall your offspring be." He did not weaken in faith when he considered his own body, which was as good as dead (since he was about a hundred years old), or when he considered the barrenness of Sarah's womb. No distrust made him waver concerning the promise of God, but he grew strong in his faith as he gave glory to God, fully convinced that God was able to do what he had promised. That is why his faith was "counted to him as righteousness." (Rom. 4:16–22)

Abraham is a model of Christian faith—the faith that justifies—because he trusted in God's promise without reservation. Certainly empirical investigation of the natural possibilities would have concluded that Abraham and Sarah were too old to beget a son. But Abraham trusted God's word *rather than* the empirical evidence. Indeed, this kind of faith is characteristic of Abraham's life: He left his home in Ur to go to a country quite unknown to him. He was even willing to sacrifice Isaac, the son of the promise, on the authority of God's word. (In accepting both God's promise and God's command to sacrifice Isaac, Abraham indicated his faith that God could raise the dead, Heb. 11:19.) His faith lapsed, to be sure, in Egypt (Gen. 12:10–20) and in Gerar (20:1–18); he was not sinlessly perfect. But Scripture commends the remarkable instances in his life when he believed God despite temptations to doubt.

Even righteous Job had to learn this lesson. He had asked for an interview with God, in which he could demand an answer from God, a reason why God had allowed him to suffer, a vindication of divine justice (Job 23:1–7; 31:35–37). But when God does appear, it is God who asks the questions, God who brings accusations. Job meekly submits:

And the Lord said to Job:

"Shall a faultfinder contend with the Almighty?
    He who argues with God, let him answer it." (Job 40:1–2)

Then Job answered the Lord and said:

"Behold, I am of small account; what shall I answer you?
    I lay my hand on my mouth.
I have spoken once, and I will not answer;
    twice, but I will proceed no further." (Job 40:3–5; cf. 38:1–3; 42:1–4)

Second, God's authority is also absolute in the sense that his covenant *transcends all other loyalties*. We are to have no other gods before the Lord (Ex. 20:3). We are to love him with *all* our heart; there should be no competing loyalties (Deut. 6:4–5; Matt. 22:37). The Lord is the head of the covenant, and he forbids us to grant lordship to anyone else.

Jesus strikingly claims deity by demanding the same kind of exclusive loyalty for himself. "Honor your father and your mother" (Ex. 20:12) is one of the fundamental commandments of the law, one that Jesus fully honors and urges against those who would dilute its force (Matt. 15:1–9). Nevertheless, Jesus demands of his disciples a loyalty that transcends the loyalty that we owe to our parents. In Matthew 8:19–22 and 10:34–38, he teaches that the demands of discipleship take priority over duties to our parents. Only God can legitimately make such a demand.

The principle *sola Scriptura* follows from this teaching. No other authority may compete with God's own words. No words may be added to God's or put on the same level of authority (Deut. 4:2; 12:32; Isa. 29:13; Matt. 15:8–9). It is wrong to bind the consciences of God's people by mere human traditions. Only the word of God has ultimate authority.

Third, God's authority is absolute in the sense that it *covers all areas of life*. The law of Moses governs every aspect of the lives of Israelites: not only their religious life, narrowly considered, but also affairs of calendar, diet, politics, economics, law, marriage, divorce, sex, war, and many other areas. It is sometimes assumed that the NT is less demanding, that it tells us to look to Christ and forget about rules and regulations. But Jesus did say, "If you love me, you will keep my commandments" (John 14:15).[29] And if anything, the NT is even more explicit than the OT about the application of God's Word to all areas of life (Rom. 14:23; 1 Cor. 10:31; 2 Cor. 10:5; Col. 3:17, 23–24). Note the universal language in these verses: *whatever, all, everything, every*. The Lord's authority extends to every aspect of human life.

To reflect a moment on recent controversy, we can see that it is wrong to try to restrict the infallible authority of God's Word in Scripture to some narrowly defined religious area, or to "matters of salvation" as opposed to other matters.[30] Certainly Scripture centers on Christ and redemption. But its applicability is not limited to the preaching of the fundamental gospel. Having created and redeemed us as our covenant Lord, God claims the authority to direct all our thinking and all our decisions. The Lord is totalitarian, as only he has a right to be.[31]

The relation between the Lord's control and his authority illumines the relation of God's sovereignty to human responsibility. Though more can be said about it, fundamentally this problem reduces to the relation between God's control and his authority. When people talk about God's sovereignty, they usually refer to God's control over all things.[32] When we speak of human responsibility, we are describing how we are under God's authority. Seen in this way, there is no conflict between divine sovereignty and

29. Note the many verses to this effect in the Johannine literature, mentioned earlier. This is one of the major themes of the Johannine writings.
30. See chapter 26 on the comprehensiveness and sufficiency of Scripture.
31. Remember that it is God's totalitarian authority that frees us from bondage to human authorities. It is therefore a law of freedom.
32. I prefer, however, to speak of God's sovereignty as a synonym for his lordship and therefore as including all three of the lordship attributes.

human responsibility. In fact, the two fit together easily.[33] The One who controls all things has the right to demand our obedience.

When we later discuss God's covenants with human beings (chapter 4), I will stress that each of them is both unconditional and conditional. They are unconditional in that God will surely accomplish his purposes through the covenants. They are conditional in that human beings receive the blessings of the covenant through obedient faith. This does not mean that human beings *earn* blessings through obedience but that God accomplishes his sovereign purposes by bringing about a faithful human response.

Presence

The presence of God, the third of the lordship attributes, may be seen as a consequence of his control and authority. When we speak of God's presence, we are not, of course, speaking of a physical presence, for God is incorporeal. What we mean, rather, is that he is able to act on and in the creation and to evaluate authoritatively all that is happening in the creation. Since God controls and evaluates all things, he is therefore present everywhere, as present as an incorporeal being can be.

But in this chapter, we are interested in something more than mere presence. For God is not only present in the world; he is *covenantally* present. He is *with* his creatures to bless and to judge in terms of the standards of his covenant. That is the concept that we will explore at this point.

Reviewing the elements of the suzerainty treaty form, we recall that the historical prologue emphasizes God's control, and the stipulations (commandments) emphasize his authority. In the next section, the sanctions (blessings and curses) show that God is not an absentee landlord, but continues to be with his people, both to bless their faithfulness and to judge their disobedience.

Commentators on Exodus 3 have often argued that *Yahweh* means, among other things, that God "is there," present to deliver his people from Egypt. As Peter Toon puts it, "Yahweh is God-with-his-people."[34]

The texts we have cited that have as part of their purpose to expound the name *Yahweh* focus on his commitment to his people, his solidarity with them, his intention to be with them. In Exodus 3, before giving his name in verse 14, God answers another question of Moses:

> But Moses said to God, "Who am I that I should go to Pharaoh and bring the children of Israel out of Egypt?" He said, "But I will be with you." (Ex. 3:11–12a)

Moses asks God who Moses is, before he asks God in verse 13 who God is. God's answer to the first question is similar to his answer to the second. The second answer, as we saw, was *ehyeh asher ehyeh*, "I AM WHO I AM." The first answer is *ehyeh immak*, "I will be with you," or "I am with you." We might think that "I will be with you" does not really

33. For more discussion of this matter, see chapter 35.
34. Peter Toon, *Our Triune God* (Wheaton, IL: Victor Books, 1996), 89.

answer Moses' question, "Who am I?" Moses asks about himself, Moses; God replies by speaking of himself, God. But of course, God more than answers Moses' question. Who is Moses? He is the man with whom God is. God has covenanted to stand with Moses in his confrontation with Pharaoh. So Moses is Yahweh's man; that's who he is.

Then Moses asks in verse 13 the name of God, so that he can report it to Israel. The "I AM" in verse 14 connects God with Israel as the "I AM" in verse 12 connects God to Moses. God is with the Israelites to deliver them.

God with us! Immanuel (Isa. 7:14; Matt. 1:23)! This is one of the most precious concepts in Scripture. The essence of the covenant is that God is *our* God and we are *his* people. To Abraham, God said:

> And I will establish my covenant between me and you and your offspring after you throughout their generations for an everlasting covenant, to be God to you and to your offspring after you. (Gen. 17:7)

At the end of redemptive history, this purpose is fulfilled:

> And I heard a loud voice from the throne saying, "Behold, the dwelling place of God is with man. He will dwell with them, and they will be his people, and God himself will be with them as their God. He will wipe away every tear from their eyes, and death shall be no more, neither shall there be mourning, nor crying, nor pain anymore, for the former things have passed away." (Rev. 21:3–4)

Between beginning and end, God dwells with Israel in the tabernacle and temple, and supremely in Jesus, God living with his people in the tabernacle of flesh (John 1:14; 2:21), Immanuel. Through Christ, God's people themselves are his temple, the dwelling of his Spirit (1 Cor. 6:19).

All these images reinforce the truth that God is committed to his people, that he will aid and deliver them, that he will be "with" them. This is a frequent theme in God's relationship to Abraham, Isaac, and Jacob. King Abimelech seeks a treaty with Abraham, recognizing that "God is with you in all that you do" (Gen. 21:22). Another Abimelech says to Abraham's son Isaac, "We see plainly that the LORD has been with you" (26:28). With Isaac's son Jacob, God renews the covenant in the same terms as he has presented it to Abraham and Isaac, concluding:

> Behold, I am with you and will keep you wherever you go, and will bring you back to this land. For I will not leave you until I have done what I have promised you. (Gen. 28:15; cf. 31:3, 5, 42)

Jacob's son Joseph also receives the testimony of a pagan master, this time as a slave in Egypt:

His master saw that the LORD was with him and that the LORD caused all that he did to succeed in his hands. So Joseph found favor in his sight and attended him. (Gen. 39:3–4)

Covenant presence, then, means that God commits himself to us, to be our God and to make us his people. He delivers us by his grace and rules us by his law (so covenant presence presupposes control and authority; we have seen earlier that they imply presence), and he rules not only from up above, but with us and within us.

Perspectives on Our Covenant Lord

I have suggested that the three lordship attributes presuppose and imply one another. If God controls all things, then his commands are authoritative, and his presence inescapable. If his commands are supremely authoritative, then God can command all things, thereby exercising control, and since we cannot escape from his authority (Ps. 139:7–12), he is necessarily present to us. Further, God's presence is a presence of divine control and authority. So it is not as if God could be divided between three parts,[35] each representing one attribute. Rather, each of the lordship attributes describes God as a whole, from a different perspective.

We will see that often in the Bible a subject is discussed not according to different parts, but according to different perspectives. Often these multiple perspectives are closely related to the lordship attributes of God. I will often illustrate threefold perspectival relationships using a triangular diagram; see fig. 2.1.

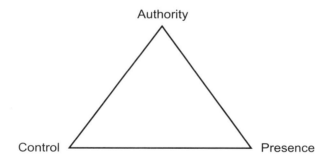

Fig. 2.1. The Lordship Attributes

The triangle as a whole represents divine lordship. To understand God's lordship, you can start from any corner. If you begin with control, you will inevitably have to account for God's authority and presence as well. Similarly with the other two corners. So each of the three concepts is not an independent part, but a perspective on the whole. And each concept is a perspective on the other two.

---

35. As we will see in chapter 20, God is not made of parts, but is "simple."

Lordship and Knowledge

Epistemology is a division of philosophy that deals with human knowledge. It studies such questions as these: "What is knowledge?" "How can we know anything?" "What are the roles of various human faculties, such as reason, sensation, intuition, and imagination?"[36]

Recognizing God's lordship affects the way we understand the world. If God is in *control* of the world, then the world is under his control. If God is our supreme *authority*, then he has the right to tell us what to believe. And if he is *present* everywhere, our attempts to know the world ought to recognize that presence. The most important fact about anything in the world is its relationship to God's lordship.

Philosophical epistemologists have often tried to identify (1) the rules or norms for knowledge (such as logic), (2) the facts that we are seeking to know, and (3) the subjective equipment (reason, senses, intuition, imagination, etc.) by which we gain knowledge.

The nature of God's lordship is that (1) the highest rules or norms of knowledge come from him; (2) the course of nature and history is under his control, so that the facts are his facts; (3) our knowledge faculties are gifts of God and operate in his very presence. We can illustrate this by a lordship triangle similar to the one we discussed earlier; see fig. 2.2.

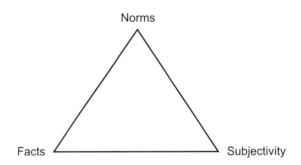

Fig. 2.2. Aspects of Knowledge

The whole created world is (1) a revelation of God (Ps. 19:1), (2) the facts that God has brought to pass, and (3) a set of experiences that God has given us. Ultimately these three are the same. To fully understand God's revelation is to understand the facts of the created world and our inner experiences. To understand fully the facts of the world is to understand it as God's revelation and as our inner experience. To understand our experience is to understand it as God's revelation and as objective fact.

So the nature of God's lordship suggests that we can know the world from three perspectives, corresponding to the three lordship attributes. In the *normative perspective*, we understand the whole world as a revelation of God, governing our thought.

36. I have discussed many of these questions in *DKG*.

In the *situational perspective*, we understand the whole world as the factual situations that God as controller has brought to pass. In the *existential perspective*, we understand the world as a set of personal experiences granted by God, who is present with us and within us. See fig. 2.3.

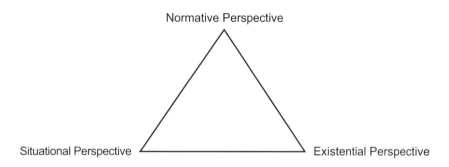

Fig. 2.3. Perspectives on Knowledge

So knowledge is always, simultaneously, (1) an application of God's norms for knowledge, (2) an understanding of the facts of God's creation and providence, (3) use of our God-given cognitive faculties. These three are interrelated and mutually dependent. Right application of God's norms will give us the right understanding of the facts and will enable us to make proper use of our subjective faculties. Proper understanding of the facts will include a proper understanding of God's norms and of our subjective faculties. And proper use of our subjective faculties will give us knowledge of God's norms and the facts of the world.

In theology as in all other forms of human knowledge, we must take these three perspectives into account, which is simply to take God's lordship into account.[37]

Key Terms
Central theme
Perspective
Autonomy
Covenant
Suzerain
Mosaic covenant
Suzerainty treaty
Name (as element of covenant)
Historical prologue
Stipulations
Sanctions

37. I will have more to say about the three perspectives as an analysis of human knowledge in chapters 29–32.

Lordship attributes
Control
Authority
Presence
Epistemology
Norms
Facts
Subjectivity
Normative perspective
Situational perspective
Existential perspective

Study Questions

1. What are some of the advantages in using divine lordship as a central theme in a systematic theology? Do you see any disadvantages? Explain.
2. Why are some writers critical of the concept of divine lordship? Reply to them.
3. Frame says, "The main problem is that we live in a world obsessed by autonomy." Explain; evaluate.
4. Describe the role of the written treaty in the covenant. Compare the Decalogue with the general pattern of a suzerainty treaty.
5. "God rules over all things as Lord of a covenant before his covenant with Israel, even before his covenant with Adam and Eve." Give biblical evidence.
6. Show how other biblical descriptions of believers' relationship to God (friend, wife, son) are related to our covenant servanthood.
7. Present biblical evidence to show that God's control of the creation is part of the meaning of his covenant lordship. Same for his authority and his presence.
8. "*Control* and *authority* are not synonyms, but they imply each other." Explain; evaluate.
9. In what senses is God's authority absolute?
10. Show how the three lordship attributes are related to the "I AM" of Exodus 3:14.
11. "So each of the three concepts is not an independent part, but a perspective on the whole. And each concept is a perspective on the other two." Explain; evaluate.
12. Describe the three epistemological perspectives and explain how they relate to one another.

Memory Verses

Ex. 3:13–15: Then Moses said to God, "If I come to the people of Israel and say to them, 'The God of your fathers has sent me to you,' and they ask me, 'What is his name?' what shall I say to them?" God said to Moses, "I AM WHO I AM." And he said, "Say this to the people of Israel, 'I AM has sent me to you.'" God also said to Moses, "Say this to the people of Israel, 'The LORD, the God of your fathers, the God of Abraham, the God of Isaac, and the God of Jacob, has sent me to you.' This is my name forever, and thus I am to be remembered throughout all generations."

Rev. 21:3–4: And I heard a loud voice from the throne saying, "Behold, the dwelling place of God is with man. He will dwell with them, and they will be his people, and God himself will be with them as their God. He will wipe away every tear from their eyes, and death shall be no more, neither shall there be mourning, nor crying, nor pain anymore, for the former things have passed away."

Resources for Further Study

Frame, John M. *DG*. The first seven chapters present a fuller exegetical defense of my triperspectival understanding of divine lordship.

———. *DKG*. This book develops in detail my triperspectival epistemology, in contrast with non-Christian views of knowledge.

CHAPTER 3

GOD'S LORDSHIP AS A UNIQUE WORLDVIEW

TO REGARD GOD AS LORD is to see him as utterly unique. He is unique both (1) in his radical differences from anything in creation and (2) in his equally radical differences from anything else that is called a god or that is falsely worshiped as a god. These two forms of uniqueness are connected. The false gods that people worship are always created beings. The very nature of idolatry is to worship a created thing as if it were God.[1]

The Scriptures often emphasize that God is radically different from any other god (see, e.g., Deut. 32:39; Isa. 40:18–20, 25–26; 41:21–24; 43:11–13; 44:6–7; 45:5–7; 46:5–7; 48:12). In these passages, the name *Yahweh*, "Lord," often marks the uniqueness of God, how he is different from all false gods. For example:

> "I, I am the LORD,
> and besides me there is no savior.
> I declared and saved and proclaimed,
> when there was no strange god among you;
> and you are my witnesses," declares the LORD, "and I am God." (Isa. 43:11–12)

---

1. These differences dictate a unique biblical worldview. Philosophers typically distinguish between ontology (study of being, sometimes called *metaphysics*), epistemology (study of knowing), and value theory (such as ethics and aesthetics). In the previous chapter, I argued that God's lordship determines a uniquely biblical epistemology. In this chapter, I will claim that God's lordship determines a unique ontology or worldview. In *DCL* I develop the argument that God's lordship determines a unique theory of value.

The study of worldview has undergone some vicissitudes over recent decades, challenged lately by the post-modern critique of *metanarrative*. Appropriating some of this sentiment, evangelicals have sometimes argued that we should look at Scripture only as a "redemptive history," not at all as a worldview. But I am unapologetic. Scripture is not philosophical in its language, and it does focus on redemptive history. But its history begins before redemption, in the unfallen world, and that history is unintelligible apart from the unique worldview that it always presupposes. If consideration of worldview is unfashionable in our time, it will not be long before a generation of thinkers comes to recognize that we cannot do without it.

How, then, is the Lord different from other alleged supreme beings? Certainly no mere theologian can exhaustively describe his uniqueness. Everything about him is unique, so to describe his uniqueness is to describe everything that he is. His power is different from any other power, his love different from any other love. In this book I will often be contrasting his attributes and actions to those of other alleged supreme beings. But it is possible to summarize some fundamental ways in which the biblical God is unique and therefore different from the gods and absolutes of all other religions and philosophies. These summary-descriptions are general categories from which many specific kinds of uniqueness can be derived.

The Lord Is Absolute

To say that God is absolute is to say that (1) his attributes possess the highest possible degree of perfection. His power can never be surpassed or defeated (Job 23:13; Isa. 43:13). His understanding is without limit (Ps. 147:5), so that "no wisdom, no understanding, no counsel can avail against the LORD" (Prov. 21:30). His love is immeasurable (Eph. 3:19).

(2) God's attributes and actions set the standard for all other beings. God's love is the measure of our love (Eph. 5:2, 25; 1 John 3:16). His wisdom is the standard of our wisdom and rebukes our foolishness (1 Cor. 1:18–30). It is his power that exposes the vast powers of nature (Ps. 65:6–7) and man (Ps. 21:13; 1 Cor. 1:24–25) to be weak. So God's goodness is the standard of our goodness, his mercy the standard of ours. This is part of what it means for us to be the image of God.

(3) God is self-existent and self-sufficient (a se). He is not dependent on any being outside himself for his existence or sustenance. Implicitly, his attributes are also a se. His power, love, and knowledge do not depend on anyone or anything other than himself (Acts 17:25). We do not worship God in order to supply some need of his; indeed, he has no needs (Acts 17:25). Rather, we worship him because he deserves it, and because he has promised to bless those who worship him in spirit and truth (Ps. 50:8–15). For more discussion of God's aseity, see chapter 19.

The Lord Is Tripersonal

The name *Yahweh*, most obviously, is the name of a personal being, a proper name. The Lord is not an impersonal force or principle. When God reveals his name to Moses, he presents himself as One who speaks and acts. He commits himself to deliver Israel from Egypt. He promises redemption and threatens judgment. He empowers Moses and Aaron to accomplish his purposes. He is not, therefore, an impersonal force to be manipulated by human ingenuity. He has his own purposes, his own standards, his own delights and hatreds. He loves Israel and seeks the people's love and obedience. He takes his own initiatives, rather than merely responding to events.

Each of us relates to him as one person to another. Rather than taking him for granted, as we do with impersonal things and forces, we must always take his concerns into account, responding to him in repentance, love, thanksgiving, worship.

Scripture rarely if ever uses the word *person* to describe God, or even to refer to the Father, Son, and Holy Spirit as persons. But like *Trinity*, *person* is an extrabiblical word that is very nearly unavoidable for us. It is the word in our vocabulary that applies to beings who think, choose, speak, act intentionally, and so on. The biblical term *living* reinforces this picture. God is the living God, over against all the dead gods of the nations (see, e.g., Deut. 5:26; Josh. 3:10; 1 Sam. 17:26, 36; 2 Kings 19:4, 16; Pss. 42:2; 84:2; Jer. 10:10; Matt. 16:16; 26:63; Acts 14:15; Rom. 9:26). Frequently oaths in Scripture begin with "as the Lord lives" (as in Judg. 8:19; Ruth 3:13; 1 Sam. 14:45).[2]

Certainly, the God of the Bible is much greater than any finite person. That very greatness tempts us to think of him as impersonal, for we have been taught that the great natural forces governing the universe are impersonal. (But have we forgotten that God makes his angels winds and fire, Heb. 1:7?[3]) God is, to be sure, the greatest of all forces or principles. But if we ask Scripture whether in the final analysis God is personal or impersonal, the answer must surely be that he is personal. We move away from Scripture's pervasive emphasis if, with Paul Tillich, we deny that God is "a" person, but affirm only "that God is the ground of everything personal and that he carries within himself the ontological power of personality."[4] An impersonal principle could fit the terms of Tillich's formula.

Thus, we learn something very important about the biblical worldview. In Scripture, the personal is greater than the impersonal. The impersonal things and forces in this world are created and directed by a personal God. Naturalistic thought believes that all persons in the world are the product of impersonal forces, and that they can best be understood by reducing them to impersonal bits of matter and energy or, monistically, as aspects of an impersonal oneness. In these views, persons are reducible to the impersonal. In the biblical view, the impersonal reduces to the personal. Matter, energy, motion, time, and space are under the rule of a personal Lord. All the wonderful things that we find in personality—intelligence, compassion, creativity, love, justice—are not ephemeral data, doomed to be snuffed out in cosmic calamity; rather, they are aspects of what is most permanent, most ultimate. They are what the universe is really all about.

Only in biblical religion is there an absolute principle that is personal. Other religions have personal gods, but those gods are not absolute.[5] Other religions and philoso-

---

2. Paul K. Jewett points out that anthropomorphic references to God in terms of body parts should be understood as confirmations of his personal character. See *God, Creation, and Revelation* (Grand Rapids: Eerdmans, 1991), 187.

3. In one of the first philosophy courses I took at college, the professor once asked the students to judge between two hypotheses: (1) the rustling of the leaves in the tree outside is caused by wind; (2) the rustling is caused by angels. Being a logical positivist, he expected us to conclude that only the first hypothesis deserved serious consideration, for the second hypothesis was scientifically unverifiable. As a Christian, I responded differently. And since that time I have always wondered whether there were angels in that tree making the wind blow, or even rattling the leaves themselves.

4. Paul Tillich, *Systematic Theology* (Chicago: University of Chicago Press, 1951), 1:245.

5. Sometimes polytheistic religions supplement their personal (but finite) gods with an impersonal absolute, such as the Greek "fate." See Carl F. H. Henry, *Remaking the Modern Mind* (Grand Rapids: Eerdmans, 1948), 175–97.

phies (Hinduism, Aristotle, Spinoza, Hegel) seek to affirm something like an absolute principle, but those principles are impersonal.[6] Islam believes in an unknowable God who can (inconsistently) be described in personal terms. The extent to which Allah is considered personal is due to Muhammad's original respect for "the book" of Scripture and to the Arab polytheism described in the Hadith. Other sects also hold to some level of personality in God because of the influence of the Bible on their founders. But such groups as the Mormons and Jehovah's Witnesses, like the Muslims, are inconsistent, to say the least, in their confession of God's absolute personality.

A significant aspect of God's personality is that God is a *speaking* God. He is not "mute" like the idols (1 Cor. 12:2), but he addresses both himself and his creatures. And those words are, necessarily, absolute words—words with absolute truth and authority. An impersonal absolute cannot talk to us. So *the word of God* is an important topic of our theology (chapters 23–28).

And none of the other religions and philosophies confess what is most significant about the biblical God, that he is not only personal, but *tri*personal. As I will indicate in more detail later on (chapters 20–22), God is three persons in one, Father, Son, and Holy Spirit. God's triunity is necessary to our salvation. For when God saves us from sin, he sends his Son to die for us and the Spirit to apply Jesus' sacrifice to our hearts.

God's Trinitarian existence means that his attributes are not only personal, but interpersonal. His love should be defined not as a mere self-love (though self-love is entirely appropriate to his nature), but as the love of the Father for the Son, the Son's love for the Father, and so on. He did not make human beings because he was lonely and needed someone to love. He has no needs, as we saw from Acts 17:25. He is a love complete in himself. And it is this interpersonal love that serves as a model for our love. His love is exhaustively defined within himself. So we see that God's tripersonality supports his absoluteness.

The Lord Is Transcendent

In theology and philosophy, there is a common distinction between God's transcendence and immanence. Roughly, God's transcendence means that he is "up there," and his immanence means that he is "down here." The concept of transcendence builds on biblical texts that describe God as "Most High" (Gen. 14:18–22; Deut. 32:8; Pss. 7:17; 9:2) or "high and lifted up" (Isa. 6:1). It also depends on texts speaking of heaven as God's dwelling place (1 Kings 8:30–49) and as the place from which God speaks (Heb. 12:25–26).

Heaven in Scripture sometimes refers to the sky above, but often it refers to a specific place. When God revealed to Moses the plan for the Israelite tabernacle and later to Solomon the plans for the permanent temple, the builders had to follow the plan to the letter, because that plan was an image of the heavenly tabernacle (Ex. 25:40; Heb.

---

6. There is, nevertheless, a tendency in such religions and philosophies to refer to the impersonal absolute in personal terms, inconsistent though that may be, which, in the view of Carl F. H. Henry, "reflects an intuitive awareness of a personal deity." Henry, *God, Revelation and Authority* (Waco, TX: Word Books, 1982), 5:143.

8:1–7), where God himself dwells. Although God is omnipresent as we will see, he intensifies his presence in local areas, such as the burning bush of Exodus 3, the meeting with Israel at Mount Sinai (Ex. 19), the Most Holy Place in the tabernacle, and the Most Holy Place in the temple. God dwells preeminently in Jesus, the highest temple (John 1:14), and because of Jesus he dwells in believers as his temples (1 Cor. 3:16–17; 6:19; Eph. 2:21). The greatest intensity of divine presence is found in heaven. All these holy places are reflections of God's heavenly presence.

From a human viewpoint, heaven is "up there." When Jesus returned to the heavenly glory following his resurrection, he was "lifted up," and the disciples lifted their eyes (Acts 1:9–11). So we think of transcendence as the otherworldly existence of God. But when Scripture speaks of God's being "on high" or "in heaven," it does not refer mainly to God's location. The idea that God lives in a different part of the universe from man would not in itself justify the religious awe that accompanies the exaltation language.

We should, I think, see these expressions primarily as describing his royal dignity. God is "exalted" not mainly as someone living miles above the earth, but as One who is on a throne. The expressions of transcendence refer to God's rule, his kingship, his lordship (Isa. 66:1). Often this meaning is explicit in texts that use transcendence language:

> Who is like the LORD our God,
>   who is seated on high,
> who looks far down
>   on the heavens and the earth? (Ps. 113:5–6)

> To you I lift up my eyes,
>   O you who are enthroned in the heavens! (Ps. 123:1)

> But the LORD of hosts is exalted in justice,
>   and the Holy God shows himself holy in righteousness. (Isa. 5:16)

In the gospel of John, Jesus frequently says that he has come "from heaven" or "from above." This means that he has been with God from eternity (John 1:1) and he has been sent to earth to testify concerning what he has seen of God (3:13). So there is a reference to locality in these expressions. But more: coming from above also means, therefore, that his words have supreme authority (3:31–34). And when Jesus ascends again to heaven, he ascends to God's *throne*, to the "Majesty on high" (Heb. 1:3). He sits at the "right hand of Power" (Matt. 26:64), fulfilling the prophecy of Psalm 110:1–2:

> The LORD says to my Lord:
>   "Sit at my right hand,
> until I make your enemies your footstool."

The LORD sends forth from Zion
   your mighty scepter.
   Rule in the midst of your enemies!

Cf. Acts 2:33–34; 7:55–56. At God's right hand, Jesus intercedes for his people and calls on his Father to act with royal power (Rom. 8:34).

So the transcendence of God is best understood not primarily as a spatial concept, but as a reference to God's kingship. God's transcendence means that he is sovereign over his creatures. Thus, the term *transcendence* combines the terms *control* and *authority* that we considered in the previous chapter. Transcendence is God's rule, and he rules by controlling all things and by commanding his will to be done.

When philosophers and theologians speak of divine transcendence, they often interpret it to mean that God is so far from us that he can have little to do with our thought or experience.[7] On this view, we cannot know God. Indeed, God cannot reveal himself to us in clear ideas, words, and sentences. Although this view can appear to be a pious recognition of God's mystery, it actually fits best with claims to human autonomy. If God is so far from us that he cannot interact with us, cannot reveal himself, cannot speak to us, then practically speaking there is no God. We must then learn to live our lives without consulting God, that is, by our own autonomous thought.

But such ideas sharply contradict Scripture. We will see that according to Scripture God identifies himself clearly in nature, in history, and in words, spoken and written. He is mysterious, to be sure, incomprehensible. But as we will see (chapter 29), his incomprehensibility does not contradict his knowability. And if God is not knowable, he cannot save us from sin. For to have eternal life is nothing less than to know the only true God, and Jesus Christ, whom he has sent (John 17:3).

The Lord Is Immanent

If we understand God's transcendence as I have suggested, then there is no conflict between his transcendence and his immanence. Heaven, the focal point of his transcendence, is a place where he is *present*, immanent. So the images of his heavenly throne such as the ark of the covenant in the tabernacle, are places where he draws near to his people. Indeed, many texts emphasizing transcendence describe God's immanence in the same context:

> Know therefore today, and lay it to your heart, that the LORD is God in heaven above and on the earth beneath; there is no other. (Deut. 4:39)

> Behold, to the LORD your God belong heaven and the heaven of heavens, the earth with all that is in it. Yet the LORD set his heart in love on your fathers and chose their offspring after them, you above all peoples, as you are this day. (Deut. 10:14–15)

---

7. I have listed a number of these contentions in *DG*, 107–10.

For the LORD your God, he is God in the heavens above and on the earth beneath. (Josh. 2:11b)

For thus says the One who is high and lifted up,
    who inhabits eternity, whose name is Holy:
"I dwell in the high and holy place,
    and also with him who is of a contrite and lowly spirit,
to revive the spirit of the lowly,
    and to revive the heart of the contrite." (Isa. 57:15)

There is . . . one God and Father of all, who is over all and through all and in all. (Eph. 4:4–6)

Immanence can be a synonym for God's omnipresence. Like *transcendence*, then, it can designate location: everywhere, as distinct from "up there." But like *transcendence*, it is best used as a theological term. As *transcendence* refers to God's rule as the Sovereign Lord, so *immanence* refers to his *presence* in the world he has made, which we considered in the previous chapter. He not only rules over us, but is "with" us. The deepest sense in which God is present is in Jesus, God incarnate. Jesus is *Immanuel*, the name given to him in Isaiah 7:14 and Matthew 1:23. To say that God is present or with us is not merely to describe his location but to describe his saving purpose. He comes among us, not just to be among us, but to deliver us from sin and its consequences.

As with transcendence, the biblical concept of God's immanence has often been distorted by philosophers and modern theologians. There has been some tendency to deny divine immanence altogether (as in the deism of Lucretius and of some seventeenth- and eighteenth-century rationalists such as Herbert of Cherbury, John Toland, Anthony Collins, Matthew Tindal, and Thomas Paine). But abolishing God's involvement in history grants sovereignty to finite forces, deifying them. Man's intellect becomes the ultimate authority in determining truth, and natural law becomes the ultimate cause of events in nature and history. So even the deists acknowledge an immanent god, an immanent absolute, but one different from the God of Scripture. Creation itself, particularly man, becomes the immanent god.

Another alternative is pantheism, as in Xenophanes, Spinoza, Hegel, and others. In this view God is the world, taken as a whole, and the world is God. Divine immanence for such thinkers means that the world itself is divine. So the world is its own ultimate cause and the ultimate authority for thought. The immanence of God means that God has given his power and authority over to the world. Divine immanence is the autonomy of creatures. Pantheism and deism thus agree on the existence and importance of human autonomy.

Modern process theology claims to have a position distinct from both deism and pantheism, namely, *panentheism*. Pantheism says that the world is God and God is the world. Panentheism says that the world is "in" God. But of course, there are different ways in which creatures can be "in" God. Paul on Mars Hill in Athens quotes the

Greek poets Epimenides and Aratus as saying that "in him we live and move and have our being" (Acts 17:28). In his letters he often speaks of believers as being "in Christ." These expressions represent, I believe, various forms of God's presence with us and of our consequent presence to him. But in the process view, we are ourselves constituents of God's "consequent nature," and we therefore influence his nature, decisions, and actions.[8] Process theology denies transcendence in the biblical sense, and its view of immanence gives powers to creatures that Scripture ascribes to God alone.

Relations between Transcendence and Immanence

Often, philosophers and theologians have tried to achieve balance between the false concepts of transcendence and immanence that I have described. In first- and second-century Gnosticism, God is beyond all human thought and language; but nevertheless the primary worldview of Gnosticism is monistic: God and the world are one reality, related to each other on a continuum, so that the world is divine, albeit with a lower degree of divinity.[9] In Scripture, of course, there are no degrees of divinity. God is divine, the world is nondivine, and that is that. But for Gnosticism, the concept of a continuum is the only way in which a completely transcendent God can be brought into contact with the world. Obviously, this kind of thinking generates contradictions, which church fathers such as Irenaeus, despite the difficulties of their own formulations, were quick to notice.

For Immanuel Kant (1724–1804), God, the human soul, and the world (as a unified whole) are "noumenal," beyond any possible human experience, and therefore unknowable. So Kant's god is transcendent in the sense I criticized in the previous section. In the "phenomenal" world, we can gain knowledge on the basis of our experience. But the basic features of the phenomenal world—space, time, the "categories of the understanding" such as causality, unity, and plurality—are the product of the human mind, as is the moral law. In many ways, in Kant's philosophy, man replaces God as both the ultimate source and the ultimate interpreter of reality. So Kant regards God both as an unknowable transcendent and as an immanent being identical with man.

Much theology since Kant has been Kantian in its structure: in Barth, for example, God is both "wholly other" (wholly hidden) and "wholly revealed."[10] God is not revealed through the definite words and sentences of the Bible, but through ineffable divine actions that theologians struggle to interpret however they will. Barth's theological concern in all of this, stated often in his writing, is to avoid any human attempt to "possess," "control," or "manipulate" God. He wants a doctrine of transcendence that makes it impossible for human beings to control the deity in any way, so he makes God

8. See, for example, John Cobb and David Ray Griffin, *Process Theology: An Introduction* (Philadelphia: Westminster Press, 1976), 192.

9. Peter Jones, *Spirit Wars: Pagan Revival in Christian America* (Escondido, CA: Main Entry Editions, 1997), 170–71.

10. See *CVT*, 353–69; Cornelius Van Til, *Christianity and Barthianism* (Philadelphia: Presbyterian and Reformed, 1962).

wholly hidden. It would have been better if Barth had solved the problem differently: by focusing on God's sovereignty rather than his hiddenness. It is God's rule, not his hiddenness or absence from the world, that keeps us from controlling him. And what of divine immanence? Barth wants to say that God is "wholly revealed" in Christ, so that there is no secret will of God that might contradict the gospel promise. But if God is wholly revealed, then we in effect know him exhaustively and our knowledge equals his.[11] So for Barth as for other modern theologians, divine immanence deifies created beings.

Some more recent theologians identify God's transcendence with the "future." Jürgen Moltmann developed this view extensively in his *Theology of Hope*,[12] emphasizing that God is not transcendent in the sense of being "up there" in a different realm from ourselves, but is transcendent to us as the future is transcendent to the present. The future brings all our experience to us, but it is not under our control, so, Moltmann thinks, it is an appropriate category by which to describe God's own transcendence. Moltmann, however, does not hold that the future is already written in God's plan, but that the future is open, undetermined. As with Bultmann, the open future is the arena of human freedom. So as with the Gnostics, transcendence implies ineffability. But in theological futurism there is also a sense in which transcendence and immanence coincide. Indeed, there are hints in Moltmann and other futurists, influenced as they are by Hegel and process thought, that the divine nature is incomplete, that God becomes what he will be as he responds to the flow of the historical process, much of which is within the capacity of our autonomous choice. So God is transcendent as the future transcends the present, but he is immanent in that the divine future depends on us to become what it will be.

We may summarize by the following diagram the biblical and nonbiblical concepts of transcendence and immanence that we have surveyed; see fig. 3.1.

The left side of the rectangle represents the biblical views of transcendence and immanence that we have discussed. View 1 is biblical transcendence: God's rule. Included in God's rule are his lordship attributes of control and authority. View 2 is biblical immanence: God's covenant presence. The right side of the rectangle represents the unbiblical views that we have surveyed. View 3 is nonbiblical transcendence: that God is so far "above" us that we cannot know him or identify him in history. As Barth would say, he is wholly hidden or wholly other. View 4 is nonbiblical immanence: that the immanence of God is in effect the autonomy of creatures, God as wholly revealed.

The diagonal lines are lines of opposition. Views 1 and 4 are contradictory: for to say that creatures are autonomous (4) is to contradict the assertion that God is the supreme ruler of the world (1). Views 2 and 3 are also opposed, because to insist that

11. For Barth, a person cannot be said to receive revelation unless he responds correctly to that revelation, in faith. So if God is wholly revealed to someone, he must be wholly known to that person.

12. New York: Harper and Row, 1965. Moltmann cites Rudolf Bultmann as a source for his view that "Spirit may be called the power of futurity" (212).

God cannot be identified in history (3), that he is unknowable and unspeakable, contradicts the biblical teaching concerning God's presence (2).

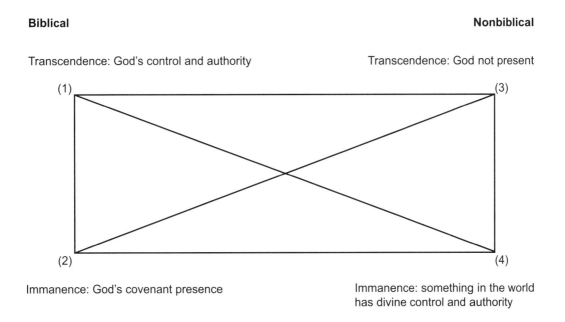

Biblical   **Nonbiblical**

Transcendence: God's control and authority   Transcendence: God not present

Immanence: God's covenant presence   Immanence: something in the world has divine control and authority

Fig. 3.1. Transcendence and Immanence: Rectangle of Opposition

The vertical lines draw our attention to the relative consistency of the two approaches. The biblical view is consistent and without tension.[13] The nonbiblical view is full of tension: for how can God be both ineffable and identical with the world, as in Gnosticism? How can he be wholly hidden and wholly revealed, as in Barth? But although this system is contradictory, we can understand how this view of transcendence *generates* this particular view of immanence, and vice versa. If God is the nameless beyond, then necessarily we are left as masters of our own destiny. For, practically speaking, he cannot rule us. We cannot take account of him in our values, our decisions, or our worldviews. Still, we cannot live without ultimate values, so we become god ourselves. The universe cannot exist without ultimate powers of causation, so it becomes its own cause. Removing God from the world enables human autonomy. And, conversely, if our goal is to be autonomous,[14] then we must either deny God's existence altogether[15]

13. This is not to deny that there is mystery. Our knowledge of God is not exhaustive. But what God reveals of himself is not contradictory.

14. Remember that Scripture teaches that autonomy is always the goal of fallen man. So it is not arbitrary to ascribe this sort of thinking ultimately to human rebellion against God.

15. Atheism is an extreme version of transcendence (3). For it asserts that God is *so* far from the real world in which we live that he should not even be counted among real beings.

or convince ourselves that he is too far beyond us to have any practical influence in our lives. So views 3 and 4 require each other in a sense, even though bringing them together creates tension and paradox.

The horizontal lines lead us to consider the similarity of the two ways of thinking at the verbal level. Both views of transcendence appeal to the biblical language of God's exaltation and height. Both views of immanence describe his involvement in all things. But beneath the verbal similarity, there are enormous conceptual differences, indeed contradictions, as we have seen, between the two systems. The verbal similarities indicate why the nonbiblical positions have attracted many Christians. But these issues are so important that we must penetrate beneath the surface similarities to recognize the antithesis between these two ways of thinking.

The God of the Bible is not a nameless, unknowable absolute removed from the course of human history. Nor is he one who gives his power and authority over to the world he has made. He dwells everywhere with us as the covenant Lord.

The important thing about the discussion of transcendence and immanence in modern theology is not[16] that theologians have differed over the *degree of emphasis* to be placed on transcendence or immanence. It is, rather, that modern theologians have adopted *views* of both transcendence and immanence that are sharply opposed to those of the Bible.

The two views of transcendence and immanence are not mere differences of opinion. The views identified above as 3 and 4 constitute the fundamental worldview of unbelief. One who rejects the God of the Bible necessarily believes the opposite of biblical theism. One cannot be neutral on this question: you are either for God or against him.

If you deny God's transcendence, his control and authority, then you must believe that ultimate control and authority are vested in the finite world—that is, that the finite world is divine. This is view 4. If you deny the presence of God in creation, then you must believe that God is absent. That is view 3.

Epistemological Parallels

Each of these two worldviews implies an epistemology. In chapter 2, I set forth the triperspectival epistemology implicit in the biblical concept of divine lordship. Non-Christian epistemology opposes this and embraces two alternatives: rationalism, irrationalism, or both. One who believes that God is absent will question the possibility of rational thought, for he will doubt whether there is any rational structure or meaning to the world at all. He will be an irrationalist. But one who believes that the finite world is divine will believe that something in the finite world, maybe the human mind itself, constitutes a supreme authority for human knowledge. He will be a rationalist. He will seek to think autonomously.

16. As Stanley Grenz and Roger Olson often seem to suppose, in their book *Twentieth-Century Theology: God and the World in a Transitional Age* (Downers Grove, IL: InterVarsity Press, 1992).

Rationalism and irrationalism are opposed to each other, but they are also parasitic on each other. Rationalism is an irrational commitment, based on a desire to avoid the demands of the true God. Irrationalism is a rationalist position because it pretends to be based on human autonomy.

Earlier, I used a rectangular diagram to show the differences between Christian and non-Christian thinking about transcendence and immanence. Now we can see how the same diagram can be interpreted epistemologically. A biblical epistemology will recognize (1) the limitations of human reason, because it must be subject to the transcendent God, and (2) the powers of human reason, because reason is a good gift of God, suited to appropriate God's revelation. Non-Christian epistemology, however, is (3) irrationalistic, denying the existence of divine revelation or of any ultimate source of knowledge outside man, and (4) rationalistic, claiming that human reason must function autonomously, without the authority of the transcendent God.

Of course, this looks different to non-Christian thinkers. For them, it is the Christians who are rationalists and irrationalists. In their eyes, view 1 is irrationalistic because it requires our reason to be subordinate to God, a sacrifice of the intellect intolerable to autonomous thought. And for them, view 2 is rationalistic because it claims that we can know truth with certainty. See fig. 3.2.

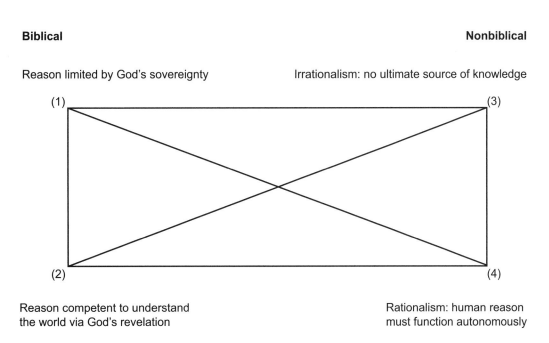

Biblical   **Nonbiblical**

Reason limited by God's sovereignty   Irrationalism: no ultimate source of knowledge

(1)   (3)

(2)   (4)

Reason competent to understand   Rationalism: human reason
the world via God's revelation   must function autonomously

Fig. 3.2. Rationalism and Irrationalism: Rectangle of Opposition

Cornelius Van Til pointed out that the rationalist-irrationalist tension began in the garden of Eden. Eve would not take God's Word as her ultimate authority; she looked at

God's speech, Satan's, and her own, as if the three were equal. But that is to imply that there is no final truth about anything: irrationalism. Nevertheless, required to choose, Eve claimed the right to decide for herself, over against God: autonomous rationalism.

We will explore further (especially in chapters 29–32) the epistemological implications of biblical theism. My present point is that the non-Christian views of transcendence and immanence—the non-Christian metaphysics—imply a non-Christian epistemology as well.

But even more fundamentally, the difference is religious. We must choose whether to recognize God as Lord or not. Those who do not recognize him exchange the truth for a lie (Rom. 1:25), and they lose the basis for finding truth. Although they know many things, they gain knowledge only by borrowing principles from Christian theism.

So we are not talking here about mere differences of opinion, but about spiritual warfare. It is these two opposite worldviews that contend today for the hearts of all people.

The Lord Is Creator

We have seen that as the Lord, God is absolute, tripersonal, transcendent, and immanent. Taken in biblical senses, these are unique characteristics, both in the sense that God is different from anything else in creation and in the sense that the doctrine of God in Scripture is different from any other worldview or philosophy.

Another way to speak of the Lord's uniqueness is by invoking the Creator-creature distinction. Creation is a unique act of God, by which, as we will see later, he brings being out of nothing and arranges everything on earth according to his will. In Genesis 1, God calls light to appear out of darkness, when light was still nonexistent (v. 3). He is the God who "calls into existence the things that do not exist" (Rom. 4:17). Nobody else can do this. And so in Scripture there is a sharp distinction between Creator and creature, between the One who makes all things and the beings that he makes. Cornelius Van Til believed that the Creator-creature distinction distinguished the Christian worldview from all others. In his classroom, he frequently drew on the board two circles; see fig. 3.3.

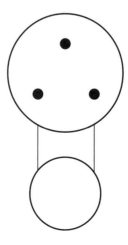

Fig. 3.3. Creator-Creature Distinction

The upper circle represented God, the lower circle creation. Often Van Til would put three dots in the upper circle to represent the Trinity and two lines between the two circles to indicate lines of communication. The lines did not, however, represent anything existing *between* Creator and creature. Everything is either Creator or creature. There is no third realm of being.

Van Til understood this to be a diagram of the Christian worldview. There are two levels of being: God and the world. The two are distinct. God can never become the world, for he can never lose his status as the world's Creator. The world can never become God, because it can never undo the fact that it is created. And there is no third category.

But what of Jesus, who is both God and man? Even in him, Van Til contended, deity and humanity are not confused. For, as the Council of Chalcedon (A.D. 451) taught, even in Jesus the divine and human natures were not confused or changed into each other. Nor are they separated or divided. In Jesus, divinity and humanity are as intimately close together as they can possibly be. But even in him, the two are distinct.[17]

In the doctrine of creation, therefore, we can see both God's transcendence and his immanence in the biblical senses noted earlier. He is transcendent to his creation, for he is always distinct from the world. But he is immanent, for there is nothing standing between himself and the world. There is always an intimate connection (which we call divine omnipresence), but never a confusion between the two. One never changes into the other.

Van Til believed that all non-Christian thought could be summarized in a one-circle diagram; see fig. 3.4.

Fig. 3.4. The One-Circle Position

That is, in non-Christian thought, God and the world are on the same level, made of the same stuff, meaning, of course, that there is no God at all in the biblical sense. Essentially, they are the same reality, viewed from different perspectives. This diagram is obviously useful for illustrating pantheistic thought. But deism, too, restricts God's sovereign power over the world and excludes him from the course of history. All non-Christian thought gives autonomy to creatures in some measure.[18] It denies that an absolute, tripersonal God has the authority to govern human thought and life.

---

17. See further in chapter 37.

18. In speaking of "non-Christian thought," Van Til understood that religions and philosophies influenced by the Bible, such as Judaism and Islam, maintained some characteristics of a biblical worldview. But insofar as they departed from Scripture, they denied God's sovereignty as the Creator.

The two-circle diagram is a way to illustrate the biblical and unbiblical doctrines of transcendence and immanence that we considered earlier. That the two circles are distinct and irreducible indicates God's transcendence. That there is no third category means that there is nothing separating the creation from God, so that he is necessarily present to everything and everyone that he has made. The one-circle diagram indicates the unbiblical doctrines of transcendence and immanence. Here, immanence can mean only identity, and transcendence can mean only something unintelligible, a being beyond being itself.

Conclusion

To summarize: We have seen that the biblical worldview is radically different from all other worldviews, whether religious or secular. The Bible teaches (1) that this world is created and governed by an absolute person, in fact an absolute tripersonality; (2) that this God is both transcendent and immanent in his relationship to the world—his transcendence is his covenant control and authority, and his immanence is his covenant presence; (3) that divine revelation provides and limits human access to the knowledge of God and his world; and (4) that Creator and creature are radically distinct from one another, but that the Creator is always close to his creation.

Key Terms

Worldview
Absolute
Personal
Tripersonal
Self-existent
Self-sufficient
A se
Impersonal
Living God
Monism
Transcendence (biblical)
Immanence (biblical)
Heaven
Transcendence (nonbiblical)
Immanence (nonbiblical)
Pantheism
Panentheism
Process theology
Noumenal
Phenomenal
Wholly hidden
Wholly revealed

Rationalism

Irrationalism

Creator-creature distinction

Study Questions

1. "God's attributes and actions set the standard for all other beings." Explain; evaluate.

2. "In Scripture, the personal is greater than the impersonal." How? Explain.

3. "Only in biblical religion is there an absolute principle that is personal." Explain; evaluate.

4. "So the transcendence of God is best understood not primarily as a spatial concept, but as a reference to God's kingship." Is this true? Give biblical evidence.

5. Compare the biblical view of God's transcendence and immanence to that of Immanuel Kant; with that of Karl Barth; with that of Jürgen Moltmann.

6. Draw Frame's rectangular diagram and explain each line and corner, interpreting it first metaphysically, then epistemologically.

7. "So we are not talking here about mere differences of opinion, but about spiritual warfare." How do the differences between Christian and non-Christian views of metaphysics and epistemology constitute spiritual warfare?

8. How does the Creator-creature distinction show the uniqueness of the biblical worldview? Does Christ's incarnation compromise that distinction? Why or why not?

9. "Divine revelation provides and limits human access to the knowledge of God and his world." Explain; evaluate.

Memory Verses

Isa. 5:16: "But the Lord of hosts is exalted in justice,
    and the Holy God shows himself holy in righteousness."

Isa. 43:11–12: "I, I am the Lord,
    and besides me there is no savior.
I declared and saved and proclaimed,
    when there was no strange god among you;
    and you are my witnesses," declares the Lord, "and I am God."

Isa. 57:15: For thus says the One who is high and lifted up,
    who inhabits eternity, whose name is Holy:
"I dwell in the high and holy place,
    and also with him who is of a contrite and lowly spirit,
to revive the spirit of the lowly,
    and to revive the heart of the contrite."

Resources for Further Study

Frame, John M. *DG*, 103–15. This is my most elaborate discussion of divine transcendence and immanence. I should warn you that in the original printing the diagram on page 113 is misnumbered.

Jones, Peter R. *One or Two: Seeing a World of Difference.* Escondido, CA: Main Entry Editions, 2010. An excellent recent popular attempt to defend the biblical Creator-creature distinction against the monism of modern neopaganism.

Van Til, Cornelius. *The Defense of the Faith*, edited by K. Scott Oliphint. Phillipsburg, NJ: P&R Publishing, 2008. The early pages excellently set forth the nature of the Christian faith as a worldview.

PART 2

THE BIBLICAL STORY

BEFORE WE BEGIN our detailed study of the theology of Scripture, we should make a preliminary sweep over its landscape, to get the broader context of Scripture's specific teachings. Scripture is often described as a *story* or *narrative*, and it will be helpful for us to understand at this point what the story is about—its beginning, ending, and middle. In chapter 1, I described this kind of narrative analysis as *biblical theology* as opposed to other kinds of theology such as *systematic theology*. This book is primarily a systematic theology, but there is no reason why its systematic discussion should not be prefaced by a biblical theological treatment. Indeed, the division between the two disciplines is somewhat artificial. There is no reason why a systematic theology should not explore traditional biblical theological concepts such as covenant, kingdom, and genealogy-family. Nor, for that matter, is there any reason why a biblical theologian should not explore the attributes of God or the hypostatic union of Jesus' two natures, since the narrative presupposes a system of truth including these concepts.

So in the next three chapters I will be describing the biblical story, first as a history of divine-human covenants, second as a narrative of the advancement of God's kingdom, and finally as a genealogy of the family of God.

CHAPTER 4

THE LORD'S COVENANTS

IN SYSTEMATIC THEOLOGY, or any other kind of theology, context is vitally important. Systematic theology, in a study of some topic (such as Jesus' humanity, or the believer's adoption), might gather together the teaching of many Bible passages, scattered through all parts of Scripture: one text from Deuteronomy, one from 2 Kings, one from Psalm 34, one from Ephesians. This procedure is sometimes called *proof-texting*, and it is often criticized for its failure to take the contexts of the passages adequately into account. I think proof-texting, taken in itself, is a perfectly legitimate procedure. The Westminster Assembly developed proof texts for its confession and catechisms. Their purpose was to give to their readers some idea of where in the Bible their formulations came from. That is perfectly right. Anyone who seeks to validate a theological idea must be willing to show where his idea comes from in Scripture. Of course, there is always the danger that a theologian will misuse a text when he makes it a proof text. But that danger is vitiated when the writer is able to analyze the texts he appeals to, rather than merely cite them. So systematic theologians, and occasionally confessional documents, do present exegesis of many of their proof texts, seeking to set forth their meaning in their contexts.

Note that I said *contexts*, not *context*. Each particular verse of Scripture has many contexts: the verses on either side, the book it is part of, the section of Scripture in which it is found, other passages dealing with the same topic, other books by the same author, other books (even extrabiblical books) of the same genre, other writings that come from the same setting. In the end, however, the most important context of any verse is the Bible as a whole. Every theologian writes out of a general perspective, an idea of the purpose and thrust of the Scripture as a whole. So in this part of the book, I will try to indicate the type of Book that Scripture is, and its overall message.

Genres of Biblical Literature

As a whole, the Bible is not an example of any *genre* of literature. It is *sui generis*. It does contain literature that is like literature outside the Bible: hymns, wisdom, narratives, letters, apocalyptic. But no other book includes all of these in one volume, written over many centuries, understood to be the Word of God. And the portions of Scripture that fall into various genres are unique within those genres.

The narratives have the purpose not merely of recording facts or interpreting events, but of telling what the unique, true God has done. And these stories are also unique in that they are situated in real calendar time and geographic places. There are, to be sure, other stories from the ancient world of gods' interacting with human beings. These are myths, stories without date and time that make no historical claim but try to convey a moral lesson. But the biblical narratives present the actions of one absolute personal being who acts in real times and places, just as historical as Nebuchadnezzar and Augustus Caesar. They are not myth.[1]

But they are not merely history either, as we usually think of it. Their purpose is not merely to describe and interpret world events. Rather, they tell us what God has done. And they tell us this not from a merely human point of view, but from God's own point of view. And they tell us these events not only because of their world-historical importance, but for the sake of our salvation, to restore our own fellowship with God.

No other religion contains narrative like this, unless (such as Judaism, Islam, and some others) it is deeply influenced by the Bible. Religions such as Buddhism, Hinduism, and Taoism do not depend on historical events. There are stories about the Buddha, especially about his enlightenment. But for a Buddhist, these stories are not the heart of his religion. For him, the heart of Buddhism is a series of eternal truths (e.g., life is suffering) that would be true even if the Buddha had never lived. But Christianity depends on historical events: God's dealings with Israel, the incarnation of Christ, his atonement, resurrection, and ascension. If Jesus is not risen from the dead, says Paul, our faith is "futile" (1 Cor. 15:17).

So even though Scripture contains narrative that is in some ways like extrabiblical narrative, it is a unique narrative. We may not interpret it merely by applying the rules we use for other examples of the narrative genre.

The same is true for other genres of literature in Scripture. The Psalms are songs, but unique songs, songs that narrate God's history, songs that express praise, lament, joy, peace, in our relationship with God. Biblical wisdom literature is like extrabiblical wisdom literature, but it calls us to trust in God and not in our own understanding (Prov. 3:5–6). Psalms and wisdom are indeed words of the true God, to be integrated into our hearts and lives. The letters of the apostles, too, are not like other letters. They, too, are the very Word of God (1 Cor. 14:37–38).

The fact that Scripture is the Word of the only true God, a fact that we will dwell on at a later point (chapters 23–28), sets it apart from all other books, even books considered holy by other religions. The uniqueness of God dictates the uniqueness of

---

1. There are in Scripture, to be sure, narratives that are not situated in specific times and places, such as Jesus' parables. The purpose of a parable is not to tell what really happened, but to set forth a scenario for purposes of moral and spiritual instruction. But we should heed Peter, who affirms in 2 Peter 1:16 that in the apostolic testimony about Jesus, "we did not follow cleverly devised myths."

Scripture. This fact defines Scripture as a unique genre, and all parts of it as unique within their genres. We can learn some things about how to interpret Scripture from interpreting other literature. But interpreting Scripture will never be entirely like interpreting anything else.

Narrative and Worldview

And Scripture is not only a set of unique literary genres. It also sets forth a unique message. That message includes a historical narrative, as we have seen, set amid songs, wisdom, prophecy, letters, and apocalyptic. But it also includes a general view of the world, a general ontology presupposed in all its other contents. That view, as we saw in chapters 2–3, presents God as Lord of all creation, controlling all things, exercising ultimate authority, and dwelling with his creation. He is absolute, tripersonal, transcendent, immanent, Creator. This worldview is the setting for the story, and the story makes no sense if readers try to place it within a different worldview.

Many writers today hold to views of transcendence and immanence, for example, that contradict the views of Scripture. As we saw in chapter 3, this unbiblical ontology has epistemological implications: the unbiblical form of transcendence leads to epistemological irrationalism, and the unbiblical form of immanence leads to rationalism. But it is plain in the biblical narrative that, contrary to irrationalism, God and his truth can be known, for he has revealed himself clearly to us (Rom. 1:19–20). And contrary to rationalism, autonomous reasoning is foolishness (Prov. 3:5–8; 1 Cor. 1:20–30). If we approach the Bible with an autonomous epistemology, we will not be able to make sense of it. Rationalism will twist it into something that satisfies the ego of human beings. Irrationalism will remove its challenge to our sinful hearts.

Since the mid-1600s, many biblical scholars, theologians, and philosophers have tried to force the Bible into a mold that can be accommodated to autonomous reasoning. Typically, that has led to a denial of miracles and the supernatural.[2] One who reasons autonomously cannot accept the supernatural; but one who accepts God as Lord over his creation cannot argue against it, for if this world is God's, he can do whatever he wants with it and in it. In fact, the Bible is supernatural through and through: not only in its miracle stories, but in everything it says about God's acts in history for our salvation. God's deliverance of Israel from Egypt was a supernatural act, as were the incarnation, atonement, resurrection, and ascension of Jesus.

It is not possible to expound the narrative of redemptive history as it really happened, without the worldview that history presupposes. But once we have embraced that worldview, we see the redemptive story as credible, though still wonderful. And

---

2. By "supernatural" events here I am referring to acts of God in the natural world and in human history. I do not define supernatural or miraculous events as "exceptions to natural law," as has often been done both in Christian and in non-Christian thought. See my discussion of miracle in chapters 7 and 8.

when we see the redemptive story for what it is, we can see that it could happen only in a world where God is Lord.[3]

Now, I think the biblical story can be usefully expounded in three perspectives: the Lord's covenants (normative), the kingdom of God (situational), and the family of God (existential); see fig. 4.1.

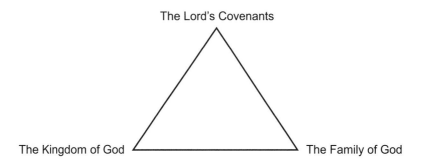

Fig. 4.1. Three Central Biblical Themes

In this chapter, we will consider the normative perspective: the biblical story as a succession of covenants between God and his creatures. Under this perspective, the biblical story is a story of God's making covenants and the outworking of those covenants in history.

In this chapter, I will summarize the history of these covenants, focusing particularly on three themes: (1) the relationship in these covenants between God's sovereignty and our obedience, (2) the individualism and universality of the covenants, and (3) the triad of divine word (normative), land (situational), and seed (existential).[4] See fig. 4.2.

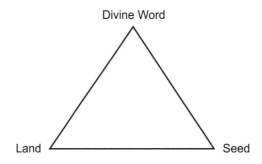

Fig. 4.2. The Eternal Covenant of Redemption

3. I resist, therefore, the movement that would confine theological discussion to "redemptive history" and leave worldview aside. Certainly Scripture is more like a history than like a philosophical metaphysics. But the metaphysics, ontology, or worldview is the setting in which the history takes place, and it is essential to rightly understanding the history.

4. This triad corresponds somewhat to the covenant-kingdom-family triad.

The Eternal Covenant of Redemption

The events of the biblical story do not begin in history, or even with God's first act of creation in Genesis 1:1. Other passages tell us things that happened before[5] that creative act. So the story of Scripture begins with God existing in the eternal, glorious fellowship of the Holy Trinity (John 17:5).

I will later discuss the actions that God performs in eternity, what we call his *eternal decrees* (chapter 11). Every event in history is something that God has planned, and the planning goes back to eternity. For now I am particularly interested in one particular decree, the agreement between the Father and the Son, often called the *covenant*[6] *of redemption*, or in Latin the *pactum salutis*. In this covenant, before the world was even made, God the Father gave a people to his Son, chosen "in him before the foundation of the world" (Eph. 1:4). It was then that "he predestined us for adoption as sons through Jesus Christ, according to the purpose of his will" (v. 5; cf. John 10:29; 17:6).

The Holy Spirit is also a party to this agreement, for the Father and the Son (John 15:26; Rom. 1:4) agreed to send the Spirit into the world to bear witness of Christ, to teach people about him (John 14:26), and to declare to them things to come (John 16:13). The Spirit will be the Author of regeneration (John 3:5; Rom. 2:29), who sets God's people free from sin (Rom. 8:2). (See chapters 39–45.) All the Spirit does for God's people was planned before the foundation of the world.

The Bible, then, is the story of how God seeks these people (John 4:23), to make them his Son's prized possession. Mysteriously, God's story also includes the fall of man into sin. So God's work to bring his people to his Son is a redemption, a reconciliation between sinners and himself. From eternity, God reaches into time to redeem them, even after they have rebelled against him and lost all claim to his eternal blessings (see Rom. 5:8). In this way, God glorifies his lordship in our salvation.

Now I will expand the three themes that I distinguished earlier in this chapter as pertaining to all the covenants, as they apply to the *pactum salutis*:

1. *Sovereignty and Obedience*: As a covenant, the *pactum* is verbal, a word of God, a communication between the members of the Trinity that they all affirm. The Son and Spirit willingly accept their servant role. So even though their activity is eternally

---

5. Since, as I believe, time itself is a created thing, then, strictly speaking, there were no temporal categories "before" the creation: no before, no after, no simultaneity. But the expression *before creation* has often served theologians (and biblical writers, too, as John 17:5) in their attempts to locate the eternal life of God. We should remember, though, that God's eternal intra-Trinitarian life continues after creation, throughout creation, and into eternity future. It might be more precise (though still figurative) to say that God's eternal actions take place *above* time, rather than before, during, or after it. See chapter 17 for further discussion of these matters.

6. The term *covenant* usually refers to an agreement between a superior and an inferior, between a lord and a servant. Hence documents of covenant agreement are often called *suzerainty treaties*. But there are also *parity covenants*, covenants between equals, as between Laban and Jacob in Genesis 31:44. In the eternal fellowship of the Trinity, the Father and the Son are equals, and in that sense the *pactum salutis* is a parity covenant. But we should remember that part of the content of this covenant is that the Son accepts the role of a servant. So there is here something analogous to the lord-servant covenants that predominate in Scripture. Indeed, the lord-servant relation of the *pactum* is the eternal model for the suzerainty covenants that God makes in history. Jesus is the Servant of the Lord prophesied in Isaiah 52:13 and elsewhere.

determined, they receive their mandate in faithful obedience. God's blessings on his elect therefore come both through the sovereign determination of the Father and through the faithful obedience of the Son and the Spirit. In this covenant there is no discrepancy between these. We will see that the harmony between the Lord's actions and the servant's obedience is a regular feature of the divine covenants.

2. *Individual and Universal*: The *pactum salutis* focuses, of course, on God's elect people, those who are finally saved. In that sense its object is particular, not universal. But Scripture often indicates that salvation has a cosmic dimension. When man falls, he brings the rest of creation down with him (Gen. 3:17–19). Creation will not be delivered from this curse until the consummation of redemption, so it longs and groans for that day (Rom. 8:18–22). Through Jesus, God reconciles all things to himself (Col. 1:19–20) and makes "all things new" (Rev. 21:5). So the *pactum* has a universal meaning.

3. *Blessing, Seed, and Land*: Because that universality includes blessings for the earth as well as its inhabitants, we can find in the *pactum* three elements that we will note in all the covenants: (a) divine blessing (normative), (b) land (cosmic reconciliation) (situational), and (c) seed (the people given by the Father to the Son) (existential).

The Universal Covenant

That universal perspective persists when we move from eternity into time, when we consider God's covenant with the created world.

God is Lord, the King[7] over all the earth. Usually when God is called *King* in the Psalms, his covenant with Israel is in view, which we will consider later (Pss. 18:50; 29:10–11; 44:4; 48:2). But God's kingship is not limited to Israel. He is able to deliver Israel from all her enemies because he rules all the earth (Ps. 47:2, 7). The psalmist recognizes God as "my King," and he calls God to remember his covenant with Israel; but God can answer this prayer because his lordship is not only over Israel, but over all creation, even over all of Israel's enemies.

> Yet God my King is from of old,
>   working salvation in the midst of the earth.
> You divided the sea by your might;
>   you broke the heads of the sea monsters on the waters.
> You crushed the heads of Leviathan;
>   you gave him as food for the creatures of the wilderness.
> You split open springs and brooks;
>   you dried up ever-flowing streams.
> Yours is the day, yours also the night;
>   you have established the heavenly lights and the sun.
> You have fixed all the boundaries of the earth;

7. In this book, I will generally use *lordship* and *kingship* synonymously, though there are differences of nuance. *Lord* focuses on a covenant relationship, *king* on rule within that relationship. But rule is an aspect of covenant, and kingship (when legitimate) arises out of a covenant relationship. So chapter 5 will emphasize the vocabulary of kingship.

you have made summer and winter.

Remember this, O Lord, how the enemy scoffs,
    and a foolish people reviles your name.
Do not deliver the soul of your dove to the wild beasts;
    do not forget the life of your poor forever.

Have regard for the covenant,
    for the dark places of the land are full of the habitations of violence.
Let not the downtrodden turn back in shame;
    let the poor and needy praise your name. (Ps. 74:12–21)

For the Lord is a great God,
    and a great King above all gods.
In his hand are the depths of the earth;
    the heights of the mountains are his also.
The sea is his, for he made it,
    and his hands formed the dry land. (Ps. 95:3–5)

So he says through Isaiah:

Thus says the Lord:
    "Heaven is my throne,
    and the earth is my footstool;
what is the house that you would build for me,
    and what is the place of my rest?" (Isa. 66:1)

Through Isaiah, God mentions two levels of his kingship: his rule from heaven over the whole earth, and his rule over Israel, centered in the temple. The second depends on the first and is limited by the first. The people of Israel should not presume that God is their God only, or that he will always be on their side regardless of their behavior.

Anything God creates is necessarily under his lordship: under his control, subject to his authority, confronted by his presence. So his covenant lordship does not begin with the creation of man. In the creation account, from the first of the six days of Genesis 1, God controls everything as he makes the world. Creation is not a battle between God and some other deity or force. There is no struggle in Genesis 1, as there is in the creation accounts of other nations. In Genesis 1:3, God simply commands, and the light appears.

These commands indicate not only God's control, but also his authority. He speaks, and even the inanimate creation must obey his powerful word. Here, we cannot draw a line between control and authority. God controls by speaking authoritatively, and we can see the authority of his words in that everything obeys him.

Control, authority, and also, of course, presence. During the whole creation process, God is there, with the things he has made. Underscoring that presence is the reference in Genesis 1:2 to the Holy Spirit "hovering over the face of the waters."

So God is the Lord, the King, over all the earth, before man comes on the scene. The created world is his servant. And of course, when you have a lord and a servant, you have a covenant.[8] When Adam is created, he automatically comes under the jurisdiction of this covenant, for he, too, is a creature of God. Before God even speaks to him in Genesis 1:28, God has surrounded him with testimonies to his sovereignty and his requirements. So the universal covenant has a moral content, and we may assume that there are blessings for obedience to God's statutes and curses for disobedience.

So, recalling the three themes mentioned earlier: (1) God is fully sovereign over all things within the creation, but he blesses obedience and punishes disobedience. (2) The covenant is universal, but binds all individuals. (3) The covenant gives to living beings possession of the land, to fill it with their descendants, a divine blessing to all (Ps. 104).

When God through Isaiah indicts people of the whole earth because they have "transgressed the laws, violated the statutes, broken the everlasting covenant" (Isa. 24:5), he may be referring to the Edenic covenant, which I describe below, or to the universal covenant. I'm inclined to favor the latter, though the references in context of the curses on the earth as well as mankind could fit either covenant. The covenant-breakers here include the "host of heaven" according to verse 21, which, in contrast to the "kings of the earth," probably refers to the rebellious angels. The angels would not be included under the Edenic covenant, but they would be part of the universal covenant. Actually, however, it doesn't matter much what covenant Isaiah 24:5 specifically refers to, since the Edenic covenant and all later covenants are applications of the universal covenant to the human race.

Compare also Jeremiah 31:35–37 and 33:20, 25, where *berith* applies to "God's ordering of the world of nature as described in Gen. 1."[9] Kline also refers to the term *hesed*, God's covenant faithfulness, used not only in references to God's covenants with human beings, but also in relation to his care for the natural world (Pss. 33:5; 36:5, 10; 119:64).

The Edenic Covenant

God's relationship to human beings is different in many ways from his relationships to other creatures, but it is nevertheless covenantal in character. God is Lord, and human beings are his subjects.

---

8. I am not discussing God's covenant lordship over angelic and demonic beings, simply because Scripture tells us very little about it. Scripture affirms often that there are such beings, and they play a surprisingly large role in the spiritual warfare that accompanies redemptive history. See Eph. 6:10–20. Satan and his "angels" (Matt. 25:41) are beings who rebelled against God and were cast out of heaven, eventually to end in the "lake of fire" (Rev. 20:10). I know of no specific reference to a covenant made between God and these supernatural beings. But clearly the angels were under obligation to honor God as Lord. Some fulfilled that obligation and were blessed; others did not and were cursed. Certainly God's relationship with the angels indicates his control and authority over them and his presence to bless and curse. Angels are, at the very least, subjects of God's universal covenant. For a few reflections on the value of this biblical teaching for our lives, see *DCL*, 253–56, and chapter 33 of the present volume.

9. Meredith G. Kline, *Kingdom Prologue* (Eugene, OR: Wipf and Stock, 2006), 14.

I believe that the existence of a covenant specifically between God and man is implicit in Genesis 1–2, though there is no record of God's formally announcing it as in other covenants. God made Adam and Eve on the last of the six days of creation as the consummation of his creative work. In the narrative, God, in a remarkable conference with the heavenly host, makes a special announcement of this particular creative act (Gen. 1:26), and he makes human beings in his very image (v. 27), distinguishing them from all other created beings. In verse 28 he gives them distinct responsibilities, often called the *cultural mandate*, empowering them by his blessing:

> And God blessed them. And God said to them, "Be fruitful and multiply and fill the earth and subdue it and have dominion over the fish of the sea and over the birds of the heavens and over every living thing that moves on the earth."

So God as Lord defines the role of human beings as God's vassal kings over the world he has made.

Note here the triad I mentioned earlier: in this verse, there is a statement of divine *blessing*, a gift of *land* (the whole earth) to be filled with human *seed*.

This fundamental mandate pushes the human family beyond the boundaries of the garden, to the whole world. So the worldwide perspective of God's eternal covenant of redemption and of his universal covenant enters the covenants of human history. The Edenic covenant also, however, requires Adam to carry out some duties at home. He must "work" and "keep" the garden (Gen. 2:15), which is his home as well as God's holy dwelling. Further, Adam is responsible to keep God's *creation ordinances* (labor, 1:28; 2:15; marriage, 2:23–25; Sabbath, 2:1–3; Ex. 20:11)—ordinances that define human ethics for all history.[10]

So the covenant is individual (with Adam and Eve in their home) and universal (extending to the whole world).

Finally, the covenant contains one specific command:

> And the LORD God commanded the man, saying, "You may surely eat of every tree of the garden, but of the tree of the knowledge of good and evil you shall not eat, for in the day that you eat of it you shall surely die." (Gen. 2:16–17)

Here is a special test of Adam's covenant faithfulness, one that Adam failed. Theologians have asked what would have happened if Adam had kept this special commandment, rather than disobeying it. Typically covenants issue in blessings for obedience as well as curses for disobedience. The curses for Adam's disobedience are quite explicit in Scripture, as we will see. But strangely, this text does not explicitly mention any blessing for obedience.

But of course, merely to avoid the curse is a blessing. At minimum, the blessing is life, since death is the curse. And in the context there are some suggestions that this life-blessing

---

10. For more discussion of the creation ordinances, see *DCL*, 202–3.

is not just a continuation of Adam's present life, but something higher, a kind of consummate state. Genesis 3:22 implies that at some point an obedient Adam might have been invited to eat the fruit of the Tree of Life (2:9) and thereby live forever. The Sabbath ordinance (Gen. 2:3; Ex. 20:11) might also have introduced a forward-looking emphasis into human labor, suggesting that our work would lead into a consummation state that would relate to our present life as rest relates to work. The text, however, is not clear or explicit about these blessings, and we do well to avoid speculation. Even if we take the hints that God offers a consummation blessing to Adam, we should not assume that this blessing will come through Adam's obedience to the specific command of Genesis 2:17, rather than from his general obedience to all of God's commands.[11] It does not even say in any clear way that the prohibition is for a limited time, or, if it is, for how long it will be in effect.

Some theologians have thought that the covenant blessing is even more detailed than a general promise of life. They refer to a life in confirmed righteousness, a life in which Adam is no longer able to sin. But the text does not say this. The idea of a blessing of confirmed righteousness comes not from Genesis 1–2, but from the blessings associated with redemption: life in the new heavens and new earth. But the history of Genesis 1–3 is distinct from the history of redemption. Although the Edenic covenant is parallel in some ways to the later redemptive covenants, it represents an earlier stage in God's dealings with human beings, a stage in which we should be careful to respect God's limitations on our knowledge. It is wise to be content with what is obvious: if Adam had obeyed this command, he would have been able to continue on as God's covenant servant, enjoying whatever rewards God chose to give, if only the continuing favor of his Father. There is, after all, no greater reward than God's continuing favor, given in the form he thinks best for us.

Many theologians have described the covenant in Eden as the *covenant of works*. This phrase is found in WCF 7.2, which reads:

> The first covenant made with man was a covenant of works, wherein life was promised to Adam; and in him to his posterity, upon condition of perfect and personal obedience.

WLC 20 (cf. WSC 12) speaks of God's

> entering into a covenant of life with [Adam], upon condition of personal, perfect, and perpetual obedience.

In the WLC, we find *covenant of life* rather than *covenant of works*. These titles, however, are essentially the same, the former emphasizing the covenant blessing, the latter the means of attaining it. Earlier Reformed statements such as the Belgic, French, and Second Helvetic Confessions and the HC do not use the language of covenant but make clear that Adam disobeyed God's commandment and thereby lost God's blessing. In chapter 14 of the Belgic Confession, we read:

11. The Sabbath ordinance pertains to all of man's work, not only to his obedience to the command of Genesis 2:17.

> For the commandment of life, which [Adam] had received, he transgressed; and by sin separated himself from God, who was his true life; having corrupted his whole nature; whereby he made himself liable to corporal and spiritual death.

I don't think there is much difference between the actual teaching of the WCF and the Belgic Confession. The advantage of using the covenant terminology as in the WCF is to reiterate what we have been emphasizing, that all of God's relations with creatures are covenantal.

The disadvantage of the phrase *covenant of works* is that it has led to a controversy over the nature of the covenant agreement between God and Adam. Two problems especially have entered the discussion: (1) The terminology is reminiscent of a commercial exchange. This suggests that eternal life is a kind of commodity, and that if Adam pays the price, "perfect obedience," "works," or "merit," God will turn that commodity over to Adam and his posterity. (2) The works are Adam's works, not God's, so one gets the impression that Adam is left entirely on his own. These two contentions are used to maintain a clear contrast between *works* and *grace*.[12]

Certainly the focus of the Edenic covenant is on what Adam does rather than on God's action as the ground of Adam's blessing or curse. And certainly whatever blessing Adam received would have been appropriate to his obedience: he would have *deserved* the blessing. But it would be wrong to claim as in issue 2 above that had Adam successfully resisted temptation, God would have had nothing to do with it. It was God who created Adam and all his surroundings. God made him in his image and made him his vassal king over the earth. God gave him abundant food and drink, a wife, and above all fellowship with himself. And indeed Adam's decision was foreordained by God, as we will see. As for issue 1, Adam did not earn any of these things by his works. These were gifts of God's unmerited favor. So if Adam had passed his test successfully, he would not have boasted as if he had done it all on his own. He would have praised God for his unmerited favor. The term *covenant of works*, therefore, may mislead us by suggesting that Adam possessed an autonomy that no other creature has ever possessed. Best to regard this covenant, like the others, as a sovereign blessing of God, calling Adam and Eve to respond in obedient faith.

There is, however, nothing wrong with what the Westminster Standards actually say about the covenant of works. So we say nothing wrong when we use the phrase as did the Westminster divines. But when we choose extrabiblical language to describe biblical truths, we should take into account the impressions that this language would be likely to make on contemporary readers. And indeed there are some problems of possible misunderstandings and misuses of this language, such as issues 1 and 2 above. I do not, therefore, object to the phrase *covenant of works* as long as the use of that

---

12. *Grace* in Protestant theology usually refers to unmerited divine favor where wrath is deserved. On that definition, grace presupposes sin, and there can be no grace before the fall. But there is no reason to deny that God showed unmerited favor (apart from deserved wrath) before the fall, before God's wrath came into play. Some, speaking somewhat loosely in my judgment, define grace as unmerited divine favor without reference to deserved wrath. On that looser definition, God did give grace before the fall. For Adam did not merit or deserve his creation, his surroundings, his vassal kingship, or his fellowship with God. Those were God's gifts to him.

phrase is kept within the limits of the Westminster definitions, but I prefer to refer to the covenant under discussion as the *Edenic covenant.*

But Genesis 3 tells the tragic story of how Adam and Eve, tempted by Satan, violated this command, bringing a curse on themselves and on the earth itself (Gen. 3:1–19; Rom. 8:19–23). God expels the guilty couple from Eden, and from this point their labor becomes toilsome and their childbearing painful.

Does the Edenic covenant continue today? Since Adam and Eve are expelled from the garden, human beings no longer have the responsibility to work and keep it. Nor do we need to worry about eating prematurely from the Tree of the Knowledge of Good and Evil, for that, too, is closed off from us. But the creation ordinances continue, and Scripture demands faithfulness in our work (as 2 Thess. 3:10), marriages (Ex. 20:14), and Sabbath observance (Ex. 20:8–11; Mark 2:27–28). And Scripture never repeals the mandate defined as the very purpose of our existence in Genesis 1:26–28; indeed, God reiterates that mandate in Genesis 9:1.

Negatively, since Adam was the federal head of the human race, we have sinned "through" him (Rom. 5:12–21). This means that his sin is our sin (v. 19), his guilt our guilt (vv. 16–17). So, with Adam, we are part of the Edenic covenant, as covenant-breakers, condemned to death. Cf. chapter 36.

The Covenant of Grace

We cannot be saved from sin and its consequences by keeping the creation ordinances, for such obedience can never erase the sin of Adam in which we are implicated. And as I said earlier, God never intended these ordinances to be a means by which Adam would somehow *purchase* eternal life for himself. So after the fall, Adam could not achieve divine forgiveness by keeping God's commands.

But following the narrative of the fall, Scripture indicates that God intends to save his fallen people. There is good news mixed with the bad. God curses Satan, the serpent (Gen. 3:14–15), but at the end of this curse he indicates that Satan will be crushed by a child of Eve (v. 15). Though labor and childbearing are to be painful, they will preserve the human race until the time when the special child of the woman will gain this victory and save his people. Adam and Eve received this promise in faith. Adam named his wife *Eve,* "mother of all living" (3:20), expressing his confidence that God would keep mankind alive until the Deliverer should come, and Eve named her first son *Cain,* honoring childbirth as a gift of God (4:1). So the promise of seed (the child promise) correlates with the promise that Adam's work will continue to feed the human race (the land promise), bringing God's blessing out of curse.

The good news that a child would be born to redeem mankind is the same gospel by which we today may be saved from God's wrath. As Adam and Eve looked forward to that child, we look back upon him, Jesus Christ, who died for our sin, rose again, and ever lives to intercede for us. This is the gospel, the good news of God's grace. Though we are doomed by our disobedience, and though we cannot save ourselves, God promises in Genesis 3 that he will give salvation as a gift, the gift of the child.

So there is a covenant of grace. We are saved from the death we deserve because of sin, not by anything we do, but by God's sheer gift of the Redeemer child. In Genesis 3, it is a covenant of promise. Adam and Eve simply believe that God will give his gift. Death and sin remain in the world, and eventually Adam and Eve will die without seeing the child of the promise. So they live by faith, not by sight (as 2 Cor. 5:7).

But their faith in this covenant was a living and active faith,[13] not a dead orthodoxy. Their second son, Abel, by faith

> offered to God a more acceptable sacrifice than Cain, through which he was commended as righteous, God commending him by accepting his gifts. And through his faith, though he died, he still speaks. (Heb. 11:4)

God saves his people apart from their works, but they must respond in faith. Cain responded with hatred and murder, bringing God's rebuke.[14] But Abel's sacrifice brought God's commendation. Grace does not eliminate responsibility. In every covenant there are blessings for obedience, curses for disobedience. This is true even within the covenant of grace.

God's covenants are unconditional in the sense that God will always carry out the purposes for which he made the covenants. In the covenant of grace, God the Father will certainly save all those he has given to belong to his Son. But they are conditional in that those who would receive those blessings must respond to God with a living and active faith (James 2:14–26). By God's sovereign plan, however, he sees to it that the conditions are met in those he has ordained for salvation.

As I indicated in chapter 2, the covenants are unconditional because of God's lordship attribute of complete control over the creation. They are conditional because of God's lordship attribute of authority, his right to command and be obeyed.

So as in all of God's covenants, we see here (1) God's sovereignty, now manifested as grace, but received by a living and obedient faith; but also (2) God's way of saving individual people as the means of redeeming the whole creation; and (3) God's blessing coming through land and seed.

God's Covenants with Noah

The covenant of grace continues throughout Scripture, to its account of the final judgment. Salvation from sin is always by God's grace, not by human works. But God always demands a living and active faith as a human response. While the covenant

---

13. The phrase *living and active faith* is a recurring phrase, even a theme, in the writings of my former colleague Norman Shepherd. Although I don't agree with all of Shepherd's formulations, I mean to support his basic contentions, that (1) biblical faith is a working faith, but (2) the works of faith do not *earn* salvation for us. See Shepherd, *The Call of Grace: How the Covenant Illuminates Salvation and Evangelism* (Phillipsburg, NJ: P&R Publishing, 2000), and *The Way of Righteousness* (La Grange, CA: Kerygma Press, 2009).

14. I don't mean here to suggest that Cain was a saved person. First John 3:12, to the contrary, describes him as "of the evil one." But he was part of the original family that received God's covenant of grace. Cain's lack of faith showed that God had not elected him to salvation.

of grace continues in effect through Scripture, God makes additional covenants to further his redemptive purposes.

Cain's descendants continued and increased his disobedience, until God determined to judge the human race (Gen. 6:5–7). There had been a few faithful ones, particularly Seth and his descendants (4:26–5:32). But in the end, God's favor rested only on Noah and his family (6:8). God establishes a covenant with Noah (6:18), promising to save them from the waters of judgment. Noah, by his living and active faith, "constructed an ark for the saving of his household" (Heb. 11:7). After the flood, Noah brings an offering to God (Gen. 8:20–22) and God promises never again to destroy the earth by a flood (8:21–22; 9:15–17). In 9:1 and 7, he renews the cultural mandate given to Adam in the Edenic covenant.

God makes this covenant not only with Noah and his family, but with "every living creature of all flesh" (Gen. 9:16). Again, we see that God's historical covenants continue his universal covenant.

Some have thought, following Meredith G. Kline, David VanDrunen, and others,[15] that Genesis 4–9 establishes a secular order, not subject to the requirements of special divine revelation, but only to "natural law." These writers think that the purpose of the Noachic covenant is secular as opposed to sacred, that it establishes a civil, not a religious, society. But there is no suggestion in the text of any such purpose. God's postflood covenant follows Noah's act of building an altar and sacrificing animals to God, certainly a religious act (8:20–22). Indeed, Scripture regards all human activities as religious, in the sense of being governed by all of God's words (Matt. 4:4; 1 Cor. 10:31). The Noachic covenant, embracing all flesh, certainly embraces all human beings as well, whether believers or not. In that sense it is a *covenant of common grace*.[16] But it is not indifferent as to how they respond to God. Even Noah's grandson Canaan receives a curse for the lack of respect shown to Noah by Canaan's father Ham (Gen. 9:20–27). Unbelievers within the covenant are called to become believers and to walk by faith as Noah did. And the passage never mentions natural law or natural revelation, though we may assume that these continue to convey the same moral content as they do in the universal covenant. In the Noachic covenant, God sets the standards of the covenant by his own words, his "special revelation."

In the NT, the flood is a type of God's final judgment on sin (Matt. 24:37–39; Heb. 11:7; 1 Peter 3:20; 2 Peter 2:5; 3:5–6), and also of the baptism of believers (1 Peter 3:21). Noah is for us a model of saving faith. By constructing an ark, "he condemned the world and became an heir of the righteousness that comes by faith" (Heb. 11:7). God's promise to Noah is an encouragement to believers that the apparent delay of Jesus' return is part of God's redemptive plan (2 Peter 3:4–13).

15. Kline, *Kingdom Prologue*; David VanDrunen, *A Biblical Case for Natural Law* (Grand Rapids: Acton Institute, 2006). See my reviews of these and other books of this school of thought in my *The Escondido Theology* (Lakeland, FL: Whitefield Media, 2011).

16. Common grace is God's favor and gifts given to those who will not be finally saved (see chapter 12).

All of this is religious through and through, even on the narrowest definition of what constitutes religion.

The Noachic covenant continues the covenant of grace as well as the universal covenant. God saves the human race by his grace, promises that there will not be another universal destruction by water, and calls on Noah and his descendants to live by obedient faith. God brings life out of death, anticipating the work of Christ. So he preserves the human race until the Redeemer child should complete the work of redemption and the Holy Spirit should draw all the elect into the kingdom.

Again we note the themes of divine sovereignty and human obedient faith, God's dealings with individuals to bring redemption to the whole world, and the triad of *blessing, seed* (Noah's descendants), and *land* (the renewal of the cultural mandate in Genesis 9:7).

God's Covenant with Abraham

We have seen that God's purpose for mankind has always been that they should fill the earth. He commanded Adam and Eve to fill the earth (Gen. 1:28), and he renewed that command to Noah (9:1, 7). The story of the Tower of Babel, however (11:1–9), indicates man's sinful reluctance to obey this command. Those who built the tower preferred to huddle together in a central place, and God judged them for it.

Again, God chooses a single family to carry out his covenant purpose. His blessing, as with Noah, however, is not for that family alone, but through them to bless "all the families of the earth" (Gen. 12:3). As with previous covenants, God's perspective is both individual and worldwide. So the Abrahamic covenant carries forward the interests of God's universal covenant.

It also carries forward, like the Noachic covenant, the interests of God's covenant of grace. Notice the intense emphasis in the covenant on what God will do, the *I wills* in the following quotation:

> And I will make of you a great nation, and I will bless you and make your name great, so that you will be a blessing. I will bless those who bless you, and him who dishonors you I will curse, and in you all the families of the earth shall be blessed. (Gen. 12:2–3)

Three times in the Abraham story God makes promises of what he will do for Abraham and his family. The second is in Genesis 15:

> Then the LORD said to Abram, "Know for certain that your offspring will be sojourners in a land that is not theirs and will be servants there, and they will be afflicted for four hundred years. But I will bring judgment on the nation that they serve, and afterward they shall come out with great possessions. As for yourself, you shall go to your fathers in peace; you shall be buried in a good old age. And they shall come back here in the fourth generation, for the iniquity of the Amorites is not yet complete." (Gen. 15:13–16)

The four-hundred-year span between this promise and its fulfillment indicates that the blessing will come about through God alone, for only he controls history over such a great expanse of time. In the third group of covenant promises, note again the *I wills*:

> Behold, my covenant is with you, and you shall be the father of a multitude of nations. No longer shall your name be called Abram, but your name shall be Abraham, for I have made you the father of a multitude of nations. I will make you exceedingly fruitful, and I will make you into nations, and kings shall come from you. And I will establish my covenant between me and you and your offspring after you throughout their generations for an everlasting covenant, to be God to you and to your offspring after you. And I will give to you and to your offspring after you the land of your sojournings, all the land of Canaan, for an everlasting possession, and I will be their God. (Gen. 17:4–8)

Nevertheless, God expects Abraham to respond with living and active faith. In Genesis 12 and 17, in fact, God's command precedes his promise. Genesis 12 begins:

> Now the LORD said to Abram, "Go from your country and your kindred and your father's house to the land that I will show you. And I will make of you a great nation, and I will bless you and make your name great, so that you will be a blessing." (Gen. 12:1–2)

Abraham must obey God's command if he is to receive his inheritance in the Land of Promise. Similarly, God's formulation of the covenant in Genesis 17 begins not with the section quoted above, but with this:

> When Abram was ninety-nine years old the LORD appeared to Abram and said to him, "I am God Almighty; walk before me, and be blameless, that I may make my covenant between me and you, and may multiply you greatly." (Gen. 17:1–2)

Given the emphasis on grace, it is hard to understand why God's command would come before his promise. In these two passages, indeed, Abraham's obedience is actually a condition of God's making his promise. Genesis 26:5 says that God would fulfill the covenant "because Abraham obeyed my voice and kept my charge, my commandments, my statutes, and my laws."

But as we have seen, all covenants require obedient faith. This is not a condition of one covenant or another; it is essential to all human dealings with God, simply by virtue of who God is. It is a requirement of what I have called the universal covenant. Individual covenants require specific forms of obedience, but obedience itself, springing from faith, is simply a requirement of all relations between God and human beings. This requirement is implicit in the very distinction between Creator and creature.

So it is not the case, as some have argued, that in the Abrahamic covenant God's promises are *unconditional*, as opposed to the Mosaic covenant in which the promises are *conditional*. One argument to this effect is that the Abrahamic covenant is a "land-grant" type of treaty, God's giving the Promised Land to Abraham and his seed. Some scholars believe that land-grant treaties are unconditional, but many do not.[17]

In any case, it is clear that the Abrahamic covenant in Scripture is conditional, simply because God himself attached conditions to it. Besides the general requirements of obedience noted above, God demanded that Abraham circumcise his household (Gen. 17:9–14). And Scripture is very specific in saying that God demanded from Abraham a response of obedient faith (Gen. 15:6; 26:4–5; Heb. 11:8–12, 17–19; James 2:21–23).[18]

This emphasis on faithful obedience does not compromise grace at all. For we can never begin to earn God's forgiveness of our sins through good works, and the blessings that God promises to Abraham are far beyond what any human being could accomplish. God will give to Abraham and Sarah a child when they are far beyond the time of child-bearing. He will make of Abraham a great nation, and that nation will bring blessing to all the nations of the world. These promises will be fulfilled by God's grace alone.

Nor does the emphasis on obedience compromise the biblical emphasis that we are saved by faith and not by works. Indeed, Abraham is the great example in the NT of saving faith in Christ. Abraham did not earn his salvation by doing good works. He was saved by faith in God's promise. In Romans 4:16–17, Paul explains that God promised that Abraham would be the father of many nations, a promise that (given the ages of Abraham and Sarah) could not be fulfilled on the basis of human expectations. So his faith was counted to him as righteousness (Gen. 15:6; Rom. 4:3, 22). He knew that his relationship with God could not be purchased, only received as a promise. The promise is Christ, for it is in Christ that God completes Abraham's family (Rom. 4:16, 23–25; Gal. 3:6–9, 14, 16, 29).

Paul contrasts faith and law in Romans 10:3–6 and Galatians 3:12 in arguing against Jews and Judaizing Christians who urge law-keeping as a method of salvation apart from Christ or in addition to Christ. To disparage Christ in this way is to reject God's promise to Abraham and to substitute for that promise salvation by works. When we try to keep the law as a substitute for Christ, or when we think our law-keeping must supplement the work of Christ, the law is "not of faith" (Gal. 3:12). When we turn from such law-righteousness and trust Christ alone, "Christ is the end of the law for righteousness to everyone who believes" (Rom. 10:4).

So like all the other covenants, the Abrahamic covenant is unconditional in the sense that in it God declares that he will certainly accomplish his own purpose, the blessing of the nations through Abraham. But it is conditional in that those who would receive that blessing must trust and obey. As sovereign controller, God is the God of grace. As sovereign authority, he demands obedience of his covenant partners.

---

17. See Gary Knoppers, "Ancient Near Eastern Royal Grants and the Davidic Covenant: A Parallel?," *Journal of the American Oriental Society* 116, 4 (October–December 1996): 670–97, referenced by Richard Pratt in "Reformed Theology Is Covenant Theology," available at http://old.thirdmill.org/newfiles/ric_pratt/ric_pratt.RTiscovenant.html.

18. My argument here is dependent on Shepherd, *The Call of Grace*, 13–22.

In this section, I have focused on the theme of divine sovereignty-grace and the human response of obedient faith. We have also seen the twin emphases of individuality (Abraham) and universality (to bless all nations). Note also the triadic structure of the promise: a divine blessing, focusing on seed (Abraham's descendants) and land (the Promised Land of Canaan).

God's Covenant with Israel under Moses

The book of Genesis continues with accounts of Abraham's family, particularly his son Isaac, his sons Esau and Jacob, and Jacob's twelve sons. At the end of the book, Jacob dies, and the family lives in Egypt. They had gained favor with the Egyptians because of the influence of Jacob's son Joseph.

But over the "four hundred years" that God described to Abraham (Gen. 15:13), the book of Exodus says:

> But the people of Israel were fruitful and increased greatly; they multiplied and grew exceedingly strong, so that the land was filled with them. (Ex. 1:7)

A new king arose in Egypt, who did not know Joseph, and he feared the power of this new nation. So he "set taskmasters over them to afflict them with heavy burdens" (Ex. 1:11) and decreed that male Israelite babies should be killed (v. 16). But they cried to God, and God delivered them under the leadership of Moses. The people left Egypt under God's miraculous protection. And when they arrived at Mount Sinai, the dwelling place of God, God made a covenant with them. He charged Moses to say to them:

> You yourselves have seen what I did to the Egyptians, and how I bore you on eagles' wings and brought you to myself. Now therefore, if you will indeed obey my voice and keep my covenant, you shall be my treasured possession among all peoples, for all the earth is mine; and you shall be to me a kingdom of priests and a holy nation. These are the words that you shall speak to the people of Israel. (Ex. 19:4–6)

Notice here that the covenant begins with the grace of God, his sovereign work in delivering Israel from Egypt and bringing her to himself. God's deliverance to Israel is not based on Israel's numbers or impressiveness (Deut. 7:7–8) or Israel's righteousness (9:5–6), but on God's love and on the wickedness of the Canaanite nations. But this covenant is conditional in the same way that the Abrahamic covenant was. *If* Israel is obedient, *then* she will be God's treasured possession.

I do not agree with the theory of Meredith G. Kline[19] that under the Mosaic covenant people were saved from sin by divine grace, but that their temporal blessings within the land of Canaan had to be earned by works. That idea draws a parallel between the Edenic covenant and the Mosaic that misunderstands the former. And it disregards the

---

19. Kline, *Kingdom Prologue.*

fact that all of God's covenants contain sovereign divine promises, but require human responses of faith.[20] If we acknowledge both these aspects of the covenant, we need not think up special reasons why some part of this particular covenant (the temporal blessings) demands obedience. The biblical text, further, never says that the spiritual and temporal blessings of Israel come from different sources. The relation between God's grace and human obedience in the Mosaic covenant is the same as that in the other covenants.[21]

In Exodus 19:7–8, the people promise to obey all of God's words. The Mosaic covenant, then, is a fulfillment and extension of the Abrahamic:

> And God heard their groaning, and God remembered his covenant with Abraham, with Isaac, and with Jacob. (Ex. 2:24)

Before telling Moses his mysterious name *Yahweh*, he identifies himself to Moses as "the God of your father, the God of Abraham, the God of Isaac, and the God of Jacob" (Ex. 3:6), and later Moses identifies God to Israel in the same terms (v. 15).

In Genesis and Exodus, there is a process of God's narrowing, in one sense, the scope of the covenant: to the family of Noah, to that of Abraham, to that of Jacob. But God has not forgotten his universal purpose, to bless all nations. The covenant with Israel is an extension of that with Abraham, the purpose of which was to bless all nations (Gen. 12:1–3). Israel, therefore, was to be God's witness to all the nations of the world (Isa. 43:10–12; 44:8). The nations are to admire the laws that God has given to Israel, and the wisdom and understanding of the people that these laws elicit (Deut. 4:5–8). The fulfillment of Israel's covenant will bring Israel together with the other nations, particularly her worst enemies:

> In that day there will be a highway from Egypt to Assyria, and Assyria will come into Egypt, and Egypt into Assyria, and the Egyptians will worship with the Assyrians.
>   In that day Israel will be the third with Egypt and Assyria, a blessing in the midst of the earth, whom the LORD of hosts has blessed, saying, "Blessed be Egypt my people, and Assyria the work of my hands, and Israel my inheritance." (Isa. 19:23–25)

When God establishes his covenant with Israel, he draws near to the people in terrifying majesty (Ex. 19:16–25) and declares to them in audible words the Ten Commandments (20:1–17). Later, Moses brought down from Sinai "the two tablets of the testimony, tablets of stone, written with the finger of God" (31:18). These tablets were the covenant in written form, the suzerainty treaty between God and Israel. This was

---

20. They never demand that human beings *earn* God's favor.

21. This theory is often put in this way: that the Mosaic covenant is a "republication of the covenant of works." That description misunderstands the theory above, which does not assert that the Mosaic covenant is a covenant of works, but only that Israel's blessings in the land were based on works. Further, it greatly misleads readers on the basis for salvation in the Mosaic covenant, which is not human works at all, but the grace of Christ mediated through the priesthood and temple sacrifices.

the written constitution of the nation of Israel, placed in the ark of the covenant, the holiest place in Israel (25:16).

Israel's life under the Mosaic covenant fills out the rest of the OT. At the Sinai meeting, God has the people build a tabernacle under a pattern that Hebrews identifies as the likeness of the true tabernacle in heaven (Heb. 8:5). In that place Moses met with God, and the people brought sacrifices to the priests, of whom the first was Moses' brother Aaron. Centuries later, under King Solomon, God replaces the tabernacle with the temple, a permanent location for God to meet with his people.

God adds to the Ten Commandments many laws concerning sacrifices, ritual cleanness, and uncleanness. There are three annual feasts (Passover, Pentecost, and Tabernacles) and dietary restrictions. There are ethical requirements, many to help the poor in Israel.

As the narrative continues, the people distrust God's promise that they will conquer the nations in the Land of Promise, and so God condemns the whole nation to wandering in the wilderness until the unbelieving generation has been replaced by a new one. Under the leadership of Joshua, Moses' successor, Israel achieves spectacular victories in the conquest of Canaan, by the power of God; but the people's disobedience leads to some setbacks. By the time of Joshua's death, the conquest of Canaan is still incomplete. Israel gains some victories under judges appointed by God, but her unfaithfulness places her again and again under the dominion of other nations. Only when the Israelites repent and turn back to God do they again prevail.

Like the other covenants, then, the Mosaic covenant is unconditional, in that God certainly achieves the purposes for which he made the covenant. But it is conditional, in that Israel receives the blessings only by a living, obedient faith.

The covenant is particular, focused on a single nation. But it is also universal, God's means of carrying his blessings to all nations. Looking back, we can say that the primary purpose of the Mosaic covenant is to provide an environment in which Jesus, the Son of God, would be born, teach his people, perform mighty works, die, be raised, and ascend to heaven, for the forgiveness of our sins. From this environment the gospel of Christ would go forth to all the nations of the world.

And in the Mosaic covenant, like the others, we can see the threefold pattern of God's *blessing* his people, placing his *seed* in a *land* that he promised to Abraham.

In what sense, if any, do new covenant believers participate in the Mosaic covenant? It is significant that of all the covenants, this is the only one that has a terminus. The blessings and obligations of all other covenants continue through history until the final judgment. Scripture speaks of an "end" only to the Mosaic covenant: after quoting Jeremiah 31:31–34, the writer to the Hebrews says:

> In speaking of a new covenant, he makes the first one obsolete. And what is becoming obsolete and growing old is ready to vanish away. (Heb. 8:13)

It is the Mosaic covenant that is becoming obsolete and ready to vanish. The book of Hebrews banishes all nostalgia of Jewish Christians' wanting to return to the old ways of the Mosaic era. The writer shows that all the Mosaic institutions—the priesthood, the sacrifices, the tabernacle, and the temple—are fulfilled in Jesus in such a way that they are to be set aside in their original form. Even the law must undergo change, because much of the Mosaic law had to do with priests and sacrifices (Heb. 7:12). This doesn't mean that the Ten Commandments are no longer normative; Jesus himself (Matt. 5:17–48) and Paul (Rom. 13:9–10) affirm them. They are essentially a republication of the creation ordinances. But some of the specific laws given for Israel's ceremonial and judicial life are obsolete.

There is both continuity and discontinuity between the Mosaic covenant and the new covenant (which I will discuss below). The promises given to Israel are fulfilled to us in Christ. The promise of divine forgiveness belongs to us. He is the Passover Lamb sacrificed for us (John 1:29, 36; 1 Cor. 5:7; 1 Peter 1:19). He is our Priest, our Temple, our King. We are the heirs of Israel, receiving the blessing of Abraham (Gal. 3:9). Indeed, we are the Israel of God (Gal. 6:16). Paul describes even Gentile Christians as wild branches grafted into the tree of Israel in place of the unbelieving branches that have been cast out (Rom. 11:11–24). So the Mosaic covenant is for us, but in a consummate way, so that many of the institutions of that covenant have passed away.

God's Covenant with David

When Samuel, last of the judges, becomes old, the elders of Israel demand that he appoint for them a king "like all the nations" (1 Sam. 8:5). God had indeed promised Abraham (Gen. 17:6, 16) and later Jacob (Gen. 35:11) that their covenant family would include kings. In Deuteronomy 17:14–20, God through Moses speaks of kings as a natural development in the conquest of the land and places certain requirements on the office. The king must be an Israelite (v. 15), must not acquire many horses (for that would require him to go back to Egypt, v. 16). Nor should he acquire many wives, or silver, or gold (v. 17). He is to be a student of God's law and must never turn aside from it (vv. 18–20).

But Scripture is ambivalent about the actual workings of human kingship. The short kingship of Abimelech, son of Gideon, in Shechem (Judg. 9:1–57) showed how bad a king could be. He murdered all but one of his seventy brothers and came himself to a wretched end. Jotham, his one surviving brother, spoke a parable in which the trees sought a king and only the bramble, threatening destruction, accepted the job (vv. 7–21). Similarly, when Israel asks Samuel to appoint a king, God gives this verdict:

> Obey the voice of the people in all that they say to you, for they have not rejected you, but they have rejected me from being king over them. According to all the deeds that they have done, from the day I brought them up out of Egypt even to this day, forsaking me and serving other gods, so they are also doing to you. Now then, obey their voice; only you shall solemnly warn them and show them the ways of the king who shall reign over them. (1 Sam. 8:7–9)

Samuel tells them, as did Jotham, that kingship will lead to tyranny (Judg. 9:10–18). Nevertheless, he proceeds to anoint a king for them, chosen by God (1 Sam. 9:16). The king is Saul, son of Kish, of the tribe of Benjamin.

Saul *looks* like a king:

> Saul [was] a handsome young man. There was not a man among the people of Israel more handsome than he. From his shoulders upward he was taller than any of the people. (1 Sam. 9:2)

Yet he shows a becoming modesty at the honor he receives (1 Sam. 9:21). In the early days of his kingship, Saul leads Israel to victory against the Ammonites (11:1–11) and shows mercy on his Israelite opponents (vv. 12–15). But later Saul violates a command of God, and God declares that his kingdom will not continue but will pass to a man after God's own heart (13:14). After this, Saul's relationship to God continues to deteriorate.

The man after God's own heart is David, the greatest king of Israel. He enters Saul's service, defeats the giant Goliath, becomes a great warrior, provoking Saul's jealousy to the point that Saul tries to kill David (1 Sam. 19–20). Yet when David has an opportunity to kill Saul, he refuses to lift his hand against God's anointed (24:1–7; 26:1–12).

Saul takes his own life in battle with the Philistines (1 Sam. 31), and David mourns his death (2 Sam. 1). Then the elders, first of his own tribe of Judah (2:1–4), then of all Israel (5:1–5), anoint him king. Like Saul, David sins grievously against God; but unlike Saul, David repents of his sin (2 Sam. 11–12; cf. 24:1–25; Ps. 51). God forgives him, but the end of his reign is disturbed by two rebellions and much grief. Still, under David, Israel reaches a point of great prominence among the nations. From the viewpoint of the biblical writers, David is the most deserving of respect among all the kings of Judah and Israel.

God's covenant with David establishes his throne, and that of his descendants, forever:

> Thus says the LORD of hosts, I took you from the pasture, from following the sheep, that you should be prince over my people Israel. And I have been with you wherever you went and have cut off all your enemies from before you. And I will make for you a great name, like the name of the great ones of the earth. And I will appoint a place for my people Israel and will plant them, so that they may dwell in their own place and be disturbed no more. And violent men shall afflict them no more, as formerly, from the time that I appointed judges over my people Israel. And I will give you rest from all your enemies. Moreover, the LORD declares to you that the LORD will make you a house. When your days are fulfilled and you lie down with your fathers, I will raise up your offspring after you, who shall come from your body, and I will establish his kingdom. He shall build a house for my name, and I will establish the throne of his kingdom forever. I will be to him a father,

and he shall be to me a son. When he commits iniquity, I will discipline him with the rod of men, with the stripes of the sons of men, but my steadfast love will not depart from him, as I took it from Saul, whom I put away from before you. And your house and your kingdom shall be made sure forever before me. Your throne shall be established forever. (2 Sam. 7:8–16)

God's grace will establish David's throne forever. But he will also discipline David's heirs when they commit sin. Again, the themes of divine sovereignty and human responsibility, of grace and faithful obedience, join together.

Also, the Davidic covenant continues the theme of universality. In Psalm 72:8–11, a messianic text, Solomon prays for the Davidic king:

> May he have dominion from sea to sea,
>   and from the River to the ends of the earth!
> May desert tribes bow down before him
>   and his enemies lick the dust!
> May the kings of Tarshish and of the coastlands
>   render him tribute;
> may the kings of Sheba and Seba
>   bring gifts!
> May all kings fall down before him,
>   all nations serve him!

The reign of David's son Solomon exceeded that of David in earthly power and glory. Solomon had asked God for wisdom, rather than long life, riches, or the life of his enemies. God gave him wisdom, and power and riches as well (1 Kings 3:1–14). But these gifts were conditional. God said that Solomon had to "walk in my ways, keeping my statutes and my commandments" (v. 14). In keeping these conditions, Solomon was inconsistent, as his father was. He built the temple, a permanent dwelling for God and for the worship of God's people. But his own heart was turned from the Lord by foreign women, so that he built places for the worship of their gods as well (11:7–8).

When he died, the Israelites told his son Rehoboam that Solomon had "made our yoke heavy" (1 Kings 12:4). They urged Rehoboam to lighten that load, but Rehoboam chose, rather, to be harder on the people than his father was: "My father disciplined you with whips, but I will discipline you with scorpions" (v. 11). So the northern tribes chose another king, Jeroboam, and turned away from the Davidic dynasty. Rehoboam did maintain rule over the tribe of Judah in the south.

So until the exile, Israel was divided into two nations. The southern kingdom was ruled by descendants of David, the northern by a succession of individual kings and dynasties. In both kingdoms, most of the rulers receive a negative verdict from Scripture, but occasionally, especially in the south, there was a king who sought, at least for part of his reign, to be faithful to the Lord.

During this time, God raised up prophets to confront the sins of the kings and the people. A prophet is a man with God's word in his mouth (see Deut. 18:18–22, and its exposition in our chapter 24), as was Moses. The prophets were God's "covenant prosecutors" who accused Israel of breaking his covenant and declared judgment. But besides judgment, there was also grace. God through the prophets renewed the promise of the woman's child, who would bring to God's people a full redemption from sin:

> For to us a child is born,
>   to us a son is given;
> and the government shall be upon his shoulder,
>   and his name shall be called
> Wonderful Counselor, Mighty God,
>   Everlasting Father, Prince of Peace.
> Of the increase of his government and of peace
>   there will be no end,
> on the throne of David and over his kingdom,
>   to establish it and to uphold it
> with justice and with righteousness
>   from this time forth and forevermore.
> The zeal of the LORD of hosts will do this. (Isa. 9:6–7)

In Isaiah 53, we read of a Servant of God who will come to bear our sins:

> Surely he has borne our griefs
>   and carried our sorrows;
> yet we esteemed him stricken,
>   smitten by God, and afflicted.
> But he was wounded for our transgressions;
>   he was crushed for our iniquities;
> upon him was the chastisement that brought us peace,
>   and with his stripes we are healed.
> All we like sheep have gone astray;
>   we have turned—every one—to his own way;
> and the LORD has laid on him
>   the iniquity of us all. (Isa. 53:4–6)

The Servant suffers God's wrath so that his people might be healed from sin. Yet he is the King, a king like David. So the NT identifies Jesus as the great son of David (Matt. 9:27; 12:23; 20:30–31; 21:9, 15; 22:42).

But Israel did not hear the prophets, and she turned further and further away from God. The northern kingdom was conquered by Assyria in 722 B.C., and the southern kingdom by Babylonia in 597. Both conquerors forced many Israelites from their homes in Canaan to live in exile.

Since believers today are in Christ, we, too, are part of the Davidic covenant. God's promises to David are fulfilled in Christ and therefore given to us. We are to reign with Christ over God's creation (2 Tim. 2:12; Rev. 5:10; 22:5).

The psalms of David are the songs of our hearts. With David we trust God's provision each day as our only comfort in life and death.

Christ is King over all, the *seed* of the woman ruling the *lands* of the earth, spreading God's *blessing* to God's people.

The New Covenant

So Jesus Christ is the main theme of Scripture. Jesus said to his Jewish opponents:

> You search the Scriptures because you think that in them you have eternal life; and it is they that bear witness about me, yet you refuse to come to me that you may have life. (John 5:39–40)

Luke describes an encounter between Jesus and a couple of disciples who were confused by recent reports about Jesus' death and resurrection:

> And he said to them, "O foolish ones, and slow of heart to believe all that the prophets have spoken! Was it not necessary that the Christ should suffer these things and enter into his glory?" And beginning with Moses and all the Prophets, he interpreted to them in all the Scriptures the things concerning himself. (Luke 24:25–27)

All previous revelation, all previous covenants, are fulfilled in him. He is the Prophet greater than Moses (John 1:1–14; Heb. 3:1–6), the Priest who replaces the priests of the temple (Heb. 4:14–5:10; 7:1–8:7), the King greater than David (Mark 12:35–37). Jesus' sacrifice on the cross fulfills and replaces the animal sacrifices of the temple, for only his sacrifice took away the sins of his people (Heb. 10:1–18). It is in Jesus' death that his people have died to sin, and in his resurrection we, too, have been raised to newness of life (Rom. 6:1–11).

New covenant is the name for the new relationship that we have with God through Christ. Remarkably, in the Gospels Jesus comes as the Lord of the covenant, taking the place of Yahweh as the head of the covenant. Only God can take this role, so Jesus identifies himself clearly as God in the flesh, the Lord of the covenant come to deliver his people from their sins.

The Sabbath day in the OT was the day that belonged especially to the Lord. It is "a Sabbath to the LORD your God" (Ex. 20:10). But Jesus declares that the Sabbath belongs to him: "So the Son of Man is lord even of the Sabbath" (Mark 2:28). Jesus is the head of the covenant, a role that only Yahweh could play. The cup of the Lord's Supper is "the new covenant in my blood" (1 Cor. 11:25).

God had told the prophet Jeremiah that he would make a new covenant with his people:

Behold, the days are coming, declares the LORD, when I will make a new covenant with the house of Israel and the house of Judah, not like the covenant that I made with their fathers on the day when I took them by the hand to bring them out of the land of Egypt, my covenant that they broke, though I was their husband, declares the LORD. But this is the covenant that I will make with the house of Israel after those days, declares the LORD: I will put my law within them, and I will write it on their hearts. And I will be their God, and they shall be my people. And no longer shall each one teach his neighbor and each his brother, saying, "Know the LORD," for they shall all know me, from the least of them to the greatest, declares the LORD. For I will forgive their iniquity, and I will remember their sin no more. (Jer. 31:31–34)[22]

Verse 32 speaks of the covenant God made with the people of Israel through Moses. In that covenant, he commanded them to write his words on their heart (Deut. 6:6; 11:18; 32:46). They were to obey God, not grudgingly, but as their greatest delight. But they failed to keep that covenant. In the new covenant, God himself will write his words on the hearts of his people. His law will be "within them." By his grace, they will indeed delight to do his will. Those without the divine writing on their hearts, who are Jews in name only (Rom. 2:28–29; 9:6), will not receive the blessings of the covenant.

In the Mosaic covenant, the people brought animal sacrifices to the priests to deal with their sins. But it was impossible for the blood of bulls and goats to take away sins (Heb. 10:4). The animal sacrifices were only shadows (v. 1) of the final sacrifice of Christ. When God forgave the sins of Israelites, it was not because of the deaths of animals, but because of the death of Christ, symbolized by the animal offerings.

The same is true of salvation under the Abrahamic covenant (Rom. 2:25–27; 9:7–13). And the promise of the Noachic covenant that the earth would not be destroyed before the final judgment is based on the fact that before the judgment, those belonging to Christ must be saved (2 Peter 3:9).

So the work of Christ is the source of all human salvation from sin: the salvation of Adam and Eve, of Noah, of Abraham, of Moses, of David, and of all of God's people in every age, past, present, or future. Everyone who has ever been saved has been saved through the new covenant in Christ. Everyone who is saved receives a new heart, a heart of obedience, through the new covenant work of Christ. So though it is a new covenant, it is also the oldest, the temporal expression of the *pactum salutis*.

Like the other covenants, the new covenant establishes a body of believers in covenant with the Lord. Those who enter the church with a living faith in Christ receive all the blessings of the covenant. The new covenant is unconditional in that its very

---

22. Compare God's promise to give his people a "new heart" in Ezekiel 11:19–21 and 36:24–38. Chapter 37 on God's Spirit's making the dry bones live is also a new covenant promise.

content is God's unconditional gift of a new heart, fulfilling all covenant conditions. But it is conditional in that those conditions are real and necessary. We are justified by faith alone, not by any effort to earn our salvation (Rom. 3:23–24; Eph. 2:8–9). But the faith by which we are justified is a living and obedient faith (Gal. 5:6; Eph. 2:10; James 2:14–26).

So as with the other covenants, it is possible for someone to join the new covenant community externally without the new heart that defines that covenant. He may be baptized and profess Christian doctrine. But if he lives a life of sin, he shows that he does not have the new heart that is the mark of the new covenant. He has wrongly entered the covenant community and ought to be disciplined by the body. He has become a Christian externally, but without inward change.

So the new covenant features both grace and responsibility, as we have seen in all the covenants. Addressing the new covenant community, Scripture contains warnings of judgment to those who would presume on God's grace (Heb. 6:1–12; 10:26–39).

The new covenant also emphasizes the principle of universality. God's grace saves people as individuals. But the main directive of Jesus sends them out into the world to make disciples of all the nations, fulfilling the promise of God to Abraham (Matt. 28:18–20). Note in this Great Commission (1) the *blessing* of Jesus' presence, (2) the spread of the gospel to all *lands*, (3) to be filled with the *seed* of baptized believers.

Only when all of God's elect (those given to the Son in the *pactum salutis*) are saved will Jesus return, utter the final judgment, and establish the new heavens and new earth (2 Peter 3:9–13). So the blessing will be full: the seed of the woman (Christ and his people) ruling over all of God's new creation.

This is the story of the Bible: God the Father securing the fellowship of those he has given to his Son. For those people, Christ the Son atones for their sin, and the Spirit gives them new hearts to love God and one another. So God glorifies his lordship in the salvation of his people.

Covenants and Perspectives

Of the covenants that we have discussed, most are time-specific. The Noachic covenant begins at a specific time, when Noah builds an altar to the Lord after the flood (Gen. 8:20–9:17). Before that, there was no Noachic covenant, though we all benefit from its provisions until the final judgment. Similarly for the covenant of grace (Gen. 3:14–19), the Abrahamic covenant (Gen. 12:1–3; 15:1–21; 17:1–21), the Mosaic covenant (Ex. 19:1–9; 20; 21), and the Davidic covenant (2 Sam. 7:4–17).

But three of the covenants that I have described above are not time-specific in this way: the eternal covenant of redemption (the *pactum salutis*), the universal covenant, and the new covenant. All believers partake equally in the benefits of these three covenants, regardless of when in time they live.

The eternal covenant of redemption is entirely supratemporal, so it has no beginning in time, no datable ratification ceremony. Its benefits come to all of those of all times who are elect in Christ. The universal covenant also has no temporal restriction. God is always Creator and Lord, so this covenant is always in effect.

The new covenant does have a temporal inauguration. Covenants are typically inaugurated by the shedding of blood, and that is certainly the case with the new covenant, by the blood of Christ, the blood that fulfills all the blood of bulls and goats in the other covenants.

> But when Christ appeared as a high priest of the good things that have come, then through the greater and more perfect tent (not made with hands, that is, not of this creation) he entered once for all into the holy places, not by means of the blood of goats and calves but by means of his own blood, thus securing an eternal redemption. For if the blood of goats and bulls, and the sprinkling of defiled persons with the ashes of a heifer, sanctify for the purification of the flesh, how much more will the blood of Christ, who through the eternal Spirit offered himself without blemish to God, purify our conscience from dead works to serve the living God. (Heb. 9:11–14)

This passage follows the writer's quotation from the new covenant passage in Jeremiah (Heb. 8:8–12). So the shedding of Jesus' blood, a datable historical event, is the substance of the new covenant, the covenant that purifies not only the flesh, but the conscience, the heart.

Nevertheless, as we saw earlier, the efficacy of the new covenant, unlike that of previous covenants, extends to God's elect before Jesus' atonement. When believers in the OT experienced "circumcision of the heart," or when they were Jews "inwardly," they were partaking of the power of the new covenant.

So there are three covenants that extend to all of God's people. Not all believers benefit specifically from the Noachic, Abrahamic, Mosaic, or Davidic covenant. But all benefit from the eternal, the universal, and the new covenants.

It may be useful to give some further attention to these time-transcending covenants. The eternal covenant of redemption is nothing less than the triune God's eternal plan for history. It determines that history will be the outworking of a story of creation, fall, and redemption. In that covenant, the Father gives a people to the Son, to be renewed by the Spirit. All history must follow that plan. So the eternal covenant is *normative*, as I defined it in chapter 2.

The universal covenant is the prerogative of God to be Lord over everything he creates. By that creation, he establishes the setting in which the story of the eternal covenant will be played out. Creation as a whole is the *situation* for the fulfillment of the *pactum salutis*. This covenant, then, is the *situational* perspective in relation to the *pactum salutis*.

The new covenant determines that on the basis of the work of Christ, God's people will be saved to the uttermost, given a new heart of complete faithfulness to the Lord. This is the *existential* perspective of God's great plan. See fig. 4.3.

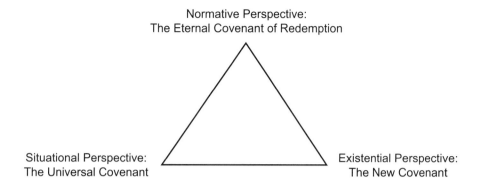

Normative Perspective:
The Eternal Covenant of Redemption

Situational Perspective:
The Universal Covenant

Existential Perspective:
The New Covenant

Fig. 4.3. Time-Transcending Covenants

These three covenants are related perspectivally. (1) The eternal covenant (normative) ordains the role that the universal and new covenants are to play. (2) The universal covenant (situational) displays God's relationship to every fact in creation, including the hearts of his people (existential), with the interpretation of those facts that extends into eternity (normative). And (3) the new covenant guarantees, based on the universal and eternal covenants, that nothing can separate the heart of the believer from the love of Christ (Rom. 8:35–39). So one cannot define any of these three without reference to the others. And to understand each is to understand all. The three are perspectives for thinking about God's comprehensive redemptive lordship: an eternal plan formulated by God's eternal wisdom, carried out by God's mighty power in history, applied to the hearts of the people whom the Father has given to the Son.

The other covenants apply these to different historical situations, announcing what God has determined in his eternal plan (normative), for each situation (situational), for the benefit of his people (existential).

Living in God's Covenant

In chapter 2, I indicated the typical elements of biblical covenants, following the suzerainty treaty pattern: the name of the lord, the historical prologue, and so on. These not only are formal elements of a literary genre, but are directions for the lives of God's covenant servants.

The Name of the Lord: The Lord is the One with whom we have to do. In every decision, we should take account of the fact of who he is. Our life is, as Calvin said, *coram deo*, in the presence of the living God. This means that Christian ethics is profoundly personal, the outworking of our relationship with an absolute person.[23]

The Historical Prologue: The redemptive history of God's covenants speaks of grace. As the Lord brought Israel out of the house of bondage (Ex. 20:2), so Jesus has brought

---

23. See *DCL*, 251–53, on the ethical importance of God as the most important fact of our life-situation.

us out of slavery to sin, into the freedom of the glory of the children of God (Rom. 8:21). This is our motivation to obey God's commands. We love because he first loved us (1 John 4:19).

The Stipulations: These are the laws of the covenant. They tell us what to do. Grace doesn't replace the law; rather, as we have seen, grace motivates our obedience to God's law. God's laws vary somewhat from one age to the next. In the new covenant, for example, we do not bring sacrificial animals to worship, as did those under the Mosaic covenant. But in every age, God's law is "holy and righteous and good" (Rom. 7:12), a delight to the wise man (Ps. 1:2).[24] It is not a terror and threat except to one intending to rebel against God.[25]

The Sanctions: These are the blessings for obedience and curses for disobedience. One in covenant with God knows that our decisions have consequences, and the Lord is right to impose those consequences upon us.

Administration: God's covenants are not abstract ideas, but they function in the real world. So in the covenants are roles for covenant mediators, judges, elders, kings, priests, prophets, apostles, elders, deacons, and so on. Our life in the covenant is not merely between the individual and God. It is a humble service in which we work with others, honor those who rule, and accept the structures and procedures that govern our relationship with God and with others.

Key Terms

Proof text
Genre
Myth
Narrative
Worldview
Individualism
Universality
Autonomous reasoning
Supernatural
Suzerainty treaty
Eternal covenant of redemption
Pactum salutis
Universal covenant
Edenic covenant
Cultural mandate
Covenant of works
Covenant of life

24. For more on the role of law in the Christian life, see ibid., 176–250.

25. Here I am opposing Martin Luther's law-gospel distinction. See my *The Escondido Theology*, 45–46 and elsewhere; *DCL*, 182–92; and P. Andrew Sandlin, *Wrongly Dividing the Word: Overcoming the Law-Gospel Distinction* (Mount Hermon, CA: Center for Cultural Leadership, 2010).

Covenant of grace
God's covenants with Noah
Common grace
God's covenant with Abraham
God's covenant with Israel under Moses
God's covenant with David
New covenant

Study Questions

1. Is there any value in citing proof texts for doctrinal formulations? What are the dangers associated with this?

2. "As a whole, the Bible is not an example of any *genre* of literature. It is *sui generis.*" Explain; evaluate.

3. Frame says that the biblical stories are not myth. Respond.

4. He also says that "they are not merely history either, as we usually think of it." Explain; evaluate.

5. Does the Bible teach a unique worldview? If so, why is this worldview important to its message?

6. In each of the biblical covenants, describe the relationship between God's blessings and human obedience.

7. In each of the biblical covenants, describe its individualism and universality.

8. In each covenant, describe the elements of blessing, seed, and land.

9. In each covenant described in this chapter, list the parties, the terms, the promises, and the threats.

10. Why does Frame hesitate to say that the Edenic covenant promised to Adam a life of confirmed righteousness if he remained faithful?

11. Should the Edenic covenant be described as a covenant of works? Explain your answer.

12. Does the Noachic covenant establish a *secular* order? Explain and argue your position.

13. Is the Abrahamic covenant unconditional? Explain; evaluate.

14. Do you believe that the temporal blessings of the Mosaic covenant were to be earned by works? Why or why not?

15. How does each of the biblical covenants point forward to Christ?

16. Distinguish the three covenants that are not time-specific.

17. Frame says that the eternal, universal, and new covenants are perspectives on God's entire redemptive work. Explain; evaluate.

18. Summarize how the covenantal character of our relation to God affects the Christian life.

Memory Verses

Isa. 66:1: Thus says the LORD:
"Heaven is my throne,
  and the earth is my footstool;
what is the house that you would build for me,
  and what is the place of my rest?"

Jer. 31:33: But this is the covenant that I will make with the house of Israel after those days, declares the LORD: I will put my law within them, and I will write it on their hearts. And I will be their God, and they shall be my people.

John 5:39–40: You search the Scriptures because you think that in them you have eternal life; and it is they that bear witness about me, yet you refuse to come to me that you may have life.

Rom. 4:19–22: [Abraham] did not weaken in faith when he considered his own body, which was as good as dead (since he was about a hundred years old), or when he considered the barrenness of Sarah's womb. No distrust made him waver concerning the promise of God, but he grew strong in his faith as he gave glory to God, fully convinced that God was able to do what he had promised. That is why his faith was counted to him as righteousness.

Eph. 1:3–4: Blessed be the God and Father of our Lord Jesus Christ, who has blessed us in Christ with every spiritual blessing in the heavenly places, even as he chose us in him before the foundation of the world, that we should be holy and blameless before him.

Resources for Further Study

Kline, Meredith G. *Kingdom Prologue*. Eugene, OR: Wipf and Stock, 2006. My review of this book in *The Escondido Theology* takes issue with his view of the covenants at several points, but I have learned much from Kline.

Murray, John. *The Covenant of Grace*. London: Tyndale Press, 1950. See also his essay "Covenant Theology," in his *MCW*, 4:216–40, which deals with the history of these ideas in the Reformed tradition.

Shepherd, Norman. *The Call of Grace: How the Covenant Illuminates Salvation and Evangelism*. Phillipsburg, NJ: P&R Publishing, 2000. Shepherd's view is opposed to Kline's at many points. See also his *The Way of Righteousness*. La Grange, CA: Kerygma Press, 2009.

CHAPTER 5

THE KINGDOM OF GOD

WE HAVE SEEN that the Bible story can be told as the story of covenants that God has made, within the Trinity and with his creatures. But there are other ways in which the story can be told, other perspectives from which it can be seen. One of these is *the kingdom of God*. I think of covenants as normative, the kingdom as situational. The covenants establish the normative constitution of God's people. The kingdom describes the dynamic movement of history.

For some readers, that may be a surprising way to describe the kingdom. Often we think of *kingdom* as a geographical sphere of rule, such as the United Kingdom or the Hashemite Kingdom of Jordan. Of course, God's rule is over everything he has made. And his rule remains constant; he always rules everything. So what dynamism is there in the kingdom image?

But Geerhardus Vos formulated Jesus' view of the kingdom as follows:

> To him the kingdom exists there, where not merely God is supreme, for that is true at all times and under all circumstances, but where God supernaturally carries through his supremacy against all opposing powers and brings men to the willing recognition of the same.[1]

On this definition, the kingdom is dynamic, indeed dramatic. It is a world-historical movement, following the fall of Adam, in which God works to defeat Satan and bring human beings to acknowledge Christ as Lord. It is, preeminently, the *history* of salvation.

God could have remedied the fall in an instant, sending his Son in an accelerated time frame, bringing him to death, resurrection, ascension, and triumphal return in a matter of seconds. Or he might have accomplished this work in a matter of decades, allowing for a somewhat more normal kind of historical development. But instead he determined a process spread over millennia. He spent centuries narrowing the messianic line to a chosen family, bringing them into the Land of Promise, ordaining

---

1. Geerhardus Vos, *The Teaching of Jesus concerning the Kingdom of God and the Church* (Grand Rapids: Eerdmans, 1958), 50.

the birth of his Son in the "fullness of time" (Gal. 4:4), accomplishing redemption in thirty-three more years, and sending his disciples on a journey of several thousand years at least to bring this good news to all the nations.

Why he chose to stretch out the drama of salvation over so long a time is a mystery. The length of this time is related to other mysteries of Scripture, such as the problem of evil. We would not cry, "How long, O LORD?" (Pss. 6:3; 13:1; 80:4; 90:13; Hab. 1:2; Zech. 1:12; Rev. 6:10), if God had determined to complete his purposes in an instant, and the sting of pain and suffering would be much less if God were to abbreviate his story to a few decades. But God's decision is clear: that the history of redemption will take millennia, leaving space for dramatic movements, ups and downs, twists and turns, longings and astonishments. Salvation is to be a great epic, not a short story. God will glorify himself, not by measuring his kingdom in time spans appropriate to human kings, but by revealing himself as "King of the ages" (Rev. 15:3 NIV).

So in Scripture one event will picture, foreshadow, even motivate another event a thousand years later. The rebellion of Israel against God in the wilderness (Num. 14) is a warning to Christian believers in the first century A.D. (Heb. 3:7–19). Indeed, the accounts of that ancient history have the purpose of edifying believers in the new covenant period (Rom. 15:4).

The Two Ages

At every point in this great history, then, we look backward and forward. We look back on what God has already done, and we look forward to the fulfillment of his promises in the future. So at every stage of redemption, there is (to employ the theological jargon) an *already* and a *not yet*.

Biblical theology, which focuses on the history of redemption, has emphasized especially the "two-age" structure of the NT. In Matthew 12:32, Jesus speaks of a sin that will not be forgiven "either in this age or in the age to come." Paul also refers to these two ages in Ephesians 1:21. The first of the two ages is "this age" (*ho aion houtos*), the period of time in which we live, a period that is to end at the second coming of Christ and the final judgment (Matt. 13:39–40, 49; 24:3; 28:20). This is the age in which sin and the curse continue in the earth, before God's final victory. So Scripture describes this age in ethical terms. It is "the present evil age" (Gal. 1:4) from which Christ's redemption delivers us.

Nonbelievers are caught up in the affairs of "this age," unwilling to be bothered by the demands and promises of God. Jesus speaks of "the sons of this age" (Luke 20:34), Paul of "the debater of this age" (1 Cor. 1:20), the "rulers of this age" (1 Cor. 2:8), and the "wise in this age" (1 Cor. 3:18).

Some Christians, to be sure, are "rich in this present age" (1 Tim. 6:17), that is, they have acquired things that are valued by this age. That is not necessarily sinful, but Timothy must give them a special charge "not to be haughty, nor to set their hopes on the uncertainty of riches, but on God, who richly provides us with everything to enjoy." So all believers must take heed "to live self-controlled, upright, and godly lives in the present age" (Titus 2:12). The present age, even to believers, is a source of temptation.

The "age to come," however, is the age of fulfillment. Jesus contrasts the "sons of this age" (Luke 20:34) with "those who are considered worthy to attain to that age and to the resurrection from the dead" (v. 35). In the understanding of those Jews who believed in resurrection, "that age" follows our death and God's final judgment. In "the age to come," God's people have "eternal life" (Mark 10:30).

But the remarkable thing about NT teaching, in contrast with the Jewish conception, is that in one sense the "age to come" has already appeared in Christ. Believers in Christ are those "on whom the end of the ages has come" (1 Cor. 10:11). The closing of the holy places in the temple to worshipers is symbolic of the present age, so that when the veil is torn and we enter boldly into God's presence through Christ, another age has begun (Heb. 9:8–9). Christ "has appeared once for all at the end of the ages to put away sin by the sacrifice of himself" (9:26). For believers, then, the "coming age" has begun in Christ. He has dealt with sin once for all.

The resurrection of Jesus is the crucial sign that the "last days" are here. The Pharisees associated the last days with the resurrection of the righteous and the wicked. So Jesus associates that time with resurrection in John 6:39–40, 44, 54. But when the grieving Martha says that her brother Lazarus "will rise again in the resurrection on the last day" (John 11:24), Jesus replies, "I am the resurrection and the life. Whoever believes in me, though he die, yet shall he live, and everyone who lives and believes in me shall never die" (vv. 25–26). Then he proceeds to raise Lazarus from the dead, indicating that the life-giving power of the age to come is present in himself. So in Luke 17:21 Jesus tells the Pharisees that the kingdom is already in their midst, certainly referring to himself. Wherever Jesus is, there is the age to come.

After Jesus himself has risen, and signs of the Spirit's presence abound (sent from the throne of Christ), Peter announces that Joel's prophecy of the "last days" has been fulfilled (Acts 2:17). The writer to the Hebrews proclaims in the past tense that "in these last days [God] has spoken to us by his Son" (Heb. 1:2).

The same conclusion follows from NT teaching on the kingdom of God. Recall the definition of the kingdom that I quoted earlier from Vos. The kingdom of God, long awaited, has come in Christ (Matt. 3:2; 4:17; 12:28). The gospel is the gospel of the kingdom (4:23; 9:35; 10:7); the Sermon on the Mount, the ethic of the kingdom (5:3, 10, 19, 20; 6:33); the Lord's Prayer, the prayer of the kingdom (6:10); the parables, the mysteries of the kingdom (13:11). The church has the keys of the kingdom (16:19). The kingdom of God has come. Christ the King has been raised to God's right hand, where he has authority over all things (28:18).

Yet some biblical expectations for the last days and the kingdom are still unfulfilled. The bodily resurrection of the just and unjust has not taken place. The return of Christ and the final judgment remain future. The saints pray, "Thy kingdom come" (Matt. 6:10 kjv). That prayer assumes that the coming of the kingdom is future to some extent, though the prayer contains petitions for the near future, not only for the ultimate consummation.

Sin and the curse continue on the earth. Indeed, these "last days" are "times of difficulty" (2 Tim. 3:1; cf. 2 Peter 3:3). They are times in which false teaching abounds, in which unscrupulous people try to undermine the doctrine and holiness of God's people. Indeed, they are times when "all who desire to live a godly life in Christ Jesus will be persecuted" (2 Tim. 3:12).

So the biblical data is somewhat paradoxical. On the one hand, the last days are here in Christ. On the other hand, much remains future. The age to come is present; the present age lingers. From Jesus' ministry until his return, the two ages exist simultaneously. Our present existence is, as Vos put it, "semi-eschatological."

Below is Vos's diagram of the two ages.[2] "This age" runs from the fall of Adam to the return of Christ (parousia). "The age to come" runs from the resurrection of Christ through all eternity. During the period between the resurrection and the parousia, the two ages exist side by side. See fig. 5.1.

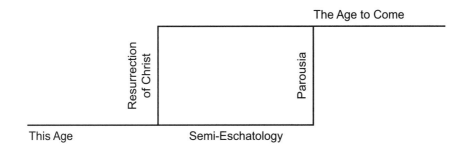

Fig. 5.1. The Two Ages

It is important for us to understand the dynamic and the tension of the semi-eschatological age in which we live. Our salvation is complete in Christ, but sin will not be destroyed until his return. Or again, as biblical theologians often put it, salvation is *already*, but also *not yet*. Christ has all authority, but Satan still has some power. We can draw confidently on the power and love of God, yet there are perils in the way. We have died to sin and have been raised to righteousness in Christ (Rom. 6), and yet we must "put to death . . . what is earthly in you" (Col. 3:5). The battle is won, but there is much mopping up to be done.[3]

This historical paradox is a current form of the larger paradox of the relation of divine sovereignty and human responsibility. God has saved us through Christ, by his

2. Geerhardus Vos, *The Pauline Eschatology* (Phillipsburg, NJ: Presbyterian and Reformed, 1986), 38.

3. Oscar Cullmann used World War II language to illustrate this paradox: Christ's atonement and resurrection are like D-Day, his return and the final judgment V-Day. But of course, the resurrection of Jesus guarantees its final outcome in a way that D-Day could not.

own sovereign power. We must rely on him for all our provision. But this fact does not allow us to be passive. There is a battle to be fought (Eph. 6:10–20), a race to be run (1 Cor. 9:24–27). We are not to "let go and let God." Rather, as Paul says, "work out your own salvation with fear and trembling, for it is God who works in you, both to will and to work for his good pleasure" (Phil. 2:12–13). God's sovereign action does not discourage, but rather motivates us to fight the spiritual battle, confident that ultimate victory is God's.

Some theologians present the semi-eschatological age as a time of suffering, pain, and defeat. Others present it as a time of victory for the gospel. In fact, both positions are correct. The history of the church has been full of suffering and persecution. But the blood of the martyrs has been the seed of the church, and often the worst persecutions have given rise to the strongest churches. And through history, Christian people have brought profound change to society, in the treatment of widows and orphans, the growth of learning, and the development of democracy, to mention only a few areas.

The *already* of the kingdom is not only the work of Christ in the past (his death, resurrection, and ascension). It is also what he is doing now, through the Spirit, in the church. The kingdom is to be "on earth as it is in heaven" (Matt. 6:10). It is like yeast, or a seed, that grows large through a temporal process (Matt. 13:24–33). In this time, believers do suffer defeats. The growing kingdom brings growing pains to its subjects. But they also experience the wonderful blessings of living under God: the green pastures, still waters (Ps. 23:2), the table that God prepares for us in the presence of our enemies (v. 5), the return of houses, brothers, sisters, mothers, children, and lands (Mark 10:30). And believers become "salt" and "light" to the rest of creation (Matt. 5:13–14).

God the King

The kingdom of God (defined as a historical program, as we have done) is essentially the coming of the King. Very close to the image *Lord* is the image *king*. The Hebrew and Greek words for *king* occur over twenty-eight hundred times in Scripture. Add to those the references to *kingdom*, the corresponding verbs, and related forms, and we can see that kingship is indeed pervasive in Scripture. These references include, of course, references to human kings as well as to the divine one. But as images, human kingship and divine kingship influence each other. Human kingship is to some extent an image of the divine. But negatively also: God's kingship stands in contrast with the corruption and tyranny of earthly kings.

That God is King is a major theme of Scripture, from Exodus 15:18 on. The Psalms speak often of the rule of God. Psalms 93–99, especially, provide concentrated reflection on the fact that God reigns over all. He is especially the King of Israel (Isa. 41:21) and over Israel's human king (Pss. 5:2; 145:1; and elsewhere). When the Israelites ask Samuel to appoint them a king "such as all the other nations have" (1 Sam. 8:5 NIV), the Lord tells Samuel, "It is not you they have rejected, but they have rejected me as their king" (v. 7 NIV).

Recall from chapter 2 that the covenant relation is between a great king and a lesser king. So God rules by virtue of his covenant. In this context, *king* and *lord* are close synonyms. The lord is the head of the covenant, the supreme norm; the king is the supreme power, the controller, who leads his people to battle against the foe. So it makes sense to relate covenant to kingdom as authority to power, as normative and situational perspectives. And we should always remember that the Lord is the King, and the King is the Lord (Pss. 10:16; 24:8, 10; 29:10; 47:2; 84:3; 98:6).

God's throne is the ark of the covenant, between the cherubim and beside the book of the covenant (1 Sam. 4:4; Ps. 99:1; cf. Isa. 6:1–5). As the Lord, the King controls his realm and speaks with authority. He also stands with his people, to protect and defend them, to provide justice and mercy.

But God is King not only of Israel, but of all the nations, indeed of the whole earth (Ex. 15:18; Pss. 22:28; 96–99; 145). God rules all because he is God and brings all things to pass, but also, as I indicated in chapter 4, because he is related to the whole creation by covenant.

His kingdom is eternal (Ex. 15:18; Ps. 93:2), but also historical and temporal. God is King eternally by virtue of his divine nature. But the narrative of Scripture is a history of the coming of the kingdom.

God is not an absentee King. He is also the Warrior who defends his people Israel against his and their enemies (Ex. 15:3; cf. Deut. 33:26; Ps. 68:5). He is the "Lord of hosts," as we have seen, the Lord of the angelic armies. When Israel is faithful to the Lord, she does not need to worry about her own resources (Deut. 20; Judg. 7:1–8). God fights for his people, often with no effort on their part (as 1 Sam. 7:10–13). Israel's victories are notable mainly for the supernatural assistance given to her. So the spiritual warfare is one that is fought by the "whole armor of God" (Eph. 6:10–20), the armor of faith, God's Word, righteousness, peace, salvation, and especially prayer. God himself wore this armor (Isa. 59:15–17) because there was no man who could deliver Israel from her sins. So Jesus, who delivers from sin, is the rider on the white horse, the Faithful and True, who "judges and makes war" (Rev. 19:11).

Christ the King

God advances his kingdom by choosing the families of Noah, Abraham, Isaac, and Jacob as his special people, through whom all the nations of the earth would be blessed and would come to know that he is Lord. So in the Psalms, the earthly king, David, advances the work of Yahweh, the King over him. As we saw in chapter 4, the Davidic covenant is the covenant of the kingdom. But David must also confess his sin (Pss. 32; 51). He looks forward to a greater King, One who is both his son and his Lord (Ps. 110:1). God is to set his King upon his holy hill, to rule all the nations (Pss. 2:1–12; 45; 72).

Jesus confounds the Pharisees by asking them how the messianic son of David could also be David's Lord (Matt. 22:41–46). It is evident that Jesus himself is the son of David greater than David himself. In him, God himself comes to rule his people. So, following John the Baptist (3:2), Jesus begins his preaching ministry by proclaiming, "The kingdom of heaven is at hand" (4:17). It is he who will carry through God's "supremacy against all opposing powers and [bring] men to the willing recognition of the same."

The wise men who visit Jesus at his birth identify him as the "king of the Jews" (Matt. 2:2). Jesus resists the public demand that he become an earthly king (John 6:15), but in Luke 19:38, his disciples welcome him to Jerusalem with the song "Blessed is the King who comes in the name of the Lord!" When Pontius Pilate asks him whether that title is appropriate, he responds affirmatively (Matt. 27:11). Pilate and the Roman soldiers then use that title to taunt the Jews (Matt. 27:29, 37; Mark 15:9, 12), and in time the Jewish leaders themselves turn the taunt against Jesus (Mark 15:32). And the Jews formulate Jesus' claim as a challenge to Rome, justifying his crucifixion (John 19:12, 15).

During his earthly life, Jesus did not reign in such a way as to challenge the political supremacy of Rome. But because of his atonement and resurrection, Paul is able to say:

> Therefore God has highly exalted him and bestowed on him the name that is above every name, so that at the name of Jesus every knee should bow, in heaven and on earth and under the earth, and every tongue confess that Jesus Christ is Lord, to the glory of God the Father. (Phil. 2:9–11)

And Jesus himself announces, after his resurrection:

> All authority in heaven and on earth has been given to me. Go therefore and make disciples of all nations, baptizing them in the name of the Father and of the Son and of the Holy Spirit, teaching them to observe all that I have commanded you. And behold, I am with you always, to the end of the age. (Matt. 28:18–20)

He is King of kings and Lord of lords (Rev. 19:16; cf. 17:14).

Since Jesus' ascension, the kingdom of God is the work of God through his people, bringing Jesus' kingship to bear on the whole world. It is bringing people to bow the knee to him, and every tongue to confess his lordship. It is turning people into disciples, baptizing, and teaching them to observe everything that Jesus has taught us. Note that our teaching is not just any "teaching" (*didasko*), but a teaching "to observe" (*tereo*). The focus is not on propositions, but on actions. The discipleship class leads not only to "knowing that," but to "knowing how." Insofar as the teaching remains at the intellectual level, the work is not done. The teaching is to be kept, observed, applied.

So the Great Commission is a program for cultural change. As individuals bow the knee to Christ, they discover that worshiping Jesus must lead to action, bringing Jesus' teachings to bear on everything. So the kingdom brings individuals to Christ and also brings those individuals to exalt him in every area of life. It is both individual and social change, until God consummates the kingdom at the return of Jesus to judge the living and the dead.[4]

4. In this respect I differ strongly from the view of the Escondido theologians that the kingdom in the present age is limited to the sermons and sacraments of the institutional church. See my *The Escondido Theology*

The Gospel of the Kingdom

As the disciples go to all the nations, teaching them the things of Christ, their words are "good news," "gospel." Paul writes to the church of Corinth:

> Now I would remind you, brothers, of the gospel I preached to you, which you received, in which you stand, and by which you are being saved, if you hold fast to the word I preached to you—unless you believed in vain. (1 Cor. 15:1–2)

In the OT, the phrase "good news" often refers, as in English, to any kind of welcome report, or any report that one might expect to be welcome (2 Sam. 4:10; 18:27; 1 Kings 1:42; 2 Kings 7:9). The prophecy of Isaiah, however, is the most important background for the NT gospel, for there the good news is specifically of divine redemption:

> Get you up to a high mountain,
>   O Zion, herald of good news;
> lift up your voice with strength,
>   O Jerusalem, herald of good news;
>   lift it up, fear not;
> say to the cities of Judah,
>   "Behold your God!" (Isa. 40:9)

> I was the first to say to Zion, "Behold, here they are!"
>   and I give to Jerusalem a herald of good news. (Isa. 41:27)

> How beautiful upon the mountains
>   are the feet of him who brings good news,
> who publishes peace, who brings good news of happiness,
>   who publishes salvation,
>   who says to Zion, "Your God reigns." (Isa. 52:7; cf. Nah. 1:15; Rom. 10:15)

> The Spirit of the Lord GOD is upon me,
>   because the LORD has anointed me
> to bring good news to the poor;
>   he has sent me to bind up the brokenhearted,
> to proclaim liberty to the captives,
>   and the opening of the prison to those who are bound;
> to proclaim the year of the LORD's favor,
>   and the day of vengeance of our God;
>   to comfort all who mourn. (Isa. 61:1–2)

At Jesus' birth, the angel proclaims this gospel to the shepherds:

(Lakeland, FL: Whitefield Media, 2011).

> Fear not, for behold, I bring you good news of great joy that will be for all the people. For unto you is born this day in the city of David a Savior, who is Christ the Lord. (Luke 2:10–11)

The gospel, then, is the good news of redemption through Christ. But this redemption is specifically through Christ as King. It is the message "your God reigns" (Isa. 52:7) and the royal act of freeing captives and executing vengeance (61:1). The angels' message presents Christ as the new David, David's son and David's Lord. Jesus' coming is the coming of the Lord, the coming of the King.

So the first preaching of the NT, by John the Baptist (Matt. 3:2) and by Jesus (4:23), is the "gospel of the kingdom," that is, "Repent, for the kingdom of heaven is at hand" (4:17).[5] The first preaching by Jesus' disciples is the same (10:7). Throughout the NT, the kingdom is the focus of the good news: see Matt. 9:35; 24:14; Luke 8:1; Acts 1:3; 8:12; 19:8; 20:25; 28:23, 31.

But the kingdom in the NT is *already* and *not yet*. When Jesus chose to read Isaiah 61:1–2 in the synagogue at Nazareth, his hometown, according to Luke 4:16–21, announcing that the passage was fulfilled in him, he ended his reading before "and the day of vengeance of our God." Jesus, at his first coming, does not carry out God's vengeance, but only "the year of the Lord's favor." The Lord's favor is *already*, his vengeance *not yet*.

"The Lord's favor" is preeminently Jesus' death on the cross, bearing our sins, and his resurrection, in which we rise to newness of life (Rom. 6:4). So when Paul formulates the contents of the gospel in 1 Corinthians 15:1–11, he focuses on Jesus' atonement and resurrection:

> Now I would remind you, brothers, of the gospel I preached to you, which you received, in which you stand, and by which you are being saved, if you hold fast to the word I preached to you—unless you believed in vain. For I delivered to you as of first importance what I also received: that Christ died for our sins in accordance with the Scriptures, that he was buried, that he was raised on the third day in accordance with the Scriptures. (1 Cor. 15:1–4)

Indeed, Paul can say that when he first preached the gospel at Corinth, he "decided to know nothing among you except Jesus Christ and him crucified" (1 Cor. 2:2). Similarly, Paul in Acts 20:24 describes his preaching as "the gospel of the grace of God."

Theological writers have not always found it easy to reconcile the *kingdom* emphasis in the gospel with its *grace* emphasis. But it is not difficult to bring the two together. Kingdom is a broader concept than grace, for it includes both grace and vengeance. Even Paul, who stresses grace, speaks of

> that day when, according to my gospel, God judges the secrets of men by Christ Jesus. (Rom. 2:16)

---

5. "Kingdom of heaven" is the phrase preferred by Matthew, "kingdom of God" by the other NT writers. There is no reason to think of these as anything but synonymous. Perhaps Matthew's Jewish readers were more comfortable avoiding direct reference to "God."

Paul's gospel, like the gospel of Isaiah, John the Baptist, and Jesus, is a gospel of the whole kingdom, both grace and judgment. Acts 14:22; 19:8; 20:25; 28:23; and 28:31 describe Paul's preaching as a kingdom gospel.

So in the Great Commission, Jesus sends his disciples through the world to make disciples, not only teaching them about the cross and resurrection, important as those are, but also "teaching them to observe all that I have commanded you" (Matt. 28:20). The kingdom is *already* and *not yet*, but also growing through the world, like grain sown in a field (13:1–9), a mustard seed growing into a large tree (vv. 31–32), yeast growing through bread (v. 33), as Jesus' disciples apply to their lives all the things that Jesus taught. Today, in our own experience, people are finding the kingdom as a hidden treasure (v. 44) and as a costly pearl (vv. 45–46). They are caught up (with, to be sure, nonelect people) in God's dragnet (vv. 47–50). The kingdom is established in the work of Jesus and will be consummated at his return to judge at the end of this age. But the kingdom is also something that expands through the world between those two great events. The growth of the kingdom, its expansion, is a present reality. That growth is given by God's sovereign grace, through the work of believers as they obey Jesus' Great Commission.

Law and Gospel

Much has been said in the theological literature about the relationship of gospel to law. Martin Luther, for example, argued for a very sharp distinction between these. He said that God's law tells us what we must do to be right with God. But the gospel tells us how we can be saved from God's wrath against those who have not kept his law. God's law includes all his commands; the gospel contains all his promises. Luther warned against any confusion of law and gospel. In his view, there should be no gospel in the law, no law in the gospel. For him, what is most important in theology is to "properly distinguish" law and gospel. John Calvin also spoke of the law-gospel distinction, but the distinction never became as central in Reformed theology as in Lutheran theology. Indeed, Lutherans regularly criticized Calvinists for confusing law and gospel.[6]

It makes sense to say that we should not confuse God's demands with his promises. Nevertheless, the kind of sharp distinction that Luther proposed is not biblical. For one thing, biblical proclamations of gospel include commands, particularly commands to repent and believe (Mark 1:15; Acts 2:38). And God gave his law to the children of Israel in a context of gospel: he had delivered them out of Egypt; therefore, they should keep his law (Ex. 20:2–17). The law is a gift of God's grace (Ps. 119:29). There is more to be said, evidently.[7]

6. The law-gospel distinction plays a central role in the Lutheran Formula of Concord, but it rarely if ever appears in Reformed confessions, the Second Helvetic being an exception. There is a similar difference between Lutheran and Reformed systematic theologies.

7. For my analysis, see *DCL*, 182–91. See also the booklet by P. Andrew Sandlin, *Wrongly Dividing the Word: Overcoming the Law-Gospel Distinction* (Mount Hermon, CA: Center for Cultural Leadership, 2010).

Traditionally, Lutherans and Calvinists have distinguished three "uses" of the law: (1) to restrain evil in society, (2) to terrify sinners in order to drive them to Christ, and (3) to provide guidance to those who believe to live the Christian life. (Sometimes the first use is called the second and vice versa.) There have been controversies among Lutherans about the legitimacy of the third use, and a number of Calvinists[8] have also been uncomfortable with it, thinking that the third use leads to legalism or moralism. But in fact, the Bible abounds with commands that God expects believers to obey. We are not saved by keeping the law, but we are always obligated to keep the law, and once we are saved and raised from death to life, we desire to keep the law out of love for God and for Jesus. The law not only is a terrifying set of commands to drive us to Christ, but also is the gentle voice of the Lord, showing his people that the best blessings of this life come from following his will.

In the preaching of the kingdom, law and gospel come together. The coming of the kingdom is the coming of a King to enforce his law on a disobedient world, that is, to enforce his covenant against covenant-breakers. But the King who comes is full of love and forgiveness. So his coming is good news, gospel, not only because he judges the wicked, but because he brings redemption, forgiveness, and reward to his redeemed people. When God brought Israel out of Egypt, he spoke good news to her: "I am the LORD your God, who brought you out of the land of Egypt, out of the house of slavery" (Ex. 20:2). And then, very naturally, he proclaimed his commandments: "You shall have no other gods before me. You shall not make for yourself a carved image," and on through the tenth commandment (vv. 3–17). The commandments were indeed terrifying to the Israelites (vv. 18–21), but they were part of the good news, setting forth a way of life for Israel in fellowship with her Lord and Savior. As I said in the previous chapter, the Decalogue was a covenant between God and Israel, and Israel was to receive it by a living, obedient faith.

One Kingdom or Two?

Having drawn a sharp distinction between law and gospel, Luther also distinguished two kingdoms, in effect a kingdom of law and a kingdom of gospel. The kingdom of law was the civil order, ruled by the state. The kingdom of gospel was the order of salvation, ruled by the church. The civil order is secular, the church sacred. The civil order is governed by natural law, the sacred order by Scripture. Every believer belongs to both kingdoms, but the two do not overlap in their functions. So modern advocates of the Two Kingdoms theory maintain that the church should never (or very rarely) try to influence the secular world, nor should it allow itself to be influenced by secular culture.

It should be evident from our study so far that Scripture speaks of only one kingdom of God. That kingdom is the historical program of God coming to overcome his enemies, to redeem his people, and to bring his lordship to bear on all areas of created

---

8. For examples, see my book *The Escondido Theology*, cited earlier.

reality. There is no "secular kingdom," no kingdom ruled only by natural law and not by Scripture. All people, all institutions, all spheres of human life have a responsibility to hear God's Word, to respond to it obediently, and to accept the renewal of God's grace.[9]

After Cain killed his brother Abel (Gen. 4:1–15), his family moved to Nod, east of Eden, and built up cities and culture. These people ignored and disobeyed God, to such an extent that eventually their wickedness came to characterize the human race as a whole, to such an extent that God determined to destroy it, except for righteous Noah and his family. But even after the flood, even after God's covenant with Noah (8:21), human beings drifted far from God. It would be wrong to describe their cultures as *secular*. These cultures were religious, but devoted to false gods. *Secular* societies, societies that pretend to exist without religion, are a modern phenomenon. But even modern secular culture is rebellion against God. It is not a religiously neutral social order, as Luther and others have evidently imagined. For there is no neutrality. A society that tries to live without God inevitably worships something, whether a false god, an ideology, human reason, or the state. These are idols as certainly as were Baal and Astarte. To develop a culture apart from God's Word is sin. And sin is always religious. It is rebellion against the true God, embracing an idol.

Crime is always the expression of false religion. A criminal rejects God's law and places himself above it. That is a religious choice. Similarly, righteousness involves a choice to worship God in one's actions. Wickedness and righteousness are religious through and through.

So Scripture never remotely suggests that such a neutral order is possible. We should not imagine that God commanded such neutrality as a means of restraining sin. Such societies may indeed restrain sin to some extent (as agents of God's common grace), but they cannot be justified for that reason. The kingdom of God asserts God's rule over all people, all areas of their lives, all human institutions, all human culture. Anyone who is not on God's side is against him.

Life in the Kingdom

In Matthew 6:33, Jesus tells his disciples to "seek first the kingdom of God and his righteousness, and all these things will be added to you." "These things" are things such as food and clothing mentioned in the preceding context. So Jesus sets the kingdom as the goal of human life. Believers ought to make it their highest goal to contribute to the historical program of the kingdom of God. They should carry out the Great Commission, to make disciples for Jesus. They should do what they can to defeat evil and all that opposes God in the world and bring people to a willing recognition of Christ as King of kings.

Jesus devotes much of his oral teaching to our life in the kingdom. The Sermon on the Mount begins with the "Beatitudes," the blessings given to his kingdom disciples:

---

9. Recall that in chapter 4, I argued against those who think that God's covenant with Noah is a secular order.

comfort in the midst of mourning, inheritance for those who are meek, mercy to the merciful (Matt. 5:1–11). Those in the kingdom are to be salt and light in the earth (vv. 13–16). They keep the law, not just externally, but from the heart (vv. 17–48). Note that the kingdom and law are not opposed. The law continues as the standard of kingdom life, the normative perspective. But the kingdom provides direction, prioritization, a situational perspective.[10]

The kingdom begins in Jesus himself and in the working of the Spirit, bringing people to acknowledge him as King. So the headquarters of the kingdom is the church, the community of those who worship and follow God in Jesus. But God's intention is that believers will not keep the kingdom to themselves, but will bring it into all spheres of human life: Paul says, "Whether you eat or drink, or whatever you do, do all to the glory of God" (1 Cor. 10:31). As believers take their faith into their workplaces and culture, they take the kingdom with them. They reach unbelievers with the gospel, as Jesus commanded. But even when their associates remain unconverted, they seek to do their work in line with Jesus' standards, and this brings about changes in culture. I hesitate to use the term *transform* to describe these changes, for often the changes are small and fragmentary. Only at the Lord's return will the transformation of the creation be complete. But it begins now. Jesus compares the kingdom to little things that grow large: a mustard seed (Matt. 13:31), leaven (13:33). He compares them to common things that have uncommon importance: believers are salt (5:13) and light (5:14) in the world. He teaches his disciples to pray, "Your kingdom come, your will be done, on earth as it is in heaven" (6:10): the coming of the kingdom here is not only the final judgment, but the growing influence of God's will on earth, paralleling the obedience of angels and departed saints in heaven.

The Two Kingdoms view maintains that the kingdom came in Jesus and will come again in Jesus' return, but that it is confined to the church in the period between Jesus' two advents. That view goes against the passages cited above. Clearly, the kingdom has in fact deeply affected human culture over the centuries: in the sciences, the arts, the treatment of orphans and widows, education, and every other area of importance to human beings. We must continue to seek the kingdom of God (Matt. 6:33) every day as Jesus has commanded, and we should expect to see the results in divine blessing.

Key Terms

Kingdom of God (Vos)
History of salvation
The two ages
Already and *not yet*
Parousia
This age
The age to come

---

10. For elaboration, see chapters 9–17 of *DCL*.

Semi-eschatology
Gospel
Kingdom emphasis
Grace emphasis
Three uses of the law
Two Kingdoms view
Secular
Neutrality

Study Questions

1. "Why did God choose to stretch out the drama of salvation over so long a time?" Show why this question is important and respond to it.

2. "So in Scripture one event will picture, foreshadow, even motivate another event a thousand years later." Give an example.

3. "But the remarkable thing about NT teaching, in contrast with the Jewish conception, is that in one sense the 'age to come' has already appeared in Christ." Explain; evaluate.

4. Reproduce Vos's diagram of the two ages and explain every line.

5. Describe the nature of Jesus' kingship. To what extent is he like or unlike earthly kings?

6. Describe the tension between the "kingdom emphasis" and the "grace emphasis" in the gospel. How can that tension be resolved?

7. Describe and evaluate Martin Luther's view of the relationship between law and gospel.

8. "In the preaching of the kingdom, law and gospel come together." Explain; evaluate.

9. Respond to the Two Kingdoms view.

10. "But even modern secular culture is rebellion against God." Why is it important to remember this?

11. "And sin is always religious. It is rebellion against the true God, embracing of an idol." Explain; evaluate.

12. Summarize how the kingdom makes a difference in the Christian life.

Memory Verses

Isa. 52:7: How beautiful upon the mountains
    are the feet of him who brings good news,
who publishes peace, who brings good news of happiness,
    who publishes salvation,
    who says to Zion, "Your God reigns."

Matt. 6:33: But seek first the kingdom of God and his righteousness, and all these things will be added to you.

Matt. 28:18–20: All authority in heaven and on earth has been given to me. Go therefore and make disciples of all nations, baptizing them in the name of the Father and of the Son and of the Holy Spirit, teaching them to observe all that I have commanded you. And behold, I am with you always, to the end of the age.

1 Cor. 15:1–4: Now I would remind you, brothers, of the gospel I preached to you, which you received, in which you stand, and by which you are being saved, if you hold fast to the word I preached to you—unless you believed in vain. For I delivered to you as of first importance what I also received: that Christ died for our sins in accordance with the Scriptures, that he was buried, that he was raised on the third day in accordance with the Scriptures.

Resources for Further Study

Frame, John M. *DCL*, 131–313.

———. *The Escondido Theology*. Lakeland, FL: Whitefield Media, 2011.

Ridderbos, Herman N. *The Coming of the Kingdom*. Vineland, ON: Paideia Press, 1979. Comprehensive biblical treatment.

Sandlin, P. Andrew. *Wrongly Dividing the Word: Overcoming the Law-Gospel Distinction*. Mount Hermon, CA: Center for Cultural Leadership, 2010.

Vos, Geerhardus. *The Teaching of Jesus concerning the Kingdom of God and the Church*. Grand Rapids: Eerdmans, 1958.

CHAPTER 6

THE FAMILY OF GOD

SOME PEOPLE HAVE QUESTIONED why I chose God's lordship, rather than his fatherhood, as the main theme of my four-book series. At one level, the question was easy to answer. In Scripture, *Lord* is far more frequent than *Father* as a title of God. *Father*, applied to God, is rare in the OT, becoming common only in the NT; but God's covenant lordship is a theme that pervades both Testaments, OT no less than NT.

At another level, however, the question is a serious one. *Father*, though infrequent in the OT as a title of God, emerges in the NT as Jesus' own name for the One who sent him. (He does not address God as *Lord* or as *King*.) The relation of the Father to the Son reveals the communion of the Trinity itself.

But then, Jesus also authorizes his disciples to call on God as their Father (Matt. 6:9). So *Father* is the name of God most closely associated with Jesus. Further, this is our most intimate way to speak of, and with, God. It is the child's expression *Abba* (Mark 14:36; Rom. 8:15; Gal. 4:6), sometimes interpreted "Daddy." So the question becomes: Shouldn't theology focus on the name of God most associated with Christ himself and most richly evocative of the special relation between God and the NT believer?

This is a persuasive argument, but not persuasive enough to make me change the theme of the Theology of Lordship series of books or of this one. Nevertheless, God's fatherhood must receive our full appreciation. In this book I will treat it as a perspective on God's relation to us, coordinate with his lordship and his kingship. God's lordship is the normative perspective, which stresses God's authority as head of the covenant. His kingship is the situational perspective, identifying God as the One who pursues the purposes of his redemptive history. His fatherhood is the existential perspective, his intimate, personal relationship to each of his people.

Corresponding to these titles of God are three titles of God's people. Corresponding to God's lordship, we are servants. Corresponding to his kingship, we are subjects. Corresponding to his fatherhood, we are his family, his sons and daughters. See fig. 6.1.

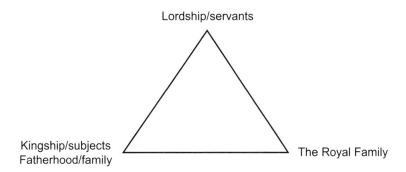

Fig. 6.1. Titles of God's People

Although *Father* is not a frequent name of God in the OT, Scripture from the beginning presents the history of redemption not only as the history of covenants or of the kingdom, but of the royal family. The cultural mandate of Genesis 1:28 included a command to reproduce, so that the seed of our first parents was to "fill the earth." God renewed that command to Noah's family after the flood (9:7). Through reproduction, indeed, was to come the One who would deliver mankind from sin, the offspring of the woman (3:15). So Scripture is full of genealogies, indicating not only the development of culture through the nations, but also the progress of the history of redemption, the ancestors of the family from which the Deliverer would come.[1]

And so the history of redemption moves from generation to generation within that family. Its focus moves from the family of Adam to that of Noah, to Abraham, Isaac, and Jacob, to Israel as that family become a nation. Then, as we saw in chapters 4 and 5, David's family becomes especially prominent during his lifetime and later, and much is said about Christ's belonging to David's line. David is important as the subject of God's messianic covenant, as the model head of the kingdom of God, and as the most illustrious ancestor of Jesus' genealogy.

Then in the NT, believers are God's family, under his fatherhood. *Brother* is the most common way of referring to a believer after Jesus' resurrection. The term distinguishes the believer from the world. For example, in 1 Corinthians 5:9–11, Paul tells the church that he has no objection to their associating with immoral people in the world. But he says:

> I am writing to you not to associate with anyone who bears the name of brother if he is guilty of sexual immorality or greed, or is an idolater, reviler, drunkard, or swindler—not even to eat with such a one. (1 Cor. 5:11)

---

1. Not only are there literal genealogies in Scripture, lists of names indicating who begat whom, but the history of redemption itself can be described as a genealogy or generation. The book of Genesis is divided into sections headed by the phrase "these are the generations of" (Gen. 2:4; 5:1; 6:9; and so on). The "generations of the heavens and the earth" (2:4) show what transpired on the earth after it was created. The "generations of Adam" (5:1) describe Adam's descendants and tell stories concerning them. The history of Genesis is a family history. Luke's genealogy of Jesus traces him back to Adam and identifies Adam as "the son of God" (Luke 3:38).

The name *brother* (which, of course, includes sisters) is a precious title, indicating fellowship in the holy family. We should not give any credence to those who claim the name of brother and yet engage in immorality.

Paul extends the family metaphor to refer to himself as father:

> I do not write these things to make you ashamed, but to admonish you as my beloved children. For though you have countless guides in Christ, you do not have many fathers. For I became your father in Christ Jesus through the gospel. (1 Cor. 4:14–15; cf. Philem. 10)

This may appear contrary to Jesus' criticism of the Pharisees:

> They do all their deeds to be seen by others. For they make their phylacteries broad and their fringes long, and they love the place of honor at feasts and the best seats in the synagogues and greetings in the marketplaces and being called rabbi by others. But you are not to be called rabbi, for you have one teacher, and you are all brothers. And call no man your father on earth, for you have one Father, who is in heaven. Neither be called instructors, for you have one instructor, the Christ. (Matt. 23:5–10)

But Jesus here speaks somewhat hyperbolically to say that the error of the Pharisees, claiming a level of authority that belonged to God alone, should never be found among his disciples. In 1 Corinthians 4:14–15, Paul does claim authority, but only the authority of the One who first brought the gospel to the church and who through that gospel brought the church into fellowship with Christ. Here the father image conveys gentleness and love rather than domination.

The family image also indicates that in salvation God calls not only individuals, but families, households, even nations. God's covenant with Noah was also a covenant with his family. The same was true of Abraham, indicated especially by God's command to Abraham to circumcise all the males in his household (Gen. 17:8–14). When Abraham's family grows into the nation of Israel, God insists that their children be circumcised as well (Ex. 4:24–26; Lev. 12:3; Josh. 5:2). In the same spirit, Peter on the day of Pentecost says:

> For the promise is for you and for your children and for all who are far off, everyone whom the Lord our God calls to himself. (Acts 2:39)

So in the new covenant also, God is calling families, and explicitly children (Matt. 19:14),[2] to himself. Conversions in the NT are commonly of household units (Acts 11:14; 16:15, 31–34; 1 Cor. 1:16). The church's meetings were commonly in someone's house (Rom. 16:5; 1 Cor. 16:19; Col. 4:15; Philem. 2).[3]

---

2. When Jesus lays hands on the children and blesses them, he is performing a priestly act, placing the name of God upon them, as in Numbers 6:22–27.

3. The fact that God calls families to himself in both Testaments and the household nature of both circumcision and baptism are relevant to the question of the subjects of baptism, which I will discuss in chapter 49 of

So the church is not only the covenant people of God, and the subjects of the king, but also the family of God. Through Christ, our Father "sets the lonely in families" (Ps. 68:6 NIV). So clearly it is appropriate for this family to address God as Father, as Jesus taught us to do.

The Fatherhood of God

How is God's fatherhood related to his lordship and kingship? The line between political and family images in Scripture is not sharp. The human race began as a family, with the father or patriarch playing the roles of prophet, priest, and king. As the human race increased in numbers, these roles became more differentiated. When the family of Israel became a nation, Moses, on the advice of Jethro his father-in-law, set up a system of judges over "thousands, hundreds, fifties and tens" (Ex. 18:21 NIV), with himself at the top of the hierarchy.[4] So civil government in Scripture is an expansion of family government. And, appropriately, Scripture uses *father* as a metaphor for civil and military rule (Gen. 45:8; Judg. 5:7 [mother!]; 2 Kings 5:13; Isa. 49:23). Indeed, the metaphor extends to prophets, wisdom teachers, and church leaders (2 Kings 2:12; 13:14; Ps. 34:11; Prov. 1:8, 10, 15; 1 Cor. 4:15; Gal. 4:19 [mother, again]. Paul presses the analogy to say that a man should not be an elder in the church if he is not a good father (1 Tim. 3:4–5; Titus 1:6). So the Westminster catechisms understand the fifth commandment, "Honor your father and your mother," as a principle applying to all human relationships.[5]

So in Scripture God's fatherhood is not sharply distinct from his lordship. Sometimes it is linked with creation, as in Deuteronomy 32:6, where God rebukes Israel for its corruption:

Do you thus repay the LORD,
    you foolish and senseless people?
Is not he your father, who created you,
    who made you and established you?

Cf. Mal. 2:10. Similarly in Acts 17:28, where Paul quotes the words of the pagan Aratus, "We are indeed his offspring." God is Father of all by virtue of creation.

But God exercises a special kind of fatherhood toward his chosen people by virtue of his covenants with them. In such contexts, Scripture emphasizes more specifically the qualities of a good family head: the father as protector, provider, and guide (Deut. 1:31), showing compassion to his children (Ps. 103:13), especially toward the fatherless (Ps. 68:5). The Father is the Redeemer (Isa. 63:16).[6] He reaches out with joy to the

---

this book.

4. See *DCL*, 593–602, for a longer account of the relation between family and state.

5. WLC 123–33; WSC 63–66.

6. But in the context of Isaiah 63:16, the prophet knows that redemption has not yet been accomplished. He calls God to cease withholding his tenderness and compassion.

returning prodigal (Luke 15:11–32). Discipline, too, is important (Prov. 3:11–12; Heb. 12:4–11). Though sometimes painful, it is evidence of the Father's love. Indeed, without it, we would not be children of God at all, but illegitimate (Heb. 12:8). Even as a Father, God is not to be trifled with. Intimate and compassionate as he is, he requires the honor of the fifth commandment (Mal. 1:6): "If then I am a father," he asks, "where is my honor?" Cf. Jer. 3:4–5, 19.

The father image, applied to God, is somewhat rare in the OT, as we have seen, but it becomes quite central to the NT, because of Jesus' teaching and because of his special relationship to God.[7] Regularly, he refers to God as "the Father" and "my Father," and to himself as "son." Jesus is "Son of God" in a unique sense, one that can be expounded only in terms of the doctrine of the Trinity.[8] In the case of Jesus, the Son of God is no less than God.

But remarkably, Jesus teaches his disciples also to address God as Father, as in the Lord's Prayer: "Our Father in heaven" (Matt. 6:9). God is not our Father in the same sense as he is the Father of Jesus; we are not God. Jesus delicately distinguishes the two fatherhoods of God when he speaks with Mary Magdalene after his resurrection: "I am ascending to my Father and your Father, to my God and your God" (John 20:17). Elsewhere in the NT, the term *adoption* is used to describe our relation to the Father (Rom. 8:15, 23; 9:4; Gal. 4:5; Eph. 1:5). Jesus is the Son by nature; we are sons by adoption. Jesus is the eternal Son, but God confers sonship upon us in time (cf. John 1:12–13). But the distinction is not a separation. We are "fellow heirs with Christ" (Rom. 8:17). We "suffer with him in order that we may also be glorified with him."[9]

We are sons for Jesus' sake, because of him, and in him. He has redeemed us so that we might receive the rights of sons (Gal. 4:5). All believers in Christ, therefore, are sons of God; none are more or less so. In the body of Christ, the Gentiles are coheirs with the Jews (v. 7).

So to know God as *Father* is a special privilege of God's family, of those who know Christ. A special sign of this relationship is the intimate Aramaic word *Abba*, sometimes described as a child's word for "Daddy," used among the early Christians. Jesus used the term (Mark 14:36), and Paul teaches that God has sent upon us the Spirit of his Son, of Jesus, enabling us also to address God in that way (Gal. 4:6; cf. Rom. 8:15).

In a related family image, God is also related to his people as *husband*.[10] To the barren woman, deserted by her husband, Isaiah says that "your Maker is your husband, the LORD of hosts is his name" (Isa. 54:5). God is the One who found Israel "wallowing in your blood" (Ezek. 16:6), abandoned. He said to her, "Live!," saved her life, and married her. But she was unfaithful. Adultery images idolatry, and in Hosea 1–3 the

---

7. Of course, the concept of adoption, of God's taking a people to bear his name, is not foreign to the OT, as we saw in the previous chapter. But in the NT the image of God's fatherhood to describe this relationship is far more pervasive.

8. See my discussion in chapters 21–22 of this book.

9. See the discussion of adoption in chapter 42.

10. Both *father* and *husband*. Biblical teachings are always consistent with one another, but biblical images are not necessarily so.

prophet himself becomes the image, marrying a prostitute, taking her back despite her unfaithfulness. In the NT, Christ is the Bridegroom, the church the bride:

> Husbands, love your wives, as Christ loved the church and gave himself up for her, so that he might sanctify her, having cleansed her by the washing of water with the word, so that he might present the church to himself in splendor, without spot or wrinkle or any such thing, that she might be holy and without blemish. (Eph. 5:25–27)

As father and husband, God identifies himself as head of the family. They are terms of authority, but also of love, compassion, and grace.

Father and Mother?

Much recent theology has focused on the appropriateness of feminine language for God. The late evangelical theologian Paul K. Jewett made this question central to his *God, Creation, and Revelation.*[11] Although he denied in his preface that "I have any thought of accommodating the exposition of the Christian faith to the canons of modernity,"[12] he sometimes used *she* to refer to God[13] and gave much space to the defense of feminist arguments. Elizabeth Johnson's *She Who Is,*[14] a comprehensive treatise on the doctrine of God, has as its main thesis the necessity of using feminine language (more or less exclusively, for the time being[15]) in reference to God. These titles are typical of many.

This question is certainly not a major concern of Scripture itself, nor is it a high priority of this volume. But since theology is application, it is important for us to apply biblical principles to issues of concern to contemporary people. And there certainly are biblical principles that are relevant to this question.

What Would a Female God Be Like?

First, we should be clear that this question is a question about *imagery.* No one argues that God is literally male or female, for the general consensus among Christians (and, in my view, the biblical teaching) is that God is incorporeal.[16] Elizabeth Johnson does believe that God is physical in the panentheistic sense: God's body is the world.[17] But even she does not base her argument for the femininity of God on physical characteristics.

Further, although Scripture sometimes represents God anthropomorphically by using images of bodily parts, those parts never include sexual organs.[18] So sexuality as

---

11. Grand Rapids: Eerdmans, 1991.

12. Ibid., xvi.

13. Ibid., 336 and following unit.

14. New York: Crossroad Publishing, 1996. I will interact with some of Johnson's arguments in this section.

15. Ibid., 54.

16. See my later discussion of God's incorporeality, chapter 25.

17. Johnson, *She Who Is*, 230–33. She introduces her panentheism toward the end of the book. Her main arguments don't depend on it in any obvious way.

18. The Hebrew verb *racham* ("have compassion") is related to the noun *rechem* ("womb"). So some have thought there was an allusion to God's "womb" in Psalm 103:13 and Jeremiah 31:20. Similarly with the corresponding

such is not part of Scripture's *visual* imagery. The issues concerning "feminine images of God," therefore, are subtle. They are questions about analogies between God's status, character, personality, and actions and those we associate with women.

The very nature of this question raises problems for feminism. Are there traits of character or personality distinctive to women in some degree? Sometimes feminists have said no. In their view, all human character and personality traits are common to men and women, and to think otherwise is to engage in stereotypes. Other times, they have recognized that there are differences (in degree, at least), but have wanted society to give greater honor to those traits associated with women.

Johnson and some others want to have it both ways. Johnson insists that our notion of the feminine (and therefore the feminine God) should include "intellectual, artistic," and "public leadership," even "pride and anger."[19] She praises the religion of Ishtar (in the OT, Astarte or Ashtoreth, the wife of Baal, Judg. 2:13; 10:6; 1 Sam. 7:3–4; 12:10) for finding in its goddess "a source of divine power and sovereignty embodied in female form," who wages war and exercises judgment.[20] On this basis, male and female traits are essentially the same. What society needs to understand is that they can be found in women as well as men.[21]

This emphasis conflicts, however, with Johnson's distaste for the notions of "power-over,"[22] rule, and submission.[23] She sees these as typically male characteristics that feminist theology should avoid ascribing to God. Is "power-over" a male trait that feminist theology would displace in favor of female traits? Or is it a trait that feminists should embrace as properly feminine and find its archetype in a female deity?

It is not clear, therefore, what kind of god a female deity would be. Would she be far more nurturing, kind, hospitable, friendly than the male deity of patriarchal theology? Or would she be just as powerful, dominant, aggressive as any male, but nevertheless somehow female? Johnson usually seems to favor the latter alternative, with some inconsistency, as we have seen. But then what is distinctively female about this female deity? If her femininity is not physical, we can judge her sexuality only by traits of character and personality. But on Johnson's description, the goddess's traits are common to males and females. So it is hard to judge what Johnson really means to assert in saying that God is female.

Feminine Images of God in Scripture

Nevertheless, we should proceed to look at the biblical data. It should be agreed that though God is the Creator and therefore the exemplar of both "masculine" and

NT term *splanchnizomai*. This term and its cognate forms never clearly refer to a womb in the NT. I believe this argument presses etymology too far.

19. Johnson, *She Who Is*, 53. Cf. 181–85, 256–59.

20. Ibid., 55–56. Johnson frequently appeals to non-Christian religions to commend their theology of gender. That practice raises legitimate questions about the biblical integrity of her theology.

21. Note also her critique of stereotypes in ibid., 47–54.

22. As in ibid., 21, 69, 269–71.

23. Ibid., 69.

"feminine" virtues (however these are defined), the biblical images of God, insofar as sexuality is relevant to them, are predominantly masculine. The pronouns and verbs referring to God in Scripture are always masculine, and the images used of him (Lord, King, Father, husband, etc.) are typically masculine.[24]

There are, however, some feminine images of God in the Bible. In Deuteronomy 32:18, God through Moses rebukes Israel, saying:

> You deserted the Rock, who fathered you;
>   You forgot the God who gave you birth. (NIV)

In this image, God plays both male and female roles in Israel's origin. In Numbers 11:12, Moses, frustrated by the grumbling of the Israelites, denies before God that he (Moses) had conceived these people and brought them forth. So he asks, "Why do you tell me to carry them in my arms, as a nurse carries an infant?" (NIV). Perhaps the thought of Deuteronomy 32:18 lies in the background of Moses' words: it is God who conceived Israel and gave her birth, and so God is the One who should be her nursemaid. These two passages are often mentioned in the feminist literature, but the female imagery is very brief in the contexts of the verses. Nothing much is made of the fact that God gives birth or might be nursemaid. The imagery here is less striking than that of Galatians 4:19, where the apostle Paul describes himself as being in the pains of childbirth for the church, and 1 Thessalonians 2:7, where he says that the apostles were "gentle among you, like a nursing mother taking care of her own children." No one ever suggests because of these passages that we should regard Paul as female, or as "mother." Nor do Numbers 11:12 and Deuteronomy 32:18 require us to rethink God's gender.[25]

In Isaiah 42:14–15, God declares impending judgment:

> For a long time I have held my peace;
>   I have kept still and restrained myself;
> now I will cry out like a woman in labor;
>   I will gasp and pant.
> I will lay waste mountains and hills,
>   and dry up all their vegetation.

Feminist writers often present this passage as a feminine image of God. The image here is certainly feminine. An expectant mother may spend many months in modest

24. The image *judge* has one female exemplar, Deborah (Judg. 4–5).

25. Nor, even more obviously, should we draw such a conclusion from Isaiah 46:3. The passage mentions Israel's conception and birth, but does not suggest at all that God conceived and bore the nation. Of course he did, in a way, and the passage may recall Deuteronomy 32:18; but Isaiah 46:3 certainly does nothing to strengthen the theological case for a feminine God. The same should be said of Isaiah 49:15, often mentioned in the feminist literature. In this passage, God places his love for his people far above and beyond the love of a mother for her baby. There is a resemblance between God and the mother, but the note of contrast is more predominant. In the verse God claims not to be a mother, but to be far greater than any mother. And in Isaiah 66, it is Zion who is in labor (v. 8) and who will nurse (vv. 11–12). God's only motherly function in the passage is to comfort (v. 13).

quietness, but when her time comes to give birth she will scream! So God delays his judgment, but when the right time comes he will certainly make his presence known. Of course, Scripture often mentions the pain of childbirth as God's curse (Gen. 3:16) and, proverbially, the worst pain imaginable. So as metaphor it applies naturally and frequently to both men and women. Psalm 48:4–6 reads:

> For behold, the kings assembled;
>   they came on together.
> As soon as they saw it [Zion], they were astounded;
>   they were in panic; they took to flight.
> Trembling took hold of them there,
>   anguish as of a woman in labor.

The kings are male, but they tremble like a woman giving birth. Cf. Isa. 13:8; 21:3; 26:17; Jer. 4:31; 6:24; Mic. 4:9. So although we should acknowledge Scripture's use of this feminine metaphor for God, we should not derive any broader consequences from this fact. This image gives us no encouragement whatever to think of God as female. The feminine imagery used for God in Isaiah 42:14–15 is common in Scripture, often used for male persons.

In Luke 15:8–10, Jesus tells a parable about a woman who lights a lamp, sweeps the house, and searches carefully to find a lost coin. When she finds it, she calls her friends together to rejoice. Some believe the woman represents God, perhaps specifically in the person of Jesus, as do the shepherd and the father in the other two Luke 15 parables, though the point of the parable focuses more on the rejoicing of the friends (= the angels, v. 10) than on the homemaker's efforts. In Matthew 23:37, Jesus compares himself to a hen who gathers her chicks under her wings. A feminine metaphor, but certainly not one that calls into question the gender of Jesus.

Beyond these specific passages, there are some broader biblical ideas thought by some to presuppose a feminine element of some kind in God. One is the use of *racham* and *splanchnizomai* for divine compassion, a use that I discussed briefly in footnote 18. See chapter 12 for more discussion.

Another is the use of *Spirit* (Heb. *ruach*, Gr. *pneuma*). *Ruach* is a feminine noun, and Genesis 1:2 may picture the Spirit "brooding" as a mother bird. Scripture also represents the Spirit as the Giver of Life (Ps. 104:30), particularly new birth (John 3:5–6).

Not much can be derived from the grammatical point. Feminine nouns do not necessarily denote female persons,[26] and the corresponding Greek term *pneuma* is neuter. "Brooding" is a possible interpretation of the word *rachaf* in Genesis 1:2. The word *born* (*gennao*) can mean "beget" as well as "bear," so it can refer to the male role in reproduction as well as to the female. Nevertheless, the interpretation "bear" is preferable in John 3:5 because of Nicodemus's response in verse 4. I would conclude that there

---

26. Since examples can sometimes help to get us out of the habit of relying too much on etymology, I point out here that the Latin *uterus* ("womb," as in English) is masculine.

are a couple of feminine images of the Spirit in Scripture, but that is not sufficient to suggest as some do that the Spirit is the feminine person of the Trinity.[27] If the group of images that we discussed earlier is insufficient to justify talk of divine femininity, certainly these two images are not sufficient to prove the femininity of the Spirit.

Another concept under discussion is that of *wisdom* (Heb. *hokmah*, Gr. *sophia*). Both Greek and Hebrew terms are feminine nouns, and in Proverbs, wisdom is personified as a woman (Prov. 7:4; 8:1–9:18). Wisdom is a divine figure in Proverbs 8:22–31, and the NT identifies it with Christ (1 Cor. 1:24, 30; Col. 2:3; cf. Isa. 11:2; Jer. 23:5), as it also uses the closely related term *Word* (John 1:1–18). So some have concluded that the second person of the Trinity is feminine.[28]

But that is a poor argument. For one thing, Jesus is unquestionably male. The suggestion, therefore, that the nature of wisdom requires female embodiment is simply wrong. As for the female personification of wisdom in Proverbs, there is a perfectly obvious reason for that, one that has nothing to do with a female element in the Godhead. Proverbs 1–9 presents the reader with two women, sometimes called "Lady Wisdom" and "Lady Folly." Lady Folly is the harlot who entices a young man to immorality. Lady Wisdom also cries out to men in the city (8:1–4), urging on them the alternative, a godly life. Wisdom is a lady, not because the writer wants to assert a feminine element in the Godhead, but simply as a literary device presenting a positive alternative to the obviously female prostitute.

My conclusion from these biblical references is that there are indeed feminine images of God in Scripture, but they are rather few and suggest no sexual ambivalence in the divine nature. They do not necessitate, or even encourage, the use of *mother* for God, or the use of feminine pronouns for him. Nor do they justify attempts to suppress the masculine images or pronouns.

Theological Importance of Masculine Imagery

But the feminist might reply here that since God is not literally male, and Scripture contains some female imagery as well as male, we should be free to speak of God in either male or female terms. Johnson asks, "If it is not meant that God is male when masculine imagery is used, why the objection when feminine images are introduced?"[29]

This reply would be cogent if the biblical preponderance of male imagery were theologically unimportant. So feminists often argue that Scripture places little importance on the maleness of Jesus, or on the importance of speaking of God in masculine terms. The masculine imagery, they argue, is understandable in view of the patriarchalism of ancient culture, but it makes no difference to the essential message of Scripture.

There are, however, a number of reasons to think that the overwhelming preponderance of masculine imagery has some theological importance:

27. For some references, see Johnson, *She Who Is*, 50–54. Johnson herself prefers not to limit the femininity of God to the person of the Spirit, though she discusses the Spirit extensively (124–49).

28. Ibid., 150–69.

29. Ibid., 34.

1. As we have seen, God's names are of great importance theologically. They reveal him. There is no reason to assume that the proportions of male and female imagery are not part of this revelation of his nature. As Johnson and others insist, a change of the balance of sexual imagery is not a theologically neutral change; it does change our concept of God.[30] Do we have the right to change the biblical concept of God?

2. To underscore the last point, it is also important to recognize that in Scripture God names himself. His names, attributes, and images are not the result of human speculation or imagination, but of revelation.[31] He has not authorized change in the balance of male and female imagery, and we should not presume to make such changes on our own authority.[32]

3. Female deities were well known to the biblical writers. Ashtoreth (Judg. 10:6; 1 Sam. 7:4; 12:10) was worshiped by the Canaanites as the wife of Baal. The coupling of male and female deities was an important aspect of pagan fertility worship. So in writing about Yahweh, the OT writers did not choose masculine language unthinkingly, unaware of any alternative. They were not determined by a unanimous cultural consensus. Rather, they distinctly rejected worship of a goddess or of a divine couple.

4. As we will see in chapter 10, creation is a divine act that produces a reality outside of God himself, a *creaturely other*. The world is not divine, nor is it an emanation from his essence. Nor does God create by "making room 'within' himself for the nondivine."[33] As a metaphor for this biblical view of creation, the male role in reproduction is superior to the female.

5. In Scripture, the most central name for God is *Lord*, which indicates his headship of the covenants between himself and his creatures. In Scripture, rule in the covenant community is typically a male prerogative. Kings, priests, and prophets are generally male. Authority in the church is given to male elders (1 Cor. 14:35; 1 Tim. 2:11–15).[34]

---

30. So they really do not believe, though they sometimes claim to, that sexual imagery concerning God is unimportant.

31. Johnson's view is different. In her view, God is a great mystery and no language is entirely appropriate to describe him (see ibid., 6–7, 44–45, 104–12). He has "many names" (117–20), so we should be as open to feminine as to masculine names for him. Here I see the nonbiblical concept of transcendence that I opposed in chapter 3. In my view, God has revealed himself in language appropriate to his nature.

32. I do not mean to say here, of course, that we must reproduce the emphasis of Scripture with mathematical precision. Theology and preaching always change the emphasis of Scripture, for they apply biblical truth to people, rather than simply reading the Bible. But it would not be good application to speak of God regularly as *she*, or to raise the level of feminine imagery to, say, 80 percent of our references to God.

33. Ibid., 234. Johnson is quoting William Hill, *The Three-Personed God* (Washington, DC: Catholic University of America Press, 1982), 76n53. This is, of course, the panentheistic model of God's relation to the world.

34. I cannot, of course, begin here to enter the controversy surrounding this point. I do believe there is room for debate about whether, and in what circumstances, a woman may "speak in church" (1 Cor. 14:35), and whether women may be deacons. But it seems to me obvious from these passages that women are not admitted to that office that makes the final decisions on the affairs of the church. For sound discussions of these issues, see Susan Foh, *Women and the Word of God* (Phillipsburg, NJ: Presbyterian and Reformed, 1979); James B. Hurley, *Man and Woman in Biblical Perspective* (Grand Rapids: Zondervan, 1981); Orthodox Presbyterian Church, General Assembly Committee Report on Women in Office (Minutes of the General Assembly, 1987–88); John Piper and Wayne Grudem, eds., *Recovering Biblical Manhood and Womanhood* (Wheaton, IL: Crossway, 1991); Mil Am Yi, *Women and the Church: A Biblical Perspective* (Columbus, GA: Brentwood Christian Press, 1990).

The husband is the head of the covenant formed by marriage.[35] A switch to feminine imagery for God would certainly dilute the strong emphasis on covenant authority that is central to the biblical doctrine of God. This is one reason why, as I indicated in chapter 2, some feminist theologians, including Johnson, actually oppose the idea of God's lordship.

6. As we saw earlier in this chapter, God relates to his people as husband to wife. Obviously, this profound image would be obscured if we were to regard God as female. This is important not only for the doctrine of God, but also for the doctrine of man, theological anthropology. It is important for both male and female Christians to know, and to meditate deeply on the fact, that in relation to God they are female—wives called to submit in love to their gracious husband. It is the church, not God, that is feminine in its spiritual nature.[36]

7. One frequent suggestion of compromise is that we eliminate *all* sexually distinctive language, either male or female, in referring to God. Instead of *Father*, we would then refer to God as *Parent* or *Creator*.[37] Unisex language, however, inevitably suggests that God is impersonal, and that is completely unacceptable from a biblical standpoint.[38] Certainly to eliminate *Father* in favor of more abstract terms would be to eliminate something very precious to Christian believers.[39]

8. Has the use of preponderantly male imagery for God resulted in the oppression of women?[40] There is a deep divide between feminist and nonfeminist Christians as to what constitutes oppression. In traditional Christianity, it is not degrading for a woman to be submissive to her husband and excluded from the office of elder in the church. Often in the view of feminist writers, it is degrading for anybody to be subject to the authority of other persons, even of God. But submission to the

35. Marriage is a covenant in Scripture (Ezek. 16:8, 59; Mal. 2:14) strongly analogous to the covenants between God and man. In marriage, the husband is head of the wife (1 Cor. 11:3; Eph. 5:23). Feminists sometimes argue that *head* means "source" and has no connotations of authority. But see Wayne Grudem's strong argument to the contrary: "The Meaning of *Kephale*," app. 1 in Piper and Grudem, *Recovering Biblical Manhood and Womanhood*, 425–68. And in any case, Scripture asserts the authority of the husband over the wife in many places, even when the word *head* is not used. See Num. 30:6–16; Eph. 5:22; Col. 3:18; 1 Tim. 3:12–13; Titus 2:5.

36. Thanks to Jim Jordan (in correspondence) for this observation.

37. Some have made the suggestion that we describe the persons of the Trinity by titles such as *Creator*, *Redeemer*, and *Sanctifier*, respectively, for Father, Son, and Spirit. But this proposal is mistaken: (1) because it reduces the ontological Trinity (the eternal persons, Father, Son, and Spirit) to the economic (the actions of these persons in and for the world), and (2) because it ignores the *circumincessio*, the involvement of each person in every act of the others.

38. Even more obvious is the impersonalism that would result if we substituted neuter for masculine pronouns. But something must be done with the pronouns if our goal is to eliminate sexually distinctive language for God. Or do we try the impossibly awkward course of avoiding pronouns altogether?

39. One author (I apologize for not remembering who) comments that we do not, after all, address our own fathers as "parent." Indeed, the connotations of such an address would be entirely inappropriate to the relationship.

40. "Wittingly or not, it undermines women's human dignity as equally created in the image of God." Johnson, *She Who Is*, 5. Note her examples on 23–28, 34–38. She wants to argue that the use of feminine language for God is actually truer than the alternative, for it will convey the biblical truth that women are not to be oppressed. In my view, that truth is important; but it should be expounded by biblical texts that are actually relevant to the issue, not by distorted renderings of the biblical imagery for God.

authority of others is unavoidable in human life, for both men and women; this is one of the hardest lessons that fallen human beings have to learn. Much more can be said on this issue. Certainly men have abused women to a terrible extent through history. And certainly both men and women have sometimes justified this abuse by a misunderstanding of male headship and of the Bible's male imagery for God. But it would be hard to show that any better understanding of God, or any more whole-some relationship between the sexes, would result from the substitution of female or impersonal imagery for male.

My conclusion, then, is that we should follow the Bible's pattern of predominantly male imagery for God, with occasional female imagery. I would not object to a preach-er's occasionally saying that God is the "mother" of the church. As in Deuteronomy 32:18, we can observe that although our physical birth comes from two sources, our spiritual birth comes from only one: Yahweh, who is both mother and father to us. Nor is it wrong to use childbirth, homemaking, mother birds, and even extrabiblical female images as images of God and illustrations of his actions. And as we will see, I think much more should be made of the submission of the persons of the Trinity to one another, as the archetype of the godly wife's submission to her husband. But there is no biblical justification for using predominantly female imagery for God or representing him with female pronouns.

Living in God's Family

The story of the Bible is the family history, the story of how the family was founded, nurtured, and disciplined, and the extraordinary things that happened to it and through it. It is our genealogy, showing how we became children of God, our book of generations, showing what the family has done over the years. Like *kingdom*, *family* is a dynamic metaphor. Our sonship today is different in important ways from the sonship of OT Israel. Paul speaks of the Mosaic covenant as a time of imprisonment (Gal. 3:22–23), captivity (v. 23), guardianship (v. 24). To Paul, these restrictions leave little distinction between sonship and slavery (4:1–3). But in Christ, we become free:

> But when the fullness of time had come, God sent forth his Son, born of woman, born under the law, to redeem those who were under the law, so that we might receive adoption as sons. And because you are sons, God has sent the Spirit of his Son into our hearts, crying, "Abba! Father!" So you are no longer a slave, but a son, and if a son, then an heir through God. (Gal. 4:4–7)

The new covenant age is a time of maturity for the family. We are no longer little children, but adults, though we need to be reminded of this (Gal. 4:8–11). That means that we are closer to our inheritance, the new heavens and the new earth.

Because we are members of God's family, we are called to love God and obey him, but also to love one another. The spiritual gifts of each member are for the use of the whole body (Rom. 12:1–8; 1 Cor. 12:1–13:13; Eph. 4:1–16).

And he gave the apostles, the prophets, the evangelists, the shepherds and teachers, to equip the saints for the work of ministry, for building up the body of Christ, until we all attain to the unity of the faith and of the knowledge of the Son of God, to mature manhood, to the measure of the stature of the fullness of Christ, so that we may no longer be children, tossed to and fro by the waves and carried about by every wind of doctrine, by human cunning, by craftiness in deceitful schemes. Rather, speaking the truth in love, we are to grow up in every way into him who is the head, into Christ, from whom the whole body, joined and held together by every joint with which it is equipped, when each part is working properly, makes the body grow so that it builds itself up in love. (Eph. 4:11–16)

There should be among us no spirit of competition or jealousy, but a desire to "stir up one another to love and good works" (Heb. 10:24).

So we practice the faith always in community. Our brothers and sisters play a vital role in building us up in Christ, and their needs have a special call on our compassion. As we have a special responsibility to support our families (1 Tim. 5:8), so we should use our resources and gifts to support our Christian brothers and sisters. Paul says:

So then, as we have opportunity, let us do good to everyone, and especially to those who are of the household of faith. (Gal. 6:10)

Key Terms
Abba
Divine fatherhood (Trinitarian)
Divine fatherhood (over human beings)
Servants of God
Subjects of God
Family of God
Generations (in Genesis)
Adoption
God as husband

Study Questions
1. Is divine fatherhood a better concept than divine lordship as an organizing concept for systematic theology? Why or why not?
2. How does Frame understand the relationship between God's lordship, kingship, and fatherhood? Evaluate.
3. Summarize the history of redemption as a family history.
4. Paul speaks of himself as a father to the Corinthian church. Does he thereby violate Jesus' command to "call no man your father"?
5. "Like *kingdom*, *family* is a dynamic metaphor." Explain; evaluate.
6. Describe some respects in which the NT family of God is different from that in the OT.

7. Are there feminine images of God in Scripture? Mention some references defending your answer. If there are feminine images, should we use them and the masculine images equally often? Why or why not?

8. Describe ways in which belonging to God's family makes a difference in the Christian life.

Memory Verses

Ps. 68:5–6: Father of the fatherless and protector of widows
   is God in his holy habitation.
God settles the solitary in a home;
   he leads out the prisoners to prosperity,
   but the rebellious dwell in a parched land.

Ps. 103:13–14: As a father shows compassion to his children,
   so the LORD shows compassion to those who fear him.
For he knows our frame;
   he remembers that we are dust.

Mal. 1:6: A son honors his father, and a servant his master. If then I am a father, where is my honor?

Matt. 6:9: Pray then like this:

"Our Father in heaven,
hallowed be your name."

Acts 2:39: For the promise is for you and for your children and for all who are far off, everyone whom the Lord our God calls to himself.

Rom. 8:14–17: For all who are led by the Spirit of God are sons of God. For you did not receive the spirit of slavery to fall back into fear, but you have received the Spirit of adoption as sons, by whom we cry, "Abba! Father!" The Spirit himself bears witness with our spirit that we are children of God, and if children, then heirs—heirs of God and fellow heirs with Christ, provided we suffer with him in order that we may also be glorified with him.

Resources for Further Study

Clowney, Edmund P. *The Church.* Downers Grove, IL: InterVarsity Press, 1995.

Murray, John. "Adoption." In *Redemption Accomplished and Applied,* 132–40. Grand Rapids: Eerdmans, 1955. See also his "Adoption." In *MCW,* 2:223–34.

Poythress, Vern S. "The Church as a Family: Why Male Leadership in the Family Requires Male Leadership in the Church as Well." In *Recovering Biblical Manhood and Womanhood*, edited by John Piper and Wayne Grudem, 237–50. Wheaton, IL: Crossway, 1991. The volume is available as a .pdf file at http://www.cbmw .org/images/onlinebooks/rbmw.pdf. The article alone is available at http://www.frame-poythress.org.

Poythress, Vern S., and Wayne Grudem. *The Gender-Neutral Bible Controversy*. Nashville: Broadman and Holman, 2000.

PART 3

THE DOCTRINE OF GOD

CHAPTER 7

THE ACTS OF THE LORD: MIRACLE

IN THE BIBLE EVERYTHING BEGINS with God. Its first verse is: "In the beginning, God created the heavens and the earth" (Gen. 1:1), and John, speaking of God the Son, tells us, "In the beginning was the Word" (John 1:1). God is the ultimate context of the biblical story. In that story, everything is "from him and through him and to him," and therefore to his glory forever (Rom. 11:36).

In chapter 2, we learned that God is the Lord, and that we can understand his lordship by way of three lordship attributes: control, authority, and presence. In chapter 3, we saw that God's lordship defines a worldview that is uniquely biblical: God is the absolute tripersonality, the Creator of all things, always transcendent to the world, yet immanent in the world. His transcendence is his control and authority, his immanence his covenant presence.

Since God's lordship is his headship over his servants in a covenant, we discussed in chapter 4 the biblical story as a story of covenants. In these covenants, God creates and redeems a people to glorify him. Chapter 5 discussed the closely related concept of God's kingship and kingdom, and chapter 6 God as Father. So we have already explored many of the most important things that Scripture teaches us about God. But in part 3 we must look more closely at him. We must gain a better understanding of who he is and what he does.

Given the discussions in chapters 4–6, it would be possible to discuss God's acts and attributes triperspectivally, in terms of lordship, then kingship, then fatherhood. But that would be repetitious and unnecessary, since these three concepts are already perspectivally related. That is to say that the three designate the same divine being, and each, as presented in Scripture, incorporates the other two. So I will be focusing on God's lordship through most of the remainder of the book (as in my four-volume Theology of Lordship series), sometimes bringing in ideas that evoke the other two perspectives. Of the various images of God in Scripture, his lordship, again, is the most pervasive, so it will be prominent in our theological account.

So as we pursue a more detailed understanding of God, we will emphasize that God is the Lord. When Moses asked what he should say to the Israelites who asked the name of God, God said to Moses:

> Say this to the people of Israel, "The Lord, the God of your fathers, the God of Abraham, the God of Isaac, and the God of Jacob, has sent me to you." This is my name forever, and thus I am to be remembered throughout all generations. (Ex. 3:15)

Everything that Scripture says about God, therefore, is about *this* God, about the Lord. So I noted in chapter 2 that Scripture tells us over and over that God performs his mighty deeds so that people "will know that I am the Lord" (Ex. 14:4; cf. 6:7; 7:5, 17; 14:4; many other passages).

Scripture teaches us about the Lord in three ways: (1) it narrates his mighty acts, (2) it describes God directly and authoritatively (his names, images, and attributes), and (3) it portrays God's inner life as a relationship between Father, Son, and Spirit. His mighty acts persuade us that he is the Lord. The direct biblical descriptions of God emerge out of the narration of his mighty acts and describe various aspects of his lordship. Then the biblical doctrine of the Trinity brings us as closely as possible to the inner life of our Lord.

In general, item 1 focuses on God's control (situational), 2 on his authority (normative), and 3 on his presence (existential), though of course all three lordship attributes are found wherever God is, in whatever he does, and in all aspects of his being. See fig. 7.1.

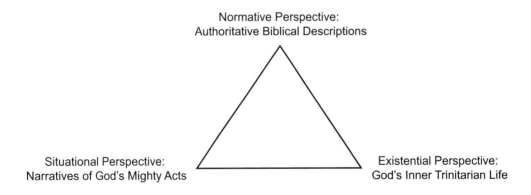

Fig. 7.1. Ways in Which Scripture Teaches Us about God

In this and the next few chapters, we will look at God's acts, the mighty deeds he performs so that all will know that he is the Lord. In later chapters, we will consider the Bible's authoritative descriptions of God and God's Trinitarian inner life. Some theologians have preferred different orders of topics. Some have made the case that you need to know who God *is* before you can understand what he *has done*. There is some truth in this, but as we will see, Scripture often (in the Psalms, for example) derives God's attributes from God's acts.

I myself have little interest in questions about the order of topics in theology. As we saw in chapter 1, theology does not put the facts of Scripture into some kind of "proper order." Rather, theology is the application of Scripture, so the order of its discussions will be determined by the needs it addresses as much as by the order of topics in Scripture itself. It will always differ from the order of Scripture itself because it is not Scripture.

In fact, our knowledge of God's attributes (what he is) depends on our knowledge of what he has done (his acts), and vice versa. Still, we need to make a choice of where to start the discussion. I choose to start with the acts of God because Scripture often does that and because it seems that contemporary readers are more interested in narrative (God's deeds) than in metaphysics (God's being). But I hope to show that God's deeds are such that they reveal who he is and thus move every believer to praise him for his attributes (his might, wisdom, and love).[1]

So this chapter will begin to describe the acts of God narrated in Scripture. Those acts can be organized theologically under six different headings: miracles, providence, creation, redemption, God's eternal decrees, and his intra-Trinitarian actions such as eternal generation and procession. These categories reflect God's lordship attributes. We may think of God's eternal decrees as normative, for they dictate the plan that all other events follow. Miracle, providence, and creation are situational, describing God's workings in the world within which redemption takes place. Redemption is existential, the divine action of restoring fellowship between God and sinners, reconstituting the heart of sinful man as his dwelling place. I will not discuss redemption systematically in this chapter, since that is the main theme of Scripture and of the rest of this book. See fig. 7.2.

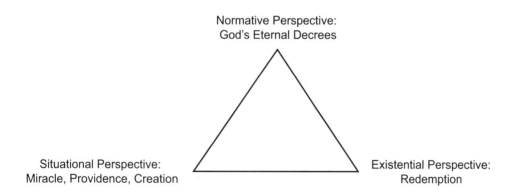

Fig. 7.2. Divine Acts

1. One critic of my *DG* described this as an approach "from below" rather than "from above." "From below" is used by some contemporary theologians to describe a theology that begins with autonomous human rational analysis of experience and draws implications for our knowledge of God, as opposed to a theology "from above" that begins with divine revelation. That critic had no understanding of what I was trying to do. In the vocabulary of the contemporary discussion, my method is entirely "from above," relying fully on the words of God himself in his Word. But that Word, of course, speaks of events of history as well as eternity, and I have chosen to begin with Scripture's teaching about God's acts in history and later move to its teaching about God's heavenly and eternal existence.

In considering God's acts, we will look at miracle, followed by providence, creation, and eternal decrees, in that order. In the larger plan of part 3, this chapter will discuss miracle. Chapters 8 and 9 will deal with providence. Together, miracle and providence constitute God's actions in history. Chapter 10 will deal with creation, God's act at the beginning of history. Chapter 11 will treat his eternal decrees, actions that are "before" and "above" history. After a discussion of God's nature and attributes (chapters 12–19), we will then consider God's actions within his Trinitarian existence (chapters 20–22).

Defining Miracle

I believe that a biblical definition of miracle will go far to deal with problems that arise in connection with this topic, such as the relation of miracle to science and the credibility of miracle stories in Scripture. In my judgment, the best definition of the word *miracle* is "an extraordinary manifestation of God's covenant lordship."

Defining *miracle* is not an easy task because the term is rarely found in English translations of Scripture. A number of Hebrew and Greek terms designate events that we call miracles, but there is no one-to-one correspondence between any term in Hebrew or Greek and the English term *miracle*. Whether a particular Hebrew or Greek term should be translated "miracle" depends on the context, but that is to say that whether a biblical event is a miracle must be determined by factors other than the vocabulary used. We must make up our minds whether an event is a miracle *before* deciding whether to translate an original-language term as "miracle."

I think the best procedure is first to think about the meaning of the English term, in order to clarify what we are looking for in the biblical narratives when we look for miracle. The English term also has its ambiguities, but uniformly we use it to describe events that are highly unusual, so unusual that we would otherwise consider them impossible. I propose this as our *preliminary definition of miracle*. On this definition, we easily apply the term to biblical events such as Israel's crossing of the Red Sea on dry land, Jesus' turning water to wine, his feeding five thousand people with a few loaves and fishes, and the like.

But theologians often are not satisfied with such a simple way of understanding the term. They want to know whether there is some deeper philosophical or theological principle in the distinction between miracles and other events.

Miracle and Natural Law

One proposal of this sort is to define miracle in relation to natural law, as a violation of it (David Hume), an interruption of it (Norman Geisler), or an interference with it (C. S. Lewis). But what is natural law? *Natural law* is not a biblical term any more than *miracle* is. Here are some possible ways of defining it:[2]

2. I will ignore here the use of *natural law* in ethics, to indicate ethical standards knowable to human beings by reason and conscience alone, apart from Scripture. That use is not relevant to the definition of miracle, though it is related to some of the concepts of natural law discussed here. I discuss natural law in the ethical sense in *DCL* and in *The Escondido Theology* (Lakeland, FL: Whitefield Media, 2011).

1. *The ultimate processes that govern the world.* In a biblical worldview, these are nothing less than the decrees of God himself. In this sense, natural laws are never broken, and miracle should not be seen as any kind of exception to natural law.

2. *The regular processes by which God usually governs creation.* These are the regularities in the natural world that scientists seek to describe with formulae and theories. Theologically, they are expressions of God's covenant with Noah to keep the seasons regular "while the earth remains" (Gen. 8:22). The deists and Hume believed that natural laws in this sense were absolute, operating without exception. But Scripture gives us no assurance that these laws hold at all times. God is free to work either through or outside of these natural laws.

In many cases, miracles are exceptions to natural law in this sense—but not in every case. For example, God dried up a portion of the Red Sea by sending "a strong east wind" (Ex. 14:21). This was a natural process, although the timing of it was quite astonishing. So "suspension of natural law" in this sense should not be included in the definition of miracle. Nor is it clear how this concept goes beyond our preliminary definition. For to say that an event is an exception to the "regular processes" of God's providence (*regular*, of course, being a relative term) is no more than to say that the event is extraordinary or unusual.

3. *Human expectations concerning the workings of nature.* This concept of natural law is flexible, since different people have different expectations. These expectations vary greatly from person to person, place to place, and time to time. So to say that miracles contradict human expectations is to say something true, but not very interesting. Nor is this fact worthy of being included in a definition of miracle. To define miracle this way is to make it subjective and therefore relative: what is a miracle to one person will not be a miracle to another. Such a definition fails to identify any single characteristic that objectively distinguishes miracles from other events. And that search is the main reason why theologians have wanted to advance beyond our preliminary definition.

4. *The basic mechanical structure of the universe.* Some writers, both Christian and non-Christian, have thought of the universe as subject to a network of mechanisms that govern all events. The mechanism is not God's will as such (as definition 1 above), nor God's personal choices (2), nor something in the human mind (3), but something created into the structure of the world itself. On this view, miracles would be events that suspend these mechanisms. But Scripture never speaks of natural laws in this sense, and I know of no reason to suppose that they exist. Scripture ascribes the events of nature directly to God. As we will see later in this chapter, it is God himself who brings the snow and rain. The concept of world-mechanisms is deistic rather than biblical. In Scripture, God's actions in the world are thoroughly personal.

Further, the example of Exodus 14:21, noted earlier, is relevant here as well. If the movement of the wind is an example of a natural mechanism, then God is able to perform a miracle without violating, but rather incorporating, that mechanism.

Finally, even if there are such mechanisms, none of us knows for sure what they are. Science (ancient or modern) has never reached a complete and incorrigible formulation of all the laws that govern the universe. And certainly unscientific observers, such as the biblical writers for the most part, could not have identified what events violate these mechanisms and which ones don't. So on this definition they could not have identified what events are miracles. Indeed, to identify an event as a miracle on this basis, one would have to be omniscient, for he would have to know that in all the universe no law, no mechanism, could account for it.

So I don't believe it is scriptural or helpful to define miracle in terms of natural law, on any of the interpretations of natural law above. Indeed, this discussion also calls into question the common understanding of miracle as "supernatural" as opposed to providence, which is "natural."

Immediacy

Another approach to defining miracle is to identify it as an "immediate" act of God, an event performed without the use of means.[3] But Scripture does not explicitly distinguish between some events in which God uses means and others in which he does not. I think it is a reasonable inference from Scripture that God uses means in many cases (Ex. 14:21, again, as an example), and that in others he does not (e.g., creation out of nothing, regeneration). But Scripture never identifies miracles as immediate acts of God as opposed to mediate. Exodus 14:21, again, is an example of a miracle in which God uses means. And just as the biblical writers would have been incompetent to identify miracles by citing natural laws, so they could not possibly have known with certainty which events God brought about mediately and which he brought about immediately.

Of course, a miracle cannot be fully accounted for by natural means alone. At some point, the power of God himself must be engaged. Yet that is true not only of miracles, but of all other events as well.

Attestation of Prophecy

We have seen that theologians have tried to enhance our preliminary definition of miracle by reference to natural law (in various senses) and to immediacy. Another suggested theological enhancement is this: that a miracle always attests God's messengers, particularly the prophets, Jesus, and the apostles.

Unlike the first two elaborations, this one is based on a genuine emphasis of Scripture. We recall the staff of Moses that turned into a snake and back again (Ex. 4:1–5). God enabled Moses to work this miracle in response to the anticipated skepticism of Israel to the claim that God had spoken to Moses (v. 1). So the miracle verifies Moses' status as God's prophet. Another example is 1 Kings 17:24, in which the mother of the son resurrected through the word of Elijah testifies, "Now I know that you are a man of God, and that the word of the LORD in your mouth is truth." The miracle attests Elijah

---

3. See, for example, B. B. Warfield, "The Question of Miracles," in *Selected Shorter Writings of Benjamin B. Warfield* (Nutley, NJ: Presbyterian and Reformed, 1973), 2:178; J. Gresham Machen, *What Is Christianity? and Other Addresses* (Grand Rapids: Eerdmans, 1951), 55.

as a prophet of God. See also Ex. 7:9–13; Matt. 9:6; 11:4–6; Luke 4:18–21; John 5:19–23, 36; 10:24–26, 38; 20:30–31; Acts 2:22; 14:3; Rom. 15:18–19; 2 Cor. 12:12; Heb. 2:3–4.

There can be no doubt, then, that a major purpose of biblical miracles is to accredit prophets and apostles, and even the Son of God, as God's messengers. And since miracle attests the prophet, it also attests his prophecy as God's truth.

In a broad sense, we may even say that all biblical miracles[4] have this function. For the purpose of Scripture in general is to bring us God's Word, with the rationale of that Word. The Word itself provides us with the evidence of its own truth. And miracles constitute a substantial portion of that evidence. Every miracle of Scripture serves the gospel of redemption, by reporting God's activity in support of that message.

On the other hand, this is not the only purpose of miracles in Scripture. The flood of Genesis 6–9 did accredit Noah as a prophet, certainly. But when the rain came, it was too late for that accreditation to lead anyone to faith, outside of Noah's family. Scripture does tell us that Noah was a prophet (2 Peter 2:5), but it is silent about any events that might have accredited his prophecies to his contemporaries. The main purpose of the flood was not accreditation, but judgment.

Jesus' incarnation is a miracle, certainly, and it does accredit his words in a way. But a better perspective is to note that Jesus' words (and works) verify his incarnation, rather than the other way around. The incarnation is not primarily a means of validating a message but rather the very means of our salvation. It, together with the atonement and resurrection, is the very content of the message.

Jesus' healings attested his words, but he did not heal *merely* to accredit himself as a prophet. In Matthew 14:14, we read, "When he went ashore he saw a great crowd, and he had compassion on them and healed their sick." The nature of this miracle was an expression of Jesus' divine compassion, to meet the needs of people. Cf. Matt. 20:34; Mark 1:41. Jesus also feeds the four thousand because of his compassion for the multitudes (Matt. 15:32–39). Of course, that very compassion attested Jesus as God's Messiah. In a general sense, everything Jesus did displayed his godly character and therefore to some extent vindicated his claims and message. But in that sense miracles do not attest Jesus' prophetic office more fully than any of his other actions do.

Miracles also serve to advance God's cause in the spiritual warfare. God gives strength to his people beyond their own, in order to give them victory over great nations, as in Israel's exodus and conquest of Palestine. God opens the hearts of Gentiles supernaturally to bring the gospel to the ends of the earth (Acts 13:48; 16:14). He overcomes opposition to plant his church in all nations.

Should we, then, include "attestation of prophecy" in the definition of miracle? Since all biblical miracles do attest God's Word, at least in a general way, it is not easy to argue against this proposed addition. But there are some disadvantages in this refinement. Notice that we do have some freedom in choosing what to include in a definition. Scripture says nothing explicit about how we should *define* these events, and

---

4. Of course, we have to exclude from this generalization miracles of false prophets (Deut. 13:2; 2 Thess. 2:9).

of course it does not require any specific definition of the English word *miracle*. It does not tell us what biblical content to include in the definition and what content should remain for later description. On these matters, we should weigh the advantages and disadvantages of different proposals. Since there is no perfect correspondence between the English *miracle* and any of the Greek or Hebrew terms of Scripture, all proposed definitions will have some disadvantages.

I think that is also true with definitions of miracle that include "attestation of prophecy." Those who advocate this refinement to our minimal definition usually construe this attestation to be roughly contemporary with the first articulation of the prophecy. So *prophecy* here is *new* prophecy, *recent* prophecy, *new* special revelation. Now, obviously, miracles during the time of the writing of Scripture were attestations of new prophecy, because that was a time in which some prophecy was new. But to define miracle as attesting new special revelation prejudices the question whether God might do similar things in our own time, not to attest *new* special revelation, but to attest revelation given long ago, or for one or more of the other purposes of miracle noted earlier. Scripture itself doesn't discuss this question because it was written during a time when God was adding new special revelation to the canon.

Every event in Scripture, not only the unusual ones, attests the truth of God's Word, the truth of prophecy. That is to say, one purpose of Scripture is to accredit itself. It is "self-authenticating." Every event in Scripture is part of a narrative that, as a whole, attests the credibility of God's messengers. For example, the stoning of Stephen in Acts 7 is not a miracle; but Stephen's willingness to speak boldly of Christ in the face of his murderers is a powerful witness to the truth of the gospel message, a truth newly given to the church by the events of Jesus' atonement and resurrection. All martyrdoms in Scripture have the purpose of accrediting revelation in this way. But it would be wrong, of course, to say that we should *define* martyrdom as an act that bears witness to the truth of new special revelation. And it would, of course, be stupid to claim that martyrdoms therefore cease when new special revelation ceases,[5] at the end of the apostolic age. Martyrdoms continue into the present as powerful witnesses to the truth of *old* special revelation, the truth delivered once for all to the saints.

Similarly, the heroism of David's mighty men (as in 2 Sam. 23:13–17) is a powerful witness to their faith in God's covenant with David. All heroism in Scripture, similarly, bears witness to prophecy, as in the examples of Hebrews 11. But it would not be right to define *heroism* as a witness to new special revelation and then to draw the conclusion that after the completion of the canon, heroism no longer exists.

For these reasons, I am not inclined to add "attestation of prophecy" to our basic definition of miracle, though I grant that this is a very important, even central, element in the theological function of miracle during the biblical period. If we do add such a qualification to the definition, we must remember that such a decision does not really address, except in a verbal way, the question of the cessation of miracle. On

---

5. I am assuming that the canon of special revelation is closed.

a definition including "attestation of new prophetic revelation," miracles do cease at the end of the apostolic period. But that fact does not rule out the possibility of other divine works after that period (properly given some name other than *miracle*), which are *like* miracles except that they do not bear witness to new special revelation.

We have seen that miracles are unusual events, brought about by God. That is our preliminary definition. I have argued that attempts to identify miracles with suspensions of natural law, or with immediate rather than mediate acts of God, are not biblically warranted. And although I grant that biblical miracles attest special revelation, I have resisted attempts to add such attestation to the definition of miracle.

A More Biblical Definition

But now we must ask positively what the main emphases of Scripture's own teaching concerning miracles are. Those, I think, can be summarized in the statement: "Miracles are extraordinary manifestations of God's covenant lordship." If I were asked to provide a theologically enhanced definition of miracle, this would be it.

As we saw earlier, God performs his mighty acts so that people will know that he is Lord. We should expect, then, that miracles draw our attention to those attributes that define his lordship: his control, authority, and presence. In fact, this is very much the case. I do not base my argument on word studies, but it is interesting that even the biblical miracle vocabulary in Hebrew and Greek contains these three emphases; see fig. 7.3.

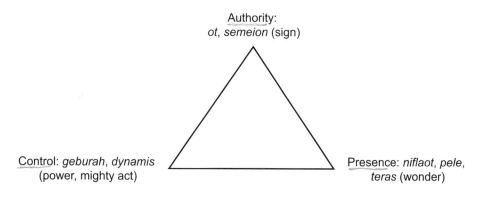

Fig. 7.3. Perspectives on Miracle

As mighty acts, miracles display the great power of the Lord to control his creation. As signs, they authoritatively reveal him. As wonders, they create in the hearts of people a religious awe, because in miracles they find themselves in the presence of the living God. Let us look at these aspects more closely:

1. *Control*: Miracles are, perhaps most obviously, the result of enormous power, the power of God. After crossing the sea on dry land, Moses and the Israelites sing praise for the great redemptive power of God (Ex. 15). Note:

Your right hand, O Lord, glorious in power,
   your right hand, O Lord, shatters the enemy. (Ex. 15:6)

This power is the power that worked "wonders" (v. 11). In Egypt, God won the contest of power against the magicians and against Egypt's gods (Ex. 7:8–13; 8:19; 12:12; 15:11). Israel is confident that that same power will terrify the leaders of the Canaanites when God brings his people to the Promised Land: "because of the greatness of your arm, they are still as a stone" (15:16).

Throughout Scripture, miracles are among the "mighty works" for which God's people praise him.

In Mark 5:24b–34, a woman touches Jesus' garment and is immediately healed of a bleeding ailment that she has had for twelve years. Jesus realizes that "power had gone out from him" (v. 30). According to Luke 5:17, "the power of the Lord was with him to heal." In Luke 6:19, "all the crowd sought to touch him, for power came out from him and healed them all." The apostles also heal—by God's power, not their own (Acts 3:12). Simon the sorcerer is called the "Great Power" (8:10 NIV), but he must bow before a greater (vv. 18–24).

2. *Authority*: Miracles are "signs," and therefore revelation. Revelation from God always bears his supreme authority.

By his mighty deeds, says Moses, Yahweh has "begun to show your servant your greatness and your mighty hand" (Deut. 3:24). Miracles not only accomplish great things; they display God to us. They teach us about him. So God feeds his people in the wilderness, "that he might make you know that man does not live by bread alone, but man lives by every word that comes from the mouth of the Lord" (8:3).

In Mark 2:1–11, Jesus heals a paralytic and thereby reveals that he has the authority to forgive sins. John's gospel especially focuses on the "signs" of Jesus' ministry. Toward the end, John indicates his purpose in presenting the signs:

> Now Jesus did many other signs in the presence of the disciples, which are not written in this book; but these are written so that you may believe that Jesus is the Christ, the Son of God, and that by believing you may have life in his name. (John 20:30–31)

In the first sign, Jesus changed water to wine at Cana. John comments that thereby he "manifested his glory. And his disciples believed in him" (John 2:11). The water of Jewish ceremonial washings becomes the wine of the messianic banquet. The Lord who brings the consummation of redemption has arrived on earth. Jesus' miracles often parallel the works of Yahweh in the OT, such as miraculous feedings (Ex. 16; John 6:1–14), stilling of the storm (Ps. 107:29; Mark 4:35–41), raising the dead (1 Kings 17:7–24; Luke 7:11–17; John 11:1–44), healing the blind, deaf, lame, and mute (Isa. 35:5; Luke 7:18–23). In Luke 7, Jesus lists these miracles to renew the confidence of John the Baptist that indeed Jesus is "the one who [was] to come" (v. 20). The miracles bear powerful witness as to who Jesus is. The feeding of the five thousand reveals him as the bread of life (John 6:1–71). His raising of Lazarus reveals him as the resurrection and the life (11:25–26).

The point is not only that miracles attest revelation, although we saw earlier that that is an important aspect of miracles. It is also the case that miracles *are* revelation. They show the character of God (power, care, compassion), the person and work of Jesus, the blessings of redemption, and its fulfillment in the messianic banquet.

3. *Covenant Presence*: Miracles are also *wonders*: that is, typically they provoke a powerful subjective response from those who observe them. Of course, there are some who respond wrongly—persisting in their unbelief, or even ascribing the miracles to Satan (Matt. 12:24–28). But the appropriate and usual response is one of awe.

The awe is religious awe, arising from the sense that God is present. The exodus leads to worship: the praise-hymn of Exodus 15. God's mighty acts motivate the Psalms, in which God's people express their awe, wonder, and joy in his presence.

The miraculous catch of fish in Luke 5:1–10 is very much a religious experience for the disciples. Peter's response seems odd at first, but on reflection we can see that it is entirely appropriate: "Depart from me, for I am a sinful man, O Lord" (Luke 5:8). What does a miraculous catch of fish have to do with Peter's sin? In the miracle, Peter experiences a theophany. Jesus is God in the flesh, who rules the earth and sea. And like Isaiah, when the prophet "saw the Lord" (Isa. 6:1), Peter is reminded of his unfitness to be in God's presence. Isaiah said, "Woe is me! For I am lost; for I am a man of unclean lips, and I dwell in the midst of a people of unclean lips; for my eyes have seen the King, the LORD of hosts!" (v. 5). This is how Peter felt. But as with Isaiah, God gives to Peter a prophetic commission, "from now on you will be catching men" (Luke 5:10). To see the miracle rightly is to recognize God's presence in the miracle.

As displays of God's control, authority, and presence, miracles may be defined as extraordinary manifestations of God's lordship. On this understanding there is no need to be concerned about the relation of miracle to natural law, or whether miracles are mediate or immediate. And this definition provides a perspective in which we can understand the role of miracles in attesting prophecy. Attesting prophecy is one of various ways in which miracles reveal God's nature and will.

Have Miracles Ceased?

Given the definition of miracle that I have developed above, I don't think it can be demonstrated from Scripture that miracles do not occur today. Rather, given that miracles are extraordinary demonstrations of God's lordship, they may well occur in our time, but only at God's own initiative.

I do intend to argue later (chapter 25) that the canon of Scripture is closed, and I believe, somewhat less firmly, that God has removed from the church the word-gifts of tongues and prophecy,[6] although I also agree with Vern S. Poythress that those gifts are analogous to works of the Spirit in the church today.[7] Now, it is sometimes assumed that those who hold to the cessation of these charismata must also hold to the cessation of all miracles after the time of the apostles. But that conclusion does not follow. Granting that tongues and prophecy are miraculous, and that they have ceased, it does not follow that *all* miracles have ceased.

At the same time, I do not believe that the more spectacular miracles (walking on water, stilling a storm by a word, healing instantly by a word) are a normal part of Christian experience today, nor do I believe that we should feel guilty if we have not experienced such wonders.

Although the Bible seems full of miracles, these events were not common even during the biblical period. Of course, by definition miracles are uncommon, "extraordinary." But even in the biblical period, in which many miracles took place, these events were not evenly distributed through time. Many centuries went by (as between Noah and Abraham, Abraham and Moses, Malachi and Jesus) without many miracles' being recorded. In Abraham's life, there were theophanies, and of course the miraculous birth of Isaac. But Abraham lived many years without seeing any miracle. Through most of his life he was made to wait, anticipating the fulfillment of the promise to come. That he was, for the most part, patient during this waiting period is one of the exemplary features of Abraham's faith. And Moses spent forty years in the wilderness before God appeared to him in the burning bush and inaugurated a new era of miracles. So God evidently reserves miracles for special occasions, certainly among them the attestation of his messengers, as we have seen.

Miracle and Apologetics

In debates between Christians and non-Christians, miracles have often played an important role. These discussions tend to focus on three questions: (1) Are miracles possible and probable? (2) Is there evidence for miracle? (3) Are miracles evidence for the truth of the Christian faith?

Are Miracles Possible?

In the context of a Christian worldview, the answer is obvious. Miracles are possible because the world is under God's sovereign control. It is God who, by his nature and decrees, determines what is possible. The regularities of nature are his covenantal gift to us, and they do not at all limit his ability to work in the world as he pleases.

We need not get into discussions of the supposedly random behavior of elementary particles to provide some small possibility of very unusual events taking place.

---

6. Richard B. Gaffin's *Perspectives on Pentecost* (Phillipsburg, NJ: Presbyterian and Reformed, 1979) makes a strong case for the cessation of the charismata, but not, in my estimation, a watertight one.

7. Vern S. Poythress, "Modern Spiritual Gifts as Analogous to Apostolic Gifts: Affirming Extraordinary Works of the Spirit within Cessationist Theology," *JETS* 39, 1 (1996): 71–101. Also available at http://www.frame -poythress.org. See also his *What Are Spiritual Gifts?* (Phillipsburg, NJ: P&R Publishing, 2010).

According to present-day science, the smallest particles/waves of matter behave "counterintuitively"; but there is no known path by which these bits communicate their strangeness to processes involving much larger bodies. These observations have not moved many, if any, naturalistic scientists to believe in miracles. To rest the case for miracles on the whims of photons and quarks is to trust a frail reed. Rather, miracles are possible because God exists.

Are miracles probable? Of course they are unlikely, because they are by definition extraordinary. But that fact does not reduce their probability to zero. Probability, like possibility, is determined by God. In a Christian-theistic worldview, our question becomes how likely it is that God will bring about miracles. To answer that question, we must know something about God, particularly about his intentions and goals.

God announced to Noah that the course of nature would proceed in a way that is generally regular (Gen. 8:22). But God's higher intention is to redeem a people for himself, and to do that, it is appropriate for him to perform unusual works, to accomplish salvation, apply it, and attest it. If the world were governed by impersonal forces, there would be no reason to expect departures from the basic functions of those forces.[8] But ours is a world ruled by a person, and he seeks fellowship with us. That is sufficient reason to expect that he will identify himself in the natural order, as the ruler of that order. And since he has ordained miracle as a mark of his lordship and an attestation of his revelation, we can say that miracle is significantly probable.

Is There Sufficient Evidence for Believing in Biblical Miracles?

David Hume says, in his famous essay "Of Miracles":[9]

> A miracle is a violation of the laws of nature; and as a firm and unalterable experience has established these laws, the proof against a miracle, from the very nature of the fact, is as entire as any argument from experience can possibly be imagined.[10]

I have rejected Hume's definition of miracle and therefore consider the rest of this quotation to be irrelevant. Even granted his definition, however, he begs the question when he says that "a firm and unalterable experience has established these laws." If this argument is to stand as a proof against miracle, the experience establishing the laws must be universal and without exception. Therefore, Hume begins his argument by saying that nobody has ever had experience of exceptions to these laws, experiences of miracle. But that is precisely the question that needs to be resolved.[11]

But Hume does not quite want to argue that because natural laws are universal, miracles are metaphysically impossible. At least he does not want his argument to

---

8. On the other hand, there would in that case be no reason to expect regularity either.

9. David Hume, *An Inquiry concerning Human Understanding* (New York: Liberal Arts Press, 1955), 117–41.

10. Ibid., 122.

11. Compare the bottom of 122: "But it is a miracle that a dead man should come to life, because that has never been observed in any age or country." Never? Here he dismisses the apparent counterexamples of Scripture.

appear to assume that. An "argument from experience," as he explains earlier in the essay, is never absolutely certain, but is always more or less probable. We determine the level of probability by weighing one experience against another, and, importantly, one *testimony* against another. So the rest of Hume's argument is about the credibility of testimony. His assumption (above) about the laws of nature leads him to say this about the level of testimony needed to establish a miracle:

> No testimony is sufficient to establish a miracle unless the testimony be of such a kind that its falsehood would be more miraculous than the fact that it endeavors to establish.[12]

He then argues that no report of a miracle has ever fulfilled this criterion. In no case, he thinks, has a miracle report come from witnesses who are absolutely trustworthy.[13] He believes that miracle reports tend to come from emotional excess and therefore exaggeration.[14] These reports tend to come from "ignorant and barbarous nations,"[15] are opposed by those of different religious persuasions,[16] and even at best should be rejected because of the "absolute impossibility or miraculous nature of the events which they relate."[17]

In this last quotation, Hume tips his hand. He wants us to believe that he is not begging the question by assuming at the outset the impossibility of miracle. But in the last quotation he clearly seems to be making that assumption. In his view, there simply cannot be any "violation of the laws of nature." His argument, essentially, is that no testimony can establish a report of something impossible.

Applied to the reports of miracles in Scripture, Hume's arguments are unpersuasive unless we assume a priori the impossibility of miraculous events. There is no reason to suppose that the biblical reports of miracles stem from emotional excess or exaggeration, and shouldn't the biblical writers be considered innocent at least until proven guilty? Nor is biblical Israel fairly described as an "ignorant and barbarous nation." The most that can be said is that the biblical writers lived before the advent of modern science. But clearly they understood that axe-heads do not normally float, that one cannot normally feed multitudes with a few loaves and fishes, and that men don't normally rise from the dead. They knew that Satan counterfeits God's miracles (Ex. 7:11–12, 22; 8:7; Deut. 13:1–3; Matt. 24:24; 2 Thess. 2:9; Rev. 13:13) (and sometimes fails, Ex. 8:17–18), and so they had a proper skepticism about such things. And they also knew that unless miracles are unlikely, they cannot do what God intends for them to do.

And as for the opposition of contrary parties, we have no knowledge of such opposition in the OT context. So far as we know, nobody questioned whether the plagues of

12. Ibid., 123.
13. Ibid., 124.
14. Ibid., 125–26.
15. Ibid., 126.
16. Ibid., 128.
17. Ibid., 133.

Egypt took place, whether Elijah raised the son of the widow of Zarephath, or whether the axe-head really floated. In the NT period, the opponents of Christianity either resorted to transparent rationalizations (such as that the disciples must have stolen the body of Jesus) or else conceded the miracle and attributed it to Satan.

But the more fundamental criticisms of Hume's argument are epistemological:

1. He assumes a nontheistic view of the possibility and probability of miracles. For him, possibility and probability are determined entirely by autonomous human experience, without any consideration of who God is and what God's intentions are. His argument, indeed, assumes that the God of Scripture does not exist; for if God did exist, one would have to take him into account in judging the possibility and probability of miracle, as we did in the previous section.

2. Hume assumes at the outset that divine revelation plays no role in determining whether miracles have taken place. For the Christian, however, writers such as Moses, Luke, John, and Paul are perfectly credible witnesses, not because they are completely unprejudiced, sophisticated, scientific, and civilized, but because they are themselves prophets of God, inspired by God's Spirit. It is significant that although Paul in 1 Corinthians 15 appeals to numerous witnesses of the resurrection of Jesus (including five hundred, most of whom are still living—a significant evidentiary point), his main argument for belief in the resurrection is that it is an integral part of the gospel he preached, a gospel that he received by revelation (Gal. 1:11–12). So if the dead do not rise, then

> our preaching is in vain and your faith is in vain. We are even found to be misrepresenting God, because we testified about God that he raised Christ, whom he did not raise if it is true that the dead are not raised. (1 Cor. 15:14–15)

The Corinthians should believe in resurrection because it is a central element in the gospel *revelation*.

Hume does not even consider the possibility of knowledge by divine revelation. Doubtless he would consider revelation, too, to be a miracle and therefore impossible and incredible. But in so dismissing the possibility of revelation, he cuts himself off from any communication from the God who is the only ground of rational discourse. If the testimony concerning miracles is the testimony of God himself, then it would fulfill his condition quoted earlier. For the falsehood of God's testimony would certainly be more miraculous (in Hume's sense) than the facts that the testimony establishes.

The same must be said of many, including many scholars, who study the Bible with the presupposition that miracles, including revelation, never take place. The mainstream of modern biblical criticism began with writers such as Baruch Spinoza, Hermann Reimarus, and D. F. Strauss, who made precisely that assumption. They therefore routinely denied the historicity of anything in Scripture that appeared to them to be supernatural, and they sought to reconstruct the history of Israel and the story of Jesus in line with that assumption—an assumption precisely contrary to the assumptions of the biblical writers themselves[18] and logically incompatible with all the distinctive teachings of Christianity.

More recent Bible critics in the liberal tradition have sought to break away from such naturalistic assumptions, and they have been successful in various degrees. But they have not reconciled themselves to the fact that God as covenant Lord rules his people by a written Word, of which he is the Author. So they, like Hume, have often operated on the assumption that the biblical writings reflect only the level of human knowledge typical of the culture of the human writers. These critics have not taken a firm stand on the Scriptures as the very *criterion* of historical truth. But that, nothing less, is the presupposition of Christian faith, the stance of the covenant servant of God.

Are Miracles Evidence for the Christian Faith?

Are miracles an apologetic problem or an apologetic resource? In the theological and philosophical literature, they have been both. There have been arguments about whether miracles have happened (their possibility, probability, and actuality), such as those that we have considered above. But miracles have also been used as evidence for the truth of Christianity.

Certainly the miracles that occurred in the Bible were intended to convince. They do not merely "propose a decision,"[19] but they obligate their audience to make the right decision, to recognize and believe God. We saw earlier that miracles attest prophets. That miracles warrant belief in Christ is a frequent theme in John's gospel. Jesus says:

> If I am not doing the works of my Father, then do not believe me; but if I do them, even though you do not believe me, believe the works, that you may know and understand that the Father is in me and I am in the Father. (John 10:37–38)

> If I had not done among them the works that no one else did, they would not be guilty of sin, but now they have seen and hated both me and my Father. (John 15:24)

Many see the miracles and don't believe (John 12:37–38), yet they *ought* to believe on the basis of the miracles. And many do (2:23; 4:53; 6:2, 14; 7:31; etc.). This is John's purpose in recording the signs: "that you may believe that Jesus is the Christ, the Son of God, and that by believing you may have life in his name" (20:31).

Peter addresses the Jews on the day of Pentecost, announcing:

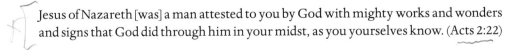

> Jesus of Nazareth [was] a man attested to you by God with mighty works and wonders and signs that God did through him in your midst, as you yourselves know. (Acts 2:22)

---

18. See, for example, Robert Strimple's account of the history of criticism in his *The Modern Search for the Real Jesus* (Phillipsburg, NJ: P&R Publishing, 1995).

19. G. C. Berkouwer, *The Providence of God* (Grand Rapids: Eerdmans, 1952), 225.

The letter to the Hebrews also cites "signs and wonders and various miracles" by which God testified to the salvation of Christ (Heb. 2:4). These statements clearly imply that those who experienced the miracles are thereby obligated to believe in Jesus as Lord. Thus, miracles are evidence, indeed decisive evidence, of the truth of Jesus.

The greatest miracle, the resurrection of Jesus, is particularly important as a warrant for belief. Jesus prophesied it in answer to the Jews' question, "What sign do you show us for doing these things?" (John 2:18). Peter on Pentecost, again, referred to the resurrection in calling the Jews to faith (Acts 2:24–36). If Christ is not raised, therefore, our faith is vain (1 Cor. 15:14).

Christianity is based on historical events, and God's mighty works in history warrant faith. Miracles are an embarrassment to many intelligent Buddhists because Buddhism is not based on historical events. If Buddhism is true, it is true by virtue of its timeless wisdom, not by virtue of historical events. But Christianity in this respect differs from Buddhism, Hinduism, and many other world religions. In Scripture, God's miraculous deeds are important to our salvation and to our knowledge of salvation.

To say that miracles warrant faith is not to say that miracles automatically bring people to faith. As we have seen, many people saw the miracles of Jesus and did not believe. Some were hardened by God, as we saw in chapter 4, so that they could not see the truth (John 12:37–40).

Nor is it always legitimate for people to demand miraculous evidence. Jesus regularly rebuked the Jews' demands for more and more signs (Matt. 12:38–45; 16:1–4; John 4:48; 6:30–40; cf. 1 Cor. 1:22). Abraham in Jesus' parable tells the rich man in hell that he should not ask someone to rise from the dead to bring his brothers to repentance: "If they do not hear Moses and the Prophets, neither will they be convinced if someone should rise from the dead" (Luke 16:31).

Miracles are revelation, but they are not the only form of revelation. All creation reveals God (Rom. 1:18–21), and Scripture ("Moses and the Prophets") is his written revelation. In these sources, there is enough revelation to make us all responsible to believe. Paul in Romans 1 exposes unbelief as willful and culpable. So no one can claim that because God has not shown him a miracle, he has an excuse for unbelief. Certainly the Jewish opponents of Jesus, who had already seen many signs,[20] had no right to demand more. No one may say that he will not believe without a miracle. In that sense, miracles are epistemologically superfluous. We don't absolutely need them, but in them God gives us more evidence than we strictly need. He piles on the evidence, to underscore the cogency of his Word and our own responsibility to believe.

That fact is especially important to us today, because for the most part we have not directly experienced the more spectacular kinds of miracles. The "argument from miracle" today is really an argument from miracle-*reports*, from testimony. In the earthly ministry of Jesus, his miracles and words were somewhat independent sources of knowledge, each attesting the other (see John 10:38; 14:11), though of course these

---

20. Some said, "When the Christ appears, will he do more signs than this man has done?" (John 7:31).

were also interdependent and mutually interpreting in many ways. But for us, Jesus' works and words are found in the same place, the pages of Scripture. For us, Jesus' words to "doubting Thomas" are especially appropriate:

> Have you believed because you have seen me? Blessed are those who have not seen and yet have believed. (John 20:29)

The miracle of the resurrection brought Thomas to faith. But no one may demand from God a similar individual miraculous attestation. Moses and the Prophets, with the NT, are sufficient.

My point is not that miracles themselves are irrelevant, since we are now left with only a written Word. Miracle is part of the persuasive power of the Word itself, illumined by the Spirit. The Bible is not just any old book; it is a Book of miracles—miracles that accomplish and attest God's salvation. When Paul appeals to many witnesses in 1 Corinthians 15, those witnesses are part of Scripture's self-authentication. The miracles of Scripture play a significant role in persuading us that Scripture is true.

Some may find a circle here: we believe the miracles because of Scripture, and Scripture because of the miracles. It is true that Scripture is our ultimate standard—the covenant constitution of the people of God. And an ultimate standard cannot be proved by any standard other than itself. But the circularity does not render the argument unpersuasive. We do not say merely, "The Bible is the Word of God because it is the Word of God," although that syllogism is strictly valid and sound. But we recognize the specific ways in which Scripture attests itself, by presenting content that is wonderfully persuasive and cogent. And miracle is a large part of that.[21]

Reading Scripture thoughtfully, under the Spirit's illumination, we find credible accounts of miracles that reinforce our confidence in the scriptural truths that those miracles attest. And we gain confidence that the miracles really happened, as we gain greater understanding of God's inspiration of the writers who report the miracles. And then, fortified with greater confidence that the miracles really happened, we gain a greater confidence in biblical inspiration. It is a spiral process, in which two realities reinforce one another, as we compare them again and again. That is the way of faith.

Key Terms
Frame's *preliminary definition of miracle*
Natural law (four meanings)
Supernatural
Natural
Immediacy

21. On the question of circularity, see *DKG*, 130–33; *AGG*, 9–14; *CVT*, 299–309; and my articles in Steven B. Cowan, ed., *Five Views on Apologetics* (Grand Rapids: Zondervan, 2000). The next-to-last sentence in my paragraph sets forth the distinction I have made elsewhere between a "narrow" circle and a "broad" circle. See also chapter 31 of this volume.

Attestation of prophecy
Frame's *theologically enhanced definition of miracle*
Signs
Powers
Wonders
Naturalistic assumptions

Study Questions

1. "Scripture teaches us about the Lord in three ways." What are these? How are they perspectivally related?

2. What is the order of topics in part 3? Explain and evaluate Frame's rationale for following this order.

3. How can you define an English term such as *miracle* when it doesn't correspond directly to any term in Hebrew or Greek?

4. Why does Frame object to defining miracle as an exception to natural law? Evaluate his arguments.

5. Evaluate attempts to define miracles as immediate, rather than mediate, acts of God.

6. Should "attestation of prophecy" be part of our definition of miracle? Why or why not?

7. Explain and evaluate Frame's theologically enhanced definition of miracle.

8. Have miracles ceased? Evaluate arguments on both sides.

9. Why have some believed that miracles were impossible? Reply to them.

10. Is there sufficient evidence for believing in biblical miracles? Reply to David Hume on this point.

11. Are miracles evidence for the Christian faith? Reply to those who say that they are not.

12. "We believe the miracles because of Scripture, and Scripture because of the miracles." Is this a circular argument? Can it be defended? How, or why not?

Memory Verses

Ex. 15:6: Your right hand, O LORD, glorious in power,
    your right hand, O LORD, shatters the enemy.

Luke 5:8–10: But when Simon Peter saw it, he fell down at Jesus' knees, saying, "Depart from me, for I am a sinful man, O Lord." For he and all who were with him were astonished at the catch of fish that they had taken, and so also were James and John, sons of Zebedee, who were partners with Simon. And Jesus said to Simon, "Do not be afraid; from now on you will be catching men."

John 20:29: Have you believed because you have seen me? Blessed are those who have not seen and yet have believed.

John 20:30–31: Now Jesus did many other signs in the presence of the disciples, which are not written in this book; but these are written so that you may believe that Jesus is the Christ, the Son of God, and that by believing you may have life in his name.

1 Cor. 15:13–14: But if there is no resurrection of the dead, then not even Christ has been raised. And if Christ has not been raised, then our preaching is in vain and your faith is in vain.

Heb. 2:3–4: How shall we escape if we neglect such a great salvation? It was declared at first by the Lord, and it was attested to us by those who heard, while God also bore witness by signs and wonders and various miracles and by gifts of the Holy Spirit distributed according to his will.

Resources for Further Study

Berkouwer, G. C. *The Providence of God*. Grand Rapids: Eerdmans, 1952. Pp. 188–231.

Kuyper, Abraham. *You Can Do Greater Things than Christ: Demons, Miracles, Healing and Science*, translated by Jan H. Boer. Jos, Nigeria: Institute for Church and Society, 1991. Presents a view that differs both from typical Reformed views and from my own.

Lewis, C. S. *Miracles*. New York: Macmillan, 1947.

Warfield, B. B. *Miracles: Yesterday and Today, True and False*. Grand Rapids: Eerdmans, 1965. Arguments for the cessation of miracles after the apostolic age.

CHAPTER 8

THE ACTS OF THE LORD: PROVIDENCE, PART 1

PROVIDENCE AND MIRACLE together constitute the acts of God in the created world. If miracles are "extraordinary" manifestations of God's lordship, then events of providence are more "ordinary" by comparison. But there is more to be said.

The term *providence*, like the term *miracle*, is not often found in English translations of Scripture. Nevertheless, in Reformed theology, the definition of providence is far less controversial than that of miracle. Most Reformed confessions and theologies agree with this simple formulation:

> God's works of providence are, his most holy, wise, and powerful preserving and governing all his creatures, and all their actions.[1]

Providence and Miracle

In this definition, miracle is a subdivision of providence, one way in which God preserves and governs his creatures and their actions. To some writers, it is important that miracle and providence be sharply distinct from each other. This view is often motivated by the desire to argue the cessation of miracles at the end of the apostolic age.[2] Those arguing the cessation of miracles must show that there are distinguishing characteristics of miracle, so that miracles can cease, although providence continues. If we cannot clearly distinguish miracles from other events, we cannot explain what it is that ceases at the end of the apostolic age. As we have seen, among those allegedly distinguishing characteristics are such concepts as "exceptions to natural law," "immediate acts of God," and "attestations of new special revelation."

---

1. WSC 11.

2. I think there is also, often, an apologetic motive. It is thought that if miracles are not distinct from providence, they cannot serve as a proof for the truth of Christianity. Miracles have to be distinctive, special events to serve that purpose. I discussed the apologetic significance of miracles in the previous chapter. Here I will note also that providence, too, is a proof of God's reality (Ps. 19:1; Rom. 1:18–21). So we do not need to draw a sharp distinction between providence and miracle in order to use these concepts in apologetics.

As my own discussion of the nature of miracles indicates, however, I do not believe that Scripture warrants a sharp distinction between providence and miracle. Indeed, in Scripture, the language of miracle is used for providential events, and the events of providence have much the same significance as miracles.

Psalm 107, for example, is a series of testimonies about the "wonders" of the Lord. Verses 4–9 arguably refer to Israel's wilderness experience, and verses 10–22 may refer to God's chastisements of his sinful people and his response to their repentance. But verses 23–43 refer to God's general providence, rather than the history of redemption specifically. God rescues sailors from storms at sea when they cry to him (vv. 23–32). He gives to his people water and food (vv. 33–43). These are also among God's wonders.

Psalm 136 also lists "wonders" of the Lord (v. 4), including creation (vv. 5–9), the events of the exodus (vv. 10–24), and, almost as an afterthought, the fact that God "gives food to all flesh" (v. 25). General providence is a wonder of God, alongside all his miraculous deeds of creation and redemption. In Psalm 145 also, God's "wondrous works" (v. 5) and "awesome deeds" (v. 6) include God's compassion to all (v. 9).[3] The psalmist observes:

> The eyes of all look to you,
>   and you give them their food in due season.
> You open your hand;
>   you satisfy the desire of every living thing. (Ps. 145:15–16)

Again, providence is among God's wondrous works. Cf. also Job 37:5–24; 42:3.

We see that the psalmist is not straitjacketed by overly rigid theological distinctions. He meditates on God's wonderful deeds, and then at the end it occurs to him that, after all, general providence is pretty wonderful, too! Does it take any more power or wisdom to create the world than to feed all the creatures? Is God's division of the seawaters any more wonderful than his feeding all the humans, animals, and plants on the face of the earth? Evidently, providence, too, is a wonder, a miracle.

It is meditation on miracle that brings the psalmist to consider providence as a work and a revelation of God. Miracle rather shakes up one's mental composure, reminding us that this world does not just drift along on its own, but is the place where a great person lives and acts.[4] But if that is the case, that person's influence is not only local and temporary. The God who brought the plagues on Egypt and divided the sea must be no less than the God of all nature. It is thus that our minds move from miracle to providence.

The reason, of course, is that providence, too, is God's act, and it, too, manifests his control, authority, and presence. If we must distinguish between providence and miracle, we should perhaps contrast the latter as "extraordinary manifestations of God's lordship" with the former as "ordinary manifestations of God's lordship." But even that is not quite

---

3. Reinforced in verse 8 by an allusion to the exposition of the divine name in Exodus 34:6–7.

4. When we contemplate the regularities of nature, we are tempted to attribute them to impersonal laws. Regularities suggest analogies with machines, natural forces, and the like. Miracles, being relatively irregular, tend more easily to suggest *personal* causation.

right; for in the eyes of the psalmist, providence itself is rather extraordinary. Only one person, after all, is able to feed all living things on earth. At any rate, we should normally place miracle on the "more extraordinary" side of the spectrum. My only point at present is that there is a spectrum, a continuum, not a sharp distinction, between providence and miracle. And there is, then, a sense in which all is miracle.

Providence and God's Control

There are many ways in which providence, like miracle, amazes us. I will discuss these in terms of God's lordship attributes, for providence, like miracle, is a demonstration of God's lordship.

Efficacy

The catechism definition of providence uses the term *powerful*, along with other descriptions that we will consider later. To say that the power of God's providence is efficacious is simply to say that it always accomplishes its purpose. God never fails to accomplish what he sets out to do. Creatures may resist, to be sure, but they cannot prevail. For his own reasons, God sometimes wishes to delay the fulfillment of his intentions, even over a period of years (though, of course, for him a thousand years are as a day). Through that period, he may allow himself to suffer apparent defeats. But as we will see later in our discussion of the problem of evil (chapter 14), each apparent defeat actually makes God's eventual victory all the more glorious. The cross of Jesus is, of course, the chief example of this principle.

Nothing is too hard for God (Jer. 32:27); nothing seems marvelous to him (Zech. 8:6); with him nothing is impossible (Gen. 18:14; Matt. 19:26; Luke 1:37). So his purposes will always prevail. Against Assyria, he says:

> "As I have planned,
>   so shall it be,
> and as I have purposed,
>   so shall it stand,
> that I will break the Assyrian in my land,
>   and on my mountains trample him underfoot;
> and his yoke shall depart from them,
>   and his burden from their shoulder."

> This is the purpose that is purposed
>   concerning the whole earth,
> and this is the hand that is stretched out
>   over all the nations.
> For the LORD of hosts has purposed,
>   and who will annul it?
> His hand is stretched out,
>   and who will turn it back? (Isa. 14:24–27; cf. Job 42:2; Jer. 23:20)

When God expresses his eternal purposes in words, through his prophets, those prophecies will surely come to pass (Deut. 18:21–22; Isa. 31:2).[5] God sometimes even represents his word as his active agent that inevitably accomplishes his bidding:

> [As the fruitful rain,] so shall my word be that goes out from my mouth;
>   it shall not return to me empty,
> but it shall accomplish that which I purpose,
>   and shall succeed in the thing for which I sent it. (Isa. 55:11; cf. Zech. 1:6)

So the wise teacher reminds us:

> No wisdom, no understanding, no counsel can avail against the Lord. (Prov. 21:30; cf. 16:9; 19:21)

God always accomplishes his purpose, counsel, pleasure, or will:

> God declar[es] the end from the beginning
>   and from ancient times things not yet done,
> saying, "My counsel shall stand,
>   and I will accomplish all my purpose." (Isa. 46:10)

> All the inhabitants of the earth are accounted as nothing,
>   and he does according to his will among the host of heaven
>   and among the inhabitants of the earth;
> and none can stay his hand
>   or say to him, "What have you done?" (Dan. 4:35)

> At that time Jesus declared, "I thank you, Father, Lord of heaven and earth, that you have hidden these things from the wise and understanding and revealed them to little children; yes, Father, for such was your gracious will." (Matt. 11:25–26)

> He chose us in him before the foundation of the world, that we should be holy and blameless before him. In love he predestined us for adoption as sons through Jesus Christ, according to the purpose of his will. (Eph. 1:4–5; cf. v. 9)[6]

---

5. Not every prophecy in Scripture is an expression of God's eternal purpose. Some prophecies indicate what God will do in various *possible* situations. Sometimes, therefore, he announces judgment, but "relents" when people repent (see Jer. 18:5–10). I will discuss this issue again (chapter 17) in connection with God's unchangeability. See also Richard Pratt, "Prophecy and Historical Contingency," at http://www.thirdmill.org.

6. Scripture also contains, to be sure, many examples of creatures who fail to please God, by disobeying his commands and thereby failing to measure up to his standards. Here the traditional Reformed distinction between God's decretive and preceptive wills (or, here, pleasures) is important. God always accomplishes what he ordains to happen, but he does not always ordain that his precepts, his standards, be followed. In other words, he is sometimes pleased to ordain his own displeasure, as when he ordains sinful actions of human beings (see later in this chapter for examples, and my longer discussion of God's will, chapter 16.)

Scripture also speaks of the efficacy of God's purposes in our lives by the image of the potter and the clay (Isa. 29:16; 45:9; 64:8; Jer. 18:1–10; Rom. 9:19–24): as easily as the potter molds his clay, makes one vessel for one purpose, another for another, so God deals with people. His purpose will prevail, and the clay has no right to complain to the potter about it.

This emphasis on the general efficacy of God's purpose stands as the background for the Reformed doctrine of *irresistible grace*. As we mentioned earlier, sinners do resist God's purposes; indeed, that is a significant theme in Scripture (Isa. 65:12; Matt. 23:37–39; Luke 7:30; Acts 7:51; Eph. 4:30; 1 Thess. 5:19; Heb. 4:2; 12:25). But the point of the doctrine is that their resistance does not succeed against the Lord. When God intends to bring someone to faith in Christ, he cannot fail, although for his own reasons he may choose to wrestle long with a person before achieving that purpose.[7] We will see later in this chapter that God's election always precedes, and is the source of, our response of faith. And we will also see that God calls sinners effectually into fellowship with him. Of course, we will have to discuss further the nature of human resistance in our later consideration of creaturely responsibility and freedom (chapter 35) and in our discussion of perseverance (chapter 44).

But Scripture regularly teaches that when God elects, calls, and regenerates someone in Christ, through the Spirit, that work accomplishes his saving purpose. When God gives his people a new heart, it is certain that they will "walk in my statutes and keep my rules and obey them" (Ezek. 11:20; cf. 36:26–27). When God gives new life (John 5:21), we cannot send it back to him. Jesus said, "All that the Father gives me will come to me" (John 6:37). If God foreknows (= befriends; see later) someone, he will certainly predestine him to be conformed to the likeness of Christ, to be called, to be justified, to be glorified in heaven (Rom. 8:29–30).

> Blessed is the one you choose and bring near,
>   to dwell in your courts!
> We shall be satisfied with the goodness of your house,
>   the holiness of your temple! (Ps. 65:4)

> [God] has mercy on whomever he wills, and he hardens whomever he wills. (Rom. 9:18, quoting Ex. 33:19)

> For God has not destined us for wrath, but to obtain salvation through our Lord Jesus Christ. (1 Thess. 5:9)

Like his Word, therefore, God's grace will never return void.

---

7. There are also situations in which people who appear to be elect turn away from God and prove themselves not to be among his people. There are also cases in which God chooses someone without the intention of giving him the full benefits of salvation. Judas is one example (John 6:70), as is national Israel, which, because of unbelief, loses its special status as God's elect nation.

We can summarize the biblical teaching about the efficacy of God's rule in the following passages, which speak for themselves:

> The counsel of the LORD stands forever,
>   the plans of his heart to all generations. (Ps. 33:11)

> Our God is in the heavens;
>   he does all that he pleases. (Ps. 115:3)

> Whatever the LORD pleases, he does,
>   in heaven and on earth,
>   in the seas and all deeps. (Ps. 135:6)

> Also henceforth I am he;
>   there is none who can deliver from my hand;
>   I work, and who can turn it back? (Isa. 43:13)

> The words of the holy one, the true one, who has the key of David, who opens and no one will shut, who shuts and no one opens. (Rev. 3:7)

Universality

I will now try to show that God exercises such efficacious control over everything that happens in the world, in accordance with his universal covenant (see chapter 4). We will note events in various aspects of creation.

The Natural World

The natural world, first of all, is God's creation. Scripture emphasizes that fact frequently: Gen. 1:1–31; Ex. 20:11; Pss. 33:6, 9; 95:3–5; 146:5–6; Jer. 10:12; 51:15–16; Acts 17:24; Col. 1:16. He has made it according to his own wisdom, his own plan. He knows it inside and out and has planned all the laws and principles by which it operates.

The biblical writers do not hesitate to ascribe the events of the natural world directly to God:

> You visit the earth and water it;
>   you greatly enrich it;
> the river of God is full of water;
>   you provide their grain,
>   for so you have prepared it.
> You water its furrows abundantly,
>   settling its ridges,
> softening it with showers,
>   and blessing its growth.
> You crown the year with your bounty;
>   your wagon tracks overflow with abundance. (Ps. 65:9–11; cf. 135:5–7; 147:15–18)

Cf. also Gen. 8:22; Job 38–40; Pss. 104:10–30; 107:23–32; 145:15–16; 147:8–9; 148:8; Jer. 5:22; 10:13; 31:35; Jonah 4:6–7; Nah. 1:3; Acts 14:17. Notice the monergism in these statements: these are things that God *does*, because they please him. He does not merely allow them to happen; rather, he makes them happen. *God* waters the land. *God* drenches the furrows. *God* makes the clouds rise. *God* thunders (Jer. 10:13). *God* makes it snow or rain. *God* sends the frost and the ice, and then, when he pleases, he melts it. As he created all things by his word, so he sends his command, his word, to govern the events of nature.

Even those events that appear to be most random are under God's sovereign control. "The lot is cast into the lap, but its every decision is from the LORD" (Prov. 16:33). Throw dice or draw straws; God controls the result. He decides the numbers to be drawn in the lottery. Indeed, in some cases he reveals his will through the drawing of lots (Jonah 1:7; Acts 1:23–26).[8] What we call "accidents" come from the Lord (Ex. 21:13; Judg. 9:53; 1 Kings 22:34).

Scripture also teaches the sovereignty of God by showing his purposeful discrimination in natural events. Before bringing Israel out of Egypt, God brings plagues on the Egyptians; so Israel has known Yahweh as the Lord of nature. In Exodus 9:13–26, he brings a terrible hailstorm upon the Egyptians, but leaves one area untouched: the land of Goshen, where the Israelites lived. God is the One who gives rain to one town and withholds it from another (Amos 4:7). He sends prosperity and famine (Gen. 41:28–32).

Jesus emphasizes that this divine control extends to the smallest details. He teaches us that our heavenly Father not only makes the sun rise and sends rain (Matt. 5:45), but also feeds all the birds (6:26–27),[9] clothes the lilies (6:28–30), and accounts for the falling of the sparrows and the number of our hairs (Matt. 10:29–30; Luke 12:4–7). And he demonstrates his unity with the Father by calming the sea, by his own command (Matt. 8:23–27; Mark 4:35–39; Luke 8:22–25).

So the biblical view of the natural world is intensely personalistic. Natural events come from God, the personal Lord. He also employs angels and human beings to do his work in the world. But the idea that there is some impersonal mechanism called *nature* or *natural law*[10] that governs the universe is absent from the Bible. So is the notion of an ultimate "randomness" postulated by some exponents of quantum mechanics.[11] Now, obviously, there are such things as natural forces—gravity and electricity, for

8. I am not advising Christians today to ascertain God's will by lot. In the case of Jonah, I think it was wrong for the sailors to try to find the culprit by lot, although they were, of course, desperate, and ultimately they expelled Jonah not because of the lot, but because of his own confession of sin against God. As for the apostles in Acts 1, I assume that Joseph and Matthias were so alike in their qualifications that the lot was the only way to choose. Nevertheless, in both passages God uses the lot to reveal his will. Certainly Acts 1:24–26 represents the apparently random decision as God's answer to prayer.

9. Of course, he feeds the lions, too (Ps. 104:21), and sometimes shuts their mouths (Dan. 6:22).

10. Compare my discussion in chapter 7.

11. Quantum mechanics may demonstrate a randomness in the finite world, that is, events without finite causes. But it can never demonstrate negatively that those events have no causation at all, that is, that they are independent even of God's determination.

example. Scripture indeed mentions the natural forces of the weather. But it is plain that in the view of the biblical writers, any impersonal objects or forces are only secondary causes of the course of nature. Behind them, as behind the rain and the hail, behind even the apparent randomness of events, stands the personal God, who controls all things by his powerful word.

Human History

Scripture doesn't tell us about God's work in nature merely to satisfy our curiosity. Rather, as always, God in his Word intends to teach us about ourselves. God made us of dust (Gen. 2:7), so we are a part of nature and very dependent on the rain, the sunshine, the crops, and the animals. Without the cooperation of the "lower creation," we could not exist. When Jesus talks about God's providing for the sparrows and lilies, it is part of an a fortiori argument: *how much more* does he care for you? We are "of more value than many sparrows" (Matt. 10:31).

Nor could we exist without a vast accumulation of apparently random events. We all owe our existence to the combination of one sperm and one egg out of a vast number of possible combinations, and to equally improbable combinations that produced each of our parents and our ancestors back to Adam. And consider how many natural events enabled each of our ancestors to survive to maturity, marry, and reproduce. All these things, plus the improbable events of our own life experience, have made us what we are.

So if God controls all the events of nature, then certainly he also controls the course of our own lives. And we do not need to infer that conclusion from the preceding discussion; rather, Scripture teaches it explicitly. The apostle Paul tells the Athenian philosophers:

> And he made from one man every nation of mankind to live on all the face of the earth, having determined allotted periods and the boundaries of their dwelling place. (Acts 17:26)

God is King not only over Israel, but over all the nations, over all the earth (Pss. 2:6–12; 47:1–9; 95:3; cf. Gen. 18:25). He governs the events of human history for his purposes. So the psalmist says:

> The LORD brings the counsel of the nations to nothing;
>   he frustrates the plans of the peoples.
> The counsel of the LORD stands forever,
>   the plans of his heart to all generations. (Ps. 33:10)

We can see God's comprehensive rule in the life of Joseph, who was betrayed by his brothers, sold into slavery in Egypt, and elevated to a position of prominence there, and who delivered his family from deadly famine. At every point in the story, God is the One who brings about the events of the narrative. God gave to Joseph the power to interpret dreams (Gen. 41:16, 28, 32). And it was God who determined that Joseph's brothers would betray him (Gen. 45:5–8). Later, Joseph says to them:

> As for you, you meant evil against me, but God meant it for good, to bring it about that many people should be kept alive, as they are today. (Gen. 50:20)

Again and again, it is God who brings about each event, good or evil, for his good purposes. God did not merely allow Joseph to be sent into Egypt; rather, God himself sends him, though certainly the treacherous brothers are responsible. Throughout the Scriptures, God stands behind each great historical event.

As we saw in the discussion of miracle, it is Yahweh who brings the people out of Egypt, by his strong arm. Then he puts terror into the hearts of Israel's enemies as his people take their inheritance in the Promised Land (Ex. 23:27; Deut. 2:25; cf. Gen. 35:5). After Joshua's conquests,

> the Lord gave them rest on every side just as he had sworn to their fathers. Not one of all their enemies had withstood them, for the Lord had given all their enemies into their hands. Not one word of all the good promises that the Lord had made to the house of Israel had failed; all came to pass. (Josh. 21:44–45)

Later, the nations did seek to destroy God's people. The nations are gathered against Israel, says the Lord,

> but they do not know
>   the thoughts of the Lord;
> they do not understand his plan. (Mic. 4:12)

So Israel is often at war, but God decides who will prevail:

> The horse is made ready for the day of battle,
>   but the victory belongs to the Lord. (Prov. 21:31)

God promises to give victory to Israel, as Israel is faithful to him. He tells Israel to allow liberal exemptions from military service, for God can win with many or few (Deut. 20:1–15; Judg. 7:1–8; 1 Sam. 14:6). The outcome is always in the Lord's hands (Deut. 3:22; Josh. 24:11; 1 Sam. 17:47; 2 Chron. 20:15; Zech. 4:6). But he will also bring defeat on Israel to show his displeasure against Israel's disobedience (Josh. 7:11–12).

Indeed, God's people prove unfaithful to the covenant. So Yahweh raises up the Assyrian power to judge his people in the northern of the two kingdoms. The Assyrians do not intend to do God's bidding, but they do it, for their own reasons, after which God judges their sins as well (Isa. 10:5–12; 14:24–25; 37:26). Isaiah's prophecy about Assyria concludes:

> This is the purpose that is purposed
>   concerning the whole earth,
> and this is the hand that is stretched out
>   over all the nations.
> For the LORD of hosts has purposed,
>   and who will annul it?
> His hand is stretched out,
>   and who will turn it back? (Isa. 14:26–27)[12]

Similarly with the Babylonians, who invade the southern kingdom and lead the people into exile (Hab. 1:6–11). Again, it is God who raises up the conquerors.

So God sends his people into exile, using the Assyrians and Babylonians as his tools, but he will restore them again (Jer. 29:11–14). He will stir up the Medes, in turn, to destroy Babylon (Jer. 51:11). He "removes kings and sets up kings" (Dan. 2:21). The chastened Nebuchadnezzar concludes:

> His dominion is an everlasting dominion,
>   and his kingdom endures from generation to generation;
> all the inhabitants of the earth are accounted as nothing,
>   and he does according to his will among the host of heaven
>   and among the inhabitants of the earth;
> and none can stay his hand
>   or say to him, "What have you done?" (Dan. 4:34b–35)

But there is more. The Persian Empire supplants the Babylonian, and God chooses Cyrus, the Persian ruler, as his instrument to bring Israel back to the Land of Promise (Isa. 44:28; 45:1–13). On the conservative understanding of the chronology implied by the biblical text, God through Isaiah calls Cyrus by name, centuries before Cyrus is born. Then through the edict of this pagan king (Ezra 1:2–4), God ends Israel's exile. Her return is at every point the work of God:

> [God] says of Cyrus, "He is my shepherd,
>   and he shall fulfill all my purpose";
> saying of Jerusalem, "She shall be built,"
>   and of the temple, "Your foundation shall be laid." (Isa. 44:28)

Cyrus is a free agent, and doubtless he made up his own mind for his own reasons to let Jerusalem be rebuilt. But God says here that Cyrus was doing God's good pleasure, and that Cyrus would certainly make the decision that God had predicted long before. The book of Ezra tells us that "the LORD stirred up the spirit of Cyrus" (Ezra 1:1) to order the return of Israel from exile (cf. 2 Chron. 36:22; and later in regard to Darius, Ezra 6:22; and Artaxerxes, 7:27). Note also the repeated *I wills* in Jeremiah's prophecy of restoration (Jer. 30:4–24).

---

12. Compare the prophecy of Cyrus, below.

Thus God sets the stage for the center point of human history. It is to restored Israel that God grants the visit of his Son, Jesus:

> But when the fullness of time had come, God sent forth his Son, born of woman, born under the law, to redeem those who were under the law, so that we might receive adoption as sons. (Gal. 4:4–5)

Again, God brings everything about. Jesus' conception is supernatural. Everything he does fulfills prophecy.[13] Everything he does is in obedience to his Father's will.[14]

But he is betrayed:

> This Jesus, delivered up according to the definite plan and foreknowledge of God, you crucified and killed by the hands of lawless men. God raised him up, loosing the pangs of death, because it was not possible for him to be held by it. (Acts 2:23–24; cf. 3:18; 4:27–28; 13:27)

Judas made a personal decision to betray Jesus, for which he is fully responsible. Nevertheless, the betrayal and execution of Jesus takes place "as it has been determined" (Luke 22:22; cf. Matt. 26:24; Mark 14:21). God's purpose stands behind Jesus' betrayal and death. He intended it to be an atoning sacrifice for our sins (Mark 10:45; Rom. 3:25; 1 John 4:10), recalling his words to Isaiah:

> "I, I am the LORD,
>   and besides me there is no savior.
> I declared and saved and proclaimed,
>   when there was no strange god among you;
>   and you are my witnesses," declares the LORD, "and I am God.
> Also henceforth I am he;
>   there is none who can deliver from my hand;
>   I work, and who can turn it back?" (Isa. 43:11–13; cf. v. 25)

The gospel of John teaches that Jesus' death happened at a particular "hour" determined by the Father (John 2:4; 7:6, 30, 44; 8:20; 12:23, 27; 13:1; 16:21; 17:1). Before that hour, nobody could kill Jesus (7:30, 44), though they wanted to. He died only at the time planned by the Father.

It was God's act that raised Jesus from the dead. It was God in Christ who by the power of the Holy Spirit sent the new Christian church to proclaim Jesus' name throughout the earth (Matt. 28:19–20; Acts 1:8). And it was God who ordained that few Jews and many Gentiles would believe (Rom. 9–11). God also told Paul, the apostle to the Gentiles, that he would have to suffer for the sake of Jesus (Acts

---

13. This is a pervasive theme in Matthew's gospel (1:22; 2:15; 3:3; 4:14; 16:21; etc.; see also Luke 13:31–33; Acts 13:29).

14. A major theme of John's gospel (4:34; 5:30; 6:38; 7:16–18; etc.).

9:16, 23) and that the Jews in Jerusalem would bind him and hand him over to the Romans (21:10–11).

It is God the Father who has planned the day and hour of Jesus' return in glory (Matt. 24:36). Jesus will come in his sovereign power and glory (1 Thess. 4:16). Jesus himself is Lord, as we will see, and salvation is his work, as it is the Father's. In the book of Revelation, the twenty-four elders sing to Jesus, the Lamb in the center of the throne:

> And they sang a new song, saying,
>
> "Worthy are you to take the scroll
>   and to open its seals,
> for you were slain, and by your blood you ransomed people for God
>   from every tribe and language and people and nation,
> and you have made them a kingdom and priests to our God,
>   and they shall reign on the earth." (Rev. 5:9–10)

Overwhelmed by his vision of God's plan of salvation, Paul responds:

> Oh, the depth of the riches and wisdom and knowledge of God! How unsearchable are his judgments and how inscrutable his ways!
>
> "For who has known the mind of the Lord,
>   or who has been his counselor?"
>
> "Or who has given a gift to him
>   that he might be repaid?"
>
> For from him and through him and to him are all things. To him be glory forever. Amen. (Rom. 11:33–36)

Through the centuries of redemptive history, *everything* has come from God. He has planned and done it all. He has not merely set boundaries for creaturely action; he has made everything happen.

I conclude that God rules the whole course of human history. Scripture, of course, focuses on the great events of the history of redemption: God's election of Israel, the incarnation, death, resurrection, ascension, and return of Jesus. But we have seen that for these great events to take place, God had to be in control of all the nations: Egypt, Babylon, Assyria, and Persia, as well as Israel. Indeed, his mighty deeds prove him to be no less than King over all the earth.

Individual Human Life

But God does not only control the course of nature and the great events of history. As we have seen, he is also concerned about details. So we find that in Scripture God controls the course of each human life. How could it be otherwise? God controls all natural events in detail, even including "random" events. He controls the history of nations and of human salvation. But these, in turn, govern to a large extent the events of our daily lives; and, conversely, if God does not control a vast number of individual human lives, it is hard to imagine how he would be able to control the great developments of history.

In fact, Scripture does also teach explicitly that God controls the course of our individual lives. That control begins before we are conceived. God says to Jeremiah:

> Before I formed you in the womb I knew you,
> and before you were born I consecrated you;
> I appointed you a prophet to the nations. (Jer. 1:5)

Is Jeremiah an exception to the general rule because he is God's prophet, or does God know us all before conception? If God knew Jeremiah before his conception, then God must have arranged for one particular sperm to reach one particular egg to produce each of Jeremiah's ancestors back to Adam, and then Jeremiah himself. So God is in control of all the "accidents" of history to create the precise person he seeks to employ as his prophet.[15] God's foreknowledge of an individual implies comprehensive control over the human family. And Paul says of all believers that God "chose us in [Christ] before the foundation of the world" (Eph. 1:4).

So the whole history of human procreation is under God's control, as he acts intentionally to bring about the conception of each of us (Gen. 4:1, 25; 18:13–14; 25:21; 29:31–30:2; 30:17, 23–24; Deut. 10:22; Ruth 4:13; Pss. 113:9; 127:3–5). And of course, God is also active after the child's conception, as he is formed in the womb:

> For you formed my inward parts;
>   you knitted me together in my mother's womb.
> I praise you, for I am fearfully and wonderfully made.
> Wonderful are your works;
>   my soul knows it very well.
> My frame was not hidden from you,
> when I was being made in secret,
>   intricately woven in the depths of the earth.
> Your eyes saw my unformed substance;
> in your book were written, every one of them,
>   the days that were formed for me,
>   when as yet there was none of them. (Ps. 139:13–16)

So our very existence as human beings is by God's gift of life. Further, we are who we are individually by God's providence. Modern genetic science continues to discover

---

15. The same must be said of Cyrus, discussed earlier. Also, according to 1 Kings 13:1–3, an unnamed prophet told wicked King Jeroboam that a son of David named Josiah would kill his idolatrous priests. As with Cyrus, the prophet mentions Josiah by name, and his activities, long before his birth (1 Kings 13:1–3).

more and more things about us that arise because of our genetic makeup, through the incredibly complex programming of the DNA code.[16] How could anything but a person account for such information technology within every living cell? God is that person, and by controlling our genetic makeup and gestation, he makes us to be the physical beings we are, before we are even born.[17]

After birth, too, the events of our lives are in God's hands. Exodus 21:12–13, a law concerning the taking of life, reads:

> Whoever strikes a man so that he dies shall be put to death. But if he did not lie in wait for him, but God let him fall into his hand, then I will appoint for you a place to which he may flee.

Note how the law ascribes what we would call "accidental" loss of life to the agency of God. Naomi, the mother-in-law of Ruth, sees the hand of God in the deaths of her two sons:

> No, my daughters, for it is exceedingly bitter to me for your sake that the hand of the LORD has gone out against me. (Ruth 1:13)

In the prayer of Hannah, mother of Samuel, she recognizes that

> the LORD kills and brings to life;
>   he brings down to Sheol and raises up.
> The LORD makes poor and makes rich;
>   he brings low and he exalts. (1 Sam. 2:6–7)

The psalmist recognizes that

> the steps of a man are established by the LORD,
>   when he delights in his way;
> though he fall, he shall not be cast headlong,
>   for the LORD upholds his hand. (Ps. 37:23–24)

So God plans the course of our lives: our birth, our death, and whether we prosper or fall.

The differences between us, our relatively different natural and spiritual abilities, come from God (Rom. 12:3–6; 1 Cor. 4:7; 12:4–6).

James offers wisdom about the planning of our lives:

---

16. I do not believe, however, that the genetic code accounts for everything we are. There are complex relationships between body and spirit.

17. Compare Paul's statement in 1 Corinthians 12:18 ("But as it is, God arranged the members in the body, each one of them, as he chose") and 15:35–41, where God gives to every creature precisely the kind of body that he wants it to have. If someone wants to make an issue of the fact that these passages mention bodies but not minds, see the next section. But recall at this point that there is a close relation (in my view not identity) between mind and brain. Injury to the brain often impairs thinking. So if God controls the brain, he thereby controls much of our thinking function as well. The rest, of course, he also controls, but by other means.

Come now, you who say, "Today or tomorrow we will go into such and such a town and spend a year there and trade and make a profit"—yet you do not know what tomorrow will bring. What is your life? For you are a mist that appears for a little time and then vanishes. Instead you ought to say, "If the Lord wills, we will live and do this or that." As it is, you boast in your arrogance. All such boasting is evil. (James 4:13–16)[18]

Clearly, for James, all the events of our lives are in God's hands. Whatever we do depends on God's willing it to happen.

Human Decisions

We now approach a more controversial area, that of human decisions. Does God bring about our decisions? Some of them? Any of them? In chapter 35, I will discuss the nature of human responsibility and freedom, which are genuine and important. But here we must face the fact that our decisions are not independent of God, and therefore that our definition of freedom must be, somehow, consistent with God's sovereignty over the human will.

In our survey of the history of redemption, we have already seen that God brought about the free decisions of certain people, such as Joseph's brothers (Gen. 45:5–8), Cyrus (Isa. 44:28), and Judas (Luke 22:22; Acts 2:23–24; 3:18; 4:27–28; 13:27). So we should not be prejudiced by the unbiblical but popular notion that God *never* foreordains our free decisions.

Further, we have seen that God ordains the events of nature and the events of our daily lives. How can such pervasive divine involvement in our lives not profoundly influence our own choices? It is God who has made us inside and out. To make us who we are, he must control our heredity. So he has given us the parents we have, and their parents, and their parents. And to give us the parents we have, God must control many of their free decisions, such as the free decisions of Jeremiah's parents to marry, and of their parents, and their parents. Further, we have seen that it is God who has placed us in our environment, in the situations that require us to make decisions. It is God who decides how long we will live, who brings about our successes and failures, even though such events usually depend on our free decisions as well as on factors outside us.

Negatively, God's purposes *exclude* many free decisions that would otherwise be possible. Since God had planned to bring Joseph to Egypt, his brothers were, in an important sense, not free to kill him, though at one point in the story they planned to do so. Nor could Goliath have killed David, nor could Jeremiah have died in the womb.[19] Nor could the Roman soldiers have broken Jesus' legs when he hung on the cross, for God's prophets had declared otherwise.

---

18. For a negative example, see Jesus' parable of the rich fool, Luke 12:13–21. Cf. also Jer. 10:23: "I know, O Lord, that a man's life is not his own; it is not for man to direct his steps" (NIV).

19. See Gordon H. Clark, *Predestination in the Old Testament* (Phillipsburg, NJ: Presbyterian and Reformed, 1978), 5–6.

But over and above these inferences,[20] Scripture teaches directly that God brings about our free decisions. God does not merely foreordain what happens to us, as we have seen earlier, but also foreordains what we choose to do.

The root of human decision is the *heart*. Jesus says:

> The good person out of the good treasure of his heart produces good, and the evil person out of his evil treasure produces evil, for out of the abundance of the heart his mouth speaks. (Luke 6:45)

A thornbush cannot bear figs, because to bear figs would be contrary to its very nature. So the heart is the center of human life, our fundamental nature and character. But that heart is under God's control: "The heart of man plans his way, but the Lord establishes his steps" (Prov. 16:9; cf. 21:1). Certainly this is what God did with Cyrus, as we have seen. Also with the pharaoh of the exodus (Rom. 9:17; cf. Ex. 9:16; 14:4), as we will see in the next section.[21]

God directs the hearts not only of kings, but of all people (Ps. 33:15). So he controls the decisions not only of Pharaoh, but also of the Egyptian people, giving them a favorable disposition toward Israel (Ex. 12:36). Scripture underscores that this change was the Lord's work, for it mentions that God had predicted it in his meeting with Moses at the burning bush (3:21–22).

God who forms the purposes of our heart also decides the steps we will take to carry out those purposes, as in Proverbs 16:9, quoted above (cf. 16:1; 19:21).

According to many Scripture passages, God controls free decisions and attitudes, often predicting those decisions far in advance. He declares that when the Israelites go up to Jerusalem for the annual feasts, the enemy nations will not covet their land (Ex. 34:24). God is saying that he will control the minds and hearts of these pagan peoples so that they will not cause trouble for Israel at these times.

When Gideon, judge of Israel, leads his tiny army against the Midianite camp, "the Lord set every man's sword against his comrade and against all the army" (Judg. 7:22). During the exile, God causes a chief Babylonian official "to show favor and sympathy to Daniel" (Dan. 1:9 niv). After the exile, the Lord "filled [Israel] with joy by changing the attitude of the king of Assyria" (Ezra 6:22 niv).

The soldiers at Jesus' crucifixion freely decided not to tear Jesus' garment, but instead to cast lots for it. God foreordained this decision:

> This was to fulfill the Scripture which says,

---

20. Another inference may be made on the basis of God's exhaustive knowledge of the future. If God knows our free decisions before we are born, then certainly we are not the ultimate source of them. Many today, however, have denied God's exhaustive foreknowledge, including process theologians and "open theists." So I will argue the matter later, in chapter 15. If that argument is cogent, then God knows our free decisions from eternity and therefore, since he is the only being who exists in eternity past, he is the cause of those decisions.

21. See also 1 Samuel 10:9 on Saul, 1 Kings 3:12 on Solomon.

"They divided my garments among them,
    and for my clothing they cast lots."

So the soldiers did these things. (John 19:24, quoting Ps. 22:18; cf. 19:31–37)

John's point is not only that God knew in advance what would happen. Rather, the event took place *so that* the Scripture might be fulfilled. Whose intention was it to fulfill Scripture through this event? It was not the intent of the soldiers, but the intent of God, the Primary Cause of their decision.

The Gospels tell us over and over again that things happen so that Scripture may be fulfilled. Many of those events involve free decisions of human beings. Meditate on Matthew 1:20–23; 2:14–15, 22–23; 4:12–16; and many others. In some, human beings (such as Jesus himself in 4:12–16) may have consciously intended to fulfill Scripture. In other cases, they either had no such intention or did not even know they were fulfilling Scripture (e.g., Matt. 21:1–5; 26:55–56; Acts 13:27–29). In any case, the Scripture *must* be fulfilled (Mark 14:49).[22]

The picture given to us by this large group of passages is that God's purpose stands behind the free decisions of human beings. Often God tells us, sometimes long before the event, what a human being will freely decide to do. But the point is not merely that he foreknows, but that he is fulfilling his own purpose through the event. That divine purpose imparts a certain necessity (Gk. *dei*, as in Matt. 16:21; 24:6; Mark 8:31; 9:11; 13:7, 10, 14; Luke 9:22; 17:25; 24:26; and many other texts) to the human decision to bring about the predicted event.[23] We will, of course, have to discuss later (chapter 35) how this necessity is compatible with human freedom.

Sins

This section will raise even more serious difficulties than the last. If it is hard for us to accept God's foreordination of human decisions in general, it is even harder to accept his foreordination specifically of our sinful actions. The former raises questions about human freedom and responsibility; the latter raises questions about God's own goodness. For how can a holy God bring about sin?

We will deal with that problem in chapter 35. But for now, it is important to see that God does in fact bring about the sinful behavior of human beings, whatever problems

22. In this passage, Jesus says that Scripture was fulfilled both in the failure of his enemies to arrest him in the temple courts and in their decision to arrest him in the garden. Both, of course, were their free decisions.

23. The nature of "fulfillment" in reference to prophecy is rather complex. Sometimes, as in Deuteronomy 18:21–22 and Daniel 7:1–28, prophecy straightforwardly predicts future events and is fulfilled when those events take place. Other times, as in Matthew 2:14–15, the relation between prophecy and fulfillment is not as evident. When Matthew quotes Hosea 11:1, "Out of Egypt I called my son," he is not claiming, I think, that Hosea *predicted* the Messiah's sojourn in Egypt, but rather that that sojourn is symbolically appropriate to Jesus' role as the faithful remnant of Israel. But in all cases, the text suggests that God was bringing about an event that in one way or another (literally, allusively, symbolically) brings out the depth of meaning in the prophecy. In these fulfillment passages, there is always a sense of divine necessity.

that may create in our understanding. However we answer the notorious problem of evil,[24] our response must be in accord with Scripture, and therefore with the great number of Scripture passages that affirm God's foreordination of everything, even including sin. Many attempts to solve the problem deny this premise—but scripturally, the premise will not be denied.

We have already seen that God controls the free decisions of human beings, particularly by controlling the heart, the center of human existence. But the hearts of fallen people are sinful, as God says through Jeremiah:

> The heart is deceitful above all things,
>   and desperately sick;
>   who can understand it? (Jer. 17:9)

Such hearts freely choose to do evil, but they are no less under God's control than the hearts of the righteous.

So we saw that God sent Joseph into Egypt to preserve the lives of his family in a time of famine, accomplishing that purpose by means of the sinful actions of Joseph's brothers, who sold him into slavery. Between the time of Joseph and Moses, the pharaohs turned against Israel. The psalmist does not hesitate to attribute the Egyptians' hatred to God:

> And the Lord made his people very fruitful
>   and made them stronger than their foes.
> He turned their hearts to hate his people,
>   to deal craftily with his servants. (Ps. 105:24–25)

When God met with Moses to deliver Israel from Egypt, he told Moses in advance what Pharaoh's decision would be (Ex. 3:19): Pharaoh would not let Israel go unless constrained by "a mighty hand." Then God hardened the heart of Pharaoh to create that unwillingness (4:21; 7:3, 13; 9:12; 10:1, 20, 27; 11:10; 14:4, 8[25]). Note the sustained emphasis on God's agency. It is also true that Pharaoh hardened his own heart (8:15), but in the narrative God's hardening of him is clearly prior and receives the greater emphasis. To harden one's heart is to refuse God's commands, even refusing to listen to them or take them seriously. Clearly, it is a sin. God warns against it (see Ps. 95:7–8). But in this case God made it happen, for his own specific purpose (Rom. 9:17). Having

---

24. The problem of evil concerns both *natural* evil (events that bring human suffering) and *moral* evil (sinful actions of rational creatures). Certainly God is sovereign over natural evil, for as we have seen, he manifests his judgments in history. He often deals with human sin by bringing disaster and death (see, e.g., Eccl. 7:14; Isa. 54:16; Amos 3:6). In Christian theology, natural evil is God's judgment upon moral evil (Gen. 3:14–19), so moral evil has the primacy. Moral evil is therefore the more serious problem, both because it stands behind all other evil and because it raises questions about God's own character. I discuss the problem more fully in chapter 14.

25. Compare Exodus 14:17–18, where God hardens the hearts of the Egyptian army, that they might know that he is Yahweh.

discussed God's dealings with Pharaoh, Paul summarizes: "So then he has mercy on whomever he wills, and he hardens whomever he wills" (9:18).[26]

No doubt Pharaoh was a wicked man before this time, and God's hardening could be seen humanly as a natural extension of Pharaoh's previous attitudes, or even as a divine punishment for previous sin. (To get beyond a "human" viewpoint, we would have to ask in the light of the rest of Scripture how God was involved with Pharaoh's heredity, environment, character, and decisions before the exodus period.) That is true of all the other hardening passages in Scripture; God doesn't harden people who have been good and faithful to him. But the hardening, when it happens, nevertheless, *comes from God*. So God does deal with sinners by causing them to become more sinful.[27]

Pharaoh is not the only example, by any means. Frequently in Scripture, we read of God's "hardening hearts." Sihon, king of Heshbon, would not allow Israel to pass through his land on the way to Canaan because "the LORD your God hardened his spirit and made his heart obstinate, that he might give him into your hand, as he is this day" (Deut. 2:30; cf. Josh. 11:18–20; 1 Sam. 2:25; 2 Chron. 25:20). God sent upon Saul a "harmful spirit" that tormented him (1 Sam. 16:14). Later, God sent another spirit who would cause the false prophets to lie, in order to lead wicked King Ahab to the battle in which he would die (1 Kings 22:20–23).[28]

God hardens the people of Israel as well as their evil kings. This was the mission of Isaiah the prophet:

And he said, "Go, and say to this people:

"'Keep on hearing, but do not understand;
keep on seeing, but do not perceive.'
Make the heart of this people dull,
    and their ears heavy,
    and blind their eyes;
lest they see with their eyes,
    and hear with their ears,
and understand with their hearts,
    and turn and be healed." (Isa. 6:9–10)

Later, Isaiah asks:

O LORD, why do you make us wander from your ways
    and harden our heart, so that we fear you not?

26. Paul also quotes in this context one of the passages we mentioned earlier that defines the meaning of *Yahweh*: "And I will be gracious to whom I will be gracious, and will show mercy on whom I will show mercy" (Ex. 33:19). In hardening Pharaoh, God sovereignly withheld his mercy.

27. Romans 1:24–32 describes how God "gave up" sinners so that they would commit greater sins.

28. On the theme of God's sending evil or deceitful spirits, cf. Judg. 9:23; 2 Kings 19:5–7. In 2 Thessalonians 2:11–12, we are told that before the coming of Christ Satan will work counterfeit miracles and that "therefore God sends them a strong delusion, so that they may believe what is false, in order that all may be condemned who did not believe the truth but had pleasure in unrighteousness."

> Return for the sake of your servants,
>   the tribes of your heritage. (Isa. 63:17)

He complains that

> there is no one who calls upon your name,
>   who rouses himself to take hold of you;
> for you have hidden your face from us,
>   and have made us melt in the hand of our iniquities. (Isa. 64:7)

Other nations, too, are objects of God's hardening. God's prophets sometimes foretell that nations and individuals will rebel against God. As we have seen, Isaiah prophesies that God will send the Assyrians to plunder and trample Israel (Isa. 10:5–11). The Assyrian comes to do vile things, but he comes, says God, because "I send him" (v. 6). See also Ezekiel 38:10: Gog, like Pharaoh and Sihon, will sinfully attack God's people, "that the nations may know me, when through you, O Gog, I vindicate my holiness before their eyes" (Ezek. 38:16). The prophecy indicates God's purpose: he will bring about the sin of the people in order to glorify himself in the way he deals with it.

Sometimes, without mention of prophecy, Scripture indicates that God brought about a sinful action. Samson sought a Philistine woman to be his wife, though God had forbidden his people to marry people from the nations of Canaan. His parents were properly indignant, but the writer says, "His father and mother did not know that it was from the LORD, for he was seeking an opportunity against the Philistines" (Judg. 14:4). In 2 Samuel 24, the LORD incites David to conduct a census, for which God later judges him and for which David repents.

Several times in the OT, God prevents certain people from following wise counsel. He ordained that Absalom, rebel son of David, would not listen to the wise counselor Ahitophel, "for the LORD had ordained to defeat the good counsel of Ahitophel, so that the LORD might bring harm upon Absalom" (2 Sam. 17:14). Later, King Solomon's son and successor, Rehoboam, also ignored wise counselors and the pleas of the people, and sought to establish himself as a fearsome despot, which led to the secession of the northern tribes from his rule. Why did he not listen to wiser men? The biblical writer answers:

> So the king did not listen to the people, for it was a turn of affairs brought about by the LORD that he might fulfill his word, which the LORD spoke by Ahijah the Shilonite to Jeroboam the son of Nebat. (1 Kings 12:15)

God also prevents Amaziah, king of Judah, from obeying wise counsel, since God intended to bring judgment on him (2 Chron. 25:20).

Moving to the NT: Jesus quotes the Isaiah 6 passage in Matthew 13:14–15 to explain why he uses parables: to enlighten the disciples but also to harden the wicked. He mentions it also in John 12:40 to explain why the Jews disbelieved despite miraculous signs. So when God's word brought a response of unbelief and rebellion, it did not fail. God's word never fails to achieve its purpose (Isa. 55:11). Rather, in these cases the word was accomplishing precisely what God intended, difficult as that may be for us to accept.

Jesus, too, mentions sinful actions necessitated by prophecy. He excludes his betrayer from his blessing:

> I am not speaking of all of you; I know whom I have chosen. But the Scripture will be fulfilled, "He who ate my bread has lifted his heel against me." (John 13:18, quoting Ps. 41:9)

Jesus knows who the betrayer is before the betrayal. He indicates that God, through Scripture, has made betrayal necessary. In John 15:25, Jesus explains why the Jews irrationally disbelieved in him despite many signs and wonders: "But the word that is written in their Law must be fulfilled: 'They hated me without a cause.'"

Paul speaks of the apostles' ministry in the same way as Isaiah 6 (2 Cor. 2:15–16), as does Peter (1 Peter 2:6–8).[29] In Scripture, God's Word typically brings light and salvation. But in some cases it brings hardening: darkness and unbelief.

Paul also regards God's hardening as the reason for the unbelief of the Jews:

> What then? Israel failed to obtain what it was seeking. The elect obtained it, but the rest were hardened, as it is written,
>
> "God gave them a spirit of stupor,
>   eyes that would not see
>   and ears that would not hear,
> down to this very day." (Rom. 11:7–8, alluding to Isa. 29:10)

Paul argues in context (Rom. 9–11) that the unbelief of Israel is a necessary prerequisite for the ingathering of the Gentiles, that God had to bring about the former in order to accomplish the latter. See 9:22–26 and 11:11–16, 25–32, followed by Paul's great hymn to the incomprehensible purposes of God.

Preceding Israel's hardening, however, was God's hardening of the Gentiles. God had plainly revealed himself to all nations through the creation (Rom. 1:19–20), but the nations had rejected God's revelation, refusing to glorify God, worshiping idols, exchanging the truth for a lie (vv. 21–25). God's response was to harden them:

> Therefore God gave them up in the lusts of their hearts to impurity . . . . For this reason God gave them up to dishonorable passions. . . . God gave them up to a debased mind to do what ought not to be done. (Rom. 1:24–28)

The culmination of the theme of God's sovereignty over human sin is God's fore-ordination of what John Murray called in his lectures "the arch crime of history," the

---

29. Peter adds, about the unbelievers, that they disobey "as they were destined to do."

murder of the Son of God. As we have seen, Judas's betrayal,[30] the Jews' murderous hatred of Jesus, and the horrible injustice of the Romans were all due to God's "definite plan and foreknowledge" (Acts 2:23). These did what God's "hand and your plan had predestined to take place" (4:28; cf. 13:27; Luke 22:22). The crucifixion of Jesus could not have happened without sin, for Jesus did not deserve death. For God to foreordain the crucifixion, he had to foreordain sinful actions to bring it about.

And in the book of Revelation, when the evil beast sets up his satanic rule, we read of the nations of the world that

> God has put it into their hearts to carry out his purpose by being of one mind and handing over their royal power to the beast, until the words of God are fulfilled. (Rev. 17:17)

In summary, the wisdom teacher says:

> The LORD has made everything for its purpose,
> even the wicked for the day of trouble. (Prov. 16:4)[31]

Faith and Salvation

In some ways, this section will be much happier than the one preceding, for it deals with the positive side of God's sovereignty rather than the negative. But we should remember that the two sides are quite inseparable; they reinforce each other. If saving faith is a gift of God, then the lack of saving faith, sinful unbelief, comes from God's withholding of that blessing.[32] In that way, this section will reinforce the previous one.

Nevertheless, we should rejoice that "salvation belongs to the LORD!" (Jonah 2:9). We saw in our discussion of the history of redemption that God is the One who sovereignly rescues his people from sin and its consequences. And we saw in our earlier discussion of irresistible grace that God breaks down our resistance to bring us into his fellowship.

Without God's salvation, we were all once without hope, "dead in . . . trespasses and sins" (Eph. 2:1), "by nature children of wrath" (2:3). But, says Paul, God

> raised us up with him and seated us with him in the heavenly places in Christ Jesus, so that in the coming ages he might show the immeasurable riches of his grace in kindness toward us in Christ Jesus. For by grace you have been saved through faith. And this is not your own doing; it is the gift of God, not a result of works, so that no one may boast. For we are his workmanship, created in Christ Jesus for good works, which God prepared beforehand, that we should walk in them. (Eph. 2:6–10)

---

30. The parallel with Joseph's betrayal by his brothers is significant.

31. As often in Scripture, however, this verse about God's control of wickedness precedes another emphasizing the responsibility of the wicked for their own actions: "The LORD detests all the proud of heart. Be sure of this: They will not go unpunished" (Prov. 16:5 NIV).

32. Note Deuteronomy 29:4: "But to this day the LORD has not given you a heart to understand or eyes to see or ears to hear."

This is the gospel, the central message of Scripture, that God came in Christ to reconcile us to himself by grace—by God's unmerited favor to those who deserve wrath. As we see, grace is opposed to works as a means of salvation. Salvation comes not through what we do, but through what God does for us. We have nothing to boast about. We are hopeless, guilty sinners, whose only hope is God's mercy.

So salvation is God's work—not only in its broad historical outlines, as we saw earlier, but also for each of us as individuals. It is an exercise of God's sovereign control over his world and his creatures. That control begins before we were conceived, indeed before the world was made. For Paul tells us that God

> chose us in [Christ] before the foundation of the world, that we should be holy and blameless before him. In love he predestined us for adoption as sons through Jesus Christ, according to the purpose of his will, to the praise of his glorious grace, with which he has blessed us in the Beloved. (Eph. 1:4–6)

He also informs us that God

> saved us and called us to a holy calling, not because of our works but because of his own purpose and grace, which he gave us in Christ Jesus before the ages began. (2 Tim. 1:9)

Here we learn of God's choice (*election* is the theological term) of a people for himself, before the foundation of the world. We will consider election in more detail under the topic of God's decrees in chapter 11. For now, it is enough to recognize that election is a biblical truth and that therefore salvation is ultimately by divine appointment, divine choice (cf. 1 Thess. 1:4; 5:9; 2 Thess. 2:13–14).

Certainly there is also a human choice, a choice to receive Christ, to believe in him (John 1:12; 3:15–16; 6:29, 40; 11:26).[33] Without this choice, there is no salvation (3:36). There are also human decisions to follow Jesus, to obey his commandments, decisions that Scripture continually urges us to make (14:15, 21, 23, etc.). This is the question that we will explore in this section: Which choice comes first? Does God choose us for salvation and then move us to respond? Or do we first choose him and thereby motivate him to choose us for salvation?

The second alternative is quite impossible, since it violates the very idea of grace. If our choosing God moves him to save us, then salvation is based on a work of ours, and we have something to boast about.[34]

---

33. Some Calvinists have used John 15:16, "You did not choose me, but I chose you," to prove that there is no human choice at all. That claim is, of course, nonsense in the light of the many passages that indicate the importance of human decision in our relation to Jesus. In John 15:16, Jesus is not saying that the disciples made no decision to follow him; rather, he is indicating that his choice, not theirs, marked the beginning of their relation to him as disciples and apostles.

34. The Arminian response to this argument is to deny that faith is a work. It is true that faith has no merit that would move God to save us. That is true of anything and everything we do. But the Arminian wants to have it both ways. He wants to say that faith has no merit, but he also wants to say that our faith somehow motivates

Further, God's choosing takes place in eternity past, before we are even conceived. Before we began to exist, God's plan for us was fully formulated. We can no more change God's decision than we can change our grandparents.

But Arminian theology nevertheless claims that God chooses us because he knows in advance that we will choose to believe in him. On this view, our choice is the cause, God's choice the effect. We are the first cause, God the second. Some have supported this understanding by Romans 8:29 and 1 Peter 1:2, which say that election is based on "foreknowledge." But the foreknowledge in these passages is not foreknowledge that we will choose God. Often in the biblical languages, as in English, when "know" has a noun rather than a fact-clause as its object,[35] it refers to a personal relationship rather than a knowledge of information. In Psalm 1:6, for example, we learn that "the LORD knows [NIV: watches over] the way of the righteous." This does not mean that God knows what they are doing, something rather obvious, but that he guards and keeps those who walk in his path. Cf. Amos 3:2:

> You only have I known
>   of all the families of the earth;
> therefore I will punish you
>   for all your iniquities.

The NIV translates for the word *known* the word *chosen*. That is correct. God is not confessing ignorance of all the families other than Israel. Rather, he is claiming a special covenant relation with Israel, a covenant that in context the people have broken. Cf. Hos. 13:5; Matt. 25:12; John 10:14; Rom. 11:2 (*foreknew*); 1 Cor. 8:3; 1 Thess. 5:12 (where *know* is translated "respect"); 1 Peter 1:20 (literally, *foreknown*, again translated "chosen"). So in Romans 8:29, God's "foreknowledge" means that he has established a personal relationship with believers (one that, according to Ephesians 1:4–5, begins in eternity past). *Foreknew* could be translated "befriended," or even "chose" or "elected."

So Scripture teaches all believers as Jesus taught his disciples, "You did not choose me, but I chose you and appointed you that you should go and bear fruit and that your fruit should abide, so that whatever you ask the Father in my name, he may give it to you" (John 15:16). God's choice precedes our choice, our response, our faith. How could it be otherwise, considering all we have already observed about God's sovereignty throughout nature, history, and human life in general? Can it be that the choice to believe in Christ is the one choice that is outside God's control? Is salvation the one area in which we should *not* give God the praise?[36]

Many passages explicitly teach that our response is God's gift. Jesus teaches that "all that the Father gives me will come to me" (John 6:37); "no one can come to me unless

---

God to save us, that God chooses us on the basis of our choosing him. If our faith motivates God to save us, then it must have merit in his eyes.

35. This is the difference between "knowing him" and "knowing that." For example, consider the difference between "I know Bill" and "I know that Bill is 43 years old."

36. Thanks to Vern Poythress for suggesting to me this profound question.

the Father who sent me draws him. And I will raise him up on the last day" (v. 44);[37] "this is why I told you that no one can come to me unless it is granted him by the Father" (v. 65). It is the Spirit by whom we call on God as our Father, our Abba (Rom. 8:15).

When Paul and Silas first bring the gospel to the city of Philippi, one of their listeners is a woman named Lydia. "The Lord opened her heart to pay attention to what was said by Paul" (Acts 16:14), whereupon she and her household were baptized. The language is quite straightforward: her faith came from God. Earlier, in Pisidian Antioch, a number of Gentiles come to faith in Christ, and we read that "as many as were appointed to eternal life believed" (13:48).[38] The divine appointment came first; belief (faith) was the result.[39] Therefore, it is when God's hand is with the apostles that people believe (11:21); their conversion is evidence of God's grace (v. 23). In 18:27, also, converts are those "who through grace had believed." Cf. Rom. 12:3; 1 Cor. 2:5; 12:9; Eph. 6:23; Phil. 1:29; 1 Thess. 1:4–5.

Repentance, too, is the work of God in us. It is the opposite side of faith. Faith is turning to Christ; repentance is turning away from sin. You cannot have one without the other.[40] As with faith, it is God who grants repentance. We noticed earlier that God sometimes hardens hearts, in effect keeping them from repentance. God also acts positively to give the spirit of repentance. In a passage vividly anticipating the sufferings of Christ, God announces through Zechariah that

> I will pour out on the house of David and the inhabitants of Jerusalem a spirit of grace and pleas for mercy, so that, when they look on me, on him whom they have pierced, they shall mourn for him, as one mourns for an only child, and weep bitterly over him, as one weeps over a firstborn. (Zech. 12:10)

So Jesus is exalted from the cross to God's right hand: "God exalted him at his right hand as Leader and Savior, to give repentance to Israel and forgiveness of sins" (Acts 5:31). Later, the Christians give thanks that "God has granted repentance that leads to life" (11:18; cf. also 2 Tim. 2:25).

37. *Draw* (*helko*) is a strong word, sometimes translated "drag." The one dragged may resist, but not successfully. See John 18:10; 21:6, 11; Acts 16:19; 21:30; James 2:6. Arminian theologians point out that in John 12:32 Jesus promises to "draw all people" to himself. Here, too, the drawing is efficacious. But in context (esp. vv. 20–22), he is promising to draw people of all nations, not only Jews, a regular theme in John's gospel (1:12–13; 10:16; 11:51–52). First Timothy 2:1–6 is a possible parallel, but I will later present a somewhat different understanding of that passage. At any rate, in John 12:32 Jesus is not promising to draw every single human being.

38. This principle throws light on John 10:26, when Jesus tells the Jews, "But you do not believe because you are not part of my flock." To be Jesus' sheep is to be elect, to be appointed for eternal life. "I give them eternal life, and they will never perish, and no one is able to snatch them out of the Father's hand" (v. 28). Again, election precedes believing. Note the same relation in John 17, where Jesus speaks of the disciples as those whom the Father has given to him (vv. 2, 6). He tells the Father that he has taught these elect people and as a result they have believed (vv. 6–8).

39. So we can understand, when God tells Paul to remain at Corinth despite persecution, "for I have many in this city who are my people" (18:10), God is not speaking of people who have already believed, but of those who will believe through Paul's one-and-a-half-year ministry there. The people already belong to God, but they will come to believe through Paul's preaching.

40. See chapter 41.

Many biblical teachings underscore the sovereignty of God in salvation. We will look at some of these later when we consider the doctrine of human salvation, chapters 39–45. But we should mention them here. There is the doctrine of effectual calling, by which God efficaciously summons people into union with Christ (Rom. 1:6–7; 8:30; 11:29; 1 Cor. 1:2, 9, 24, 26; 2 Thess. 2:13–14; Heb. 3:1; 2 Peter 1:10). *Calling* does not always refer to effectual calling; it does not in Matthew 22:14, where "many are called, but few are chosen." In these latter passages it refers to the universal offer of salvation through Christ, an offer that many refuse. But in the passages mentioned earlier, the *called* are those whom God has sovereignly brought from death to life.[41]

There is also the doctrine of regeneration, the new birth.[42] The new birth, like effectual calling, is an act of God, not something that we can bring about.[43] In the classic passage, John 3, Jesus tells Nicodemus that to be born again is to be born by the Spirit of God (vv. 5–6). In the new birth, the Spirit works as he pleases, invisibly, like the wind (v. 8).[44] How is the new birth a birth? It is the beginning of new spiritual life. We recall Paul's telling us that by nature we are "dead in . . . trespasses and sins" (Eph. 2:1). The new birth brings life out of that death. Without this new birth, we cannot even see the kingdom of God (v. 3), because our spiritual eyes are dead. Paul teaches in Romans 1 that sinners suppress the truth and exchange it for a lie. So the new birth marks the beginning of spiritual understanding, as well as the beginning of obedient discipleship.

Other passages also emphasize that our spiritual understanding is a gift of God. In Matthew 11:25–27, we learn that God, Father and Son, hides spiritual insight from some and reveals it to others. "No one knows the Father," says Jesus, "except the Son and anyone to whom the Son chooses to reveal him" (v. 27). John tells us that "the Son of God has come and has given us understanding" (1 John 5:20); compare his words about the anointing of the Spirit (2:20–21, 27). Paul talks about the wisdom of Christ, hidden for a time, "which God decreed before the ages for our glory" (1 Cor. 2:7). He goes on to say that no one can understand the wisdom of Christ without God's Spirit (vv. 12–16). And when Paul speaks about the power of his preaching to bring faith, he regularly ascribes that persuasive power to God's Spirit (1 Cor. 2:4–5; 1 Thess. 1:5; 2 Thess. 2:14).[45], [46] Unless God has given us a mind to understand, we will not appreciate his message (Deut. 29:4; cf. our previous discussions of Isa. 6:9–10). So we ask God

41. For more on calling, see chapter 40.

42. For more on regeneration, see chapter 41.

43. This is part of the thrust of the birth metaphor. Clearly, we had no part in bringing about our physical birth. Our physical life came from others. Similarly, the new life comes from another, by divine grace.

44. Other passages emphasizing divine sovereignty in regeneration: John 1:13; 1 John 2:29; 3:9; 4:7; 5:1, 4, 18.

45. On the internal testimony of the Spirit, see John Murray, "The Attestation of Scripture," in *The Infallible Word*, ed. Ned Stonehouse and Paul Woolley, 40–52 (Grand Rapids: Eerdmans, 1946); my *DWG*, 304–16, 615–40; and chapter 28 of the present volume.

46. So knowledge of God is part of the new life in Christ. It is not merely intellectual, but its intellectual aspect is part of an overall covenantal relation. "The fear of the LORD is the beginning of wisdom" (Ps. 111:10; cf. Deut. 4:6; Prov. 1:7; 9:10; 15:33; Isa. 33:6). See *DKG* and chapters 28–32 of this book for the implications of this for the Christian theory of knowledge.

for wisdom, knowing that for Jesus' sake he is willing to give it and that he is the only ultimate source of spiritual knowledge (James 1:5; cf. Eph. 1:17–19; Col. 1:9).

Scripture also employs other ways of describing how God brings us from death and ignorance to life and spiritual perception: God circumcises our hearts (Deut. 30:6), writes his law on our hearts (Jer. 31:31–34), gives us new hearts (Ezek. 11:19; 36:26), gives us hearts to know God (Jer. 24:7), washes and renews us (Titus 3:4–7), creates us anew (2 Cor. 5:17), shines his light into our darkness (2 Cor. 4:6),[47] raises us from the dead with Christ to new life (Rom. 6:4), begins a good work in us (Phil. 1:6). These expressions do not always refer to initial regeneration, the very beginnings of spiritual life, but they do refer to all our spiritual life and knowledge as the work of God.

So our continuing life with God is like its beginning: we are constantly dependent on the Lord for the resources to live obediently. Without him, we can do nothing (John 15:5). We saw earlier that God is sovereign over the free decisions of people, including decisions to commit sin. And in the outworkings of saving grace, it is God who motivates his people to obey him. Sanctification as well as regeneration is his work, though of course we are responsible for what we do.

So we recall Ephesians 2, where verse 10 teaches:

> For we are his workmanship, created in Christ Jesus for good works, which God prepared beforehand, that we should walk in them.

We know that without God's grace, we are dead in sin (Eph. 2:1; Rom. 7:18; 8:6–8). We cannot do anything good on our own. So as we work out our salvation, we know that "it is God who works in you, both to will and work for his good pleasure" (Phil. 2:13). It is the Lord who sanctifies, who makes his people holy (Lev. 20:8). He is the One who makes his people willing to work for him (Hag. 1:14), who stirs them to generous giving and devotion to the Lord's work (1 Chron. 29:14–19). Though we are not sinlessly perfect in this life (1 John 1:8–10), he is working to perfect in us the image of Christ (Jer. 32:39–40; Eph. 5:25–27). So we pray that God will enable us to please him, for we know that this is his will, and only he can make it happen (Col. 1:10–12).

God is also the source of any success we may have in proclaiming his Word. Paul himself admits that his confidence in his ministry is not based on anything in himself: "Not that we are sufficient in ourselves to claim anything as coming from us, but our sufficiency is from God" (2 Cor. 3:5). And "we have this treasure in jars of clay, to show that the surpassing power belongs to God and not to us" (4:7; cf. 10:17). God uses us to minister to others, by means of his gifts (Rom. 12:3–8; 1 Cor. 4:7; 12:1–11; Eph. 4:1–13). These passages emphasize over and over that these are gifts of God, in Christ, by the Spirit.

So God's grace is the source of every blessing that we have as Christians. Truly, as Jesus said, "apart from me you can do nothing" (John 15:5). We have nothing that we have not received (1 Cor. 4:7). Even our response to his grace is given by grace. When

---

47. Paul here draws a parallel with the original creation of light in Genesis 1:3. There is light, when before there was *only* darkness.

God saves us, he takes away every possible ground of boasting (1 Cor. 1:29; Eph. 2:9). All the praise and glory belong to him.

Summary Passages

I do not apologize for including such a large number of Scripture passages in this chapter. Nothing is more important, especially at this point in the history of theology, than for God's people to be firmly convinced that Scripture teaches God's efficacious, universal control over the world, and teaches it over and over again. Scripture mentions and implies this control in many different historical and doctrinal contexts and applies it to our own life with God in a great number of ways. This sheer quantity and variety of teaching on the subject is a large part of the point of this chapter.

I have listed these passages with little comment, for I think they speak for themselves. Today there are large theological movements that would deny the universality of God's control over the universe, particularly over the free decisions of man. I have mentioned briefly a few of the arguments of these thinkers and will discuss their position further at later points in the book. But it ought to be evident now to the reader that even if there are interpretative difficulties in some of these passages, it is quite impossible to escape the cumulative force of all of them. As B. B. Warfield said about the evidences of biblical inspiration, the total evidence is like an all-devouring avalanche. One may avoid one rock or a few by deft movements, but one cannot escape them all.

This pervasive emphasis sets the context in which we should consider the relatively few passages that are explicitly universal, those that state that God controls everything that comes to pass. In view of what we have seen, we should not expect these passages necessarily to be limited in their application. We have already shown that everything that happens in this world—creation, providence, history, redemption (both large, historical movements and tiny details)—is under God's sovereign control. The passages that explicitly teach universal predestination only summarize, with the helpful redundancy characteristic of Scripture, this large amount of biblical data.

Let us now look at four passages that explicitly teach the universality of God's control over the world. First, let us note Lamentations 3:37–38:

> Who has spoken and it came to pass,
>   unless the Lord has commanded it?
> Is it not from the mouth of the Most High
>   that good and bad come?

Here the scope of God's decree is universal: all calamities and all good things. Nobody can make anything happen unless God has decreed it to happen.

Then, observe what Paul teaches in Romans 8:28:

> And we know that for those who love God all things work together for good, for those who are called according to his purpose.

Paul has been talking about the sufferings that Christians must endure in hope of the glory to come. The sufferings have a cosmic dimension: "For we know that the whole creation has been groaning together in the pains of childbirth until now" (Rom. 8:22). The sufferings, therefore, include not only persecutions for the sake of Christ, but all the sufferings introduced into the creation by the fall of Adam (Gen. 3:14–19): the pain of childbirth, the thorns and thistles in the world. These sufferings "are not worth comparing with the glory that is to be revealed to us" (Rom. 8:18), but for the moment they are difficult to bear. The good news is that Jesus' atonement has cosmic dimensions: in time it will counteract all the effects of the fall as well as sin itself, so that "the creation itself will be set free from its bondage to corruption and obtain the freedom of the glory of the children of God" (v. 21). Therefore, God is now working in all things, not only when we suffer for the gospel, to bring good—good for those who have been effectually called into fellowship with Christ. For our purposes, the conclusion is that every event is part of God's great plan to bring the richest blessing to his people. We do not often see how the sufferings of this world will enhance the joy to come, but we trust that God is bringing about just that result, since he works in, and therefore controls, all things.

It is that confidence that God is working in *all things* that leads to the great hymn of confidence, which ends:

> For I am sure that neither death nor life, nor angels nor rulers, nor things present nor things to come, nor powers, nor height nor depth, nor anything else in all creation, will be able to separate us from the love of God in Christ Jesus our Lord. (Rom. 8:38–39)

Let us look now at Ephesians 1:11, which reads:

> In [Christ] we have obtained an inheritance, having been predestined according to the purpose of him who works all things according to the counsel of his will.

This is, of course, not the first reference in this chapter to God's sovereign predestination. Verse 4 mentions election, 5 predestination to adoption as sons. The first part of verse 11 ("chosen," "predestined") recapitulates the teaching of the earlier verses. But the reference to the "purpose of him who works all things" must go beyond that recapitulation. It is unlikely that Paul would repetitively say that we have been elected and predestined according to the plan of him who elects and predestines. Rather, Paul is saying that God's saving election and predestination are part of something larger than themselves. Salvation is part of God's overall control of the world he has made. Salvation will certainly be consummated, because the Savior is the One who controls all things.

Finally, we return to Romans. Paul teaches in Romans 9–11 that God has hardened the hearts of many of the Jews, in order to open the door of God's blessing to Gentiles. After all has been said, much remains mysterious. Paul's response is not to question God's fairness or love. He answers these sorts of complaints with the potter-clay analogy (Rom. 9:21–24): what right has the clay to question the rights of the potter? But obviously much mystery remains. Overwhelmed, Paul praises God's very incomprehensibility:

> Oh, the depth of the riches and wisdom and knowledge of God! How unsearchable are his judgments and how inscrutable his ways!
>
> "For who has known the mind of the Lord,
>   or who has been his counselor?"
>
> "Or who has given a gift to him
>   that he might be repaid?"
>
> For from him and through him and to him are all things. To him be glory forever. Amen. (Rom. 11:33–36, quoting Isa. 40:13; Job 41:11)

Verse 36 ascribes to God everything in creation. It is not referring just to "things" as material objects, but also to events: the "judgments" and "ways" of verse 33, God's judgment of Israel and his grace to the Gentiles. God's involvement with his world is threefold: as Creator ("from him"), Governor ("through him"), and ultimate purpose ("to him") of the whole world. God controls all things.

Key Terms
Providence (catechism definition)
Providence (in relation to God's lordship)
Efficacy
Universality
Irresistible grace
Monergism
Foreknowledge (two meanings)
Election

Study Questions
1. Do the Scriptures draw a sharp distinction between miracle and providence? Mention some texts that show what these concepts have in common.
2. Mention some passages that show how God's providential intentions are efficacious.
3. "The biblical writers do not hesitate to ascribe the events of the natural world directly to God." Evaluate this assertion, citing relevant texts. What does this imply for the idea of *natural law* discussed in chapter 7?
4. "Even those events that appear to be most random are under God's sovereign control." Evaluate, citing biblical passages.

5. "I conclude that God rules the whole course of human history." Evaluate Frame's argument for this statement, citing biblical texts.

6. "God's foreknowledge of an individual implies comprehensive control over the human family." Evaluate Frame's argument for this statement, citing Scripture.

7. Does God bring about human free decisions? Discuss, citing Scripture. What if these decisions are sinful?

8. Does God foreordain human faith? Discuss from Scripture.

Memory Verses

Isa. 14:27: For the LORD of hosts has purposed,
  and who will annul it?
His hand is stretched out,
  and who will turn it back?

Rom. 11:33–36: Oh, the depth of the riches and wisdom and knowledge of God! How unsearchable are his judgments and how inscrutable his ways!

"For who has known the mind of the Lord,
  or who has been his counselor?"

"Or who has given a gift to him
  that he might be repaid?"

For from him and through him and to him are all things. To him be glory forever. Amen.

Eph. 2:8–10: For by grace you have been saved through faith. And this is not your own doing; it is the gift of God, not a result of works, so that no one may boast. For we are his workmanship, created in Christ Jesus for good works, which God prepared beforehand, that we should walk in them.

Resources for Further Study

Berkouwer, G. C. *The Providence of God*. Grand Rapids: Eerdmans, 1952.

Boettner, Loraine. *The Reformed Doctrine of Predestination*. Grand Rapids: Eerdmans, 1957.

Frame, John M. *DG*, 274–88.

Helm, Paul. *The Providence of God*. Leicester: Inter-Varsity Press, 1993.

THE ACTS OF THE LORD: PROVIDENCE, PART 2

WE HAVE SEEN THAT IN PROVIDENCE God expresses his lordship attribute of control over the created world. God's control is both efficacious and universal. But that isn't all. Confessional and theological accounts of providence (with biblical support) also describe God's providential control of the world in terms of *government* and *preservation*.

Government

We saw that God is the great King of all the earth, who controls all things in his domain. As a subdivision of providence, government speaks of that rule, but emphasizes particularly that the rule is *teleological*. That is to say, God governs all events for a purpose. The English word *govern* comes from the Latin *gubernare*, "to steer a ship." That dynamic emphasis on directing the motion of something toward a goal remains in the traditional theological use, though it is lost in the more common use of *govern* today, which is merely political. Nature and history, like ships, are moving. They have a direction, a destination, and everything works toward that end. When Hebrews 1:3 speaks of Christ's "sustaining all things by his powerful word" (NIV), *sustain* is the Greek verb *phero*, "bear" or "carry." The picture is not one of Christ as a kind of Atlas carrying the world on his shoulders ("upholding," KJV), but a dynamic image of him carrying the world from one point to another through time. There is a destination, and Christ's purpose is to bring the world process to that goal, that conclusion.

God's rule of the world, then, is distinctively personal, not mechanical or merely causal. Other passages also stress the *telos* or goal of providence. In Ephesians 1, Paul speaks of God's good pleasure,

> which he set forth in Christ as a plan for the fullness of time, to unite all things in him, things in heaven and things on earth.

> In him we have obtained an inheritance, having been predestined according to the purpose of him who works all things according to the counsel of his will. (Eph. 1:9b–11)

See also in this connection Rom. 8:18–25, 28–30. Scripture speaks over and over of God's purpose: to glorify himself, to defeat evil, to redeem a people to give him eternal praise. It presents to us again and again the promise of final consummation.

That consummation is not only the goal that God pursues, but also the motivation for the Christian life. It is a pity that the church's teaching on eschatology, the last days, has been concerned mostly with arguments about the order of events. In Scripture itself, the primary thrust of eschatology is ethical, in several ways:

1. We live in tension between this age and the age to come. In Christ, the age to come has already arrived, but the present age, dominated by sin, will not completely expire until Christ returns. Christ has delivered us from the "present evil age" (Gal. 1:4), so in Christ we already have the blessings of the age to come. But sin remains in us until the present age comes to an end (1 John 1:8–10). So we are risen with Christ, but we must also seek the things that are above (Col. 3:1–4). We have died to sin (v. 3), but we must "put to death" the sins of this life (v. 5). So the Christian life is an attempt motivated by God's grace to live according to the principles of the age to come. Thus, we are motivated by the goal toward which God steers the ship of history.

2. Since the present age is to end and the things of this world are to be dissolved, the Christian ought to have a set of priorities radically different from those of the world (1 Cor. 7:26, 29; 2 Peter 3:11). We must not be conformed to the pattern of this world (Rom. 12:2; *world* is, literally, *age*). We are to "seek first" the kingdom of God[1] and his righteousness, rather than the pleasures, even the necessities, of this life (Matt. 6:33).

3. Since we eagerly await the return of Jesus, we will anticipate it even now by purifying ourselves as he is pure (2 Peter 3:12; 1 John 3:3).

4. Since the resurrection of Christ has decisively established that new age, we are confident that our labors for his kingdom will not be in vain, but will inevitably prevail (1 Cor. 15:58).

5. We look to the return of Christ as our deliverance from tribulation and thus as a source of hope (Luke 21:28).

6. Knowing that Christ is coming, but not knowing the day or hour, we must always be ready to meet him (Matt. 24:44; 1 Thess. 5:1–10; 1 Peter 1:7; 2 Peter 3:14).

7. The rewards that God will give his people also serve as motivation (Ps. 19:11; Matt. 5:12, 46; 6:1; 10:41–42; Rom. 14:10; 1 Cor. 3:8–15; 9:17–18, 25; 2 Cor. 5:10; Eph. 6:7–8; Col. 3:23–25; 2 Tim. 4:8; James 1:12; 1 Peter 5:4; 2 John 8; Rev. 11:18). I have engaged in some textual overkill here, because some Christians think it unseemly to consider the rewards that God offers to his faithful servants. Certainly our works do not merit the rewards of

---

1. *Kingdom of God* is, of course, another way in which Scripture speaks of God's goal for the creation, and it, too, "comes" over a period of time. See chapter 5 of this volume. It came in Jesus, it comes gradually through the period between the two advents of Christ, and it comes in consummate form at his return. It has come, but we pray for it to come in the future (Matt. 6:10).

heaven, but God promises them to us, and he often uses them to motivate our service. The Christian ethic is not a Kantian deontologism, an ethic of duty for duty's sake, with no consideration of blessing. In Scripture, what glorifies God also glorifies man. God's best interest is also ours. Scripture calls us to sacrifice our own interests for God's and those of one another, but only in the short run. In the long run, our interests and God's coincide.

Preservation

If God is to direct the creation toward his intended goal, he must, of course, preserve its existence at least until it reaches that goal. Preservation, therefore, is an aspect of God's government of the world and, like government, an expression of God's lordship attribute of control.

Preservation has several senses in the theological vocabulary, and I will distinguish them in the subsections to follow:

1. *Metaphysical preservation* is God's act to keep the universe in being. It is more of a "good and necessary consequence" (WCF 1.6) than an explicit teaching of Scripture, though I think the inference is unavoidable in Colossians 1:17b: "and in [Christ] all things hold together." Without God, nothing would exist; that is the doctrine of creation. Without God, nothing would continue to exist; that is the doctrine of metaphysical preservation. The world continues to exist by God's permission. Were he to withdraw his permission, there would be no world. So his permission here, as with evil (chapter 14), is an "efficacious permission."

Unfortunately, theologians have often formulated metaphysical preservation according to a theory of the continuum of being, in which the universe "tends toward nonbeing" because it does not have as much being as God has. On this view, God's metaphysical preservation remedies this tendency. This view, of course, consistently developed, puts God and the world on a continuum as well: the world lacks being, because the world is less divine than God himself. This theory has roots in Gnosticism and neo-Platonism, but it compromises the biblical teaching of the relationship between Creator and creature. Scripturally, there are no degrees of being or of divinity. The universe is not divine in any degree, and it does not lack some degree of being.

Rejecting the continuum theory, however, does not entail that we should reject metaphysical preservation as such. To say that God metaphysically preserves the world is simply to say that the world is radically contingent. It depends on God for everything, and without his permission it could not continue to exist. To say this is merely to be consistent with our confession that the world is completely under the control of its Sovereign Lord.

2. *Redemptive-historical preservation* is God's temporary preservation of the world from final judgment, so that he can bring his people to salvation.

In Genesis 2:17, God told Adam that he should not eat the forbidden fruit, for "in the day that you eat of it you shall surely die." When Adam and Eve ate the fruit, however, they did not die immediately. Death did enter history at that point (Gen. 3:19; Rom. 5:12), as did human pain and the curse on the earth (Gen. 3:16–19). But by the standards of strict justice, Adam and Eve should have died immediately after their disobedience. That God allowed them to continue living is already an indication of grace. God was already blessing them far more than they deserved. God gave them life when they deserved death.

The woman is to have pain in childbearing (Gen. 3:16), but there will be children. Not only will God preserve the lives of the first couple, but he will give them descendants as well. And even more wonderfully, one of those descendants will crush the head of the devil-serpent (v. 15). So immediately after the fall, God gives grace, based on his intention to redeem his people through Christ. The man is to labor, in order to feed and therefore sustain the human family (vv. 17–19) as it awaits the coming of the Deliverer. Thus begins God's preservation of the world and the human race in redemptive history. The continuation of the natural world and of human history provides the context for the history of redemption to unfold.

Redemptive-historical preservation is, however, limited and temporary. The biblical image of this limitation is the story of the great flood in Genesis 6–9. In Genesis 4:15, God places a mark on the murderer Cain to preserve his life. But Cain's descendants abuse their preservation and fall more deeply into sin, rejoicing in their disobedience without even showing the degree of remorse that Cain displayed (4:23–24; cf. v. 13). Yet God's patience continues. Chapter 5 records a genealogy of patriarchs with very long lives. But in Genesis 6:3, in response to very serious sin,[2] God significantly reduces the life span of human beings. His patience is drawing to an end.

Yet man does not heed this warning. Human life reaches a peak of sinful rebellion, and

> the LORD saw that the wickedness of man was great in the earth, and that every intention of the thoughts of his heart was only evil continually. (Gen. 6:5)

So God destroys all but one family in a great flood. Now, the flood displays, as no other event, the necessity of God's preservation of the earth. In Genesis 7:11–12, we read:

> On that day all the fountains of the great deep burst forth, and the windows of the heavens were opened. And rain fell upon the earth forty days and forty nights.

We should recall that on the first three days of creation, God divided the heaven, the earth, and the sea (Gen. 1:3–13), and the waters "under the expanse" from the waters above it (1:7). So the event of 7:11–12 is an image of de-creation. What God divided in Genesis 1, he now brings back together. At God's word, the creation collapses in on itself. The waters above and the waters below again meet, and God's judgment falls on all, except for the one family who "found favor in the eyes of the LORD" (6:8).

After the flood comes God's covenant with Noah, a covenant of preservation. God says:

---

2. I will not discuss here the nature of this sin, which is disputed. Cases have been made that the sin was (1) mixed marriage (of Cainites and Sethites), (2) sexual relations between women and angelic beings, (3) royal polygamy. I incline toward the third hypothesis. See Meredith G. Kline, "Divine Kingship and Genesis 6:1–4," *WTJ* 24, 2 (1962): 187–204.

> And when the LORD smelled the pleasing aroma, the LORD said in his heart, "I will never again curse the ground because of man, for the intention of man's heart is evil from his youth. Neither will I ever again strike down every living creature as I have done. While the earth remains, seedtime and harvest, cold and heat, summer and winter, day and night, shall not cease." (Gen. 8:21–22)

It is not that man's sin has been washed away in the flood. Rather, the flood proves that historical judgments alone cannot deal with sin. The indictment of the inclinations of man's heart in Genesis 8:21 is essentially the same as the terrible indictment of preflood mankind in 6:5. The flood proves that that sinfulness has infected the whole human race. It is in Noah's family as much as in the families that were destroyed (cf. 9:20–24).[3] Noah's family is saved by God's grace, not by their goodness.

So God promises to preserve the earth and the regularities of the seasons. He will again be patient. But his patience is again limited. The seasons will continue "as long as earth endures," and there is no guarantee that it will endure forever.

Now, redemptive-historical preservation has two biblical reference points, like the two foci of an ellipse. One is the flood, the other the return of Christ. Jesus taught that the time of his return would be "as it was in the days of Noah" (Matt. 24:37 NIV). Peter carries the comparison further, pointing out that

> the heavens existed long ago, and the earth was formed out of water and through water by the word of God, and that by means of these the world that then existed was deluged with water and perished. But by the same word the heavens and earth that now exist are stored up for fire, being kept until the day of judgment and destruction of the ungodly. (2 Peter 3:5b–7)

Peter says that there will be another de-creation, by fire rather than by water. He presents an image of total destruction:

> The heavens will pass away with a roar, and the heavenly bodies will be burned up and dissolved, and the earth and the works that are done on it will be exposed. (2 Peter 3:10)

God's preservation of the natural order, then, is characteristic of the time between the two great judgments: the typical judgment of the flood, and the antitypical judgment of the final catastrophe. The time in between is the time of God's patience.

The Noachic covenant[4] is sometimes called the *covenant of common grace*, God's non-saving grace to his enemies. It is that, but it is also, and more significantly, a provision of special grace, of salvation. For during this time God is preserving the world to give people time to repent of their sins and believe in Christ:

---

3. Hence the Reformed doctrine of *total depravity*. Cf. Rom. 3:10–23; 6:17; 8:5–8.
4. Compare the account of this covenant in chapter 4.

The Lord is not slow to fulfill his promise as some count slowness, but is patient toward you, not wishing that any should perish, but that all should reach repentance. (2 Peter 3:9)

So Paul, in his evangelistic preaching at Lystra (Acts 14:17) and Athens (17:25–28), points to God's providence as evidence of his patience with sinners.[5] The world is being preserved because God has redeeming work to do. It is Christ, the Redeemer, in whom all things "hold together" (Col. 1:17), for he intends to "reconcile to himself all things" (v. 20).

We saw that miracle is more of a redemptive-historical category in Scripture than a metaphysical one. It is a declaration of God's covenant lordship, *contra peccatum* rather than *contra naturam*. Preservation is the same. Although metaphysical preservation may be inferred from biblical teachings, redemptive-historical preservation is much more explicit, indeed pervasive, in the biblical texts. And when we think of preservation in redemptive-historical terms, we draw together more closely in our minds the concepts of providence and miracle.

The regular passing of the seasons and God's providing food for his creatures should lead men to repent, and it should motivate Christians to sense anew the urgency of evangelism. For Christians know that God's patience will again come to an end. There will again be a time like the days of Noah, and God will come in judgment when men least expect it.

In preserving the earth, then, God displays himself powerfully as the Lord of the covenant. He controls all things so that the world will not be destroyed. During that time, he proclaims authoritatively the gospel of salvation. And he accomplishes the purpose of his lordship: to gather a people to be his, to be with them in his covenant presence.

3. *Covenant preservation* refers to God's preserving the lives of believers and the church as part of his covenant blessing. Scripture often refers to this kind of preservation:

And now do not be distressed or angry with yourselves because you sold me [Joseph] here [to Egypt], for God sent me before you to preserve life. (Gen. 45:5)

Cf. Ex. 20:12; Deut. 6:1–2, 24; Josh. 24:17; Pss. 16:1; 31:23; 37:28; 66:9; 121:5–8; 138:7; 143:11. God protects his people, as their shield (Gen. 15:1; Pss. 3:3; 5:12; 28:7). He is their refuge (Deut. 33:27; Pss. 9:9; 14:6; 18:2). They rest under his everlasting arms (Deut. 33:27). He delivers them from their enemies (Deut. 33:27; Ps. 18:17). These are frequent themes in the Psalms and elsewhere (e.g., Isa. 43:2–7); I have given only a few of many examples.

Long life is a blessing of God's covenant (Ex. 20:12), and God stands with his people in this life in their struggle against death and danger. As does the psalmist in Psalm 107, every believer can testify of God's loving care through the afflictions of this world. And even in the more comfortable times of life, God provides what we need to live.

---

5. Preachers, note that there is biblical precedent for sermons using natural revelation as their texts.

As he feeds and clothes the sparrows, he clothes us (Matt. 6:25–34; 10:28–30). Thus he preserves our lives, and indeed the lives of all living things (Pss. 36:6; 145:15–16; 147:8–9). In him we live and move and have our being (Acts 17:28).

Covenant preservation is corporate, as well as individual. Christ builds his church on a rock, "and the gates of hell shall not prevail against it" (Matt. 16:18).

This kind of preservation is closely related to the last, redemptive-historical preservation. For as God preserves the earth to bring the lost to himself, he preserves his people on earth as his witness. And he saves them from sickness, oppression, and death as a witness of his power and a display of his lordship. When he saves the lives of his people, they give him praise. So providence, like miracle, is a display of God's lordship. God proves faithful to his covenant promise.

But like redemptive-historical preservation, covenant preservation has a limit. Death is still in the world, and God has ordained that all of us will experience it (Gen. 3:19), except for a few special recipients of grace such as Enoch (Gen. 5:22) and Elijah (2 Kings 2:11–12). Jesus suffered and died for our sins, and indeed, God has promised that believers will suffer persecution (2 Tim. 3:12) for Jesus' sake. That has often meant martyrdom. The complete fulfillment of covenant preservation, therefore, is not in this life but in the next. As with Jesus, God does not abandon us to the grave or let us see decay (Ps. 16:10).

I will discuss the problem of evil later, in chapter 14, under the topic of God's goodness. For now, let us note that evil is not a refutation of God's good purposes for creation or of his love for his people. The evil of this world serves God's long-term purpose to glorify himself and to do good for his people. Even persecution is a privilege; believers rejoice "that they were counted worthy to suffer dishonor for the name" (Acts 5:41; cf. Matt. 5:12; John 15:21). God preserves his people through persecution and honors their suffering by uniting it to the sufferings of Christ (2 Cor. 1:5; 4:10; Gal. 6:17; Phil. 3:10; Col. 1:24; 1 Peter 4:13).

Covenant preservation is what most believers mean by *providence*, rather than government, concurrence, or metaphysical preservation. God is Jehovah Jireh, our *Provider* (Gen. 22:14).

4. *Eternal preservation* is redemption itself. When God revealed himself to Abraham in Genesis 22:14 as "The LORD will provide," what he provided was a ram for sacrifice, in place of Isaac, Abraham's dear son and bearer of the covenant promise. So God's ultimate providence to his people is redemption itself. And when God provides salvation to his people, he preserves them, so that they will not fall away, for all eternity.

Jesus says:

> Truly, truly, I say to you, whoever hears my word and believes him who sent me has eternal life. He does not come into judgment, but has passed from death to life. (John 5:24)

He is speaking of people living on earth. But when one of them believes, his eternal destiny is assured. He will not be condemned at the final judgment. He has crossed from death to life, and will not cross back again. Such believers are Jesus' sheep, of whom he says:

My sheep hear my voice, and I know them, and they follow me. I give them eternal life, and they will never perish, and no one will snatch them out of my hand. My Father, who has given them to me, is greater than all, and no one is able to snatch them out of the Father's hand. I and the Father are one. (John 10:27–30)

This is the Reformed doctrine of the *perseverance of the saints*. This doctrine does not teach that everybody who makes a *profession* of faith is eternally saved. Scripture is fully aware that some professing Christians apostatize, turn away from the truth. Judas Iscariot is the paradigm case. In John, many who "believe" in Jesus later turn away (John 6:66; 8:31–59). There are solemn warnings about apostasy and apostates in Hebrews 6:4–8; 10:26–30; 1 John 2:19. The apostates, at one time, shared in the life of the church, and therefore in the blessings of the Holy Spirit. Judas himself cast out evil spirits and healed diseases in Jesus' name (Matt. 10:1–4). But they turned from the Lord and suffered God's condemnation.

Those who persevere are those in whom God begins a work of saving grace (Phil. 1:6). And they persevere, imperfectly to be sure, in faith and holiness until in heaven they are perfected in Christ.

Revelation

In this chapter and the previous one, I have described God's providence in terms of his lordship attribute of control. His providential control of the world is efficacious and universal, and it can be seen in his government and preservation of the world he has made. But providence also expresses the other two lordship attributes that I have ascribed to God: his authority and his presence.

I expounded the basic biblical idea of divine authority in chapter 2. Here I will argue more specifically that providence includes an authoritative revelation of God. This fact represents another parallel between miracle and providence.

We can see that idea in the fact that providence, like creation, is by God's word:

He sends out his command to the earth;
    his word runs swiftly.
He gives snow like wool;
    he scatters hoarfrost like ashes.
He hurls down his crystals of ice like crumbs;
    who can stand before his cold?
He sends out his word, and melts them;
    he makes his wind blow and the waters flow.
He declares his word to Jacob,
    his statutes and rules to Israel.
He has not dealt thus with any other nation;
    they do not know his rules.
Praise the Lord! (Ps. 147:15–20; cf. 148:5–8)

The psalmist here draws a correlation between the "command" and "word" that control the course of nature and the "word" that God revealed to Israel. These "words" come from the same mouth. They have the same power, the same truth, and they reveal the same God.[6]

Providence also displays the *wisdom* of God (Ps. 104; Prov. 8:22–36). *Wisdom* and *word* are closely related in Scripture. God's works declare the marvelous mind of God that has planned everything to happen according to his will. He understands all the animals, the weather, the plants, the sea creatures (Job 38–42).

Providence, then, reveals God's lordship. It reveals his power and his presence in the world he has made. It also declares his wrath against sin (Rom. 1:18), clearly reveals "his eternal power and divine nature" (v. 20), and communicates "God's decree that those who [sin] deserve to die" (v. 32). From God's providence, people should know that they should not worship men (Acts 14:14–17) or worship God by idols (Rom. 1:23; cf. Acts 17:22–23, 29–31) or engage in sexual impurity, including homosexuality (Rom. 1:24–27).

As miracle is an extraordinary demonstration of God's lordship, providence is an ordinary one in some respects; but its universality and pervasiveness make it important as a form of revelation. It is the one means that many people have now to know God. And it is the revelation by which all of us are left without excuse (Rom. 1:20).

Does providence provide guidance to us? Yes, in the sense that God's providence provides some opportunities and closes others to us. Yes, in that providence, through our spiritual gifts, heredity, environment, education, temperament, and interests, suggests to us how we can best serve God. A wise person takes his environment and his own nature into account in making decisions. Providence supplies the "situation" to which the Word of Scripture must be applied. We should remember, however, that providence is not a text as the Bible is. One cannot "read" providence as one reads Scripture, to find out specifically what we *ought* to do. The Puritan John Flavel commented that "the providence of God is like a Hebrew word—it can only be read backwards!"[7] It is much easier to see how God has used providence to lead us in the past than to figure out how he will use it to lead us in the present and future. And in any case, we can rightly interpret providence only through the spectacles of Scripture.[8]

Concurrence

We have looked at providence as government, preservation (these focusing on God's control), and revelation (focusing on God's authority). Now we will look at concurrence, which focuses on God's presence in and with all his creatures.[9]

6. See a similar correlation between nature and Scripture in Psalm 19:1–11.

7. Quoted by Sinclair Ferguson in *A Heart for God* (Colorado Springs: NavPress, 1985), 145.

8. For more observations on guidance, see the discussions of God's will in chapter 16. For more on God's revelation through providence, see chapter 24.

9. Forms 2–4 of preservation also focus on God's covenant presence. Perhaps I could have written this chapter so as to make clearer correlations between the kinds of providence and the lordship attributes, but my higher goal

Louis Berkhof defines *concurrence* as

> the cooperation of the divine power with all subordinate powers, according to the pre-established laws of their operation, causing them to act and to act precisely as they do.[10]

The concept emerges out of the discussion of the relation between the divine Primary Cause and the secondary causes of events in the world. The Jesuits, Socinians, and Remonstrants argued that God determines the natures of all beings and forces in the world, but does not determine the specific actions that these beings perform.[11] Their theory fits well with the libertarian view of free will, which we will discuss in chapter 35.

On the contrary, most Calvinists have affirmed concurrence more or less in Berkhof's sense, and I will defend that view here.

The relevant biblical data are those we discussed in chapter 8: that God controls nature, history, and individual persons (including their free decisions) in minute detail. Note that in those passages God determines not merely the major trends in the world, but the smallest events as well: the falling of a sparrow, the fall of a lot, and so on. And some Scripture passages, such as Romans 8–11 and Ephesians 1, teach that he controls absolutely everything.

Now, let's assume, for example, that God makes a golf ball go into a hole, using a golfer as secondary cause. But what about the golfer's swing? Scripture tells us that God brings that about, too, for he controls everything. But there are secondary causes of the golfer's swing also: movements in the golfer's muscles, neurons, brain, and so on. The verses we have studied imply that God causes those as well. We can press this analysis into the world of molecules, atoms, and subatomic particles. Are any of their movements independent of God? Certainly not.

So the doctrine of concurrence is merely an application of the general principle that God brings all things to pass. Concurrence teaches that God causes events on the micro level as well as on the macro level. He uses second causes, but none of the second causes work without him. He uses second causes, but he is always working in and with those second causes.

So there is an *immediacy* to God's causality in the world. As I said in chapter 7, *immediate* does not distinguish miracles from nonmiraculous events, because every event is caused by God immediately. Nothing can be completely explained by finite causes alone. God's will explains all events, both large and small.

The main objection to concurrence is that it makes God the author of sin, since it makes him not only the remote cause, but also the proximate cause of sin. Later, I will discuss further

---

was clarity, and I think the present organization is most conducive to that. It always consoles me to remember that the three perspectives are, after all, perspectives, which means that anything we say about God can be said under any of the three categories.

10. Louis Berkhof, *Systematic Theology* (London: Banner of Truth, 1941), 171.

11. A. A. Hodge, *Outlines of Theology* (1879; repr., Grand Rapids: Zondervan, 1972), 271.

the remote-proximate distinction and the concept of *authorship*. *Author* in these discussions means not a mere cause of sin, but a *doer* of sin. And as I will argue, it is not clear that mere causal proximity to a sinful act makes God a *doer* of sin. Nor is it clear that making God a remote cause rather than a proximate cause answers those who would blame him for sin.

Another objection to concurrence is that it makes second causes superfluous. God becomes the sufficient cause of each event, and the second cause doesn't really cause anything. Later, I will discuss in more detail the paradox that although God controls everything, he has created a universe that is significantly different from himself, operating on the basis of its own nature and the laws of its being. At every moment it is dependent on God, yet it operates out of its own God-given resources. In the narrative of nature and history, almost all[12] events in the story have two causes: divine and creaturely. The creaturely causes are genuine. Creatures bring about the events they cause, and the events would not come about without those causes. The same, however, can be said of the divine causes. Creation is like a book written by a gifted novelist, who creates a story-world in which events have causes within the story, but in which every event is brought about by the volition of the author.[13]

Key Terms

Providence as government
Providence as preservation
Metaphysical preservation
Redemptive-historical preservation
Covenant preservation
Eternal preservation
Providence as revelation
Providence as concurrence
Perseverance of the saints
Author of sin
Proximate cause
Secondary causes

Study Questions

1. Show from Scripture that God's government of the world is teleological.
2. "In Scripture itself, the primary thrust of eschatology is ethical." Evaluate, referring to biblical texts.
3. "Scripturally, there are no degrees of being or of divinity." Explain this statement and tell why it is important.
4. "Now, redemptive-historical preservation has two biblical reference points, like the two foci of an ellipse." What are the two foci? Explain; evaluate.

---

12. Exceptions: acts of God that are truly "immediate" in the sense of having no secondary cause at all, such as the incarnation, regeneration, the act of creation itself, and whatever other immediate acts of God there may be.

13. For more on the author-character model of divine-human interaction, see chapters 14 and 35.

5. How does providence display God's lordship? Cite Scripture texts in this connection.

6. Does providence provide guidance to us? If so, how? If not, why not?

7. Does Scripture teach divine concurrence? Explain your answer. Does concurrence imply that God is the author of sin? That there is no role for secondary causes?

Memory Verses

Gen. 45:5: And now do not be distressed or angry with yourselves because you sold me [Joseph] here [to Egypt], for God sent me before you to preserve life.

Ps. 147:15–20: He sends out his command to the earth;
   his word runs swiftly.
He gives snow like wool;
   he scatters hoarfrost like ashes.
He hurls down his crystals of ice like crumbs;
   who can stand before his cold?
He sends out his word, and melts them;
   he makes his wind blow and the waters flow.
He declares his word to Jacob,
   his statutes and rules to Israel.
He has not dealt thus with any other nation;
   they do not know his rules.
Praise the Lord!

John 10:27–30: My sheep hear my voice, and I know them, and they follow me. I give them eternal life, and they will never perish, and no one will snatch them out of my hand. My Father, who has given them to me, is greater than all, and no one is able to snatch them out of the Father's hand. I and the Father are one.

Eph. 1:11: In [Christ] we have obtained an inheritance, having been predestined according to the purpose of him who works all things according to the counsel of his will.

2 Peter 3:5b–7: The heavens existed long ago, and the earth was formed out of water and through water by the word of God, and . . . by means of these the world that then existed was deluged with water and perished. But by the same word the heavens and earth that now exist are stored up for fire, being kept until the day of judgment and destruction of the ungodly.

Resources for Further Study

Berkouwer, G. C. *The Providence of God*. Grand Rapids: Eerdmans, 1952.

Frame, John M. *DG*, 274–88.

Helm, Paul. *The Providence of God*. Leicester: Inter-Varsity Press, 1993.

THE ACTS OF THE LORD: CREATION

WE HAVE SEEN GOD'S LORDSHIP displayed in his mighty acts, and in those mighty acts we have discovered the God who rules the entire course of nature and history. Now, if God is Lord over the course of events, can he be anything less than Lord at the *beginning* of the world order? Surely the beginning can be no exception to the general principle that God works all things in conformity with the purpose of his will (Eph. 1:11). So we turn our attention from miracle, to providence, and now to creation.

Defining Creation

Theologians have differed on the basic meaning of the concept of creation. To Thomas Aquinas, creation is "the very dependency of the created act of being upon the principle for which it is produced."[1] But as we have seen, the world depends on God every moment, not only at the moment of its origination. So many theologians have argued that creation is continuous, that it takes place every moment. In creation God produces being. But on this view, he gives being every moment, so every moment he creates anew.

Aquinas held this position in part because he could not overcome by natural reason Aristotle's arguments for the eternity of the world. Aquinas conceded, in effect, that God's creation of the world at the first moment in time could not be proved by natural reason. It had to be an article of faith.[2] But he thought creation in the broader sense, creation as the continuous dependence of the world on God for its being, could be proved through a cosmological argument: at any point in time, the beings in the world require a First Cause in God, a cause operating in the present. So Aquinas, followed by the Thomist tradition, adopted continuous dependence as his basic concept of creation and supplemented it with the biblical teaching that God made the world

1. Aquinas, *SCG*, 2.18.2.
2. Aquinas, *ST*, 1.46.2.

with the beginning of time. Some Reformed thinkers have also regarded providence as continuous creation.[3]

More recent thinkers have found this view attractive, perhaps in part because it doesn't require the effort to locate creation in calendar time or to reconcile it with modern science.[4]

I do not doubt, of course, that the world depends on God for every moment of its existence. But I prefer to discuss that point under the headings of metaphysical preservation and concurrence, as I did in the previous chapter. In this book I wish to stick as closely as possible to biblical uses of terms. And in Scripture, *creation* generally refers to the events of Genesis 1 when God created heaven, earth, sea, and all that is in them.[5] Our definition of creation should not be influenced by what can or cannot be proved by Aristotelian natural reason, or by what can or cannot be reconciled with modern science and philosophy. In Scripture, there is a "beginning" of all things, and that beginning is when God created the world (Gen. 1:1; Job 38:4; Pss. 90:2; 102:25; Isa. 40:21; 41:4; 46:10; John 1:1; Heb. 1:10; 1 John 1:1; Rev. 1:8; 3:14; 21:6; 22:13). That beginning is a legitimate subject of theological discussion, and the doctrine of creation is the logical place to take it up.

As we look at Genesis 1, we find that we must make a distinction between the creation of the heaven and earth (Gen. 1:1) and God's later acts of creation within the already-existing world order (vv. 3, 6, 9, 16, 21, 27). Theologians have traditionally described these as *original* and *subsequent* creation, respectively. Original creation is, strictly speaking, the only creation *ex nihilo*, "out of nothing." Subsequent creation presupposes already-created realities. Genesis 1:24 mentions that God commanded the already-existing land to bring forth living creatures. Genesis 2:7 represents God as forming man from the dust.

Nevertheless, it is plain that even those beings that God created after the event of Genesis 1:1 owe their existence entirely to his creative act. Unless God had determined to create them, they would not exist. So we may bring original and subsequent creation together in the following definition: *Creation is an act of God alone, by which, for his own glory, he brings into existence everything in the universe, things that had no existence prior to his creative word.*

---

3. Heinrich Heppe cites Braunius, Ursinus, and Heidegger in *RD*, 251. Benjamin Wirt Farley cites Cocceius and Ames in *The Providence of God* (Grand Rapids: Baker, 1988), 28. Jonathan Edwards developed well-known arguments for this position. See John H. Gerstner, *The Rational Biblical Theology of Jonathan Edwards* (Orlando, FL: Ligonier Ministries, 1992), 190–202.

4. For example, Friedrich Schleiermacher, *The Christian Faith* (New York: Harper, 1963), 1:xviii; H. P. Owen, "God, Concepts of," in *The Encyclopedia of Philosophy*, ed. Paul Edwards (New York: Macmillan and The Free Press, 1967), 3:344–48; Howard Van Till, opponent of "creation science," applauds David Kelsey's concept of creation as metaphysical dependence in his review of *Evolution and Creation*, ed. Ernan McMullin, *Faith and Philosophy* 5, 1 (January 1988): 104–11.

5. An exception might be Psalm 104, where the writer describes God's providence for the world (and continuous production of new life) in terms of creation (v. 30). But the psalm as a whole is an echo of Genesis 1, drawing important analogies between God's original creative work and his current activity in the natural world. And as we will see, *creation* in Scripture also refers to redemptive re-creation. But even in that usage there is always an implicit comparison to the events of Genesis 1.

Creation and Worship

As in miracle and providence, God creates the world as the Lord. I emphasized in chapters 2–3 that God reveals himself centrally as Lord, and we will see in chapter 13 that the Lord is a *holy* being, One before whom we must bow in worship. Indeed, many references to creation in Scripture are liturgical: they present creation as a reason for worshiping God. Creation itself, including the inanimate objects, worships God (Pss. 19:1–4; 50:6; 89:5; 98:7–9; 148:1–14; Isa. 55:12). And when we think of God as Creator, we encounter his holiness, and we are moved to worship.

Scripture presents various connections between creation and worship. God's work of the six days entitles him to consecrate a seventh day of holy rest for himself and a seventh day of the human week made holy for himself, a day of worship (Ex. 20:11). Indeed, God made the heavens and earth to be his temple. In Isaiah's prophecy, God compares the created world to Israel's temple:

> Thus says the LORD:
> "Heaven is my throne,
>   and the earth is my footstool;
> what is the house that you would build for me,
>   and what is the place of my rest?" (Isa. 66:1)[6]

In the Psalms and elsewhere in Scripture, consideration of creation leads to worship (of many examples, see Neh. 9:6; Pss. 8:3–9; 33:6–9; 95:3–7; 146:5–6; Rev. 14:7). Paul tells the Gentiles at Lystra and Athens that the true God has created all things, and that therefore they ought not to worship men or idols (Acts 14:15; 17:24–25). How absurd it is that men "worshiped and served the creature rather than the Creator, who is blessed forever! Amen" (Rom. 1:25). Creation also motivates the heavenly hymnody of Revelation (Rev. 4:11; 14:7). In worship, we thank our Creator (Ps. 136:3–9), turn to him for help (121:2; 124:8; 146:5–6), and seek his blessing (134:3).

God intended such worship from the beginning, which is to say that God created the world, as in our definition, for his own glory, to bring praise to himself:

> The heavens declare the glory of God,
>   and the sky above proclaims his handiwork. (Ps. 19:1)

> I will say to the north, Give up,
>   and to the south, Do not withhold;
> bring my sons from afar

---

6. See the discussion of the creation as God's temple, in the image of the divine glory-cloud theophany, in Meredith G. Kline, *Images of the Spirit* (Grand Rapids: Baker, 1980), 20–26. In his more recent *Kingdom Prologue* (Eugene, OR: Wipf and Stock, 2006), 18, he finds temple imagery used for the creation also in Psalms 11:4; 93; 103:19; 104:1–3; Isaiah 40:21–23; Micah 1:2–3; Matthew 5:34–35.

and my daughters from the end of the earth,
everyone who is called by my name,
     whom I created for my glory,
          whom I formed and made. (Isa. 43:6–7; cf. 60:21; 61:3)[7]

For from him and through him and to him are all things. To him be glory forever.
Amen. (Rom. 11:36)

Cf. also Prov. 16:4; 1 Cor. 11:7; Rev. 4:11.

Creation and God's Lordship

In other ways, too, creation reveals God's lordship. It establishes God's *ownership* of all things, and therefore his lordship over all his creation (Ps. 24:1–2). Because God has created all things, he has the right to do as he wishes with his own (see my discussion in chapter 5).

Creation also displays God's lordship attributes. It displays his control, because it establishes that he rules the world not only throughout history, but at the beginning of history as well. Scripture underscores this point by emphasizing the universal scope of creation. God created, and therefore owns and rules, absolutely everything. Scripture expresses this universality by the expression "heaven and earth" or "heaven, earth, and sea":

For in six days the LORD made heaven and earth, the sea, and all that is in them. (Ex. 20:11a)

You are the LORD, you alone. You have made heaven, the heaven of heavens, with all their host, the earth and all that is on it, the seas and all that is in them; and you preserve all of them; and the host of heaven worships you. (Neh. 9:6)

Blessed is he whose help is the God of Jacob,
     whose hope is in the LORD his God,
who made heaven and earth,
     the sea, and all that is in them,
who keeps faith forever. (Ps. 146:5)

Cf. also Acts 14:15; 17:24; Col. 1:16; Rev. 4:11; 10:6; 14:7. What amazing power belongs to the One who made absolutely everything in heaven, earth, and sea!

Creation also demonstrates God's lordship attribute of authority, for creation is by God's *word*. How did God make the world? By speaking. He said, "Let there be light," and there was light (Gen. 1:3). He is like a commander issuing orders to his servants

---

7. It may be that *creation* in these Isaiah verses refers to redemptive re-creation rather than initial creation. But of course, Scripture regularly presents re-creation as analogous to creation. When God re-creates human beings to bring him glory, he redeems them to serve again the purpose for which they were originally created. So see such texts as 1 Sam. 12:22; Isa. 43:6–7; 46:13; 61:3; 62:3–5; Ezek. 36:22–23; Zeph. 3:17–18; Eph. 1:11–12; 2 Thess. 1:10.

and gaining their instant obedience. And even more remarkably, they obey him before they even exist.[8] They spring into existence by his command. His speaking is not an incidental part of his creative work. The psalmist takes special note of it:

> By the word of the LORD the heavens were made,
> and by the breath of his mouth all their host. . . .
> For he spoke, and it came to be;
> he commanded, and it stood firm. (Ps. 33:6, 9)[9]

In John 1:1, the apostle identifies Jesus with the word that God spoke "in the beginning" (cf. Gen. 1:1) and therefore recognizes him as the One through whom "all things were made . . . , and without him was not any thing made that was made" (1:3; cf. Col. 1:15–16). Jesus demonstrates his lordship by his word of power to still the waves (Mark 4:35–41) and bring healing (Luke 7:1–10).

God's word also *interprets* his creation. After he creates the light, we read that "God called the light Day, and the darkness he called Night" (Gen. 1:5). Similarly in verses 8 and 10. *Calling* or *naming* in the ancient Near East was not merely labeling. These names were not arbitrary designators, or chosen merely for aesthetic reasons as we often choose names for our children. These names said something about the thing that was named. In giving names to his creatures, and later in asking Adam to name the animals (2:19–20), God established a linguistic system in which the true nature of everything could be expressed. As he has by his plan preinterpreted all things, so in creation he applies that interpretation to the world and makes that interpretation authoritative for all creatures. That interpretation includes evaluation. God looks on his creations and declares them good (1:4, 12, 18, 21, 25, 31).

Since creation is by God's word, it is also by God's wisdom (Ps. 104:24; Prov. 3:19; 8:1, 22–36; Jer. 10:12; 51:15). The wisdom of God's work is evident to the psalmist (104:1–35), and it boggles the mind of Job (38–42). So creation is a revelation, however mysterious, of the great mind of God. Since creation is universal, every fact of our experience reveals God to us.

So Scripture correlates God's creative word with the written Word of Scripture. As the heavens consistently declare the glory of God (Ps. 19:1), so his law is perfect, restoring the soul (v. 7). As his creative word stands firm in the heavens (Ps. 119:89–90), so his laws endure and stand as our authority (verse 91, in the context of the psalm as a whole).

Creation also manifests the lordship attribute of covenant presence. This is perhaps less obvious than the other two, until we remind ourselves of the alternatives to creation. Recall particularly the unbiblical concept of transcendence from chapter 3,

---

8. I am, of course, speaking ironically here. This metaphor is, I think, implicit in the text. I am not suggesting that created things exist before they exist, except in the mind of God. My point is not metaphysical. I am using it only to underscore, as the text does, the radical authority by which God commands.

9. Hebrews 11:3 and 2 Peter 3:5 also emphasize creation by the word. Note also allusions in Isaiah 48:13; Amos 9:6.

the scholastic idea that the world "tends toward nonbeing," implying a continuum of being from God to the world (chapter 9).

In the neo-Platonic-Gnostic scheme, God is so far removed from the world that human beings cannot even speak truly of him, though creatures are also somehow essentially divine. In this scheme, God is connected to the world by a chain of semi-divine mediators. He is too exalted to create a material world. The material world comes from a lesser being. (In some Gnostic representations, the material world is a mistake, the product of a clumsy aeon, rather low on the scale of being.) Later, in the fourth century, the Arian heretics, who believed that the Son of God was a created being, used a similar argument: God the Father could not have created the world by himself. For the purpose of creation, he had first to create a semidivine being, the Son or Word, who, in turn, would make the world.

The church fathers responded to this cosmology by emphasizing the doctrine of creation. Irenaeus[10] replied to the Gnostics, and Athanasius[11] to the Arians, that God does not need any mediator to create the material world. He is not defiled by touching matter directly. So creation is *direct*. It is a point at which God's finger touches the world. Yes, God the Father creates together with the Son and the Spirit. But Son and Spirit are not inferior beings, as Arius thought. They are fully God. So creation is the work not of an inferior being, not of a semidivine creature, but of God himself.

So in creation, God acts as Lord. He needs no helpers; he need not fear that creation will somehow harm him. He cannot be confused with the world, for it does not emanate from his essence but has its own distinct nature. He controls all, interprets all, and thereby enters into an intimate relationship with his world. Before the creation week in Genesis 1, the Holy Spirit is "hovering" over the waters (Gen. 1:2). He confronts the world as one distinct being confronts another, and he embraces it as his own good world. Thus Scripture lays a firm foundation for the parallel between creation and redemption, creation and new creation. For in redemption, God again makes something new and embraces it as his own.

In all these ways, God shows by his creative acts that he is Lord. Cf. also Jer. 33:2; Amos 4:13; 5:8; 9:6.

Creation and Redemption

Salvation is of the Lord (Jonah 2:9). Since creation is such a vivid revelation of God's lordship, we should expect significant parallels between creation and salvation. And of course, Scripture does not disappoint that expectation.

The Genesis creation narrative itself, written in my view by Moses, reflects/anticipates God's redemption of Israel from Egypt. As in Exodus, God commands all the forces of nature. He brings light to the earth as he later brought darkness to Egypt (Gen. 1:3–5; Ex. 10:15). He divides the waters of the earth (Gen. 1:6–10) as he later

---

10. Irenaeus, *Against Heresies*.
11. Athanasius, *De Decretis*, 3.7; *Discourse II against the Arians*, 17.

divided the waters of the Red Sea. He makes the earth to teem with living creatures (Gen. 1:20–25) as he later inundated Egypt with frogs, gnats, flies, and locusts (Ex. 8:1–32; 10:1–20).[12] He celebrates his creative work in a Sabbath of rest (Gen. 2:3; Ex. 20:8–11), as he later called Israel to celebrate redemption from Egypt by keeping the Sabbath day (Deut. 5:15). In both creation and redemption, God displays himself as the Lord of all the earth. Creation, redemption, and judgment are similar events, requiring the same sovereign power, authority, and presence (see, e.g., Isa. 42:5–6; 45:11–13).

Creation establishes God's ownership of the world and of the human race, and therefore his right and power to redeem, to buy back, his creation (Isa. 43:1–7, 14–21; 44:21–26).

Creation, too, is a covenant, in which God as Lord rules the day and night (Jer. 33:20–25). As Lord, God in creation rules all his creatures by calling them into being, establishing their function, and seeing that they maintain it. He is the power behind creation, its authoritative interpreter, and its faithful maintainer. So, says Jeremiah, God will be faithful to his covenant with David. (Note also the comparison between creation and the Davidic covenant in Psalm 89.)

So Scripture often speaks of salvation in terms of creation. In Psalm 74, Asaph calls on God to deliver Israel from oppression, recalling that "God my King is from of old, working salvation in the midst of the earth" (v. 12). He describes God's saving power in terms of creation, with allusions to the exodus (vv. 13–17). In the prophecy of Isaiah, God speaks as the One who "created" and "formed" Israel, and then describes Israel's redemption (Isa. 43:1–7, 14–15).

Salvation itself, then, is a new creation, a frequent theme in Paul's writings. In 2 Corinthians 4:6, he writes (quoting Gen. 1:3):

> For God, who said, "Let light shine out of darkness," has shone in our hearts to give the light of the knowledge of the glory of God in the face of Jesus Christ.

Compare John's identification of Christ with the light in 1:4 of his gospel, following his statement that through Christ all things were made. In both Paul and John, darkness represents sin.[13] When God illumines us to receive the truth, it is like creation *ex nihilo*—for before God's creative word, there was no light in us; we *were* darkness (Eph. 5:8). Indeed, we were *dead* in sin (2:1), until by God's grace we were "created in Christ Jesus for good works" (2:10). So:

---

12. The plagues show God's sovereignty specifically against elements of nature that were objects of worship in Egypt. In Exodus 12:12, God proclaims his judgment, in the Passover night, against all the "gods of Egypt."

13. Paul tends to speak of "new creation" in the sorts of contexts where John speaks of new birth or regeneration. Both figures connote the immensity of change wrought by God's grace. Light from darkness, life from death. Paul's figure is better suited to present personal transformation in a context of cosmic renewal.

> If anyone is in Christ, he is a new creation. The old has passed away; behold, the new has come. (2 Cor. 5:17)

As God made Adam in his image (Gen. 1:27), so he newly creates believers into the image of Christ, giving us a new knowledge, righteousness, and holiness (Eph. 4:24; Col. 3:10). These are not our inheritance from fallen Adam; for these, God must create us anew. As we have borne Adam's image, so we will bear the image of the second Adam, Jesus (1 Cor. 15:45–49). And the new creation establishes a new community, not divided by circumcision into Jew and Gentile, but an "Israel of God," one in Christ (Gal. 6:15–16).

New creation is not only a symbolic way of talking about human ethical transformation, though it is that. Our new creation is the beginning of a cosmic renewal, a renewal as comprehensive as was the original creation. Our transformation by the grace of God is only the beginning of a new heavens and new earth (Isa. 65:17–18; 66:22; 2 Peter 3:10–13; Rev. 21:1–4) in which dwells God's righteousness. Believers are the beginning of a work of Christ, by which he will eventually reconcile "all things" to himself (Col. 1:15–20). The present creation, cursed by man's fall (Gen. 3:16–19),

> waits with eager longing for the revealing of the sons of God. For the creation was subjected to futility, not willingly, but because of him who subjected it, in hope that the creation itself will be set free from its bondage to corruption and obtain the freedom of the glory of the children of God. (Rom. 8:19–21)

It is not as if the new creation were a "plan B" to replace an original creation that God had somehow failed to keep on course. Redemption was God's plan before the creation of the world (1 Cor. 2:7; Eph. 1:5–11; 2 Tim. 1:9; Titus 1:2). The new creation represents the *telos*, the goal, of the old. Recall Romans 11:36, in which Paul, having described the course of redemption and the relation of Israel to the Gentiles, proclaimed that "from him and through him and to him are all things." The "from him" may represent the original creation. But that original creation (as we saw with providence in chapter 9) had a goal, a purpose; it was "unto him." The history of redemption, then, completes the purpose of the original creation. We may perhaps even say that the new creation completes the old, even though in the end that completion will be a drastic reconstruction (2 Peter 3:12; cf. 1 Cor. 3:12–15).

So Christians would do well to meditate on creation. To trust God's salvation is like believing in creation:

> By faith we understand that the universe was created by the word of God, so that what is seen was not made out of things that are visible. (Heb. 11:3)

To the writer to the Hebrews, this faith in creation is, in essence, the same as the faith of Abel, Enoch, Noah, Abraham, and the other great saints of the OT. The point of comparison seems to be that in both cases, faith is directed to the *invisible*. Faith trusts God in the absence of sight (cf. 2 Cor. 5:7). Abraham trusted God, even though he did not see the fulfillment of God's promises. So the faith of Hebrews 11:3 trusts simply on God's say-so that the world comes from him. We could not as scientists trace the elements of the world back to some visible starting point, for there is none. The visible world has an invisible basis.

The allusion to creation *ex nihilo* is even stronger in another NT reference to Abraham's faith, Romans 4:17:

> As it is written, "I have made you [Abraham] the father of many nations"—in the presence of the God in whom he believed, who gives life to the dead and calls into existence the things that do not exist.

Paul goes on to explain how Abraham's faith, the great model for Christian faith, the faith "counted to him as righteousness" (Rom. 4:22), was a faith in God's promise despite apparently impossible odds, a faith that God could bring life from death. God is the God of creation, who calls things that are not as though they were, who by his word brings being out of nothingness, light out of darkness. We can trust his Word, his promise, therefore, even when we do not see any visible evidence of the fulfillment.

So creation reassures us of God's faithfulness to his covenant. As day and night continue, so God's promises are steadfast. Creation assures us that he will provide for our needs. Our help is in the Lord, who made heaven and earth (Pss. 121:2; 146:5–10). The One who created all things never gets weary, and he will supply new strength to his weary people (Isa. 40:26–31). The Creator is faithful to those who suffer for him (1 Peter 4:19). As his new creation endures, so will his people (Isa. 66:22).

And such reassurance should renew our own commitment to be faithful as God's covenant servants. We should "continue to do good" even in the midst of persecution (1 Peter 4:19 NIV). We should seek his wisdom, too, for that wisdom was his agent of creation (Prov. 8).

Creation out of Nothing

Having sketched the basic thrust of the biblical doctrine of creation, we now move to some more problematic areas. First, the concept of creation *ex nihilo*, out of nothing. This doctrine replies to the question, "What is the material cause of the universe?"—that is, "What did God make the world out of?" And the answer to the question is, "Nothing."

Creation *ex nihilo* is difficult to define. What is *nothing*, after all? Any definition or conceptualization of *nothing* will make it into something; so such definition is, strictly speaking, impossible.

Further, in trying to visualize creation out of nothing, we tend to picture God's putting things into empty space. But in the doctrine of creation *ex nihilo*, space itself is created. Imagine making, say, a stone, when you have nothing to make it out of, and not even a place to put it![14]

Some have thought it would be better to speak of creation *into* nothing, rather than creation *out of* nothing. But in my mind the two expressions have equal advantages and disadvantages. Both ideas are important: creation is neither "out of" a preexisting material nor "into" a preexisting place. That is, we must oppose both the Aristotelian notion of an eternal "matter" and the Platonic notion of an eternal "receptacle."

Plato and Aristotle themselves understood to some extent the problems of accounting for the world by preexistent realities. For how can we account for the preexistent realities themselves? Only by making them, in some sense, nothing. Both Plato's "receptacle" and Aristotle's "matter" are receivers of form, thus essentially unformed, and therefore in one sense nonbeing. Yet they must have some sort of being if they are to receive form, indeed if we are even to speak of them.

The pre-Socratic philosopher Parmenides sensed the problem and tried to eliminate the concept of nothingness or nonbeing from his philosophical system, even to the point of eliminating the word *not* from his philosophical vocabulary. But *not* is quite indispensable to human language, and indeed to logic itself.

We will see how some thinkers have considered evil a form of nonbeing. In chapter 9 I mentioned the related view of some that the whole universe "tends toward nonbeing." Here we encountered the idea of "degrees of being," a continuum between being and nonbeing. On this view, nothingness is really something, and all somethings are partly nothing. But as we have seen, that sort of view creates terrible conceptual and theological difficulties.

So when we speak of creation out of nothing, we should not think of nothing as a kind of stuff out of which God made the world. Indeed, one of the main purposes of the doctrine is to contradict that idea. To say that God created the world from nothing is to say that God created the world without any preexisting material or medium. He merely spoke and things appeared, along with space and time for them to occupy. To say that requires no definition of *nothing*. It simply denies the view that God made the world from preexistent stuff.

The doctrine also denies pantheism or monism, the view that creation is made of God's own being, a kind of emanation from him, as light from the sun, by which the creation is itself divine. It is true that creation is in a sense *de deo* (Edwards, Gerstner), since God is the exclusive source of creation. I prefer not to use that language, however, because of its suggestion of pantheistic emanationism.

So the doctrine of creation *ex nihilo* is perhaps best understood as a negative doctrine. It does not attempt, positively, to explain the process of creation but leaves that mysterious. Its whole meaning is to deny two false views: creation from preexisting reality and emanation from the divine essence. Since there are no other conceivably

---

14. And if time, too, is a creation, you have not one moment in which to accomplish your task.

possible sources for the material being of the world, we say that there is no such source or, in other words, that the source is *nothing*, confusing as that expression may be.

Now, granted that understanding, why should we believe in creation out of nothing? There are no biblical texts that teach it in so many words. Hebrews 11:3 says that God did not make "what is seen" out of "things that are visible." That language is certainly consistent with creation *ex nihilo* and even suggests it, but it leaves open the possibility that God might have created the world out of what was invisible, out of some invisible preexisting material. Romans 4:17; 1 Corinthians 1:28; and 2 Corinthians 4:6 also suggest the idea of creation *ex nihilo*, but they don't actually teach it. In the apocryphal book 2 Maccabees, there is an expression *ouk ex onton*, "not from things that are" (7:28), the equivalent of "from nothing." Hebrews 11:3 and other NT texts might allude to this passage. But the passage itself, of course, is not part of the biblical canon.

Nevertheless, very soon after the closing of the NT canon, the language of creation from nothing became common currency in the church. The early postapostolic work *Shepherd of Hermas* uses it.[15] Later in the second century, it was articulated by Theophilus of Antioch, Aristides, and Irenaeus. This doctrine was important to the church's polemic against Gnosticism. Evidently these men thought it was the clear teaching of Scripture. But what was the basis of that conviction?

Some have tried to derive the doctrine of creation *ex nihilo* from the meaning of the Hebrew *bara'*, the word translated "create" in Genesis 1:1 and elsewhere. Certainly, of all the Hebrew words translated "create" or "make," *bara'* is the most appropriate to designate creation *ex nihilo*. It almost always has God as its subject.[16] In Isaiah and Jeremiah, it is the normal word for God's redemptive re-creation, which as we have seen bears significant parallels to creation *ex nihilo*. And *bara'* never takes an "accusative of material," that is, a direct object designating the material from which something else is made, as in "Mary made the dough into cookies." In Genesis 12:2, God tells Abraham, "I will make of you a great nation": Abraham is the material out of which the nation will be made. But in that verse, the word *make* is *asah*, not *bara'*. *Bara'* is not used in such a way. Thus, *bara'* tends to be used in sentences that make no mention of the material ingredients from which something is made, if there are such things.

So *bara'* is an appropriate term, I think the most appropriate Hebrew term, to designate creation out of nothing. But it does not always refer to that concept. In Genesis 1:21 and 27, it refers to God's making sea creatures and man, respectively, and both these creations (man explicitly, Gen. 2:7) presuppose preexisting material. So *bara'* does not *mean* creation out of nothing, and therefore we cannot derive the doctrine out of the mere definition of the Hebrew term.

Nevertheless, several considerations require us to affirm creation *ex nihilo* as a good and necessary inference from the biblical doctrine of creation:

---

15. See Vision 1:6; Mand. 1.

16. An exception is in Joshua 17:15, 18. But in the Qal and Nifal, the most common active and passive voices in Hebrew, God is always the subject.

1. The world had a beginning, as we have seen (Gen. 1:1; Job 38:4; Pss. 90:2; 102:25; Isa. 40:21; 41:4; 46:10; John 1:1; Heb. 1:10; 1 John 1:1; Rev. 1:8; 3:14; 21:6; 22:13). Before that beginning,[17] there was no world, only God. So there was then no material out of which the world could be made. God is, as I will argue in chapter 18, not a material being, so there is no material in him by which he made the world.

2. As we have seen, creation is universal: everything in heaven, earth, and sea is God's creation. That includes, surely, all material that can be used to make other things. So all such material is itself created. None of it existed before creation. So God did not make the world out of preexisting material.

3. As we saw earlier, God creates as the Lord. He brings the world forth by his power and command. He is Lord; the creation is his servant. So Scripture teaches a clear distinction between Creator and creature. The world is not the lower end of a continuum with God at the top. It is not essentially divine, as on the Gnostic scheme. So creation is not an emanation of the divine essence.

Recall that the doctrine of creation *ex nihilo* is essentially a negative doctrine, denying (a) the idea of creation from preexisting substance and (b) the idea of emanation of the world from God's essence. Considerations 1 and 2 above eliminate (a); 3 eliminates (b). Since Scripture denies everything that creation *ex nihilo* intends to deny, we may take creation *ex nihilo* as an implication of Scripture.

Or, to put it differently: The world was made neither from a preexisting finite substance nor from God's being. There is no third alternative. So the world was not made from anything. It was made from nothing.

The Six Days

Genesis 1 and 2 teach that God made the world in six days and rested on the seventh. There has been much controversy in the church, especially in the last hundred years, over the length of those days, and over whether the text intends to teach a literal chronological sequence.

The three major views being discussed today among evangelicals are (1) the *normal-day* view, that the days are around twenty-four hours each, succeeding one another chronologically,[18] (2) the *day-age* view, that the narrative gives a chronological history of God's creative acts, but that the "days" are of indefinite duration, most likely periods

---

17. I will argue in chapter 17 that time itself is created, so that there is literally no temporal *before*. (*Before* is sometimes used in nontemporal senses, as in "the number 1 comes before the number 2," and "the king stood before the crowd to address them.") But we must at times use this language (as in Psalm 90:2; Ephesians 1:4; and elsewhere) to refer to God's actions in eternity. It is difficult for us to conceptualize such actions, except in temporal terms.

18. See, e.g., Noel Weeks, *The Sufficiency of Scripture* (Edinburgh: Banner of Truth, 1988), 95–118; Robert Reymond, *A New Systematic Theology of the Christian Faith* (Nashville: Thomas Nelson, 1998), 392–94. The best recent argument for this view is James B. Jordan, *Creation in Six Days* (Moscow, ID: Canon Press, 1999). Jordan deals persuasively with a broad range of recent literature on the subject.

of many years,[19] and (3) the *framework* view, that the passage describes God's creative acts topically, and that the succession of days is a literary device for presenting those topical categories, not asserting a chronological sequence.[20]

I have no new insight on these issues, nor even any view on the matter that I could argue with confidence. I would direct readers to the many other scholars who are producing articles and books on these subjects. Frankly, I tend to be persuaded by the last person I have listened to (Prov. 18:17)! But the following points seem to me to be important as we seek resolution of these questions:

1. This discussion concerns the interpretation of Genesis 1 and 2. The question is not whether we should abandon the teaching of these chapters to accommodate secular science. The question is: what does this passage actually say? It is an exegetical issue. I am convinced that the main advocates of all three views are seeking to be true to the teaching of the passage.

2. I am not denying that secular science has influenced this debate. The claims of scientists that the universe has existed for billions of years have certainly motivated theologians to go back to the text, in order to see whether these claims are consistent with Scripture, and that has meant rethinking traditional positions. In my view, that is entirely right and proper. We should not assume at the outset that the scientists are wrong. It is also possible that our interpretation of Scripture is wrong, though it is not possible for Scripture itself to be wrong. We must be humble enough, self-critical enough, to reexamine these questions, even under the stimulus of scientific claims with which we may be initially unsympathetic. This is part of our apologetic mandate to bring every thought captive to Christ. In that sense, it is right for our exegesis to be "influenced by science."

3. But there are also wrong ways of being influenced by science. In reexamining traditional views, we should not be governed by any principles of reasoning inconsistent with Scripture. We should not, for example, assume the absolute uniformity of natural laws, the impossibility of miraculous events, or the absolute validity of currently accepted procedures for determining dates of origin.

4. Defenders of the framework view have presented much evidence of literary devices in Genesis 1–2. Day 1 corresponds with day 4, 2 with 5, 3 with 6, by designating realms and inhabitants,[21] respectively. The presence of a literary structure, however, does not exclude chronological sequence or normal days. Scripture often uses literary devices in narratives that are clearly historical, such as the "signs" of the gospel of John, the "generations" of Genesis 2:4; 5:1; 6:9, and so on. The use of a literary device in a historical narrative

---

19. See Edward J. Young, *Studies in Genesis One* (Philadelphia: Presbyterian and Reformed, 1964); Davis A. Young, *Creation and the Flood* (Grand Rapids: Baker, 1977).

20. See Henri Blocher, *In the Beginning* (Downers Grove, IL: InterVarsity Press, 1984); Mark D. Futato, "Because It Had Rained," *WTJ* 60, 1 (1998): 1–21; Meredith G. Kline, "Because It Had Not Rained," *WTJ* 20, 2 (1957–58): 146–57; Meredith G. Kline, "Space and Time in the Genesis Cosmogony," *Perspectives on Science and Christian Faith* 48 (1996): 2–15; N. H. Ridderbos, *Is There a Conflict between Genesis 1 and Natural Science?* (Grand Rapids: Eerdmans, 1957).

21. Or, as Kline puts it, realms and rulers.

sometimes renders the narrative incomplete,[22] and the literary intentions of the gospel writers do sometimes lead them to present events in orders other than chronological.[23] But such literary devices and intentions do not *exclude* either completeness or chronology, for many narratives within these literary structures are chronological.

5. The broad literary structure of Genesis 1–2 proposed by the framework theory is not incompatible with a chronological sequence. There is nothing absurd in the idea that God created the world in a sequence of events in which he first made the realms, then the inhabitants of those realms.

6. Framework theorists do urge other considerations against a chronological interpretation. One is that natural processes were at work during the creation week, so that the days of creation cannot have been normal days. In Genesis 2:4–7a, we are told:

> These are the generations of the heavens and the earth when they were created, in the day that the LORD God made the earth and the heavens. When no bush of the field was yet in the land and no small plant of the field had yet sprung up—for the LORD God had not caused it to rain on the land, and there was no man to work the ground, and a mist was going up from the land and was watering the whole face of the ground—then the LORD God formed the man.

The framework view argues that the watering of the earth refers to day 3 of the creation week, when Genesis 1 says that God made plants (vv. 11–12). If the third day were a normal day, there wouldn't have been time for the plants to grow up in response to the natural process of watering. So the third day must be figurative, says the framework theory.

The framework theorists are correct to say that until day 3 the prerequisites for plant growth did not exist, and that until day 6 the prerequisite for cultivated grains[24]—human farmers—did not exist. But these observations do not imply that day 3 was long enough for all the plants to be watered and to grow up by natural process. Rather, the impression the text gives in 1:11 is that once the prerequisite of rain was available, the land produced mature plants, miraculously, at God's command, as with the other commands of God during the creation week. The water didn't bring the plants into being, but it enabled them to continue growing and to reproduce.[25] Similarly, the grain most likely existed before God created men, but there were no cultivated fields.

22. Certainly this is the case in the scheme of fourteens in Matthew 1:2–17.

23. Plainly there is nonchronological narrative in either Genesis 1 or Genesis 2, or both, for the orders of events differ in the two chapters.

24. I recognize that the Hebrew terms translated "shrub" and "plant," respectively, may refer to different kinds of plants. Futato's interpretation is that the former means "wild vegetation" and the latter means "cultivated grain." See Futato, "Because It Had Rained," 10.

25. Unless one posits abiogenesis, the naturalistic development of life from nonlife, God must have performed *some* special creative acts in regard to the plants. He either made the seeds or made the mature plants, which then continued to grow by natural means. And between the options of God's making seeds and God's making mature plants, the text certainly favors the latter. Note the repetitive language in verses 11–12: God made plants with seeds in them.

None of this implies that the creation week included natural processes that would take many years. Even if the rain were part of the efficient cause for the growth of the first plants, it is not hard to imagine God's miraculously accelerating that process.

Consider this parallel: I presume that when God made the stars to light the night, he did not have to wait millions of years for their light to reach the earth. Rather, he created light waves to illumine the earth that would be replenished by a light source, the stars. Similarly, when he created plants, he created them mature and nourished, together with a source for their continued nourishment, the rain. This is the regular pattern of the creation week: mature heavenly bodies, mature plants, mature animals, an adult man and woman, placed in an environment where they could continue to carry out their divinely given mandates. What Genesis 2:5 says is that at one time in the creation week, God refrained from making the mature plants because he had not yet created the means for their continued life.

7. So I am not persuaded by arguments that the days of Genesis 1 *must* be nonchronological or that they must be ages long.

8. There are reasons for taking the days as normal days: (a) The word *day* does not always refer to a twenty-four-hour period, but it does most often, especially when accompanied by numerals. The phrase *evening and morning* also suggests a twenty-four-hour period (see Ex. 18:13; 27:21). (b) In the Sabbath commandment (Ex. 20:8–11), we are told to work six days and rest one, in imitation of God's creative activity. But if the days are not normal days, it is not clear what we should imitate. (c) Further, the plural *days*, used in Exodus 20:11, is never used figuratively elsewhere.

9. On the other hand, I am not persuaded that figurative views should be considered heresy, because of the following: (a) Although the literal view seems the most natural way to take Genesis 1, it does not seem to me that the argument is sufficiently strong as to absolutely exclude a figurative view, especially if points 10 and 11 below are taken seriously. (b) There have long been differences among Christians on this matter, and various views have been accepted in the church. Only recently has there been a movement to make the literal view a test of orthodoxy.[26] (c) It is not clear to me that any other doctrines rest logically on a literal view of the days of Genesis. A figurative view does not, I think, imperil our confession of biblical inerrancy or the historicity of Genesis, for the figurative views under discussion claim to be derived precisely from the text. A figurative view of the days does not as such warrant an evolutionary view of man's ancestry. Nor does it compromise the literal historicity of the fall of Adam and Eve, or any of the truths concerning our new creation in Christ. Normally we do

26. Augustine in *The City of God*, 11.7, expresses puzzlement as to what kind of days these were. His view was that God created everything at once. Anselm in *Cur Deus Homo*, 18, follows him. The Reformers generally held that the creation days were twenty-four hours long, but conservative American Presbyterians, including Charles and A. A. Hodge, B. B. Warfield, J. Gresham Machen, Oswald T. Allis, and Edward J. Young, have often held other views. See the statement "Westminster Theological Seminary and the Days of Creation," affirmed on June 1, 1998, by the faculty of Westminster Theological Seminary in Philadelphia, to which I am indebted for the other references in this note.

not make literal exegesis a test of orthodoxy,[27] and I do not see why the days of Genesis should be an exception.

10. In all this discussion, we should remind ourselves that God, speaking through Moses in Genesis 1–2, has a purpose, namely, to display God's glory in his creative work and to provide background for the narrative of the fall. It is certainly not the primary purpose of the narrative to tell us precisely how God made the world, when he did it, how long it took, and how all of this relates to the theories of modern science. It may be that the narrative is such that it answers some of these questions on the way to achieving its primary purpose. Certainly we must assume that its statements are consistent with what really happened, with a true cosmogony. But there may not be sufficient data in the passage to determine a detailed cosmogony in the language of modern science. And we should not demand that God give us more than he has given.

11. As we have seen, divine creation (both original and subsequent) is unique. It is analogous to human production of things, but it is an *absolute* or *ultimate* productivity such as is impossible for human beings. This point is even more obvious if we assume, as I have argued we should, that God creates things in a mature state. The analogy as presented in Genesis 1 suggests a temporal analogy as well, that as human production takes various periods of time, so God's productive work in creation also takes time. But I think it unwise to dogmatize on just how far to take this analogy, that is, how precisely to take the correspondence between God's workdays[28] and ours. I myself see no reason to suppose that the creation week was longer than a normal week. But I see no reason either to require that view as a test of orthodoxy.

The Age of the Earth

I am even less well equipped than in the last case to deal adequately with the remaining "hot-button" issues, namely, the age of the earth and evolution. The reason, alongside the fact that I tend to leave hot-button issues to other people, is that I don't have much scientific training, aptitude, or knowledge.[29] Of course, I don't think theological conclusions should be based on scientific theories. But someone who writes on the age of the earth and on evolution is entering areas of vigorous debate about scientific claims. One cannot deal with these questions in a satisfying way unless he is able to relate his exegetical conclusions to the scientific discussion. In that respect, my treatment of these issues here will be inadequate.

My exegetical position at the moment is that the earth is young, rather than old. I argued above that the creation narrative suggests a week of ordinary days, and that

27. Clearly, the atonement and resurrection of Jesus, for example, must be understood as literal events, at the price of invalidating one's confession of Christ. But there are many passages in Scripture that some interpret literally and others figuratively, concerning which mutual tolerance is the rule.

28. This language is taken from C. John Collins, "How Old Is the Earth?," *Presbuteron* 20 (1994): 109–30; and "Reading Genesis 1:1–2:3 as an Act of Communication," in *Did God Create in Six Days?*, ed. Joseph Pipa Jr. and David Hall (Oak Ridge, TN: Covenant Foundation, 1999), 131–51.

29. Or, perhaps, interest. I do have a fairly normal, healthy layman's interest in such questions, but I admit that I have a hard time concentrating on complicated discussions of these matters.

there is no compelling evidence against that interpretation. That week begins a series of genealogies: Adam, Seth, and their descendants (Gen. 5) leading to Noah, and the descendants of Noah's sons (Gen. 10) leading to Abraham. These genealogies may well be incomplete. Certainly that is true of the Matthean genealogy of Jesus (Matt. 1). But I doubt that there are enough gaps or omissions in these genealogies to allow for millions of years of human existence.

I think the only way, then, that one could biblically argue for an old earth, billions of years old, given a creation week of normal days, is to posit a gap between Genesis 1:1 and 1:3. Some theologians have argued that the text *permits* a long period of time there, though of course it is impossible to prove from the text the existence of such a period. The trouble is that during such a period the heavens and earth would have existed (1:1), but there would have been no light (1:3) or heavenly bodies (1:14–19). But most scientists would deny that such a situation ever existed. Therefore, the gap theory, whatever its exegetical merits, creates more problems with science than it solves.

A young-earth view implies the proposition that God created the world with an appearance of age. The Genesis 1 narrative certainly indicates that God created Adam and Eve, for example, as adults. They would have appeared to be, say, twenty years old, when they were actually fresh from the Creator's hand. Some have said that creation with apparent age amounts to God's deceiving us, but that is certainly not the case in any general way. Normally, when we see adult human beings we can estimate their age by certain physical characteristics. The adult creation of Adam and Eve implies only that these estimates are not *always* true. It shows us (as I argued in connection with miracle) that the world is only *generally* uniform, not absolutely so. God does not tell us in natural revelation that *every* mature person has existed more than ten years. So he cannot be charged with lying to us when he miraculously produces an exception to this general rule.

Some have argued that God would be "lying" to us if he made stars that appear to be billions of years old, but whose origin was actually only ten thousand years ago. Yet God has never told us that the methods that scientists use to calculate the age of stars are absolutely and universally valid. It is not as if the stars were a book that literally tells us their age. Rather, they are data by which scientists believe they can learn the age of bodies in many cases.[30] Reading that data requires not only the data itself, but a whole body of scientific theory and methods by which to interpret that data. What scientists may learn from Genesis is that these methods do not work for objects specially created. So scientists may need to read Genesis in order to refine their methods to a higher level of precision. Of course, it is a general principle that science may not claim that its theories are without exceptions, unless it claims at the same time divine omniscience.

30. What starlight "tells" us about the age of stars depends on your perspective. On the common scientific theory, what we see in the stars really happened many years ago, when their light began its journey to the earth. So on the scientific view, what we see in the stars appears more recent than it really is. That is, if theology presents us with an "apparent age" theory of the stars, current astronomical theory tells us that starlight presents "apparent novelty." Thanks to Steve Hays for this observation.

Anyone who admits to any special creations at all must grant in general the reality of apparent age. Assume that God simply made a bunch of rocks out of nothing and left them floating in space to generate the rest of the universe: even in this case, were a geologist to look at those rocks ten minutes after the creation, he would certainly conclude that they were many years old.

Or what if God made the world by a "big bang," by the explosion of a "singularity"? Many scientists today think that we cannot get behind the big bang, since the big bang is the beginning of time and space as we know them. But the tendency of science is to ask "why?" and that question is not easily restrained. So some today are asking, and certainly more in the future will ask, where the big bang came from, how it came about. To them, even the elementary particles present at the big bang have an ancestry. Such scientists will pursue evidences in those particles (like the rings of the trees in Eden) that suggest a prior existence. Thus, even those particles, to those scientists, will appear "old." My point is simply that any view of origins at all implies apparent age. If there is an origin, the things at that origin will appear to be older than the origin.

There are problems with the apparent-age view. One concerns astronomical events such as supernovas. Judging from the time it takes visual evidence of a supernova to reach the earth, most scientists would judge that these events happened long before what young-earthers regard as the time of creation. Why would God make it appear as if a great event took place when, indeed, that event could not have happened in the time available since creation? Here, though, we must remind ourselves that *all* apparent age involves this problem. Any newly created being, whether star, plant, animal, or human being, if created mature, will contain data that in other cases would suggest events prior to its creation. If Adam and Eve were created mature, their bodies would suggest that they had been born of normal parents by sexual reproduction. Their bodies would suggest (on the presupposition of the absolute uniformity of physical laws and processes) that events had taken place that in fact never happened. Why the apparent supernovas? From God's point of view, just another twinkle in the light stream for the benefit of mankind.

If that is not a sufficient answer, we should simply accept as a general principle that God creates beings in a way that is consistent with their subsequent role in the historical process. If Adam had a navel, that navel suggested an event that did not occur. But it also made him a normal human being, in full historical continuity with his descendants. Similarly, the starlight that God originally created would contain the same twinkles, the same interruptions and fluctuations, that would later be caused by supernovas and other astral events.

I find the type of explanation given above satisfactory as an answer to most problems of apparent age. One problem I find more difficult to deal with is the existence of fossils that seem to antedate by millions of years any young-earth date for creation. If God at the creation planted fossilized skeletons in rock strata, skeletons of organisms that never lived, why would he have done so except to frustrate geologists and biologists?

James B. Jordan has made some observations worth considering in this respect:

But what about dead stuff? Did the soil [during the original creation week—JF] have decaying organic matter in it? Well, if it was real soil, the kind that plants can grow in, it must have had. Yet the decaying matter in that original soil was simply put there by God. Soil is a living thing, and it lives through decaying matter. When Adam dug into the ground, he found pieces of dead vegetation.

This brings us to the question of "fossils" and "fossil fuels," like oil and coal. Mature creationists have no problem believing that God created birds and fish and animals and plants as living things, but we often quail at the thought that God also created "dead" birds and fish and animals and plants in the ground. But as we have just seen, there is every reason to believe that God created decaying organic matter in the soil. If this point is granted, and I don't see how it can be gainsaid, then *in principle* there is no problem with God's having put fossils in the ground as well. Such fossils are, *in principle*, no more deceptive on God's part than anything else created with the appearance of age.[31]

Jordan's comments are bound to be controversial in some circles, but I think they deserve a thoughtful hearing. Other Christians believe the fossils can be completely accounted for by the dynamics of a worldwide flood. But I must exit the discussion here, to leave it in the hands of scientists operating with biblical presuppositions.

This discussion may, however, send us back to consider again the possibility of a nonliteral creation week. As I indicated, the text *suggests* a literal week and does not *necessitate* a nonliteral view. But as I said, the nonliteral view is not *excluded*. And as I have argued, it is not wrong, in the face of scientific challenge, to reconsider our exegesis, though our ultimate conclusion must be governed by Scripture, not by secular science.

Evolution

I reject the theory of evolution on the following grounds:

1. In Genesis 2:7, it is a special act of God (inbreathing) that made Adam a "living creature" (*nephesh chayah*). God did not take an already-existing living creature and make him specifically human, as in theistic evolution. Rather, he took dust and gave it life. Adam came to life by the same divine action by which he became man.[32] The description of the creation of woman in Genesis 2:21–22 is even more obviously a supernatural divine act.

2. The frequent repetition of "according to their kinds" and "according to its kind" in Genesis 1:11–12, 21, 24–25 indicates that there are divinely imposed limitations on what can result from reproduction. I do not know how broadly these "kinds" should be construed, or how they relate to modern biological classifications such as family, genus, and species. But whatever a kind is, these passages evidently imply that plants and animals of one kind do not produce plants or animals of another. But that is what must happen if the theory of evolution is to be true.

3. Although I am not well equipped to judge scientific evidence, I will simply add that as a layman I am not convinced by the evidence presented to me for evolution.

31. James B. Jordan, "Creation with the Appearance of Age," *Open Book* 45 (April 1999): 2.
32. This argument is condensed from *MCW*, 2:5–13.

Doubtless there has been what is sometimes called *microevolution*: variations in the distribution of genetic possibilities within a species, due to natural selection. So in some environments fruit flies of a certain color become more preponderant, and in other environments those of a different color, as color proves in different ways to be an aid to survival and reproduction. But this amounts to variation within species of already-existing genetic possibilities, rather than a process that produces a new species, that is, a new set of genetic possibilities. Nor does it come anywhere near to proving the existence of a process that could derive all present living forms from a single cell. Evidence for macroevolution, the derivation of all living organisms from the simplest by natural selection and mutation, seems to me to be sketchy at best.

4. Further, I agree with Phillip Johnson[33] that the real persuasive power of the theory of evolution is not based on evidence, but rather on its being the only viable naturalistic alternative to theism. Of course, that consideration carries no weight with me, nor should it influence any other Christian to view the theory favorably. Indeed, it should make us very open to criticism of the theory.

I agree with Johnson and many others that the theory of evolution has brought great harm to society, leading it to deny the biblical view of human nature as the very image of God, the awful nature and consequences of sin, and our need for the redemption of Christ. I am encouraged that opponents of Darwinism in academic circles have recently been given a far better hearing than would have been possible fifty years ago. More than any other single figure, Johnson has led this new assault on evolutionary dogma, with careful argumentation and gentle prodding of the establishment rather than with stridency and dubious hypotheses. We are all greatly in his debt.[34]

Key Terms

Creation (Aquinas)
Creation (Frame)
Original creation
Subsequent creation
New creation
Creation *ex nihilo*
Day-age theory
Framework hypothesis
Old earth
Young earth
Apparent age
Living creature
According to their kind

33. Phillip Johnson, *Darwin on Trial* (Downers Grove, IL: InterVarsity Press, 1993); Phillip Johnson, *Reason in the Balance* (Downers Grove, IL: InterVarsity Press, 1995).

34. For discussion of the recent controversy about whether mankind could have descended from a single couple, see chapter 34.

Theory of evolution
Microevolution

Study Questions

1. Describe some of the biblical connections between creation and worship.

2. How does creation display God's lordship attributes? Cite biblical passages.

3. "Scripture correlates God's creative word with the written Word of Scripture." How does it do this? Give references from Scripture.

4. Describe from Scripture some relationships between creation and redemption.

5. Is it better to speak of creation "out of" nothing, or creation "into" nothing? Describe Frame's position, then your own.

6. "So when we speak of creation out of nothing, we should not think of nothing as a kind of stuff out of which God made the world." Why not? Explain.

7. "So the doctrine of creation *ex nihilo* is perhaps best understood as a negative doctrine." What does it negate? Evaluate this suggestion.

8. Should we take the six days of Genesis 1 literally? If not, how? And why?

9. Do you believe in an old-earth or a young-earth view? Why? Do you think your view should be made a test of orthodoxy in the church? Why or why not?

10. If God made the stars recently, but made them appear billions of years older, would he thereby be lying to us? Why or why not?

11. Do you believe in evolution? If so, on what basis? If not, why not?

12. "The real persuasive power of the theory of evolution is not based on evidence, but rather on its being the only viable naturalistic alternative to theism." Explain; evaluate.

Memory Verses

Gen. 1:1: In the beginning, God created the heavens and the earth.

Ps. 33:6; 9: By the word of the Lord the heavens were made,
    and by the breath of his mouth all their host. . . .
For he spoke, and it came to be;
    he commanded, and it stood firm.

2 Cor. 4:6: For God, who said, "Let light shine out of darkness," has shone in our hearts to give the light of the knowledge of the glory of God in the face of Jesus Christ.

Col. 1:16: For by him [Christ] all things were created, in heaven and on earth, visible and invisible, whether thrones or dominions or rulers or authorities—all things were created through him and for him.

Heb. 11:3: By faith we understand that the universe was created by the word of God, so that what is seen was not made out of things that are visible.

Resources for Further Study

Gilkey, Langdon. *Maker of Heaven and Earth*. Garden City, NY: Doubleday, 1959. Gilkey was a fairly liberal theologian, but this early book contains some biblical insight.

Johnson, Phillip. *Darwin on Trial*. Downers Grove, IL: InterVarsity Press, 1993. Johnson is a follower of the "intelligent design" movement, opposed to evolution.

Jordan, James B. *Creation in Six Days*. Moscow, ID: Canon Press, 1999. Jordan argues that the days of Genesis 1 are literal.

Kline, Meredith G. *Images of the Spirit*. Grand Rapids: Baker, 1980. Pp. 20–26. On creation as God's temple.

Young, Davis A. *Creation and the Flood*. Grand Rapids: Baker, 1977. Old-earth, figurative understanding of the Genesis days.

CHAPTER 11

THE ACTS OF THE LORD: GOD'S DECREES

WE HAVE SEEN THAT GOD acts as Lord in miracle, providence, and creation. Now, according to Scripture, all these actions are the result of thought. We saw that God performs miracles with distinct purposes in mind, and he governs the course of nature and history with a goal in view. He creates the world, also, for his own glory and according to his own wisdom. So there is thought behind all of God's actions, a plan. Is it possible that God acts as Lord in miracle, providence, and creation, but not in the planning of these events? Certainly not. So as biblical logic leads us from God's lordship in miracle to that of providence and creation, so now it leads us beyond history, "before" creation, to consider God's lordship in the planning stages of his great historical drama.

This chapter, then, will mark a transition in our discussion from history to eternity. We have been considering God's actions in history, and in the next chapters we will consider his eternal nature. In this chapter, we will think about decisions that God makes in eternity that govern history.

So in this chapter, we will consider God's lordship in his wise plan, his eternal decrees.[1] I have already discussed many matters that theologians normally include under the doctrine of the decrees. In addition to the points reviewed in the previous paragraphs, we should recall especially chapter 8, in which I summarized the efficacy and universality of God's control of the world. There I concluded that God controls all things and all the events of nature and history. Later on (chapters 14, 35), I will expound the author-character model of God's involvement with the world: God does not control the world merely by setting limits for the world's free activity, as a teacher "controlling" his classroom. Rather, like the author of a well-wrought novel,

---

1. *Decree* can be used either in the singular or in the plural, *decrees*. The singular and plural are more or less interchangeable. The former considers God's plan for the whole creation as a unity. The latter focuses on the fact that within that single plan, God has a plan for every individual thing and every individual event.

he conceives and brings about every event that happens, without compromising the integrity of his *creaturely others*.

Also, the doctrine of providence (chapters 8, 9) and the doctrine of the decrees are perspectivally related. Under providence, we considered God's sovereign direction of nature and history from below: he works in and with every event to bring it about according to his purpose. Under the decrees, we consider the same data from above, focusing on the purpose itself for which God brings about all things. God's sovereign working is not only from above (as in deism) nor only from below (as in pantheism), but both. God directs his creation both in his transcendence and in his immanence (chapter 7). The decree is God's purpose in eternity; creation, providence, and redemption are the execution of God's decree in time.[2]

So it might seem that our actual chapter on the decrees could be rather short. Indeed, it will not take long now to develop the biblical concept of God's decrees, but there is much more to say about one particular decree, the decree of election, by which God chooses some to enjoy the benefits of salvation.

God's Plan

God's decrees are the wise, free, and holy acts of the counsel of [God's] will, whereby, from all eternity, he hath, for his own glory, unchangeably foreordained whatsoever comes to pass in time, especially concerning angels and men. (WLC 12)

The decrees of God are his eternal purpose, according to the counsel of his will, whereby, for his own glory, he hath foreordained whatsoever comes to pass. (WSC 7)

God from all eternity, did, by the most wise and holy counsel of his own will, freely, and unchangeably ordain whatsoever comes to pass: yet so, as thereby neither is God the author of sin, nor is violence offered to the will of the creatures; nor is the liberty or contingency of second causes taken away, but rather established. (WCF 3.1)

Such are Reformed confessional definitions of God's decrees. *Decree*, referring to a divine determination, is rarely found in English translations of Scripture. (Psalms 2:7 and 148:6 are two notable exceptions.[3]) But Scripture speaks much of God's *plans*, *counsel*, *purposes*, and so on. We saw in chapter 8 that God has plans and that those plans are efficacious: what he purposes will surely come to pass. We considered many passages, such as this one:

The counsel of the LORD stands forever,
    the plans of his heart to all generations. (Ps. 33:11)

2. I will not argue here, though I will assume, that God's decrees are eternal in the supratemporal sense. For that, see the discussion in chapter 17 on God's eternity. But it should be obvious that God's decree "precedes" creation in some sense (Eph. 1:3). If time itself is a creation, then the decree is "before" time, that is, supratemporal.

3. The term *decree* is certainly justifiable because it arises from the biblical picture of God as King, as Lord. The decrees are the sovereign commands of the Lord of all.

We also saw that these plans are universal: they govern all the affairs of nature, history, and individual lives, including sin and salvation.

> I am God, and there is none like me,
> declaring the end from the beginning
> and from ancient times things not yet done,
> saying, "My counsel shall stand,
> and I will accomplish all my purpose." (Isa. 46:9b–10)

The efficacy of God's purpose is as universal as his knowledge, from the beginning to the end, from distant past through all the future.

In these verses, God's decree is his "plans" or "counsel" (*'etzah*), his "purposes" (*machsheboth*), what "pleases" him (*chaphetz*). The NT expresses this idea with terms such as *boule* ("will," "counsel"), *thelema* ("will," "intention"), *eudokia* ("pleasure"), *prothesis* ("purpose"), *proorismos* ("foreordination"), *prognosis* ("foreknowledge" in the sense of commitment to bring about an event or a personal relationship[4]). For a sampling of passages that speak of God's purpose in these terms, see the following: Matt. 11:26; Acts 2:23; 4:27–28; Rom. 8:29; 9:11; Eph. 1:5, 9, 11; 3:11; 2 Tim. 1:9; Heb. 6:17; 1 Peter 1:2.

God's plan is also *eternal* (Isa. 37:26;[5] 46:9–10; Matt. 25:34; 1 Cor. 2:7; Eph. 1:4; 3:11; 2 Tim. 1:9). As we will see, God's plans can be historical and temporal in the sense that he wills for things to happen at one time rather than another. And sometimes he ordains something to happen temporarily. But the plan by which he ordains these temporary states of affairs is nevertheless eternal. Therefore, his plan is *immutable*, "unchangeable." Although he wills for things to change in history, his plan for such change cannot be changed (Ps. 33:11; Isa. 14:24; 46:10; James 1:17). In our discussion of God's eternity later, we will see how God does sometimes announce policies conditionally, as when he announces judgment and then withholds it upon repentance (Ex. 32:14; Jer. 18:7–10; 26:13; 36:3; Jonah 3:8–10). But the whole course of this interaction is governed by God's eternal decree.

The Decrees and God's Lordship

God's decrees display his lordship attributes. In an obvious way, they display his control, for they are efficacious and universal. God's intentions will certainly be fulfilled, and they will be fulfilled for everything in the created world.

---

4. See our discussion of foreknowledge in chapter 15. William F. Arndt and F. Wilbur Gingrich translate *prognosis* in 1 Peter 1:2 as "predestination." *A Greek-English Lexicon of the New Testament and Other Early Christian Literature* (Chicago: University of Chicago Press, 1957), 710. Although some Greek lexicons translate "foreknowledge," following the etymology of the term, the idiomatic usage often breaks with the etymological root, so that the term can be simply translated "choice."

5. "Long ago" and "days of old" might not connote to everybody the theological concept of eternity, but this is typical OT language referring to an indefinite time in the past. The important point is that God's plan is not a response to current events or even based on short-term foresight of current events, but comes from far in the distant past. The NT references expand this concept, indicating that God's plan goes back before creation.

They also display his authority, for they are meaningful thoughts, wise plans, or counsels for the world. As such, they *interpret* the world; they determine the meaning and significance of everything that God makes. God's interpretations, of course, are always supremely authoritative. When he declares the significance of something for his purpose, that is the significance it has. So the doctrine of the decrees implies that God has authoritatively preinterpreted everything and every event. As Cornelius Van Til emphasized, the interpretation of the facts precedes the facts. Our world is a world that is exhaustively meaningful, because it is the expression of God's wisdom. Among human beings, interpretation is not the work of trying to assess for the first time the significance of uninterpreted facts. Rather, ours is a work of secondary interpretation, the interpretation of God's interpretation.

God's decrees also manifest his covenant presence with his creatures. For the doctrine of the decrees means that in his mind, God has established a personal relationship with every creature that reaches back into eternity. Of course, creaturely existence always has a beginning; it is not itself eternal. But to say that God decrees the course of nature and history is to say that God knows us before we begin to exist, and that even then he established his purpose for each of us, his relationship to us.

So God says to Jeremiah:

> Before I formed you in the womb I knew you,
> and before you were born I consecrated you;
> I appointed you a prophet to the nations. (Jer. 1:5)

Paul says in Ephesians 1:4 that God "chose us in [Christ] before the foundation of the world, that we should be holy and blameless before him."

Historical Election[6]

With many persons and groups, that eternal covenant presence of God takes the form of *election*. *Election* simply means "choice"; so in Ephesians 1:4, the word *chose* describes divine election. Election, therefore, is one kind of divine decree, so we can add to our list of terms indicating God's "purpose" and "intention" the biblical vocabulary of divine choice: *bachar* ("choose"), *hibdil* ("set apart"), *eklegomai* ("choose"), *proetoimazo* ("prepare before"), and *prognosis* ("foreknowledge," "choice").[7]

Ephesians 1:4 describes God's electing people to salvation, but God also chooses people for specific tasks, as in Jeremiah 1:5, quoted above. In Luke 6:13, Jesus "called his disciples and chose from them twelve, whom he named apostles." Cf. John 6:70; 15:16, 19; Gal. 1:15–16. God's election of people for his service does not necessarily imply that those people will finally receive the blessings of salvation. God chose Saul to be king (1 Sam. 9:17) and prophet (10:5–11), but Saul disobeyed God and came to a

---

6. Both historical and eternal election should be understood in the context of the *pactum salutis*, the eternal covenant of redemption, which I discussed in chapter 4.

7. See the earlier discussion in this chapter.

disgraceful end. Scripture does not affirm that Saul died in fellowship with God; it leaves his personal salvation uncertain. Jesus chose Judas the betrayer to be an apostle, but Jesus says of him:

> "Did I not choose you, the Twelve? And yet one of you is a devil." He spoke of Judas the son of Simon Iscariot, for he, one of the Twelve, was going to betray him. (John 6:70–71)

> But woe to that man by whom the Son of Man is betrayed! It would have been better for that man if he had not been born. (Matt. 26:24)

> While I was with [the disciples], I kept them in your name, which you have given me. I have guarded them, and not one of them has been lost except the son of destruction, that the Scripture might be fulfilled. (John 17:12)

Like Saul, Judas committed suicide (Matt. 27:3–5; Acts 1:18–20), and the condemnations of Scripture preclude his salvation.

God also chose the nation Israel for his redemptive purpose. He chose Abraham out of Ur of the Chaldees (Neh. 9:7) and chose Isaac over Ishmael, Jacob over Esau (Rom. 9:6–13). After the exodus, Moses says to Israel:

> He loved your fathers and chose their offspring after them and brought you out of Egypt with his own presence, by his great power. (Deut. 4:37)[8]

> For you are a people holy to the LORD your God. The LORD your God has chosen you to be a people for his treasured possession, out of all the peoples who are on the face of the earth. (Deut. 7:6; cf. 10:15; 14:2; Ps. 33:12; Isa. 41:8–9; 44:1; 45:4; many other passages)

God's choice of Israel is by grace, not merit:

> It was not because you were more in number than any other people that the LORD set his love on you and chose you, for you were the fewest of all peoples, but it is because the LORD loves you and is keeping the oath that he swore to your fathers, that the LORD has brought you out with a mighty hand and redeemed you from the house of slavery, from the hand of Pharaoh king of Egypt. (Deut. 7:7–8)

> Do not say in your heart, after the LORD your God has thrust them out before you, "It is because of my righteousness that the LORD has brought me in to possess this land," whereas it is because of the wickedness of these nations that the LORD is driving them out before you. . . .
>
> Know, therefore, that the LORD your God is not giving you this good land to possess because of your righteousness, for you are a stubborn people. (Deut. 9:4, 6)

---

8. Note in this passage the Lord's authority (his loving choice), his control ("power"), and his presence.

God chose Israel to glorify his name and to be a blessing to all the nations (Gen. 12:3). Israel was the nation through whom the Redeemer would come, and from whom the message of salvation would go out to all other nations of the world. But throughout the OT the Israelites remain "stiff-necked." They worship idols, they oppress widows and orphans, they show contempt for God's law. So through his prophets God threatens judgment. Nevertheless, he also promises grace and forgiveness.

The interchange in the prophetic writings between the theme of judgment and the theme of grace and forgiveness is remarkable. Often the prophet moves from judgment to grace with no transition, with little indication of the reason for the change. But we can understand the relationship between the two themes in general terms.

In Isaiah 1:1–17, God expresses his displeasure at Israel's rebellion. Through the prophet, he brings a "covenant lawsuit" against Israel for her violation of his covenant law. He compares Israel with Sodom and Gomorrah, the wicked cities that he thoroughly destroyed in the time of Abraham and Lot (Gen. 18:16–19:29; cf. Ezek. 16:49–58). He says that he hates the people's offerings and holy feasts. He will not answer their prayers. But then in the midst of the condemnation comes the word of forgiveness:

> Come now, let us reason together, says the LORD:
> though your sins are like scarlet,
>   they shall be as white as snow;
> though they are red like crimson,
>   they shall become like wool. (Isa. 1:18)

In this case, God offers forgiveness at the price of repentance. If the Israelites turn from their evil ways and obey the Lord, they will receive the blessings of the covenant, but if not, they will receive the curses:

> If you are willing and obedient,
>   you shall eat the good of the land;
> but if you refuse and rebel,
>   you shall be eaten by the sword;
>   for the mouth of the LORD has spoken. (Isa. 1:19–20)

But how likely is their repentance? Even in Exodus (33:5), God had called them "stiff-necked." They had worshiped a golden calf while Moses was speaking to God on Mount Sinai (Ex. 32:1–35). They wandered in the desert forty years because they had not believed God's promise of victory over the Canaanites. Again and again, God charged them with wickedness. Yet somehow God is going to "purge away your dross and remove all your impurities" (Isa. 1:25 NIV).

> "And I will restore your judges as at the first,
>   and your counselors as at the beginning.

> Afterward you shall be called the city of righteousness,
>   the faithful city."
>
> Zion shall be redeemed by justice,
>   and those in her who repent, by righteousness.
> But rebels and sinners shall be broken together,
>   and those who forsake the LORD shall be consumed. (Isa. 1:26–28)

Evidently there will be "a few survivors" (Isa. 1:9) from the divine judgment who will be faithful to the Lord and will be the foundation of the new city of righteousness. The Assyrians will bring disaster, but there will be a remnant (10:20–34). The remnant will return from their exile, and they will return to the Lord (10:21). It is this remnant that is the real continuation of Israel; it is they who receive the fulfillment of the covenant promises (11:11–12:6; 41:8–20; 43:1–7; Jer. 23:3–4; 31:7–14).

The books of Ezra and Nehemiah describe the return of the exiles, the remnant, back to the Promised Land. But God's glorious promises to the remnant through Isaiah and Jeremiah are not fulfilled. The people must confess the sin of intermarrying with the pagan nations (Ezra 9:1–10:44; Neh. 13:23–27). The end of their prayer of repentance reminds God:

> And its rich yield goes to the kings whom you have set over us because of our sins. They rule over our bodies and over our livestock as they please, and we are in great distress. (Neh. 9:37)

During the intertestamental period, some in Israel rebel against the foreign rulers, but ultimately they are unsuccessful. During the earthly ministry of Jesus, Israel is under the domination of Roman emperors, and in his teaching Jesus speaks like Isaiah of the unbelief and disobedience of Israel. Those returned from exile are not the *faithful* remnant. Neither the Israel of Ezra and Nehemiah nor the first-century Israel is the city of righteousness of which Isaiah spoke. Rather, Israel has again become like Sodom and Gomorrah, and worse (Matt. 11:20–24).

Who, then, is the faithful remnant who inherits the promises of God to Abraham and through whom all the nations of the earth are blessed? After the remnant passage in Isaiah 10:20–34, we read:

> There shall come forth a shoot from the stump of Jesse,
>   and a branch from his roots shall bear fruit.
> And the Spirit of the LORD shall rest upon him,
>   the Spirit of wisdom and understanding,
>   the Spirit of counsel and might,
>   the Spirit of knowledge and the fear of the LORD.
> And his delight shall be in the fear of the LORD. (Isa. 11:1–3a)

The righteous Branch will rule justly for the poor and needy and will slay the wicked (Isa. 3b–5). The result will be a wonderful time of peace, when the wolf will lie down with the lamb, and:

> They shall not hurt or destroy
> in all my holy mountain;
> for the earth shall be full of the knowledge of the LORD
> as the waters cover the sea. (Isa. 11:9)

It is under the rule of the righteous Branch that God's people are gathered from all the nations (Isa. 11:12–16) and join in praise to God for salvation (12:1–6).

Similarly, in the remnant promises of Isaiah 41:8–20 and 43:1–7, the people do not repent out of their own moral strength. Rather, there is a new visitation of the divine presence, a redemptive re-creation, pointing to the work of the Servant of the Lord in 52:13–53:12. Of him, the prophet says:

> Surely he has borne our griefs
> and carried our sorrows;
> yet we esteemed him stricken,
> smitten by God, and afflicted.
> But he was wounded for our transgressions;
> he was crushed for our iniquities;
> upon him was the chastisement that brought us peace,
> and with his stripes we are healed.
> All we like sheep have gone astray;
> we have turned—every one—to his own way;
> and the LORD has laid on him
> the iniquity of us all. (Isa. 53:4–6)

And in Jeremiah's prophecy of the remnant, again we see the righteous Branch (Jer. 23:5–6), whose name is "The LORD is our righteousness" (v. 6).

Ultimately, then, elect Israel is Jesus Christ. He is the faithful remnant, the righteous Branch. Through him alone comes forgiveness of sins, for he bears God's judgment in the place of his people. The OT gives us a perplexing picture, for the judgment theme seems inconsistent with the theme of grace and forgiveness. If God is fully just, then it seems that nobody can receive his blessing; all will be destroyed. On the other hand, if God's mercy fulfills the terms of his promises, it seems that his forgiveness of sin would have to violate his moral order. But through Jesus, God's justice and mercy meet together in wonderful harmony. Jesus bears the full judgment of God, so that through him God's mercy suffices to bring eternal life to all his people.

And in Christ, by his grace, all believers belong to the remnant (Rom. 11:1–6). This remnant includes both Gentiles and Jews, for God has "grafted" Gentiles into the tree of Israel (11:17–21), having removed some of the (Jewish) "natural branches." But the Gentiles should not boast:

> They were broken off because of their unbelief, but you stand fast through faith. So do not become proud, but fear. For if God did not spare the natural branches, neither will he spare you. (Rom. 11:20–21)

As not all Israel are Israel (Rom. 9:6), so not all members of the Christian church are regenerate believers. Some are elect only as the unbelieving Israelites were: historically elect, rather than eternally elect. Like Saul and Judas, they are chosen only temporarily; they can become nonelect. So the election of the visible Christian church is similar to the election of OT Israel. It is an election that temporarily includes some within its bounds who will never come to true faith and will never have eternal life. This parallel between the church and Israel should not be surprising, because of course the church and Israel are, contrary to the views of dispensationalism, the same body. The tree of redemption is one, and God prunes it and grafts branches on to it, as he will. So the visible church participates in the "election of Israel."

Now let us consider some frequently asked questions about the election of Israel:

1. Is the election of Israel the election of a corporate entity, or is it the election of individuals? I would say both. God chooses Israel as a family, a nation. But he also chooses *within* that family. He chooses Abraham, but not his parents and brothers. He chooses Isaac, not Ishmael. He chooses Jacob, not Esau.

> But it is not as though the word of God has failed. For not all who are descended from Israel belong to Israel, and not all are children of Abraham because they are his offspring, but "Through Isaac shall your offspring be named." This means that it is not the children of the flesh who are the children of God, but the children of the promise are counted as offspring. (Rom. 9:6–8, quoting Gen. 21:12)

He also chooses the remnant, not the entire nation, to receive his blessing. And ultimately, God's choice is of one individual, Jesus.

Jesus establishes another corporate entity, the church. The church is elect in Christ. But as in Israel, some apostatize, they turn away from Jesus, and there is no more hope for them (Heb. 6:1–12; 10:26–31; 1 John 2:18–19). As Paul says, God sometimes breaks off even newly ingrafted branches. The writer to the Hebrews warns his Jewish Christian readers not to turn away from God as Israel did in the wilderness (Heb. 3–4). So in the NT, too, there is an election within an election, and we will discuss that further below.

2. Is the election of Israel to salvation or to service? Again, I would say both. God calls Israel as his servant (Isa. 44:1), his witnesses (43:10, 12). But as God's servant, Israel has great privileges:

> Then what advantage has the Jew? Or what is the value of circumcision? Much in every way. To begin with, the Jews were entrusted with the oracles of God. (Rom. 3:1–2)

They are Israelites, and to them belong the adoption, the glory, the covenants, the giving of the law, the worship, and the promises. To them belong the patriarchs, and from their race, according to the flesh, is the Christ who is God over all, blessed forever. Amen. (Rom. 9:4–5)

These are all blessings of salvation, the blessings of people who have turned from worshiping idols to serve the living and the true God. Not all individuals in Israel are eternally saved. But as we have seen, the true Israel is Christ and those who are in him. Those who belong to the true Israel are indeed eternally saved. This fact is the root of the second concept of election to be discussed in the next section.

3. Is the election of Israel based on works or grace? As we saw in Deuteronomy 7:7–8 and 9:4–6, it is not because of Israel's numbers (power, influence) or righteousness, but wholly because of God's unmerited love, that is, his grace. (See also Deut. 4:37; 8:17–18; 10:15; Ezek. 16:1–14.) On the other hand, Israel's continued status in God's covenant depends on obedience. God told the people at Mount Sinai, during the covenant-making:

Now therefore, if you will indeed obey my voice and keep my covenant, you shall be my treasured possession among all peoples, for all the earth is mine; and you shall be to me a kingdom of priests and a holy nation. (Ex. 19:5–6a)

Jeremiah later reminds Israel:

But this command I gave them: "Obey my voice, and I will be your God, and you shall be my people. And walk in all the way that I command you, that it may be well with you." (Jer. 7:23)

The covenant relationship itself, here, is conditioned on obedience.[9]

In Hosea, God even announces that Israel as a whole is no longer elect, that Israel is "not my people" (Hos. 1:9). Yet (in another strange movement from judgment to grace) he immediately announces:

In the place where it was said to them, "You are not my people," it shall be said to them, "Children of the living God." (Hos. 1:10)

Israel loses its election and regains it again. God also judges many individuals in Israel, removing covenant blessings from them because of their disobedience.

This pattern does not exist only in OT Israel. We belong to Christ wholly by grace (Eph. 2:8–9). But judgments come upon faithless people in the NT church as in Israel:

---

9. Obviously, obedience is required for Israel to receive the blessing sanctions of the covenant rather than the curses. But these passages say more: that obedience is the condition on which the covenant itself exists. Compare my discussion of the Abrahamic covenant in chapter 4. But perhaps the difference is only perspectival. The ultimate meaning of the covenant curse is that God is not our God and we are not his people. The covenant curse is covenant excommunication.

Judas, Ananias and Sapphira (Acts 5:1–10), Simon the sorcerer (8:9–25). And we have seen the warnings of Hebrews against turning away from God's grace in Christ and thereby falling into condemnation.

So although the election of Israel is by grace, there is an important place for continued faithfulness. In this historical form of election, people can lose their elect status by faithlessness and disobedience. Branches can be broken off "because of their unbelief" (Rom. 11:20).

When we consider this divine rejection, we should not argue that the discarded branches were "never really elect." There is a place for such reasoning, but it pertains to a different kind of election that we will discuss in the following section. Here, however, we are talking about historical election. And in this context, it is possible to lose one's election. The discarded branches were indeed elect at one time, for they were part of the tree of Israel. Israel as a nation was really elect, before God declared her to be "not my people"; and she became elect again, when God declared the Israelites to be "children of the living God."

The same is true of the NT church. It would not be right to say that Judas, Ananias, or the apostates of Hebrews 6 and 10 were never elect in any sense. These were elect in the sense that Israel was elect. Indeed, when Calvinists worry about the implications of Hebrews 6 and 10, it is useful for them to consider that the apostates in these passages are very much like OT Israel: They have

> once been enlightened, . . . tasted the heavenly gift, . . . shared in the Holy Spirit, . . . tasted the goodness of the word of God and the powers of the age to come. (Heb. 6:4–5)

Israel experienced all these things throughout OT history and particularly in the earthly ministry of Jesus. But the people rejected him and joined those who crucified the Son of God. So those church members who turn away from Christ "are crucifying once again the Son of God to their own harm and holding him up to contempt" (Heb. 6:6).

Note how Hebrews 6:4–6 emerges out of the references to Israel in chapters 3 and 4. The Israelites, blessed as they were with God's enlightenment, his heavenly gift, the Holy Spirit, the Word of God, and the powers of the coming age, nevertheless hardened their hearts against the Lord (3:7–11, 15). The writer urges Christians to

> strive to enter that rest, so that no one may fall by the same sort of disobedience. (Heb. 4:11)

So God continues to break branches off the tree of redemption. Even those freshly ingrafted can be broken off because of unbelief.

Eternal Election

But in Scripture there is also an election that cannot be lost and that is not at all conditioned on human faithfulness or works. We saw earlier that the election of Israel is in an ultimate and final sense the election of Jesus Christ as the faithful remnant. Though branches of the tree of redemption can be broken off, Christ himself can never, since the cross, lose his fellowship with the Father. He was "chosen before the creation of the world" (1 Peter 1:20 NIV).

So those who are "in" Christ, who belong to him inwardly and not merely outwardly, who are the true Israel, can never lose their salvation. They are *elect* in a stronger sense than was the nation of Israel as a whole and in a stronger sense than is the general membership of the visible Christian church.

This kind of election, like that of Israel as a nation, is covenantal: in it God chooses some to be his covenant people. But the covenant is different in character. In the prophecy of Jeremiah, the Lord describes it thus:

> Behold, the days are coming, declares the LORD, when I will make a new covenant with the house of Israel and the house of Judah, not like the covenant that I made with their fathers on the day when I took them by the hand to bring them out of the land of Egypt, my covenant that they broke, though I was their husband, declares the LORD. But this is the covenant that I will make with the house of Israel after those days, declares the LORD: I will put my law within them, and I will write it on their hearts. And I will be their God, and they shall be my people. And no longer shall each one teach his neighbor and each his brother, saying, "Know the LORD," for they shall all know me, from the least of them to the greatest, declares the LORD. For I will forgive their iniquity, and I will remember their sin no more. (Jer. 31:31–34)

The writer to the Hebrews quotes this passage in 8:8–12 and 10:16–17, and indicates that the new covenant is the covenant sealed with Jesus' blood, which puts an end to all other sacrifices. Cf. Isa. 42:6; Zech. 9:11; Luke 22:20; 1 Cor. 11:25; 2 Cor. 3:6. Hebrews 9:15 summarizes:

> Therefore he is the mediator of a new covenant, so that those who are called may receive the promised eternal inheritance, since a death has occurred that redeems them from the transgressions committed under the first covenant.

The difference between the old and new covenants is that the blood of the new covenant, the blood of Christ, actually cleanses from sin. The blood of bulls and goats under the old covenant did not actually cleanse from sin but only symbolized the coming work of Jesus. All those in the OT period who received God's forgiveness received it on the basis of Christ's atoning sacrifice, which of course to them was still future. They were saved by faith in God's promise of the Messiah. So there were new covenant believers during the OT period. Abraham is an example, for, as Jesus taught:

> Your father Abraham rejoiced that he would see my day. He saw it and was glad. (John 8:56)

The blessings unique to the new covenant are (1) the forgiveness of sins and (2) God's writing his law on their hearts. One who has the law written on his heart obeys God willingly. He wants, in the inmost center of his being, to love God and keep his commandments. God, in other words, creates a new disposition in his new covenant people, a desire to serve him. That is the new creation I described in chapter 10.

Membership in this covenant is, of course, by God's choice, God's election. Election in the new covenant is similar to election in the old, but there are differences appropriate to the differences between the two covenants. Most significantly, for those chosen to be "in Christ," eternal salvation is certain:

> For those whom he foreknew he also predestined to be conformed to the image of his Son, in order that he might be the firstborn among many brothers. And those whom he predestined he also called, and those whom he called he also justified, and those whom he justified he also glorified. (Rom. 8:29–30)

The logic is inevitable. Anyone whom God savingly foreknows,[10] he predestines to be conformed to the likeness of Christ. (That is, he writes the Word on his heart.) And anyone so predestined receives an effectual call from God sometime in his life, a summons into fellowship with Christ, an order that he cannot decline.[11] Those whom God calls he justifies: he declares them righteous for Jesus' sake. And those he justifies, he glorifies. No one who is foreknown, predestined, called, and justified can escape glorification. Final salvation is certain.

So Paul continues in Romans 8:31–39 in a great hymn based on the theme of the certainty of salvation for those in Christ. If God is for us, nobody can be against us (vv. 31–32), so God will certainly give us all things. No one can bring any charge against us before God (vv. 33–34), so there can be no condemnation (cf. v. 1). No one can separate us from the love of Christ (vv. 35–39), nothing in earth or heaven. The elect are Jesus' sheep, of whom none can perish or be plucked from his hand (John 10:28–29).

This kind of election is also the focus of Ephesians 1:3–14. These elect are chosen "in [Christ] before the foundation of the world, that we should be holy and blameless before him" (1:4). The elect here will inevitably become holy and blameless. God decided that they would be, before he created the heavens and the earth. He determined to redeem them by the blood of Christ and thereby to forgive their sins (v. 7). It is inevitable that they will hear the gospel of salvation (v. 13) and believe. And:

> In him you also, when you heard the word of truth, the gospel of your salvation, and believed in him, were sealed with the promised Holy Spirit, who is the guarantee of our inheritance until we acquire possession of it, to the praise of his glory. (Eph. 1:13–14)

---

10. I take "foreknew" in this passage to mean "befriended beforehand" or "elected." See the argumentation for this understanding in chapter 4.

11. Review the brief discussion of effectual calling in chapter 4.

God guarantees, then, the salvation of these elect.

Other Scripture passages speak of the election of individuals to salvation (see Matt. 24:22, 24, 31; Mark 13:20–22; Luke 18:7; Acts 13:48; 1 Cor. 1:27–28; Eph. 2:10; Col. 3:12; 1 Thess. 1:4–5; 2 Thess. 2:13; 2 Tim. 1:9; 2:10; Titus 1:1; James 2:5).

This kind of election is *unconditional*. As we saw in chapter 4, God chooses us before we choose him. Our faithful response is a gift of his grace. So election to salvation is not based on anything we do. It is entirely gracious. It is also *eternal*: "before the foundation of the world" (Eph. 1:4), "from the beginning" (2 Thess. 2:13 NIV), "before the ages began" (2 Tim. 1:9).

As *election* has two different meanings, based on the distinction between old and new covenants, so does the biblical concept of the *book of life*. In Exodus 32:33, after Israel has been found worshiping a golden calf, God says to Moses, "Whoever has sinned against me, I will blot out of my book."

In Psalm 69, the writer asks God to judge the wicked in Israel:

> Add to them punishment upon punishment;
>   may they have no acquittal from you.
> Let them be blotted out of the book of the living;
>   let them not be enrolled among the righteous. (Ps. 69:27–28)

Here the psalmist envisages a book in God's presence containing the names of those he has chosen for covenant blessing. Initially, it seems, the list contains everybody in Israel. But God will blot some of them out because of their sin, for not all who are descended from Israel are Israel.[12] The image of people's being blotted out of the book of life is parallel to Paul's image of natural branches' being broken off from the tree of redemption. Cf. Rev. 3:5.

So the *book of life* image can be an image of historical election, the election of Israel. But like the term *election* itself, the book-of-life image can also represent election in a stronger sense. In Revelation 17:8, those not in the book of life are excluded from it "from the foundation of the world," and, implicitly, those written in the book were written in it from the world's foundation. This expression precludes the notion that one could be listed in the book and later blotted out because of something that happens in history. In Revelation 3:5 (in contrast, to be sure, with Psalm 69:28), no one can be blotted out of the book. Revelation 13:8 should also be taken this way, as is suggested by the correlation between the writing of the book and the "Lamb that was slain from the creation of the world" (NIV).

So election has two senses. I call the first *historical election*, because in that sense elect persons can become nonelect as a result of their unfaithfulness through human history. The second, by way of contrast, is *eternal election*, because in that sense the number of the elect is fixed from eternity. This terminology might mislead some, because the

---

12. Compare Ezekiel 13:9, in which the lying prophets "shall not be in the council of my people, nor be enrolled in the register of the house of Israel."

first no less than the second is the result of an eternal divine decree. But in the first, God may decree that some lose their covenant status, and in the second he decrees no such change. With that understanding, I will continue to use this language.

Historical election and eternal election are distinct, but they cannot be entirely separated. Note the following:

1. Both historical and eternal election are aspects of God's saving purpose. The election of Israel and the temporary election of individuals in history are means by which God gathers together those who will receive his final blessing.

2. As we have seen, the "remnant" of historical election is no less than Jesus Christ. Jesus himself is eternally elected by God (1 Peter 1:20), together with those God has chosen to be in him. So in the end, historical and eternal election coincide.[13] In history, they do not; for historical election is a temporal process and eternal election is forever settled before creation.

All the eternally elect are historically elect, but not vice versa. Historical election is the process in time by which God executes his decree to save the eternally elect. As God judges the reprobate through history, the difference narrows between the historically elect and the eternally elect. In the end, the outcome of historical election is the same as that of eternal election.

3. Thus, historical election is a mirror of eternal election. God elects Israel by grace, as he elects believers eternally by grace. He promises blessings to her that are essentially the blessings of salvation, ultimately the presence with her of the living God. God's covenant presence with Israel in the tabernacle and temple is an image of his presence with eternally elect believers in Christ. The chief difference, of course, is that among the historically elect there are some who will not be finally saved. But even the historical rejection of unbelievers from the covenant images eternal election, for it pictures the final separation between the elect and the reprobate.

4. We may think of historical election as the visible and temporal form of eternal election. We cannot see another's heart to know for sure whether he is eternally elect. But we can see whom God has led to unite with his visible body, the church. We can see who has given a credible profession of faith in Christ. By observing the process of historical election in the light of Scripture, we gain a limited knowledge of eternal election—the best knowledge possible for us today.

5. Those who join the church are historically elect, in the way that Israel was historically elect. It is possible for people in the church to apostatize, to renounce their profession. Church membership, therefore, does not guarantee membership in the new covenant. But the church is a new covenant institution in that it proclaims God's eternal election in Christ and the forgiveness of sins through Jesus' atonement. In that sense, Israel was also a new covenant institution. So the book of Hebrews reminds

---

13. Note that in Revelation 20:15, those whose names are "not found written in the book of life" are thrown into the lake of fire. Is this the historical book of life, from which names can be blotted out? Or is it the eternal book of life, written before the creation? We cannot tell. For by the day of judgment, all blotting will have been done, and the names in the historical book will be the same as the names in the eternal book.

its Jewish Christian readers of the new covenant to which they are called, and it also warns them not to fall away as did Israel in the wilderness.

Reprobation

If God has chosen some for salvation, and he has not chosen everyone, then it follows that some are not elect. Since only the elect are saved, the nonelect are ultimately lost. So God's election of some implies his rejection of others. This rejection is called *reprobation*. Traditionally, within reprobation theologians have distinguished between *preterition*, in which God determines not to choose certain persons for salvation, and *precondemnation*, in which he determines to justly punish them for their sin.

This is a hard doctrine, because it seems to conflict with God's loving and merciful nature and with his desire that all be saved (Ezek. 18:23, 32; 33:11; 1 Tim. 2:4; 2 Peter 3:9). As to the apparent conflict with God's love, see my discussion in chapters 12–14 of God's goodness and the problem of evil. Arguably, the problem here is the most difficult form of that problem. See also our later chapters on God's love and on his will (chapters 12, 16). We will discuss there in what sense God loves the reprobate and in what sense he wills or desires to save them. I believe that there are biblical senses in which God loves and desires to save all people.

Here I will only observe that the doctrine of reprobation is scriptural. We saw in chapter 8 that God does foreordain human sin and therefore foreordains its consequence, which is always death (Rom. 6:23). God works all things after the counsel of his will, and the ultimate destiny of the lost is certainly among those things.

Like election, reprobation has both historical and eternal meanings. Historical Israel is elect in contrast with all the other nations (Deut. 4:37; 7:6; 14:2). In choosing Israel, God rejects the others. Nevertheless, some from other nations join themselves to Israel, and ultimately God's purpose is for Israel to fulfill his promise to Abraham, to be a blessing to all nations (Gen. 12:3; 22:18; 26:4). He intends to graft the wild branches of the nations into the tree of Israel. So God's rejection of the nations is temporary, though it is part of his eternal plan. So Paul writes to Gentile Christians:

> Remember that you were at that time separated from Christ, alienated from the commonwealth of Israel and strangers to the covenants of promise, having no hope and without God in the world. But now in Christ Jesus you who once were far off have been brought near by the blood of Christ. (Eph. 2:12–13)

Indeed, we must remember that all believers were once rejected by God, objects of wrath (Eph. 2:1–3). That rejection was genuine; we all deserved eternal punishment. But we thank God that that rejection was only temporary, for his eternal plan was to lead us to Christ.

But in addition to historical reprobation, Scripture also teaches an eternal reprobation. God has foreordained that some will not have eternal life. Scripture teaches this doctrine by implication: for if eternal life is by God's election, his grace, and his means of grace in history, then eternal death can only be, ultimately, the result of God's with-holding his electing grace. Surely when he withholds grace he is no less intentional than when he gives it. The former is no less planned than the latter. And so eternal rejection, as eternal election, is by an eternal divine plan. This, too, is among the "all things" that God works according to the counsel of his will (Eph. 1:11).

Scripture also teaches this doctrine explicitly. As there is a book of life, there is also a book of condemnation. Jude 4 refers to certain men "who long ago were designated for this condemnation."

We know that people perish because of unbelief. But people cannot believe unless God chooses them (John 8:47; 10:26; 12:39–40). God gives to some to "know the secrets of the kingdom of heaven" (Matt. 13:11), but not to others. The others' hearts are closed by God's decision. So Jesus speaks in parables to conceal the truth from those who are not chosen to know it (Matt. 13:13–14; cf. Isa. 6:9–10). God hides the truth from the wise and learned and reveals it to his children, "for such was your gracious will" (Matt. 11:26).

The central passage on reprobation is Romans 9. The passage deals with both his-torical and eternal reprobation, and that fact has confused some readers. But we must acknowledge at the outset that the primary issue that Paul faces here is that of Israel's salvation. He says:

> I have great sorrow and unceasing anguish in my heart. For I could wish that I myself were accursed and cut off from Christ for the sake of my brothers, my kinsmen according to the flesh. (Rom. 9:2–3)[14]

In the ministries of Jesus, the apostles, and Paul himself, salvation is offered "to the Jew first and also to the Greek" (Rom. 1:16). But most of the Jews rejected the gospel, and the church became increasingly Gentile. Paul himself is a Jew, and he is in anguish over the unbelief of his fellow Israelites. The issue is no minor thing; their eternal sal-vation is at stake. Paul's wish, *per impossibile*, that he could be cut off from Christ for the sake of Israel implies that unless God acts in a new way, the Israelites themselves will be cursed and cut off from Christ. So the issue is not just that Israel will lose its historical election as God's distinctive people. That in itself is cause for rejoicing, for it means that God now calls all nations to himself. Rather, the problem is that individual Israelites will be cut off eternally from God.

Has God's Word failed (Rom. 9:6)? Normally the Word is "the power of God for salvation to everyone who believes" (1:16). We should expect that as Paul and others preach the Word, this divine power will bring salvation to Israel. But so far, that does not seem to be happening. But no, says Paul, the Word of God does not fail.

How can the Word be powerful to salvation when its hearers do not believe? Paul's answer is that not all Israel are Israel (Rom. 9:6): not all are elect (vv. 11–12).

---

14. Cf. Rom. 10:1: "Brothers, my heart's desire and prayer to God for them [the Israelites] is that they may be saved." Again, the issue is their eternal salvation.

Now, Paul's illustrations of election are from the sphere of historical election. Isaac is chosen over Ishmael (Rom. 9:7–9), Jacob over Esau (vv. 10–13). We cannot say on the basis of Scripture that either Ishmael or Esau, or the national groups formed by their descendants, is eternally reprobate. But Paul is not intending to distinguish between historical and eternal election. He is, rather, focusing on the principles that these two forms of election have in common: in both cases, election is by grace, apart from works (v. 11). In all these cases, election is by God's purpose (v. 11) and calling (v. 12). Esau is reprobate (whether historically or eternally) before he is born (v. 11), hated by God (v. 13). It is impossible to avoid the conclusion that Paul is making the same point concerning the eternal election of the unbelieving Israelites:[15] they reject Christ because God has not called them. They are reprobate by the sovereign decision of God.

Otherwise, the question of Romans 9:14, "What shall we say then? Is there injustice on God's part?" makes no sense. The question can arise only because on Paul's view Israel's unbelief is due to God's sovereign decision. If Israel's unbelief were due only to the people's free decision, no one would say that God was unjust to condemn them. And Paul emphasizes that it is God's decision (v. 15; cf. v. 18) by quoting Exodus 33:19:

> And I will be gracious to whom I will be gracious, and will show mercy on whom I will show mercy.

And he adds, "So then it depends not on human will or exertion, but on God, who has mercy" (v. 16).

Then Paul brings up the example of Pharaoh. God says that he raised him up

> that I might show my power in you, and that my name might be proclaimed in all the earth. (Rom. 9:17b)

Again a question arises:

> You will say to me then, "Why does he still find fault? For who can resist his will?" But who are you, O man, to answer back to God? Will what is molded say to its molder, "Why have you made me like this?" Has the potter no right over the clay, to make out of the same lump one vessel for honorable use and another for dishonorable use? (Rom. 9:19–21)

Paul might have said that God is just because Pharaoh and the others made a free decision to reject God. That would have been true, as far as it goes. But Paul wants to present a deeper answer because it is also his answer to the question of Israel's unbelief.

15. One cannot, of course, assume that all those Israelites who disbelieved the preaching of Paul were eternally reprobate. Paul doubtless realized that some might come to Christ at a later time. His concern is with the great number of the Jews who have rejected the gospel. And his answer is that God has first rejected them: some perhaps temporarily, some permanently.

His answer is that Israel's unbelief comes from God's sovereign decision. In that light we can also understand the next question:

> What if God, desiring to show his wrath and to make known his power, has endured with much patience vessels of wrath prepared for destruction[?] (Rom. 9:22)

None of this compromises Israel's own responsibility. Paul stresses that, too, in Romans 9:30–10:21. But then in 11:1–10, he emphasizes again God's sovereignty. The remnant is "chosen by grace" (v. 5). The others are hardened by God's giving them a spirit of stupor (vv. 7–10).

We should note three points about what the doctrine of reprobation does *not* teach:

1. The doctrine of reprobation does not prejudice the free offer of the gospel to all. We do not know who is elect and who is reprobate, so we must proclaim the gospel freely to all. And it remains entirely true that if anybody receives Christ, he will be saved (John 1:12–13; 3:16). Jesus brings together God's sovereignty and our responsibility when he says:

> All that the Father gives me will come to me, and whoever comes to me I will never cast out. (John 6:37)

2. Nor does the doctrine of reprobation prejudice our assurance of salvation. That assurance is not based on our reading of the eternal decrees of God, which are secret unless God reveals them, but on the promises of God.

3. Nor does this doctrine imply that election and reprobation are parallel in every respect. They are "equally ultimate," in the sense that both decrees of God are ultimately efficacious.[16] Yet there is between them what has been called an *asymmetry*. The blessings ordained by God's eternal election are entirely by God's grace, apart from human works. But the curses ordained by God's eternal reprobation are fully earned, based on the sins of the reprobate.[17]

The Order of the Decrees

Many theologians have tried to establish an "order" among God's decrees. They agree that this order is not an order in time, for the decrees are all eternal. Rather, the order is a "logical" order, in some sense. These theologians ask us to try to picture the process of God's thinking before he created the world. When human beings make plans, they plan to do A so that they can accomplish B: they proportion means to ends. Some ends have a higher priority than others. So we "order" our plans by such principles

---

16. The concept *equal ultimacy* is confusing. To some writers, such as G. C. Berkouwer, it appears to deny the asymmetry mentioned in the next sentence. In Van Til's writings, however, it simply means that both election and reprobation are efficacious decrees of God; they accomplish their purpose. See *CVT*, 86–88; see also G. C. Berkouwer, *The Triumph of Grace in the Theology of Karl Barth* (Grand Rapids: Eerdmans, 1956), 390; G. C. Berkouwer, *Divine Election* (Grand Rapids: Eerdmans, 1960), 172–217.

17. See Canons of Dordt, First Head of Doctrine, 6.

as means to end and high priority to low priority. Those arguing for an order of the decrees call us to imagine the process of God's thinking the same way, as we consider the plans lying behind God's creation and redemption of human beings.

Another kind of order is that in which decree A creates the conditions for carrying out decree B. This appears to be the order that Paul follows in Romans 8:29–30:

> For those whom he foreknew he also predestined to be conformed to the image of his Son, in order that he might be the firstborn among many brothers. And those whom he predestined he also called, and those whom he called he also justified, and those whom he justified he also glorified.

God's foreknowledge[18] created the relation between himself and his people so that he could predestine them to be conformed to Jesus' likeness. His predestination grounds his calling of them, and so on.

It is true that God does things with goals and purposes in mind. Genesis 3:22–23 says that God banished Adam and Eve from the garden of Eden so that they would not eat from the Tree of Life. On that basis, thinking along the lines of the post-Reformation Reformed theologians, one might say that God's decree to prevent Adam and Eve from eating of the Tree of Life "preceded" his decree to banish them from the garden. *Precede* here does not have its normal temporal meaning, but rather indicates that the first decree is the end, the second the means.

It is also true that God sets priorities. Not everything is equally important to him. Jesus speaks of some matters of God's law being more important than others (Matt. 23:23). God's Word is a "centered" Book, in which creation, fall, and redemption are events far more important than anything else that happens. So those arguing "orders" of decrees rightly ask us to imagine God's setting priorities.

And certainly God does plan event A in order to provide conditions for the realization of event B. I doubt, however, that Romans 8:29–30 is intended to teach such an order. Strictly, all that the passage teaches is that the group of people who are foreknown is coextensive with the group that is predestined, and so on. Furthermore, Paul does not speak here of a series of divine decrees, but of a series of divine actions. Some of these actions (foreknowing and predestining) are decrees, but the others (calling, justification, glorification) occur in history. They are the results of decrees, but Paul does not speak of the decrees that govern them. His purpose is not to give us a look inside God's thought process, but to give us the assurance that all elect persons will persevere to the end, that everybody whom God foreknows will be predestined, called, justified, glorified.

From these considerations, two problems emerge in talk of orders of the decrees: (1) there are different kinds of orders: means-end orders, priority orders, condition-realization orders. (2) Scripture rarely, if ever, attempts to give a broad summary of the order of God's thoughts. It does present ends and means in particular cases, priorities in others, conditions-realizations in others. But it never, to my knowledge, presents us with

---

18. See our account of foreknowledge in chapter 15, summarized in footnote 4 of this chapter.

any general map of God's mind. We may reasonably say on the basis of Scripture that God's highest purpose is to glorify himself. But beyond that, I think little can be said.

In Reformed theology, the two main views of the order of the decrees are *supralapsarianism* and *infralapsarianism*. The proposed orders are:

Supra

1. To elect some creatable people for divine blessing.
2. To create.
3. To permit the fall.
4. To send Christ to provide atonement.
5. To send the Spirit to apply the atonement to the hearts of believers.
6. To glorify the elect.

Infra

1. To create.
2. To permit the fall.
3. To elect.
4–6. Same as supra.

The controversy centers on the different orders of decrees 1–3, and about the odd notion in the supra order of a divine decree to elect a "creatable" people.

For defenders of the supra view, the important point is that God's foremost concern in his decrees is to display his grace in a chosen people. Everything else is, roughly, a means to that end. In order to give grace to those people, he must create them, permit the fall, and redeem them. So item 1 is related to the others as end to means. But items 2 and 3 are probably best construed as each providing the conditions necessary for the decrees that come after them to be accomplished. So there is no consistent pattern of "order" through the list. Perhaps the reason for giving priority to 1 over the others is that for supras God's care for the elect is so much more profound than his concern with the rest of creation that the other decrees are of far lesser importance.

The infra view makes no judgment as to God's foremost concern. It simply calls us to imagine the process as if God were thinking, "First I will create, then I will permit the fall," and so on. Here the governing principle is mostly what I have called *condition-realization*. It is therefore important to understand that the meaning of *order* differs between the two lists.[19]

For infras, the important point to remember is that God elects people out of the race of *fallen* people and conceives them as fallen even in his planning before the creation.

---

19. For a somewhat more elaborate account of this issue, see *DKG*, 264, in the context of the chapter.

The supras reply that to conceive of election this way is to make election less ultimate in God's mind than it should be; it makes election somehow subordinate to creation and fall.

I believe that we should not take any position on the debate between infras and supras. In urging such agnosticism, I am standing with Herman Bavinck,[20] though my reasons are somewhat different from his:

1. The two positions equivocate on the meaning of *order* and therefore can't be precisely compared with each other.

2. Scripture never explicitly presents a complete and definitive order of thoughts in God's mind, in any of the relevant senses of *order*.

3. On the contrary, Scripture warns us against trying to read God's mind. His thoughts are not our thoughts (Isa. 55:8). This discussion runs great risks of engaging in speculation into matters that God has kept secret. For example, to cite a principle commonly urged in the literature, do we really know that in God's decrees the "last in execution is the first in intent"?[21] But it is not necessarily true of a symphony that the most important chords are the last ones. Nor is the last scene of a novel necessarily the most important. Is the final judgment more important than Jesus' atonement? Surely in these areas it is dangerous to presume that we can make value judgments. Why do we think we know so much about God's mind?

4. Surely in one sense all of God's decrees presuppose each other and exist for the sake of each other (see our discussion of *creaturely otherness* in chapter 35). God formulates each decree with all the others in view. Each influences the others. This fact makes it very difficult to list decrees according to any of the proposed principles of order.

5. In God's mind, where all decrees take all others into account, all may be considered ends and all may be considered means. They are all ends because they all represent things that God intends to do. They are all means because each decree supports the accomplishment of the others.

6. There are therefore *reciprocal* relationships among the purposes of God. God works miracles to attest prophecy, but he also ordains prophets to attest his mighty works. Creation provides the backdrop for redemption, but redemption restores creation. Redemption presupposes creation, but creation itself is in the image of redemption (see chapter 10).

7. I know of nothing in Scripture that settles the question whether God in eternity views the elect as "creatable" or as "created." I think the most likely answer is "both." He views us as creatable because before creation we haven't yet been created, and because he might have chosen not to create us. Since our creation at that point (eternity past) is only possible, not actual, God thinks of us as creatable. But he also views us as created (a) because he has in fact eternally decreed to create us, and (b) because only after the decree of creation is accomplished can anything else happen to us. God views us in all states, actual and possible.

20. *BRD*, 2:361–66, 388–92.
21. I take it that "first in intent" here means "of first importance," "of highest priority."

8. Does God envisage his elect as taken from a fallen humanity, or somehow apart from the fall? I'm not sure that I understand the question. Certainly God foreordains that his elect will be redeemed from Adam's fallen race, but I can't imagine that the supras would actually deny this.[22] And, equally certainly, God knows what they would be like without the effects of the fall. So we should not imagine either (a) God's thinking about the elect while somehow putting the fall out of his mind, or (b) that God does not have a purpose for his elect that transcends the particular pattern of history that he brings to pass. Infras are particularly concerned to avoid (a) and supras to avoid (b). But these two concerns are not inconsistent with each other, and they should not have led to the creation of two parties in the Reformed churches.

9. Although points 4–6 above suggest a relatively equal standing for all divine decrees, I do not deny that God has priorities. His own glory, of course, has the highest priority. The eternal blessing of the elect in Christ is certainly an important means to that goal and may itself be described as the goal of history. I argued in chapter 9 that the consummation state will be so great as to eliminate all sadness over evil. Earlier in this chapter, I argued that the goal of historical election is to manifest eternal election. So all of God's decrees are ends, but some ends are higher than others. The truth stated somewhat inchoately by the supralapsarians should be honored, that the glorification of the elect in Christ, the fulfillment of the kingdom of God, is the goal of history.

10. When one tries to see the practical relevance of all of this, it seems to boil down to a question of the meaning of the fall or, more generally, the problem of evil. The supra position is in danger of making moral evil seem tame, as a mere step upward toward the glorification of the elect. The infra position understands better the horrible, inexplicable character of evil, but infras find it more difficult to understand evil as part of a harmonious divine plan.[23] I will discuss the problem of evil at greater length in chapter 14.

11. Supras focus on the lordship attribute of control, emphasizing that even the fall has an intelligible role to play in God's eternal plan. Infras focus more intently on the lordship attribute of authority, as if to say that we should not demand of God a rationale for evil, but should simply take him at his word that he is dealing with it in his own way. Both these responses are biblical, as we saw in chapter 9. Perhaps our present need is not to debate these positions as if they were alternatives, but to ask God to cure the discomforts that create such questions, to deal with our hearts, as the Lord who is present in blessing and judgment.

Key Terms
Decree
Author-character model

22. Perhaps the problem is that the supras fear that this understanding makes predestination to depend on God's *foresight*, in this case of the fall. But (1) I will argue later that God's foreordination should not be completely separated from his knowledge, as if his foreordination were in ignorance. (2) Both positions correlate predestination with God's foresight in certain ways. The supras see God as decreeing creatable people, conceived as unfallen. But that, too, is a kind of foresight.

23. Thanks to Vern Poythress for suggesting to me this observation and the next.

Decrees
Election
Historical election
Eternal election
Remnant
New covenant
Book of life
Reprobation
Preterition
Precondemnation
Equal ultimacy
Free offer of the gospel
Order of the decrees
Supralapsarian
Infralapsarian
Unconditional election

Study Questions

1. Explain the "biblical logic" that leads from miracle, to providence, to creation, to the decrees.
2. "The doctrine of providence and the doctrine of the decrees are perspectivally related." Explain.
3. "Although he wills for things to change in history, his plan for such change cannot be changed." Explain and evaluate, referring to Scripture.
4. Summarize how the decrees of God reflect his lordship attributes.
5. Show from Scripture how Christ is the faithful remnant.
6. Is the election of Israel based on works or grace? Discuss.
7. What is new about the new covenant? What blessings are unique to the new covenant?
8. What is the biblical basis for the doctrine of reprobation? Evaluate it.
9. Frame believes there are two problems that invalidate talk of an order of God's decrees. Describe those problems and evaluate Frame's argument.

Memory Verses

Ps. 33:11: The counsel of the Lord stands forever,
   the plans of his heart to all generations.

Isa. 46:9–10: I am God, and there is none like me,
declaring the end from the beginning
   and from ancient times things not yet done,
saying, "My counsel shall stand,
   and I will accomplish all my purpose."

Rom. 9:19–21: You will say to me then, "Why does he still find fault? For who can resist his will?" But who are you, O man, to answer back to God? Will what is molded say to its molder, "Why have you made me like this?" Has the potter no right over the clay, to make out of the same lump one vessel for honorable use and another for dishonorable use?

Eph. 1:4: [God] chose us in [Christ] before the foundation of the world, that we should be holy and blameless before him.

Resource for Further Study

Bavinck, Herman. *BRD*, 2:337–405.

CHAPTER 12

GOD'S ATTRIBUTES: LOVE AND GOODNESS

AS I INDICATED IN CHAPTER 7, Scripture teaches us about God in three ways: by narrating his acts, by presenting him directly in authoritative descriptions, and by portraying his inner life as Father, Son, and Spirit. In chapters 7–11, I have discussed God's acts of miracle, providence, creation, and decree. Now I wish to proceed to the second kind of teaching: Scripture's authoritative descriptions of God. In these descriptions, Scripture comes right out and tells us directly who God is, rather than asking us to derive his nature from his actions.

In *DG*, I further subdivided these descriptions into (1) *names* of God, (2) *images* of God, and (3) *attributes* of God.[1] God's names are words such as *Yahweh* and *elohim*, as well as compound terms such as *el shaddai* ("God Almighty"). In this volume, I have said quite a bit about *Yahweh*, the name of God's covenant lordship (chapters 2–3). Images of God include terms such as *King, Shepherd, Light, Shield,* and *Father.* I have discussed *King* and *Father* in this book, in chapters 5 and 6, respectively.[2] In this chapter, I will begin our discussion of the divine attributes.

An attribute is a concept expressed by an adjective (as *eternal*) or a noun (as *eternity*) used to describe a person or thing. The Bible uses many of these terms, such as *love, righteousness, holiness, grace, knowledge, truth,* and *eternity,* to describe God, and there are others not specifically mentioned in Scripture (such as *simplicity, immensity, aseity,* and *personality*) that can be deduced from the biblical teachings.

Some of God's attributes are necessary to his being, so that without those attributes he would not be God. Examples of these are his love, knowledge, eternity. God would have these attributes even if he had never created the world. I will call them *necessary* or *defining* attributes. Other attributes of God depend on his free decision to create beings outside himself. Among these would be "Father of Bill Jones." If God had not

---

1. See *DG*, 343–86.
2. Note especially my discussion in chapter 6 of feminine images of God in Scripture.

freely chosen to create Bill, he would not have that attribute. That God is the Father of Bill might be true, but it is not *necessarily* true of God. If he had chosen not to create Bill, he would still be God. I will call these *relative* attributes. In this sense, *Lord* is a relative attribute. For without servants there is no Lord. God would not be Lord of anything if he had not chosen to create servants and ordained a covenant with them.

Sometimes, however, God's relative attributes are grounded in his necessary attributes. Although God's lordship is a relative attribute, it is grounded in his omnipotence and supreme wisdom. We can, indeed, say that God has the following necessary attribute: that whenever he creates something other than himself, he is necessarily Lord over it. Thus, although lordship in itself is a relative attribute, it is grounded in a necessary attribute. So I defend my decision to present the biblical doctrine of God as a description of his lordship. And my account of his attributes will continue that theme. Although God's lordship is a relative attribute, it is supremely important to our relationship with God. Everything else we know about God must be understood in terms of that relationship.

We saw that God performs his acts so that people would know that he is the Lord (Ex. 14:4; cf. 6:7; 7:5; 8:22; etc.). From his acts, we learn about his nature, his attributes, and therefore his attributes set forth the nature of his lordship. They describe his lordship from various perspectives. Therefore, I will present God's attributes as manifestations of his lordship attributes: his control, authority, and presence.

The Bible, of course, does not directly authorize a scheme for classifying the attributes. Some classification is necessary, however, so that we can proceed through them in an orderly way for pedagogical purposes. Theologians have chosen different approaches. The most common in Presbyterian circles has been the distinction between *communicable* and *incommunicable* attributes. The former are attributes that God and man can share in common, the latter attributes that they do not share. But in one sense there are no communicable attributes. Human love at its best is analogous to divine love, but it is not the same thing, for God's love is original and ours is derivative from his. On the other hand, no attributes of God are entirely incommunicable, for we are his image in a comprehensive sense, as we will see. Our love, at its best, is the love of God imaged in our own lives. So in presenting the attributes of God, Scripture does not emphasize the contrast between communicable and incommunicable. My lordship classification, by contrast, is based on themes that Scripture itself stresses.

So I will be using two threefold classifications that reflect God's control, authority, and presence. I distinguish attributes of love, knowledge, and power, and interface these with classifications of control, authority, and presence; see fig. 12.1.

This diagram will not serve as a detailed map of my discussions, and I don't intend to put much emphasis on it. But if readers are interested in the reasons I discuss one attribute before another, or why I present certain attributes together, this diagram may be of some help.[3]

---

3. *DG*, 394–401, gives an extended rationale for the chart.

	Love	Knowledge	Power
Control Dynamic; Content	Goodness Love Grace Mercy Patience Compassion Jealousy Wrath	Speech	Eternity Immensity Incorporeality Will Power Existence (*Esse*)
Authority Static; Form, Structure	Justice Righteousness	Truth	Aseity Simplicity Essence
Presence Integrity; Involvement	Joy Blessedness Beauty Perfection Holiness	Knowledge Wisdom Mind	Glory Spirituality Omnipresence

Fig. 12.1. Classification of Divine Attributes

I will begin with those attributes that stress God's ethical character: his love, goodness, righteousness, and holiness. Theological treatments of the doctrine of God tend more typically to begin with the attributes of power. But when Scripture comes closest to defining God, it tends to focus on love (1 John 4:8, 16), light (1:5), and holiness (Isa. 6:3). The OT expounds the name *Yahweh* in terms of God's mercy, grace, and loving-kindness (Ex. 33:19; 34:6–7; Ps. 103:8–10). So love is not less fundamental to God's nature than his power, aseity, or eternity. God's love is bedrock. There is nothing more basic to his nature. When we know that God is love and understand fully what that means, then we know what God really and truly is.

Goodness

In describing God's ethical character, I will be focusing on love, but I will begin with the broader concept of *goodness*, which includes love and many other divine attributes such as grace, patience, faithfulness, mercy, and justice.

Good is, first of all, a general term of commendation. We describe as good any kind of excellence, including beauty, economic value, practical usefulness, skillfulness—indeed, anything that evokes from us a favorable response. In theology we tend to focus on moral goodness, but there are many other kinds of goodness as well. We may describe someone as a "good plumber" or a "good pianist" even though he is morally wretched. A dinner, computer, or hammer can be good, even though inanimate objects are not subject to moral evaluation. So we may distinguish between moral goodness and nonmoral goodness. Nonmoral goodness often means "good for something," so we often describe it as "teleological goodness." In this sense, God says that the light is good, in Genesis 1:4. For more discussion of the difference between teleological and moral goodness, see *DCL*, 14–15.

Theologians have sometimes understood God's goodness as including both moral goodness and other kinds of excellencies (or *perfections*). So God's perfections of eternity and aseity, for example, are forms of his goodness. Scripture, however, uses the term most often for distinctively moral excellence.

In a broad sense, goodness is conduct (by man or by God himself) that measures up to God's standards (e.g., Gen. 3:5; Lev. 5:4; Num. 24:13; Rom. 2:10; 3:12). As such, it is more or less synonymous with *righteousness*.

The question of standard, or criterion, is an important issue, and I should say a bit about it here. In Plato's dialogue *Euthyphro*, the question arises as to whether piety is what the gods say it is, or whether they command piety because of its intrinsic nature, apart from their own wishes. In the dialogue, Socrates argues what is evidently Plato's position, that the gods command piety because of its intrinsic nature. So piety, then, is something independent of the gods, something impersonal and objective, or, in Plato's system, a *form*.

The same question has been asked about goodness and its relation to the biblical God. The biblical answer is that goodness is, first of all, God's own character. It is an attribute of God himself. So it is as objective as Plato wished it to be, but it is a personal quality, rather than an impersonal form. God commands his creatures to imitate his behavior (Lev. 19:1–2; Matt. 5:48), so for us goodness is based on his commands. But his commands are not arbitrary, since they are grounded in his eternal nature. Of course, there are some things that God may do that he forbids his creatures to do. For example, God may take human life at his own discretion; we may not. But both his responsibility and ours are grounded in God's goodness and his high valuation of human life.

So goodness is conduct that meets God's standards. But Scripture usually speaks of goodness in a narrower sense, as benevolence. A good person is one who acts to benefit others. For examples of God's goodness in this sense, see these verses: Gen. 50:20; Num. 10:29; Deut. 30:5; Josh. 24:20. God is the source of all blessings (Ps. 34:8–10; James 1:17). Truly, he is good to Israel (Ps. 73:1). From the righteous, God withholds no good thing (Pss. 84:11; 85:12; 103:5; Matt. 7:11). One important blessing is God's mercy, often paired with goodness in the Psalms (Pss. 100:5; 106:1; 107:1; 109:21; 118:1; 136:1). And God's good mercies include the forgiveness of sins (86:5).

To whom is God good? Psalm 145:9 says that he is "good to all, and his mercy is over all that he has made." He is good to his people (73:1), but is good to them even before they become his people, before they embrace him as Lord (Rom. 5:8). What of those who never embrace him, who always remain God's enemies? Scripture teaches that he is good to them as well (Matt. 5:45), sending rain and sunshine on the just and the unjust.

This is not to say, however, that God gives the *same* blessings to everyone. He is not obligated to do that, and he does not do it. His goodness to the elect, for example, is very different from his goodness to the reprobate (chapter 11). But even the reprobate receive God's blessings of rain and sunshine. These blessings are substantial, so much that they ought to motivate repentance (Acts 14:17; Rom. 2:4), though the reprobate refuse to give heed.

An important conclusion to this discussion is that nobody can complain that God has not been good to him. Even the lost in hell cannot complain that God has never done anything good to them. In Jesus' parable of the rich man in Hades, the "good things" that the rich man received in life (Luke 16:25) bear witness against him.

Love

The Language of Love

The concepts *goodness* and *love* overlap considerably in Scripture. Goodness, as we have seen, is a very broad concept, conduct that meets God's standards, but we saw that in Scripture God's goodness is most often specifically focused on benevolence. Love is not so much about God's general standards of conduct as it is about benevolence. But though love is a narrower concept, it is also theologically richer. God's love is the heart of the biblical story, especially precious to the hearts of God's people.

Jack Cottrell offers an excellent definition of God's love:

> His self-giving affection for his image-bearing creatures and his unselfish concern for their well-being, that leads him to act on their behalf and for their happiness and welfare.[4]

We note that although *goodness* applies to the creation generally, *love* is distinctly a relation between persons. This definition also brings out well that God's love includes both affection and action, both feelings and deeds. The biblical emphasis is on God's deeds. But the terms for *compassion*, *pity*, *mercy* (especially *raham*, *hamal*, *splanchnizomai*, *oiktiro*), as aspects of God's love, connote strong emotion, as do the parallels between God's love and human marriage (Ezek. 16:1–63; Hos. 1:2–11; 3:1–5). These emotions are, to be sure, emotions of jealousy (leading to wrath) as well as tenderness.

I will not make much of the differences between the various Hebrew and Greek words for *love*. Much has been said about the differences between the Greek terms *eros* (erotic love—not used in the NT), *philia* (friendship), and *agape* (the NT word normally used for the love of God and for love among believers).[5] There may be some intentional wordplay between the verbs *phileo* and *agapao* in John 21:15–17, but if there is, the force

4. Jack Cottrell, *What the Bible Says about God the Redeemer* (Joplin, MO: College Press, 1987), 336.

5. See, for example, C. S. Lewis, *The Four Loves* (London: Geoffrey Bles, 1960); and the more technical study, Anders Nygren, *Agape and Eros*, trans. Philip Watson (London: SPCK, 1953).

of it isn't entirely clear to me. Otherwise, the NT does not make much of the differences between these terms, though it uses *agapao* regularly for the idea of redemptive love.

Of course, both *philia* and *agape* are sharply different from *eros*, simply because *eros* is distinctly sensual. So theologians have said much about how *eros* is acquisitive, egocentric, desiring something from its object, and how *agape* by contrast is spontaneous, unmotivated, indifferent to the present value of the object, and self-giving. There is some truth in this contrast. Clearly, *eros* would have been inappropriate to designate God's love, and certainly the love of God is self-giving.[6] But the self-giving nature of God's love is not found so much in the word *agape* as in the teaching of Scripture about God's love.[7] The main reason, I think, that the NT writers chose the unusual word *agape* to refer to God's love is that the LXX translators used this word to translate the Hebrew *ahabah*.[8] Therefore, the NT use of *agape* reiterates and expands the concept of the love of God in the OT. Its nuances, therefore, are best discovered through Bible study, rather than a study of Greek lexical stock.[9]

Related to the recent discussions of *eros* and *agape* is the traditional theological distinction in God's love between benevolence, beneficence, and complacency. Francis Turretin explains:

> A threefold love of God is commonly held; or rather there are three degrees of one and the same love. First, there is the love of benevolence by which God willed good to the creature from eternity; second, the love of beneficence by which he does good to the creature in time according to his good will; third, the love of complacency by which he delights himself in the creature on account of the rays of his image seen in them. The two former precede every act of the creature; the latter follows (not as an effect its cause, but as a consequent its antecedent). By the love of benevolence, he loved us before we were; by the love of beneficence, he loves us as we are; and by the love of complacency, he loves us when we are (viz., renewed after his image). By the first, he elects us; by the second, he redeems and sanctifies us; but by the third, he gratuitously rewards us as holy and just. John 3:16 refers to the first; Eph. 5:25 and Rev. 1:5 to the second; Is. 62:3 and Heb. 11:6 to the third.[10]

Not all of Turretin's references use the word *love*, but the distinction reflects a genuine variation of scriptural usage. The references to divine compacency show that God's

6. I am not convinced that it is in every sense "unmotivated" and "indifferent to the present value of the object."

7. This is a good example of what James Barr identified as a confusion between words, concepts, and teachings. See Barr, *The Semantics of Biblical Language* (London: Oxford University Press, 1961).

8. Perhaps the translators were moved in part by the fact that these two terms sound somewhat alike. But the more significant reason may have been that when the LXX was translated, "*agapan* was becoming the standard verb for 'to love' because *philein* had acquired the meaning 'to kiss.'" Moisés Silva, *Biblical Words and Their Meaning* (Grand Rapids: Zondervan, 1983), 96.

9. In 2 Samuel 13:15, the LXX uses *agape* to refer to an incestuous rape. This is within the possible range of the term, considered simply as a Greek word. It is the nature of God's love that leads the biblical writers to use the term mostly for noble affections.

10. Francis Turretin, *Institutes of Elenctic Theology* (Phillipsburg, NJ: P&R Publishing, 1992), 1:242.

love is not always "indifferent to the qualities of its objects." God loves the righteous, according to Psalms 37:28 and 146:8. Certainly in these passages the fact that they are righteous motivates his love. Israel's obedience motivates God's love for her in Deuteronomy 7:13, although God also loved her *before* she was obedient and in spite of her disobedience (Deut. 9:4–6). So in Proverbs, God's wisdom says, "I love those who love me" (Prov. 8:17), even though in 1 John 4:19, "we love because he first loved us" (compare the broader context in verses 7–21). For more examples of God's love of complacency, see John 14:21, 23. An adequate understanding of God's love must deal with all three aspects of it. Bringing them together, we may say that God loves us first (benevolence and beneficence), and then loves us because of his work in us (complacency), including our response of obedience.

The Extent of God's Love

As with goodness, God's love extends to everyone, but in different ways. God loves himself in his Trinitarian society. The Father loves the Son (Matt. 3:17; 17:5; John 17:24, 26); the Son loves the Father (John 14:31). The love between the three persons is eternal. So he would have been a loving God even if he had not created the world. His love is a *necessary* attribute, one without which he would not be God. As 1 John 4:8 and 16 teach us, God *is* love.

God also loves everything that he has made, including his enemies (Matt. 5:43–48), as we have seen. His gift of Christ is also universal in one sense: "For God so loved the world, that he gave his only Son, that whoever believes in him should not perish but have eternal life" (John 3:16). In this verse, although only believers receive eternal life, God's love in sending Christ is directed to the world as a whole. In John's writings, the world is the object of salvation, not only in 3:16, but also in 1:29; 3:17; 4:42; 6:33, 51; 8:12; 9:5; 12:47; and 17:21, 23. The work of Christ is the redemption, re-creation, reconstitution of the whole world.

This usage does not imply universal salvation. John makes it perfectly clear that not everyone in the world is saved, but only those who believe in Christ. When Christ comes to save the world, it is only "whoever believes in him" (John 3:16) who will not perish (cf. 1:12; 3:17–21, 36). Those who do not believe are condemned (3:18–21). So Jesus, before his death, prays for his disciples and, specifically, *not* for the world (John 17:9).[11]

My conclusion is that God sent his Son, motivated by his love for the whole world. Jesus comes as "Savior of the world" (John 4:42; 1 John 4:14), although not every individual in the world will be saved. Through Christ, God will lift the curse from the creation, and the creation will again be under the dominion of those who love God. God will banish those who serve Satan, the "ruler of this world" (John 12:31; 14:30; 16:11; cf. Eph. 2:2), from the world to come.

Does the coming of Christ benefit the reprobate? Certainly the general cultural benefits of Christianity benefit all. So to the providential benevolence of God to all

---

11. I will discuss in chapter 50 the reward of the elect and the punishment of the reprobate.

people, we should add that God blesses all human beings by the coming of Jesus and the Spirit. And the reprobate are also blessed by the fact that God gives them an *opportunity* to turn from their wickedness and believe in Christ. None of these benefits are accidental. God intends them for good, and so they come from God's love.

To be sure, all these benefits (both providential and redemptive-historical), on the last day, bring greater condemnation on the reprobate, on those who never do believe. Some Calvinists conclude that these benefits, therefore, have nothing to do with God's love, but only with his wrath. But divine attributes are not easily separable.[12] And it is important for us to take history seriously. Before they come to faith, believers are under the wrath of God, real wrath (Eph. 2:3). Similarly, in the time before the last judgment, unbelievers, even the reprobate, experience the love of God, real love. God's grand historical novel (see chapters 14 and 35) is not concerned only with endings, but also with beginnings and middles. His love to the reprobate is real love, even though it leads later to wrath. God judges the wicked because they have despised his *kindness* (Rom. 2:4). That kindness must be real kindness if it is to be a valid ground of condemnation.

Some Calvinists hesitate to say to unbelievers, "God loves you," for they think God loves only the elect, and it is impossible to know whether any particular unbeliever is elect. Obviously, such a phrase can be misunderstood. But in Deuteronomy 7, God tells Israel that he "set his love on you" (v. 7) and "chose" her (v. 6; cf. 4:37; 10:15; 23:5; 33:3; Ps. 44:3; Jer. 31:3; Hos. 11:1; Mal. 1:2), even in a context where it is evident that there have been, are, and will be unbelievers within Israel. His covenant with her is a "covenant of love" (Deut. 7:12 NIV). The prophets tell the people of God's love for them to motivate their faithfulness.[13]

And Paul witnesses to unbelievers of God's kindness to them, in Acts 14:17, as well as implicitly in Acts 17:26–30 and Romans 2:4. We certainly are well within the limits of Scripture when we point out to non-Christians that God has loved them in many ways, by giving them life, health, and various measures of prosperity. And we can add, as I will explain later (chapter 16), that God desires their salvation (Ezek. 18:23; 33:11; 1 Tim. 2:4; 2 Peter 3:9). In his patience, he has given time for repentance (2 Peter 3:9; Rev. 2:21). These kindnesses should motivate the unbeliever to turn to the Lord.

On the basis of John 3:16, we can also say, "God loves you because you are his handiwork, his image. God sent his Son to die, to redeem a people from this fallen world. So he gave you a priceless opportunity: if you believe, you will be saved. If you do believe, you will enjoy the fullness of God's blessing. If you do not, you have only yourself to blame." I grant that such an appeal "sounds Arminian." It appears to say that God sent Jesus only to make salvation hypothetically possible for all, but that the final determination is made by man. But the appeal does not say that at all. The final determination is by God; but here as in many other cases God's sovereignty does not negate human responsibility, but makes it all the more important. God makes the final

---

12. We will look more closely at God's wrath at a later point.
13. Thanks to Norman Shepherd for suggesting this point to me.

determination as to who is saved, but one may not be saved unless he believes (John 1:12; 3:15–16, 36; 5:24; 20:31), and those who disbelieve die for their own sins.

The full story is this: God sent his Son with both hypothetical and categorical intentions. Categorically, Christ died only for his elect, *limited atonement*.[14] Hypothetically, he died so that *if* anyone at all should believe, he would be saved. His death makes that hypothetical statement true.[15] So Christ died to guarantee salvation to the elect and to provide the opportunity of salvation for all.[16]

Some may say that this "opportunity" is meaningless for the nonelect, for God has predetermined that they will never avail themselves of it. But that is to think unhistorically. As we saw earlier, when God sends rain and sunshine on the unjust (including the reprobate), these are genuine benefits, even though in the end it increases their condemnation. The rain and sunshine are not curses, but in the cases of the reprobate they become so, because they are blessings spurned. These must be genuine blessings if they are indeed to increase the sinner's condemnation.

God's natural blessings in Scripture are means by which he calls sinners to repent and believe (Acts 14:14–18; Rom. 2:4). The opportunity to believe in Christ is also a genuine blessing of God that should motivate repentance and faith. It, too, must be a genuine blessing if the rejection of it increases the condemnation of the nonelect. And it is: God's free offer of the gospel is entirely sincere and true—if anyone believes in Jesus, he will certainly be saved.[17]

God's Saving Love

So there are various ways in which God loves everyone, whether elect or nonelect. But the form of divine love most central to Scripture's message is the love of God in saving sinners. This is the gospel of Christ, the good news. We have seen already that it is the Father's love for the world that sent Jesus to save sinners (John 3:16). Here we focus on God's special love for the people whom Jesus came to save.

Throughout Scripture, redemption comes from God's love. As we saw in the previous section, God chose[18] Israel because he *loved* her, not because she was more numerous than other peoples (Deut. 7:7–8) or because she was more righteous (9:4–6). That love began with the oath he swore to Abraham (v. 8). God's love sovereignly instituted the covenant relationship, so it preceded any love that man offered to God. In the OT as in the NT, "we love because he first loved us" (1 John 4:19). But God's sovereign love motivates our response of obedience, which leads to more divine love:

14. See my discussion of this doctrine in chapter 38.

15. For more on the argument that the atonement brought salvation both categorically for the elect and hypothetically for all, see my review of Brian Armstrong, *Calvinism and the Amyraut Heresy*, WTJ 34, 2 (May 1972): 186–92.

16. I am assuming the common Reformed view that the atonement is efficient for the elect, but sufficient for all. As my friend Mark Horne points out, it would be bizarre to imagine that Jesus could have saved a few more people if he had suffered a bit longer or more intensely. His sacrifice was perfect.

17. I will discuss the "free offer of the gospel" later in my discussion of the will of God, chapter 16.

18. Note the correlation between love and "choice," that is, election, here and in Deuteronomy 4:37; 10:15. The reference here is to historical election. But Paul correlates God's love also with eternal election in Ephesians 1:4. This relationship underscores the sovereignty of God's love.

> And because you listen to these rules and keep and do them, the LORD your God will keep with you the covenant and the steadfast love that he swore to your fathers. (Deut. 7:12)

So God's love both initiates the covenant and continues as his people respond in obedience. It initiates the covenant unconditionally, but its continuance is conditional on human obedience (compare my discussion in chapter 4).

For believers, of course, all conditions are met by Jesus, guaranteeing salvation for them and motivating their continued obedience. The OT could not in the nature of things focus as sharply on the cross as could the NT. But in the OT also, redemption is the motivation for obedience. Israel is to keep the Ten Commandments because God delivered the people from the land of Egypt, the house of bondage (Ex. 20:2); and Israel is to imitate God's redemptive activity. As God freed Israel from Egypt, Israel is to give rest to its servants (Deut. 5:12–15). And when Israel fails to obey, she must bring sacrifice, and look to the coming sacrifice of the Messiah (Isa. 52:13–53:12).

The NT typically defines love (both the love of God and the love required of believers) by reference to the cross of Christ. We have already seen this in John 3:16. "God *so* loved" means that God loved the world in this particular way; God's sending his Son shows the very nature of his love for us. Note also:

> Greater love has no one than this, that someone lay down his life for his friends. You are my friends if you do what I command you. (John 15:13–14)[19]

> But God shows his love for us in that while we were still sinners, Christ died for us. (Rom. 5:8)

Cf. Gal. 2:20; Eph. 5:2, 25; 1 John 3:16; 4:9–10 (following the "God is love" of verse 8); Rev. 1:5b.

In Romans 8:35, the love of Christ from which nobody can separate us is the love of him who "did not spare his own Son but gave him up for us all" (v. 32). In Ephesians 2:4, God's "great love with which he loved us" is salvation from sin, particularly his shed blood (v. 13). Compare other passages where Jesus' atonement is a model for our behavior toward one another: Matt. 20:25–28; 2 Cor. 5:14–15; Phil. 2:1–11; 1 Peter 2:21–25.

So God's expectation of us is to imitate, to image, him. We might respond by saying that of all of God's acts, Jesus' atonement is the one that we are least able to imitate—and in a way that is true. Only Christ could lay down his life as an atonement for sin. But we should, like Jesus, be willing to lay down our lives so that others might live. That standard, to be sure, is intimidating. The cross as a model for human ethics shows us how sinful we still are, how very far from God's standards. But by faith and through God's Spirit, we can make a start. My present point, however, is simply that the atonement is a profound representation of God's very nature. "God is love"

---

19. In terms of Turretin's distinctions, verse 13 represents beneficence, verse 14 complacency.

implies that God will go to the uttermost to bless his people. He will give himself to the greatest extent. And if the cross represents God's character in such profundity, it cannot help but be the standard for our own lives.

But God's saving love for us did not begin at the cross. As we have seen, it was the love of God that sent Jesus to earth. And even before the incarnation, God's love for us reaches back to eternity (Eph. 1:4–5). So God's saving love motivates even the eternal election of God's people.[20] Then it reaches out to us in time, through the atonement, bringing us into God's family:

> See what kind of love the Father has given to us, that we should be called children of God. (1 John 3:1; cf. Eph. 1:5)

So Paul waxes eloquent, praising the vastness of God's love, its incomprehensibility. God's love is great because God is.

> [I pray] that you, being rooted and grounded in love, may have strength to comprehend with all the saints what is the breadth and length and height and depth, and to know the love of Christ that surpasses knowledge, that you may be filled with all the fullness of God. (Eph. 3:17b–19)

To know God's love is to be filled with his very fullness.

God's Love and His Lordship

We have seen various ways in which God's love is a covenantal concept. It is God's love that initiates his covenant with Israel and, indeed, all his covenants with men. His love chooses us for salvation before the foundation of the world. So his love is controlling, sovereign.

Process theologians and open theists object to the idea that God's love controls people. They argue that love never controls, that it works *persuasively* rather than *coercively*.

God's love does certainly coerce some people. God coerces his enemies when he judges them for the sake of his beloved. Thus, God's love acts in wrath. It is also possible to see coercion sometimes in the conversion of sinners. The vision of Christ on the road to Damascus blinded Saul.

But the issue is most clearly focused in this question: Does God violate our free will in converting us? Yes and no. He makes us believe in him, something that we resist apart from grace. In that sense, he forces us to believe against our will. But when we believe, surely, we are doing something we want to do, for God's grace also changes our wants. In that sense, we believe willingly. In conversion, then, God brings us to act contrary to our depraved will, and in accord with a new will given by grace.

So *coercion* is not the best word to describe what happens in conversion. The problem is not that *coercion* connotes too much divine control, but rather too little. God

---

20. This is also true of historical election (recalling the distinction of chapter 11 between historical and eternal election). Note the parallels between God's love and his choice of Israel in Deuteronomy 4:37; 7:6–7; 10:15.

does not need to coerce, for he has control of our hearts and thus makes us to believe without any sense of being forced. So *control* and *coercion* are not the same thing, as I shall emphasize in our later discussion of free will in chapter 35.

What of *persuasion*? Well, God does persuade us to believe in the sense that he makes us want to believe. But in doing this, he works changes in us far deeper than the term *persuasion* suggests. He creates in us a new heart.

God's love is also the authoritative norm for our behavior, for we are to image God's very redemptive love in Christ. And it is his love that leads him to be present with us.

Grace

Grace in Scripture refers to God's benevolence, as do *goodness* and *love*, but with different perspectives and nuances.

The KJV translates the Hebrew *hen* (verb *hanan*) as "grace"; the ESV translates the word often as "favor," sometimes as "mercy" and in other ways. Often in human relationships, the question arises about one person's attitude toward another: will he welcome me, be open to a request, be friend or foe? A positive attitude is called *favor*. Typically in the OT it occurs in the phrase "find favor in his eyes" and variants. For example, Laban says to Jacob, "If I have found favor in your sight, I have learned by divination that the LORD has blessed me because of you" (Gen. 30:27; cf. 32:5; 33:8, 10, 15; 34:11; etc.).

When used to describe human favor, *hen* does not presuppose any details about why the favor is needed or granted. The use of the term does not prejudice the question whether the favor is merited or not, or what motivates the one who gives it. We must search the context for that additional information, if it is available.

Weighty theological issues, however, enter the picture when God is the One who shows *hen*. Since man is fallen and cursed, any favor shown by God to him is surprising. This is especially true with regard to the first reference in Scripture to God's *hen*. Before the great flood, as we learn in Genesis, the wickedness of man had become very great, so that "every intention of the thoughts of his heart was only evil continually" (Gen. 6:5).[21] But amazingly, we read in verse 8 that "Noah found favor [*hen*] in the eyes of the LORD." Here it is plain, not from the general use of *hen*, but from the context of Genesis 6, that this favor of God was not based on Noah's goodness. Surely God included Noah in the terrible judgment of verse 5. For his own reasons, God was favorable to Noah. But the reasons do not include Noah's merit. Although he may have been more godly than other men, his godliness did not *entitle* him to divine deliverance. But God gave him a warning, and he responded by faith (Heb. 11:7).

---

21. This verse is a powerful testimony to the *total depravity of man*. Note the universal indications, *every, only, all the time*. And not only man's actions are wicked (obvious in the context), but also his *thoughts*, and not only those, but the *inclinations* of his thoughts. And the thoughts reveal the quality of his *heart*. And lest anyone think the flood solved the problem of human sin, Genesis 8:21 speaks the same way of man after the flood: "the intention of man's heart is evil from his youth." That is God's postfall judgment of Noah's family. Compare our discussion of sin in chapter 36.

In Genesis 33:11, Jacob tells his brother Esau that God has dealt "graciously" with him, so that he can present his brother with lavish gifts. The soteriological meaning of *grace* is not as evident here as in Genesis 6 and Hebrews 11, but the term summarizes the way in which God has fulfilled his promises to Abraham, Isaac, and Jacob, enabling them to prosper in the Land of Promise. Jacob was a schemer; he did not deserve God's blessing, but he received it by grace. So Jacob's son Joseph, when he sees his beloved brother Benjamin after many years of exile. He is overcome with joy, but is unable to reveal his true identity. So he pronounces on Benjamin a benediction, "God be gracious to you, my son!" (Gen. 43:29).

The next reference to divine grace is in Exodus 33:12–17, where Moses asks God to teach him and to be present with Israel (cf. 34:8). He bases his plea on the fact that God knows Moses by name and Moses has "found favor" (33:12) with him, and he makes his request so that God will show continued favor (v. 13). God must be present with Israel so that the world will know that God is "pleased" (*hen* again) with Moses and with Israel (v. 16). The Lord grants the request because "you have found favor in my sight, and I know you by name" (v. 17). Then God displays his glory to Moses, and promises to proclaim his name *Yahweh* to him. He follows with the phrases that we have looked at before as a central exposition of the divine name: "I will have mercy [*hanan*] on whom I will have mercy, and I will have compassion [*raham*] on whom I will have compassion" (v. 19 NIV). In Romans 9:15, as we have seen, Paul quotes this passage to indicate God's absolute sovereignty in redemption.

God's grace is also prominent in the next biblical exposition of the name *Yahweh*, Exodus 34:6: "The LORD, the LORD, a God merciful [*rahum*] and gracious [*hannun*], slow to anger, and abounding in steadfast love and faithfulness."

In these passages as in Genesis, God chooses people (here, Moses individually and Israel as a nation) in order to show them favor. Like Noah, Jacob, and Benjamin, Israel is undeserving. She is "stiff-necked." Exodus 33 and 34 follow Israel's disobedience with the golden calf, a disobedience that continues (with periodic revivals) throughout the biblical history. God's favor to Israel, therefore, is not based on Israel's righteousness, as God later tells the people:

> Do not say in your heart, after the LORD your God has thrust them out before you, "It is because of my righteousness that the LORD has brought me in to possess this land," whereas it is because of the wickedness of these nations that the LORD is driving them out before you. Not because of your righteousness or the uprightness of your heart are you going in to possess their land, but because of the wickedness of these nations the LORD your God is driving them out from before you, and that he may confirm the word that the LORD swore to your fathers, to Abraham, to Isaac, and to Jacob.
>
> Know, therefore, that the LORD your God is not giving you this good land to possess because of your righteousness, for you are a stubborn people. (Deut. 9:4–6)

If this passage seems repetitious, we should conclude that the point is important, and that God took special pains to communicate it to a stiff-necked people.

God's grace to men, then, appears in spite of man's unrighteousness, and by God's utterly sovereign decision ("I will have mercy on whom I will have mercy"). It is legitimate, therefore (though not implicit in the *hanan* vocabulary as such[22]), to define God's grace theologically as his "sovereign, unmerited favor, given to those who deserve his wrath."

We can also see from these references that God's grace, like his love, is *covenantal*. It is implicit in the covenant name of God. Yahweh initiates the covenant, by choosing undeserving people to bear his name: Noah, Abraham, Isaac, Jacob, Moses, Israel as a nation. That is grace. Then God shows more grace to his chosen people, based on his covenant promises to Noah, Abraham, and the others. We sometimes ask the question: if God's grace is not based on human merit, what is the reason for it? Is it arbitrary? No; as I said in connection with Genesis 6, God has his own reasons, but they are not based on human merit. Rather, they are based on his decision to save men from sin by way of covenants, by making promises and fulfilling them. This is the basic shape of God's historical drama.

So the priestly benediction, in which Aaron and his sons "put my name on the Israelites," invokes God's grace:

> The LORD bless you and keep you;
> the LORD make his face to shine upon you and be gracious [*hanan*] to you;
> the LORD lift up his countenance upon you and give you peace. (Num. 6:24–26)

Israel bears God's name; he is her Lord, Yahweh, present with her. So he shows favor not because of Israel's righteousness, but because he is her covenant Lord. Grace, therefore, is utterly *personal*. It is the Lord's own attitude of favor toward his people.

In the NT, the vocabulary of grace (now the Greek *charis*[23] and variants) appears rarely in the Gospels, though John emphasizes the point that grace and truth come through Jesus Christ (John 1:14–17). In the book of Acts, the term appears in 4:33 indicating the divine influence that moved the church to care sacrificially for its poor. Here, grace is not only an attitude of favor on God's part, as in the OT, though it certainly is that. It is also an active power, enabling people to do the works of God.

When many Gentiles believe in Christ at Antioch, Barnabas arrives and sees "the grace of God" (Acts 11:23). Here again, God's grace is his power, bringing about faith. God favors these Gentiles and therefore enables them to believe. Compare Acts 18:27, which says that Apollos "greatly helped those who through grace had believed." As we saw in chapter 8, faith is a gift of God's grace.

Thus, the "grace of God" in Acts 13:43 refers to the gospel. Paul and Barnabas urge their hearers to "continue in the grace of God." So the gospel is the "word of his grace" (14:3; 20:32), the "gospel of the grace of God" (20:24).

In Acts 15, the concept of grace enters the polemics between early Christianity on the one hand, and the Jews and Judaizers on the other. Some Christians of Pharisaic

---

22. For example, Luke 2:40 tells us that Jesus increased in "favor" (*charis*, the NT equivalent of *hen*) with God and man. But clearly we should not assume that God's favor on Jesus was undeserved.

23. This term translates *hen* in the LXX, and also *hesed*, which we will consider later.

background had insisted that it was "necessary to circumcise them and to order them to keep the law of Moses" (Acts 15:5); that is, the Gentiles must become Jews in order to become Christians. Peter advises otherwise: God brought the Gentiles to faith, making no distinction between them and the Jewish Christians (compare Peter's vision and experience with Cornelius in chapters 10 and 11).

> Now, therefore, why are you putting God to the test by placing a yoke on the neck of the disciples that neither our fathers nor we have been able to bear? But we believe that we will be saved through the grace of the Lord Jesus, just as they will. (Acts 15:10–11)

From this point on in the NT, *grace* is not only God's favor, not only God's power to change hearts, but also salvation apart from the works of the law. Such is the emphasis of Paul's writings.

> But now the righteousness of God has been manifested apart from the law, although the Law and the Prophets bear witness to it—the righteousness of God through faith in Jesus Christ for all who believe. For there is no distinction: for all have sinned and fall short of the glory of God, and are justified by his grace as a gift, through the redemption that is in Christ Jesus. (Rom. 3:21–24; cf. 4:4, 16; 11:6; Gal. 2:21)

Paul contrasts grace not only with obedience to the law of Moses, but with any reliance on our own works as a means of salvation:

> For by grace you have been saved through faith. And this is not your own doing; it is the gift of God, not a result of works, so that no one may boast. (Eph. 2:8–9)

> [God] saved us and called us to a holy calling, not because of our works but because of his own purpose and grace, which he gave us in Christ Jesus before the ages began. (2 Tim. 1:9)

In 2 Timothy 1:9, God gives us his grace in our eternal election (chapter 11).[24] So his grace cannot possibly be based on our works. Rather, it gives us the power to do good works (2 Cor. 9:8; Eph. 2:10). Indeed, it is God's grace that gives us the abilities we need to preach the gospel and to do his will (Rom. 12:3, 6; 1 Cor. 3:10; 15:10; 2 Cor. 8:7; Gal. 2:9; Eph. 3:7–8; 4:7). So as in the OT, God's saving grace is *unmerited*, given to us for God's reasons, not because of anything good in us.[25]

---

24. Compare Romans 11:5, in which the remnant is chosen, elected, by grace.

25. Once we are saved, however, God continues to give gifts and blessings. These, too, are grace, and they are certainly not merited, but they do sometimes take into account the previous works of God in us. James 4:6 and 1 Peter 5:5 quote Proverbs 3:34, "God opposes the proud, but gives grace to the humble." God gives additional gifts of grace to those to whom he has first given the grace of humility. We saw earlier that God loves his people unconditionally; but he also loves them more and more, in response to their obedience. The same may be said of grace.

Also as in the OT, grace appears in the benediction, the blessing of God. The apostolic greetings (Rom. 1:7; 1 Cor. 1:3, etc.) and benedictions (Rom. 16:20, 24; 1 Cor. 16:23; and esp. 2 Cor. 13:14) always emphasize grace. In Numbers 6:24–26, Aaron's sons declared God's grace in putting his name on the people. In 2 Corinthians 13:14, Paul does the same as he places upon the churches God's threefold name:

> The grace of the Lord Jesus Christ and the love of God and the fellowship of the Holy Spirit be with you all.

So all the blessings of God come to us by God's sovereign grace. Without his grace we are nothing. By grace comes the forgiveness of our sins, the power to do good works, and the ability to serve the people of God. And all of these come from the most amazing grace of all:

> For you know the grace of our Lord Jesus Christ, that though he was rich, yet for your sake he became poor, so that you by his poverty might become rich. (2 Cor. 8:9)

Common Grace and God's Patience

We have seen that although God directs his goodness and love especially to believers, there are also senses in which God's goodness and love are universal. "The LORD is good to all" (Ps. 145:9), and he loves even his enemies by sending them rain and sunshine (Matt. 5:44–45). So many have thought that the same may be said of grace, that there are forms of divine grace that God gives to the nonelect.

To my knowledge, Scripture never uses *hen* or *charis* to refer to his blessings on creation generally or on nonelect humanity. So it would perhaps be better to speak of God's common goodness, or common love, rather than his common grace. The word *grace* in Scripture tends to be more narrowly focused on redemption than *goodness* and *love*, though the latter terms also have rich redemptive associations.

But we should not quarrel over words at this point. As I said in the previous section, the redemptive focus is not necessarily or always a part of the use of *hen* and *charis*. Certainly in Luke 2:52, where Jesus grows in *charis* with God and man, the term does not imply redemption from sin. *Hen* and *charis* simply refer to God's favor, and obviously his goodness and love are forms of his favor. So if God's goodness and love apply universally in some senses, the same is true of God's favor, his grace.

And of course, Scripture teaches us about God's grace even in some places where *hen* and *charis* are absent. Clearly, the parable of the prodigal son (Luke 15:11–32) is about grace, though the specific terms for *grace* are missing from the passage.

The use of *grace* here, rather than *goodness* or *love*, may be related to a tendency of some Reformed writers to restrict the definition of common grace to the beneficial effects of the gospel on society, or at least to place their major focus there. But the broader discussion of the concept, in the writings of John Calvin[26] and the later monumental treatment by Abraham Kuyper,[27] sees the concept more broadly.[28] John Murray defines *common grace* as *"every favour of whatever kind or degree, falling short of salvation, which this undeserving and sin-cursed world enjoys at the hand of God."*[29] The terms *favour, undeserving*, and *sin-cursed* show the relation that Murray sees between these common blessings and the grace of God.

Within this general definition, theologians have distinguished various aspects of common grace:

1. *God restrains sin*: God forbids fallen men from doing all the wrong they could do (Gen. 4:15; 11:6; 20:6; 2 Kings 19:27–28; 2 Thess. 2:7).

2. *God restrains his wrath*: God might have destroyed the human race after Adam and Eve ate the forbidden fruit. But instead he allowed human life to continue, promising redemption by the offspring of the woman (Gen. 3:15). And throughout history it is plain that God does not allow us to receive the full punishment we deserve (Matt. 19:8; Acts 17:30; Rom. 3:25). Scripture sometimes refers to this restraint as God's *patience* (*'erek 'af, makrothymia*). We find this important divine attribute in the exposition of the divine name in Exodus 34:6 and elsewhere (Num. 14:18; Ps. 86:5; Rom. 2:4).

3. *God gives temporal blessings to all*: These are the blessings I mentioned earlier under the categories of God's universal goodness and love, such as his provision of rain and sunshine for all creatures (Matt. 5:45; cf. Pss. 65:5–13; 104; 136:25; 145:9, 15–16).

4. *Unregenerate people do good*: In one sense, no one can do good apart from the saving grace of God. We have seen that man is depraved (Gen. 6:5; 8:21; Rom. 3:9–18). "Those who are in the flesh [instead of God's Spirit] cannot please God" (Rom. 8:8). *Good* here is good in the highest sense: good works done to the glory of God, obedient to the Word of God, motivated by faith and love for God.[30] But Scripture does attribute good, in lesser senses, to the unregenerate, such as King Jehu (2 Kings 10:29–31). Jesus said that even the wicked do good things to those who do good to them (Luke 6:33).

5. *Unregenerate people know truth*: In Scripture, knowledge is ethical, something that we engage in either obediently or disobediently (see chapters 29–32). So although all people know God (Rom. 1:21), they suppress that knowledge. Cf. 1 Cor. 1:18–2:15. But Jesus says the Pharisees, for all their disobedience, are able in some measure to teach correctly (Matt. 23:2–3).

6. *Unregenerate people experience some blessings of the Holy Spirit*: Murray puts it this way:

> Unregenerate people receive operations and influences of the Spirit in connection with the administration of the gospel, influences that result in experience of the

26. See *Institutes*, 2.2.16; 2.3.4; other references in Herman Kuiper, *Calvin on Common Grace* (Netherlands and Grand Rapids: Oosterbaan and Le Cointre, Goes, and Smitter Book Co., 1928).

27. Abraham Kuyper, *De Gemeene Gratie*, 3 vols. (Kampen: Kok, 1945), so far untranslated into English.

28. The narrower view can be found in Charles Hodge, *Systematic Theology* (Grand Rapids: Eerdmans, 1952), 2:654, and in A. A. Hodge, *Outlines of Theology* (Grand Rapids: Zondervan, 1972), chap. 28, sec. 13. John Murray discusses this issue in the excellent article "Common Grace," in *MCW*, 2:93–119.

29. Murray, "Common Grace," 96 (his italics). Much of what follows is dependent on Murray's treatment.

30. Cf. WCF 16.7.

power and glory of the gospel, yet influences which do not issue in genuine and lasting conversion and are finally withdrawn.[31]

Examples in the OT are Balaam (Num. 22:1–24:25) and King Saul (1 Sam. 10:9–11). In the NT is the example of Judas Iscariot, Jesus' betrayer, who nevertheless preached the coming of the kingdom, healed the sick, raised the dead, and drove out demons (Matt. 10:5–8). It is in this pattern that we should understand Hebrews 6:4–6:

> For it is impossible, in the case of those who have once been enlightened, who have tasted the heavenly gift, and have shared in the Holy Spirit, and have tasted the goodness of the word of God and the powers of the age to come, and then have fallen away, to restore them again to repentance, since they are crucifying once again the Son of God to their own harm and holding him up to contempt.

Sometimes, then, the blessings of God's common grace look very much like the blessings of salvation itself. But God sees the heart of the nonbeliever and knows that beneath his surface piety there is no authentic repentance or faith.

Covenant Love

The Hebrew term *hesed* is difficult to translate into English. The usual renderings have been "mercy" (KJV), "lovingkindness" (ASV), "steadfast love" (RSV, ESV). The NIV uses "kindness" and "love" in various contexts. In Exodus 34:6, the KJV translates it "goodness." The LXX translates by *eleos*, "mercy," which enters the NT in passages employing the *hesed* concept. *Eleos*, however, also seems to be used in a more general sense like our English word *mercy*: "the goodness of God when shown to those in misery."[32] I have often felt that *loyalty* and *faithfulness* are sometimes good terms for translating *hesed*, although those terms overlap considerably with *'emeth* and *'emunah*, which are often found together with *hesed*.

Despite the difficulty of translation, *hesed* represents one of the most important divine attributes, found in around 245 verses of Scripture. Over and over, God's people praise him, "for his *hesed* endures forever" (1 Chron. 16:34, 41; 2 Chron. 7:3, 6; 20:21; as a repeated refrain in Pss. 107; 118; 136). Like other attributes of goodness, *hesed* is part of the definitive exposition in Exodus 34:6 of the name of Yahweh.

The key to the meaning of *hesed* is the concept *covenant* that we have explored often in this book (see especially chapters 2–4), *Lord* being God's covenant name. In Deuteronomy 7:9, 12, Moses exhorts Israel:

> Know therefore that the LORD your God is God, the faithful God who keeps covenant and steadfast love with those who love him and keep his commandments, to a thousand generations . . . .

31. Murray, "Common Grace," 109.
32. *BRD*, 2:213.

And because you listen to these rules and keep and do them, the Lᴏʀᴅ your God will keep with you the covenant and the steadfast love that he swore to your fathers.

Love in the phrase "covenant and steadfast love" is *hesed*, in a Hebrew phrase that closely identifies *hesed* with the covenant itself. Similarly, in 1 Samuel 20:8, David says to Jonathan, "As for you, show kindness [*hesed*] to your servant, for you have brought him into a covenant with you before the Lᴏʀᴅ" (ɴɪᴠ).[33] Cf. also Neh. 1:5; 9:32. Notice also the close connection between *hesed* and God's promises to Jacob and Abraham, "as you have sworn to our fathers" (Mic. 7:20), and the connection of *hesed* with David (Ps. 18:50; Isa. 55:3).[34] God made covenants with Abraham (including Isaac and Jacob) and David that included promises of *hesed*.

We discussed in chapter 2 the suzerainty treaty form that underlies the biblical covenants:

1. Name of the Great King
2. Historical Prologue (past blessings of the great King toward the vassal)
3. Stipulations (laws, vassal's obligations)
   a. General: Exclusive loyalty
   b. Specific, detailed
4. Sanctions
5. Continuity

In this model, the general stipulation of 3a, exclusive loyalty, was sometimes called *love*.[35] Covenant loyalty may seem to us to be a "political" concept of love, not capturing the rich emotional meaning of the term. But of course, when we are covenantally loyal to God, we consecrate to him everything we are, loving him with heart, soul, strength, and mind (Deut. 6:5; Matt. 22:37)—including, of course, all our emotion. It is not surprising, then, that Scripture regards marriage as a covenant (Ezek. 16:8; Mal. 2:14) and that marriage is an image of the relation of God to his people (Hos. 1–3; Ezek. 16; Eph. 5:22–33).

Hesed in Scripture refers to this covenant loyalty, both in covenants on the human level (for example, David and Jonathan in 1 Samuel 20:8) and in covenants between God and man. But *hesed* also refers to *God's* covenant loyalty: the commitment of the Lord to the covenant relationship.

---

33. Sometimes *hesed* appears in the context of personal relations similar to that between David and Jonathan, without mention of a formal covenant. In 2 Samuel 10:2, "David thought, 'I will show kindness [*hesed*] to Hanun son of Nahash, just as his father showed kindness [*hesed*] to me'" (ɴɪᴠ). Cf. 1 Kings 2:7; 1 Chron. 19:2; 2 Chron. 24:22. If these loyalties and reciprocities are not formally covenantal, there is nevertheless a strong analogy between them and covenantal relationships.

34. Note how three times in Matthew, people cry out to Jesus as son of David to have "mercy" on them (Matt. 9:27; 15:22; 20:30).

35. Note that on this model, there is no opposition between love and law, since love is part of the law. Nor is there any antithesis between grace and law, since law is the vassal's response to the grace described in the historical prologue.

For God to show *hesed* is for him to keep the promises of his covenant. So Scripture often couples the term with *'emeth* ("truth," "faithfulness") (Gen. 24:27, 49; 47:29; Ex. 34:6; Josh. 2:14; Ps. 26:3; many other references) or *'emunah* ("faithfulness") (Deut. 7:9; Pss. 89:2; 92:2). These terms interpret one another, becoming together virtually one concept. *Hesed* is God's faithfulness to his covenant promise, the fact that he is true to his word, the fact that he will bless his people as he says he will. So to plead God's "mercies" (*hesed*) is to plead the promises of the covenant (Pss. 6:4; 31:16; 69:16).

Hesed may sometimes (rarely), however, refer to curses rather than blessings. "Kindness" may be a misleading translation of *hesed* in 1 Samuel 20:8. In context, David suggests that Jonathan's *hesed* might lead him to kill David, if indeed David has been unfaithful to him and to Saul.[36] Covenants in Scripture are often two-sided: they include blessings to those who obey the covenant law, curses to those who disobey. *Hesed* requires the fulfillment of both kinds of sanction.

Now, we saw earlier in this chapter that God's love sovereignly initiates his covenants. The word *ahabah* refers to this love in Deuteronomy 7:8. Typically, *hesed* (as in 7:9) refers not to the love of God that initiates covenants, but to a divine love that presupposes a covenant's present existence. God's *ahabah* creates the relation; his *hesed* fulfills and completes it.[37] So of the two terms, *ahabah* tends to be more closely equivalent to grace: it is not a response to human obedience.[38] But *hesed* does frequently presuppose human obedience to the covenant stipulations.[39] Note in Deuteronomy 7:9 that God keeps his covenant of *hesed* "with those who love him and keep his commandments, to a thousand generations." *Hesed* can be God's response to repentance (Deut. 4:30–31; Ps. 51:1).[40] Note also 2 Samuel 22:26 (cf. Ps. 18:25):

> With the merciful [*hasid*, from the *hesed* root] you show yourself merciful;
> with the blameless man [*tamim*] you show yourself blameless.

Psalm 25:10:

> All the paths of the LORD are steadfast love [*hesed*] and faithfulness,
> for those who keep his covenant and his testimonies.

Psalm 62:12:

> and . . . to you, O Lord, belongs steadfast love [*hesed*].

36. Compare 2 Timothy 2:11–13, which extols the faithfulness of the Lord, but which includes the warning, "If we deny him, he will also deny us" (v. 12).

37. Compare the relation of *ahabah* and *hesed* in Jeremiah 31:3: "I have loved you with an everlasting love [*ahabah*]; I have drawn you with loving-kindness [*hesed*]" (NIV).

38. In the suzerainty treaty formula, *ahabah* would be found at points 1 and 2.

39. This is the case in the quasi-covenantal uses of *hesed* within relationships on the human level, as we saw earlier in 2 Samuel 10:2 and other verses.

40. Psalm 103:3–4, where *hesed* follows forgiveness, healing, and redemption.

> For you will render to a man
> according to his work.

Hesed, then, is typically conditional, in a way that *ahabah* is not.

Typically, then, God's *hesed* is given to those who obey him. This fact should not, however, be used to justify a doctrine that we are saved by works. As we have seen, God's sovereign love (*ahabah*) initiates the covenant relation, and *hesed* is based on God's promises. As R. T. France puts it, "It is love (*ahabah*) that launches a marriage, but it is *hesed* that makes a go of it."[41] So God's love pervades our covenant life, from beginning to fulfillment.

The intensely covenantal context of *hesed* suggests that *hesed* might be limited to the covenant people of God, without the more general applications we have made of the concepts *goodness*, *love*, and *grace*. Even *hesed*, however, describes God's love to his creation as a whole. In Psalm 36, the psalmist contrasts the wickedness of men (vv. 1–4) with the *hesed* of God (vv. 5–10):

> Your steadfast love [*hesed*], O LORD, extends to the heavens,
> your faithfulness to the clouds.
> Your righteousness is like the mountains of God;
> your judgments are like the great deep;
> man and beast you save, O LORD.
>
> How precious is your steadfast love [*hesed*], O God!
> The children of mankind take refuge in the shadow of your wings.
> They feast on the abundance of your house,
> and you give them drink from the river of your delights.
> For with you is the fountain of life; in your light do we see light.
>
> Oh, continue your steadfast love [*hesed*] to those who know you,
> and your righteousness to the upright of heart!

This passage, like the other *hesed*-passages that we have examined, is full of covenantal language. Again we see the coupling of *hesed* and *'emunah* in verse 5, and with righteousness and justice in verse 6. The "house" of the Lord (v. 8) often refers to the temple in Scripture, or more broadly to the people of God. The pictures of feasting and drinking (v. 8) typically refer to God's appointed feasts and to the blessings of fellowship with the Lord. But here the reference is not merely to Israel, but to animals (v. 6) and "high and low among men" (v. 7 NIV).

I take it that since creation itself is covenantal (chapters 4, 10), a temple of God, and since the preservation of the earth is a promise of God's covenant to Noah (Gen. 8:21–22), his providential preservation of life is his *hesed*.[42] Or perhaps the psalmist is thinking

---

41. R. T. France, *The Living God* (London: Inter-Varsity Press, 1970), 90.
42. Thanks to Prof. Mark Futato for this suggestion. Of course, I take responsibility for the formulation here.

specifically of God's *hesed* to Israel, and he sees that *hesed* in God's providential preservation of life throughout the earth. In any case, God's blessings to all his creatures are *hesed*. So God loves Israel, but in loving Israel he loves the whole world. The purpose of God's covenant with Abraham, after all, was that in him all the nations would be blessed (Gen. 12:3). So there is common *hesed*, as there is common goodness, love, and grace.

Compassion

"Compassion" is perhaps the best general way to translate *racham, hamal, splanchnizomai, oiktiro,* and *metriopatheo*[43] as used in Scripture. *Hamal* is sometimes translated "pity" or "love," *raham* as "be merciful." These words indicate a sympathetic view of another's distress, motivating helpful action. *Raham* and *splanchnizomai* relate etymologically to the inner body, particularly to the womb. Perhaps for that reason they often have strongly emotional connotations. I will argue later that God does have emotions, although they are not physically based. Call them *attitudes* rather than *emotions* as you prefer, but these terms convey well the intensity of God's love and concern.

Raham is the *mercy* of both Exodus 33:19 and 34:6, which I have identified as significant expositions of the divine name. So "merciful and gracious" (34:6) (*gracious* is *hannun*, related to *hen*) resounds through Scripture as a basic characterization of God (see 2 Chron. 30:9; Neh. 9:17, 31; Pss. 86:15; 103:8; 111:4; 112:4; 145:8; Joel 2:13; Jonah 4:2). Since *compassion* expounds his covenant name, we are not surprised to find him showing compassion for the sake of his covenant (2 Kings 13:23).

God often shows compassion for his people after they have rebelled and he has judged their sin (as Deut. 13:17; 30:3). So compassion motivates him to forgive their sins (Ps. 78:38).

Matthew tells us that on several occasions Jesus was moved by compassion for people to heal and feed them (Matt. 9:6; 14:14; 15:32; 20:34). Readers familiar with the OT find in these references the compassion of Yahweh.

So like the other attributes of God that we have discussed, God's compassion is a model for ours: "But if anyone has the world's goods and sees his brother in need, yet closes his heart [*splanchna*] against him, how does God's love abide in him?" (1 John 3:17).

How wicked to be forgiven a great debt, and to have so little compassion as to demand small debts owed to us (Matt. 18:21–35). Compassion is a necessary ingredient of the love of Christ (see also 1 Peter 3:8; Jude 22).

Other Forms of God's Goodness

God's "gentleness," "meekness," or "humility" (*anaw, prautes, epieikeia*) is mentioned in 2 Samuel 22:36 and Psalm 18:35, and Scripture often commends this virtue in human beings: see Num. 12:3; Pss. 22:26 ("afflicted" in ESV); 25:9; 2 Cor. 10:1 (Paul mentions the "meekness and gentleness" of Christ to those who criticized him as meek in their presence, but bold when away); Gal. 5:22; 1 Thess. 2:7; 2 Tim. 2:24; Titus 3:2; James 3:17.

---

43. Used only once in Scripture, at Hebrews 5:2, describing Jesus' ability as man to sympathize with his people.

To refer to God as meek or gentle is a bit surprising, and this usage is, of course, rare. But there is some theological importance in this language, as well as importance for the Christian life. In Matthew 20:20–26, Jesus teaches the nature of leadership in his kingdom: not being served, but serving; being great by being a slave. And he presents himself as the example: "even as the Son of Man came not to be served but to serve, and to give his life as a ransom for many" (v. 28). As we saw in our discussion of love, the love of Christ is the standard of the Christian life. Now we see that such love involves humility, a self-abasement that does not destroy us but fulfills what God meant us to be.

There is something mysterious here, but as I grope for words, I conclude that Jesus' self-abasement reveals something about the very lordship of God.[44] For all his mighty power, he is a Lord who serves his people. Note the remarkable reference to his service in Luke 12:37. This divine service does not compromise his power or authority; rather, it is the form that his power takes. He makes all things work for good, not only his own good, but the good of *those who love him* (Rom. 8:28).

My perception is that gentleness and humility are among the virtues least practiced by Christians today. If God himself can serve his creatures, surely we, who can boast of nothing except the cross, should be able to serve without seeking constantly to maintain or improve our own status and reputation.

There are a few references to the "beauty" of the Lord (KJV) (Pss. 27:4; 90:17) (*no'am*), and others to the "beauty of holiness" (KJV) (1 Chron. 16:29; 2 Chron. 20:21; Ps. 29:2) (*hadarah*). God designed the temple to be a beautiful place indeed, and as we have seen, the temple is itself an image of the heavenly temple, the theophany itself. So God's image is found in aesthetic as well as ethical ways. The beauties of the earth and of human art bear significant analogy to the Creator of all. And of course, as with all other attributes, God's beauty serves as a norm for ours.[45]

God *rejoices* (*shamah*) in the creation (Ps. 104:31) and in people (*ratzah*, Ps. 149:4). We also often read about what does and does not *delight* him (*hafetz*). We will look again at this concept under the category of God's will, with which his *pleasure* is partly synonymous. But it is refreshing to know that joy is a divine attribute and that when the Spirit plants joy in us (Gal. 5:22), we are becoming more like God. We should not think of God, or the ideal Christian, as constantly disapproving or dour.

Peace (*shalom, eirene*) in Scripture refers mostly to a quality of human life given by God as a blessing of salvation. But by implication it is certainly also a divine attribute. God is called the "God of peace" in Romans 15:33; 16:20; 2 Corinthians 13:11; and Hebrews 13:20. In chapter 17, we noted the compound name *Yahweh Shalom* in Judges 6:24: "The LORD Is Peace." The Messiah is Prince of Peace in Isaiah 9:6, and "of the increase of his government and of peace there will be no end" (v. 7).

Peace is a very common term in Scripture. "Peace be to you" (Judg. 6:23; 19:20; Ps. 122:8; Luke 10:5; 24:36) is the common Hebrew greeting and "go in peace" the common

44. And also about the relationships between the persons of the Trinity, as we will see later.

45. *How* it serves as a norm is a difficult question. But at least, insofar as art conveys a "message," that message ought to be consistent with God's revelation.

farewell (Luke 8:48). Theologically, it represents the fullness of the blessings of salvation: peace as opposed to war, but also completeness, wholeness, prosperity. The Lord promises peace to his redeemed people (Pss. 4:8; 29:11; 37:11; 119:165; Isa. 26:3; Luke 2:14; John 14:27; Rom. 5:1). The gospel is the message of peace (Acts 10:36). So the Aaronic benediction pronounces the blessing of peace upon God's people (Num. 6:26), and the apostolic greetings and benedictions of the NT regularly include "grace and peace" or "grace, mercy, and peace" (Rom. 1:7; 2 Cor. 1:2; Gal. 6:16). These phrases may attempt to bring together the OT emphasis on peace with the NT emphasis on grace.

Peace comes from God alone, since the fall has made us prone to wars and fightings (James 4:1–3). Peace, as all other blessings of salvation, makes us like God. So like all other blessings of salvation and Christian virtues, peace among men is the reflection of God's own nature; it is a divine attribute. God is completely at peace with himself. We often experience struggles between contradictory impulses within us. God, on the contrary, is completely in harmony with himself. His three persons glorify and serve one another willingly and cheerfully. So he is "whole," "well," and "prosperous," blessed, happy.

Blessedness occurs in expressions such as "God be blessed" (*eulogetos*, Rom. 1:25; 9:5; 2 Cor. 1:3; etc.), and *blessed* (*makarios*) is a divine attribute in 1 Timothy 1:11 and 6:15. We can easily understand what it means for God to bless us, namely, to give us benefits. But what does it mean for us to bless God?

Although as we will see God has no needs, nevertheless creation benefits him by displaying his attributes (grace, goodness, wisdom, power, and so on), glorifying his name (we recall that he does his mighty works so that people will know that he is Lord), eliciting the praises of his creatures. *Eulogetos* can be translated "praised," so to bless God is to praise him. In Psalm 103:1, the ESV translates *barak* as "bless," the LXX "*eulogeo*," the NIV "praise."

But there may be more to God's blessedness than merely the praises of his creatures. *Makarios* is often found in *beatitudes*: teaching beginning with "blessed is"—e.g., Ps. 1:1; Matt. 5:3–11; James 1:12; Rev. 14:13. It is sometimes translated "happy," though in modern English *happy* tends to refer to mere emotional satisfaction. Happiness in Aristotle, for example, is overall good fortune, a good life in every sense. The beatitudes of Scripture indicate the components of such happiness, as well as the happiness that is a consequence of such behavior.

God is supremely blessed because he is the full embodiment, indeed the archetype, of the virtues described in the beatitudes and elsewhere in Scripture. Those virtues bring about the very best life possible, including supreme satisfaction, and that satisfaction belongs to God.

Of course God is grieved, as we will see, by the works of Satan and human sin. But as he sees the end from the beginning, he is able to see the course of history in its full context, from its widest perspective. So although he grieves about particular evils, he is simultaneously able to rejoice that his overall plan is wonderful, that it achieves all his purposes.

So God's blessedness shows us that the greatest possible happiness is to be found only by imaging the blessedness of God himself. We can see this image perfectly in the embodied life of Jesus.

Appropriately, we began this chapter with *goodness/perfection* and we now come full circle, ending with *blessedness*, that quality of life possessed by One who embodies all perfections. What a wonderful God we have!

Key Terms
Names of God
Images of God
Attributes of God
Necessary attributes
Relative attributes
Communicable attributes
Incommunicable attributes
Good
Moral goodness
Nonmoral goodness
Teleological goodness
Love
Benevolence
Beneficence
Complacency
Persuasive
Coercive
Grace
Common grace
Covenant love (*hesed*)
Compassion
Gentleness
Peace
Blessedness

Study Questions
1. "So love is not less fundamental to God's nature than his power, aseity, or eternity." Explain; evaluate.
2. What is "the *Euthyphro* problem"? Respond to it.
3. To whom is God good? Are there differences in the goodness that God shows to different recipients? Discuss.
4. List the chief Greek terms for *love* in Scripture, and show how these differ from one another.
5. Whom does God love? Discuss the differences in the love that God shows to different recipients.
6. Should we ever say "God loves you" to a group containing non-Christians? Discuss.

7. Can we imitate the love that Jesus showed us in the cross? How? Explain.

8. Does God's love ever coerce people into the kingdom? Explain.

9. "So all the blessings of God come to us by God's sovereign grace." Defend this statement from Scripture.

10. Distinguish different aspects of common grace.

11. Discuss the nature of *hesed*. To whom does God show *hesed*?

12. "There is something mysterious here, but as I grope for words, I conclude that Jesus' self-abasement reveals something about the very lordship of God." What does it reveal?

Memory Verses

Ps. 25:10: All the paths of the LORD are steadfast love and faithfulness, for those who keep his covenant and his testimonies.

Ps. 145:9: The LORD is good to all, and his mercy is over all that he has made.

John 3:16: For God so loved the world, that he gave his only Son, that whoever believes in him should not perish but have eternal life.

Eph. 2:8–9: For by grace you have been saved through faith. And this is not your own doing; it is the gift of God, not a result of works, so that no one may boast.

Eph. 3:17–19: That Christ may dwell in your hearts through faith—that you, being rooted and grounded in love, may have strength to comprehend with all the saints what is the breadth and length and height and depth, and to know the love of Christ that surpasses knowledge, that you may be filled with all the fullness of God.

Resources for Further Study

Kuiper, Herman. *Calvin on Common Grace*. Netherlands and Grand Rapids: Oosterbaan and Le Cointre, Goes, and Smitter Book Co., 1928.

Lewis, C. S. *The Four Loves*. London: Geoffrey Bles, 1960.

Murray, John. "Common Grace." In *MCW*, 2:93–119.

CHAPTER 13

GOD'S ATTRIBUTES: RIGHTEOUSNESS AND HOLINESS

IN THIS CHAPTER, we continue our discussion of God's attributes of goodness: his attributes in the general sphere of ethics. God's righteousness is a form of his goodness. But righteousness raises different issues and requires us to explore other themes. And then our consideration of both goodness and righteousness will force us to ask some serious questions about the wrath of God, his jealousy, even his hatred.

If you review the chart of the attributes hesitantly proposed in chapter 12, you will note that when we move from goodness to righteousness, we are moving from a *control* cell to an *authority* cell. The main idea of divine righteousness is that God acts according to a perfect internal standard of right and wrong. All his actions are within the limits (if we can use that term reverently) of that standard. So righteousness is the form, the structure of God's goodness, and his goodness is the concrete, active embodiment of his righteousness.

The chart, however, exaggerates the difference between goodness and righteousness, part of the reason for my hesitation in proposing the chart. To say that God is good implies that God is righteous. So goodness includes righteousness, rather than being separate from it. And Scripture often presents God's righteousness, as we will see, not merely as an authoritative standard, but as an active power bringing salvation. In other words, righteousness, like goodness, can itself be an active, dynamic benevolence, not just the static structure of benevolence. Recall also from the previous chapter that God's goodness, like his righteousness, is an authoritative standard for the corresponding human virtues. Love also, particularly as we see it in Christ, is a standard for our conduct, indeed, the very mark of the Christian (John 13:34–35). So goodness and righteousness are not separable in God's actual being and action. Both describe God's dynamic actions to save his people, and both serve as standards of conduct.

We should remind ourselves again that all these divine attributes are just different ways of describing a *person*. When this person does mighty works in our history and experience, all his attributes come with him. Whatever he does, he simultaneously reveals his benevolence and his authoritative standards.

The Hebrew *tzedeq* and the Greek *dikaiosune* are translated "righteousness," "rightness," "justice," "lawfulness." The terms are therefore in the forensic sphere, the sphere of law and the courtroom, the sphere in which one advocates or defends behavior. This is why I put *righteousness* where I did in the chart of chapter 12. Because God's covenant contains law (the *stipulations*, chapter 2), God's relation to us inevitably has a forensic side. Our God makes demands of us; he expects us to act according to his standards, and therefore to be righteous. Liberal theologians have sometimes sought to eliminate law from this relationship, thinking that it conflicts with the biblical emphasis on love. But law and righteousness permeate the Scriptures, and as we have seen, love itself requires us to keep God's commandments (as 1 John 5:3).

Note that the same terms in the original language can be translated either "righteousness" or "justice." In English there is some difference between these two terms. *Righteousness* comes from a German root (*Recht*), *justice* from a Latin one (*justitia*). In English, *right* and *righteous* tend to apply more often to individuals, *just* and *justice* to institutions, societies, and rulers—but that generalization has many exceptions. Both can refer either to persons or to actions.[1] The Hebrew and Greek terms can include any of these nuances, depending on the context. The Hebrew *mishpat*, "judgment," however, can sometimes be translated "justice," rarely if ever "righteousness."

The older theologians made a number of distinctions within God's righteousness that can be presented in a Ramist[2] outline:

1. Internal (God's moral excellence)

2. External (the rectitude of his conduct)
   a. rectoral or legislative (promulgating just laws for his creatures)
   b. distributive (administering rewards and punishments)
       i. remunerative (distribution of reward)
       ii. retributive (distribution of punishment)

Scripture nowhere enumerates these distinctions in so many words, and its actual way of presenting God's righteousness is very different from this chart, as we will see. Still, this outline does enumerate a number of genuinely biblical uses of the concept. My own triadic approach would look more like this:

1. Existential (God's moral excellence, the quality of his own character and actions) (1 on the Ramist outline)

---

1. In general, ethical predications pertain to persons, actions, and attitudes. I'm not aware of places in Scripture where *righteousness* pertains to attitudes.

2. Named for Petrus Ramus (1515–72), an influential French Protestant philosopher. He believed that the proper method in studying a subject was to divide that subject into two parts, and each of them into two parts, until one reaches the supposedly ultimate elements of the subject matter. Of course, we now know that he was incorrect. The proper method in theology is not to divide everything into twos, but rather into threes!

2. Normative (God's own standards for himself and creation) (includes but goes beyond 2a on the Ramist outline)
3. Situational (God's actions, by which he makes his righteousness prevail) (includes 2b on the Ramist outline)[3]

Number 1 essentially equates God's righteousness with his goodness, so I will not add further discussion of it here, though I will be stressing that 2 and 3 arise from God's own character. The other two categories also overlap with goodness, but in those areas I would like to present more biblical data. See fig. 13.1.

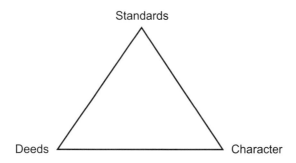

Fig. 13.1. God's Righteous Standards

God reveals his standards to us in his deeds and personal self-revelation, but most explicitly in his revealed law. His law is not arbitrary, but is based on his own nature. The moral law is not something above him, that has authority over him. Nor is it something that he has created, as though (as nominalism would have it) he could change it at will (making adultery to be virtuous, for example). Rather, his moral standard is simply himself, his person, his nature. His acts are righteous because he is a righteous God. Righteousness, therefore, is his desire, his pleasure. The standard of our moral behavior is not an abstract concept, but an infinite person, God himself.

Of course, God has certain rights that we do not have: the right to take human life as he sees fit, the right to act autonomously without honoring someone higher than himself, and so on. But for the most part, his law to us calls us to imitate his own character and conduct. He made us in his image, to be like him. When we sinned in Adam, he called us back to imitate him. The main principle of the law of Moses is: "You shall be holy, for I the LORD your God am holy" (Lev. 19:2). The Ten Commandments call Israel to a lifestyle that is a suitable response to God's great deliverance: "I

---

3. This, like number 2, may go beyond the Ramist chart, for it would include necessary acts of God, acts of God within his Trinitarian self-existence, which don't refer to the creation. But this area is mysterious, and I have no biblical guidance here as to what sorts of acts these might be. Still, I believe that God in his essence is active, and that he always acts righteously. Those statements would be true of his eternal existence as well as of his actions in time.

am the LORD your God, who brought you out of the land of Egypt, out of the house of slavery" (Ex. 20:2). So as God worked six days and rested on the Sabbath, Israel is to do the same (vv. 8–11). As God gave the Israelites rest from their bondage, they are to give rest to their families, servants, and animals (Deut. 5:15). The same principle exists in the NT. Jesus tells his disciples, "You therefore must be perfect, as your heavenly Father is perfect" (Matt. 5:48), and Peter applies Leviticus 19:2 directly to the church in 1 Peter 1:15–16.

Imitating God implies imitating Christ.[4] The Christian life arises from our renewal in the image of Christ (Eph. 4:22–24; Col. 3:10). As we have seen, this imitation of God includes loving one another as Christ loved us (John 13:34–35; 15:12; Eph. 5:2; 1 John 4:10–11).

So the righteousness that God expects from us is essentially to image his own ethical character, his love, his holiness, his own righteousness.

We can find the basic standards of God's righteousness, making allowance for those areas of discontinuity between God's rights and our own, in the laws of Scripture. What he commands of us is what he himself is and does. God seeks his own glory, so he forbids us to worship other gods (Ex. 20:3), to make idols (vv. 4–6), or to misuse his name (v. 7). He has chosen to act in a historical pattern of work and rest, so he calls us to imitate that (vv. 8–11). He makes covenants and respects their terms, including structures of authority (v. 12). He loves life (v. 13) and fidelity (v. 14). He demands respect for his ownership of the world and for the secondary ownership that he confers upon us (v. 15). He loves truth (v. 16) and purity of heart (v. 17). The other laws in Scripture spell out the meanings of the Ten Commandments more fully and apply them to various specific situations. God intended some of those secondary laws, like the requirements of animal sacrifice, for the specific situation existing before the coming of Christ. They are no longer literally binding after the final sacrifice of Jesus. But they continue to instruct us about God's character, about what things are of great concern to him.

The penalties given in the laws also teach us about God's righteousness. The chief principle governing them is set forth in Obadiah 15:

> As you have done, it shall be done to you;
>   your deeds shall return on your own head.

Cf. Jer. 50:29; Joel 3:4, 7; Hab. 2:8; and the "law of talion," "eye for eye, tooth for tooth" (Ex. 21:24).[5] The death penalty for murder is similar: "Whoever sheds the blood of man, by man shall his blood be shed" (Gen. 9:6). See also Matt. 7:2; Rev. 16:6; 18:6–7.

---

4. Notice how virtually everything we say about God can be said of Christ as well. So the biblical doctrine of God supplies pervasive and comprehensive proof of the deity of Christ. I will take note of this fact in chapter 21, but the reader should notice these references as we go along and let the depth of Scripture's testimony to the deity of Christ overwhelm him.

5. The law of talion was never intended as an excuse for personal vengeance, but was, as Vern Poythress puts it, "a directive to judges making decisions regarding penalties in cases of injury." See Poythress, *The Shadow of Christ in the Law of Moses* (Brentwood, TN: Wolgemuth and Hyatt, 1991), 123, available at http://www.frame

One theme of the wisdom of God in Proverbs is that the wicked fall into the snares they set for the righteous:[6]

> But these men lie in wait for their own blood;
>> they set an ambush for their own lives.
> Such are the ways of everyone who is greedy for unjust gain;
>> it takes away the life of its possessors. (Prov. 1:18–19)

> Whoever digs a pit will fall into it,
>> and a stone will come back on him who starts it rolling. (Prov. 26:27)[7]

Cf. Pss. 35:8; 141:10; Prov. 1:31; 10:16; 11:8; 28:10; 29:6. There is a "poetic justice" in God's providence. It doesn't happen with mechanical regularity. At times the wicked prosper and the righteous seem forsaken. But the schemes of the wicked, in the end, will be seen to have heaped up judgment for the wicked themselves. As they have done, it will be done to them. On the last day, God will right all wrongs, and as we will see in the next chapter, there will be no more complaints against his justice.

So righteousness is a kind of elemental fairness. As we sow, so shall we reap. As we want others to do to us, we should do to them. This principle sums up "the Law and the Prophets" (Matt. 7:12).[8]

God's own judgments are fair in the most perfect way. In pleading for his nephew Lot, Abraham asks rhetorically, "Shall not the Judge of all the earth do what is just?" (Gen. 18:25). The Song of Moses proclaims:

> The Rock, his work is perfect,
>> for all his ways are justice.
> A God of faithfulness and without iniquity,
>> just and upright is he. (Deut. 32:4; cf. Ps. 92:15)

> The Lord is righteous in all his ways
>> and kind in all his works. (Ps. 145:17)

All his judgments are righteous (Pss. 9:8; 50:4–6; 51:4; 96:10, 13; 98:9), as is his law, the standard by which his judgments are made (Deut. 4:8; Pss. 19:7–9; 119:138, 142; Isa. 42:21). The fact that he judges all things in heaven and earth implies that his standards are the highest standards of righteousness.

-poythress.org. This book is an excellent analysis of biblical law, to which I am indebted for much of the information in this discussion.

6. One can hardly think about this principle today without reference to the cartoon figure Wile E. Coyote, whose schemes to trap the Road Runner inevitably backfire on him.

7. Or, as we say today, "what goes around, comes around."

8. This passage, often called the *Golden Rule*, is therefore equivalent to the "two greatest commandments of the law," the commandments to love God and to love our neighbor as ourselves. Jesus teaches that these, too, sum up the law (Matt. 22:37–40).

God's Righteous Deeds

We may well expect, then, when we move from the normative to the situational perspective, that God's actions in history will apply his righteous standards and ensure their triumph. Indeed, that is the case, as indicated in the passages I quoted on God's judgment. But under the situational perspective we note something else as well, which gives us a much richer picture of God's righteousness.

Righteousness in Scripture is not only a standard governing conduct, but also a means of salvation. In 1 Samuel 12:6–11, Samuel enumerates God's "righteous deeds" (v. 7) as his deliverances, both from Egypt and during the time of the judges. This use of *righteous* is a bit surprising. We can understand how the deliverance of God's people from Egypt (the OT paradigm of redemption) is an act of God's grace, or his love. And certainly this deliverance is also righteous, in the sense that it is according to his perfect standards ("you have kept your promise, for you are righteous," Neh. 9:8). But *how* does this deliverance accord with God's standards? Israel is a sinful, disobedient people. Surely she doesn't *deserve* to be saved. Indeed, as we saw in chapter 11, God doesn't choose Israel because of her numbers or her righteousness. So why should this deliverance be evidence of God's *righteousness* in particular? Does it not indeed pose a problem for God's righteousness, calling it into question?

In Psalm 9:7–8, the psalmist reflects on God's rule:

> But the LORD sits enthroned forever;
>   he has established his throne for justice,
> and he judges the world with righteousness;
>   he judges the peoples with uprightness.

Then he adds:

> The LORD is a stronghold for the oppressed,
>   a stronghold in times of trouble. (Ps. 9:9)

Here we want to ask: does verse 9 simply change the subject, moving from the forensic sphere to that of divine protection? Or is there a connection between these topics?

Even more striking is Isaiah 46:12–13:

> Listen to me, you stubborn of heart,
>   you who are far from righteousness:
> I bring near my righteousness; it is not far off,
>   and my salvation will not delay;
> I will put salvation in Zion,
>   for Israel my glory.

Here God brings his righteousness and his salvation to bear on Israel in the same event. He saves Israel by bringing his righteousness near. And he does this in a context that fully acknowledges Israel's unrighteousness. Righteousness and salvation are parallel concepts also in Psalms 40:10; 85:9–10; 98:2–3; Isaiah 45:8; 51:5.

And God's righteousness even brings forgiveness of sins. We learn in 1 John 1:9, "If we confess our sins, he is faithful *and just* to forgive us our sins and to cleanse us from all unrighteousness." Again, forgiveness comes through God's righteousness. But why righteousness, rather than grace or love, which would seem more appropriate here?

The background of this usage can be found in the biblical teaching that God rescues the righteous from their oppressors. In Psalm 34:15–22, we read:

> The eyes of the LORD are toward the righteous
>> and his ears toward their cry.
> The face of the LORD is against those who do evil,
>> to cut off the memory of them from the earth.
> When the righteous cry for help, the LORD hears
>> and delivers them out of all their troubles.
> The LORD is near to the brokenhearted
>> and saves the crushed in spirit.
>
> Many are the afflictions of the righteous,
>> but the LORD delivers him out of them all.
> He keeps all his bones;
>> not one of them is broken.
> Affliction will slay the wicked,
>> and those who hate the righteous will be condemned.
> The LORD redeems the life of his servants;
>> none of those who take refuge in him will be condemned.

The "righteous" here are not sinlessly perfect, but they are *tamim* ("relatively perfect," "upright"). Further, they are "in the right" over against their enemies who would seek to destroy them. But they cannot rescue themselves, so they cry out to God. God then acts to vindicate the cause of the righteous over against the wicked. These divine acts are not only acts of goodness, grace, and love; they are also the righteousness of God.

In other passages, those here called "righteous" are called "afflicted," "oppressed," "weak," "poor," or "needy." In Psalm 72:1–4, the writer prays for the messianic King:

> Give the king your justice, O God,
>> and your righteousness to the royal son!
> May he judge your people with righteousness,
>> and your poor with justice!
> Let the mountains bear prosperity for the people,
>> and the hills, in righteousness!
> May he defend the cause of the poor of the people,
>> give deliverance to the children of the needy,
>> and crush the oppressor!

Cf. Pss. 10:14; 35:10; 68:5; 82:3; 113:7; 140:12; 146:7–9; Jer. 22:16. Note the emphasis on righteousness and the King's righteous judgment for the afflicted over against their oppressors. In Psalm 82:3–4, God berates human rulers because they show partiality to the wicked. He tells them:

> Give justice to the weak and the fatherless;
>   maintain the right of the afflicted and the destitute.
> Rescue the weak and the needy;
>   deliver them from the hand of the wicked.

The Messiah obeys the Lord:

> He shall not judge by what his eyes see,
>   or decide disputes by what his ears hear,
> but with righteousness he shall judge the poor,
>   and decide with equity for the meek of the earth;
> and he shall strike the earth with the rod of his mouth,
>   and with the breath of his lips he shall kill the wicked.
> Righteousness shall be the belt of his waist,
>   and faithfulness the belt of his loins. (Isa. 11:3b–5; cf. Pss. 7:6–13, 17; 143:1–4, 11)

When Jesus the Messiah comes into the world, his coming is good news for the poor, for he is to exalt the lowly and bring down the proud (Isa. 40:4; Luke 1:51–53;[9] 4:18–19).

God's righteousness saves the afflicted from their powerful oppressors. The Lord is particularly concerned with those who have the least power in society: widows, orphans, and aliens. In Exodus 22:22, God commands, " You shall not mistreat any widow or fatherless child." Deuteronomy 10:18 says of God, "He executes justice for the fatherless and the widow, and loves the sojourner, giving him food and clothing."[10] Israel is to be compassionate toward them:

> When you reap your harvest in your field and forget a sheaf in the field, you shall not go back to get it. It shall be for the sojourner, the fatherless, and the widow, that the LORD your God may bless you in all the work of your hands. (Deut. 24:19; cf. 26:12–13)

So Isaiah 1:17:

> Learn to do good;
> seek justice,
>   correct oppression;

---

9. Compare the Song of Hannah, 1 Samuel 2, especially verses 3–8.

10. In modern society, the clearest application of this principle is to the unborn, who have no voice, and who are being murdered by the millions every year.

bring justice to the fatherless,
 plead the widow's cause.

Lacking earthly power, opposed by those rulers who should be defending them, the afflicted turn to the Lord:

"Because the poor are plundered, because the needy groan,
 I will now arise," says the Lord;
 "I will place him in the safety for which he longs." (Ps. 12:5)

As for me, I am poor and needy,
 but the Lord takes thought for me.
You are my help and my deliverer;
 do not delay, O my God! (Ps. 40:17)

We are reminded of the situation of the nation Israel as a whole, before the exodus. They were enslaved, in severe pain and suffering, oppressed by the most powerful ruler of the time. They had no human hope of escaping that oppression. So they cried out to the Lord, who heard them and delivered them, triumphing over Pharaoh, his soldiers, and his gods. This salvation was not only grace, but also righteousness. God vindicated his righteous people against their wicked oppressors.

But later in their history, some Israelites themselves became oppressors. Against them, God intervened to save his afflicted ones, who could do nothing but cry out to him for mercy. In time, the oppressors grew more numerous, the afflicted less so. But the afflicted were the true *remnant* (see chapter 11), God's elect within the larger nation.

Although their cause is righteous, compared to that of their oppressors, God delivers them, not because of their own good works, but because they cry to God for mercy. They are therefore justified by faith in God's righteousness, not their own. In Isaiah 45:24, they confess, "Only in the Lord, it shall be said of me, are righteousness and strength; to him shall come and be ashamed all who were incensed against him."

Liberation theology has made much of this biblical theme, saying that God is "on the side of the poor."[11] But liberation theologians tend to take *poor* in a largely economic sense. Certainly it is true that in Scripture widows, orphans, and aliens tend to be economically destitute. It is also true that the "oppression" condemned in Scripture was often economic oppression. Scripture calls God's people in many ways to care for the poor.[12]

---

11. As Gustavo Gutierrez, *A Theology of Liberation* (Maryknoll, NY: Orbis, 1973).
12. This was a central concern of the apostles, for example (Acts 6:1–4; Gal. 2:10), and of the early church as a whole (Acts 2:44–45; 4:32–35). The OT mandated care for the poor through (1) protection of private property (Ex. 20:15; 22:1–15) (not abolition, as in the Marxist agendas of liberation theologians), (2) allowing the poor to glean in the fields (Lev. 19:9–10; Deut. 24:19–22), (3) immediate payment of wages (Lev. 19:13), (4) willing, compassionate lending (Ex. 22:25–27; Deut. 15:7–11), (5) fairness in economic dealings (Ex. 22:22–24), (6) impartiality in the courts (Ex. 23:6–9), (7) Hebrew "slavery"—actually a kind of "household service" for those who cannot pay

But God doesn't deliver people merely because they have a low level of income or wealth. The "sluggards" of Proverbs 6:6, 9; 10:26; 13:4; 20:4; 26:16, the lazy people who won't work for their living, are not the recipients of God's deliverance. And of course, God delivers some who are economically wealthy: Abraham, Moses, David.[13] God delivers "the poor" because (1) they are unjustly oppressed, whether economically or otherwise, and (2) they turn to God: they trust and hope in God alone.

God tells judges not to be on the side of the poor, but to be impartial:

> You shall do no injustice in court. You shall not be partial to the poor or defer to the great, but in righteousness shall you judge your neighbor. (Lev. 19:15; cf. Deut. 1:16–17; 16:18–20; 25:1)

But of course, the problem in Israel was not that judges tended to favor the poor, but that they tended to favor the rich. So God emphasizes justice to the poor:

> You shall not pervert the justice due to your poor in his lawsuit. Keep far from a false charge, and do not kill the innocent and righteous, for I will not acquit the wicked. (Ex. 23:6–7)

God's own impartial justice, which does not respect persons (Rom. 2:11; Eph. 6:9; Col. 3:25; 1 Peter 1:17), will certainly "give justice to his elect, who cry out to him day and night" (Luke 18:7).

So God's righteous salvation is covenantal, given to the elect remnant who trust in his promises. Scripture never suggests that God's righteousness requires an equal distribution of wealth in society, as on the Marxist and liberationist accounts. Rather, it requires equality of all people before the law and fairness in our dealings with one another.

God's righteousness as the salvation of the afflicted is the background of Paul's doctrine of justification. In Romans 1:17, Paul indicates why he is "not ashamed of the gospel":

> For in it the righteousness of God is revealed from faith for faith, as it is written, "The righteous shall live by faith."

To Martin Luther, this verse posed a problem. As a Roman Catholic monk, he was accustomed to thinking of God's righteousness only as the divine standard of judgment. God's righteousness, therefore, was a fearsome thing. How could the revelation of God's righteousness be "good news" (*gospel*)? Even more perplexing, how could it be "the power of God for salvation to everyone who believes" (Rom. 1:16)? Luther

---

their debts (Ex. 21:1–11; Lev. 25:39–55; Deut. 15:12–18), (8) giving rest to servants on the Sabbath (Ex. 20:10; 23:12), (9) allowing the poor to take freely from the fields during the sabbatical year (Ex. 23:10–11; Lev. 25:1–7), (10) remitting debts in the sabbatical year (Deut. 15:1–6), (11) returning sold property in the year of Jubilee (Lev. 25:13–17).

13. David identifies himself as "poor and needy" in Psalm 40:17. David endured suffering, indeed oppression, at different times through his life, but that oppression never, so far as we know, was focused on his material wealth.

eventually concluded that God's *righteousness* here is not the righteousness by which he judges men on the last day, but the righteousness he *gives* us, *imputes* to us in this life, by grace through faith. This meaning is clear in chapter 3:

> But now the righteousness of God has been manifested apart from the law, although the Law and the Prophets bear witness to it—the righteousness of God through faith in Jesus Christ for all who believe. (Rom. 3:21–22a)

As our sin and condemnation came through the one man Adam, so our righteousness, justification, and life come through the one man Jesus (Rom. 5:12–19). His righteousness comes not through our works, but only through God's free gift, his grace (3:24). Christ "became to us . . . righteousness" (1 Cor. 1:30). And:

> For our sake he made him to be sin who knew no sin, so that in him we might become the righteousness of God. (2 Cor. 5:21)

Though this gift of righteousness is free to us, it is not free to God. An awful price has been paid, the sacrifice of God's only Son,

> whom God put forward as a propitiation by his blood, to be received by faith. This was to show God's righteousness, because in his divine forbearance he had passed over former sins. It was to show his righteousness at the present time, so that he might be just and the justifier of the one who has faith in Jesus. (Rom. 3:25–26)

So we see now why the gospel of Christ is a revelation of God's *righteousness*, not only of his goodness, grace, and love. The gospel tells us what God has done so that he can declare us righteous, not because of our works, but because of the sacrifice of Christ.

But it also vindicates God's own righteousness (Rom. 3:26). How could God declare sinners to be righteous? Is this not precisely a perversion of justice, that he should "clear the guilty"? Is that not, indeed, a violation of his own name (Ex. 34:7)? But the perfect sacrifice of Jesus is the basis of our righteousness, and when God clears our guilt for Jesus' sake, he is acting justly. So through Christ, God is able both to justify the ungodly (us) and to defend himself against any charge of injustice.

So like the salvation of the poor and needy in the OT, our salvation in Christ is by God's *righteousness*. Jesus himself is the ultimate remnant, the poor and needy one, oppressed, crying out to God alone. Though Father and Son are estranged for a time, God hears his prayer and raises him gloriously from the dead. And when God raises Jesus, he raises us in him (Rom. 6:3–14).

Now we understand why God is not only faithful, but also just, to forgive our sins (1 John 1:9). And we understand that the righteousness of God is not only law, but also gospel. It is not only a standard of conduct, but the power of God unto salvation.

As with God's goodness, love, and grace, therefore, God's righteousness has both general and particular aspects. In the sense of fairness, God treats all creatures in righteousness. He never violates his standards of conduct. But in the active redemptive sense, God's righteousness saves only those who are righteous by faith.

And as we will see with God's holiness, his righteousness is both fearsome and loving, both a forbidding transcendence and a redemptive immanence.

God's Jealousy

Now I will be considering some divine attributes that, in the view of some, conflict with God's goodness, love, grace, and righteousness. We will be looking at God's jealousy, hatred, and wrath.

Jealousy (Heb. *qanna'*, Gk. *zelos*) is a passionate zeal to guard the exclusiveness of a marriage relationship, leading to anger against an unfaithful spouse. In Numbers 5:11–31, Moses describes a "grain offering of jealousy" (v. 15) and a test of fidelity to be made when a man suspects his wife of unfaithfulness. To my knowledge, Scripture never presents jealousy as a negative trait. It may seem so in the KJV translation of Song of Solomon 8:6 ("jealousy is cruel as the grave"), but that text takes on a different appearance in the more accurate ESV rendering. In context, the ESV reads:

> For love is strong as death,
>   jealousy is fierce as the grave.
> Its flashes are flashes of fire,
>   the very flame of the LORD. (Song 8:6)

Here, fiery jealousy is part of love, the prerogative of love that is strong as death. The writer compares it to that of the Lord. It is the proper attitude of a man toward his wife (cf. also Prov. 6:34). It is entirely right for him to be zealous for her purity and for the exclusiveness of her love to him. *Qanah* can also be used (as *jealousy* in modern English) for the sin of envy (Gen. 26:14; 30:1; Ps. 37:1), but Scripture treats jealousy and envy as distinct concepts.

Jealousy is an important attribute of God:

> You shall not make for yourself a carved image, or any likeness of anything that is in heaven above, or that is in the earth beneath, or that is in the water under the earth. You shall not bow down to them or serve them, for I the LORD your God am a jealous God, visiting the iniquity of the fathers on the children to the third and the fourth generation of those who hate me, but showing steadfast love to thousands of those who love me and keep my commandments. (Ex. 20:4–6; cf. Deut. 5:8–10)

The reason for the prohibition of idolatry (and possibly for the first commandment as well) is that God is jealous. God's jealousy is always directed against idolatry in Scripture. (See Deut. 32:16, 21; Josh. 24:19–20.) But note the close connection between the divine jealousy and his name, "the LORD your God." In Exodus 34:14, Yahweh says, "For you shall worship no other god, for the LORD, whose name is Jealous, is a jealous

God." Seven verses earlier (v. 7), in what I have argued is a definitive exposition of the name *Yahweh*, we find the same jealousy-language as in 20:5:

> [Yahweh] will by no means clear the guilty, visiting the iniquity of the fathers on the children and the children's children, to the third and the fourth generation.

God's jealousy is *for* his great name in Ezekiel 39:25. For his name's sake he will not give his glory to another (Isa. 42:8; 48:11).

So jealousy is an attribute of God, a description of the divine nature. By nature, he deserves and demands exclusive worship and allegiance.

In the Bible's emphasis on God's jealousy, we see that there is a profound analogy between God's covenant and the marriage relation. Idolatry is like adultery. The same attitude of covenant disloyalty lies behind both sins. Husbands should love their wives as Christ loves the church (Eph. 5:25). That love is exclusive in both cases. So God's jealousy clearly manifests his lordship.

As in the passages above, God's jealousy is closely connected to his wrath and judgment. Moses associates God's jealousy with the figure of "consuming fire" (Deut. 4:24; cf. Heb. 12:29) and the burning of his anger (Deut. 6:15).

From this discussion we can see that God's jealousy is not inconsistent with his love or goodness. On the contrary, his jealousy is part of his love. Although, as we have seen, God has some love for all his creatures, he has an exclusive love for his own people, and he demands the same of them. When they violate that love, he behaves as a godly husband: he becomes jealous. There is nothing wrong with that jealousy. It reflects the intensity of his care for the love-relationship. When a man's beloved wife turns away and loves another man, he is rightly jealous. If he were not, that would be evidence that he does not care for her. In Scripture, adultery is serious business: a capital crime in the OT (Lev. 20:10), a ground for divorce in the NT (Matt. 19:9). Idolatry similarly (Deut. 13:1–5).

God's Hatred

More difficult to reconcile with God's love and goodness is God's attribute of *hatred* (Heb. *sane'*, Gk. *miseo*[14]). Proverbs 10:12 contrasts hate and love:

> Hatred stirs up strife,
> but love covers all offenses.

The law of love, as we have seen, is the norm of human conduct, so Leviticus 19:17 urges, "You shall not hate your brother in your heart."[15] Scripture often urges us,

---

14. In the NIV, some passages, such as Proverbs 11:20, also speak of God's "detesting" something or regarding something as an "abomination" (*to'evah*). *Qutz* is "abhor" in Leviticus 20:23 and elsewhere.

15. Significantly, the verse adds: "but you shall reason frankly with your neighbor, lest you incur sin because of him." A frank airing of differences guards love, rather than destroying it. So the NT urges us to swift and open discussion of differences, leading to reconciliation (Matt. 5:23–26; 18:15–20; Eph. 4:26). When we do not seek quick resolution, we tend to harbor grudges, and that turns love into hate.

however, to hate evil (Pss. 97:10; 101:3; 119:104, 128, 163; Amos 5:15; Jude 23; Rev. 2:6). And godly hatred is directed not only against evil deeds, ways, falsehoods, but also against some people: "I hate the double-minded, but I love your law" (Ps. 119:113).[16] The psalmist asks:

> Do I not hate those who hate you, O Lord?
>> And do I not loathe those who rise up against you?
> I hate them with complete hatred;
>> I count them my enemies. (Ps. 139:21–22)

Scripture, then, seems to recommend hatred in some contexts, to deplore it in others. So we must look more closely to see whether there are different kinds of hatred, or different situations in which it is and is not appropriate. First, let us note that *hate* in Scripture does not always refer to hostility. Jacob loved Rachel, but hated Leah (Gen. 29:31, in Hebrew; NIV says "not loved"). His love for Rachel was, of course, an erotic love (vv. 17–18), and most likely that kind of love is what he lacked for Leah; the term *hate* doesn't need to be taken any more strongly than that. Verse 30 says simply that "he loved Rachel more than Leah." If there was also hostility between Jacob and Leah, it would be hard to prove it from the passage.

Similarly, Jesus calls us to hate our family and even our own lives in comparison to our love for him (Matt. 10:37; Luke 14:26; John 12:25), even though he strongly endorses the fifth commandment ("honor your father and your mother") in Matthew 15:3–9. Here *hate* and *love* measure relative priorities: we are to love Jesus far more than anyone here on earth.

Further, even when hatred includes hostility, that hostility should be understood essentially as a policy of opposition. Just as love in Scripture is both act and feeling, so the same can be said of hate. To hate someone means to oppose his goals, and to take action if possible to prevent him from succeeding. This hatred may include emotional revulsion, of course. Indeed, we should be emotionally disgusted with wickedness. But one may hate the wicked in the sense of opposing (intellectually, volitionally, and emotionally) his policies and plans, without emotional disgust for the person himself. (Similarly, one may love another person by seeking to help to meet the person's needs, without emotional passion for that person.) Hatred may also include desiring the worst for someone else, but it does not necessarily mean that.

The meaning of *hate*, therefore, like the meaning of *love*, varies in different biblical contexts. Emotional disgust, practical opposition, relative priorities, lack of romantic attraction, seeking the worst for somebody: some or all of these may be involved in *hatred* in different proportions in different contexts. In some contexts, hatred excludes love (and *love* also has various senses); in some it does not.

---

16. It is not, therefore, true in every sense that we are to "hate the sin, but love the sinner." In some senses, God calls us to hate sinners as well.

So although Proverbs 10:12 contrasts love and hate (and certainly they should be contrasted in most contexts!), the two are not always or in every respect incompatible. If love is a disposition to seek the good of someone else, and hate is opposition to the values and plans of someone, then it is certainly possible both to love and to hate the same person.[17] For example, it is possible to hate some vicious despot (Adolf Hitler, Josef Stalin, Idi Amin, Pol Pot, Slobodan Milosevic, Saddam Hussein) in the sense of opposing his plans and calling God to judge him, indeed even being emotionally disgusted by his character and actions, while at the same time desiring his conversion. We should always keep that qualification in mind when we pray the imprecatory psalms, those psalms that call down judgments on the enemies of God and of the psalmist.

God also hates wickedness and the wicked themselves (Lev. 20:23; Deut. 25:16; Pss. 5:5; 11:5; Prov. 6:16–19; 11:20; 16:5; 17:15; Jer. 12:8; Hos. 9:15; Zech. 8:17; Rev. 2:6, 15). His hatred has awful consequences, of course. Ultimately God will destroy his enemies and send them to hell. But God's present enmity is not always his final word. All of us were once "by nature children of wrath" (Eph. 2:3) because of sin. As I argued in chapter 12, God's wrath upon us then was genuine wrath. We were wicked, and God really hated us. We were headed for hell. But God loved us in Christ (Eph. 2:4). Since that love went back before the creation of the world (1:4), evidently there was a period of time when God loved and hated us simultaneously. Before an elect person is converted, God both loves and hates him: God opposes him, prevents him in the long term from achieving his wicked purposes; but for such a one, God also has glorious blessings in store.

Now, in Malachi 1:3 and Romans 9:13, we read, "Jacob I loved, but Esau I hated." Paul traces God's attitudes toward the two men back before their birth (Rom. 9:11), "that God's purpose of election might continue." As I said in chapter 11, it is difficult to interpret this passage because it uses illustrations from God's historical election of Israel to teach us about God's eternal election. I don't believe we can determine from this passage whether or not Esau was ultimately a saved man. Historically, however, God chose Jacob, not Esau, to inherit the promises given to Abraham. Jacob receives, therefore, God's special covenant love, his *hesed*, as God separates his family from all the nations and promises special blessings to him and to his seed. God does not give that particular kind of love to Esau, and he never intended to. God planned before Esau's birth that he would not have it. In this context, Esau is "hated."

It is important for Paul's readers to know that God does discriminate between people before those people are born. It is not necessarily or always a discrimination between eternal salvation and eternal punishment. In Esau's case, I have no reason to think that it was. But it is, in other cases. Paul teaches that this eternal divine discrimination explains the unbelief of Israel. If the unbelief of many Jews continues to

17. This point is similar to the one I made about the ambiguity of *favor* in chapter 12's discussion of common grace.

their deaths, we must conclude that God's sovereign discrimination explains their eternal condemnation. In that case, God's hatred for them would have more serious consequences than his hatred for Esau.

What, then, should we conclude about God's love? His hate and his love do not exclude each other in every respect, so the attribute of hatred does not in itself compromise Scripture's teaching that "God is love." God does love and hate some people at the same time, in different respects.

There are some, of course, who eventually receive no love from God: the devil and his angels, and the lost in hell. But "God is love" does not require that God's love be distributed equally to everybody and everything in creation. God's punishment of Satan and his followers shows the greatness of his love to the saved: to rid their world of evil and to establish his justice. Indeed, in all that he does, he advances the purposes of his love. God is love.

But this point raises a further question: can we also say, "God is hate"? Is hate, like love, a defining attribute of God, and therefore a way of describing his essence?

We could perhaps answer this question simply by denying that God's hate is a defining or essential attribute. (See the distinction in chapter 12.) Certainly Scripture does not emphasize God's hatred in the way it emphasizes his love. And it is certainly difficult to imagine how there could be any hatred in God apart from the creation. There are no enmities in the Trinity, only love between the persons. So perhaps hatred is only an accidental or relational attribute, an attribute arising from God's relation to the creation, like "God of Moses."[18]

But this solution to the problem misses some nuances. God cannot love goodness without hating evil. The two are opposite sides of the same coin, positive and negative ways of describing the same virtue. In the mind of God before creation, evil exists only as an idea in his mind, only as a possibility. But surely God regards that possibility with hostility. Even though he intends to bring evil into existence (see chapter 14), he regards it as something to be overcome, rather than as something to be honored.

"God is love," then, implies that from eternity past, God has an implacable hatred of evil. That hatred is not separable from his perfect nature. It is a necessary and defining attribute, not a mere accidental or relational one. "God hates evil" gives us a profound description of his character. "God is hate" is of course not a helpful way of making this point, since it would create terrible confusion. But once we specify the objects of God's hate, we can state clearly that it is a divine attribute.

As we have seen, "God is love" can also be misunderstood by people who don't know the objects of God's love and the type of love in view. But the apostle John accepted that risk in 1 John 4:8. There are greater risks, I think, in speaking of God's hatred. But we need to accept those as well, in order to communicate the full teaching of God's Word on this important matter.

---

18. We might be tempted to say the same thing about God's jealousy if the OT were not so emphatic in identifying jealousy with God's own name.

In the final analysis, then, it is biblical and edifying to say that God by nature is throughout eternity passionately opposed to evil. This hatred pervades all his thoughts and actions. God is the supreme hater of wickedness.

God's Wrath

The biblical vocabulary for God's *wrath* is extensive: in Hebrew, *'af, 'ebrah, haron, qetzef, hemah,* in Greek *orge* and *thymos,* in various forms. These are also translated "anger," "fury," and so on.

Jesus teaches that being angry with one's brother violates the sixth commandment:

> You have heard that it was said to those of old, "You shall not murder; and who-ever murders will be liable to judgment." But I say to you that everyone who is angry with his brother will be liable to judgment; whoever insults his brother will be liable to the council; and whoever says, "You fool!" will be liable to the hell of fire. (Matt. 5:21–22)

So anger can be found in a number of NT lists of sins (Gal. 5:20; Eph. 4:31; Col. 3:8; 1 Tim. 2:8; James 1:19–20). On the other hand, Ephesians 4:26–27 says:

> Be angry and do not sin; do not let the sun go down on your anger, and give no opportunity to the devil.

Paul suggests that the sin is not so much in the anger itself as in our tendency to nurse that anger rather than seeking reconciliation. Jesus displayed anger (*zelos,* from the jealousy-vocabulary that we considered earlier) when he cleansed the temple of money-changers (John 2:14–17). We can assume, I believe, that anger, like hatred, is appropriate when directed against God's enemies. Jeremiah tells his hearers that he is "full of the wrath of the LORD; I am weary of holding it in" (6:11).

So Scripture speaks often of the wrath of God as his response to sin. Wrath dif-fers from jealousy and hatred, in that (1) jealousy is more focused on the specific sin of idolatry; wrath opposes our sin in general; (2) jealousy and hatred are motives for wrath; wrath actually executes punishments.

It is interesting to note that many Bible texts simply speak of "wrath" without men-tioning God as the source of the wrath. For example:

> But the Levites shall camp around the tabernacle of the testimony, so that there may be no wrath on the congregation of the people of Israel. (Num. 1:53)

Cf. Num. 18:5; Josh. 9:20; 22:20; 1 Chron. 27:24; 2 Chron. 19:10; 24:18; Matt. 3:7; Luke 21:23; Rom. 4:15; 5:9; 9:22; 13:4–5; Eph. 2:3; 1 Thess. 1:10; 2:16; 5:9.[19] In Leviticus 10:6;

---

19. In some of these passages, the NIV, ESV, and other modern translations supply a name of God or a pronoun to indicate the source of the wrath. I am following the original languages here.

Numbers 16:46; and Romans 2:8, "wrath" is also used somewhat impersonally, though the divine source is mentioned in the context.

C. H. Dodd, in his commentary on Romans,[20] argued that for Paul, *wrath* is a kind of impersonal force or a natural law by which transgressions automatically receive their consequences. Dodd evidently felt that this view mitigated the problem of evil somewhat and enabled us to think more consistently of God as love. But Dodd's view exaggerates the implications of these data:

1. There is no shortage of verses that ascribe wrath directly to God: e.g., Num. 11:33; 2 Kings 22:13; John 3:36; Rom. 1:18; Eph. 5:6; Col. 3:6; Heb. 3:11; 4:3; Rev. 14:10, 19; 15:1, 7; 16:1; 19:15. Note also the striking, ironic phrase "the wrath of the Lamb" in Revelation 6:16–17. The biblical writers are not in doubt about whose wrath it is.

2. When Scripture describes the actual course of God's wrath in history, it speaks very personally of God's action. As we have seen, Dodd finds in Romans a number of impersonal formulations; but these refer back to the personal phrase "wrath of God" in 1:18. Then Romans 1 describes God's wrathful actions against those who suppress his truth: he "gives them up" (vv. 24, 26, 28) to greater sin. At each point, God takes personal initiative. Indeed, as we have seen, the process of reprobation depends on God's very personal *hatred* (9:13). Paul leaves no doubt that the salvation and judgment of men are based on God's personal decisions.

3. As I indicated in chapters 7–9, Scripture does not teach that God runs the universe by a system of impersonal "natural laws" that are somehow independent of his immediate action. Indeed, nothing happens without God's personal ordination (chapter 8). Dodd's construction, on the contrary, is essentially deist.

4. As I will argue in chapter 14, we should not try to solve or mitigate the problem of evil by compromising God's causation of all things.

5. There is a better way to understand the relatively impersonal references to wrath. God in Scripture can be terrifying:[21] "It is a fearful thing to fall into the hands of the living God" (Heb. 10:31). God's wrath can come on men in surprising and sudden ways, though he reveals them to us in retrospect as righteous and wise. After God appoints Moses to be Israel's deliverer, we read, "At a lodging place on the way the Lord met him and sought to put him to death" (Ex. 4:24), because he had failed to circumcise his son. After God delivered the Israelites from Egypt, he met them at Mount Sinai. These were the people he had chosen in love (Deut. 7:8), yet he warned them not to

---

20. C. H. Dodd, *The Epistle of St. Paul to the Romans* (New York: Harper, 1932), 21–23, and elsewhere. See, on the contrary, Leon Morris, *The Cross in the New Testament* (Grand Rapids: Eerdmans, 1965), 189.

21. I believe that Jesus takes away that terror from his people, since he has torn in two the veil of the temple (Matt. 27:51) and called us to enter boldly into the "holy places" (Heb. 10:19). This does not, of course, relieve us of the need to show "reverence and awe" in God's presence (12:28). But the wrath of God in Scripture is against those who are not trusting in Jesus, and in the book of Hebrews it is threatened against those who renounce Christ and return to Judaism. For these, "there no longer remains a sacrifice for sins, but a fearful expectation of judgment, and a fury of fire that will consume the adversaries" (10:26b–27a). It is in this context that the author affirms the dread of falling into the hands of God (v. 31). So the wrath of God is still terrifying to those who experience it, and when believers contemplate it, they should recognize that dimension of it.

ascend the mountain "lest [Yahweh] break out against them" (Ex. 19:24). Like C. S. Lewis's Aslan, God is good, but he is not tame. There is something wild, mysterious, and threatening about God's wrath, which is not always easy to reconcile with what we know of God's love.

The Jews were sparing in their use of divine names in any case, and the biblical writers naturally tended to use abbreviated terms so as not to dwell too much on the perplexing, mysterious, and frightening aspects of God's nature. But they were not consistent in this pattern. We should confess honestly that we do the same. Though Scripture abounds in references to God's wrath and in teaching about the final judgment, we tend to abbreviate it. In our teaching, the proportion of our references to God's love and to his wrath is not nearly the same as the proportion in Scripture. I include myself in this generalization. I don't think this is necessarily or always wrong; we do, after all, have some biblical precedent, in the brusque references to "the wrath." In this usage, we can feel the writer cringe, look away. And that teaches us something about how terrible the wrath of God really is. "Our God is a consuming fire" (Heb. 12:29; cf. Ex. 24:17; Lev. 10:2; Deut. 4:24; 9:3; Ps. 97:3; Isa. 33:14; 2 Thess. 1:8).

God's wrath is terrible, but in the course of history the Lord is eager to defer that anger, to forgive those who turn from sin. We have seen in the last chapter that he is patient (*'arek*), and we note now that he is *'arek 'af*, "slow to anger" (Ps. 103:8; Joel 2:13; Jonah 4:2). He gives sinners many opportunities to repent (2 Peter 3:9). As we will see in our discussion of God's will, he does not desire the death of the wicked. His love postpones his wrath. This patience is part of his name in Exodus 34:6–7, and God tells us through Isaiah:

> For my name's sake I defer my anger,
>   for the sake of my praise I restrain it for you,
>   that I may not cut you off. (Isa. 48:9)

So God delays his wrath for the sake of his love. But there remain serious questions about how God's wrath is related to his love, and to his other ethical attributes. How can God be love at all, if he ever brings his wrath against his creatures?

The relationship between God's love and his wrath can best be seen by way of two intermediate concepts: God's righteousness and his jealousy.

We have seen that God's love always observes the boundaries of his righteousness. Even in redemption, God takes enormous pains so that in showing love he may be just (Rom. 3:26). The sacrifice of Christ ensures that God's redemption is both loving and righteous, so that Scripture can even appeal to God's righteousness as a ground for the forgiveness of sins, and thus God's righteousness becomes a form of his love. But it is also God's righteousness that ensures the final punishment of those who reject his love, that is, his wrath against them. Without the wrath of God against those who finally disbelieve, God's love is no longer righteous. So God's righteousness binds together his love and his wrath. God's righteous love must be wrathful, if at the end of history there remain any unrepentant people.

We can also move from God's love to his wrath by means of his jealousy. God's love is covenantal. It creates a special relationship between God and his creatures: a marriage, in effect. So when people reject him, he is filled with holy jealousy, and the result is wrath. When we see God's love not as a mere sentimental affection, but as a covenant commitment, we see it as a jealous love that leads to wrath when abused.

So God's love and his wrath are not at odds with each other. If we think they are, we have not understood God's love. Perhaps it is unnecessarily paradoxical to say that "God's wrath is a form of his love." Some theologians have said that sort of thing in order to hint (or teach overtly) that God's wrath may not be as severe as the church has historically believed. I have no such intention. God's wrath is terrible to contemplate—no doubt worse than we might imagine from the biblical figures of fire and worm.[22]

Some have also argued that God's anger is a mere moment in the course of his love, based on passages such as Psalm 30:5:

> For his anger is but for a moment,
>   and his favor is for a lifetime.
> Weeping may tarry for the night,
>   but joy comes with the morning.

But the psalmist here speaks explicitly to God's "saints":

> Sing praises to the LORD, O you his saints,
>   and give thanks to his holy name. (Ps. 30:4)

Sadly, for those who are not saints, Scripture makes clear that it is weeping, not rejoicing, that will come in the morning (Matt. 8:12; 22:13; 24:51; 25:30), and God's favor will remain only for a night (recall our discussion of common grace in chapter 12).

But God's wrath is nevertheless an outworking of his love. Once we understand God's love, we know it as a tough love, one that respects God's standards of righteousness and that burns in jealousy against those who betray it. So God's wrath serves the purposes of his love, and God's love is the richer for it: it bestows on his beloved the ultimate blessing of a sin-free world.[23]

God's Holiness

God's holiness is another of his ethical attributes, but it is also much more.

We are not to meet God as an ordinary friend or enemy, but as One who is radically different from us, before whom we bow in reverent awe and adoration. God's holiness, then, indicates the fundamental distinction between Creator and creature (see chapter 3).

---

22. I will defend the doctrine of eternal punishment in chapter 50.

23. "God is wrath," of course, is as misleading an expression as "God is hatred." But Deuteronomy 4:24; 9:3; and Hebrews 12:29 identify God with the "consuming fire" of Exodus 24:17 NIV (cf. Num. 11:1–3; Ps. 97:3; Isa. 33:14; 2 Thess. 1:7–8).

When Yahweh first meets with Moses, he says to Moses from within the burning bush:

> "Do not come near; take your sandals off your feet, for the place on which you are standing is holy ground." And he said, "I am the God of your father, the God of Abraham, the God of Isaac, and the God of Jacob." And Moses hid his face, for he was afraid to look at God. (Ex. 3:5–6)

The ground is "holy" not because there is something special or dangerous about the ground as such, but because Yahweh is there, the supremely Holy One. God's messenger is to stand back, to remove his shoes in respect. He is afraid to look at the face of God.

When redeemed Israel meets with God at Mount Sinai, the whole mountain is holy ground (Ex. 19:23). The people must draw back; anyone who touches the mountain must be put to death (vv. 12–13).

The concept of "holy ground," the intensive presence of the Lord, continues through Scripture, though it exists in different degrees. The innermost court of the tabernacle and temple is the "Most Holy" (Ex. 26:33; see Heb. 9:8). Compared to it, the "Holy Place" (Ex. 26:33) is less holy, but still holy. Similarly, the whole temple is holy, but not as holy as the Most Holy Place. The radiation of God's holiness also extends in diminished intensity to the holy mountain, the holy city, the holy land (Zech. 2:12), and indeed to the whole creation (Isa. 6:3; 66:1). We may note these different degrees and extensions of holiness by a diagram of concentric circles; see fig. 13.2.

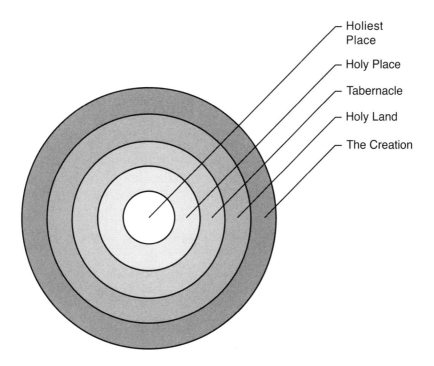

Holiest Place

Holy Place

Tabernacle

Holy Land

The Creation

Fig. 13.2. Degrees of Holiness

So it is not the case that "holy" and "common" designate a simple bifurcation of the universe, so that one is in either "the sphere of the holy" or "the sphere of the common."[24] In different respects and with different intensity, all of creation is holy, and all of creation is common.[25], [26]

Centuries after Moses, when the prophet Isaiah meets the Lord in the temple, the seraphs call to one another, "Holy, holy, holy is the LORD of hosts; the whole earth is full of his glory!" (Isa. 6:3).[27] Perhaps it is this experience that motivates him to speak regularly of God as "the Holy One of Israel" (1:4; 5:19; 10:20; 12:6; 17:7; and so on). In the NT, Jesus is regularly called holy (Luke 1:35; 4:34; Acts 2:27; 3:14; etc.), as is, of course, the Holy Spirit.

Holiness, then, is God's capacity and right to arouse our reverent awe and wonder. It is his uniqueness (Ex. 15:11; 1 Sam. 2:2), his transcendence as our Creator. It is his majesty, for the holy God is like a great king, whom we dare not treat like other persons. Indeed, God's holiness impels us to worship in his presence.

Because we are sinners as well as creatures, God stands over against us, not only as transcendent, but as ethically pure. It is particularly as sinners that we fear to enter God's holy presence. When Isaiah heard the seraphs cry, "Holy, holy, holy," he immediately remembered his own sin:

> Woe is me! For I am lost; for I am a man of unclean lips, and I dwell in the midst of a people of unclean lips; for my eyes have seen the King, the LORD of hosts! (Isa. 6:5)

And before he could hear God's call to prophesy, a seraph laid a live coal on his lips, symbolically communicating God's forgiveness.

So holiness is ethical as well as metaphysical. The Lord's holiness transcends us not only as creatures, but especially as sinners.

Thus, the holy Lord tells us to back away. But amazingly, he also draws us to himself and makes us holy as well. Israel becomes his "holy nation" (Ex. 19:6; see 22:31). The Israelites will be holy, "for I the LORD your God am holy" (Lev. 19:2; cf. 1 Peter 1:16). They participate in a holy assembly (Ex. 12:16), keep a holy day (16:23), sacrifice at a holy place (26:33), through a holy priest, anointed with holy oil (30:25), wearing holy garments (31:10).[28] They learn God's will through the "holy Scriptures" (Rom. 1:2; see 2 Tim. 3:15). NT Christian believers are "saints," holy ones (Rom. 1:7; 1 Cor. 1:2).

Israel's holiness, like God's, is both separation and moral purity. She is separated from all the other nations as God's special people (Deut. 7:1–6), and she is to image God's ethical perfection (Lev. 19:2).

God's holiness, then, which initially seems so forbidding and judgmental, is the means of our salvation. God draws us to his presence, making us his friends. Those

24. As argued in Meredith G. Kline, *Kingdom Prologue* (Eugene, OR: Wipf and Stock, 2006).
25. Even the Most Holy Place in the temple is common compared to the heavenly sanctuary (Heb. 9:23–24).
26. Compare the discussion of the universal covenant in chapter 4 of this volume.
27. In the Bible, holiness is the only divine attribute proclaimed in threefold repetition. Cf. Rev. 4:8.
28. And God's promise is that one day they will cook in holy pots (Zech. 14:20–21).

drawn into God's circle are holy, in contrast to the profane world. So in Hosea 11:9, God's holiness is ground for his mercy:

> I will not execute my burning anger;
>   I will not again destroy Ephraim;
> for I am God and not a man,
>   the Holy One in your midst,
>   and I will not come in wrath.[29]

The psalmist-Messiah in Psalm 22:1–5 invokes God's holiness as the reason why God should deliver him:

> My God, my God, why have you forsaken me?
>   Why are you so far from saving me, from the words of my groaning?
> O my God, I cry by day, but you do not answer,
>   and by night, but I find no rest.
>
> Yet you are holy,
>   enthroned on the praises of Israel.
> In you our fathers trusted;
>   they trusted, and you delivered them.
> To you they cried and were rescued;
>   in you they trusted and were not put to shame.

As the Holy One, God has for centuries delivered his people from death and destruction. There must be a reason why this Holy One has now forsaken the psalmist.

Holiness, then, is a very rich concept. It speaks of God's transcendence and separation from finite and sinful creatures. But it also speaks of how God draws them to himself, making them holy. Holiness marks God's transcendence, but also his immanence, his presence to redeem us. He is not only "the Holy One," but "the Holy One among us," "the Holy One of Israel." And as both transcendence and immanence, judgment and salvation, law and gospel, God's holiness drives us to worship him. Yahweh is the Lord who moves us to worship him with reverence and awe (Heb. 12:28).

In this respect, God's holiness is very similar to his righteousness, which we considered earlier in this chapter. Both of these attributes represent God in his transcendence and immanence, his forbidding, awesome majesty, and his loving approach to human beings.

Key Terms
Attributes of goodness
Righteousness (the "main idea")

29. Compare other passages in which God's holiness is redemptive: Isa. 41:14; 43:3, 14; 49:7.

Ramist chart
Internal righteousness
External righteousness
Rectoral righteousness
Distributive righteousness
Remunerative righteousness
Retributive righteousness
Existential righteousness
Normative righteousness
Situational righteousness
Nominalism
Law of talion
Jealousy
Hatred
Imprecatory psalms
Wrath, anger
Holiness
Common

Study Questions

1. "To say that God is good implies that God is righteous. So goodness includes righteousness, rather than being separate from it." Explain; evaluate.

2. "And Scripture often presents God's righteousness, as we will see, not merely as an authoritative standard, but as an active power bringing salvation." Explain, citing biblical examples.

3. Describe God's righteousness, using the Ramist chart and Frame's threefold analysis.

4. "The standard of our moral behavior is not an abstract concept, but an infinite person, God himself." Explain; evaluate. Describe the dilemma that this formulation attempts to resolve.

5. "Notice how virtually everything we say about God can be said of Christ as well." Give an example. Why is this fact important?

6. "There is a 'poetic justice' in God's providence." Explain, pointing out Frame's qualifications of this statement.

7. "Righteousness in Scripture is not only a standard governing conduct, but also a means of salvation." Explain, citing biblical examples.

8. Frame believes that God's concern for "the afflicted" in the OT provides backgrounds for his salvation of the ungodly in the NT. Explain, citing biblical texts.

9. Is God "on the side of the poor"? Present a biblically balanced view.

10. "God's jealousy is part of his love." Explain.

11. "Scripture, then, seems to recommend hatred in some contexts, to deplore it in others. So we must look more closely to see whether there are different kinds of hatred, or different situations in which it is and is not appropriate." Summarize the biblical teaching on this question, citing biblical passages.

12. Is it right to say that God "hates the sin, but loves the sinner"? Discuss the biblical data.

13. Some Scripture passages seem to present "wrath" as something impersonal. How should we understand this phenomenon?

14. "But God's wrath is nevertheless an outworking of his love." Explain; evaluate.

15. "In different respects and with different intensity, all of creation is holy, and all of creation is common." Explain, citing Scripture.

16. "Because we are sinners as well as creatures, God stands over against us, not only transcendent, but as ethically pure." Explain.

17. "God's holiness, then, which initially seems so forbidding and judgmental, is the means of our salvation." Explain. How is this like God's righteousness?

Memory Verses

Ex. 34:14: For you shall worship no other god, for the Lord, whose name is Jealous, is a jealous God.

Ps. 145:17: The Lord is righteous in all his ways
and kind in all his works.

Prov. 26:27: Whoever digs a pit will fall into it,
and a stone will come back on him who starts it rolling.

Isa. 6:3: Holy, holy, holy is the Lord of hosts;
the whole earth is full of his glory.

Obad. 15: As you have done, it shall be done to you;
your deeds shall return on your own head.

Rom. 1:17: For in [the gospel] the righteousness of God is revealed from faith for faith, as it is written, "The righteous shall live by faith."

Rom. 9:13: Jacob I loved, but Esau I hated.

Resources for Further Study

Bavinck, Herman. *BRD*, 2:178–255.

Frame, John M. *DG*, 27–29, 446–68.

CHAPTER 14

THE PROBLEM OF EVIL

FOLLOWING OUR DISCUSSION of God's moral attributes, it is necessary to take up the most important challenge to God's goodness and righteousness, the so-called problem of evil.[1] Indeed, this is probably the most difficult problem in all of theology, and for many atheists it is the Achilles' heel of the theistic worldview. In a nutshell, the problem is this: How can there be any evil in the world, if God exists? Or to put it more formally:

1. If God is omnipotent, he is able to prevent evil.
2. If God is good, he wants to prevent evil.
3. But evil exists.
4. Conclusion: either God is not omnipotent, or he is not good.

As I have formulated it, the argument assumes that God exists. But the conclusion is often taken as a *reductio ad absurdum* of that assumption. To say that God is not omnipotent or not good is to say that the God of the Bible does not exist.

The syllogism above is sometimes called the *logical problem of evil*, for it accuses the theistic worldview of logical inconsistency. The charge is that theists believe in an omnipotent, good God, but inconsistently believe also that evil exists. Often, of course, the problem of evil is felt, rather than argued. The *emotional problem of evil* is simply the agony we feel when we experience tragedy in life, and we cry out, "Why, Lord?"

Another distinction that we should initially make is between natural and moral evil. The former includes anything that brings suffering, unpleasantness, or difficulty into the lives of creatures. Earthquakes, floods, diseases, injuries, and death are examples of natural evil. Moral evil is the sin of rational creatures (angels and men). According to Scripture, moral evil came first. Satan's temptations and the disobedience of Adam and Eve led to God's curse on the earth:

---

1. I have discussed the problem of evil in *AGG*, 149–90; *CVT*, 83–86; and *DG*, 160–82. I have not changed my view in any substantive way since writing these previous books, so there will be some overlap, indeed repetition, between them and the present chapter. But any systematic theology worth its salt must discuss this topic.

And to Adam he said,

"Because you have listened to the voice of your wife
    and have eaten of the tree
of which I commanded you,
    'You shall not eat of it,'
cursed is the ground because of you;
    in pain you shall eat of it all the days of your life;
thorns and thistles it shall bring forth for you;
    and you shall eat the plants of the field.
By the sweat of your face
    you shall eat bread,
till you return to the ground,
    for out of it you were taken;
for you are dust
    and to dust you shall return." (Gen. 3:17–19)

God will remove this curse only on the final day, the consummation of Jesus' redemption, when God executes his final judgment and this world is replaced by a new heavens and new earth. In the meantime, the creation "groans" in the pain of childbirth (Rom. 8:22) "with eager longing for the revealing of the sons of God" (v. 19).

Scripture, therefore, gives us an explicit answer to the problem of natural evil. Natural evil is a curse brought on the world because of moral evil. It functions as punishment to the wicked and as a means of discipline for those who are righteous by God's grace. It also reminds us of the cosmic dimensions of sin and redemption. Sin brought death to the human race, but also to the universe over which man was to rule. God has ordained that the universe resist its human ruler until that ruler stops resisting God. So in redemption, God's purpose is no less than "to reconcile to himself all things, whether on earth or in heaven, making peace by the blood of his cross" (Col. 1:20). The unanswered question is the problem of moral evil: how can sin exist in a theistic universe? I will therefore focus on moral evil for the rest of this chapter.

I will assume in this chapter a strong concept of divine omnipotence, based on the discussion to appear in chapter 16, and on our previous discussion (chapter 8) of the efficacy and universality of God's sovereign control over the creation. Granted what we have already seen about God's sovereignty, the various attempts to show that God is too weak to prevent evil[2] do not seem promising. I will also assume the goodness, righteousness, and holiness of God (chapters 12–13). Note especially that the exposition of the divine name in Exodus 34:6–7 teaches the righteousness of God, as does Deuteronomy 32:4: "The Rock, his work is perfect, for all his ways are justice." He does not

---

2. As in the book by Rabbi Harold Kushner, *When Bad Things Happen to Good People* (New York: Schocken, 1981), but also in the literature of process theology. See David Ray Griffin, *God, Power, and Evil* (Philadelphia: Westminster Press, 1976), and his *Evil Revisited* (Albany, NY: State University of New York Press, 1991), reviewed by me in *CTJ* 27, 2 (November 1992): 435–38.

take pleasure in evil (Ps. 5:4). His eyes are too pure to look on evil; he cannot tolerate it (Hab. 1:13).[3] So I will not consider solutions that call these attributes into question.

Common defenses[4] against the problem may be divided into three general types, the first focusing on the nature of evil, the second on the ways in which evil contributes to the overall good of the universe, and the third on God's agency in regard to evil. I will consider these in succession.

The Nature of Evil

The Christian Science sect and some forms of Hinduism maintain that evil is an *illusion*. If so, of course, the problem of evil dissolves. But this claim is easily refuted. Even if evil does not exist in the world outside ourselves, it certainly exists in our own minds and feelings. Even Christian Scientists and Hindus will concede that much. If it is an illusion, it is a deeply troubling one, and the very pain of it raises the problem of evil again. How can a good and omnipotent God allow us to be troubled by such illusions? So this proposal merely shifts the problem of evil to another level and thereby fails as a solution. It also fails as a claim about the world, for illusions are, after all, themselves real evils. The fact that human beings often fail to distinguish between illusion and reality is itself an evil that must be dealt with. So if evil is an illusion, it is not an illusion. The illusionist view refutes itself.

Another view that attempts to put evil into a shadowy metaphysical category is the view that evil is a *privation*. This view is far more widespread than the first within Christendom, having been advocated by Augustine, the Catholic and post-Reformation scholastic traditions, and many modern apologists and theologians. To say that evil is a privation is not to say that it is an illusion. It is rather to say that it is something negative rather than positive. It is a lack, a defect in a good universe. It is an absence of good, rather than the presence of something not good. Further, it is an absence of good where good should be. We do not consider it evil that a tree is unable to see, but we do pity a human being who lacks sight. Evil is therefore not a mere absence of good, but a privation or deprivation.

These thinkers begin with the biblical premise that all being is good (Gen. 1:31; 1 Tim. 4:4). So evil is nonbeing, not a "something," not a substance or object. It is a lack of being, a deprivation of being. It is "negative and accidental."[5]

Étienne Gilson, the Thomist scholar, expounds the concept as follows:

---

3. Of course, Habakkuk brings up this principle in order to ask God why he *has* been tolerating evil. In effect, Habakkuk is raising the problem of evil.

4. Alvin Plantinga, in *God, Freedom, and Evil* (Grand Rapids: Eerdmans, 1974), makes a useful distinction between a *defense* and a *theodicy*. The latter has the goal of justifying God's ways to men, of demonstrating the goodness of all his actions. The former merely seeks to show that the problem of evil does not disprove the God of the Bible.

5. Étienne Gilson, *The Spirit of Medieval Philosophy* (New York: Charles Scribner's Sons, 1940), 113. Karl Barth's view of sin and evil as "nothingness" (*Das Nichtige*) is similar, except that for Barth the nothingness is an aspect of *Geschichte*, that highest reality shared by God and man in Christ, in which alone God is truly God and man is truly man. See my *CVT*, 359–65.

It is very certain that all things God has made are good; and no less certain that they are not all equally good. There is the good, and the better; and, if the better, then also the less good; now in a certain sense the less good pertains to evil.[6]

Later, he adds:

But what we must especially note is that these very limitations and mutabilities for which nature is arraigned, are metaphysically inherent in the very status of a created being as such. . . . Things, in short, are created *ex nihilo*, and because created they are, and are good; but because they are *ex nihilo* they are essentially mutable . . . . The possibility of change is a necessity from which God Himself could not absolve his creation; for the mere fact of being created is the ultimate root of that possibility . . . . Everything that exists in virtue of the creative action and endures in virtue of continued creation, remains radically contingent in itself and in constant peril of lapsing back into nothingness. Because creatures are apt not to be they tend, so to speak, towards nonbeing.[7]

On Gilson's view, natural evil is (1) the defects in the lesser goods that God has made in creating a many-valued universe and (2) the "mutability" of creation, the tendency of all the good things of creation to "lapse back into nothingness," a kind of metaphysical entropy. Remember that Gilson equates being with goodness. Since God created all things good, everything is good insofar as it has being. But as things slip back into nonbeing, they lose their goodness as well as their being. So this metaphysical lapse means that things tend to lose their perfections unless God acts to sustain them.

What of moral evil? Gilson argues that rational beings, angels and men, are also mutable.

The whole problem now stands on a new footing: all that needs to be made in order that it may be, is always tending to unmake itself, so much so that what now permanently threatens the work of creation is literally, and in the full rigour of the term, the possibility of its *defection*. But only a possibility, be it noted, nothing more; a possibility without real danger as far as concerns the physical order which has no control over itself, but a very real and practical danger indeed in the moral order, that is to say when men and angels are concerned; for in associating them with his own divine government, their Creator requires them also to keep watch with Him against their own possible defection.[8]

Rational beings, like other creatures, tend to slip into nonbeing, to "unmake" themselves, and therefore to become less perfect than God made them to be. The difference between rational and nonrational beings is that rational beings have some control over

6. Gilson, *Spirit*, 113.
7. Ibid., 113–14.
8. Ibid., 114–15.

their own metaphysical stability. They can keep themselves from losing their perfections. Gilson goes on to explain that to maintain themselves in perfection, God gave to men free will (I gather in a libertarian[9] sense). But men used their free will wrongly and fell into sin.

> For all evil comes of the will; this will was not created evil, nor even indifferent to good or evil; it was created good, and such that it needed only an effortless continuance in good to attain to perfect beatitude. The only danger threatening such a nature lies therefore in that metaphysical contingence inseparable from the state of a created being, a pure *possibility*, without the least trace of actual existence, a possibility that not only could have remained unactualized but ought to have done so . . . [so] it seems we may justly claim for Christian thought that it has done everything necessary to reduce [evil] to the status of an avoidable accident, and to banish it to the confines of this fundamentally good universe.[10]

What is God's relation to evil in this view?

> Lastly, we may proceed to this final conclusion to which we must hold firmly, however strange it may appear: viz. The cause of evil lies always in some good, and yet, God, who is the Cause of all good, is not the cause of evil. For it follows clearly from the preceding considerations, that, when evil is reducible to a defect in some act, its cause is always a defect in the being that acts. Now in God there is no defect, but, on the contrary, supreme perfection. The evil caused by a defect in the acting being could not, therefore, have God for its cause. But if we consider the evil which consists in the corruption of certain beings, we must, on the other hand, assign its cause to God . . . . Whatever being and action is observable in a bad act, is attributable to God as to its cause, but whatever defectiveness is contained in the act, is attributable to the defective secondary cause, and not to the almighty perfection of God.
>
> Thus, from whatever angle we approach the problem, we always come back to the same conclusion. Evil as such is nothing. It is, therefore, inconceivable that God could be its cause. If asked, further, what is its cause, we must reply that it reduces itself to the tendency of certain things to return to nonbeing.[11]

To some extent, Gilson's reply to the problem of evil is a form of the free-will defense, which I will mention later, very briefly. He tries, however, to get behind human freedom

9. To anticipate a later discussion (chapter 35), libertarian freedom in human choice means that when a person chooses, he may always have chosen otherwise. On this view, no human choice is determined by a cause, whether that cause be God, something in the person's environment, heredity, moral disposition ("heart"), or desire. I believe that Scripture denies that human beings have libertarian freedom so defined. Human beings do have *compatibilist* freedom, freedom to choose according to their desires, whether or not those desires are caused by something outside themselves. The term *compatibilism* indicates that such freedom is compatible with causation, even determinism.

10. Gilson, *Spirit*, 121–22.

11. Étienne Gilson, *The Philosophy of St. Thomas Aquinas*, trans. Edward Bullough (New York: Arno Press, 1979), 161–62.

to show how a wrong use of human freedom is grounded in a metaphysical principle: the tendency of creatures to become less perfect. Every creature has this tendency. Rational creatures can guard against it, but they don't necessarily do this. When they don't, they are responsible for allowing themselves to become imperfect. God doesn't cause moral evil, but he does cause the existence of corruptible beings. He creates corruptible beings because he intends these to add to the overall perfection of the universe. But he is not responsible for the failures of rational beings to guard against their own corruption. Evil is nonbeing, and God does not create nonbeing, only being.

I do not find this to be a cogent response to the problem of evil, for the following reasons:

1. It seems to assume libertarian freedom, which I will reject in chapter 35 of this book. Some Reformed thinkers have held the privation theory although rejecting libertarian freedom: God is the efficient cause of everything good, but only the "effectually permissive cause of evil." He "merely permits" evil, because it "has not true being at all."[12] But I confess that I don't know the difference between effectual permission and efficient causation, and I don't know why God should be responsible for what he causes efficiently, but not for what he permits effectually. More on that later in the chapter.

2. When someone freely chooses to allow himself to become imperfect, that choice (assuming that it is libertarian) is not itself the product of metaphysical entropy. That choice itself is evidently something other than a privation of good, for on Gilson's account it is prior to the privation; it is a choice to make the privation happen. But then the privation theory is quite irrelevant, an unnecessary complication to the argument. Why not simply adopt a conventional free-will defense and say that free will itself explains moral evil, rather than free will plus privation?

3. If God cannot prevent the corruption of rational beings, then how is he able to make some creatures incorruptible (angels and glorified saints)? If he can, but chooses not to, then the problem of evil recurs at a different level: why did he choose not to prevent the fall?

4. Should we regard evil as "nothing," a mere limitation or privation of goodness? Many seem to think it obvious that we should, but I am not persuaded. Black could be seen as the negation of white (or of any color), but one could also say that white and color are the negation of black. It seems a good general practice to regard opposites on the same ontological level. Males and females are opposites, but neither is a *mere* negation of the other. Both are substantial beings. Why should good and evil be any different?

It is true that good is prior to evil in some ways: (a) Good came first in history, as creation preceded fall. (b) Good has positive value in itself; evil has positive value only to the extent that it enhances good. (c) Good will receive God's blessing, evil his curse. But it is not clear to me that any of these require us to say that evil is nonbeing, or a mere negation or privation. Is there some other asymmetry between good and evil that requires us to regard evil as nonbeing? I have not been able to find suggestions of

12. Polan, in *RD*, 143.

that sort in the literature. Without them, I must assume that good and evil, though opposite, are both forms of being.[13]

5. I know no biblical reason to assert that created things by nature tend to slip into nonbeing, to lose their being, or to become corrupt.[14] Scripture says nothing of the kind, and in the absence of scriptural warrant I know of no other reason to say such a thing. This assertion assumes that there are degrees of being, and that created things can slip from higher degrees to lower degrees. The idea that being admits of degrees comes from the philosophy of Plato, in which the Forms or Ideas are "real," with the Form of the Good as the most real entity and others as lesser degrees of reality. It also fits Aristotle's view that things in the world are combinations of form and matter, but that matter is essentially a kind of nonbeing that inhibits form in various degrees. But in the Bible, there is no hint that some things have more being than others. God and his creations are; everything else is not; and that is the end of it. God is not more *real* than created beings, though he is very different from them in other ways. Further, in a biblical worldview there is no reason to suppose that things have an inherent tendency to become less perfect, less good, or less real.

6. Granting, however, Gilson's view that evil is a lack or privation of being, a kind of nonbeing, why would that absolve God of blame for evil? The picture of God that Gilson presents is crudely analogous to a maker of doughnuts. The doughnut maker shapes the dough into the familiar O-shape. When someone says, "I see what ingredients you use for the doughnut, but what do you make the holes out of?" the baker takes it as a bad joke. There are no "ingredients" for holes. The hole is simply an emptiness in the dough that appears when the pastry is created. When the baker makes one, behold, the hole is there, too! Making doughnuts is not a two-step procedure in which one first makes and shapes the dough, and then makes the hole; at least it doesn't have to be. The hole is not something that one must make in addition to the solid doughnut; it is only a lack or privation of dough.

Agreed. But doughnuts do, after all, have holes. The doughnut maker could have made his dough into a solid pastry without a hole, but he chose to include a hole. Shouldn't he receive blame for a hole that is too small, too large, or misshapen? Or credit for one that is just the right size? Should he not take responsibility for his choice to make doughnuts rather than solid pastries?

13. The relation between being and nonbeing has, of course, been a difficult philosophical issue since Parmenides. It is difficult to describe, or even refer to, nonbeing without making it look like a kind of being. But if evil is not an illusion, but something real, as these theologians all maintain, then what other conditions must it fulfill to be regarded as being? I don't believe that question has been answered.

It may be, as one of my correspondents suggests, that Augustine's adoption of the privation theory comes out of reaction to his original Manichaeism. The Manichees saw good and evil as equally powerful realities, in constant warfare. When Augustine became a Christian, he saw clearly that in God's world, good is the ultimate being and evil is not. But what is it? Perhaps Augustine thought he could best reject the *ultimacy* of evil by denying to it the status of being. I find this move understandable, but not persuasive.

14. One can, of course, discuss the concept of physical entropy in this connection, but the arguments for that are scientific rather than biblical, and the concept has little to do with the *moral* corruption that we are concerned with here, though Gilson draws an analogy between the two.

Similarly, if God is Creator of all the being in the universe, is he not also the source of whatever lacks or privations or negations of being there may be in the world? We saw in chapter 8 that Scripture represents God as bringing about some sinful human actions. It does not seem to me to matter much whether we regard these sins as being or nonbeing. If they come from God, they come from God, and the problem of evil remains.

7. What is evil, on a biblical view? As we have seen, natural evil is God's curse, the pains brought into the world by the fall of man. Moral evil is sin, transgression of God's law (1 John 3:4). Scripture does not speculate whether or these evils are "being" or "nonbeing" or where they fit into the metaphysical structure of the world.

Indeed, from a biblical point of view, there are dangers in reducing evil to metaphysics, reducing the righteousness-sin relation to the being-nonbeing relation.[15] Cornelius Van Til often warned against "reducing ethics to metaphysics," or "confusing sin with finitude,"[16] for such reduction depersonalizes sin. In such reduction, sin becomes a defect in creation itself (ultimately, contra Gilson, a defect in God's creative act) rather than the rebellion of created persons against their personal Creator. And this conception grants sinners a new excuse, their created finitude and mutability.

Further, this view encourages views of salvation in which the goal is to get rid of our finitude and become divine, rather than to become obedient. These dangers are not at all hypothetical. They represent a definite tendency in the history of thought, especially systems such as those of Plotinus, the Gnostics, Medieval and Eastern Mysticism, and much modern New Age thought. As we saw in chapter 3, these systems replace the biblical Creator-creature distinction with a continuum of divinity, and salvation is ascent toward the top of the ontological continuum, toward divinity.

Some Good Things about Evil

Another approach to the problem is to claim that the presence, or at least the possibility, of evil in the world is good, when seen from a broader perspective. Even human beings are sometimes called to inflict pain for a good purpose: surgery to heal, punishment of children to discipline them. So it doesn't seem impossible to imagine that God has a good purpose in permitting evil, one that outweighs the suffering and pain, one that, in the end, makes this a better world than it would have been without the intrusion of evil. Such observations have been called the *greater-good defense* against the problem of evil.

Some have argued that the possibility of evil is necessary for an orderly universe.[17] An orderly universe, in this view, is a universe governed predictably by natural law.

---

15. In one sense, the privation theory seeks to avoid this very problem. It tries to remove evil from the metaphysical sphere by removing it from the sphere of being. But I think that in fact it actually encourages the metaphysicalizing of sin.

16. These two formulations are more or less synonymous.

17. Ronald Nash, *Faith and Reason* (Grand Rapids: Zondervan, 1988). He cites discussions by F. R. Tennant, Michael Peterson, and Richard Swinburne advocating this approach.

But natural laws are impersonal. The law of gravity, for example, takes no account of persons. If someone jumps from a high cliff, he will be hurt, whether he is righteous or wicked. If God miraculously protected everybody (or those otherwise righteous) who took foolish chances, it would be difficult to predict the events of nature scientifically. So if we are to have an orderly, predictable universe, so the argument goes, we must be willing to accept a certain amount of pain and suffering.

Others have argued that a certain amount of evil in the world is necessary for "soul making."[18] John Hick argues that we are born morally immature, and we need some hard knocks to gain moral fiber.

The most common form of the greater-good defense is the *free-will defense*, which argues that God rightly risks the possibility of evil to allow human beings the great benefit of libertarian freedom of choice. See chapter 35 on human freedom, or my brief remarks in the last section of this chapter, for my negative response.

Some have noticed that there are virtues that could not exist or manifest themselves except as responses to evil: compassion, patience, courage, seeking justice, and the redemptive love by which one dies for his friends (John 15:13). Sometimes these have been called "second-order goods" that are dependent on "first-order evils."[19]

We can think of other positive uses of evil. In Scripture, God uses evil to test his servants (Job; James 1:3; 1 Peter 1:7), to discipline them (Heb. 12:7–11), to preserve their lives (Gen. 50:20), to teach them patience and perseverance (James 1:3–4), to redirect their attention to what is most important (Ps. 37), to enable them to comfort others (2 Cor. 1:3–7), to enable them to witness powerfully of the truth (Acts 7), to give them greater joy when suffering is replaced by glory (1 Peter 4:13), to judge the wicked both in history (Deut. 28:15–68) and in the life to come (Matt. 25:41–46), to bring reward to persecuted believers (Matt. 5:10–12), and simply "that the works of God might be displayed" (John 9:3; cf. Ex. 9:16; Rom. 9:17).

The thrust of all these arguments is that although evil is to be deplored in itself, there are some respects in which it makes the world in general a better place. Some have argued, therefore, that evils contribute to a "greater good." Some have even argued that even with all its evil, this world is the "best possible world." The philosopher G. W. Leibniz[20] argued that an omnipotent, omniscient, omnibenevolent God could create no less.

It is certainly true that when God brings pain and suffering on people, he has a good purpose. "As for you, you meant evil against me, but God meant it for good" (Gen. 50:20). And in a context dealing with the sufferings of Christians, Paul says that "for those who love God all things work together for good, for those who are called according to his purpose" (Rom. 8:28). Recognizing and affirming this principle is an essential element in any Christian response to the problem of evil. For it is essential

---

18. John Hick, *Evil and the God of Love* (London: Collins, 1966). He cites the church father Irenaeus as the source of his approach.

19. Which are, of course, ultimately, the abuses of first-order goods.

20. G. W. Leibniz, *Theodicy* (New Haven, CT: Yale University Press, 1952).

to realize that even though God does bring evil into the world, he does it for a good reason. Therefore, he does not *do* evil in bringing evil to pass.

I would quarrel with some of the arguments mentioned above in this connection. The idea that some human pain must be endured in any orderly universe does not take account of the biblical teachings about the prefall world and about the postconsummation heaven, in which "he will wipe away every tear from their eyes, and death shall be no more, neither shall there be mourning, nor crying, nor pain anymore, for the former things have passed away" (Rev. 21:4). Certainly heaven will be an orderly place, but God is clearly able to maintain that order without human suffering.

Hick's Irenaean "soul-making" theodicy overlooks the fact that in Scripture Adam was created good, not morally immature with a need to develop character through suffering. It is true that God uses evil to sanctify us, but the true making of souls, in both old and new creations, is by divine grace.

As for Leibniz's theory, many have doubted whether there could be such a thing as a "best possible world." Given any possible universe, can we not always imagine another that includes one more good or one less evil? Indeed, Scripture tells us explicitly that the present world is inferior to the world to come. If God is able to make a world that is less-than-best for a temporary period, why can't he create a world that is never the absolute best? And is it not possible that God wants to display his grace by giving existence to beings that are less than perfectly excellent?

Nevertheless, there is a valid insight in the greater-good defense. Scripture provides many examples of God's bringing good out of evil. And we know that in the last day, God's justice, mercy, and righteousness will be so plain to all that nobody will accuse him of wrongdoing. Rather:

> All nations will come
>   and worship you,
> for your righteous acts have been revealed. (Rev. 15:4b)

When all of God's actions are added up, it will be plain that the sum total of his works are righteous. From the evils of history he has brought unquestionable good, worthy of the highest praise.

Remember the following, however:

1. It is important for us to define *greater good* theistically. The greater good should be seen, first of all, not as greater pleasure or comfort for us, but as greater glory to God. Certainly there are events that are hard to justify as benefits to the people involved, the chief one being eternal punishment. But God is glorified in the judgment of sinners, and that is a good thing, not an evil. Nevertheless, God has promised that what brings glory to him will, in the long run, also bring benefits to believers. So Romans 8:28 says that "for those who love God all things work together for good, for those who are called according to his purpose."

2. Unless God's standards govern our concept of goodness, there can be no talk of good or evil at all. If there is no personal absolute, values must be based on impersonal things and forces, such as matter, motion, time, and chance. But values cannot be based on any of these. They arise only in a context of personal relationships, and absolute standards presuppose an absolute person. Thus, the Christian may turn the tables on the unbeliever who raises the problem of evil: The non-Christian has a *problem of good*. Without God, there is neither good nor evil.[21]

3. If we are to rightly evaluate God's actions, we must evaluate them over the full extent of human history. The Christian claim is not that the world is perfect as it is now; in fact, Scripture denies that it is. But the full goodness of God's plan will be manifest only at the end of redemptive history. For his own reasons, God has determined to "write" history as a story taking place over millennia of time.[22] Evil would not be such a problem if it were created and overcome supratemporally (as in Barth's *Geschichte*) or in a period of, say, three seconds. The problem is with the long wait for God's salvation.[23] But for him, of course, a thousand years are as a day (Ps. 90:4). And when we look back upon our sufferings in this world, they will seem small to us as well, "not worth comparing with the glory that is to be revealed to us" (Rom. 8:18). It is then that we will see how God has worked in all things for our good (8:28). Paul, who underwent much more suffering than most of us, even says that "this light momentary affliction is preparing for us an eternal weight of glory beyond all comparison" (2 Cor. 4:17).

4. God often surprises us by the ways in which he brings good out of evil. Certainly Joseph was surprised at the means God used to lift him from a status as slave and prisoner to that of Pharaoh's prime minister. Certainly the children of Israel were surprised at the miracles by which God brought them out of Egypt and sustained them in the wilderness. But the chief example of God's astonishing ways is found in the cross of Jesus. The prophets promised God's judgment on Israel's disobedience, but simultaneously promised that God would forgive and bless. How could he do both? The Israelites' disobedience merited nothing less than death. How could God be just in dealing with their sin and still bring them his promised blessings? Certainly this problem was quite impenetrable, until Jesus died in our place. His atonement was at the same time judgment and grace: judgment upon Jesus for our sin, and grace to the true Israel, those of us who are elect in him. My present point is this: that if God acted so wonderfully and surprisingly to bring good out of evil, when it seemed most impossible, can we not trust him to bring good out of the remaining evils that we experience?

5. Since the ultimate theodicy is future, we must now deal with the problem of evil by faith. We cannot total up the present evils against the present goods and from that calculation exonerate God of blame. But our inability to do this does not require us

---

21. See *AGG*, 89–102, for a fuller treatment of this argument.

22. Later, I will draw an analogy between the relation of God to the world and the relation of an author to his characters.

23. Recall the discussion of God's "presence in time," in chapter 6 of *DG*, and the many texts urging patience in waiting for God's time. Among them: Hab. 2:3; Matt. 6:34; Rom. 8:25; Phil. 4:6–7; Heb. 10:36; James 1:3–4; 5:7–11.

to surrender to those who use the problem of evil to deny the existence of God. For the burden of proof is, after all, not on us. It is the objector who must show that the evils of this world *cannot* be part of an overall good plan. I have shown many ways in which God brings good out of evil, even when it seems impossible for the good to prevail. Can the objector *prove* that God is unable to integrate the present evils into an overall good plan? This burden of proof is a heavy one, for the objector must prove a negative: that there is *no* way for God to vindicate his justice on the last day. I do not believe that burden has been met.

6. Does the greater-good defense presuppose that the end justifies the means? It does say that God's good purposes justify his use of evil. When we criticize someone for holding that "the end justifies the means," we mean that he thinks a noble end will justify means that would otherwise be accounted wicked. But that is precisely the question before us: is God's act to bring about evil normally a wicked action, which God justifies ad hoc because of his noble purpose? But how would we judge in this context what is "normally" the case? If God brought about moral evil in some sense, that act was unique. Ultimately, evil came into the world only once. Other "hardenings" of people's hearts in history are actions that only God can perform. Who are we to say that such actions are "normally" wicked, rather than to confess that they are a unique divine prerogative? When a man kills an innocent person, his act is normally murder. But when God takes human life, he acts within the proper authority of his lordship. Why should we not say the same thing about his agency in bringing evil to pass?[24] At least, we must say again that the burden of proof is on the objector.

7. Since the burden of proof is on the objector, it is not necessary for us to come up with a full theodicy, a justification of God's ways. In this world, we walk by faith, not by sight (2 Cor. 5:7). We will see later that sometimes seeking a theodicy can be sinful—when people demand of God an explanation for the ills that have befallen them.

My conclusion on the greater-good defense, then, is that God certainly does will evil for a good purpose. The good he intends will be so great, so wonderful and beautiful, that it will make present evils seem small. But we are not under obligation to show in every case *how* God's past and present actions contribute to the final good, and the unbeliever has no right to demand such an explanation.

Although the greater-good defense is basically sound, it leaves us with a sense of mystery. For it is hard to imagine *how* God's good purpose justifies the evil in the world.

Evil and God's Agency

We have seen that natural evil is a curse that God placed on the world in response to man's sin. We also saw earlier, in chapter 8, that God does harden hearts, and through his prophets he predicts sinful human actions long in advance, indicating that he is in control of human free decisions. Now, theologians have found it difficult to formulate in general terms how God acts to bring about those sinful actions. Earlier in

---

24. I will argue later that the ontological difference between God and man lies behind these moral distinctions.

the chapter, we saw Gilson arguing that God is not the cause of sin and evil because evil is nonbeing and therefore has no cause. Gilson is willing to say that God is the *deficient cause* (which sounds like a contrast to *efficient cause*), meaning that God creates mutable beings, but does not determine the specific defects that constitute sin. I found his privation theory, and his view of libertarian freedom, inadequate. But the discussion brings out an issue that we all must think about. Do we want to say that God is the "cause" of evil? That language is certainly problematic, since we usually associate cause with blame. Consider Mike, who made Billy put graffiti on the school door. Billy, of course, made the marks, but Mike caused him to do it. And so, most of us would agree, Mike deserves the blame. So it seems that if God causes sin and evil, he must be to blame for it.

Therefore, there has been much discussion among theologians as to what verb best describes God's agency in regard to evil. Some initial possibilities: *authors, brings about, causes, controls, creates, decrees, foreordains, incites, includes within his plan, makes happen, ordains, permits, plans, predestines, predetermines, produces, stands behind, wills.* Many of these are extrascriptural terms; none of them are perfectly easy to define in this context. So theologians need to give some careful thought to which of these terms, if any, should be affirmed, and in what sense. Words are the theologian's tools. In a situation such as this, none of the possibilities is fully adequate. There are various advantages and disadvantages among the different terms. Let us consider some of those that are most frequently discussed.

1. The term *authors* is almost universally condemned in the theological literature. It is rarely defined, but it seems to mean both that God is the efficient cause of evil and that by causing evil he actually does something wrong.[25] So the WCF says that God "neither is nor can be the author or approver of sin" (5.4). Despite this denial in a major Reformed confession, Arminians regularly charge that Reformed theology makes God the author of sin. They assume that if God brings about evil in any sense, he must therefore approve it and deserve the blame. In their view, nothing less than libertarian freedom will serve to absolve God from the charge of authoring sin.

But as we will see in chapter 35, libertarian freedom is incoherent and unbiblical. And as we saw in chapter 8, God does bring about sinful human actions. To deny this, or to charge God with wickedness on account of it, is not open to a Bible-believing Christian. Somehow, we must confess both that God has a role in bringing evil about and that in doing so he is holy and blameless. In the previous section, I tried to show how the greater-good defense, properly understood, supports this confession. God does bring sins about, but always for his own good purposes. So in bringing sin to pass, he does not himself commit sin. If that argument is sound, then a Reformed doctrine of the sovereignty of God does not imply that God is the author of sin.

---

25. Lest there be confusion over language: the "author-story" model of God's relation to creatures, which I mentioned earlier and will expound later, does not make God the "author of sin" in this sense. Nothing about that model implies that God commits or approves of sin. In fact, I will argue later that it provides us a reason to deny that.

2. *Causes* is another term that has led to much wrestling by theologians. As we recall, Gilson, with the Thomistic tradition, denies that God is the cause of evil[26] by defining evil as a privation. Reformed writers have also denied that God is the cause of sin. John Calvin teaches, "For the proper and genuine cause of sin is not God's hidden counsel but the evident will of man,"[27] though in context he also states that Adam's fall was "not without God's knowledge and ordination."[28] Some other examples:

> See that you make not God the author of sin, by charging his sacred decree with men's miscarriages, as if that were the cause or occasion of them; which we are sure that it is not, nor can be, any more than the sun can be the cause of darkness.[29]

> It is [God] who created, preserves, actuates and directs all things. But it by no means follows, from these premises, that God is therefore the cause of sin, for sin is nothing but *anomia*, illegality, want of conformity to the divine law (1 John iii. 4), a mere privation of rectitude; consequently, being itself a thing purely negative, it can have no positive or efficient cause, but only a negative or deficient one, as several learned men have observed.[30]

Canons of Dordt 1:5 says that "the cause or blame for this unbelief, as well as for all other sins, is not at all in God, but in man."

In these quotations, *cause* seems to take on the connotations of the term *author*. For these writers, to say that God "causes" evil is to say, or perhaps imply, that he is to blame for it. Note the phrase "cause or blame" in the Canons of Dordt, in which the terms seem to be treated as synonyms. But note above that although Calvin rejects *cause*, he affirms *ordination*. God is not the "cause" of sin, but it is by his "ordination." For the modern reader, the distinction is not evident. To ordain is to cause, and vice versa. If causality entails blame, then ordination would seem to entail it as well; if not, then neither entails it. But evidently in the vocabulary of Calvin and his successors, there was a difference between the two terms.

For us, the question arises whether God can be the efficient cause of sin, without being to blame for it. The older theologians denied that God was the efficient cause of sin (a) because they held the privation theory, and (b) because they identified cause with authorship. But if, as I recommend, we reject the privation theory, and if, as I believe, the connection between cause and blame in modern language is no

26. Except, of course, as a *deficient* cause.

27. John Calvin, *Concerning the Eternal Predestination of God* (London: James Clarke and Co., 1961), 122. Calvin accepts the privation theory, as evident on page 169.

28. Ibid., 121.

29. Elisha Coles, *A Practical Discourse on God's Sovereignty* (17th c.; repr., Marshallton, DE: National Foundation for Christian Education, 1968), 15.

30. Jerome Zanchius, *Observations on the Divine Attributes*, in *Absolute Predestination* (Marshallton, DE: National Foundation for Christian Education, n.d.), 33. Compare the formulations of post-Reformation dogmaticians Polan and Wolleb in *RD*, 143, and of Mastricht on 277. All of these base their arguments on the premise that evil is a mere privation.

stronger than the connection between ordination and blame, then it seems to me that it is not wrong to say that God causes evil and sin. Certainly we should employ such language cautiously, however, in view of the long history of its rejection in the tradition.

It is interesting that Calvin does use *cause*, referring to God's agency in bringing evil about, when he distinguishes between God as the "remote cause" and human agency as the "proximate cause." Arguing that God is not the "author of sin," he says that "the proximate cause is one thing, the remote cause another."[31] Calvin points out that when wicked men steal Job's goods, Job recognizes that "the Lord gave and the Lord has taken away; may the name of the Lord be praised." The thieves, proximate cause of the evil, are guilty; but Job doesn't question the motives of the Lord, the remote cause. Calvin does not, however, believe that the proximate-ultimate distinction is sufficient to show us *why* God is guiltless:

> But how it was ordained by the foreknowledge and decree of God what man's future was without God being implicated as associate in the fault as the author and approver of transgression, is clearly a secret so much excelling the insight of the human mind, that I am not ashamed to confess ignorance.[32]

He uses the proximate-remote distinction merely to distinguish between the causality of God and that of creatures, and therefore to *state* that the former is always righteous. But he does not believe the distinction solves the problem of evil. Indeed, it does not, for as in the Billy-Mike example we have good reason in many situations to associate remote causality (Mike) with blame, sometimes to the exclusion of blame for the proximate cause (Billy). It would be wrong to generalize from the Billy-Mike example to prove that God is to blame for human sin. Certainly God's motives are very different from those of Mike in our example. But we cannot prove that God is *not* to blame, merely by pointing out that he is only the remote cause.

At least, the discussion above does indicate that Calvin is willing in some contexts to refer to God as a cause of sin and evil. Calvin also describes God as the sole cause of the hardening and reprobation of the wicked:

> Therefore, if we cannot assign any reason for his bestowing mercy on his people, but just that it so pleases him, neither can we have any reason for his reprobating others but his will. When God is said to visit mercy or harden whom he will, men are reminded that they are not to seek for any cause beyond his will.[33]

3. Consider now the term *permits*. This is the preferred term in Arminian theology, in which it amounts to a denial that God causes sin. For the Arminian,

---

31. Calvin, *Eternal Predestination*, 181.
32. Ibid., 124.
33. *Institutes*, 3.22.11. Cf. 3.23.1.

God does not cause sin; he only permits it. Reformed theologians, however, have also used the term, referring to God's relation to sin. The Reformed, however, insist contrary to the Arminians that God's "permission" of sin is no less efficacious than his ordination of good. Calvin denies that there is any "mere permission" in God:

> From this it is easy to conclude how foolish and frail is the support of divine justice afforded by the suggestion that evils come to be not by [God's] will, but merely by His permission. Of course, so far as they are evils, which men perpetrate with their evil mind, as I shall show in greater detail shortly, I admit that they are not pleasing to God. But it is a quite frivolous refuge to say that God otiosely permits them, when Scripture shows Him not only willing but the author of them.[34]

God's "permission" is an *efficacious* permission. Heinrich Heppe describes it as *voluntas efficaciter permittens* and quotes Martin Heidegger:

> Nor whether he is willing or refusing is God's permission like man's permission, which admits of an eclipse which he neither wills nor refuses, as the Lombard and with him the Scholastics assert. It is effective, mighty, and not separate from God's will at all. Otiose permission of sin separated from God's will is repugnant both to the nature of the First Cause and to the divine and almighty foresight, to His nature and to Scripture.[35]

If God's permission is efficacious, how does it differ from other exercises of his will? Evidently, the Reformed use *permits* mainly as a more delicate term than *causes*, and to indicate that God brings about sin with a kind of reluctance born of his holy hatred of evil.

This usage does reflect a biblical pattern: When Satan acts, he acts, in an obvious sense, by God's permission.[36] God allows him to take Job's family, wealth, and health. But God will not allow Satan to take Job's life (Job 2:6). So Satan is on a short leash, acting only within limits assigned by God. And in this respect all sinful acts are similar. The sinner can go only so far, before he meets the judgment of God.

It is right, therefore, to use *permission* to apply to God's ordination of sin. But we should not assume, as Arminians do, that divine permission is anything less than sovereign ordination. What God permits or allows to happen will happen. God could easily have prevented Satan's attack on Job if he had intended to. That he did not prevent that

---

34. Calvin, *Eternal Predestination*, 176. The term *author* raises questions. I take it, in Calvin's usual line of thinking, to mean that God authors the evil happenings without authoring their evil character. But the use of *author* here indicates something of the flexibility of language in Calvin's formulations, in contrast with its relative rigidity in his successors.

35. *RD*, 90. Compare my earlier reference to Polan on *RD*, 143.

36. In this use, and in the Reformed theological use, *permission* has no connotation of moral approval, as it sometimes has in contemporary use of the term.

attack implies that he intended it to happen. Permission, then, is a form of ordination, a form of causation.[37] That it is sometimes taken otherwise is a good argument against using the term, but perhaps not a decisive argument.

I will not discuss other terms on my list (except *wills*, which we will discuss in chapter 16). The above should be sufficient to indicate the need of caution in our choice of vocabulary, and also the need to think carefully before condemning the vocabulary of others. It is not easy to find adequate terms to describe God's ordination of evil. Our language must not compromise either God's full sovereignty or his holiness and goodness.

None of these formulations solves the problem of evil. It is not a solution to say that God ordains evil, but doesn't author or cause it (if we choose to say that). This language is not a solution to the problem, but only a way of raising it. For the problem of evil asks *how* God can ordain evil without authoring it. And as Calvin pointed out, the distinction between remote and proximate cause is also inadequate to answer the questions before us, however useful it may be in stating who is to blame for evil. Nor is it a solution to say that God permits, rather than ordains, evil. As we have seen, God's permission is as efficacious as his ordination. The difference between the terms brings nothing to light that will solve the problem.

I should, however, say something more about the nature of God's agency in regard to evil. Recall from earlier in this chapter the model of the author and his story: God's relationship to free agents is like the relationship of an author to his characters. Let us consider to what extent God's relationship to human sin is like that of Shakespeare to Macbeth, the murderer of Duncan.

I borrowed the Shakespeare/Macbeth illustration from Wayne Grudem's excellent *GST*. But I do disagree with Grudem on one point. He says that we could say that either Macbeth or Shakespeare "killed King Duncan." I agree, of course, that both Macbeth and Shakespeare are responsible, at different levels of reality, for the death of Duncan. But as I analyze the language that we typically use in such contexts, it seems clear to me that we would *not* normally say that Shakespeare killed Duncan. Shakespeare wrote the murder into his play. But the murder took place in the world of the play, not the real world of the author. Macbeth did it, not Shakespeare. We sense the rightness of the poetic justice brought against Macbeth for his crime. But we would certainly consider it very unjust if Shakespeare were tried and put to death for killing Duncan.[38] And no one suggests that there is any problem in reconciling

37. Traditional Arminians agree that God is omnipotent and can prevent sinful actions. So we wonder how they can object to this argument. If God could prevent sin, but chose not to, must we not say that he has ordained it to happen? Some more recent Arminians claim that God created the world without even knowing that evil would come to pass. But doesn't this representation make God, in the words of one of my correspondents, like a kind of "mad scientist," who "throws together a potentially dangerous combination of chemicals, not knowing if it will result in a hazardous and uncontrollable reaction"? Does this view not make God guilty of reckless endangerment?

38. Think how many writers of TV programs would be taken from us if such a legal basis were valid. No further comment.

Shakespeare's benevolence with his omnipotence over the world of the drama. Indeed, there is reason for us to praise Shakespeare for raising up this character, Macbeth, to show us the consequences of sin.[39]

The difference between levels, then, may have moral significance as well as metaphysical.[40] It may illumine why the biblical writers, who do not hesitate to say that God brings about sin and evil, are not tempted to accuse him of wrongdoing. The relation between God and ourselves, of course, is different in some respects from that between an author and his characters. Most significantly: we are real; Macbeth is not. But between God and ourselves there is a vast difference in the *kind* of reality and in relative status. God is the absolute controller and authority, the most present fact of nature and history. He is the Lawgiver, we the law receivers. He is the head of the covenant; we are the servants. He has devised the creation for his own glory; we seek his glory, rather than our own. He makes us as the potter makes pots, for his own purposes. Do these differences not put God in a different moral category as well?

The very transcendence of God plays a significant role in biblical responses to the problem of evil. Because God is who he is, the covenant Lord, he is not required to defend himself against charges of injustice. He is the Judge, not we. Very often in Scripture, when something happens that calls God's goodness into question, God pointedly refrains from explaining. Indeed, he often rebukes those human beings who question him. Job demanded an interview with God, so that he could ask God the reasons for his sufferings (Job 23:1–7; 31:35–37). But when he met God, God asked the questions: "Dress for action like a man; I will question you, and you make it known to me" (38:3). The questions mostly revealed Job's ignorance about God's creation: if Job doesn't understand the ways of the animals, how can he presume to call God's motives into question? He doesn't even understand earthly things; how can he presume to debate heavenly things? God is not subject to the ignorant evaluations of his creatures.[41]

---

39. As my friend Steve Hays points out in correspondence, the dark aspects of Shakespeare's dramas also add to his stature as an artist. Our admiration of Shakespeare is partly based on his understanding of the sin of the human soul and his ability to expose and deal with that sin, not trivially, but in ways that surprise us and deepen our understanding.

40. The metaphysical difference between the Creator God and the world of which evil is a part may indicate the true connection between the ethical and metaphysical, as opposed to the false connection of the "chain of being" thinkers mentioned earlier in this chapter. It may also indicate a grain of truth in the privation theory: there is a metaphysical difference between good and evil, but it is not the difference between being and nonbeing, but rather the difference between uncreated being and created being.

41. To say this is not to adopt the view of Gordon H. Clark that God is *ex lex*, or outside of, not subject to, the moral law. See Clark's *Religion, Reason, and Revelation* (Philadelphia: Presbyterian and Reformed, 1961), where he argues that because God is above the moral law, he is not subject to it. Certainly God has some prerogatives that he forbids to us, such as the freedom to take human life. But for the most part, the moral laws that God imposes on us are grounded in his own character. See Ex. 20:11; Lev. 11:44–45; Matt. 5:45; 1 Peter 1:15–16. God will not violate his own character. What Scripture denies is that man has sufficient understanding of God's character and his eternal plan (not to mention sufficient authority) to bring accusations against him.

It is significant that the potter-clay image appears in the one place in Scripture where the problem of evil is explicitly addressed.[42] In Romans 9:19–21, Paul appeals specifically to the difference in metaphysical level and status between the Creator and the creature:

> You will say to me then, "Why does he still find fault? For who can resist his will?" But who are you, O man, to answer back to God? Will what is molded say to its molder, "Why have you made me like this?" Has the potter no right over the clay, to make out of the same lump one vessel for honorable use and another for dishonorable use?

This answer to the problem of evil turns entirely on God's sovereignty. It is as far as could be imagined from a free-will defense. It brings to our attention the fact that his prerogatives are far greater than ours, as does the author-character model. Therefore, although we may reverently ask God why he brings suffering into our lives, we have no right ever to bring accusations against him. God is well within his rights when, as often in Scripture, he does not respond to implicit or explicit charges of wrongdoing. Indeed, when he is charged with doing wrong, he typically turns the accusations against the plaintiff (as Matt. 20:15–16; Rom. 9:19–21).[43]

One might object to this model that it makes God the author of evil. But that objection, I think, confuses two senses of *author*. As we have seen, the phrase *author of evil* connotes not only causality of evil, but also blame for it. To "author" evil is to do it. But in saying that God is related to the world as an author to a story, we actually provide a way of seeing that God is *not* to be blamed for the sin of his creatures.

This is not, of course, the only biblical response to the problem of evil. Sometimes God does not respond by silencing us, as above, but by showing us in some measure what evil contributes to his plan, what I have called the *greater-good defense*. The greater-good defense refers particularly to God's lordship attribute of control, that he is sovereign over evil and uses it for good. The Romans 9 response refers particularly to God's lordship attribute of authority. And his attribute of covenant presence addresses the emotional problem of evil, comforting us with the promises of God and the love of Jesus from which no evil can separate us (Rom. 8:35–39), and promising us that on the last day our hearts will confess, even sing, of God's righteousness, without being troubled by evil (Rev. 15:3–4).

Valid responses to the problem of evil, then, can be arranged triperspectivally; see fig. 14.1.

---

42. The problem is raised, of course, in the book of Job and many other places in Scripture. But to my knowledge, Romans 9 is the only passage in which a biblical writer gives an explicit answer to it. Job, of course, never learns why he has suffered.

43. I have sometimes referred to this defense against the problem of evil as the *"shut-up" defense*, as in the Ring Lardner line, "'Shut up,' he explained."

1. Normative: Human beings have no right to bring accusations against God.
2. Situational: God will always bring good out of evil.
3. Existential: God will comfort us so that our hearts are fully assured of the justice and rightness of his actions.

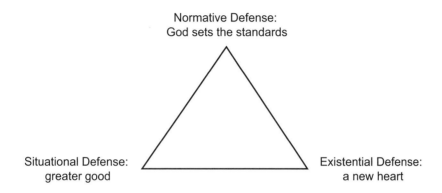

Fig. 14.1. Defenses against the Problem of Evil

Key Terms

Logical problem of evil
Emotional problem of evil
Natural evil
Moral evil
Evil as illusion
Evil as privation
Orderly-universe defense
Soul-making defense
Free-will defense
Libertarian freedom
Compatibilist freedom
Best-possible-world defense
Greater-good defense
Author of evil
Cause of evil
Permission of evil
Author-character model

Study Questions

1. "Scripture, therefore, gives us an explicit answer to the problem of natural evil." What is that answer? Discuss.

2. "Granted what we have already seen about God's sovereignty, the various attempts to show that God is too weak to prevent evil do not seem promising." Explain; evaluate.

3. Summarize the three general types of defenses against the problem of evil.

4. Summarize the privation defense and reply to it.

5. "But I confess that I don't know the difference between effectual permission and efficient causation." Explain this observation and show how it bears on the discussion of evil.

6. "Granting, however, Gilson's view that evil is a lack or privation of being, a kind of nonbeing, why would that absolve God of blame for evil?" Explain this question as a critique of the privation view, using Frame's illustration of the doughnut maker.

7. "Cornelius Van Til often warned against 'reducing ethics to metaphysics,' or 'confusing sin with finitude.'" Explain Van Til's use of these expressions and show how they bear on the privation view of evil.

8. Evaluate the greater-good defense and various forms of it, such as the orderly-universe, soul-making, free-will, and best-possible-world defenses.

9. "Unless God's standards govern our concept of goodness, there can be no talk of good or evil at all." Explain; evaluate.

10. How should we speak of God's relation to evil: authorship, cause, permission, or some other? Explain.

11. Does the author-character model help us in dealing with the problem of evil? How, or why not?

12. "The very transcendence of God plays a significant role in biblical responses to the problem of evil." How? Give some examples.

13. Frame suggests that biblical responses to the problem of evil can be arranged triperspectivally. Show how he does this, and evaluate.

Memory Verses

Gen. 18:25: Far be it from you to do such a thing, to put the righteous to death with the wicked, so that the righteous fare as the wicked! Far be that from you! Shall not the Judge of all the earth do what is just?

Gen. 50:20: As for you, you meant evil against me, but God meant it for good, to bring it about that many people should be kept alive, as they are today.

Rom. 8:28: And we know that for those who love God all things work together for good, for those who are called according to his purpose.

Rom. 9:19–21: You will say to me then, "Why does he still find fault? For who can resist his will?" But who are you, O man, to answer back to God? Will what is molded say to its molder, "Why have you made me like this?" Has the potter no right over the clay, to make out of the same lump one vessel for honorable use and another for dishonorable use?

Rev. 15:3–4: And they sing the song of Moses, the servant of God, and the song of the Lamb, saying,

"Great and amazing are your deeds,
    O Lord God the Almighty!
Just and true are your ways,
    O King of the nations!
Who will not fear, O Lord,
    and glorify your name?
For you alone are holy.
    All nations will come
    and worship you,
for your righteous acts have been revealed."

Resources for Further Study

Lewis, C. S. *The Problem of Pain*. New York: HarperOne, 2001. Lewis uses some arguments I don't like, such as the free-will defense, but he writes well and has helped many readers. This book should be read alongside his later *A Grief Observed* (New York: HarperOne, 2001), in which he details his personal grief over the loss of his wife and becomes less certain of the adequacy of his arguments.

Tada, Joni Eareckson, and Stephen Estes. *When God Weeps*. Grand Rapids: Zondervan, 1997. Describes real sufferings and practical ways of relating these to God's love.

CHAPTER 15

GOD'S ATTRIBUTES: KNOWLEDGE

WE WILL NOW consider another group of God's attributes, those concerned with God's knowledge and knowability, sometimes called the *intellectual* or *epistemological* attributes. In the chart of chapter 12, I arranged five attributes in this category. I will treat two of them, God's speech and his truth, in chapter 23, which deals with the word of God. In chapter 29 I will deal with two others, God's incomprehensibility and knowability (not on the chart of chapter 12), which have to do with God's accessibility to our own knowledge. Here I will focus on God's own knowledge of himself and the world, postponing until later the nature of his communication with us, and our ability to receive that communication.

God's Knowledge

Many philosophers have defined *knowledge* as "justified, true belief." Although some have found problems with this definition,[1] it is still the starting point for many philosophical discussions. There is, however, no consensus among philosophers as to what constitutes *justification* in this definition, so knowledge remains somewhat mysterious to epistemologists.[2] The question of justification is, of course, the question of what norms should properly govern and evaluate claims to knowledge. So knowledge has an ethical dimension: items of knowledge are not only beliefs, but beliefs we *ought* to have. But the ethical dimension of knowledge shows that knowledge cannot be grounded only in finite reality. It must presuppose God, who is the only adequate source of norms.[3] See fig. 15.1.

---

1. Edmund Gettier, "Is Justified True Belief Knowledge?" *Analysis* 23 (1963): 121–23, began the recent discussion. See, for example, John Pollock, *Contemporary Theories of Knowledge* (Totowa, NJ: Rowman and Littlefield, 1986), 180–93.

2. For my thoughts, see *DKG*, 104–68, and my "Christianity and Contemporary Epistemology," *WTJ* 52, 1 (1990): 131–41.

3. See my *PWG*, 39–56, for an argument to this effect, also the "moral argument" in *AGG*, 93–102, and the argument on 102–4 that rationality itself is value-based. In *DKG*, I present the larger epistemological perspective warranting these arguments. I am glad that some recent thinkers are discussing the question of normativity

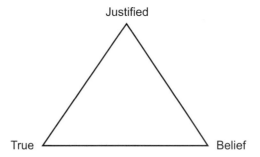

Fig. 15.1. Traditional Philosophical Definition of Knowledge

Another problem with the definition of knowledge as justified, true belief is that this definition is suited only to the knowledge of propositions, items of information ("knowing that"). What about the knowledge of skills ("knowing how") or of persons? Knowing how to do something cannot be reduced to a knowledge of propositions. One may memorize thousands of truths about playing football; but that knowledge, in itself, will not make someone a skilled quarterback. Similarly, knowing a friend is not merely knowing propositions about him.[4] I may know more true propositions about the president of the United States than about the boy who delivers my newspaper. But I may yet truthfully claim that I know the newsboy, and I do not know the President.[5] See fig. 15.2.

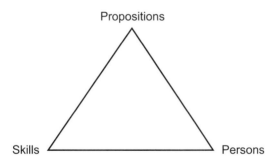

Fig. 15.2. Objects of Knowledge

in knowledge. See especially Alvin Plantinga, *Warrant: The Current Debate* (New York: Oxford University Press, 1993), and *Warrant and Proper Function* (New York: Oxford University Press, 1993). *Warranted Christian Belief* (New York: Oxford University Press, 2000), the third volume in Plantinga's trilogy, deals with the relation of epistemic warrant to God.

4. On the other hand, factual knowledge about a friend does not necessarily decrease the existential quality of a friendship. Normally it is beneficial, contrary to Emil Brunner, *Truth as Encounter* (Philadelphia: Westminster Press, 1964). On the knowledge of persons, compare the usage in Scripture in which knowledge refers to sexual intercourse, as Genesis 4:1.

5. Although these are not reducible to one another, it is still true that each depends on the other two. You cannot know propositions unless you have the skill to achieve knowledge, and unless you know the divine person who understands all things. Similarly for the other two. So in one sense, the three are perspectivally related. Propositions are, perhaps, normative; skills, situational; personal knowledge, existential.

In the view of Scripture, the most important kind of knowledge is the knowledge of God. Knowing God is the key to all other knowledge: "The fear of the LORD is the beginning of knowledge" (Prov. 1:7). So knowledge is fundamentally knowledge of a person. It is also covenantal, since the personal God is our covenant Lord. He calls us to seek knowledge as his obedient servants.[6]

God made and preinterpreted all things in the universe, as we saw in chapter 10. Our task in knowing the world is to think God's thoughts after him, so propositional knowledge is based on knowledge of a person. He supplies the *norms*, the *justifications*, that are missing in secular accounts of knowledge, as well as the truths that we are to believe and the mental capacity for us to come to knowledge.[7] It is God also who enables us to learn skills: "Blessed be the LORD, my rock, who trains my hands for war, and my fingers for battle" (Ps. 144:1).

Knowledge (Heb. *da'ath*, Gk. *gnosis, epignosis*)[8] is also a divine attribute:

> The LORD is a God of knowledge,
> and by him actions are weighed. (1 Sam. 2:3)

> Does he who teaches man lack knowledge? (Ps. 94:10 NIV)[9]

If human knowledge is dependent on God, then God's own knowledge depends on God. That is, it is self-attesting, self-referential, self-sufficient.[10] His knowledge is the ultimate *justified, true belief*: He is the ultimate *justification* of knowledge, the standard for creaturely knowledge and his own.[11] He is the ultimate *truth*: the truth is what he is and what he has decreed to be. And this justification and this truth are enclosed in God's ultimate mind, ultimate subjectivity, ultimate *belief*. So as many theologians have taught, God's knowledge depends only on himself. God knows all things by (1) knowing himself, and (2) knowing his own plan for the universe.

Since both these objects of thought are eternal, God's knowledge is eternal; he

> declar[es] the end from the beginning
> and from ancient times things not yet done,
> saying, "My counsel shall stand,
> and I will accomplish all my purpose." (Isa. 46:10)

---

6. Note the correlations between obedience and knowledge in many passages of Scripture. In Jeremiah 22:16, the two are virtual synonyms. See *DKG*, 43–45.

7. So the triad *justified, true belief* is triperspectival. Justification is normative; truth is situational (the facts as they really are), and belief (a subjective state) is existential. See *DKG* for elaboration.

8. I will also refer to some verses employing the Hebrew *bin* root (*tabun*, etc.), often rendered "understanding." The Greek *eidenai*, along with *ginosko* (the root of *gnosis*), is also translated "to know."

9. "Lack knowledge" is missing, but understood, in the Hebrew text. The ESV leaves it unexpressed, which is not wrong, but the NIV more fully brings out the meaning.

10. This is God's *aseity*, his self-existence and self-sufficiency, with respect to knowledge. In chapter 19, I will discuss aseity in more general terms.

11. On the circularity implicit in this formulation, see chapters 28–32 on our knowledge of God.

God's Knowledge and His Lordship

Scripture draws a number of connections between God's knowledge and his lordship. We saw in chapters 8 and 11 that God's knowledge of people often refers not to propositional knowledge, not knowledge *about* them, but rather to his choice, his election of them as his covenant servants. Here "knowledge" is like "befriending." In Amos 3:2, God says to Israel, "You only have I known of all the families of the earth; therefore I will punish you for all your iniquities." The word translated "known" in the ESV is translated "chosen" in the NIV. Clearly, God does not here intend to express ignorance of the nations other than Israel. But his special covenant relation with Israel is here called "knowledge."

If, as I have argued, God is covenant Lord (in different ways, to be sure) to everything in creation, then he knows everything covenantally. He has, in other words, chosen everything for his own purposes. And this purposeful choice implies propositional knowledge. If God creates and directs the whole course of nature and history, and if that creation and direction presuppose his wise purpose, then God knows everything: himself and everything in creation.

So Scripture connects God's knowledge with his control: creation and providence.

> Who has measured the waters in the hollow of his hand
>   and marked off the heavens with a span,
> enclosed the dust of the earth in a measure
>   and weighed the mountains in scales
>   and the hills in a balance?
> Who has measured the Spirit of the LORD,
>   or what man shows him his counsel?
> Whom did he consult,
>   and who made him understand?
> Who taught him the path of justice,
>   and taught him knowledge,
>   and showed him the way of understanding? (Isa. 40:12–14)

These are, of course, rhetorical questions. Those in verse 12 have as their answer "only the Lord," and those of 13–14, "no one." Since God has created all things, he has all knowledge of them. That knowledge is self-contained; he did not learn it from anyone. Cf. also Ps. 139:1–24. God made the world by his wisdom (Ps. 104:24; Prov. 3:19; 8:27; Jer. 10:12; 51:15).[12]

The lordship attribute of authority can be seen in the way Scripture connects God's knowledge with his judgments. As Donald Carson puts it:

> Yahweh can well judge all men and nations (Ps. 67:5), for not only is he all-powerful, he is all-knowing. His omniscience is not infrequently associated with the certainty

12. For more references on God's knowledge exhibited in creation and providence, review chapters 8–11. In Psalm 104, note all the details of the course of nature ascribed to God's wisdom.

and exhaustive nature of his impending judgment (e.g., Isa. 29:15f; Jer. 16:16–18; Ezek. 11:2, 5; Ps. 139:1ff; Prov. 5:21; 24:2).[13]

God knows exhaustively what sinners do, and he evaluates their actions rightly. His evaluations are the very standard of truth; they cannot be wrong. He is the teacher, we always the pupils; so: "Does he who teaches man lack knowledge" (Ps. 94:10b NIV[14])? Certainly not. So the fullness and accuracy of his knowledge cannot be questioned.

Both God's control and his authority are found in his decrees and plans for the universe, as in Isaiah 46:10, quoted earlier. Since God will certainly accomplish his purpose, and since that purpose encompasses all of time, the end from the beginning, he is able to make known whatever will come to pass. And such revelation, of course, presupposes knowledge.

And God's knowledge also emerges, obviously, from his lordship attribute of presence. Because God is everywhere, no one can hide from him (2 Chron. 16:9; Ps. 139:1–24; Prov. 5:21; 15:3; Jer. 23:24; Acts 17:24–28; Heb. 4:13). He knows everything we do, including our secret sins (2 Kings 6:12; Pss. 10:10–14; 33:13–15; 90:8; Prov. 24:12; Ezek. 8:12; Hos. 5:3). Indeed, he knows our hearts and our thoughts (1 Sam. 16:7; 1 Kings 8:39; 2 Kings 6:12; Pss. 94:11; 139:2, 23–24; Prov. 15:11; 21:2; Jer. 17:10; 20:12; Ezek. 11:5; Luke 16:15; John 2:25; Acts 1:24; Rom. 8:27; 1 Cor. 4:5; 1 Thess. 2:4; Heb. 4:12–13; 1 John 3:20; Rev. 2:23).[15]

Omniscience

It should now be obvious that the extent of God's knowledge is universal. God controls the whole course of nature and history (above, and chapters 8–10), and controls everything by a wise plan (chapter 11). He is the "author" of the text of history (chapter 14). His wise plan constitutes knowledge, knowledge of everything, omniscience.[16] His knowledge is just as extensive as his lordship. As we saw in the preceding section, his control, authority, and presence are universal and therefore presuppose universal knowledge.

13. Donald A. Carson, *Divine Sovereignty and Human Responsibility* (Atlanta: John Knox Press, 1981), 25. First Thessalonians 2:4 and Hebrews 4:12–13 are other passages that correlate omniscience with judgment.

14. See footnote 9 above.

15. Note that John 2:25 and Revelation 2:23 ascribe this same knowledge to Jesus. Note, too, that a number of these references also deal with the lordship attribute of authority, because they refer to God's sovereign judgment against sin.

16. More formally, God's omniscience may be defined as his knowledge of all actual and possible states of affairs, and/or of the truth value of all propositions. (I will discuss his knowledge of possibilities in a later section.) We should not say that God *asserts* or *utters* all true propositions. When Joe Smith says, "I am a sinner," he expresses a true proposition. God knows that that proposition, spoken by Joe, is true, and he knows the state of affairs of which Joe speaks. But God does not *assert* that proposition in so many words, because he is not Joe, and he is not a sinner. A point like this should be obvious, but it has actually generated considerable philosophical discussion. For instance, some have said that God cannot know that "today is Tuesday" (uttered by Joe on Tuesday) if he is supratemporal. They have argued that view as a refutation of God's supratemporality. More on this issue at a later point.

Our confession of God's omniscience is not, however, based only on the arguments above. Scripture states it quite explicitly, and often.

> Great is our Lord, and abundant in power;
>   his understanding is beyond measure. (Ps. 147:5)

> [Peter] said to him, "Lord, you know everything; you know that I love you." (John 21:17b; cf. 2:24–25)

> For the word of God is living and active, sharper than any two-edged sword, piercing to the division of soul and of spirit, of joints and of marrow, and discerning the thoughts and intentions of the heart. And no creature is hidden from his sight, but all are naked and exposed to the eyes of him to whom we must give account. (Heb. 4:12–13)

> God is greater than our heart, and he knows everything. (1 John 3:20b)

God knows all about the starry heavens (Gen. 15:5; Ps. 147:4; Isa. 40:26; Jer. 33:22), and about the tiniest details as well (Pss. 50:10–11; 56:8; Matt. 10:30). "God knows!" is an oathlike utterance (2 Cor. 11:11; 12:2–3). It certifies the truth of human words, because it presupposes that God's knowledge is exhaustive, universal, and infallible. God's knowledge is absolute knowledge, a perfection: so it elicits religious praise (Ps. 139:17–18; Isa. 40:28; Rom. 11:33–36).

Wicked people often think that God will not notice what they do—but they will find that God does know, and that he will certainly condemn their sin (Pss. 10:11; 11:4; 73:11; 94:7; Isa. 29:15; 40:27; 47:10; Jer. 16:17–18; Ezek. 8:12). To the righteous, however, God's knowledge is a blessing of the covenant (Ex. 2:23–25; 3:7–9; 1 Kings 18:20–40; 2 Chron. 16:9; Pss. 33:18–20; 34:15–16; 38:9; 145:20; Matt. 6:32). He knows what is happening to them, he hears their prayers, and he will certainly answer.

God's Knowledge of the Future

Does God's omniscience include knowledge of the future? Certainly it does, in the view of Scripture. We have seen that God foreordains the whole course of history by his eternal plan. If he plans and foreordains all things, surely he knows them, a fortiori.

But some professing Christians have expressed doubts that God has "exhaustive" knowledge of the future. Lelio (1525–62) and Fausto (1539–1604) Socinus (uncle and nephew), together with their followers, are best known for their denials of the deity of Christ and of substitutionary atonement. But they also "held to a heretical doctrine of God."[17] Robert Strimple explains:

---

17. Robert B. Strimple, "What Does God Know?," in *The Coming Evangelical Crisis*, ed. John H. Armstrong (Chicago: Moody Press, 1996), 140.

The Socinian doctrine can be stated very briefly, and it must be contrasted with both Calvinism and Arminianism. Calvinism (or Augustinianism) teaches that the sovereign God has *foreordained* whatsoever comes to pass, and therefore He *foreknows* whatsoever comes to pass. Arminianism denies that God has foreordained whatsoever comes to pass but wishes nevertheless to affirm God's foreknowledge of whatsoever comes to pass. Against the Arminians, the Socinians insisted that logically the Calvinists were quite correct in insisting that the only real basis for believing that God *knows* what you are going to do next is to believe that he has *foreordained* what you are going to do next. How else could God know ahead of time what your decision will be? Like the Arminians, however, the Socinians insisted that it was a contradiction of human freedom to believe in the sovereign foreordination of God. So they went "all the way" (logically) and denied not only that God has foreordained the free decisions of free agents but also that God foreknows what those decisions will be.[18]

Although contemporary "free-will theists"[19] or "open theists" claim to be Arminian in their theology, they have in fact become Socinian[20] in their view of God's knowledge.[21] For Arminians, God's foreknowledge plays a very important role, because it is central to their attempt to maintain a doctrine of divine sovereignty together with their doctrine of libertarian free will.[22] Open theists abandon this attempt, holding that God does not have exhaustive knowledge of the future. They argue that if God knows the future completely, the future must be fixed, and man cannot be really free (that is, free in the libertarian sense).

Much of the open theists' argument for their proposal depends on assuming the libertarian view of human freedom. To those who, like me, reject that position, the open-theist argument from Scripture is not very persuasive. Nevertheless, since there is quite a bit of controversy over this matter today, I should give some broad attention to the Scripture teaching on the subject of God's foreknowledge.[23]

---

18. Ibid., 140–41.

19. For examples of this type of theology, see Richard Rice, *God's Foreknowledge and Man's Free Will* (Minneapolis: Bethany House, 1985); Clark Pinnock et al., *The Openness of God* (Downers Grove, IL: InterVarsity Press, 1994).

20. As Strimple points out, one of the "selling points" of open theism is that it is a *new* position. But in fact it is an old heresy, rejected by the church four hundred years ago.

21. The same is true of the "moral government theology" of Gordon C. Olson and others. See E. Calvin Beisner, *Evangelical Heathenism* (Moscow, ID: Canon Press, 1996).

22. On libertarianism, see chapter 35 of this book.

23. Earlier in this chapter, I argued that "knowledge" in Scripture often refers not to knowledge of facts, but to personal relationships. Cf. chapter 35 as well. In my view, the same can be said of God's *foreknowledge* of men in Romans 8:29; 11:2; and 1 Peter 1:2. These verses don't speak primarily of God's knowing facts in advance, but of his establishing relationships with people before the world was made. Nevertheless, foreknowledge in this sense entails foreknowledge in the sense of knowing facts in advance. So I believe that these verses are relevant to our present concerns as they were to earlier topics of discussion. In this section, I will use *foreknowledge* in the more common sense, to mean "knowledge beforehand," the current focus of our attention.

Another problem in the use of the term *foreknowledge*: Some would argue that since God is timelessly eternal, the word *foreknowledge* is inappropriate. God's knowledge, on this view, is timeless, and therefore not "before" anything. I will discuss God's relation to time under the topic of eternity (chapter 17). For now, let us just say that the term *foreknowledge* simply means this: that before any event transpires, it is true for us to say that God

God's Knowledge of the Future in General

God's knowledge of the future is important in Scripture, both as an aspect of his sovereignty, as we have discussed, and as a foundation for prophecy. Note the test of a true prophet in Deuteronomy 18:21–22:

> And if you say in your heart, "How may we know the word that the LORD has not spoken?"—when a prophet speaks in the name of the LORD, if the word does not come to pass or come true, that is a word that the LORD has not spoken; the prophet has spoken it presumptuously. You need not be afraid of him.

A true prophet has God's words on his lips (vv. 18–20). When his prophecies predict future events, God's word gives him supernatural knowledge. If the event does not happen, the prophet is proved false. Deuteronomy 18 does not even consider the possibility that God himself might have been in error, and that the prophet faithfully proclaimed the divine errors to the people. God himself does not err. He is omniscient, as we have seen. In Deuteronomy 18, God's omniscience is the presupposition. The text banishes from the outset any consideration that God might be wrong. God is *necessarily* right. And this passage shows us that his omniscience extends to future events.[24]

Knowledge of the future is not only the test of a true prophet. It is also the test of a true God. In the contest between Yahweh and the false gods of the ancient Near East, a major issue is: which deity knows the future? This is a frequent theme in Isaiah 40–49, a passage that focuses on the sovereignty of Yahweh over against the absurd pretensions of the false gods:

> Set forth your case, says the LORD;
>   bring your proofs, says the King of Jacob.
> Let them bring them, and tell us
>   what is to happen.
> Tell us the former things, what they are,
>   that we may consider them,
> that we may know their outcome;
>   or declare to us the things to come.
> Tell us what is to come hereafter,
>   that we may know that you are gods;
> do good, or do harm,
>   that we may be dismayed and terrified. (Isa. 41:21–23; cf. 42:9; 43:9–12; 44:7; 45:21;
>   46:10; 48:3–7)

knows it. On this reading, the timelessness of God's knowledge warrants the use of *foreknowledge*, rather than calling that term into question.

24. There is an interesting confirmation to this point in the story of Micaiah and Ahab, 1 Kings 22:1–28. Micaiah's final word sums up the teaching of the passage on the nature of prophecy: "If you return in peace, the LORD has not spoken by me" (v. 28; see also Dan. 2:22; Amos 3:7).

Prediction of future events is not the only aspect of prophecy. Prophets also interpret history, exhort to repentance and faithfulness, proclaim God's standards. As we will see in a discussion of God's unchangeability (chapter 17), some prophecies that apparently predict the future are actually conditional. God announces the destruction of Nineveh, for example, but then retracts that announcement when the Ninevites repent (Jonah 3:4, 10; see also 4:1–2, alluding to Exodus 34:6–7, and the general principle of Jeremiah 18:7–10).

Nevertheless, amid the diverse elements of prophecy, one crucial element is prediction of the future. Knowledge of the future is a defining mark of the true God and of his true prophets. Prophecies often indicate in general terms the coming of God's judgment, as:

> Behold, the day of the LORD comes,
>   cruel, with wrath and fierce anger,
> to make the land a desolation
>   and to destroy its sinners from it. (Isa. 13:9)

They describe the coming of the Messiah (Isa. 9:6–7; 11:1–9), and the coming of Gentiles to seek the Lord (Acts 15:15–18). But sometimes prophets describe the future in even more specific terms. The prophet Samuel tells young King Saul that Saul will meet two men who will tell him that his lost donkeys have been found; then he will meet three men going to Bethel carrying three goats, three loaves of bread, and a skin of wine. Then he will meet a procession of prophets near Gibeah, and so on (1 Sam. 10:1–8). These events take place exactly as the prophet indicated (vv. 9–11).

In the NT, the writers emphasize over and over again that various events take place in order to fulfill Scripture (Matt. 2:15, 17; 3:3; 8:17; 12:17; etc.). In some cases, these fulfillments may involve Jesus' deliberate intention to fulfill prophecy. In other cases, the fulfillment may be a mere parallel between an event in the history of Israel and an event of Jesus' life (as Matt. 2:15), a literary device intended to underscore the evangelist's assertion that Jesus is the true remnant of Israel. But in many cases, the gospel writers clearly intend to ascribe to the OT prophets a supernatural knowledge of the future, as when Micah predicted that the Messiah would be born in Bethlehem (Mic. 5:2; Matt. 2:6).

God's Foreknowledge of Free Human Decisions and Actions

Now, the open theists do not deny the reality or importance of predictive prophecy. But they believe that when God reveals future events, he is doing one of the following: (1) announcing his own plans, what *he* intends to do, (2) speaking in very general terms that could be fulfilled by a great many states of affairs, (3) announcing events that are necessary (or highly probable?) consequences of past and present states of affairs, or (4) announcing what will take place if certain conditions obtain.[25] What the

---

25. See Richard Rice, "Biblical Support for a New Perspective," in Pinnock et al., *The Openness of God*, 50–53.

open theists are concerned to deny, however, is that God foreknows the free decisions of human beings. On the open theists' libertarian view, such divine foreknowledge destroys human freedom.

As Robert Strimple points out, to deny that God knows the free decisions of men is no small reduction in the church's traditional view of God's knowledge. It is not a "modest" or "limited" proposal, as Clark Pinnock and Richard Rice seem to think:

> Either they are disingenuous, or they have not thought through sufficiently the implications of their position.
>
> Think about it. Just how "limited" is the part of the world's ongoing history that we are asked to see as not under God's control, nor even within his present knowledge? How many truly significant occurrences in our world are *not* the actions of human beings or the consequences of such actions? Pinnock and Rice give us surprisingly few specific examples of such occurrences—preferring to speak vaguely of "divine actions that are not dependent upon circumstances in the creaturely world." Perhaps the fact that the sun will shine on my picnic tomorrow would be one such event. But even a "natural" phenomenon such as whether or not tomorrow will be sunny in Southern California may well be determined by how much smog has been produced by how many automobiles whose drivers decided to turn on the ignition key in the past several days. And, of course, at a global level, how could God know it as absolutely certain that someone would not have made this planet uninhabitable before tomorrow by recklessly unleashing a nuclear holocaust?[26]

In the following discussion I shall mention some passages that in my opinion cannot be understood in terms of the above four categories[27] and that show God's absolute foreknowledge of human free acts. In my list must be included the passages in chapter 8 that show God as *foreordaining* free acts of human beings. If he foreordains, again, he must foreknow.[28] But note also the following.

In Genesis 9:24–27, Noah, speaking as a prophet of God, indicates the future of two sons and a grandson. Clearly, the prophecy is intended to describe not the earthly lives of these individuals, but the history of their descendants. The grandson, Canaan, is to be a slave of Noah's sons Shem and Japheth. Yahweh is to be blessed as "God of Shem," and Japheth will live in the tents of Shem. The importance of this prophecy in Moses'

---

26. Strimple, "What Does God Know?," 143. In a footnote, he points out that Pinnock denies that God has preordained, or even permitted, "evil events in our lives, such as destructive earthquakes or ravaging floods." So, he says, "it is not clear how Pinnock can even affirm that God controls all purely 'natural' events."

27. Of course, in one sense every predictive prophecy falls under category 1. The free actions of men are under God's control, so that his knowledge of human free actions is also a knowledge of his own action. I am here expounding my own position, however, not that of the open theists. They presume a very sharp distinction between God's knowledge of his own actions and his knowledge of men's actions. In this section, I assume that distinction for the sake of argument and show that God foreknows actions of men that, on the libertarian view, are not caused by divine actions.

28. And of course, foreknowledge proves foreordination. This is why Isaiah invokes divine foreknowledge—to prove God's sovereignty, in contrast with the false gods.

history is certainly that the Shemites (Semites, Israel) will conquer Canaan and that all the nations (Japhethites) will be blessed (cf. Gen. 12:3) through Shem. This prophecy does not begin to be fulfilled until Israel's conquest of Canaan many centuries later, and the specific form of the blessing to Japheth does not become evident until Jesus sends his disciples to bring the gospel to "all nations" (Matt. 28:19).

So the prophecy of Noah predicts events many centuries in advance. But it also anticipates free actions of human beings. The prophecy cannot be fulfilled unless the family of Shem develops into a nation capable of defeating the family of Canaan in battle. For that to happen, countless marriages and births must take place, as well as much cultural development, geopolitical events putting Israel and Canaan into proximity, hostility between them, military power in Israel, and above all, Israel's putting its faith in the true God.[29] And the blessing on Japheth presupposes that the Japhethites will hear of the God of Israel and will freely put their trust in him. So the fulfillment of Noah's prophecy requires millions of free human decisions. In giving Noah those words, God foreknew that those free decisions would take place.

So God's covenant with Abraham also anticipates free human decisions:

> Then the LORD said to Abram, "Know for certain that your offspring will be sojourners in a land that is not theirs and will be servants there, and they will be afflicted for four hundred years. . . . And they shall come back here in the fourth generation, for the iniquity of the Amorites is not yet complete." (Gen. 15:13–16)

As we learn from later narratives in Genesis, Abraham's descendants, several centuries later, become "strangers" in Egypt because of the betrayal of Joseph by his brothers, Joseph's walk with God that elevates him to a position of authority, Jacob's decision to move to Egypt, and the rise of a pharaoh hostile to the Jews. All these events take place through the free decisions of human beings: of Joseph, his brothers, Jacob, the pharaohs. And of course, the return of Israel to Canaan is also a complicated story about human free decisions, a story written by the hand of God (Gen. 45:5–8; 50:20). When God predicts these events, he is also predicting the human free decisions necessary to bring these events about.

Similarly the prophecies of Isaac (Gen. 27:27–29, 39–40) and Jacob (who gathers his children "that I may tell you what shall happen to you in days to come," 49:1), the Balaam oracles (Num. 23–24), the Song of Moses (Deut. 32:1–43), and the blessing of Moses on the tribes of Israel (Deut. 33:1–29).

First Samuel 10:1–7 is Samuel's prophecy of very specific events that we saw earlier. Note now that these events require free human decisions. Samuel says that Saul will meet two men near Rachel's tomb (v. 2): not three, not one. Evidently each man made

---

29. As we have seen, of course, faith is God's gift. But when God gives faith, he foreordains that we will freely believe. The divine gift precedes the human response; but there is a human response, human responsibility (see our later discussion). So in this section, I will assume that when God or his prophet foretells that someone will believe, he is foretelling a free human act.

a free decision to travel that road, and the two freely agreed to walk together. They also freely decided what to say to Saul, but Samuel knew in advance what they would say. Then Samuel identifies the next group that will meet Saul: exactly how many there will be, exactly what they will be carrying, and what Saul will do in response. Again, Samuel knows in advance (because the Lord knows in advance) what free decisions these people will make. Similarly through the narrative.

In 1 Samuel 23:12, God tells David that if he stays in Keilah, the citizens will turn him over to Saul. Presumably, the decision of the inhabitants of Keilah is a free one. But God knows what that free decision would be. Now, this is a "conditional" prophecy, and thus might be thought to be in the open theists' category 4.[30] David's betrayal will occur only on the condition that he stays in Keilah. But God is not here saying what he, God, will do on that condition; rather, he is saying what the Keilahites will do, what their free decision will be. God's knowledge, even conditional knowledge, of a human free act does not cohere with the system of open theism.

In 1 Kings 13:1–4, an unnamed prophet from the southern kingdom of Judah comes to Jeroboam, ruler of the northern kingdom of Israel, and rebukes his false worship:

> O altar, altar, thus says the LORD: "Behold, a son shall be born to the house of David, Josiah by name, and he shall sacrifice on you the priests of the high places who make offerings on you, and human bones shall be burned on you." (1 Kings 13:2)

Jeroboam reigned in approximately 931–910 B.C., Josiah 639–609; so the prophecy foretells an event three hundred years in the future, mentioning Josiah by name, foretelling his actions. The prophecy also implies much about Josiah's values. He is to be a champion of the true worship of Yahweh. The prophecy anticipates many human free decisions: the marriages, conceptions, and births that lead to Josiah, the name given to him, the plot that elevated him to the kingship (2 Kings 21:23–24), Josiah's training and character, his decision to repair the temple (22:1–7), his response to the rediscovery of the law (vv. 11–20), his renewal of the covenant (23:1–3).

In 2 Kings 8:12, the prophet Elisha sadly tells Hazael, king-to-be of Syria, that Hazael will do great harm to Israel: "You will set on fire their fortresses, and you will kill their young men with the sword and dash in pieces their little ones and rip open their pregnant women." These are to be Hazael's free decisions, foreknown by God. Hazael himself considers them unlikely (v. 13). Perhaps the open theist will object that any Syrian king would do these things, granted the historical circumstances; so this passage would fall under category 3 of the four listed earlier: these are human decisions rendered necessary by historical situations. If the open theist takes this option, however, he thereby concedes that Hazael's decisions were not free in the libertarian sense, and that therefore Hazael was not morally responsible for his heinous actions. One hopes that open theists are not so generous to more recent practitioners of genocide. But the

---

30. And of course, in context of the narrative, the condition is not fulfilled. David does not stay in Keilah, and so the people of Keilah do not in fact deliver him up.

passage illustrates well a dilemma facing the open theist: he must conclude from this passage either that God foreknew Hazael's free decision or that Hazael was not a free agent. Neither conclusion is consistent with the theory of open theism.

According to Psalm 139:4, God knows our words "altogether" before they are on our tongues. Also:

> In your book were written, every one of them,
>   the days that were formed for me,
>   when as yet there was none of them. (Ps. 139:16b)

Does this mean that God foreknows all the events of the days of our lives? Or only that he knows the number of days allotted to us? Even if the psalmist intends only the latter in this passage, he is attributing to God a profound foreknowledge of human free decisions. Length of life depends on a great many human decisions: decisions of our parents and caregivers during our childhood, our decisions affecting health and diet, decisions to become involved in dangerous activities, decisions creating friendships and enmities, decisions of friends to rescue us from danger, decisions of enemies to pursue aggression, and, most of all, decisions as to our values: for divine wisdom brings length of life (Prov. 3:2).

We saw that 1 Kings 13:1–4 refers to Josiah by name, three hundred years before his birth. Similarly, Isaiah 44:28–45:13 (and most likely 46:11) refers to Cyrus, the Persian king who authorized the return of Israel from exile to Canaan. Isaiah prophesied in Judah during reigns of Uzziah, Jotham, Ahaz, and Hezekiah (1:1), in the eighth and seventh centuries B.C. Cyrus conquered Babylon around 539 B.C. and ruled it until around 530, the late sixth century. So Isaiah's prophecy anticipates Cyrus's birth, name, conquest, rule, character, and numerous free decisions, over a century in advance.

In Jeremiah 1:5, Yahweh says that he knew the prophet before his conception, and appointed him as a prophet. So God knew that of all the marriages in Israel and all the various combinations of sperm and egg, one would produce a specific individual named Jeremiah equipped in advance to be a prophet. Many free human decisions led to the conception of Jeremiah in his mother's womb, and God knew all those decisions in advance.

Jeremiah himself, in 37:6–10, reports in advance the free decisions of the Egyptian and Babylonian military leaders, opposing the predictions of rival pundits (vv. 9–10).[31] For similar prophecies, see 25:9; 39:15–18. In 25:11, he says that Judah's captivity will last seventy years. Ezekiel also sets forth some future actions of the king of Babylon in great detail (21:18–23; 26:1–14; 30:10). And Daniel's predictions of the history of empires (Dan. 2, 9, and 11) anticipate innumerable free decisions, by rulers, soldiers, peoples, giving timetables for sequences of historical events centuries in advance.

---

31. Again, the open theist has the option of regarding these military decisions as historically determined and the prophecy as based on God's knowledge of the determining conditions. But as I noted before, it would be ironic to find free-will theists resorting to determinist explanations of human behavior in order to validate their theory.

In the NT, Jesus teaches that his Father knows the day and hour of his coming (Mark 13:32). But that day, we learn, will not come until after other events have taken place, events involving human free decisions (13:1–30). So God knows in advance that those decisions will be made, and he knows when they will have been made. Compare Jesus' prophecy of the destruction of the temple in Matthew 24:2: Jesus knew in advance that some people would freely decide to destroy God's house.

Jesus also knew in advance who would betray him (Matt. 26:24). In this passage, the open theist may not respond that Judas's acts were determined by existing conditions known by Jesus and therefore were not free. For Jesus makes it clear that Judas is responsible for his action. So on the open-theist theory, Judas's act must have been free and therefore unpredictable. But in fact Jesus predicted it. Cf. John 6:64; 13:18–19. In John 13:38, Jesus also predicts Peter's threefold denial, an act for which Peter later takes full responsibility.

So in Acts 2:23, Peter ascribes the events of Jesus' death to "the definite plan and foreknowledge of God," noting also the responsibility of the "lawless men" (cf. Acts 4:27–28).

Jesus knows in advance what kind of death Peter will die (John 21:18–19). Before his death, Peter will be dressed and led somewhere against his will. So again, Jesus indicates his foreknowledge of free human actions.

Passages Alleged to Teach Divine Ignorance

So there really is a great amount of evidence in Scripture that God knows in advance the free decisions of human beings. Indeed, one wonders how, in the face of so much biblical data, the open theists can maintain their position. One of their main arguments is philosophical rather than exegetical: they maintain that the future is inherently unknowable because it is not a proper object of knowledge. On this view, statements about the future are either false or neither true nor false.[32] The argument is that the future is not presently *real*, and therefore cannot be an object of knowledge. There is, I think, some truth in this assertion.[33] But the same is true of the past, since we are not directly acquainted with it. So if true statements can refer only to what is presently real, statements about the past are in the same boat as statements about the future.

And the argument also applies to what we call "the present." Some have seen the present as a knife-edge between past and future that vanishes before we can conceptualize it, in which case no statement can be strictly a statement about the present. Usually we think of "the present" as a part of the past, recently available to our experience. But then our statements about the present are as problematic as those about the

---

32. This assertion, of course, violates our usual understanding of statements about the future. If I say that the San Diego Padres will win the pennant, and later they do, normally my statement would be considered true, otherwise false. One must, I think, be strongly committed to a libertarian metaphysic to abandon this commonsense understanding.

33. Future states of affairs are not real in the present. But God's plan for the future is a reality today. Statements about the future are statements (either true or false) about the nature of God's plan for the future.

past, which are in turn as problematic as those about the future. So the argument that purports to show the unknowability of the future entails the unknowability of past and present as well, that is, the unknowability of anything.

The discussion can get very technical and complicated, but as I see it, those who argue for the unknowability of the future are mainly interested in finding a view of knowledge consistent with libertarian freedom, which I have given reason for us to reject. I doubt that any theist who rejected libertarian freedom would ever have been tempted to think of the future as unknowable. This position is in any case certainly unscriptural, for as we have seen, according to the Bible, God does know the future and he reveals some of it to his prophets.

Open theists, however, do propose biblical arguments as well. Without giving very much consideration to the huge number of passages we looked at above and in chapter 8, they point out some examples of texts that in their view suggest divine ignorance.

In Genesis 3:9, after Adam and Eve have eaten the forbidden fruit, God calls to Adam, "Where are you?" Does this question indicate that God could not locate Adam's hiding place (v. 8)? If so, the passage would prove too much from an open-theist perspective. For it would show that God is ignorant not of the future, but of some events in the past and facts about the present. In fact, however, the passage does not teach God's ignorance of anything. "Where are you?" is the first question (out of four: the other three in verses 11 and 13) of God's cross-examination. God intends for them to admit their wrongdoing by answering his questions. His probing questions reveal ignorance no more than do the questions of any skillful prosecuting attorney.[34]

The same is true of Genesis 11:5, in which "the LORD came down to see" the tower that sinful men were building in defiance of his will. Was the Lord ignorant of the tower before he came down? In that case, one wonders why he chose to come down to that particular place. And in that case, God is ignorant of the *present*; the passage teaches nothing of any divine ignorance about the future. But in fact there is no divine ignorance here. As in Genesis 3:9, God is visiting sinful men in preparation for judgment. When God "draws near" to men in Scripture, it is for blessing and/or judgment. In this case, the Lord creates confusion of language, dooming the tower project to failure, and scattering the people over the face of the earth.

Genesis 18:20–21 speaks of another time when God drew near to judge, in this case the cities of Sodom and Gomorrah. Here, however, a somewhat stronger case can be made for divine ignorance than in Genesis 3:9 and 11:5. God says:

> I will go down to see whether they have done altogether according to the outcry that has come to me. And if not, I will know. (Gen. 18:21)

Does God here admit that his visit to Sodom will help him to gain information that he did not already know? Several points need to be made here:

---

34. Recall our earlier discussion of the relation between God's knowledge and his judgments. He is omniscient because he is the ultimate Judge of all.

1. Note again that this passage concerns God's knowledge of the present, not of the future.

2. As in the two earlier passages, the emphasis is not on God's gaining information to complete his own understanding of the situation, but rather on God as prosecutor gathering evidence to present an indictment. Chapter 19 vindicates God's judgment: the two angels not only know the wickedness of Sodom, but actually *experience* it. The evidence is very specific and concrete. It is in that sense that the divine visit adds to the knowledge relevant to the judgment.

3. Nevertheless, taken literally,[35] the verse does describe an increase in God's knowledge. Traditionally, this description has been understood as an *anthropomorphism*: a description of divine knowledge in terms literally appropriate only to human knowledge. On this view, God does not gain knowledge by his visit to Sodom, but he *appears* to gain it. Anthropomorphisms in descriptions of God are appropriate, as we will see.

Thus, the tradition accommodates the language of Genesis 18:20–21 to the broader biblical teaching about God's omniscience. The alternative, of course, is to take passages such as this one literally and to accommodate the broader teaching to this one (and to the few passages like it), regarding the omniscience texts as somewhat hyperbolic.[36] But the latter alternative, I think, is not warranted. (a) For one thing, the sheer number of omniscience texts is vastly greater than the number of apparent-ignorance texts. (b) For another, God's omniscience, as we have seen, is a fundamental ground for the confidence of God's people in the Lord's power and promises. If God is not literally omniscient, then that ground of confidence becomes null and void. (c) In the theophanic context of this passage, there are good reasons for taking the text anthropomorphically. When God appears as a man, he has special reason to describe his knowledge in human terms.

4. But there may be something more here than anthropomorphism. In the theophany of Genesis 18, there is an anticipation of the greater theophany of God in Jesus Christ. Orthodox Christians believe that the incarnate Son of God has two natures, divine and human. According to his divine nature, he is fully omniscient. According to his human nature, he "increased in wisdom and in stature" (Luke 2:52). As we have seen, Jesus was omniscient during his days on earth (John 16:30). But he also gained knowledge by asking people questions, by having new experiences. At times he was amazed at what took place (as in Luke 7:9). The theophanic incarnation of Genesis 18 also presents us with a being who is divine in some ways, human in others. There

---

35. Of course, nobody takes the passage literally in every respect. A perfectly literal reading, as Douglas Wilson points out, would leave us with a God "who has to walk to get places" (Gen. 18:2–3), who gets his feet dirty (v. 4), who gets tired (v. 4), and so forth. See Douglas Wilson, *Knowledge, Foreknowledge, and the Gospel* (Moscow, ID: Canon Press, 1997), 30. Such a conclusion would be the result of saying that God must be limited in all the ways in which he appears to be limited by his theophanic form. But if God transcends that form in some ways, why not in all ways? (Note the parallel discussed below between incarnation and theophany. Christ's divine nature transcended his material form, without compromising his true humanity.)

36. This discussion reflects Paul Helm's structuring of the problem in *The Providence of God* (Leicester: Inter-Varsity Press, 1993), 51–52.

may be significant analogies between this theophany and Christ. It is best for us to be cautious in attempting to conceptualize the theophany.

5. Considerations 3 and 4 may be grounded in a still broader principle. In chapters 2 and 3, we saw that God is not only transcendent, but also fully present in space and time. God's presence in time does not detract from his transcendence or his omniscience. Nevertheless, in each time he knows what time it is. As he is with me now as I write, he experiences with me the transition from 11:09 to 11:10 A.M. And he is aware of how the world is different at 11:10 from the way it is at 11:09. In other words, the immanent God does experience change,[37] though he himself is unchanging. And since every change brings something new, God *experiences* newness (as the angels experienced the wickedness of Sodom; recall comment 2 above). This divine experience is evidently similar in these ways to our experiences of learning new things. God knows the end from the beginning. But he also understands what it is like to experience something that hasn't happened before.

I conclude, therefore, that God's immanence in time necessitates that his knowledge-in-immanence be significantly analogous to human knowledge, however difficult that fact may be for us to describe. Our difficulties in describing it are similar to the difficulties we have in describing the knowledge of Christ (4 above). The language of God's learning new things is therefore anthropomorphic, but not *merely* anthropomorphic (3 above). In this case, the anthropomorphism reveals a genuine likeness between human knowledge and God's knowledge in his immanence.

In Genesis 22:12, God tells Abraham, "Now I know that you fear God, seeing you have not withheld your son, your only son, from me." Abraham was willing to sacrifice his son Isaac at God's command, but God provided a ram as a substitute (v. 13). Before this test, was God ignorant about what Abraham would do? I think not, because of the many texts that teach divine omniscience. The reference to an *apparent* increase in God's knowledge may be accounted for by the previous principles:

(a) Again, the issue is more judicial than epistemological. God is looking for *evidence* of Abraham's faithfulness, his fear of God. So James says that Abraham was "justified by works when he offered up his son Isaac on the altar" (James 2:21).

(b) Again, it is legitimate for us to speak of anthropomorphism here. But that anthropomorphism is grounded in the nature of God's involvement in the temporal sequence.

The same considerations bear on Deuteronomy 13:3, "For the LORD your God is testing you, to know whether you love the LORD your God with all your heart and with all your soul." Note how often the language of "finding out" appears in the context of *testing*. This is the case also in the Psalms where God is said to "search" his people (Pss. 44:21 KJV; 139:1, 23). God knows how the test, the search, will come out, but that fact does not make the actual test superfluous. Scripture stresses the importance of both divine sovereignty and human responsibility. In some senses, God responds to our

37. I will discuss this assertion in greater length and (I hope) depth under the topic of God's eternity and unchangeability.

responses to him. So our responses to tests are important to God. The gospel itself is such a test, and our response to it is crucial to our relationship with God.

In Jeremiah 26:2–3, the Lord tells Jeremiah to preach his Word to the temple worshipers and then adds, "Perhaps they will listen and each will turn from his evil way. Then I will relent and not bring on them the disaster I was planning because of the evil they have done" (NIV). I will discuss the divine *relenting* under the topic of God's unchangeability (chapter 17).[38] Here let us simply note that God sometimes announces judgment not for the purpose of describing his eternal plan, but to *test* the response of people. That test is not complete, of course, until the response actually takes place. Until then, the test is not finished, the results not sealed. Positive and negative responses are still possible.[39] So there is an element of uncertainty that God here expresses by the term "perhaps." That term should be understood similarly in Ezekiel 12:3. This principle also accounts for the legitimacy of the questions raised by the king of Nineveh in response to Jonah's preaching: "Who knows? God may turn and relent and turn from his fierce anger, so that we may not perish" (Jonah 3:9). Who knows?

There is also a group of passages that speak of God's "remembering" (Gen. 9:15–16; Ex. 6:5) or "forgetting" (Pss. 9:18; 13:1; Jer. 23:39). "Remember" in these texts simply means to fulfill the covenant promises. Human beings are prone to think that God forgets his promises, because the fulfillments are often delayed. So when the fulfillment comes, it is as when (note anthropomorphism) a man remembers something he had forgotten. But Scripture makes it clear that God never actually forgets his covenant.[40] Forgetting, then, is the temporary delay as seen from a human point of view. Forgetting can also be, as in Jeremiah 23:39, God's casting someone out of the covenant fellowship.[41]

Among those passages claimed to support a doctrine of divine ignorance, we are left with only one closely parallel group: Jeremiah 7:31; 19:5; and 32:35, where God says:

> [The people of Israel and Judah] built the high places of Baal in the Valley of the Son of Hinnom, to offer up their sons and daughters to Molech, though I did not command them, nor did it enter into my mind, that they should do this abomination, to cause Judah to sin.

38. The word *perhaps* or its equivalent (Heb. *'ulay*) often occurs in texts where people are hoping uncertainly that God will bring them some benefit (e.g., Gen. 18:24–30; Ex. 32:30; Isa. 37:4). The present passage may be construed anthropomorphically as God's taking their own way of speaking on his own lips.

39. In one sense, only one response is possible, the response that God has foreordained. But given other perspectives, other abilities and preventers, we may speak of things being possible that are contrary to God's eternal plan. It is, for example, *logically* possible that Christ would not have died for sinners. But that possibility was excluded by God's plan.

40. Wilson on Genesis 8:1, "God remembered Noah": "Does God smack his forehead in this passage? 'Oh, yeah! *Noah!*'" Or in Exodus 6:5: "Man, that was close! I almost forgot. The *covenant!*" *Knowledge*, 39.

41. Since *knowing* can mean inclusion in covenant fellowship (as Amos 3:2), exclusion can be *forgetting*.

Given our long discussion, then, do there remain, after all, three passages of Scripture that attribute ignorance to God? I think not. *Mind* here is *lev*, *heart* in Hebrew. *Heart* is a frequent word in Scripture, but rarely found in reference to God. In reference to men, phrases with *lev* translated "come into the mind" or "come into the heart" indicate not just the presence of an idea in the mind, but an intention or desire of the heart, as in 2 Chronicles 7:11; Nehemiah 7:5. In Jeremiah 32:35, "nor did it enter into my mind" is parallel to "I never commanded." So it is most reasonable to conclude that these passages do not assert divine ignorance, but rather deny in the most emphatic terms that human sacrifice was God's intention or the desire of his heart.[42]

Indeed, Leviticus 18:21 and Deuteronomy 18:10 make it obvious that the thought of human sacrifice did enter God's mind as an item of knowledge. Also in God's mind was the knowledge that Israel might engage in such a horrid practice and therefore needed to be warned against it.

I conclude, then, that although these passages raise interesting issues and suggest new perspectives about God's knowledge-in-immanence, they do not teach divine ignorance of any sort. Our earlier conclusion stands: God is omniscient, and his omniscience includes exhaustive knowledge of the future.

God's Knowledge of Possibilities

God knows not only what is actual in the past, present, and future, but also what is not actual, but only possible. He knows not only what is, but also what is not, but could be. And of course, he also knows what could not be. In Jeremiah 26:3 ("It may be they will listen, and every one turn from his evil way"), considered in the previous section, the "may be" indicates a possibility that may or may not become actual. There is a sense in which nothing "can" happen unless God has eternally planned to make it happen. But there are other kinds of possibility,[43] based on different kinds of abilities and preventers, so that there are senses in which states of affairs are possible even though God has sovereignly determined not to bring them about. Many events, for example, are logically possible even though God has ordained that they will not occur. Similarly, events can be physically possible, economically possible, politically possible, and so on, even though they are impossible from the standpoint of God's decree. God has determined, by his nature and his creative activity, all the things, properties, and relationships that govern possibility in these senses, and so of course he knows what is possible and what is not.

God's knowledge of what is possible is sometimes called his *necessary knowledge*, *natural knowledge*, or *knowledge of intellect*, as opposed to his *free knowledge* or *knowledge of vision*. For ultimately what is possible is what is compatible with

---

42. Of course, this interpretation raises the question of how God could decree, or even allow to happen, a practice contrary to his intention and desire. The answer is to be found in the distinction between decretive and preceptive wills, which we will consider in chapter 16.

43. See the "excursus on ability" in chapter 35.

God's own nature. Since God knows his nature necessarily, he knows possibilities necessarily. This is true of what we might call *metaphysical* possibility, in which the only preventer is incompatibility with the divine nature. But of course, the other kinds of possibility—physical, economic, legal, and so on—depend not only on God's nature, but also on God's decisions to create the world a certain way. Physical possibility, for example, is not merely what is consistent with the divine nature, but what is consistent with the laws of physics (or, alternatively, consistent with the powers of the human body). Physical possibility, then, presupposes God's decision to create the world in a certain way. Metaphysical possibility, therefore, is the kind of possibility that theologians have in mind when they speak of God's necessary knowledge of possibility.

Free knowledge and *knowledge of vision* refer to God's knowledge of actualities, the things that he has decided to actualize at some point in the history of the creation. It is called *free* because creation is a free act of God, rather than a necessary act. God has knowledge of the world because he has freely decided to create the world.

The distinction between *intellect* and *vision* draws an analogy between divine and human knowledge. On some accounts of human knowledge, the "intellect" knows what is merely possible (for example, logical and mathematical relationships), and our "sense perception" (including vision) tells us which possible states of affairs actually exist. For example, the intellect tells us that if we have only three pencils, we have fewer than four. But sense perception tells us whether or not we actually have three pencils. This distinction between intellect and sensation is, however, in my view, somewhat oversimplified. I have argued in *DKG* that even in human knowledge, intellect and sensation are mutually dependent. Certainly it would be unwise to make a sharp distinction between what *God* knows by his intellect and what he knows by his senses. Literally speaking, for one thing, God has no sense organs.

In Reformed theology, God knows what is possible by knowing his nature. He knows created actuality by knowing his eternal decree. Knowledge of his nature is necessary; knowledge of his decree is free.

God's Knowledge of Contingencies: *Middle Knowledge*

Now, between necessary and free knowledge some theologians have defined a third category of divine knowledge that they have called *middle*. William Lane Craig distinguishes the three forms of divine knowledge as follows:

1. *Natural Knowledge*: God's knowledge of all possible worlds. The content of this knowledge is essential to God.
2. *Middle Knowledge*: God's knowledge of what every possible free creature would do under any possible set of circumstances and, hence, knowledge of those possible worlds which God can make actual. The content of this knowledge is not essential to God.

3. *Free Knowledge*: God's knowledge of the actual world. The content of this knowledge is not essential to God.[44]

These distinctions were first developed by the Spanish Jesuit Luis Molina (1535–1600) and adopted by other Jesuits, Socinians, Arminians, some Lutherans, and the Amyraldian Calvinists of Saumur. Thomists and mainstream Reformed theologians have generally rejected the notion. In recent years, a number of Christian philosophers have adopted the concept, such as Craig and Alvin Plantinga.[45]

Given Craig's definition, it is difficult to see at first why Reformed theologians have objected to the concept. Certainly God does know what every free creature would do in every possible circumstance.[46] The most frequently cited biblical examples are appropriate. In 1 Samuel 23:7–13, David is staying in a town called Keilah, when Saul comes seeking his life. He asks the Lord whether, if he stays in Keilah, the inhabitants will deliver him to Saul. God answers, "They will surrender you" (v. 12), so David leaves. Here God expresses knowledge not of what actually happens (for the Keilahites never get the opportunity to betray David), but of what *would* happen given other circumstances. So God knows what the Keilahites would do under circumstances other than the actual. As philosophers sometimes put it, he knows the truth of a contrary-to-fact conditional: "*If* David stays, the Keilahites will betray him."

The other text often cited in this connection is Matthew 11:20–24. Here Jesus says that if the inhabitants of Tyre, Sidon, and Sodom had seen the miracles of Jesus, they would have repented.[47] In fact, they did not see the miracles of Jesus and did not, therefore, have that opportunity to repent. But Jesus knows what they *would* have done in other circumstances. So Jesus here expresses knowledge of a contrary-to-fact conditional truth.

These passages, of course, are not intended to make technical theological points about God's eternal knowledge. Perhaps we should not insist on precisely literal interpretations. But granting the previous arguments of this book, it is plain that God, governing all things by his eternal decree, knows what each thing is capable of, and knows what would result from any alteration of his plan.

Indeed, God in Scripture often speaks of what would happen in conditions other than those that actually occur. God says over and over again in different ways that if Israel is faithful, she will receive all of God's blessings in the Land of Promise. That statement is true, but it is a contrary-to-fact conditional. In fact, Israel never displays that faithfulness (except, of course, in the remnant, Jesus Christ). It is also true that if Paul, say, had not repented and believed in Christ, he would have been lost. Scripture often pictures contrary-to-fact possibilities in order to display the grace and justice of God.[48]

44. William Lane Craig, *The Only Wise God* (Grand Rapids: Baker, 1987), 131.

45. Alvin Plantinga, *The Nature of Necessity* (Oxford: Clarendon Press, 1974), 169–80.

46. Heinrich Heppe notes Gomarus, Walaeus, Crocius, and Alsted as Reformed theologians who held to "middle knowledge" in this sense. See *RD*, 79. See also *BRD*, 2:198–203.

47. In comparison, of course, with the cities of Chorazin, Bethsaida, and Capernaum, which saw the works of Jesus but still did not believe.

48. It may also be possible to infer from Scripture what would have happened to mankind if Adam and Eve had not sinned—hence the many theological discussions of that contrary-to-fact conditional.

From a Reformed point of view, however, it is difficult to see why this kind of divine knowledge must be isolated as a third kind of knowledge alongside necessary and free. Note that in Craig's definition, necessary knowledge is a "knowledge of all possible worlds," and middle knowledge is a "knowledge of those possible worlds which God can make actual." What is the difference between these? Are there worlds that are genuinely possible, that God cannot make actual? What is a "possible world" if it is not a world that God can make actual?

And why should we not include the possible actions of free creatures (in definition 2) as ingredients of the possible worlds of definition 1? When God knows possible worlds, does he not, by virtue of that knowledge, also know all possible free creatures and their possible actions? So from a Reformed point of view, there is no reason why we shouldn't regard God's knowledge of contingencies under the category of necessary knowledge.

So we should reject Craig's assertion that this knowledge is "not essential to God." It does, of course, deal with creatures, and creatures are not essential to God. But it deals with *possible* creatures, not actual ones, and with their actions under *possible* circumstances, not actual ones. So it does not depend on God's decree to create the actual world. God knows what creatures and what creaturely actions are possible, simply because he knows himself. He knows what he can bring about. God knows these possibilities simply by knowing his own nature. And his knowledge of his own nature is essential.

But this approach to God's knowledge of contingencies was not satisfactory to Molina or to other historical and modern exponents of middle knowledge. To understand why, we should note that the term *free* in Craig's definition 2 refers to libertarian freedom. And indeed, the main defenders, historical and modern, of middle knowledge have held libertarian views. Indeed, much of their enthusiasm for middle knowledge has been that it provides a vocabulary for speaking about God's knowledge of creaturely actions that are free in the libertarian sense.

Now, if libertarianism is true, then middle knowledge is indeed distinct from God's necessary knowledge. For on this view God does not know the possible free actions of creatures merely by knowing himself. Since he does not cause their free actions, he cannot know their free actions, or possible free actions, without knowing the creatures themselves.

I will argue in our discussion in chapter 35 that libertarianism is false, indeed incoherent. Here, I should add that libertarianism brings incoherence into this discussion as well. To see this, let us follow Craig's argument further:

> By his middle knowledge God knows all the various possible worlds which he could create and what every free creature would do in all the various circumstances of these possible worlds. For example, God knew that Peter, if he were to exist and be placed in certain circumstances, would deny Christ three times. By a free decision of his will, God then chose to create one of those possible worlds . . . . Thus, God is able to know future free acts on the basis of his middle knowledge and his creative will.[49]

49. Craig, *The Only Wise God*, 133.

On Craig's view, God considers all possible worlds by his middle knowledge, and then chooses to create one of them. In the world that he chooses to create, someone named Peter exists, who in these created circumstances *will* deny Christ three times. Note that I said *will*, not *could* or *might*. Once God creates a world (including a world history) that includes Peter's denial, that denial is inevitable.

So what room is there in this scenario for libertarian freedom? Once Peter is created, his denial is inevitable: determined, one might say. Craig has employed the concept of middle knowledge in order to maintain libertarian freedom together with divine foreknowledge. But at the moment of Peter's terrible decision, how can he be said to have libertarian freedom? Rather, he can only deny Jesus, because he is living in a world in which that denial is an ingredient. God determined before Peter was born that he would betray Jesus.

Craig doesn't see it this way. He believes that God has decided to create this world, based on his knowledge of what creatable Peter would freely (in the libertarian sense) choose, and on his knowledge of other creatable creatures in this creatable world. But how can Peter make a libertarian free choice, when he is part of a world that contains his denial as an event, when the events of his life have been decided before his birth?

Indeed, when God chooses "to create one of those possible worlds," is he not in that very act foreordaining everything that comes to pass in that world? Craig may say that God's choice is motivated by his knowledge of Peter's libertarian free choices; but God's choice itself cannot help but limit Peter's freedom, so that Peter no longer has that kind of free will.

Libertarian free choices are choices with absolutely no preventers, choices that are fully within the power of the agent. Defenders of libertarianism often fail to understand the diversity that exists among the kinds of freedom, depending on different kinds of goals, abilities, and preventers. They tend to think that the only alternatives are *some prevention* and *no prevention*. Craig here fails to notice that God's creation of a possible world is in fact a preventer to the libertarian free choices of the creatures. If God has chosen to make the world a certain way, no creature can thereafter freely choose to make the world different. There may be other preventers that are missing from Peter's situation, but God's foreordination of a particular world in fact prevents him from deciding in any way other than as he does.

Craig would like to believe that middle knowledge reconciles divine sovereignty with libertarian freedom.[50] In fact, it does not. If "divine creation on the basis of middle knowledge" means anything, it means that libertarianism is excluded. Craig is inconsistent to affirm both libertarianism and the divine act of actualizing a complete possible world, including all creaturely choices.

If we abandon libertarianism, we abandon the traditional meaning of *middle knowledge*, and as I said earlier, there is no reason to distinguish God's knowledge of contingencies from his necessary knowledge of himself. It is still important, however, that we affirm God's knowledge of the possible actions of possible and actual creatures, of what they will or would do in all circumstances. I suggest that this knowledge is

50. Ibid., 133–38.

indeed part of the rationale of creation. God creates the world according to his eternal plan; but that plan presupposes his knowledge of creatable, possible worlds and, indeed, his foreknowledge of the actual world. God's plan foreordains everything that comes to pass, but God does not foreordain in ignorance. He knows and understands what he foreordains and what he chooses not to foreordain. Therefore, the integrity of creatures is part of God's plan from the beginning.

God's Wisdom

Wisdom (Heb. *hokmah*, Gk. *sophia; phronimos* is also translated "wise" in the NT) is a kind of heightened knowledge, a knowledge that penetrates to deep significance and practical relevance. We are sometimes encouraged to think of wisdom as "knowledge put into practice," but knowledge itself can also be practical, and wisdom can be theoretical. Herman Bavinck probably separates the two too sharply when he says:

> Knowledge and wisdom are rooted in different human capacities. We acquire knowledge by study, wisdom by insight. The former is achieved discursively; the latter, intuitively. Knowledge is theoretical; wisdom is practical and goal-oriented. Knowledge is a matter of the mind apart from the will; wisdom, though a matter of the mind, is made subservient to the will. Knowledge, accordingly, is often totally unrelated to life, but wisdom is oriented to, and closely tied in with, life. It is ethical in nature; it is "the art of living well"; it characterizes the conduct of those who make the right use of their greater store of knowledge and match the best means to the best ends.[51]

There is some truth here, but wisdom can involve study, knowledge, discernment, and so on. And when we consider wisdom as a divine attribute, we should not separate it sharply from other divine attributes such as knowledge.

In Scripture, we first hear of God's giving wisdom to human beings in Exodus 28:3; 31:3, 6; etc., where the wisdom amounts to skill in craftsmanship for the building of the tabernacle and its furnishings (cf. 1 Kings 7:14). Note here that wisdom involves "knowing how," not just "knowing that." It is a knowledge of skills as well as facts. God also gives wisdom to rulers as judges (Deut. 34:9; 1 Kings 3:28; Prov. 1:3). But wisdom also includes many other forms of knowledge. Solomon, the OT paradigm of wisdom,

> spoke 3,000 proverbs, and his songs were 1,005. He spoke of trees, from the cedar that is in Lebanon to the hyssop that grows out of the wall. He spoke also of beasts, and of birds, and of reptiles, and of fish. (1 Kings 4:32–33)

Praising the wisdom of God, Daniel speaks about the "deep and hidden things" that God reveals (as, in context, the nature and interpretation of Nebuchadnezzar's dream) (Dan. 2:22). So wisdom can include revealed secrets.

---

51. *BRD*, 2:203.

But most often in Scripture, *wisdom* has an ethical meaning. "I have taught you the way of wisdom; I have led you in the paths of uprightness," says the wisdom teacher in Proverbs 4:11, calling his son to forsake wickedness. God proclaims the wisdom of the laws he gives to Israel in Deuteronomy 4:6–8 (cf. Ps. 19:7). James asks:

> Who is wise and understanding among you? By his good conduct let him show his works in the meekness of wisdom. But if you have bitter jealousy and selfish ambition in your hearts, do not boast and be false to the truth. This is not the wisdom that comes down from above, but is earthly, unspiritual, demonic. For where jealousy and selfish ambition exist, there will be disorder and every vile practice. But the wisdom from above is first pure, then peaceable, gentle, open to reason, full of mercy and good fruits, impartial and sincere. And a harvest of righteousness is sown in peace by those who make peace. (James 3:13–18)

Here, as in Proverbs and Ecclesiastes, wisdom is the skill of godly living. Wisdom walks "in the way of righteousness, in the paths of justice" (Prov. 8:20). Those who live wisely, then, reap the covenant blessing of prosperity: "granting an inheritance to those who love me, and filling their treasuries" (v. 21).

Wisdom is also God's way of salvation. When Stephen witnessed of Christ to the Jews, "they could not withstand the wisdom and the Spirit with which he was speaking" (Acts 6:10). The gospel is the wisdom of God, foolish to the world, but the power of God to salvation (Rom. 1:16; 1 Cor. 1:18–2:16; 3:18–23; 8:1–3). Ultimately, God's wisdom is Christ (1 Cor. 1:30; Col. 2:3; cf. Isa. 11:2).

So wisdom is exceedingly precious. More so than gold or silver (Ps. 19:10; Prov. 16:16).

In all these cases, wisdom is God's gift. It was God's Spirit who came upon the tabernacle artisans and on Joshua as he succeeded Moses as Israel's leader. Solomon asked God for wisdom and received it, together with riches and long life. It was God who revealed secrets to Daniel. Stephen spoke with wisdom and the "Spirit." To James, true wisdom "comes down from above" (James 3:15). James also reminds us that if someone lacks wisdom, "let him ask God, who gives generously to all without reproach, and it will be given him" (1:5), and he promises that such prayers will be answered. And the gospel of Christ is the "hidden wisdom of God" (1 Cor. 2:7), "not taught by human wisdom but taught by the Spirit, interpreting spiritual truths to those who are spiritual" (v. 13). That is the most important thing to know about true human wisdom.

So the "fear of the LORD is the beginning of wisdom" (Ps. 111:10; cf. Prov. 9:10; 15:33) (and of knowledge, too: Prov. 1:7). Wisdom can be found in God's Word, and we are wise when we obey God's teaching (Ps. 119:98–100; Eccl. 12:13; Col. 3:16; 2 Tim. 3:15).

Scripture refers also to the "wise men" of other countries, the pagan wisdom teachers. Sometimes it grants their genuine insight. First Kings 4:31 presents Solomon's wisdom as greater than that of several wise men of the nations of his time. The language here is not antithetical; the difference is one of degree. But when the pagan wise men compete with God, their efforts are pitiful (Gen. 41:8; Ex. 7:11–12; Jer. 8:9; 10:7).

Taken as a whole, the body of ungodly wisdom is indeed antithetical to the wisdom of God's Word. God proclaims against the "wise" of unfaithful Israel:

> The wisdom of their wise men shall perish,
>   and the discernment of their discerning men shall be hidden. (Isa. 29:14b)

Paul says of unbelievers, "Claiming to be wise, they became fools" (Rom. 1:22). And in 1 Corinthians 1:18–2:16; 3:18–23; and 8:1–3, he shows the sharp opposition between the wisdom of the world and the wisdom of God. If the fear of the Lord is the *beginning* of wisdom, then wisdom that rejects the Lord is not wisdom at all, but foolishness. In the passage from James quoted above, false wisdom is "demonic."

The discussion above can help us understand the nature of wisdom as a divine attribute. God's wisdom is the source of his words and laws. It is the source and standard for all of the world's knowledge and skills, for godly living, and for the way of salvation in Christ. All of God's work in creation and providence reveals his wisdom (Pss. 104:24; 136:5; Prov. 3:19; Jer. 10:12; 51:15), reinforcing what we said in chapter 11, that everything in nature and history is according to God's wise plan, his decree. God's wisdom not only inspires crafsmen; it is a craftsman (Prov. 8:30).

Proverbs 8–9 personifies God's wisdom, anticipating the NT identification of wisdom with Christ.[52] Much of what the passage says about wisdom applies to Christ, being ascribed to him elsewhere in Scripture. Proverbs 9:1–4 compares interestingly with Matthew 11:28–30, where Jesus, in the wisdom tradition, calls all who are weak and heavy laden to learn of him and to bear his gentle yoke. One problem with this identification, however, is Proverbs 8:22:

> The LORD possessed me at the beginning of his work,
>   the first of his acts of old.

"Possessed," *qanah* in Hebrew, has been taken to mean "created" or "gave birth." The Arian heretics of the fourth century A.D. used this verse as a proof text to teach that the Son of God was a created being. But *qanah* need not bear this meaning. It is the same word translated "get" when the wisdom teacher advises his son to "get wisdom," in 4:5, 7; 16:16; 17:16. Proverbs 8:22 simply means that when God began his creative work, he did what he advises men to do: he "got wisdom."

Meditation on God's wisdom drives his people to praise him. In Romans 11:33–36, the apostle Paul, having surveyed the history of salvation, falls down in amazement at all that God has done and the wisdom revealed in it:

52. *Wisdom* and *Word* are closely related in Scripture. God's Word is also the craftsman who makes the world and governs the course of nature and history. In John 1 and elsewhere, Jesus is identified with the Word of God, in a context dealing with the creation. So Jesus as *logos* reinforces the identification of Jesus as *sophia*. See chapter 23.

Oh, the depth of the riches and wisdom and knowledge of God! How unsearchable are his judgments and how inscrutable his ways!

"For who has known the mind of the Lord,
    or who has been his counselor?"

"Or who has given a gift to him
    that he might be repaid?"

For from him and through him and to him are all things. To him be glory forever. Amen.

God's Mind

Theologians, especially in the scholastic tradition, are fond of talking about God's *intellect* or *reason*, but these terms are rare or nonexistent in English translations of Scripture. These translations do use the term *mind* occasionally of God, representing by this term a wide variety of Hebrew and Greek expressions: *peh* ("mouth," Lev. 24:12 KJV), *nephesh* ("soul," 1 Sam. 2:35), *lev* ("heart," Jer. 19:5; 32:35; 44:21), *phronema* ("thoughts," "purposes," Rom. 8:27), *nous* (the usual Greek term for "mind," Rom. 11:34; 1 Cor. 2:16). Certainly the Bible has no interest in isolating a divine faculty called the *intellect* and discussing its relation to another divine faculty, such as *will* or *imagination*, in the manner of scholastic philosophy. The use of *soul* and *heart* to describe the location of God's thoughts indicates that thought belongs to his whole self, his whole being, rather than to some faculty within him, distinguished from other faculties. Certainly that is what the doctrine of simplicity, which I will discuss in chapter 20, would suggest.[53]

The passages dealing with God's mind are more concerned with the contents and expressions of God's mind, his thoughts, than with the faculty that produces them. That is the case in all the passages cited above. As we will see, this data is similar to the biblical data about God's will (chapter 16). Of course, Scripture speaks of God's will much more often than it speaks of his mind. But in both cases it is concerned with contents and expressions rather than the source of these in some inner faculty. God's will is his decrees and his precepts. God's mind is his thoughts. If we are to speak of some mental or volitional faculty in God, that faculty can be nothing less than God's whole being. God is a willing God and a thinking God. So it is proper to deal with these concepts under the category of divine attributes.

Even though biblical references to God's mind are somewhat scarce, there is no doubt that God thinks. We have seen that everything that happens in the world is by a divine plan; planning is a form of thinking. Speech, knowledge, and wisdom, which we have considered in this chapter, all presuppose thought. So does God's justice, for it requires precise evaluation of creaturely action. And his faithfulness presupposes that he remembers his covenant and acts in accord with it. God's thought permeates the

---

53. See *DKG*, 328–46, for a similar treatment of human faculties.

creation, and it fills his revealed Word. So it amazes us, so as to drive us to praise (Rom. 11:33–36). It is incomprehensible (chapter 11). God's thoughts are not ours (Isa. 55:8).

Is God's thought rational? logical? Certainly it is both. Logic involves two things: (1) the validity of arguments, and (2) consistency between propositions. God often presents arguments to people in Scripture, giving them reasons to obey him. "If then you have been raised with Christ, seek the things that are above" (Col. 3:1). So God imposes on us the responsibility to think logically, to think consistently with his revelation.[54] And of course, that responsibility images God's own nature.

God also speaks and acts consistently. We see this in his eternal plan, as he arranges the objects and events of the universe in a consistent narrative. We see it in his speech,[55] for his Word is always true. Truth is always consistent with itself; it always excludes falsehood. God's righteousness entails that he will be consistent in his judgments, impartial. His faithfulness means that he will speak and act consistently with his covenant promises. And his knowledge also is logically consistent, for knowledge is true belief, excluding all falsehood.

So God acts and thinks in accordance with the laws of logic. This does not mean that he is "bound by" these laws, as though they were something "above" him that had authority over him. The laws of logic and rationality are simply the attributes of his own nature. As he is righteous, so he is logical. To be logical is his natural desire and pleasure. Nor does he create the laws of logic, as if they were something that he could change at will. Rather, they are necessary attributes, inalienable qualities of all his thinking and acting.

To say this is not to say that God's revelation is always in accord with some particular human *system* of logic. Systems of logic are developed by human beings to try to catalogue and describe the factors that generate validity and invalidity, consistency and inconsistency. They recommend methods for testing validity and consistency and for constructing valid arguments and consistent sets of propositions. But because these systems are human, they are fallible. Just as one generation of scientists tries to improve on the knowledge of previous generations, so logicians try to improve on the systems of logic that they have inherited. So, for example, Bertrand Russell thought he had discovered some faults in Aristotle's system of logic, and Russell's work led to systems of greater sophistication and complexity. But even if Russell was right, future logicians might find fault in his system, as future scientists might find fault with contemporary quantum theory. No human system of logic, then, necessarily measures up to the mind of God. God's logic is perfect, the standard for all human logic.

---

54. So logic may be seen as a subdivision of ethics. See *DKG* for a development of this idea.

55. I would not translate *logos* as "logic" in John 1:1, as Gordon H. Clark recommends in *The Johannine Logos* (Nutley, NJ: Presbyterian and Reformed, 1972), 19. In Scripture (as opposed to some of the philosophical sources that Clark mentions), the emphasis is on communication rather than rationality or logic as such. But there is no doubt that God's *davar, logos, rema* is meaningful and intelligible. It is not a numinous, ineffable power that comes upon men, as in some modern theologies.

Therefore, it is at least possible that something in God's revelation might appear contradictory according to all the best current logical systems, and yet be quite consistent in terms of the ultimate nature of logical truth.[56]

It is also the case, as I emphasized in *DKG* (242–301), that some of God's revelation may seem inconsistent to us not because of defects in our logical system, but because we fail in some measure to understand what God has revealed. Someone might think, for example, that God is being inconsistent in telling the Jews under Joshua to kill the Canaanites, and to tell NT believers to love their enemies. But this apparent inconsistency is resolved when we understand the difference between Joshua's situation and ours, and the differences between the duties of armies and those of private individuals.

The doctrines most often described as "apparently contradictory" are divine sovereignty/human freedom, the problem of evil, and the Trinity. Cornelius Van Til believed that these doctrines involve "apparent contradictions" that can never be reconciled by the human mind.[57] I see no scriptural basis for such a claim. I don't think Scripture tells us what apparent contradictions are reconcilable by creatures and which are not. On the three doctrinal issues mentioned above, I have tried in this book to state them nonparadoxically, in ways that remove the appearance of contradiction, while preserving, of course, the mystery of God's relation to the world. I may have succeeded or failed. But I see no reason why we should stop trying. Some apparent contradictions can, I think, like the Joshua example, be removed by careful study of God's Word. Others, perhaps, await future increases in our Bible knowledge, or even, perhaps, future developments in the science of logic itself. Others, perhaps, await our vastly increased knowledge of God (1 Cor. 13:8–12; 1 John 3:2) when we meet him in glory. And still others may be such that creaturely minds can never reconcile them.

If there are some apparent contradictions that we cannot reconcile (now, in the future, or ever), we should simply try to hold both sides of the paradox, as best we can, and walk by faith. If divine sovereignty and human responsibility seem contradictory to us, we may and should, nevertheless, both continue to regard God as sovereign and accept responsibility for our thoughts and actions. Our faith does not depend on our being able to reconcile all apparent contradictions. Rather, it rests on the solid foundation of God's revelation of himself, in all creation, in Scripture, and in Christ. So we walk by faith rather than by sight.

---

56. If the Bible's teaching about God did not stretch our minds, we would be tempted to doubt its truthfulness. How can the Lord of all creation be perfectly understandable to us? But we need to be more humble, recognizing how small our minds really are. I heard an interesting illustration: imagine a tribe of two-dimensional people living on a flat surface. A cube intersects the plane of their existence so that it appears to the tribe as a square with four corners. But then a revelation comes to them that the figure actually has eight corners, and what appear to be corners on the plane aren't really corners at all. The people would surely accept that revelation, if they did accept it, as a challenge to their very rationality. But how much greater is the difference between God and man than the difference between three-dimensional and two-dimensional reality?

57. See my *CVT*, 151–60.

Key Terms

Knowledge (philosophical definition)
Justification (of knowledge)
Omniscience
Socinianism
Open theism
Foreknowledge
Natural knowledge
Necessary knowledge
Free knowledge
Knowledge of intellect
Knowledge of vision
Metaphysical possibility
Physical possibility
Middle knowledge
Libertarianism
Wisdom
Intellect
Mind
Reason
Logic
Contradiction
Inconsistency

Study Questions

1. "Knowledge has an ethical dimension." Explain; evaluate.
2. "So knowledge is fundamentally knowledge of a person." Explain; evaluate.
3. "If human knowledge is dependent on God, then God's own knowledge depends on God. That is, it is self-attesting, self-referential, self-sufficient." Explain; evaluate.
4. How does Scripture relate God's knowledge to his control, authority, and presence? Discuss.
5. Does God's omniscience include knowledge of the future? To what extent? Cite Scripture in your answer.
6. Describe the differences between Calvinists, Arminians, and open theists on the extent of God's foreknowledge.
7. To what extent does God know in advance the free decisions of human beings? Discuss various views, Scripture references.
8. Note some Scripture passages alleged to teach divine ignorance. How do you understand these? Discuss.
9. State and evaluate William L. Craig's argument for divine middle knowledge.

10. *"Wisdom* has an ethical meaning." Explain; evaluate.

11. "Is God's thought rational? logical?" Discuss.

12. What should we do when doctrines of Scripture appear contradictory to us?

Memory Verses

Rom. 11:33–36: Oh, the depth of the riches and wisdom and knowledge of God! How unsearchable are his judgments and how inscrutable his ways!

"For who has known the mind of the Lord,
    or who has been his counselor?"

"Or who has given a gift to him
    that he might be repaid?"

For from him and through him and to him are all things. To him be glory forever. Amen.

Heb. 4:13: And no creature is hidden from his sight, but all are naked and exposed to the eyes of him to whom we must give account.

James 3:17–18: But the wisdom from above is first pure, then peaceable, gentle, open to reason, full of mercy and good fruits, impartial and sincere. And a harvest of righteousness is sown in peace by those who make peace.

Resources for Further Study

Anderson, James. *Paradox in Christian Theology.* Eugene, OR: Wipf and Stock, 2007.

Calvin, John. *Institutes,* 1.1.1. Here, Calvin argues that our knowledge of God and of ourselves are interconnected.

Frame, John M. *DKG.* In this book, I discuss what it means for us to know God, and how our knowledge of God begins in God's knowledge of himself. I have summarized much of this material in the present volume, chapters 28–32.

———. *NOG.* My critique of open theism.

Piper, John, Justin Taylor, and Paul K. Helseth. *Beyond the Bounds: Open Theism and the Undermining of Biblical Christianity.* Wheaton, IL: Crossway, 2003. Includes extensive bibliography on the subject.

Poythress, Vern S. *Logic: A God-Centered Approach to the Foundation of Western Thought.* Wheaton, IL: Crossway, 2013.

Wilson, Douglas. *Knowledge, Foreknowledge, and the Gospel.* Moscow, ID: Canon Press, 1997.

CHAPTER 16

GOD'S ATTRIBUTES: POWER, WILL

WE WILL NOW TURN TO consider the attributes of power. In the chart of chapter 12, we are moving ahead to the third column.

Certainly the immensity of God's power made a huge impression on believers during the biblical period. Consider:

> Lift up your heads, O gates!
> And be lifted up, O ancient doors,
> that the King of glory may come in.
> Who is this King of glory?
> The LORD, strong and mighty,
> the LORD, mighty in battle! (Ps. 24:7–8)

[I pray that you,] having the eyes of your hearts enlightened, . . . may know what is the hope to which he has called you, what are the riches of his glorious inheritance in the saints, and what is the immeasurable greatness of his power toward us who believe, according to the working of his great might that he worked in Christ when he raised him from the dead and seated him at his right hand in the heavenly places, far above all rule and authority and power and dominion, and above every name that is named, not only in this age but also in the one to come. And he put all things under his feet and gave him as head over all things to the church, which is his body, the fullness of him who fills all in all. (Eph. 1:18–23)

Now to him who is able to do far more abundantly than all that we ask or think, according to the power at work within us, to him be glory in the church and in Christ Jesus throughout all generations, forever and ever. Amen. (Eph. 3:20–21)

In chapter 2, I dealt with God's control as an attribute of his lordship, and in chapter 8 we looked at many passages indicating the efficacy and universality of God's control

335

over creation. God's control of all things in creation, providence, and redemption displays his wisdom, as we have seen, and also his mighty power. That he does all these things astounds and overwhelms human beings. Such power drives us to worship. No one else has nearly as much power as God. This is also an important element in the biblical teaching concerning miracle: in his mighty works, God displays his power, his lordship as control (chapter 7).

Nobody can frustrate him:

> O Lord, God of our fathers, are you not God in heaven? You rule over all the kingdoms of the nations. In your hand are power and might, so that none is able to withstand you. (2 Chron. 20:6)

> But he is unchangeable, and who can turn him back?
>   What he desires, that he does. (Job 23:13)

> No wisdom, no understanding, no counsel
>   can avail against the Lord. (Prov. 21:30)

> Also henceforth I am he;
>   there is none who can deliver from my hand;
>   I work, and who can turn it back? (Isa. 43:13)

> All the inhabitants of the earth are accounted as nothing,
>   and he does according to his will among the host of heaven
>   and among the inhabitants of the earth;
> and none can stay his hand
>   or say to him, "What have you done?" (Dan. 4:35)

He can subdue anybody who resists him, and eventually he will. On the way to the cross, Jesus says to his captors:

> Do you think that I cannot appeal to my Father, and he will at once send me more than twelve legions of angels? (Matt. 26:53)

Paul speaks of God,

> who will transform our lowly body to be like his glorious body, by the power that enables him even to subject all things to himself. (Phil. 3:21)

He does things that are proverbially impossible: raising from the stones children for Abraham (Matt. 3:9), bringing what is out of what is not (Heb. 11:3). He makes *all* things work together for good to those who love him (Rom. 8:28).

So his name is not only "the Holy One of Israel" (Isa. 1:4; etc.), but also "the Mighty One of Israel" (Isa. 1:24; cf. 49:26; 60:16). He is *el shaddai, Pantokrator*, God Almighty.

There is in Scripture, therefore, a pervasive emphasis on God's mighty power, contrary to those modern theologians who object to the notion of a God who has "power over" others.[1]

God's Omnipotence

The greatness of God's power is ground for religious praise, as we saw in the passages quoted from the Psalms, Ephesians, and elsewhere. False gods are weak and beggarly (Gal. 4:9). In such praise, the believer regards God's power as an absolute, the very standard of power. (As often, metaphysical assertions grow out of the stance of worship, not out of mere rational analysis.) To attribute weakness to God is incompatible with the stance of worship. God is always powerful, always competent.

So arises the doctrine of omnipotence as such. The term *omnipotence* is not in Scripture, but the term is appropriate to refer to two biblical ideas, closely related to each other:

1. *God can do anything he pleases.*

> But he is unchangeable, and who can turn him back?
>   What he desires, that he does. (Job 23:13)

> Our God is in the heavens;
>   he does all that he pleases. (Ps. 115:3)

> The LORD of hosts has sworn:

> "As I have planned,
>   so shall it be,
> and as I have purposed,
>   so shall it stand,
> that I will break the Assyrian in my land,
>   and on my mountains trample him underfoot;
> and his yoke shall depart from them,
>   and his burden from their shoulder."

> This is the purpose that is purposed
>   concerning the whole earth,
> and this is the hand that is stretched out
>   over all the nations.
> For the LORD of hosts has purposed,
>   and who will annul it?

1. As Jürgen Moltmann, *The Trinity and the Kingdom* (San Francisco: HarperCollins, 1981), 56; Elizabeth Johnson, *She Who Is* (New York: Crossroad Publishing, 1996), 20.

> His hand is stretched out,
>   and who will turn it back? (Isa. 14:24–27)

Cf. Ps. 135:6; Isa. 55:11; Dan. 4:35.[2] See also the section of chapter 8 dealing with the efficacy of God's control.

2. *Nothing is too hard for God.* The difference between this idea and the previous one is that it explicitly describes what God can do in universal terms: not only can he do what he wants to do, but *nothing* is too hard for him, or, conversely, all things are possible for him. Note:

> Is anything too hard for the LORD? At the appointed time I will return to you, about this time next year, and Sarah shall have a son. (Gen. 18:14)

Literally, the first sentence reads, "Is any word [*davar*] too wonderful [*pele*, a miracle-term] for the Lord?" The angel who announces to Mary the coming birth of Jesus echoes this language: "For nothing will be impossible with God" (Luke 1:37).

In Numbers 11:23, "the LORD said to Moses, 'Is the LORD's hand shortened? Now you shall see whether my word will come true for you or not.'" Again, God gives a promise that seems impossible: a supply of meat in the desert. But of course, Israel should not measure the probability of God's word being true over against the unlikelihood of the event. God's word is supremely authoritative, and Israel should trust it as the very standard of truth. So the question "Is the LORD's arm shortened?" is rhetorical. Ascribing weakness to God contradicts the very nature of lordship and the authority of his word. So *of course* this task is not too hard for the Lord.

Face to face with God, brought to an end of himself, first by his sufferings and then by God's amazing knowledge and power, Job admits, "I know that you can do all things, and that no purpose of yours can be thwarted" (Job 42:2). God can do *all things.* Cf. also Jer. 32:17, 27; Zech. 8:6; Matt. 19:26 (Mark 10:27; Luke 18:27). And before his death on the cross, Jesus prayed:

> Abba, Father, all things are possible for you. Remove this cup from me. Yet not what I will, but what you will. (Mark 14:36)

We should not exaggerate the difference between the texts under the first principle and those under the second. Even the passages in the second list (with the significant exception of Mark 14:36) refer in context to actions that God actually carries out. But the believers' confidence in the second list of passages is based on a universal premise: God can fulfill his promise to me because he can do *anything.* So in these passages, "God can do all things" is a normative premise that should govern the thinking of his people. When God promises something seemingly impossible, God's people should

---

2. These are the words of Nebuchadnezzar, king of Babylon. But it is evident in context that here he is telling the truth, having been humbled by the Lord.

be thinking not only that "God's Word is always true," but also that "God can do all things." So the realm of possibility for God is wider than the realm of actuality. God *can* do things that he does not actually do. We should never restrict our view of God's power only to what he does, or has done, in history. God does not exhaust his power in his work of creation and providence.

What God Can't Do

The "all things," however, requires some interpretation. The problem of defining it has engendered much controversy. The reason is that there are clearly some things that God *can't* do, such as lying, stealing, making another God, making a square circle, making a stone so big that he cannot lift it, and so on. Therefore, philosophers and theologians have tried in one way or another to qualify the "all" in "God can do all things," to find some alternative way of defining the concept, or to reject it altogether.

Let us look at some of the classes of actions that God cannot perform.

1. *Logically contradictory actions*, such as ultimately saving and condemning the same individual, making a round square (i.e., an object that is both square and not square at the same time and in the same respect), or making a rope with only one end.[3] As we saw in the previous chapter, God is a logical, rational being, though he does not necessarily conform to the laws of any human system of logic. The laws of logic are an aspect of his own character. Being logical is his nature and his pleasure. So the fact that he cannot be illogical is not a weakness. It may not be fairly described as a lack of power. Indeed, it is a mark of his great power that he always acts and thinks consistently, that he can never be pushed into the inconsistencies that plague human life.

We note here, as we will do with other "qualifications of omnipotence," that there are problems of language in this discussion. Not every "inability" is a lack of power; indeed, again, some inabilities are marks of extraordinary power. Imagine a baseball player who hits a home run whenever he comes to the plate. Someone might say of him, "He can't hit singles or doubles." That *sounds* like a weakness, until you look at the broader context.

Remember also my point in the previous chapter that abilities presuppose possible barriers (sometimes called *preventers*) that the abilities overcome. In the case of God's inability to be illogical, what prevents his illogicality is his righteousness, faithfulness, truth, rational speech, knowledge, and wisdom. God's incapacity here is not due to illness, injury, lack of strength, a crowded schedule, and so on. It is due to traits that are wholly admirable. This sort of reasoning will help us to see how alleged divine inabilities are really strengths. The term *inability*, therefore, is misleading in this context, though it is literally applicable. *Inability* is usually a pejorative, but in this case there is nothing deserving of criticism.

---

3. Assuming the principle that it is logically impossible to generate an actually infinite object out of finite material parts.

2. *Immoral actions*, such as lying, stealing, coveting, breaking his promises. God is *apseudes* (Titus 1:2), nonlying:[4]

> God is not man, that he should lie,
>   or a son of man, that he should change his mind.
> Has he said, and will he not do it?
>   Or has he spoken, and will he not fulfill it? (Num. 23:19)

Balaam's questions are obviously rhetorical. It is unthinkable that God should lie or fail to keep his promise. He "cannot deny himself" (2 Tim. 2:13). He "cannot be tempted with evil" (James 1:13). God does, of course, have some moral prerogatives that human beings do not have, such as the right to take human life for his own reasons. But for the most part, human morality is an imaging of God: "You shall be holy, for I am holy" (1 Peter 1:16, quoting Lev. 11:44; cf. Lev. 11:45; 19:2; 20:7; Matt. 5:48). God is the standard for human morality, so he cannot be less than perfect in his holiness, goodness, and righteousness.

Again, we may speak of God's inability here, but we are really talking about something admirable—moral excellence and consistency. These are the only qualities that "prevent" God from engaging in immoral actions. So again, the term *inability* is misleading.

3. *Actions appropriate only to finite creatures*, such as buying shoes, celebrating his birthday, taking medicine for a cough. Again, God's inability to do these things is not due to any lack of power. Remember, however, that God is quite capable of taking on human form and doing all these things. His "inability" exists only in his disincarnate existence.

4. *Actions denying his own nature as God*, as making another god equal to himself, abandoning his divine attributes, absorbing the universe into his own being. God necessarily exists as the one true God. If God were to perform any of these actions, he would no longer exist as the one true God. The world would then no longer be a theistic universe, but rather a chaos. But in fact, there could be no such world. So these actions are impossible. Even God cannot perform them. But that fact is good for everybody. It does not deserve the pejorative *inability*.

5. *Changing his eternal plan*: His eternal plan is unchangeable (see chapter 11). There has been some discussion about whether God can change the past. I prefer to deal with this issue without getting into the complications of current scientific theories about time. The most relevant point is simply that just as God's eternal plan has determined what will happen in the future (to us), so he has determined once for all the events of time that to us is past. Since that plan does not change, God cannot change the past or the future.

---

4. One can argue whether this means one "that *cannot* lie" (KJV) or merely one "who *does not* lie" (NIV). But clearly, *apseudes* characterizes all of God's actions. A god who lies is not the God of the Bible. So I take *apseudes* as an essential attribute. Thus the KJV translation is appropriate.

6. *Making a stone so large that he cannot lift it*: This is the famous "paradox of the stone," beloved of philosophers.[5] We are at first inclined to say that this is a logically contradictory action, such as making a round square. What gives us pause is that (a) the description is not formally contradictory in any obvious way, and (b) this is in fact an action that some human beings can perform. There is no incoherence in the idea of a human being's making an object too big to lift. People do it all the time. So why should this action be incoherent in the case of God? And is this a case in which human beings can do something that God can't do?

But we have seen in 3 above that there are many acts that are appropriate only to finite beings: getting medical treatment, studying books to gain knowledge, paying taxes, and so forth. The act in question here is, I think, one of those. I mentioned earlier that when God takes on human form, he may do any number of these things, and that is also true in this case. Indeed, Jesus himself, during his days as a carpenter, might have made an object (say a house) that as man he was unable to lift. The question is really whether God could do this in his nonincarnate state.

So the preventer here, what keeps him from making the stone, is God's infinity—not a weakness, but a strength. But the issues of 1 and 4 enter here, too. For *God* to make an object so large that he cannot lift it would involve either a contradiction of his omnipotence (1) or an abandonment of it (4). For God is omnipotent, and however we choose to define *omnipotence*, it certainly entails that he can lift any stone of any weight. So the preventer here is his infinity, together with his logical nature or his power itself. These are all, of course, strengths, rather than weaknesses. Perhaps what makes this puzzle so fascinating is that the three issues of power, logic, and infinitude need to be sorted out before a satisfying solution can be found.

Definitions of Omnipotence

But how, then, shall we define *omnipotence*, granted all these qualifications? Some philosophers have decided that because of the complications mentioned above, *omnipotence* cannot be defined. It must be either denied or replaced by a different concept.[6]

We are tempted, perhaps, to say that *omnipotence* means that God can do anything with the exceptions of the classes of actions listed in 1 to 6. But that would be a rather unwieldy definition, and it certainly would not express clearly that insight into God's power that drove the biblical saints to worship.

---

5. Some of the significant essays in the recent discussion are gathered in Linwood Urban and Douglas N. Walton, *The Power of God* (New York: Oxford University Press, 1978), 131–68, by George I. Mavrodes, Harry G. Frankfurt, C. Wade Savage, and others. The same considerations mentioned here, I think, bear also on the question whether God can "make a chair not made by God," and similar examples. This action is coherent and possible for human beings, but it is not appropriate for God. Were he to perform it, it would compromise his nature as God.

6. See, for example, Anthony Kenny, *The God of the Philosophers* (Oxford: Clarendon Press, 1979), 95–96.

Anthony Kenny[7] discusses some of the alternative definitions available in the philosophical literature. Here is my own list with comments, influenced somewhat by his, avoiding too much technical complication.

1. *God is able to do whatever he wants.* But this is also true of the elect angels and glorified saints, whom we would not describe as omnipotent.

2. *God is able to do anything logically possible.* But some of the actions excluded in the previous discussion are logically possible.

3. *God can do what is possible.* This definition would incorporate different kinds of possibility, other than logical possibility. But possible for whom? Not creatures, because in Scripture God's omnipotence includes actions that are *impossible* for creatures. Possible for God, then? But this definition would be tautological: God can do what God can do. That definition would be true, but not informative.[8]

4. *God has infinite power.* *Infinite power* requires further definition, if it is not to include power to perform the actions excluded earlier. So this phrase doesn't help us.

5. *God has power over all things.* Certainly he does have this power, according to Scripture. He is supreme, in control, the Lord of all. But this attempted definition really changes the subject. Our original question was: what can God *do*, in the course of exerting this power?

6. *God has more power than anyone else.* Also scriptural, but it poses the same problem as 5.

7. *God can do anything compatible with his attributes.* This is Kenny's solution,[9] and I think it is the best available at present. There is a problem here, however, and that is that all of God's attributes can be construed as powers, as I illustrate in this volume.[10] So this definition (like 3 on the second interpretation) lands in tautology, telling us that God can do what he can do.

This, however, is the same kind of circularity we considered in chapter 12, in the section dealing with the *Euthyphro* problem. There we saw that God's goodness, for example, is defined by his whole nature, and also that God's whole nature is good. Good is what he is, says, and does; but what he is, says, and does is good. Here we are saying the same about God's power. His power is defined by his whole nature, as in Kenny's proposal. But his whole nature should be defined as power; for power is not ultimately something abstract, but a concrete divine person. God's power is everything that he is; all his attributes manifest his power.

7. Ibid., 91–99.

8. Alvin Plantinga illustrates this problem by reference to Mr. McEar, who is capable only of scratching his ear. If omnipotence means that someone can do anything possible for him to do, then McEar is omnipotent. See Alvin Plantinga, *God and Other Minds* (Ithaca, NY: Cornell University Press, 1967), 170.

9. My formulation is, of course, a simplified paraphrase. Kenny's version: "the possession of all logically possible powers which it is logically possible for a being with the attributes of God to possess." *God of the Philosophers*, 98. I consider logic itself to be an attribute of God, so the references to logical possibility are superfluous.

10. Kenny says, in parentheses, "If the definition is not to be empty 'attributes' must here be taken to mean those properties of Godhead which are not themselves powers: properties such as immutability and goodness." Ibid., 98. But is it not the case that immutability is God's power to remain the same through change in the world, and that goodness is his power to do good and avoid evil?

The reason for this problem is that there is no one or no thing higher than God by which to define his attributes. Nor are his attributes really separable from one another; each is a perspective on his whole nature. This is the *doctrine of simplicity*, which I will expound in a chapter 20.

So our definition boils down, in one sense, to "God can do what he can do." The definition is circular, as, ultimately, are all definitions of divine attributes. But the circle need not be a *narrow* circle.[11] For we learn of God's nature through his revelation, which is rich in content. God's righteousness is "everything he is," but it is also his mighty acts to redeem his people from unjust oppression. Similarly, God's power is "everything he is." But it is also his marvelous work of creation, providence, and redemption, as well as his power to conceptualize possibilities beyond the actual world.

In the end, we cannot define precisely what God is able to do. But we are confident that he can do everything Scripture describes him as doing, and much more. And we know that the only "preventers" are his own truth, righteousness, faithfulness, and so on. That fact should assure us that God is entirely competent to accomplish all his righteous, loving purposes.

Omnipotence and Redemption

All the controversy about the definition of omnipotence and the various theological distinctions made about it may distract us from the actual purposes of God in revealing his power to us. God does not reveal his omnipotence merely so that we can engage in philosophical games or speculate on what he might or might not do. As with all his revelation, God wants the doctrine of omnipotence to edify his people (2 Tim. 3:16–17).

As I said earlier, God's power drives his people to worship. It also warns us against governing our lives by our own expectations of what is possible, leaving God out of account. We may, for example, like the disciples, wonder how certain classes of people could be saved: the very rich (as in Luke 18:23–27), hardened criminals, persecutors of Christians, and so on. So we may be tempted to ignore such people in the course of our gospel witness, focusing only on those who from our human perspective we deem to be "winnable." But the words of the Lord Jesus would turn us from such despair and favoritism: "What is impossible with men is possible with God" (Luke 18:27).

Redemption itself contradicts all human expectations. It is God's mighty power entering a situation that from a human viewpoint is hopeless. God comes to Abraham, who is over a hundred years old, and to Sarah, far beyond the age of childbearing, and he promises them a natural son. Sarah laughs. But God asks, "Is anything too hard for the LORD?" (Gen. 18:14). God's omnipotence intervenes, and Isaac is born. The omnipotence is the power of God's covenant promise: the Hebrew literally reads, "Is

11. In discussing apologetics, I have often made a distinction between broad and narrow circularity, as in *DKG*, 131; *AGG*, 14. A "narrowly" circular argument would be a tautology such as "Scripture is true because Scripture is true." A "broadly" circular argument enlarges the circle by mentioning facts, as "Scripture is true because Jesus' resurrection is verifiable." Within a biblical worldview, however, the second argument is as circular as the first, for it assumes that Scripture is the chief criterion for determining what is verifiable.

any word of God void of power?" God's powerful word comes into our world of sin and death and promises salvation. Isaac will continue the covenant, and from him in God's time will come the Messiah, who will save his people from their sins. When the Messiah comes, he will be born not to a barren woman like Sarah, but to a virgin—an even greater manifestation of God's omnipotence. So the angel echoes to Mary God's promise to Abraham: "nothing will be impossible with God" (Luke 1:37).

So God's Word never returns to him void (Isa. 55:11). It is God's omnipotence, doing for us what we could never do for ourselves. Apart from God's power, we could expect only death and eternal condemnation. But God brings life in the place of death. So the resurrection of Christ becomes a paradigm of divine power in Ephesians 1:19–23, quoted earlier. A God who can raise people from the dead can do *anything*. He is a God worthy of trust.

Power and Weakness

I have so far emphasized, as Scripture does, the obvious forms of divine power as seen in creation, providence, miracle. But by focusing on such spectacular exhibits of God's power, we might tend to think of God's power as a kind of brute strength that can overpower any obstacle by sheer force. As Paul Helm says:

> It is tempting to think of God as a Herculean figure, able to outlift and out-throw and outrun all his opponents. Such a theology would be one of physical or metaphysical power; whatever his enemies can do God can do it better or more efficiently than they.[12]

But, he adds, we should resist this temptation, "for the Christian view of providence reveals not only the power of God, but his weakness also."[13] How is God weak? Paul says in 1 Corinthians 1:25 that "the weakness of God is stronger than men." He is thinking here of the cross of Christ (see 1:18, 23–24). Jesus was delivered up to death by wicked men, so that God would raise him up in glory, having made him an offering for the sins of his people (Acts 2:23).

Jesus refuses to be an earthly ruler, or to bring in his kingdom by the sword. Rather than kill his enemies, he dies at their hand. All of this gives every appearance of weakness. But Paul says that the cross is "the power of God and the wisdom of God" (1 Cor. 1:24). Clearly, God used this time of weakness to accomplish his most amazing, indeed his most powerful, work: bringing life from death and defeating Satan and all his hosts.

So also in our own time, the most powerful work of God, the gathering of people out of Satan's clutches into Christ's kingdom, comes not through warfare or politics, not through the influence of money or fame, but through "the folly of what we preach" (1 Cor. 1:21). Jesus sends his people through the world, to all nations, bearing only his

---

12. Paul Helm, *The Providence of God* (Leicester: Inter-Varsity Press, 1993), 224. Much of my discussion in this section is based on Helm's, with thanks.

13. Ibid.

Word (Matt. 28:18–20). But that Word is the "power of God for salvation to everyone who believes" (Rom. 1:16). God's power lies in the humble medium of preaching, and indeed in the suffering of his people (1 Peter 2:13–3:22; 4:12–19). They defeat Satan through the armor that God supplies: truth, righteousness, the gospel of peace, faith, salvation, the Word of God, prayer (Eph. 6:10–20). Thus we are "strong in the Lord and in the strength of his might" (v. 10).

Some writers today believe that God is weak in the sense that he is unable to do what he would like. On this view, he cannot eradicate evil, though he would like to, and he cannot make any progress without our help.[14] Scripture does not teach the weakness of God in this sense. Indeed, such a view of God contradicts a vast amount of biblical teaching on God's sovereignty, control, and power.

But it is important for us to recognize that God's sovereign, controlling power appears not only in spectacular displays like the miracles of Jesus, but also in events in which people perceive him as weak. As I indicated in *DG*,[15] the spectacular in Scripture is typically preparation for the "ordinary." But God is at work in the ordinary as much as in the extraordinary. He often works behind the scenes, and he often does his most wonderful works through apparent defeats. So he tells Paul that "my power is made perfect in weakness" (2 Cor. 12:9). And Paul says:

> Therefore I will boast all the more gladly of my weaknesses, so that the power of Christ may rest upon me. For the sake of Christ, then, I am content with weaknesses, insults, hardships, persecutions, and calamities. For when I am weak, then I am strong. (2 Cor. 12:9b–10)

God's Will

God's power works according to his will. Theologians tend to regard God's will as his faculty for making decisions, as they regard his mind as his faculty of thought. But as we saw in the preceding chapter, Scripture rarely if ever speaks of a divine faculty of thought in distinction from the thoughts themselves, or in distinction from other faculties such as will. Similarly, though Scripture often refers to God's will (much more often than to God's mind), it does not typically speak of the will as some metaphysical or psychological entity in God that enables him to make decisions and exercise power. Rather, God's will is the decisions themselves. The decision-maker, as we would expect from the doctrine of simplicity, is not some part of God, or some faculty within God; it is God himself, the person. God is the One who acts; his will is what he decides.

Although, as we will see, God's will has many dimensions, a simple but accurate definition would be this: God's will is anything he wants to happen.

OT English translations rarely use "will" in reference to God, though *ratzon* ("plea-sure," "delight," "favor") is so translated in Psalms 40:8 and 143:10. In the NT, *thelema*

---

14. Note the references to Rabbi Kushner and the process theologians in chapter 14 for examples of this view.
15. *DG*, 264–66.

("wish," "will") is used fairly often in this way, *boule* and *boulema* ("counsel") much less so. But the concept is often expressed also by the term "pleasure" (or "good pleasure"), found predominantly as translations of the Hebrew root *hafetz* (as Isa. 44:28; 46:10) and the Greek *eudokeo* (as Eph. 1:5, 9; Phil. 2:13). God's will is what pleases him. The vocabulary of "thinking" and "planning" (Heb. *hashav*) and "choosing" (*bachar*) is also relevant. And "way" (Heb. *derek*, Gk. *hodos*) is found many times in Scripture referring to God's will (almost always in the preceptive sense; see below). And (also in the preceptive sense) "will" and "way" are often interchangeable (though not entirely synonymous) with the broad vocabulary of revelation: "ordinances," "testimonies," "laws," "statutes," "commandments," "words," and so forth.

These terms are used more or less interchangeably. The differences of nuance between the terms are not, I think, of doctrinal importance. One could not argue, for example, that one term more typically denotes God's will as decree and another God's will as precept. If this distinction is legitimate (see below), both sides of it are expressed by each of the biblical terms.

Decree and Precept

Among human beings, there are many different kinds of wants and pleasures, and of course we tend to arrange them in priorities. Some things we want more than other things. Some we cannot achieve, so we settle for others. We postpone fulfilling some desires until others are realized. Sometimes one must be realized before another. Some are not compatible with others, so we must choose between them. For these reasons, some of our desires are unfulfilled, temporarily or permanently.

Here we see some analogy to the complexities of God's will. God, too, has many desires, variously valued and prioritized. Some of God's desires he achieves immediately. But since he has determined to create a world in time and has given to that world a history and a goal, some of his desires, by virtue of his own eternal plan, must await the passing of time. Further, there are some good things that, by virtue of the nature of God's plan, will never be realized.

So theologians have made various distinctions within the larger concept of the will of God. God's will is, of course, one; but since it is complex, some have distinguished different aspects of it as *wills*, plural. We should be careful with this language, but it does make it easier for us to consider the complications of our topic.

One distinction is between God's *antecedent* and *consequent* wills. God's general valuation of some things as good we may call his *antecedent will*; his specific choices among those goods (in view of the overall nature of the world that he intends to make) may be called *consequent*. That distinction is legitimate, since God's eternal plan respects the integrity of the beings that he intends to create and takes them into account. Again, God might genuinely value many states of affairs that are simply not compatible with the "story" that he has chosen to tell.

God's thinking, of course, is not a temporal process. All his thoughts are simultaneous, as we will see in the following chapter. Nevertheless, it is helpful to represent God's thought *as if* it were in two stages: (1) God evaluates every possible state of affairs, and (2) God chooses among these values, rejecting some and accepting others for the sake of his historical drama.

But Roman Catholic, Lutheran, and Arminian theologians have used the antecedent-consequent distinction to make a place for libertarian freedom. On their view, God's antecedent will includes the salvation of all men. His consequent will, however, awaits the (libertarian) free decisions of human beings. Those who choose to believe, God blesses; those who do not, he condemns to eternal punishment. These blessings and curses come by his consequent will.

In my view, these theologians are right in saying that God antecedently wants everyone to be saved. We will look more closely at this question later, but certainly universal salvation is a good, a desirable state of affairs. They are also right to claim that in view of the actual historical situation, God does not bring that result to pass. There is no harm in calling this second volition *consequent*. In his eternal plan, God does determine not to achieve certain goods, at least partly because of the nature of the creatures that he intends to create.

The Roman Catholic, Lutheran, and Arminian theologians are wrong, however, in saying that God's consequent will is dependent on the (libertarian) free decisions of man. I have given reasons (chapter 14) for denying the truth of libertarianism and will present many more in our discussion of the doctrine of man (chapter 35).

Reformed theologians have typically rejected the antecedent-consequent distinction because of its association with libertarian freedom. But they have adopted a rather similar distinction, between God's *decretive* and *preceptive* wills. God's *decretive will* is simply what in chapter 11 we called God's decree. It is his eternal purpose, by which he foreordains everything that comes to pass. God's *preceptive will* is his valuations, particularly as revealed to us in his Word (his *precepts*). The decretive will focuses on God's lordship attribute of control, the preceptive will on the lordship attribute of authority. God's decretive will cannot be successfully opposed; it will certainly take place. It is possible, however, and often the case, for creatures to disobey God's preceptive will.

The decretive will is sometimes called the *will of God's good pleasure* (*beneplacitum*). This is somewhat misleading, because Scripture speaks of God's "pleasure" in both decretive and preceptive senses—decretive, for example, in Psalm 51:18 and Isaiah 46:10 KJV, preceptive in Psalms 5:4 NIV and 103:21 KJV. Some have also called the decretive will God's *hidden* or *secret* will, but that, too, is misleading, since God reveals some of his decrees through his Word.

For that reason I hesitate also to call the preceptive will the *revealed* will (*signum*, "signified" will), though that language has often been used for this concept. *Preceptive* is also somewhat misleading, for it does not always have to do with literal precepts (God's laws, commandments). Sometimes God's preceptive will refers not to precepts but to states of affairs that God sees as desirable, but that he chooses not to bring about (as Ezek. 18:23; 2 Peter 3:9). Still, I will use *preceptive* because of customary usage, and because I don't know of superior terminology available.

How is this distinction similar to the antecedent-consequent distinction? God's preceptive will, like the antecedent will, consists of his valuation of every possible and actual state of affairs. His decretive will, like the consequent will, determines what will actually happen. The difference is that the concept *decretive* is intended to exclude libertarianism. God's decision as to what will actually happen is not based on his foreknowledge of the libertarian free choices of men. It is rather based on his own decision to write his historical drama in a certain way.

It is therefore disingenuous for Arminians to criticize Calvinists for teaching "two wills" in God. Arminianism, indeed all theologies, recognizes some complexity in God's will (though confessing its ultimate unity), and theologians of all persuasions have sometimes talked about multiple wills in God. Arminians and even open theists also like to distinguish God's *will of permission*, concerning which Paul Helm says:

> Suppose . . . there are areas of human action (including human evil action) which God not only does not will, but which he does not know will happen until the events occur. Nevertheless, the events in these areas are *permitted* by God, albeit in a very loose and weak sense. For if God did not allow them, and in some sense support them, then they would not occur . . . . God then wills (permits) what he does not will (command) . . . . So it is not an advantage of that view that it avoids having to think of God having two "wills."[16]

Does Scripture warrant this distinction? Below are some passages using the vocabulary of "thought," "intent," "pleasure," "purpose," "counsel," and "will" to refer to God's decretive will:

> As for you, you meant evil against me, but God meant it for good, to bring it about that many people should be kept alive, as they are today. (Gen. 50:20)

> At that time Jesus declared, "I thank you, Father, Lord of heaven and earth, that you have hidden these things from the wise and understanding and revealed them to little children; yes, Father, for such was your gracious will." (Matt. 11:25–26)

Cf. Pss. 51:18; 115:3; Isa. 46:10; Jer. 49:20; 50:45; Dan. 4:17; Acts 2:23; Rom. 9:18–19; Eph. 1:11; James 1:18; Rev. 4:11. I would say that God's "ways" in Romans 11:33 should also be taken in the decretive sense, though elsewhere the term is almost always preceptive.

---

16. Helm, *Providence of God*, 132. The Arminian exegete I. Howard Marshall admits the duality within the will of God in "Universal Grace and Atonement in the Pastoral Epistles," in *The Grace of God and the Will of Man*, ed. Clark Pinnock (Grand Rapids: Zondervan, 1989), 56: "We must certainly distinguish between what God would like to happen and what he actually does will to happen, and both of these things can be spoken of as God's will."

Here are some instances of these same terms used in a preceptive sense:

> Not everyone who says to me, "Lord, Lord," will enter the kingdom of heaven, but the one who does the will of my Father who is in heaven. (Matt. 7:21)

> Therefore do not be foolish, but understand what the will of the Lord is. (Eph. 5:17; cf. 6:6)[17]

Cf. Pss. 5:4; 103:21; Matt. 12:50; John 4:34; 7:17; Rom. 12:2; 1 Thess. 4:3; 5:18; Heb. 13:21; 1 Peter 4:2. These passages literally refer to "precepts" of God. The following refer not to precepts, but to desirable states of affairs that God does not ordain, states of affairs that I include within the general category *preceptive*:

> Have I any pleasure in the death of the wicked, declares the Lord GOD, and not rather that he should turn from his way and live? (Ezek. 18:23)

> The Lord is not slow to fulfill his promise as some count slowness, but is patient toward you, not wishing that any should perish, but that all should reach repentance. (2 Peter 3:9)

Note other passages where God desires repentance from human beings, which may or may not be forthcoming: Isa. 30:18; 65:2; Lam. 3:31–36; Ezek. 33:11; Hos. 11:7–8.

Does God Desire the Salvation of All?

If God desires for people to repent of sin, then certainly he desires them to be saved, for salvation is the fruit of such repentance. Some Calvinists, however, have denied this conclusion, reasoning that God cannot possibly desire something that never takes place. But I have dealt with that objection already. Scripture often represents God as desiring things that never take place. As we have seen, he wants all people to repent of sin—but we know that many people never repent. And there are many, many other examples. God desires that all people will turn from false gods and idols, hold his name in reverence, remember the Sabbath, honor their parents, and so on. But those desires are not always fulfilled.

The reason is that God's "desires" in this sense are expressions of his preceptive will, not his decretive will. His decretive desires always come to pass; his preceptive desires are not always fulfilled. So there is nothing contrary to Calvinistic theology in the assertion that God wants everyone to be saved.

Further, there are specific passages that lead to this conclusion. We saw in chapter 12 that in some senses God is gracious and loving to all his creatures, including those that are unrighteous (Matt. 5:44–48).[18] God sends rain and fruitful

---

17. "Will" here is *thelema*, which in Ephesians 1:11 is clearly decretive.

18. For further discussion of these passages, see John Murray, "The Free Offer of the Gospel," in *MCW*, 4:113–32. In this section I am much indebted to Murray's article.

seasons to everybody and even fills their hearts with gladness (Acts 14:17). God desires the best for his creatures, and of course, what is the very best for them is salvation in Christ.

Then in Deuteronomy 5:29, God expresses his desire in passionate terms:

> Oh that they had such a mind as this always, to fear me and to keep all my commandments, that it might go well with them and with their descendants forever!

Cf. Deut. 32:29; Ps. 81:13–14; Isa. 48:18. In these passages God expresses an intense desire not only for obedience, but also for the consequence of obedience, namely, the covenant blessing (cf. Ex. 20:12) of long life and prosperity. Ultimately the covenant blessing is nothing less than heaven itself, eternal fellowship with God.

Divine passion is even more obvious in Matthew 23:37 (Luke 13:34), where Jesus weeps over Jerusalem, saying:

> O Jerusalem, Jerusalem, the city that kills the prophets and stones those who are sent to it! How often would I have gathered your children together as a hen gathers her brood under her wings, and you would not!

The gathering here certainly includes the blessings of salvation. Jesus wants the people of Jerusalem to be gathered to him.

In the prophecy of Ezekiel, God's desire for human repentance is also a desire that the repentant one will have life. "Life" is often a biblical summary of God's salvation that brings us out of death (as Eph. 2:1–7). Through Ezekiel, God says:

> Have I any pleasure in the death of the wicked, declares the Lord God, and not rather that he should turn from his way and live? (Ezek. 18:23; cf. vv. 31–32; 33:11)

In Isaiah 45:22, God again cries out:

> Turn to me and be saved,
>   all the ends of the earth!
>   For I am God, and there is no other.

Murray argues[19] that the range of this plea is not universal in a merely ethnic sense (all nations, but not all individuals), but embraces all individuals. Part of his argument is based on the fact that the verse (and the context) emphasizes the uniqueness of the true God and his prerogatives over his entire creation. His plea must be as broad as his own lordship authority.

Second Peter 3:9 teaches the same desire on the part of God:

---

19. Ibid., 4:126–27.

The Lord is not slow to fulfill his promise as some count slowness, but is patient toward you, not wishing that any should perish, but that all should reach repentance.

Those wanting to limit the reference of this passage to the elect sometimes focus on the "you," suggesting that this limits the reference to believers. Like other NT letters, this one is written to the church, and it presumes faith on the part of its readers. Yet, also like other letters, this one recognizes that professing believers are subject to many temptations in this life and that some do fall away. When they fall away permanently, they thereby show that they never had real faith. So in addressing believers, Peter is not assuming that all his readers are among the elect. And "patient" (*makrothumei*) here is an attitude that, according to other passages, God shows to the reprobate (Rom. 2:4; 9:22). The passage itself makes no distinction between elect and reprobate.

So in 2 Peter 9b, Peter may be expressing God's desire that everyone in the church will come to repentance; but if his focus is thus on the church, he is not distinguishing between elect and reprobate within the church. My own view, however, is that his thought in this verse goes beyond the church: The "any" and "all" of verse 9b are not necessarily included among the "you." So after describing God's patience with his people in the church, Peter looks beyond them, asserting God's desire for *universal* human repentance.

Murray does not deal with 1 Timothy 2:4, but it is much discussed in this connection. That verse speaks of God, "who desires all people to be saved and to come to the knowledge of the truth." It is certainly plausible to take the "all" here to refer to ethnic universalism[20] (see above in the discussion of Isaiah 45:22), especially since verses 1 and 2 urge prayer "for all people, for kings and all who are in high positions, that we may lead a peaceful and quiet life, godly and dignified in every way." Reformed commentators typically insist that verses 1–2 cannot be universal except in the sense "all sorts." They then draw the conclusion that God desires the salvation of "all men without distinction of rank, race, or nationality,"[21] but not the salvation of every individual.

But the parallel between the language here and that of passages such as Isaiah 45:22 might lead us to question this interpretation. And in my view, verses 1–2 do not have to be taken *only* as a universalism of classes of people. To pray for a king is at the same time to pray for his people as individuals. William Hendriksen thinks it impossible that in verses 1–2 Paul could be asking prayer for *"every person on earth."*[22] There is no time, he thinks, to do this in more than a "very vague and global way." But it would also be impossible to pray specifically for every king and magistrate on the face of the earth. In any case, Paul's desire is simply that we pray for the nations in the spirit of

20. Of course, there are many passages of Scripture in which "all" does not refer to every human being. "All" is often limited by its context. Examples: Mark 1:37 KJV; 5:20 NIV; 11:32; Luke 3:15; John 3:26; Rom. 5:18; 1 Cor. 15:22; Titus 2:11.

21. William Hendriksen, *A Commentary on the Epistles to Timothy and Titus* (London: Banner of Truth, 1960), 95.

22. Ibid., 94 (emphasis his).

God's blessing to Abraham, that God's grace will be applied to all people throughout the world and produce peace.

The real barrier to taking 1 Timothy 2:4 in a way similar to the other passages we have discussed is not verses 1–2, but verses 5–6:

> For there is one God, and there is one mediator between God and men, the man Christ Jesus, who gave himself as a ransom for all, which is the testimony given at the proper time.

If we see 2:4 as indicating God's desire for the salvation of every individual, must we not then take Jesus' "ransom" also in a universalistic sense, contrary to the Reformed doctrine of limited atonement? But the point of verses 5–6 in my view is very similar to the point made in Isaiah 45:22 and its context. Notice how in both Isaiah 45:22 and 1 Timothy 2:4–6, the thought moves from God's desire that all be saved to the exclusiveness of God's prerogatives and saving power. My own inclination is to take verses 5–6 not as enumerating those for whom atonement is made, but as describing the *exclusiveness* of the atonement, of God's saving work in Christ. His is a ransom *for all men* in the sense that there is no other.

If we read the passage this way, there is no reason, dogmatic or exegetical, why we should not take verse 4 (which is so like the other verses we have explored) to indicate God's desire for the salvation of everyone. I am inclined to take this position, though I don't regard the question as fully closed. My main point, however, is that we should not allow our exegesis of this passage to be prejudiced by the dogmatic view that God *cannot* desire the salvation of all. If this passage does not teach such a desire, many other passages do.

Which Is the *Real* Will of God?

Herman Bavinck says:

> Roman Catholics, Lutherans, Remonstrants, and others, proceed from the "revealed" or "signified" [preceptive] will. This is then the "true" will, which consists in that God does not will sin but only wills to permit it; that he wills the salvation of all humans and offers his grace to all, and so on. Then, after humans have decided, God adjusts himself to that decision and determines what he wants, salvation for those who believe and perdition for those who do not believe. The "consequent will" follows the human decision and is not the actual and essential will of God, but the will of God occasioned by the conduct of humans. The Reformed, by contrast, proceeded from the will of God's good pleasure [decretive], viewing this as the actual and essential will of God. That will is always carried out, always effects its purpose; it is eternal and immutable. The "expressed" or "signified" will [preceptive], on the other hand, is God's precept, concretely stated in law and gospel, the precept that serves as the rule for our conduct.[23]

---

23. *BRD*, 2:243.

Bavinck here presents an adequate summary of the differences between the Reformed and their major opponents. I cite him only to dissent from both parties in their desire to identify what will of God is the "real" will.

God's decrees and his precepts both represent divine values. It is true that the decrees always take effect; the precepts do not necessarily do so. That seems to give special honor to the decrees above the precepts. But one can also argue the other way: God's precepts represent his ideals, ideals that describe states of affairs often far more excellent than the present world as it has been decreed. God's precepts, for example, demand a world in which everyone honors the true God, in which everybody honors his parents, in which there is no murder—or murderous anger, and so forth. Would not such a world be better than the one we now live in?[24]

God's precepts also express goals, to which his decrees are means. The new heavens and new earth are a place where righteousness dwells (2 Peter 3:13; cf. Matt. 6:33). So one could argue that God's preceptive will is his "real" will, the one that he seeks to achieve in this world through the history of redemption.[25]

But I will not argue that point. Rather, I will insist that Scripture does not value one will above another, or compare one unfavorably to the other. The fact is that both these precepts and decrees are divine desires and should be given the highest honor. God's precepts are an object of worship in the Psalms (Ps. 56:4, 10), and are worthy of the most profound meditation (Ps. 1) and obedience (Ps. 119). God's decrees represent his control, his precepts his authority. We honor both equally as we honor the Lord.

A Third Will?

Christians have, however, often spoken of "God's will" in ways that escape the classifications *preceptive* and *decretive*. A typical case is when a church member asks his pastor how he can find "God's will for my life." In answering this question, the pastor would be rather unkind to take it decretively ("God's will for your life is whatever happens"). And to take it preceptively ("God's will for you is found entirely in the Bible, *sola Scriptura*") seems to miss the point. The parishioner is not asking for God's law or gospel. He is asking whether and how he can get guidance from God in making practical decisions: whether or whom to marry, what to study in school, what field of work to enter, and so on. So we ask: is "God's will for my life" a third aspect of God's will, coordinate with the other two?

This kind of question has opened the door to dangerous subjectivism. Christians have sometimes been told that the will of God in this sense comes through a strong feeling given by God. I do believe that feeling plays an important role in human

---

24. See chapter 14 for an argument that this is not necessarily the "best of all possible worlds."

25. I have argued in previous chapters that God's decision to make a world in time lies behind some of the more difficult problems of theology. See chapter 14 on the relevance of this consideration to the problem of evil. So here we should note that the temporality of creation has some bearing on the problem of understanding the duality of will in God.

knowledge,[26] in our knowledge both of Scripture and of other things. But *sola Scriptura* means that Scripture alone is the complete transcript of God's words to us. Emotions (together with reason, imagination, sense-perception, etc.) can help us to understand and apply Scripture to our circumstances, but they cannot add anything to the words of God in the Bible. That is to say that emotions can sometimes make us aware of data relevant to a decision. But apart from Scripture, they cannot obligate us to make one decision rather than another. Only Scripture provides divine norms, norms establishing an ultimate obligation.

Further, Scripture itself never advises God's people to expect God to lead through feelings apart from his Word. To walk in God's ways is to walk according to his testimonies, his ordinances, his words.

It would be wrong, however, to tell an inquirer that God does not guide his people in making specific life decisions. Scripture has much to say about *wisdom*, which God gives liberally to his people (James 1:5). As we saw in the preceding chapter, wisdom begins with the fear of the Lord (Ps. 111:10) and the following of his precepts. A godly person seeks, through wisdom given by the Spirit, to *apply* the precepts of the Lord to the circumstances of life.[27]

Sometimes wisdom dictates or rules out a particular course of action: a wise person will not fail to worship the true God, and he will not commit adultery, for example. But sometimes wisdom leaves open a range of options: it calls for a man to support his family (1 Tim. 5:8), but it does not dictate precisely what kind of shelter, clothing, or food to provide for them. One reason for the confusion about "God's will for my life" is that the phrase suggests only one possible course of action. We might think that if we have a choice between living in San Diego or Philadelphia, God will require one choice and forbid the other. But as a matter of fact, either choice might well be acceptable to God. If our motives are right and neither move would involve us in conflict with God's law, then we can assume that either decision is within the will of God.

But that choice may need some refinement. For example, my choice to live in Philadelphia may not conflict with God's Word in any big, obvious ways. But after prayerful meditation it may become evident that I could make much better use of my gifts in San Diego. Or it may be that the situation in Philadelphia would offer more temptations to sin, temptations that, knowing myself, I would be best off avoiding. Or it may be that there are better opportunities for Christian growth or service in one place or the other. All of these must be weighed in the decision, and there might be several pluses and minuses on each side.

Wisdom is not only obeying Scripture in the big, obvious ways. It is also, according to Proverbs, intelligence, knowledge, skills, understanding circumstances (including their likely consequences), self-knowledge, understanding of other people. It is a discernment that comes through reading Scripture, but a reading arising out of spiritual

---

26. See *DKG*, 152–64, 335–40.

27. For discussion of the concept *application*, see *DKG*, 81–85, 93–98, and *DCL*, passim.

maturity and experience.[28] Thus, it is the ability to weigh pluses and minuses of the alternatives before us. This, too, is obeying Scripture, for Scripture requires us to be wise, to redeem opportunities.[29]

God wants us, then, to make our decisions as wisely as possible. This is his preceptive will. In the example above, taking into account all the pluses and minuses of moving to Philadelphia or San Diego, it may well be that one decision is wiser than the other. That is not necessarily the case; perhaps neither choice is wiser than the other, as we saw above. When I choose one cabbage over another in the supermarket, it usually is the case that neither choice is wiser than the other. But if one decision *is* wiser than the other, then it is correct to say that that choice is the will of God, in the preceptive sense. For God's preceptive will includes not only the words of Scripture itself, but the "good and necessary consequences" of Scripture.[30] When one choice is wiser than the other, God's preceptive will tells me to make the wiser choice.

On the other hand, if the two possible decisions are indistinguishable in terms of wisdom, then we may say that either decision is *within* God's will.

It is thus that God guides his people: through Spirit-given wisdom, based on Scripture, wisdom that enables us to understand what is at stake in our choices and to evaluate those circumstances in a godly way. Through such guidance God reveals to us our *vocation*, to invoke a good Reformation term.

I do not, therefore, believe that we absolutely need a third category in addition to *decretive* and *preceptive*. But we should not oversimplify our understanding of God's preceptive will. It includes not only the explicit words of Scripture, but the words of Scripture applied to each of us, using the God-given gifts of intelligence, spiritual discernment, and so on.

But though a third category is not strictly necessary, it might be helpful. We do, after all, have some leeway as to how to divide the pie of biblical teaching. Strictly speaking, of course, only one category is needed: God's "wants" or "desires." But as we have seen, God has many different kinds of desires, so that some analysis is helpful. Scripture does not explicitly distinguish between decrees and precepts, but as we look at Scripture, we see that it speaks of God's will in these two ways. So to help students of theology, we create the categories *decretive* and *preceptive*. Perhaps it would be helpful to make *wisdom* or *vocation* a third category, in order to avoid misunderstandings. After all, it would be wrong, as we have seen, to tell an inquirer that God's will includes only his decrees and the Bible, as if to imply that God does not guide us in specific ways.

So I suggest the following teaching for such inquirers: God guides us through his decrees, his written Word, and Spirit-given wisdom: (1) By his decrees, he opens doors

28. See such passages as Romans 12:1–2; Ephesians 5:8–10; Philippians 1:9–10; Hebrews 5:12–14, in which knowledge of God's will comes through regeneration, sanctification, and testing. I discuss this in *DKG*, 153–55.

29. For more helpful discussion on the ways in which God leads us to make such choices, see Edmund P. Clowney, *Called to the Ministry* (Philadelphia: Westminster Theological Seminary, 1964), and James C. Petty, *Step by Step* (Phillipsburg, NJ: P&R Publishing, 1999).

30. WCF 1.6. On the inclusion of applications among these consequences, see *DKG*, 84.

and closes them, giving us some opportunities and withholding others; but those circumstances of our lives do not in themselves tell us how to behave. (2) By Scripture, he tells us what he wants us to do, showing us how to respond to these circumstances. (3) By Spirit-given wisdom, God enables us to *apply* Scripture to circumstances.

Scripture uses the idea of *God's will* to describe the outcome of the wisdom in category 3, in the passages mentioned in footnote 28: Rom. 12:2; Eph. 5:10; Phil. 1:9–10; Heb. 5:14. Certainly God knows what kind of life we would live if all our decisions were as wise as possible. We should not hesitate, then, to describe that life as God's will. This is not to say that if we make an unwise decision, we have "missed out" forever on God's will for our lives. After we make an unwise decision, we should turn to God's wisdom again, confident that it will lead us in the path of blessing.

These three categories, *decree*, *precept*, and *wisdom*, are perspectivally related. God decrees to act according to his precepts and his wisdom. His precepts include the teaching that we should bow before God's sovereign decrees and seek his wisdom. And his wisdom is displayed both in his decrees and in his Word. In terms of the overall triadic structure of my Theology of Lordship series, the decree is situational, the precept normative, and wisdom existential. See fig. 16.1.

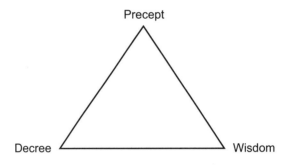

Fig. 16.1. Perspectives on the Will of God

Key Terms
Omnipotence
Paradox of the stone
Circularity
Narrow circle
Preventers
Antecedent will
Consequent will
Decretive will
Preceptive will
Wisdom

Study Questions

1. Name the two biblical ideas that evoke the concept of God's omnipotence. Cite texts that present these ideas.

2. Is there anything that God cannot do? If so, list some of them. Do these threaten the doctrine of God's omnipotence? Why or why not?

3. What is the "paradox of the stone"? Respond to it.

4. Frame says that the definition of *omnipotence* is circular. In what way? Does that cause a problem? Respond.

5. "In the end, we cannot define precisely what God is able to do." Explain; evaluate.

6. How is God's omnipotence important to our redemption?

7. Is there any sense in which God is weak? Discuss.

8. "It is therefore disingenuous for Arminians to criticize Calvinists for teaching 'two wills' in God." Why? Discuss.

9. Cite some Bible passages speaking of God's will in a decretive sense; a preceptive sense.

10. Does God desire the salvation of all? Cite Scripture texts to this effect. If so, does that affect the Reformed doctrine of limited atonement? How?

11. Which is the "real" will of God? Discuss.

12. A friend asks you, "How can I find God's will for my life?" Respond.

Memory Verses

Num. 23:19: God is not man, that he should lie,
  or a son of man, that he should change his mind.
Has he said, and will he not do it?
  Or has he spoken, and will he not fulfill it?

2 Chron. 20:6: O Lord, God of our fathers, are you not God in heaven? You rule over all the kingdoms of the nations. In your hand are power and might, so that none is able to withstand you.

Ps. 115:3: Our God is in the heavens;
  he does all that he pleases.

Matt. 23:37: O Jerusalem, Jerusalem, the city that kills the prophets and stones those who are sent to it! How often would I have gathered your children together as a hen gathers her brood under her wings, and you would not!

Rom. 12:2: Do not be conformed to this world, but be transformed by the renewal of your mind, that by testing you may discern what is the will of God, what is good and acceptable and perfect.

2 Cor. 12:9: But he said to me, "My grace is sufficient for you, for my power is made perfect in weakness." Therefore I will boast all the more gladly of my weaknesses, so that the power of Christ may rest upon me.

Eph. 1:11: In him we have obtained an inheritance, having been predestined according to the purpose of him who works all things according to the counsel of his will.

Eph. 3:20–21: Now to him who is able to do far more abundantly than all that we ask or think, according to the power at work within us, to him be glory in the church and in Christ Jesus throughout all generations, forever and ever. Amen.

Resources for Further Study

Bavinck, Herman. *BRD*, 2:242–49.

Helm, Paul. *The Providence of God*. Leicester: Inter-Varsity Press, 1993. Christian philosopher discusses some of the problems noted in this chapter.

Kenny, Anthony. *The God of the Philosophers*. Oxford: Clarendon Press, 1979. Note his discussion of omnipotence.

Murray, John. "The Free Offer of the Gospel." In *MCW*, 4:113–32. Standard Reformed discussion of the free offer and of God's desire that all men might be saved.

Urban, Linwood, and Douglas N. Walton. *The Power of God*. New York: Oxford University Press, 1978. Philosophical treatments.

GOD'S ATTRIBUTES: LORD OF TIME

IN THIS CHAPTER, I WILL CONTINUE my discussion of God's attributes of power. Here we will look at his attributes of infinity, eternity, immensity, temporal omnipresence, and unchangeability. These have to do with God's relationships to time.

Theologians do not generally refer to these as attributes of power, but as *metaphysical* attributes (God's relations to the metaphysical structure of creation), *incommunicable* attributes (since none of these can be predicated of creatures), attributes of *transcendence* (since they indicate God's transcendence over time), and so on. The term *metaphysical*, however, might seem to suggest that these attributes relate to "God in himself" in contrast with God in relation to the creation. But in fact all our knowledge of God is in relation to creation, in the sense that it is *our* knowledge, and we are creatures. Like all of God's attributes, these describe God's relation to various aspects of the world he has made, and that relation is always one of lordship. For my critique of the incommunicable-communicable distinction, see chapter 12.

I also object to calling these attributes of transcendence. The concept of transcendence commonly used here uncomfortably reminds me of the non-Christian concept of transcendence described in chapter 3. For example, theologians have often described God's eternity as his absence from the temporal world. While there is some truth in this description, I think it is more biblical to understand God's eternity as his lordship (control, authority, and presence) over time and therefore his presence in time as much as his transcendence over it, his lordship over the whole temporal sequence.

So this chapter will continue the emphasis of the previous one: here I will present God as Lord of time. He is Lord of all creation in terms of all his covenants with creatures, particularly the universal covenant that I expounded in chapter 4.

God's Infinity

I will say little about God's *infinity*, for the word is almost never used in Scripture, and what can be said about it is best said under other headings. Only the KJV translation of Psalm 147:5 can be said to regard infinity as a divine attribute, and there it is specifically infinity of his "understanding," for which see our discussion of omniscience in chapter 15.

In Greek philosophy, infinity is either a negative concept (absence of definite characteristics) or a positive one (existing so far beyond reality that it cannot be named). Both of these concepts reflect what I have called the non-Christian view of transcendence, and as such they are alien to biblical thought.

It is, however, common in theology to use the term adjectivally: infinite power, infinite knowledge, and so on. In these contexts, *infinite* can substitute for the *omni-* prefix in *omnipotence* and *omniscience*, and I have discussed in previous chapters what these terms should be taken to mean. It can also be used to express the "perfection" of God's attributes. So we will in effect explore God's infinity as we discuss his other perfections.

We should therefore understand God's infinity in either or both of these ways: (1) God is free from the limitations implicit in creaturely existence, and (2) God's attributes are supremely perfect, without any flaw.[1]

God's Eternity

The terms *eternity* and *eternal* in Scripture represent several Hebrew (*'ad*, *'olam*, *qedem*) and Greek (*aidios*, *aion*, *aionios*) terms. These terms can refer to finite periods of time or to long or endless duration through time. Whether they can also refer to a radical transcendence over time itself is a possibility that we will explore below. *Aion*, when not used to refer to a finite period of time, tends to be found as the genitive *ton aionon* ("of the ages"), the adjective *aionios*, or phrases such as *eis ton aiona* ("to the age," "forever"), *eis tous aionas*, and *eis tous aionas ton aionon* ("to the ages of the ages," "forever and ever").

In the Bible, *eternal* usually refers not to God's nature, but to the quality of life or punishment that awaits human beings: eternal life or eternal death. But here are some of the rare uses of these terms as divine attributes, or referring to God's other attributes or decrees:

> Abraham planted a tamarisk tree in Beersheba and called there on the name of the Lord, the Everlasting [*olam*] God. (Gen. 21:33)

> The eternal [*qedem*] God is your dwelling place,
>   and underneath are the everlasting arms. (Deut. 33:27a)

> For his invisible attributes, namely, his eternal [*aidios*] power and divine nature, have been clearly perceived, ever since the creation of the world, in the things that have been made. So they are without excuse. (Rom. 1:20)

---

1. Neither of these has much to do with mathematical infinity. Introducing that concept into discussions of God's nature is usually, in my view, not helpful.

This was according to the eternal [*ton aionon*] purpose that he has realized in Christ Jesus our Lord. (Eph. 3:11)

Cf. also 1 Tim. 1:17 (the "King eternal," NIV) and Heb. 9:14 (the "eternal Spirit").

Now, there has been a long debate as to the definition of eternity as a divine attribute. Greek philosophers Parmenides, Plato, and Plotinus understood "eternal" reality to be timeless—beyond or outside time. For Parmenides' *Being*, Plato's *Forms*, and the *One* of Plotinus, there is no change, no before or after.

Christian theologians also spoke of God as timeless, as existing before[2] time, and so on. This language became especially common during the Arian controversy of the fourth century A.D., as orthodox theologians opposed the Arian contention that there was a "time when the Son was not."[3] No, they replied, both the Son and the Father existed before time. Time is their creation. So they are essentially timeless.[4] Augustine says to God in his *Confessions*:

Thy present day does not give way to tomorrow, nor indeed, does it take the place of yesterday. Thy present day is eternity.[5]

The classic statement of God's atemporal eternity is found in Boethius's *Consolation of Philosophy*, 5.6. There he defines God's eternity as "the simultaneous and perfect possession of infinite life." This definition held sway in the church for many centuries. We can find its equivalent in Anselm[6] and Aquinas[7] (but not in Duns Scotus and William of Occam), and in the major post-Reformation theologies.[8]

The Socinians opposed this view. They held that God's eternity meant merely that God has no beginning or end, not that he is above or outside of time. This position may be called *temporalist*, and on this view God experiences temporal succession as we

2. Strictly speaking, it is improper to speak of something occurring before time, because *before* is itself primarily a temporal expression. Without time, there is no before or after. But it is convenient for those who believe time is part of the creation to refer to God's eternal nature apart from creation by the phrase *before time*. There are spatial uses of *before* as well, as in "stand before the king," and perhaps we can think of God "standing before time" in that sort of way.

3. More precisely, the Arians asserted a *when* (*pote*) when the Son was not, rather than a *time* (*chronos*). The difference, in my judgment, is rhetorical rather than substantial.

4. Hilary of Poitiers' *On the Trinity* is a particularly strong example. In 8.40, he says, "Again, let him who holds the Son to have become Son in time and by His Incarnation, learn that through Him are all things and we through Him, and that His timeless Infinity was creating all things before time was."

5. Augustine, *Confessions*, 11.3.

6. *Proslogium*, chap. 19, and *Monologium*, chap. 22, in *St. Anselm Basic Writings*, ed. S. N. Deane (La Salle, IL: Open Court, 1974).

7. *SCG*, 1. He says (section 3) "There is, therefore, no *before* or *after* in Him; He does not have being after non-being, nor non-being after being, nor can any succession be found in his being."

8. Martin Luther and John Calvin themselves did not concern themselves much with the definition of eternity, or in general with defining divine attributes. But their successors resumed the discussion, following the Boethian-Augustinian approach by and large. See *RD*, 65. Francis Turretin's discussion is representative, in *Institutes of Elenctic Theology* (Phillipsburg, NJ: P&R Publishing, 1992), 1:202–4.

do. Such a position was, of course, a necessary implication of their denial of exhaustive divine foreknowledge, which I discussed in chapter 15.

More recently, theologians and philosophers, even some of Reformed conviction, have sometimes attempted to qualify the atemporalist tradition. The views of James H. Thornwell and Charles Hodge on this question are not entirely consistent, in my view. James Oliver Buswell taught that God was fully in time. Oscar Cullmann and Nicholas Wolterstorff also challenged the Augustinian-Boethian view, but James Barr said that it was exegetically defensible, and Paul Helm's *Eternal God: A Study of God without Time*[9] presented a vigorous defense of divine timelessness.[10]

As with the denial of exhaustive divine foreknowledge (chapter 15), the strongest motive of those who deny divine timelessness, in my opinion, is the desire of these thinkers to make room for libertarian freedom. If God is timelessly eternal, it is difficult to argue that he is ignorant of what to us is future, for he sees all times equally from his eternal vantage point. And if God knows exhaustively what to us is future, then he knows the free acts of human beings before[11] they take place. And if he knows these actions in advance, it is hard to argue that they are free in a libertarian sense.

On the other hand, Scripture often presents God as acting *in* time, so it certainly is not possible to exclude God from time altogether. Evidently the issue is more complicated than a simple decision between whether God is "in" or "out" of time, as an object might be inside or outside of a box.

Scripture on God and Time

As with all other theological questions, Scripture alone can ultimately resolve the question of the nature of God's eternity.

One cannot derive either a temporalist or an atemporalist view of God from the use of *aion* in its various forms. In this respect I follow Barr rather than Cullmann. The frequent use of *aionios* to refer to the eternal life of God's people should not be taken in an atemporal way. Nothing in Scripture suggests that human beings will ever transcend time.[12] Eternal life is life without end, in fellowship with the eternal God. So one would naturally think that the term has the same meaning when applied to God. A number of passages speak of God as having no beginning or end (Deut. 32:40; Pss. 33:11; 93:2; 102:24, 27; 145:13; 146:10), and in the absence of other evidence it would seem best to say only that God is *everlasting*: persisting through time rather than transcending it.

We should remember, of course, that the biblical writers did not have in mind our modern scientific concept of time, or even (most likely) the Platonic philosophical

---

9. Oxford: Clarendon Press, 1988.

10. See *DG*, 547–48, for specific discussion of these thinkers. I discuss some of their arguments specifically on pages 548–53.

11. The *before* is, of course, from our temporal point of view.

12. Some have taken Revelation 10:6 ("there should be time no longer," kjv) to indicate a nontemporal existence for the creation in the eschaton. But the context speaks rather of impending judgment, so I think the niv is correct to translate "there will be no more delay." That is the only verse I know that has been used to suggest that our eternal life is nontemporal.

distinction between time and eternity. Their understanding of time was more immediate and practical. They understood that God gives us a certain number of years of
life before we die, but that his years never fail (Ps. 90:9–10; Heb. 1:12). There is no
reason to suppose that they thought much about the "nature" or "essence" of time or
the relations sustained to time (so defined) by God and man.[13] Certainly they didn't
see time primarily as a kind of "box" that a person can be either inside or outside of.

So perhaps we should back away a bit from the original terms of our question. It may
not be possible to derive from Scripture an explicit answer to the question whether God
is temporal or supratemporal. But I do think there is biblical reason to conclude that
God's relation to time is very different from our own. For the biblical God transcends
a number of limitations associated with our experience of temporality:

The limitation of beginning and end: In the passages cited above, Scripture teaches that
God has no beginning or end. Temporalists and atemporalists agree on that proposition. But it is also significant that the world has a beginning, and that God exists *before*
that beginning. Genesis begins with "the beginning" (*reshit, arche*), and many other
passages refer to the initial creation as the beginning (Isa. 40:21; 41:4, 26; 46:10; Matt.
19:4; Heb. 1:10; etc.). But the Creator precedes the creation. In John 1:1, the creative
Word existed, not only at the beginning. One translation that brings out the durative
force of the verb reads: "when all things began, the Word already was" (NEB).

James Barr argues, contrary to Cullmann, that this *beginning* can be taken as the
beginning of time itself:

> In general there is a considerable likelihood that the early Christians understood the
> Genesis creation story to imply that the beginning of time was simultaneous with
> the beginning of the creation of the world, especially since the chronological scheme
> takes its departure from that date.[14]

The "chronological scheme" includes not only the six days of creation (however liter-
ally or figuratively they are to be taken), but also the establishment of day and night
(Gen. 1:5) and the creation of the heavenly bodies "to separate the day from the night.
And let them be for signs and for seasons, and for days and years" (v. 14).

This argument does not prove absolutely from Scripture that time itself had a beginning. It would be possible, certainly, for time to exist in the absence of days and nights
demarcated by heavenly bodies. But certainly the biblical writers saw God as having his

---

13. Ludwig Wittgenstein discusses in *Philosophical Investigations* a quotation from Augustine on the subject.
Platonist that he was, Augustine admitted difficulty in defining time. "If nobody asks me, I know; but if somebody asks me, I don't know." Wittgenstein took this as an example of how philosophical problems arise. We
use words such as *time* very naturally, without perplexity, until somebody asks us the "definition" or "essence."
Then we are bewildered or "bewitched," and we find it necessary to consult philosophers. Wittgenstein's own
suggestion is that if we are able to use the word *time* in its everyday settings, then we understand it sufficiently. It
may not be possible to define it, to reduce all its uses to one essence. Nouns in language are not always amenable
to essence-description. See Ludwig Wittgenstein, *Philosophical Investigations* (New York: Macmillan, 1968), 89.

14. James Barr, *Biblical Words for Time* (Naperville, IL: Alec R. Allenson, 1969), 75.

own existence beyond and prior to the history of the material creation and the human race. And it is problematic to try to imagine what role time would play in a situation before the creation, in which there are no bodies in motion, but only the unchanging God. What we *know* as time, measured by the heavens, affecting our practical lives, certainly began with the creation. If God experienced time before the creation, his experience of it was certainly very different from ours today.

The limitation of change: I have chosen to discuss God's unchangeability in a separate section below. But clearly God is unchangeable in some respects (Mal. 3:6), and however one interprets it, his unchangeability gives him an experience of time different from ours.

The limitation of ignorance: Through time, our memories of the past grow dim, and our anticipation of the future is always highly fallible. But as I argued in chapter 15, God knows perfectly what to us are past, present, and future, seeing them, in effect, with equal vividness. This does not mean that all times are indistinguishable for him. He knows that one event happened on Monday, another on Tuesday, and he knows the process by which one event flowed into the next. Thus, I consider it misleading to say that there is no "succession of moments" in God's consciousness.[15] But he does see all events laid out before him, as one can see an entire procession from a high vantage point.

The procession analogy[16] is a frequent illustration of an atemporal consciousness. An atemporal being would see all events equally vividly. Since God can do this, his experience of time, in still another sense, is very different from ours. Indeed, his relation to time is unique.

The limitation of temporal frustration: To us, time often seems to pass too slowly or too quickly. Too slowly, trying our patience as we wait for something to happen; too quickly, as we try to complete a task by a deadline. For God, however, time never passes too slowly:

> For a thousand years in your sight
>   are but as yesterday when it is past,
>   or as a watch in the night. (Ps. 90:4)

But neither does time pass too quickly for God:

> With the Lord one day is as a thousand years, and a thousand years as one day.
> (2 Peter 3:8)

I am not here trying to make a point about time traveling at multiple speeds in God's consciousness. I doubt that these passages have in mind anything so abstruse.

---

15. God does not sense one moment of his own transcendent consciousness flowing into another. But he fully understands the process by which time flows in the creaturely world.

16. Or one could use the analogy of a movie film. When one watches the film projected onto the screen, he watches one frame at a time, each moving into the next. But if one could look at the film itself (only short ones, I gather, are suitable for this illustration), stretched out before one's field of vision, he could see all frames at once, and therefore all "times" in the film.

Rather, the point is that God is so completely in control of the temporal sequence that he is able to accomplish precisely what he wants.

The same point can be made through reflection on the "fullness of time" (NIV: "when the time had fully come") in Galatians 4:4. God has structured the whole history of the world to accomplish precisely his own purposes. (See chapters 8 and 11 for more biblical evidence of God's divine control in the accomplishment of his eternal purpose.)

Again, we must conclude that God's experience of time is very different from ours. He looks at time as its Lord, as his tool in accomplishing his purposes; we look at it as a limit on our choices. He is Lord of time. The dates of history are "times or seasons that the Father has fixed by his own authority" (Acts 1:7; cf 17:26; Mark 13:32).

What conclusion follows from these four ways in which God transcends limitations associated with time? Shall we say that God is merely "in" time, or is he in some way "outside of" time?[17] Well, try to imagine what it would be like to have a consciousness without beginning and end, without change, with perfect knowledge of all times, and with complete sovereignty over temporal relationships. What would that feel like?

When we talk about ourselves being "in time," part of what we mean, I think, is that to us time is a limit. It is a sort of box that we cannot get out of; it limits our knowledge and our choices. To God, time is clearly not that sort of box. A much better metaphor is the atemporalist one, that he looks down on time from a lofty height. So it seems to me that God's experience of time, as Scripture presents it, is more like the atemporalist model than like the temporalist one.

I cannot present the above as a watertight argument for divine atemporality. But it seems to me that once we deny the existence of libertarian freedom, all the relevant considerations favor atemporality, and none favor temporality.

More important than the question of temporality, however, is God's lordship over time. In chapter 3 and since, I have argued that God's transcendence in Scripture is not his being outside or beyond history, but rather his being Lord and King, in control of all things and speaking with authority over all things. So God's special relation to time, whether temporal or atemporal, should not be defined first in terms of temporality, but in terms of lordship.

Some temporalists have used the phrase "Lord of time" as an alternative to calling him atemporal.[18] But temporalists who espouse libertarian freedom (that is, most temporalists) need to ask how libertarianism can possibly be consistent with divine lordship as Scripture presents it.

---

17. Later, I will argue that God is in time as immanent. Here, however, I am concerned with the nature of his transcendence with respect to time, his eternity. The question: does that transcendence imply that he is outside time in some sense, or not?

18. Oscar Cullmann, *Christ and Time* (Philadelphia: Westminster Press, 1950), 69; Nicholas Wolterstorff, "God Everlasting," in *God and the Good*, ed. Clifton Orlebeke and Lewis Smedes (Grand Rapids: Eerdmans, 1975), 203; Otto Weber, *Foundations of Dogmatics* (Grand Rapids: Eerdmans, 1983), 2:456–58.

God's Temporal Omnipresence

We have not, however, exhausted the biblical teaching on the relation of God to temporal reality. So far we have focused on the nature of God's transcendence in relation to time. Now we must look at his temporal immanence.

I disagree with Nicholas Wolterstorff's general position on this matter, but I appreciate one of his arguments, to the effect that God's redemptive actions in Scripture are temporally successive and that the biblical writers regard God as having a time-strand of his own. This is certainly right. I mentioned earlier that God accomplishes his purposes in the fullness of time. That fact is a testimony to his sovereignty, but also to the importance of temporal relationships in the divinely ordained course of history.

The biblical narrative is a historical succession of events—events of creation, fall, and redemption. I mentioned in chapter 5 that, as Cullmann, Geerhardus Vos, and others have pointed out, the NT tells us of two *ages*: the old age and the new. The old is the age of fallen humanity, running from the fall to the final judgment. The new is the age of salvation, beginning with the coming of Christ and running into eternity future. We now live in a time of overlap between the two ages. So history is a linear pattern of events, beginning at creation, reaching a climax in the work of Christ, continuing on to the final judgment and the eternal state.

The work of Christ is *once for all*. Its *pastness* is important to the NT writers. The *presentness* of the time of decision is also important: "Behold, now is the favorable time; behold, now is the day of salvation" (2 Cor. 6:2b). And the *futurity* of the consummation is important: suffering now, glory later (1 Peter 1:3–7; etc.).

All these events are God's works, so God works in a temporally successive pattern. The sequence is foreordained by God's decree, but he brings it to pass in time. Now, Wolterstorff takes this temporal pattern to imply that God has "a time strand of his own" and therefore that God is temporal.

In one sense, Wolterstorff is correct. We saw in chapter 2 that covenant presence is an important element of God's lordship. And covenant presence means both that God is *here* and that God is *now*. Israel in Egypt needed to learn that God was present not only to the patriarchs four hundred years before, but to them as well, in their current experience. So it is not only the case that God *works* in time; it is also the case that he is *present* in time, at all times.

I believe that too little attention has been paid to God's temporal omnipresence in the discussion over God's temporality. Much of what some writers want to gain by a temporalist view (other than, of course, libertarian freedom) can be as easily secured through sufficient recognition of God's temporal covenant presence. For example, a covenantally present God, like a temporalist God, can know (and assert) temporally indexed expressions such as "the sun is rising *now*." He can feel with human beings the flow of time from one moment to the next. He can react to events in a significant sense (events that, to be sure, he has foreordained). He can mourn one moment and rejoice the next. He can hear and respond to prayer in time. Since God dwells in time, there is give-and-take between him and human beings.[19]

As I indicated in chapter 9, God's providence operates on the world both from above (government) and from below (concurrence). And in the incarnation of Jesus Christ, we see again how the eternal God enters time. In Christ, God enters not a world that is otherwise strange to him, but a world in which he has been dwelling all along.

But this temporal immanence does not contradict his lordship over time or the exhaustiveness of his decree. These temporal categories are merely aspects of God's general transcendence and immanence as the Lord. The "give-and-take" between God and the creation requires not a reduced, but an enhanced view of God's sovereignty. We must recognize God as Lord in time as well as Lord above time.

So God is temporal after all—but not *merely* temporal. He really is "in" time, but he also transcends time in such a way as to have an existence "outside" it. He is both inside and outside of the temporal box, a box that can neither confine him nor keep him out. That is the model that does most justice to the biblical data.

God's Unchangeability

Another attribute describing God's relation to time is that of *unchangeability* or *immutability*. Whether we think of change as the measure of time or time as the measure of change, the two are closely related.

From the time of the ancient Greek philosophers, intellectuals have tried to understand change. Many have concluded that there must be something unchanging, a reference point from which we can measure and therefore understand the changes around us. In Christian thought, the ultimate vantage point has always been God.[20]

Scripture refers to God as unchanging:

> Of old you laid the foundation of the earth,
>   and the heavens are the work of your hands.
> They will perish, but you will remain;
>   they will all wear out like a garment.
> You will change them like a robe, and they will pass away,
>   but you are the same, and your years have no end. (Ps. 102:25–27; cf. Mal. 3:6;
>   James 1:17)

One particular emphasis is that God does not break his word or change his mind (KJV: "repent"):

> God is not man, that he should lie,
>   or a son of man, that he should change his mind.

---

19. More on this interaction in the next section.

20. Cornelius Van Til and others have argued that only the Christian God, as absolute person, is able to provide the presuppositions of meaningful experience. See my *CVT*, 51–78, 311–22; *AGG*, 57–147.

> Has he said, and will he not do it?
> Or has he spoken, and will he not fulfill it? (Num. 23:19; cf. 1 Sam. 15:29)

Compare Psalm 110:4 (Heb. 7:21); Jeremiah 4:28; Ezekiel 24:14, in which God says in specific cases that he will not change his mind. So as we have seen in earlier chapters, God's counsel stands firm; his purpose certainly will come to pass (Deut. 32:39; Ps. 33:11; Isa. 43:13; etc.). The image of the *rock* underscores Yahweh's stability, the sureness of his purposes.

A God Who Relents

Nevertheless, a number of problems arise in discussions of God's unchangeability. For example, we should note that there are many passages of Scripture in which God does appear to change his mind. In Genesis 2:17, God tells Adam that in the day he eats of the forbidden fruit, he will surely die. Yet, in the first biblical indication of God's grace, Adam and Eve do not die after eating the fruit, but God rather proclaims his intention to defeat Satan (3:16).[21]

In Exodus 32:9–10, God announces judgment against the children of Israel for their false worship:

> And the LORD said to Moses, "I have seen this people, and behold, it is a stiff-necked people. Now therefore let me alone, that my wrath may burn hot against them and I may consume them, in order that I may make a great nation of you."

But Moses seeks God's favor, calling on him to "relent" (v. 12). "Relent" here is *nacham*, the same word translated "change his mind" in Numbers 23:19 and 1 Samuel 15:29 NIV (KJV: "repent").[22] And God does relent:

> And the LORD relented from the disaster that he had spoken of bringing on his people. (Ex. 32:14)

Six verses from 1 Samuel 15:29, which denies that God relents, we read:

> And Samuel did not see Saul again until the day of his death, but Samuel grieved over Saul. And the LORD regretted that he had made Saul king over Israel. (v. 35)

"Regretted" is *nacham*. So in these six verses we learn that God does not *nacham*, but that he "*nachamed*" that he had made Saul king. The passage appears contradictory. Similarly, before the flood, God "was sorry [*nacham*] that he had made man on the

---

21. We may, of course, say that man's *spiritual* death (Eph. 2:1, 5) dates from the fall. But I believe that the threat of Genesis 2:17 was to Adam's physical as well as his eternal state. Human death did, in general terms, begin with the fall, but in my view God did not fully carry out the terms of the threat in 2:17.

22. When used of God, *nacham*, of course, cannot mean to repent of sin, so the KJV translation is misleading here. It can mean "relent," "change one's mind," or "be grieved" (usually of an intense grieving).

earth" (Gen. 6:6). It seems again that God has changed his mind: from joy in creating man to grief.

The prophet Joel calls on Israel to repent:

> "And rend your hearts and not your garments."
> Return to the LORD your God,
>   for he is gracious and merciful,
> slow to anger, and abounding in steadfast love;
>   and he relents over disaster.
> Who knows whether he will not turn and relent,
>   and leave a blessing behind him,
> a grain offering and a drink offering
>   for the LORD your God? (Joel 2:13–14)

This passage is especially interesting because it quotes one of the definitive expositions of the divine name *Yahweh*, the one in Exodus 34:6–7, but it adds to this exposition that the Lord is One who "relents" (*nacham*). (I assume that this is a conclusion from the emphasis on forgiveness in Exodus 34.) So relenting is part of his very nature as the Lord. He is the Lord who relents.

The prophet Amos records a dialogue between himself and the Lord:

> This is what the Lord GOD showed me: behold, he was forming locusts when the latter growth was just beginning to sprout, and behold, it was the latter growth after the king's mowings. When they had finished eating the grass of the land, I said,
>
> "O Lord GOD, please forgive!
>   How can Jacob stand?
>   He is so small!"
> The LORD relented concerning this:
>   "It shall not be," said the LORD.
>
> This is what the Lord GOD showed me: behold, the Lord GOD was calling for a judgment by fire, and it devoured the great deep and was eating up the land. Then I said,
>
> "O Lord GOD, please cease!
>   How can Jacob stand?
>   He is so small!"
> The LORD relented concerning this:
>   "This also shall not be," said the Lord GOD. (Amos 7:1–6)

We are reminded here of Abraham's intercession for Lot in Sodom, in Genesis 18:16–33, and Moses' calling on God to spare Israel, as we have seen it in Exodus 32:9–14. In both passages, the intercessor gets his way. The Lord relents; he retreats from the judgment that he had originally announced.

When he finally arrives at Nineveh after some delay, Jonah announces, "Yet forty days, and Nineveh shall be overthrown!" (Jonah 3:4b). This is God's word, given through the prophet. But Nineveh is not overturned. God relents from his purpose. Jonah is not surprised, however:

> But it displeased Jonah exceedingly, and he was angry. And he prayed to the LORD and said, "O LORD, is not this what I said when I was yet in my country? That is why I made haste to flee to Tarshish; for I knew that you are a gracious God and merciful, slow to anger and abounding in steadfast love, and relenting from disaster." (Jonah 4:1–2)[23]

Like Joel, Jonah quotes Exodus 34:6–7, drawing from that passage the conclusion that God relents. This connection with the name *Yahweh* again suggests that relenting belongs to God's very nature: he is "a God who relents." Relenting is a divine attribute.

But how can this be, in the face of passages such as 1 Samuel 15:29 that appear to deny that God relents?

In the light of Joel 2:13–14 and Jonah 4:1–2, it is not a mere game with words to say that relenting is part of God's unchangeable divine nature. In Jeremiah 18:5–10, God indicates that such relenting is part of his general way of working:

> Then the word of the LORD came to me: "O house of Israel, can I not do with you as this potter has done? declares the LORD. Behold, like the clay in the potter's hand, so are you in my hand, O house of Israel. If at any time I declare concerning a nation or a kingdom, that I will pluck up and break down and destroy it, and if that nation, concerning which I have spoken, turns from its evil, I will relent of the disaster that I intended to do to it. And if at any time I declare concerning a nation or a kingdom that I will build and plant it, and if it does evil in my sight, not listening to my voice, then I will relent of the good that I had intended to do to it."

Cf. Jer. 26:3, 13, 19 (referring to Isa. 38:1–5); 42:10. Here the Lord states a general policy: many prophecies of judgment and blessing (see below for exceptions) are *conditional*. God reserves the right to cancel them or reverse them, depending on people's response to the prophet. As Calvin puts it, speaking of Jonah's prophecy:

> Who now does not see that it pleased the Lord by such threats to arouse to repentance those whom he was terrifying, that they might escape the judgment they deserved for their sins? If that is true, the nature of the circumstances leads us to recognize a tacit condition in the simple intimation.[24]

Some prophecies, then, that appear to be straightforward predictions are, according to the principle of Jeremiah 18:5–10, really warnings, with "tacit conditions" attached.

23. Cf. also 1 Chron. 21:15.
24. *Institutes*, 1.17.14.

Sometimes, as in the passages from Jeremiah, Joel, and Jonah, those tacit conditions have to do with obedience or disobedience, repentance or complacency. Sometimes, as in Genesis 18:16–33, Exodus 32:9–14, and Amos 7:1–6, prayer is such a condition. As the prophet intercedes for his people, God relents from the judgment he announced. The prophet stands before the throne of God himself and pleads for God's people, and God answers by relenting.

How is all this compatible with the sovereignty of God? Note the following:

1. Jeremiah 18:5–10 follows a passage (vv. 1–4) in which God compares himself to a potter and Israel to clay, a radical image of God's sovereignty. God's relenting is his sovereign decision. His right to withdraw his announced judgments and blessings is part of his sovereignty.

2. If we interpret these passages (as did Jonah) according to the principle of Jeremiah 18, we are interpreting them as expressions of his preceptive will, rather than his decretive (chapter 16): as warnings, not as predictions of what will certainly happen. So there is no question of his decretive will failing. His preceptive will, of course, unlike the decretive, can be disobeyed, but at great cost.

3. Even God's decretive will, his eternal plan, takes human actions and prayers into account. God's decretive will in the book of Jonah is not to judge Nineveh at that time. But he has eternally determined to accomplish that through Jonah's prophecy and the repentance of the Ninevites.[25] It is God's eternal intention to forgive Israel in the situation of Amos 7:1–6. But he does this through the power of Amos's intercession, and not without it.

Another problem: how is all this compatible with the authority of the prophetic word? For in Jonah 3:4, God through his prophet announces something that does not take place: the destruction of Nineveh. In Deuteronomy 18:21–22, the test of a true prophet is this:

> And if you say in your heart, "How may we know the word that the Lord has not spoken?"—when a prophet speaks in the name of the Lord, if the word does not come to pass or come true, that is a word that the Lord has not spoken; the prophet has spoken it presumptuously. You need not be afraid of him.

On this criterion, should not Jonah have been denounced as a false prophet? No, because God had revealed that such prophecies have "tacit conditions." What Jonah said to Nineveh was really, "Yet forty days and Nineveh will be destroyed, *unless* you repent of your sins and turn to the Lord." Jonah himself understood (Jonah 4:2) that God might forgive Nineveh despite the apparently categorical language of the prophecy. The Ninevites understood it, too. The king said:

> Who knows? God may turn and relent and turn from his fierce anger, so that we may not perish. (Jonah 3:9)

---

25. This is an example of what I mentioned earlier in the chapter: the give-and-take between human beings and God in his temporal immanence.

Jonah was a true prophet, announcing God's judgment with tacit conditions. His words were God's, his tacit conditions God's tacit conditions.

But then does Deuteronomy 18:21–22 become a dead letter? Not at all. Not all prophecies are conditional. Sometimes prophets do make straightforward predictions of events to come. Obviously, in 1 Samuel 10:1–7, for example, there is no conditionality. Samuel simply tells Saul a number of events that will take place in the immediate future, and they happen exactly as Samuel said. (For other examples, see the general treatment of providence in chapter 8 and the discussion of divine foreknowledge in chapter 15.) We must determine from the context which principle is operative: straightforward prediction, or conditional proclamation.

Some prophecies, too, are qualified by assurances. In Jeremiah 7:15, God says that the exile is certain, so certain that, according to verse 16, the prophet is not even to pray for the people, "for I will not hear you." Here, God makes known his decretive will. What he has predicted will certainly come to pass, whatever the conditions. In Amos 1:3, 6, 9, 13; 2:1, 4, 6, God announces judgments to come and says that these will certainly come to pass; he will not turn back his wrath. For other examples, see the following: Isa. 45:23; Jer. 4:28; 23:20; 30:24; Ezek. 24:14; Zech. 8:14. Sometimes, indeed, God takes a solemn oath to indicate the certainty of the predicted events: Ps. 110:4; Isa. 14:24; 54:9; 62:8; Jer. 44:26; 49:13; 51:14; Amos 4:2; 6:8; 8:7. Sometimes the phrase "as I [the Lord] live" pledges the unconditional truth of the prophecy (Ezek. 5:11; 14:16, 18, 20; 20:3, 31, 33; 33:27; 35:6, 11). In these examples God declares his unchangeable decretive will.[26]

In what sort of context are we likely to find "tacit conditions"? In prophecies of blessing and judgment, according to Jeremiah 18:5–10. To be sure, some such prophecies are unconditional, as those mentioned in the previous paragraph. But most of them are conditional, and most conditional prophecies are prophecies of blessing and judgment. Blessing and judgment are the twin sanctions of God's covenants. Often the prophet serves as the prosecuting attorney for God's "covenant lawsuit." In the covenant, God offers two alternatives: blessing for obedience, cursing for disobedience (see chapter 2). It is the job of the prophet to hold out both alternatives. This is the theological reason why prophecies of blessing and judgment are often conditional: they are proclamations of God's covenant. So it should not surprise us either to find that "relenting" is part of God's covenant name.

So to say that much prophecy is conditional is not to say that "anything can happen" following a prophecy. Even conditional prophecy limits what can happen and what cannot. The covenant itself is sealed by God's oath, so its curses and blessings will certainly come to pass granted the relevant conditions. The result will not be neutral; it will be *either* curse *or* blessing. Most of these prophecies are imprecise, to be sure; they don't describe exactly what kind of blessing or curse, or the timing of them. But they speak the truth.[27]

---

26. The fact that many passages have these explicit assurances, however, suggests that prophecy does not always have this unconditional character. So these passages, too, reinforce our impression that many prophecies in Scripture are conditional.

27. In this section, I am greatly indebted to Richard Pratt's important article "Historical Contingencies and Biblical Predictions," available at http://reformedperspectives.org/newfiles/ric_pratt/TH.Pratt

How Is God Unchanging?

We have seen that *unchanging* needs some definition beyond the obvious, since Scripture attributes to God some kinds of changes, even changes of mind. There are also questions that arise of a philosophical sort. Say that Susan becomes a Christian on May 1, 1999. Before that date, we could not say of God that he was "believed in by Susan," but after that date we could say that. A change has taken place, one that can be interpreted as a change in God.

Philosophers sometimes call these "Cambridge changes"[28] to distinguish them from "real changes." On the human level, consider that Mary has the property of being taller than her son Justin on January 1, 1998, then loses that property on January 1, 1999. She has remained the same height, but Justin has grown taller. Normally we would say that Mary has not changed in this respect, but Justin has. If we are in a philosophical state of mind, however, we can formulate the event as a change in Mary, namely, of losing a property and/or gaining one. We might call this a "Cambridge change" as opposed to a "real change."

It is not perfectly easy in some cases to distinguish the two,[29] but most of us would grant intuitively that there is a distinction to be made. Hence, theologians have often said that God does not change "in himself," but does change "in his relations to creatures." When Oviedo experiences a heat wave, it is not because the sun has grown hotter, but because Oviedo stands in a different relation to it (outside cloud banks, etc.). When God "changes" his attitude from wrath to favor, it is because the creature has moved from the sphere of Satan to the sphere of Christ.

Some "changes in God" can be understood in this way, but it would be wrong, I think, to understand all of them according to this model. For one thing, Reformed theology insists that when a person moves from the sphere of wrath to that of grace, it is because God has moved him there. God's "change" in this context (from wrath to grace) is not the product of creaturely change; rather, the creaturely changes come by God's initiative. Wolfhart Pannenberg says that in medieval theology,

> because of God's immutability any change in God's attitude to sinners has to begin with a change on our side. This was the main impulse behind the development of the Scholastic doctrine of a *gratia creata*. Only when the soul in its creaturely reality is adorned with this grace can the unchanging God have a different attitude toward it.[30]

Certainly the biblical doctrine of God's unchangeability is not intended to lead to such conclusions. But how do we avoid them?

.Historical_Contingencies.html. Pratt distinguishes (1) prophecies qualified by conditions, (2) prophecies qualified by assurances, and (3) predictions without qualifications. He analyzes each group most helpfully.

28. It evidently means that there are some kinds of events that only subtle philosophers would regard as changes.

29. See, e.g., Helm, *Eternal God*, 45.

30. Wolfhart Pannenberg, *Systematic Theology* (Grand Rapids: Eerdmans, 1988), 1:437. He refers to Johann Auer, *Die Entwicklung der Gnadenlehre in der Hochscholastik*, vol. 1, *Das Wesen der Gnade* (Freiburg: Herder, 1942).

I will not here take up the difficult and probably unedifying task of distinguishing Cambridge changes from real changes. If such a distinction turns out to be impossible, then it won't hurt us to concede that indeed God does change in some of these relational ways, just as we have conceded that God changes his mind in some senses. But Scripture does clearly teach that God is immutable in some important ways. So we do need to spend some time thinking about what changes, specifically, Scripture intends to exclude when it speaks of God's unchangeability. As I see it, they fall into the following categories. God is unchanging:

1. *In his essential attributes.* The WSC's answer to question 4 says that "God is a Spirit, infinite, eternal, and unchangeable in his being, wisdom, power, holiness, justice, goodness, and truth." Hebrews 13:8 (speaking specifically of Christ) and James 1:17 speak of God's being in general terms as unchangeable. Notice also in Hebrews 1:10–12 (quoting Ps. 102:25–27):

And,

"You, Lord, laid the foundation of the earth in the beginning,
    and the heavens are the work of your hands;
they will perish, but you remain;
    they will all wear out like a garment,
like a robe you will roll them up,
    like a garment they will be changed.
But you are the same,
    and your years will have no end."

Here the writer underscores the fundamental contrast between Creator and creature, and he characterizes it this way: Creatures change, but God does not. The passage does not merely say that God is without end, though that is true. Rather, unlike nature, which is worn out from one season to the next, God always remains the same. And remarkably, the author applies this teaching not specifically to God the Father, but to Christ. Note also that in Hebrews 5:8 he says of Christ, "Although he was a son, he learned obedience through what he suffered." Note the "although" (*kaiper*). The writer considers it somewhat anomalous that the Son of God should actually suffer and increase in knowledge. (The church deals with that anomaly, of course, under the category of Christology, distinguishing between Jesus' divine and human natures.) The author's main conception, therefore, is that God (Father or Son) does not change.

God's wisdom and knowledge are unchanging because, as we have seen in chapter 15, they are exhaustive. Since God knows all things in all times, from all eternity, his knowledge neither increases nor decreases. Nor does his power change, for as we saw in chapter 16, God is omnipotent, and there are no degrees of omnipotence. The same must surely be said of God's goodness and truth, for as we have seen, God is supremely perfect in these attributes, indeed the standard for the corresponding attributes in human beings.

2. *In his decretive will.* Psalm 33:11 reads:

> The counsel of the LORD stands forever,
>   the plans of his heart to all generations.

As we saw in earlier chapters, God governs all things by the story that he has written, his eternal decree that governs the entire course of nature and history. That story has been written already; it cannot and will not be changed.

3. *In his covenant faithfulness.* When God says, "For I the LORD do not change; therefore you, O children of Jacob, are not consumed" (Mal. 3:6),[31] he is telling them that he will surely fulfill his covenant promises despite Israel's disobedience. He is the Lord of the covenant, and he will not forsake his people. In Micah 7:19–20, the prophet says of God:

> He will again have compassion on us;
>   he will tread our iniquities underfoot.
> You will cast all our sins
>   into the depths of the sea.
> You will show faithfulness to Jacob
>   and steadfast love to Abraham,
> as you have sworn to our fathers
>   from the days of old.

The covenant continues through time. As we saw in chapter 4, this is an important biblical theme: God's presence with his covenant people through many generations, despite the people's temptation to relegate the covenant to a past age. So God says, in Psalm 89:34–37:

> I will not violate my covenant
>   or alter the word that went forth from my lips.
> Once for all I have sworn by my holiness;
>   I will not lie to David.
> His offspring shall endure forever,
>   his throne as long as the sun before me.
> Like the moon it shall be established forever,
>   a faithful witness in the skies.

And in Isaiah 54:10:

> "For the mountains may depart
>   and the hills be removed,

31. This verse might also refer to the unchanging nature of God's being. Divine lordship, as we have seen, is not only a description of God's relations to creatures, but also a key to his nature as God.

> but my steadfast love shall not depart from you,
> and my covenant of peace shall not be removed,"
> says the LORD, who has compassion on you.

We can see that in these contexts the unchanging character of God's covenant is vitally important to the biblical doctrine of salvation. It is this covenantal immutability that comforts us, that reassures us that as God was with Abraham, Isaac, and Jacob, so he will be with us in Christ. So Jesus is the same, yesterday, today, and forever (Heb. 13:8).

The writer to the Hebrews does say that God's covenant with Israel is "obsolete": "In speaking of a new covenant, he makes the first one obsolete. And what is becoming obsolete and growing old is ready to vanish away" (Heb. 8:13). Does God's covenant, then, change after all? No; the first covenant is obsolete not because God will violate its terms, but because he will fulfill those terms in a far more glorious manner than the Jews imagined. God's promises endure; through Jesus, all the nations of the earth are blessed:

> So when God desired to show more convincingly to the heirs of the promise the unchangeable character of his purpose, he guaranteed it with an oath, so that by two unchangeable things, in which it is impossible for God to lie, we who have fled for refuge might have strong encouragement to hold fast to the hope set before us. We have this as a sure and steadfast anchor of the soul, a hope that enters into the inner place behind the curtain, where Jesus has gone as a forerunner on our behalf, having become a high priest forever after the order of Melchizedek. (Heb. 6:17–20)

4. *In the truth of his revelation.* What God declares to be true was true from the beginning and always will be (Isa. 40:21; 41:4; 43:12; 46:10). So his ancient words remain our infallible guide, despite the passing of time and the changes in human culture (Rom. 15:4; 2 Tim. 3:16–17).

Unchangeability and Temporal Omnipresence[32]

Obviously, God is unchangeable in his atemporal or supratemporal existence. But when God enters time, as theophany, incarnate Son, or merely as present in time, he looks at his creation from within and shares the perspectives of his creatures. As God is with me on Monday, he views the events of Sunday as in the past, and the events of Tuesday (which, to be sure, he has foreordained) as future. He continues to be with me as Monday turns into Tuesday. So he views the passing of time as we do, as a process.

Theologians have sometimes described God's relenting as "anthropomorphic." There is some truth in that description, for divine relenting is part of the historical interaction

---

32. Thanks to Vern Poythress for suggesting to me many of the ideas of this section. I take full responsibility for the formulations.

between God and his people, an interaction in which God's activity is closely analogous to human behavior. In the exchange, for example, between God and Amos in Amos 7:1–6, God engages in a temporal conversation with a man, as an actor in history. The Author of history has written himself into the play as the lead character, and interacts with other characters, doing what they do.

That is one perspective on the situation. The other is the atemporal perspective: God has eternally decreed that he will forgive Israel, by means of Amos's intercession. This decree never changes.

But the historical process does change, and as an agent in history, God himself changes. On Monday, he wants something to happen, and on Tuesday, something else. He is grieved one day, pleased the next. In my view, *anthropomorphic* is too weak a description of these narratives. In these accounts, God is not merely *like* an agent in time. He really *is* in time, changing as others change. And we should not say that his atemporal, changeless existence is more real than his changing existence in time, as the term *anthropomorphic* suggests. Both are real.

Neither form of existence contradicts the other. God's transcendence never compromises his immanence, nor do his control and authority compromise his covenant presence. God stirs up "one from the east" to subdue nations and kings (Isa. 41:2). This is God as a historical agent. But the prophecy concludes in verse 4:

> Who has performed and done this,
>   calling the generations from the beginning?
> I, the LORD, the first,
>   and with the last; I am he.

God has planned from the beginning that the eastern scourge would devastate Palestine. That is God as an atemporal agent, controlling all by his decree.

The difference between God's atemporal and historical existences begins not with the creation of man, but with creation itself. In Genesis 1, note that God creates the light and darkness, and then names them "Day" and "Night" (v. 5). Here, God is acting in a sequence. Then on the second day he makes the expanse to divide the waters, and names it "sky" (v. 8 NIV). On the third day he gathers the sea and lets dry land appear, defining "Earth" and "Seas" (v. 10), "and God saw that it was good." That last phrase is especially interesting. God acts, and then he evaluates his own work. He acts, and then he responds to his own act.[33]

God's historical novel, remember, is a logical, temporal sequence, in which one event arises naturally out of the one before. When God himself becomes an actor in the drama, he acts according to that sequence. He sends the rains; then he brings the harvest. At one time, his interest is producing rain; at another, harvest. Thus do his interests *change* over time, according to his unchanging plan.

---

33. If we take a nonchronological view of the days of Genesis 1, we must still recognize that God's creative work precedes his rest in chronological sequence.

Some Modern Views

Process Theology

My approach bears a superficial resemblance to process theology, which also recognizes two modes of existence in God, transcendent and immanent, sometimes called the "primordial and consequent natures of God." John B. Cobb and David Ray Griffin explain the process view as follows:

> For Charles Hartshorne, the two "poles" or aspects of God are the abstract essence of God, on the one hand, and God's concrete actuality on the other. The abstract essence [which Whitehead called God's *primordial nature*—JF] is eternal, absolute, independent, unchangeable. It includes those abstract attributes of deity which characterize the divine essence at every moment. For example, to say that God is omniscient means that in every moment of the divine life God knows everything which is knowable at that time. The concrete actuality [or *consequent nature*—JF] is temporal, relative, dependent, and constantly changing. In each moment of God's life there are new, unforeseen happenings in the world which only then have become knowable. Hence, God's concrete knowledge is dependent upon the decisions made by the worldly actualities. God's knowledge is always relativized by, in the sense of internally related to, the world.[34]

This position is deeply unscriptural, and it should not be confused with that of this book. Note the following differences:

1. For Hartshorne, God's primordial nature is abstract. In my view, God exists atemporally as a concrete person.

2. For Hartshorne, even God's primordial nature is temporal. In the definition above, God's primordial omniscience is defined by what he knows "in every moment of the divine life." In my view, God transcends time.

3. For process thought, God in his consequent nature is relative to the world and dependent on it. I maintain that God is self-contained and sovereign, both as transcendent and as immanent.

4. Process theologians teach that God does not have exhaustive knowledge of the future. Scripture says that he does (see chapter 15).

5. For process thought, there is no unchanging standpoint from which change can be identified and measured. Since the "eternal objects" (equivalent to God's primordial nature) are abstract rather than concrete, possible rather than actual, they cannot serve as such a standpoint. But in Scripture, God, as concrete actuality, stands exalted as the unchanging Lord of time.

There are many problems in process theology, besides its manifest unscripturality, that I cannot take time here to discuss. I will say that process theology does not teach a credible doctrine of divine transcendence. For these thinkers, God as primordial is

---

34. John B. Cobb and David Ray Griffin, *Process Theology: An Introductory Exposition* (Philadelphia: Westminster Press, 1976), 47–48.

a mere abstraction, not a concrete actuality. To say that God is primordial or transcendent, on this view, is simply to say that every possible universe will include some kind of process deity. On the other hand, God-as-consequent, in process thought, is not clearly distinct from the world and is relative to it. Although process thought seeks to distinguish itself from pantheism (it prefers to be called *panentheism*: all is *in* God), it is not clear to me what there is in this God that is not also in the world. So in this view there is no meaningful Creator-creature distinction and no Sovereign Lord.

Futurism

Most thinkers who limit God to the temporal process limit him (as human beings are limited) to existence in the present. Some theologians, however, impressed by the eschatological dimension of Scripture, think of his existence as primarily future. For them, God is transcendent, not as one who lives in a realm above us, nor (as I have maintained) as one who rules the world as Lord, but as future time that inevitably overwhelms the present. This is not to say that the future has a fixed character—for these writers, the future is *open*; this is part of the reason for its transcendence. We cannot predict it or control it; we can only receive it as blessing or judgment.

This position was set forth in some detail by Jürgen Moltmann in *Theology of Hope*.[35] In a later work, he says simply that God is "the power of the future."[36] He finds some anticipations of his view in Rudolf Bultmann,[37] who also emphasizes the openness of the future and future as the nature of God. Similarly, Wolfhart Pannenberg said that "an existent being acting with omnipotence and omniscience would make freedom impossible,"[38] and so made this suggestion:

> The future seems to offer an alternative to an understanding of reality which is concentrated upon what is existing. For what belongs to the future is not yet existent and yet it already determines present existence.[39]

Stanley Grenz, an evangelical with some sympathy for this position, says:

> The future orientation suggested by thinkers such as Pannenberg and Moltmann provides a promising starting point for conceiving of the divine reality. God is best conceived not as standing behind us or above us, but in front of us. For systematic theology, this basic outlook means that we no longer seek to answer theological questions from the perspective of the past—from the decisions God made before the creation of the world. Rather we engage in the theological enterprise by viewing reality from the perspective of the future—from God's ultimate goal for creation.[40]

35. New York: Harper and Row, 1967.
36. Jürgen Moltmann, *The Experiment Hope* (Philadelphia: Fortress, 1975), 51.
37. Moltmann, *Theology of Hope*, 190, 212, 283.
38. Wolfhart Pannenberg, *The Idea of God and Human Freedom* (Philadelphia: Westminster Press, 1973), 109.
39. Ibid., 110.
40. Stanley Grenz, *Theology for the Community of God* (Nashville: Broadman and Holman, 1994), 104–5.

Scripture does teach that God is the "coming one," and it puts major emphasis on the future. But that future is not a perfectly open future, as at least Bultmann and Moltmann believe, but a future conceived in God's eternal plan. Further, it is simply wrong biblically to identify God with the future, as over against the present and past, and as opposed to an atemporal existence. God rules past, present, and future and exists independently of all three. He is the beginning and the end, the Alpha and the Omega. Scripture looks back on God's mighty works of the past, praises him as the One who is with us today, and looks forward to the certain fulfillment of his promises in the future. Thus, biblical faith honors God as the chief agent in history and as the One who stands above history. Contrary to futurism as expounded by Grenz, we should seek to answer theological questions multiperspectivally, from the standpoint of the future, from the standpoints of past and present, and from the standpoint of the "decisions God made before the creation of the world," such as that mentioned in Ephesians 1:4.

And futurism raises serious questions about the very existence of God in the present time. If God is not an "existent being acting with omnipotence and omniscience" in the present, but one who is coming to be in the future, then it is simply the case that in the world as we know it God does not exist.[41] That perspective is entirely contrary to that of Scripture.

Pannenberg and Moltmann have not, in my opinion, maintained this sort of view consistently, especially in their later works, though they continue to hint at it. They often speak of God as existing in the past and present. The qualifications they have made on their general futurist position are too complicated to go into here. But insofar as they make God a temporal being, insist on an open future, promote libertarian views of freedom, and question the full reality of God's atemporal, past, and present existence, they have turned far from the biblical doctrine of God.

Key Terms

Metaphysical attributes
Incommunicable attributes
Attributes of transcendence
Attributes of power
Infinity (in Greek philosophy)
Infinity (Frame's two definitions)
Atemporal eternity
Temporalism
Temporal omnipresence
Procession analogy
Relent

41. Pannenberg is deeply influenced by Hegel, for whom God is the absolute reality, coming to self-consciousness in the world.

Cambridge changes
Anthropomorphic
Process theology
God's primordial nature
God's consequent nature
Pantheism
Panentheism
Futurism

Study Questions

1. Why does Frame describe such divine attributes as *eternity* and *unchangeability* under the category *attributes of power*? Evaluate.

2. Why does Frame prefer to say little about divine infinity?

3. Why does Frame back away from the question whether God is in time or outside time? Comment.

4. "The biblical God transcends a number of limitations associated with our experience of temporality." What are these?

5. "It seems to me that once we deny the existence of libertarian freedom, all the relevant considerations favor atemporality, and none favor temporality." Explain; evaluate.

6. "I believe that too little attention has been paid to God's temporal omnipresence in the discussion over God's temporality." What would we gain from more attention to this concept?

7. Does God change his mind? Make biblical distinctions.

8. In what specific ways is God unchangeable?

9. "But the historical process does change, and as an agent in history, God himself changes." Explain; evaluate.

10. "Thus do [God's] interests *change* over time, according to his unchanging plan." Explain; evaluate.

11. Respond biblically to the claims of process theology.

12. Same for futurism.

Memory Verses

Deut. 33:27a: The eternal God is your dwelling place,
    and underneath are the everlasting arms.

Ps. 102:25–27: Of old you laid the foundation of the earth,
    and the heavens are the work of your hands.
They will perish, but you will remain;
    they will all wear out like a garment.
You will change them like a robe, and they will pass away,

but you are the same, and your years have no end.

Isa. 54:10: "For the mountains may depart
  and the hills be removed,
but my steadfast love shall not depart from you,
  and my covenant of peace shall not be removed,"
  says the LORD, who has compassion on you.

Gal. 4:4–5: But when the fullness of time had come, God sent forth his Son, born of woman, born under the law, to redeem those who were under the law, so that we might receive adoption as sons.

2 Peter 3:8: With the Lord one day is as a thousand years, and a thousand years as one day.

Resources for Further Study

Bavinck, Herman. *BRD*, 2:153–70.

Helm, Paul. *Eternal God: A Study of God without Time.* Oxford: Clarendon Press, 1988.

Pratt, Richard. "Historical Contingencies and Biblical Predictions." Available at http://reformedperspectives.org/newfiles/ric_pratt/TH.Pratt.Historical _Contingencies.html.

GOD'S ATTRIBUTES: LORD OF SPACE, MATTER, LIGHT, AND BREATH

THERE ARE ANALOGIES between God's relation to time (which we discussed in the previous chapter) and his relation to space. Many arguments against divine atemporality are analogous to arguments that might be used to show that God is spatial.[1] In this chapter, I will specifically discuss the question of God's relation to space (*immensity, spatial omnipresence*), along with the related questions of his relation to matter (*incorporeality*), light (*invisibility, glory*), and breath (*spirituality*).

God's Immensity

Divine immensity is to space what God's atemporal eternity is to time. It does not mean merely that God is omnipresent in space, but that he transcends space altogether. As I argued in the preceding chapter that God is both atemporal and omnipresent in time, I will here maintain that he is both aspatial (immense) and also omnipresent *in* space.[2] We can establish God's immensity from the following considerations:

Explicit Scripture Texts

Unlike *eternity*, *immensity* is not a biblical term. But it has enjoyed much use in theology for God's spatial transcendence. Theologians have derived the concept from the following texts:

At the dedication of the temple, King Solomon asks:

> But will God indeed dwell on the earth? Behold, heaven and the highest heaven cannot contain you; how much less this house that I have built! (1 Kings 8:27; cf. 2 Chron. 2:6)

1. See *DG*, 550–51, in relation to the arguments discussed on 548–51.
2. Some theologians have identified immensity and omnipresence; others have distinguished them. See *RD*, 66. I believe the distinction indicated between these terms is a useful one.

Solomon implies that God not only fills the heavens and the earth, but transcends them altogether. The totality of the heavens and the earth constitutes the totality of space. So no space can contain God. Similarly, God says through Isaiah:

> Thus says the LORD:
> "Heaven is my throne,
>   and the earth is my footstool;
> what is the house that you would build for me,
>   and what is the place of my rest?
> All these things my hand has made,
>   and so all these things came to be,
>   declares the LORD. (Isa. 66:1–2a)

Heaven is God's throne, but the King is greater than the throne he sits on. Again, if heaven and earth exhaust what we call space, God is greater than space, beyond it, immense.

An Ethical Focus

This metaphysical point is closely related to an ethical one, each implying the other. Israel was often tempted to believe that the presence of God in the temple made her immune to invasion or conquest. Some Israelites thought God was bound to help them, no matter how wicked they were, because the temple was his home. He was bound to the temple and therefore to the people of Israel:

> Its heads give judgment for a bribe;
>   its priests teach for a price;
>   its prophets practice divination for money;
> yet they lean on the LORD and say,
>   "Is not the LORD in the midst of us?
>   No disaster shall come upon us." (Mic. 3:11)

There was some truth in this supposition. Israel was, after all, God's covenant people. The covenant indeed was a "bond" between them. But the covenant contained curses for disobedience as well as blessings for obedience. At the very making of the covenant in Exodus 19–20, God made it plain that he was not bound to take Israel's side if she forsook him. To those who would worship idols, he declares:

> For I the LORD your God am a jealous God, visiting the iniquity of the fathers on the children to the third and the fourth generation of those who hate me, but showing steadfast love to thousands of those who love me and keep my commandments. (Ex. 20:5b–6)

In Amos 3:2, God invokes the covenantal bond as the basis for his punishments:

> You only have I known
> > of all the families of the earth;
> therefore I will punish you
> > for all your iniquities.

On another occasion, God tells Jeremiah to stand near the temple and say:

> Hear the word of the LORD, all you men of Judah who enter these gates to worship the LORD. Thus says the LORD of hosts, the God of Israel: Amend your ways and your deeds, and I will let you dwell in this place. Do not trust in these deceptive words: "This is the temple of the LORD, the temple of the LORD, the temple of the LORD."
>
> For if you truly amend your ways and your deeds, if you truly execute justice one with another, if you do not oppress the sojourner, the fatherless, or the widow, or shed innocent blood in this place, and if you do not go after other gods to your own harm, then I will let you dwell in this place, in the land that I gave of old to your fathers forever. (Jer. 7:2b–7)

The people thought they were safe (v. 10) to do things God detests. He reminds them that he destroyed a previous "dwelling for my Name" at Shiloh (v. 12 NIV) and will do the same to the existing temple (v. 14). Similarly, in Acts 7:49–50, Stephen quotes Isaiah 66:1–2, followed by this indictment: "You stiff-necked people, uncircumcised in heart and ears, you always resist the Holy Spirit. As your fathers did, so do you" (v. 51).

So it is important to say that although God manifests his presence in a special way in various places, even to the point that a place can be called his "dwelling," he is not bound to any place. He cannot be confined. He is greater than any place where he may be said to dwell, including the heaven and earth themselves.

Biblical Personalism

Another consideration invokes the principle of biblical personalism. God is covenantally present with his creatures in space and time. But if he is extended through space, he cannot be present as a whole person to every creature. Rather, he will be divided into parts, so that part of him is present to one person, another part to another. That is not the biblical doctrine of God's omnipresence. In Scripture, God is present as a whole person to all. That implies that he is as fully present to one point in space as to any other. But if God is fully present to every point in space, he cannot be spatially extended. "He is *totus* in all *res*, *totus* in single things, *totus* in himself."[3]

Lordship and Space

We can think about God's immensity the same way we thought about his atemporal eternity. Clearly, God's relation to space is different from ours. We are limited by our bodies to a certain portion of space; God is not. The time, expense, and effort of travel

3. Salomon Van Til, quoted by Heinrich Heppe in *RD*, 64.

limit our ability to visit different places. That is not true of God. We are not sovereign over the material universe. We are subject to many things beyond our control, such as weather, earthquakes, climate, soil conditions, pollution. These limitations are in part due to our finitude, in part due to the curse brought by God on the world and ourselves after the fall of Adam. But God is not subject to any of these limits. He created the world and completely controls it. Past, present, and future are written in his eternal plan.

So God is sovereign over spatial reality, the Lord of space. That is the primary biblical meaning of immensity as God's aspatiality. As we will see, the point is not that God is excluded from space, but rather that he sovereignly controls it. He is not *in* space as if space were a kind of box confining him.

God's Spatial Omnipresence

In chapters 2 and 3, I expounded *covenant presence*, or *immanence*, as a lordship attribute of God. As we saw there, God's presence is both *now* and *here*, with all his creatures at all times and places. In chapter 17, I described God's presence *now* under the rubric *temporal omnipresence*. In this chapter, we focus on the corresponding spatial attribute, *spatial omnipresence*.

If, as I will argue, God is not a corporeal being, spatial omnipresence cannot mean that God is a physical substance spread through the material universe. What it means, rather, is that God's power, knowledge, and ability to act in the finite world[4] are universal. God can instantly act at any place; he knows everything that happens, and he personally governs and directs everything in the universe (from above and from below, as we saw in chapter 9). So omnipresence is a direct implication of God's lordship, in his control and authority, as well as his covenant presence. We discussed the universality of his power, knowledge, and involvement with his world in other contexts, and so nothing more really needs to be said to establish the doctrine of divine omnipresence.

But we should note Bible texts that teach the doctrine explicitly. For example, David says to the Lord:

> Where shall I go from your Spirit?
>   Or where shall I flee from your presence?
> If I ascend to heaven, you are there!
>   If I make my bed in Sheol, you are there!
> If I take the wings of the morning
>   and dwell in the uttermost parts of the sea,
> even there your hand shall lead me,
>   and your right hand shall hold me. (Ps. 139:7–10)

David is not saying that God just happens to be wherever David chooses to go. Rather, David understands that the very nature of God as Lord makes him inescapable. The

---

4. Note that this triad corresponds to the lordship attributes.

One who made and controls heaven and earth is necessarily present everywhere in the world he has made.

Similarly, Paul says to the Athenian philosophers:

> For
>
> "In him we live and move and have our being";
>
> as even some of your own poets have said,
>
> "For we are indeed his offspring." (Acts 17:28)

For Paul as for David, God's omnipresence is an implication of his lordship. God created everything and determined the course of history so that he would be available to all:

> The God who made the world and everything in it, being Lord of heaven and earth, does not live in temples made by man, nor is he served by human hands, as though he needed anything, since he himself gives to all mankind life and breath and everything. And he made from one man every nation of mankind to live on all the face of the earth, having determined allotted periods and the boundaries of their dwelling place, that they should seek God, in the hope that they might feel their way toward him and find him. Yet he is actually not far from each one of us. (Acts 17:24–27)

God is everywhere present, because he is the source of everything and of every person on the earth, and because he is the controller of nature and history. And he has controlled history in such a way that he is inevitably present to all.

Scripture does, however, sometimes speak of God as being absent from or far from some people. So we must get busy making distinctions again. God's *presence* can mean several things:

1. It can mean that God is present to every place, which is the doctrine of omnipresence proper, as in the texts above.

2. It can refer to God's presence in special *holy* places (chapter 13), such as the burning bush (Ex. 3:5–6), Mount Sinai (Ex. 19:10–13, 20–23), the tabernacle, and the temple. Jesus is, of course, the fulfillment of these holy places (as in John 1:14; 2:21), the true temple. And through him, God's people themselves become temples of the Holy Spirit (1 Cor. 6:19), for they are members of Christ himself (6:15).[5], [6] Cf. Eph. 3:17; Col. 1:27.

Heaven is a place in which God's presence is localized supremely. Scripture sometimes represents God as in heaven, looking down on the earth (Deut. 26:15; Pss. 11:4;

---

5. There are also references in the OT to God's indwelling his people (see Isa. 63:11; Hag. 2:5). The OT, however, does not explicitly distinguish between God's corporate dwelling with Israel (in the tabernacle and temple) and his dwelling in believers as individuals.

6. Compare Ephesians 1:22–23, which combines the idea of Christ's special dwelling in his people with the idea of his filling all things.

33:13–14; 115:3). The risen Jesus, still man as well as God, is in heaven now at God's right hand. In that sense he is absent from us now and will return on the last day. But in the Spirit he is with us always (Matt. 28:20).

This language does not mean that God's power, knowledge, and freedom to act are greater in the holy places than elsewhere on earth. But we might say that in these places his presence is more intense, more intimate, and the penalties for disobedience are more severe. When God makes his "dwelling" in a place, that place becomes his throne. We show special deference to him there, and we become more aware of his power to bless or curse.

3. God's presence also has an ethical meaning in Scripture. This meaning is related to point 2, but it is more general. God is present with the righteous, absent from the wicked:

> But your iniquities have made a separation
>   between you and your God,
> and your sins have hidden his face from you
>   so that he does not hear. (Isa. 59:2)

So:

> The Lord is far from the wicked,
>   but he hears the prayer of the righteous. (Prov. 15:29)

God calls the wicked to "draw near" to him by repenting of their sin (James 4:8), and he calls the righteous to draw near to him in worship and obedience (Ps. 73:28; Heb. 10:22). On this account, God is absent from the wicked, present with the righteous. His presence is proportional to our ethical kinship with him.

Or God can be said to be present with the wicked, in judgment. This is not a contradiction, just different language making the same point. The consequences for the wicked are the same:

> If they dig into Sheol,
>   from there shall my hand take them;
> if they climb up to heaven,
>   from there I will bring them down.
> If they hide themselves on the top of Carmel,
>   from there I will search them out and take them;
> and if they hide from my sight at the bottom of the sea,
>   there I will command the serpent, and it shall bite them. (Amos 9:2–3; cf. Jer.
>   23:23–24)

Note the interesting parallels with Psalm 139:7–10, quoted earlier. In Psalm 139, God's presence was blessing to David (though also a caution). Here God's presence means judgment to the wicked.

But in a special way, God dwells with those with a contrite heart:

> For thus says the One who is high and lifted up,
>   who inhabits eternity, whose name is Holy:
> "I dwell in the high and holy place,
>   and also with him who is of a contrite and lowly spirit,
> to revive the spirit of the lowly,
>   and to revive the heart of the contrite." (Isa. 57:15)

God's special presence with the righteous is his blessing on them that entails his special providences in their earthly lives and his gift of eternal life. Therefore, to the righteous, God is a "very present help in trouble" (Ps. 46:1). The only way in which human beings can be righteous, of course, is through the grace of Jesus Christ. Those who are in Christ can never be separated from God's love (Rom. 8:38–39; cf. Ps. 16:11; John 14:23; Rom. 8:9–10; 2 Cor. 3:17).

God's Incorporeality

I don't know of any Scripture verse that actually says that God is incorporeal or immaterial. Perhaps there is some hint of it in the resurrection appearance of Jesus in Luke 24:36–40:

> As they were talking about these things, Jesus himself stood among them, and said to them, "Peace to you!" But they were startled and frightened and thought they saw a spirit. And he said to them, "Why are you troubled, and why do doubts arise in your hearts? See my hands and my feet, that it is I myself. Touch me, and see. For a spirit does not have flesh and bones as you see that I have." And when he had said this, he showed them his hands and his feet.

This passage may be seen to contrast spirit with corporeality. Then when John 4:24 tells us that "God is spirit," we may deduce from that statement that God is not a body. On the other hand, (1) I'm inclined to think the NIV is right to see the issue in Luke 24 as ghostliness, not spirituality as such. (2) As I will indicate later, I think the point of John 4:24 is not God's immateriality, but his possessing the qualities of the Holy Spirit. So perhaps it would not be wise for us to try to prove God's incorporeality from John 4:24 and Luke 24:36–40.

Nevertheless, God's incorporeality is clearly a good and necessary consequence of biblical teachings that we have already considered. Certainly God in his atemporal and/or aspatial existence cannot be a physical being.

But what of God as immanent, as omnipresent in space and time? We saw in chapter 17 that when God enters time, he responds appropriately to the changing events of the world, approving some things, disapproving others. In one sense he may be said to change, as he responds to change. In some ways, then, when God enters time, he takes on some characteristics of a changing being. Similarly, when God enters space, he experiences the world in ways analogous to those of a spatial being. For example, he feels directly everything that happens in the universe; he can directly move any object in the universe; he looks out from every location; he responds appropriately to every event that takes place in the world.[7]

Still, it would not be right to say that God has a physical being such that the universe is his body (pantheism) or that he is one part of the physical universe, for the following reasons:

1. God is not to be identified with any physical being, for he is transcendent over space and time.

2. Further, as we will see (chapter 20), God is a simple being, incapable of being divided into parts. But physical beings can be divided into parts.

3. As omnipresent in space and time he cannot be a *particular* physical being, for such a being could not inhabit all times and places equally.

4. If God has a physical existence, then, his body would have to be the entire universe. But we must not *identify* him with the universe. That would be pantheism, and we have seen good reasons to disavow that view. In Scripture, Creator and creature are distinct. God is not the creation; he is the Creator, the Lord of creation. We should not forget that God as omnipresent is at the same time transcendent.

5. Nor, for the same reason, should we think of the world as *part* of God's being (*panentheism*, "all is *in* God"). Everything in the world is created by God, so nothing in the world is divine.

6. Nevertheless, God is present *in* the world he has made. And in his immanent, temporal, and spatial omnipresence, God experiences the world in ways similar to the ways we do. His experience of the world is *analogous* to the experience of one for whom the universe is his body. Indeed, we can say more than this. God experiences the world not only from his transcendent perspective and from the perspective of the whole universe, but also from every particular perspective within the universe. Since he is with me, he experiences the world from my perspective, as well as from the perspective of every other being in the universe. True omniscience must include a knowledge of every such perspective.[8]

We should not be surprised that there are significant analogies between God's experiences of the world and our own. Scripture tells us that we were made in his image.

Theophany and Incarnation

The discussion above provides useful background in considering Scripture's teachings about theophany and incarnation. We have seen that God is capable of viewing the world from finite perspectives, in ways analogous to the experiences of finite beings. The doctrines of theophany and incarnation show us that God is

---

7. In these descriptions of physical existence, I have drawn on the description by Richard Swinburne in *The Coherence of Theism* (Oxford: Clarendon Press, 1977), 102. Swinburne, in turn, summarizes formulations by Jonathan Harrison. Compare my longer discussion of these matters in *DG*, 583–85.

8. Compare my discussion of "Passages Alleged to Teach Divine Ignorance" in chapter 15.

able to take on a physical form. In that physical form, his relation to the world is even more closely analogous than in his general omnipresence to the experience of a physical person.

The theophany is a visible manifestation of God to human beings. God may appear to them in the form of an angel (Gen. 32:22–32, esp. v. 30) or of a man (18:16–33). Most often he appears as the *glory-cloud*, as the fiery cloud that led Israel through the wilderness and settled upon the sanctuary. Meredith G. Kline explains:

> When the inner reality veiled within the theophanic cloud is revealed, we behold God in his heaven. The world of the Glory theophany is a dimensional realm normally invisible to man, where God reveals his presence as the King of glory enthroned in the midst of myriads of heavenly beings.[9] It is the realm into which the glorified Christ, disappearing from human view, entered to assume his place on the throne of God. It is the invisible (or "third") heaven brought into cloud-veiled visibility.[10]

Kline finds this theophany in Genesis 1:2, the brooding of the Spirit over the waters, and in other texts dealing with the Spirit. So he identifies the Spirit with the glory-cloud as well.

We saw earlier that though God is everywhere, he sometimes reveals himself in particular holy places where his presence is especially intense. The theophany is this kind of holy space. So appropriately, the theophanic glory-cloud descends upon the tabernacle, and the bright "cloud" envelops Jesus, Moses, Elijah, and the disciples on the Mount of Transfiguration (Matt. 17:5).

Insofar as the glory is God's "address" or geographical location, we can understand better the texts we noted earlier in which God "looks down from heaven" on the sons of men. That he uniquely inhabits heaven implies that heaven is a privileged perspective from which God views the creation. But since God's heavenly dwelling does not contradict his general omnipresence, his heavenly perspective does not cancel out the fact that God views the world from all other perspectives as well.

The incarnation of the Son of God in Jesus Christ is, of course, unique in human history. Jesus is a theophany (as Jesus tells Philip, "anyone who has seen me has seen the Father," John 14:9), but much more. Only in the case of Jesus did God become flesh permanently, being conceived in the body of a woman, experiencing a human infancy and growth, increasing in wisdom and stature, subject to the sufferings of this life and to death itself.

9. Kline refers in a footnote to Ezekiel 1:1ff.; 3:12ff.; 10:1ff.; 11:22ff.; and 43:2ff. He says that these are "a good place to start, but once it is determined that the Glory is a revelational modality of heaven, every biblical unveiling of the scene of the heavenly throne and the divine council becomes a source for our envisaging of the divine presence within the cloud-theophany." Meredith G. Kline, *Images of the Spirit* (Grand Rapids: Baker, 1980), 17n. The theophany of Isaiah's famous vision in Isaiah 6:1–13 and the visions of John in Revelation also display these features.

10. Ibid., 17.

There is great mystery here. Jesus never abandons his divine attributes. He is omniscient, omnipotent, omnipresent.[11] Yet he suffers and thirsts, displays ignorance. Christians have understood these facts in terms of the "two natures of Christ" defined by the Council of Chalcedon in A.D. 451. Jesus has a complete divine nature and a complete human nature (cf. chapter 37). The two natures are distinct, not mixed or turned into one another (for the Creator-creature distinction must be affirmed even in Christ, in which the Creator and creature are most intimately joined); but neither are they separated or divided in their functions.

But the two natures are united in one person. That person is a divine person, the very Son of God in human flesh. In Christ, God "in every respect has been tempted as we are, yet without sin," so he can "sympathize with our weaknesses" (Heb. 4:15). Certainly in Christ, God perceives the world not only from his transcendent perspective, not only from all creaturely perspectives, but uniquely from one particular creaturely perspective. The body of Jesus is God's body in Jonathan Harrison's sense. But at the very same time, God (the Son, as well as the Father and the Spirit) has an existence that transcends all physical limitation.

God is not, therefore, to be defined as a physical being. (Even the incarnate Son of God had a divine sovereignty over space and time.) But as Lord of all things material and physical, he is supremely able (1) to understand the world from the perspective of every physical being, (2) to reveal himself in any physical form he chooses, and (3) to become flesh, so that he has his own body, without abandoning his transcendent existence.

I argued that it is perhaps better to say that God is Lord of time and Lord of space than to say merely that God is atemporal and aspatial. Though he does have atemporal and aspatial existence, he is also temporally and spatially omnipresent. His sovereignty does not mean that he is excluded from time and space, but that he acts toward them as Lord, not as one who is limited by them. The same point can be made about God's incorporeality. This doctrine does not exclude God from physical reality. Rather, it teaches that he relates himself to physical reality as the Lord, transcending it and using it as he chooses.

God's Invisibility

The same approach will help us to understand better the biblical teaching concerning God's invisibility. To say that God is invisible is not to exclude God from the realm of the visible, but to regard him as the Lord of visibility, the Lord of light.

Several biblical texts speak of God as invisible (Gk. *aoratos*): Rom. 1:20; Col. 1:15; 1 Tim. 1:17; Heb. 11:27. The Johannine literature says in a number of places that no one has ever seen God (John 1:18; 5:37; 6:46; 1 John 4:12, 20).

As we have seen, however, God has revealed himself by theophany and incarnation, both highly visible means. In a real sense, to see the theophany or the incarnate Christ is to see God.

---

11. "Kenosis" Christologies, of course, do maintain that when the Son of God became man, he set aside some or all of his divine attributes. But God cannot be God, as we have seen, without his attributes. If the incarnate Christ lacked any essential divine attribute, then he was not God in the flesh.

In the presence of theophany, the question is not whether God can be seen, but rather whether any human being can survive after seeing him. In Exodus 33, Moses asks to see God's "glory" (v. 18). God promises Moses an experience of his *goodness* and an exposition of his *name* (v. 19). "But," he adds, "you cannot see my face, for man shall not see me and live" (v. 20). Typically, God's people are terrified to look upon God (Ex. 3:6; Job 13:11; Isa. 6:5).

But some do in fact see God, and amazingly their lives are preserved. Hagar, cast out of Abraham's house by Sarah after the birth of Ishmael, meets God and responds:

> So she called the name of the LORD who spoke to her, "You are a God of seeing," for she said, "Truly here I have seen him who looks after me." (Gen. 16:13)

Jacob, having wrestled with the theophanic Angel of the Lord, names the place of his encounter *Peniel*, saying, "For I have seen God face [*panim*] to face, and yet my life has been delivered" (Gen. 32:30). Manoah and his wife, parents of Samson, experience a theophany and exclaim, "We shall surely die, for we have seen God" (Judg. 13:22)— but they do not die. After the exodus and the giving of the law, God asked the priests and elders of Israel to "come up to the LORD" (Ex. 24:1). They went up "and they saw the God of Israel" (v. 10). Verse 11 significantly adds, "And he did not lay his hand on the chief men of the people of Israel; they beheld God, and ate and drank." Isaiah (6:1) and Amos (9:1) also "saw the Lord."

From the cleft of a rock, God grants to Moses an image of his "back," but "my face [*panim*] shall not be seen" (Ex. 33:23). We wonder, did God reveal his *panim* to Jacob, but not to Moses? And if so, why the apparent difference? And what is the difference between merely seeing God and seeing his "face"? The mystery concerning Moses' experience of God includes the use of the term *temunah*. In Deuteronomy 4:15, God speaks to Israel through Moses and grounds the prohibition of idolatry in the fact that "you saw no form on the day that the LORD spoke to you at Horeb out of the midst of the fire." Yet in Numbers 12:8, when Miriam and Aaron are contesting Moses' primacy over them as a prophet, God says:

> With [Moses] I speak mouth [*peh*, "mouth," not *panim*] to mouth, clearly, and not in riddles, and he beholds the form [*temunah*] of the LORD. Why then were you not afraid to speak against my servant Moses?

So Moses saw God's *temunah*, but Israel did not see it.[12] Apparently, too, Moses received revelation by *peh*, but not *panim*, though Jacob actually saw God's *panim*.

---

12. I disagree with Herman Bavinck's statement that God is "unpicturable (Ex. 20:4; Deut. 5:8); since he is without form (Deut. 4:12, 15)." *BRD*, 2:182. Deuteronomy does not say that God is without form, only that God did not display his form to Israel on Mount Sinai. And God is certainly not unpicturable in any straightforward sense. He images himself in theophany; Christ is his image par excellence (Col. 1:15; Heb. 1:3), and man is his image as well (Gen. 1:27). God prohibits worship by images not because he cannot be pictured, but because (1) the old covenant was founded on the revelation of God in his invisibility, and (2) God intends to assert his exclusive right to make images of himself.

The language of divine visibility applies often in the NT to the incarnate Christ. The apostle John insists that though no one has seen God, Jesus has made him known (John 1:18). And Jesus makes God known in highly visible ways. To Philip, Jesus says, "Whoever has seen me has seen the Father" (14:9). John's first letter glories in the visibility and tangibility of the revelation of Jesus:

> That which was from the beginning, which we have heard, which we have seen with our eyes, which we looked upon and have touched with our hands, concerning the word of life—the life was made manifest, and we have seen it, and testify to it and proclaim to you the eternal life, which was with the Father and was made manifest to us. (1 John 1:1–2)

Compare Acts 1:3; 1 Corinthians 15:3–8; and 2 Peter 1:16–18 in their emphasis on the visibility of Christ in his transfiguration and resurrection. The apostles appeal to "eyewitnesses" to vindicate the gospel.

We do not now literally see Jesus since his ascension to the Father's right hand. But, evidently reminiscing about the visibility of his earthly ministry, the author to the Hebrews speaks about how we "see" Jesus:

> But we see him who for a little while was made lower than the angels, namely Jesus, crowned with glory and honor because of the suffering of death, so that by the grace of God he might taste death for everyone. (Heb. 2:9)

These biblical emphases, both on God's invisibility and on his visibility, sometimes come together, forming paradoxes:

> We look not to the things that are seen but to the things that are unseen. For the things that are seen are transient, but the things that are unseen are eternal. (2 Cor. 4:18)

> By faith [Moses] left Egypt, not being afraid of the anger of the king, for he endured as seeing him who is invisible. (Heb. 11:27)

It is a bit difficult to know how, precisely, to bring these biblical data together into a theological formulation. I confess that I am not able to unravel the distinctions between *panim*, *peh*, and *temunah*. Nor can I determine precisely the nature of the visual revelation given to Jacob, Moses, Miriam, Aaron, the elders of Israel, the nation of Israel, Isaiah, and others, and how these revelations differed from one another. But of some points we can be fairly confident:

1. God is *essentially invisible*. This means not that he can never be seen under any circumstances, but rather that, as Lord, he sovereignly chooses when, where, and to whom to make himself visible. He controls all the matter and light in the universe so that he alone determines whether and how he will be visible to his creatures. So his relation to visibility (to light and matter) is similar to his relation to time and space.

2. God has often made himself visible, in theophany and in the incarnate Christ, so that human beings may on occasion truly say that they have "seen God." The glory-cloud theophany (see the preceding section) is a permanent visible revelation of God, located in heaven, but sometimes visible from earth. And at God's right hand in heaven stands Jesus, who remains both God and man and therefore a permanently visible divine person.

3. "No one has ever seen God" means that no one has ever seen God apart from his voluntary theophanic-incarnational revelation: "the only God, who is at the Father's side, he has made him known" (John 1:18).

4. It is right to be terrified in the presence of theophany. The theophany is always holy ground. In the vicinity of theophany, God will severely judge any lack of proper reverence. And as with Adam and Eve in the garden, God often "comes" to us for the purpose of judging sin. But as we have seen, some people do see God without losing their lives. So we see the grace of God, preserving life, though we have forfeited the right to live.[13] When God hides Moses in the "cleft of the rock" so that Moses can see his "back" (Ex. 33:22–23), the difference between back and face is somewhat obscure. But in the cleft of the rock the church is right to see an anticipation of Christ.

5. There is a rather notable difference in this respect between the inauguration of God's covenant with Moses and the beginning of the new covenant in Christ. In the former, God stresses that the people saw no form (*temunah*). The reason is not that there was no *temunah* to be seen, for Moses saw God's *temunah*, according to Numbers 12:8. Rather, although the Sinai revelation included many visible phenomena, God withheld from Israel the intimate vision he granted to Moses, the vision of God's *temunah*. But the NT writers positively exult over the visibility of Jesus' coming. The incarnate Christ is as emphatically visible (as in 1 John 1:1–3) as Yahweh in the Mosaic covenant was emphatically invisible. The new covenant begins with a revelation of profound visibility.

6. The visibility of God often has an eschatological thrust in Scripture. The new covenant, with its highly visible revelation of God, is the beginning of the "age to come" in which God sets all things right. This new age overlaps the old age of sin's dominion until the second coming of Jesus and the final judgment. Then the old age ("this age") ends, and God consummates the "age to come." The visibility of Jesus is the beginning of the end, in which God will be profoundly visible in theophany and incarnation. So the theophanies through Scripture anticipate our heavenly fellowship with God. Note the following:

> Blessed are the pure in heart, for they shall see God. (Matt. 5:8)

> For now we see in a mirror dimly, but then face to face. Now I know in part; then I shall know fully, even as I have been fully known. (1 Cor. 13:12; cf. Zech. 12:10; 1 John 3:2; Rev. 1:7)

---

13. So God's warning, "man shall not see me and live" (Ex. 33:20), is like the conditional prophecies that we examined in chapter 15. Though God prescribes death to sinners who look upon him, he reserves the right to extend the grace of forgiveness.

God's Glory

We have seen that although God is essentially invisible, there are important ways in which he makes himself visible. God's *glory*, as a divine attribute, is related to his visibility, so it is appropriate here to discuss it.

Glory, with the verb *glorify* and adjective *glorious*, is one of the most common terms in the Christian vocabulary, but one of the hardest to define precisely. What does it actually mean to "glorify" God or to "seek God's glory"?

Glory and its other forms represent several Hebrew (*kabod, tiphara, hod, hadar*) and Greek (*doxa, time, eulogia*) terms. *Kabod* and *doxa* are the most common of these. *Kabod* is also translated "wealth" or "riches," as the Greek *time*. Both terms can be translated "reputation," "splendor," or "honor."[14]

The Glory-Theophany

To see how these meanings fit together, we can perhaps start with the idea of a great light shining from God's theophanic presence. As we saw in the discussion of theophany above, the cloud that led Israel through the wilderness and settled on the tabernacle is called the *glory*. One of the earliest references to the glory of the Lord occurs in Exodus 16 when the Israelites, newly released from Egypt, began to grumble about the lack of food. God promises manna; then

> Moses and Aaron said to all the people of Israel, "At evening you shall know that it was the Lord who brought you out of the land of Egypt, and in the morning you shall see the glory of the Lord, because he has heard your grumbling against the Lord. For what are we, that you grumble against us?" And Moses said, "When the Lord gives you in the evening meat to eat and in the morning bread to the full, because the Lord has heard your grumbling that you grumble against him—what are we? Your grumbling is not against us but against the Lord."
>
> Then Moses said to Aaron, "Say to the whole congregation of the people of Israel, 'Come near before the Lord, for he has heard your grumbling.'" And as soon as Aaron spoke to the whole congregation of the people of Israel, they looked toward the wilderness, and behold, the glory of the Lord appeared in the cloud. (Ex. 16:6–10)

The "glory" here is certainly the bright theophany in the cloud. So as we have seen, Kline calls this theophany the *glory-cloud*.

Glory as God's Presence

In a great many passages, therefore, *glory* is simply the created light that emerges from the theophany. One could argue from these passages that *glory* is something that accompanies God, rather than a divine attribute as such. In the glory-cloud, however, God is with his people, immanent, covenantally present. So *glory* can refer not only

---

14. There is also the verb *kauchaomai*, often translated "glory" in the KJV, but better translated "boast" as in the NIV.

to the created light surrounding God in the theophany, but to God himself, present with his people. So it appears regularly in contexts of praise:

> Yours, O Lᴏʀᴅ, is the greatness and the power and the glory and the victory and the majesty, for all that is in the heavens and in the earth is yours. Yours is the kingdom, O Lᴏʀᴅ, and you are exalted as head above all. (1 Chron. 29:11; cf. Ps. 24:7. Eph. 1:6)

Jesus (the fulfillment of the tabernacle and the temple) shares the very glory of God, a remarkable testimony to his deity. He says:

> And now, Father, glorify me in your own presence with the glory that I had with you before the world existed. (John 17:5)

Cf. Matt. 25:31; John 1:14; 2:11; 17:22, 24. He is called "the Lord of glory" in 1 Corinthians 2:8 and James 2:1. He is particularly glorious in what would seem least glorious, his death for sin. Referring to his coming death, he says:

> The hour has come for the Son of Man to be glorified. (John 12:23)

> Now is the Son of Man glorified and God is glorified in him. (John 13:31)

Cf. Rev. 5:11–12; 7:9–12. In his death, of course, and for most of his earthly life, Jesus did not emit a visible light. (The transfiguration, of course, was a literal glorification.) The death of Christ is glorious in that, like the glory-theophany, it reveals One who is supremely worthy of praise.

God's Glory in Creation

So the glory is God himself, covenantally present. But God's presence glorifies the creation, too. Creation is not divine, but it is his finite glory-light. God has made the world to be his temple, so it declares his glory (Ps. 19:1). Adam is not only the image of God, but the glory of God as well (Ps. 8:5; 1 Cor. 11:7).

In these passages, glory is not a literal light. The created qualities of the universe, and of human beings, may not have literally glowed; but as the image of God the world was something *splendid*, a product that enhanced the revelation of his beauty.

God's Reputation

Adam's sin, however, mars his glory, as it mars the image of God in which he is made. But redemption restores that glory in this life:

> And we all, with unveiled face, beholding the glory of the Lord, are being transformed into the same image from one degree of glory to another. For this comes from the Lord who is the Spirit. (2 Cor. 3:18)

Redemption especially restores that glory in the life to come (Rom. 8:18; 1 Cor. 2:7; 2 Cor. 4:6, 17; Heb. 2:10).

It is God's intention for the creation to return glory back to him. When our lives image the attributes of God, others see the glory of God's presence in us as his temples. So we bring God's glorious reputation to the eyes of others. Thus, we ourselves are part of the light that goes forth from God over the earth.

In this ethical sense, Scripture calls on us to *glorify* God. In one sense, of course, we cannot increase God's glory. But when we speak truly of him and obey his Word, we enhance his reputation on earth (and among the angels, Eph. 3:10), and we ourselves become part of the created light by which people come to know God's presence. So Jesus says that his disciples, like himself, are the "light of the world" (John 8:12; see also Matt. 4:14–16).

We can also understand glorifying God as giving praise to him. *Doxa* is sometimes translated "glory," sometimes "praise." The two ideas are closely related. Our words and our lives bring praise to God, which shows his glory-light to the world. To glorify God, then, is simply to obey him, and therefore to proclaim his greatness by our words and deeds.

Glory and the Trinity

We have seen how God glorifies his creation and the human race, and how creation, in turn, glorifies God. The circle of glorification, however, does not begin with creation. There is also a circle of glorification within the Trinity itself.[15] The Father glorifies the Son (John 8:50, 54; 13:32; 14:13; 17:1, 5), and the Son glorifies the Father (John 7:18; 13:31; 17:4). The Spirit glorifies the Son (John 16:14), and therefore glorifies the Father through the Son.

In this context, we learn also that Christian believers glorify Christ (John 17:10) and that he gives glory to us (v. 22):

> The glory that you have given me I have given to them, that they may be one even as we are one.

There is great mystery here as we gain a glimpse of the intra-Trinitarian being of God. More discussion of the Trinity will come later in the book (chapters 20–22; cf. 39). At least, we can say that in the Trinity there is a mutual glorification: each person glorifies the others. As we explore the mysterious inwardness of the Godhead, we are no longer talking about a glory-light in a literal sense. Rather, each member of the Trinity speaks and acts in such a way as to enhance the reputations of the other two, to bring praise and honor to the other persons. There is here a mutual deference, a willingness to serve one another. That is the "mind of Christ" (1 Cor. 2:16) that motivated the Son of God to become a sacrifice for the sins of men.

---

15. Thanks to Jeff Meyers for drawing my attention to this pattern.

The Father does glorify himself (John 12:28), but he does this by glorifying the Son and Spirit, and by glorifying his people. Though he deserves all glory and praise, he serves others, and thereby attracts even more glory to himself.

Jesus prays in John 17:22 that his people may be "one even as we are one." How can the church possibly be one as God himself is one? The church is not divine, and so it can never achieve the perfect oneness of the Father, Son, and Spirit. But the passage does help the church to set some goals to achieve with God's help. One way toward a oneness that reflects the Trinity is for us to *glorify one another* as do the persons of the Trinity. That means loving one another, serving one another, praising one another, honoring one another. If we sought to really glorify one another, we would seek, even across denominational and traditional lines, to make one another *look good*, to enhance one another's reputations, rather than to make ourselves look good at everyone else's expense.[16]

God's Spirituality

We will, of course, have much more to say later about the Holy Spirit as the third person of the Trinity (chapters 20–22, 39). But in this section I am interested in *spirit* or *spirituality* as an attribute of God, as in John 4:24, where Jesus says, "God is spirit, and those who worship him must worship in spirit and truth." Here Jesus is, I believe, not referring specifically to the Holy Spirit, but to spirituality as an attribute of the triune God. We will see, however, that there is a close relation between the qualities of the Holy Spirit and the spirituality of the triune God.

Theologians have sometimes defined *spirituality* negatively as "incorporeality" and/ or "invisibility." Herman Bavinck does this, though he also adds a more positive definition.[17] Scripture does hint that spirit is by nature immaterial, in Isaiah 31:3, and in Luke 24:36–43, which I discussed earlier under the topic of incorporeality. But I doubt that incorporeality and invisibility constitute an adequate biblical definition of *spirit*.

As we have seen, Scripture identifies the glory-theophany with the Spirit of God. Kline says:

> There is indeed a considerable amount of biblical data that identify the Glory-cloud as particularly a manifestation of the Spirit of God. Here we will cite only a few passages where the functions performed by the Glory-cloud are attributed to the Spirit— Nehemiah 9:19, 20; Isaiah 63:11–14; and Haggai 2:5—and mention the correspondence of the work of the Holy Spirit at Pentecost to the functioning of the Glory-cloud at the exodus and at the erection of the tabernacle.[18]

16. For more on this subject and the applications of John 17, see my essay "Walking Together," available at http://www.frame-poythress.org.

17. *BRD*, 2:186. His positive definition is that as spirit, God is "the hidden, simple (uncompounded), absolute ground of all creatural, somatic and pneumatic, being." I'm not sure what this means, or how it can be derived from the biblical data concerning spirit.

18. Kline, *Images*, 15. He cites also Meredith M. Kline, "The Holy Spirit as Covenant Witness" (Th.M. diss., Westminster Theological Seminary, 1972), and his own *Structure of Biblical Authority* (Grand Rapids: Eerdmans, 1975).

Note that Kline says that the glory-cloud is "a manifestation" of the Spirit. Kline's association of the Spirit and the cloud is helpful, and it implies that everything I said earlier about the glory-cloud pertains to the Spirit as well. But like *glory*, Scripture refers to the working of the Spirit even in the absence of a theophany.

The glory-cloud provides a model for the broader and less literal senses of *glory*: God's glory is an "outshining" from him, not only of literal light, but also of creative power and ethical qualities. So the glory-cloud provides a model that helps us to understand the work of the Spirit in other contexts. As the glory-cloud rested on the tabernacle and entered the temple, so the Spirit indwells believers, who are "temples of the Holy Spirit." As God's presence in the cloud empowered his people, gave them direction, and accompanied them with blessing and judgment, so the Spirit acts throughout Scripture.

In general, God's Spirit is his presence in the world, performing his work as Lord. Later we will see that, like God's Word (John 1:14) and God's fatherhood, Spirit is both a divine attribute and a person of the Trinity. But for now, let us focus on the ways in which *spirit* describes God's actions in the world.

Spirit represents words in Hebrew (*ruach*) and Greek (*pneuma*) that can both also mean "wind" or "breath." *Wind* and *breath* are regular biblical metaphors for the work of the Spirit. As wind blows invisibly and unpredictably, so the Spirit gives new birth (John 3:5–8). As words cannot be communicated without breath, so the Spirit regularly accompanies the Word of God to its destination (2 Sam. 23:2; Isa. 59:21; John 6:63; 1 Thess. 1:5; 2 Tim. 3:16; 1 Peter 1:12; 2 Peter 1:21). This is true not only of prophecy, but of creation as well:

> By the word of the LORD the heavens were made,
>   and by the breath of his mouth all their host. (Ps. 33:6)

For pedagogical purposes, it is convenient to distinguish the connotations of *spirit* along the lines of the lordship attributes: power, authority, and presence in blessing and judgment. I will then say a bit about the role of God's Spirit in redemptive history.

Power

Like a mighty, rushing wind, the Spirit exerts the great power of God. The prophet Micah says:

> But as for me, I am filled with power,
>   with the Spirit of the LORD,
>   and with justice and might,
> to declare to Jacob his transgression
>   and to Israel his sin. (Mic. 3:8)

We have seen the Spirit's involvement in the great work of creation (Gen. 1:2; see also Pss. 33:6; 104:30). The *ruach* is also the power behind the cherubim (Ezek. 1:12, 20) and the power behind the unusual strength of Samson (Judg. 13:25) and others (Judg. 14:6, 19; 15:14). The Spirit lifts people up and carries them away (2 Kings 2:16; Ezek. 3:12, 14; 8:3; 11:1, 24; 37:1; 43:5; Acts 8:39–40; figuratively, 2 Peter 1:21). The Spirit gives power to preaching (Luke 4:14; Rom. 15:19; 1 Cor. 2:4; 1 Thess. 1:5).

Authority

As already suggested, it is the Spirit who appoints prophets and brings the word of God to them. The Spirit is the breath behind the word. Among the many passages connecting the Spirit with prophecy, see these: Gen. 41:38; Num. 24:2; 1 Sam. 10:6, 10; 2 Kings 2:9, 15–16; Neh. 9:30; Isa. 61:1; Ezek. 2:2; 3:24; Joel 2:28; Luke 1:17; 1 Peter 1:11. It is the Spirit also who speaks through Jesus, his apostles, and the NT prophets, bringing the new covenant revelation (Matt. 10:20; Luke 4:14; John 3:34; 14:16–17; 15:26; 16:13; Acts 2:4; 6:10; 1 Cor. 2:4, 10–14; 7:40; 12:3; 1 Thess. 1:5; Rev. 2:7; 19:10).

It is the Spirit who gives wisdom (see chapter 15): both practical skills and ethical understanding (Ex. 28:3; 31:3; 35:31; Deut. 34:9). So the Spirit raises up men with the wisdom to rule and win battles (Num. 11:17, 25–29; Judg. 3:10; 6:34; 11:29; 14:6, 19; 15:14; 1 Sam. 11:6; 16:13). And he gives gifts to the church to edify the body (1 Cor. 12:1–11).

The anointing of prophets, priests, and kings with oil symbolized their investiture by the Spirit. Kline writes about the garments of the priests as replicating the Glory-Spirit[19] and about "the Prophet as Image of the Glory-Spirit."[20] Jesus the Messiah (the Anointed One), the ultimate Prophet, Priest, and King, is therefore richly endued with the Spirit (Isa. 11:2; 42:1; Matt. 3:16; 4:1; 12:18; Luke 4:16–21 [fulfilling Isa. 61:1–2]).

Presence in Blessing and Judgment

The Spirit is also God with us. David asks:

> Where shall I go from your Spirit?
>   Or where shall I flee from your presence? (Ps. 139:7)

In Israel he made his home in the tabernacle and temple. Christians are temples of the Spirit, and therefore have the Spirit dwelling within (1 Cor. 3:16; Gal. 4:6; 5:16–26; 1 Peter 1:2). As the "breath" of God gave life to Adam (Gen. 2:7), so the Spirit gives new spiritual life (John 3:5–8; 6:63; 1 Cor. 15:45; 2 Cor. 3:6; 1 Peter 3:18; 4:6). And the Spirit enables the believer to grow in righteousness (Rom. 8:1–17).

So the Spirit is present to bless God's people. But as is less widely acknowledged, the Spirit is active in judgment as well. Kline argues, rightly I think, that *ruach hayyom* in Genesis 3:8a should not be translated "cool of the day" but as "Spirit of the day"—"day" being a kind of anticipation of the final day of judgment. Kline finds this use of "spirit" also in Isaiah 11:1–4; 2 Thessalonians 2:8; 1 Peter 4:13–16.[21]

---

19. Kline, *Images*, 35–56.
20. Ibid., 57–96.
21. Ibid., 97–131.

The Spirit in Redemptive History

As we have seen, the Spirit has never been absent from the world, or from God's people. But the Spirit's presence is not merely a constant feature of the world's landscape. Rather, as always with the immanent God, the Spirit acts in different ways at different times. He is active in all the changes that take place through the history of redemption. The major change in the NT period is the Spirit's "coming" on the Day of Pentecost (Acts 2), empowering the church to bring the gospel of Christ to Jerusalem, Judea, Samaria, and "the end of the earth" (Acts 1:8).

This special presence of the Spirit is always in the forefront of the NT writings. So when Jesus declares in John 4:24, "God is spirit, and those who worship him must worship in spirit and truth," he is not, I think, saying merely that God is invisible and incorporeal. Nor is the point of the verse that in worship we should be preoccupied with immaterial rather than with material things. Rather, Jesus is speaking of the great coming event ("the hour is coming," v. 23), when at his behest the Spirit comes with power upon the church. When the Spirit comes, worship, like evangelism, will be "in Spirit." The great power of the Spirit will motivate the prayer and praise of God's people.

That worship will also be in "truth." In context, I think that "truth" is not merely truth in general as opposed to falsehood. The worship of the old covenant, as God ordained it, was not false. But Jesus here refers to the truth he came to bring: the truth of salvation through the blood of his cross, the gospel of grace. Therefore, worship in Spirit is Christ-centered. The Spirit bears witness to Christ, and he motivates God's people to sing the praises of Jesus.

To say that "God is spirit," then, is to say that true worship of God is directed to the Son by the Spirit. God identifies himself with the Spirit and tells us here that the qualities and acts of the Spirit are indeed the qualities and acts of God. God's *spirituality*, then, means not only that God is invisible and immaterial, but that he bears all the characteristics of the Spirit who dwells with his people.

Key Terms

Immensity
Aspatiality
Spatial omnipresence
Incorporeality
Invisibility
Glory
Spirituality
Presence (different meanings)
Heaven
Theophany
Peh
Panim

Temunah
Incarnation
Glory-cloud
Essential invisibility
Glory
Spirit

Study Questions

1. Describe the "ethical focus" of the doctrine of divine immensity.

2. "God is present as a whole person to all." Explain. Relate to the idea of "biblical personalism," and to immensity as a divine attribute.

3. How is God's relation to space different from ours? Compare immensity and eternity in this regard.

4. What is the difference between God's general omnipresence and his presence in special locations? Is this fact important? Discuss.

5. Formulate and discuss the "ethical meaning" of God's spatial omnipresence. What does it mean to say that God is "absent" from some people?

6. What is the biblical basis for saying that God is incorporeal? Discuss.

7. How does God's presence in the physical world affect his incorporeality? Does he take on a physical nature, even apart from the incarnation? Does he treat the world as his body? Discuss.

8. How is the incarnation like and unlike divine theophanies? Discuss the significance of that.

9. How is incorporeality a form of God's lordship?

10. Same for invisibility.

11. Is God unpicturable? Why or why not? (See footnote 12 about Herman Bavinck's view.)

12. "The visibility of God often has an eschatological thrust in Scripture." Explain; evaluate.

13. "The circle of glorification, however, does not begin with creation. There is also a circle of glorification within the Trinity itself." Explain; evaluate.

14. "For pedagogical purposes, it is convenient to distinguish the connotations of *spirit* along the lines of the lordship attributes." Show how Frame does this. Evaluate.

15. Explain the statement of John 4:24 that "God is spirit, and those who worship him must worship in spirit and truth."

Memory Verses

1 Kings 8:27: But will God indeed dwell on the earth? Behold, heaven and the highest heaven cannot contain you; how much less this house that I have built!

Ps. 139:7–10: Where shall I go from your Spirit?
    Or where shall I flee from your presence?
If I ascend to heaven, you are there!
    If I make my bed in Sheol, you are there!
If I take the wings of the morning
    and dwell in the uttermost parts of the sea,
even there your hand shall lead me,
    and your right hand shall hold me.

Prov. 15:29: The LORD is far from the wicked,
    but he hears the prayer of the righteous.

Matt. 5:8: Blessed are the pure in heart, for they shall see God.

John 4:24: God is spirit, and those who worship him must worship in spirit and truth.

2 Cor. 3:18: And we all, with unveiled face, beholding the glory of the Lord, are being transformed into the same image from one degree of glory to another. For this comes from the Lord who is the Spirit.

2 Cor. 4:18: We look not to the things that are seen but to the things that are unseen. For the things that are seen are transient, but the things that are unseen are eternal.

1 John 1:1–2: That which was from the beginning, which we have heard, which we have seen with our eyes, which we looked upon and have touched with our hands, concerning the word of life—the life was made manifest, and we have seen it, and testify to it and proclaim to you the eternal life, which was with the Father and was made manifest to us.

Resources for Further Study

Bavinck, Herman. *BRD*, 2:164–70, 182–91.

Kline, Meredith G. *Images of the Spirit*. Grand Rapids: Baker, 1980.

GOD'S ATTRIBUTES:
THE SELF-CONTAINED GOD

IN THIS CHAPTER, I WILL EXPLORE two closely related attributes of God: *aseity* and *impassibility*.

God's Aseity

The term *aseity* comes from the Latin phrase *a se*, meaning "from or by self." Herman Bavinck defines it by saying that God "is what he is through or by his own self."[1] He derives this attribute from the "I AM" of Exodus 3:14, which he takes in the sense "I will be what I will be."[2] This is the first divine attribute that Bavinck discusses, and he considers it central: "All other perfections were derived from this name."[3] It is commonly viewed as "the first of the incommunicable attributes."[4]

Nevertheless, Bavinck prefers the term *independence* to the term *aseity*:

Among the Reformed this perfection of God comes more emphatically to the fore, though the word "aseity" was soon exchanged for that of "independence." While aseity only expresses God's self-sufficiency in his existence, independence has a broader sense and implies that God is independent in everything: in his existence, in his perfections, in his decrees, and in his works.[5]

1. *BRD*, 2:151.
2. Ibid. (emphasis his). Of course, I take Exodus 3:14 somewhat differently, as setting forth the control, authority, and presence of the covenant Lord (chapters 2–3). But as we will see, I take that lordship to *imply* aseity.
3. Ibid. Bavinck agrees that the other attributes are included in this one because by this description God is recognized as *God* in *all* his perfections. He adds that we cannot derive these attributes by means of logic, but only by revelation. But note Gordon H. Clark's attempt to derive them by logic, using, of course, biblical premises, in "Attributes, The Divine," in *Baker's Dictionary of Theology* (Grand Rapids: Baker, 1960), 78–79. Since God's thought is logical (chapter 15), we should not see revelation and logic as a simple antithesis. But it is right to insist that arguments of this sort be based on biblical premises.
4. *BRD*, 2:152.
5. Ibid., 2:144–45.

I am unable to verify this distinction between *aseity* and *independence*. One could argue that *aseity* is the better term because it refers to God "as he is in himself," apart from creation, while *independence* presupposes a created world (at least in God's plan) from which he is independent. On that account, aseity is more fundamental. God is independent of the world because in himself he is *a se*. And, contra Bavinck, I don't think *aseity* need be limited to existence; like *independence*, it can be freely applied to everything God is and does, to his attributes, decrees, and works. So for practical purposes, I would consider the two terms interchangeable, noting that *aseity* takes the concept to a deeper level.

We can therefore use these as synonyms for *aseity*: *independence, self-existence, self-sufficiency,* and *self-containment*.[6] The term *self-caused* (*causa sui*), sometimes used as another synonym, is misleading. Since efficient causation requires some priority of the cause to the effect, nobody can literally bring about his own existence. Taken nonliterally, as usual in theology, the phrase means that God (1) is uncaused, and (2) has within himself sufficient reasons or grounds for his existence. *Absolute* is another term that I will sometimes use as a synonym for *a se*, though with certain divine attributes it can also mean "infinite" or "unqualified." When I spoke of God as *absolute personality* in chapter 3, *absolute* had the sense of *a se*.

In chapter 3, I suggested that the phrase *absolute personality* was useful in defining the biblical God over against the gods of pagan religions and secular philosophies. Non-Christian thought often acknowledges personal gods that are nonabsolute, or absolute principles that are not personal. Only Scripture presents consistently the reality of a God who is both personal and absolute.[7] It is appropriate that we have discussed God's personality toward the beginning of the book, and now we look at his absoluteness toward the end of our discussion of the divine attributes. Everything in between has shown the interaction of these. We have seen that all of God's other attributes are absolute, that he is self-sufficient in his goodness, righteousness, wisdom, relations to time and space, and so on. But all these attributes also characterize him as a *person*. They are not abstract, impersonal principles. Rather, God's righteousness is everything he is and does as a person, and similarly for other attributes.

Theologians have usually treated aseity as a metaphysical attribute, that is, one that focuses on the independence of God's being over against other beings. It seems to me, however, that the same basic concept is equally important in the epistemological and ethical areas. That is to say, God is not only self-existent, but also *self-attesting* and *self-justifying*. Not only does he exist without receiving existence from something else, but

---

6. Cornelius Van Til liked to refer to God as *self-contained*, meaning that "God is in no sense correlative to or dependent upon anything besides his own being." *The Defense of the Faith*, ed. K. Scott Oliphint (Phillipsburg, NJ: P&R Publishing, 2008), 11. Van Til agreed with Bavinck's estimate of the centrality of aseity and Bavinck's view that all the other divine virtues were included in aseity. See Van Til's *An Introduction to Systematic Theology* (Nutley, NJ: Presbyterian and Reformed, 1974), 206.

7. I owe this insight to Van Til. See my *CVT*, 51–61.

he gains his knowledge also from himself (his nature and his plan), and he serves as his own criterion of truth. And his righteousness is self-justifying, based on the righteousness of his own nature and on his status as the ultimate criterion of righteousness.[8]

So I agree with Bavinck and others that aseity is a very important attribute (though for reasons mentioned in previous chapters I hesitate to call it *the* central attribute). But though Reformed writers agree as to the importance of divine aseity, they have often failed to offer substantial and precise biblical support for the doctrine. Bavinck lists a great many texts[9] to show God's independence from the world, but he offers no argument to show that that independence is an *absolute* independence, or that God is absolutely self-existent and self-sufficient in all things.

As we work our way toward such an argument, we should recall the emphasis of this book on God's lordship and therefore on his absolute control, authority, and presence in blessing and judgment. As we have seen, God's control is such that every event takes place at his initiative; he is never moved to act by anything outside himself. His authority is the ultimate standard of truth and right; he looks to nobody outside himself to define that standard. And he is present in all the world he has made; nobody can shut him out.

God's control is absolute in that both his atemporal decree and his concurrent working in time (chapters 8, 9, 11, 17) govern the world exhaustively, so that even within time and space he is the One on whom everything else depends. He determines the course of history before anything is created, so his decree is not dependent on the world. That decree is unchangeable, not subject to the influence of creatures.[10]

God's authority is absolute in that he is self-sufficient in his goodness, righteousness, truth, wisdom, and knowledge, the unchanging standard of all the corresponding creaturely virtues. Creaturely truth, for example, would be meaningless without his, but his truth does not depend on the world he has made. He knows all things through himself: by knowing his nature and by knowing his eternal plan, and he creates the truth about the actual world by his creation and providence. Our knowledge depends on his (Ps. 36:9), but his does not depend on anything except himself.

God's presence is absolute in that he acts as a whole person at all times and places. The creation cannot continue to exist without God's continued preservation and concurrent providence in the smallest details of nature and history. But he can exist in all his perfections without the world.

The specific texts used to support the general concept of divine aseity can be brought into an argument as follows:

1. *As Lord, God owns all things.* He is "possessor of heaven and earth" (Gen. 14:19, 22).[11]

---

8. For discussion of the issue of circularity raised by this formulation, see chapter 16; also *DKG*, 130–33.

9. *BRD*, 2:150–52.

10. Remember, however, what I said before about how God's knowledge of creatable persons influences his plan (chapter 15). But here one part of God's plan influences another part; it is not that creatures modify God's plan on their initiative.

11. "Possessor" is the KJV translation of *qanah*. The NIV translates "create," but "possess" is the more frequent meaning of *qanah*, and other words are far more commonly translated "create."

The earth is the LORD's and the fullness thereof,
    the world and those who dwell therein. (Ps. 24:1)

For every beast of the forest is mine,
    the cattle on a thousand hills.
I know all the birds of the hills,
    and all that moves in the field is mine.

If I were hungry, I would not tell you,
    for the world and its fullness are mine. (Ps. 50:10–12)

Cf. Ex. 19:5; Deut. 10:14; 1 Chron. 29:11; Job 41:11; Pss. 82:8; 89:11.

2. *Everything possessed by creatures comes from God.* Scripture emphasizes the universality of creation, as we saw in chapter 10. God has created everything in the heavens, earth, and sea (Ex. 20:11a; Neh. 9:6; Ps. 146:5–6; etc.). So "every good gift and every perfect gift is from above" (James 1:17).

3. *When we give something back to God, we give him only what he has first given us* (evident from point 2). We are stewards of God's land (Luke 12:42; 16:1–8; Titus 1:7), accountable to use these blessings to his glory. Everything in creation remains his, even after he has given it to us, so even our own possessions are his.

4. *When we give something back to God, he is not obligated to recompense us.*

So you also, when you have done all that you were commanded, say, "We are unworthy servants; we have only done what was our duty." (Luke 17:10)

5. *So God owes nothing to any creature.*

Who has first given to me, that I should repay him?
    Whatever is under the whole heaven is mine. (Job 41:11)

And Paul later quotes Job:

"Or who has given a gift to him
    that he might be repaid?"

For from him and through him and to him are all things. To him be glory forever. Amen. (Rom. 11:35–36)

Now, of course, as we have seen, God does bring himself under obligation to creatures by making covenants and promises, and by displaying to them the constancies of his nature. But these obligations, based on his nature and his voluntary covenants, are self-imposed, not forced on him by creatures. What Paul tells us is that God is not only the First Cause, but the First Giver. He does recompense people for their obedient service. But it is he that has first given them the privilege of serving him and of receiving that reward.

6. *So God has no needs.* God gives to us not so that we will help him to repair some lack in his being and life, but because he is the First Giver. He is not dependent on us, for then he would *owe* his existence or his well-being to us. This truth has important relevance to the worship of God's people. Look at a bit more of Psalm 50, which I began to quote above:

> Not for your sacrifices do I rebuke you;
>   your burnt offerings are continually before me.
> I will not accept a bull from your house
>   or goats from your folds.
> For every beast of the forest is mine,
>   the cattle on a thousand hills.
> I know all the birds of the hills,
>   and all that moves in the field is mine.
>
> If I were hungry, I would not tell you,
>   for the world and its fullness are mine.
> Do I eat the flesh of bulls
>   or drink the blood of goats?
> Offer to God a sacrifice of thanksgiving,
>   and perform your vows to the Most High,
> and call upon me in the day of trouble;
>   I will deliver you, and you shall glorify me. (Ps. 50:8–15)

Biblical worship, unlike much pagan worship, is not intended to meet the *needs* of its God. The purpose of animal sacrifice in the OT was not to satiate God's hunger, but symbolically to atone for human sin. As verses 14 and 15 make clear, in worship we offer our thanks for the fact that God has met *our* needs. Through vows we incur *our* obligations to him. And we call on him to meet our needs in the future.

So God speaks against idolatry through Isaiah's satiric wit:

> An idol! A craftsman casts it,
>   and a goldsmith overlays it with gold
>   and casts for it silver chains.
> He who is too impoverished for an offering
>   chooses wood that will not rot;
> he seeks out a skillful craftsman
>   to set up an idol that will not move. (Isa. 40:19–20; cf. 41:7; 46:6; Jer. 10:3–5; Hab.
>   2:18–20)

And in Isaiah 44:15–17, we read of a carpenter who cuts down some wood:

> Then it becomes fuel for a man. He takes a part of it and warms himself; he kindles a fire and bakes bread. Also he makes a god and worships it; he makes it an idol and falls down before it. Half of it he burns in the fire. Over the half he eats meat; he roasts it and is satisfied. Also he warms himself and says, "Aha, I am warm, I have seen the fire!" And the rest of it he makes into a god, his idol, and falls down to it and worships it. He prays to it and says, "Deliver me, for you are my god!"

The idol is dependent on man. Therefore, it is ridiculous that a man should worship it. To make an idol, you must be skillful. You must know what wood to use, because you don't want your god to rot on you; and you must make it carefully, because you don't want your god to topple. And of course, it is your choice as to what wood you want to burn and what you want to worship. You are the one who saves the god from flaming destruction. So the Lord mocks the kind of worship in which the god is dependent on the worshiper, in which the worshiper meets the god's *needs*.

So Paul, when he encounters idolatry in Athens, sets forth the nature of true worship:

> The God who made the world and everything in it, being Lord of heaven and earth, does not live in temples made by man, nor is he served by human hands, as though he needed anything, since he himself gives to all mankind life and breath and everything. And he made from one man every nation of mankind to live on all the face of the earth, having determined allotted periods and the boundaries of their dwelling place, that they should seek God, in the hope that they might feel their way toward him and find him. Yet he is actually not far from each one of us, for
>
> "In him we live and move and have our being";
>
> as even some of your own poets have said,
>
> "For we are indeed his offspring."
>
> Being then God's offspring, we ought not to think that the divine being is like gold or silver or stone, an image formed by the art and imagination of man. The times of ignorance God overlooked, but now he commands all people everywhere to repent. (Acts 17:24–30)

Note that God is not worshiped by men's hands "as though he needed [*prosdeomai*] anything." God is worshiped by men's hands, but the hands are raised in praise and thanksgiving, not to supply the needs of God. Rather, he is the One who has given us everything: life, breath, times, and places. It is in him that we live and move and have our being: we depend utterly on him; he does not depend at all on us.

7. *So God is by nature a se.* A being with no needs is an extraordinary being, to say the least. We can see that here, as elsewhere in the doctrine of God, we are forced to draw metaphysical conclusions from the nature of worship. If worship is what Scripture

says it is, then the object of worship must be utterly without any needs, independent of his worshipers.

Scripture rarely uses metaphysical language, but in Galatians 4:8–9, Paul says:

> Formerly, when you did not know God, you were enslaved to those that by nature are not gods. But now that you have come to know God, or rather to be known by God, how can you turn back again to the weak and worthless elementary principles of the world, whose slaves you want to be once more?

Note the phrase "that by nature are not gods" (*tois phusei me ousi theois*). Paul agrees with our previous statement that a being worthy of worship must have a nature worthy of worship. But the false gods are "weak" (*asthene*) and "worthless" (*ptocha*, "poor," "begging"). A god who depends on his worshipers to remedy his weaknesses and poverty does not deserve worship. So the true God is One who is not weak in any respect, nor is he poor. He is God by nature: self-existent and self-sufficient, *a se*.

So although aseity is a metaphysical idea, our knowledge of it is, as for all other divine attributes, grounded in the practical reality of God as covenant Lord. We confess his aseity because such a confession is implicit in the very act of worship, the reverence that the worshiper has for his Lord.

With this background, we can understand how Paul's praise to God in Romans 11:36 entails the metaphysical claim that God is self-existent, self-sufficient, *a se*:

> For from him and through him and to him are all things. To him be glory forever. Amen.

He has created and provided all things ("from him"); nothing happens without his power ("through him"); and he receives everything back to himself ("to him"). He has no needs; he is self-sufficient.

In all traditions of thought, secular as well as religious, there has been a search for something *a se*: an ultimate cause of being, an ultimate standard of truth, an ultimate justification of right. In the realm of being (metaphysics), it may be a deity, a system of abstract forms, or natural law. In the realm of knowledge (epistemology), the standard may be a religious or secular authority, human subjectivity, sense experience, reason, or some combination of these (see *DKG*). In the realm of ethics, it may be a system of duties, calculation of consequences, or human inwardness.[12] Ideally, the metaphysical absolute, the epistemological norm, and the ethical norm should all be grounded in one being, since these three are correlative to one another. But non-Christian thought has usually found it impossible to locate all these ultimates in a single principle. Part of the problem is that non-Christian thought is determined that its absolute be impersonal. But an impersonal being cannot serve as a norm for knowledge and ethics, nor can it be a credible first cause. So many non-Christians have given up the quest for an absolute

---

12. See *DCL*, chaps. 5–8.

altogether, preferring to embrace meaninglessness and chaos. The non-Christian substitutes for God have failed, just as the idols of Psalm 50 and Isaiah 40. Only the *a se* God of Scripture can give unity and meaning to human thought and experience.

So aseity is essential to a credible doctrine of God, not a mere bit of abstract theorizing. It is also important to note that aseity does not isolate God's being from the world, but rather enables God to enter our history without confusing his being with the being of the world. If God entered the world out of need, then he would be dependent on the world; then there would be no clear distinction between Creator and creature. Yet he enters our world not out of need, but as the *a se* Lord of all.

Does God Have Feelings?

Theological literature has sometimes ascribed to God the attribute of *impassibility*. This concept has been used to deny (1) that God has emotions or feelings and (2) that God suffers. These two issues are related to each other in various ways, but I would like to discuss them sequentially: the question of emotion here, and the question of suffering in the next section.

The aseity of God enters into both these questions, because it has been argued that both emotions and suffering are inappropriate to One who is utterly self-sufficient, independent, and autonomous, not to mention unchangeable.

On the question of divine emotions, we have seen that Scripture ascribes many attitudes to God that are generally regarded as emotions. In previous chapters, we have discussed biblical references to God's compassion, tender mercy, patience, rejoicing, delight, pleasure, pity, love,[13] wrath, and jealousy. I noted in chapter 17 that *nacham* is sometimes properly translated "be grieved" (as of God in Genesis 6:6), and Ephesians 4:30 tells us not to "grieve" the Holy Spirit of God.

Beyond all of that, we should note that God's Word, through prophets and in writing, regularly expresses emotion and appeals to the emotions of its hearers. Certainly we feel the passion in God's words when he addresses Israel, "Turn back, turn back from your evil ways, for why will you die, O house of Israel?" (Ezek. 33:11b), or when Paul turns from his logical exposition of God's plan of salvation and bursts forth in praise (as, for example, in Romans 8:31–39 and 11:33–36).

But emotion is present even in language that is relatively calm. That is true of both divine and human language. Calmness itself is an emotion. And even a matter-of-fact statement such as "in the beginning, God created the heavens and the earth" (Gen. 1:1) is intended not only to inform us, but to give us a certain feeling about the event described. Indeed, it might not be possible to distinguish the intellectual force of language from its emotional force. Intellectual communication intends, among other things, to give the hearer a *feeling* of "cognitive rest,"[14] an inner satisfaction that the communication is true.

---

13. Love is not *merely* emotional, but it certainly has an emotional component to it.
14. See *DKG*, 152–53, in the context of 149–62, and also 335–40.

Scripture does not distinguish the emotions as a part of the mind radically different from intellect and will. As I said in chapters 15 and 16, Scripture does not speak of God's mind and will as faculties interacting in various ways, only of the thoughts and decisions that God makes. The same may be said of God's emotions. Scripture refers to God's individual emotions, but it doesn't specify any metaphysical or categorical difference between these, on the one hand, and his thoughts and decisions on the other.

Nevertheless, some theologians have drawn a sharp line between emotions and other kinds of mental content, and they have put biblical references to God's emotions into the category of anthropomorphisms. On this view, when Scripture says that God knows his people, for example, he really knows them; but when Scripture says that God is angry, he is not "really" angry.

Why is it that theologians have sometimes thought emotions to be unworthy of God? Donald Carson comments:

> In the final analysis, we have to do with the influence of certain strands of Greek metaphysical thought, strands which insist that emotion is dangerous, treacherous, and often evil. Reason must be set against emotion, and vulnerability is a sign of weakness. One may trace this line from Aristotle's "unmoved mover" through platonic and neo-platonic writings to the Stoics. The conclusion must be that "God is sensible, omnipotent, compassionate, *passionless*; for it is better to be these than not to be" (so Anselm in *Proslogium*, chapter 6).[15]

I think Carson is right, and certainly these strands of Greek metaphysical thought are not biblical. So they cannot be a ground for denying divine emotions. A few more observations might help to clarify the issue:

1. Emotions in human beings often have physical accompaniments and symptoms: tears, queasy stomach, an adrenaline flow, and so on. Since God is incorporeal (chapter 18), his emotions are not like man's in that respect. Of course, we should not forget that God did become incarnate in Christ, and that Jesus really did weep (Luke 19:41; John 11:35). But God's incorporeality gives us no reason to deny in some general way that God has emotions, even apart from the incarnation. In human beings, thinking is also a physical process, linked to the brain. But we would never dream of denying that God can think on the ground that he is incorporeal.

2. Doctrines such as God's eternal decree, his immutability, and his aseity sometimes lead us to think that God can never "respond" to what happens in the world. Responding seems to assume passivity and change in God. Now, emotions are usually responses to events. They are, indeed, sometimes called *passions*, a term that suggests passivity. This consideration is one reason why theologians have resisted ascribing emotions to God.

But although God's eternal decree does not change, it ordains change. It ordains a historical series of events, each of which receives God's evaluation. God evaluates

15. Donald A. Carson, *Divine Sovereignty and Human Responsibility* (Atlanta: John Knox Press, 1981), 215.

different events in different ways. Those evaluations themselves are fixed in God's eternal plan. But they are genuine evaluations of the events. It is not wrong to describe them as responses to these events.[16]

Further, we have seen that God has not only an atemporal and aspatial transcendent existence, but also an immanence in all times and spaces. From these immanent perspectives, God views each event from within history. As he does, he evaluates each event appropriately, when it happens. Such evaluations are, in the most obvious sense, responses.

Does such responsiveness imply passivity in God? To say so would be highly misleading. God responds (both transcendently and immanently) only to what he has himself ordained.[17] He has *chosen* to create a world that often grieves him. So ultimately he is active rather than passive. Some might want to use the term *impassible* to indicate that fact: God is ultimately active rather than passive.

3. As suggested in observation 2, much of what we are inclined to call *emotion* in God is his *evaluation* of what happens in history. He rejoices in the good and grieves over the evil. There should be no doubt that God, in his lordship attribute of authority, is the supreme and exhaustive evaluator of everything that happens in nature and history. His evaluations are always true and appropriate.

Now, sometimes, in order to be appropriate, an evaluation must include some superlatives, some exciting language.[18] For example, it is not enough to say merely that God rules; to express the full truth of the matter, we need expressions such as "King of kings and Lord of lords." When we find such colorful expressions, we are inclined to say that they express emotion, that they have emotional content. Indeed, they are emotional expressions, but they are also the sober truth. They represent an infallible evaluation of the fact. Again we see a kind of coalescence between emotion and intellect, and an argument in favor of asserting divine emotions: without emotions, God would lack intellectual capacity, and he would be unable to speak the full truth about himself and the world.

4. There are, of course, emotions that are inappropriate to God. God is never homesick, anxious about tomorrow, inwardly troubled by divided intentions, compulsive, or addicted. Nor is he like human beings who are regularly overcome by waves of passion, who make decisions on the basis of momentary feelings, whose passions lead

---

16. There is a role for God's knowledge in the very formulation of his eternal plan. God knows the things he plans, and each element of his plan takes the others into account. So his eternal plan itself includes God's responses to all the elements of that plan.

17. Recall the discussion of God's temporal omnipresence in chapter 17. In Genesis 1, even before man is created, God responds to his own creative actions.

18. I wish this point were better understood by young preachers. Too often they try to convey truth without passion, which often means without making it interesting for the hearers. Sometimes they defend this by saying that they want to convey only the "objective" truth, not mixing it up with "subjective" emotion. But they fail to realize that a dispassionate exposition of God's Word often falsifies it. We do not rightly expound Romans 11:33–36 unless we somehow convey to our hearers Paul's sense of amazement and wonder. The same point applies to commentators and theologians.

them to false judgments. God doesn't have *such* kinds of emotions. But this fact is not an argument for denying to God those emotions ascribed to him in Scripture.

Can God Suffer?

Recently a number of theologians have questioned the traditional view of the church that God is unable to suffer.[19] Richard Bauckham summarizes Jürgen Moltmann's "three reasons for speaking of God's suffering."[20] The first is *the passion of Christ*. Moltmann sees his argument as following the tradition of Martin Luther's "theology of the cross," which "makes the cross, for all its stark negativity, the basis and criterion of Christian theology."[21] Moltmann believes that the doctrine of impassibility in the church fathers was based on Greek philosophy rather than trying to "understand the being of God from the event of the cross."[22]

Moltmann's second reason for attributing suffering to God is *the nature of love*. In Moltmann's view, divine love entails "reciprocity" between God and creation. It must be possible for him to be "affected by the objects of his love." So God must be vulnerable to suffering. This argument is based not on a mere analogy between divine and human love, but on the nature of divine love revealed in the cross.[23]

Third, Moltmann appeals to *the problem of human suffering*.[24] He finds no adequate answer to the problem of evil except to say that God suffers with suffering human beings. Again, he does not merely argue from human suffering to divine suffering, but rather argues from God's suffering with Jesus on the cross. This event has soteriological implications: "all suffering becomes God's *so that he may overcome it*."[25]

I have argued earlier in this chapter that God experiences grief and other negative emotions, not only in the incarnate Christ, but in his nonincarnate being as well. Isaiah expresses God's grief in terms of distress or affliction (*tzar*):

> In all their affliction he was afflicted,
> and the angel of his presence saved them;

19. Of seminal importance is Kayoh Kitamori, *Theology of the Pain of God* (Richmond, VA: John Knox Press, 1965), followed closely by Jürgen Moltmann, *The Crucified God* (London: SCM Press, 1974; repr., San Francisco: HarperSan Francisco, 1990). Compare Eberhard Jüngel, *God as the Mystery of the World* (Grand Rapids: Eerdmans, 1983), which emphasizes "the identification of God and the crucified Jesus." Feminist theology generally supports this paradigm; e.g., Elizabeth Johnson, *She Who Is* (New York: Crossroad Publishing, 1996), 246–72. For recent statements of the traditional view, see Richard Creel, *Divine Impassibility* (Cambridge: Cambridge University Press, 1986); Millard Erickson, *God the Father Almighty* (Grand Rapids: Baker, 1998); Thomas G. Weinandy, *Does God Suffer?* (Notre Dame, IN: University of Notre Dame Press, 2000).

20. Richard Bauckham, "In Defence of *The Crucified God*," in *The Power and Weakness of God*, ed. Nigel M. de S. Cameron (Edinburgh: Rutherford House Books, 1990), 93.

21. Ibid., 94.

22. Ibid., 95. The traditional view is that Jesus suffered on the cross as man, but not as God, and that no suffering should be attributed to God the Father. The tradition rejected the idea that God the Father suffered the pain of Christ on the cross, the position called *patripassianism*.

23. Ibid., 95–96.

24. Ibid., 96–99.

25. Bauckham quotes Moltmann, *The Crucified God*, 246 (emphasis Moltmann's).

> in his love and in his pity he redeemed them;
>> he lifted them up and carried them all the days of old. (Isa. 63:9)

God is the compassionate God, who knows the agonies of his people, not only as the transcendent Author of history, but as the Immanent One who is with us here and now. In Christ he draws yet nearer, to be "made like his brothers in every respect, so that he might become a merciful and faithful high priest" (Heb. 2:17). Thus, the Son of God empathizes with us:

> For we do not have a high priest who is unable to sympathize with our weaknesses,
> but one who in every respect has been tempted as we are, yet without sin. (Heb. 4:15)

This emotional empathy can be called *suffering*, though that is perhaps a misleading term. There is no reason in these passages to suppose that God suffers any injury or loss. The same is true of the biblical references to God's *weakness* (see my discussion of that in chapter 16).

But is there any sense in which God suffers injury or loss? Certainly Jesus suffers these on the cross. And I agree with Moltmann that Christ's sufferings are the sufferings of God. The Council of Chalcedon (451), which defines Christian orthodoxy on the subject of Christology, says that Jesus has two complete *natures*, divine and human, united in one *person*. We may say that Jesus suffers and dies on the cross "according to his human nature." But what suffers is not a *nature*, but the person of Jesus. And the person of Jesus is nothing less than the second person of the Trinity, who has taken to himself a human nature. His experiences as man are truly his experiences, the experiences of God.

Are these experiences only of the Son, and not of the Father? The persons of the Trinity are not divided, but the Son is in the Father and the Father in the Son (John 10:38; 14:10–11, 20; 17:21). Theologians have called this mutual indwelling *circumcessio* or *circumincessio*.

I do not, however, conclude that the Father has exactly the same experiences of suffering and death that the Son has. Although they dwell in each other, Father and Son play different roles in the history of redemption. The Son was baptized by John; the Father was the voice from heaven. The Son is crucified; the Father is not. Indeed, during the crucifixion the Father forsakes the Son as he bears the sins of his people (Matt. 27:46). Was the Father, nevertheless, still "in" the Son at that moment of separation? What exactly does it mean for the Father to be "in" the Son when he addresses the Son from heaven? These are difficult questions, and I have not heard any scripturally persuasive answers to them. But we must do justice to both the continuity and the discontinuity between the persons of the Trinity. Certainly the Father empathizes with, agonizes with, and grieves over the death of his Son. But it is wrong to insist that the Father must experience death in the same way that the Son does.

But God the Son does die, and of course he rises again. So in his incarnate existence, God suffers, even dies; yet his death somehow does not leave us with a godless universe. Beyond that, I think we are largely ignorant, and we should admit that ignorance.

To summarize, let us distinguish, as we have earlier, among four modes of divine existence:

1. In God's atemporal, aspatial transcendent existence, God ordains grievous events to his glory and evaluates them appropriately. In that sense he grieves, but he does not suffer injury or loss.

2. In his temporal and spatial omnipresence, he grieves with his creatures, and he undergoes temporary defeats on his way to the complete victory that he has foreordained.

3. In his theophanic presence, he is distressed when his people are distressed (Isa. 63:9), but he promises complete victory and vindication both for him and for his faithful ones.

4. In his incarnation, the Son suffers injury and loss: physical pain, deprivation, and death. The Father knows this agony, including the agony of his own separation from his Son. He regards this event as the unique and awful tragedy that it is, but also as his foreordained means of salvation. What precise feelings he experiences we do not know, and we would be wise not to speculate.

Moltmann is right to find divine suffering in the cross in the senses mentioned above. But he is wrong, I think, to conclude that the doctrine of God's impassibility is merely a remnant of Greek philosophy. As we have seen, the doctrine of impassibility should not be used to deny that God has emotions, or to deny that God the Son suffers real injury and death on the cross. But God in his transcendent nature cannot be harmed in any way, nor can he suffer loss. In his eternal existence, "suffering loss" could only mean losing some attribute, being defeated in his war with Satan, or otherwise failing to accomplish his eternal plan. Scripture assures us that none of these things will happen—so they cannot happen. In this sense, God is impassible.

In conclusion, I will offer some comments on Moltmann's three points noted earlier. As we will recall from Bauckham's summary, Moltmann's view comes from a particular methodology, his application of Luther's "theology of the cross." Certainly our theology should be centered on the redemption accomplished by Christ. As Paul says, in one sense we should "know nothing . . . except Jesus Christ and him crucified" (1 Cor. 2:2). We should proclaim Jesus' atonement and victory in all our theological work. As we have seen, however, the event of Jesus' crucifixion is in many ways mysterious, especially in regard to the relations between Son and Father in Jesus' death. What Moltmann does, I fear, is to insist very dogmatically on one dubious interpretation of this mystery (namely, that the Father suffers metaphysical loss in the death of Jesus) and to use that as a paradigm for interpreting everything else in the Bible, even to the point of denying some other biblical emphases. I do not think such a procedure can rightly claim justification in the theology of the cross.

As to Moltmann's second point, I would agree that love involves reciprocity. God's love, both in the eternal fellowship of the Trinity and in the world of creatures, is responsive in the ways I have previously indicated. I do not agree that love requires "vulnerability" in the sense of susceptibility to injury and loss. Is it really impossible to love someone who cannot be ultimately harmed? Millions of Christian believers over the centuries would affirm that it is possible. The psalmists typically express their love to God as their strength and deliverance (Pss. 18:1; 31:2–3; 116:1–4); it doesn't occur to them to say that they love God because he is vulnerable. Paul praises the omnipotence of God's love: it is such a powerful love that nothing can separate us from it (Rom. 8:35–39).

So in regard to Moltmann's third point, the idea that God shares our sufferings in order to overcome them: Yes, he does, in Jesus.

> He was despised and rejected by men;
>   a man of sorrows, and acquainted with grief;
> and as one from whom men hide their faces
>   he was despised, and we esteemed him not.
>
> Surely he has borne our griefs
>   and carried our sorrows;
> yet we esteemed him stricken,
>   smitten by God, and afflicted. (Isa. 53:3)

As we have seen from Hebrews, Christ is made like us so that he can be a merciful and faithful High Priest, empathizing with the feeling of our infirmities. He takes away sin, the cause of those infirmities, and he hears our prayers with understanding. But this principle should not be magnified into a metaphysical assertion about God's vulnerability, for as we have seen, God's eternal nature is invulnerable, and that invulnerability is also precious to the believer.

God's suffering love in Christ, therefore, does not cast doubt on his aseity and unchangeability. It is, however, ground for rejoicing. I close with words of B. B. Warfield:

> We have a God who is capable of self-sacrifice for us. . . . Now, herein is a wonderful thing. Men tell us that God is, by very necessity of His nature, incapable of passion, incapable of being moved by inducement from without; that he dwells in holy calm and unchangeable blessedness, untouched by human sufferings or human sorrows for ever—haunting
>
> The lucid interspace of world and world,
> Where never creeps a cloud, nor moves a wind,
> Nor ever falls the least white star of snow,
> Nor ever lowest roll of thunder moans,
> Nor sound of human sorrow mounts to mar
> His sacred, everlasting calm.
>
> Let us bless our God that it is not true. God can feel; God does love. We have Scriptural warrant for believing, as it has been perhaps somewhat inadequately but not misleadingly phrased, that moral heroism has a place within the sphere of the divine nature: we have Scriptural warrant for believing that, like the hero of Zurich, God has reached out loving arms and gathered to his own bosom that forest of spears which otherwise had pierced ours.

But is not this gross anthropomorphism? We are careless of names: it is the truth of God. And we decline to yield up the God of the Bible and the God of our hearts to any philosophical abstraction. We have and we must have an ethical God—a God whom we can love, in whom we can trust.[26]

Key Terms

Aseity
Independence
Self-existent
Self-attesting
Self-justifying
Absolute
Impassibility
Passions
Circumincessio

Study Questions

1. Develop an argument for the aseity of God, using biblical texts. Evaluate it.
2. "God must be *a se* to be worthy of worship." Evaluate this statement, using biblical texts. Is it possible to derive statements about God's metaphysical nature from the nature of worship? Cite relevant Scripture texts.
3. "Only the *a se* God of Scripture can give unity and meaning to human thought and experience." Explain; evaluate.
4. "It is also important to note that aseity does not isolate God's being from the world, but rather enables God to enter our history without confusing his being with the being of the world." Explain; evaluate.
5. Does Scripture ascribe emotions to God? Reply, referring to specific texts.
6. God is the chief evaluator of the world. Relate this fact to the question of God's emotions.
7. Does God suffer? Distinguish different meanings of *suffer*. Relate the question of divine suffering to (a) the incarnation and cross, (b) the persons of the Trinity.

Memory Verses

Ps. 50:10–12: For every beast of the forest is mine,
the cattle on a thousand hills.
I know all the birds of the hills,
and all that moves in the field is mine.

26. B. B. Warfield, "Imitating the Incarnation," sermon on Philippians 2:5–8, in *The Person and Work of Christ* (Philadelphia: Presbyterian and Reformed, 1950), 570–71. Thanks to Jeff Meyers for drawing my attention to this passage.

> If I were hungry, I would not tell you,
>   for the world and its fullness are mine.

Isa. 63:9: In all their affliction he was afflicted,
>   and the angel of his presence saved them;
> in his love and in his pity he redeemed them;
>   he lifted them up and carried them all the days of old.

Ezek. 33:11b: Turn back, turn back from your evil ways, for why will you die, O house of Israel?

Acts 17:24–25: The God who made the world and everything in it, being Lord of heaven and earth, does not live in temples made by man, nor is he served by human hands, as though he needed anything, since he himself gives to all mankind life and breath and everything.

Rom. 11:35–36: "Or who has given a gift to him
>   that he might be repaid?"

For from him and through him and to him are all things. To him be glory forever. Amen.

Heb. 4:15: For we do not have a high priest who is unable to sympathize with our weaknesses, but one who in every respect has been tempted as we are, yet without sin.

Resources for Further Study

Bauckham, Richard. "In Defence of *The Crucified God.*" In *The Power and Weakness of God*, edited by Nigel M. de S. Cameron, 93–99. Edinburgh: Rutherford House Books, 1990.

Bavinck, Herman. *BRD*, 2:151–53.

Macleod, Donald. *Behold Your God*. 2nd ed. Fearn, Ross-shire, UK: Christian Focus, 1995.

Warfield, B. B. "Imitating the Incarnation." Sermon on Philippians 2:5–8. In *The Person and Work of Christ*, 570–71. Philadelphia: Presbyterian and Reformed, 1950.

CHAPTER 20

GOD, THREE IN ONE

EARLIER, I INDICATED that Scripture reveals God to us (1) by declaring his acts, (2) by giving us authoritative descriptions of him, and (3) by giving us a glimpse of his inner triune life. These forms of revelation correspond to the categories situational, normative, and existential, respectively.

We now move to consider the third of these. Point 3 is not radically distinct from 2: contrary to some writers, I don't believe it is necessarily wrong to think of God's triunity as an attribute (and therefore as God's nature).[1] And the doctrine of the Trinity also continues our study of God's acts, for I will discuss here the acts of eternal generation and procession within the Godhead,[2] as well as acts of love and communication among the three persons. Theologians describe these acts as God's acts *ad intra*, acts that "terminate within the Godhead." But we will consider other acts specific to each of the three persons that have effects within the creation—divine acts *ad extra*.

But though we will continue here to describe God's nature and actions as we have in previous chapters, we can almost sense that when we discuss the Trinity, we are reaching a new level of depth in our understanding of God. Gerald Bray says:

> The revelation of the Trinity, as opposed to the implied unitarianism of Judaism, can be explained only by the transformation of perspective brought about by Jesus. The Trinity belongs to the inner life of God, and can be known only by those who share in that life. As long as we look at God on the outside, we shall never see beyond his unity; for, as the Cappadocian Fathers and Augustine realized, the external works of the Trinity are undivided (*opera Trinitatis ad extra sunt indivisa*). This means that an outside observer will never detect the inner reality of God, and will never enter the communion with him which is promised to us in Christ. Jews may recognize God's existence and know his law, but without Christ they cannot penetrate the mystery of that divine fellowship which Christians call the Holy Trinity.[3]

1. This is wrong only if one insists on some highly technical definitions of *attribute* and divine *nature*, definitions that are not required by Scripture. I prefer to take these terms in a more commonsensical way.

2. *Godhead* is an old term for *divine being* or *nature*, often used especially when one wishes to contrast the one divine nature with the three persons.

3. Gerald Bray, *The Doctrine of God* (Downers Grove, IL: InterVarsity Press, 1993).

We must, of course, distinguish between Judaism on the one hand and God's OT revelation on the other. Unlike Judaism, the OT should not be charged with implied unitarianism; and certainly OT revelation does not teach the sufficiency of knowing God's existence and his law. Despite the veil of the temple, God invited his people in the OT to an intimate relationship with him: "I will take you to be my people, and I will be your God" (Ex. 6:7). "The LORD is my shepherd; I shall not want" (Ps. 23:1). "I have loved you with an everlasting love; therefore I have continued my faithfulness to you" (Jer. 31:3).

Yet Bray is right to emphasize that something new appears in the NT revelation. The tearing of the temple veil through the atoning work of Christ certainly brings us to a greater level of fellowship with God: "and [God] raised us up with [Christ] and seated us with him in the heavenly places in Christ Jesus" (Eph. 2:6). As we stand before the Father in the Son, we enjoy a knowledge of God's intra-Trinitarian fellowship that was not available to the OT saints. The OT anticipates the doctrine of the Trinity in many ways, and its teaching is fully compatible with that doctrine. Indeed, it provides many useful materials for the study of the Trinity, as we will see. But to understand this theme in the OT, we must read it from a NT vantage point.[4]

So in this part of the book, I will explore this biblical glimpse into God's inner life and therefore into the life that believers share with him. We should remind ourselves from time to time that it is only a glimpse. God has withheld much in this area that we would like to know. The mysteries before us here are especially intractable. But this study can be enormously rewarding. In sharing with us even a little of his triune existence, God has given the church a great blessing.

As Sinclair Ferguson points out, it is before he goes to the cross (John 13–17) that Jesus has the most to say to his disciples about the Trinity, about his relation to the Father and to the Spirit.[5] It is the cross that enables us to share the unity and love that exists eternally between the Father and the Son (John 17:11, 22–26). It is the cross, resurrection, and ascension of Christ that bring to us the full power and knowledge of the Holy Spirit (John 14:16–17, 26; 15:26; 16:13). Such are the blessings we learn of

---

4. Otto Weber, in *Foundations of Dogmatics* (Grand Rapids: Eerdmans, 1981), 1:349–53, offers some valid warnings to theologians like me who deal with the being and attributes of God before discussing the Trinity. In this respect, my order of discussion is fairly traditional. Certainly in the traditional procedure there are dangers of developing a doctrine of God based on philosophical abstractions rather than on the relation of God to us in Christ. As Weber admits, however, his preference for discussing the Trinity first may not be made into an absolute requirement. To make it such would be to invalidate the order of Scripture itself, which presents God in the OT primarily (though not exclusively) as a singular being, and only in the NT as an explicitly Trinitarian one. My focus on God as covenant Lord has, I believe, answered Weber's concerns and prepares the way, as does the OT doctrine of covenant lordship, to discuss Christ and the Spirit as Yahweh. In any case, as I indicated in chapter 1, it is unwise to take too seriously questions about the order in which theological topics should be discussed. So I oppose Paul K. Jewett's statement that "the location of the Trinity in the table of contents tells the discerning student more about a treatise on systematics than anything short of reading the book itself." *God, Creation, and Revelation* (Grand Rapids: Eerdmans, 1991), 265. There and on 266, Jewett suggests that to put the discussion of the Trinity toward the end of a systematic theology is to go the way of the subjectivist Friedrich Schleiermacher: guilt by association. I plead not guilty.

5. Sinclair Ferguson, *A Heart for God* (Colorado Springs: NavPress, 1985), 18–37.

when we study the doctrine of the Trinity. The study can at times be technical and dry, but the rewards are great.

Trinitarian Basics

Far from being an abstruse philosophical speculation, the doctrine of the Trinity attempts to describe and account for something biblically obvious and quite fundamental to the gospel. That fact is this: Scripture testifies from beginning to end that God is one; but it also presents three persons who are God: the Father, the Son, and the Holy Spirit. As we will see, there is no legitimate argument over the deity of these three persons. Their deity pervades Scripture and assures us that our salvation is from beginning to end a *divine* salvation, the work of God himself. Nor can it be debated whether the biblical God is one. Indeed, his oneness is also important to our salvation. He is God alone; there is none beside him. So none can prevent him from bringing eternal salvation to his people.

So God is one but somehow also three. This fact is difficult to understand, but it is quite unavoidable in Scripture and central to the biblical gospel.

The doctrine of the Trinity attempts to account for this fact and to exclude heresies that have arisen on the subject. Its basic assertions are these: (1) God is one. (2) God is three. (3) The three persons are each fully God. (4) Each of the persons is distinct from the others. (5) The three are related to one another eternally as Father, Son, and Holy Spirit. I will discuss these assertions in this order, beginning with the first two in this chapter. Chapter 21 will address the third assertion. And chapter 22 will treat assertions 4 and 5.

God Is One

The doctrine of the Trinity teaches both God's threeness and his oneness. The adjective *triune* refers to God as both three (*tri*) and one (*une*). So we begin our study of the Trinity by focusing on God's oneness. This is the order followed in Scripture itself: the OT puts most emphasis on God's oneness; the NT focuses far more clearly on the personal distinctions within God's being.

Theologians speak of God's unity in several senses: (1) his simplicity, which I discuss later in this chapter, (2) the unity of the persons within the Trinity, (3) the uniqueness of God's nature, sometimes called his *generic* unity, and (4) God's *numerical* oneness: the fact that there is only one of him. I will be discussing sense 2 in later contexts. Senses 3 and 4 seem to me to coalesce. When Scripture says that there is only one God, it clearly has in mind a very definite kind of God. To say that God is numerically one is to say that there is only one being with that unique nature.[6], [7] In this section, therefore, I will discuss God's unity in this sense.

---

6. I reject, therefore, the view of Paul K. Jewett, among others, that "numeric oneness" is an unwarranted addition to "generic oneness." *God, Creation, and Revelation*, 295. I also reject Jürgen Moltmann's view that "the unity of the divine tri-unity lies in the *union* of the Father, the Son and the Spirit, not in their numerical unity." *The Trinity and the Kingdom* (San Francisco: HarperSanFrancisco, 1991), 95.

7. This is also true in the finite world. Nothing can be numerically one unless it is somehow different from other beings.

In chapter 2 I mentioned the *shema* of Deuteronomy 6:4–5, the fundamental OT confession of God's covenant lordship:

> Hear, O Israel: The LORD our God, the LORD is one. You shall love the LORD your God with all your heart and with all your soul and with all your might.

Note that verse 4 is also a confession of God's oneness. That oneness is important to the covenant. There is only one covenant Lord. This passage brings together senses 3 and 4 above. God is one being (quantitatively) because there is only one Lord (qualitatively). The Lord's acts reveal his uniqueness:

> For ask now of the days that are past, which were before you, since the day that God created man on the earth, and ask from one end of heaven to the other, whether such a great thing as this has ever happened or was ever heard of. Did any people ever hear the voice of a god speaking out of the midst of the fire, as you have heard, and still live? Or has any god ever attempted to go and take a nation for himself from the midst of another nation, by trials, by signs, by wonders, and by war, by a mighty hand and an outstretched arm, and by great deeds of terror, all of which the LORD your God did for you in Egypt before your eyes? To you it was shown, that you might know that the LORD is God; there is no other besides him. (Deut. 4:32–35; cf. v. 39)

This passage, too, reveals God's unity, both numerically ("there is no other") and generically (the God who did uniquely great and awesome deeds). Similarly in Deuteronomy 32:39:

> See now that I, even I, am he,
>   and there is no god beside me;
> I kill and I make alive;
>   I wound and I heal;
>   and there is none that can deliver out of my hand.

God's oneness is related to all his lordship attributes. Only one being can be fully in control of all other beings, so that no one can deliver out of his hand. He is the God of all things in heaven, earth, and sea (Deut. 4:39; 2 Kings 19:15) because he created them all (Neh. 9:6; Mal. 2:10).

Similarly with the lordship attribute of authority:

> Thus says the LORD, the King of Israel
>   and his Redeemer, the LORD of hosts:
> "I am the first and I am the last;
>   besides me there is no god.
> Who is like me? Let him proclaim it.
>   Let him declare and set it before me,

since I appointed an ancient people.
　　Let them declare what is to come, and what will happen.
Fear not, nor be afraid;
　　have I not told you from of old and declared it?
　　And you are my witnesses!
Is there a God besides me?
　　There is no Rock; I know not any." (Isa. 44:6–8; cf. 45:21)

Only God speaks authoritatively of the past and the future. And he is the one ultimate Lawgiver and Judge (James 4:12).

God also is unique as Lord in his presence with human beings:

I am the Lord, and there is no other,
　　besides me there is no God;
　　I equip you, though you do not know me,
that people may know, from the rising of the sun
　　and from the west, that there is none besides me;
　　I am the Lord, and there is no other. (Isa. 45:5–6)

So God is the only Savior:

Turn to me and be saved,
　　all the ends of the earth!
　　For I am God, and there is no other. (Isa. 45:22)[8]

Much NT reflection on the unity of God focuses on the fact that he is God of both Jews and Gentiles, the only Savior of men, the only One who can truly bless all the nations, as he promised Abraham. See Rom. 3:29–30; Gal. 3:20;[9] 1 Tim. 2:5 (cf. Isa. 37:16). All nations are to know that he alone is God (2 Kings 19:19).

So besides the Lord, there is "no other" (cf. 2 Sam. 7:22; 1 Kings 8:60; Isa. 46:9; 1 Cor. 8:4). There is "none like [him]" (Ps. 86:8). He alone is God (2 Sam. 22:32; 2 Kings 19:19; Pss. 18:31; 86:10; Isa. 37:16). He is the only One who does wondrous works (Ps. 72:18), the only "true God" (Jer. 10:10; John 17:3; 1 Thess. 1:9), the "only wise God" (Rom. 16:27; 1 Tim. 1:17 KJV; Jude 25 KJV), the only true Father (Matt. 23:9), the only One who is good (Mark 10:18), the only source of spiritual gifts (1 Cor. 12:4–6; Eph. 4:4–6).[10]

From our previous study of the doctrine of God, it is not difficult to see that all his attributes imply his unity. Only one being can be the standard of perfection, goodness,

8. Cf. Zech. 14:9; Acts 9–10. These all teach that since there is only one God, he is God of all the nations.

9. This is a difficult passage, but I take it to mean that God worked through mediators to bring the law to Israel, conditioning blessings on Israel's response; but that in the covenant with Abraham he worked alone, unilaterally promising to bless all nations in Abraham's seed.

10. These are Trinitarian passages, distinguishing the three persons of the Godhead as the source of spiritual gifts. Note how these Trinitarian distinctions appear in passages stressing the unity of God. It is remarkable that the NT writers do not see the Trinitarian distinctions as compromising God's unity, but as reinforcing it.

love, knowledge, truth, and so on. Only one being can be the owner of all things (Gen. 14:19, 22; Ps. 24:1; etc.). All of God's attributes are unique: for example, his love is not the same as creaturely love, for it is the source and standard of all creaturely love. And all his actions are uniquely his own: only one being could be the Creator of all and the One who governs the whole course of nature and history. Only one being could govern all things by his own eternal decree.

Remarkably, Jesus Christ, God the Son, also is a divine unity, the one and only Savior and Lord. He is the way, the truth, and the life (John 14:6), the only name by which we must be saved (Acts 4:12). Eternal life is "that they know you the only true God, and Jesus Christ whom you have sent" (John 17:3).[11]

The unity of God profoundly affects the religious life of the believer. The nature of the covenant is that the vassal be exclusively loyal to one Lord. The first and second commandments of the Decalogue proscribe worship of anyone other than Yahweh, or worship of Yahweh by the use of idols. We are to worship him alone (Ex. 22:20; Isa. 42:8–9), serve him only (1 Sam. 7:3), trust him alone (2 Kings 19:19; Ps. 71:16), seek honor from him alone (John 5:44). God's unity, therefore, is not merely a numerical fact, but a central concern of piety. Before God's presence we confess that he alone is God.

God and the Gods

Scripture does sometimes refer to "gods" other than Yahweh. For example:

> Who is like you, O Lord, among the gods?
>   Who is like you, majestic in holiness,
> awesome in glorious deeds, doing wonders? (Ex. 15:11)

Cf. Ex. 18:11; 20:3, 23; 23:13; Deut. 29:26; Judg. 11:24; 1 Sam. 26:19; 2 Kings 5;[12] Pss. 82:1, 6; 96:4–5; 1 Cor. 8:5. On the basis of such passages, some writers have claimed that there are in Scripture traces of *henotheism* or *monolatry*: acknowledging the existence of many gods, but worshiping only one of them.[13]

Significantly, these writers claim that there are only *traces* of henotheism in Scripture. Clearly, the pervasive doctrine of Scripture, as we saw in the preceding section,

---

11. Note again how the Trinitarian distinction does not compromise John's emphasis on the singularity of the source of eternal life.

12. I list this passage among the others, but I really cannot understand why some writers think it teaches henotheism. Naaman does receive some kind of indulgence with regard to his (slight and forced) participation in Rimmon worship (2 Kings 5:18–19). But the real climax of the story is Naaman's *repudiation* of henotheism in verse 15: "Behold, I know that there is no God in all the earth but in Israel." He brings Israelite soil with him back home to Aram (v. 17) not, I think, because of a henotheistic belief that God's presence is limited to the land of Israel, but because he believes correctly that there is a *special* presence of God in the Holy Land and that therefore the Holy Land is the proper place to offer sacrifice. Further, even if the writer of 2 Kings represents Naaman as a henotheist, he certainly does not represent God as a henotheistic deity. The chapter begins with the affirmation that Yahweh, not Rimmon, had given victory to Aram (v. 1).

13. For example, Heinz R. Schlette, "Monotheism," in *Sacramentum Mundi: An Encyclopedia of Theology*, ed. Karl Rahner et al. (New York: Herder and Herder, 1970), 979–81. See also Weber, *Foundations of Dogmatics*, 1:355.

is that there is only one true God who rules all things. But are there a few exceptions to this pervasive emphasis? I think not. The following points are decisive:

1. If the doctrine of God's oneness means that only one being has ever been called *God*, or that only one being has ever been worshiped, then of course it is false, as these passages indicate. But as we have seen, the numerical oneness of God is also a qualitative oneness: there is only one Supreme Being and therefore only one being who truly deserves worship. In that sense, all of Scripture bears consistent witness to God's oneness.

2. The passages that refer to "gods" make this very point: God is far greater than the "gods," and he is sovereign over them. This is true even in Judges 11:24, where Jephthah seems to acknowledge that the god Chemosh gave certain lands to the Ammonites. In verse 27, Jephthah commits the dispute to the judgment of Yahweh, and Yahweh's victory is devastating to Ammon (vv. 32–33).

The term *gods* in these passages clearly means not beings that have the same nature as the true God, but beings that are far less. If *God*, therefore, refers to a being that is truly supreme in his attributes and powers, these passages, like those presented in the preceding section, teach that there is only one God.

3. The actual ontological status of the "gods" is not always clear.[14] Does Chemosh actually exist, according to Judges 11:24? Or is Jephthah speaking ironically, or by way of concession to the Ammonites' way of thinking? When Elijah challenges the priests of Baal on Mount Carmel, he refers to Baal sarcastically:

> And at noon Elijah mocked them, saying, "Cry aloud, for he is a god. Either he is musing, or he is relieving himself, or he is on a journey, or perhaps he is asleep and must be awakened." (1 Kings 18:27)

But clearly we should not derive any ontological conclusions from such prophetic humor. Many of these beings may be simply fictional, but we do not need to assume that this is always the case. Paul equates false gods with demons in 1 Corinthians 10:20. The important thing is that we recognize that these beings, fictitious or real, are those who "by nature are not gods" (Gal. 4:8). Though they are *called* "gods" (1 Cor. 8:5), they do not deserve that name and do not deserve the worship of human beings.

4. Every part of Scripture opposes the view that there are other beings somehow equal to God. In Genesis, God is the sole Creator of all things, the One who alone destroyed the earth in a flood, the One who promises to bless all the families of the earth through Abraham (Gen. 12:3) and who works all things for good (50:20) for the redemption of his people. Exodus narrates a contest between Yahweh and the "gods" of Egypt (Ex. 12:12) and declares Yahweh to be incomparable (15:11). The same is true of the conquest narratives of Joshua and Judges and of God's dealing with Israel and the nations throughout Scripture. Jesus is King of kings and Lord of lords (Rev. 19:16).

---

14. Note also that in Psalm 82:1, 6, *elohim* evidently refers to human beings in positions of authority. In that sense, of course, there are many gods; but that is not the sense at issue here.

Contemporary Critiques of Monotheism

Most dictionaries define *monotheism* somewhat as follows: "the doctrine or belief in the existence of only one God." In the primary biblical use of the term *God* to refer to the one true God, clearly Scripture is monotheistic in this sense.

Given the strong, pervasive biblical affirmation of monotheism in this sense, it is strange to see that theologian Jürgen Moltmann has engaged in "A Criticism of Christian Monotheism."[15]

He develops this critique by defining monotheism as the *monarchia* of Greek philosophy: something like the *One* of Plotinus, which excludes any plurality and therefore anything like biblical Christology. He finds a parallel between this monarchy and the nature of Allah in Muslim thought.

I agree with Moltmann that monarchy of the Plotinian/Islamic type is unbiblical. In terms of my earlier discussion, this sort of divine unity is a form of unbiblical transcendence (chapter 3), and it rules out the biblical doctrine of the Trinity as I expound it here.

But why does Moltmann insist on such an odd definition of monotheism? Evidently because he wants to draw a further equation—between the *monarchia* of Greek philosophy and the idea of an "almighty ruler of the universe."[16] But we have seen that the biblical God is exactly that: the almighty ruler of all. He is not only that; "almighty ruler" describes only his control, perhaps also his authority, but not his covenant presence. But almighty rule is clearly one aspect of his lordship, and Moltmann clearly does not want to acknowledge a God who is Lord in this sense. For him, monotheism is wrong because it implies divine lordship. So I reject his argument and similar arguments of others, and affirm biblical monotheism as I have just described it.[17]

God Is Simple

Theologians also speak of God's oneness in another sense: his *simplicity*.

Simplicity is the first divine attribute that Thomas Aquinas discusses after his proofs for God's existence in *ST*,[18] and it is frequently a basic premise in his later arguments. But I believe that the truth in these classic treatments like that of Aquinas might be

---

15. Moltmann, *The Trinity and the Kingdom*, 129–50. Cf. Weber, *Foundations of Dogmatics*, 1:353–55. Wolfhart Pannenberg, to his credit, takes issue with Moltmann's polemic against monotheism, saying that Moltmann is "guilty of a wrong terminological decision," in *Systematic Theology* (Grand Rapids: Eerdmans, 1988), 1:336n.

16. Moltmann, *The Trinity and the Kingdom*, 192. This is odd, because the One of Plotinus is identical with the universe, not the ruler over it.

17. For a longer discussion of Moltmann's argument for his position, see my *DG*, 627–31.

18. In *SCG*, after the existence of God comes an account of the importance of the way of remotion, followed by a chapter on eternity, and then a long series of chapters denying the presence in God of such things as passive potency, matter, and composition. These are all examples of the way of remotion (including eternity, which means that God has no beginning or end, and no before or after). In this series of chapters, Aquinas denies many kinds of divisions in God, and thereby establishes the divine simplicity. Indeed, even eternity is, in Aquinas's view, a form of simplicity, since it denies that God's experience of time is divided into any succession of moments.

more easily ascertained, stated, and argued from a biblical standpoint than from the standpoint of scholasticism's own natural theology.

To say that God is simple, in the scholastic philosophy, is to say that there is no *composition* in his being. Specifically, there is no composition of physical parts, form and matter, actual and potential, genus and differentia, substance and accident, God and his essence, essence and attributes, attributes and one another, essence and *esse*. God is not, then, in any sense made up of parts.

Granted that God is not a physical being, it is obvious that he is not made up of *physical* parts. Nor can he be divided into form and matter, or actuality and potentiality, since he has no matter or (passive) potentiality. Nor is he made up of genus and differentia, since he is not in a genus, nor is he a genus (godhood) differentiated by species (various gods). Nor is he made up of substance and accidents, because there are no accidents in him.[19] Since God has no accidents, everything in him is essential to his being; so he is, in a sense, his essence.

But the other claims require further consideration. It is not, indeed, entirely apparent what is meant by *parts* or *divisions* in a nonphysical being. In what way could a spiritual being conceivably be *divided* or *composed*? What would be the difference, specifically, between a spiritual being whose attributes are parts of him, and a spiritual being in which his attributes are not parts, but somehow equivalent to himself?

For Aquinas, parts are always something less than the whole, and parts can be understood and can function to some extent apart from the whole. They are in some measure independent of the whole. If they are united into a whole, they can also, because of their independence, be removed from the whole. And if they are united to a whole, this union is a process by which a potential union is caused to be actual.

Why can't there be such parts in God? (1) Because there can be nothing in him that is less, that is less noble, than himself. (2) Nothing in him can be removed from him, for nothing in him can not-be. (3) The fact that he has many attributes is not something caused, for he is the First Cause. (4) In God there can be no process of potentiality becoming actuality, because he is pure act, with no passive potentiality.[20]

So God's attributes are not parts or divisions within the Godhead in Aquinas's fairly technical sense of *parts*, but each attribute is necessary to God's being. Each is essential to him, and therefore his essence includes all of them. God cannot be God without his goodness, his wisdom, his eternity. In other words, he is necessarily good, wise, eternal. None of his attributes can be removed from him, and no new attribute can be added to him. And therefore, none of the attributes exist without the others. So each attribute *has* divine attributes; each is qualified by the others. God's wisdom is

---

19. God does, however, enter into relationships with creatures, as we have seen. These relationships are not essential to his being, for he would be God even if he had not chosen to create the world. I am assuming, therefore, that it is possible to distinguish between God's *necessary* or *defining* attributes (essential to his being) and other predications that describe God in his relationships with creatures. I have made this distinction at various points in our study of the divine attributes.

20. These arguments are paraphrased from Aquinas, *SCG*, 1.18.

an eternal wisdom, his goodness a wise goodness and (importantly) a just goodness. And his *esse* is a necessary existence, necessary to his essence. Granted who God is, he cannot fail to exist.

Note that these arguments do not rule out all complexity within the divine nature. Imagine a distinguishable aspect of God's nature (such as an attribute or a person of the Trinity) that is no less noble than himself, that cannot be removed from him, that necessarily belongs to him apart from any causal process, that is not the result of a movement from potentiality to actuality. It would not be inconsistent with the doctrine of simplicity above for God to have many such aspects. Indeed, since simplicity in this sense does not rule out all multiplicity, it might be less confusing to use the term *necessary existence* rather than the term *simplicity*.

But Aquinas sometimes seems to deny any complexity at all in God. He argues, for example,[21] that unity must always be prior to multiplicity, so that God, who is prior to everything, must have no multiplicity. Elsewhere in *SCG*,[22] he argues that the different names we use for God are not synonymous, though they refer to God's simple being. He denies that such names compromise God's simplicity, not by arguing that there are genuine complexities and pluralities in God, to which the different names refer, but by arguing that the plurality is in our minds: we must conceive of the simple being of God by "diverse conceptions." On this view, it is not enough to say that God's attributes, for example, are necessary to his being; rather, the multiplicity of attributes is only apparent. In reality, God is a being without any multiplicity at all, a simple being for whom any language suggesting complexity, distinctions, or multiplicity is entirely unsuited.

That is essentially the Plotinian neo-Platonic view, in which the best name of God is *One*. In the preceding section, I criticized Moltmann for equating this notion with monotheism. For Plotinus, even the name *One* is inadequate, since God is utterly beyond the descriptive power of human language. But *One* is the best we can do, since unity is prior to multiplicity and more noble than multiplicity.

Aquinas argues well for the necessity of God's being. But his argument for a total absence of multiplicity in God is quite inadequate. A biblical Trinitarian cannot argue, for example, that in every respect unity is prior to multiplicity. Nor can he argue that diversity in God is only apparent, only a diversity within our own minds. In Scripture, as we will see, God is one and many, and the balance of unity and diversity in God ensures the balance of unity and diversity within the created world.

Aquinas does, of course, affirm the creedal statements concerning the Trinity. His analysis of the Trinity in terms of subsistent relations, however (as we will see later), plays down the distinctions between the Trinitarian persons. Thomists argue that their view of simplicity is consistent with the Trinity because simplicity pertains not to the three persons, but to the divine nature that they all share. But Aquinas's concept

---

21. Ibid.
22. *SCG*, 1.35.2.

of simplicity influences his understanding of the Trinitarian persons, and I don't see how that can really be avoided. I do not believe we can make such a neat separation between nature and persons.

Certainly the persons are essential to God's being, just as essential as any attribute. It is not evident to me why *triunity* should not be considered an attribute of God along with the others. Certainly it is true to say that God's being is triune.

Where does our discussion leave us, then? With a doctrine of God's necessary existence rather than a doctrine of simplicity as such. But if we turn away from the scholastic metaphysics and look to Scripture, we might be able to learn something more.

Consider how Scripture sometimes employs the language of divine attributes: "God is spirit" (John 4:24), "God is light" (1 John 1:5), "God is love" (4:8, 16). These expressions state what God really and truly is. In other words, they describe his essence, not merely what he happens to be on some occasions. But note that there are three of these attributions, not just one. So God's essence can be described in three different ways. I am inclined to say that these expressions describe the whole divine essence from three different perspectives.[23]

Is it likely that God's holiness, for example, is less essential to his being than spirit, light, and love? In Psalm 89:35 and Amos 4:2, God swears by his holiness. Certainly he is not here swearing by something lower than himself, and he can swear by nothing higher. For God to swear by his holiness can be nothing more or less than for him to swear by himself (see Heb. 6:13). He is the Holy One.

Similarly, God's truth and his character as the "living" God distinguish him from all false gods (e.g., Jer. 10:10). So these, too, tell who he essentially is. He *cannot* prove false (Num. 23:19; 2 Tim. 2:13; Titus 1:2; Heb. 6:18). And obviously, he cannot die.

Is it possible, then, that God could renounce, or be robbed of, his lordship? Could he be the same God without his control, authority, and presence? I think not. The biblical passages dealing with these and related attributes such as his personality, goodness, loving-kindness, and so on present these as qualities that can never fail, without which God would not be God.[24]

God's essence is not some dark, unrevealed entity behind God's revealed character. Rather, God's revelation tells us his essence. It tells us what he really and truly is.

---

23. Herman Bavinck approaches a perspectival formulation when he says that "we cannot possibly form a picture of the infinite fullness of God's essence unless it is displayed to us now in one relationship, then in another, and now from one angle, then from another." *BRD*, 2:127. He cites Augustine, P. Vermigli, and B. de Moor in this connection.

24. I realize, of course, that lordship and the lordship attributes are relational attributes: attributes that characterize God's relationship with creatures. It might be argued, therefore, that these are not part of God's essence. Had God determined not to create the world—and he was free to make that choice—he would not have been Lord. True. But the essence of God is such that in his creation, in relation to his creatures, he cannot be anything other than Lord. So his lordship, with its lordship attributes, though not necessary in themselves, is grounded in God's essential nature. We can say that lordship is an essential attribute of God in that it is the quality of his nature by which he necessarily is Lord to any creature.

The passages above do not show that *all* of God's attributes are necessary to his being and perspectives on that being, but they do provide a pattern and a way of thinking about divine attributes to which it is hard to find plausible exceptions.

But does this pattern justify talk of simplicity? If the attributes are perspectives on a single reality, that reality will be simple by comparison, though also complex, as I must keep insisting. And evidently, since there are many attributes that all characterize God's essence, these attributes are not separate from one another. Indeed, all of God's attributes have divine attributes! God's mercy is eternal, his creative power wise. So the biblical teachings about God's attributes suggest a profound unity in God's nature and among the attributes that characterize his nature.

This is not to say that God's attributes are synonymous. They all refer to God's essence, but they describe different aspects of it. God really is good *and* just *and* omniscient. The multiple attributes refer to genuine complexities in God's essence.

But it is important to see the unity within this complexity. And to see it, we should remind ourselves that our covenant Lord is a person. What is God's *goodness*? Is it something *in* God? It is more accurate, I think, to say, that *divine goodness*, though it sounds like an abstract property, is really just a way of referring to everything God is. For everything God does is good, and everything he is is good. All his attributes are good. All his decrees are good. All his actions are good. There is nothing in God that is not good.[25]

To praise God's goodness is not to praise something other than God himself. It is not to praise something less than God, a part of him, so to speak. It is to praise him. God's goodness is not something that is intelligible in itself apart from everything else God is.

God's goodness is the standard of our goodness. We are to image God's goodness. Does that mean that we are to image some abstract property that is somehow attached to God or present *in* God somewhere? No; it means that we are to image God himself. Our moral standard is not an impersonal, abstract property.[26] It is a person, the living God. The center of biblical morality is that we should be like him. As I argued earlier in this book, covenant lordship means personalism. The personal is prior to the impersonal. God's personal goodness defines any legitimate abstract concept of goodness.

God relates to us as a whole person, not as a collection of attributes. The attributes merely describe different things about that person. They are a kind of shorthand for talking about that person. Everything he says and does is good, right, true, eternal, wise, and so on.

As we will see, the triunity of God does not conflict with his simplicity, understood as I have described it. Each of the three persons is "in" the other two (*circumincessio*),

25. Eberhard Jüngel, in *God as the Mystery of the World* (Grand Rapids: Eerdmans, 1983), 314, says strikingly that if we do not *define* God as love, then the essence of God is unloving and God is a monster.

26. Some have objected that the doctrine of simplicity, by which God's attributes are identical with himself, makes God equivalent to abstract properties. But the equation can point us in the other direction: not that God is reduced to *goodness*, but that *goodness* is seen to be God himself. Of course, the equation is between God and his own goodness, divine goodness, not between God and goodness in general.

and therefore each exhausts the divine nature, just as every attribute includes the whole divine nature. But each of the three persons is distinct from the other two, as each attribute is distinct from the others. Of course, there are important differences between God's attributes and the distinctions of persons within the Trinity. Attributes and persons are not the same.[27] But the relationship between unity and multiplicity is the same in regard to persons as it is in regard to attributes.

It seems to me, therefore, that there is a legitimate biblical motive in the doctrine of simplicity. We might be surprised to find that it is not an abstract, obscure, philosophical motive, but a very practical one. Those emerging from the murky waters of scholastic speculation might be surprised to find that the doctrine of simplicity is really fairly simple. It is a biblical way of reminding us that God's relationship with us is fully personal.

So the simplicity of God, like all his other attributes, sets forth his covenant lordship. It reminds us of the unity of our covenant Lord, and the unity that he brings into our lives as we seek to honor him and him alone. The Christian is not devoted to some abstract philosophical goodness, but to the living Lord of heaven and earth.

To my mind, the biblical approach to this issue is far more edifying and persuasive than the scholastic natural theology such as we saw in Aquinas. In Scripture, there is no compromise of the Trinity, no compromise of the centrality of God's covenant lordship.

God Is Three

But alongside biblical monotheism there is another biblical theme that stresses that God is not a *mere* oneness. He is not like the *One* of Plotinus, who lacks any complexity at all. Though God is numerically one and simple, he has many attributes, as we have seen, thinks a vast number of thoughts, and performs innumerable actions. His attributes are one, but a oneness that can be characterized in many ways. His thoughts are one, but they are thoughts about innumerable objects. His actions are one, but they have vast numbers of effects in the world. His life is the ultimate in richness and fullness. Scripture expresses this richness in various ways, eventually bringing into focus its specifically Trinitarian character.

We will begin with phenomena found mostly in the OT, and then move on to see the fulfillment in the NT of this incipient Trinitarianism. B. B. Warfield's comment about the nature of the OT testimony is valuable:

> The Old Testament may be likened to a chamber richly furnished but dimly lighted; the introduction of light brings into it nothing which was not in it before; but it brings out into clearer view much of what is in it but was only dimly or even not at all perceived before. The mystery of the Trinity is not revealed in the Old Testament; but the mystery of the Trinity underlies the Old Testament revelation, and here and there almost comes into view. Thus the Old Testament

---

27. As we will see, however, the relationship between attributes and persons in Scripture is very close. See the discussion of hypostatizations in the next section.

revelation is not corrected by the fuller revelation which follows it, but only perfected, extended and enlarged.[28]

Plurals

The very greatness of God, the richness of his inner life, entails some kind of plurality within him. Perhaps that multifaceted greatness, the sheer vastness of his power and wisdom, has something to do with the use of plural nouns for him in the OT: not only *elohim* but also *panim* ("face," "presence"), as in Exodus 33:11. In *DG*, chapter 17, I analyzed the plural form of *elohim* in terms of "abstraction" and "amplification": *elohim* refers to God as generic deity, but also, perhaps, as the ultimate or supreme, rich in being. *Elohim* usually takes a singular verb, but takes plural verbs in the following verses: Gen. 20:13; 35:7; Ex. 32:4; Neh. 9:18; Isa. 16:6. Note also the plural forms of *'adon* in Malachi 1:6, of *Creator* (two Hebrew terms) in Psalm 149:2 ("Maker," esv, niv) and Ecclesiastes 12:1, and of *ba'al* (referring to God as "husband") in Isaiah 54:5. The "seven spirits" of Revelation 1:4; 3:1; 4:5; and 5:6 are evidently an intensive reference to the Holy Spirit.

God also sometimes speaks in the plural as in "Let us make man in our image" (Gen. 1:26; cf. 3:22; 11:6). Perhaps we are to understand this language as a consultation of the heavenly council, the glory-cloud that we discussed in chapter 18. But even that is to underscore the fact that when God appeared to human beings in the OT, he appeared as a rich diversity of form, movement, and sound, interacting dynamically with the heavenly beings and with his spatiotemporal creation.

We should not try to derive any precise doctrinal content from these grammatical peculiarities. In every language, plural forms sometimes denote singular realities (such as *pants* in English). I do think it significant, however, that the writers and characters of the OT, emphatic monotheists, do not object to these plural forms or try to avoid them, even though the language offered them alternatives. In the text, there is no evident embarrassment. That suggests that they regarded God not as a bare unity, but as a unity of many things.

Hypostatizations

The OT refers to a number of beings that are somehow identical to, yet distinguished from, God. These are sometimes described as *hypostatizations* or *personifications* of divine attributes.

The *word* of God is certainly divine (see chapter 23), an object of praise (Ps. 56:4, 10). Yet it is also God's tool in his making and governing of the world: *by* the word of the Lord were the heavens made (Ps. 33:6). He "sends" his word (Ps. 147:18; cf. Pss. 107:20; 148:8). His word "goes out" of his mouth to accomplish his purposes (Isa. 55:11). So the OT establishes a unity and difference between God and his word. In intertestamental and Hellenistic Judaism, *Word* becomes a kind of intermediary between God and the

---

28. B. B. Warfield, "The Biblical Doctrine of the Trinity," in *Biblical Doctrines* (Grand Rapids: Baker, 1981), 141–42. This is an enormously helpful article on the subject, of which I have made much use in writing this section.

world, a link in the great chain of being.[29] But the NT restores it to the fully divine status it deserves, identifying the Word with Christ (John 1:1–14). So the OT hypostatization is fulfilled in NT Trinitarianism.

In Scripture there is a close relationship between God's *word* and his *wisdom*. The OT also hypostatizes God's wisdom in Proverbs 3:19: "The Lᴏʀᴅ by wisdom founded the earth; by understanding he established the heavens." Wisdom is a divine attribute, but it is also that *by which* God made the world. Also, in Proverbs 8:1–9:12, God's wisdom takes the form of a lady (see chapter 15), calling men to fear the Lord and hate evil. Cf. also Jer. 10:12; 51:15. As with *Word*, the NT identifies *wisdom* with Christ (1 Cor. 1:30), so again the hypostatization anticipates somewhat the doctrine of the Trinity.

God's *name* is another example of this phenomenon. The name of God is God himself,[30] but he saves us *by* his name (Isa. 30:27; 50:10), guides us for his name's sake (Ps. 23:3), and makes his name to dwell in a place (Deut. 12:5). Jesus is the fulfillment of God's name, the name to which every knee will bow (Phil. 2:10).

God's *glory*, as we saw in chapter 18, is a divine attribute, but also a visible form by which God manifests himself to creatures. God exists above time and space, but his glory resides in heaven, and also in earthly places of his choosing (Deut. 26:15; Ezek. 43:4–7).

Divine Persons in the Old Testament

God's *Spirit* is closely related to his glory, as we saw in chapter 18. Clearly, the Spirit is divine; he is God at work in the world. But the OT also makes a distinction between God and the Spirit, as in Genesis 1:2, when God creates and the Spirit hovers over the waters. The Spirit is the *breath* (*ruach*) by which the Word accomplished its creative purpose (Ps. 33:6). God creates *by* his Spirit (Job 26:13). As with the Word, God *sends* the Spirit to do his bidding (Ps. 104:30). The Spirit enters the prophets so that they can hear and speak God's word (2 Sam. 23:2; Ezek. 2:2; cf. Zech. 7:12). Obviously, this use of *Spirit* finds its fulfillment in NT Trinitarianism, as the Spirit comes upon the church from the Father and the Son.

The phrases *angel of the Lord* and *Angel of God* (even, sometimes, simply *angel*) often refer to a divine being. Not every angel in Scripture is divine: in Revelation 19:10 and 22:9, an angel refuses worship and tells John to worship God instead.[31] But in many cases, the angel is God. Appearing to Hagar, the angel speaks as God, making covenant

---

29. *Great chain of being* refers to a theme of philosophy, especially among the Greeks: that the relation between the supreme being and the world is not creation, but emanation. In emanation, the supreme being makes the world by sending forth his own essence or being, so that the world is essentially divine. The "chain" is the whole series of divine emanations.

30. See *DG*, chap. 17.

31. My list of passages in which the angel is a divine being would, however, be somewhat longer than Bavinck's in *BRD*, 2:262. I am not as certain as he that "an ordinary angel is meant" in 2 Samuel 24:16; 1 Kings 19:5–7; and other passages. In 2 Samuel 24:16, to be sure, God tells the angel to cease his destruction, but that is not inconsistent with a relation between God and a divine angel.

with her and her children (Gen. 16:6–13; 21:17–20). In Genesis 22:11–12, the angel tells Abraham that "you have not withheld your son, your only son, from *me*." In 31:11–13, the angel identifies himself as "the God of Bethel." In 32:30, Jacob says of the man (called an "angel" in Hosea 12:4) who wrestled with him that "I have seen God face to face, and yet my life has been delivered." See also Gen. 48:15–16; Ex. 3:2–22; 13:21 (14:19; 32:34); 23:20–23; Num. 20:16; Isa. 63:8–9; Zech. 1:8–12; Mal. 3:1. But in Exodus 23:20 and 32:34, God distinguishes himself from the divine angel. The angel is one whom God is "sending" (23:20).

The *Messiah* is a human deliverer, a son of David, but also God. He is the servant of the Lord who suffers to bear the sins of his people (Isa. 52:13–53:12). But in the final analysis, no mere human can save Israel from its sins. Only God's own arm can bring salvation (Isa. 59:15–20; cf. 43:3, 11; 45:15, 21; 49:26; 60:16; 63:8). Salvation is of the Lord (Jonah 2:9). So the coming King is called God in Psalm 45:6, but is distinguished from God in verse 7. And in Psalm 110:1, a verse applied to Christ several times in the NT, David's messianic son is also his Lord:

> The LORD says to my Lord:
>   "Sit at my right hand,
> until I make your enemies your footstool."

Triads in the Old Testament

So far we have considered various attributes and personal beings in the OT that are divine, yet distinguished from God. But the number three, essential to the doctrine of the Trinity, has not yet entered the discussion.

There is something mysteriously captivating to the human mind about the number three. Threefold repetitions and distinctions abound in human life and speech, both in Scripture and outside it. I have a file containing hundreds of these, including not only theological triads such as *Prophet*, *Priest*, and *King*, but also physical ones such as *solid*, *liquid*, *vapor*, mental ones such as Augustine's *memory*, *understanding*, *will*, and so on, not to mention, of course, the lordship attributes (*control*, *authority*, *presence*) and my three perspectives, *normative*, *situational*, and *existential*.[32]

I'm not sure how all this is related to the doctrine of the Trinity, but I would be surprised were I to discover that there is no significant connection at all. I will explore later some of the connections that I consider valid and helpful. Nevertheless, as we survey some triads in the OT, it would not be wise for us to take all of them simply as adumbrations of the Trinity. To some extent, these triads are like the plural forms that we discussed earlier: they serve to "amplify" what is being said, to raise the language to a level worthy of deity. The threefold formulation suggests completeness, fulfillment. We sense fulfillment when manifoldness (two) terminates in completeness (three).

---

32. For a list of these, see Appendix A of *DG*.

But of course, that amplification, that completeness, itself finds its fulfillment in the doctrine of the Trinity. God is the threefold God, life at its greatest amplification, its greatest fulfillment. God's full nature and attributes are best displayed in the unity of love, knowledge, and power among the three persons.

Earlier, we considered some OT divine attributes and personal theophanies that find fulfillment in NT Trinitarianism. From a NT vantage point, we can align these with the Father, Son, and Spirit: clearly, *Word* and *Messiah* should be identified with the Son, *Spirit* with the Spirit. But *glory* surely pertains to all three persons, as does *wisdom*. In any case, the OT does not place these attributes and personal theophanies into a distinctly triadic order.

Nevertheless, we can find triads of various sorts in the OT. As with the other OT texts that we have considered, these do not imply a precise or detailed doctrine of the Trinity, but they are important for what they contribute to the full Trinitarian doctrine of the NT.

The Aaronic benediction, by which God places his name on Israel, is threefold:

> The Lord bless you and keep you; the Lord make his face to shine upon you and be gracious to you; the Lord lift up his countenance upon you and give you peace. (Num. 6:24–26)

Note the threefold repetition of "Lord."[33] This passage may be the model of the explicitly Trinitarian apostolic benediction of 2 Corinthians 13:14:

> The grace of the Lord Jesus Christ and the love of God and the fellowship of the Holy Spirit be with you all.

In Isaiah 6:3, the angels sing, "Holy, holy, holy is the Lord of hosts." The threefold repetition amplifies God's holiness, indicates that God's holiness is vast, far beyond any creaturely holiness.

In Isaiah 33:22, the prophet says:

> For the Lord is our judge; the Lord is our lawgiver;
>   the Lord is our king; he will save us.

This is a threefold repetition of "Lord," ascribing to him three offices that, interestingly, correlate with the three functions of modern governments.[34] His government of the world is all-encompassing. For other threefold references to God, see Jeremiah 33:2 and Daniel 9:19. Cf. Rev. 1:4–5; 4:8.

---

33. Note also that the concepts of *grace* in the second clause and *peace* in the third anticipate the typical NT apostolic blessing: "Grace be to you and peace."

34. These also correlate with the lordship attributes: King = control, Lawgiver = authority, Judge = present in blessing and judgment.

Old Testament Triads of Divine Beings

We saw earlier some beings, such as *word* and *wisdom*, that are divine, yet somehow distinct from God. So God is able to "send forth" his word or to create the world "by" his wisdom. God and his word are one, but also two. Same with regard to God and his wisdom. But there are also passages where three such divine beings are brought together. These passages anticipate the doctrine of the Trinity in a special way.

In Psalm 33:6, we read:

> By the word of the LORD the heavens were made,
>   and by the breath of his mouth all their host.

Here we find together the Lord, his word, and his breath (= Spirit, *ruach*). This is what I have sometimes called the *linguistic model of the Trinity*. The Father is the speaker, the Son the word (John 1:1–14), and the Spirit the breath that carries the word to the hearer.

Isaiah 48:16 reads:

> "Draw near to me, hear this:
>   from the beginning I have not spoken in secret,
>   from the time it came to be I have been there."
> And now the Lord GOD has sent me, and his Spirit.

The speaker is Yahweh, as the preceding context indicates. But the verse says that Yahweh has been sent by someone else called "the Lord GOD," together with another called "his Spirit." From a NT vantage point, we can see this text as a Trinitarian one. Interestingly, the following verse adds: "Thus says the LORD, your Redeemer, the Holy One of Israel," a threefold self-description corresponding somewhat to the Trinitarian persons (cf. 44:6).

In Isaiah 63:9–10, we read:

> In all their affliction he was afflicted,
>   and the angel of his presence saved them;
> in his love and in his pity he redeemed them;
>   he lifted them up and carried them all the days of old.
>
> But they rebelled
>   and grieved his Holy Spirit;
> therefore he turned to be their enemy,
>   and himself fought against them.

Here we read of Yahweh, the angel of his presence, and his Holy Spirit. The angel, of course, is the divine being who, we noted earlier, led Israel through the wilderness.

In Haggai 2:5–7, Yahweh says:

[I am with you] according to the covenant that I made with you when you came out of Egypt. My Spirit remains in your midst. Fear not. For thus says the LORD of hosts: Yet once more, in a little while, I will shake the heavens and the earth and the sea and the dry land. And I will shake all nations, so that the treasures of all nations shall come in, and I will fill this house with glory, says the LORD of hosts.

Here the Lord affirms that his Spirit remains in Israel and that the "treasures of all nations," the Messiah, will come, bringing glory to the temple. The Lord, the Messiah, and the Spirit correspond to the Trinity of the NT.

Divine Persons in the New Testament

For all the adumbrations of Trinity in the OT, much therein remains unclear. For example, from the data of the OT alone, it would be difficult, if not impossible, to determine how many divine beings there are. One might well ask whether *word, wisdom, name, glory, angel, Messiah,* and *spirit* designate seven distinct divine beings and, if not, what the relationships among them are. Is the triad *Lord, word, breath* (Ps. 33:6) the same as the triad *Lord, angel, Spirit* (Isa. 63:7–10)?

In the NT, however, the writers are clearly settled on the existence of three divine persons, called *Father, Son,* and *Spirit.* To the *Son* applies what the OT ascribed to *word, wisdom, name, Messiah,* and, most likely, the *divine angel* as well. So the NT brings vastly more clarity into our understanding of these persons. In that way the NT is very different from the OT. Yet as Warfield points out, the NT writers sense no tension between their teaching and that of the OT:

> To their own apprehension they worshiped and proclaimed just the God of Israel; and they laid no less stress than the OT itself upon His unity (John 17:3; 1 Cor. 8:4; 1 Tim. 2:5).[35] They do not, then, place two new gods by the side of Jehovah as alike with him to be served and worshiped; they conceive Jehovah as at once Father, Son, and Spirit. In presenting this one Jehovah as Father, Son, and Spirit, they do not even betray any lurking feeling that they are making innovations. Without apparent misgiving they take over OT passages and apply them to Father, Son, and Spirit indifferently.[36]

There is, then, no controversy in the NT that its Trinitarianism is consistent with the OT. Indeed, for the NT writers, as Warfield also points out, the Trinity is settled doctrine:

35. I would note, though Warfield doesn't do so here, the remarkable fact that these passages, which stress divine unity, also distinguish between two or more persons of the Trinity (note vv. 5–6 after 1 Cor. 8:4; cf. also Eph. 4:3–6). One might have thought that the writers would avoid making Trinitarian distinctions when they are writing about God's oneness, out of fear that to mention God's threeness in such a context would obscure the point being made. Yet the NT writers not only think that Trinitarianism is consistent with divine unity, but also seem to think that God's threeness somehow *underscores* his unity. Perhaps the thought is that we can see the oneness of God even more clearly when we see him as three persons working in perfect harmony.

36. Warfield, "The Biblical Doctrine of the Trinity," 142.

> If they betray no sense of novelty in so speaking [of God as a Trinity], this is undoubtedly in part because it was no longer a novelty so to speak of Him. It is clear, in other words, that, as we read the New Testament, we are not witnessing the birth of a new conception of God. What we meet within its pages is a firmly established conception of God underlying and giving tone to the entire fabric. It is not in a text here and there that the New Testament bears its testimony to the doctrine of the Trinity. The whole book is Trinitarian to the core; all its teaching is built on the assumption of the Trinity; and its allusions to the Trinity are frequent, cursory, easy and confident. It is with a view to the cursoriness of the allusions to it in the New Testament that it has been remarked that "the doctrine of the Trinity is not so much heard as overheard in the statements of Scripture." It would be more exact to say that it is not so much inculcated as presupposed. The doctrine of the Trinity does not appear in the NT in the making, but as already made.[37]

So in the NT there is no systematic, point-by-point exposition of the doctrine of the Trinity, like the exposition of justification in Romans 3–5. The NT gives systematic attention to doctrines that were controversial in the early church. Evidently the Trinity was not. It appears there "in full completeness,"[38] accepted by all.

So something remarkable has happened between the completion of the OT and the first writings of the NT. What was vaguely intimated in the OT has become a clear, settled doctrine in the NT, needing no elaborate definition or defense. Of course, what happened is obvious: the Son of God became flesh, and the Holy Spirit came upon the church with power. The events of Christmas and Pentecost changed everything. Jesus "came from the Father" (John 16:28), and he sent the Spirit from the Father (15:26). All the blessings of salvation come through those three persons. Jesus died for sinners, rose again, and ascended to glory. The Spirit empowered the church for its universal mission. It was these epochal events that brought all the OT divine attributes, hypostatizations, triads, and persons together in Father, Son, and Spirit. So the church naturally came to praise, thank, and worship these three. And its teaching about salvation continually revolved around the work of the Father, the Son, and the Spirit.

So everything in the NT is about the Father, Son, and Spirit.[39] In the birth narratives, Jesus is conceived by the Holy Spirit (Matt. 1:18, 20; Luke 1:35) and thus comes to be "God with us" (Matt. 1:23), the "Son of God" (Luke 1:35). At his baptism, the three persons are present: Jesus, the Spirit descending as a dove (Matt. 3:16; Luke 3:22), and the Father speaking from heaven, "This is my beloved Son, with whom I am well pleased" (Matt. 3:17; cf. Matt. 17:5; Luke 3:22).

In Matthew 4 and Luke 4, the Spirit leads Jesus into the wilderness, where Satan tempts him. The temptation is essentially an invitation to Jesus (as to Adam in Genesis 3) to serve Satan rather than the Father (see Matt. 4:4, 7, 10). Jesus then returns to

---

37. Ibid., 143.
38. Ibid., quoting Gunkel.
39. I can only scratch the surface in this survey of NT Trinitarian teaching. I will enter into more depth later in my discussions of the deity of Christ and the Holy Spirit and of other Trinitarian issues (chapters 28–29).

Galilee "in the power of the Spirit" (Luke 4:14) and announces in the synagogue that he fulfills Isaiah 61:1–2: The Spirit of the Lord is upon him (Luke 4:18) to proclaim the year of the Lord's (the Father's) favor (v. 19). He casts out devils by the Spirit of God (Matt. 12:28) to show that the kingdom of God (the Father) has come. Compare Acts 10:38, where Peter speaks of "how God anointed Jesus of Nazareth with the Holy Spirit and with power. He went about doing good."

The richest Trinitarian teaching in the Gospels is in the Johannine discourses preceding Jesus' atoning death. Here Jesus expresses eternal intimacy with the Father (John 17, esp. vv. 5, 10–11, 22, 26) and promises to send upon the church the Holy Spirit from the Father (and his own coming to them *in* the Spirit) (14:16–18, 26; 15:26; 16:13–15; 20:21–22).

After his resurrection, Jesus commissions his disciples to make disciples and baptize them "in the name of the Father and of the Son and of the Holy Spirit" (Matt. 28:19). One name, applying to three divine beings, coordinate with each other. Remember that baptism in the NT is into the name of God, not into the name of any creature (1 Cor. 1:14–15).

In Acts 2:33, Jesus fulfills his promise:

> Being therefore exalted at the right hand of God, and having received from the Father the promise of the Holy Spirit, he has poured out this that you yourselves are seeing and hearing.

So Peter urges the people:

> Repent and be baptized every one of you in the name of Jesus Christ for the forgiveness of your sins, and you will receive the gift of the Holy Spirit. For the promise is for you and for your children and for all who are far off, everyone whom the Lord our God calls to himself. (Acts 2:38–39)

The Father offers the Holy Spirit to all who embrace the Son in faith. Cf. also Acts 9:17–20 (in the conversion of Saul).

Paul makes a rich use of Trinitarian formulations. It is helpful to remember that in his usual vocabulary, *theos* (God) represents the Father, *kyrios* (Lord) or *huios* (Son) the Son, and *pneuma* the Spirit. So a passage such as 1 Corinthians 12:4–6 or Ephesians 4:4–6 that distinguishes "one Spirit . . . one Lord . . . one God" is deeply Trinitarian.[40]

The first part of Paul's letter to the Romans may be said to have a Trinitarian structure: the judgment of God the Father upon sin (1:18–3:20), the atoning work of the Son

---

40. This vocabulary explains why Paul distinguishes Jesus from *theos*, "God." Paul does this not to cast any doubt on the full deity of Christ, but simply to distinguish the Son from the Father. Indeed, I believe that he does sometimes use *theos* for Christ (Rom. 9:5; 2 Thess. 1:12; Titus 2:13), but his general practice is not to do so. Nevertheless, the term that he typically applies to Christ, *kyrios*, is as strong a divine title as *theos*, perhaps even more so, in the light of its connection with *Yahweh* in the LXX translation of the OT. See later discussion of the deity of Christ.

by which God justifies and sanctifies the ungodly (3:21–7:25), and the freedom and assurance of the Spirit (8:1–39). Paul mentions the three persons together in 1:1–4; 5:1–5, 5–8; 6:4;[41] 8:1–4, 8–9, 11, 14–17; 15:16 and 30. See also 1 Cor. 6:11; 8:6; 12:4–6; 2 Cor. 1:21–22; 3:3–4; 13:14,[42] Gal. 4:6;[43] Eph. 1:3–14;[44] 2:18, 22; 3:2–5, 14–17; 4:4–6; 5:18–20; Phil. 3:3; Col. 1:6–7; 3:16–17; 1 Thess. 1:2–6; 5:18–19; 2 Thess. 2:13–14; 1 Tim. 3:15–16; Titus 3:4–6.

Other NT writers also bring together the persons of the Trinity in their accounts of God's salvation: Heb. 2:3–4; 6:4–6; 9:14; 10:29–31; 1 Peter 1:2; 4:13–19; 1 John 4:2, 13–14; 5:6–12; Jude 20–21; Rev. 1:4–5.[45] Notice also in Revelation 13 a satanic counterfeit of the Trinity: (1) a dragon, (2) a beast (healed of a fatal wound) who receives great power and authority from the dragon (vv. 2–3), and (3) a second beast (vv. 11–18) who makes everyone worship the first beast, and who works miraculous signs.

The NT also contains many passages in which two of the three persons appear as the common source of blessing: Father and Son (Rom. 6:4; 1 Cor. 15:24–28); Christ and the Spirit in close parallel (John 14:16, 18, 23; Acts 16:7; Rom. 8:2, 9; 2 Cor. 3:17; Gal. 4:6; Phil. 1:19; 1 Peter 1:10–11; cf. Gal. 3:3; 5:16, 25). Note the apostolic greetings and benedictions in the following passages: 1 Cor. 1:3; 2 Cor. 1:2; Gal. 1:3; Eph. 1:3; 6:23–24; 1 Thess. 1:1; 2 Thess. 1:2; 1 Tim. 1:2; 2 Tim. 1:2; Titus 1:4. These blessings are always from God our Father and our Lord Jesus Christ (except 2 Corinthians 13:14, where Paul names all three persons).

In the following chapter, I will take a closer look at the biblical teaching concerning the deity of Christ and the Spirit, and those studies will reinforce the pervasiveness of Trinitarian teaching in the Scriptures. I will also examine something of the distinct ministries of the persons and their unity in these ministries. But it should already be evident that the NT holds a profoundly Trinitarian view of God.

The main thrust of these passages is that all three persons bring us salvation and equally deserve our praise and thanks. They are together in the ministry of the prophets and in Jesus: in his words and miracles, his resurrection from the dead. And they are together in the Spirit's work of illumination, conviction, adoption, sanctification, and glorification. As Warfield pointed out, these passages are not formal teaching about the Trinity. Rather, they teach about other matters, but almost subconsciously take on a Trinitarian form. So the doctrine of the Trinity is "overheard." Let us take one passage as an example. In 1 Corinthians 12:4–6, Paul says:

41. Here Paul uses *glory* rather than *Spirit*; but as we have seen, these concepts are closely related.

42. A benediction, threefold as in Numbers 6:24–26, coordinating the three persons as the ultimate source of all spiritual blessings.

43. The NIV titles Galatians 3:26–4:7 "Sons of God," 5:1–15 "Freedom in Christ," and 5:16–26 "Life by the Spirit." I think these titles are appropriate to the content. The intervening sections 4:8–20 ("Paul's Concern for the Galatians") and 4:21–31 ("Hagar and Sarah") are arguably subdivisions of the "Sons of God" theme.

44. Note the focus on the Father's election in Ephesians 1:3–6 (recapitulated in verses 11–12), the work of Christ in verses 7–10, the seal of the Spirit in verses 13–14.

45. This passage presents several intensive triadic structures: a threefold reference to the Father as he "who is and who was and who is to come," an intensively plural reference to the Holy Spirit as "the seven spirits who are before the throne," and a threefold reference to Jesus, "the faithful witness, the firstborn of the dead, and the ruler of kings on earth."

Now there are varieties of gifts, but the same Spirit; and there are varieties of service, but the same Lord; and there are varieties of activities, but it is the same God who empowers [*energematon*] them all in everyone.

Warfield comments:

It may be thought that there is a measure of what might be called artificiality in assigning the endowments of the church, as they are graces to the Spirit, as they are services to Christ, and as they are energizings to God. But thus there is only more strikingly revealed the underlying Trinitarian conception as dominating the structure of the clauses: Paul clearly so writes, not because "gifts," "workings," "operations," stand out in his thought as greatly diverse things, but because God, the Lord, and the Spirit lie in the back of his mind constantly suggesting a threefold causality behind every manifestation of grace. The Trinity is alluded to rather than asserted; but it is so alluded to as to show that it constitutes the determining basis of all Paul's thought of the God of redemption.[46]

The full proof of the proposition "God is three" awaits our study of the deity of Christ and the Spirit, to which we now proceed. But from our present study we should expect to find a common status for the Father, Son, and Spirit. All three stand together as Creator and Savior. Scripture joins them together in contexts of praise and thanksgiving. They are the ultimate object of the believer's trust and hope. What else can they possibly be than one somehow threefold God?

Key Terms
Ad intra
Ad extra
Godhead
Simplicity
Generic unity
Numerical oneness
Monotheism
Henotheism
Monolatry
Monarchia
Way of remotion
Hypostatizations
Personifications
Great chain of being
Emanation

46. Warfield, "The Biblical Doctrine of the Trinity," 159. Concerning 2 Corinthians 13:14, he comments, "[Paul] . . . does not say, as he might just as well have said, 'The grace and love and communion of God be with you all,' but 'The grace of the Lord Jesus Christ, and the love of God, and the communion of the Holy Spirit, be with you all.' Thus he bears, almost unconsciously but most richly, witness to the trinal composition of the Godhead as conceived by him" (160).

Study Questions

1. List the five "Trinitarian basics" and explain their meaning.

2. "So in this part of the book, I will explore this biblical glimpse into God's inner life and therefore into the life that believers share with him. We should remind ourselves from time to time that it is only a glimpse." Did you note any writers cited in this chapter who neglected this reminder? Discuss.

3. Show how God's unity is related to the lordship attributes.

4. "The unity of God profoundly affects the religious life of the believer." How? Discuss.

5. Who are the "gods" in Scripture? Are they real beings?

6. Why would a Christian theologian deny monotheism? Discuss the issues raised by Jürgen Moltmann in this connection.

7. Describe and evaluate Thomas Aquinas's view of divine simplicity. Should we reject the idea that God is simple? Why or why not?

8. "God's essence is not some dark, unrevealed entity behind God's revealed character. Rather, God's revelation tells us his essence. It tells us what he really and truly is." Explain; evaluate.

9. What does B. B. Warfield mean by his comparison between the OT and a "chamber . . . dimly lighted"?

10. Do the plural words for God in the OT have Trinitarian implications? Discuss.

11. What can we learn about the Trinity from OT hypostatizations?

12. Discuss triadic formulae, triads of beings, and triads of personal beings in the OT. How do these bear on the doctrine of the Trinity?

13. Warfield says that in the NT, as distinguished from the OT, the Trinity is "settled doctrine." Do you agree? Why? If this is true, what happened since the OT period to settle this issue?

Memory Verses

Ex. 15:11: Who is like you, O Lord, among the gods?
Who is like you, majestic in holiness,
awesome in glorious deeds, doing wonders?

Num. 6:24–26: The Lord bless you and keep you; the Lord make his face to shine upon you and be gracious to you; the Lord lift up his countenance upon you and give you peace.

Isa. 45:5–6: I am the Lord, and there is no other,
besides me there is no God;
I equip you, though you do not know me,
that people may know, from the rising of the sun
and from the west, that there is none besides me;
I am the Lord, and there is no other.

Isa. 63:9–10: In all their affliction he was afflicted,
  and the angel of his presence saved them;
in his love and in his pity he redeemed them;
  he lifted them up and carried them all the days of old.

But they rebelled
  and grieved his Holy Spirit;
therefore he turned to be their enemy,
  and himself fought against them.

2 Cor. 13:14: The grace of the Lord Jesus Christ and the love of God and the fellowship of the Holy Spirit be with you all.

1 John 4:8b: God is love.

Resources for Further Study

Bavinck, Herman. *BRD*, 2:95–334.

Warfield, B. B. "The Biblical Doctrine of the Trinity." In *Biblical Doctrines*. Grand Rapids: Baker, 1981.

CHAPTER 21

THE THREE ARE GOD

WE WILL NOW CONSIDER the third of the five propositions by which in the preceding chapter I summarized the doctrine of the Trinity. We have seen that God is one, and that God is three. Now we must focus more closely on the deity of the three persons.[1] Of course, this discussion considerably overlaps that of the second proposition. To show the threeness of *God*, it is necessary to show that the beings mentioned in the triads are actually divine. I began to show that concept in the previous chapter by citing texts showing that all the works of creation and salvation, distinctively works of God, have a threefold source. But many other texts undergird this conclusion, and we should look at them here at least in a summary way.

Summary is the appropriate term. I cannot begin, in one chapter, to duplicate or surpass the thoroughness of B. B. Warfield's *The Lord of Glory*[2] or Robert Reymond's *Jesus, Divine Messiah*.[3] Because of these and many other comprehensive studies of the deity of Christ, I believe that a summary here will be sufficient.

These volumes also support the main point I want to make here: that the deity of the divine persons is a *pervasive* teaching of the NT (supported in important ways by the OT). The deity of Christ, for example, is not to be found in only a handful of controversial verses. It is found in one way or another on nearly every page of the NT. Even a book-length treatment is scarcely sufficient to do justice to the evidence. Christians do injustice to the subject when they focus exclusively on the relatively few (but

---

1. The deity of the Father may, of course, be taken for granted, so our discussion will focus on the deity of the Son and the Spirit. In considering the deity of the Son, we will focus on the NT data concerning the incarnate Christ, for that is where we learn most about the person of the eternal Son.

2. New York: American Tract Society, 1907; repr., Grand Rapids: Baker, 1974.

3. Phillipsburg, NJ: Presbyterian and Reformed, 1990. In this masterful volume, Reymond not only exegetes relevant passages, but also interacts with recent critical scholarship to establish the authenticity of those NT texts to which he appeals. He shows that even on the assumptions of the most skeptical biblical critics, it is possible to derive from the NT a high Christology, indeed a full doctrine of Jesus' deity. I will not enter into those arguments here, but will rather simply presuppose, as I have throughout this volume, the truth of Scripture as God's Word. That assumption, of course, immediately opens up to us *all* the NT data, regardless of the critics' evaluation of these data. But I do regard Reymond's discussions as very valuable, and I commend them to the reader.

very significant, as we will see) passages in the NT where Jesus is called *theos*, "God." These passages are only the tip of the iceberg.

In the preceding chapter, we noted Warfield's point that the doctrine of the Trinity in the NT is "not so much inculcated as presupposed." The NT writers have no need to prove the Trinity; the comings of Christ and the Spirit for our salvation have adequately proved that doctrine for both writers and the original readers of the NT. So for us modern readers, the doctrine is "not so much heard as overheard." But we overhear it everywhere. In that sense, it is pervasive. Warfield makes the same point in regard to the deity of Christ. He notes that

> the late Dr. R. W. Dale found the most impressive proofs that the Apostles themselves and the primitive churches believed that Jesus was one with God, rather in the way this seems everywhere taken for granted, than in the texts in which it is positively asserted.[4]

The same point holds true in this case because, of course, the doctrines of the deity of Christ and the Spirit are parts of the overall doctrine of the Trinity. So like the larger doctrine, these doctrines were not controversial among first-century Christians. The NT writers rarely, if ever, try to prove them. But they *mention* and *imply* them again and again. They presuppose them, and as Cornelius Van Til used to say in another connection, often presupposition is the best proof.

Taking Jesus' Deity for Granted

Here are some examples from the NT in which the deity of Christ is "taken for granted" rather than "positively asserted."

1. Jesus' teaching in the Gospels is remarkably egocentric. In the Sermon on the Mount, the last beatitude describes the blessedness of those persecuted "on my account" (Matt. 5:11). This persecution is like the persecution of the OT prophets (v. 12) for Yahweh. In the comparison, the apostles are prophets and Jesus is Yahweh.

In verse 17, he denies that he has come to "abolish the Law or the Prophets." But what human teacher might even be suspected of doing that? Only God could abolish these. The question does not even arise unless Jesus is God. In fact, he does not abolish them, but he does speak with astonishing authority (7:28–29), contradicting the traditions of the elders, and claiming that his own words represent the foundation of human life (7:24–27). He says that he has the right to determine who enters the kingdom of heaven (7:21–23). He determines who will know the Father (11:27). He demands that people be willing to lose all in order to follow him (16:25). He speaks of "his angels" (13:41; 16:27; 24:31). It is he who will reward and punish the deeds of men (16:27–28; 25:31–46); and the basis of the judgment will be the relation of men to him.

Jesus' egocentrism is even more obvious in the gospel of John. There he draws attention to himself over and over, with his "I ams": He claims to be the bread of life (6:48),

4. Warfield, *The Lord of Glory*, 1.

the light of the world (8:12), the resurrection and the life (11:25), the way, the truth, and the life (14:6), and so on. Later, we will consider the relation of these to Exodus 3:14.

Over and over again, Jesus calls people to "follow me" (Matt. 4:19; 8:22; 9:9; 16:24; 19:21; John 10:27; 12:26; 13:36; 21:19, 22). In most of these passages, Jesus' call is to men who are to be his special followers; but in Matthew 16:24, John 10:27, and John 12:26, it is a general command to all who would believe in him.

In Matthew 19:16–21, the Lord assumes for the sake of argument that the rich young man has kept the commands of the Decalogue that deal with his responsibility to other human beings. But the young man still lacks something. Instead of referring him to the first four commands, his duty to God, Jesus calls him to sell his goods, give to the poor, and "come, follow me." Jesus here calls the young man to follow him, when we might have expected an exhortation to worship God. The two here are functionally equivalent.

No OT prophet ever drew attention to himself in this way as the source of all divine blessing and the standard of all divine judgment. God's teachers typically turn attention away from themselves, to God. If Jesus is not God, his egocentric teaching is prideful, indeed blasphemous. Only if he is God is it admirable.

Jesus even places loyalty to himself above family loyalty. In Matthew 10:37, Jesus announces:

> Whoever loves father or mother more than me is not worthy of me, and whoever loves son or daughter more than me is not worthy of me.

In Luke 14:26, he puts it even more strongly:

> If anyone comes to me and does not hate his own father and mother and wife and children and brothers and sisters, yes, and even his own life, he cannot be my disciple.[5]

Family loyalty is a very high value in Scripture, enshrined in the fifth commandment, "Honor your father and mother," and later in the apostolic injunction:

> But if anyone does not provide for his relatives, and especially for members of his household, he has denied the faith and is worse than an unbeliever. (1 Tim. 5:8)

Jesus himself rebuked the Pharisees and teachers of the law because they allowed people to dishonor their parents by making special gifts to God (Mark 7:11). Nevertheless, of course, there is certainly a sense in which God deserves greater honor than parents. But only God—certainly not any human teacher. But in Matthew 10:37, Jesus claims an honor due only to God.

So believers do all things (including suffering) for the name of Jesus (Acts 9:16; Rom. 15:30; 2 Cor. 12:10; 3 John 7).

---

5. Recall, however, our discussion of hatred in chapter 13. It does not necessarily involve hostility, and it can be a relative expression.

In none of these passages does Jesus *teach* that he is God. He simply assumes divine status, functions, and prerogatives.

2. Negative evidence: As D. James Kennedy points out,[6] Jesus in the Gospels never withdraws or modifies a statement, never apologizes or repents (though among human beings such behavior is a mark of greatness), never seeks advice, never asks prayer for himself. He sometimes behaves strangely (sleeping in the boat during a storm, Matt. 8:24; allowing Lazarus to die, John 11:37), but does not explain his actions. These facts can be considered virtues only in God himself. But these texts do not teach Jesus' deity; they presuppose it.

3. In Galatians 1, Paul defends his apostleship against Judaistic critics. So he identifies himself as

> Paul, an apostle—not from men nor through man, but through Jesus Christ and God the Father, who raised him from the dead. (Gal. 1:1)

In Galatians 1, Paul is vitally concerned with the Creator-creature distinction. His apostolic call comes, emphatically, from God and not from men. Note, however, that in the context of this sharp distinction, Paul places Christ on the side of the Creator: Paul is an apostle sent not by a man, but by *Jesus Christ*. Jesus is on the side of the Creator. Jesus is the sending God.[7]

Paul does not, of course, intend to deny the humanity of Jesus. He stresses it emphatically elsewhere (as 1 Tim. 2:5). Indeed, he might have said even here that he was an apostle sent not by an ordinary man, but by that most extraordinary man, Jesus Christ. But in this passage he decides almost unselfconsciously, casually, to set Jesus sharply over against any human source for his apostleship. Jesus is God.

Paul makes the same contrast in Galatians 1:10 and 12:

> For am I now seeking the approval of man, or of God? Or am I trying to please man? If I were still trying to please man, I would not be a servant of Christ. . . . For I did not receive [the gospel] from any man, nor was I taught it, but I received it through a revelation of Jesus Christ.

Christ is a man, to be sure. But Paul serves Christ, receives his gospel from Christ, *rather than* any man. In this passage, Paul is not *teaching* the doctrine of the deity of Christ. That doctrine is not a point of disagreement between himself and his detractors. Paul assumes that doctrine as something conceded by all sides. It is taken for granted.

4. The salutations and benedictions that we noted in the previous chapter (such as "Grace to you and peace from God our Father and the Lord Jesus Christ," Rom. 1:7) are easy to overlook, since they occur so frequently. But they assume nothing less than a divine role for Jesus. In Romans 1:7, grace and peace represent all the benefits of

---

6. D. James Kennedy, *Truths That Transform* (Old Tappan, NJ: Fleming H. Revell, 1974), 57.

7. On this point, see J. Gresham Machen, *Machen's Notes on Galatians* (Nutley, NJ: Presbyterian and Reformed, 1972), 202.

salvation, benefits that come only from God.[8] But as we saw in the preceding chapter, these benefits have a twofold (threefold in 2 Corinthians 13:14) source. Only God is Savior (Isa. 43:11), but Father and Son are both the saving God.

Christ, the Covenant Lord

But the most fundamental biblical datum, in my view, is the way Jesus stands in the place of Yahweh as the Lord of the covenant. In the early chapters of this book, we saw how important covenant lordship is to the biblical doctrine of God. *Yahweh*, *Lord*, is the name by which God wishes his people to know him. The Lord is the One who controls all things, speaks with absolute authority, and enters creation to draw creatures into covenant relation with him. The most concise, and arguably most fundamental, summary of OT teaching is "Yahweh is Lord." But the NT, over and over again, represents Jesus as Lord in the same way that Yahweh is Lord. The most fundamental summary of NT teaching is "Jesus Christ is Lord" (Phil. 2:11; see also Rom. 10:9; 1 Cor. 12:3).

Jesus' blood is "my blood of the covenant, which is poured out for many for the forgiveness of sins" (Matt. 26:28), represented by the wine of communion. The cup, he says, is "the new covenant in my blood" (1 Cor. 11:25). "New covenant" alludes to God's promise in Jeremiah 31:31. The letter to the Hebrews speaks of Jesus as the "mediator" of the new covenant (12:24; see also 8:8, 13). As the God-man, he is the Mediator. But he is more than the Mediator; he is the *Lord* of the covenant.

So we focus on the NT use of *kyrios*, "Lord." *Kyrios* is the most common title of Christ in the NT. In some passages it may be a polite form of address or acknowledgment of his rabbinic status (Matt. 8:21; 15:27; 17:15; 18:21).[9] But more passages by far employ the term as a divine title, identifying Jesus with Yahweh, the Lord of the OT.

The LXX regularly uses *kyrios* to translate both the name *Yahweh* and the term *'adon*, "Lord." Some have argued that this use of *kyrios* occurs only in copies of the LXX from Christian sources. It is true that the only copies from demonstrably non-Christian sources use the Hebrew tetragram *YHWH*, rather than *kyrios*, for *Yahweh*. This fact, of course, does nothing to refute the thesis that *kyrios* was the normal Greek rendering of *Yahweh*, or to support the thesis that this use of *kyrios* represents a Christian distortion of the OT text. In the non-Christian sources, *Yahweh* is left untranslated, rather than given a translation other than *kyrios*. So the question remains open as to how the writers of those copies of the LXX referred to Yahweh in Greek. And other linguistic evidence certainly affirms the use of *kyrios* for Yahweh. Carl F. H. Henry says:

---

8. "Grace" (*charis*) resembles a Greek greeting; "peace" (*eirene*) is the equivalent of the Hebrew *shalom*. So these terms summarize the benefits of salvation and also welcome both Greeks and Jews who believe in Jesus.

9. I am not, however, willing to concede all vocative uses of *kyrios* to this polite usage, as does David Wells in *The Person of Christ* (Westchester, IL: Crossway, 1984), 75. It seems to me, for example, that in Matthew 8:8, the extraordinary faith of the centurion, who believes that Jesus can heal by a mere word, may well have included an extraordinary understanding of Jesus' lordship. And our view of the disciples' use of *kyrie* depends somewhat on our assessment of the maturity of their understanding.

Yet it must be granted that not only Philo and Josephus, but also apocryphal OT books like Wisdom of Solomon use KYRIOS for YAHWEH, an identification that was also made in Greek-speaking synagogues. Christians acquainted with Greek-speaking Jewry therefore would readily use the term KYRIOS to include the connotation of God Almighty.[10]

Some have claimed that the pagan use of *kyrios*, either the language of the mystery religions or that of the emperor cult, or both, also influences the NT. That *kyrios* was accepted by many in the ancient world as, in some contexts, a divine title certainly aided the Christian proclamation of Jesus as Lord, though of course, this fact also challenged Christian evangelists to distinguish their concept of lordship from that of the general culture. In this respect, *kyrios* played a role similar to *theos*.

But the main influence on the NT use of *kyrios* is clearly the OT. That is such an overwhelming influence that there is no need to look for any other, and it yields a concept of divine lordship incompatible with any pagan notion. As Christopher Kaiser says of the confession "Jesus is Lord" (1 Cor. 12:3):

> The form of this confession may have been designed as a direct counter-statement to the civic confession, "Caesar is Lord" (*kyrios kaisar*), but the content is clearly Hebraic in its allusion to Yahweh, the Lord of the OT.[11]

The OT looks forward to a Deliverer, somehow distinct from Yahweh, yet who also bears the title *Lord*. In Psalm 110:1, David declares:

> The LORD says to my Lord:
>   "Sit at my right hand,
> until I make your enemies your footstool."

In Jeremiah 23:5–6, Yahweh promises:

> Behold, the days are coming, declares the LORD, when I will raise up for David a righteous Branch, and he shall reign as king and deal wisely, and shall execute justice and righteousness in the land. In his days Judah will be saved, and Israel will dwell securely. And this is the name by which he will be called: "The LORD is our righteousness."

To the NT writers, the Lord our righteousness is Jesus. They clearly equate the lordship of Jesus to that of Yahweh. Frequently they cite OT passages that speak of Yahweh and refer those to Jesus. In Matthew 3:3, the writer quotes Isaiah 40:3 in reference to John the Baptist:

> For this is he who was spoken of by the prophet Isaiah when he said,

10. Carl F. H. Henry, *God, Revelation and Authority* (Waco, TX: Word Books, 1976), 2:236. Cf. I. Howard Marshall, *The Origins of New Testament Christology* (Downers Grove, IL: InterVarsity Press, 1976), 99.

11. Christopher Kaiser, *The Doctrine of God* (Westchester, IL: Crossway, 1982), 29. In a note, he refers to the discussion of "Jesus is Lord" in J. N. D. Kelly, *Early Christian Creeds* (London: Longman, 1972), 14–15.

> "The voice of one crying in the wilderness:
> 'Prepare the way of the Lord;
>   make his paths straight.'"

Lord in Isaiah is *Yahweh*, but in Matthew 3:3 (cf. Mark 1:3; Luke 1:76; John 1:23) the citation refers to the One for whom John paved the way (by his own admission, Matt. 3:11–17), namely, Jesus. In Matthew 21:16, Jesus quotes Psalm 8:2 to defend the praises of the children directed to him. But in Psalm 8 (see v. 1), the praises are directed to Yahweh. Cf. also:

- Isa. 6:1–10; Matt. 13:14–15; John 12:37–41
- Ps. 110:1; Matt. 22:44–45
- Mal. 3:1; Luke 1:76
- Ps. 23:1; John 10:11
- Isa. 8:14; Rom. 9:32–33
- Joel 2:32; Rom. 10:9–13
- Isa. 45:23; Rom. 14:11; Phil. 2:10–11
- Jer. 9:24; 1 Cor. 1:31
- Isa. 40:13; 1 Cor. 2:16
- Ps. 68:18; Eph. 4:8–10
- Isa. 2:10, 19, 21; 66:15; 2 Thess. 1:7–9
- Ps. 130:8; Titus 2:14
- Ps. 102:25–27; Heb. 1:10–12
- Isa. 51:6; Heb. 1:11
- Ps. 34:8; 1 Peter 2:3
- Isa. 8:13; 1 Peter 3:15
- Zech. 12:10; Rev. 1:7
- Jer. 17:10; Rev. 2:23
- Ps. 62:12; Rev. 22:12
- Isa. 40:10; Rev. 22:12

So the NT writers regularly use *kyrios* as a divine title of Christ.[12] That usage antedates even the birth of Jesus. When Mary, mother of Jesus, visits Elizabeth, mother of John, in Luke 1:43–44, Elizabeth asks:

> And why is this granted to me that the mother of my Lord should come to me? For behold, when the sound of your greeting came to my ears, the baby in my womb leaped for joy.

Surely the leaping of baby John was a supernaturally given response, appropriate to a divine visitation; Elizabeth's use of "Lord" should be taken in a similarly exalted sense. Then to the shepherds in the field, the angel announces:

---

12. They also use *kyrios*, as in the OT, to refer to God the Father, further confirmation that they regarded the term as a divine title. See Matt. 1:20; 9:38; 11:25; Acts 17:24; Rev. 4:11.

For unto you is born this day in the city of David a Savior, who is Christ the Lord. (Luke 2:11)

The angel announces that the long-expected Messiah, Christ, is born, and that he bears the title *Lord*.

So the Baptist comes to "prepare the way of the Lord" (Mark 1:3, quoting Isa. 40:3). In Isaiah, the verse clearly announces the coming of Yahweh; John applies it to Jesus.

In Mark 2:28, Jesus claims to be "lord [*kyrios*] even of the Sabbath." This is an astonishing claim. In the OT, the Sabbath was the day that Yahweh claimed for himself, over against all human interests:

Six days you shall labor, and do all your work, but the seventh day is a Sabbath to the LORD your God. (Ex. 20:9–10a)

It is holy to him (Ex. 20:8, 11). So through Isaiah God chastises the people for "doing your pleasure on my holy day" (Isa. 58:13). The Sabbath belongs to the Lord alone and not to any man. But in Mark 2:28, Jesus claims lordship over it. Clearly, this use of *kyrios* is a claim to deity.

The Sabbath is God's dwelling in time, the temple his dwelling in space. As with the Sabbath, Jesus is greater than the temple, the dwelling place of God (Matt. 12:6). It is his house, as the Sabbath is his day (Matt. 21:12–13). He is the Lord himself, come to his temple to purge it (Mal. 3:1). In the theology of the NT, believers are a temple "in the Lord" (Eph. 2:21), and in the end the final temple is the Lord God Almighty himself, and the Lamb (Rev. 21:22).

In Mark 5:19–20, the gospel writer identifies *kyrios* with deity more subtly. Jesus tells the healed demoniac to

go home to your friends and tell them how much the Lord has done for you, and how he has had mercy on you.

This is language from the Psalms and elsewhere typically used of divine blessings. But the demoniac

went away and began to proclaim in the Decapolis how much Jesus had done for him, and everyone marveled.

Note how "Jesus" in verse 20 replaces the clearly divine *kyrios* in verse 19.

Following the miraculous catch of fish, Peter fell down at Jesus' knees, saying, "Depart from me, for I am a sinful man, O Lord" (Luke 5:8). This is the response of a sinner before the holy God, like Isaiah's:

Woe is me! For I am lost; for I am a man of unclean lips, and I dwell in the midst of a people of unclean lips; for my eyes have seen the King, the LORD of hosts! (Isa. 6:5)

Later Jesus teaches that the title *kyrios* grants him such authority that disobedience to him is unthinkable: "Why do you call me 'Lord, Lord,' and not do what I tell you?" (Luke 6:46). As with Yahweh in the OT, authority is a lordship attribute of Jesus. When he speaks, people are amazed at his authority, far beyond that of any earthly teacher (Matt. 7:28–29; cf. Matt. 13:54; 22:33; Mark 1:22; 6:2; Luke 4:32; John 7:46).[13]

The climax of the Gospels' use of *kyrios* is the passage in Matthew 22:43–46 (cf. Mark 12:35–37; Luke 20:41–44), where Jesus silences his Jewish critics by quoting Psalm 110:1:

> The LORD says to my Lord:
> "Sit at my right hand,
> until I make your enemies your footstool."

Jesus then asks them how the Christ, the Messiah, the son of David, could also be David's *Lord. Kyrios* here is covenant Lord even over David; he takes the place of Yahweh, to the amazement and scandal of Jesus' enemies.

Similarly those uses of *kyrios* that present Jesus as the Judge of all on the last day (Matt. 7:21–23; 25:37, 44), and the remarkable confession of Thomas (see below) that Jesus is "My Lord and my God" (John 20:28).[14] Peter preaches to Cornelius's household that Jesus is "Lord of all" (Acts 10:36; cf. Rom. 10:12).

For Paul, as we saw in the preceding chapter, *kyrios* is the distinctive name of the second person of the Trinity (as in 1 Cor. 8:6; 12:4–6; 2 Cor. 13:14; Eph. 4:4–6). So Paul's occasional contrast between *theos* and *kyrios* does not make *kyrios* less than God; it simply distinguishes Father from Son, two persons of the Godhead. So for Paul, the fundamental Christian confession is *kyrios Iesous*, "Jesus is Lord" (Rom. 10:9; 1 Cor. 12:3; Phil. 2:11). He is the Lord on whom we call for salvation (Rom. 10:12–13; cf. Joel 2:32; Acts 2:21), whose message brings faith (Rom. 10:17). He is, indeed, "the Lord of glory" (1 Cor. 2:8; cf. James 2:1).

So Paul is *doulos*, a bondservant of Christ, his Lord (Rom. 1:1; Gal. 1:10). Christians are "called to belong to Jesus Christ" (Rom. 1:6).

We should note that Jesus' resurrection marks a change in the nature of his lordship. In the terms of traditional Reformed theology (cf. WSC 27–28), the resurrection marks the end of Jesus' "state of humiliation" and the beginning of his "state of exaltation," in which he exercises his sovereign authority from the courts of heaven (see chapter 38). In this state, he has gained title to all the kingdoms of the earth, not only by virtue of his deity, but also by virtue of his historical victory over Satan, sin, and death. So although Jesus is always Lord, there is a sense in which he *receives* lordship in a higher

---

13. In Matthew 7:28–29, the reference to Jesus' authority introduces two events in which Jesus heals by his mere *word*. The faith of the centurion in Matthew 8:5–13 is great because he believes that Jesus can "speak by a word" (note the redundant expressions in the Greek) and bring healing, just as the centurion himself can command soldiers to do his bidding. Similar contexts can be found in the other references listed above to the authority of Jesus' teaching.

14. See a later section in this chapter for the use of *theos* in this verse. The presence of both *theos* and *kyrios* here requires us to take *kyrios* as a divine title.

sense, as a gift from the Father upon completion of redemption. So the risen Christ tells his disciples, "All authority in heaven and on earth has been given to me" (Matt. 28:18). Paul in Romans 1:4 speaks of his being "declared to be the Son of God in power according to the Spirit of holiness by his resurrection from the dead," and in 14:9 says:

> For to this end Christ died and lived again, that he might be Lord both of the dead and of the living.

And a yet higher form of lordship awaits Jesus. He now sits at the right hand of God, his priestly work completed, waiting for his enemies to be made his footstool (Heb. 10:12–13; cf. 1 Cor. 15:25–28).

When Scripture talks of Jesus' lordship during his earthly ministry, it is not always clear whether it speaks of Jesus' lordship as God incarnate, or whether it speaks by anticipation of his coming lordship in redemptive history. In my view, the biblical writers do not always clearly distinguish these. For some purposes, the distinction is unimportant; divine lordship is divine lordship. In any case, it is important to remember that the historical process by which Jesus acquires power over the world does not detract at all from the eternal lordship that Jesus holds by virtue of being God. The former represents his immanence, the latter his transcendence. As God incarnate, Jesus experiences change that includes increased power and authority. As God eternal and transcendent, Jesus is always the Sovereign Lord.

Besides the use of *kyrios* and *doulos*, the NT speaks of Christ's covenant lordship by making even more direct allusion to Exodus 3:14, the "I AM." The "I AM" is the source for the name *Yahweh* and therefore of the concept of covenant lordship.

In the gospel of John, Jesus often takes the "I AM" on his lips. Sometimes he uses it with significant predicates: "I am the bread of life" (6:35), "I am the light of the world" (8:12). Cf. 10:7–11; 11:25; 14:6; 15:1. Even more significantly, he uses "I AM" without predicate to indicate (as in Exodus 3:14) his presence to bless and judge. To the woman of Samaria, he says, "I who speak to you am he" (John 4:26 NIV). But there is no "he" in the Greek, which reads literally "I am [*ego eimi*], who speaks to you." It is not wrong to supply the "he," though its absence is significant. And even the phrase "I am he" recalls Exodus 3:14 by way of the "I am he" (*ani hu*) passages in Deuteronomy 32:39–40; Isaiah 41:4; 43:10–13; etc. See chapter 2.

In John 8:24, Jesus tells the Jews:

> I told you that you would die in your sins, for unless you believe that I am he you will die in your sins.

"He" has been added by the ESV translators. The original reads, "If you do not believe that I am, you will indeed die in your sins." Again, it is not necessarily wrong to complete the phrase so as to read "I am he" or "I am the Messiah." But the simple *ego eimi* indicates already that the claim Jesus makes is momentous indeed. He is no ordinary

Messiah. Similarly in John 8:28 and 13:19. We are even more impressed at the momentousness of these statements in 18:5–6 (cf. v. 8):

> They answered him, "Jesus of Nazareth." Jesus said to them, "I am he." Judas, who betrayed him, was standing with them. When Jesus said to them, "I am he," they drew back and fell to the ground.

Here (and implicitly, therefore, in the earlier instances), the "I AM" is a powerful word that repels the Lord's enemies.

The climax of the "I AM" theme in John is found at the end of the eighth chapter:

> "Your father Abraham rejoiced that he would see my day. He saw it and was glad." So the Jews said to him, "You are not yet fifty years old, and have you seen Abraham?" Jesus said to them, "Truly, truly, I say to you, before Abraham was, I am." (John 8:56–58)

Abraham came into being (*ginomai*); Jesus simply *is*. In context, the passage speaks of Jesus' transcendence over time: Abraham looked to him, and he existed before Abraham. But the emphasis here is not merely on preexistence, which could have been expressed by "before Abraham *was*, I *was*." The "I AM," especially in the light of other such references in John, clearly identifies Jesus with the "I AM" of Exodus 3:14, with Yahweh himself. The Jews understand: in John 8:59 they pick up stones to kill him. From their point of view, this statement was blasphemy. From ours, if it is not blasphemy, it can be nothing less than a claim to deity in the fullest sense.[15]

Jesus is no less than the covenant Lord, Yahweh come in the flesh.

Christ, the Son of God

Like the other divine titles of Christ,[16] *Son of God* can also be used for finite beings: angels (Job 1:6; 2:1; and most likely Pss. 29:1; 89:6), kings (2 Sam. 7:14; Pss. 2:7; 89:26–27), priests (Mal. 1:6; cf. Heb. 5:5–6), Israel (Deut. 14:1; Isa. 63:8 KJV; Jer. 31:9, 20; Hos. 1:10; 11:1), Adam (Luke 3:38), Christian believers (Matt. 5:9; John 1:12; Rom. 8:14–16, 19, 23; Gal. 3:26–4:7; Eph. 1:5; 1 John 3:1–2; Rev. 21:7). Acts 17:28 also implies that God is Father over all people by virtue of creation. In these passages, *son* (*huios* or *teknon*) connotes various facts about the nature, function, origin, and inheritance of the persons in view.

But Scripture applies *Son of God* to Jesus in a unique sense. Of course, Jesus fulfills the sonships of Adam, of Israel, and of its officers in important ways, and for him, too, his sonship reveals facts about his nature, function, origin, and inheritance. But his sonship is of a different order from that of anyone else. He is *the* Son of God (Luke 1:31–32; John 1:34; 1 John 5:20). He is God's *own* Son (Rom. 8:3, 32), and God is his *own*

---

15. For more on the "I AM," refer to my earlier discussion in chapters 2–3, which incorporates some NT references to Jesus.

16. We have seen how *kyrios* can be a form of polite address. Even *theos* (= *elohim*) refers to human judges in Exodus 21:6; 22:7–9; Psalm 82:1, 6; John 10:34.

Father (John 5:18). He speaks of God as *my* Father (Matt. 25:34; 26:29; Luke 24:49; John 14:23), and in other passages he speaks of his Father in ways that indicate the uniqueness of this relationship:

> For whoever is ashamed of me and of my words in this adulterous and sinful generation, of him will the Son of Man also be ashamed when he comes in the glory of his Father with the holy angels. (Mark 8:38; cf. 13:32; 14:36)

Jesus taught the disciples to pray, "Our Father" (Matt. 6:9), but he did not join in that prayer with them. He never uses *our* to identify his relationship to God with that of the disciples. Indeed, after his resurrection, he informs them that "I am ascending to my Father and your Father, to my God and your God" (John 20:17). Here he distinguishes between his own relationship to God and theirs, between his sonship and theirs. Of course, there is a strong analogy between the two. Jesus' intimate "Abba, Father" (Mark 14:36) becomes part of the piety of the early church as well (Rom. 8:15; Gal. 4:6), for the Spirit of Jesus himself moves the disciple to speak to God this way.

Jesus' sonship, indeed, is prior to ours. We can become sons of God only if he gives us authority to do so (John 1:12; cf. 14:6; 17:26). And as we saw above, we cry out "Abba, Father" because the Spirit of Jesus moves us to pray as he did.

The terms *only-begotten* Son (*monogenes*)[17] (John 1:14, 18; 3:16, 18; 1 John 4:9) and *beloved* Son (*huios agapetos*) (Matt. 3:17; 7:5; Mark 1:11; 9:7; 12:6) also indicate the uniqueness of Jesus' sonship, as do other passages that display the intimate relationship of the two divine persons. Matthew 11:25–27 is one of these:

> At that time Jesus declared, "I thank you, Father, Lord of heaven and earth, that you have hidden these things from the wise and understanding and revealed them to little children; yes, Father, for such was your gracious will. All things have been handed over to me by my Father, and no one knows the Son except the Father, and no one knows the Father except the Son and anyone to whom the Son chooses to reveal him.

Even more remarkable is Jesus' High Priestly Prayer in John 17, which begins:

> When Jesus had spoken these words, he lifted up his eyes to heaven, and said, "Father, the hour has come; glorify your Son that the Son may glorify you, since you have given him authority over all flesh, to give eternal life to all whom you have given him. And this is eternal life, that they know you the only true God, and Jesus Christ whom you have sent. I glorified you on earth, having accomplished the work that

---

17. Most scholars today have concluded that *monogenes* comes from *genos* ("kind") rather than *gennao* ("beget," "bear") and thus should be translated "only" or "unique," rather than "only-begotten" as in the older translations. I am not convinced of this conclusion. For example, it seems to me that the translation "God the One and Only" in John 1:18 NIV doesn't make much sense. See chapter 22 for more discussion of this issue, in the section on the eternal generation of the Son.

> you gave me to do. And now, Father, glorify me in your own presence with the glory that I had with you before the world existed." (John 17:1–5)

Here we get a glimpse of the remarkable eternal fellowship between Father and Son: their mutual knowledge, mutual love, mutual glorification. We see here the obedience of the Son in the unique work of redemption, assigned him by the Father. And in John 5:18–23:

> This was why the Jews were seeking all the more to kill him, because not only was he breaking the Sabbath, but he was even calling God his own Father, making himself equal with God.
>
> So Jesus said to them, "Truly, truly, I say to you, the Son can do nothing of his own accord, but only what he sees the Father doing. For whatever the Father does, that the Son does likewise. For the Father loves the Son and shows him all that he himself is doing. And greater works than these will he show him, so that you may marvel. For as the Father raises the dead and gives them life, so also the Son gives life to whom he will. The Father judges no one, but has given all judgment to the Son, that all may honor the Son, just as they honor the Father. Whoever does not honor the Son does not honor the Father who sent him."

Here the fellowship between Father and Son implies that the Son shares his Father's knowledge, love, powers, and prerogatives.

Compare also John 1:18, in which the only-begotten God is "at the Father's side,"[18] and the exhaustive mutual knowledge of Father and Son in John 10:15.

Clearly, Jesus' unique sonship implies his ontological deity. To Jews, a "son of" someone (or figuratively of something) shares the nature of his parent. And we have seen that Jesus and his Father share distinctively divine love, knowledge, powers ("the Father . . . shows him all that he himself is doing," including the power to raise the dead), and prerogatives (to judge the world, to receive divine honor). Cf. Matt. 28:18. NT references to Jesus' sonship typically emphasize his equality with the Father, as in the texts above and John 3:35; 10:37–38. His sonship is above that of the angels (Heb. 1:5).[19]

The Jews of Jesus' day understood that his claim to sonship implied equality with God (John 5:18; 10:30–31). It was this claim that led to the Jews' charge of blasphemy against him (Matt. 26:63–66), which led to his crucifixion. Jesus never denies this claim or its meaning; indeed, he affirms it before his accusers (Matt. 26:64).

---

18. Compare also the *pros ton theon* of John 1:1.

19. The writer to the Hebrews, of course, is interested in showing the superiority of Christ to all other beings, and therefore the superiority of the Christian gospel to OT Judaism. Note 5:8: "Although he was a son, he learned obedience through what he suffered." The concessive "although" (*kaiper*) suggests that, unlike earthly sons, there is something anomalous about the Son of God's having to learn obedience through suffering. Clearly, in the mind of the writer, Jesus' sonship implies divine attributes prima facie inconsistent with learning obedience through suffering. The anomaly, of course, arises from the nature of the incarnation. Thanks to Dennis Johnson for this insight.

As with Jesus' lordship, his sonship has various historical dimensions. As he became Lord in a higher sense by virtue of his resurrection, so he is, by the resurrection, "declared to be the Son of God in power according to the Spirit of holiness by his resurrection from the dead" (Rom. 1:4). God's statement of Psalm 2:7, "You are my Son; today I have begotten you," is applied to the day of resurrection in Acts 13:33. But Scripture also calls Jesus Son of God by virtue of his supernatural birth in Luke 1:35. As with lordship, Jesus' sonship describes his eternal nature, revealed progressively through different events of redemptive history. Jesus was Son before he was sent into the world (John 3:17; 17:5; Rom. 8:3; Gal. 4:4; Col. 1:3–17; Heb. 5:5–6).

As with his lordship, Jesus' sonship is prominent in the confession-like passages of the NT. Peter's confession is that Jesus is "the Christ, the Son of the living God" (Matt. 16:16). Cf. also John 11:27; 20:31; Acts 8:37; Heb. 4:14; 1 John 2:23; 4:15; 5:5; Jesus' own confession before the Sanhedrin (Matt. 26:63–64); and the Father's confession of his Son from heaven (Mark 1:11; 9:7).

There is considerable overlap between the concepts *Lord* and *Son*. Both indicate Jesus' rule over the covenant people (as Son, he is the covenant King of Psalm 2:6). Both indicate Jesus' powers and prerogatives as God, especially over God's people: in other words, divine control, authority, and presence. We can describe the difference between them as perspectival: *Son* emphasizes Jesus' relationship to his Father, *Lord* his relationship to his people. But each encompasses the emphasis of the other. Lordship presupposes sonship, and sonship implies lordship.

Jesus, the Christ

Christ or *Messiah* means "anointed one." In the OT, prophets (1 Kings 19:16), priests (Ex. 29:7; 30:30–33), and kings (1 Sam. 10:1; 16:13; 24:10) were anointed with oil as they assumed office. The Jewish messianic expectation at the time of Jesus' earthly ministry focused on a royal figure, a descendant of David (Matt. 22:42), who would liberate Israel from Rome and reestablish Israel as a great power.

But the OT itself anticipates the coming of One who is far more than a political deliverer. It rarely uses the term *Messiah* (Ps. 2:2; Dan. 9:25–26), but it does speak often of a coming King far greater than David. The sons of Korah sing of the coming King, addressing him thus:

> Your throne, O God, is forever and ever.
>   The scepter of your kingdom is a scepter of uprightness. (Ps. 45:6)

Through Isaiah, God characterizes the coming Savior:

> For to us a child is born,
>   to us a son is given;
> and the government shall be upon his shoulder,
>   and his name shall be called

> Wonderful Counselor, Mighty God,
>   Everlasting Father, Prince of Peace. (Isa. 9:6)

And through Micah:

> But you, O Bethlehem Ephrathah,
>   who are too little to be among the clans of Judah,
> from you shall come forth for me
>   one who is to be ruler in Israel,
> whose coming forth is from of old,
>   from ancient days. (Mic. 5:2)

Through Zechariah (2:8–11), God speaks of himself both as One sending and as One sent to live with his people. We also noted earlier Psalm 110:1, in which the Davidic king is also David's Lord.[20]

The coming of the Messiah, therefore, is also the coming of God. The OT often looks forward to a day of the Lord, when Yahweh will come to set things right. In Isaiah, again, we read:

> Truth is lacking,
>   and he who departs from evil makes himself a prey.
> The LORD saw it, and it displeased him
>   that there was no justice.
> He saw that there was no man,
>   and wondered that there was no one to intercede;
> then his own arm brought him salvation,
>   and his righteousness upheld him.
> He put on righteousness as a breastplate,
>   and a helmet of salvation on his head;
> he put on garments of vengeance for clothing,
>   and wrapped himself in zeal as a cloak. (Isa. 59:15–17)

Paul's "whole armor of God" (Eph. 6:10–18) was first the armor worn by God himself. No one but God can institute justice on earth and bring salvation from all the effects of sin.

We have seen how OT passages about the lordship of God refer to Jesus in the NT. So quite literally the coming of the Christ is the coming of Yahweh. As Zechariah foresaw, the humble King riding on a donkey brings with him all the power of the Sovereign Lord to bring peace and judgment (Zech. 9:9–17).

---

20. I will not enter the exegetical controversies surrounding these passages, controversies that have been vigorous. For any Bible-believer, however, it is plain that (1) in the NT, Christ is a divine figure, and (2) the NT writers found in the OT a divine Messiah. Clearly, for example, the writer of Hebrews 1:8 reads Psalm 45:6 as teaching that the Messiah is God.

At a number of points in the Gospels, Jesus directly claims to be the Messiah (Matt. 16:16–17; Mark 14:62; John 4:25–26; 11:25–27).[21] *Messiah* (*Christos* = "Christ") is also, like *Lord* and *Son*, an element of NT confessional language. It is, with "Son of God," the focus of Peter's confession in Matthew 16:16 and that of Martha in John 11:27. Note the negative words in 1 John 2:22, against those who deny that Jesus is Christ, and the identification in 5:1 of those who are born of God with those who believe that Jesus is the Christ. John writes his gospel "so that you may believe that Jesus is the Christ, the Son of God, and that by believing you may have life in his name" (John 20:31).

In much of the NT, *Jesus Christ* becomes a proper name, the title attached almost inseparably to Jesus' given name. Obviously, the affirmation that Jesus is the Messiah is central to the biblical gospel.

As Christ, Jesus fulfills all the OT expectations of deliverance. He is son of David and Son of God, the final Prophet, Priest, and King. Once the OT expectation, and man's true need, are rightly understood, it is plain that *Christ*, like *Lord* and *Son*, is a divine title.

Jesus Christ Is God

There are ten places or so where the NT directly identifies Jesus as God (*theos, morphe theou, theotes*). These have been contested exegetically, but I think these disputes have been due less to genuine difficulties in the texts than to theological resistance against Jesus' claims. So the followers of Arius in the fourth century and many others down to the Jehovah's Witnesses and some liberal theologians of our time have sought to minimize the meanings of these passages. That effort, in my view, is not difficult to refute, and it is also futile: even if it can be shown that none of the passages below identifies Jesus as God, there are countless passages that identify him by divine titles *Lord*, *Son of God*, and *Christ*, and others that we will consider later that teach his deity in other ways. The deity of Christ is a *pervasive* teaching of Scripture.

The identification of the Messiah with *theos* begins in the OT, where the Messiah is *elohim* (Ps. 45:6; cf. Heb. 1:8), *Immanuel* (Isa. 7:14; cf. Matt. 1:23), and *el gibbor* (Isa. 9:6). But let us now consider the NT data:

John 1:1

This verse is the most famous and most hotly disputed of the passages we will consider. For convenience of discussion, I will number the three clauses.

1. In the beginning was the Word,
2. and the Word was with God,
3. and the Word was God.

---

21. Robert Reymond also notes other passages in which the claim is made "obliquely": Matt. 22:42–45; 23:10; 24:5; Mark 9:41; 12:35–37; 13:21–22; Luke 24:44–46; John 10:24–25. See his excellent discussion of Jesus' messiahship in *Jesus, Divine Messiah*.

Clearly, "Word" here refers to Christ, since verse 14 says that "the Word became flesh and dwelt among us." Thus, the passage identifies Jesus with the Word by which God created the heavens and the earth.[22]

At the very least, then, the passage teaches that Jesus existed before creation. The verb "was" in the first clause (Gk. *en*) is in the imperfect tense, which indicates a duration before the "beginning." So the first clause might be translated "when all things began, the Word was already in existence." The second clause, therefore, teaches that before creation (in timeless eternity, as I argued in chapter 17), Jesus the Word was "with God" (*pros ton theon*), in eternal fellowship with him.

Even without looking at the third clause, we can discern clear evidence of Jesus' deity here. As we saw in chapter 3, the biblical cosmology is bilevel: there is the Creator and the creature, nothing between. The Word in this passage is not creature, but Creator. It is the divine Word that existed before creation, by whom all things were made (v. 3). Indeed, the divine Word is, as we will see in our discussion of the Word of God, an attribute of God, a perspective on the whole divine nature, and therefore fully divine.

We must, however, look more closely at the third clause. In the Greek, the subject and predicate are in reverse order, literally "God was the Word." But the English translations are correct. Greek often places the subject of a sentence after the predicate, and in this case "Word" is clearly the subject, as indicated by parallels with the other clauses, and also by the definite article, preceding "Word" and absent from "God." Thus, clause 3 reverses the order of clause 2, which places subject before predicate.

Why the reversal? Some have argued that the reverse order emphasizes the predicate, "God," in the third clause: The Word was *God*! This point is correct, I think, but it is part of a larger pattern. Clauses 2 and 3 are a Hebrew chiasm. Chiasm is a device found often in Hebrew writing and in other writing influenced by Hebrew, in which ideas, concepts, words, or themes are structured in an A B B A order, or A B C C B A, and the like. Here the two clauses feature the nouns "Word," "God," "God," "Word." The chiastic structure does indeed emphasize the middle term, in this case "God." A major intent of the verse, therefore, is to set forth the relation of the Word to God.

The absence of the definite article from "God" in the third clause, however, has led some to argue that here "God" does not entail deity in the fullest sense, but only divine qualities or even godlike qualities, so that *theos* should be translated "a god" or "divine" (in a loose sense). But that conclusion does not follow, for the following reasons:

1. The absence of the article may be "a purely grammatical phenomenon."[23] When, as here, a Greek sentence uses *to be* to connect a subject and a predicate noun, the predicate noun normally lacks the article even when it is definite. So the absence of an article implies nothing about the precise sense of *theos*.

2. This argument is even stronger in passages like ours where the predicate precedes the subject. The *Colwell rule* states that in such a *to be* sentence, when the predicate

22. "In the beginning" draws our attention back to Genesis 1:1, and verse 3 indicates that the Word was the agent of creation. God made the world by *speaking*. Cf. Ps. 33:6, 9.

23. C. H. Dodd, "New Testament Translation Problems II," *Bible Translator* 28 (January 1977): 103.

precedes the subject, the predicate noun usually lacks the article even though it is definite, but the subject of the sentence, if definite, will employ the definite article.[24] So again the phenomenon has a grammatical explanation and does not presuppose any change of meaning between "God" in clause 2 and "God" in clause 3.

3. As we have seen, in such constructions the predicate noun usually or normally lacks the article. Following that normal practice here might have also served the author's purpose to draw additional attention to the term "God," the center of the chiasm. Dropping the article focuses on the noun itself, and it brings the two occurrences of *theos* closer together in the chiasm. That consideration weakens the need for further explanation of the construction.

4. In similar verses where *theos* is a predicate noun lacking the definite article, the reference to God in the fullest sense is indisputable: Mark 12:27; Luke 20:38; John 8:54; Rom. 8:33; Phil. 2:13; Heb. 11:16.

5. There are many other verses, some in the same first chapter of John's gospel, in which *theos* lacks a definite article, but in which the reference to God in the fullest sense is indisputable. Nobody would claim a reduced meaning of *theos*, for example, in John 1:6, 13, or 18.

6. Even if we grant that *theos* without the definite article puts some emphasis on the *qualities* of God rather than his *person*, this supposition does not entail that *theos* in the third clause has a reduced sense. If one tries to prove otherwise, he needs to show that the qualities emphasized are something other than the essential attributes of God. If the qualities are essential qualities, then the third clause identifies the Word with God in the highest sense.

7. A very strong argument is needed to prove that the meaning of *theos* changes between clause 2 and clause 3. That burden of proof has certainly not been met.

John 1:18

Our next passage reads, "No one has seen God at any time; the only begotten God who is in the bosom of the Father, He has explained Him" (NASB).

Here the question is what textual tradition we should follow. Some ancient Greek manuscripts read *huios* instead of *theos*: "only-begotten Son," rather than "only-begotten God." But those manuscripts usually considered to be of higher quality (Aleph, B) and many citations from church fathers use *theos*. Internal evidence confirms this conclusion. In textual criticism, one principle often followed is that the most difficult reading should be preferred, since a scribe is more likely to soften the reading than to make it more difficult.[25] Here the more difficult reading is certainly *monogenes theos*; we can understand how a scribe would be tempted to replace it with the more usual

---

24. For a recent discussion of this grammatical point, see Lane C. McGaughy, *Toward a Descriptive Analysis of EINAI as a Linking Verb in New Testament Greek*, Society of Biblical Literature Dissertation Series 6 (Missoula, MT: Society of Biblical Literature for the Linguistics Seminar, 1972), esp. 49–53, 73–77.

25. My experience in proofreading my own work does not consistently bear out this principle, for whatever that observation may be worth.

and more easily understandable *monogenes huios*. So both the manuscript tradition and the principle of difficulty favor the reading *monogenes theos*, "only-begotten God."

On that reading comes this interpretation: No one has seen God (presumably the Father), but the only-begotten God (in context, the Word or the Son) has made him known. Here again, Jesus is called God.

John 20:28

In this verse, Thomas, having seen the risen Christ, cries out, "My Lord and my God!" (*Ho kyrios mou kai ho theos mou*). Some have interpreted this as an oathlike expression of surprise, as profane people today sometimes say, "My God!" But this interpretation is quite impossible. It is not a vocative expression. And clearly, in context, the author's intent is to present a cogent confession of faith by one of the first witnesses of the resurrection. Three verses later, John tells us that "these are written so that you may believe that Jesus is the Christ, the Son of God, and that by believing you may have life in his name" (v. 31).

So the point of verse 28 is that Thomas now discerns who Jesus really is; he believes that Jesus is the Christ, the Son of God.

Acts 20:28

Here Paul exhorts the elders of the church of Ephesus:

> Pay careful attention to yourselves and to all the flock, in which the Holy Spirit has made you overseers, to care for the church of God, which he obtained with his own blood.

The antecedent of "he" is "God"; but "he" clearly refers to Jesus, who bought the church with his own blood.

Romans 9:5

In the context of this verse, Paul mourns the unbelief of Israel. Reflecting on God's former blessings to the Israelites, he says, "To them belong the patriarchs, and from their race, according to the flesh, is the Christ who is God over all, blessed forever. Amen." Some have wanted to read it "the human ancestry of Christ, the one who is over all. May God be forever praised![26] Amen." On the second translation, Christ is not called God, though the "over all" does grant his messianic dominion. On that reading, Paul pauses in his discussion to utter a doxology.

Against the doxological interpretation: (1) In a doxology, one would expect "praised" (*eulogetos*) to precede "God" (*theos*), as in 2 Corinthians 1:3 and Ephesians 1:3, rather than to follow it as here. (2) The ESV translation fits better into the context. There, Paul speaks of the human ancestry of Christ, followed naturally by a reflection on

---

26. The Greek term sometimes translated "blessed" and sometimes "praised" is *eulogetos*.

his divine nature. So there seems no reason except theological prejudice to adopt the doxological interpretation.

It is, to be sure, unusual for Paul to refer to Jesus as *theos*. As I mentioned earlier, Paul's usual Trinitarian terminology restricts *theos* to the Father and uses *kyrios, huios,* or *Christos* for the Son. But the meaning of this passage, a contrast between Jesus' human origins and divine nature, makes the exception logical at this point. Certainly Paul believed in the deity of Christ; that is evident in his use of *kyrios*. So it is not contrary to his theology, though it is somewhat contrary to his usual vocabulary, to speak of Jesus as *theos*.[27]

2 Thessalonians 1:12; Titus 2:13; 2 Peter 1:1

In Titus 2:13, Paul exhorts his readers to live godly lives, "waiting for our blessed hope, the appearing of the glory of our great God and Savior Jesus Christ." On this translation, Paul calls Jesus Christ "God." The alternative translation is "the great God and our Saviour Jesus Christ" (KJV), which identifies Jesus as Savior, but not as God.

As with John 1:1, a rule of Greek grammar, in this case the *Granville Sharp rule*, is relevant:

> When the copulative *kai* connects two nouns of the same case, if the article *ho* or any of its cases precedes the first of the said nouns or participles, and is not repeated before the second noun or participle, the latter always relates to the same person that is expressed or described by the first noun or participle, i.e., it denotes a farther description of the first-named person.[28]

This rule fits Titus 2:13, in which the definite article precedes *theos* and is not repeated before *soter*, and the two nouns are joined by *kai*. So we should conclude that *theos* and *soter,* "God" and "Savior," denote the same person, Jesus Christ.

In confirmation of this view, the passage speaks of the "appearing" (*epiphaneia*). In the NT, this term is used only of Christ, not of God the Father. The other uses, all pertaining to Christ, are found in 2 Thessalonians 2:8; 1 Timothy 6:14; 2 Timothy 1:10; 4:1, 8. So the appearing here, too, is that of Christ who is God, not of God *and* Christ. Here, too, then, *theos* refers to Christ.

The Granville Sharp rule also makes *theos* refer to Christ in 2 Peter 1:1, "Simeon Peter, a servant and apostle of Jesus Christ, To those who have obtained a faith of equal standing with ours by the righteousness of our God and Savior Jesus Christ." Note the parallel with "Lord and Savior" in verse 11, which certainly refers to Christ.

---

27. Among exegetes holding this position, see Bruce Metzger, "The Punctuation of Rom. 9:5," in *Christ and Spirit in the New Testament*, ed. Barnabas Lindars, Stephen S. Smalley, and C. F. D. Moule (Cambridge: Cambridge University Press, 1973), 95–112; also commentaries on Romans by Cranfield, Fitzmyer, and others.

28. H. E. Dana and Julius R. Mantey, *A Manual Grammar of the Greek New Testament* (New York: Macmillan, 1955), 147. Others favoring this interpretation of these verses: Nigel Turner, *Grammatical Insights into the New Testament* (Edinburgh: T. and T. Clark, 1977), 15–16; Murray J. Harris, *Jesus as God* (Grand Rapids: Baker, 1992), 174–85; also commentaries by I. Howard Marshall, Michael Green, Douglas Moo, Gordon H. Clark.

For the same reason, 2 Thessalonians 1:12, "that the name of our Lord Jesus may be glorified in you, and you in him, according to the grace of our God and the Lord Jesus Christ," is better translated omitting the definite article before "Lord."

1 Timothy 3:15–16

Here, Paul says:

> If I delay, you may know how one ought to behave in the household of God, which is the church of the living God, a pillar and buttress of the truth. Great indeed, we confess, is the mystery of godliness:
>
> He was manifested in the flesh,
>   vindicated by the Spirit,
>   seen by angels,
> proclaimed among the nations,
>   believed on in the world,
>   taken up in glory.

The nearest antecedent of "He" in verse 16 is "God" in 15. But verse 16 clearly describes the incarnate life of Christ.

Hebrews 1:8

This verse quotes Psalm 45:6 and applies it to Christ to show that Christ is above the angels: "But of the Son he says, 'Your throne, O God, is forever and ever, the scepter of uprightness is the scepter of your kingdom.'" Clearly, the writer to the Hebrews believes that *theos* here refers to Jesus.

1 John 5:20

John tells his readers:

> And we know that the Son of God has come and has given us understanding, so that we may know him who is true; and we are in him who is true, in his Son Jesus Christ. He is the true God and eternal life.

"Christ" is the antecedent of "he." John identifies Christ with the "true God" and (as in John 14:6 and 17:3) with eternal life.

Philippians 2:6

We should also look briefly at two texts that do not directly use *theos* to refer to Christ, but that use forms of the term in such a way as to clearly affirm Jesus' deity. In Philippians 2:1–11, Paul exhorts the church to have the mind of Christ: an attitude of humility, putting others ahead of self. He uses the example of Christ, who humbled himself by leaving the divine glory and suffering death for human beings. In verse 6, Paul indicates the essential nature of Jesus and therefore his right to full divine honor:

> [Jesus], though he was in the form of God, did not count equality with God a thing to be grasped.

The NIV correctly translates *hos en morphe theou huparchon* as "being in very nature God." There is some dispute over the meaning of the phrase *morphe theou*, translated "form of God" in the ESV. Most interpreters have agreed with the assessment of M. R. Vincent that *morphe* here is "that expression of being which is identified with the essential nature and character of God, and which reveals it."[29] More recent writers have sought to read *morphe theou* as either "image of God" or "glory of God," but the linguistic case for these options is weak.[30] The parallel between *morphe theou* and *morphe doulou* in verse 7 forces us to take *morphe* in the sense of "essential qualities." So Paul is teaching that Jesus was fully God, but humbled himself to the point of death to save us from sin.[31]

Colossians 2:9

In this text, Paul affirms, "For in him the whole fullness of deity dwells bodily." "Fullness," *pleroma*, may be a response to Gnostics for whom the *pleroma* was a system of many deities that were somehow emanations of one supreme being. Paul affirms that Jesus is not one of many *aeons* as the Gnostics would have it, but contains in himself the entire fullness of deity. There can be no question but that this text teaches the deity of Christ in the strongest possible sense. *Pleroma* rules out any mitigation of the meaning of *theotes*, "deity." This language is, if possible, even stronger than the texts that merely apply to Jesus the term *theos*.

Epilogue

Someone might ask why references to Christ as God in the NT are so few and so often controversial. As for the controversy, it is not surprising that people want to find ways to reject the stupendous claim made about him by Jesus himself and his apostles. His deity has long been a stumbling block to unbelief.

Nevertheless, we might well wish that these references were more frequent in the NT. Ignatius, bishop of Antioch (d. A.D. 110–15), refers to Jesus as God fourteen times in his seven letters to churches, so that use seems well established in the postapostolic generation. But it surprises us that the NT writers themselves seem to take so little notice of the astounding fact that a man was God.

We should remember, however, that *theos*, "God," is not the only term that indicates the deity of Christ. As I have mentioned, Paul uses *theos* rarely of Christ,

---

29. M. R. Vincent, *The International Critical Commentary: A Critical and Exegetical Commentary on the Epistles to the Philippians and to Philemon* (New York: Scribner, 1897), 57–58.

30. See Wells, *The Person of Christ*, 63–64, for a brief rebuttal of these positions.

31. For the controversy over the "emptying" (*kenosis*) of verse 7 (NASB), see chapter 37.

because he prefers the divine title *kyrios*. And as we have seen, *kyrios* is no less a divine title than *theos*. If anything, *kyrios* is the stronger term. *Theos* is more or less the NT equivalent of *elohim*, *kyrios* the NT equivalent of *Yahweh*. And *Yahweh* not only names God, but focuses on his relation to his people as Lord of the covenant. And of course, Jesus is called *kyrios* in the NT far more often than he is called *theos*.

We should also remember that the NT is more interested in redemption than in ontology per se. *Yahweh* and *kyrios* are divine names, but focused particularly on God's redemptive covenant, rather than the divine nature as such. Certainly it is remarkable that Jewish monotheists like the apostles came to believe that a man was God. But for them it was even more astonishing that in this God-man all the redemptive promises of God had been fulfilled. This wonderful fulfillment of redemption is better expressed by the *Yahweh-kyrios* vocabulary than by *elohim-theos*.

And the NT also witnesses to the deity of Christ by the titles *Son* and *Christ*, as well as in other ways to be discussed below, reinforcing the conclusion that the deity of Christ is a *pervasive* doctrine of Scripture.

Other Titles of Christ

1. *Son of Man* is the title that Jesus uses most often of himself. Others use it of him only in Acts 7:56; Revelation 1:13; and 14:14. In general, a "son of man" is a man, just as the "Son of God" (in the unique sense noted earlier) is God. So "son of man" is the regular phrase by which God addresses the prophet Ezekiel.[32] But there is much more to be said about the NT use, which regularly alludes to Daniel 7. In that passage, Daniel sees God, the "Ancient of Days," on his throne of judgment, surrounded by thousands of attendants. Then

> I saw in the night visions,
>
> and behold, with the clouds of heaven
>   there came one like a son of man,
> and he came to the Ancient of Days
>   and was presented before him.
> And to him was given dominion
>   and glory and a kingdom,
> that all peoples, nations, and languages
>   should serve him;
> his dominion is an everlasting dominion,
>   which shall not pass away,
> and his kingdom one
>   that shall not be destroyed. (Dan. 7:13–14)

32. So in Psalm 8:4–8; but note here, as in the Christological use, the emphasis on the dominion and authority of the son of man, over all other creatures. Similarly Psalm 80:17.

Who is this being who is "like a son of man"? The interpretation of the vision equates the son of man with "the saints":

> These four great beasts are four kings who shall arise out of the earth. But the saints of the Most High shall receive the kingdom and possess the kingdom forever, forever and ever. (Dan. 7:17–18)

They possess the kingdom because the Ancient of Days pronounces judgment in their favor (Dan. 7:22).

Jesus' self-designation as Son of Man, however, certainly distinguishes him from other men, even from "the saints." For in the NT passages, the Son of Man is not the church as a whole, but an individual who rules both the church and the world. *Son of man* is equivalent to other Christological titles: The Son of Man is Christ, the Son of God (Matt. 16:13–16), Lord (even of the Sabbath) (Matt. 12:8; Mark 2:28). When the Son of Man is lifted up in crucifixion, says Jesus, "then you will know that I am" (John 8:28, a verse that as we have seen may contain an allusion to the "I AM" of Exodus 3:14).

In a broader biblico-theological context, we may understand that the Son of Man is related to the saints as their *representative*. He is the second Adam (1 Cor. 15:22, 45–49). It is because of his perfection that God pronounces, as in Daniel 7:22, a judgment in favor of the saints rather than against them. As Son of Man, he has the power to forgive sins (Mark 2:5–10; Luke 5:20–24; 7:47–49; Acts 5:31). Appropriately, it is the Son of Man who "gather[s] his elect" when he returns in glory (Mark 13:27), for it is he who planted them as "good seed" on the earth (Matt. 13:37).

He is perfect not only in his own character, but also in that he lays down his own life as a perfect sacrifice for sin. So Jesus often associates the title *Son of Man* with his sufferings (Matt. 8:20), death (Mark 8:31; 9:12, 31; 10:33, 45; 14:21, 41; John 3:14–15; 8:28), burial (Matt. 12:40), resurrection (Mark 8:31; 9:9, 31; 10:34), and glorious return (Matt. 16:27; 24:44; 25:31; 26:64; Mark 8:38; 13:26; 14:62; Luke 19:10; John 6:62). The references to the return of the Son of Man on the clouds bring us full circle back to the picture in Daniel 7:13–14. So like Daniel's son of man, Jesus receives power and authority, participating in the final judgment (Mark 8:38). He has authority to judge *because* he is Son of Man (John 5:27).

Son of Man, therefore, refers in the first instance to Jesus' humanity as the representative of God's elect who saves them from sin. But as we have seen, only God can save (Jonah 2:10). The Son of Man is a transcendent, heavenly figure, as in Daniel 7, who like Yahweh comes "with the clouds" (recall our earlier discussion of the divine glory-cloud in chapter 18) and rules with power and authority. He is *Lord* of all things human, including the Sabbath day (Matt. 12:8; Mark 2:28). So Jesus as Son of Man is human, but not merely human. As Son of Man, he shares divine powers and prerogatives.

2. *Word* is a title of Christ in John 1:1–14 (which we considered earlier) and Revelation 19:13. It is implicit in Colossians 1:15–18, which describes Jesus as the agent of creation, the OT role of God's word (Gen. 1; Ps. 33:6, 9), and Hebrews 1:2–4, in

which Jesus is the final revelation of God. As we will see in chapter 23, *word* is an attribute of God, and from our earlier discussion of John 1 it is evident that *Word* is there a divine title.[33]

3. *Image of God* applies, of course, to all human beings (Gen. 1:27) in Scripture, but like other titles that we have considered, it applies to Jesus in a higher sense. He is the light of God that no sinner has in himself; all of us need to see his glory if we are to be saved (2 Cor. 4:4). He is *the* image of God, and thus he has special prerogatives over the world—prerogatives of God, not of a mere man. He is the Creator, the One in whom all things hold together, supreme over all (Col. 1:15–20). He is

> the radiance of the glory of God and the exact imprint of his nature, and he upholds the universe by the word of his power. (Heb. 1:3)

The writer to the Hebrews describes Jesus in these ways to show that he is higher than the angels.

4. *Savior* (similarly *Redeemer, Deliverer*) is a term that we often associate properly with Jesus' mission on earth. But we should remember that this term is a divine title in the OT. It is also associated with human deliverers (Judg. 3:9, 15; 6:36; Isa. 19:20), but in one sense salvation is *exclusively* divine. Only God can save us from our worst predicament: "I, I am the LORD, and besides me there is no savior" (Isa. 43:11; cf. 45:15, 21; 47:4; 49:26; 60:16; 63:1–8; Hos. 13:4; Luke 1:47; 1 Tim. 2:3; 4:10; Titus 1:3; 3:4; Rev. 19:1).

The NT makes it clear that Jesus is Savior in this highest sense. When the angel announces to the shepherds the birth of Jesus, he speaks of a "Savior" who is "Christ the Lord" (Luke 2:11). The Samaritans confess that Jesus "is indeed the Savior of the world" (John 4:42). Peter announces that "God exalted him at his right hand as Leader and Savior, to give repentance to Israel and forgiveness of sins" (Acts 5:31). In such contexts, Jesus is *the* Savior, the One who brings the final deliverance from sin. Cf. Acts 13:23; Eph. 5:23; Phil. 3:20; 2 Tim. 1:10; Titus 1:4;[34] etc.

5. *Holy One* is a divine title in the OT (as 2 Kings 19:22; Pss. 71:22; 78:41, 89:18–19; often in Isaiah and later prophets). In the NT, the demons themselves bear witness that Jesus is the "Holy One of God" (Mark 1:24; Luke 4:34). He is the Holy One of Psalm 16:10, who cannot see corruption (Acts 2:27; 13:35). Though all of God's people are holy, the term applied to Jesus is certainly singular, distinct. He is *the* Holy One. Similar points can be made about the title *Righteous One* (Acts 3:14; 7:52; 22:14).

6. *Alpha and Omega, beginning and end*, is also a divine title. In Isaiah 44:6, God says, "I am the first and I am the last; besides me there is no god." There can be only one "first and last," and that One can be only God. Cf. Rev. 1:8. But the book of Revelation

---

33. The use of *Word* as a divine title can also be found in extrabiblical Jewish literature. See the Onkelos Targum on Genesis 3:8, 10, 24, which describes the voice of the Word (*memra*) walking in the garden; also in Deuteronomy 33:27.

34. Note the alternation between "God our Savior" in Titus 1:3 and "Christ Jesus our Savior" in 1:4. Both phrases are common in the later books of the NT, virtually interchangeable.

often applies these phrases to Jesus, indeed from the lips of the risen Christ himself (see Rev. 1:17–18; 2:8; 21:6; 22:13).

Other Evidence for Jesus' Deity

I believe that the evidence for Jesus' deity presented above is overwhelming. But there is much more. In *DG*, chapter 28, I discuss at length other lines of biblical support for this conclusion:

1. Jesus bears divine attributes: holiness, perfect truth, wisdom, almighty power, eternity, immutability, glory.
2. Jesus performs divine acts: creation, providence, miracle, forgiveness of sins, final judgment.
3. Jesus in Scripture is an object of faith and worship.

In the same chapter, I discuss Bible passages that allegedly pose difficulties for faith in Jesus' deity—e.g., Prov. 8:22; Mark 10:18; John 14:28; 17:3; 1 Cor. 8:6; 11:3; 15:28; Col. 1:15–18.

The Deity of the Holy Spirit

As with Christ, some have argued against the full deity of the Holy Spirit. The ancient Arians, followed by modern cultists, made the Son by nature less than God and the Spirit less than the Son. But it is not difficult to show that Scripture regards the Spirit, like the Son, to be fully God. My treatment of this issue will be parallel to my treatment of the deity of Christ, but briefer, because the biblical references are fewer, and because the arguments here closely parallel arguments already discussed.

We have already seen that in the Trinitarian triadic texts, the Spirit stands alongside the Father and Son: Matt. 28:19; Rom. 15:19; 2 Cor. 13:14; Eph. 2:21–22; 4:4–6; Phil. 3:3; Rev. 1:4–5; 2:7. It is inconceivable that in these texts that identify the divine name, specify the ultimate source of spiritual blessing, and speak of God in worshipful terms, one of the members should lack full divine status. There are also a number of texts that mention two members of the Trinity. We saw earlier some texts that mention Father and Son, but there are also several that mention the Son and Spirit as equal partners[35] (see Acts 9:31; Rom. 15:30; 1 Cor. 6:11; Phil. 2:1; Heb. 10:29; Rev. 2:18, 29 [where both Son and Spirit speak God's words to the churches]). In these passages as well, it is impossible that one partner should be divine and the other nondivine.

As with Jesus, there are many places where NT writers refer to OT texts dealing with Yahweh and apply them to the Holy Spirit. Words ascribed to Yahweh in Jeremiah 31:33–34 are ascribed to the Spirit in Hebrews 10:15–17. Consider similar parallels in:

---

35. I don't know of any passages where Father and Spirit are mentioned without the Son. Why are these lacking? Perhaps because of the very close relation between Son and Spirit: the Spirit comes to bear witness to the Son (John 14:26; 15:26; 16:13).

- Lev. 16:1, 15–34; Heb. 9:8
- Ps. 95:7–11; Heb. 3:7b–11
- Isa. 6:9–10; Acts 28:25–28
- Isa. 64:4; 1 Cor. 2:9

Scripture actually refers to the Spirit as "God" in Acts 5:3–4. Ananias lied to the Holy Spirit (v. 3); therefore, he has lied to God (v. 4). In 1 Corinthians 3:16–17; Paul says that believers are the temple of God because the Spirit of God dwells in us (cf. 6:19–20).

In Mark 3:28–29, Jesus speaks of a blasphemy against the Holy Spirit—but in Scripture, blasphemy is always against God.

As with Jesus, the Spirit has divine *attributes*. The Messiah's own divine qualities can be represented as being due to the Spirit's endowment:

> And the Spirit of the LORD shall rest upon him,
>   the Spirit of wisdom and understanding,
>   the Spirit of counsel and might,
>   the Spirit of knowledge and the fear of the LORD. (Isa. 11:2)

He is the *grace and love* of God given to man, motivating believers to godliness (Rom. 5:5; 15:30; 2 Cor. 6:6; Gal. 5:16–17; Phil. 2:1; Col. 1:8). As such, he is the living water, the fullness of divine blessing (Luke 11:13; John 4:10; 7:38–39; Rev. 22:1, 17). He is the *power* of God (Judg. 14:6; 1 Sam. 11:6–7; Isa. 11:2; 40:6–7 KJV; Mic. 3:8; Luke 1:35; Acts 1:8; 10:38; Rom. 15:13, 19).

Like the Father and the Son, the Spirit is *eternal* (Heb. 9:14), *omniscient* (Isa. 40:13; 1 Cor. 2:10–11), *wise* (Isa. 11:2), *omnipresent* (Ps. 139:7–10; Acts 1:8), *incomprehensible* (Isa. 40:13). Scripture calls him *holy* nearly a hundred times, and clearly his holiness is the holiness of God, not the derivative holiness of a creature.

Like the Son, the Spirit performs all the *acts* of God. He is the *Creator* (and therefore not a creature) (Gen. 1:2; Pss. 33:6;[36] 104:30). Like Father and Son, he is the *Judge* of creatures (John 16:8–11). He is the *Giver of Life*, both physical and spiritual (Gen. 2:7; Job 33:4; Ps. 104:30; John 3:5–8; 6:63; Rom. 8:11; 1 Cor. 15:45; 2 Cor. 3:6; cf. earlier references to the living water, the water of life). He makes us aware of our *adoption* by God (Rom. 8:15). Through him, we are *washed, sanctified, and justified* (1 Cor. 6:11). The Spirit confers *gifts* on God's people so that they can serve him in many ways (Judg. 3:10; 6:34; 11:29; 1 Cor. 12:6, 11). He is the *Paraclete*, the believer's advocate (John 14:16, 26; 15:26; 16:7). He is "another" Paraclete, for Jesus himself is the original. The Spirit, then, shares in the work of Jesus, standing to defend God's people.

He is also the *Teacher* of the church, the One who speaks the Word of God.[37] Regularly in the OT, the Spirit "comes upon" prophets, enabling them to speak

---

36. Recall that in Hebrew, *breath* and *spirit* are the same word: *ruach*. The Spirit is the powerful breath of God that accomplishes God's purposes, though as we will see, he is also personal.

37. The Trinitarian picture here is that the Father is the speaker, the Son the Word, and the Spirit the powerful breath that carries the Word to its hearers and brings about their response.

God's words (Num. 11:25; 24:2; 1 Sam. 10:10; 18:10; 19:23; 2 Kings 2:9; 2 Chron. 18:23; 24:20; Isa. 61:1; Ezek. 2:2; Mic. 3:8). So to Paul, the Scriptures of the OT are *theopneustos*, breathed out by God's Spirit (*pneuma*) (2 Tim. 3:16). Jesus promises that the Spirit will give his words to the disciples (Matt. 10:20; Luke 12:12). So when the Spirit comes upon the apostles in the book of Acts, they speak of Jesus. John even says that because of the anointing of the Spirit, God's people need no human teachers (1 John 2:27).[38]

These considerations also go to show that the Spirit is a *person*, not an impersonal force. In the Trinitarian triadic texts, it is impossible to imagine that the Father and Son are personal, but that the Spirit is something else. Further, the divine attributes of the Spirit and the divine acts that the Spirit performs make it clear that the Spirit is personal.

So we see that God is one, but that he is also three persons, each of them fully divine.

Key Terms
Kyrios
Christ
Son of God
Monogenes
Son of man
Word
Image of God
Savior
Colwell rule
Granville Sharp rule
pleroma

Study Questions
1. "The doctrine of the Trinity in the NT is 'not so much inculcated as presupposed.'" Explain; evaluate. Cite some passages where Jesus' deity is "taken for granted."
2. Is it wrong to speak of Jesus' *egocentrism*? Explain the term and show how it fits into the discussion of Jesus' deity.
3. Review some of the "negative evidence" for Jesus' deity.
4. The term *kyrios* is "a divine title, identifying Jesus with Yahweh, the Lord of the OT." Explain; evaluate, citing some relevant texts.
5. Mention some OT passages referring to Yahweh that the NT relates to (a) Jesus and (b) the Holy Spirit.

---

38. I presume that John speaks here of the basic teachings of the gospel that, as he says, his readers already know. Elsewhere, the NT does make provision for human teachers in the church and calls Christians to listen to those teachers, as in Hebrews 13:7, 17.

6. Mention some passages referring to Jesus by the term *theos* and/or its derivatives. Explain their likely meaning.

7. How would you reply to a Jehovah's Witness who denied that John 1:1 identifies Jesus with God?

8. Make a case for the deity of the Holy Spirit, citing biblical texts.

Memory Verses

Isa. 9:6: For to us a child is born,
    to us a son is given;
and the government shall be upon his shoulder,
    and his name shall be called
Wonderful Counselor, Mighty God,
    Everlasting Father, Prince of Peace.

John 1:1: In the beginning was the Word, and the Word was with God, and the Word was God.

John 8:57–58: So the Jews said to him, "You are not yet fifty years old, and have you seen Abraham?" Jesus said to them, "Truly, truly, I say to you, before Abraham was, I am."

John 20:28: My Lord and my God!

Col. 2:9–10: For in him the whole fullness of deity dwells bodily, and you have been filled in him, who is the head of all rule and authority.

Resources for Further Study

Frame, John M. *DG*, chapter 28.

Reymond, Robert. *Jesus, Divine Messiah*. Phillipsburg, NJ: Presbyterian and Reformed, 1990.

Warfield, B. B. *The Lord of Glory*. New York: American Tract Society, 1907; repr., Grand Rapids: Baker, 1974.

C H A P T E R 2 2

FATHER, SON, AND SPIRIT

IN CHAPTER 20, I PRESENTED a summary formulation of the doctrine of the Trinity: (1) God is one. (2) God is three. (3) The three persons are each fully God. (4) Each of the persons is distinct from the others. (5) The three are related to one another eternally as Father, Son, and Holy Spirit. Chapter 20 introduced the subject and developed theses 1 and 2. Chapter 21 defended thesis 3. In this chapter, I will deal with 4 and 5, focusing on the distinctions and relations among the three persons.

In this chapter, I will give more attention than before to the church's creedal formulations and to the history of theological reflection on these subjects, since that tradition has raised and answered important questions about the Trinity that bear especially on theses 4 and 5. I will therefore be giving more consideration here to the technical terminology by which the Trinitarian distinctions have been expressed.

The Distinctness of the Persons

Some theologians, impressed with the biblical emphasis on the unity of God, have minimized the distinctions between Father, Son, and Spirit. Herman Bavinck explains:

> The precursors of Sabellianism in the second and third centuries A.D. were Noetus, Praxeas, Epigonus, and Cleomenes, who taught that in Christ, the Father himself had been born and had suffered and died; that the "Father" and the "Son" were names for the same person in different relations, namely, before and during his incarnation, both for the same person as such as well as in his historical manifestation; or also that the *divine* nature in Christ was the Father and the *human* nature, the flesh (*sarx*), the Son. Now, in the third century this monarchianism, patripassianism,[1] or modalism was promulgated and further developed by Sabellius. The Father, Son, and Spirit are the same God; they are three names for one and the same being. Calling this being *"Huiopator,"*[2] he applied the name to its three successive energies or stages. God consisted first of all in the person (*prosopon*), the appearance or mode of the Father,

---

1. Literally, *Father-suffering*, from their belief that the Father suffered on the cross.
2. Literally, *Son-Father*.

namely, as Creator and Lawgiver; next, in the *prosopon* of the Son as Redeemer, from the time of his incarnation to the moment of his ascension, and finally in the *prosopon* of the Holy Spirit as the Vivifier.[3]

This position holds that God is one person, with three masks (*prosopa*), playing three roles. For Sabellius, the roles were historically successive, but for some modalists they are simultaneous, each a kind of aspect or revelation of God. For modalists, as with Gnostics and Arians, the divine nature itself is hidden from us because it is transcendent. We know God only through various roles that he plays in history, but none of these roles presents us with God as he really is. (Recall my discussion in chapter 3: this is a form of unbiblical transcendence.)[4]

Thus is the doctrine of the Trinity related to the doctrines of God's transcendence and immanence and, in turn, to the doctrines of divine lordship and revelation. If God's transcendence removes him from our knowledge, then of course we have no rational basis for making Trinitarian distinctions within God's being. But if God is transcendent as the *Lord*, involved in our history and revealing himself in his Word, then we can make the distinctions that he himself has revealed to us.

We can understand, then, why modalism appealed especially to later thinkers (Erigena, Abelard, Joachim of Floris, Servetus, Boehme, Swedenborg, Kant, Schleiermacher, Schelling, Hegel) whose thought was governed more by speculation than by Scripture.[5] Apart from revelation, the human mind would never conceive of the Trinity.[6] Apart from revelation, God is an unknown, a mystery, about which nothing more can be said. So if there are differentiations or distinctions to be made within such a being, we cannot know them. We are therefore shut up either to modalism or to a view such as Arianism, in which all "divine distinctions" are actually within the creaturely realm.

In Scripture, however, it is clear, as we have seen, that Father, Son, and Spirit are all divine and, further, that they are distinct from one another. That should be obvious from all the many personal transactions among the persons. The Father appoints the Son to a place of honor (Pss. 2:7; 110:1). Father and Son know each other (Matt. 11:27), but the Son is somehow ignorant of something the Father knows (Mark 13:32). The Word is *with* God, as well as being God (John 1:1–2). The Father gave his Son to die for sinners (John 3:16; Gal. 4:4–6). Jesus prays to the Father (Mark 14:36; John 17;

---

3. *BRD*, 2:290.

4. Compare also the discussion in Helmut Thielicke, *The Evangelical Faith* (Grand Rapids: Eerdmans, 1977), 2:146–49; Otto Weber, *Foundations of Dogmatics* (Grand Rapids: Eerdmans, 1981), 1:366–71.

5. Karl Barth has often been accused of modalism because he objects to the idea that God has three "centers of consciousness," and he interprets the Trinity merely as an expression of the freedom of God as Lord "to become wholly different from Himself and then to return to Himself." See Cornelius Van Til, *The New Modernism* (Philadelphia: Presbyterian and Reformed, 1946, 1973), 222; cf. 221–30, 145–59. See also Leonard Hodgson, *The Doctrine of the Trinity* (New York; Scribner, 1944, 1963), 229. Barth rejected this criticism, however. See *CD*, 4.4:19–23.

6. There have been, however, some modalists of evangelical background who have attempted the impossible task of defending this position by Scripture, such as the "Jesus only" Pentecostals. See, e.g., John Miller, *Is God a Trinity?* (Hazelwood, MO: Word Aflame Press, 1975). But Miller, like the liberal rationalists, frequently urges that orthodox Trinitarianism contradicts reason.

many other places), making requests, giving thanks, expressing love.[7] He teaches the disciples to pray to the Father in the name of Jesus (John 16:23). Jesus asks the Father to send the Spirit, who is "another" Paraclete distinct from Jesus himself (John 14:16). The Father speaks from heaven, testifying to the Son (Matt. 17:5). Jesus ascends to the Father (John 20:17) and sits down with the Father on the Father's throne (Rev. 3:21). The angelic chorus ascribes salvation to God *and* to the Lamb (Rev. 7:10). None of this makes sense on a modalistic basis. The members of the Godhead are distinct persons.

The Distinct Personality of the Spirit

Clearly, then, Father and Son are distinct persons.[8] But questions have been raised as to whether the Spirit is a third person coordinate with Father and Son, or whether the Spirit is a kind of impersonal force or power associated with God.

We are often inclined to equate spirit with the nonmaterial realm, so that *spirit* amounts to a force that animates matter. But *spirits* in Scripture, human as well as divine, are persons, not impersonal forces. And as I indicated in chapter 18, God's spirituality is not *merely* power, but the personal qualities of the Holy Spirit.

Certainly Scripture connects the Spirit closely with the power of God (see Mic. 3:8; Zech. 4:6; Luke 1:17, 35; 4:14; Acts 1:8; 10:38; Rom. 1:4; 15:13, 19; 1 Cor. 2:4; 1 Thess. 1:5; 2 Tim. 1:7). But the power of God is never impersonal. It is a power directed by God's intelligent plan to accomplish his purposes. The Spirit, therefore, represents not only God's power, but his wisdom as well (Ex. 28:3; 31:3; 35:31; Deut. 34:9; Isa. 11:2; Dan. 5:11, 14; Luke 1:17; 2:40; Acts 6:10; 1 Cor. 2:4; 12:8; Eph. 1:17). The Spirit has a "mind" (Rom. 8:27). Often it is quite impossible to substitute "power" for "spirit" (see, e.g., Acts 10:38; Rom. 15:13; 1 Cor. 2:4). The Holy Spirit is not a mere power; he is the *personal bearer* of divine power.

Spirit (*pneuma*) is a neuter word in Greek (though the corresponding Hebrew term, *ruach*, is feminine), but the biblical writers often use masculine pronouns with it, emphasizing the personality of the Spirit. In John 14:17, Jesus speaks of

> the Spirit of truth, whom the world cannot receive, because it neither sees him nor knows him. You know him, for he dwells with you and will be in you.

Cf. John 14:26; 16:14; 1 Cor. 12:11. The Spirit speaks using the first-person "I" in Acts 10:20; 13:2. He performs acts that only persons perform: comforting, revealing, inspiring, speaking, witnessing, hearing, sending, knowing, teaching, guiding, striving, interceding.

As we have seen, the Spirit is divine, coordinate with Father and Son as a bearer of the divine name (Matt. 28:19; 2 Cor. 13:14). So he cannot be different from them in

---

7. Modalists sometimes reply that in his prayers, Jesus in his human nature (the Son) is conversing with his divine nature (the Father). But natures are not personal beings. They do not converse with one another. Only *persons* enter personal transactions. So either Jesus is two persons (the heresy ascribed to Nestorius) or he is a person distinct from the person of the Father.

8. For the technical definition of *person* in this context, see later discussion.

nature. But for the same reason, he must be distinct from them, as Father and Son are distinct from each other.

Second Corinthians 3:17–18 has sometimes been thought to compromise the distinction between the Spirit and Christ. Paul says there:

> Now the Lord is the Spirit, and where the Spirit of the Lord is, there is freedom. And we all, with unveiled face, beholding the glory of the Lord, are being transformed into the same image from one degree of glory to another. For this comes from the Lord who is the Spirit.

Here, Paul makes a clear allusion to Exodus 34:34, in which Moses removes a veil from his face when he enters the presence of the Lord (that is, Yahweh). In the Exodus passage, the "Lord" to whom we turn (2 Cor. 3:16) is Yahweh, without explicit Trinitarian distinction. Yahweh is, as we have seen, Father, Son, and Spirit in one. The Lord *is* the Father, the Son, and also the Spirit. So to cite here an identity between the Lord and the Spirit causes no Trinitarian confusion. For Paul, it is important to identify Yahweh specifically with the Spirit here, because he is considering the Spirit's ministry of giving life, as opposed to the law's ministry of death (v. 6). When we turn to the Lord, Yahweh, we turn to the Spirit. The Lord (Yahweh) is spirit (cf. John 4:24), not law, so he opens our hearts (2 Cor. 3:15) and gives spiritual life (v. 6), freedom (v. 17), and glory (v. 18).

The problem in 2 Corinthians 3:17–18 emerges because *Lord* (*kyrios*) is also, as we have seen, Paul's normal term for Jesus Christ, and in his application of Exodus 34, "turn[ing] to the Lord" (2 Cor. 3:16) is "turning to Jesus." This application is appropriate because of course Yahweh *is* Jesus; to turn to Yahweh is to turn to Jesus. "The Lord" in 2 Corinthians 3:17–18 is, I would say, primarily a reference to Yahweh, but there is certainly some connotation here of Christ as Lord, especially since the passage deals with the contrast between law and grace. And since Yahweh is the Spirit, and Jesus is Yahweh, in one sense Jesus is the Spirit.

This creates some awkwardness with the standard Trinitarian language,[9] but it is plain here that Paul is not concerned to make precise Trinitarian distinctions, nor certainly to repudiate distinctions that he makes elsewhere between the three persons.

We do see here some of the mystery of the Trinity. Though the doctrine is not irrational, there are aspects of it that are very difficult to understand. Generally, we say that things identical to the same thing (here, Jesus and the Spirit to Yahweh) are identical to each other (so the Lord is the Spirit). In 2 Corinthians 3:17–18, that logical inference is allowed. But we know from other Scriptures that that is not the whole story, and the "identity" here is not an identity in every sense, but an identity of nature or essence.[10]

Of course, this passage does imply a very close relationship between Christ and the Spirit in ways other than commonness of nature, as we see elsewhere in biblical phrases

9. I recall the traditional Sunday school illustration: "the Father is God, the Son is God, the Spirit is God; but the Father is not the Son, nor the Son the Spirit, nor the Spirit the Father."

10. Later in this chapter, I will discuss Vern Poythress's Trinitarian use of logic, which bears on this question.

such as "Spirit of Christ." Christ accomplishes his work by a special endowment of the Spirit (Isa. 61:1; Matt. 3:16; 12:18; Luke 4:18), and the work of the Spirit is to bear witness to Christ (John 15:26). But these phrases themselves reflect a distinction between Christ and the Spirit, as even here in 1 Corinthians 3:17, the phrase "Spirit *of* the Lord."

The passage recalls 1 Corinthians 15:45, where Jesus, as second Adam, is made "a life-giving spirit." In that function of giving life, the Son and Spirit are both so intimately involved that they are scarcely distinguishable. Another passage that intertwines references to Christ and to the Spirit in their life-giving work is Romans 8:9–11:

> You, however, are not in the flesh but in the Spirit, if in fact the Spirit of God dwells in you. Anyone who does not have the Spirit of Christ does not belong to him. But if Christ is in you, although the body is dead because of sin, the Spirit is life because of righteousness. If the Spirit of him who raised Jesus from the dead dwells in you, he who raised Christ Jesus from the dead will also give life to your mortal bodies through his Spirit who dwells in you.

But of course, this fact doesn't prevent biblical writers in other contexts from making distinctions between Son and Spirit, as we saw above, just as biblical writers make personal distinctions within the being of Yahweh. Jesus prays that the Father will send the Spirit (John 14:16), *another* Counselor, and he will not come in power until Jesus ascends to the Father.

Circumincessio

Scripture therefore presents a delicate balance between the distinctness of the persons and their mutual involvement, and I must now say more about the latter. *Circumincessio*, *circumcessio*, *circumcession*, *perichoresis*, and *coinherence* are technical terms for the mutual indwelling of the persons: the Father in the Son and the Son in him (John 10:38; 14:10–11, 20; 17:21), both in the Spirit and the Spirit in both (Rom. 8:9). To see Jesus is to see the Father (John 14:9), for he and the Father are one (10:30). When Jesus departs from the earth, he "come[s]" in the Spirit to be with his people (John 14:18).[11]

All three persons are involved in all the works of God in and for creation.[12] As we have seen, Father (Gen. 1), Son (John 1:3; Col. 1:16), and Spirit (Gen. 1:2; Ps. 104:30) are involved in the work of creation. Similarly providence and, in many ways, redemption and judgment. This is not to say that the three persons play identical roles in these events. The Father, not the Son, sent Jesus into the world to redeem his people; the

---

11. Remarkably, Jesus also draws an analogy between the mutual indwelling of the members of the Trinity and (1) the dwelling of the divine persons in believers, and (2) the unity of believers with one another (John 17:21–23). This is, of course, an analogy, not an identity: we cannot be one *exactly* as God is one. But we are called to support one another, indeed to glorify one another, as the members of the Trinity do. For more applications of this principle to the Christian life, see my "Walking Together," available at http://www.frame-poythress.org.

12. These are the *opera ad extra* in the traditional terminology, the works of God that terminate outside himself. There are acts that God performs within his own being (*opera ad intra*) in which only one person is involved, such as the Father's begetting of the Son. I will discuss these later.

Son, not the Father or Spirit, became incarnate to die on the cross for our sins. At the moment of death, indeed, he was, in some mysterious way, even estranged from his Father (Mark 15:34). The Spirit, not the Father or Son, came on the church with power on the day of Pentecost (he was *sent by* the Father and Son, John 14:15–21), though the Son comes to us *in* and *by* the Spirit.

According to Peter (1 Peter 1:1–2), the Father is the One who foreknows, the Son the One who sprinkles blood, and the Spirit the One who sanctifies. This is a useful generalization about the distinctive roles of the persons: the Father plans, the Son executes, the Spirit applies. But of course, Peter does not intend here to describe a precise division of labor. He knows that all these events require the concurrence of all three persons.

Mutual Glorification

That concurrence is a profound indication of the unity of the persons. There is no conflict in the Trinity. The three persons are perfectly agreed on what they should do and how their plan should be executed.[13] They support one another, assist one another, promote one another's purposes. This intra-Trinitarian "deference," this "disposability"[14] of each to the others, may be called *mutual glorification*.[15]

In the gospel of John, the Father glorifies the Son (John 8:50, 54; 12:23; 17:1) and the Son the Father (7:18; 17:4). The Spirit glorifies the Son (16:14), who in turn glorifies the Father.

To my knowledge, no text says precisely that the Father or Son glorifies the Spirit, but Father and Son do honor the Spirit in his particular work. In John 16:7, Jesus tells the disciples:

> It is to your advantage that I go away, for if I do not go away, the Helper will not come to you. But if I go, I will send him to you.

The Spirit, the Helper, has his special work, which is different from that of the Son. The Spirit can do that work only after the Son has ascended to the Father. So the Son defers to the Spirit. He "goes away," so that the Spirit may come. Jesus testifies, indeed, that after he is gone and the Spirit is come, the disciples will do "greater works" than

13. As man, Jesus prays to the Father that he will not have to drink the cup of the Father's wrath (Matt. 26:39). Does this desire express a disagreement in the Godhead? I think not. His request is a legitimate request, as surely the Father recognizes; for to drink the cup of wrath is something that anyone should shrink from. And Jesus also recognizes that if the cup cannot be avoided, he must accept it (v. 42); the Father's will must be done. There is a mysterious tension between Father and Son in this prayer, anticipating the Father's estrangement from Jesus at the cross, but there is no disagreement between them as to what must happen. In this time of prayer, the eternal agreement of Father and Son becomes a temporal process, in which the elements of agreement come together in time.

14. Royce Gruenler, *The Trinity in the Gospel of John* (Grand Rapids: Baker, 1986), 21 and passim.

15. In addition to Gruenler and others, I am indebted in this section to personal correspondence with Dr. Peter Leithart and the Rev. Jeffrey Meyers.

the works Jesus performed on earth (John 14:12). So Jesus pays honor to the Spirit: he rejoices that in one sense the Spirit's ministry will be greater than his own. So the Father and Son glorify the Spirit by giving to him a distinctive and great role in the work of redemption.

The mutual deference of the persons of the Trinity is a major theme in the gospel of John. The Son is always subject to the Father (5:30; 6:38; 7:18; 9:4; 10:18), but the Father defers to the Son, by answering his prayers, by granting him authority, by testifying on his behalf (John 3:35; 5:22–23, 26–27; 6:37, 43–44; 11:41–42; 12:26; 14:10; 15:2, 8).

Jesus is disposable to believers as well (John 6:49–51, 55–56; 10:7–9; etc.). He lays down his very life for them. Amazingly, the Lord is their servant (John 13:1–17; cf. Matt. 20:26–28; Luke 12:37; 22:26), and this servanthood is to be a model for relationships among believers in the church. Those in authority are not to rule for their own benefit, as the "lords" of the Gentiles, but they are to serve those under their authority, as Jesus served them. So the mutual disposability of the members of the Trinity for one another carries over into their relationships with human beings and serves as a model for their own behavior.

Certainly there are senses in which believers can never be one as the Trinity is one, and yet Jesus calls us into the oneness of the Father and Son (John 17:22). Clearly, Jesus does not intend to erase the distinction between the Creator and the creature. But the concept of mutual glorification suggests an important way in which Christians can be like the members of the Trinity: we, too, are called to defer to one another in this way, to glorify one another, to be disposable to one another's purposes, that is, to love one another as God loved us.

Substance and Persons

The main outlines of the biblical doctrine are now before us. But we must also look at various questions about this doctrine that have arisen in church history and that are still with us. One of these asks us to define ontologically or metaphysically what it means to be a member of the Trinity. How are Father, Son, and Spirit to be distinguished or identified with the one true God? Or, to put it differently, when we say that God is one and that God is three, what is it that is one, and what is three? One what? Three what?

We should be cautious in discussing such questions, to avoid speculation beyond Scripture. Scripture itself does not use technical terms for God's oneness and threeness, and as we saw, for example, in our discussion of 2 Corinthians 3:17, it is not always concerned with terminological precision in describing the relations of the three persons. Thinking about these matters is important, however, if only to avoid unbiblical formulations like those of Sabellianism and Arianism, and so that we can benefit from the important reflections on this subject by past generations.

In answering the questions "one what?" and "three what?" the church came to adopt the following terminology; see fig. 22.1.

	Greek	Latin	English
One	*Ousia,* *Physis*	*Substantia,* *Essentia*	Being, Substance, Essence, Nature
Three	*Hypostases,* *Prosopa*	*Personae*	Persons, Subsistences, Modes of subsistence

Fig. 22.1. Trinitarian Terminology

In general, these terms have served the church well. But they have also raised additional questions and caused some misunderstandings. A number of points need to be made, therefore, to promote clarity, and to describe further the circumstances by which the church came to adopt this language.

1. These are not biblical terms, but are taken from various secular uses, philosophical, legal, and otherwise. We should not, therefore, take them as sacrosanct. I doubt that we will find better terms at this juncture in history, but we should not cringe at the thought that these terms may be problematic to some people.

Many important Christian thinkers have expressed reservations about this language. Augustine said, "The answer 'three persons' is given, not that something should be said, but so as not to remain wholly silent."[16] John Calvin observed:

> Where names have not been invented rashly, we must beware lest we become chargeable with arrogance and rashness in rejecting them. I wish, indeed, that such names were buried, provided all would concur in the belief that the Father, Son, and Spirit, are one God, and yet that the Son is not the Father, nor the Spirit the Son, but that each has his peculiar subsistence. I am not so minutely precise as to fight furiously for mere words. For I observe, that the writers of the ancient Church, while they uniformly spoke with great reverence on these matters, neither agreed with each other, nor were always consistent with themselves.[17]

Calvin goes on to note inconsistencies in terminology between Jerome, Hilary, and other writers.

2. At the same time, we should not be unwilling to use extrabiblical terms when they are theologically helpful. The work of theology is not to repeat the language of Scripture, but to *apply* the language of Scripture to our thought and life.[18]

16. Augustine, *On the Trinity*, 5.9.10; translation from David Brown, "Trinitarian Personhood and Individuality," in *Trinity, Incarnation, and Atonement*, ed. Ronald J. Feenstra and Cornelius Plantinga (Notre Dame, IN: University of Notre Dame Press, 1989), 48. Cf. 7.4.9.

17. *Institutes*, 1.13.5.

18. See my discussion of *theology as application* in *DKG*, esp. 76–85, and in chapter 1 of this volume. Compare Bavinck: "Scripture, after all, has not been given us simply, parrotlike, to repeat it, but to process it in our own

3. In the Greek language prior to the Trinitarian use of these terms, and even in early Christian theology, *ousia* and *hypostasis* were not clearly or consistently distinguished. Christopher Kaiser says that "*hypostasis* and *ousia* were originally synonyms in patristic thought and remained so well into the fourth century."[19] Indeed, the original Nicene Creed anathematizes those who say that "he, the Son of God, is of a different *hypostasis* or *ousia*" (from the Father).[20] But later discussions, particularly the work of the Cappadocian fathers, led to a distinction between these two terms, and it became orthodox to say that Father and Son were different *hypostases*, but not different *ousiai*. To some extent this decision was arbitrary. Theologians needed a term for the divine unity, and they picked *ousia*; they needed a different term for the divine plurality, and they picked *hypostasis*. Nothing in the nature of these terms themselves *required* the church to use *ousia* for the unity, and *hypostasis* for the plurality, of God.

Gordon Clark, after citing an instance in which he believes Augustine identifies person and substance,[21] says:

> In spite of all the linguistic confusion, . . . [Augustine] made it quite clear that the Godhead was one in one sense and three in a different sense. Whether this difference be called *person* or *substance* is inconsequential. . . . Although it is not familiar to our ears, one could say that God is one person and three substances. In fact, translate *substance* back into Greek and it is most orthodox to say that the Godhead is three substances. It makes no difference what term one uses, provided that he clearly states that they are not synonymous. God is one and three in different senses.[22]

Elizabeth Johnson carries this line of thought a bit further:

> In explaining Augustine's point, Edmund Hill suggests that we try referring to the persons as three *x*'s in God, or as A, B, C, so unknown is the threesomeness to which the term refers. Centuries later Anselm of Canterbury will even speak of "three something-or-other," "three I know not what" (*tres nescio quid*).[23]

I agree with Anselm that when we use terms such as *substance* and *person* to refer to God, we do not entirely understand what we are talking about, but we should not embrace total agnosticism on this matter. We should avoid deductions based on the extrabiblical philosophical uses of these terms alone. Use of the terms is legitimate, but only as markers to be filled with biblical content. To say that God is three *persons*

---

minds and to reproduce it in our own words." *BRD*, 2:296.

19. Christopher Kaiser, *The Doctrine of God* (Westchester, IL: Crossway, 1982), 66. Cf. *BRD*, 2:297.

20. From the original version of the creed, from A.D. 325. The more familiar version was ratified by the Council of Constantinople of 381 and does not contain these anathemas.

21. I read the Augustine passage somewhat differently from Clark.

22. Gordon H. Clark, *The Trinity* (Jefferson, MD: Trinity Foundation, 1985), 52–53.

23. Elizabeth Johnson, *She Who Is* (New York: Crossroad Publishing, 1996), 203. She refers to Edmund Hill, *The Mystery of the Trinity* (London: Chapman, 1985), 59–60; and Anselm, *Monologium*, 78, in *St. Anselm: Basic Writings*, ed. S. N. Deane (La Salle, IL: Open Court, 1974), 142.

does not add anything to what we learn in Scripture about the Father, Son, and Spirit. Rather, the concept *person* should include all and only the content of the biblical teachings. *Person* is simply a label for the ways in which Father, Son, and Spirit are alike, in distinction from the Godhead as a whole.

It would be wrong for us to think that a careful historical study of the uses of these terms would yield the essence of the relationships between the one triune God and his three persons. What we know about these relationships (and in this area we often know less than we think we do) comes not from a study of these technical terms, but from the teachings of Scripture. The terms serve merely to label the concepts we derive from the Bible.

4. By etymology and use, the Greek *hypostasis* and the Latin *substantia* were more or less equivalent. But the Greeks used *hypostasis* for the plurality of God, and the Latins used *substantia* for God's oneness. This fact led to much misunderstanding, and all the more so because the Latin "one substance" sounded Sabellian to the Greeks: for it seemed that what the Greeks numbered as three, the Latins numbered as one. And similarly, the Greek "three hypostases" sounded Arian or even tritheistic to the Latins: as if the Latins believed in one divine substance, one God, and the Greeks believed in three.[24] These suspicions were even more encouraged by the fact that Sabellianism was predominantly a Western-Latin heresy and Arianism predominantly Eastern-Greek. And the Latins preferred *persona* (originally, *mask*) to denote the threeness of God, a term with a significant history in Sabellianism. Understandable as these suspicions were, most scholars would agree that it was possible to express orthodox Trinitarianism using either the Greek or the Latin terminology, and indeed many writers did. The confusion warns us against pursuing theological controversy based wholly on the individual words that people employ, and it provides further ground for a limited agnosticism concerning the precise meanings of these terms.

5. *Substance, nature, being,* or *essence,* in this context, is simply what God is, everything he is. J. Theodore Mueller defines *ousia* and *essentia* as "the divine nature with all its attributes."[25] Understood thus, it is evident that there can be only one divine substance, for there can be only one God.

6. The term *person* has had many meanings over the centuries, and there has been much theological controversy over what it *ought* to mean. Johnson says that *hypostasis* is

> a philosophical term that is virtually untranslatable into modern English. Its approximate meaning connotes a firm base from which an existing thing stands forth and develops; or a full-stop to a nature; or the fundamental subsistence of a thing.[26]

24. Partly for this reason, Augustine preferred the term *essentia* to *substantia*. But in Augustine's time, *essentia* was a new term, not generally used in Latin.

25. J. Theodore Mueller, *Christian Dogmatics* (St. Louis: Concordia, 1934, 1955), 153. In Aristotle's philosophy, substance is what "exists in itself" as the bearer of attributes.

26. Johnson, *She Who Is,* 203. *Subsistence* refers to a *way* in which something exists.

As noted earlier, the Latin term *persona* (equivalent to the Greek *prosopon*) could mean "mask" or "role," a meaning congenial to Sabellianism. It has also been used to refer to a legal entity, a being with rights and obligations. Sometimes writers also used the term the way in which modern writers speak of persons. That was natural, since Scripture certainly pictures the members of the Trinity as having personal interactions with one another. But not until Boethius (475–524) defined *person* as "an individual substance of a rational nature"[27] did a "modern" definition of *person* become generally accepted. Boethius himself, however, recognizes a difficulty here: that if the persons of the Trinity are "individual substances," how can it also be said, as in the traditional Latin vocabulary, that God is "one substance"?[28] And some modern writers have argued that this concept of *person*, applied to the Trinity, is tritheistic.[29] Nevertheless, as we will see later, many today advocate something like the Boethian definition in their defense of "social Trinitarianism."

7. Many writers have defined *person* as a *relation* within God, a definition that seeks to avoid tritheism, but poses difficulties of understanding. Gerald Bray finds this to be "a basic concept in Augustine's trinitarianism,"[30] and it becomes quite central to the understanding of Thomas Aquinas, who says:

> Distinction in the Godhead occurs only through relations of origin [paternity, filiation, procession]. . . . But a relation in the Godhead is not like an accident inhering in a subject. Instead, it is the divine essence itself. For that reason it is subsistent, just as the divine essence subsists. Therefore, just as deity is God, so divine paternity is God the Father, who is a divine person. "Divine person," therefore, signifies a relation as subsisting.[31]

Cornelius Plantinga notes that Thomas also presents the persons as "real persons, just as they are in the Gospel of John."[32] But he finds Aquinas's "relation" doctrine to be inconsistent with his Johannine realism. Aquinas does, to be sure, indicate that the relations are different from one another: paternity is different from filiation, and so forth. But, says Plantinga,

> Thomas simplifies things so aggressively that even that difference is eventually washed out. For each person is identical with his relation: the Father just is paternity; the

27. Boethius, *A Treatise against Eutyches and Nestorius*, 3, in *Boethius: The Theological Treatises*, ed. and trans. H. F. Stewart and E. K. Rand (Cambridge, MA: Harvard University Press, 1926), 85.

28. Edmund J. Fortman points out some further inconsistencies and hesitations in Boethius's own use of *substantia*, both for God's oneness and for his threeness. See Fortman, *The Triune God* (Grand Rapids: Baker, 1972), 163–64. Thomas Aquinas substituted the term *subsistence* for the term *substance* in this definition, in *ST*, 1.29.1.

29. Fortman refers to Karl Barth (*Triune God*, 261), Karl Rahner (299), and others who oppose the idea of three "centers of consciousness" in God and consider it tritheistic. Cf. also Johnson, *She Who Is*, 203. For Barth, see *CD*, 4.1:204–5.

30. Gerald Bray, *The Doctrine of God* (Downers Grove, IL: InterVarsity Press, 1993), 173.

31. *ST*, 1.29.4c; cf. 1.32.2–3.

32. Cornelius Plantinga, "The Threeness/Oneness Problem of the Trinity," *CTJ* 23, 1 (April 1988): 47.

Son just is filiation; the Spirit just is procession. Further, these relations themselves, Thomas explicitly says, are all really the same thing as the divine essence. They differ from it only in intelligibility, only in perception, only notionally, not ontologically. For everything in the universe that is not the divine essence is a creature.[33]

As we saw in chapter 20, the doctrine of divine simplicity plays a large role in Aquinas's thought. Nothing in God is distinct from the divine essence—neither his attributes nor his Trinitarian persons. But if the persons are just alternative names of the divine essence, Plantinga objects, Aquinas's view is indistinguishable from modalism. And when we take *Father*, *Son*, and *Spirit* as names of relations (paternity, filiation, spiration), are we not reducing concrete persons to abstract ideas, denying the real personalism of the biblical accounts?

I agree with Plantinga that we should reject Aquinas's view that the three persons are distinct only notionally, only in our minds. That position is, in my view, indistinguishable from Sabellianism. There is real distinction, real complexity in God, as I discussed in chapter 20. There I argued that God is not simple in the sense of lacking all complexity, but in the sense that each of his necessary attributes exhausts his being. We saw that each necessary attribute is a way of looking at God's complete nature. Each attribute, indeed, includes all the others (his love is eternal, his mercy just, etc.). But this kind of mutual perspectivalism does not exclude, but presupposes, complexity in the Godhead. For it is true to say that God is merciful, just, *and* eternal. His being is so complex that these and all his other attributes truly characterize him.

So we can now take a similar approach to the persons of the Trinity. Each exhausts the divine being; each bears all the divine attributes, and indeed, each is *in* the other two (*circumincessio*). So when we encounter one person, we are encountering the triune God. But when we learn that the divine being contains everything described by the divine attributes, and everything in the three persons as well, we are impressed with the wonderfully rich *complexity* that is God. There is a real difference between the Son, praying in the garden to his Father, and the Father, hearing him in heaven. But both Son and Father belong to the rich complexity that is the divine essence, and both exhaust that essence.

With Plantinga I also question Aquinas's definition of the persons as the relations of paternity, filiation, and spiration within the Godhead. Aquinas's concept of a "subsistent relation" is most odd. Relations do not subsist on their own, apart from the things they relate. Paternity doesn't exist by itself, apart from the persons (Father, Son) related to one another by paternity. And to suggest that *relation* is somehow a better term than *person* to designate the members of the Trinity is, I think, wrong. The persons are not "really" relations, rather than true persons. They are persons standing in relation.

Unlike Plantinga, I do believe in a doctrine of divine simplicity sufficient to justify the identity of the persons, their relations, and the whole divine nature. We may say,

---

33. Ibid. Thanks to Ralph A. Smith for his excellent critical summary of Plantinga's argument in *Paradox and Truth* (Tokyo: Covenant Worldview Institute, 2000).

then, that the persons are identical to their relations; but on my view it is also true to say that the relations are identical to the persons. The doctrine of simplicity should not entail reductionism. The persons are identical to their relations, but they are not *reducible* to their relations; they are not *mere* relations. The persons are no more reducible to relations than the relations are reducible to the persons. The persons and the relations both exist together, both categories exhausting the divine nature, both expressing the complexity that exists as the divine nature.

Plantinga argues that to define persons as relations implies reducing concrete personal beings to impersonal abstractions such as *paternity*. My proposal, however, is that both persons and relations can be defined in terms of one another, belonging as they do to the fullness of the Godhead. Both ultimately encompass the whole Godhead, and the whole Godhead is concrete and personal, not abstract and impersonal. So the ultimate identity of persons and relations means not that persons are "really" abstractions, but that the abstractions are "really" personal.[34] Paternity, for example, is simply the Father, standing in relation to the Son.

8. So we can see that there are important relations between *person* in the Trinitarian sense and *person* as an attribute of the divine nature (recall our discussion of God's absolute personality in chapter 3), though there are important distinctions to be made between these. Some theologians have maintained that in a sense the whole triune God is one person. B. B. Warfield, for example, argues that in the OT (which contains only hints of the Trinitarian distinctions), "the great thing to be taught the ancient people of God was that the God of all the earth is one person."[35] A full account of the Trinity would have confused the ancient Hebrews, Warfield says, in the great battle between monotheism and polytheistic idolatry.

Cornelius Van Til says:

> It is sometimes asserted that we can prove to men that we are not asserting anything that they ought to consider irrational, inasmuch as we say that God is one in essence and three in person. We therefore claim that we have not asserted unity and trinity of exactly the same being.
>
> Yet this is not the whole truth of the matter. We do assert that God, that is, the whole Godhead, is one person.[36]

---

34. In *DG*, chap. 12, I made the same point with regard to divine attributes. To identify God with his attributes is not to say that he is an abstraction or a collection of abstract qualities. It is, rather, to insist that his attributes are fully personal. Interestingly, the argument that divine simplicity implies an abstract God was made by Cornelius Plantinga's brother, philosopher Alvin Plantinga, in *Does God Have a Nature?* (Milwaukee: Marquette University Press, 1980).

35. B. B. Warfield, "The Spirit of God in the OT," in *Biblical and Theological Studies* (Philadelphia: Presbyterian and Reformed, 1952), 153.

36. Cornelius Van Til, *An Introduction to Systematic Theology* (Nutley, NJ: Presbyterian and Reformed, 1974), 229. See my discussion of this passage in my *CVT*, 65–71. Aquinas also says (in a rather obscure discussion of number) that in one sense God is one person: see *ST*, 1.30.3. And of course, more recent thinkers such as Barth and Rahner, who object to the idea of three "centers of consciousness" in God, would agree. See *CD*, 1.1:400, 414–15; Otto Weber, *Foundations of Dogmatics* (Grand Rapids: Eerdmans, 1981), 1:377.

Van Til is not teaching here the contradictory position that God is one person and three persons in the same sense of *person*, although Gordon Clark accused him of doing that.[37] In the quoted passage, Van Til's "we" joins himself to those who "claim that we have not asserted unity and trinity of exactly the same being." He only wishes to say that "this is not the whole truth of the matter." And indeed it is not, if only because the whole truth is beyond human understanding.

As I said in chapter 3, we should not deny that *personality* is an attribute of God. That God is personal, rather than impersonal, is a central teaching of Scripture, over against nonbiblical religions and philosophies. And if God is personal, and God is one, then surely in a sense he is one person. Indeed, through most of the OT, except for some Trinitarian adumbrations, God acts as a single person: planning, creating, governing, speaking, redeeming, judging.

When we speak of God as a person, or as personal, we are using *person* in a different sense from its Trinitarian use. The personality of the Godhead does not add a fourth person to the three, nor another *relation*, in the technical sense. The two senses are related, however, especially if we interpret the Trinitarian *person* in a somewhat Boethian sense. For each of these persons exhausts the Godhead, and each person is in and with the other two. The Godhead is personal because it is tripersonal. Being three persons, the Godhead cannot help but be personal, rather than impersonal, in character.

9. And as God's substance is personal, so his persons are substantival. They are each a subject of predication. They are distinct from one another, and each has some property that distinguishes it from the others. In the traditional vocabulary, these properties are unbegottenness (the Father), begottenness (the Son), and passive spiration (the Spirit).[38] Theologians have taken care to call these *personal properties* rather than *attributes of God*. Attributes, in the usual theological vocabulary, belong to the whole divine nature and to all three persons, while personal properties belong to one person in distinction from the others and from the whole Godhead.

But the properties are attributes grammatically and metaphysically. Certainly Father, Son, and Spirit are *beings*, subjects of predication, just as is the Godhead as a whole. The persons are, in the Greek terminology, *hypostases*. Boethius was not unreasonable (though he was terminologically awkward) in calling them *substances*. And the personal properties are predicates of those substantival subjects, attributes of the persons. And since each person exhausts the divine nature, the personal properties are predicates of the divine nature, attributes of God. God is a Father (Mal. 1:6; John 5:18; 1 John 3:1), a Son (John 1:1, 14, 18), and a Spirit (John 4:24).

But how can the three persons be distinct from each other when each is coterminous with the whole divine being? I believe that my account of divine simplicity, in which the identity of everything divine with the divine being indicates (rather than negates)

---

37. Clark's criticism was presented in a taped lecture. See the formulation of John Robbins, Clark's disciple, in *Cornelius Van Til: The Man and the Myth* (Jefferson, MD: Trinity Foundation, 1986), 20, a booklet that I do not generally recommend as an analysis or critique of Van Til.

38. For more on these, see below on eternal generation and procession.

the complexity of this being, is of some help. Simplicity embraces distinctness, rather than canceling it out. That God is a Father, a Son, and a Spirit indicates real complexity in God's nature, a nature that encompasses real distinctions. *Father*, *Son*, and *Spirit* are not synonyms. Each says something different, something distinct, about God. And each refers to something different about God. But we do not know the precise nature of that complexity-in-unity.

That is, again, merely to acknowledge our ignorance of the precise distinction between substance and person in God and of the precise interactions between these. God has given us, in Scripture, a glimpse into his inner life, but only a glimpse.[39] The Trinity is not an irrational doctrine, but it is highly mysterious. It is not contradictory, but we do not always see clearly how apparent contradictions can be resolved.

I fear that theologians have often made global statements about God's ineffability, his "wholly otherness," but in the details of their theology have claimed micro- and macroscopic knowledge of the divine being. I prefer that we make no global statements asserting God's unknowability, but that we be more modest in admitting, concretely and specifically, what we do not know. Trinitarian theology seems to me to be a locus where that sort of warning is especially needed.

Ontological and Economic

The *ontological* Trinity (sometimes called *immanent*[40] Trinity) is the Trinity as it exists necessarily and eternally, apart from creation. It is, like God's attributes, what God necessarily *is*. The *economic* Trinity is the Trinity in its relation to creation, including the specific roles played by the Trinitarian persons through the history of creation, providence, and redemption. These are roles that the persons of the Trinity have freely entered into; they are not necessary to their being.[41]

Sabellianism denies that the Trinity is ontological; for the modalist, Father, Son, and Spirit are not the nature of God, but are roles that God assumes in history. Arianism, similarly, teaches that the three persons are not necessary to the being of God, but are rather creations of the one true God, the Father, who is monopersonal. But the biblical position, as we have seen, is that the Trinity is what God eternally and necessarily is, as well as the roles by which he relates to creatures.

Many recent theologians, such as Barth and Rahner, have argued that the ontological-economic distinction is faulty, creating too large a separation between God's nature

39. Vern S. Poythress puts it better, perhaps, by saying that these concepts should be used "analogically," in "Reforming Ontology and Logic in the Light of the Trinity," *WTJ* 57, 1 (1995): 216. I will describe this article and Poythress's concept of analogy later in this chapter.

40. Do not confuse this use of *immanent* with the *immanence of God* discussed in chapter 3. The two concepts are nearly opposite to each other. *Immanent Trinity* is the Trinity apart from creation; *immanence of God* as a lordship attribute is the triune God's involvement with his creatures. Trinitarian immanence is the presence of God with himself, rather than with creation, although of course the immanent Trinity does enter relations with creation. In entering these relations, it does not become anything other than it is immanently or ontologically.

41. Compare our distinctions between God's necessary and free attributes (necessary and free will, knowledge, speech) in other chapters.

and his revelation of himself in history. Some of the principles that they wish to guard by this critique are important, particularly these: (1) God reveals himself as he really and truly is. His economic dealings with us, particularly his revelation in Scripture, do not distort his true nature. (2) The incarnate life of Jesus is itself an aspect of the life of Jesus as eternal Son of God. The actions and experiences of Jesus in time are actions and experiences of God. (3) The economic roles played by the three persons must be roles appropriate to their natures. That the Son, rather than the Father or the Spirit, became incarnate was a free decision among the persons of the Trinity, but not an arbitrary one.

I believe, however, that it is too much to say, with Rahner, that "the 'economic' Trinity is the 'immanent' Trinity and the 'immanent' Trinity is the 'economic' Trinity."[42] There is a difference between what God is necessarily and what he freely chooses to do in his plan for creation.

Eternal Generation

In human life, a child's existence begins in an event called *begetting* or *generation*. The same was true of the incarnate Christ: Jesus was *begotten* in the womb of Mary by the power of the Holy Spirit. Now, many theologians have asked whether there is an analogous event in the eternal realm. As we have seen, Jesus is Son of God not only in his earthly life, but also eternally. His sonship is *ontological*, rather than merely *economic*. Jesus' begetting in the womb of his mother is a historical event, an *economic* event. The question before us is this: is there also an *ontological* begetting, an *eternal* generation, to which he owes his eternal sonship?

Many have dismissed this question (and the theological answers to it) as speculative, and I think there is some truth in this criticism. But we should give attention to this discussion because of its prominence in the history of doctrine, and also because it deals with real concerns of faith.

Our faith moves us to worship Jesus as Son of God, in the power of the Spirit. So it is legitimate for us to ask: what does it *mean* for Jesus to be Son, and for the Spirit to be Spirit? As we have seen, these titles, biblically understood, imply that both persons are divine. But do they teach us anything more than that?

The divine Son and Spirit are analogous to human sonship and spirituality. But how far does the analogy reach? Human sons are younger than their fathers; but this is not true of the divine Son, who exists in eternity alongside his Father. Human sons are born weak, ignorant, sinful; not so the divine Son, who shares his Father's perfections through all eternity. So our concept of divine sonship must be refined, purged of connotations inappropriate to an infinite being. But after all the refining, what is left? Does Jesus' sonship have anything in common with ours?

A common answer has been: yes, both divine and human sonship are the result of *generation*, of *begetting*. The Nicene Creed (revised 381) confesses faith

---

42. Karl Rahner, *The Trinity* (New York: Seabury Press, 1974), 22. Cf. *CD*, 1.1:8–15, 358.

in one Lord, Jesus Christ, the only-begotten Son of God, begotten from the Father
before all time, Light from Light, true God from true God, begotten, not created.

But what is this *begetting*? The idea of begetting, like the idea of sonship, must be
refined if it is to refer to God. Among human beings, begetting normally occurs in a
sexual relationship. It occurs in time, so that a human being who did not exist at one
time exists at a later time by virtue of being begotten. But eternal begetting is surely
neither sexual nor temporal, nor, certainly, does it confer existence on someone who
otherwise would not have existed; for God is a necessary being, and the three persons
share the divine attribute of necessary existence.

After we have refined the concept, then, what is left of the idea of eternal begetting?
Or should we discard that idea as part of our refining of the term *Son*?

Some have described eternal generation as the "origin" or "cause" of the Son.[43] But
that notion poses serious problems.[44] God has no origin or cause; and if the Son is
fully God, then he has no origin or cause either. He is *a se*. He has within himself the
complete ground of his existence. Is begetting the cause of the Son in the sense of the
divine act that *maintains* his existence, so that he constantly depends on the Father?[45]
But this idea would imply that the Son's existence was contingent, rather than necessary; it, too, would compromise the aseity of the Son.

Most insist that the notion of causality or origin must be distinguished from causes
and origins in the finite world: It is not temporal. It is not by the Father's choice or will,
but by his nature. Or it is by his necessary will, rather than his free will.

Certainly creation *ex nihilo* is inappropriate within the Godhead, as the church
insisted over against the Arians. But then what is it that eternal generation generates?
If eternal generation does not confer *existence* on the Son, what does it confer? Some
claimed that by it the Father communicates to the Son not existence, but the divine
nature. Zacharias Ursinus wrote, "The Son is the second person, because the Deity is
communicated to him of the Father by eternal generation."[46] Calvin, however, attacked
that position, arguing that "whosoever says that the Son has been given his essence
from the Father denies that he has being from himself."[47] If the Son's deity is derived,[48]

43. *RD*, 115: "This intrapersonal relationship results in the distinction of the divine persons according to
origin, order and operation. . . . As therefore the Son has his existence from the Father, and the H. Spirit His from
the Father and from the Son, so too in divine action the Father's will takes precedence." See also, for example,
the statement of Eastern Orthodox theologian Vladimir Lossky, quoted in Fortman, *Triune God*, 280: "The Father
is called the cause of the Persons of the Son and the Holy Spirit," though, Lossky adds, "this unique cause is not
prior to his effects. . . . He is not superior to his effects." These are, Lossky says, "relations of origin."

44. Speaking of the Cappadocian theology, Gerald Bray says, "It is difficult to see what 'cause' can mean when
speaking of an eternal person, and all too easy to reflect that the word represents a lingering trace of pre-Nicene
subordinationism, which held that there was a time when the Son (and the Spirit) did not exist." *Doctrine of God*, 159.

45. This idea would be similar to the idea of creation as a continuous process; see chapter 10.

46. Zacharias Ursinus, *Commentary on the Heidelberg Catechism* (Cincinnati: T. P. Bucher, 1851), 135.

47. *Institutes*, 1.13.23. Compare B. B. Warfield's discussion in *Biblical Doctrines* (Edinburgh: Banner of Truth,
1988), 171.

48. "Derived deity" is oxymoronic.

then, says Calvin, the Son is not *a se*. But if he is not *a se*, *autotheos*, "God in himself," he cannot be divine.

But then what is it that the Father confers upon the Son in eternal generation? According to Calvin, what the Son receives from the Father is not his being, not his divine essence, but his *person*:

> Therefore we say that deity in an absolute sense exists of itself; whence likewise we confess that the Son since he is God, exists of himself, but not in relation to his Person; indeed, since he is the Son, we say that he exists from the Father.[49]

I take it that what Calvin is saying is that the Son receives from the Father neither his existence nor his divine nature, but his *sonship*. He is Son because the Father has made him Son. But what does that mean? It could be taken to mean merely that *Father* and *Son* are reciprocal terms. A person cannot be a son unless he has a father. And since the reverse is also true, we could say that just as the Son receives his sonship from the Father, the Father receives his fatherhood from the Son. That would be a clear understanding of the relationship, and rather obvious, but trivial. Certainly it does not suggest anything closely analogous to human begetting.

But Calvin and others in the Reformed tradition seem to have a more unidirectional concept in mind: the Father is the *origin* of the Father-Son relation, in some way that the Son is not. But what does it mean to be the originator or creator of a relationship in which one stands necessarily and eternally? Certainly we should not imagine that God the Father is fundamentally a unitarian God who by executing some eternal process became triune. Nor should we imagine that the Father, existing eternally with two other unnamed beings, somehow acted to make them his Son and Spirit, respectively.

The very terms *Father* and *Son* bring to our minds the idea of *begetting*. But when we try to apply that idea to the divine being, words fail us. When we try to refine it, to make it appropriate to the divine being, its meaning seems to slip away from us.

Can Scripture help us to formulate a clearer concept of eternal generation? Let us explore some of the biblical data used by theologians to prove and explain the doctrine.

1. Many have emphasized, as I did in the preceding chapter, that Jesus' sonship is eternal and ontological, not merely temporal. So, they have concluded, he must have been *begotten* not only temporally, but eternally as well. But what does *begetting* mean in this context? If it is merely a verbal form of the noun *Son*, taking *Son* to mean "one begotten," then the conclusion follows trivially. Eternal sonship implies eternal begetting, because that is what sonship means. But this reasoning doesn't tell us anything about eternal begetting beyond what we already know about sonship. On this basis, sonship and begetting are simply alternative ways of saying the same thing: to be a Son is to be begotten, and to be begotten is to be a Son. The doctrine of eternal generation on this basis is verbally superfluous.

49. *Institutes*, 1.13.25.

On the other hand, if begetting is an event prior to sonship, one that brings sonship into being, then the conclusion does not follow at all. The fact that Jesus' incarnate sonship is due to an act of begetting (Luke 1:35) does not imply that Jesus' eternal sonship is also the result of begetting. Obviously, there are major differences between the origin of Jesus' earthly sonship and the origin of his eternal sonship. As I indicated earlier, the concept of sonship is subject to theological refinement. For example, no one would argue that since Jesus' earthly sonship began in the body of a woman, his eternal sonship must also begin there (or even somewhere analogous). The idea of begetting is, prima facie, also inappropriate to God. Should it not also be dropped in the interest of theological refinement? Apart from other biblical data, there is no reason to conclude that begetting is more appropriate to the ontological Trinity than gestation in the womb.

2. Some have argued from the term *monogenes* as Scripture applies it to Christ (John 1:14, 18; 3:16; etc.) that the Son is eternally begotten. The kjv translates this term "only begotten." Recent translations, however, have preferred such translations as "only," "unique," or "One and Only." The debate concerns both etymology and usage. The etymological question is whether the *genes* in *monogenes* comes from the verb *gennao* ("beget") or from *genos* ("kind," "genus"). In my view, a good case can still be made for the older view of the etymology.[50] On the question of usage, I agree with Lee Irons[51] and John V. Dahms[52] that the uses of *monogenes* in John should be taken in the traditional way, based on considerations of context and intelligibility. On John 1:18, "the only begotten God, who is in the Father's bosom, has made him known" (Irons' translation), Irons comments:

> The niv completely misses the point ("God the One and Only . . . has made him known"), for it is not the fact that the Son is the only God (as opposed to another god) but the fact that he is begotten of God (and thus truly God) which enables him to make God known.[53]

The other *monogenes* texts, in my view, are also consistent with this understanding of the term.

These considerations, then, justify the language of eternal generation.[54] But what do the *monogenes* texts tell us about the nature of that generation? I think very little.

---

50. See Lee Irons, "The Eternal Generation of the Son," available at http://members.aol.com/ironslee /private/Monogenes.htm, 1–2. As Irons points out, however, the usage of the term is far more important than the etymology in determining meaning—a point definitively argued by James Barr in *The Semantics of Biblical Language* (Oxford: Oxford University Press, 1961).

51. Irons, "Eternal Generation of the Son," 1–2.

52. John V. Dahms, "The Johannine Use of *Monogenes* Reconsidered," *New Testament Studies* 29 (1983): 222–32. F. F. Bruce also, in *The Gospel of John* (Grand Rapids: Eerdmans, 1984), 65n26, says that the evangelist may himself have associated (informally, not as an expert on etymology) *monogenes* with *gennao*, drawing parallels with *our* new begetting/birth from God.

53. Irons, "Eternal Generation of the Son," 1–2.

54. Yet the understanding of *monogenes* underlying this argument is controversial. So I do not believe the doctrine should be made a test of orthodoxy on the basis of this argument.

"Begotten" is little more than a synonym for "Son." If it suggests or presupposes an event prior to Christ's sonship by which he became Son, it certainly does not describe that event. "Only begotten" stresses[55] the unique status of this Son over against all creatures, over against any other being that might be called a son of God, but the "only" adds nothing to our understanding of the *nature* of divine begetting. Certainly the texts employing *monogenes* will not enable us to decide whether the generation is of existence, divine essence, or person, or what a communication of personhood, if that is the nature of eternal generation, might mean.

3. A third consideration, only hinted at in the literature, is this: Although it is improper to assume a one-to-one correspondence between aspects of human sonship and aspects of divine sonship, nevertheless the former ought to be *appropriate* to the latter. That the Son, rather than the Father or Spirit, became incarnate was not an accident or a chance event. Rather, it was part of an all-wise divine plan. So there must have been some reason why it was more appropriate for the Son to become incarnate than for either of the other two persons to do so.

Thus, the fact that Jesus was begotten and born in history does give us some hints as to his eternal nature. His earthly begetting images something of his eternal relationship with the Father. I suggest that perhaps the phrase *eternal generation* could be taken to designate that parallel. To say that the Son is eternally generated from the Father is to say that something about his eternal nature makes it appropriate for him to be begotten in time.

As we thus meditate on the nature of Jesus' eternal sonship, we should not confine our attention to his begetting. As Wolfhart Pannenberg says:

> Relations among the three persons that are defined as mutual self-distinction cannot be reduced to relations of origin in the traditional sense. The Father does not merely beget the Son. He also hands over his Kingdom to him and receives it back from him. The Son is not merely begotten of the Father. He is also obedient to him and he thereby glorifies him as the one God. The Spirit is not just breathed. He also fills the Son and glorifies him in his obedience to the Father, thereby glorifying the Father himself. In so doing he leads into all truth (John 16:13) and searches out the deep things of Godhead (1 Cor. 2:10–11).[56]

So with the Son's eternal generation we can also speak of his eternal obedience and eternal glorification of the Father. But these assertions (including the assertion of eternal generation) should not be the subject of microscopic analysis and rigid enforcement as tests of orthodoxy. They are biblical *hints* as to the nature of the eternal relationship between Father and Son.

To summarize: the biblical data do authorize us to speak of the eternal generation of the Son, and it is certainly appropriate for the church to confess the statements of the

---

55. This stress, of course, is shared by the interpretation of *monogenes* that derives it from *genos*.

56. Wolfhart Pannenberg, *Systematic Theology* (Grand Rapids: Eerdmans, 1991), 1:320.

Nicene Creed quoted earlier. But they do not describe this eternal relationship in any detail. We know at least that *Son* is not an arbitrary title; the eternal Son is analogous to human sons in some way. Negatively, we should reject some false interpretations: (1) that the Father gives existence to the Son by a creative act, and (2) that the Father confers divine essence upon the Son, giving him a derived deity. Whether we confess that the Father confers sonship upon the Son should await further clarification of the idea.

A certain amount of reverent agnosticism is appropriate here. There is much that the Bible does not reveal about the relation of the Son to the Father. Charles Hodge says:

> The relation, therefore, of the Second Person to the First is that of filiation or sonship. But what is meant by the term, neither the Bible nor the ancient creeds explain. It may be sameness of nature; as a son is of the same nature as his father. It may be likeness, and the term Son be equivalent to *eikon, apaugasma, charakter,* or *logos,* or revealer. It may be derivation of essence, as a son, in one sense, is derived from his father. Or, it may be something altogether inscrutable and to us incomprehensible.[57]

And Robert Dabney:

> [This doctrine] seems to me rather a rational explanation of revealed facts, than a revealed fact itself. On such a subject, therefore, none should dogmatize.[58]

Earlier, Dabney expresses his concerns more strongly:

> The discussions and definitions of the more formal and scholastic Theologians, concerning the personal distinctions in the Godhead, have always seemed to me to present a striking instance of the reluctance of the human mind to confess its own weakness. For, let any read them with the closest attention, and he will perceive that he has acquired little more than a set of terms, whose abstruseness serves to conceal from him their practical lack of meaning.[59]

What the Bible reveals is that there is one God in three persons, persons related to one another as Father, Son, and Spirit. Much of the rest of Trinitarian theology, one suspects, is an attempt to get beyond this fundamental truth by multiplying forms of *Father, Son,* and *Spirit.* When we are told, for example, that there are four "relations" in the Godhead, namely, *paternity, filiation,* and *active and passive spiration (procession),* we get the impression that we are being taught something beyond the meaning conveyed by *Father, Son,* and *Spirit.* But is that impression correct? Does *eternal generation*

---

57. Charles Hodge, *Systematic Theology* (Grand Rapids: Eerdmans, 1952), 1:468. He adds, "The Nicene fathers, instead of leaving the matter where the Scriptures leave it, undertake to explain what is meant by sonship, and teach that it means derivation of essence."

58. Robert Lewis Dabney, *Lectures in Systematic Theology* (Grand Rapids: Zondervan, 1972), 205.

59. Ibid., 202.

mean anything more than that the Father is eternally Father and the Son is eternally Son? Do we know anything more about eternal generation than that? Much of this reflection, it seems to me, really amounts to putting the names of the three persons into different forms, without any increase in knowledge or edification. I have tried to treat these discussions with respect and to point out what I think can be gained from them. But I confess that I cannot escape the notion that at least some of this discussion amounts to playing with words.

Eternal Procession

The same question arises in the case of the Holy Spirit. The Father and the Son *send* the Spirit to earth (on Pentecost and other occasions), so that he *proceeds* from them. The names of the Spirit in the original languages, *ruach* and *pneuma*, suggest the image of divine breath: the Spirit *proceeds* from God as our breath proceeds from our mouths. Now the question arises: is there an *eternal* procession of the Spirit from the Father (the Eastern view) or from the Father and Son (the Western view) analogous to his processions in history?

The church has used the word *procession* (= *ekporeusis, emanatio*), rather than *generation* or *begetting* as in the case of the Son, to designate the Spirit's eternal "relation of origin." The words differ because *begetting* obviously pertains to the Son (especially as *monogenes*), but not to the Spirit, and because *procession* corresponds somewhat to the biblical ideas of *sending* and *breathing*. *Procession* is a somewhat broader term than *generation*, conveying less specific imagery. But many theologians have expressed ignorance as to how procession differs from generation. Heinrich Heppe quotes Sohnius as saying:

> What the property [procession] is and, as it were, the formal distinction between generation and procession . . . the doctors of the Early Church *Augustine* and the *Damascene* and others admit their ignorance since it has not been expressly defined in God's Word.[60]

Alting adds, *"Ekporeusis* is distinguished from generation. But how, we don't know."[61]

As with the eternal generation of the Son, questions arise about the meaning of the eternal procession of the Spirit. Does it refer to a derivation of existence? Of deity? Of personhood? And if the latter, what, in turn, does that mean? These questions have not been discussed as much in regard to the Spirit as in regard to the Son, but they are equally difficult in the present discussion, and they lead to similar conclusions or nonconclusions. My discussion of them would essentially repeat my treatment of eternal generation, so I will not say more on these topics here.

What is the biblical evidence for the eternal procession of the Spirit? That, too, is parallel to the discussion in the previous section:

60. *RD*, 130. See also *BRD*, 2:313–14.
61. Quoted in *RD*, 130.

1. It would be odd if Scripture were to present generation as the relation between Son and Father, but presented no similar relation between Spirit and the others. So we should perhaps expect to find in Scripture some similar relation, such as the theological tradition finds in *procession*. Of course, "what we expect to find" may not be made a theological standard or a ground for a particular exegesis.

2. The name *Spirit* and the primary biblical model of the Spirit (that is, *breath*) suggest derivation. But as with *Son*, this suggestion does not answer specific questions about the Spirit's eternal relation to the other persons. As with the Son's generation, we want to ask what is being derived: Existence? Deity? Spirithood? And we want to know the meanings of these. But Scripture doesn't tell us much, if anything, that enables us to describe the nature of procession, beyond the mere name.

3. Although there is no biblical term applied to the Spirit comparable to *monogenes*, there is one biblical text that has often been thought to teach the Spirit's eternal procession, namely, John 15:26, where Jesus says:

> But when the Helper comes, whom I will send to you from the Father, the Spirit of truth, who proceeds from the Father, he will bear witness about me.

The "sending" here is, of course, temporal rather than eternal. But "proceeds" is the Greek *ekporeutai* and is in the present tense, so it does not refer to the future sending (= Pentecost) of the previous clause. Many writers, therefore, have taken this verse as teaching the eternal procession of the Spirit. That interpretation, however, is by no means obvious. In my view, the present-tense *ekporeusis* may simply refer to the regular way in which the Spirit enters the world to do God's business. Jesus is saying that he will send the Spirit, whom the Father regularly sends into the world (upon prophets, kings, Jesus himself), on a special future occasion to bear witness to him. As the Spirit has gone out from the Father to rest on Jesus, so the Spirit will come to the apostles at Jesus' behest. On this interpretation, John 15:26 does not explicitly teach the eternal procession of the Spirit.

4. As in the previous section, however, I suggest here that the historical processions of the Spirit are *appropriate* to the Spirit's eternal existence. The Spirit is the member of the Trinity whom the Father and Son send, over and over again, to do their business on earth. Unlike the Son, he is not generated or born into a human body. He comes like breath or wind (John 3), invisibly, but with an intimate relation to creatures. He transforms them from within. We should regard this sort of ministry as appropriate to the Spirit, as generation is appropriate to the Son. It is not an accident, not an arbitrary divine choice, that the Spirit is regularly the One who is *sent*, who *descends*, who *comes* into our world from the Father and the Son. So perhaps there is value in defining eternal procession as that quality of the Spirit that makes it appropriate for him to receive these missions from the Father and Son and to proceed as he does into the temporal world.[62]

---

62. The reader should review the quote from Pannenberg in the previous section: the Spirit's distinctive property is not only procession, but also filling and glorifying the Son, leading into all truth, and so on.

But as with generation, Scripture gives us no detailed information about the nature of the Spirit's eternal procession. Again, exhortations to theological modesty are in order.

Filioque

The Nicene Creed as formulated at the Council of Constantinople in A.D. 381 confesses faith "in the Holy Spirit, the Lord and life-giver, Who proceeds from the Father." John Leith notes:

> In the West the original text "who proceeds from the Father" was altered to read "from the Father and the Son" [*filioque*]. This alteration is rooted in the theology of the Western Church, in particular the theology of Augustine. The procession from the Son was vigorously affirmed by the Council at Toledo in 589 and gradually was added to the creed, though it was not accepted as part of the creed at Rome until a number of centuries had passed.[63]

The Eastern church did not look with favor upon this change and thought it arrogant of the Western churches to alter an ecumenical statement of faith without consulting their Eastern brothers. This doctrinal issue was one of the main causes of the schism between Eastern and Western churches that began in A.D. 1054 and continues to the present.

I am inclined to agree with the Eastern Christians that the Westerners should not have modified the creed without the consent of the whole church. But in this book I am, of course, concerned with the doctrinal issues rather than the issues of church polity. So I will consider the question whether the Spirit proceeds from the Father only, or from the Father and the Son.

I will say more later about the relative differences in focus between Eastern and Western theologies in this area. The East, following the lead of the Cappadocian fathers, focuses on the Father as the "fountain of deity" and then asks how the other persons are related to him. The Western thinkers, following Augustine, focus more attention on the whole Godhead, the simple divine nature, and then ask how within that simple nature there can be three persons and how those persons may be related to one another. As we have seen, the Western tradition has been tempted in a Sabellian direction, to reduce the concrete persons to "relations." But the Westerners have sometimes charged the Easterners with subordinationism (as in Calvin's critique of the notion of "derived deity").

So the Western thinkers have wanted to see everything in God in relation to everything else, emphasizing the *circumincessio* (which, to be sure, is also affirmed in the East). So for them, at least as the Easterners see it, the existence of the Son and the Spirit is due primarily to their necessary existence as God, not to a particular act of the Father, although the Westerners also frequently affirm that the Father is the "fountain of deity."

---

63. John Leith, *Creeds of the Churches* (Richmond, VA: John Knox Press, 1973), 32.

So the Eastern theologians tend to see the Western position as compromising the concreteness and integrity of the persons—as if the Spirit's existence comes not from the Father or Son or both as concrete persons, but from the divine nature generally.

I will have something to say later about the two different Trinitarian models that here confront one another. In general, my view is that both are legitimate and that neither, as a model, resolves the specific question before us. But these models are important to the controversy, for they indicate, I think, why some of the more specific arguments weigh more heavily in the Eastern theology and others in the Western. Let us consider some of those more specific arguments:

1. The Eastern theologians claim that John 15:26 refers the Spirit's procession (*ekporeutai*) exclusively to the Father. The Westerners point out that in that very verse it is Jesus who is "sending" the Spirit to the disciples. I have argued that the reference of *ekporeutai* to eternal procession has not been established. If my understanding is correct, then both the procession and the sending mentioned in the verse take place in history. Now, that understanding does not make the verse irrelevant to the doctrine of eternal procession, for as we have seen it is legitimate to find an analogy between the historical and the eternal relationships among the persons of the Trinity. But if both the procession and the sending of John 15:26 take place in time, that would support, by analogy, the view that the Spirit's eternal procession is from both Father and Son.

2. Some Western theologians claim that the Eastern view separates the Spirit from Christ. If the Spirit proceeds only from the Father, rather than from Jesus, they say, then we can come to the Father by the Spirit apart from Jesus, leading to a kind of mysticism rather than a cross-centered piety. Some Eastern theologians, in turn, charge that it is the West that encourages mysticism, for Western theology ascribes eternal procession, in the end, to a vague, abstract "Godhead," rather than to the concrete person of the Father. Yet: (a) Mysticism has arisen in both Eastern and Western churches; I have seen no evidence that views of eternal procession have had much influence in motivating or deterring mysticism. (b) Eastern Christians do make Jesus a central object of devotion. Practically speaking, there is no reason to think that they approach God apart from Christ. (c) Eastern theologians have been willing to say that the Spirit proceeds from the Father *through* the Son, or from the Father *to rest on* Christ (after the model of Jesus' baptism).[64] Both of these models, it seems to me, encourage Christ-centered piety. (d) Western theology, despite its particular concern for the unity of the Godhead, does not teach that the Spirit proceeds from the Godhead, but rather from the Father and Son.

3. Western thinkers have sometimes criticized the Eastern view as subordinationist, for in the procession of the Spirit, Father and Son are not equal. But why? Is it subordinationist to draw any distinction at all between the activities of Father and Son? Surely not. Why, then, does this particular distinction indicate subordinationism? Even on the Western view, the roles of the persons in generation and procession are not identical to

---

64. See, for example, Bray, *Doctrine of God*, 157.

one another, hence the theological distinctions between the persons by the "personal properties" of generation, filiation, and passive spiration.

4. I believe that the analogy between the eternal and temporal proceedings of the Spirit favors the Western view. As we have seen, the Son as well as the Father sends the Spirit into the world, and Scripture frequently refers to the Spirit both as the "Spirit of God" and as the "Spirit of Christ." It refers once to the "Spirit of your Father" (Matt. 10:20). The mission of the Spirit is to testify of Christ (John 15:26).

5. But it is dangerous to develop doctrines based on analogy alone. And even if John 15:26 constitutes a proof text for one position or the other, the church has usually not seen fit to create tests of orthodoxy on the basis of one proof text. Although I somewhat prefer the Western formulation, I think both East and West were unwise to have made this a church-dividing issue. Neither view should have been made a test of orthodoxy.

6. We should remember that (a) Scripture gives us no precise definition of *person* or *substance*, (b) it gives us no precise definition of either *generation* or *procession*, or of how these two concepts differ, and (c) the best arguments for eternal generation and procession are based on analogy, rather than explicit biblical teachings or strict logical consequences of biblical teachings. These considerations, like those in point 5, should moderate our advocacy of either position. Again, theological humility is in order. God has given us a glimpse of his inner life, not a map or a treatise.

Subordination

The fourth-century battle in the church over the Trinity focused mostly on the *subordinationism* of the Arian party. The Arians taught that the Son and Spirit were creatures and thus were not of the same nature (*homoousios*) as the Father, but subordinate beings. Orthodox Nicene Trinitarianism denied that the Son and Spirit were subordinate in this sense, that is, ontologically. They are divine in the same sense the Father is, equal to the Father in glory, sharing with him the divine nature with all the divine attributes.

But although the church has officially denied the *ontological* subordination of Arianism, it has affirmed *economic* subordination among the persons of the Trinity. That is, the persons of the Trinity voluntarily subordinate themselves to one another in the roles they perform in respect to creation. As we have seen, the Father *sends* the Son into the world, and the Son joyfully obeys his Father's will. On earth, the Son does only what his Father gives him to do (even *knows* only what the Father gives him to know, Matt. 24:36). In the end, he delivers up the kingdom to his Father (1 Cor. 15:24) and himself becomes one of the subjects in his Father's kingdom (v. 28). When the Spirit enters the world, he does not speak of himself (John 16:13), but speaks only what he hears (presumably from the Father and Son). And as I pointed out in the section "Mutual Glorification" above, the Father also defers to the Son and Spirit in various ways.

So we may summarize by saying that biblical Trinitarianism denies ontological subordination, but affirms economic subordination of various kinds. But there is a third kind of subordination that has been discussed for many centuries and has played a major role in the contemporary literature. That might be called eternal subordination of *role*.

Both Eastern and Western thinkers have regularly affirmed that God the Father has some sort of primacy over the other two persons. Theologians have used phrases such as *fons deitatis* ("fountain of deity") and *fons trinitatis* ("fountain of the Trinity") to describe the Father's distinct *role* in the Trinity.[65] That the Father has some sort of primacy is implicit in the name *Father* in distinction from *Son* and *Spirit*, and of course, the doctrines of eternal generation and procession suggest that the Father has some sort of unique "originative" role. So the church has generally spoken of the persons as "first, second, and third." Further, if, as I have claimed, the economic activities of the persons present clues to, or analogies of, their eternal relationships, then the forms of economic subordination mentioned above suggest a pattern. The Son and Spirit become voluntarily subordinate to the commands of the Father, because that kind of subordination is appropriate to their eternal nature as persons. (But, we should recall, the Father *defers* to the Son and Spirit, honoring and glorifying them as they honor and glorify him.)

This kind of subordination is not the ontological subordination of Arius rejected by the church. Nor is it merely economic, for it has to do with the very eternal nature of the persons, their "personal properties" that distinguish each from the others. Dahms calls it "essential and eternal,"[66] but perhaps "essential" is misleading in this context, since it suggests a difference in nature, but orthodox theology teaches that the three persons have the same nature, essence, being. But it is right to describe this difference of role as eternal. We may put it this way: (a) There is no subordination within the divine nature that is shared among the persons: the three are equally God. (b) There is subordination of role among the persons, which constitutes part of the distinctiveness of each. (c) Because of (b), the persons subordinate themselves to one another in their economic relationships with creation.

But how can the one person be subordinate to another in his eternal role while being equal to the other in his divine nature? Or, to put it differently, how can subordination of role be compatible with divinity? Does not the very idea of divinity exclude this sort of subordination?

The biblical answer, I think, is no. Scripture presents God, even the Father, as One who serves, who accepts affliction for his people. See my discussion of God's power in weakness, chapter 16, of God's suffering love in chapter 19, and of the mutual glorification earlier in this chapter. Even more obviously, the incarnate Son comes into the world as the Lord, but not as the lords of the Gentiles (Matt. 20:25–28). He is the Servant King, who rules for the benefit of his people, and who calls the rulers of his church to do the same. Subordination, in the sense of serving others in love, is clearly a divine attribute, and one that serves as an explicit model for our behav-

---

65. This is a central point in the theology of the Cappadocian fathers. See, e.g., Fortman, *Triune God*, 76. Among Reformation thinkers, see Ursinus, *Heidelberg Catechism*, 135.

66. John V. Dahms, "The Subordination of the Son," *JETS* 37, 3 (September 1994): 351–64.

ior. Such service does not compromise the full deity of the Son and Spirit; rather, it manifests their deity.

It may be that this eternal hierarchy of role accounts for some of the language in Scripture about the Father's being "greater" than the Son (John 14:28), about the Son's being able to do nothing of himself (John 5:19), and so on. See my discussion of these in chapter 28 of *DG*.

Subordination of role has become an important topic in recent evangelical theological discussion, largely in relation to feminism. Some have argued that there is no subordination of any sort within the Godhead, and that therefore the Trinity is a completely egalitarian society. Thus, on this view, the Trinity provides a model for an egalitarian society among human beings, in which gender, for example, plays no part in determining a person's role in family, church, or society.[67] They insist that any distinction of role based on gender demeans those in subordinate roles.

In reply, other writers have made the case for the "eternal subordination" of Son and Spirit as I have done above.[68] They argue that there is a hierarchy *of role* within the Trinity and that that hierarchy does not compromise their equality of nature, glory, and honor. So hierarchies of role in human society, even those based on gender, do not demean those who are subordinate to higher authorities.

Again, we should be careful of trying to derive too much by way of analogy between the historical appearances of the Trinitarian persons and their eternal relations. But I do think that analogy at least suggests eternal roles of submission within the Trinity, which do not detract in the least from the intrinsic deity of each person.

Should we regard this Trinitarian hierarchy as a model for human society? Scripture does teach that human beings are in the image of God and ought to be like God in the conduct of their lives. It also calls us, as in Matthew 20:25–28 and John 13:1–17, to be like Jesus in serving one another. I hesitate to place much ethical weight on the intra-Trinitarian role relation, which is based only on biblical analogy. But certainly we have plenty of direct biblical teaching that we should follow the example of Jesus in history. And that example is, I believe, a reflection of his intra-Trinitarian life.

The notion that subordination to authority demeans a person is absurd on the face of it. All of us are subordinate to some authorities beyond ourselves: government, employers, church governments, and so forth. Even "absolute monarchs" must please their subjects, if not out of the principle of servant-leadership, at least to protect themselves against coups and assassinations. Ultimately, we are all under the authority of God. To rebel against submission as such is to rebel against God himself. He places us under authority not to oppress us, but so that we can fulfill our callings. We should not be at all surprised to find that such submission reflects the very life of the Trinity.

67. For this argument, see Gilbert Bilezikian, *Beyond Sex Roles* (Grand Rapids: Baker, 1985), and particularly Bilezikian's "Hermeneutical Bungee-Jumping: Subordination in the Godhead," *JETS* 40, 1 (1997): 57–68.

68. See Stephen D. Kovach and Peter R. Schemm Jr., "A Defense of the Eternal Subordination of the Son," *JETS* 42, 3 (September 1999): 461–76; Dahms, "The Subordination of the Son," 351–64. For other titles and a brief summary of the debate, see *GST*, 251.

Trinitarian Models

I have said that God gives us only a glimpse of his inner Trinitarian life. But as we have seen, it has proved difficult for theologians to be satisfied with a mere glimpse. So a certain amount of sheer curiosity, plus the laudable desire to make the mystery of the Trinity as clear as possible, within the limitations of revelation, has led theologians to illustrate the Trinity in different ways. There have been many attempts to illustrate the Trinity, but in this section I will consider the two historically predominant models that have been used to describe the nature and relationships of the persons.

The first is the nature of the human mind, the second the nature of human social relationships. The first type of model, often called *psychological*, is especially connected with the name of Augustine, who expounded it at great length in *On the Trinity*. He finds oneness and threeness in the faculties of the mind: intellect, memory, will. He also explores the phenomena of self-knowledge, in which we find the unitary person functioning in three ways: the knower, the known, and the knowledge. He also explores the nature of self-love: the lover, the beloved, and the love between them. So although he often speaks of the three persons as different centers of consciousness, persons in the modern sense, he tends, when he wishes to define the nature of the Trinity theologically, to picture God as a single mind, and the persons as if they were aspects of that mind, like memory, imagination, and will.

Thomas Aquinas, although he insisted that the Trinity was a matter of faith, not natural knowledge, nevertheless made the concepts of self-knowledge and self-love mentioned above into a virtual *proof* for the Trinity, starting with the data of natural reason. He tries to prove from natural theology that God exists and that he has the attributes (among others) of knowledge and love. But then he argues that God's knowledge and love both require adequate objects and that these can be no less than divine persons—or, as he describes them, subsistent relations.[69] And because God's intellectual activity consists entirely of knowledge and love, there can be only two persons in addition to the Father.

The problem with these models, of course, is that they do not account for the NT data, in which the persons of the Trinity are actual centers of consciousness, entering into various transactions with one another: the Father sends the Son, the Son prays to the Father, the Father answers the prayers of the Son, the Father and Son together send the Spirit. Indeed, the Augustinian-Aquinas type of model veers toward Sabellianism.[70] Certainly Augustine and Aquinas were quite aware of that danger and sought to avoid it in various ways, by various detailed distinctions. But when you stand back and look at the big picture they present, the dangers become apparent.

---

69. The argument, in effect, is that the Father's self-knowledge is so perfect that it constitutes another person exactly like him (the Son). (Similarly with love and the Spirit.) The thought is intriguing. But what of the Son's equally perfect self-knowledge? Does that generate still another person? And what of the Son's perfect knowledge of the Father? Does that generate another Father? I think this is another example of what Dabney called "the reluctance of the human mind to recognize its own weakness." Dabney, *Lectures in Systematic Theology*, 202.

70. Recall that I indicated the same danger with regard to the Western teaching that equates the persons with "subsistent relations."

The difficulty is to get sufficient *distinction* into a model based on the individual human mind. If you try to emend the model to include such distinction, you might consider the pathology of multiple personality in human psychology, popularly described in *The Three Faces of Eve* and *Sybil*. In these cases, there do seem to be distinct persons living in one body. The different personalities may have different talents, different levels of knowledge, and different levels of maturity, and they may behave very differently. Some of them may be ignorant of the existence of the others. Yet in some situations these have been "integrated," eventually, into one personality.

Of course, in many respects, multiple personality is a very poor analogy of the Trinity. For example, the mutual ignorance among the multiple personalities, indeed their frequent multiple hostility, shows something very different from the harmony of Father, Son, and Spirit. But if we consider a situation in which there are distinct personalities, which are entirely conscious of one another and in complete harmony, one might have a promising illustration.

We all display different "faces" to the world. We use different vocabularies with different people; we write in different styles. Our sense of humor often varies depending on whom we are with. This is not just playacting (as on a fully Sabellian analogy). In these variations we display different real aspects of ourselves.

Indeed, there are various situations in which we hold internal conversations—conversations that are not redundant, but actually informative. Consider situations in which we try to conjure up memories of things. The memory is part of us, but it is also something for which we search. Consider the phenomenon of dreaming: part of us creates the dream; another part observes, and is sometimes surprised by what transpires. Have you ever had the experience of dream reading? One part of you creates a text; another part of you reads it. Thus you dream that you are reading. And there are, we are told, various transactions that take place within us from right brain to left brain and vice versa. Sometimes (often, to be sure, in pathological cases) one part of the brain hears a *voice* produced by another part.

Again, conceive of a mind that has infinitely more complexity than the human mind, but that is perfectly harmonious and self-aware. Perhaps then you will have something approaching an adequate analogy of the Trinity.

The second type of model is taken from interpersonal relationships on the human level. This is often called *social Trinitarianism*. Social Trinitarians cite as their theological mentors not Augustine, but the Cappadocian fathers: Basil of Caesarea, Gregory Nazianzen, and Gregory of Nyssa. Augustine began with the unity of God and tried to find pluralities within the unity; the Cappadocians, on the other hand, started from the three persons and sought to describe various kinds of unity among them. They began by describing the Father (the *fons deitatis*), and his various motives for eternally begetting the Son and for sending forth the Spirit. The Boethian definition of *person* as an "individual substance of a rational nature" (to say nothing of the biblical picture itself) might have led to a more social view in the West, but in its formal theological definitions Western theology retained, for many centuries, the Augustinian psychological model as its main point of reference. One significant exception was Richard of St. Victor (d. 1173), who departed from medieval Augustinian formulations to set forth a kind of social Trinitarian doctrine.

But recent theology has seen a resurgence in social Trinitarianism, particularly in the past forty or fifty years. Earlier in the twentieth century, we may recall, both Barth and Rahner denied emphatically that there were "three centers of consciousness in God." But more recently the pendulum has swung almost entirely to the other side. Leonard Hodgson's[71] pioneering work has been followed by similar formulations by Jürgen Moltmann,[72] Wolfhart Pannenberg,[73] Colin Gunton,[74] Cornelius Plantinga,[75] Royce Gruenler,[76] and many others. Some have used the social model in the interest of "open theism,"[77] an approach rejected earlier in this volume; but Gruenler and others have used the social model without evident sympathies with open theism.

The great strength of social Trinitarianism is the weakness of psychological Trinitarianism: the transactions between the divine persons in the Scriptures. The NT, especially the gospel of John, presents the Trinity not as three aspects of a single mind, but as real persons, conversing, loving, sending, and so on. The weakness of the social model, however, is the difficulty of finding adequate unity among the persons to justify a confession of monotheism.[78] As Sabellianism was a danger to Western theology, so tritheism (particularly in its Arian form) was a danger to the Eastern theologians.[79]

Here, as with the psychological model, I think that godly speculation can have an edifying function. For it may be that among human beings there is more unity than appears on the surface. Things could be said about ESP experiences and statements of recent scientists (supposedly based on subatomic physics; certainly I cannot verify it) that all minds may be united at a deep level. But more significantly, we should reflect on the solidarity of the human race in Adam and of the elect in Christ. Certainly this solidarity is federal and representative. But is that all? The representative model has always been troubled by the specter of arbitrariness. Certainly God has a right to appoint Adam as my representative, but does that appointment have any basis in God's justice

71. Leonard Hodgson, *The Doctrine of the Trinity* (New York: Scribner, 1944, 1963).

72. Jürgen Moltmann, *The Trinity and the Kingdom* (San Francisco: HarperCollins, 1981).

73. Pannenberg, *Systematic Theology*, 1:259–336.

74. Colin Gunton, *The Promise of Trinitarian Theology* (Edinburgh: T. and T. Clark, 1991).

75. Plantinga, "The Threeness/Oneness Problem of the Trinity," 38–52; Cornelius Plantinga, "Social Trinity and Tritheism," in *Trinity, Incarnation, and Atonement*, ed. Ronald J. Feenstra and Cornelius Plantinga (Notre Dame, IN: University of Notre Dame Press, 1989), 21–47. Note his popular treatment, "The Perfect Family," in *Christianity Today*, March 4, 1988, 24–27.

76. Gruenler, *The Trinity in the Gospel of John*.

77. Clark Pinnock, "Systematic Theology," in *The Openness of God*, ed. Clark Pinnock et al. (Downers Grove, IL: InterVarsity Press, 1994), 107–9.

78. Recall from our discussion in chapter 20 that monotheism is controversial among some theologians.

79. Indeed, as we saw earlier, the very terminology used suggested these dangers. The Westerners, saying that God had one substance (*substantia*) and three persons (*personae*, originally *masks*), sounded Sabellian to the Easterners, who said that God had one being (*ousia*) and three substances (*hypostaseis*). And the Easterners sounded tritheistic or Arian to the Westerners.

and wisdom? I suspect that representation is rooted in something deeper than itself. I am not impressed with attempts to base this solidarity in a kind of Platonic realism, or to draw metaphysical conclusions from our seminal presence in Adam's loins. But I can't avoid the conclusion that at some level the human race (and its successor, the Christian church) is far more "one" than might appear on the surface.[80]

And it may be even more unified in the future. When we are in heaven, no doubt we will retain our individual characteristics. But the earthly family will be transcended by the people of God, so that there will be no more marrying or giving in marriage. And the evident unity among that family will be greater than that of the earthly family: a union that will take away any potential grief over the loss of sexual pleasure. No doubt we will share knowledge and talents on a scale unprecedented in this life. Could such a social system be an adequate analogy of the Trinity? It does seem to me to point in that direction.

So it seems to me that these two models, the psychological and the social, both contain some important biblical truth, and it is possible that they both glimpse parts or aspects of what we may one day see more clearly. Certainly in Scripture God does often behave as a single individual, as I indicated in my discussion of *person*. This is the predominant OT perspective, though the OT does hint at personal distinctions in the Godhead. The predominant NT picture is social, though the NT reaffirms that God is one. We should not expect, certainly in this life, to reduce this mysterious biblical teaching to the confines of a single model. But both these pictures help us somewhat to focus our glimpse.

Trinitarian Analogies

Besides these general models, theologians have tried to illustrate the Trinity by triadic structures found in nature, history, and philosophy. These illustrations are sometimes called by the technical term *vestigia trinitatis*, vestiges, images, or evidences of the Trinity in the created world.

If all of creation reflects God's invisible nature, his power and glory, is there any way in which creation reflects the Trinity as such? Karl Barth denied emphatically the existence of *vestigia trinitatis*, as part of his critique of natural theology, and Aquinas, too, insisted that one could know the Trinity only by revelation. But we saw above that Aquinas was not entirely consistent in this claim.

I know of nothing in Scripture that rules out the possibility of *vestigia trinitatis*. We have seen that the world as a whole reflects God's glory, and that glory is the glory of the triune God. So the whole creation is a *vestigium trinitatis*. But are there specific ways in which we can show analogies or evidences of the Trinity in the world?

Certainly there are many phenomena that are three in one sense, one in another (or, more broadly, one-and-many). Saint Patrick's shamrock is as good an example as

---

80. But of course, not "one" in such a way as to compromise the antithesis between believers and unbelievers and ultimately between elect and nonelect.

any. But are there phenomena that can be more specifically related, in edifying ways, to the Trinitarian unity and diversity?[81]

The number three seems omnipresent in Scripture, nature, philosophy, and religion. I have catalogued hundreds of triads, including many that might be thought to reflect the Trinity in one way or another.[82] Some of the parallels, to be sure, are far-fetched. But in order to evaluate these analogies, we should recall the general roles played by the three persons in the economy of creation and redemption. Although all three persons are involved in all acts of God, we saw that there was a general division of labor as follows: the Father plans, the Son accomplishes, the Spirit applies.

The persons of the Trinity also correspond roughly to the three main events of the biblical story: creation (in which the emphasis is on the Father), redemption accomplished (the Son's incarnation, perfect life, atonement, and resurrection), and redemption applied (the Spirit's application to our hearts of the Son's redemptive work).

These roles suggest a correspondence between the persons of the Trinity and the lordship attributes expounded in this book. The Father is the authority; the Son controls all things, obedient to the Father's authoritative plan; and the Spirit represents God's presence with the world as the divine plan unfolds.

Or should we say, rather, that the Father is the controller, the Son the authority (because he is the Word), and the Spirit the presence? I am somewhat torn between the two models, but I now prefer the first, since it better fits the patterns of mutual glorification and eternal role-subordination that we have seen in the Trinity. But the choice between these two alternatives is not urgently important: (1) all persons of the Trinity have all the lordship attributes; (2) each person is "in" the other two (*circumincessio*), so that the location of the lordship attributes is only a question of emphasis. And most importantly, (3) all the lordship attributes presuppose the Trinity. God's control is the control by which each person sovereignly employs the creation to glorify the others. His authority is that of a speaker (the Father) uttering a Word (the Son) and carrying it to his hearers by his powerful breath (the Spirit). And God's presence is the presence of God the Father in the Son, by the Spirit.

As with the doctrine of the Trinity, the lordship attributes include one another. God exercises his control by speaking with authority in the presence of his creation. His authority controls all things in his presence, and his presence is a presence in authoritative blessing and judgment that ultimately determines the creature's destiny.

All of God's activities in the world, therefore, are Trinitarian—the result of the complex interplay between the three persons. And all the covenantal triads that I have employed in the Theology of Lordship books arise out of the unity and complexity of God's Trinitarian being, such as the history, law, and sanctions of the suzerainty

81. Everything, of course, reflects God's glory and therefore his triune nature in a general way. Thus, Van Til relates the Trinity, as we will see, to the overall unity and diversity of the created world. But I am asking here what particular phenomena offer instructive analogies to the Trinity.

82. In Appendix A of *DG*, I have collected around a hundred of these. See also Appendix A of this volume in which I have gathered the triadic distinctions made throughout the present book.

treaties; knowledge of world, law, and self in *DKG*;[83] situational, normative, and existential perspectives; and so on.

So the covenant structure of Scripture reveals many analogies of the Trinity. I believe that we can also find analogies of the Trinity elsewhere in Scripture and outside it, especially (1) where beginning moves to accomplishment and then to application-consummation, (2) where categories in a group (especially a group of three) coinhere, (3) where there are significant analogies to the lordship attributes or the three perspectives that emerge out of them, (4) when three categories exhaust their universe of discourse, (5) when there seems to be an emphatic, intentional repeating of the number three as often in biblical law, narrative, and theology.

I think that one or more of these principles applies to the *vestigia* noted in Appendix A of *DG*. The reader might profitably look through that appendix for examples.

Philosophical Analogies

Philosophers, too, have found it hard to resist threefold formulations. Georg Hegel and other idealist philosophers are famous for their triadic understanding of reality as *dialectical*—self-negating and consummating: (1) an idea or state of affairs (2) negates itself, then (3) reintegrates with its negation, bringing the process to a higher level. When I have an idea, for example, I often upon reflection find truth in its negation. But when I find a way to combine the truth of the original idea with the truth of the negation, I see more of the truth than I saw before.[84] Hegel believed that both human thought and human history followed this pattern. In history, one social order succumbs to another, but civilization rises to a higher level when a culture incorporates value from both the original order and its negation. Hegel saw this process as the true meaning of the reality for which the Trinity is a symbol.

Hegel's understanding is far from that of Scripture. What Scripture presents as a triune God, Hegel presents as a structure of multiple triads in reality in general. I also resist Hegel's notion that the Son negates the Father (though it can at least be said that the Son is *not* the Father), to be rejoined by the consummating Spirit. In the biblical view, all three persons contrast with one another, and all three are united by a common nature, including a mutual love.

Cornelius Van Til regarded all the world as a *vestigium trinitatis*, in its remarkable diversity-in-unity, which has baffled philosophers through the years. Realists have thought that the reality of the world is its oneness, for we know the world by bringing things together under concepts. The concepts are what is rational, not the particular things. On the other hand, nominalists have thought that what is real are particular

---

83. *DKG*, 62–73.

84. Plato's thought is also called *dialectical*, usually for the simple reason that Plato wrote dialogues rather than treatises. But there is a kinship between Plato and Hegel here. For Plato evidently believed that dialogue was not a mere form, but a valuable tool in gaining truth. In dialogue, one character argues a thesis, another (usually Socrates) refutes it, and then they try to reach a greater understanding based on the progress of the argument: thesis, antithesis, synthesis.

things (sometimes even little particles of things), and that concepts are mental constructions. Realists reduce particulars to universal concepts; nominalists do the reverse. But in fact, it is impossible to think of particular things apart from universal qualities, or to justify assertions about universals without reference to particulars.

So unbelieving philosophers will always fail in their attempt to gain an exhaustive knowledge of the world by reducing it to some dimension that they think their reason can handle. The universe is irreducibly one-and-many. The one cannot be understood without reference to the many, or vice versa. The universe is one-and-many because God is also one-and-many. He has made the world in his triune image. So the doctrine of the Trinity serves as a rebuke to would-be autonomous epistemology.[85]

Vern S. Poythress carries this argument still further. He finds a Trinitarian analogy in the triad of physical science—particle, wave, and field—applied to linguistics by Kenneth Pike's concepts of feature mode, manifestation mode, and distribution mode.[86] Poythress adopts the terminology of contrast, variation, and distribution: to find meaning, we seek to find how a linguistic unit is distinctive, differing from others (contrast), how it may vary in sound and form while remaining the same word (variation), and the contexts in which it functions (distribution). (In my terms, these are normative, existential, and situational, respectively.)

More recently, Poythress has written "Reforming Ontology and Logic in the Light of the Trinity: An Application of Van Til's Idea of Analogy." Here he ascribes to the persons of the Trinity three aspects: the *instantiational*, the *associational*, and the *classificational*, which he explains as follows:

> Each Person of the Godhead is particular. Let us call this particularity the *instantiational* aspect. Each Person is an instantiation of God. Second, God exists in fellowship and communion. The Persons of the Godhead exist in association with other Persons, in context of fellowship with other Persons. We may call this aspect the *associational* aspect. Third, the Persons of the Godhead are all God. They are classified using the category "God." We may call this aspect the *classificational* aspect.
>
> The *classificational* aspect expresses the fact that the three Persons share common attributes and are all God. Thus it is closely related to the *unity* of the three Persons in one God. The *instantiational* aspect expresses the particularity of each Person, and in this way is closely related to the *plurality* of Persons in the Godhead. But of course each Person is one Person, with unity. And this God is three Persons, with diversity. Unity and diversity are "equally ultimate" as Van Til reminds us.
>
> The classificational aspect reflects the character of God the Father, who is the same through all the dynamicity of God's historical actions. The instantiational aspect

85. For a somewhat longer account of Van Til's use of the Trinity to solve the *one-and-many problem*, see my *CVT*, 71–78.

86. Poythress, "Reforming Ontology"; Vern S. Poythress, "A Framework for Discourse Analysis," *Semiotica* 38, 3/4 (1982): 289–90; Kenneth Pike, *Language in Relation to a Unified Theory of the Structure of Human Behavior* (The Hague and Paris: Mouton, 1967), 84–93; Kenneth Pike, *Linguistic Concepts: An Introduction to Tagmemics* (Lincoln: University of Nebraska Press, 1982), 41–65.

reflects the character of God the Son, who became flesh for us. The associational aspect of mutual fellowship and indwelling reflects the character of God the Holy Spirit, who indwells us.[87]

He stresses, however, that the three persons coinhere, each existing in and with the others, so none of these aspects is limited to any one person.

Since creation reflects the Trinity, human language, thought, communication, and logic also have these aspects. Poythress reiterates Van Til's critique of realism and nominalism by showing that realism (both Platonic and Aristotelian) exalts the classificational aspect above the others, trying to find "pure categories" untainted by particular instantiations and contextual associations. Empiricism absolutizes the instantiational, subjectivism the associational. These reductionisms are plausible because the aspects coinhere: each encompasses the other two. But in fact, there are no pure universals, pure particulars, or pure relationships. Trying to reduce knowledge to one aspect is idolatrous. It is trying to find an absolute starting point in creation rather than in God's triune existence.

Poythress analyzes communication similarly, into expressive, informational, and productive aspects, a triad that intersects the former one so that we can ask, for example, "how the classificational aspect displays the expressive, informational, and productive purposes of God."[88] Nevertheless, this triad also corresponds to the persons of the Trinity:

> In sum, we may say that the eternal Word is the archetypal speech of God. This archetypal speech enjoys three aspects: in its *expressive* aspect, it is the speech of God the Father; in its *informational* aspect, its specific content is God the Son; in its *productive* aspect, it is "searched" and carried into effect in God the Holy Spirit. By analogy, God's speech to us displays these three aspects. It is expressive of who God is, and in it we meet God himself; it is informational and contains specific statements and commands; it is productive in us in blessing and curse—in sanctification, or in punishment, or in judgment. These three aspects are coinherent and presuppose one another, as we would expect. Each is a perspective on the whole. Together they form a perspectival triad analogically related to the Trinitarian character of God.[89]

Now, logical syllogisms are usually said to depend for their validity on the univocal use of terms: a term must have the same sense in premises and conclusion. For practical purposes, many logical syllogisms have sufficient continuity of meaning to generate valid conclusions. But, says Poythress, there is no such thing as a univocal term. All terms are analogical. That is to say that, as in the Trinity, there is no pure instantiation apart from association and classification. Say that someone were to propose the syllogism:

---

87. Poythress, "Reforming Ontology," 190–92. He cites Cornelius Van Til's *Defense of the Faith* (Philadelphia: Presbyterian and Reformed, 1963), 25.

88. Poythress, "Reforming Ontology," 202.

89. Ibid., 201.

1. Whatever the Father does, the Son also does. (John 5:19)
2. The Father begets the Son.
3. Conclusion: The Son begets the Son.

The syllogism would appear to follow the rules of logic, but the instantiation of premise 2 as a particular case of premise 1 is not appropriate. Such instantiation must take account of the distinctive nature of the associations and classifications within the persons of the Trinity. Similarly, instantiation in logical reasoning about earthly matters cannot involve merely mechanical substitutions of concepts, but must take into account the distinctive nature of those concepts and their association with other realities in the world.[90] Logic requires the activity of a *person*, relating his premises and conclusions to his entire range of experience and knowledge.[91] Those who claim that there are logical contradictions in Scripture (including the doctrine of the Trinity itself), Poythress argues, fail to understand the terms they use in proper scriptural senses, determined by all the biblical data.[92] Biblical use of logic is "conditioned by redemptive history."[93] All of this suggests a conclusion bearing on all reasoning: In a Trinitarian universe, only God himself, by his revelation, can give us the stability of meaning by which we reason logically.

Poythress also discusses logical circularity, alternative views of logic, the use of logic in apologetics, and implications for linguistics and other sciences. His proposal is a powerful one, with implications for all of human life.[94]

Trinity and the Lordship of God

Does the doctrine of the Trinity have anything to do with the main theme of this book, the lordship of God? Yes, I believe that a large part of the significance of this doctrine is its relationship to God's lordship. The doctrine of the Trinity is not given to relieve our curiosity. It is given to make us better covenant servants and children of God's family.

The battle for the Trinity during the fourth century was about the lordship of Jesus. The question was whether Jesus was fully Lord, as much entitled to that designation as God the Father.

The real passion of that battle was not over metaphysics or technical language. It was over the practical religious realities of worship and salvation. Should we worship Jesus? And is he the Lord who comes to save his people? *Worship* and *salvation* can be used to summarize the subject matter of Scripture. Worship is our chief duty as creatures, salvation our chief blessing as sinners saved by grace. In both of these areas, the doctrine of the Trinity plays a major role, both in Scripture and in the historical debate about the Trinity.

---

90. Ibid., 200–207.
91. Ibid., 210–11.
92. Ibid., 211–13.
93. Ibid., 214–15.
94. See Poythress, *Logic* (Wheaton: Crossway, 2013).

Worship: Athanasius, the great defender of Nicene orthodoxy, put the question of worship very pointedly: if the Arians are right, then for centuries Christians have been worshiping a creature; and worshiping a creature is the very biblical definition of idolatry. And Scripture agrees with Athanasius, not only with his doctrine, but also with his focus on worship. As we have seen, much of the Trinitarian language of Scripture appears in liturgical texts: the baptismal formula of Matthew 28:19, the apostolic greetings and benedictions (Rom. 16:27; 2 Cor. 13:14), the polemic against idolatry (1 Cor. 8:4–6), the call to prayer (Rom. 15:30).

Salvation: And Athanasius also made the point that if Jesus was a mere creature, as on the Arian view, then we are not saved. Only the Lord can save. As we have seen, "Savior" is an exclusive divine title in Isaiah (43:11; 45:21; etc.). And again, Athanasius tapped into a major concern of Scripture itself. For much of the Trinitarian teaching in the NT comes in contexts where the writers wish to enumerate the richness of the blessings of salvation: see, e.g., John 17:3; 1 Cor. 12:4–6; Eph. 3:5–7; 4:4–6; 2 Thess. 2:13–14; 1 Peter 1:2; 1 John 5:5–6. Can it be that it is eternal life to know a mere creature (John 17:3)? Can it be that the gifts of salvation are the gifts of mere creatures (1 Cor. 12:4–6; Eph. 4:4–6)?

And as we meditate on the different but unified roles of the three persons in saving us, we are driven back to worship. We are saved by the eternal purpose of the Father, by the atoning work of the Son, through the power and wisdom of the Spirit. We grow in our understanding of God's grace as we see how each person of the Trinity interacts with the others to bring us out of darkness, into the light.

So the doctrine of the Trinity powerfully supports the lordship of Jesus, the eternal Son. But it also supports the lordship of the Father and Spirit. To see this more clearly, let us look again at the lordship attributes:

Control: The Arians wanted to worship a big God, a God who was truly transcendent, beyond our knowing. But in the end, their God was dependent on the world. For, they reasoned, if God were to come into direct contact with the world, his deity would be threatened. Therefore, God had to create and redeem the world through semidivine mediators, the Son and the Spirit. That was God's weakness: the world was capable of threatening his deity.

On the contrary, in biblical Trinitarianism, God has nothing to fear from the world. God is the Lord, who can create the world with his own finger. His needs no finite associates, only his own Son and Spirit, who are themselves fully divine. So Trinitarianism reinforces the lordship attribute of sovereign control.

Authority: The doctrine of the Trinity reminds us that God is the One who authoritatively defines himself. We might imagine that God's love, for example, is defined as a relation between himself and the world. But then a divine attribute would be dependent on the world: God would have needed the world in order to have an adequate object for his love. His divine attribute of love would have depended on the world. But Trinitarianism teaches us that God's love is defined not by the world, but by the eternal love between Father and Son.[95] God would have been a loving God even if he

---

95. See how important it is that the Son be fully God.

had chosen not to create the world. So God is sovereign in defining his own nature.[96] And he is sovereign not only in defining his love, but in exercising it. He loves the world not because he must, but because he chooses freely to do so.

The important corollary is that we must think of God not on the basis of our own autonomous philosophies, but on the basis of his revelation of himself. Matthew 11:25–27, an important passage for understanding the relation of the Son to the Father, teaches us that we can know the Father only through the Son's revelation of him; and 1 Corinthians 2:10–15 says the same about the Spirit. Since God himself determines what he is (by his nature and by his free decisions), his words about himself must constrain our thoughts about him. He is the authoritative Lord.

Presence: I mentioned that the doctrine of the Trinity is connected to a view of the Creator-creature relation: God is not forced to relate to the world by semidivine mediators. He can and does touch the world directly, in creation, providence, redemption, and judgment.

And the persons of the Trinity do indeed enter our history in all these ways. They reveal themselves in the world so clearly that they can be models for us. So Jesus exhorts us to be holy as the Father is holy (Matt. 5:48). We are to love one another as Christ loved us (John 13:34–35). We are to be fit dwellings of the Holy Spirit, his temples (1 Cor. 6:19).

Even more remarkably, the persons of the Trinity relate to us in ways analogous to the ways in which they relate to one another. Remarkably, God is not only the Father of Jesus, but also the Father of believers (Matt. 6:9; John 20:17). We become one with the Father "as" the Son and the Father are one (John 17:11, 21–23). We become spiritual as we are indwelt by the divine Spirit (1 Cor. 2:15–16; Gal. 6:1).

Seen somewhat differently, the lordship attributes reflect the distinctive actions of the three persons of the Trinity. The Father ordains the eternal plan that governs nature and history (authority). The Son, obediently to his Father, carries out that plan by his mighty power, often exercised in weakness (control). And the Spirit applies that plan to the hearts of God's people (presence).

So the doctrine of the Trinity is quite integral to the doctrine of divine lordship. It reinforces God's sovereign control, his aseity, the sovereignty of his love and knowledge, the authority of his Word, the intimacy of his relationship to the creation, the richness of salvation. It is not an incidental addition to the doctrine of God; it is rather the doctrine of God as a whole, seen from an intradivine vantage point, as God gives us a glimpse of his own inner life.

Key Terms

Sabellianism
Modalism
Arianism

---

96. A similar point could be made about God's knowledge. God's knowledge is first of all his intra-Trinitarian knowledge of himself. He knows the world by knowing himself and knowing his plan. So his knowledge is not dependent on the world, but is fully sovereign.

Huiopator
Circumincessio
Opera ad intra
Opera ad extra
Ousia
Physis
Hypostasis
Prosopon
Substantia
Essentia
Personae
Subsistence
Mode of subsistence
Subsistent relation
Ontological Trinity
Immanent Trinity
Economic Trinity
Eternal generation
Eternal procession
Monogenes
Filioque
Subordinationism
Psychological model
Social model

Study Questions

1. "Thus is the doctrine of the Trinity related to the doctrines of God's transcendence and immanence and, in turn, to the doctrines of divine lordship and revelation." How is it related to these?
2. Show from Scripture that the persons of the Trinity are distinct from one another.
3. Is the Spirit a mere force, or a person? Cite biblical evidence.
4. In what sense does Paul say that "the Lord is the Spirit" in 2 Corinthians 3:17?
5. In John 17, Jesus prays that the disciples will be one even as the Father and Son are one. How is that possible?
6. Why should we distinguish *ousia* ("being") from *hypostasis* ("person") in God, given that these Greek terms were originally synonymous?
7. Is it helpful to speak of the three persons as "relations" in God? Why or why not?
8. Is it ever justified to speak of God as "one person"?
9. Should we affirm the doctrine of eternal generation? In what sense? Cite biblical evidence.

10. "Does *eternal generation* mean anything more than that the Father is eternally Father and the Son is eternally Son?" What more might it mean? Discuss.

11. Should the *filioque* have been used as a test of orthodoxy? Why or why not?

12. Is there any form of subordinationism that is biblically acceptable?

13. How is the doctrine of the Trinity related to the lordship attributes? To worship and salvation?

Memory Verses

John 10:30: I and the Father are one.

John 14:16–17: And I will ask the Father, and he will give you another Helper, to be with you forever, even the Spirit of truth, whom the world cannot receive, because it neither sees him nor knows him. You know him, for he dwells with you and will be in you.

John 15:26: But when the Helper comes, whom I will send to you from the Father, the Spirit of truth, who proceeds from the Father, he will bear witness about me.

John 17:11b: Holy Father, keep them [the disciples] in your name, which you have given me, that they may be one, even as we are one.

Resources for Further Study

Augustine. *On the Trinity.*

Bavinck, Herman. *BRD,* 2:256–334.

Bray, Gerald. *The Doctrine of God.* Downers Grove, IL: InterVarsity Press, 1993.

Gruenler, Royce. *The Trinity in the Gospel of John.* Grand Rapids: Baker, 1986.

Poythress, Vern S. "Reforming Ontology and Logic in the Light of the Trinity." *WTJ* 57, 1 (1995): 187–219. Poythress develops this argument further in his *Logic: A God-Centered Approach to the Foundation of Western Thought.* Wheaton, IL: Crossway, 2013.

Van Til, Cornelius. *An Introduction to Systematic Theology.* Nutley, NJ: Presbyterian and Reformed, 1974.

Warfield, B. B. "The Spirit of God in the OT." In *Biblical and Theological Studies.* Philadelphia: Presbyterian and Reformed, 1952.

PART 4

THE DOCTRINE OF
THE WORD OF GOD[1]

---

1. The following discussion uses *word of God* (and like phrases) and *word* (as shorthand for *word of God*) in a variety of ways. When *word of God* or *word* refers to the written, inscripturated Word of God, *Word* is capitalized. *Word* is also capitalized when it refers to Christ as the Word incarnate. Otherwise, *word of God* and *word* are lowercased. This distinction is followed throughout the book.

CHAPTER 23

GOD AND HIS WORD

GOD IS THE FOUNDATION of everything and therefore of theology. In part 3 I have spoken of him as Lord of all and therefore as the foundation of all being (sometimes called *principium essendi*). The I AM is the bedrock of all existence, by his necessary being, his eternal plan, his creation of the universe, and his providence in all nature and history. In parts 4 and 5, I will present the necessary consequence, that he is the origin of our *knowledge* of him and of his creation, the *principium cognoscendi*.

God's ability to communicate is not a frequent topic in theological treatments of the divine attributes. But it would be hard to find a subject more frequent in Scripture than the *word of God*. Again and again, we read that "the word of the Lord came to" a prophet. Hundreds of times, the prophets proclaim, "Thus says the Lord." So we need to consider how the word of God arises from God's own nature, as we have so far expounded it.

God's Speech

Certainly God's speech is one of his important actions. I have devoted an entire book to it, *DWG*. In the present volume, I have already stressed the element of revelation (that is, of divine speech)[1] in all the acts of God described in chapters 7–11, by emphasizing how these acts express God's lordship attribute of authority, together with the other lordship attributes. All these actions reveal him, for through them we know that he is the Lord. They communicate his truth authoritatively.

So God's words are among his mighty acts, and his mighty acts convey his word. But in Scripture there is also a kind of alternation between word and act, which suggests that God's words deserve separate treatment. God's words announce what he will do; then he acts; then by further words he interprets what he has done and announces further actions. For example, in Genesis 6:9–21, God tells Noah of the coming flood. In

---

1. In revelation, God makes himself known. Speech can be understood as a narrower category, his action to make himself known. Or it can be understood as something broader: God expressing himself in ways that bring about knowledge but also other effects. But there is no revelation without divine speech, for all revelation is by his initiative, his action.

519

7:1–8:19, the flood comes and subsides. Then in 8:20–9:28, God interprets the implications of the flood, initiates a new covenant, and declares future events. This alternation is the macrostructure of Scripture: the OT announces the coming of Christ to redeem his people. The Gospels narrate the fulfillment of that announcement. The rest of the NT interprets that event and announces further events to come.

Of course, God's words and acts are also related perspectivally. For (1) all his acts reveal his word, his plan, (2) all his words are themselves acts, (3) our knowledge of God's acts is entirely and exclusively through his Word, so that for us to know God's words and to know his acts are the same thing. So the alternation model may mislead us concerning the full relation between word and act. But at least that model helps us to see the value of looking at history from both perspectives, rather than from only one.

I discuss these matters and many more at length in *DWG*, and I will take up a number of them here in part 4 of this volume. In this chapter, I would like to explore the nature of the word of God. Is the word of God a divine attribute? A divine act? A divine person? An ineffable mystery? A divine book? Some combination of these?

God's word (Heb. *davar*, Gk. *logos*, *rema*[2]), according to Scripture, is his speech, by which he expresses and therefore reveals himself. Scripture itself is God's Word in this sense (2 Tim. 3:16[3]), but the speech of God is not limited to written revelation. In Genesis 1, God creates all things by speaking, a fact that arouses the awe and praise of later biblical writers:

> By the word of the LORD the heavens were made,
>   and by the breath of his mouth all their host.
> He gathers the waters of the sea as a heap;
>   he puts the deeps in storehouses.
>
> Let all the earth fear the LORD;
>   let all the inhabitants of the world stand in awe of him!
> For he spoke, and it came to be;
>   he commanded, and it stood firm. (Ps. 33:6–9)

Cf. also Ps. 148:5; Prov. 8:22–30;[4] John 1:1–3, 10; Heb. 1:2; 11:3; 2 Peter 3:5–7.

God's word also directs the course of providence. God not only brings the world out of nothing by his word, but also commands its course of action after that (Gen. 1:9, 11, 22; 8:22). So:

---

2. Of course, we also find this concept in the many words in both languages for *speak*, *command*, and the like, as well as the rich redundancy of terms in Psalm 119 and elsewhere referring to God's *testimonies*, *statutes*, *laws*, *ordinances*, *ways*, *precepts*, *decrees*, *commands*, and so on.

3. The Greek term *theopneustos* here means "breathed out by God," in other words, "spoken by God."

4. Here the subject is personified wisdom, not the word as such. But *wisdom* and *word* are closely related in Scripture. So the writer of Proverbs 8 alludes to creation by God's word in Genesis 1 to underscore his point that all of God's works are done in wisdom.

> He sends out his command to the earth;
>> his word runs swiftly.
> He gives snow like wool;
>> he scatters hoarfrost like ashes.
> He hurls down his crystals of ice like crumbs;
>> who can stand before his cold?
> He sends out his word, and melts them;
>> he makes his wind blow and the waters flow. (Ps. 147:15–18)

Cf. Job 37:12;[5] Pss. 18:15; 29:3–9; 148:6–8; Matt. 8:26–7; Heb. 1:3; 2 Peter 3:5–7.

The word is living (Heb. 4:12) and active also, obviously, in judgment (Gen. 3:17–19; 6:7; 11:6–7; etc.) and in grace. It is God's word that heals, saves, and delivers us. Note the emphasis on the word when Jesus heals the centurion's son in Luke 7:1–10[6] (cf. Ps. 107:20). Scripture describes God's saving acts as words of God, speeches of God. Salvation begins when God speaks his *decree* before time. He executes that decree by sending the living Word, Jesus (John 1:1–14; 1 John 1:1–3). He draws us to himself by the word of *effectual calling* (Isa. 43:1; see chapter 4), and by the *gospel*. Paul says:

> For I am not ashamed of the gospel, for it is the power of God for salvation to everyone who believes, to the Jew first and also to the Greek. (Rom. 1:16; cf. Phil. 2:16; 1 Thess. 1:5; 2:13; 2 Tim. 1:10)

He calls us by a new name (Isa. 62:2; 65:15).

God's word, then, is involved in everything God does: his decrees, creation, providence, redemption, and judgment, not only in revelation narrowly defined. He performs all his acts by his speech.

Further, God and his word are always *present* together. Where God is, the word is, and vice versa. Note the many biblical correlations between God's word and his Spirit:[7] Gen. 1:2–3; Ps. 33:6 (cf. Ps. 104:30); Isa. 34:16; 59:21; John 6:63; 16:13; Acts 2:1–4 (the coming of the Spirit leads to Spirit-empowered words); 1 Thess. 1:5; 2 Thess. 2:2; 2 Tim. 3:16 (the scriptural Word is *theopneustos*, coming from the divine breath or spirit), 2 Peter 1:21 (the breath or Spirit of God carrying the biblical writers where he

---

5. To be sure, this is part of a speech of Elihu, one of Job's friends, who do not speak truly of him. My understanding of the book of Job is that Job's friends usually do speak truth, but not about Job. They utter truths about God, but they wrongly apply those truths to Job. That, I think, is the intention of the author. So I don't think it wrong to quote Elihu in this connection, especially since his words are corroborated by many other texts.

6. In verse 7, the centurion, through his friends, asks Jesus to *eipe logo*—literally, "speak by a word"—to heal his servant. "Speak" would have been sufficient, but the friend adds "by a word," a redundancy giving special emphasis to the centurion's faith that Jesus, like only Yahweh, is able to heal simply by *speaking*. Then comes the comparison between Jesus and the centurion himself: Jesus has authority to command disease as the centurion is able to command his soldiers. Jesus commends the centurion's faith as greater than any that he has found in Israel. This faith is specifically faith in the *word* of Jesus.

7. *Spirit* in Scripture is *ruach* (Heb.) and *pneuma* (Gk.). Both these terms can also mean "breath" or "wind." The image is that when one person speaks to another, his breath carries the words to the other person. So the word and the Spirit must be joined if we are to receive God's revelation.

wanted them to go). So in Israel, the nearness of God was the nearness of the word (Deut. 4:5–8; 30:11–14), and in Romans 10:6–8, that nearness is the nearness of Christ.

So in the word of God we see all of God's lordship attributes represented. We see his control in the word's powerful actions,[8] his authority in his words addressed to us, and his presence in the inseparability of his word and Spirit. So God's word is inseparable from his lordship.

We have reason, then, to see God's speech as an essential attribute of his nature. Note also:

1. Scripture distinguishes the true God from all the false ones because he *speaks*; he is not *dumb* like the idols (1 Kings 18:24–46; Pss. 115:5–8; 135:15–18; Hab. 2:18–20; 1 Cor. 12:2).

2. One biblical picture of the Trinity is that the Father is the speaker (references above), the Son the Word he speaks (John 1:1–14; Rom. 10:6–8 [alluding to Deut. 30:11–14]; 2 Cor. 1:20; Heb. 1:1–3; 1 John 1:1–3; Rev. 19:13), and the Spirit the breath that carries that word to its destination (Ps. 33:6; see footnote 7).

3. The speech of God has divine attributes: righteousness (Ps. 119:7), faithfulness (119:86), wonderfulness (119:129), truth (119:142; John 17:17), eternity (Ps. 119:89, 160), omnipotence (Gen. 18:14; Isa. 55:11; Luke 1:37), perfection (Ps. 19:7–11).

4. God's word is an object of worship (Pss. 56:4, 10; 119:120, 161–62; Isa. 66:5). Many times Scripture calls us to praise the "name" of the Lord (e.g., Pss. 9:2; 34:3; 68:4; 138:2). There is a close relation in Scripture between God's name, his word, and his being.

5. The word is God,[9] and therefore it is his "self-expression" in the very highest sense. This must be so if God's word is to be an object of worship, or to have divine attributes, or to model the Trinity, or to distinguish God from idols. And John 1:1 says this in so many words.[10] In point 2 above, I listed a number of verses equating Christ with the Word of God. In John 1:1, however, the Word of God is not only Christ, but also the means by which God created the heavens and the earth. "In the beginning" of verse 1 clearly alludes to Genesis 1:1, and the reference to creation in verse 3 again recalls the creation narrative in which God creates by word. By implication, all the words by which God decrees, creates, provides, judges, and saves are divine.[11]

---

8. The *power* of the word is a major theme in Scripture. See Isa. 55:11; Rom. 1:16; 1 Thess. 1:5; Heb. 4:12; and many of the other passages listed in this section. In Jeremiah 1:9–12, God's word in the prophet's mouth gives him power "over nations and over kingdoms, to pluck up and to break down, to destroy and to overthrow, to build and to plant." But the word is not a bare power or brute force; it is also *meaning*. It always *says* something intelligible, contrary to many liberal and neoorthodox theologians. God not only creates the world by his word, but also interprets it, by giving names and evaluations (Gen. 1:5, 8, 10, 12, etc.). So God's words express his authority as well as his power and presence.

9. There is some Jewish precedent for this identification. *Memra* ("Word") in the Targums is one of many terms that the Jews of the time used to avoid direct use of the divine name.

10. For more discussion of this passage, focusing on its implications for the deity of Christ, see chapter 21.

11. Another important passage identifying God and his word is Hebrews 4:12–13. In verse 12, we learn that the word is living and active, judging the human heart. Verse 13 refers to God's omniscience. In the NIV there appears to be a change of subject between these two verses: the word in verse 12, God in verse 13. But in the Greek there is no change of subject. The word is the omniscience of God himself.

John 1:1 also distinguishes the Word from God: "the Word was *with* God." Here we find ourselves in the midst of Trinitarian mystery. The same paradox exists in the Bible's teachings concerning Jesus. Jesus is the Word—so the Jesus-Word is God, but is also distinct from God. God is one, but he exists, as we have seen, in three persons. So sometimes we read that the Word and God are the same; sometimes we read that the word is God's tool (as in "*by* the word of the LORD the heavens were made," Ps. 33:6). We have seen this unity and complexity of God's nature in other contexts (see chapter 20). As with the persons of the Trinity, God's attributes are both identified with him and distinguished from him in Scripture.

For now, however, the important point is that by his very nature God is a *speaking* God. His speech is a divine attribute as much as love, omniscience, or eternity. In chapter 3, I indicated that only in biblical religion is there such a thing as a personal absolute. The same may be said of God's speech, an aspect of his personality. Only in biblical religion is there a God who is absolute and who also *speaks* to his creatures. The absolute beings of Hinduism, Buddhism, and Greek and modern philosophy do not *speak* to human beings. But the biblical God does. And in his speech, he brings himself to us.

So the word of God is a great treasure. We should rejoice that our God is not dumb, like the gods of the nations, but has shared with us his laws, his wisdom, and his love.[12] And God is always with and in his word. When we read the Word, we encounter him; when we encounter him, we hear his word.

It is also good to know that God not only speaks to us, but also speaks to himself, since he is word by nature. The Father, Son, and Spirit search one another's hearts (1 Cor. 2:10–11). They express love and glorify one another eternally (John 17:24). God exhaustively knows himself. We creatures do not have perfect self-knowledge. In our hearts, souls, and bodies are hidden depths that we do not understand. Often our thoughts and actions (to say nothing of our physical conditions) surprise us; often they reveal things about ourselves that we had not known and would perhaps just as soon not have known. But there are no unexplored depths in God's nature. He does not surprise himself. He is word. His word exhaustively expresses his being to himself, among the persons of the Trinity. Our God has perfect knowledge of who he is and of what he does.

I conclude that God's word, his speech, is an essential attribute, inseparable from God's being.[13] It is his capacity for speech, as a speaking God. It is particularly identical to the second person of the Trinity,[14] but all three persons are involved in God's speech, and the word of God exists wherever God is. So we may define *word of God* as

12. For perspective buffs, law is normative, wisdom situational, love existential.

13. Karl Barth and other theologians in the mid-twentieth century commonly said that God's word (or "revelation") is God himself, justifying such slogans as "God doesn't reveal propositions; he reveals himself." My discussion here agrees with the idea that God reveals himself. But his self-revelation includes revelation about everything he is and everything he has made, in nature and history.

14. There is no scriptural reason why it cannot be identical both to the whole Godhead and to one of the three persons. "Spirit" is both a particular person of the Trinity and a characterization of the whole divine nature (John

(1) an attribute of God, identical to his being, (2) the second person of the Trinity, and (3) any and all of his specific communications, addressed either to Trinitarian persons or to creatures.

God's Truth

In *DG*, I discuss both God's speech and his truth among his attributes of knowledge (chapter 15 in this book). Here I am giving the word of God, God's attribute of speech, independent attention. Together with that, it is important to discuss the divine attribute of truth. God is himself true. All his words are true. His word *is* truth (John 17:17; cf. 2 Sam. 7:28; 1 Kings 17:24; Pss. 119:43, 89–90, 142, 151). So, as in the chart of chapter 12, speech is the content of God's knowledge, and truth is the internal standard that governs God's speech.

Herman Bavinck distinguishes three different meanings of *truth* (Heb. *'emeth*, *'emunah*, Gk. *aletheia*[15]) in Scripture: metaphysical, logical (I would say *epistemological* or *propositional*), and ethical.[16] In the metaphysical sense, to say that something is true is to say that it is "all that it is supposed to be."[17] "True" gold is the genuine article, as opposed to "fool's gold." In Scripture, God is the *true* God as opposed to the idols. God says through Jeremiah:

> Beaten silver is brought from Tarshish,
>   and gold from Uphaz.
> They are the work of the craftsman and of the hands of the goldsmith;
>   their clothing is violet and purple;
>   they are all the work of skilled men.
> But the LORD is the true God;
>   he is the living God and the everlasting King.
> At his wrath the earth quakes,
>   and the nations cannot endure his indignation. (Jer. 10:9–10)

And through Paul: "For they themselves report concerning us the kind of reception we had among you, and how you turned to God from idols to serve the living and true God" (1 Thess. 1:9). Jesus says that eternal life is "that they know you the only true God, and Jesus Christ whom you have sent" (John 17:3).

We may also describe as metaphysical a somewhat different but related usage, in which *truth* denotes what is ultimate in comparison with other realities. John Murray says:

4:24). "Father" is the name of the first person of the Trinity, but Scripture also teaches that the whole triune God bears a fatherly relation to his people (chapter 6).

15. The LXX sometimes uses *pistos*, "faithful," to translate the Hebrew terms. The KJV translates *pistos* as "true" in 2 Corinthians 1:18, but more recent translations do not follow it here. But as we will see, *faithful* and *true* are closely related in Scripture.

16. *BRD*, 2:208–9.

17. Ibid., 209. Thus Thomas Aquinas equated Being and Truth, developing his equation between God and Being. For him, being, unity, truth, beauty, and goodness are all ultimately the same, both in God and in the creation. These are the "transcendental" concepts that frequently enter his theology.

We should bear in mind that "the true" in the usage of John is not so much the true in contrast with the false, or the real in contrast with the fictitious. It is the absolute as contrasted with the relative, the ultimate as contrasted with the derived, the eternal as contrasted with the temporal, the permanent as contrasted with the temporary, the complete in contrast with the partial, the substantial in contrast with the shadowy.[18]

Like the other divine attributes, metaphysical truth pertains not only to God the Father, but also to his Son, Jesus Christ. Jesus says, "I am the way, and the truth, and the life. No one comes to the Father except through me" (John 14:6). As in the contrast between the true God and the idols, Jesus here sets aside all the other religions of the world and presents himself as the only genuine Mediator between God and man (cf. 1 Tim. 2:5). First John 5:20 identifies the Son and the Father by means of the attribute of truth:

> And we know that the Son of God has come and has given us understanding, so that we may know him who is true; and we are in him who is true, in his Son Jesus Christ. He is the true God and eternal life.[19]

The Spirit is also "the truth" in 1 John 5:6.

Epistemological or propositional truth can be seen as an implication of metaphysical truth.[20] It is a property of language, rather than reality in general. But true language is language that rightly represents reality, that expresses the way something "really is." Truth in this sense is the proper correlation between language and reality. A true statement is one on which we can rely; it will not mislead us. The same can be said of commands (Ps. 119:142, 151) and promises (2 Sam. 7:28; Heb. 10:23).[21] So in the verses cited at the beginning of this section, God's *words* are truth.[22] He cannot lie (Num. 23:19; Titus 1:2; Heb. 6:18), nor can he be in error (Heb. 4:12–13). So he is true, even when every man is a liar (Rom. 3:4).

18. John Murray, *Principles of Conduct* (Grand Rapids: Eerdmans, 1957), 123. He points out that in John 1:17, "For the law was given through Moses; grace and truth came through Jesus Christ." John is not saying that the law is false or untrue; rather, it is incomplete, compared to the fullness of God's revelation in Christ. So Christ is the *true* light (John 1:9). Other examples of this use of *true* and *truth*: John 6:32; 15:1; 17:3; Heb. 8:2. In this sense, *true* approaches the meaning "perfect."

19. Clearly, the antecedent of "He" in the last sentence is "Jesus Christ." So this verse clearly teaches the full deity of Christ. Compare the discussion of this passage in chapter 21. The emphasis on metaphysical truth makes this identification all the more emphatic.

20. It is not always easy to distinguish whether a particular Scripture passage is speaking of metaphysical or propositional truth. Revelation 3:7 and 6:10 refer to Jesus as the One who is "true," probably both in the metaphysical sense and in the sense that what he says is always reliable. Same for the reference to the Spirit in 1 John 5:6. First John 5:20 combines and connects these meanings.

21. Modern philosophers sometimes distinguish propositions, commands, promises, questions, and the like as different "speech acts," among which only propositions, strictly speaking, can be true or false. On this view, only propositions make truth claims, and so only propositions may be judged as to their truth. But of course, other sorts of speech acts often presuppose truth claims, and they often communicate propositional knowledge alongside their other functions. "Johnny, put the dog down" is a command, but it assumes that there is a dog, that Johnny is carrying him, and so on.

22. See also Deut. 17:4; 1 Kings 10:6; Eph. 4:24.

His truth, like all his attributes, is of the highest perfection. So in his lordship attribute of authority, he is the very *standard* of truth for his creatures. As with goodness and righteousness (chapters 12, 13), truth is what God is and therefore what he says. There is no higher standard than God against which his truth may be measured. So God's metaphysical ultimacy implies that he is the standard of propositional truth.

There are times when God in judgment sends upon men a "lying spirit" (1 Kings 22:22) or "strong delusion" (2 Thess. 2:11). Such is the mystery of evil (chapter 14). And it is at least arguable that he does not condemn lying in defense of human life, as in the case of the Hebrew midwives (Ex. 1) and Rahab (Josh. 2).[23] Such is the difficulty of living in a fallen world. But there is no case in Scripture of God's own word ever proving false.[24]

The importance of propositional truth in Scripture cannot be denied. Since its seventeenth-century beginnings, liberal theology has denied the possibility of "propositional revelation," revelation in which God reveals words and sentences that agree with reality. The older liberalism (through the time of Wilhelm Herrmann and Adolf von Harnack) simply denied the divine authority of Scripture, treating the Bible as a collection of merely human religious writings. Thus, these thinkers were able to maintain the autonomy of their own thought, denying the need to place their scholarship under the authority of God's Word. The neoorthodoxy of Karl Barth and Emil Brunner said much about the authority of the Word, but they conceived of God's Word as a kind of gracious divine power that did not convey any propositional truth.[25] So the neoorthodox, like the older liberals, justified autonomous human thought and acknowledged the freedom of Bible critics from any divine constraints.

But clearly in the Bible God reveals himself not only through personal confrontations and events in history, but also through words, which he speaks directly to his people (Ex. 20:1–17; Deut. 4:12; Matt. 3:17; 17:5) and through prophets who bear his full authority (Deut. 18:17–22;[26] Jer. 1:10–12; John 16:13; 1 Cor. 14:37). And as we saw in the previous section, he also provides written words given by the Spirit. These words are among those that have the quality of divine truth. Is the Bible *inerrant*, then? Certainly, if *inerrant* means "true" in the propositional sense. But I will have more to say about that in chapter 26.

The third kind of truth, ethical truth, emerges naturally from the other two. Metaphysical truth is genuineness; epistemological truth faithfully represents what is genuine; ethical truth is faithfulness in all areas of life. We represent the truth not only in

---

23. See my treatment of the ninth commandment in *DCL*, 830–40.

24. There are cases, as with the Ninevites in the book of Jonah, in which God announces judgment but retracts that announcement later upon repentance. See the discussion of God's unchangeability in chapter 17. Even in such cases, when God announces judgment, that announcement is true in the sense that judgment does impend against his enemies.

25. The older liberals were concerned about truth, but did not see it as divinely revealed. The neoorthodox were concerned with revelation, but they did not see that revelation as conveying propositional truth. So the liberals believed in *aletheia* without *logos*, the neoorthodox *logos* without *aletheia*.

26. The test of a prophet in verse 22 is whether or not the prophecy comes *true*.

words, but in the language of our actions. It is our deeds that tell the world what we really believe to be true. So God calls us not only to speak the truth, but also to live it. One who lives, walks in (2 John 4), or does (1:6) the truth, in whom the truth exists (2:4), is reliable, trustworthy, faithful, first to God, and therefore to reality. He does not lie (1:6; 2:21, 27) or deceive himself (1 John 1:8). And he also keeps God's commandments in other areas (2:4). Jesus said that if we love him, we must keep his commands (John 14:15); so to be faithful, we must be obedient. Love must also be true: "Little children, let us not love in word or talk but in deed and in truth" (1 John 3:18).[27]

God is true also in the ethical sense. As we saw in chapter 12, *'emeth* is a close synonym and frequent companion to *chesed*, "covenant love" or "faithfulness." *'Emunah*, also:

> Know therefore that the LORD your God is God, the faithful God who keeps covenant and steadfast love with those who love him and keep his commandments, to a thousand generations. (Deut. 7:9; cf. Deut. 4:31; 2 Sam. 7:16; Ps. 40:11; Hos. 12:1)

By nature he is "a God of faithfulness" (Deut. 32:4; cf. 1 Cor. 1:9; 10:13; 1 Thess. 5:24; 2 Thess. 3:3; Heb. 10:23; 11:11; 1 John 1:9). He is reliable, dependable, the "rock" (1 Sam. 2:2; Pss. 18:2; 62:2; see also Isa. 26:4). As Bavinck says, "he is a perfectly reliable refuge for all his people, Ps. 31:6; 36:5."[28]

I have indicated how propositional truth arises out of metaphysical truth, and ethical out of propositional.[29] But there are also relationships in the other direction. One's ethical reliability requires him to seek and speak propositional truth, and one's view of what is propositional truth dictates his view of what is. The three kinds of truth are perspectivally related in the sense that none can exist without the others, and each determines how we view the others. So the three kinds of truth coalesce in God's being, with one another, and with the other divine attributes.

God's Word to Us

In the previous two sections, I have focused on the word of God as an aspect of his own nature. But of course, we observe God's nature from our own position as finite beings, so we cannot help but note some of the implications of this teaching for our own life with God. In this section, I will summarize what it means for God to speak to creatures and specifically to us.

I have argued as the main theme of this book that God relates to creatures as their covenant Lord. We can describe this relationship in terms of the three lordship attributes: control, authority, and presence. We have seen that all of God's actions, attributes,

---

27. Other examples: Neh. 9:33; Pss. 15:2; 25:5; 26:3; 51:6; 86:11; Ezek. 18:9; Hos. 4:1; John 3:20f.; Gal. 5:7.

28. Herman Bavinck, *The Doctrine of God* (Grand Rapids: Baker, 1951), 200.

29. Gordon H. Clark derives metaphysical and ethical truth from propositional in *Baker's Dictionary of Theology* (Grand Rapids: Baker, 1960), 532–33, reinforcing his generally intellectualist approach to theology. But he does not consider the possibility that similar deductions can be made in the opposite direction or that these meanings of truth may be *mutually* dependent.

and Trinitarian persons express these attributes, and certainly God's speech expresses them as well. So as we have already noted to some extent, God's word manifests his controlling power, his supreme authority, and his presence with his creatures. Let us consider these further.

Controlling Power

I indicated earlier that God accomplishes all his mighty acts by speech. This includes his eternal plan, the eternal deliberations of the persons of the Trinity (Matt. 11:25–27; John 4:34; 5:19–30; 17:1–26), his work of creation (Gen. 1; Ps. 33:6–9), providence (Ps. 147:15–18), judgment (Gen. 3:17–19), and grace (Luke 7:7–9; Rom. 1:16; Phil. 2:16).

And when the apostles bring the gospel of Christ to the world, they rejoice that it is not only a content, but also a power (Rom. 1:16; 1 Thess. 1:5; 2:13). Not only is it accompanied by signs of God's power (Rom. 15:19), but the word itself changes hearts and strengthens believers (Rom. 16:25). It is the "word of life" (Phil. 2:16; see also John 1:1), the gospel that brings life and immortality to light (2 Tim. 1:10).

So the word of God is powerful both in judgment and in blessing. These are the twin covenant sanctions. In the covenant, the Lord promises blessing to the obedient, judgment to the disobedient (Deut. 27–28). So the commandments of God have a double edge; they can be blessing (Ex. 20:12) or curse (v. 7). Obedience to God's commands is the path of life (Lev. 18:5; Deut. 8:3; Pss. 19; 119:25, 50), but the commandments themselves can give opportunity for sin (Rom. 7:7–25). God tells Isaiah that his message will be mostly one of hardening and curse: "Make the heart of this people dull, and their ears heavy, and blind their eyes; lest they see with their eyes, and hear with their ears, and understand with their hearts, and turn and be healed" (Isa. 6:10). God sends Isaiah to people who doubtless have already hardened their hearts against the Lord. But in this context it is Isaiah's words, the words of God, that bring the hardening. Jesus and the apostles invoke the words of Isaiah 6 to characterize their own preaching (Matt. 13:14–15; Mark 4:11–12; Luke 8:10; John 12:37–40; Acts 28:26–28; Rom. 11:8; cf. John 15:22).

The power of the Word brings wonderful blessings to those who hear in faith, with a disposition to obey. But it hardens those who hear it with indifference, resistance, or rebellion. In considering this biblical teaching, I often warn my seminary students to pay heed to what God is telling us here. For seminarians typically spend two or more years intensively studying Scripture. It is so important that they hear in faith, lest the Word actually harden their hearts and become a fire of judgment to them. God's Word never leaves us the same. We hear it for better or worse. So we should never hear or read God's Word merely as an academic exercise. We must ask God to open our hearts, that the Word may be written on them as well as in our heads.

So God accomplishes all his works by his powerful word: creation, providence, judgment, grace.[30]

---

30. If we add God's eternal plan to this list, we have a good summary of all the works of God reported in Scripture. God's eternal plan is also an exercise of his word. It is the agreement between Father, Son, and Spirit to

The power of the word is the power of God's Spirit (1 Thess. 1:5), though the Spirit is not always mentioned in contexts that speak of the word's power (as 1 Thess. 2:13). That is to say that the power of the word is personal, not impersonal. So when the word of the gospel leads one hearer to faith and hardens another, that is God's sovereign decision. The difference is not that some hearers are better able to resist God's word than others, as some Lutherans have claimed. That would mean that the word, like an impersonal force of electricity or gravity, works uniformly on everyone, and that the only differences in response come from those who hear. Scripture, however, teaches that God himself determines who will respond favorably to his word. That is Paul's argument in Romans 9:1–28.

To say this is not to say that the word is powerful only when the Spirit accompanies it and is powerless otherwise. The word is never powerless, as we have seen from Genesis 18:14 and Isaiah 55:11. That implies that the word is never without the power of the Spirit. But sometimes that power effects a blessing, sometimes a curse, depending on God's sovereign intent.

How powerful is the power of the word? The power of God's word is nothing less than his own omnipotence. As we saw earlier, *no* word of God is too hard for him to accomplish. In Isaiah 55:11, we read, "So shall my word be that goes out from my mouth; it shall not return to me empty, but it shall accomplish that which I purpose, and shall succeed in the thing for which I sent it." What God says with his mouth he fulfills with his hand (2 Chron. 6:15; cf. Ezek. 1:3; 3:22).

As you read God's Word, always remember that it is something *active*, that it is *doing* something to you, for better or worse. When we hear or read the Word, we are not above it, using it for our own purposes. Rather, in the Word, God is doing something to us.

Meaningful Authority

As we saw earlier, the word is a power, but not a "raw" power. It is a power that moves things in a meaningful direction, determined by God's plan. So, for example, not only does God create the world by his word, but he also interprets created things, using words to describe what they are (Gen. 1:5, 8, 10).

So in the early chapters of Genesis, God speaks *to* Adam and Eve, declaring their dominion over the earth and the task they are to perform (1:28–30), announcing their probation (2:16–17), and setting forth the consequences of the fall (3:8–23). His speech to them is not only meaningful, but authoritative. That is to say, it imposes on them an obligation to respond in an appropriate way. That is the proper definition of *authority*: an authoritative word is one that imposes obligations on those who hear. And the word of God imposes an absolute obligation.

The exact nature of the obligation depends on the context of the command. There are all sorts of divine utterances on a wide variety of topics: worship, Sabbath, family,

---

carry out their program for creation, fall, and redemption. See Pss. 2:7–9; 110; Matt. 11:25–27; John 4:34; 5:19–30; 6:38; 17:1–26.

marriage, faith, and so on. There are different kinds of speech as well: commands, assertions, promises, and the like. When God commands, we are to obey. When he asserts, we are to believe him. When he promises, we are to embrace and trust those promises. Thus, we respond to the sheer authority of God's word.

Adam and Eve had no way of testing what God told them about the forbidden fruit. They couldn't work any experiment that would show them whether God had rightly predicted the effects of the fruit. They simply had to take God at his word. Satan interposed a contrary interpretation, but the first couple should not have taken his opinion seriously. They should simply have believed God. They did not, of course. They sided with Satan rather than God—or, perhaps better, they claimed that their own authority transcended God's. That is to say, they claimed *autonomy*. They claimed that they themselves were the highest authority, the ultimate criterion of truth and right.

The NT praises Noah (Heb. 11:7), Abraham (Rom. 4:1–25; Heb. 11:8–19), and many others because of their faith, and their faith was grounded in God's word. They simply believed what God said and obeyed him. So for new covenant believers: if they love Jesus, they will do what he says (John 14:15, 21, 23; 15:7, 10, 14; 17:6, 17; 1 John 2:3–5; 3:22; 5:2–3; 2 John 6).

So we should think of God's word as a personal communication from him to us. In *DWG*, I presented this as a general way of thinking about the word of God: the *personal-word model*. Think of God speaking to you as a real person would—as directly as your parents, your spouse, your children, your friends. Many in Scripture heard such speech from God, such as Noah, Abraham, and Moses.

And when God speaks, his word carries authority. This means that it imposes obligations. When God commands, he expects us to obey. When he brings information, we are to believe him. When he promises, we should embrace his promises.

If God really talked to you, as he did to Abraham, you would not (if you know what is best for you) criticize his words or disagree with him. Paul says of Abraham:

> No distrust made him waver concerning the promise of God, but he grew strong in his faith as he gave glory to God, fully convinced that God was able to do what he had promised. (Rom. 4:20–21)

Abraham was strong in faith even though God's words to him were hard to take. God told him to leave his home and go to a place he did not know (Gen. 12:1–3), to believe God's promise that he would beget a son in his old age (17:15–21), and later to sacrifice his son Isaac on a mountain altar (22:1–2). Often God's words to us pose problems that we cannot solve. But God expects us to be like Abraham, not like Adam and Eve, to hear what he says, to be strong in faith, without wavering.[31]

---

31. So we should reject theories of revelation, such as those of Baruch Spinoza, Immanuel Kant, and Wolfhart Pannenberg, that insist that we subject God's Word to the evaluation of would-be autonomous human reason. See *DWG*, chaps. 3 and 4, for a more detailed discussion.

Personal Presence

Since, as we saw, God's word is God himself, God is wherever his word is. Scripture is very specific about this. In Deuteronomy 4:7–8 and 30:11–14, God says that his nearness to Israel is the nearness of his statutes. Paul appropriates this theme in Romans 10:6–8:

> But the righteousness based on faith says, "Do not say in your heart, 'Who will ascend into heaven?'" (that is, to bring Christ down) or "'Who will descend into the abyss?'" (that is, to bring Christ up from the dead). But what does it say? "The word is near you, in your mouth and in your heart" (that is, the word of faith that we proclaim).

Here the dwelling of Christ in us is the dwelling of his word. Christ is near us in the word of faith, and as we grasp hold of it, we grasp hold of Christ, so we are saved (Rom. 10:9–10).

The Holy Spirit, too, is closely linked with the word. Where the Spirit is, the word is. As God created the world by his word, the Spirit hovered over the waters (Gen. 1:2). Psalm 33:6 couples God's "word" and "breath" as the sources of creation. God's breath is his Spirit (cf. Isa. 34:16; 59:21). Jesus says that his words are Spirit and life (John 6:63; cf. 1 Thess. 1:5; 2:2). The written Word is "breathed out" by God (2 Tim. 3:16; cf. 2 Peter 1:21). The Spirit inspires the Word and teaches it (1 Thess. 1:5; 1 John 2:27) to God's people.

So the personal presence of God always accompanies the Word, speaking the Word to our hearts. Where the Word is, God is, and where God is, the Word is. We should never try to seek fellowship with God apart from the Word. And when we do hear or read the Word, we should understand that we are entering the temple of God himself. That is to say, God's Word is *holy* (2 Tim. 3:15).

Key Terms

Principium essendi
Principium cognoscendi
Divine speech
Divine revelation
Word of God
Truth
Metaphysical truth
Epistemological or logical truth
Ethical truth
Propositional truth
Propositional revelation
Raw power
Memra
Autonomy
Authority
Personal-word model

Study Questions

1. Describe the relations between God's words and his acts.

2. "God's word, then, is involved in everything God does: his decrees, creation, providence, redemption, and judgment, not only in revelation narrowly defined. He performs all his acts by his speech." Explain; evaluate, using biblical references.

3. "The word is not a bare power or brute force." Explain; evaluate. What is it, then?

4. "So in the word of God we see all of God's lordship attributes represented." Explain; evaluate.

5. Frame says that one biblical picture of the Trinity employs the concept of the word of God. Explain; evaluate.

6. "The speech of God has divine attributes." Explain; evaluate, using biblical texts.

7. "God's word is an object of worship." Explain; evaluate, using biblical texts.

8. "The word is God." Present the biblical argument for this conclusion and evaluate.

9. "So God's metaphysical ultimacy implies that he is the standard of propositional truth." Explain; evaluate.

10. Does God give to us propositional revelation? Explain; make a case.

11. "So God accomplishes all his works by his powerful word." Present the biblical basis for this statement and evaluate.

12. "God's Word never leaves us the same. We hear it for better or worse." Explain; evaluate. Apply this principle to your own study and hearing of the Word.

13. Describe and explain the difference between Reformed and Lutherans over the power of the word. Adjudicate from Scripture.

14. "Adam and Eve had no way of testing what God told them about the forbidden fruit." Why is this important? Explain; evaluate.

15. Show how the word conveys God's lordship attributes.

16. "God's Word is *holy*." Expound.

Memory Verses

Ps. 33:6–9: By the word of the LORD the heavens were made,
and by the breath of his mouth all their host.
He gathers the waters of the sea as a heap;
he puts the deeps in storehouses.

Let all the earth fear the LORD;
let all the inhabitants of the world stand in awe of him!
For he spoke, and it came to be;
he commanded, and it stood firm.

Rom. 1:16: For I am not ashamed of the gospel, for it is the power of God for salvation to everyone who believes, to the Jew first and also to the Greek.

Rom. 4:20–21: No distrust made him waver concerning the promise of God, but he grew strong in his faith as he gave glory to God, fully convinced that God was able to do what he had promised.

Resources for Further Study

Frame, John M. *DWG*, 47–68. See also *DG*, 469–79, on God's speech and his truth.

Van Til, Cornelius. *An Introduction to Systematic Theology*. Nutley, NJ: Presbyterian and Reformed, 1974. This book presents the doctrine of revelation as based in a Christian world-and-life view, which is the only way in which this doctrine can be rightly understood.

CHAPTER 24

GOD SPEAKS TO US IN EVENTS AND WORDS

IN CHAPTER 23, I SOUGHT TO define biblically the nature of the word of God. In summary, the word of God is (1) an attribute of God, identical to his being, (2) the second person of the Trinity, and (3) any and all of his specific communications, addressed either to Trinitarian persons or to creatures. In this chapter, I will begin to discuss the *media* of the word, the ways in which the word of God comes from God's lips to our ears, minds, and hearts.

We are familiar today with the term *media* as it is used for radio, television, films, newspapers, and magazines, and we often express some trepidation about the effects of the media on our culture. The problem, of course, is not with the media themselves, but with fallen man's use of them. That there are pure and righteous ways to employ media becomes evident when we consider that God himself makes use of media to communicate his word.

We are concerned here with *created* media. Certainly God's intra-Trinitarian communication does not require created media, so in terms of this discussion, we should refer to the intra-Trinitarian communication as *unmediated*. But I'm inclined to think that when God speaks with human beings, he almost always uses one medium or other. We sometimes speak of God's revealing himself "directly," as when he spoke on Mount Sinai to all Israel, or when he spoke to a prophet such as Moses "mouth to mouth" (Num. 12:8). But even in those situations, God evidently uses created media. God's voice on these occasions used the atmosphere to carry sound waves to the ears of his audience and thence to their brains. He uses the Hebrew language, or some ancestor of it: a language of creatures, certainly not the divine language by which the persons of the Trinity communicate with one another. So even when God's revelation is "direct," it employs created media.

Perhaps there is an exception when and if God determines to place a message immediately into a person's mind, without any seeing, hearing, or reasoning. God certainly has the power to do this. In one sense, I think the work of the Spirit to impress God's truth on our hearts (Matt. 11:25–27; Eph. 1:17) is immediate, though even that is a witness to God's word and therefore in one sense mediated by God's word. In any case, it is clearly important for us to consider the nature of mediation.

I distinguish three categories of revelation media: events, words, and persons. These categories correspond roughly to the lordship attributes: events are brought about by God's controlling power; words bear God's meaningful authority; and persons embody the personal presence of the Lord. But we should not press the parallel too far. It would be wrong, for example, to say that event-revelation embodies God's control, but not his authority or presence. Rather, through all the media of revelation, God expresses all the aspects of his lordship. In event-revelation, God reveals himself not only as the supremely powerful controller, but also as the supremely meaningful authority and the supremely personal presence. Similarly for word-revelation and person-revelation. Scripture treats all of God's revelation as supremely powerful, authoritative, and personal; see fig. 24.1.

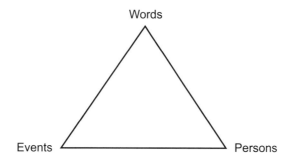

Fig. 24.1. Modes of God's Revelation

Indeed, the three kinds of media are inseparable from one another and perspectivally related. We gain our knowledge of event-revelation by means of word-revelation, words narrating and explaining the events. But God's giving of words is also an event. And the words have no value to us except as they convey to us the events of creation, fall, and redemption. Further, the narrative of events expressed in words is a narrative about persons, divine, angelic, and human. So the events, words, and persons are all necessary to one another; indeed, they constitute one another.

These three forms of revelation also explain and interpret one another. One cannot fully understand revelation in events without the commentary of God's verbal revelation. On the other hand, one cannot fully understand the verbal revelation of the Bible without understanding something of biblical languages, ancient history, and culture, which requires a study of extrabiblical event-revelation. Similarly, event-revelation and word-revelation cannot be understood without an understanding of revelatory persons, and vice versa.

So all these media are essential to the revelation that God has chosen to give us. It is not our place to pick and choose among them what we would prefer to hear, to believe, or to obey. To question the words is to question the events described in the words and the persons who participated in those events. Similarly for the other media.

Certainly it would be wrong to say that the media of revelation somehow detract from the power, authority, and divine presence of the revelation. The media are inseparable from the revelation. If they are defective, there is no way for us to reclaim an uncorrupted version of God's truth. If we are to accept God's revelation, we must accept what we hear and see through his media.

So we must never regard the media as barriers to God's communication. God is never prevented by the limitations of creation, or the finitude of people, from saying what he wants to say to them. Rather, the media are God's chosen instruments for bringing his absolute power, authority, and presence to the attention of finite hearers.

This is the fundamental answer to the question whether the "humanity" of revelation detracts from its divine character. It is often pointed out that God's revelation through prophets, apostles, and biblical writers is human as well as divine.[1] But human beings do make mistakes. So, the argument goes, we should expect mistakes in the revelation, not because of God, but because of the human instruments. But note:

1. Human beings do not *necessarily* err. Even unregenerate people sometimes speak the truth. So we should not think it impossible that God could reveal himself through human agents, keeping them from error, without violating their humanity.

2. If humanity necessarily entails error, then *all* of God's revelation in Scripture, every sentence, is erroneous, for all of it comes through human mediation. Nobody has ever argued such an extreme position.

3. Christ was fully human, but he did not speak error.

4. Almost all the biblical statements we noted in chapter 23 about the power, authority, and presence of God in revelation pertain to revelation through the mediation of human beings. There is no suggestion in any of these passages that human media somehow detract from or compromise the divine quality of the message; indeed, these passages exclude that possibility.

5. On the argument that human *language* is somehow incapable of truly referring to God, see my article "God and Biblical Language."[2]

6. In general, the humanity of God's word is not a liability, but a perfection. God's intent in revelation is to communicate with people. To do that, he must speak their language so that they may understand it. This language, therefore, must be a fully human language. Scripture shows that God has indeed succeeded in putting his word into human words—words that human prophets, apostles, and biblical writers utter as their own. For that, he deserves praise, not suspicion.

Revelation through Events

First, we consider *event-media*, the revelation of God through the mediation of events. We may further distinguish events of nature and events of history. Nature is the whole creation and everything that takes place within it. History is a set of events significant

---

1. Indeed, even the most direct revelation of God, such as his speaking from Mount Sinai in the presence of Israel, has a human element, for on such occasions he speaks a human language.

2. Appendix E of *DWG*.

to human beings. We also use the term *history* to refer to spoken or written accounts of those events. We will look at history in that sense under the second class of media, *word-media*.

History in the first sense, the set of events significant to human beings, may be divided into general history and redemptive history. General history is the usual content of secular history books: the records of the earliest humans, the rise of civilization in China, Egypt, and Babylon, and the course of civilization since. Redemptive history comprises those events by which God redeems his people from sin. Redemptive history is preeminently the work of Christ in his incarnation, atonement, resurrection, and ascension. But redemptive history also includes those earlier events that prepared for Christ, such as God's covenants with Abraham, Israel, and David, and the later events, namely, the application of Jesus' redemption in the church's mission, the return of Christ, and the final judgment.

In one sense, redemptive history is a portion of general history, but I will speak of general history in a narrower sense, namely, the nonredemptive portion of human history. This is not to deny that redemptive and nonredemptive history influence each other, each forming a context in which the other should be understood.

Nature and General History

Let us consider first nature and general history as media of revelation. Clearly, everything that God has made, and every event that takes place, reveals God in some way. For everything in the world is God's creation, and everything that happens is God's providence.[3] Indeed, no fact can be rightly understood apart from God.

So Scripture recognizes the natural world as a revelation of God. As Psalm 19:1 says, "The heavens declare the glory of God, and the sky above proclaims his handiwork." God's awesome deeds in the natural world bring the psalmists to express awe, wonder, and praise, as in Psalms 46:8–10; 65; 104. In chapter 23, I listed many Scripture passages in which the power of God displayed in nature is the power of his *word*; nature is God's self-expression. Nature behaves as it does because God's word tells it what to do.

Natural revelation is the knowledge that God conveys to human beings through nature. It is also called *general revelation* because it comes to all mankind and through all the experiences of human life.

It is important to remember that nature is not the word of God, but only a medium of the word. The word, as we saw in chapter 23, is God. It is divine, not something created. Theologians have sometimes written loosely about the "creation word" or the "word in creation." But to be precise, the word is something *above* creation that speaks *to* creation and to us *through* creation.[4]

---

3. Note the discussion of God's providence in chapters 8–9.

4. I discuss in more detail the relation between the divine word of God and the created media in Appendix D of *DWG*. This was a major issue in my debates with the followers of Herman Dooyeweerd in the 1970s.

Natural revelation shows us the kindness of God. Paul tells the pagans at Lystra that God

> did not leave himself without witness, for he did good by giving you rains from heaven and fruitful seasons, satisfying your hearts with food and gladness. (Acts 14:17; cf. Matt. 5:45)

But natural revelation can also have a negative meaning. It has a particularly important role in convicting human beings of sin. In Romans 1:18–21, Paul says:

> For the wrath of God is revealed from heaven against all ungodliness and unrighteousness of men, who by their unrighteousness suppress the truth. For what can be known about God is plain to them, because God has shown it to them. For his invisible attributes, namely, his eternal power and divine nature, have been clearly perceived, ever since the creation of the world, in the things that have been made. So they are without excuse. For although they knew God, they did not honor him as God or give thanks to him, but they became futile in their thinking, and their foolish hearts were darkened.

God has given human beings a clear revelation of himself (Rom. 1:19), including a revelation of his "invisible attributes" (v. 20), from the natural world ("in the things that have been made," v. 20). The knowledge we gain from this is not only a knowledge of information about God, but a knowledge of God himself, a personal knowledge (v. 21). That revelation has a moral content (v. 32) that requires human beings to honor God and give thanks to him (v. 21). But, Paul says, human beings fail to honor him as they should. Rather, they "suppress" the truth (v. 18), they exchange "the truth about God for a lie" (v. 25), and they do not "see fit to acknowledge God" (v. 28). Though they fail to worship God, they do not abandon religion altogether. Rather, they worship idols (v. 23), and that idolatry leads them into Paul's full catalogue of sins. He mentions first sexual sins (vv. 24–27), then "all manner of unrighteousness" (vv. 28–31). So the revelation is a revelation of the "wrath of God" (v. 18).

Natural revelation, therefore, is a clear and personal revelation of the true God, which makes authoritative demands on human beings. As in Acts 14, it displays God's kindness, his "common grace."[5] But when people betray that kindness, as they always do apart from faith in Christ, it serves as a basis for judgment, to leave them "without excuse" (Rom. 1:20). Romans 1 does not indicate that anybody can obtain God's forgiveness through natural revelation. Later on, Paul indicates that forgiveness comes through a different form of revelation, the preaching of Christ (10:14–17).

But for those who have received God's saving grace, natural revelation has a more positive meaning. Like the psalmist, we come to praise God for the revelation of him in the heavens and the earth. Nature also provides signs for redemptive covenants:

---

5. See chapter 12.

the regularity of the seasons in Genesis 8:22, the rainbow in Genesis 9:16, and "heaven and earth" in Deuteronomy 4:26; 30:19; 31:28; 32:1 serve to witness the promises and threats of God's covenants.

Nature is fallen because God placed a curse on man's labor after Adam's fall (Gen. 3:17–19). Yet it "waits with eager longing for the revealing of the sons of God" (Rom. 8:19; cf. vv. 20–23). So nature is not entirely separate from redemption, as one might suspect from Romans 1 alone. Indeed, nature is preoccupied with the hope of redemption, and it cannot rightly be understood apart from that hope.

Another blessing of natural revelation to Christian believers is this: nature is a means of applying redemptive revelation, Scripture, to our daily lives. To apply Scripture to the world, we must know some things about the world, not only about Scripture. For example, the eighth commandment tells us not to steal. But to apply that commandment to the question of cheating on taxes, we must know something about taxes (natural revelation) as well as about Scripture. So to obey God, we need to know nature as well as Scripture.

One might ask how natural revelation fits the personal-word model of revelation that I recommended in chapter 23. There is some awkwardness here, because events aren't words, at least in and of themselves. As I pointed out, natural events are not the word of God, but media of the word. In natural revelation, we do not hear a literal voice (Ps. 19:3). So some might ask whether natural revelation conveys the same power, authority, and divine presence as God's personal words.

But natural revelation does have some important characteristics of personal-word revelation. It is clear (Rom. 1:19–20) and makes clear demands of us, so that when we disobey we have no excuse (v. 20; cf. v. 32). As when we imagine God speaking directly to us, we have no right to talk back to God. His authority comes through as absolute and unconditional.

Similarly with his other lordship attributes. Many biblical texts on natural revelation stress the controlling power of God revealed therein (as Ps. 29:3–11). That power fills the believer with awe and wonder, and he ascribes glory to God. The heavens and earth become a temple for God's worship, a temple of his personal presence (Ps. 29:1–2, 10–11; cf. Isa. 66:1; Matt. 5:34–35).

So although natural revelation does not consist of literal divine words, it is an infallible *medium* of such divine words. As such, natural revelation conveys to us God's power, authority, and presence.

There is therefore no room for human autonomy in dealing with God's natural revelation. We may interpret the creation only by thinking God's thoughts after him. And this means that when we analyze the creation, we must listen to the words of God in other media, such as the written Word, if we are to understand nature as he made it to be. It is never right for us to try to interpret nature or history autonomously.[6] As

6. This is the problem with the "history-centered" theologies in the liberal tradition, such as those of Albrecht Ritschl, Karl Barth, and Wolfhart Pannenberg. These try to gain revelation from God through history, but they deny that one must interpret history within a biblical worldview and epistemology. See *DWG*, chap. 5.

John Calvin said, we are to understand the natural world through the "spectacles" of Scripture.[7] For it is the gospel message of Scripture that takes away our unrighteous desire to suppress God's truth.

Redemptive History

Redemptive history, as I defined it earlier, is that series of events by which God redeems his people from sin, a narrative fulfilled in Christ. It is the principal subject matter of Scripture. Redemptive history constitutes the mighty acts of God that he performs for the sake of his people, those acts by which people come to know that he is the Lord (Ex. 7:5; 14:18). When God brings Israel over the Red Sea on dry land, both Israel and the Egyptians come to know his lordship. In Deuteronomy 8:11–18, God tells the Israelites that when they are prosperous in the Land of Promise, they should not forget the acts of the Lord. Their wealth comes from God alone, and he can take it away if they are not faithful. God's great deeds should be warnings to the nations outside Israel (Ps. 66:5–7). God's mighty acts are a theme that resounds through the OT. For a sense of its importance to God's people, see Pss. 135; 136; 145:4, 12.

Similarly, the Gospels are preoccupied with the mighty deeds of Jesus. The gospel of John is structured according to the "signs" Jesus wrought in his earthly ministry (John 2:11; cf. Acts 2:22). Of course, the greatest of Jesus' mighty acts are his sacrificial death on the cross, his resurrection, and his ascension to God's right hand.

Jesus also performs mighty acts in the history of the early church.[8] In Acts 15:12, Barnabas and Paul relate the "signs and wonders God had done through them among the Gentiles."[9] Cf. Heb. 2:4; Rev. 15:3–4.

Redemptive history supplies what is lacking in natural revelation, the means by which God forgives sin. So it is tempting to say that natural revelation is *law*, while redemptive history is *gospel*. But the matter is more complicated than that, as we have seen. In the conventional distinction, law is unmitigated "bad news," gospel unmitigated "good news." But as we have seen, nature reveals God's kindness as well as his severity. And when believers look at natural revelation from a perspective of grace, it reinforces the gospel in many ways: in covenant signs, in its eager longing for the consummation of redemption, and in its help to believers in living the Christian life.[10]

Similarly, redemptive history contains negative as well as positive elements. It shows us the glory of Christ in his redemptive work. But it also displays the judgments of God on those who reject Christ and who will not bow before his lordship. The blessings and the judgments are inseparable: God blesses Abraham, but he curses Sodom and

---

7. *Institutes*, 1.6.1.

8. Acts 1:1 says that the gospel of Luke concerns what Jesus *"began* to do and teach," suggesting that the book of Acts presents what Jesus *continued* to do and teach.

9. "Signs and wonders" is a name for what English speakers often call *miracles*. Note my somewhat nontraditional account of miracle in chapter 7 of this book.

10. See my discussion of law and gospel in *DCL*, 182–92.

Gomorrah. He redeems Israel, but in the same act curses Egypt (and later Canaan). When Jesus returns, his people will rejoice, but the wicked will weep and wail.[11]

Redemptive history, like natural revelation, is a medium of God's word, rather than the word itself. But it conveys all the power, authority, and divine presence of God himself. The mighty redemptive acts of God are a biblical paradigm of his controlling power, especially the miraculous birth of Isaac (Gen. 18:14), God's deliverance of Israel from Egypt (Ex. 15:4–12), the cross of Christ (1 Cor. 1:18), and Jesus' resurrection from the dead (Rom. 1:4; 2 Cor. 13:4; Eph. 1:19–21; Phil. 3:10).

The mighty acts of God also bear God's lordship authority, in the sense that they demand a favorable human response. God's deliverance of Israel from Egypt ought to motivate Israel's obedience. The preface to the Decalogue is "I am the LORD your God, who brought you out of the land of Egypt, out of the house of slavery" (Ex. 20:2). Then come God's commands, "You shall have no other gods before me" (v. 3), and so on. Israel's disobedience is all the more culpable because of the powerful and clear revelation that the people have received (Deut. 29, among many passages). God gave Israel much more revelation of himself than he gave to the other nations, and "to whom much was given, of him much will be required" (Luke 12:48).

God's redemptive deeds are also a revelation of his personal presence. God does, of course, bring all events to pass (Eph. 1:11). But God's presence is all the more intense when he is acting to carry out redemption and judgment. These are "acts of God" par excellence. God's wonderful works typically elicit religious awe (as Ex. 15, many psalms). In Luke 5:1–10, Jesus grants to the disciples a miraculous catch of fish. Peter's response is surprising: "Depart from me, for I am a sinful man, O Lord" (v. 8). Peter's eyes are not on the fish, or on the event as such, but on the presence of God in Jesus. In the miracle, God himself is present.[12]

So, as with natural revelation, redemptive history is an unambiguous, clear revelation of God. This fact is contrary to the liberal views of redemptive history noted earlier. Human beings have no freedom to interpret the event as they wish. There is no role here for human autonomy. It is not as if the event were somehow "neutral," accessible indifferently to unbelief or faith. Nor is it the case that the unbelieving, secular interpretation is somehow normative. Faith is essential, of course, but faith is obligatory. Faithful interpretation of these events is the only legitimate interpretation, not one of many.

And we cannot say with the neoorthodox tradition that the historical event is only a "pointer" to a higher (*geschichtlich*) event that is the true revelation. God reveals himself precisely in the events of calendar time and space, where we live. This fact does not imply that secular historians may dictate the meaning of an event, as if calendar time

11. There is a theory that Christian preaching should focus exclusively on redemptive history. I agree, if *redemptive history* is taken broadly enough to include the whole content of Scripture. But if (as I sometimes suspect) *redemptive history* is defined as an exclusive focus on narrative, excluding the moral, wisdom, and literary content of Scripture, then I take issue. See *DCL*, chap. 16; *DWG*, chap. 35.

12. See the discussion of miracle in chapter 7.

and space were a realm where such historians could function autonomously. *Secular history* is illegitimate in any sphere of inquiry. Events of time and space can be fully understood only by those who, as with Scripture, view them through the spectacles of God's revelation.

So G. W. Lessing, who said that there was a "big, ugly ditch" between history and faith, was wrong. Rather, history necessitates faith, and history cannot be rightly understood apart from faith. There is no need for faith to retreat to some mysterious events occurring above and beyond time and space. God has acted in literal history, to redeem his people, and through that history he calls us to trust him.

Revelation through Words: The Divine Voice

The second type of medium is revelation through human words. Because of Scripture's emphasis on this kind of revelation, and because of the many theological controversies over this concept, we will focus on this particular medium for the rest of this chapter and through chapters 25–27. Then we will turn to the third type of medium, *person-revelation*, in chapter 28.

This revelation is "verbal" in two senses: it is a revelation of the word of God, and it is a revelation using human words as a medium. We will see, however, that in such revelations the word of God and the human words are not actually distinct from one another. In the verbal medium, God creates an *identity* between his own words and some human words, so that what the human words say, God says. This identity between God's words and human words is, I think, the best definition of *inspiration*.[13]

I mentioned earlier that in an obvious sense event-revelation is not verbal: events are not words, though speaking words is one kind of event. But word-revelation is precisely verbal. So there is a difference between event-revelation and word-revelation. But the difference is not great. As I indicated in the previous chapter, revelatory events bring to us clear revelation, embodying God's own lordship: his controlling power, meaningful authority, and personal presence. Revelatory events, therefore, bring to us the same kind of content that verbal revelation brings.

Why, then, does God give us both? Because of the differing potentials of the two media. We say that a picture is worth a thousand words. We could substitute *event* for *picture* in this saying. Someone who saw Jesus resurrected from the dead received revelation beyond what words could say. But there are also senses in which a group of words is worth a thousand events. For words can interpret events in ways that wordless events cannot. A witness to Jesus' resurrection saw something wonderful, overwhelming. But a verbal description and interpretation of that event could add much to the witness's understanding of what happened.

---

13. See chapter 26 for more discussion of inspiration. Some have questioned whether it is possible for a human word to be identical to a divine word: is it possible for God to speak in human language? Or is it even possible to speak truly *about* God in human language? The transcendence of God seems in some minds to be an insuperable barrier to verbal revelation. I discuss these issues in some detail in "God and Biblical Language," Appendix E of *DWG*.

And words can be preserved. Memories of events tend to fade over time. But words can be written down, even passed from generation to generation. We will see in chapter 25 the importance of *permanent* verbal revelation.

In this chapter and the following ones, we will consider several kinds of divine revelation through verbal media: the divine voice, the word through prophets and apostles, and the written Word. I intend to argue that these three forms of verbal revelation are equally the word of God, and therefore equal in divine power, authority, and presence. Put differently: as we move from the divine voice, to prophets and apostles, and to the written Word, there is no diminution of these qualities. These can be diagrammed as shown in fig. 24.2.

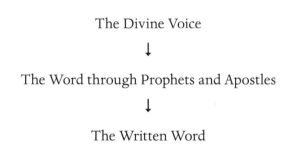

Fig. 24.2. Forms of Verbal Revelation

With some exceptions, the divine voice speaks to prophets and apostles, who present his word to people orally and by writing. I will explore those processes in what follows.

I will use the phrase *divine voice* to refer to the most direct kind of verbal revelation, in which God speaks to human beings without any human mediator. The paradigm of the divine voice can be found in Exodus 20, the only occasion on which all Israel is gathered in one place (camped around Mount Sinai) to hear words from God's own lips. God here declares the covenant (Deut. 4:13), establishing Israel as his people and himself as their God. He identifies himself as the One who delivered them from Egypt (Ex. 20:2), and he declares how they should serve him (vv. 3–17). The people are afraid and stand far off (v. 18), and they say to Moses, "You speak to us, and we will listen; but do not let God speak to us, lest we die" (v. 19). Moses accepts their request, and from then on God's revelation to Israel is largely indirect, rather than direct.

People often say that if God spoke to them directly, they would believe. And Christians sometimes imagine that hearing God directly would be the height of spiritual joy. They do not know what they are asking. For Israel, the experience was terrible, frightening. They wanted nothing more than for it to end.

Nevertheless, many other people have heard the divine voice, unmediated. Moses himself is the chief example of this. Note the description of the intimacy between God and Moses in Numbers 12:8:

> With him I speak mouth to mouth, clearly, and not in riddles, and he beholds the form of the LORD.

Unlike Moses, Israel did not "behold the form of the Lord" at Mount Sinai (Deut. 4:12),[14] but like Israel, Moses heard the word of God directly. The same, of course, was true of Adam, Cain, Noah, Abraham, and many others. The prophets regularly heard the divine voice. That indeed is part of the definition of a prophet. Like Moses, a prophet hears the word of God directly and passes it on to the people (Deut. 18:18).

Now, the divine voice is a medium for conveying God's mind to man. And there is a human-creaturely element even in the divine voice, though we have been calling it a "direct" form of revelation. For the divine voice evidently uses a human language and created elements (atmosphere, sound waves, human hearing mechanisms and brains). These created elements distinguish the divine voice from the eternal language spoken between the persons of the Trinity. The divine voice speaks in the created world, in time and space, to creatures, employing parts of the creation.

But it is not *merely* a medium. The divine voice is the word of God. It brings God before people in all his lordship attributes. The power of this voice terrified the Israelites at Sinai. Its authority was absolute. Clearly, when the divine voice speaks, God himself is personally present.

Place yourself as an Israelite hearer of the divine voice in Exodus 20. Can you imagine that you would ever find fault with what God said then? Comedians may joke about how people today translate the Ten Commandments into "ten suggestions." But of course, no Israelite would have understood them that way. When the divine voice speaks, you obey, and that is all there is to it. No authority is higher. If you disobey, you incur God's curse. If you obey, blessings abound.

The only problem here is the identification of God's voice. How do I know that it is really God speaking to me, especially if, as with Abraham, the voice tells me to do something really outrageous? The problem is exacerbated when we consider that there are counterfeits. Lying spirits have sometimes claimed to be the voice of God (1 Kings 22:20–23; cf. Matt. 24:24; 2 Thess. 2:2; Rev. 13:5–6; 16:13; 19:20; 20:10), and God sometimes permits people to be deceived by the counterfeits.[15]

Scripture doesn't tell us directly or systematically how the divine voice identifies itself. Exodus 19 tells us that God's voice at Mount Sinai followed frightening phenomena: thunders, lightnings, a thick cloud, a "very loud trumpet blast" (v. 16), and "the whole mountain trembl[ing] greatly" (v. 18). The people were cautioned "lest the LORD break out against them" (vv. 22, 24). These phenomena contributed to Israel's frightened reaction in 20:18–21. But this display of phenomena occurred on only this occasion. On other occasions there were signs: the burning bush in Exodus 3, the angelic display in Isaiah 6. Sometimes Jesus worked miracles to underscore his words.

---

14. When God reveals himself under a visible form, the revelation is called *theophany*, "divine appearance." See further *DG*, 585–87.

15. For a discussion of God's permission of evil, see chapter 14.

Nevertheless, it does not seem that such displays regularly accompanied the divine voice. No such thing is recorded in God's visits to Abraham, except for God's fire passing through the animal pieces in Genesis 15:17. God's speech to the prophets was often quiet. God seems to make a point of that with Elijah in 1 Kings 19:12: his presence is not in the wind, earthquake, or fire, but in a "low whisper." And although Jesus performed wonders that validated his claims, not every word of his was accompanied by miracles.

The conclusion seems to be that ultimately God himself identifies himself to his hearers. That is part of the revelation. Natural phenomena and miracles do impress, but Satan, too, can produce spectacle (2 Thess. 2:9). The phenomena are not our fundamental source of assurance; their main function is to underscore the nature and the seriousness of the encounter. Abraham *just knew* that God wanted him to leave Ur, that he would grant a son, that he wanted him to take his son to the mount of sacrifice.

As for the counterfeits of the divine voice, Jesus' words in Matthew 24:24 are reassuring: "For false christs and false prophets will arise and perform great signs and wonders, so as to lead astray, if possible, even the elect." He implies that the false christs and prophets will in fact deceive many, and they will try to lead astray even the elect, "if possible." But the *if*-clause is contrary to fact. The elect will not ultimately be deceived. How can that be? Evidently because assurance is supernatural. We know that the false revelation is false, just as we know that the true revelation is true—by God's sovereign self-testimony.

The importance of God's sovereignty in identifying his own word cannot be overestimated. If that is the case in regard to the divine voice, it certainly is the case for other kinds of word-media. When we discuss those, we will discuss the self-identification of the word in relation to the testimony of the Holy Spirit.

The word of God, in the end, must authenticate itself. It cannot validate itself by appealing to something higher, because there is nothing higher. It cannot appeal to a higher standard, because it is itself the highest standard, the norming norm, the criterion of criteria. So it must appeal to itself. If this appears circular, the same kind of circularity occurs whenever someone tries to validate a claim to ultimate authority. If someone believes that human reason, for example, is the ultimate authority, he can establish that only by a rational argument. Similarly, if a Muslim attempts to validate the Qur'an as ultimate authority, he must, in the final analysis, appeal to the Qur'an.

But God made our minds to think in line with his word, not some other authority. When we rebel against his word, we rebel against our own creation in his image. How can such rebels come to recognize Scripture as their highest authority? It is the work of God's saving grace in Christ to redeem us from such rebellion. Through Christ and the regenerating work of the Spirit in our hearts we come to think again as God has designed us to think, with his word as the supreme authority over our lives.

Revelation through Words: Prophets and Apostles

In the theological literature, writers often admit that God's divine voice is infallible, perfect, but they claim that imperfection necessarily enters the picture when God's word comes through human lips. Earlier in this chapter, however, I argued that in general the humanity of revelation never detracts from its divine character, for God is sovereign over all things human. There is humanity even in the language of the divine voice, but nobody would dream of saying that on that account the divine voice is imperfect or fallible. The same must be said for those cases in which the word of God comes through human lips rather than God's own, through prophets and apostles.

When the children of Israel no longer wished to hear the word of God directly from God's lips, they turned to Moses: "You speak to us, and we will listen; but do not let God speak to us, lest we die" (Ex. 20:19). So they called on Moses to speak as a prophet. A prophet is someone who has God's words on his lips, as we see from the virtual definition of *prophet* in Deuteronomy 18. In that chapter, God forbids Israel from seeking revelation from pagan fortune-tellers, wizards, necromancers, and diviners (vv. 9–14). But how are the people to learn God's will? Here, God approves Israel's desire to hear his word indirectly rather than directly, and he promises this to Moses:

> I will raise up for them a prophet like you from among their brothers. And I will put my words in his mouth, and he shall speak to them all that I command him. And whoever will not listen to my words that he shall speak in my name, I myself will require it of him. (Deut. 18:18–19)

Note that (1) the prophet's words are God's words (Deut. 18:18); and (2) God's words in the mouth of the prophet are fully authoritative, so that God will discipline anyone who refuses to "listen" (v. 19).[16]

Evidently, Moses himself is something of a model for the whole series of prophets that appear through Israel's history. Let us look further at his prophetic office.

When Moses first meets God at the burning bush, God commissions him to bring a message to Israel and to Egypt (Ex. 3:7–22). Moses complains to God, however, that he is not an eloquent speaker (4:10). God replies:

> Who has made man's mouth? Who makes him mute, or deaf, or seeing, or blind? Is it not I, the LORD? Now therefore go, and I will be with your mouth and teach you what you shall speak. (Ex. 4:11–12)

God is sovereign over Moses' speech. God will supply the words. But Moses still is not satisfied: "Oh, my Lord, please send someone else" (Ex. 4:13).

> Then the anger of the LORD was kindled against Moses and he said, "Is there not Aaron, your brother, the Levite? I know that he can speak well. Behold, he is coming out to meet you, and when he sees you, he will be glad in his heart. You shall speak

---

16. Here, "listening" is not just physical hearing, but obedient hearing. In verse 14, by contrast, God says that they may not "listen" to the wizards and diviners. The older English term *hearken* better conveys the idea of hearing with an obedient disposition.

to him and put the words in his mouth, and I will be with your mouth and with his mouth and will teach you both what to do. He shall speak for you to the people, and he shall be your mouth, and you shall be as God to him. (Ex. 4:14–16)

In this extraordinary exchange, God establishes a hierarchy: God, Moses, Aaron, Israel. God gives his words to Moses. Moses gives these divine words to Aaron. Aaron gives them to the people. Throughout the hierarchy the words are God's. Indeed, in verse 16, Moses is called "God."[17] He functions as God because he gives God's words to Aaron, his prophet. There is no decrease in authority between God himself, Moses (Aaron's God), and Aaron.[18] Moses and Aaron have the authority of God because they speak God's words.

Here, as in Deuteronomy 18, the prophet is one who has God's words in his mouth. Note similar language in the call of Jeremiah:

Now the word of the LORD came to me, saying,

"Before I formed you in the womb I knew you,
and before you were born I consecrated you;
I appointed you a prophet to the nations."

Then I said, "Ah, Lord GOD! Behold, I do not know how to speak, for I am only a youth." But the LORD said to me,

"Do not say, 'I am only a youth';
for to all to whom I send you, you shall go,
and whatever I command you, you shall speak.
Do not be afraid of them,
for I am with you to deliver you,
          declares the LORD."

Then the LORD put out his hand and touched my mouth. And the LORD said to me,

"Behold, I have put my words in your mouth.
See, I have set you this day over nations and over kingdoms,
to pluck up and to break down,
to destroy and to overthrow,
to build and to plant."

And the word of the LORD came to me, saying, "Jeremiah, what do you see?" And I said, "I see an almond branch." Then the LORD said to me, "You have seen well, for I am watching over my word to perform it." (Jer. 1:4–12)

17. Compare Psalm 82:6 in the light of John 10:35: even wicked rulers can be called "gods" because the word of God comes to them.
18. Cf. Ex. 7:1–2. This is the background of the idea that people "to whom the word of God came" may be called gods (John 10:35; see also Ps. 82:6).

Like Moses, Jeremiah pleads his own inadequacy. God remedies that inadequacy with his own adequacy: the words are to be God's own, in Jeremiah's mouth. Here the emphasis is on the power of the word, rather than its authority as in Deuteronomy 18, though of course the two are inseparable. Because Jeremiah has God's words in his mouth, he has powers that belong only to God, to build up or destroy nations. Jeremiah sees a vision of an almond branch. God interprets this vision: "I am watching over my word to perform it."[19] The word in Jeremiah's mouth is God's, and so God will see that whatever the word declares will be done. The word has the same power in the prophet's mouth as in God's own.

So the prophet is a divinely approved substitute for the divine voice itself. When Moses spoke to Israel in the name of God, his speech was less frightening than God's own, but no less authoritative or powerful. Earlier, in Exodus 19:9, God told Moses, "Behold, I am coming to you in a thick cloud, that the people may hear when I speak with you, and may also believe you forever." To hear Moses is to hear God. When Moses speaks to the children of Israel, he speaks "according to all that the Lord had given him in commandment to them" (Deut. 1:3). Moses teaches Israel the statutes of God that bear the covenant sanctions: those who obey are blessed, and those who disobey are cursed (4:1–8). Moses' statutes are God's. Cf. 5:1, 22–33; 6:1–9. Israel promises to obey all of God's words, but those are words they hear from Moses' lips, not directly from the divine voice.

Jesus himself acknowledges the authority of Moses' words. He tells the Jews:

> Do not think that I will accuse you to the Father. There is one who accuses you: Moses, on whom you have set your hope. For if you believed Moses, you would believe me; for he wrote of me. But if you do not believe his writings, how will you believe my words? (John 5:45–47)

Jesus' main point here, of course, is to testify to his own authority. But he does that by invoking and supporting the Jews' reverence for the words of Moses. Indeed, in verse 47 believing the words of Moses is a kind of prerequisite for believing the words of Jesus. Compare also Luke 16:29–31, when in Jesus' parable "father Abraham" tells the rich man that if people will not hear Moses and the Prophets, they will not be convinced even if someone rises from the dead.

So it is clearly wrong to think that there is a decrease in power, authority, or divine presence between the divine voice and the word of God in the mouth of the prophet (review, here, the diagram that I used earlier in the chapter). If we may not criticize the divine voice, no more may we criticize the prophetic word. The prophetic word is human in ways that the divine voice is not, but the additional humanity of the prophetic word does not inject any fallibility or weakness into the message. Nor does the speaker's sin impart error to the divine words. By whatever means (and such passages

---

19. The interpretation of the vision is based on a pun in the Hebrew language. Both "almond tree" and "watch" are from the root *shaqad*.

as Exodus 4, Deuteronomy 18, and Jeremiah 1 leave no question that it is miraculous), the prophet speaks God's word perfectly well, and we must not find fault with it.

Though Moses is the biblical paradigm for the office of prophet, he is neither the first nor the last to have the prophetic gift. Certainly Noah spoke prophetically when he declared many centuries in advance how God would deal with the descendants of his sons Shem and Japheth and his grandson Canaan (Gen. 9:24–27). Isaac's blessings on Jacob (27:27–29) and Esau (vv. 39–40) were prophetic, as were Jacob's final blessings on his large family (49:1–27). Whether we construe these utterances as foretelling the future (divine knowledge) or as bringing about future states of affairs (divine power), they are clearly divine words.

Elijah begins his prophetic ministry by announcing that there would be no rain "except by my word" (1 Kings 17:1). As with Jeremiah, the prophet's word has the power that only God's word has. Then "the word of the LORD came to him" (v. 2) as throughout his career. God cleanses Isaiah's lips (Isa. 6:5–7) and gives to his words the power to harden the hearts of the people (vv. 9–10; cf. Matt. 13:14–15; Mark 4:12; Luke 8:10; Acts 28:26–27).

There are also prophets in the NT church. These are numerous, and of both sexes, fulfilling the prophecy of Joel 2:28–32, which Peter cites in his Pentecost sermon (Acts 2:17–18). These prophets predicted the future (11:27–28; 21:9–14), received orders from the Holy Spirit (13:1–3), encouraged and strengthened fellow believers (15:32), identified spiritual gifts in people (1 Tim. 1:18; 4:14),[20] and witnessed for Christ amid persecution (Rev. 11:3–13). Paul urges the church at Corinth to give more emphasis in worship to the gift of prophecy, less to uninterpreted tongues, because prophecy brings edification to the congregation (1 Cor. 14:1–40). The book of Revelation is a specifically prophetic writing (1:3; 22:7). Other texts simply mention prophets, or the prophetic gift, without mentioning a specific function (Acts 19:6; Rom. 12:6; 1 Cor. 11:4–5; 12:10; 1 Thess. 5:20).

I see no reason to understand these prophets any differently from the prophets of the OT. The concept of a prophet, one who has God's word in his mouth, was familiar to Jews and Christians of the NT period. There is no explicit indication in the NT that the office of prophet had changed in any way. Certainly the presence of the word of God in their mouths adequately accounts for the functions of the NT prophets in the texts cited above,[21] and it would be difficult to account for those functions otherwise than by their unique access to God's word. But the NT does not contain a passage like Deuteronomy 18 specifically setting forth the meaning and power of the prophetic gift.

The NT, however, is more explicit about the apostles, who are certainly true successors of the OT prophets, and more.[22] Jesus at the beginning of his ministry chooses

---

20. Or did the prophets rather predict the course of Timothy's ministry? In either case, they displayed supernatural knowledge.

21. To the contrary, see *GST*, 1049–61; Wayne Grudem believes that prophecy in the NT had less authority than prophecy in the OT. He says that the NT apostles, however, are the true successors of the OT prophets, in that their word was supremely authoritative.

22. The apostles rank higher than the prophets, according to 1 Corinthians 12:28.

twelve, who are to have a special relationship to him, during his earthly ministry and beyond.[23] Anticipating their later persecution, Jesus assures them:

> When they deliver you over, do not be anxious how you are to speak or what you are to say, for what you are to say will be given to you in that hour. For it is not you who speak, but the Spirit of your Father speaking through you. (Matt. 10:19–20)

They are to have divine assistance when they are called to witness for Jesus. That assistance comes specifically in a divine gift of extraordinary speech. They are to be supported by God's people both as prophets and as righteous men (Matt. 10:40–41).

In the Johannine passion discourses, Jesus is more explicit about the apostles' role in revelation:

> But the Helper, the Holy Spirit, whom the Father will send in my name, he will teach you all things and bring to your remembrance all that I have said to you. (John 14:26)

> But when the Helper comes, whom I will send to you from the Father, the Spirit of truth, who proceeds from the Father, he will bear witness about me. And you also will bear witness, because you have been with me from the beginning. (John 15:26–27)

> When the Spirit of truth comes, he will guide you into all the truth, for he will not speak on his own authority, but whatever he hears he will speak, and he will declare to you the things that are to come. (John 16:13)

From the first two passages, we learn that the Spirit will empower the memories of the apostles, so that they will remember Jesus' words. We will see later in this chapter the great importance of Jesus' words for the salvation of his people. Jesus, as the divine voice, has given to his disciples teaching that is an absolutely necessary foundation for their life and ministry.[24] Remember Peter's "Lord, to whom shall we go? You have the words of eternal life" (John 6:68). But Jesus wrote no books. So the question is urgent as to where the words of Jesus can be found since his ascension to heaven. If we cannot identify them, we have no hope. John 14:26 and 15:26–27 answer that urgent question. The words of the apostles preserve the words of Jesus. When we seek the precious words of Jesus, it is to the apostles that we must go.

John 16:13 enlarges this view of the scope of apostolic revelation. Here the Spirit not only reminds the apostles of what Jesus said. More than that, he will guide them into all truth. And he will show to the apostles things that are to come in the future. As the prophets were both forthtellers and foretellers, so the Spirit empowers the apostles to proclaim the truth and to foretell events to come in the future. So the Spirit gives

---

23. The "beyond," of course, does not include Judas, the betrayer.

24. We will return to Jesus' function as revealer (both divine voice and Prophet) in the section at the end of this chapter.

them revelation about the past (the words of Jesus), the present ("all the truth"), and the future ("things that are to come").

When God pours out the Spirit on the day of Pentecost, the apostles begin to preach Christ.[25] The coming of the Spirit empowers the church for its worldwide witness (Acts 1:8). When the Spirit comes down in wind and fire, "they were all filled with the Holy Spirit and began to speak in other tongues as the Spirit gave them utterance" (2:4). I cannot here discuss the meaning of the gift of tongues, except to say that it enables the disciples to preach the gospel to Jews of many cultures who are gathered in Jerusalem for the feast. The tongues partially reverse the curse of Babel (Gen. 11:1–9), bringing people together under the word of God. When the Spirit comes on the Christians, they speak of Jesus. Spirit and word come together. The book of Acts often presents that correlation (4:8, 31; 6:3–5, 10; 7:55–56; 9:17–20; 13:9–10).

After his miraculous conversion in Acts 9, Paul joins the group of apostles. He is, by his own admission, "untimely born" (1 Cor. 15:8), "the least of the apostles," and "unworthy to be called an apostle" (v. 9) because he once persecuted the church. Some in the church questioned his apostolic authority, perhaps on those grounds, perhaps out of their opposition to his doctrine, an issue to which he responds in Galatians and elsewhere. But Paul has seen the resurrected Lord and is therefore a witness to the resurrection, even though he has not been with the disciples from the beginning (Acts 1:22). More significantly, he claims to be an apostle by special appointment of God himself and by the Lord Jesus Christ (Rom. 1:1; Gal. 1:1, 12). Sixteen times in his writings, he applies the title *apostle* to himself. In time, even his opponents accepted that title, so that he was able to ask them as a rhetorical question, "Am I not an apostle?" (1 Cor. 9:1). In the postapostolic age, Paul's status as an apostle was unquestioned, and it has been recognized by the church through all ages, together with his writings that constitute most of the NT.

The apostles themselves teach that their message comes from God and therefore has divine authority. In 2 Corinthians 4:1–6, Paul claims that the apostles never tamper with God's word, but rather state it openly and honestly. God who brought light out of darkness has, Paul says, "shone in our hearts to give the light of the knowledge of the glory of God in the face of Jesus Christ" (v. 6).

In Galatians 1:11–12, Paul insists against his opponents:

> For I would have you know, brothers, that the gospel that was preached by me is not man's gospel. For I did not receive it from any man, nor was I taught it, but I received it through a revelation of Jesus Christ.

Since God has appointed him an apostle, his message also comes from God by revelation. (Compare also the reference to "revelation" in Galatians 2:2.)

Speaking for all the apostles, Paul in 1 Corinthians 2:10–13 says of the wisdom of his gospel:

25. Recall in chapter 23 my discussion of the regular biblical correlation between word and Spirit.

> These things God has revealed to us through the Spirit. For the Spirit searches every-thing, even the depths of God. For who knows a person's thoughts except the spirit of that person, which is in him? So also no one comprehends the thoughts of God except the Spirit of God. Now we have received not the spirit of the world, but the Spirit who is from God, that we might understand the things freely given us by God. And we impart this in words not taught by human wisdom but taught by the Spirit, interpreting spiritual truths to those who are spiritual.

Note that for Paul the Spirit's revelation not only gives "understanding" of divine mysteries, but also provides the "words" in which the apostles teach these mysteries. Paul also appeals to the Spirit as the source of his counsel in 1 Corinthians 7:40, to revelation as the source of his knowledge of God's mystery in Ephesians 3:3.

The apostles are "stewards of the mysteries of God" (1 Cor. 4:1). "Mystery" in the NT does have some of the connotations of our modern English word—something hard to grasp, beyond our usual understanding. But it also designates more precisely those elements of God's revelation that have been hidden for centuries, now made known through the apostolic preaching and writing. See Rom. 16:25–26.

So God gives to the apostles, like the prophets of the OT, revelation in words, which they communicate in their proclamation. In this revelation, their words are words of God (1 Thess. 2:13). So they display the qualities of the divine voice itself: power (Rom. 1:16–17), authority (Gal. 1:9), and divine presence (1 Thess. 1:5). There is no decrease in any of these qualities when the word of God moves from the lips of God to the lips of the prophets and apostles.

Now, one problem arises at this point that we also discussed in connection with the divine voice earlier in this chapter. That problem is that of identifying the true revelation. We asked how Abraham knew that the One who spoke to him was the true God—and how we can identify the true voice of God among the counterfeits. In the earlier discussion, my response to that problem was to emphasize God's sovereignty in revelation. God is sovereign not only to speak as Lord, but also to assure his hearers that they are hearing the Lord.

When we pass from the divine voice to the words of prophets and apostles, a simi-lar problem emerges. Just as there are lying spirits who counterfeit the divine voice, so there are false prophets (Jer. 14:14; Lam. 2:14; Matt. 7:15; etc.) and apostles (2 Cor. 11:13; Rev. 2:2). As with the divine voice, our ultimate assurance of who speaks truth is supernatural. So Paul attributes the persuasiveness of his gospel to the Holy Spirit's testimony (1 Thess. 1:5). But Scripture also provides tests of prophetic claims that help the people of God to discern which are authentic. Recall that Deuteronomy 18 estab-lished the basic definition of a prophet: a person with the words of God in his mouth. The passage also says this:

> "But the prophet who presumes to speak a word in my name that I have not com-manded him to speak, or who speaks in the name of other gods, that same prophet shall die." And if you say in your heart, "How may we know the word that the Lord

has not spoken?"—when a prophet speaks in the name of the LORD, if the word does not come to pass or come true, that is a word that the LORD has not spoken; the prophet has spoken it presumptuously. You need not be afraid of him. (Deut. 18:20–22)

Here there are two sure marks of false prophets: (1) speaking in the name of a false god,[26] and (2) making predictions that don't come true.

These are marks of false prophets, however, not tests of true prophets. If someone speaks in the name of the true God, and he makes a prediction that comes true, does that mark him as a true prophet? Or what if he makes no predictions at all? Deuteronomy 18 does not anticipate all possible situations. It does not give us infallible marks of all true prophets of God, though it excludes some prophetic claims as false.

Beyond Deuteronomy 18, signs and wonders attested the prophetic ministry of Moses, and later of Elijah and Elisha. Certainly the same was true of Jesus' prophetic ministry. Paul speaks, too, of the "signs of a true apostle" that God performed for him (2 Cor. 12:12). But no miracles are mentioned in the ministries of many of the OT prophets or NT apostles. And as we noted earlier in this chapter, Satan counterfeits God's signs and wonders so that some (not the elect) will be deceived (Matt. 24:24). And Jesus rebukes people who *demand* a sign (Matt. 12:38–39; 16:1–4). If people will not hear Moses and the Prophets, he says, they will not believe the word of a resurrected saint (Luke 16:31).[27]

So evidently the attestation of the prophets and apostles, like the attestation of the divine voice, is fundamentally supernatural. God comes with the prophetic and apostolic word and convinces hearers that that word is his own. Miracles and predictions give the hearers a nudge, alert them that something remarkable is happening. But they are not the ultimate argument that identifies a true prophet. God's Spirit is the One who persuades.

This is all the more evident when we consider that true prophecies often seem to break the rule of Deuteronomy 18:22.[28] They make apparent predictions that do not literally come to pass; yet the prophets are accepted, by God and by God's people, as true prophets. The most obvious example is the book of Jonah, where the prophet proclaims, "Yet forty days, and Nineveh shall be overthrown!" (Jonah 3:4). But Nineveh is not overthrown, at least at that time. Rather, the king and the city repent (3:6–9), and "God relented of the disaster that he had said he would do to them, and he did not do it" (v. 10).

The apparent failure of this prophecy does not arise from the humanity of Jonah as God's messenger. The passage identifies Jonah's words in verse 4 with God's in verse 10. As is the normal pattern in Scripture, the words of the prophet are the words

---

26. Notice how 1 John 4:2–3 brings this principle into the new covenant: "every spirit that confesses that Jesus Christ has come in the flesh is from God, and every spirit that does not confess Jesus is not from God." And believing that Christ has come in the flesh includes believing in the whole apostolic witness (v. 5).

27. The relation between signs and faith is complex. See my discussion of miracles, chapter 7.

28. Compare the following discussion to the section "A God Who Relents" in chapter 17.

of God, even when that relationship is problematic. If Jonah is a false prophet, then the divine voice is also false.

But the passage offers no solution to that problem. It does, however, see this pattern as rather typical of God and his prophets. The king of Nineveh urges repentance, based on the possibility that "God may turn and relent and turn from his fierce anger, so that we may not perish" (Jonah 3:9). God's response showed that the king had supposed rightly (v. 10). Jonah himself is displeased, probably because Nineveh was a great enemy of Israel. But he himself suspected that this might happen:

> But it displeased Jonah exceedingly, and he was angry. And he prayed to the Lord and said, "O Lord, is not this what I said when I was yet in my country? That is why I made haste to flee to Tarshish; for I knew that you are a gracious God and merciful, slow to anger and abounding in steadfast love, and relenting from disaster." (Jonah 4:1–2)

Jonah here is quoting Yahweh's description of his covenant lordship in Exodus 34:6–7, adding the reference to God's "relenting." He sees God's action as typical of God, not some odd exception to God's general behavior.

Jeremiah 18:5–10 formulates this "relenting" as a general principle of God's action and of his announcements through prophets of covenant blessing and curse:

> Then the word of the Lord came to me: "O house of Israel, can I not do with you as this potter has done? declares the Lord. Behold, like the clay in the potter's hand, so are you in my hand, O house of Israel. If at any time I declare concerning a nation or a kingdom, that I will pluck up and break down and destroy it, and if that nation, concerning which I have spoken, turns from its evil, I will relent of the disaster that I intended to do to it. And if at any time I declare concerning a nation or a kingdom that I will build and plant it, and if it does evil in my sight, not listening to my voice, then I will relent of the good that I had intended to do to it."

The reversal of God's intent for Nineveh is an instance of this principle, as are similar instances in the following passages: Ex. 32:9–14; Joel 2:13–14; Amos 7:1–6. Cf. Isa. 38:1–5; Jer. 26:3, 13, 19; 42:10.

In this discussion, I am relying on Richard Pratt's important article "Historical Contingencies and Biblical Predictions."[29] In that article, Pratt discusses a wide range of biblical data that display the principle mentioned above. He argues that Israelites and NT believers regularly took account of the possibility that historical circumstances would prevent the literal fulfillment of prophetic prediction. He believes that this principle provides a possible understanding of the NT passages that appear to predict a very soon return of Jesus Christ.

But does this principle, then, make prophecy a dead letter? If prophecy does not necessarily find literal fulfillment, is it then the case that anything can happen follow-

29. http://reformedperspectives.org/newfiles/ric_pratt/TH.Pratt.Historical_Contingencies.html.

ing a prophecy? Does this mean that prophecies may safely be ignored? Pratt argues that the prophets' messages must be understood in covenantal terms. The covenant is conditional: it promises blessings for obedience, threatens curses for disobedience. The prophets are God's prosecuting attorneys, bringing the "covenant lawsuit." The people must listen because God himself, through the prophets, is calling them to repent of their disobedience. They know that the predictions of blessing and judgment are subject to historical contingency, as in Jeremiah 18. But they *must* obey the prophet's words. They must repent, or they can be sure that the worst will happen. And if they do repent, they can expect the best. Sometimes, to be sure, prophecies are qualified by divine oaths or assurances that limit the possible variations in the results of the prophecy (Amos 4:2; 6:8; 8:7). In Jeremiah 11:11, 14, God excludes even the possibility that people can save themselves by repentance. But even in these cases, the details of the fulfillment may be subject to historical contingency.

Pratt points out that the content of the prophecy limits what can happen even when historical contingencies are relevant. Jonah's prophecy indicated that *destruction*, not mere famine or defeat, would result if Nineveh did not repent. The prophecy does not specify *how* Nineveh would be destroyed, or how long it would take, or by what means. Nor does it indicate specifics about Nineveh's future if Nineveh does repent. But it does limit expectations on either alternative. It is therefore a meaningful word from God. So if a prophet predicts a range of results, blessings and cursings contingent on the behavior of his hearers, and after the people's response God's actions do not fall within that range, the prophet is a false prophet.

But of course, it is not always easy to determine when God's actions do and do not fall within such a range. On a literal reading of Deuteronomy 18:22, it seems fairly simple: if the prophet predicts something, and it doesn't happen, he is a false prophet. But on Pratt's view, a true prophet may predict something that doesn't happen, or a fairly vague range of events, because of a historical contingency. That certainly makes it harder than Deuteronomy 18:22 suggests to determine which prophets are true and which false.

We should remember here, however, that prophets are primarily forthtellers, only secondarily foretellers. Only a very small amount of biblical prophecy contains specific prediction of the future, and most of that is clearly subject to the principle of historical contingency. But at times there are specific predictions. First Samuel 10:1–7, which describes the anointing of King Saul by the prophet Samuel, is an example:

> Then Samuel took a flask of oil and poured it on his head and kissed him and said, "Has not the LORD anointed you to be prince over his people Israel? And you shall reign over the people of the LORD and you will save them from the hand of their surrounding enemies. And this shall be the sign to you that the LORD has anointed you to be prince over his heritage. When you depart from me today, you will meet two men by Rachel's tomb in the territory of Benjamin at Zelzah, and they will say to you, 'The donkeys that you went to seek are found, and now your father has ceased

to care about the donkeys and is anxious about you, saying, "What shall I do about my son?"' Then you shall go on from there farther and come to the oak of Tabor. Three men going up to God at Bethel will meet you there, one carrying three young goats, another carrying three loaves of bread, and another carrying a skin of wine. And they will greet you and give you two loaves of bread, which you shall accept from their hand. After that you shall come to Gibeath-elohim, where there is a garrison of the Philistines. And there, as soon as you come to the city, you will meet a group of prophets coming down from the high place with harp, tambourine, flute, and lyre before them, prophesying. Then the Spirit of the LORD will rush upon you, and you will prophesy with them and be turned into another man. Now when these signs meet you, do what your hand finds to do, for God is with you."

Samuel tells Saul that when he leaves, he will encounter precisely three men, bearing precisely three goats and one skin of wine. He mentions other precise details. Verse 9 tells us that "all these signs came to pass that day." Clearly, Samuel is giving to Saul a group of signs to validate the anointing of verse 1. These signs verify to Saul that Samuel is a true prophet of the Lord and that the Lord has truly anointed him to be king. Samuel's ability to describe precisely such future events vindicates his prophetic office, as Deuteronomy 18:22 indicates. The kinds of historical contingencies that we have mentioned are unlikely to affect the outcome of this particular set of predictions, so they serve as an unambiguous example of the prophet's ability to predict the future. Another example is the first recorded statement of Elijah, "As the LORD, the God of Israel, lives, before whom I stand, there shall be neither dew nor rain these years, except by my word" (1 Kings 17:1). This prediction is literally fulfilled. Prophets may have often employed literal predictions of the future in order to establish their divine credentials.

But the usual work of the prophet is different. At times it may be appropriate for him to display his power of detailed, unconditional prediction, but generally it is not. As forthtellers, prophets are covenant attorneys. The historical contingencies are understood to be part of the prophecy. So when a prophet says, "God will judge you," the audience understands implicitly: "unless you repent." Interpreting the prophecy must take this conditionality into account. So that if a prediction made by a prophet does not literally take place because of a historical contingency, believing hearers may legitimately judge that the prophecy has nevertheless "come to pass or come true" (in terms of Deuteronomy 18:22), and that result confirms the authenticity of the prophet.

So identifying true prophets is more difficult than Deuteronomy 18:22 might appear to suggest. But the ultimate test is whether the prophet truly represents God's covenant sanctions. Only then does he speak in the name of the true God (the first test of Deuteronomy 18:20), and only then do his words, understood in the covenant context, "come to pass or come true" (v. 22).

But someone who wishes to test a prophet by this means must bring to his evaluation a subtle understanding of God's covenant and the condition of the prophet's audience. There is therefore a certain level of spiritual maturity and discernment needed here, as Paul suggests in 1 Corinthians 14:29, "Let two or three prophets speak, and let the others weigh what is said." The weighing or authenticating of prophecy is not a simple task.

But that difficulty underscores the importance here of God's own witness to himself. We saw in chapter 24 that in his divine voice God not only speaks, but also identifies himself as the speaker. In prophecy, too, it is God's Spirit who identifies the true prophets and distinguishes them from the false. There are marks of true prophecy (Deut. 18; 1 John 4:1–6), but those are not always easy to apply. But as with the divine voice, so also with the prophets and apostles: somehow God drives his message home to the hearts of God's people. Would any Christian believer today seriously doubt that Isaiah was a true prophet, that Paul was a real apostle?

By his Spirit God sovereignly opens the eyes of his people to the signs of true prophecy, such as true prediction, miracles, and orthodox content (1 John 4:2–3), pressing our minds to see in these an authenticity that goes beyond mere probability, an authenticity that can only be the self-authenticating voice of God. When we receive that supernatural verification by God's grace, we confess that the words of the prophets and apostles are nothing less than the word of God, bearing supreme power, authority, and divine presence. In these lordship attributes there is no difference between the words of prophets and apostles and the voice of God himself. These words are therefore God's personal words to us.

Jesus, Divine Voice and Prophet

When Jesus came into the world, the divine voice was heard once more in the public arena. At his baptism, the Father said, "This is my beloved Son, with whom I am well pleased" (Matt. 3:17). More privately, the Father spoke from heaven to three disciples at Jesus' transfiguration, using the same words, adding: "listen to him" (Matt. 17:5). But we should also not forget that throughout his earthly ministry Jesus himself was the divine voice. He himself was the Word. And though he had the right to speak on his own authority, he spoke only what the Father required him to say (both content and manner, John 12:49). On the last day his word will judge those who reject him (v. 48).

But we need to look at Jesus here and now, for he is not only a recipient of the word, but also the Lord who speaks.

Since Jesus is both perfect God and perfect man, he is both the most authoritative speaker and the most faithful hearer of the word of God. As a human hearer, he speaks just what his Father teaches him (John 8:28; 10:18; 12:49–50; 14:10; 15:15). He does not question, contradict, or hesitate. From this relation to the Father, he passes God's words on to his hearers. So he is the greatest Prophet, the Prophet "like Moses" of Deuteronomy 18:15.

But he is also the Word of God incarnate (John 1:1, 14). We saw in chapter 23 that Jesus is the very Word of God. But this fact does not detract at all from the authority of God's personal words to human beings. In fact, Jesus himself, as the Word of God, brings verbal testimony to the truth (18:37). He presents this testimony as the reason why he came into the world. His mission was revelatory: to follow Moses' revelation of the law with a revelation of grace and truth (1:17). He has made the Father known to us (John 1:18; cf. Matt. 11:27). His mission is not *merely* revelatory. He came to accomplish redemption, not just to tell us about it. But his redemptive act reveals his grace, and the revelation of his grace interprets the redemptive act. Revelation and redemption are two aspects of, two perspectives on, his ministry to us.

Jesus' personal words are of utmost importance to the message of the NT. There is no trace of any development from a word-centered revelation in the OT to a nonverbal revelation in the NT. Quite to the contrary. Jesus' personal words are crucial to his ministry. In the community of his disciples, his word is the supreme criterion of discipleship. Jesus teaches that calling him "Lord" is meaningless unless we do the will of his Father (Matt. 7:21–23). The will of his Father is to be found in the law of Moses (Matt. 5:17–20), and also in Jesus' own words (7:24–29). Those who hear Jesus' words and do them will be like the wise man who built his house on the rock. Those who do not hear and obey will be like the fool who built his house on sand.

When he returns in glory, Jesus will be ashamed of those who have been ashamed of him—notably those who have been ashamed of his words (Mark 8:38; Luke 9:26). His mother and brothers are those who "hear the word of God and do it" (Luke 8:21).

The gospel of John, which begins by identifying Jesus with the Word of God, is, of the four, the most preoccupied with the importance of the words of Jesus. In John 6:63, Jesus says, "The words that I have spoken to you are spirit and life." Five verses later, Peter asks, "Lord, to whom shall we go? You have the words of eternal life."

In John 8:47, Jesus identifies his own teaching with the "words of God" and insists that anyone who is "of God" will hear and obey them.

John 12:47–50 is remarkable:

> If anyone hears my words and does not keep them, I do not judge him; for I did not come to judge the world but to save the world. The one who rejects me and does not receive my words has a judge; the word that I have spoken will judge him on the last day. For I have not spoken on my own authority, but the Father who sent me has himself given me a commandment—what to say and what to speak. And I know that his commandment is eternal life. What I say, therefore, I say as the Father has told me.

Note here (1) the equation between rejecting Jesus and rejecting his words (v. 48), (2) the word of Jesus (particularly in contrast with his personal presence during his earthly ministry) as the judge of men (v. 48), (3) the determination of Jesus' words by the Father, both in content ("what to say") and in form ("what to speak") (v. 49),[30] (4) the commandment of the Father (both his commands in general and his commands given to Jesus specifically) as the means and substance of eternal life (v. 50).

---

30. This seems to be the best way to render in English the Greek distinction between *ti eipo* and *ti laleso*. The first is from the verb *lego*, the second from *laleo*. These are often interchangeable and translated "to speak." But the former tends to emphasize content, the second manner—the sounds that come out of the mouth.

Some lessons from John 12: (1) If we are critical of Jesus' words, we may not appeal beyond them (neoorthodox fashion!) to Jesus himself (vv. 48–49). (2) We may not appeal to the substance or content of Jesus' words, beyond the forms in which they are presented (v. 49). (3) We may not claim eternal life while rejecting the demand of Jesus' words upon us (v. 50).

It is also the Johannine literature that identifies most clearly our love for Christ as his disciples with our obedience to his commands (see John 14:15, 21, 23; 15:7, 10, 14; 17:6, 17; 1 John 2:3–5; 3:22; 5:2–3; 2 John 6). John's visions of Revelation identify God's people as those who "keep the commandments of God and hold to the testimony of Jesus" (Rev. 12:17; see also 14:12).

Paul refers less often to the words Jesus spoke in his earthly ministry, more often, understandably, to his own apostolic revelation. But note Luke's account of his message to the Ephesian elders at Acts 20:35. And in 1 Timothy 6:3–4, Paul follows Jesus himself in making agreement with Jesus' words a test of fellowship: "If anyone teaches a different doctrine and does not agree with the sound words of our Lord Jesus Christ and the teaching that accords with godliness, he is puffed up with conceit and understands nothing."

To hear the words of Jesus, then, is the same as hearing the words of the Father. We are to hear the words of Jesus as Abraham heard the words of Yahweh, as words of supreme authority. We are not in any position to find fault with the words of Jesus. They rather create obligations on our part—to hear, believe, obey, meditate, rejoice, mourn, or whatever else the words may demand of us.

And the supremacy of the words of Jesus enhances the authority of those, the prophets and apostles, whom Jesus appointed to bring his words to us. Jesus wrote no books when he was on earth. We need his words for our salvation. But the only way for us to get his words is from the apostles, whom he appointed to remember his words and to apply them to the church's life following his ascension. We now need to ask this: where do we find the words of the apostles, who in turn will give us the words of Jesus? The answer: in their writings, to which we must now turn.

Key Terms

Media of revelation
Event-media
Word-media
Person-media
Humanity of God's word
Theophany
History
General history
Redemptive history
Nature
Natural revelation

General revelation
Inspiration
The divine voice
Prophet
Apostle
Mysteries of God
Historical contingencies

Study Questions

1. Does God ever speak to human beings without created media? Discuss from Scripture.
2. "Indeed, the three kinds of media are inseparable from one another and perspectivally related." Explain; evaluate.
3. Does the human element in revelation reduce its authority? Why or why not?
4. "It is important to remember that nature is not the word of God, but only a medium of the word." Why? Explain.
5. Describe the nature and content of natural or general revelation. How do unbelievers respond to natural revelation? How is this revelation useful to believers?
6. What did G. W. Lessing say about the relationship between history and faith? Evaluate it.
7. Describe the power, authority, and presence of the divine voice.
8. "If God spoke to me directly, I would believe." Reply.
9. Describe the problem of identifying the divine voice. Respond to it.
10. "Validating the word of God by the word of God is a circular argument." Respond.
11. "So the prophet is a divinely approved substitute for the divine voice itself." Discuss biblical evidence for this claim.
12. "So it is clearly wrong to think that there is a decrease in power, authority, or divine presence between the divine voice and the word of God in the mouth of the prophet." Explain; evaluate.
13. Evaluate Paul's claim to apostolic authority, based on his statements in Scripture.
14. Do the words of true prophets always come true? Discuss. If not, how can we recognize who is a true prophet and who is not?
15. Discuss the role of Jesus in revelation, both as divine voice and as Prophet.

Memory Verses

Ex. 4:11–12: Who has made man's mouth? Who makes him mute, or deaf, or seeing, or blind? Is it not I, the LORD? Now therefore go, and I will be with your mouth and teach you what you shall speak.

Deut. 18:18–19: I will raise up for them a prophet like [Moses] from among their brothers. And I will put my words in his mouth, and he shall speak to them all that I command him. And whoever will not listen to my words that he shall speak in my name, I myself will require it of him.

Jer. 18:7–10: If at any time I declare concerning a nation or a kingdom, that I will pluck up and break down and destroy it, and if that nation, concerning which I have spoken, turns from its evil, I will relent of the disaster that I intended to do to it. And if at any time I declare concerning a nation or a kingdom that I will build and plant it, and if it does evil in my sight, not listening to my voice, then I will relent of the good that I had intended to do to it.

John 14:26: But the Helper, the Holy Spirit, whom the Father will send in my name, he will teach you all things and bring to your remembrance all that I have said to you.

John 15:26–27: But when the Helper comes, whom I will send to you from the Father, the Spirit of truth, who proceeds from the Father, he will bear witness about me. And you also will bear witness, because you have been with me from the beginning.

John 16:13: When the Spirit of truth comes, he will guide you into all the truth, for he will not speak on his own authority, but whatever he hears he will speak, and he will declare to you the things that are to come.

Rom. 1:18–20: For the wrath of God is revealed from heaven against all ungodliness and unrighteousness of men, who by their unrighteousness suppress the truth. For what can be known about God is plain to them, because God has shown it to them. For his invisible attributes, namely, his eternal power and divine nature, have been clearly perceived, ever since the creation of the world, in the things that have been made. So they are without excuse.

1 Cor. 2:12–13: Now we have received not the spirit of the world, but the Spirit who is from God, that we might understand the things freely given us by God. And we impart this in words not taught by human wisdom but taught by the Spirit, interpreting spiritual truths to those who are spiritual.

Resources for Further Study

Frame, John M. "God and Biblical Language." Appendix E of *DWG*.

Pratt, Richard. "Historical Contingencies and Biblical Predictions." Available at http://reformedperspectives.org/newfiles/ric_pratt/TH.Pratt.Historical_Contingencies.html.

CHAPTER 25

GOD'S WRITTEN WORDS

IN THE PREVIOUS CHAPTER, I showed how God speaks to us through events, in words spoken by his divine voice, and in the words of prophets and apostles. In this chapter, I will focus on the *writings* of those prophets and apostles, and of other writers inspired by God. My general argument is that these written words have the same power, authority, and divine presence as the divine voice. Recall the diagram from that chapter, shown here in fig. 25.1.

The Divine Voice

↓

The Word through Prophets and Apostles

↓

The Written Word

Fig. 25.1. Forms of Verbal Revelation

Some have thought that there is a gradual diminishing of authority from top to bottom. But we saw that between the divine voice and the prophets/apostles there is no such diminishing. God's anointed messengers speak nothing less than the word of God himself. They are "inspired," meaning that there is an identity between their words and his. In this chapter, I will argue from Scripture that the written Word is similarly inspired, so that it has the same authority as the word through prophets and apostles and the divine voice.

It should not be surprising that, say, Paul's written words should have the same authority as his spoken words. It is not uncommon for preachers and teachers to write down their words occasionally. But written revelation from God is not just a series of casual notes by inspired writers. Written revelation plays a special, divinely appointed role in the history of redemption, and to appreciate the nature of such revelation, we must understand that theological purpose. We find that purpose in Scripture itself. Scripture itself, that is to say, teaches a doctrine of Scripture, along with all its other doctrines.

The Permanence of God's Written Word

Before we look directly at this teaching, we should consider an important assumption that underlies the Bible's doctrine of written revelation. That is that divine revelation is not just a momentary experience given to an individual. It is rather to be preserved and passed on to others and to subsequent generations. Even before the beginning of the written canon, we see this emphasis on permanence, for example, in the covenant memorials of the patriarchs. In Genesis 8:20, we read that Noah builds an altar in response to God's delivering him through the flood. God responds by reestablishing his covenant. The rainbow (9:12–17) is the sign of the covenant, a permanent witness to God's promise.[1] Abram later builds an altar in Shechem (12:7) to memorialize God's promise that his descendants would possess the land. Cf. also 13:18. After Jacob experienced his revelatory vision of God, he erected a pillar and poured oil on it (28:18), in remembrance of the divine speech to him (35:15). These stone pillars are less than written revelation, of course. But they indicate the patriarchs' desire, and God's, to leave permanent witness to God's covenantal words.

God's covenants are with families, not only with individuals. He does not renew the covenant, by divine voice, individually to each member of the covenant community. Rather, he appoints the recipients of the covenant words to preserve those words and to pass them on to later generations. Although oral tradition plays a role, the normal way of preserving words is through writing.

The same is true in the NT. As we saw in chapter 24, Jesus empowered his disciples to remember all the words he spoke to them (John 14:26). He was concerned not only for his disciples, but for those who would come to believe through the disciples' word (John 17:20). The revelation was to be "passed down" as a *tradition*, first "handed over" (*paradidomi*) from the Father to the Son (Matt. 11:27) and then "revealed" to those whom the Son chooses. The revelation of Jesus' resurrection is one that Paul "received" (1 Cor. 15:3) and then "delivered" (*paradidomi*) to the churches. So Paul exhorts the Thessalonian church, "So then, brothers, stand firm and hold to the traditions [*paradosis*] that you were taught by us, either by our spoken word or by our letter" (2 Thess. 2:15). And:

> Now we command you, brothers, in the name of our Lord Jesus Christ, that you keep away from any brother who is walking in idleness and not in accordance with the tradition [*paradosis*] that you received from us. (2 Thess. 3:6)

Later, he exhorts Timothy to "guard the deposit [*paratheke*] entrusted to you" (1 Tim. 6:20; cf. 2 Tim. 1:12–14; 2:2; 2 Peter 2:21). These passages indicate that the

---

1. Rainbows individually disappear, of course, but the *institution* of the rainbow is permanent.

gospel of Christ is a specific content, a tradition (indicated by the *paradidomi* and *paratithemi* terminology), passed from the Father, to the Son, to the apostles, to the churches. That tradition[2] serves as the criterion of discipleship, of doctrine and behavior. It is to be defended and preserved, passed from one generation to the next. As Jude says:

> Beloved, although I was very eager to write to you about our common salvation, I found it necessary to write appealing to you to contend for the faith that was once for all delivered [*paradidomi*] to the saints. (Jude 3)

The prominent twentieth-century theologian Karl Barth is well known for the view that revelation cannot be preserved, but exists only in a crisis moment, leaving us only with "recollection and expectation." He believed that if revelation becomes permanent, it then becomes something that we can possess, master, manipulate, and so forth. Intuitively, we will probably agree that some Christians, not least theologians, have fallen into the trap of treating God's Word as a commodity of which they are masters, though it is difficult to identify when this happens and to prove guilt. The only certain way to prove someone guilty of such an attitude is to read his heart. Certainly nobody ever admits guilt in this respect. In any case, Barth is right to insist that God's Word must be sovereign over us, not the other way around. But to deny the permanence of God's revelation is no help. Such a denial is unscriptural, as we have seen. And my impression is that Barthian theologians are no more or less prone than anyone else to use revelation as a tool to magnify themselves and to disrespect others, as if they were masters of the Word.

In Scripture itself, God ensures the sovereignty of his revelation, not by making it momentary and evanescent,[3] but by establishing it as a permanent part of the human landscape, like the pillars and altars of the patriarchs. God commissioned Israel to put the book of the law in the holiest part of the tabernacle (Deut. 31:26) and to have the commandments read publicly to the nation as God's witness against Israel's sins (vv. 10–11). The permanent law of God maintained God's sovereignty over his people. And later, during a time of national apostasy, Hilkiah the high priest discovered a copy of the law of God in the temple and brought it to King Josiah, leading to national repentance (2 Kings 22:8–20). Man may try to add to the word, subtract from it, ignore it, misuse it, or hide it, but man can never be sovereign over it. It will always be God's word, and its very permanence is a sign of that: "The grass withers, the flower fades, but the word of our God will stand forever" (Isa. 40:8).

---

2. Of course, in the NT there are bad traditions as well as good. The bad traditions are the merely human traditions of the Pharisees that "[make] void the word of God" (Matt. 15:6). These traditions add to and supplant the true word of God, and so we should reject them. Cf. Col. 2:8. See chapter 38.

3. Barth's approach amounts to sovereignty by retreat. In his view, for God's Word to be sovereign, it must escape the scrutiny of human beings. But such sovereignty is to no purpose. It cannot command, promise, or guide, as it must if it is to be God's covenant Word.

God's Written Words in the Old Testament

Scripture indicates that God intends his permanent revelation to take specifically verbal form. Some evidence of that intention follows:

The Generations

There are indications in the book of Genesis of revelation from that time that is specifically verbal. Genesis is divided into a number of sections, each beginning "these are the generations." This and similar phrases occur at 2:4; 5:1; 6:9; 10:1; 11:10; 11:27; 25:12, 19; 36:1, 9; 37:2 (cf. Matt. 1:1). Each serves as a summary-ending of the material that went before it. Evidently these are a literary device governing the structure of Genesis. This pattern does not continue into Exodus or the other books of the Pentateuch. That it is a literary pattern is suggested by the distinctive language of Genesis 5:1, which speaks of a *"book* of the generations of Adam." P. J. Wiseman argued that all these references to generations were in fact titles of books, sources later used by Moses.[4] If this view of the generations is true, it doesn't prove that these sources were divinely inspired. If Moses used them in his writing of the Pentateuch, however, then we may conclude that even at the times of Adam, Noah, Abraham, Isaac, and so on, God was preparing literary materials for inclusion in the eventual canon.

If the "generations" are not book titles, Moses nevertheless must have gotten the material for the book of Genesis from somewhere other than his own experience. That might have been direct divine revelation, oral tradition, or written sources other than those Wiseman supposed. On any of these alternatives, plainly God intended the stories of Noah, Abraham, and others to be permanently available to his people, eventually in written form.

The Covenant Document

God established a covenant with Israel in the time of Moses, governed by a written document. Recall that the children of Israel heard the divine voice on the "day of the assembly" (Deut. 9:10; 10:4; 18:16) but were afraid to hear it any more. They asked Moses, instead, to hear God directly and then (as a prophet) to bring God's word to the people.

But God's communication with Israel was not only through Moses' prophetic words. In Exodus 24:12:

> The LORD said to Moses, "Come up to me on the mountain and wait there, that I may give you the tablets of stone, with the law and the commandment, which I have written for their instruction."

Note that these tablets are written by God, before Moses even ascends the mountain. The words on the tablets are not only God's words, for he is the speaker throughout the document, but also God's actual writing. God here is not only the

---

4. P. J. Wiseman, *Ancient Records and the Structure of Genesis* (Nashville: Thomas Nelson, 1985).

author, but the publisher. In Exodus 31:18, there is an even more vivid picture of the divine authorship:

> And he gave to Moses, when he had finished speaking with him on Mount Sinai, the two tablets of the testimony, tablets of stone, written with the finger of God.

The very finger of God! The work is not only God's words, but God's penmanship!

This document should be seen in the context of the suzerainty treaties of the ancient Near East. Meredith G. Kline, in *The Structure of Biblical Authority,*[5] points out that in Hittite and other ancient cultures, a great king would sometimes make a treaty with a lesser king and inscribe the terms of that treaty in a written document. Kline believes that the Decalogue, the document written by God's finger on tablets of stone, shares a literary form with the Hittite suzerainty treaties. He also finds the treaty-form in the book of Deuteronomy.

In chapter 2, I noted many parallels between Moses' tablets and the Hittite suzerainty treaties. For now, the important thing to remember is that as with those treaties, God's relation to Israel is structured by a written text.

1. As the great king in the Hittite treaties began by identifying himself as the author of the document, so Yahweh identifies himself as the author, "I am the LORD your God" (Ex. 20:2), and he speaks throughout the document in the first person.

2. As with the suzerainty treaties, God unilaterally lays down the terms of his covenant. There is no negotiation.

3. As with the suzerainty treaties, the words of the document are the "words of the covenant" (Ex. 34:28). Indeed, they are identified with the covenant. Deuteronomy 4:13 says:

> And he declared to you his covenant, which he commanded you to perform, that is, the Ten Commandments, and he wrote them on two tablets of stone.

The tablets are "the tablets of the covenant" (Deut. 9:9, 11, 15). These and subsequently revealed laws are words of the covenant (Deut. 29:9, 21; 33:9).

4. The covenant words are a *holy* text. As the Hittite suzerainty treaties were placed in the sanctuaries of the great king and the lesser king, so God's covenant words were put by the ark of the covenant, the holiest place in Israel (Deut. 31:26), the most intense manifestation of God's presence. Compare Paul's description of the OT as the *holy* Scriptures in 2 Timothy 3:15. Holiness indicates a special relationship to God, and a locus of the divine presence.

5. The placing of the covenant document in the sanctuary also guards its permanence. The holy books were placed in the tabernacle, and later in the temple in Jerusalem, until the Romans destroyed the temple in A.D. 70.

6. The divine text is God's witness against Israel. In modern theology it has been common to refer to Scripture as man's witness to God. The account of God's written words in Exodus and Deuteronomy turns this upside down. God says:

---

5. Grand Rapids: Eerdmans, 1972.

> Take this Book of the Law and put it by the side of the ark of the covenant of the LORD your God, that it may be there for a witness against you. For I know how rebellious and stubborn you are. Behold, even today while I am yet alive with you, you have been rebellious against the LORD. How much more after my death! Assemble to me all the elders of your tribes and your officers, that I may speak these words in their ears and call heaven and earth to witness against them. (Deut. 31:26–28)

Far from being an account of man's opinions about God, the covenant document is God's witness against all of man's false notions and disobedience.

7. By implication, the covenant document is the highest law in Israel. It is, we may say, Israel's *constitution*. Like that of the United States of America (and unlike, for example, that of Great Britain), Israel's highest authority is a written document.

8. As with the suzerainty treaties, God orders that the law be read publicly to all Israel. In this case, it must be officially read every seven years (Deut. 31:9–13).

9. God's word is Israel's very life:

> He said to them, "Take to heart all the words by which I am warning you today, that you may command them to your children, that they may be careful to do all the words of this law. For it is no empty word for you, but your very life, and by this word you shall live long in the land that you are going over the Jordan to possess." (Deut. 32:46–47)

The Decalogue document is not the last of God's written words to Israel. Toward the end of his life, Moses writes "this law," probably including much of Deuteronomy. He gives it to the priests who carry the ark of the covenant (Deut. 31:9), and mandates that it be publicly read (vv. 11–13). Cf. vv. 24–29. The "Song of Moses," chapter 32, is especially to be preserved, taught, and heeded (31:19–22) as God's "witness."

After Moses dies and Joshua replaces him as Israel's leader, God exhorts him to follow the written law:

> Only be strong and very courageous, being careful to do according to all the law that Moses my servant commanded you. Do not turn from it to the right hand or to the left, that you may have good success wherever you go. This Book of the Law shall not depart from your mouth, but you shall meditate on it day and night, so that you may be careful to do according to all that is written in it. For then you will make your way prosperous, and then you will have good success. (Josh. 1:7–8)

At the end of his life, when Israel had conquered much of the Promised Land, Joshua

> made a covenant with the people that day, and put in place statutes and rules for them at Shechem. And Joshua wrote these words in the Book of the Law of God. And he took a large stone and set it up there under the terebinth that was by the sanctuary of the LORD. And Joshua said to all the people, "Behold, this stone shall be a witness

against us, for it has heard all the words of the Lord that he spoke to us. Therefore it shall be a witness against you, lest you deal falsely with your God." So Joshua sent the people away, every man to his inheritance. (Josh. 24:25–28)

That Joshua would add words to the sacred covenant words of God, indeed "in the Book of the Law of God," would at first glance seem arrogant, especially in light of the prohibition in Deuteronomy 4:2 and 12:32 against adding to or subtracting from the word of God. But in Joshua 24 we see that his writing was in the context of a covenant with God. Certainly this covenant was a covenant between God and Israel, with Joshua serving only as mediator. As with the words of Moses, the words of Joshua are God's words, put with the other words of God with the ark, in God's sanctuary, as God's witness against Israel. Thus a pattern is established for additions to the canon.

Written Prophecy

Prophets after the time of Moses and Joshua also produced written documents setting forth the words that God gave to them. In Isaiah 8:1–2, we read:

> Then the Lord said to me, "Take a large tablet and write on it in common characters, 'Belonging to Maher-shalal-hash-baz.' And I will get reliable witnesses, Uriah the priest and Zechariah the son of Jeberechiah, to attest for me."

Maher-shalal-hash-baz ("haste to the spoil") is the name of the son whose birth will signal the coming defeat of Damascus and Samaria by the king of Assyria. The written tablet containing the prophecy is authorized by God and witnessed (as the earlier covenant document) for authenticity. The document preserves the prophecy, so that when the event takes place it will identify Isaiah as a true prophet.

In Isaiah 30:8–11, God again authorizes written prophecy, again as a witness against Israel's unbelief. Israel will not heed the prophecy, so it takes written form "that it may be for the time to come as a witness forever." A later generation may be more attentive and will take Israel's past disobedience as cautionary.

For other references to written prophecy, see the following passages: Isa. 34:16–17; Jer. 25:13; 30:2; 51:60–61; Dan. 9:1–2. David is called a prophet in Acts 2:30, on the basis of his written text, Psalm 16. Jesus and the apostles also quote David's psalms as anticipating Jesus' work as Messiah (as Matt. 22:42–45).

In Jeremiah 36, a scroll of written prophecy plays an important role in the narrative. At God's behest, Jeremiah dictates God's words to Baruch, his scribe. Baruch reads the scroll publicly and to the Israelite officials. The unbelieving king Jehoiakim burns the scroll, but God calls on Jeremiah to write the same words on another scroll, plus divine condemnation on Jehoiakim, "and many similar words were added to them" (v. 32).

In some OT passages, one writer quotes another from what is evidently a written source. Cf. Isa. 2:2–4 with Mic. 4:1–5; Isa. 11:9 with Hab. 2:14; Jer. 26:17–18 with Mic. 3:12. A number of OT writers show familiarity with the written law of Moses (Dan.

9:9–15; Ps. 19:7; 94:12; 119:1 and throughout Ps. 119). So it is evident that during the OT period itself, a body of writings developed that could be quoted as divinely authoritative.

Wisdom

The wisdom literature (Job, Proverbs, Ecclesiastes, Song of Solomon) stands somewhat separate from the laws of Moses and the Prophets. But it, too, presupposes written revelation from God. The first four chapters of the book of Proverbs urge readers (especially young ones) to attend to wisdom as a guide to their lives. That wisdom comes from God (2:6–8), and the fear of the Lord is the beginning of wisdom and knowledge (Prov. 1:7; 9:10; 15:33; cf. Ps. 111:10). The benefits of wisdom in Proverbs, chapters 1–4 and 8–9, are essentially the same as those of God's words, statutes, and testimonies in Psalm 119. Proverbs 30:5–6 also relates God's word to wisdom:

> Every word of God proves true;
>   he is a shield to those who take refuge in him.
> Do not add to his words,
>   lest he rebuke you and you be found a liar.

The wisdom itself began in oral teaching, but was eventually, like the law, put into writing. Israel came to recognize it as written words from God and therefore of permanent importance:

> The words of the wise are like goads, and like nails firmly fixed are the collected sayings; they are given by one Shepherd. (Eccl. 12:11)

Respect for God's Written Words in the Old Testament

In none of the passages we have considered is there any suggestion that the written form of the word is less authoritative than the oral, or, for that matter, than the divine voice. In the narrative of Jeremiah 36, Jehoiakim should have taken heed to Baruch's scroll. When he burned it, he added to his condemnation. The scroll was God's personal word to him, and he despised it. When one prophet quotes the written word of another, or when Psalm 119 refers to the written law, they refer to the written words with utmost reverence, as the supreme authority for all of life.

N.B.: Contrary to many liberal writers, the concept of a written word of God does not begin with twentieth-century fundamentalism, or seventeenth-century orthodoxy, or medieval scholasticism, or postapostolic defensiveness, or late Jewish legalism.[6] It

---

6. To disparage an idea, or praise it, because it comes from a particular time or place is to commit the genetic fallacy. It's like Nathanael's early disparagement of Jesus, "Can anything good come out of Nazareth?" (John 1:46). Yet this sort of thing happens all the time in theology. There are some eras, such as the time of Paul, the Trinitarian fathers, Augustine, and the Protestant Reformation, that are supposed to be fonts of wisdom, and others (those listed above) that are considered dark days for the church. If you want to defend a theological idea, you would be wise to trace its historical pedigree to one of the favored eras. Certainly you should never claim (or admit) to have gotten an idea from twentieth-century American fundamentalists! I have often heard the idea

is not even the product of late NT documents such as 2 Timothy 3:15–17 and 2 Peter 1:19–21, which some critics dismiss as postapostolic or legalistic. It is embedded in the original constitution of the people of God and is assumed throughout Scripture.

The covenant document is the fundamental law of Israel, as the written Constitution is the fundamental law of the United States of America. N. T. Wright is critical of the tendency in the postapostolic church to regard Scripture

> as a "court of appeal," the source-book or rule-book from which doctrine and ethics might be deduced and against which innovations were to be judged.[7]

But there is no doubt that the covenant document, and the whole Torah that developed from it, served (among other functions) as a rulebook, as law, and therefore as a court of appeal in ancient Israel.

Open randomly to almost any page of Deuteronomy 4–11, and you will find admonitions such as these:

> And now, O Israel, listen to the statutes and the rules that I am teaching you, and do them, that you may live, and go in and take possession of the land that the LORD, the God of your fathers, is giving you. You shall not add to the word that I command you, nor take from it, that you may keep the commandments of the LORD your God that I command you. Your eyes have seen what the LORD did at Baal-peor, for the LORD your God destroyed from among you all the men who followed the Baal of Peor. But you who held fast to the LORD your God are all alive today. See, I have taught you statutes and rules, as the LORD my God commanded me, that you should do them in the land that you are entering to take possession of it. Keep them and do them, for that will be your wisdom and your understanding in the sight of the peoples, who, when they hear all these statutes, will say, "Surely this great nation is a wise and understanding people." For what great nation is there that has a god so near to it as the LORD our God is to us, whenever we call upon him? And what great nation is there, that has statutes and rules so righteous as all this law that I set before you today? (Deut. 4:1–8)

> Now this is the commandment, the statutes and the rules that the LORD your God commanded me to teach you, that you may do them in the land to which you are going over, to possess it, that you may fear the LORD your God, you and your son and your son's son, by keeping all his statutes and his commandments, which I command you, all the days of your life, and that your days may be long. Hear therefore, O Israel, and be careful to do them, that it may go well with you, and that you may multiply greatly, as the LORD, the God of your fathers, has promised you, in a land flowing with milk and honey.

---

of biblical inerrancy disparaged by European theologians on the ground that it is an "American" idea. (I believe myself that it is, rather, by other names, the view of the whole church before around 1650.) But even if we grant the legitimacy of such genetic reasoning, it cannot be brought against the idea of a divinely authoritative written Word, for that idea goes back to Israel's beginnings as a nation.

7. N. T. Wright, *The Last Word* (San Francisco: Harper, 2005), 65.

"Hear, O Israel: The LORD our God, the LORD is one. You shall love the LORD your God with all your heart and with all your soul and with all your might. And these words that I command you today shall be on your heart. You shall teach them diligently to your children, and shall talk of them when you sit in your house, and when you walk by the way, and when you lie down, and when you rise. You shall bind them as a sign on your hand, and they shall be as frontlets between your eyes. You shall write them on the doorposts of your house and on your gates." (Deut. 6:1–9)

And the LORD commanded us to do all these statutes, to fear the LORD our God, for our good always, that he might preserve us alive, as we are this day. And it will be righteousness for us, if we are careful to do all this commandment before the LORD our God, as he has commanded us. (Deut. 6:24–25)

You shall therefore be careful to do the commandment and the statutes and the rules that I command you today. (Deut. 7:11)

Take care lest you forget the LORD your God by not keeping his commandments and his rules and his statutes, which I command you today. (Deut. 8:11)

In Deuteronomy, the statutes, laws, commandments, ordinances, rules, words, and the like (note the eloquent redundancy) are spoken by Moses in his final addresses to the nation of Israel. They are prophetic words. But they are also permanent requirements on Israel, to be remembered and observed beyond the lifetime of Moses. And so Moses writes down the Deuteronomic law, places it with the sacred stone tablets, and arranges for its regular public reading (Deut. 31:9–13). Once that is done, the statutes are a *written* revelation, a book. So God tells Joshua to do according to the law that Moses placed in a book:

Only be strong and very courageous, being careful to do according to all the law that Moses my servant commanded you. Do not turn from it to the right hand or to the left, that you may have good success wherever you go. This Book of the Law shall not depart from your mouth, but you shall meditate on it day and night, so that you may be careful to do according to all that is written in it. For then you will make your way prosperous, and then you will have good success. (Josh. 1:7–8)

At the end of Joshua's life, he urges Israel to do the same:

Therefore, be very strong to keep and to do all that is written in the Book of the Law of Moses, turning aside from it neither to the right hand nor to the left. (Josh. 23:6)

Cf. Josh. 11:15; also Deut. 5:32; 28:14 on the language of "neither to the right hand nor to the left."

The theme of praise for God's written words is frequent in the Psalms. In Psalm 12, when David bemoans a world of lies, flattery, and oppression, corrupted by evil speech, he reflects on the one form of language that is pure:

> The words of the LORD are pure words,
>   like silver refined in a furnace on the ground,
>   purified seven times. (Ps. 12:6)

In Psalm 19, after a section on praise for God's revelation of himself in the creation, David continues:

> The law of the LORD is perfect,
>   reviving the soul;
> the testimony of the LORD is sure,
>   making wise the simple;
> the precepts of the LORD are right,
>   rejoicing the heart;
> the commandment of the LORD is pure,
>   enlightening the eyes;
> the fear of the LORD is clean,
>   enduring forever;
> the rules of the LORD are true,
>   and righteous altogether.
> More to be desired are they than gold,
>   even much fine gold;
> sweeter also than honey
>   and drippings of the honeycomb.
> Moreover, by them is your servant warned;
>   in keeping them there is great reward. (Ps. 19:7–11)

In Psalm 78, Asaph reflects on the requirement of Deuteronomy 6:6–9 that parents should saturate the minds of their children with the words of God:

> He established a testimony in Jacob
>   and appointed a law in Israel,
> which he commanded our fathers
>   to teach to their children,
> that the next generation might know them,
>   the children yet unborn,
> and arise and tell them to their children,
>   so that they should set their hope in God
> and not forget the works of God,
>   but keep his commandments;
> and that they should not be like their fathers,
>   a stubborn and rebellious generation,
> a generation whose heart was not steadfast,
>   whose spirit was not faithful to God. (Ps. 78:5–8)

With these compare Psalms 18:30; 111:7; and the many other references in the Psalms to God's laws, commandments, and the like.

Psalm 119 is, of course, the most extensive source of these references. It is the longest psalm and the largest chapter in the Bible, and its chief theme is the word of God. Nearly every verse uses one of the synonyms of our eloquent redundancy: God's law, testimonies, ways, precepts, statutes, commandments, word, rules, promise. Each of these verses brings out the perfection of God's law and the importance of not straying from it.

The psalm is not merely about obeying commands, however. It displays a highly personal relationship between the psalmist and his Lord through the word: God's testimonies are his greatest delight (Ps. 119:15–16, 24, 47), his source of wonder (v. 18), his consuming object of longing (vv. 20, 40), the means of giving him life in a desperate situation (vv. 25, 50), his strength in sorrow (v. 28), his object of worship (v. 48), his hope (v. 49), and his comfort (vv. 50, 52). He sings them (v. 54). God's law is better to him "than thousands of gold and silver pieces" (v. 72). We can continue with this type of exposition all the way to verse 176.

Recall that in chapter 23, I referred to a number of biblical passages and principles to defend the conclusion that God's word is God himself, his own personal presence. One of the arguments was that believers regard God's word as a proper object of religious worship. In that connection, I mentioned such passages as Psalms 56:4, 10; 119:48, 120, 161–62 and the worship offered to God's name in Psalms 9:2; 34:3; 68:4; 138:2.

Now, we should remind ourselves that the chief object of this religious praise, and the chief object of all the other acclaim for God's laws, statutes, commandments, and the like, is specifically the *written* Word of God. The psalmists' primary focus here is not on the divine voice heard directly, nor on the oral words of prophets, but on the written documents constituting God's law, statutes, commandments, ways, precepts, and so on.

It should be clear from this discussion that OT religion is focused on divinely authored written words. Those written words govern all aspects of the Israelite's life, and they function in many ways: as indicatives, imperatives, sources of delight, objects of worship, and so forth. No passage suggests that these written words are of less authority than the oral prophetic word or the divine voice itself. There is no suggestion that the influence of the human writer injects any falsehood or inadequacy into the sacred texts.

Israel's awareness of being subject to God's words begins in Genesis and continues throughout the OT, indeed on nearly every page, for as I said in chapter 1, the entire biblical narrative is governed by the pattern of God's speech followed by man's response.

It could not have been otherwise, for OT revelation is covenantal. It is an aspect of Israel's relationship to her Lord. The Lord-servant relationship is a relationship in which language is essential. The Lord sets forth the terms of the covenant in words; the servant accepts these and seeks to abide by them. Without words, there can be no covenant, no Lord. Further, in a covenant, the words take on permanent form, in writing, and they are preserved from one generation to another. So the very nature of covenant implies that there will be written revelation, and that that revelation will have the same power, authority, and divine presence as direct, personal revelation from the covenant Lord. So the written words of the OT are the personal words of God to his people.

Jesus' View of the Old Testament

In chapter 23, I expounded the teaching of John 1 and other passages that Jesus Christ is himself the Word of God. But in God's plan of salvation, he became a man in total subjection to the Father's will, obeying the Father's word (John 5:36; 8:42). In his earthly ministry, he did nothing merely on his own authority, but on that of his Father (10:18). He spoke only as the Father taught him to speak (8:28; 12:49), and he spoke all that the Father gave him to speak (15:15).

So in chapter 24 I emphasized that Jesus not only *is* the Word of God, but is the chief *speaker* of that word. Therefore, his words are supremely important as the criterion for Christian discipleship. Here I will argue that Jesus, the supreme speaker of God's word, validates through his word the authority of the OT as God's written Word.

The Gospels emphasize that Jesus was subject not only to the Father's direct communication to him, but also to the written words of God in the OT. He regularly and intentionally acts and speaks in such a way as to fulfill Scripture (Matt. 4:14; 5:17; 8:17; 12:17; 13:35; 26:54), and he says that the great events of his own life have taken place to fulfill Scripture (Matt. 13:14; 26:56; Luke 24:44–47). Further, he says that the OT Scriptures as a whole "bear witness about me" (John 5:39; cf. Luke 24:25–27; John 5:45–47).

Further, Jesus cites OT passages as authoritative words of God. The authority of what we call the OT was commonly accepted among the Jews of Jesus' day. It represents common ground between Jesus and his Jewish opponents. In this regard, he did not merely accommodate his views to theirs in this respect. He did not hesitate to disagree with Jewish traditions when he thought it necessary. But he never questioned the Jews' understanding of scriptural authority. There is not a shred of evidence that he personally held a view of Scripture different from theirs.

Jesus refers to the OT, describing it as "Law" and "Prophets" (Matt. 5:17–18; 7:12; 11:13; 12:5; 22:40; 23:23), which, as we have seen, reflect on the authority of the text as God's Word. The term "Scripture" (*graphe, grammata*) in citations carries the same connotation (Mark 12:10; Luke 4:21; John 7:38).[8] So the formula "It is written" (*gegraptai*) should be taken the same way (Matt. 4:4, 7, 10; 11:10; 21:13; 26:24, 31).

This understanding is consistent with Jesus' explicit reflections on the nature of the OT, the chief of which is this:

> Do not think that I have come to abolish the Law or the Prophets; I have not come to abolish them but to fulfill them. For truly, I say to you, until heaven and earth pass away, not an iota, not a dot, will pass from the Law until all is accomplished. Therefore

---

8. See B. B. Warfield, "The Terms 'Scripture' and 'Scriptures' as Employed in the New Testament," in *The Inspiration and Authority of the Bible* (Grand Rapids: Baker, 1960), 229–41.

whoever relaxes one of the least of these commandments and teaches others to do the same will be called least in the kingdom of heaven, but whoever does them and teaches them will be called great in the kingdom of heaven. (Matt. 5:17–19)

This passage serves as an introduction to Jesus' treatment of the Ten Commandments in the Sermon on the Mount. In that sermon, Jesus often differs from traditional Jewish interpretations of the commandments, indicating his disagreement by the phrase "You have heard that it was said" (Matt. 5:21 [cf. 30], 33, etc.), but he does not criticize the commandments themselves. In verse 27, he does quote the actual words of the seventh commandment "You shall not commit adultery" with the phrase "You have heard that it was said," but here he uses that phrase not to diminish the authority of the commandment, but rather to criticize those Jewish teachers who merely refer to the commandment, without acknowledging the depth of its requirement. In fact, verses 27–30 contain a strong affirmation of the authority of the seventh commandment. The seventh commandment, to Jesus, governs not only our outward behavior, but also the desires of our hearts.

In John 5:45–47, Jesus addresses the Jews as follows:

Do not think that I will accuse you to the Father. There is one who accuses you: Moses, on whom you have set your hope. For if you believed Moses, you would believe me; for he wrote of me. But if you do not believe his writings, how will you believe my words?

Here Jesus agrees with his opponents on the authority of Moses, who as we saw in chapter 24 is the very paradigm of the OT prophets. At this period of time, of course, Moses himself has been dead for centuries, so to "believe Moses" is to believe his written words. Yet Moses himself lives with God and accuses the Jews of unbelief because, according to Jesus, they do not believe Moses' writings as they claim to. Those writings, Jesus says, are about him, about Jesus. In verse 47, Jesus in effect makes believing Moses' writings to be a prerequisite for believing Jesus himself. The Jews do not *truly* believe Moses, but they must do that if they are ever to trust in Jesus. So the words of Moses have a high importance over a thousand years after they were written.

We should also note John 10:34–36:

Jesus answered them, "Is it not written in your Law, 'I said, you are gods'? If he called them gods to whom the word of God came—and Scripture cannot be broken—do you say of him whom the Father consecrated and sent into the world, 'You are blaspheming,' because I said, 'I am the Son of God'?"

Jesus here responds to the charge of blasphemy with a formal rather than substantive argument. Rather than entering into Trinitarian nuances, which his opponents could never have understood, he appeals to the broad meaning of the term "god" in the Scriptures, which his opponents would have acknowledged. His example is Psalm

82:6, which refers to the (wicked!) rulers of Israel as "gods." Jesus argues that he has far more reason than those rulers to apply the term to himself, because the Father consecrated him and sent him into the world.

In the course of his argument, Jesus calls Psalm 82:6 "your Law" (John 10:34), even though in the Jewish categories of Law, Prophets, and Writings, the Psalms were among the Writings, not the Law. This usage ascribes legal authority to this text, simply because it is part of the Scriptures (v. 35). Jesus certainly regarded it this way, and most likely the Jews did also.

In John 10:35, Jesus says that "Scripture cannot be broken." Here again, Jesus is on common ground with the Jews. Because Psalm 82:6 is Scripture, it is God's personal word, which can never become anything less. It cannot fail or lose its authority.

The Apostles' View of the Old Testament

The apostles' view of the OT does not differ from that of Jesus himself. The apostles use the same titles that Jesus used to denote Scripture, such as "Law," "Prophets," and "Scripture." They sometimes modify these titles, as with Paul's "*holy* Scriptures" (2 Tim. 3:15 NIV), which recalls the placing of the tablets of the covenant into the holiest place in the tabernacle.[9] James speaks of the "perfect law" (James 1:25), the "law of liberty" (1:25; 2:12), and the "royal law" (2:8). Paul refers to Scripture by the title "oracles of God" (Rom. 3:2; cf. Acts 7:38; Heb. 5:12; 1 Peter 4:11).[10] The oracles gave to the Jews an advantage over the Gentiles.

All of these references underscore the authority of the OT written Word. Often, to be sure, Paul uses the term *law* with a negative connotation, when he is arguing that nobody can become right with God through obedience to the law. But Paul does not doubt for a minute that the written law is God's holy Word and represents God's standard of judgment. For him, "the law is holy, and the commandment is holy and righteous and good" (Rom. 7:12).

The apostles, like Jesus, cite the OT with phrases connoting authority, such as "it is written" (Rom. 1:17; 3:4; many others). Warfield observes a remarkable pattern in these citations, particularly "Scripture says" and "It says." He notes two classes of passages:

> In one of these classes of passages the Scriptures are spoken of as if they were God; in the other, God is spoken of as if He were the Scriptures: in the two together, God and

9. We should not pass quickly over the use of "holy" in Romans 7:12 and 2 Timothy 3:15 NIV, as we often do. It is no accident that most Bibles today bear the title *Holy Bible*. The book is holy not because it engenders religious feelings, but because it stands in the closest proximity to God himself, as it did in the tabernacle and temple. It is "holy ground," like the burning bush that Moses approached on Mount Sinai, the place of God's presence (Ex. 3:5).

10. B. B. Warfield explores the meaning of this phrase in "The Oracles of God," in *The Inspiration and Authority of the Bible*, 351–407. He concludes on page 406, "We have unobtrusive and convincing evidence here that the Old Testament Scriptures, as such, were esteemed by the writers of the New Testament as an oracular book, which in itself not merely contains, but is the 'utterance,' the very Word of God; and is to be appealed to as such and as such deferred to, because nothing other than the crystallized speech of God."

the Scriptures are brought into such conjunction as to show that in point of directness of authority no distinction was made between them.[11]

In Galatians 3:8, God is spoken of as if he were the Scriptures: "And the Scripture, foreseeing that God would justify the Gentiles by faith, preached the gospel beforehand to Abraham, saying, 'In you shall all the nations be blessed.'" Romans 9:17 is similar. The other class of passages includes Matthew 19:4–5; Acts 4:24–25; 13:34–35; Hebrews 1:6; 3:7, where the NT writer cites sayings from the OT as coming from God, which in the OT context are not directly spoken by God, but by the human writer. The subjectless verbs *legei* and *phesi*, both translated "it says," "he says," and the like, cite Scripture and God interchangeably in these passages: Rom. 9:15; 15:10; 1 Cor. 6:16; 15:27; 2 Cor. 6:2; Gal. 3:16; Eph. 4:8; 5:14; Heb. 8:5; James 4:6. Warfield discusses opposing interpretations of these texts, but concludes that for the NT writers God and Scripture were interchangeable in such contexts, because the Scriptures were nothing less than the Word of God. Acts 4:25 is representative: God, "who through the mouth of our father David, your servant, said by the Holy Spirit, 'Why did the Gentiles rage, and the peoples plot in vain?'" God is the speaker, giving his utterance through the human writer (David), inspiring him to speak by the Holy Spirit. So even though David is the speaker, we may take his utterance as God's personal word to us.

This is the view of Scripture that the apostles teach when they are reflecting on the subject. James, following his brother Jesus (Matt. 7:21, 24–27), teaches that the written Word is something that we should do, not merely hear (James 1:22). For Scripture never speaks "to no purpose" (4:5). James sees great blessing in the doing of it (1:25), great dangers in neglecting any part of it. He says, "For whoever keeps the whole law but fails in one point has become accountable for all of it" (2:10). And note the following:

> Do not speak evil against one another, brothers. The one who speaks against a brother or judges his brother, speaks evil against the law and judges the law. But if you judge the law, you are not a doer of the law but a judge. There is only one lawgiver and judge, he who is able to save and to destroy. But who are you to judge your neighbor? (James 4:11–12)

There are many good reasons to avoid judging one another. But James mentions a reason that we normally don't think of: such behavior amounts to speaking evil of the law. And in James's mind, slandering the law is one of the worst things you can do. If you speak evil of the law, you are judging the law, making yourself the supreme lawgiver (i.e., claiming autonomy). You are claiming a prerogative that belongs only to God. You are seeking to replace him on the throne of the universe.

Paul agrees with James. According to Acts 24:14, he announces to the Roman governor Felix:

11. Warfield, "The Terms 'Scripture' and 'Scriptures,'" 299.

> But this I confess to you, that according to the Way, which they call a sect, I worship the God of our fathers, believing everything laid down by the Law and written in the Prophets.

In his letter to the Romans, after quoting Psalm 69:9, Paul explains his reason for appealing to the OT:

> For whatever was written in former days was written for our instruction, that through endurance and through the encouragement of the Scriptures we might have hope. (Rom. 15:4)

Here, Paul says that the Scriptures, though written centuries before his time, were written for the specific purpose of instructing and encouraging believers of the first century A.D. There are, of course, many ancient books that have the ability to instruct people centuries later. We think of the works of Aeschylus, Plato, and many others. But none of these ancient writings were written *for the purpose of* instructing people of later ages. Paul says that the Scriptures were intentionally written for the benefit of people living centuries later. If this is true, then there must have been a divine intention underlying the intentions of the human writers of the OT. Cf. here 1 Cor. 10:6, 11.

Thus we come to the most famous passage in the NT dealing with Scripture, 2 Timothy 3:15–17:

> From childhood you have been acquainted with the sacred writings, which are able to make you wise for salvation through faith in Christ Jesus. All Scripture is breathed out by God and profitable for teaching, for reproof, for correction, and for training in righteousness, that the man of God may be competent, equipped for every good work.

We should remember that Paul writes this letter late in his life, with a clear awareness that his own ministry is drawing to its end (2 Tim. 4:6–8). In the Pastoral Epistles, Paul is passing the torch to younger men. His concluding admonitions are important not only because he will soon be gone, but also because the coming times will be especially difficult (3:1–9). The church will be invaded by people "having the appearance of godliness, but denying its power" (v. 5). These are false teachers, who practice all kinds of immorality.

In this coming darkness, where does a young pastor such as Timothy turn for light? How can he determine what is true and what is false, and how can he deal with what is false? Paul gives two answers to these questions. The first: remember me (2 Tim. 3:10–14). Paul's successors should remember Paul's life and doctrine and be imitators of him.

Yes, but memories fade over time, and generations will arise who do not have personal memories of Paul. How do they discern between true teachers and "impostors"? Here

Paul's second answer becomes especially important: turn to Scripture.[12] From child-hood, raised by a Jewish mother and grandmother (2 Tim. 1:5), Timothy has known the Scriptures of the OT. These Scriptures convey wisdom (3:15) that brings salvation through faith in Christ. Paul continues, "All Scripture is breathed out by God" (v. 16). "Breathed out by God" is the ESV's literal translation of the Greek *theopneustos*, which is found only here in the Bible. Warfield defended this translation against various alternatives,[13] and I believe his argument is cogent. I take issue with Warfield on only one point. He summarizes his findings as follows:

> The Scriptures owe their origin to an activity of God the Holy Ghost and are in the highest and truest sense His creation. It is on this foundation of Divine origin that all the high attributes of Scripture are built.[14]

It seems to me, rather, that to say that Scripture is "breathed out by God" is to say more than that Scripture has a divine origin and is God's creation. Everything, after all, has a divine origin and is in some sense God's creation. What Paul says here is that the Scripture is breathed out, not created. What can that mean? Well, to breathe out words is simply to *speak* them. Paul is saying that the OT words are the *speech* of God, his personal utterances. Speech is not the same thing as creation. In chapter 23, I argued that the word is God, that it is divine, and that it is therefore precisely *not* a created thing. That is true of the living Word, Jesus Christ, and it is true of all divine utterances. The written Word is, of course, expressed on a created medium, whether stone tablets, papyrus, paper, or digital media. But the word that is written on these media is divine. It is the personal word of God himself. So "breathed out by God" means "spoken by God."

That is a fairly common biblical way of describing the inspiration of the OT. The *pneu* syllable of *theopneustos* connotes both God's breath and God's Spirit. We saw already in chapter 23 that God's word is always found with his Spirit. In that chapter, I noted the *linguistic model of the Trinity*, that the Father is the speaker, the Son the Word, and the Spirit the breath that conveys the word to its hearers. Matthew 22:43; Acts 1:16; 4:25; 28:25; Hebrews 3:7; 9:8; and other passages ascribe specific texts of the OT to the Spirit. These passages are the Spirit's words, addressed to us today.

It is important to note that *theopneustos*, often translated "inspired by God," in the one place where it occurs in Scripture, is a quality of the *written* Word. Indeed, the same is true of the list of passages above, beginning with Matthew 22:43. Theologians have often developed theories in which inspiration is a quality of human prophets, even biblical writers, but not a quality of the written text itself. Such theories are plainly

---

12. This would have been an ideal place for Paul to teach about the "apostolic succession" and the continuing teaching office of the church (*magisterium*) that on the Roman Catholic view we can consult to find authentic apostolic doctrine. Significantly, Paul does not choose this alternative.

13. Warfield, "God-Inspired Scripture," in *The Inspiration and Authority of the Bible*, 245–96.

14. Ibid., 296.

inadequate as accounts of the *theopneustos* of 2 Timothy 3:16. Even more bizarre is Barth's contention that the work of the Spirit in this verse does not produce a permanent written Word of God. In Barth's view, revelation can never be made permanent, preserved, identified with a finite object. So the "inspiration" of 2 Timothy 3:16 yields not a written Word of God, but only "recollection" of past revelation and "expectation" of revelation in the future. But this idea goes directly against Paul's purpose in this verse, to give to Timothy a permanent source of divine revelation that will enable the church at any time to discern the truth and identify error.

In verse 17 of the passage, Paul adds that the words of the OT are not only authoritative but *sufficient*: "that the man of God may be competent, equipped for every good work." We will discuss the sufficiency of Scripture in chapter 26. But while we are looking at 2 Timothy 3:17, it is interesting to note that Paul here is still talking about the OT. For him, evidently, the OT, even apart from the NT, is sufficient to identify false teaching and to equip the young pastor to do the work of God.

We come next to another famous NT passage dealing with the nature of OT Scripture, 2 Peter 1:19–21. The context of this passage is very similar to that of 2 Timothy 3:15–17. Like Paul in the latter passage, Peter in context anticipates his soon death (2 Peter 1:13–15) and seeks to prepare his successors to lead the church without him. And as with Paul, Peter anticipates hard times ahead for the church. The second chapter of the letter is very much like 2 Timothy 3:1–9, anticipating false prophets and teachers coming into the church who "secretly bring in destructive heresies" (2 Peter 2:1) and many forms of immorality (v. 14). So in effect Peter poses to his younger colleagues the same question Paul raised to his: how will you deal with this situation after I am gone? How will you distinguish true and false, right and wrong?

Interestingly, Peter gives two answers, the same as Paul's. The first is "remember me":

> For we did not follow cleverly devised myths when we made known to you the power and coming of our Lord Jesus Christ, but we were eyewitnesses of his majesty. For when he received honor and glory from God the Father, and the voice was borne to him by the Majestic Glory, "This is my beloved Son, with whom I am well pleased," we ourselves heard this very voice borne from heaven, for we were with him on the holy mountain. (2 Peter 1:16–18)

Peter's preaching of the gospel was not based on myths,[15] but on his own eyewitness experience. He refers in 2 Peter 1:17–18 to the transfiguration of Jesus, recorded in Matthew 17:1–9; Mark 9:2–9; and Luke 9:28–36.

But there will come generations of believers who do not remember Peter directly. For them, as well as for his contemporaries, Peter's second answer (again the same as Paul's) is important:

---

15. One wishes that Peter's disavowal of "myth" here (Gk. *mythos*) would make modern theologians more cautious about applying this term to the content of Scripture.

> And we have something more sure, the prophetic word, to which you will do well to pay attention as to a lamp shining in a dark place, until the day dawns and the morning star rises in your hearts, knowing this first of all, that no prophecy of Scripture comes from someone's own interpretation. For no prophecy was ever produced by the will of man, but men spoke from God as they were carried along by the Holy Spirit. (2 Peter 1:19–21)

"More sure" here is the Greek *bebaioteron*. The ESV takes the phrase "more sure, the prophetic word" to mean that the written prophetic words are more certain even than Peter's eyewitness experience. Others have taken it to mean that because of Peter's experience the prophetic word is "*made* more sure." I prefer the first interpretation, but both interpretations commend the certainty of the written Word. The "dark place" is the culture of false prophets and destructive heretics that he refers to later in chapter 2.

First Peter 1:20 denies that these written words come from a merely human source. The word "interpretation" here is misleading, though it is a permissible translation of the Greek *epiluseos*. "Interpretation" suggests that Peter's concern is about hermeneutics, about finding the meanings of difficult passages. The older translation "of private interpretation" stimulated the Roman Catholic-Protestant debate as to whether individuals could understand the Bible without submitting themselves to the church's teaching authority. But in fact the passage is not about interpretation; it is about origin—more precisely, about the basis of Scripture's authority. The passage actually tells us that the Scriptures do not originate from men who interpret reality out of their own experience, like modern-day pundits.

That is plain from 1 Peter 1:21, which denies that Scripture is produced by the will of a human being. This is not to deny that human writers were involved, but only to say that those writers were not the source of biblical authority. The human writers, rather, spoke from God, being carried along by the Holy Spirit. That is to say, they wrote what the Spirit directed them to write, not what they autonomously chose to write. The authority of their words, therefore, is the authority of the Spirit, not the authority of a mere human writer.

Second Timothy 3:15–17 and 2 Peter 1:19–21 are powerful testimonies to the authority of the OT as a written revelation of God. It is possible, however, to put too much emphasis on them in our general argument for biblical authority. Liberal writers often argue that these two passages do not actually come from Paul and Peter, and that they come from a period when the church was losing its spontaneous vitality, a time when it had a more "static"[16] focus, on church government and written standards. Thus, the argument goes, what they say is not very important for our lives today.

---

16. *Static* is a theological buzzword that comes up in many contexts, contrasted with *dynamic*. Everybody tends to honor the dynamic, to disparage the static. But this is foolish. In some situations it is good to be static, in others dynamic. For example, when undergoing surgery, it is usually best for the patient to remain static. He could cause all sorts of problems for his surgeons if he got up and started to dance.

Of course, I disagree with this view. But it is important to emphasize that these two passages don't stand alone. Indeed, they are the capstone of a theme that pervades the entire Scripture, that God rules his people by a written document. That theme begins with the stone tablets written by the finger of Yahweh on Mount Sinai in Exodus (note again Exodus 24:12 and 31:18). As we have seen, in all periods of redemptive history God urges obedience to his written Word, and psalmists extol its wisdom. Jesus concurs, as we have seen. So it should not be surprising that Paul and Peter, toward the end of their lives, call the churches back to the standard that has always ruled the people of God. The teaching of these two passages is clear and specific, but it is hardly novel.

What these two passages tell us is that there will come a time in which no one can personally recall the living voice of a prophet or apostle, and that in that time especially we should turn to the written Word. We are now living in that time. It is not a time to turn back to autonomous thinking. It is a time to read in Scripture God's personal words to us.

The New Testament as God's Written Words

There is no single NT text that teaches the authority of the NT as one complete document. That is, there is no text that speaks of the NT the way 2 Timothy 3:15–17 and 2 Peter 1:19–21 speak of the OT. That should not surprise us. In the nature of the case, the NT could not speak of itself as a completed collection, because when the NT writers wrote, the collection was still incomplete.

Nevertheless, there is plenty of biblical evidence that God intends our NT to function as his written personal words to us.

The NT cannot be considered apart from its OT context, for it claims to continue, indeed to complete, the story of Yahweh's redemption begun in the former volume. As we have seen, that former volume calls attention to itself as a written Word of God. Jesus and the apostles recognize the OT as God's own written account of his covenants with Adam, Noah, Abraham, Moses, and David. Is it likely that the greatest covenant of all, the new covenant that God made with his people in Jesus, would have no written attestation?

As I said in chapter 23, there is no reason for thinking that the new covenant is any less verbal than was the old. Covenants by their very nature are verbal transactions, in which the covenant lord identifies himself in word to the covenant servant, gives his name, cites their historical relations, sets forth his law, and so on. Jesus and the apostles revered the OT as God's Word, as we have seen, and they also identified themselves as God's prophets, bringing God's words to the world. The only remaining question for us to consider is whether they recorded that prophetic message in writing.

Remember that covenants are lasting arrangements, and therefore the covenants between God and man have always been recorded in writing. God's covenant with Moses, inscribed with his own finger, was kept in the Most Holy Place, to be read regularly to the people. The words of Jesus and the apostles were also intended to be preserved for later generations. They are the "tradition" passed from the Father, to the Son, to the apostles. It would have been anomalous in the extreme if this decisive, final revelation of God (Heb. 1:1–3) were not written down. In 2 Thessalonians 2:15, Paul identifies the traditions that he and other apostles passed on to the church "either by our spoken word or by our letter."

Or look at it this way: The words of Jesus as the divine voice and as the Prophet par excellence are absolutely crucial to the believer's life (John 6:68). As we saw, Jesus appointed the apostles to remember these words (14:26) as well as to receive additional revelation. By their own oral teaching, the apostles could preserve the memory of Jesus' words only one or two more generations. A written record would seem to be the only way in which generations of believers after the apostolic period would have access to Jesus' words. Without a written record of them, and of the apostles' testimony to them, those words would be lost to us forever. And without those words, we do not have Jesus as our covenant Lord or as our Savior. Without these words, there can be no Christianity, no Christian church. Only a written document can preserve these words as God's personal words to us.

As we saw in chapter 24, Jesus appointed his apostles to be his spokesmen. After Jesus' ascension, they presented their preaching and teaching as the word of God, given by Christ through the Spirit, not by any human source. A number of the apostles, at least, put their teaching into writing. Is it likely that this teaching is less authoritative than their oral witness? I think not. As we saw earlier in this chapter, the writings of the prophets were as authoritative as their speaking. The apostles' writings could have no less authority.

The documents themselves claim that they have full authority over their recipients. For one thing, they are not optional reading, but mandatory. Paul says to the Colossians:

> And when this letter has been read among you, have it also read in the church of the Laodiceans; and see that you also read the letter from Laodicea.[17] (Col. 4:16)

This reading took place during the worship service, as is implied by the language of this passage ("in the church") and stated later by the church fathers. To receive a letter from an apostle was a momentous event, and it was important that everyone had a chance to hear the actual letter, not just to hear the truths of the letter taught secondhand. But more than that, the reading of the letter was a *solemn* event, one to be done in worship, in the presence of the Lord himself. In 1 Thessalonians 5:27, this reading is again a solemn responsibility: Paul says, "I put you under oath before the Lord to have this letter read to all the brothers."

17. The "letter from Laodicea" may be a letter from Paul now lost, or it may be one of the Canonical Epistles under another name. This letter and Colossians were evidently intended as "round-robin" letters, to be passed from church to church, as Paul indicates here. In that case, "Laodiceans" could be the letter we know as Ephesians, a letter written about the same time as Colossians and with much parallel content. The church in Ephesus was a center for the churches in Asia Minor and may have been a clearinghouse for Paul's letters. But that is only one suggestion.

We are reminded here of the OT pattern, in which the leaders of Israel read the law publicly to the people (2 Kings 23:2; Neh. 8:1–8), as God's own witness against them (Deut. 31:19–22, 26).

In 2 Thessalonians 3:14–15, obedience to Paul's letter is a matter of discipline:

> If anyone does not obey what we say in this letter, take note of that person, and have nothing to do with him, that he may be ashamed. Do not regard him as an enemy, but warn him as a brother.

Similarly in 1 Corinthians 14:37–38:

> If anyone thinks that he is a prophet, or spiritual, he should acknowledge that the things I am writing to you are a command of the Lord. If anyone does not recognize this, he is not recognized.

The Corinthians had in their church a number of prophets and others who had, or who claimed, spiritual gifts (1 Cor. 1:7). Those who had "higher gifts" sometimes were proud and lorded it over those whose gifts were "lesser" (chaps. 12, 13). In 14:37–38, Paul says that the contents of his letter, his written word, take precedence over the authority of anyone else in the church. Indeed, Paul says, no one should be recognized as a prophet or as having a spiritual gift unless he recognizes Paul's written word as a command of the Lord. Clearly, Paul here identifies his *written* word as the word of God.

Indeed, in the time when the NT was still being written, there are indications that parts of it are regarded as *Scripture*. In 1 Timothy 5:17–18, Paul says:

> Let the elders who rule well be considered worthy of double honor, especially those who labor in preaching and teaching. For the Scripture says, "You shall not muzzle an ox when it treads out the grain," and, "The laborer deserves his wages."

The "honor" here is a payment for service, what we today call "honorarium." In support of this exhortation, Paul quotes Deuteronomy 25:4, indicating that even oxen should receive remuneration for their work. The other passage he quotes, "The laborer deserves his wages," is not found in the OT. The source is most likely Luke 10:7. So Paul quotes the gospel of Luke alongside the OT, implying that the two have the same authority.

Peter says the same about Paul's letters. In 2 Peter 3:15–16, he exhorts the people:

> And count the patience of our Lord as salvation, just as our beloved brother Paul also wrote to you according to the wisdom given him, as he does in all his letters when he speaks in them of these matters. There are some things in them that are hard to understand, which the ignorant and unstable twist to their own destruction, as they do the other Scriptures.

Peter commends Paul's writings to the church, but he admits that they can be misused. Of course, the "ignorant and unstable" misuse all the *other* Scriptures as well. By this language, Peter places Paul's writings into the category of Scripture. There are the Pauline Scriptures, and then there are also the other Scriptures.

There can be no doubt, then, that the apostles functioned as prophets, not only in their oral preaching and teaching, but in their written ministry as well. As there is an authoritative written account of the old covenant, there is also an authoritative written account of the new. These are both God's personal words to us.

The Canon of Scripture

The next logical question is this: where may we find these written words of God? In what written texts? This is the question of *canon*. *Canon* refers to the body of writing that God has given to rule the church.

Identifying the books of the canon can be made to seem like a terribly difficult task. Roman Catholics and Protestants have disputed the list of OT books since the time of the Reformation. And the list of NT books accepted by the churches as canon varied (from church to church and from time to time) in the first four centuries A.D.

The Muratorian Fragment, however, traditionally dated around A.D. 170, contains a list of NT books very close to the list we employ today. The author mentions four gospels, the last two being Luke and John (the first two missing from the manuscript). He further mentions the book of Acts, thirteen Pauline letters, the letter of Jude, two letters of John, and the book of Revelation. He does not mention Hebrews, James, or the two letters of Peter. He includes on his list Wisdom of Solomon, which is not today part of the Protestant canon.

Irenaeus, who died around A.D. 202, clearly cites in his *Against Heresies* most all the books of our present NT canon as authoritative texts. The only books he does not quote are Philemon, 2 Peter, 3 John, and Jude. He does also mention 1 Clement and Shepherd of Hermas (which the church did not finally recognize as canonical) as worth reading. He dismissed the Gnostic Gospel of Truth as heretical. So the NT canon of Irenaeus (and he was very concerned about questions of canon in his opposition to the heretic Marcion) is very close to ours.

So the claim that the church had no canon until the fourth century, or that it recognized a very different collection of books from that of the contemporary church, is clearly wrong. In the late second century, the church accepted a canon of books largely the same as ours, with a few uncertainties that would later be resolved.

Recently there has been much publicity about early documents concerning Jesus that were eventually excluded from the NT canon, such as the Gospel of Thomas and the Gospel of Judas. Some scholars have suggested that these represent a legitimate party in the early church that was disenfranchised by ecclesiastical politics, so that the process of canonization was essentially a matter of one faction trying to exclude another. Others argue that Thomas and Judas represent forms of Gnosticism rightly condemned by the church as heretical. I agree with the latter position.[18] But even books that are now well accepted in all parts of the church, such as 2 Peter, 2–3 John, and Revelation, are not found on some of the early canon lists. So some have thought that ascertaining the books that God inspired to rule the church, even given that there are such books, is a formidably difficult task. Those who accept this difficulty and seek nevertheless to undertake the task, and those who try to show that it is impossible, have produced a large amount of literature.

The present volume cannot enter into the details of this debate. My book is a systematic theological treatment, not a historical study. My purpose is not to enter into this complicated history and to determine inductively whether a canon somehow emerges from it and what books constitute that canon. Indeed, I'm inclined to think that that kind of study is unfruitful. Studies of the historical process by which the church came to identify the canon certainly do reveal interesting facts, and believers can see the hand of God throughout this process. But inductive study alone is unlikely to show us with certainty which books God has given to rule the church. My purpose here, rather, is to present the teachings of Scripture itself relevant to the doctrine of the word of God, and now relevant to the specific question of canonicity.

No biblical text sets forth a definitive list of books to be included in the Bible. We should not expect to find one, since while the biblical texts were being written the canon was not yet complete. But there are some biblical principles that direct us on a sure path.

As we have seen, it is God's intention to speak personal words to us, words that have more authority than any other. These words govern our use of all other words, of all other sources of knowledge. For God's words to have this kind of authority, they must be distinguishable from all other words, from words that are merely human. There must, therefore, be a canon, a body of divine words, that God's people can identify as his.

We have also seen that these words are not to be received as momentary experiences by individuals and then allowed to disappear into past history. Rather, they are to be kept permanently so that God can continually witness against the sins of his people (Deut. 31:24–29), both present and future generations. So God places the Ten Commandments by the holy ark of the covenant and places other words beside them. Doubtless other copies were made as well, which circulated among the people of Israel. The people knew that these were God's words, the words of supreme authority, clearly distinct from all merely human words.

So at every stage of Israel's history, there was a canon, a definite body of divine writings, that spoke to the nation and its individuals with supreme authority. The first canon was the two tablets of the covenant. A later canon added to these the Deuteronomic law of Moses (Deut. 31:24). Still a third added words of Joshua (Josh. 24:25–28).

Scripture does not continue an explicit narration of each stage in the growth of the canon. But as we have seen, it describes occasions in which prophecy was written

---

18. See, for example, Peter Jones, *Spirit Wars: Pagan Revival in Christian America* (Escondido, CA: Main Entry Editions, 1997). For my evaluation of Gnosticism and similar worldviews, see *DG*, 216–20.

down for future generations. There are also many places in the OT where one writer indicates a knowledge of the work of another, either through quotation (as Jeremiah 26:18, which quotes Micah 3:12) or through awareness of symbols, historical narrative, and themes found in previous books.[19] The NT indicates, as we noted, that during Jesus' earthly ministry he was able to appeal to the Law, Prophets, and Writings of the Hebrew Bible, which we call the OT, as common ground with his Jewish opponents. We note that although Jesus and his opponents disagreed about a great many things, they never disagreed about what texts could be authoritatively cited.

Evidently, then, we should identify the OT canon as consisting of those books acknowledged by the Jews, in the time and place of Jesus' earthly ministry. We can determine that list of books by investigating the history of the time, verifying our conclusions by looking at what texts Jesus cites and doesn't cite. In my judgment, the data indicate clearly that this canon is identical with the canon endorsed by Protestants since the Reformation.

Given God's intention to rule the church by a written document consisting of his personal words, it would be anomalous in the extreme if he put them in a place where we couldn't find them. Through OT history, God has taken pains to put these words in an *obvious* place, the tabernacle, and later the temple. Josephus says that the books kept in the temple, before its destruction in A.D. 70, were the books recognized as canonical by the Jews. Although the Jews read other books for edification, the temple books were those with fully divine authority. So there is no mystery about the extent of the OT canon. God put the books in a place where they could function as he intended, where they would be recognized as his.

The extent of the NT canon is on the surface a more difficult problem, because in the nature of the case no inspired writer could refer to the NT writings as a completed collection. But we have seen that the NT writers speak of a "tradition" that was to be passed down from generation to generation and guarded against distortion. And we have seen that there is written revelation attesting the new covenant as there was attesting the old (chapter 21). As with the OT, we should note how anomalous it would be if this revelation were hard to find. Our salvation depends on our access to the words of Jesus (John 6:68) and to the gospel preached by the apostles (Rom. 1:16; Gal. 1:6–9; Eph. 1:13).

The problem with much current literature on the canon is that it does not take account of God's expressed intentions. It seeks, rather, through autonomous reasoning (see chapters 2–3) to determine whether any first-century books deserve canonical status, and using that method it arrives at conclusions that are uncertain at best. But once we understand God's use of a canon from the time of Moses, we must approach our present problem with a presupposition: that God will not let his people walk in darkness, that he will provide for us the words we need to have, within our reach.

---

19. See John Sailhamer, *Introduction to Old Testament Theology: A Canonical Approach* (Grand Rapids: Zondervan, 1995), 212–13. This phenomenon is known as *intertextuality*.

588 THE DOCTRINE OF THE WORD OF GOD

So we reach out, and we find before us twenty-seven books—from Matthew to Revelation. God did not put them in the Jerusalem temple, for that temple is gone. He placed them in his temple the church (1 Cor. 3:16–17; Eph. 2:21; Rev. 3:12), that is, among the people of God, where, as in Deuteronomy 30:11–14, the Word is very near us.

The early church was divided by many controversies concerning basic doctrines, including the Trinity and the person of Christ. There were differences among them, too, as to what books were canonical. But it is remarkable how little they fought about this. Some of the differences had to do with geography: some books reached parts of the church before other parts. Some of them had to do with views of content and authorship. But remarkably, when in A.D. 367 Bishop Athanasius of Alexandria published a list of books accepted in his church, there was no clamor. From that time on, Christians of all traditions—Eastern Orthodox, Roman Catholic, and Protestant—agreed on the NT canon. Indeed, through the centuries since, agreement on the NT canon has been more unanimous than on the OT canon, though on the surface it might seem that ascertaining the former would have been more difficult.

What happened? Jesus' sheep heard his voice (John 10:27). Or, to put it differently, the Holy Spirit illumined the texts so that God's people perceived their divine quality. Recall that in chapter 24 I discussed a similar problem in connection with the divine voice: how can we be sure that the voice is God? The answer I proposed was that our assurance is supernatural. When God speaks, he at the same time assures us that he is speaking.[20] In the same chapter, I proposed the same answer to the problem of identifying true prophets and apostles. In this case, Scripture does give objective criteria (Deut. 18), but those criteria are difficult to apply in view of the relation between prophecy and historical contingency. Again, our ultimate assurance is supernatural. So it is, I believe, with the question of identifying canonical books.

In this case, as with the identification of prophets, the Christians used some objective criteria. Apostolic authorship was an obvious criterion. Jesus had appointed the apostles to remember his words and to lead the church into all truth. So if the Christians believed that a book was written by an apostle, they received it, without further argument, as canon.

But of course, they also received books that were not written by apostles, such as Mark, Luke-Acts, Hebrews, James, and Jude. The criterion of apostolicity was relevant to these as well, of course. These books were thought to have come from the apostolic circle, to have somehow been certified by the apostles. Mark was thought to have been a close associate of Peter, and Paul himself testifies in his writings that Luke was his associate (Col. 4:14; 2 Tim. 4:11; Philem. 24). See also the "we" sections of Acts, which indicate that Luke traveled with Paul on his missionary journeys (Acts 16:10–24; 20:5–21:18; 27:1–28:16). Hebrews was sometimes thought to be the work of Paul, though most scholars deny that today. James and Jude were most likely blood-brothers of Jesus and part of the apostolic church leadership, though not technically apostles.

20. Compare also my discussion of Abraham's revelatory experience in chapter 1.

The connection of these books with the apostles, even when indirect, is certainly in their favor. Since the apostles are the main recipients of NT revelation, we naturally look favorably on any text that they may have approved in some way. And we should grant that the first- and second-century Christians were closer to the writing of these books than we are, and they probably had more knowledge than we of who wrote the books and the grounds on which the church accepted them. But this is only a probable argument, if we look at the historical evidence alone. We cannot prove decisively that the apostles officially warranted all the books of the NT and withheld their certification from books that were excluded.

Other criteria used by early Christians were antiquity, public lection (the books read in worship), and orthodoxy of content.[21] But these criteria are also insufficient to *prove* that any book belongs in the canon, or to disprove claims to canonicity on behalf of other books.

Nor should we rest our conclusion on the testimony of the church alone, and certainly not on the testimony of a particular denomination, as in the Roman Catholic view of the matter. The Roman church has claimed that the authority of the canon rests on their pronouncement. But: (1) The church's conviction on this matter, unanimous since A.D. 367, precedes any statement by a Roman Catholic pope or council. (2) As we have seen, God intends to rule his church by a Book, not a church authority. So the authority of the church rests on the authority of the canon, not the other way around.

We should, however, join with the church of all ages (the early church and all Christian denominations since then) in the presupposition that God intended the new covenant in Christ to be attested in writing, and that the apostles were charged with bringing the written Word, as well as the oral word, before the world. Nor can we doubt that God's intention to provide such written revelation was successful. Thus does Scripture attest itself, together with the witness of the Holy Spirit. Our assurance that these books are canon, like our assurance of the divine voice and of prophecy, is supernatural. So we can be sure that the canon of twenty-seven NT books, now universally accepted in the church, is God's personal word to us today.

Is the canon "closed," or should we expect God to add more books to the canon in our time and in the future? In one sense, the canon is always closed. God forbids

---

21. Martin Luther questioned the canonicity of James, because he thought it did not set forth a clear doctrine of justification by faith alone. In this judgment, he was using a doctrinal standard to determine which books belonged in the canon. He actually held a very high view of Scripture. He questioned James precisely because he didn't think James met the very high standards he assigned to the Word of God. But the church as a whole, in all branches, has disagreed with Luther on this matter: James's teaching is indeed consistent with Paul's doctrine of justification. Like Paul, James teaches that we are saved only by a faith that is living and active (cf. Paul in Gal. 5:6). The church has agreed that the books of the canon agree with one another in doctrine. Luther's example illustrates the danger of trying to determine the canonicity of a book by applying doctrinal tests alone, and applying them in an individualistic way, without corroboration from the community. The case of James requires some hard exegetical thinking on which faithful scholars can disagree. Consistency of doctrine with other canonical books is a legitimate criterion, however, when it is used as one among others. God's written words must be in agreement with one another. But agreement and disagreement for this purpose requires discernment and corporate consensus, given by the Spirit of God.

people to add to or subtract from it (Deut. 4:2; 12:32; cf. Prov. 30:6; Rev. 22:18–19). Jesus upbraided the Pharisees for putting their traditions on a par with Scripture and therefore making "void the word of God" (Matt. 15:6). We are to be satisfied with what God has given us, and not long for more. In every age, God has given his people all the written words we need to live faithfully before him.

Nevertheless, God himself has added to the canon, as we have seen. Moses added the Deuteronomic revelation to the original Decalogue. God accepted that revelation as worthy to be placed beside the Decalogue in the Most Holy Place. Joshua added his words to those of Moses. God added the Prophets and Writings to the Law, and the NT to the OT. Of course, God has the freedom to do this, though he forbids it to any mere man.

God adds revelation as needs for it arise in history. The revelation made to Adam would not have been sufficient for Noah, since he had to prepare for the flood. The revelation made to Noah would not have been sufficient for Abraham, to define God's covenant with him. And the OT, though sufficient to meet the challenges of the NT church after Paul's demise (2 Tim. 3:17), was not sufficient to tell the whole story of Jesus.

The NT teaches, however, that with the coming of Christ, with his atonement, resurrection, and ascension, and the coming of the Spirit at Pentecost, redemptive history has reached a watershed. The work of Christ is final, in a way that the work of Abraham and Moses are not. In Christ, God has spoken (past tense, Heb. 1:2) a final word to us, attested (also past tense, Heb. 2:2) by Jesus' original hearers. As the redemptive work of Christ is once for all, so the word of Christ and the apostles is once for all. For God to add more books to the canon would be like his adding something to the work of Christ—something that Scripture teaches cannot be done.

So the canon is closed today, not only in the sense that human beings dare not add to it, but also in the sense that God himself will not add to it. The closing of the canon does not, however, put an end to revelation in general. God still communicates with us in general revelation, in the Spirit's work of writing the Word on our heart, and of course in Scripture itself. The writing of Scripture is once for all, but God continues to speak to us *through* Scripture day by day.[22]

Key Terms

Divine voice
Word through prophets and apostles
Written Word
Tradition (good and bad senses)
Generations
Book of the generations
Covenant document
Suzerainty treaty

---

22. Compare on these matters my discussion of the sufficiency of Scripture in chapter 26. There I discuss the distinction made here at greater length.

Law
Prophets
Scripture
Holy Scripture
Oracles of God
Theopneustos
Canon
Muratorian Fragment
Irenaeus

Study Questions

1. Frame says that the written Word has the same authority as the divine voice and the word through prophets and apostles. Examine his argument.

2. Describe Karl Barth's view of the impermanence of the Word of God. Is his argument sound? What does Scripture itself say on this subject?

3. What, if anything, does the book of Genesis tell us about God's revelatory intentions? Cite texts.

4. Is the Decalogue a suzerainty treaty? What does the treaty model tell us about the nature of God's revelation in Israel?

5. Is the wisdom literature an exception to the general biblical doctrine of verbal revelation? Compare the two.

6. Cite some texts indicating the kind of respect that OT writers had for the written Word of God. How do these texts bear on the broader question of the authority of verbal revelation?

7. Reply to someone who says that the idea of a written Word of God is a "modern, fundamentalist idea."

8. Cite some passages indicating Jesus' view of the OT. Evaluate the significance of these.

9. Expound 2 Timothy 3:16–17 and 2 Peter 1:19–21 in the context of the two letters.

10. In regard to the inspiration of the NT, consider (1) the parallel between OT and NT as covenants of God, (2) our need for Jesus' words, (3) specific texts indicating the authoritative nature of written words during the NT period.

11. "The problem with much current literature on the canon is that it does not take account of God's expressed intentions." Explain; evaluate.

12. Present the case for the Protestant canon of the OT and NT books.

13. Is the canon closed? Discuss.

Memory Verses

Ex. 31:18: And he gave to Moses, when he had finished speaking with him on Mount Sinai, the two tablets of the testimony, tablets of stone, written with the finger of God.

Deut. 32:46: He said to them, "Take to heart all the words by which I am warning you today, that you may command them to your children, that they may be careful to do all the words of this law. For it is no empty word for you, but your very life, and by this word you shall live long in the land that you are going over the Jordan to possess."

Josh. 1:7–8: Only be strong and very courageous, being careful to do according to all the law that Moses my servant commanded you. Do not turn from it to the right hand or to the left, that you may have good success wherever you go. This Book of the Law shall not depart from your mouth, but you shall meditate on it day and night, so that you may be careful to do according to all that is written in it. For then you will make your way prosperous, and then you will have good success.

Ps. 19:7–11: The law of the LORD is perfect,
     reviving the soul;
the testimony of the LORD is sure,
     making wise the simple;
the precepts of the LORD are right,
     rejoicing the heart;
the commandment of the LORD is pure,
     enlightening the eyes;
the fear of the LORD is clean,
     enduring forever;
the rules of the LORD are true,
     and righteous altogether.
More to be desired are they than gold,
     even much fine gold;
sweeter also than honey
     and drippings of the honeycomb.
Moreover, by them is your servant warned;
     in keeping them there is great reward.

Matt. 5:17–19: Do not think that I have come to abolish the Law or the Prophets; I have not come to abolish them but to fulfill them. For truly, I say to you, until heaven and earth pass away, not an iota, not a dot, will pass from the Law until all is accomplished. Therefore whoever relaxes one of the least of these commandments and teaches others to do the same will be called least in the kingdom of heaven, but whoever does them and teaches them will be called great in the kingdom of heaven.

1 Cor. 14:37–38: If anyone thinks that he is a prophet, or spiritual, he should acknowledge that the things I am writing to you are a command of the Lord. If anyone does not recognize this, he is not recognized.

2 Tim. 3:15–17: From childhood you have been acquainted with the sacred writings, which are able to make you wise for salvation through faith in Christ Jesus. All Scripture is breathed out by God and profitable for teaching, for reproof, for correction, and for training in righteousness, that the man of God may be competent, equipped for every good work.

2 Peter 1:19–21: And we have something more sure, the prophetic word, to which you will do well to pay attention as to a lamp shining in a dark place, until the day dawns and the morning star rises in your hearts, knowing this first of all, that no prophecy of Scripture comes from someone's own interpretation. For no prophecy was ever produced by the will of man, but men spoke from God as they were carried along by the Holy Spirit.

Resources for Further Study

Hill, Charles E. *Who Chose the Gospels? Probing the Great Gospel Conspiracy.* London: Oxford University Press, 2012.

Kline, Meredith G. *The Structure of Biblical Authority.* Grand Rapids: Eerdmans, 1972.

Kruger, Michael. *Canon Revisited: Establishing the Origins and Authority of the NT Books.* Wheaton, IL: Crossway, 2012.

Warfield, B. B. "The Terms 'Scripture' and 'Scriptures' as Employed in the New Testament." In *The Inspiration and Authority of the Bible.* Grand Rapids: Baker, 1960. See also other important articles in the same volume: "God-Inspired Scripture," "The Oracles of God," "It Says . . . Scripture Says . . . God Says."

CHAPTER 26

THE NATURE OF SCRIPTURE

IN CHAPTER 25, I DISCUSSED the development through redemptive history of a group of books identified as the written Word of God. That Word is God's very speech: no less so than the divine voice itself or the spoken words of prophets and apostles. This is Scripture's testimony about itself. And it has led the church to confess certain things about Scripture: that it is inspired, inerrant, clear, sufficient, necessary, comprehensive, and sufficient. In this chapter, I will expound these concepts.

These concepts are implications of the lordship attributes of God himself: his control, authority, and presence. For in his written Word as in all the other forms of his word, he addresses us as Lord. As we have seen, Scripture partakes in the controlling power of God's word, "the power of God for salvation" (Rom. 1:16). Scripture also speaks with God's ultimate authority. This means that it imposes ultimate obligations on its hearers and readers—obligations that we cannot avoid. It gives us information we must believe, commands we must obey, promises we must embrace, questions we must answer, and so forth. And Scripture is a temple in which God himself draws near to us (Deut. 30:11–14; Rom. 10:5–10) in all his holiness (2 Tim. 3:15).

The church's traditional descriptions of Scripture follow from the fact that Scripture is the Word of the Lord himself and therefore a bearer of God's lordship attributes. Let us now consider the traditional descriptions one by one, in this light.

Inspiration

The term *inspiration* is found only once in English translations of Scripture, in 2 Timothy 3:16. The KJV there translates the Greek *theopneustos* "given by inspiration of God." The ESV, however, prefers a literal rendering of the Greek, "breathed out by God":

> All Scripture is breathed out by God and profitable for teaching, for reproof, for correction, and for training in righteousness,

In chapter 25, I argued that to breathe out words is to speak; so *theopneustos* means that God actually *spoke* the words of Scripture. Inspiration, then, means that God takes words of human beings and makes them his own. Hence my definition: inspiration is a divine act creating an identity between a divine word and a human word.

What role, then, do the human writers play in regard to Scripture? Scripture itself does not say much about the actual process by which God inspires human words. It has been tempting to think that God's relationship to the biblical writers was like a boss giving "dictation" to his secretary. Some older writers, including John Calvin,[1] have spoken favorably of divine dictation, and others have used mechanistic analogies, such as Athenagoras's illustration: God is like the flute player, and the prophets were like flutes.[2] One can agree that dictation and flute-playing are meaningful *analogies* of the relation between God and the human authors of Scripture, however, without accepting these as literal *analyses* of inspiration.

Most theologians have rejected the dictation theory of inspiration, but in rejecting it some have shown too much zeal. In fact, there are some instances of literal dictation, as when God dictated the words of the law to Moses (Ex. 34:27; cf. Jer. 36:4; Rev. 2–3). Theologians have sometimes waxed eloquent to the effect that dictation degrades the humanity of the person receiving it. But the work of a secretary is in fact a noble calling. Think of Paul's "amanuenses," such as Tertius in Romans 16:22. To be God's secretary must be a wonderful thing indeed. Speaking for myself, I would consider it a transcendent privilege to receive dictation from God.

But of course, dictation is rare in Scripture. There is no record of Joshua, Samuel, David, Luke, or even Paul receiving literal dictation from the Lord. The regular pattern, rather, is that God appointed the biblical writers to be prophets, apostles, or associates of the apostles, and those writers wrote what they chose to write. In their writing, their individual human qualities appear vividly. David writes in a very different way from Moses. Luke's writing is very different in style from that of John, or of Paul. But as we have seen, all of these very different writers were chosen by God to convey his personal word to the world.

The result of their writing is nothing less than the Word of God, the personal word of God to us. It is *like* dictation, because what Luke writes is exactly what God wants us to hear. It is *like* mechanical inspiration, because God is in full control of the process. But how *unlike* mechanical dictation it is! God's dealings with Luke, for example, are person to person, as are all of God's other dealings with human beings. God uses Luke's gifts as a historian and as a physician, his careful accuracy, and his association with Paul to add distinctive elements to Luke's gospel and the book of Acts. He uses Luke's intellect and style to convey the truth with the nuance that he desires. God also uses the very different endowments of John and of Paul to present different perspectives on the gospel of Christ.

Abraham Kuyper and Herman Bavinck used the term *organic inspiration* to distinguish this process from dictation or mechanical inspiration. In organic inspiration,

1. *Commentary on 2 Timothy*, at 2 Tim. 3:16.
2. In Athenagoras, *Plea on Behalf of Christians*.

the diversities among the human writers are not barriers for God to overcome, but the means by which he brings us his words. Because the writers are diverse in their language, style, culture, education, interests, and abilities, God speaks through them multiperspectivally, to give us many different aspects of the truth.

Remember that God's word is not *merely* propositional. God's purpose is not merely to convey information to us, though he certainly does that. His purpose is to do for us all that can be done by language. He means to convey not only information, but tone, emotion, perspective. He means to convey his love to us, along with the sternness of his justice. Human language is rich in this way, conveying a wide variety of content. God's language is all the richer. And to communicate it, he employs a wide variety of writers with a rich diversity of personality and experience.

And the final result is exactly what he wanted to say to us. Just *like* dictation or mechanical inspiration, but with vast riches of meaning. What an amazing treasure is the written Word of God.

I have defined *inspiration* as a divine act creating an identity between a divine word and a human word. To describe the conformity of the text to God's intention, theologians have also used other technical terms. *Plenary* inspiration simply means that *everything* in Scripture is God's Word. To say this is merely to say that the entire canon is God's Word, as we have already seen. If the Bible is plenarily inspired, we may not pick and choose within the Scriptures, regarding one part as God's Word and another part as merely human.

Verbal inspiration means that the *words* of Scripture, not only the ideas of the biblical writers, are God's Word. In the light of our discussion in this book, that should be obvious. God's intention is to speak personal *words* to human beings. He has identified those words with the canonical text. We recall Peter's question, "Lord, to whom shall we go? You have the words of eternal life" (John 6:68) The emphasis on the *words* of God, Christ, and the apostles is pervasive in the NT (see Matt. 7:24–28; 24:35; Mark 8:38; 13:31; John 3:34; 5:47; 6:63; 8:47; 14:10, 24; 17:8; Acts 15:15; 1 Cor. 2:13; 1 Tim. 4:6; 6:3; 2 Tim. 1:13; 2 Peter 3:2; Jude 17; Rev. 1:3; 19:9; 21:5; 22:6–10, 18–19). In the singular, *word* can sometimes be read as designating thoughts or ideas apart from their formulation in words and sentences; but the plural, *words*, cannot be.

Our whole discussion since chapter 23 has underscored the point that God's intention is to give us *words*, personal words, not just thoughts or ideas. The divine voice, as on Mount Sinai, spoke words in the hearing of Israel. So did the voice of Jesus in his earthly ministry. So did the prophets and apostles. And so did the text of God's written Word, from covenant document to complete canon. At no point in this redemptive history is God content to give thoughts or ideas to his spokesmen, without giving them words in which to express those thoughts. Rather, he assigns them the role of speaking and writing his words.

To say that inspiration is restricted to *thoughts* or *ideas* is to give the doctrine of inspiration a very intellectualist cast. (Normally, liberals charge conservatives with intellectualist views of inspiration, but the shoe is on the other foot.) *Thought*-inspiration suggests the notion that God reveals to the writers a set of *concepts*. But as we have seen,

God wants to reveal to us a wide variety of things: not only propositions or concepts, but events, promises, feelings, tone, and the like. These don't fit very well into the notion of God's revealing *ideas*, but they fit very well into the revelation of *words*, for words (not ideas) are capable of communicating in all these ways.

Therefore, it should not be surprising that the only time we find the word *inspiration* in the English Bible (2 Tim. 3:16 KJV), it refers to the written Word—not to the ideas of prophets and apostles, not even to their oral speech, and not to the biblical writers as such, but to the very *text* of Scripture. Now, it is not wrong to ascribe inspiration to the prophets and to the writers of Scripture. The NT frequently refers to the Holy Spirit as governing the words of prophets and apostles: Matt. 10:20; 22:43; Acts 1:16; many other texts (see chapters 15, 20). There is no reason why we should not describe this influence of the Spirit as *inspiration*, using the same definition as above. But we should never say, as some have, that inspiration properly pertains to persons rather than to written texts. In Scripture, the Spirit inspires not only prophets, apostles, and biblical writers, but also *texts*. Indeed, the Spirit inspires prophets and others for the purpose of inspiring their *words*, words that regularly become texts. As we have seen, Jesus and the apostles regard the texts of the OT as fully authoritative, just as authoritative as God's direct voice. The text has no less authority than the divine voice itself, or than the prophets and apostles.

Because inspiration is verbal, it is also, often, textual. You can't put an idea or a thought exhaustively on paper, but you can put a *word* on paper. Inspiration is of words, whether spoken orally or put on a material medium (stone tablets, parchment, paper, digital media, etc.). So there is no reason to deny that God's personal words take written form in the canonical books that he has given to us.

Inerrancy, Infallibility[3]

Definitions

The terms *infallibility* and *inerrancy* introduce us to one of the most fiercely debated subjects in theology today.

It is important for us first to adopt responsible definitions of these terms to facilitate communication. *Inerrant* means simply "freedom from error or untruths."[4] *Infallible* means "incapable of erring."[5]

Some theologians have adopted different, and sometimes irresponsible, definitions of these terms, such as James Orr's definition of *inerrancy*: "hard and fast literality in

---

3. In *DWG* I present at this point in the argument (145–62) some observations on the "content" of Scripture. In the present book, however, I summarize the content of Scripture in chapters 4–6, from three perspectives (covenant, kingdom of God, and family of God). The accounts in the two books supplement one another. In *DWG*, 163–66, I respond to the discussion among the Dutch Reformed on the "relation of the authority of the Bible to its content." I reply that Scripture is authoritative because it is God's Word, not because of its particular content. But its content legitimately influences us to *receive* it as the supreme authority over our lives.

4. *The American Heritage College Dictionary*, 3rd ed. (Boston and New York: Houghton Mifflin, 2000), 695.

5. Ibid.

minute matters of historical, geographical, and scientific detail."[6] Some other theologians have thought that *infallible* is a weaker term than *inerrant*, but on the dictionary definition above, *infallible* is the stronger term. *Inerrant* means that a text has no errors; *infallible* means that it is *impossible* for the text to err. Of course, it is sometimes legitimate in theology to create new terms, or new definitions of older terms. But one should do this only to facilitate communication, not to obscure issues.

To put it more positively, *inerrant* simply means "true" in the propositional sense that I discussed in chapter 23. I could wish we could do away with both *infallible* and *inerrant* and simply say as Jesus does in John 17:17 that God's Word is truth. Unfortunately, theologians tend to want to turn *truth* into some big theological construction that has little to do with commonsense propositional correctness. So we must use other terms, such as *reliable, correct, accurate*—and, yes, *infallible* and *inerrant*—to say what we need to say.

Biblical Basis

In the dictionary senses, Scripture is both inerrant and infallible. Given our previous argument that Scripture is the Word of God and that in Scripture God speaks as Lord, it is inconceivable that it should contain error. Error comes from one of two sources: deceit or mistake. God never deceives (Num. 23:19; 2 Tim. 2:13; Titus 1:2; Heb. 6:18), and he is never mistaken (Ps. 33:13–15; Heb. 4:12–13). Since Scripture is his Word, his speech to us, it contains no errors. It is inerrant.

If anyone is unsatisfied with this deductive argument, we can get the same result by citing individual passages that say God's word is true, or truth. His word is the word of truth (Ps. 119:43, 160). His law is true (Ps. 119:142, 151). Jesus prays for his disciples, "Sanctify them in the truth; your word is truth" (John 17:17). Paul says:

> Let God be true though every one were a liar, as it is written,
>
> "That you may be justified in your words,
>   and prevail when you are judged." (Rom. 3:4, quoting Ps. 51:4)

Think as we have before of a personal conversation between you and God. If there is any disagreement between his words and our own ideas, his must prevail. And if we are so arrogant as to judge what he says, he must prevail in that judgment. One who takes this posture before God should not have any difficulty saying that the Bible is inerrant and infallible, in the senses defined above.

Inerrancy and Precision

The word *inerrancy* does have a certain disadvantage, however, suggested by Orr's rather extreme distortion of its lexical meaning. The word has come to suggest to many

---

6. James Orr, *Revelation and Inspiration* (New York: Scribner's, 1910; repr., Grand Rapids: Baker, 1969), 199.

the idea of precision, rather than its lexical meaning of mere truth. Now, *precision* and *truth* are not synonyms, though they do overlap in meaning. A certain amount of precision is often required for truth, but that amount varies from one context to another. In mathematics and science, truth often requires considerable precision. If a student says that 6 + 5 = 10, he has not told the truth. He has committed an error. If a scientist makes a measurement varying by .0004 cm of an actual length, he may describe that as an *error*, as in the phrase *margin of error*.

But outside of science and mathematics, truth and precision are often much more distinct. If you ask someone's age, the person's conventional response (at least if the questioner is entitled to such information!) is to tell how old he was on his most recent birthday. But this is, of course, imprecise. It would be more precise to tell one's age down to the day, hour, minute, and second.[7] But would that convey more *truth*? And if one fails to give that much precision, has he made an error? I think not, as we use the terms *truth* and *error* in ordinary language. If someone seeks to tell his age down to the second, we usually say that he has told us more than we want to know. The question "What is your age?" does not demand that level of precision. Indeed, when someone gives excess information in an attempt to be more precise, he actually frustrates the process of communication, hindering rather than communicating truth. He buries his real age under a torrent of irrelevant words.

Similarly when I stand before a class and a student asks me how large a textbook is. Say that I reply, "400 pages," but the actual length is 398. Have I committed an error, or told the truth? I think the latter, for the following reasons: (1) In context, nobody expects more precision than I gave in my answer. I met all the legitimate demands of the questioner. (2) "400," in this example, actually conveyed more truth than "398" would have. "398" most likely would have left the student with the impression of some number around 300, but "400" presented the size of the book more accurately.[8]

So the relation between precision and error is more complicated than many writers suggest. "What is an error?" seems like a very straightforward question, as though errors were always perfectly easy to identify once we know the facts. But actually, identifying an error requires some understanding of the linguistic context, and that in turn requires an understanding of the cultural context.[9] A child who says in his math class that 6 + 5 = 10 may not expect the same tolerance as a person who gives a rough estimate of his age or a professor who exaggerates the size of a book by two pages.

7. Even that would be somewhat imprecise. What of milleseconds and nanoseconds? Of course, when one tries to give his age that precisely, he finds that his age has changed before he gets the words out of his mouth! So in this case, absolute precision is impossible *in principle*.

8. One notes that grocery and department stores often take advantage of this psychological quirk in their shoppers, by pricing goods at $3.98, for example, rather than $4.00. The first digit of the number makes a far greater impression than the others. To encourage shoppers to buy, the stores keep that digit as low as possible. It may be too much to call this practice deception, but the plausibility of that charge indicates the extent to which precision can actually detract from truth.

9. In debates about Scripture, those who oppose inerrancy often charge those who defend it with ignorance of culture and the dynamics of language. In this case, however, the shoe is clearly on the other foot.

We should always remember that Scripture is, for the most part,[10] ordinary language rather than technical language.[11] Certainly it is not of the modern scientific genre. In Scripture, God intends to speak to everybody. To do that most efficiently, he (through the human writers) engages in all the shortcuts that we commonly use among ourselves to facilitate conversation: imprecisions, metaphors, hyperbole, and parables, to name a few. Not all of these convey *literal* truth, or truth with a precision expected in specialized contexts; but they all convey truth, and in the Bible there is no reason to charge them with error.

Inerrancy, therefore, means that the Bible is true, not that it is maximally precise. To the extent that precision is necessary for truth, the Bible is sufficiently precise. But it does not always have the amount of precision that some readers demand of it. It has a level of precision sufficient for its own purposes, not for the purposes for which some readers might employ it.

"Qualifications" of Inerrancy

Now, many writers have enumerated what are sometimes called qualifications of inerrancy: inerrancy is compatible with unrefined grammar, nonchronological narrative, round numbers, imprecise quotations, prescientific phenomenalistic description (e.g., "the sun rose"), use of figures and symbols, imprecise descriptions (as Mark 1:5, which says that everyone from Judea and Jerusalem went to hear John the Baptist). I agree with these points, but I do not describe them as "qualifications" of inerrancy. These are merely applications of the basic meaning of inerrancy: that it asserts truth, not precision. Inerrant language, in other words, is language that makes good on its own claims, not on claims that are made for it by thoughtless readers.

Take "unrefined grammar" as an example. In natural languages, there are many variations in grammar, style, and accent. Grammarians tend to elevate one group of variations as a standard. So the predominant speech in Berlin is considered to be "good German." The predominant speech of Amsterdam is "good Dutch," and so on.[12] There may be some value in this as a means of encouraging uniformity of language in public writing and speech. But it is somewhat arbitrary. We need to remember that it comes from human grammarians, not from divine revelation. There is no divine norm that requires us to speak in what grammarians may describe as "good" language. God never tells us to speak the language of the academic elite, or to disparage variations from that language as "errors."

---

10. I qualify this statement merely out of abstract scholarly caution, not because I have any actual exceptions in mind.

11. It is interesting that liberals often complain that conservatives read the Bible as a "textbook of science," imagining it to address the technical issues of modern life. Sometimes that sort of criticism is fair. But both parties should recognize that it is the genius of the inerrantist position to see the Bible as *ordinary* language, subject to *ordinary*, not technical, standards of truth. So here, as in the "ignorance of culture" charge mentioned in footnote 9, the shoe is on the other foot. For another example of anti-inerrantists' using the Bible as a "textbook of science," see the chapter "Bible Problems" in *DWG*, 183–200.

12. One suspects, however, that such "good speech" is often determined by the speech on university campuses, where the grammarians themselves feel most at home.

The NT itself is written not in the literary Greek of Thucydides and Plato, but in the *koiné*, the language of the people. Within the NT, some writers, such as Luke and the writer to the Hebrews, excel others in the impressiveness of their literary style. But Scripture never claims to be written in the most impressive language, or even in perfect grammar. What it claims is *truth*. And truth can be expressed in any dialect. In English, "I ain't goin'" is considered less proper than "I am not going." But the meaning of both phrases is clear. They say the same thing, and they can both express truth.

People sometimes think that if Scripture is the Word of God, it must be written in the most elevated language, language worthy of God. Can we imagine God speaking anything less than the King's English? But that is a misunderstanding. God's intent is to speak to ordinary people. He "accommodates," as Calvin put it; he "lisps" to us.[13] So he speaks both in the elevated language of Luke the physician and in the simpler language of the fisherman Peter. If they or anyone uses poor grammar in the judgment of modern linguists, that fact has no bearing on the Bible's inerrancy.

Consider nonchronological narrative. In modern historical writing, we assume that the author is portraying events in chronological order, unless he says otherwise, or unless there is some kind of novelistic intent. But: (1) The historical portions of Scripture (chiefly Genesis-Esther and the four Gospels) are not academic histories in the modern sense. Their purpose is to narrate the acts of God to redeem his people. (2) The Bible makes no *claim* to tell all these events in a precise chronological order. Sometimes there is such a claim for a specific group of events: for example, in Matthew 8:1, we read, "When [Jesus] came down from the mountain, great crowds followed him." This passage does make the claim that Jesus taught on the mountain, and that the crowds followed him afterward. But more often there is no such claim.

Nor does Scripture usually claim that its accounts of people's words are verbatim.[14] In ordinary language we often paraphrase the words of a speaker. Usually people understand that we are doing that, so that we don't need to claim explicitly that our quotation is imprecise. Of course, in scholarly articles, quotations of the words of others require quotation marks or indentation, footnoting, and/or bibliographical documentation. These indications constitute, among other things, an affirmation that our quotation is precise. But these conventions did not exist in the biblical period. In Scripture, there are no quotation marks; there is no apparatus for formal documentation. When Jesus quotes Moses, usually there is no reason to expect that his quotation will be precise. In ordinary language it is perfectly proper to give the gist of someone's words without precision, or even to alter the quotation to bring out something that might otherwise be ignored. And Scripture, again, is ordinary language.

---

13. Accommodation does not mean, as some have claimed, that God speaks error to us. Rather, it means that he speaks truth in such a way that we can understand it, insofar as it can be understood by human beings. Theologians often compare divine accommodation to a parent's accommodation to his young children. But a wise parent, while choosing simple language to use with his children, does not lie to them.

14. One exception is Galatians 3:16, in which Paul makes an interpretative point depending on the singular form of "seed" (ESV "offspring") in Genesis 22:18.

I conclude that Scripture is inerrant because the personal word of God cannot be anything other than true. When he gives us propositional information, and he certainly does, that information is reliable, though expressed in ordinary, not technical, language. The written Word, further, is just as inerrant as the oral message of the prophets and apostles. And their word is just as inerrant as the divine voice itself.[15]

Phenomena and Purpose

There are two major objections to the view that Scripture is inerrant. The first is that this view misunderstands the *purpose* of Scripture. The second is that it is inconsistent with the *phenomena* of Scripture.

Concerning Scripture's purpose, many have argued that Scripture is written to tell us of salvation, not about matters of history, geography, science, and so on. I have commented on this issue in chapters 4–6 and will consider it also in connection with the comprehensiveness and sufficiency of Scripture (later in this chapter). In summary, several points will help us to see the inadequacy of this view:

1. Scripture does not distinguish in any general way between the sacred and the secular, between matters of salvation and mere worldly matters.

2. Scripture speaks not only of salvation, but also of the nature of God, creation, and providence as the presuppositions of salvation. But these deal with everything in the world and with all areas of human life. So Scripture makes assertions not only about salvation narrowly considered, but about the nature of the universe.

3. The salvation that Scripture talks about is a comprehensive renewal of human life, extending to every aspect of human life and thought. So no area of human life is beyond the concern of Scripture.

4. The salvation that Scripture speaks of took place in the space-time world. The atonement and resurrection of Jesus are events of real history, which occurred in a real time and place. Our understanding of history, geography, and science must be consistent with this narrative, and with its OT prehistory.

5. Scripture is God's personal word to us. Confronted by that personal word, it is not our place to pick and choose the areas concerning which he may address us authoritatively. After he speaks to us, we may discern, in a general way, the subject matter that he chose to address. But that understanding does not give us the right to limit his speech to that subject matter or to assume that every other word of God must deal with the same subject.

For these reasons, it is not possible to draw a sharp line between one area (matters of salvation) about which Scripture speaks inerrantly and another area (the secular world) in regard to which it may err.

The other objection concerns the *phenomena* of Scripture. Phenomena are appearances, the way things look to us. Immanuel Kant distinguished between the phenomena, appearances, and the *noumena*, the world as it really is, apart from our experience. Now, when many

15. For critical interaction with other views of biblical inerrancy within evangelicalism, see my reviews of books by Peter Enns, N. T. Wright, and Andrew McGowan, Appendices J, K, and L of *DWG*.

readers look at Scripture, it *appears* to them to contain errors. So many writers have urged that we should not derive our doctrine of Scripture merely from its teachings about itself (as I have done in this discussion), but that we should take into account the phenomena. And if we take the phenomena seriously, they tell us, we will not be able to conclude that Scripture is inerrant. Developing the doctrine of Scripture from its phenomena is sometimes called an *inductive* approach, as opposed to the *deductive* approach presented earlier in this chapter, which derives inerrancy as a conclusion from Scripture's teaching about itself.

I believe the inductive method, so described, is a faulty method for determining the character of Scripture. Of course, Scripture contains "difficulties," problems, apparent errors, and we should not ignore them. But what role should these play in our formulation of the *doctrine* of Scripture? It is important to remember that *all* doctrines of the Christian faith are beset by problems. The doctrine of God's sovereignty, for example, seems in the view of many readers to conflict with the responsibility of human beings, and that apparent contradiction has led to many theological battles. The doctrine of the Trinity says that God is both three and one, and the relation between his threeness and his oneness is not easy to put into words. When speaking of Christ, we face the paradox that he is both God and man, both eternal and temporal, both omniscient and limited in his knowledge. Would anyone argue that because of these problems we should not confess that God is sovereign, that man is responsible, that God is three and one, that Jesus is divine and human?

The very nature of Christian faith is to believe God's word *despite* the existence of unresolved difficulties. When God told Abraham that he and his wife Sarah would have a child, that promise was beset by difficulty. How could a man father a child when he was over a hundred? How could a woman bear a child when she was far past the age of childbearing? From a human point of view (even in the time of Abraham), the fulfillment of such a promise seemed highly improbable. But Romans 4:19–21 says this:

> He did not weaken in faith when he considered his own body, which was as good as dead (since he was about a hundred years old), or when he considered the barrenness of Sarah's womb. No distrust made him waver concerning the promise of God, but he grew strong in his faith as he gave glory to God, fully convinced that God was able to do what he had promised.

Abraham did not weigh God's word over against the problems and conclude that God's promise could not be fulfilled. Nor did he withhold judgment, waiting for the problems to be solved before he would make a commitment. Nor did he even think that the problems decreased the *probability* of God's word being fulfilled. He did not distrust at all, despite the difficulties. He grew strong in faith and gave glory to God. He was "fully convinced." And Romans 4:22 continues, "That is why his faith was 'counted to him as righteousness.'" Paul tells us about Abraham's faith as a model for our own.[16] We, too, ought to trust God's promise, despite the difficulties.

---

16. Abraham's faith was not perfect, as is evident in Genesis 12:10–20; 16:1–4; and 20:1–18. But he did not doubt God's promise that he and Sarah would have a son, or that God would preserve the son's life (22:1–19).

So the proper method in theology is not to withhold judgment until the problems are solved. It is rather to believe God's personal word, despite the problems. We will never solve all the problems in this life. So we live by faith, not by sight. That must also be our attitude when we seek to formulate the doctrine of Scripture. When we say that Scripture is inerrant, we encounter many problems. But Scripture's claim to inerrancy is entirely clear; it is not in doubt. It is God's personal word to us. We must believe it, despite what we may be tempted to believe through an inductive examination of the phenomena.

The situation would be different if Scripture's claim were itself uncertain. If Scripture's claim to be the Word of God were itself problematic, and then we discovered from the phenomena that the biblical text is full of unsolved problems, we might well reconsider our initial assumption. But as we have seen, no one can fairly doubt that Scripture *claims* to be God's written Word. On nearly every page of Scripture, we learn that God speaks personal words to his people, words of highest authority, words that we need for our eternal salvation and our life here on earth. And we learn that those words take written form, for God intends to rule his church by means of a Book. Given the pervasiveness of this biblical teaching, we cannot question it on the basis of problems found in the phenomena.

This is not to say at all that we should ignore the phenomena, or even that we may do so. To ignore the phenomena would be to ignore the Word itself. God calls us to meditate on his Word (Ps. 1:2) and to live by every word of it (Deut. 8:3; Matt. 4:4). As we enter into a deep study of God's Word, we must investigate the problems. For when we have a problem, that means that our understanding is incomplete. We must think about the problems and solve them if possible, for our own edification and that of those we teach.

In dealing with problems, however, we must not revert to intellectual autonomy, assuming that human reason serves as the final criterion of truth. Rather, we should study the problems in faith, presupposing that God is real and that he has given us his personal words in Scripture. His Word, not our own wisdom, is to be our ultimate standard. That is true of all our activities, so it is certainly true of the study of Scripture itself.

And we must not demand that all problems be solved before we receive Scripture in faith. As we have seen in the case of Abraham, that is not how Christian faith works. In Christian faith, the Word of God determines how we should look at problems.

Once we come to faith, problems look different. Problems test our faith, but they do not carry anywhere near the weight of God's self-witness. That was true for Abraham, even though he had only a few individual encounters with God. We have had far more than that: three thousand years of history in which God has spoken to his people and attested his word (by divine voice, prophetic-apostolic proclamation, and written Word, and of course through his Son Jesus Christ) as true. Those revelations have led to the formation of a Christian way of thinking, a Christian mind. To that mind, attacks on Scripture are never credible because they must overcome a vast weight of God's own testimony.

We have problems with Scripture for two reasons: finitude and sin. Because of our finitude we have problems understanding the vast depths of God's nature and actions:

how he can be both one and three, how he can be eternal and yet enter history, how he can be good and yet permit evil, how he can be sovereign and yet hold us responsible for what we do.

Our finitude also bars us from an exhaustive knowledge of God's world, of the course of nature and history. It is difficult for us to understand cultures such as those described in the Bible, far removed from ours in space and time. It is not easy for us to understand the social workings of tribal and monarchical cultures, the customs underlying biblical stories, the nature of biblical poetry, the ways in which the meaning of texts is affected by literary practices.

When we deal with Bible problems, then, it is important for us to be aware of these limitations, that is, to read humbly. When faced with a problem, it is no dishonor to say, "I don't know how this can be resolved." Scientists do that all the time, when they encounter a phenomenon that seems to run contrary to a theory they believe. When the evidence for the theory is otherwise substantial, the scientist rightly assumes that the phenomenon can *somehow* be reconciled to the theory, even if he doesn't know how that will happen.

The other reason why we have problems with Scripture is sin. Romans 1, as we have seen, tells us that sinners "repress" the truth of God's clear natural revelation, exchanging it for a lie. They do the same with Scripture, until or unless the Spirit causes a radical change in their outlook (Luke 24:25; John 5:37–40; 2 Cor. 3:14). Because of the Spirit, believers have the means to overcome the sinful distortion of Scripture. But we are not sinlessly perfect in this life, and we are subject every day to Satan's temptation. Satan tempts us to unbelief as well as wrong behavior. Indeed, unbelief *is* wrong behavior.

So sometimes believers think like unbelievers. Often believers will ascribe authority to liberal scholarship—scholarship committed, as we have seen, to read the Bible like any human book. Such scholarship regularly assumes that the biblical worldview *cannot* be true: that miracles cannot occur, that predictive prophecy is impossible, that God cannot speak words and sentences to human beings.

The would-be autonomous kind of scholarship is often arrogant in its claims. In the past, such scholars have often spoken of the "assured results of modern scholarship." One does not hear that phrase so much these days; most of these "assured results" have been questioned. But one stands amazed at how easily modern scholars can claim that this portion of a verse in Genesis must have been written by a different author from that one, or that this sentence ascribed to Jesus in the Gospels must have originated in a setting different from that set forth in the Gospels themselves. In reply to Rudolf Bultmann's claim that the personality of Jesus was unimportant to Paul and John, C. S. Lewis, himself a scholar of ancient literature, replies:

> Through what strange process has this learned German gone in order to make himself blind to what all men except him see?[17]

17. C. S. Lewis, "Modern Theology and Biblical Criticism," in *Christian Reflections*, ed. Walter Hooper (Grand Rapids: Eerdmans, 1967), 156.

And then:

> These men ask me to believe that they can read between the lines of the old texts; the
> evidence is their obvious inability to read (in any sense worth discussing) the lines
> themselves. They claim to see fern-seed and can't see an elephant ten yards away in
> broad daylight.[18]

The difference between liberal Bible critics and believing Christians is not merely academic, a difference in point of view; nor is it merely a difference in presupposition (though
it is certainly that). It is a moral difference. The liberal reads the text with an incredibly
exalted view of his own competence to understand ancient cultures and writers in finest
detail. Christians should remember that our faith divides us from the liberal tradition
in the most profound way. We are often tempted to reply to their arrogance with more
arrogance. We should avoid that temptation, by God's grace. Often, as we will see, this
will mean that we respond to Bible problems with an honest "I don't know."[19]

Clarity

I have said that the nature of God's word, including his written Word, reflects God's
lordship attributes: his control, authority, and presence. I have discussed the first two at
length—but in what sense is Scripture a location of the presence of God? Here I focus
on the concept of *clarity* as one of the ways in which God draws near to his people in
Scripture. But we will see that the clarity of Scripture is also a consequence of God's
power and authority. See fig. 26.1.

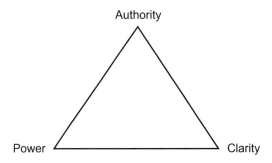

Fig. 26.1. Attributes of Scripture (First Set)

Clarity is also one of the traditional Reformed "attributes" of Scripture, usually listed
as necessity, authority, perspicuity (= clarity), and sufficiency. I will discuss necessity

18. Ibid., 157.
19. *DWG*, chapter 28, discusses a number of specific Bible problems, grouped into general types: theological
problems, ethical problems, factual problems, problems of factual consistency, problems of quotations and references, historical problems, problems of genre, scientific problems, and problems of date, authorship, and setting.

and sufficiency later in this chapter, and I have been discussing authority in various ways through chapters 23–25. So now we will discuss the clarity of Scripture.

The WCF formulates this doctrine as follows at 1.7:

> All things in Scripture are not alike plain in themselves, nor alike clear unto all: yet those things which are necessary to be known, believed, and observed for salvation, are so clearly propounded, and opened in some place of Scripture or other, that not only the learned, but the unlearned, in a due use of the ordinary means, may attain unto a sufficient understanding of them.

This is a carefully nuanced statement, with important qualifications. It is directed against the attempts in the Roman Catholic Church of the time to keep the laity from studying Scripture on their own. The Roman church feared that if laymen were to interpret Scripture for themselves, they would come up with unorthodox, even bizarre, interpretations of it. That fear, as we can now observe, was not groundless.

But Scripture itself (as in Deut. 8:3; Pss. 19:7; 119; Matt. 4:4) says that God's written Word is for everybody. We live by it. The confession, of course, agrees. But the confession's statement does not encourage autonomous or lawless Bible study. It does not make every layman an expert in Scripture. It recognizes that not every part of Scripture is equally clear to everybody. Laymen, indeed all Christians, need to watch their step in studying the Bible. There are mysteries in Scripture beyond anyone's understanding, and there are many things in Scripture that we cannot understand without more knowledge of the languages of Scripture and its cultural background.

So the confession also says that those who would study Scripture should be humble enough to seek help. The kind of Bible study it recommends is not individualistic. One should make "due use of the ordinary means." Those ordinary means include the church's preaching and teaching. That teaching is not, however, as in the Roman church, an inflexible set of conclusions with which all Bible students must agree. Rather, it seeks to guide believers into paths by which we can progress in our knowledge of God, even beyond the levels attained by our teachers.

Prayer and the Holy Spirit are also means available to every Christian in Bible study. Involvement with God himself, the Author of Scripture, draws us toward a greater understanding of the truth. So our understanding of Scripture is not directly proportional to the amount of education we have. It is for "not only the learned, but the unlearned."

A further qualification is that this level of clarity does not apply to everything in Scripture. It pertains to "those things which are necessary to be known, believed, and observed for salvation." Now, in my discussion of inerrancy and elsewhere, I have opposed distinctions between "matters of salvation" and "matters of cosmology, history, and science" in several contexts. I have opposed the idea that Scripture's purpose is redemptive in a narrow sense, so that it is not authoritative on other matters, and I will make similar points in regard to the comprehensiveness and sufficiency of Scripture. I don't think that Scripture's purpose can be defined that narrowly, and given the comprehensive nature of salvation in Scripture, I don't think it is possible to draw a sharp line in Scripture between "matters of salvation" and other matters.

Nevertheless, there is a legitimate distinction to be drawn within Scripture between what a person is required to *know* for salvation and what he is not.[20] Nobody would claim, for example, that a person will go to hell if he does not understand the difference between guilt offerings and trespass offerings in Leviticus. These are certainly "matters of salvation," but they are not matters that one must know in order to be saved. So the confession is not making the sort of distinction that I have been opposing.[21] I would say that everything in Scripture is a "matter of salvation," that is, significantly related to salvation. But a person can be saved even if he does not know or understand some things in the Bible. The clarity of Scripture pertains to those fundamentals that constitute a credible profession of Christ.

Yet my purpose in this book is not primarily to expound confessions, but biblical teaching, granted the considerable overlap between these. Does Scripture itself warrant this doctrine of the clarity of God's written Word?

Clarity and God's Control

I will consider this question in terms of the lordship attributes. First, in relation to God's control: God is fully in control of his communications to human beings. When he intends to communicate with a human being, he is always able to do it successfully. But another name for successful communication is *clarity*. An unclear word is one that does not succeed, that fails to accomplish its purpose. But we know that God's word always accomplishes its purpose (Isa. 55:10–11). Therefore, his word is always clear.

Why, then, do people fail to understand God's word? The ultimate answer is that God did not intend for them to understand. Note again God's commission to Isaiah,

20. Of course, to try to draw this line raises up a great many other issues. I agree with the confession's statement at 10.3 that "elect infants, dying in infancy, are regenerated, and saved by Christ" though they are "uncapable of being outwardly called by the ministry of the Word." It lists as proof texts Luke 18:15; Acts 2:39; and some others that are less to the point. It might also have referred to Luke 1:41, 44, in which the unborn John the Baptist leaps for joy in Elizabeth's womb when she meets Mary, the mother of Jesus. His joy in the presence of Christ indicates regeneration. But what do infants actually *know* about salvation? What do they *believe*? Propositionally, nothing. So in one sense, if we ask what is "necessary to be known, believed, and observed for salvation," the answer is "nothing." But of course, in 1.7 the confession is not thinking about the responsibilities of preborn infants, nor of "other elect persons who are incapable of being outwardly called by the ministry of the Word" (10.3), but of adults of normal intelligence. At 1.7, the confession seems to have in mind the kind of "credible confession" required for church membership, what an adult needs to confess to be recognized as a member of the body of Christ. In this sense (and I think in this sense only), we may distinguish within Scripture some matters that "are necessary to be known, believed, and observed for salvation" and others that are not. Later in this section, I will discuss other ways in which the clarity of Scripture is person-variable.

21. Indeed, as I will argue later, the confession's statement of the sufficiency of Scripture in 1.6 gives to the Bible unlimited scope: it is "the whole counsel of God concerning all things necessary for his own glory, man's salvation, faith and life." Here, Scripture is sufficient for everything.

in 6:9–10. God's word in Isaiah's mouth, oddly enough, brings dullness and a lack of understanding, not complete understanding. Jesus quotes this saying in Matthew 13:14–15 to explain why he speaks in parables. Note also verses 10–13:

> Then the disciples came and said to him, "Why do you speak to them in parables?" And he answered them, "To you it has been given to know the secrets of the kingdom of heaven, but to them it has not been given. For to the one who has, more will be given, and he will have an abundance, but from the one who has not, even what he has will be taken away. This is why I speak to them in parables, because seeing they do not see, and hearing they do not hear, nor do they understand.

Jesus says here that he intentionally speaks in parables, which enlighten the disciples as to the mysteries of the kingdom, but hide those mysteries from those outside the circle.[22] His words are clear to one group, unclear to another. They have exactly the power that he intends them to have. He intends to communicate to one group, so to them his word must be clear. To the other group, he does not intend to fully communicate, so to them the word is not clear.

The clarity of the word, therefore, is selective. It is for some, not all. It is for those with whom God intends to fully communicate.

That selectivity has further dimensions, for even disciples of Jesus do not always find the Scriptures entirely clear. For example, a six-year-old child may believe in Jesus, but have a very rudimentary understanding of Scripture. That, too, is under God's sovereign control. It is God's decision generally to communicate with us through Scripture more and more clearly as we grow in spiritual maturity. So the confession says that not everything in Scripture is equally clear to every Christian.

But "those things which are necessary to be known, believed, and observed for salvation," that knowledge by which we ascertain the authenticity of a person's Christian profession, are known by, or attainable by, all believers. Many have that knowledge by the age of six; others take longer. Few have such knowledge by age one or two. But those who belong to Jesus are able to attain such knowledge (sometimes over a period of years) "in a due use of the ordinary means."

Another way to speak of God's sovereign selectivity in revelation is to refer to the role of the Holy Spirit in bringing understanding and faith to the hearers of the word. I will write in chapter 28 about his "internal testimony," by which he illumines the text of Scripture, persuades us that it is true, and enables us to apply it to the circumstances of our lives. It is the Spirit who sovereignly decides who will understand and who will

22. In general, the dividing line is between believers and unbelievers. But that is imprecise. In Matthew 13, the line is between disciples and nondisciples so far as parables are concerned. But the disciples don't automatically understand everything for the first time. Indeed, they sometimes need to have the parables explained to them, as in Matthew 13:18–23. Among believers, as we will see, there are degrees of understanding. And unbelievers also vary in their understanding, as God sovereignly determines. Natural revelation is "clear" even to unbelievers (Rom. 1:20), though suppressed (see *DKG*, 49–61). And some enemies of God understand special revelation, too—enough to be offended by it. The Pharisees exhibit such knowledge in their response to Jesus' words.

not. I have already made the general argument that our ability to identify the true word of God is supernatural—by the Spirit (chapters 24–25).

Clarity and God's Authority

Second, let us consider the clarity of Scripture in relation to God's lordship attribute of authority. To say that God's Word has authority, as we have seen, is to say that it creates obligations in its hearers: obligations to believe what it says, to do what it commands, to write it on our hearts, and so on. The clarity of God's Word means that we have no excuse for failing to meet those obligations. To say that God's Word is clear is to say that we have no excuse for misunderstanding or disobeying it. So the clarity of Scripture has ethical implications.

In Romans 1:20, the clarity of God's revelation in nature implies that its recipients are "without excuse" for their sinful response. The same is the case with the written Word of God. Jesus says to his Jewish opponents:

> You search the Scriptures because you think that in them you have eternal life; and it is they that bear witness about me, yet you refuse to come to me that you may have life. (John 5:39–40)

The fact that they have studied the Scriptures makes it all the worse that they refuse to come to Jesus. They have no excuse. In Luke 12:47–48, Jesus says:

> And that servant who knew his master's will but did not get ready or act according to his will, will receive a severe beating. But the one who did not know, and did what deserved a beating, will receive a light beating. Everyone to whom much was given, of him much will be required, and from him to whom they entrusted much, they will demand the more.

As in modern civil law, "ignorance of the law is no excuse"—but it is a mitigating circumstance. Of course, Scripture teaches that everyone knows, in general, God's requirements for his life (Rom. 1:18–32), but there are degrees of knowledge, and those who have more knowledge incur greater obligations. So those who have studied the Scriptures ought to be more obedient than others. Of them, more will be required. God has (sovereignly, as we have seen) granted them greater knowledge, and that greater knowledge has taken away their excuses.

So the clarity of Scripture is an ethical doctrine, a doctrine about our responsibilities before God, a doctrine that ought to motivate greater obedience.

The relation of God's authority to the clarity of Scripture illumines further what I have called *selectivity*, that Scripture is not equally clear to all. We can see now that the clarity of Scripture is relative to the responsibilities that God places on each person. When a person is only one year of age, he usually has no conscious knowledge of the content of Scripture, but that accords with the fact that God does not call such children to tasks of conscious discipleship. By two years old, children can usually understand at least "Children, obey your parents" (Eph. 6:1). Their understanding is commensurate with their responsibility. As they grow older, they are able to understand what it means to believe in Jesus, to refrain from stealing, to love others. Later, a child will understand much more, but at each stage his greater understanding will be parallel to a greater level of responsibility.

The six-year-old will not likely understand the sacrificial rituals of Leviticus. But he doesn't have to. God has not given him responsibilities for which a knowledge of that material is a requisite. If he grows up to become an OT scholar, that situation will change.

I conclude this as an important principle: *Scripture is always clear enough for us to carry out our present responsibilities before God.* It is clear enough for a six-year-old to understand what God expects of him. It is also clear enough for a mature theologian to understand what God expects of him. But the clarity of Scripture (as we saw under the lordship attribute of control) is person-relative, person-specific. Scripture is not exhaustively clear to anyone. It is not clear enough to satisfy anyone who merely wants to gain a speculative knowledge of divine things. It is, rather, morally sufficient, practically sufficient, sufficient for each person to know what God desires of him.

Clarity and God's Presence

This emphasis on the personal dimension of Scripture's clarity leads us to relate it to the third lordship attribute, God's personal presence. In Deuteronomy 30:11–14, God through Moses speaks thus to the people of Israel:

> For this commandment that I command you today is not too hard for you, neither is it far off. It is not in heaven, that you should say, "Who will ascend to heaven for us and bring it to us, that we may hear it and do it?" Neither is it beyond the sea, that you should say, "Who will go over the sea for us and bring it to us, that we may hear it and do it?" But the word is very near you. It is in your mouth and in your heart, so that you can do it.

God's word is *near* to the children of Israel, *present* to them. This is literally true, for it is located in the "Book of the Law" (Deut. 30:10), the written document to be placed by the ark of the covenant, God's literal dwelling place. The Levites are to read the law to the people in an assembly every seven years (31:9–13), so that they and their children might hear and obey (cf. 6:6–9). Thus the law is to be written on their hearts (6:6).

Figuratively, too, the word is near. The questions of Deuteronomy 30:12–13—"Who will ascend to heaven?" and "Who will go over the sea?"—assume that the word cannot be appropriated without great efforts, that without strenuous pilgrimage we cannot understand and obey it. God denies this assumption. To Israel, he says, you do understand; you can do it. So the clarity of Scripture is the presence, the closeness of, Scripture.

The apostle Paul makes an interesting Christological application of Deuteronomy 30:11–14 in Romans 10:5–9:

> For Moses writes about the righteousness that is based on the law, that the person who does the commandments shall live by them. But the righteousness based on faith says, "Do not say in your heart, 'Who will ascend into heaven?'" (that is, to bring Christ down) or "'Who will descend into the abyss?'" (that is, to bring Christ up from the dead). But what does it say? "The word is near you, in your mouth and in your heart" (that is, the word of faith that we proclaim); because, if you confess with your mouth that Jesus is Lord and believe in your heart that God raised him from the dead, you will be saved.

Here Paul finds in Deuteronomy 30 something more than the promise of blessing through obedience to law. He notes that in that passage the *presence* of the law points to Christ. Moses' hearers had assumed that the word could not be appropriated without great efforts. But the *nearness* of God's word speaks of grace, not strenuous effort. In Christ, we do not need to ascend to heaven, for he has by grace come down to us. And we don't need to go down to the grave, for Christ has by grace risen from the dead. The nearness of the Word, now, is the nearness of Christ himself in the Word of faith, Paul's gospel. We meet Christ in the gospel, and as we confess and believe him, we are saved.

Here the clarity of the Word is nothing less than the presence of Christ in the Word.

Is Paul distorting the meaning of Deuteronomy 30:11–14? Superficially, it would seem that Moses' words speak of legal obedience, but Paul uses them to speak of grace. But recall that (1) the law itself proclaims the righteousness and grace of Christ (John 5:39–40).[23] And (2) Deuteronomy 30 itself counsels the Israelites to rely not on their own strenuous efforts, but on God's grace in bringing the word near them, most significantly into their hearts.[24]

The lordship attributes, as always, work together. The presence of God in the word is his sovereign choice, and it underscores the word's authority. God draws near in the word so that we can *do* the word (Deut. 30:15–20). The control and authority of God in the word bring his word to people in his covenant presence.

Necessity

In the previous section, I mentioned that necessity and sufficiency were among the "attributes" of Scripture in traditional Reformed theology. I have, however, followed a different pattern by discussing clarity not in the traditional group of four, but as part of a triad representing God's lordship attributes. In that triad, the clarity of Scripture represented God's personal presence.

---

23. Cf. "Preaching Christ from the Decalogue," in *DCL*, 400–401. Note also the message of grace in the historical prologue of the Decalogue, 403–4.

24. I will later discuss the work of the Spirit writing the words of God on our hearts as a form of revelation.

From here to the end of the chapter, I will again modify the traditional list, presenting another triad: the *necessity, comprehensiveness,* and *sufficiency* of Scripture. The second triad focuses on the relationships of Scripture to our lives: Scripture is necessary, comprehensive, and sufficient to deal with the decisions that we must make in our lives. The triad corresponds to the lordship attributes somewhat loosely, but the following summary may be of some use: necessity is a normative expression of God's authority, for it comes as a "must." Comprehensiveness focuses on God's power to control the situations of our lives, and sufficiency represents God's presence: God's Word is all we need, and we need not hunger for any other words. See fig. 26.2.

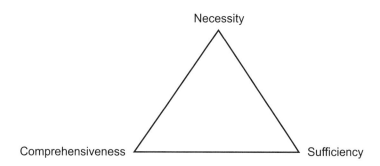

Fig. 26.2. Attributes of Scripture (Second Set)

To say that Scripture is necessary is simply to say that we need it. When Satan tempted Jesus in the wilderness, he taunted him to relieve his hunger by turning stones into bread. Jesus replied by quoting Deuteronomy 8:3: "Man shall not live by bread alone, but by every word that comes from the mouth of God" (Matt. 4:4).[25] Certainly human beings need food. But our need for God's Word is of even greater importance.

Obviously, we need the word of God in a general way. For it was by the word of God that he created all things, including ourselves (Gen. 1; Ps. 33:6, 9; John 1:3), and it is by the word that he upholds our existence continually (Ps. 147:15–18; Heb. 1:3). But Deuteronomy 8:3 and Matthew 4:4 speak specifically of the *written* Word of God, for us the Bible.

The WCF deals with the necessity of Scripture in its very first statement, 1.1:

> Although the light of nature, and the works of creation and providence do so far manifest the goodness, wisdom, and power of God, as to leave men unexcusable; yet are they not sufficient to give that knowledge of God, and of his will, which is necessary

---

25. Notice here that Jesus refers to *every* word. This (like the "all Scripture" of 2 Timothy 3:16) implies that *everything* God reveals in Scripture is necessary to our spiritual diet. This is the root of the doctrine of *plenary inspiration,* the idea that all Scripture is inspired, not just some parts of it. It is also the background of the phrase *tota Scriptura,* "by all Scripture." That phrase is often coupled with *sola Scriptura,* "by Scripture alone," which we will consider under the "Sufficiency" section below.

> unto salvation. Therefore it pleased the Lord, at sundry times, and in divers manners, to reveal himself, and to declare that his will unto his church; and afterwards, for the better preserving and propagating of the truth, and for the more sure establishment and comfort of the church against the corruption of the flesh, and the malice of Satan and of the world, to commit the same wholly unto writing: which maketh the Holy Scripture to be most necessary; those former ways of God's revealing his will unto his people being now ceased.

The confession here establishes the necessity of Scripture based on the insufficiency of other forms of revelation to give the knowledge of salvation. But Scripture is also necessary because of the nature of our relationship with God, the covenant.

The written Word is, first, necessary for our relationship with God as our covenant Lord. We have seen (chapters 2–3, 23–24) that *covenant* is a relationship between the Lord and his servants or vassals, characterized by the Lord's control, authority, and presence. In this relationship, the lord *speaks* to his vassals, defining the covenant relationship. The elements of his speech correspond to those of the suzerainty treaty form. He tells them his name, his previous deliverances and benefits (historical prologue), his laws (stipulations), his threats and promises (sanctions), and his rules for future administration of the covenant.

From this we see that the covenant is a *verbal* relationship, among other things. Without the Lord's words, there is no covenant authority; indeed, there is no covenant. "Obey my voice" and "keep my covenant" are parallel expressions in Exodus 19:5 (cf. Deut. 33:9; Ps. 89:34). The Ten Commandments are "the words of the covenant" (Ex. 34:28; 2 Chron. 34:31; cf. 2 Kings 23:3; 1 Chron. 16:15); compare the expression "tablets of the covenant" (Deut. 9:9, 11; elsewhere). In Deuteronomy 4:13, the Ten Commandments are the covenant itself:

> And he declared to you his covenant, which he commanded you to perform, that is, the Ten Commandments, and he wrote them on two tablets of stone.

Cf. 1 Kings 8:21; 2 Chron. 6:11. When the Israelites fail to keep God's words, they "break my covenant" (Lev. 26:15), the Lord says. So if there are no written covenant words, there is no covenant, nor is there a covenant Lord.

Similarly, Jesus says that if we love him, we will keep his commandments (John 14:15, 21, 23; 15:7, 10; cf. 1 John 2:3; 5:3; 2 John 6; cf. also Mark 8:38; John 12:48). Remember that his words are absolutely necessary for our lives (John 6:68). If we do not do as Jesus says, we may not call him Lord (Matt. 7:21–27). Since Jesus wrote no books, we must trust the writings of his apostles and disciples, the NT books, to mediate our covenant relationship with Jesus (cf. chapter 25).

People often claim to have a personal relationship to Christ, while being uncertain about the role of Scripture in that relationship. But the relationship that Christ has established with his people is a covenant relationship and therefore a verbal relationship, among other things. Jesus' words, today, are found only in Scripture. So if we are to have a covenant relationship with Jesus, we must acknowledge Scripture as his Word. No Scripture, no Lord. No Scripture, no Christ.[26]

And no Scripture, no salvation. Salvation is a work of God's covenant lordship, in which the Lord intervenes to deliver his people. Salvation in the ultimate sense, salvation from sin, is the result of Jesus' sacrificial death and resurrection. But it is also verbal. For we learn of it in a divine message, the gospel, and we receive salvation by faith in that gospel message. "So faith comes from hearing, and hearing through the word of Christ" (Rom. 10:17). Without that message, that gospel, there is no possibility of salvation.

The work of Christ is not something that human wisdom could have devised. Nor could a mere human report of Jesus' death and resurrection tell us what we need to know. The atonement comes out of the wisdom of God's eternal plan, and its meaning could be given only in divine words. It is God's promise that if we believe, we will be saved. A mere human promise to that effect could be dismissed as wishful thinking. Just as salvation is not by human works, it is not by human wisdom. In the message of the cross, God destroys the wisdom of the wise (1 Cor. 1:19), makes it foolish (v. 20). Paul describes his preaching thus:

> Yet among the mature we do impart wisdom, although it is not a wisdom of this age or of the rulers of this age, who are doomed to pass away. But we impart a secret and hidden wisdom of God, which God decreed before the ages for our glory. None of the rulers of this age understood this, for if they had, they would not have crucified the Lord of glory. But, as it is written,
>
> "What no eye has seen, nor ear heard,
>   nor the heart of man imagined,
> what God has prepared for those who love him"—
>
> these things God has revealed to us through the Spirit. For the Spirit searches everything, even the depths of God. For who knows a person's thoughts except the spirit of that person, which is in him? So also no one comprehends the thoughts of God except the Spirit of God. Now we have received not the spirit of the world, but the Spirit who is from God, that we might understand the things freely given us by God. And we impart this in words not taught by human wisdom but taught by the Spirit, interpreting spiritual truths to those who are spiritual. (1 Cor. 2:6–13)

Because the gospel transcends human wisdom, it must come in words "taught by the Spirit." Those words, today, can be based only in Scripture. So—no Scripture, no salvation.

Comprehensiveness

In considering biblical inerrancy, I argued that Scripture's authoritative content is not religious as opposed to secular, not about "matters of salvation" in contrast with

---

26. For a short analysis of the force of these sentences, see my "No Scripture, No Christ," Appendix N of *DWG*.

matters unrelated to salvation. Rather, Scripture addresses all of human life, as only God himself has a right to do. It applies to all the situations of our experience.[27] As we saw in chapter 4, all of human life is covenantal, governed by the word of our covenant Lord. So the comprehensiveness of Scripture represents the situational perspective in our discussion of how Scripture is important to our lives before God.

Throughout Scripture, we see God speaking to all aspects of human life, issuing commands, making promises, wooing our hearts. In the cultural mandate of Genesis 1:28, God tells Adam to fill the earth and have dominion over it—the whole earth. Everything Adam does is part of that task, everything a response to that divine command.

In God's covenant with Israel, he rules the people's calendar, holidays, diet, clothing, economy, employment practices, education, marriage and divorce, and civil government, as well as their prayers and priestly sacrifices.

One who loves God from the heart will not deny him entrance into any sector of life. Israel's fundamental law is the *shema*:

> Hear, O Israel: The LORD our God, the LORD is one. You shall love the LORD your God with all your heart and with all your soul and with all your might. (Deut. 6:4–5)

People who love God more than everything else will want to express that love in every situation. If we love God more than anything else, we will seek to know how to love him wherever we are, whatever we are doing. We will continually ask: how does my love for God make a difference—in my relationship to my family and neighbors, on the job, in my recreation?[28] And believers will want to know how to take dominion of human culture for the lordship of God: art, literature, science, medicine, government.[29]

In the NT, the believer does not face such a heavy volume of specific laws to govern his life. This is the way of maturity, a result of the passage of God's people from childhood to mature sonship (Gal. 4:1–7). But if anything, the NT is even more explicit than the OT as to the comprehensiveness of God's rule over his people. Having completed his redemptive work, Jesus rises (and we with him, Rom. 6) to receive "all authority in heaven and on earth" (Matt. 28:18). As the cultural mandate sent Adam and Eve to take dominion of the whole earth in God's name, so Christ calls his disciples to

---

27. This issue is sometimes described, especially in Dutch and Dutch-American discussions, as the issue of the *scopus* of the Bible, the subject matter that the Bible addresses. My article "Rationality and Scripture" discusses *scopus* in the Dutch-American theological context. See Appendix B of *DWG*.

28. Meredith G. Kline and others have argued that Scripture distinguishes two spheres, holy and common. The holy sphere is ruled by Scripture and God's saving grace. The common sphere is ruled by natural revelation ("natural law") and common grace. This is a kind of sacred-secular distinction, related, I think, to the medieval distinction between grace and nature and to Luther's distinction between "two kingdoms." I have argued against this type of thinking frequently through *DCL*, especially 534–40. See also *DCL*, 182–92, on the related distinction between law and gospel, and my recent volume *The Escondido Theology* (Lakeland, FL: Whitefield Media, 2011).

29. See chapters 45–49 of *DCL*, on "Christ and Culture," also Appendix E of that book, "In Defense of Christian Activism," and Appendix F, "Is Natural Revelation Sufficient to Govern Culture?" See also my discussion of the Two Kingdoms position in many places, such as *DCL*, 609–16; my review of David VanDrunen, *A Biblical Case for Natural Law* (Grand Rapids: Acton Institute, 2006), at http://www.frame-poythress.org; and *The Escondido Theology*.

go therefore and make disciples of all nations, baptizing them in the name of the Father and of the Son and of the Holy Spirit, teaching them to observe all that I have commanded you. And behold, I am with you always, to the end of the age." (Matt. 28:19–20)

The chief difference between the cultural mandate and the Great Commission is that the former precedes the fall and the work of Christ; the latter follows these. Otherwise, they are very much the same. Of course, it is not possible for people to subdue the earth for God until their hearts are changed by the Holy Spirit. So "taking dominion," following the resurrection, begins with evangelism and baptism. But baptism is not the end, and evangelism is not simply bringing people to an initial profession of faith. It is making disciples and teaching them to observe comprehensively all that Jesus has commanded, with the assurance of Jesus' continuing presence.[30] Jesus' commands do not deal with only repentance, faith, and worship. They also concern our treatment of the poor, our sexual ethics, marriage and divorce, anger, love of enemies, fasting, anxiety, hypocrisy, and many other subjects.

Jesus anticipates a kingdom covering the earth, in which people love God and their neighbors from the heart. The gospel that we preach throughout the world is the good news that the kingdom of God is at hand (Matt. 3:2; 4:17, 23; 5:3; Acts 1:3; 8:12; 19:8; 20:25; 28:23, 31). In the fundamental prayer of God's people (Matt. 6:10), we ask that God's kingdom come. That kingdom will inevitably change human institutions as well. When people are converted to believe in Christ, they bring their new faith and love into their daily work. They ask how Christ bears upon their work as historians, scientists, musicians, how this new passion of theirs affects art, entertainment, medicine, the care for the poor and sick, the justice of courts, the punishment of convicts, relations between nations. All of life is different because of grace. And indeed, Christians have influenced their societies in profound ways through the centuries: adopting babies left to die, building hospitals and orphanages, working to abolish slavery.

So Paul says, "Whether you eat or drink, or whatever you do, do all to the glory of God" (1 Cor. 10:31). "Whatever" includes everything. Other "whatever" verses include Romans 14:23: "But whoever has doubts is condemned if he eats, because the eating is not from faith. For whatever does not proceed from faith is sin." Anything we do that is not motivated by our Christian faith is sin. Note also two verses in Colossians:

And whatever you do, in word or deed, do everything in the name of the Lord Jesus, giving thanks to God the Father through him. (Col. 3:17)

And (to slaves!):

Whatever you do, work heartily, as for the Lord and not for men. (Col. 3:23)

30. On the relation between the cultural mandate and the Great Commission, see my fuller treatment in *DCL*, 307–11, and in chapter 4 of this volume.

God's lordship, therefore, is totalitarian. He rules every aspect of our lives, and he wants his lordship recognized in every corner of the earth, over every life, every family, every nation, every field of human endeavor. Of course, his lordship is totalitarian in a good way, for he intends to extend the blessing of his presence throughout the earth and on every aspect of human life as his name is honored there.

Scripture constitutes the words by which God directs us in carrying out the cultural mandate and Great Commission. It is to Scripture we go to find "every word that comes from the mouth of God" (Matt. 4:4) and "all that I have commanded you" (Matt. 28:20). Scripture shows us how to bring Christ's words to bear over the whole earth. So its content cannot be anything other than comprehensive.

Sufficiency[31]

The last of the six attributes of Scripture is sufficiency, sometimes called *sola Scriptura*, "by Scripture alone."[32] The sufficiency of Scripture is a doctrine of immense importance and a doctrine frequently misunderstood. So I will discuss it at greater length than the other attributes. My basic definition: Scripture contains all the divine words needed for any aspect of human life.

Confessional Formulation

WCF 1.6 formulates the doctrine thus:

> The whole counsel of God concerning all things necessary for his own glory, man's salvation, faith and life, is either expressly set down in Scripture, or by good and necessary consequence may be deduced from Scripture: unto which nothing at any time is to be added, whether by new revelations of the Spirit, or traditions of men. Nevertheless, we acknowledge the inward illumination of the Spirit of God to be necessary for the saving understanding of such things as are revealed in the Word: and that there are some circumstances concerning the worship of God, and government of the church, common to human actions and societies, which are to be ordered by the light of nature, and Christian prudence, according to the general rules of the Word, which are always to be observed.

Below is a commentary on this statement, phrase by phrase.

1. *The whole counsel of God concerning all things necessary for his own glory, man's salvation, faith and life.* The sufficiency of Scripture is comprehensive, in the way that I

---

31. This section is a revision of chapter 11 of *DCL*, "The Sufficiency of Scripture." Of course, the sufficiency of Scripture is an important principle of ethics (the chief concern of *DCL*) as also of the doctrine of Scripture itself (as here). The discussion in *DCL* also deals with related topics such as *adiaphora* and the relations between strong and weak believers in Romans 14 and 1 Corinthians 8–10. I will not deal with those topics here. See also my article "In Defense of Something Close to Biblicism," Appendix O of *DWG*.

32. For the companion doctrine, *tota Scriptura*, "by all Scripture," see my earlier discussion of the necessity of Scripture. Combining these with the discussion of the comprehensiveness of Scripture yields the slogan: "All Scripture, and only Scripture, for all of life."

presented the doctrine of comprehensiveness in the previous section. Everything we need to know for God's glory is in the Bible. The same is true for our own "salvation, faith and life." The confession does not understand these terms in the narrow ways that I argued against earlier. It sees salvation as comprehensive, as we can tell from the rest of the document. Similarly, "faith and life" is a comprehensive pair of concepts. The WSC says, "The Scriptures principally teach what man is to believe concerning God, and what duty God requires of man."[33] So it is reasonable to think that "faith and life" in WCF 1.6 refers to everything that we are to believe and do, the whole content of Scripture applied to the whole content of the Christian life.

Christians sometimes say that Scripture is sufficient for religion, or preaching, or theology, but not for auto repairs, plumbing, animal husbandry, dentistry, and the like. And of course, many argue that it is not sufficient for science, philosophy, or even ethics. That is to miss an important point. Certainly Scripture contains more specific information relevant to theology than to dentistry. But sufficiency in the present context is not sufficiency of specific information but sufficiency of divine words. Scripture contains divine words sufficient for all of life. It has all the divine words that the plumber needs, and all the divine words that the theologian needs. So it is just as sufficient for plumbing as it is for theology. And in that sense, it is sufficient for science and ethics as well.

2. *Is either expressly set down in Scripture, or by good and necessary consequence may be deduced from Scripture.* The sufficient content of Scripture includes not only its explicit teaching, but also what may be logically deduced from it. To be sure, logical deduction is a human activity, and it is fallible, as are all other human activities. So when someone tries to deduce something from Scripture, he may err.[34] But the WCF speaks not just of any attempt to deduce conclusions from Scripture, but of "good and necessary consequence." That phrase refers to logic done right, ideal logic. When deductive logic is done right, the conclusion of a syllogism does not add to its premises. It rather brings out content already there. In the classic syllogism, "All men are mortal; Socrates is a man; therefore Socrates is mortal," the conclusion doesn't tell you anything that you couldn't find out from the premises themselves. What the syllogism does is to make the implicit content explicit. Logic is a hermeneutical tool,[35] a device for bringing out meaning that is already there in the text. So (a) the "content of Scripture" includes

---

33. WSC 3.

34. This liability to error should caution us to be careful in the work of logical deduction. Certainly it must be done with hermeneutical wisdom. "All men have sinned (Rom. 3:23); Jesus is a man (1 Tim. 2:5); therefore Jesus sinned" may seem like a valid syllogism, but of course, it presupposes a defective Christology. (Thanks to Richard Pratt for this example.) So the right use of logic depends on many other kinds of skill and knowledge. On the other hand, the possibility of error should not lead us to abandon logical deduction. For error is not found only in logic, but also in every other activity by which we seek to understand Scripture: textual criticism, translation, interpretation, theology, preaching, and individual understanding. If our goal is to avoid making any error at all, we should not only avoid logic, but avoid all these other activities as well. But that would be an error of another kind.

35. See *DKG*, 242–301.

all the logical implications of Scripture, (b) the logical implications of Scripture have the same authority as Scripture, and (c) logical deductions from Scripture do not add anything to Scripture.

3. *Unto which nothing at any time is to be added.* Covenant documents in the ancient Near East often contained an "inscriptional curse": a prohibition against adding to or subtracting from the document. Scripture, our covenant document, also contains such language (in Deut. 4:2; 12:32; Prov. 30:6; Rev. 22:18–19; cf. Josh. 1:7). These passages do not forbid seeking information outside of Scripture. Rather, they insist that we will never need any *divine words* in addition to God's written words, words that are available to us only in the Bible. That means as well that we should never place any human words on the same level of authority as those in Scripture. That would be, in effect, adding to God's words.

4. *Whether by new revelations of the Spirit, or traditions of men.* Adding to God's words can be done either by claiming falsely to have new words from God himself or by regarding human tradition as being on the same level of authority as God's Word. The confession ascribes these errors to its two main opponents, respectively: the enthusiasts and the Roman Catholics. The enthusiasts were largely Anabaptists, who held views of continuing verbal revelation similar to some modern charismatics. The Roman Catholics defended their tradition as a source of revelation equal to the Bible. Roman Catholic theology has since changed its formulations somewhat,[36] but it still regards tradition as highly as it regards Scripture. Since the writing of the confession, it has become important also for Protestants to guard their respect for their own traditions, so that it doesn't compete with the unique respect due to Scripture.[37]

5. *Nevertheless, we acknowledge the inward illumination of the Spirit of God to be necessary for the saving understanding of such things as are revealed in the Word.* To say that Scripture is sufficient is not to deny that other things may also be necessary. We should always remember that the sufficiency of Scripture is a sufficiency of divine words. It is a sufficient source of such words. But we need more than divine words if we are to be saved and to live holy lives. In particular, we need the Spirit to illumine the Word, if we are to understand it. So no one should object that the doctrine of the sufficiency of Scripture leaves no place for the Holy Spirit.

6. *And that there are some circumstances concerning the worship of God, and government of the church, common to human actions and societies, which are to be ordered by the light of nature, and Christian prudence, according to the general rules of the Word, which are always to be observed.* On the concept of *circumstances*, see the discussion in *DCL* of the second commandment.[38] For now, let us note that the sufficiency of Scripture does not rule

---

36. Today, Roman Catholic theologians tend to speak not of "two sources" of revelation (Scripture and tradition), but of "one source," the stream of tradition of which Scripture is a part. Neither of these views, however, is compatible with the sufficiency of Scripture.

37. See my articles "In Defense of Something Close to Biblicism," Appendix O of *DWG*; and "Traditionalism," Appendix P.

38. *DCL*, 464–81.

out the use of natural revelation (the "light of nature") and human reasoning ("Christian prudence")[39] in our decisions, even when those decisions concern the worship and government of the church.

The reason, of course, is that Scripture doesn't speak specifically to every detail of human life, even of life in the church. We have seen that in one sense Scripture speaks of everything, for its principles are broad enough to cover all human actions. The principle of 1 Corinthians 10:31, *do all to the glory of God*, speaks to every human activity and grades every human act as right or wrong.

But it is often difficult to determine in specific terms what actions will and will not bring glory to God. At that point, natural revelation and Christian prudence give us important guidance. For example, Scripture doesn't mention abortion. But natural revelation tells us that abortion is a procedure that takes innocent life. That shows us that the Bible's prohibition of murder is relevant to the matter of abortion.

Note that in this example, as the confession says, there are "general rules of the Word" that are relevant to our decision. There are always general rules of the Word relevant to any human decision, as we have seen, at least the rule of 1 Corinthians 10:31. So to use the data of natural revelation in this way, though it is extrascriptural, is not to add to Scripture in the sense of Deuteronomy 4:2. To do this is not to add more divine words. It is, rather, a means of determining how the sufficient Word of Scripture should be applied to a specific situation.[40]

The fact that Scripture doesn't mention abortion, or nuclear war, or financial disclosure, or conflicts of interest, or parking meters, therefore, never means that we may abandon Scripture in considering these issues. There is always a principle of Scripture that is relevant. The only question is: specifically how does that principle apply? Recourse to natural revelation and human prudence is an attempt to answer that question.

Biblical Basis

But is this confessional doctrine itself biblical? I believe it is. I have already cited some relevant biblical passages and principles. Let us look more closely at Scripture's teaching about its own sufficiency.

As we've seen, the covenant document contains an inscriptional curse, forbidding adding and subtracting. This is to say that God alone is to rule his people, and he will not share that rule with anyone else. If a human being presumes to add his own word to a book of divinely authoritative words, he thereby claims that his words have the authority of God himself. He claims in effect that he shares God's throne.

Nevertheless, through the history of Israel some did have the audacity to set their words alongside God's. False prophets claimed to speak in God's name, even though God had not spoken to them (1 Kings 13:18; 22:5–12), a crime that deserved the death

---

39. Note the triad: *Scripture, the light of nature, Christian prudence*: normative, situational, and existential, respectively.

40. In my treatments of scriptural sufficiency in *DCL* and *DWG*, I discuss at some length the value and importance of using extrabiblical ("situational") data in applying biblical principles.

penalty (Deut. 18:20). And the people worshiped according to human commandments rather than God's:

And the Lord said:

"Because this people draw near with their mouth
   and honor me with their lips,
   while their hearts are far from me,
and their fear of me is a commandment taught by men,
therefore, behold, I will again
   do wonderful things with this people,
   with wonder upon wonder;
and the wisdom of their wise men shall perish,
   and the discernment of their discerning men shall be hidden." (Isa. 29:13–14)

Jesus applies Isaiah's words to the Pharisees, and adds, "You leave the commandment of God and hold to the tradition of men" (Mark 7:8). And it is likely that some people in Paul's time wrote letters forged in Paul's name, claiming his authority for their own ideas (2 Thess. 2:2).

God's own representatives, however, fearlessly set God's word against all merely human viewpoints. Think of Moses before Pharaoh, Elijah before Ahab, Isaiah before Ahaz, Jonah before Nineveh, Paul before Agrippa, Felix, and Festus. Consider Jesus, who spoke with the same boldness before the Pharisees, Sadducees, scribes, Herod, and Pilate. Those who are armed with God's word, the sword of the Spirit, are free from the tyranny of human opinion!

So Paul, in his famous statement about biblical inspiration, speaks of sufficiency as well:

All Scripture is breathed out by God and profitable for teaching, for reproof, for correction, and for training in righteousness, that the man of God may be competent, equipped for every good work. (2 Tim. 3:16–17)

"Every" refers to sufficiency.

General and Particular Sufficiency

We should notice that 2 Timothy 3:16–17 ascribes sufficiency to the OT. That is an interesting point, that the OT is actually a sufficient guide for NT Christians. As we saw in chapter 25, Paul recommends the OT as the criterion that Christians should use to evaluate new heresies after Paul has died. Why, then, does God give us the NT as well? That question leads to a distinction between two kinds of sufficiency.[41]

---

41. Compare here the distinction I made in connection with the closing of the canon in chapter 25.

First, *general sufficiency*. I use this phrase to refer to the principle that at any point of redemptive history, the revelation given at that time is sufficient. After Adam and Eve sinned, God revealed to them how they would be punished, and he also, remarkably, revealed to them the coming of a Deliverer, a seed of the woman, who would crush the serpent's head (Gen. 3:15). This revelation, extensive as it is, is not nearly as extensive as the revelation available to us in the completed biblical canon. Was this revelation sufficient for them? Yes, it was. Had they failed to trust this revelation, they could not have used as an excuse that it wasn't full enough. In this revelation, they had all the divine words they needed to have. So that revelation was sufficient.

Nevertheless, God added to that revelation, by speaking to Noah, Abraham, and others. Why did he add to a revelation that was already sufficient? Because Noah needed to know more than Adam did. The history of redemption is progressive. In Noah's time, God planned to judge the world by a flood, and Noah had to know that. The Adamic revelation was sufficient for Adam, but not for Noah.

Recall the principle I suggested earlier in this chapter regarding the clarity of Scripture: *Scripture is always clear enough for us to carry out our present responsibilities before God.* Like clarity, sufficiency is an ethical doctrine. It takes away excuses for disobedience. When we violate God's commandments, we cannot claim that they were unclear, or that they were insufficient.

So, like clarity, sufficiency is relative to our present duties before God. God's revelation to Adam was sufficient for him to carry out his present duties, but Noah needed more, for he had additional duties. He needed more in order to do God's will in his time.

Similarly, the revelation of the OT was sufficient for the first generation of Christians (2 Tim. 3:16–17). But God graciously provided them with much more, including the letters of Paul. In God's judgment, these were necessary for the ongoing life of the young church, and when they were collected and distributed, the believers recognized them as God's Word. Once the NT began to function as God's Word in the church, the OT was no longer sufficient in itself, but it continued to function as part of the canon that was, as a whole, sufficient.

That consideration raises the question whether God will add still more revelation to the canon. Sufficiency in itself, what I am calling *general sufficiency*, does not preclude divine additions to Scripture, though it does preclude mere human additions.

But there is an additional principle that should lead us not to expect any more divine words until the return of Christ. That is the finality of Christ's redemption, which implies what I call the *particular sufficiency* of Scripture.

When redemption is final, revelation is also final. Hebrews 1:1–4 draws this parallel:

> Long ago, at many times and in many ways, God spoke to our fathers by the prophets, but in these last days he has spoken to us by his Son, whom he appointed the heir of all things, through whom also he created the world. He is the radiance of the glory of God and the exact imprint of his nature, and he upholds the universe by the word of his power. After making purification for sins, he sat down at the right hand of

the Majesty on high, having become as much superior to angels as the name he has inherited is more excellent than theirs.

Verse 3 speaks of Jesus' purification for sins as final, for when finished he sits down at God's right hand. Verse 2 speaks of God's speech through his Son as final, in comparison with the "many times and many ways" of the prophetic revelation (v. 1). Note the past tense "has spoken." The revelation of the OT is continuous, that of the Son once for all. Nothing can be added to his redemptive work, and nothing can be added to the revelation of that redemptive work.

Hebrews 2:1–4 also contrasts the revelation of the old covenant with that of the new:

> Therefore we must pay much closer attention to what we have heard, lest we drift away from it. For since the message declared by angels proved to be reliable, and every transgression or disobedience received a just retribution, how shall we escape if we neglect such a great salvation? It was declared at first by the Lord, and it was attested to us by those who heard, while God also bore witness by signs and wonders and various miracles and by gifts of the Holy Spirit distributed according to his will.

The "message declared by angels" is, of course, the Mosaic law. The "great salvation" in Christ is something far greater. The message of this salvation was declared first by Christ, then by the apostles ("those who heard"), and then by God himself, through signs and wonders. From the writer's standpoint, these declarations are all in the past tense. Even though part of that message (at least the letter to the Hebrews) is still being written, the bulk of it has already been completed.

Scripture is God's testimony to the redemption that he has accomplished for us. Once that redemption is finished, and the apostolic testimony to it is finished, the Scriptures are complete, and we should expect no more additions to them.

The same conclusion follows from 2 Peter 1:3–11. There, Peter notes that Jesus' "divine power has granted to us all things that pertain to life and godliness, through the knowledge of him who called us to his own glory and excellence" (v. 3). All things that pertain to life and godliness, therefore, come from Jesus' redemption. After that redemption, then, evidently, there is nothing more that could contribute anything to our spiritual life and godliness. Peter then mentions various qualities that we receive through Jesus, concluding, "For in this way there will be richly provided for you an entrance into the eternal kingdom of our Lord and Savior Jesus Christ" (v. 11). This is the language of sufficiency. The virtues that come from redemption are sufficient for us to enter the final kingdom. Nothing more is needed.

So within the concept of sufficiency, I distinguish between *general* and *particular* sufficiency. As we saw earlier, the general sufficiency of Scripture excludes human additions, but is compatible with later additions by God himself. This is the sense in which the OT is sufficient, according to 2 Timothy 3:16–17. The particular sufficiency of Scripture is the sufficiency of the present canon to present Christ and all his resources.

God himself will not add to the work of Christ, and so we should not expect him to add to the message of Christ.

Challenges to the Sufficiency of Scripture

The statement earlier quoted from the WCF contrasts its doctrine of the sufficiency of Scripture with the views of its frequent opponents, the Roman Catholics and the Anabaptist enthusiasts. The Roman Catholics placed their traditions alongside Scripture as having the same authority, so the confession condemns those who would supplement Scripture by "traditions of men." The enthusiasts, somewhat like the charismatic tradition of our day, believed that God gave new revelations, of a similar type and similar authority to that of Scripture. So the confession forbids us to add anything to Scripture by way of "new revelations of the Spirit."

In traditional post-Reformation Roman Catholicism, Scripture and tradition are two sources of revelation, equal in authority. In more recent Catholicism (especially since the Second Vatican Council of the 1960s), theologians speak of "one source" of revelation, which sounds better to Protestants. But the one source is tradition, and this theology considers Scripture to be only one part of this tradition. So plainly Roman Catholicism continues to differ from the Protestant doctrine of scriptural sufficiency.

The position of charismatic theology, the successor to the Anabaptist enthusiasts, is more difficult to pin down. Most charismatics agree with orthodox Protestantism that the canon is closed. Although they believe in "new revelation" in some sense, they do not believe that it should be placed on the same level as Scripture. But if these new revelations are actually God's personal words, how can they *not* be as authoritative as Scripture? Some charismatic writers distinguish Scripture not as having greater authority than present-day revelation, but as having an official status as the governing document of the church. Certainly it is good that they recognize the nature of Scripture as the sole official constitution of the church. But one continues to wonder why it would not be possible to add the "new" revelations to the constitutional document.

A growing development in charismatic theology is the view of Wayne Grudem that the "new" revelations do not have the same authority as Scripture.[42] Grudem believes that prophets in the NT did not have the same authority as prophets in the OT. So although he believes that prophecy continues in our day, giving new revelations to believers, he thinks that such prophecy does not always turn out right and that we can be critical of it. It seems to me unlikely that the concept of prophecy would change so radically between OT and NT. And if such prophecy constitutes a personal word of God, as I have expounded that concept, then I don't see how it could be less than ultimately authoritative and inerrant.[43]

---

42. See *GST*, 1049–61. Grudem is solidly Reformed in most areas, but he takes a charismatic position on the continuance of prophecy and tongues.

43. The gift of tongues, which charismatics believe continues today, is similar to prophecy. When coupled with interpretation, tongues are equivalent to prophecy. I have nothing to add to the present discussion of tongues, except to commend the Poythress article cited in footnote 46 below.

Nevertheless, it does seem to me that there are ways in which revelation continues today, and these senses constitute talking points between Reformed and charismatic Christians.

Christians often find themselves discussing whether God will add new revelation to what we already have. In many circles, the tendency is to reply to this question with a simple yes or no: In Reformed circles, the instinct is to answer no; in some charismatic circles, the instinct is to answer yes.

But books such as this one are intended to raise such discussions to a higher level of reflection. So I would suggest the often-useful reply, "Yes in some senses, no in others."

1. God's revelation of himself in creation, *general revelation,* "revelation through events," certainly continues, and we learn new things from it every day. Every time the sun rises, the heavens declare his glory in a new way. So our knowledge of God is not a fixed quantity—"static," as theologians say. Our life with God is an ongoing drama with exciting new experiences throughout our history.

Further, we should not be intellectualistic in our understanding of how this knowledge comes to us. It may well be true that some general revelation comes to us through subconscious intuitions, through dreams, through visions, through hunches of various kinds. We simply don't know all the dimensions of human knowledge, which is to say that we don't know all the ways in which God reveals himself to us.

We should not equate such general-revelation knowledge with God's personal words in Scripture. But it does give us real knowledge of God, as I indicated in chapter 24. And we cannot understand scriptural Word-revelation without general revelation, even though the authority of Scripture, once we understand it, takes precedence over anything that we may think we have learned through general revelation.

So general revelation is real revelation, though it would not be appropriate for us to add it to the biblical canon. It may be that some claims to extrabiblical special revelation are really based on general revelation. When someone gets a "hunch" that turns out to be eerily correct, I'm inclined to say that this is what has happened. And when it does, God is certainly involved.[44]

2. Redemptive covenant revelation, sometimes called *special revelation,* has ceased. God will not be making new covenants with us, following the new covenant par excellence made with us in Christ. So there will be no more covenant words or covenant documents. This is only to say that Jesus' work is complete, once for all, and that therefore God's revelation concerning Christ is complete as well. This is the *particular sufficiency* of biblical revelation.

---

44. In this connection, theologians of the charismatic movement often refer to the phrases "word of wisdom" and "word of knowledge" in 1 Corinthians 12:8 NKJV. The *New Spirit Filled Life Bible* (Nashville: Thomas Nelson, 2002), 1596, defines the first phrase as "a spiritual utterance at a given moment *through the Spirit,* supernaturally disclosing the mind, purpose, and will of God as applied to a specific situation" (emphasis theirs). The latter phrase is "a supernatural revelation of information pertaining to a person or an event, given for a specific purpose, usually having to do with an immediate need." I am not entirely convinced of these definitions. But, accepting those definitions provisionally, what is evidently happening in both cases is divine assistance in the application of Scripture. I have no reason to deny that such events take place in our own day.

3. The *application* of Scripture to the believer continues. The Christian life is a continuing conversation with the Bible, with God's revelation in the creation, and also with the Holy Spirit, who enables us to understand and use revelation. Every day, God in Scripture speaks to us in new ways. He brings to our attention teachings, commands, promises, and questions that we had not yet seen. He points out new ways in which Scripture applies to our lives. He responds to our prayers based on Scripture. God works not only in an intellectual way, but also with our will, conforming it to his commands, and with our emotions, so that we delight to hear what he says. In these ways, God the Holy Spirit teaches us. As we will see, this teaching is called "revelation" in Ephesians 1:17 (see also Matt. 11:27). So in this sense also, revelation continues.[45]

Often, believers wish that God had revealed more to them than he has revealed in Scripture. Often, Reformed writers will respond to this need by simply telling people to read their Bibles more and more carefully. Charismatic writers often suggest that a troubled believer should listen for a fresh revelation of the Spirit. But both of these solutions are essentially intellectualistic. Both of them urge that we resolve our unease by seeking further propositional knowledge, either from Scripture or beyond Scripture. But Scripture itself tells us that often our need is not for more knowledge, but for spiritual growth, spiritual perception, the revelation of Ephesians 1:17.

4. The *preaching* and *teaching* of Scripture in the church continues, and this, too, is a kind of revelation, as we will see in the next chapter. Spirit-filled preaching has often been called *prophesying* in the Reformed tradition. When we pray for our pastor's sermon, we are asking God to take bad words away from him and to place good words in his mouth. The pastor's sermons are not the Word of God in the sense that the Bible is. But the Second Helvetic Confession, a Reformed confession, did not hesitate to say in a heading in chapter 1, "The Preaching of the Word of God Is the Word of God."

5. At the return of Christ will come the *apokalupsis*, the revelation par excellence, when every eye will see the Lord. This is revelation of an entirely different order (see Luke 17:30; Rom. 8:19; 1 Cor. 1:7; 2 Thess. 1:7; 1 Peter 1:7; 4:13). In this sense, revelation is yet to come.[46]

As we have seen, WCF 1.1 addresses the sufficiency of Scripture in contrast with the views of Roman Catholicism and Anabaptist enthusiasm, views that I have just discussed. But our present-day situation requires me to discuss a third challenge to the sufficiency of Scripture, namely, Protestant traditionalism.

The Reformers did not dismiss all church tradition in theology and worship, but the main thrust of their work was antitraditional, as was Jesus' stance against the

---

45. I will have more to say about this continuing revelation in chapters 27–28 of this book, and also the senses in which God influences the words of pastors and teachers.

46. For a discussion by a Reformed scholar of how these forms of continuing revelation may lead to experiences significantly analogous to the charismatic gifts of the NT, see Vern S. Poythress, "Modern Spiritual Gifts as Analogous to Apostolic Gifts: Affirming Extraordinary Works of the Spirit within Cessationist Theology," *JETS* 39, 1 (1996): 71–101. Also available at http://www.frame-poythress.org. See also his book *What Are Spiritual Gifts?* (Phillipsburg, NJ: P&R Publishing, 2010), published and also at the same website.

Pharisees. They used a very broad brush to eliminate from their theology and worship anything they considered contrary to Scripture or supplementary to Scripture. So the doctrine of the sufficiency of Scripture has served as a weapon against the imposition of extrabiblical notions on the conscience of the believer.

Nevertheless, nearly five hundred years has passed since the beginning of the Protestant Reformation, and during that time Protestantism itself has accumulated a large amount of tradition. Some of this is good, some bad. My present point is that it is just as important as ever to distinguish human tradition from the norms of Scripture and to fight any attempt to put the two on the same level of authority. Some cases in point:

1. In American fundamentalism, it has been common to insist on abstinence from alcoholic beverages. This insistence is understandable. Scripture itself condemns drunkenness, and in modern society the consumption of alcohol is one of the chief sources of automobile accidents. But Scripture, of course, does not teach abstinence. Indeed, Jesus and the apostles drank wine. Jesus supplied wine to the wedding at Cana (John 2:1–11). In 1 Timothy 5:23, Paul recommends wine for stomach ailments. Those who are severely tempted to abuse alcohol might well consider abstinence as a personal policy. But Scripture does not regard abstinence as a general rule, to be observed by all. Here we need to be reminded that God rules us by the Scriptures, not by the human tradition of abstinence.

2. Reformed theology rightly treasures its confessions, which are magnificent theological documents. So it is understandable that Reformed churches have often required officers, sometimes even congregations, to subscribe to these documents. It is thought that such subscription is necessary to prevent theological error from entering the church. Arguments persist, however, as to what kind of subscription is warranted. Some argue that "strict" subscription is necessary, which means either that one must not take any exceptions to the document or that one may not preach or teach in the areas where he takes exception. Others argue for a looser kind of subscription, qualified by expressions such as "subscription to the 'system of doctrine' taught in the confession."

Yet Scripture nowhere says that the church must be governed by human theological documents in addition to Scripture. Therefore, it is impossible to find biblical support for any particular view of subscription. I don't believe that Scripture *forbids* subscription to such documents. Subscription may indeed be a good means to a biblical goal, namely, soundness of teaching in the church. I do think, however, that "strict" subscriptionism violates the principle of *sola Scriptura*. If the formula of subscription is so strict that it is impossible for the church to correct a confession in the light of Scripture, then it should not be employed. There ought to be freedom within the church to rethink the confessions, reevaluating and reforming them according to the Word of God. That means that teachers, preachers, and members of the church must have the right on some occasions to teach contrary to the confession. Otherwise, the church is ruled by tradition rather than by Scripture alone.

3. Many traditions have also developed concerning worship and other aspects of church life. These concern the style and instrumentation of worship songs, the order of events in worship, degree of formality or informality, and so on. Many of these are not commanded by Scripture, but many are in accord with broad biblical principles. The problem is that church people will sometimes defend their particular practice as mandatory on all Christians, and they will criticize as spiritually inferior churches that use different styles and patterns. Often the criteria used are not scriptural, but aesthetic. People argue that this style of music is more dignified, that that liturgy is more ancient, and the like. Often these aesthetic and historical criteria are used in place of Scripture, leading to the condemnations of practices that Scripture permits and commanding of practices that Scripture does not command. That, too, in my judgment, violates the principle of *sola Scriptura*, the sufficiency of Scripture.[47]

Key Terms

Inspiration
Theopneustos
Dictation theory
Mechanical inspiration
Organic inspiration
Propositional revelation
Plenary inspiration
Verbal inspiration
Inerrancy
Infallibility
Precision
Qualifications of inerrancy
Koiné
Phenomena of Scripture
Purpose of Scripture
Inductive approach to inerrancy
Clarity
Necessity
Comprehensiveness
Sufficiency
General sufficiency
Particular sufficiency
Sola Scriptura
Tota Scriptura
Inscriptional curse

47. For more of my critique of Protestant traditionalism, see chapter 38 of *DWG*; my "In Defense of Something Close to Biblicism," Appendix O of *DWG*; "Traditionalism," Appendix P of *DWG*; and *The Escondido Theology*.

Study Questions

1. Did God inspire the biblical authors by dictating words to them? Discuss.
2. "To say that inspiration is restricted to *thoughts* or *ideas* is to give the doctrine of inspiration a very intellectualist cast." How so? Explain; evaluate.
3. "*Infallibility* is a stronger term than *inerrancy*." Explain; evaluate.
4. Present a brief argument for the inerrancy of Scripture.
5. How is the concept of inerrancy related to the biblical concept of truth?
6. Frame objects to confusions between inerrancy and precision. Explain how these concepts are related.
7. Frame thinks that *qualifications of inerrancy* is a misnomer. Mention some of these qualifications and explain Frame's assessment of them.
8. Does the purpose of Scripture qualify its inerrancy? Discuss.
9. Is it best to use an inductive approach to define biblical inerrancy, rather than a deductive approach? Explain both of these and evaluate.
10. "Once we come to faith [to Scripture], problems look different. Problems test our faith, but they do not carry anywhere near the weight of God's self-witness." Explain; evaluate.
11. Define the clarity of Scripture, its limits, and its biblical basis.
12. "*Scripture is always clear enough for us to carry out our present responsibilities before God.*" Why does Frame consider this to be an important principle? Explain; evaluate.
13. Frame says that in Romans 10, "Here the clarity of the Word is nothing less than the presence of Christ in the Word." Explain; evaluate.
14. Is Scripture sufficient for everything? Plumbing? Auto repair? Explain.
15. Frame: "Like clarity, sufficiency is relative to our present duties before God." Explain; evaluate.
16. Does the sufficiency of Scripture allow us to refer to extrabiblical data in our determination of divine duties? Explain.
17. Has revelation ceased? Explain and defend your answer. Make careful distinctions.
18. Frame believes that some Reformed people embrace a traditionalism that violates the sufficiency of Scripture. Explain; evaluate.

Memory Verses

Mark 7:8: You leave the commandment of God and hold to the tradition of men.

John 17:17: Sanctify them in the truth; your word is truth.

Rom. 3:4: Let God be true though every one were a liar, as it is written,

"That you may be justified in your words,
   and prevail when you are judged."

Rom. 4:19–21: He did not weaken in faith when he considered his own body, which was as good as dead (since he was about a hundred years old), or when he considered the barrenness of Sarah's womb. No distrust made him waver concerning the promise of God, but he grew strong in his faith as he gave glory to God, fully convinced that God was able to do what he had promised.

1 Cor. 10:31: Whether you eat or drink, or whatever you do, do all to the glory of God.

2 Tim. 3:16–17: All Scripture is breathed out by God and profitable for teaching, for reproof, for correction, and for training in righteousness, that the man of God may be competent, equipped for every good work.

Resources for Further Study

Frame, John M. *DCL*, chaps. 9–11.

————. *DWG*, chaps. 23–32, Appendices B, N, O, P.

Poythress, Vern S. *What Are Spiritual Gifts?* Phillipsburg, NJ: P&R Publishing, 2010. Also available at http://www.frame-poythress.org.

Van Til, Cornelius. *An Introduction to Systematic Theology.* Nutley, NJ: Presbyterian and Reformed, 1974.

Warfield, B. B. *The Inspiration and Authority of the Bible.* Grand Rapids: Baker, 1948. With introduction by Cornelius Van Til.

CHAPTER 27

FROM GOD'S LIPS TO OUR EARS

IN OUR STUDY OF GOD'S REVELATION in human words, we have noticed that God usually delivers his revelation to us by a process, using human speakers and writers. He sometimes speaks in a "direct voice," though even that revelation contains a human element, since God speaks in human language. But in other forms of divine speech, God's revelation takes on even more of a human dimension. He speaks to human beings, called prophets and apostles, whom he appoints to communicate to the rest of us. And they often communicate in writing. Indeed, our only present direct access to the prophetic-apostolic revelation is through the written text of Scripture.

So the process of divine communication can be illustrated by the diagram in fig. 27.1.

the divine voice

↓

prophets and apostles

↓

the written word

Fig. 27.1. Forms of Verbal Revelation

I have argued that there is no decrease in power, authority, or divine presence as we move from the divine voice, to the prophets and apostles, and to the written Word. The written Word, for example, is no less authoritative than the oral word of the prophets, or than the divine voice.

But this is only the beginning of the process by which God's personal words come from him to us. The written Word itself passes through a number of processes before it reaches our ears, our eyes, and our hearts. Here are some additional steps in the process:

- copies
- textual criticism
- translations, editions
- teaching, preaching
- sacraments
- confessions, creeds, traditions
- human reception
- interpretation, understanding

And in the following chapter, I will discuss still another level of "transmission," the work of God's bringing his Word to dwell in our hearts.

I have not put downward arrows between the items on this list, as I did on the previous list. On this list, the order is more flexible. Confessions, for example, may be based on theology, or theology on confessions. "Human reception" occurred for some readers even before any copying or translating took place. But I want to focus on present-day Christian readers. In general, I believe the list represents the sort of temporal order of events through which we usually receive the Word of God today.

A more important difference between the two lists is that on the first list, as I said, every form of the Word bears the divine lordship attributes: controlling power, authority, and presence. As we pass down the first list, there is no decrease in power, authority, and divine presence. The second list, however, is a list of fallible means by which human beings hear and assimilate the Word of God. These are works and responses of human beings, not inspired in the sense that God inspired the biblical writings themselves. These cannot claim the full power, authority, and presence of God, but they are means of conveying the Word of God, which does indeed bear these lordship attributes. In these events, the interplay between divine revelation and fallible human communication will be a major subject of my discussion.

Copying and Textual Criticism

I begin with a discussion of the *copying* of Scripture. As we saw in chapter 26, God inspires not only prophets and apostles, but also written *texts*. Second Timothy 3:16 says that all *Scripture* is inspired by God. Now, evangelicals have typically limited that inspiration to the *autographs* or *autographa*, the original manuscripts produced by the inspired writer, as opposed to copies or *apographa*.[1] As I will explain, I think this limitation is better described as a limitation to the *autographic text*, rather than to the autograph as such. I agree with this limitation, but it does raise a number of questions that we should consider here.

---

1. This limitation is not new to recent evangelicalism. Greg Bahnsen cites many writers, including Augustine, Calvin, and Baxter, who made the distinction between the truth of the autograph and errors in the copies. See his "The Inerrancy of the Autographa," in *Inerrancy*, ed. Norman Geisler (Grand Rapids: Zondervan, 1979), 156–59. Bahnsen's article is one of the best recent treatments of this issue, and much in this present chapter will reflect his arguments.

What Is an Autograph?

It may seem obvious to us that an *autograph* is simply the document written by the prophet, apostle, or other inspired writer. Any other manuscript of the same text is a *copy*. But the issue is more complicated when you consider that the biblical writer might have written more than one draft of his book or letter, and that he might have made use of an amanuensis (secretary).[2] Is the first draft the autograph? Or is it possible that the first draft required some revisions before it was sent to its destination? What if the amanuensis made some mistakes in his first draft, and the biblical writer needed to correct the manuscript?

I agree with Greg Bahnsen that the *autograph* is "the first completed, personal, or approved transcription of a unique word-group composed by its author."[3] It is a "finished product," as Bahnsen says, not a rough draft in need of perfecting. And it is certified by the author in some way so as to assure readers that this is his inspired teaching. In the case of 1 Corinthians, Paul would have certified it by declaring that he was finished with it and by sending it to Corinth by a messenger. When the messenger brought Paul's letter to Corinth, that messenger's testimony certified to the church that it was an authentic letter of Paul.

Is This Limitation Scriptural?

Common sense tells us that the content of any book consists of what the author wrote and nothing else. If I write my own ideas in the margin of Kant's *Critique of Pure Reason*, that does not make my ideas part of his book. Similarly, when Thomas Jefferson edited out many passages of the Bible that displeased him, he did not reduce the content of the Bible. The Bible is what God gave to us, not what God gave minus Jefferson's omissions. The Bible is God's own written Word, without addition or subtraction.

Scripture itself is concerned that we follow what it says, not what someone adds to it, nor a truncated version that emerged from human subtractions. So God says in Deuteronomy 4:2:

> You shall not add to the word that I command you, nor take from it, that you may keep the commandments of the LORD your God that I command you.

Cf. 12:32. In Deuteronomy, the reference is specifically to the law of God given to Moses. But Proverbs 30:5–6 presents this as a general principle, applicable to all of God's words:

> Every word of God proves true;
>   he is a shield to those who take refuge in him.
> Do not add to his words,
>   lest he rebuke you and you be found a liar.

---

2. Paul evidently used amanuenses regularly. Tertius played that role in the writing of the letter to the Romans (Rom. 16:22). In 1 Corinthians 16:21; Galatians 6:11; 2 Thessalonians 3:17; and Philemon 19, Paul writes in his "own hand" at the end of the letter, indicating that the rest of the letter was written by someone else's hand.

3. Bahnsen, "The Inerrancy of the Autographa," 190.

Very near the end of the NT, we read this:

> I warn everyone who hears the words of the prophecy of this book: if anyone adds to them, God will add to him the plagues described in this book, and if anyone takes away from the words of the book of this prophecy, God will take away his share in the tree of life and in the holy city, which are described in this book. (Rev. 22:18–19)[4]

These passages reflect the "inscriptional curses" that were found in the ancient suzerainty treaties to which I referred in chapters 2 and 25. Those treaties were the words of the great king, and it was important that the words of the great king not be confused with any other words. The presence of such curses in the Bible is consistent with our earlier-stated view that Scripture is very much like a suzerainty treaty between God and his people.

This is not to say, however, that copies are always worse than the originals. When the copy agrees with the original, without any additions or subtractions, then it is just as true as the original, indeed just as authoritative. This observation should help us to see that what is at issue is not primarily the autographic document, but the autographic *text*.[5] The *text* is a linguistic object that can be found in any number of physical media. If I type out Lincoln's Gettysburg Address on my computer and then print it out five times, there is an original autograph and five copies, but only one *text*. That same text could be reproduced on clay tablets, or papyrus, or paper, or digital media. As long as there is no change, all these copies present a single text.

Similarly with Scripture. By divine inspiration its text is found in the autograph, and when the copy is perfect, the text is found in the copy as well. It is therefore not important whether or not the autographic *document* is preserved. It is important that the autographic *text* be available to us, even though that text may be found only in copies (*apographa*) of the original.

But it is *possible* that there will be errors in the copy. Why? Because God has not promised that copies will be perfect. He has not, in other words, promised to keep all copyists from error. Like all the other items in our second list of terms, the process of copying is a fallible process. Sit down for yourself and try to copy the first chapter of Genesis. Most likely, you will make a few mistakes. Even computer printouts sometimes fail to reproduce the original text accurately. (Sometimes, for example, the printer is unable to reproduce characters given to it by a word processor.) There is no passage in Scripture, nor any biblical principle, that promises otherwise.

---

4. People sometimes ask whether this curse pertains only to the book of Revelation or to the whole Bible. I think the author intended it to apply to the book of Revelation, the book he had written; he was not thinking of a broader reference. Nevertheless, as we have seen, this text reproduces a principle that pertains to anything God says. Whenever God speaks, we should not add to it or subtract from it. So it is appropriate, and an interesting providential development, that these verses ended up nearly at the end of the Bible as the church has arranged it. It is an appropriate place to warn readers to take God's Word as it is and not try to reconstruct it.

5. Compare Bahnsen's discussion, "The Inerrancy of the Autographa," 160–62.

So the limitation of inspiration (and hence of authority, infallibility, and inerrancy) to the autographic text is a biblical limitation.

But Don't Biblical Writers Quote Copies as God's Word?

A number of writers have argued that we should not limit divine inspiration to the autograph, because Jesus and the apostles regularly quote copies, even translations and versions, as God's Word. It is true that Jesus and the apostles did not possess autographs of the texts they quote. Indeed, they often quote as God's Word the Septuagint (LXX), the Greek version of the OT commonly used among the Jews. But consider the following:

1. These quotations do not erase the fact I emphasized earlier, that Jesus and the apostles distinguished between the true Word of God and the additions and subtractions of human beings. They believed that any deviation from the original was unauthorized by God and therefore had no authority.

2. Recall that the important thing is not the autographic manuscript, but the autographic *text*. That text may exist in many copies, if those copies are accurate copies. So to cite a copy, when the copy is accurate, does not violate the sole authority of the autographic text.

3. In chapter 28 of *DWG*, I discuss the practices of Jesus, the apostles, and the NT writers in quoting or alluding to the OT. I conclude there that there is no reason to think they were quoting inaccurately or misusing the passages they quote. If that is correct, then it follows that their quotes are quotes of the autographic text. Therefore, their use of the OT is consistent with the principle that authority is limited to the autographic text.

4. Unlike the Qur'an, the Bible does not assume that God's Word is untranslatable. Rather (in keeping with the nature of Christianity as a missionary religion), the Bible itself uses multiple languages (Hebrew, Aramaic, and Greek, with further variations of style). When NT writers quote the Hebrew Bible in Greek, there is no reason to think that the differences between the two languages necessarily invalidate the quotation. The same is true when they quote the LXX. Insofar as their quotation reproduces the content of the Hebrew autographic text, it is true and authoritative.

5. In chapter 25, I indicated that biblical language is, generally speaking, ordinary, rather than technical. It is not, therefore, perfectly precise. It exhibits a level of precision appropriate to its context and purpose. Now, there are always minor differences, at least in nuance or feel, between a sentence in Hebrew and a translation of that sentence into Greek. So there are often some levels of imprecision in the NT quotes of the OT. But those do not impugn the accuracy of the quotes for their purpose. They do not negate the value of those quotations as *applications* of God's Word.

6. When theologians use NT quotations of the OT to criticize the limitation of inspiration to the autographic text, they mean to say that the autographic text is not unique in authority, that it is not uniquely inspired. On this basis, texts that are contrary to the autographic text, even erroneous ones, can be just as inspired as the autographic text.

If this is true, then an inspired text can contain error. But I have argued extensively in earlier chapters to show that this is not the case.

7. When Jesus and the apostles quote the OT using the LXX version, their intent is not to assert the authority of the LXX as a translation, but to quote what is said in the OT autographic text. The LXX is only a vehicle for accomplishing that purpose, a good means of communication to people who know Scripture primarily through the LXX.

Is This Limitation an Apologetic Dodge?

Some have claimed that the limitation of inerrancy to the autographs is a "convenient dodge" to avoid dealing with Bible problems. The argument is that when evangelicals find a problem in Scripture that they can't answer, they simply respond that "there must have been some textual error," that is, an error by a copyist.

But this criticism is unfair. In the first place, evangelicals typically arrive at this principle not from apologetic motives, but because the limitation to the autographic text is implicit in Scripture's own doctrine of Scripture.

Second, evangelical responses to Bible problems very rarely appeal to the possibility of copyists' error. There are a few places where copyist error is a likely explanation of a difficulty. One is 1 Kings 4:26, which says that Solomon had "40,000 stalls of horses for his chariots," while 2 Chronicles 9:25 says that he had only "4,000." Norman Geisler and Thomas Howe point out that these numbers are visually very similar in the Hebrew, and a scribe may well have miscopied.[6] This explanation is a reasonable one. Geisler and Howe are not bringing in the textual issue arbitrarily or inappropriately. They bring it up because there is a rational likelihood of textual corruption in this passage.

In general, it is not wise for evangelical apologists to bring up the possibility of textual corruption in the abstract. When an apologist discusses Jesus' statement in Matthew 13:31–32 about the mustard seed's being the smallest seed, it won't help to say, "Well, the text may be corrupt at that point." That reply is not cogent or even plausible, given that there is no reason to assume textual corruption in that passage. The apologetic appeal to textual corruption is cogent only where (as in 1 Kings 4:26 and 2 Chron. 9:25) there is good reason to expect textual corruption.[7]

But most evangelical apologists are wise in dealing with such matters. They don't recklessly appeal to copyists' errors whenever a problem appears.

And as I suggested in chapter 26, there is no need for evangelicals to appeal to such implausible possibilities. When we reach the end of our ability to explain, it is far better, indeed more cogent, to say honestly, "I don't know."

Does This Limitation Make Inerrancy a Dead Letter?

Another criticism is that if we limit biblical inerrancy to the autographic text, then we must make the damaging admission that our present Bibles are not inerrant. In

---

6. Norman Geisler and Thomas Howe, *When Critics Ask* (Wheaton, IL: Victor Books, 1992), 181.

7. And as I indicated in *DWG*, there is a better way to deal with the problem of the mustard seed.

that case, inerrancy pertains only to documents (the autographs) that are now lost. It makes no difference to our use of Scripture today. In reply:

1. Even if our present Bibles are not inerrant in any sense, the doctrine of inerrancy is still important. For the doctrine of biblical inerrancy, important as it is to us, is not primarily a doctrine facilitating our use of Scripture. It is primarily a doctrine about God's own truthfulness. What the doctrine of inerrancy does first of all is this: it enables us to confess the truthfulness of God. If there were errors in the autographs of Scripture, then God has not been truthful.

2. But in fact, inerrancy is not *only* a doctrine about God's truthfulness. It is also a doctrine that makes an immense difference in our own use of Scripture. As we have seen, inerrancy is limited to the autographic *text*, not to the autograph itself. Although the autographs are all missing (so far as we know), the autographic text has been transmitted through copies and editions through the centuries, down to our own time. That transmission has been imperfect, as we have seen. But it is possible, through the science of textual criticism, to determine where the imperfections are likely to be. Where there is no evidence of textual corruption, we are quite within our rights to assume that our present text is autographic and therefore to appeal to the text as the inerrant Word of God—just as Jesus and the apostles appealed to copies and versions of their day. So inerrancy is a practical doctrine as well as a theological one.

3. In fact, the biblical text has been far better preserved than any other ancient document. There are far more ancient manuscripts of Scripture and Scripture portions than of writings of the religions of Greece, Egypt, and Babylon, more than manuscripts of the Greek philosophers and poets. The manuscripts we have of Scripture are closer to the time of their original writing. And they are of higher quality. The variations among different manuscripts and manuscript families are many, but minor. They consist mainly of spelling differences, word substitutions, and minor grammatical differences that make little difference to the meaning of the passage. So the WCF rightly speaks of the "singular care and providence" (1.8) by which God has preserved the biblical text.[8]

4. Where there are significant textual problems, as in the ending of Mark, they do not affect any doctrine of the faith. In my judgment, the "long ending" of Mark (which many Bibles include as Mark 16:9–20) was not part of the original text. But nothing in that passage is contrary to anything elsewhere in Scripture.[9] And what these verses say

---

8. This singular care and providence does not imply, as some have argued, that there is one textual tradition far more reliable than the others, which we are obligated to accept. This sort of view lies behind the argument that we must use only the KJV, or other versions based on the Byzantine textual tradition, a text family that includes the majority of the ancient manuscripts, but not necessarily the oldest or most reliable. But God may have used his singular care and providence to preserve the text by distributing it through several manuscript families.

9. In Mark 16:18, Jesus promises believers that they will pick up serpents with their hands and be unharmed, and that drinking poison won't hurt them. Of course, I don't recommend these practices as a general rule. But Acts 28:3–5 describes Paul's shaking off a deadly viper without suffering harm, and I would not be surprised if God also in some situation allowed a believer to drink poison without suffering harm, as a witness of Christ's power. The other kinds of miracles mentioned here (exorcism, tongues, healing) are explicitly mentioned elsewhere in the NT. Mark 16:18 does not imply that God does such miracles anytime we choose to pick up serpents or drink poison, but it does teach, truly, that such miracles will *sometimes* happen, in the course of gospel proclamation.

is found in other passages. So that textual difficulty is actually of minor importance, though twelve verses are involved.

5. One reason why textual problems do not affect biblical doctrine is that they are almost always minor, as I've said. Another reason is that Scripture is highly redundant, in a good way. The doctrines of the Christian faith are never derived from a single text.[10] Rather, each doctrine is based on many texts, drawn together to form a consistent pattern of teaching. Scripture repeats itself over and over again, in many different literary genres, through the work of many authors, over many centuries. So when a textual problem makes it difficult to appeal to a single text, many other texts on the same subject give us assurance of the truth.

So just as Jesus and the apostles appealed to the Scriptures available to them as the Word of God, without denying biblical inerrancy, so may we.

Why Did God Allow the Autographs to Be Lost?

I have been arguing that biblical inerrancy is limited to the inspired autographic text. There is no guarantee in Scripture that copies of the original autograph will be perfect. Nevertheless, God has remarkably preserved the biblical text so that we can appeal to our present versions of Scripture as the inerrant Word of God. But, we ask, would it not have been easier if God had providentially, even miraculously, preserved the autographic manuscripts? Scripture gives us no explicit reason. But consider:

1. Many have suggested that if the original manuscripts had been preserved, they might have become objects of idolatrous worship. Given the use of relics in the history of the church, this consideration carries some weight. Recall that King Hezekiah destroyed the brass serpent that Moses had made to heal the people in the wilderness because the people had begun to worship it (2 Kings 18:4).

2. The present existence of the autograph would not help us much with the problem of understanding and applying God's Word. We have considered many debates about the inspiration, authority, and inerrancy of the biblical text. The presence of the autograph would not have stifled those debates. Nor would it have eliminated the debates about the interpretation of texts and the doctrinal use of Scripture. Very few of those debates, if any, hinge on textual questions, and they cannot be resolved by the existence of a pure text. So for God to have preserved the autographs would have been a superfluous use of his power.

Why Did God Not Give Us Perfect Copies?

A similar question is this: why did God choose not to give us perfect copies, ensuring the perfect preservation of the autographic text, though not of the autographic

---

The point of Jesus' teaching here is not that such miracles will be a normal part of every believer's experience, but that miraculous signs will *accompany* those who believe, as they bring the gospel to the world (v. 15). And in fact, God did accompany the apostles' message by signs like these, the "signs of a true apostle" (2 Cor. 12:12).

10. Occasionally, somebody will try to build an elaborate doctrinal construction on a single obscure text, as in the Mormon doctrine of baptism for the dead, supposedly based on 1 Corinthians 15:29. But this sort of thing is a mark of cultic, as opposed to orthodox, exegesis.

manuscripts? If having an inerrant Bible is so important, why didn't God determine to make *all copies* of Scripture inerrant?

We should understand, first, what such divine providence would entail. It would mean that if you sat down to write a copy of Genesis 1, you could not fail to produce a perfect replica of it. God would prevent any lapses of memory as you glanced between the original and your copy-page. He would prevent on the spot any sinful inclination you might have toward distorting the text in any way. All of that is, of course, possible for God to do. But it suggests a picture of his providence rather at odds from his usual ways of working among us.

More seriously, though, we need to consider this question from a larger perspective. Recall the second list of events that I presented at the beginning of this chapter: copying, textual criticism, translation, teaching, and so on, right down to understanding and assurance. These are all steps on the way for us to receive edification from Scripture. God intends that we will receive such edification, so he provides all these operations. But note that in each of those operations we may ask why God did not institute perfection. After all, he might have provided not only perfect copies, but also perfect textual criticism, perfect translations, perfect teaching, and so on. Indeed, he might have guaranteed that all our attempts to *understand* might be perfectly successful. He might even have determined to skip the steps between inspiring the Scripture and giving us understanding of it. For why should we go through the whole process of copying, translating, and teaching if God is able to give us an immediate understanding of his Word? Why should God institute such a process? Why should he not rather give each of us an immediate, intuitive understanding of his revelation, so that we could magically understand it all, with a glance at the Hebrew or Greek text? For that matter, why did God even bother to place his revelation in a Book? Why didn't he simply reveal it immediately to every human being?

God has not given us a clear answer to any of these questions. But they are all similar. If it seems unlikely that God would provide an inerrant Book, but consign the publication of it to fallible copyists, then is it not equally unlikely that he would turn the work of translation, teaching, and theology over to fallible human beings?[11] And if it seems likely that God would provide infallible copies of Scripture, then it is equally likely that God would provide perfect translations, and so on. If we think that God would probably not provide a perfect translation, then it is equally unlikely that he would provide us with perfect copies.

The question then becomes: why did God inspire an inerrant Word, and then consign that Word to a fallible process of distribution and appropriation? That way of putting it may suggest an answer. I think that most likely God wanted us to appropriate his personal words in a *communal* way. Had he given us perfect copies, perfect translations, and so on, each individual could have come to an understanding

---

11. The gift of tongues shows that God is able supernaturally to circumvent the normally laborious process of translation in a particular situation. So, we are asking, why did he not choose to do this on every occasion?

of Scripture without help from anyone else. He could have gone to the bookstore and bought for himself a perfect translation of Scripture, taught it to himself, and gained thereby a perfect understanding.[12] But that was not God's intention. He wanted the church to gather around the Word together, covenantally. He wanted each individual to benefit from the gifts of others in the body. Some would be gifted in languages; they would translate. Others would be gifted to teach, and they would instruct. Some would teach by words, others more by the example of their lives. Everyone would contribute something to the "edifying of the body," building up one another.[13] Each individual would rely on the gifts of others. Listening for God's Word would draw the body together.

Granted, the communal process of assimilating the Word often works in the opposite way. Churches are divided over Bible translations, interpretations, theological understanding, and so forth. Sin always messes things up. But at its best, the process of learning God's Word together is, even now, a precious one. It leads us not only to love God, but also to love one another, to honor one another's gifts, to grow in relationships as well as knowledge.

God may have additional, or completely different, reasons for his decision to give us fallible copies of an infallible Book. But certainly he has made that decision for his own reasons, and we would be unwise to second-guess him.

Isn't Any Loss a Serious Loss?

On the basis of our previous arguments, we can say that nearly all the autographic *text* of Scripture has been preserved, and through Scripture's lavish redundancy all the doctrinal teaching of Scripture is available to the church. But because the process of transmission is fallible, we must admit that *something* has been lost to us. For example, we don't know for sure how the gospel of Mark originally ended. So it may well be that we have lost a summary paragraph, or some words of Jesus. Since we live by *every* word that comes from God's mouth (Matt. 4:4), that loss is a serious loss, even if it is the loss of a mere nuance or perspective on what we already have.

But remember that losses of the word of God are not unprecedented. John tells us that many things Jesus did (doubtless including much teaching) have not been recorded in writing (John 21:25). John says there that "were every one of them to be written, I suppose that the world itself could not contain the books that would be written." So we have lost some of Jesus' teaching, teaching that would certainly have been helpful to us, even if it differed from the recorded teaching only by way of nuance or emphasis. The same is true of the prophets of the OT. Certainly the prophet Obadiah received more words of God than the brief book we have that bears his name. And there are

---

12. That we should even consider seriously such a possibility speaks to the individualism of our culture. Most peoples of the world, including first-century Jews and Christians, take the communal approach to knowledge for granted.

13. This is a fundamental NT theme (see Rom. 14:19; 15:2; 1 Cor. 8:1; 14:3–5, 12, 17, 26; 2 Cor. 10:8; 12:19; 13:10; Eph. 4:12, 16, 29; 1 Thess. 5:11).

at least two letters of Paul that have not been preserved for us (mentioned in 1 Cor. 5:9 and 2 Cor. 7:8).

God did not take care to preserve for us all his personal words through Jesus, prophets, and apostles. Some of them met needs of their original hearers, but God determined that they did not need to be preserved for us.

Certainly it would be a wonderful thing if archaeologists were to unearth a lost letter that could be authenticated as coming from Paul—or an authentic fifth gospel. But God has determined that up to now such lost revelation is not needed by the church. We should take the "every" of Matthew 4:4 to refer to the revelation that God has provided to us today, not to every word of God that has ever been uttered in history.

We should think similarly of those fragments of verbal revelation that may have been lost through the process of textual transmission. God is sovereign over this process, and he has determined what should survive and what should not. He has determined that we have all the personal words that he intends to speak to us today. In that theological sense, we have lost nothing through the process of textual transmission.

To summarize: (1) The autographic *manuscripts* of Scripture are presently lost, though we should not despair of finding at least some of them in the future. (2) The autographic *text* has been almost entirely preserved, accessible through manuscripts available to us and through the science of textual criticism. (3) The distinctive *teaching* of the Scriptures has been entirely preserved, given the beneficial redundancy of doctrinal teaching in Scripture. (4) Because of God's "singular care and providence" (WCF 1.8) over the process of transmission, we now have in Scripture all the personal words that God intends to say to us today.

Translations and Editions

The Bibles that we normally read today are not only copies, but also edited versions based on the original text. For most of us, the Bibles we read are also translations, rather than the original Hebrew, Aramaic, and Greek. Translating and editing, like copying, are fallible processes, and they do sometimes create errors in the resulting document. But as with the copying itself (discussed in the previous section), these operations, under God's providence, are suitable means for him to bring his personal words to us.

Translation is found even in the original texts of Scripture, for in those texts God speaks not in his eternal, Trinitarian, divine language, but in human language. He translates his divine language into human. Compared to this great translation, other forms of translation present negligible problems. But Scripture never suggests that this great act of translation damages the text in any way or lessens its authority.

Similarly with lesser kinds of translation. As I mentioned earlier, NT writers often quote the OT by way of the common Greek translation, the Septuagint (LXX). Many think that Jesus originally presented his sermons in Aramaic, and that the gospel writers translated them into Greek. The event of Pentecost (Acts 2:1–12), reversing the curse of Babel (Gen. 11:1–9) by making God's word known in many languages, implements the Great Commission, which calls Jesus' disciples to bring his message to all the nations of the world, and therefore into all the languages of the world. So unlike Islam, Christianity sees God's Word as *translatable*. Indeed, for the church to carry out its mission, translation is *mandatory*. And Scripture never suggests that translation in itself distorts the text in any way.

Now, of course, *bad* translation can introduce error. But just as imperfect copies can convey the autographic text of God's Word, so can imperfect translations. And the providence of God, plus the beneficial redundancy of Scripture, assures us that imperfect translations cannot prevent Scripture from telling us everything that God wants us to know.

Teaching, Preaching, and Theology

Over the centuries, more people have received the gospel through teaching and preaching than through reading. Indeed, Jesus and the apostles taught orally before any of their words were written down. So we must consider the media of teaching and preaching alongside others.

Present-day teachers and preachers do not speak infallibly as the prophets and apostles did. Nevertheless, the Bible does indicate that after the apostolic period, preaching and teaching will continue (1 Tim. 3:2; 2 Tim. 4:2).

There has been debate over the difference in meaning between *preaching* (*kerysso, keryx, kerygma*) and *teaching* (*didasko, didaskalia, didache*). C. H. Dodd argued that *kerygma* and *didache* were two very different forms of communication in the NT,[14] each with a distinctive subject matter, but that conclusion is too extreme. The *didasko* language and the *kerysso* language can refer to the same activity (as in Matt. 4:23; 9:35; 11:1; Acts 5:42; 15:35; 28:31; Rom. 2:21; Col. 1:28; 1 Tim. 2:7; 2 Tim. 1:11). The two terms differ somewhat in their connotations, so the presence of the one supplements that of the other in these passages. The *kerysso* terms represent a more dramatic form of communication, that of a herald, a proclamation. The *didasko* group refers more broadly to communication of ideas. It is fair to say that *kerygma* is a kind of *didache*, a style of *didache*. Preaching, *keryssein*, seems more appropriate to describe a dramatic discourse before a large group. Teaching, *didaskein*, seems to suggest a less formal, perhaps smaller, setting.

Preaching (*keryssein*) in the NT tends to be used most often for the proclamation of the gospel to a group for the first time, so it is associated with the most basic elements of the gospel. Jesus engaged in preaching, but the NT uses the term most often to refer to the apostolic proclamation, especially that of Paul. The apostles preached Christ to Jews in their synagogues (as Acts 9:20), to Samaritans (Acts 8:5), and to Gentiles in their cities (Acts 14:1–7).

Teaching occurs in all the same contexts, as we saw earlier. But as we've also seen, it is connected with the office of overseer as well. The *didasko* terms seem especially appropriate in a church context. The overseers are given particular responsibility for

---

14. C. H. Dodd, *The Apostolic Preaching and Its Developments* (London: Hodder and Stoughton, 1936).

teaching, but there is also a sense in which every Christian is a teacher (Eph. 4:29; Col. 3:16; Heb. 5:12; 1 John 2:27). In Reformed theology, the official teaching is said to belong to the *special office*, while the teaching of all believers is part of the *general office*, that is, the priesthood of all believers. Special-office teaching requires special gifts of character and competence (1 Tim. 3:1–7), and (as I understand 1 Timothy 2:12) that teaching is restricted to men only.[15] Women may and do participate in general-office teaching, however, as when Priscilla (mentioned first, most likely, to indicate her prominence in this activity) with her husband Aquila instructed Apollos in the Word of God (Acts 18:26), and as when Paul instructs older women to teach younger women (Titus 2:3–5).

We are accustomed to think of *preaching* as what takes place in our Sunday-morning sermons. But it is perhaps significant that the NT never uses *kerysso* terminology to refer to anything in the Christian worship service. As I have said, the line between preaching and teaching is not sharp, and that line distinguishes connotation and nuance rather than two completely distinct activities. So it is not wrong to describe teaching in worship as *preaching*. But in Reformed theology, the concept of preaching tends to be drawn from the apostolic proclamation following the ascension of Christ: a heralding, a mode of authoritative announcement rather than discussion or debate, a redemptive-historical emphasis, an address to people who are not yet committed to Christ. It would be wrong, in my judgment, to say that all those connotations necessarily carry over into the instruction that is part of Christian worship.

It is actually very difficult to find in the NT any reference to sermons as an element of Christian worship. The closest reference is in 1 Corinthians 14:26:

> What then, brothers? When you come together, each one has a hymn, a lesson, a revelation, a tongue, or an interpretation. Let all things be done for building up.

"Lesson" here is *didache*, "teaching." As we have seen, it is a broader term than *kerygma*. It does not necessarily connote a heraldic stance, an announcement mode, or a redemptive-historical emphasis. In my judgment, it does not set forth in any detail what must be said or how it should be said. Presumably it should be Christian teaching, that is, biblical content, and it should contribute to the spiritual edification of the congregation, as should every other part of worship ("let all . . . be done for building up"). But I think it would normally be inappropriate for a teacher to take the same stance in Christian worship that he might take before unbelievers in a synagogue or marketplace. Certainly we should not neglect the possibility that some unbelievers may be present in the worship service and may need to be addressed (as in 1 Cor. 14:23–25). But in the Christian meeting, the chief goal is not conversion, but the edification of people already converted.

The text does not specify in detail how the lesson brings edification. If we can rid ourselves of some common assumptions, we may note that 1 Corinthians 14:26 is less

---

15. See *DCL*, 635–44.

restrictive than many of our churches today as to the nature of teaching in worship. For example, (1) the text does not say that the lesson must be given by only one person. In fact, the pattern of 1 Corinthians 14:26, in which different members of the congregation propose worship activities, suggests that occasionally more than one member of the church might have a "lesson." (2) Nor does the passage state that only an overseer may present the lesson. The overseers should, of course, oversee. They should prevent anyone from teaching error, or from teaching matters about which he is ignorant. But as we have seen, there is a sense in which every believer is competent to teach.[16] (3) Nor does the passage say that this teaching must emulate the style and content of the apostolic sermons in Acts. The only limitation here is that the lesson ought to edify the congregation. (4) Such freedom encourages creativity. Nothing in 1 Corinthians 14:26 prevents us from considering any method or style of teaching that is consistent with biblical principles and that is educationally (i.e., edificationally) valuable, such as, perhaps: children's sermons, or sermons given to other age groups; object lessons; teaching through music or drama; visual aids; personal testimonies; fielding questions.

My purpose here, however, is not to give a detailed account of preaching and teaching in the church, but to consider the relation of these to the Word of God.

The Reformed tradition has often emphasized "the centrality of preaching." The Second Helvetic Confession, in fact, says in a heading of a section of chapter 1, "The Preaching of the Word of God Is the Word of God." That section reads:

> Wherefore when this Word of God is now preached in the church by preachers lawfully called, we believe that the very Word of God is proclaimed, and received by the faithful; and that neither any other Word of God is to be invented nor is to be expected from heaven: and that now the Word itself which is preached is to be regarded, not the minister that preaches; for even if he be evil and a sinner, nevertheless the Word of God remains still true and good.

Given this exposition and the place of this paragraph in the context of the confession's general discussion of Scripture, it is plain that "Word of God" here refers to the Scriptures, not to the preaching itself, though the heading might suggest otherwise. The Word of God is what the preacher preaches, the subject of his sermon, the content that he intends to expound. The point of the confession here is that we should not seek the word of God in some new revelation, but rather in the old revelation, the Scriptures, to which we have access through preaching.

So the confession is not saying that preaching is the word of God in the same sense that Isaiah's prophecies are the word of God. Certainly the writers of the confession recognized that preachers sometimes err. But the confession asserts that even though a preacher may be wicked, and therefore likely preaches falsehood, yet insofar as his preaching is true "the Word of God remains still true and good." That is to say: the

---

16. I do believe, for example, that sex should not be a barrier to such teaching. If a woman has something to say that the overseers regard as edifying, she should be permitted to say it.

biblical revelation loses none of its power, truth, or authority from being on the lips of a fallible, even wicked, human being. When a preacher speaks the Word truly, it is just as true, and just as authoritative, as it is on the pages of Scripture itself. It is therefore a means that God uses to bring the true Word of God to his people, just as he uses copies, translations, and editions. Insofar as the preacher brings the true Word to us, the autographic text is on his lips, just as surely as it was on the lips of Jesus and Paul. If we rebel against the Word of God that we hear on Sunday morning, it is no excuse to say, "It came from a fallible man." God uses the fallible man to bring his Word to us, and we must respect it.

So theologians have often put preaching in a central place. In Karl Barth's theology, the Word of God has three forms: Christ (who alone is revelation in the fullest sense), Scripture (which for Barth is not directly the Word of God, but is its witness and instrument), and preaching (which, in turn, is the witness and instrument by which we receive Scripture). And historically, in Protestant churches, pulpits have replaced altars in the central position in the front of the sanctuary.

I agree, of course, that preaching is an important means by which God brings the message of Scripture to us. But I have some reservations about the "centrality of preaching":

1. I see no biblical reason to put preaching above teaching as a means of communicating the Word of God. In my judgment, as I indicated earlier, these concepts overlap, and their differences don't favor either one as a means of communicating God's Word. First Corinthians 14:26 speaks of teaching, not specifically of preaching.

2. Certainly there is no reason to assume that Christian worship should be dominated by the kind of preaching defined by apostolic proclamation to unsaved Jews and Gentiles. There is no biblical evidence that that kind of preaching was part of the Christian worship service.

3. The Second Helvetic Confession implies that preaching is limited to those "lawfully called." Probably it has in mind those who hold what I have called the *special office*. Although there is wisdom in limiting the bulk of instruction in the church to those with official ordination,[17] I do not think Scripture limits teaching in the church to these. If the overseers in the church believe that an unordained person can speak words that would edify the congregation, they should permit such a person to do so. And I see no biblical reason why the words of that unordained person might not be a communication of the Word of God, just as the words of ordained persons are.

4. Indeed, I see no reason why we should not say the same thing about the words of all believers when they testify of Christ. Insofar as they communicate biblical content, their speech is the Word of God.

5. Centrality is always relative. When someone says that X is central, we may always ask: in relation to what? If X is central, what should be decentralized? In the Reformation

---

17. In my understanding, ordination gives someone the right to speak in the name of the church. That is the particular kind of authority that unordained people do not have. But that does not mean that unordained people should never teach, or that their teaching is not useful.

period, preaching became central at the expense of the sacrament. Now, I accept the Protestant critique of the Roman Mass, so I can understand why the Reformers sought to attack the Mass at its root and replace it with a preaching service. (Ulrich Zwingli took an even more extreme position, excluding music from the meeting.) But it is not obvious to me that any of the "elements" of true biblical worship is more central than any other. I have no biblical reason to think that the "lesson" (*didache*) (1 Cor. 14:26) is more central to worship than hymns, or sacraments, or prayers. And to the extent that the Reformers, in rejecting the Mass, also deemphasized the biblical sacraments, I believe they were mistaken.

Central or not, however, preaching and teaching are effective means by which God communicates his Word to us today. When these effectively communicate the meaning of Scripture, we hear Scripture. In that sense, "the preaching of the Word of God is the Word of God." Preachers sometimes get it wrong. But again, when they get it right, the Word of God is on their lips, as surely as it was on the lips of Jesus and Paul. When we hear such messages, we hear the autographic text of Scripture.

To be sure, much preaching and teaching consists of illustrations and applications of Scripture, rather than translation or paraphrase of the text itself. If, however, an illustration or application is a good one, one that truly conveys what Scripture teaches, requires, promises, and the like, it is nothing less than a communication of biblical content. So even an illustration can be a communication of the autographic text of Scripture, a personal word from God to us.

Everything I have said in this section pertains also to *theology*, which I have defined and discussed in chapter 1 of this volume. There I defined theology as "the application of the Word of God, by persons, to all areas of human life." As such, the term is a virtual synonym of *teaching* (*didache*) as set forth above.

Thus, good theology, like all good teaching, is a legitimate communication of the Word of God. This is not to say that any theologian is infallible or inerrant, any more than any other teacher or preacher. But his work is the same as theirs and has the same goal: the application of Scripture. So theology done well is a means that God uses to get his written Word into the minds and hearts of his people. That is to say, good theology is a communication of the autographic text of Scripture.

Sacraments

I will discuss the nature of the sacraments in chapter 49 of this book. But here it is important for us to note that these are, among many other things, ways in which God communicates his word to us.

In chapter 24, I distinguished three kinds of *media* by which God communicates his word to us: events, words, and persons. I discussed events in the first part of chapter 24, and words thereafter to this point, with further reflection on words yet to come. Later in the book, I will speak about the word of God in and through persons.

The sacraments are somewhat hard to place in this scheme. Literally, they are events, not words. But theological reflection on them focuses on them as a bearer of meaning.

In the Reformation, they were sometimes called *visible words*. And in one sense, they are also revelation through persons. Much discussion of the sacraments has focused on the nature of the "presence of Christ and the Spirit" in these events.

I hold, with the Reformed tradition, that there are only two sacraments: baptism and the Lord's Supper. Here is the WCF's definition of *sacrament*, a definition that certainly pertains to both ordinances:

> Sacraments are holy signs and seals of the covenant of grace, immediately instituted by God, to represent Christ, and his benefits; and to confirm our interest in him: as also, to put a visible difference between those that belong unto the church, and the rest of the world; and solemnly to engage them to the service of God in Christ, according to his Word. (27.1)

Gathering these ideas together, we can see (I trust that this isn't a surprise!) three main aspects of a sacrament, corresponding to God's lordship attributes (chapter 2) and the three perspectives based on them. The sacraments are signs, divine actions, and means of divine presence, which I assign to the categories normative, situational, and existential, respectively.

First, normatively, the sacraments are signs. That is, they are authoritative divine communications, revelations to us. They symbolize the gospel and teach us authoritatively what the gospel is. They teach us not by words, but by pictures, by actions. In baptism, not only do we hear about our cleansing, but we see and feel it, depicted dramatically. In the Supper, not only do we hear about Jesus' death for us, but we see his body given for us, and we taste, smell, and touch it. As the Reformers used to say, the sacraments are visible words. They supplement the Word of God by divinely authorized dramatic images. So the fullness of divine teaching is by Word *and* sacrament.

Second, situationally, the sacraments are God's actions on our behalf. The sacrament is not just our doing something in God's presence; it is God's doing something for us. God is really there, acting. For one thing, the sacraments are not only signs, but "seals." When we talk about a seal here, we are talking about something like the government seal on your birth certificate, which makes it official that you are a citizen of the country, with all rights and privileges appertaining. Baptism and the Lord's Supper are seals of God's covenant of grace with us in Christ, as Abraham's circumcision was a seal of his righteousness of faith (Rom. 4:11). As seals, the sacraments confirm and guarantee the covenant promises. In this respect, as I said earlier, they are visible words. As the Word of God guarantees the promises of God, so do the sacraments.

Third, existentially, the sacraments are locations of God's presence. That is implicit in what I have already said. If God is *doing* something for us in and through the sacrament, then he is, of course, present, and that itself is a wonderful blessing. So Paul speaks of the Supper as a *communion* of the body and blood of Christ (1 Cor. 10:16). The word translated "communion" in the KJV, "participation" in the ESV, is *koinonia*, "fellowship."

In his intimate presence, God helps us to grow in faith. Roman Catholics understand this process as something automatic. It happens *ex opere operato*, that is, from the very act of receiving the sacrament. But Scripture teaches that, no, our growth comes through the presence of Christ by his Spirit dealing with us personally. So the efficacy of the sacrament is by faith alone.

We can see, and we will see better from the later discussion of sacraments, that the symbolism of both sacraments is exceedingly rich. These two simple ceremonies portray salvation in Christ in an astonishing variety of ways. Baptism is about entrance to the covenant community, cleansing, forgiveness of sins, union with Christ. The Lord's Supper is about Jesus' body and blood given for us, the new covenant in his blood, table fellowship with God, and the glorious return of Jesus.

As I mentioned before, these bridge the categories of event-, word-, and person-revelation. As word-revelation, they present a large amount of biblical content. They are "visible words," as the Reformers said, but they are also words that can be touched, smelled, and tasted. All our senses are engaged, filled with biblical content.

I am not saying that the sacraments communicate the gospel apart from any words. If we had only sacraments and no verbal revelation, the meaning of the sacraments would be opaque to us. The words of Scripture provide the necessary interpretation of the sacraments, so that we can benefit from them. But if we had only words, and no sacraments, we would lose much of the force of the biblical words. God intends to communicate to us not only propositions, commands, and promises, but also visions and feelings commensurate with those words, aesthetics in a broad sense. Our participation in Christ is not merely verbal, but also visual and tactile.

And the sacraments also enliven the verbal revelation, driving its meaning into our heads and hearts. So they are a mode of verbal revelation, just as much as copies, translations, teaching, and preaching. They convey to us the teaching of Scripture in depth. So they speak to us the autographic text of Scripture, God's personal words.

I have indicated before, and will indicate again, that our appropriation of God's written words is not merely an academic task. Understanding Scripture in depth is not merely reading it with an appropriate language competence. It is a process of personal engagement with God's Spirit. That engagement comes through preaching and teaching, and also from baptism and the Lord's Supper.

Confessions, Creeds, Traditions

In this section, I will discuss some documents and practices that have gained various kinds of authority in the church. In most cases, churches regard their authority as somewhat less than Scripture, though in Roman Catholicism tradition is equal to Scripture in its authority.[18]

18. See my discussion of the Roman Catholic denial of the sufficiency of Scripture in chapter 26, under "Challenges to the Sufficiency of Scripture."

Tradition (*paradosis*) refers to words or practices "passed down" from one person or group to another. The NT distinguishes two kinds of tradition, one good and one bad. The good tradition is that revelation that God the Father "delivered unto" (*paradidomi*) Jesus his Son, to be further delivered to "anyone to whom the Son chooses to reveal him" (Matt. 11:27). This tradition is the mystery of the gospel, kept secret for ages (Rom. 16:25–26), that had been revealed to the apostles (1 Cor. 2:9–10). The apostles pass this tradition on to the church (1 Cor. 15:2–3), and the church has the responsibility to obey that tradition (2 Thess. 3:6; 2 Peter 2:21), to hold it firmly (2 Thess. 2:15; 2 Tim. 1:12–14), and to guard it against distortion (1 Tim. 6:20; Jude 3), as God gave to the Jews the responsibility to guard the oracles of God (Rom. 3:2). The church is then to pass the tradition on to "faithful men who will be able to teach others also" (2 Tim. 2:2). This tradition is God's revelation through Jesus and the apostles, now deposited permanently in Scripture (see chapter 25, our discussion of the permanence of God's written Word).

The bad tradition is the tradition of the Pharisees, which they placed on a level of authority equal to Scripture, thus "making void the word of God" (Mark 7:13). The Jewish tradition was a system of commentaries on Scripture and commandments that went somewhat beyond Scripture, so that no one would ever risk breaking any biblical commands. But they gave too much authority to this tradition, so Jesus says, "They tie up heavy burdens, hard to bear, and lay them on people's shoulders" (Matt. 23:4; cf. Col. 2:8; 1 Peter 1:18).

Roman Catholic theologians often claim that there is authentic teaching from the apostles that was never recorded in Scripture, but was communicated orally and passed on through the generations of the church over the centuries. Certainly there was such teaching. As I said earlier, the canon does not contain everything said by the prophets, Jesus, or the apostles. It does not even contain all of Paul's letters. No doubt if I were living in A.D. 60 with my present knowledge and interests, I would not hesitate to seek out an apostle's oral teaching to settle matters not clearly resolved in the written record. I would love to have asked Paul what he thought about the mode and subjects of baptism, or about the millennium. Certainly the apostles' oral teaching (see chapter 24) was as authoritative as their written teaching, that is, ultimately authoritative.

But in fact, as we have seen, God chose to rule his church permanently by a Book, not by oral tradition. And he determined for his own reasons that not everything the apostles taught orally would survive. Further, there is no way for us today to evaluate claims supposedly based on oral tradition, especially given the breakdown of trust between Protestants and Catholics. So we must reject the notion that such supposed traditions are as authoritative as Scripture, or even that they are reliable guides for Christian faith and life.

Extrabiblical tradition is not necessarily bad, however, whether or not it comes from the apostles. Indeed, such tradition is unavoidable. In the nearly two thousand years since Jesus' ascension, Christians could hardly avoid accumulating many standard ways of doing things and of formulating doctrine—ways that are not strictly required by Scripture, but are intended to facilitate the application of Scripture in various situations. For example, Scripture does not provide a liturgy, or a list of events to take place in worship. But to carry out Paul's admonition to do everything "decently and in order," many churches have agreed that worship should follow a certain standard order of events, usually allowing for variation on certain occasions. There is nothing wrong with this; it is not a violation of the sufficiency of Scripture. Since Scripture tells us to worship, but does not give us a standard liturgy, we must devise that for ourselves, trying to stay within general biblical guidelines. On the other hand, Scripture does not forbid believers to worship without a standard liturgy, and there are benefits to varying the order of worship from time to time.

What we must not do, however, is to claim that such tradition has the same authority as Scripture, or greater authority than Scripture. In the case of liturgy, no one should presume to argue that using a different order of worship necessarily violates God's will.

Theology is filled with technical terms that come from tradition, not Scripture. Scripture never says, for example, that we should refer to God as one *substance* or as three *persons*. Those terms come from philosophy, not the Bible. But those terms have entered theology as standard ways of referring to the oneness and manyness of God's Trinitarian existence. It would not be wrong to use other terms, as long as they affirmed the biblical teaching. But it is hard to imagine any other terms that would do the job as well. Today, of course, the terms we use about the Trinity not only must communicate biblical teaching accurately, but also must communicate effectively to others in the Christian community, who have adopted conventional definitions and would be misled by any unusual definitions of the standard terms.

So when the claims of a tradition are suitably modest, and that tradition facilitates the communication of the biblical Word of God, that tradition should be respected, even while being viewed with a critical eye. What we should avoid is *traditionalism*, such as (1) the view that once a tradition is established it can never be changed, (2) the notion that some tradition is just as authoritative as Scripture, (3) the notion that we should not test traditions by the Scriptures.[19]

Now, sometimes traditions are put into writing, into creeds, confessions, conciliar declarations, and so on. These have various purposes: (1) to instruct believers, especially to prepare them for baptism, (2) to present a witness to the world as to what Christians believe, (3) to declare the truth about a controversial matter and to warn against heresy, and (4) to enforce orthodoxy in the church by requiring subscription of teachers (or even church members) to a doctrinal statement, usually through an official examination.

---

19. See my "Traditionalism," Appendix P of *DWG*.

The first three purposes are fairly unproblematic.[20] They are part of the normal work of teaching in the church, addressed to the church itself and to the world. The fourth, however, is controversial.

There are passages of Scripture that may have had a creedal function in the church. Deuteronomy 6:4–5 reads:

> Hear, O Israel: The Lord our God, the Lord is one. You shall love the Lord your God with all your heart and with all your soul and with all your might.

This passage has long been used by Jews as a confession of faith in Yahweh. Later in Deuteronomy, we hear the confession of those who settle in the Promised Land and bring their firstfruits to the priest:

> And you shall make response before the Lord your God, "A wandering Aramean was my father. And he went down into Egypt and sojourned there, few in number, and there he became a nation, great, mighty, and populous. And the Egyptians treated us harshly and humiliated us and laid on us hard labor. Then we cried to the Lord, the God of our fathers, and the Lord heard our voice and saw our affliction, our toil, and our oppression. And the Lord brought us out of Egypt with a mighty hand and an outstretched arm, with great deeds of terror, with signs and wonders. And he brought us into this place and gave us this land, a land flowing with milk and honey. And behold, now I bring the first of the fruit of the ground, which you, O Lord, have given me." And you shall set it down before the Lord your God and worship before the Lord your God. (Deut. 26:5–10)

In the NT, we can mention Romans 10:9–10, in which the confession "Jesus is Lord" (cf. 1 Cor. 12:3; Phil. 2:11), together with the heart confession that Jesus is risen, defines one as a saved person. Perhaps the summary of the gospel found in 1 Corinthians 15:3–7 was also recited by the Christians as a confession of faith:

> For I delivered to you as of first importance what I also received: that Christ died for our sins in accordance with the Scriptures, that he was buried, that he was raised on the third day in accordance with the Scriptures, and that he appeared to Cephas, then to the twelve. Then he appeared to more than five hundred brothers at one time, most of whom are still alive, though some have fallen asleep. Then he appeared to James, then to all the apostles.

Paul continues to speak of Christ's appearances to him. This creed speaks of the atonement ("died for our sins"), the authority of the OT prophetic Scriptures, and Jesus'

---

20. I would quibble a bit about purpose 1. The Apostles' Creed evidently grew out of the practice of requiring a baptismal confession of basic Christian beliefs, and it is appropriate for that purpose. But longer documents such as the WSC should not in my judgment be used as "educational requirements" for baptism or confirmation. In the NT itself, people were expected to repent of their sins and confess Christ before baptism. But they were not expected to understand or articulate a complicated theology. Note how quickly converts were baptized in Acts 8:26–40 and 16:25–34.

burial and resurrection. Some have also speculated that Paul's rather lyrical treatment of Jesus' incarnation, death, resurrection, and ascension was an early Christian confession or hymn:

> Have this mind among yourselves, which is yours in Christ Jesus, who, though he was in the form of God, did not count equality with God a thing to be grasped, but made himself nothing, taking the form of a servant, being born in the likeness of men. And being found in human form, he humbled himself by becoming obedient to the point of death, even death on a cross. Therefore God has highly exalted him and bestowed on him the name that is above every name, so that at the name of Jesus every knee should bow, in heaven and on earth and under the earth, and every tongue confess that Jesus Christ is Lord, to the glory of God the Father. (Phil. 2:5–11)

Then there are the "trustworthy sayings" of Paul's pastoral letters (1 Tim. 1:15; 3:1; 2 Tim. 2:11–13; Titus 3:4–8), which may have been proverbial in the church. These are all well suited to the first three purposes of creeds that I mentioned earlier.

But in regard to the fourth purpose, there is no reason to believe that any of these statements were used as tests of orthodoxy among God's people. The statement "Jesus Christ has come in the flesh" certainly was a test of orthodoxy, according to 1 John 4:1–3, in a situation in which false prophets, docetists, were disturbing the church. But even here there is no suggestion that church members or officers had to formally confess this statement in the course of an examination in order to be in good standing. Of course, those who denied it, according to John, could not have been accepted as Christians.

Scripture speaks very strongly of the need to maintain doctrinal truth within the church. It condemns false prophets, false apostles, and false teaching in the strongest terms (Deut. 18:20–22; Matt. 7:15–20; 24:11; Luke 6:26; 2 Cor. 11:13; Gal. 2:4; 1 Tim. 6:3–5; 2 Tim. 3:1–9; 2 Peter 2:1–22; 1 John 4:1; Rev. 16:13; 19:20; 20:10), and it warns believers to turn aside from them (2 Tim. 3:5). Passages such as 2 Timothy 3:1–9 and 2 Peter 2:1–22 draw a very close parallel between false teaching and other kinds of sins. As Jesus said, "you will recognize them by their fruits" (Matt. 7:16). The problem with false teaching is not merely intellectual. Where there is false teaching, there is moral turpitude.

Presumably, then, the early church dealt with false teaching as with any other sin: by confrontation leading to the scrutiny of the church (Matt. 18:15–17) and possible sanctions including shunning and excommunication (1 Cor. 5:9–12; 2 Thess. 3:14–15; 2 John 10). This is, of course, a reactive, post facto approach. The church gives its members and teachers the benefit of the doubt until they hear something contrary to the apostolic teaching or experience the evil fruits of such heresy.

There does not seem to be evidence of a proactive, preventive approach to false teaching, such as the modern practice of requiring people to subscribe to a confession upon entering the church or entering an office. The church may well have required a confession upon baptism, perhaps a simple "Jesus is Lord," or something like the Apostles' Creed. One who becomes an overseer (bishop, elder) must be "able to teach" (1 Tim. 3:2) and able to "preach the word" (2 Tim. 4:2), which doubtless presuppose some training and examination before the candidate receives the office. But all of that can be done, of course, informally within the church, and in the absence of any formal confessional document.

So the NT church protected its orthodoxy mainly reactively, rather than proactively. I am not convinced that this model shouldn't be followed today.

In any case, the use of creeds and confessions to maintain orthodoxy in the church must be regarded as an optional method of protecting true doctrine, not a mandatory means of it. I think this point is obvious. But the discussion in various denominations about the necessity of this or that confession, or this or that form of subscription to the confession, is remarkably intense, considering that Scripture does not even require us to have such confessions.

In my judgment, there should be no confessional requirement for church members. Certainly the officers of a church should examine any person who asks to become a church member. The object of that examination should be simply to determine whether he or she can make a "credible profession of faith," a profession of trust in Christ as Savior and Lord, not contradicted by a pattern of sin. But when a church, in addition to this examination, requires the person to study and subscribe to a confession (such as the Westminster, Belgic, or Thirty-nine Articles), it requires more than Scripture requires, something beyond faith in Christ. Further, it limits church membership only to those who are well enough educated to understand the confession and master its teaching, guaranteeing that the church will be limited to a particular stratum of society. So it would close the door that Jesus opened.

It is different, of course, with regard to church officers. As I indicated above, overseers must be competent to teach, preach, and maintain orthodoxy in the church. Overseers should not be elected or appointed if they have not shown a detailed knowledge of Scripture and the gospel. One way to determine their orthodoxy is to prepare them to endorse a formal doctrinal statement. But there is no evidence that this was done in NT times.

Even though there was no confessional subscription during the biblical period, it is possible to argue the value of it in other situations pragmatically—that such a practice is the best method for ensuring orthodoxy in a church situation. If that argument can be made, then confessional subscription may be seen as an *application* of the biblical principle that church officers should be orthodox. But it cannot be shown, in my view, that this is the *only* way to ensure such orthodoxy.

Even today, I think, there is much to be said for the more reactive approach to these matters presented in the NT. Candidates for the office of overseer will show other overseers over a period of training and scrutiny that they love Jesus and his Word, that they are competent to teach and shepherd the flock, and that they believe the true gospel.[21] Then they will be received as officers by the laying on of hands and prayer (1 Tim. 4:14). From that point, if any charge against their orthodoxy is made, the burden of proof will be on the prosecution. This principle, sometimes called the *presumption of innocence*, is common to American civil law, and it is also biblical. In both Testaments, accusations must be verified by "two or three witnesses" (Deut. 17:6; 19:15; Matt. 18:16; 2 Cor. 13:1; 1 Tim. 5:19; Heb. 10:28), meaning that the accuser must have a cogent case. It is not the responsibility of the accused, faced by an unsubstantiated charge, to prove his innocence.

This form of discipline, even in the absence of an extrabiblical confessional test of orthodoxy, should be sufficient to maintain orthodoxy in the church, though it is not infallible, any more than confessional subscription infallibly ensures orthodoxy. Another benefit of such discipline is that it would also guard against false accusations. The test of accusations would be solid evidence of what took place, and the ultimate test of orthodoxy would be God's written Word itself, the only Book that God has given to rule his church.

Extrabiblical confessional documents such as the WCF have done the church good service as baptismal instruction, witness to the world, and warning against falsehood, to list the first three purposes of such documents that I named earlier. But the attempt to maintain orthodoxy in the church by confessional subscription has not, historically, achieved its goal. Many denominations that require subscription, even strict subscription, have fallen away into liberalism and other heresies.[22] And my experience has been that in churches that use confessions as tests of orthodoxy, much time has been wasted trying to exegete the confession that could have been spent exegeting the Bible.

So I maintain some skepticism about the very practice of confessional subscription. I admit, however, the unlikelihood that this practice will be abandoned in Presbyterian and Reformed churches anytime soon. So I have a fallback position. Granted that churches will continue to use confessional subscription to maintain orthodoxy, I would argue that the form of subscription should be loose enough to allow the confession to be reformed by the Word of God.

A few years ago there was a debate in the Presbyterian Church in America on the nature of confessional subscription.[23] Some argued for *strict subscription*, in which an officer must subscribe to every statement in the confession. Some strict subscriptionists allow for ministers to take exceptions to minor points of the confession, but they forbid the ministers to teach or preach their exceptions. Looser forms of subscription include *system subscription*, the present formula of the PCA, in which the minister subscribes to

---

21. I do believe that the training of church officers is best done in the most personal way possible, with a minimum of academic or ecclesiastical formality. See my "Proposal for a New Seminary," available at http://www.frame-poythress.org.

22. Arguably, the stricter the formula of subscription, the more people will be tempted to subscribe ignorantly or deceptively, keeping to themselves the parts of the confession that they don't understand, or that they doubt.

23. See, for example, David Hall, ed., *The Practice of Confessional Subscription* (Lanham, MD: University Press of America, 1995).

the confession "as containing the system of doctrine taught in the Scriptures." Usually this is understood to mean that the minister need not subscribe to every statement of the confession, but must affirm only that the confession teaches the system (the main elements) of the Bible's teaching.[24] Still looser forms are used in more liberal denominations, as when the minister agrees only to "be guided by" the confession.

In my judgment, strict subscription violates the sufficiency of Scripture. It prevents any teaching in the church that contradicts the confession. Thus, in effect, it recognizes no difference in authority between the confession and the Bible itself. If the sufficiency of Scripture is to have any meaning in the church, it must be possible to recognize error in the extrabiblical confessional document, bring that error to the church's attention, and revise the confession to make it agree with the Bible. But strict subscription guarantees that the confession will never be reformed according to the Word of God.

Nevertheless, it cannot be denied that God uses creeds and confessions to communicate his Word to us. We have seen earlier in this chapter that all authentic teaching, preaching, and theology conveys the Word of God. The creeds and confessions of the church are essentially theological teaching. They are not infallible, but when they agree with Scripture they communicate the teaching of Scripture.

Indeed, creeds and confessions have an authority above other teaching. For one thing, they represent a consensus of the church, and that consensus carries greater weight than the teaching of any individual. Individuals should be subject to others in the body of Christ, recognizing the gifts of others and the wisdom of the body as a whole. Further, that consensus is a consensus of people with special authority in the church: overseers, bishops, or elders. Though such people are not infallible, God has called them to exercise oversight of the church's doctrine and practice. Their authority should be honored, even after their death (Heb. 13:7, 17).

Each generation should rethink these documents, reforming them, where necessary, by the Word of God. But as "secondary standards," under Scripture, they should be respected. And insofar as these documents convey the true teaching of the Bible, they bring to us God's personal words.

Human Reception

As another in the series of events by which the Word of God comes to us, we now will briefly consider the human reception of Scripture. As I said before, the list is not

24. PCA candidates for ordination are asked this question: "Do you sincerely receive and adopt the *Confession of Faith* and the *Catechisms* of this Church, as containing the system of doctrine taught in the Holy Scriptures; and do you further promise that if at any time you find yourself out of accord with any of the fundamentals of this system of doctrine, you will on your own initiative, make known to your Presbytery the change which has taken place in your views since the assumption of this ordination vow?" *The Book of Church Order*, 6th ed. (n.p.: Office of the Stated Clerk of the General Assembly of the PCA, 2012), 21-5. Note that this statement not only loosens subscription by the phrase "system of doctrine," but also requires presbytery scrutiny only of views (1) that the minister himself identifies as problematic, and (2) that he considers out of accord with what he himself considers the *fundamentals* of the system of doctrine.

chronological in a general way. Certainly the human reception of Scripture began before there was theology, or teaching, or translations, or perhaps even copies. And there is human reception of Scripture in every one of these events, by the copyists, the preachers and teachers, their audiences, and so on. But the list is somewhat chronological in showing the process by which the biblical Word reaches a modern reader. So today we tend to receive the biblical message through copies, translations, editions, theology, confessions, and the like. Through these means God presents Scripture to us, and we receive it through that process.

But there has been a specific theological controversy about whether revelation exists apart from human reception of it—indeed, whether it exists apart from a human response in faith. So it is important to distinguish between (1) objective revelation, (2) subjective revelation received in unbelief, and (3) subjective revelation received in faith.

1. Objective revelation is revelation that God has made *available* for human knowledge, even to people who do not actually make use of it. In that sense, both nature and Scripture contain divine revelation addressed to everyone.

2. Subjective revelation is revelation that enters the human mind in some way. Scripture describes some examples of such revelation that is received in unbelief. Romans 1 speaks of the repression of natural revelation. Scripture speaks of the many times God spoke through the prophets, Jesus, and the apostles, to a response of rejection and rebellion. It is important for us to recognize that this is genuine revelation. Though its audience does not receive it in faith, it exists despite their reaction, and it takes away their excuses (Rom. 1:20).

3. Of course, God desires that people receive his revelation in faith. Some have argued that revelation received in faith is the only true revelation, because otherwise God's attempt to communicate has failed. Certainly there are some kinds of revelation that by definition produce a faith response (Matt. 11:27; Eph. 1:17). But this fact does not invalidate the kinds of revelation listed under points 1 and 2. Mysteriously, sometimes God's very purpose in communication is to harden hearts and to take away excuses (Isa. 6:9–10; Matt. 13:14–15; Acts 28:25–27).

Given this distinction, we can also make distinctions among the different kinds of recipients of the Word. Remarkably, God does speak to himself. There are communications among the persons of the Trinity (Gen. 1:26; Pss. 2:7–9; 45:6–8; 110; Matt. 11:25–27; John 4:34; 5:20; 6:38–39; 17:1–26; Acts 2:33–36).

There are also divine communications given to the natural world (Gen. 1:9, 20, 22, 24), to angels (Ex. 23:20; Dan. 3:28; etc.), and to the human race as a whole (Gen. 1:28–30; Rom. 1:18). The gospel of Jesus Christ is given to the apostles, but the Lord commissions them to bring it to everyone on earth (Matt. 28:19–20).

How does God want his Word to be received? I would distinguish three aspects that correlate with the lordship attributes and my epistemological perspectives: belief, obedience, and participation. See fig. 27.2.

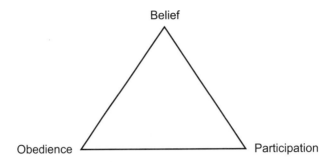

Fig. 27.2. Our Response to God's Word

Belief (normative): When God describes his mighty acts, we are expected to accept his description and interpretation. When he promises blessing or threatens judgment, we dare not call his Word into question.

Obedience (situational): What God commands must be obeyed without question.

Participation (existential): Since the Word is not exclusively propositional or imperative, God expects more from us than is easily summarized in the two points above (though either of them may be taken as a perspective on the whole of our response). Since the Word includes poetry, symbol, parable, and exhortation, among other genres of literature, God wants us to take his Word into our hearts, to let it work upon us in all the subtle ways in which these forms of language change people. The Word thus changes our interests, our emotions, our priorities, our perspectives, our preoccupations. God wants us not only to believe him and obey him, but also to be involved with him personally in a wide variety of ways.

How do we receive the Word of God? By use of the faculties that God has given us: our ability to read, hear, reason, feel. But of course, our sin makes it impossible for us to use these capacities rightly apart from his grace. What keeps us from suppressing the truth (Rom. 1:18), exchanging it for a lie (v. 25), and hardening our hearts (Isa. 6:9–10) is the Holy Spirit, who opens our eyes to perceive the full blessing of God's address to us, who enables us to rejoice in God's kindness. He opens our eyes first to see the reality of our own sin, and then to see God's forgiveness of sin for the sake of Christ.[25] So we can understand God's revelation only through the gospel. In that sense Scripture, the message of the gospel, takes primacy over all the rest of God's revelation. It becomes the "spectacles" (Calvin) by which we are enabled to see God's revelation in creation rightly.

Interpretation

Once we receive the Bible, it is our task to understand it, and to do that we must interpret it correctly. So interpretation is the next event on the list that I mentioned earlier in this chapter, though of course it occurs throughout the process by which

25. I will discuss the Spirit's work in detail in the next chapter.

Scripture reaches us. Certainly interpretation is involved at every step along the way: in confessions, theology, teaching, translation, even making copies (since many copyist errors result from misinterpretations).

The literature on interpretation is vast. Jews and Christians have been interpreting Bible passages for many centuries. But far beyond that, in the modern period, the idea of interpretation has been raised to a new level of philosophical sophistication and abstraction. Such thinkers as Schleiermacher, Dilthey, Heidegger, Gadamer, Habermas, and Ricoeur have expanded the notion of interpretation (or *hermeneutics*, as they prefer) to include the philosophy of language and communication. And because philosophy is an attempt to interpret the world, many have identified philosophy itself, indeed all forms of human knowledge, as hermeneutic.

I will not be able here to discuss hermeneutics in such an exalted way. My interest is in hermeneutics in the old, modest sense: the attempt to understand texts. And I limit that in turn, for purposes of this book, to the understanding of biblical language. Further, this discussion will be fairly elementary. I only hope to send my readers along the right track.[26]

What is interpretation, in this context? We often say that to interpret is to find the meaning of a text. But what is meaning?

We often think of meaning as translation. Here, to find the meaning of a sentence is to put it in other words that are somewhat equivalent. But why do we do that? In the case of Bible interpretation, why aren't the original words adequate?

In chapter 1, I asked a similar question about theology: why do we need theology, when we have the Bible? The answer cannot be because the Bible is inadequate in some way. Rather, the inadequacy is in us: we need theology because *we* have a problem understanding Scripture. Theology is the teaching ministry of the church, addressing that need.

Human questions about Scripture are of various kinds: what does this Hebrew word mean? What does John 1:1 mean? What is a covenant? Why did Jesus have to die? Such questions expose in us a lack of ability to use Scripture as God intended. As I indicated in chapter 27, these questions can be understood as questions of *application*. We face a text, but we lack the ability to relate it to our own lives. We may lack the ability to say it in our language, or we may lack the ability to relate it to our business decisions. In all these situations, we are trying to understand how to *apply* Scripture. So I said in chapter 27 that theology is the application of Scripture (chapter 1). In that sense, theology is equivalent to teaching and preaching (chapter 27), and they, too, can be understood as the application of Scripture. We tend to use the term *theology* to

---

26. For a much more elaborate treatment of interpretation, I recommend especially Vern S. Poythress, *God-Centered Biblical Interpretation* (Phillipsburg, NJ: P&R Publishing, 1999). Poythress has thought about these matters in great depth, and like me his chief interest is to be in accord with Scripture. Readers of my work will be especially interested in his triperspectival distinction between classificational, instantiational, and associational aspects of language, which leads to a view of meaning that balances sense, application, and import (72–74). See also my *DKG*, 169–214.

refer to an academic discipline, and *teaching* to refer to the ministry of a church. But the two are essentially the same, though they may differ in emphasis and the kinds of questions they typically address.

So now I suggest that interpretation-hermeneutics is also application. I asked earlier: when we look for the "meaning" of a passage, what are we looking for? I now answer: we are looking for an application.

Questions about meaning are of different kinds. When an English speaker asks, "What is the meaning of this Greek sentence?" a teacher often gives him an equivalent English sentence. John 1:1 begins: *En arche en ho logos.* The teacher tells the inquirer, "That means, 'In the beginning was the Word.'" So we are tempted to say that the English sentence is "the meaning of" the Greek sentence. But that is odd, for in a similar way a French speaker might find the meaning of the Greek in a French sentence, and similarly for all the other languages of the world. Is the meaning of John 1:1 to be identified with equivalent sentences from all the languages of the world?

Further, after a teacher gives the inquirer an equivalent English sentence, the inquirer may claim that he still does not know the meaning.[27] For the English itself may be as problematic as the Greek. After all, it is not obvious what it means for a "Word" to exist in the "beginning." Well, then, we seek another level of meaning—perhaps a theological explanation of the original sentence. We tell the inquirer that the "beginning" is the beginning of Genesis 1:1, the original creation. And we tell him that the "Word" is Jesus Christ (as John 1:14). So Jesus Christ was already present (*en*) when God created the world.

But even then, the inquirer might say something like this: "I understand intellectually what this means, but I don't know how it is supposed to affect my life. What does it mean *to me*?" So we move to another level of meaning. The teacher may reply, "If Jesus Christ, this Jew of Galilee, existed at the very beginning of creation, he must be pretty special. We need to put our hearts into knowing more about him and understanding who he is and what he has done." Even this answer might not satisfy the inquirer. He might want to learn more about what it means to know Christ, perhaps from a personal example rather than from a verbal formula.

But to simplify, now we have three levels of meaning: (1) an equivalent English phrase, (2) a theological explanation of the terms, (3) a program for our lives. I know of no term that better covers all these kinds of meaning (and more) than the term *application*. When we ask the "meaning" of a passage, we are simply confessing that we don't know what to do with it. When we explain meaning in various ways, we are helping people to learn what to do with the language, how to apply the language to themselves.[28]

27. I've often noticed that expressions that are problematic in Greek tend to be equally problematic in English. So switching languages doesn't necessarily help to clarify meaning.

28. As I indicated in footnote 26, Poythress correlates application with sense and import. *Sense* is the meaning of an expression that remains constant through its use in multiple contexts. *Application* is "any instantiation of a passage in word or deed." *God-Centered Biblical Interpretation*, 73. *Import* is the connection of an expression to other

Now, I used this correlation between interpretation and application in chapter 28 of *DWG* when I considered Bible problems. One problem was the apparent inappropriateness of NT quotations of the OT. I argued there that we need to have a broader view of the purposes of such quotations. They are not always quotations of predictions being fulfilled in the NT age. Sometimes they have the purpose of underscoring narrative parallels (e.g., between the life of Jesus and the history of Israel), of noting verbal parallels of some importance, and so on. We can have a better understanding of these quotations if we regard them as applications.

Now, the most common general question that people ask about biblical interpretation is: how can we understand texts from times and cultures far removed from ours? At first glance, this task may seem terribly difficult. But some considerations mitigate the problem:

1. In God's providence, human cultures are never sealed off from one another. We share with people in the ancient world our common humanity, and there are many ties between their languages and ours, their cultures and ours. There are differences between us and them, but also important similarities. These similarities are even greater between modern believers in Christ and ancient believers.

2. The greater cultural differences are bridged by the continuous existence of the church throughout the centuries. Since the time of Moses, God's people have studied Scripture and applied it to many of their own situations. We are part of that history, that interpretative process. We learn from the previous generation, and the generation before them, all the way back to Bible times. We are not, therefore, faced with a huge, empty cultural gap. That gap is filled with our own brothers and sisters in the Lord who have built bridges from the original composition of the Bible down to our own day. With their help, we can get back to the original cultural settings of Scripture by small steps.

3. Among the teachers that God has provided to the church (see our earlier discussion of *teaching*) are people gifted with expertise in these ancient cultures and languages. They are not infallible, but they can help us in a great many cases.

4. Scripture itself is the most important guide to its own interpretation, and it is an infallible guide. As WCF 1.9 says:

> The infallible rule of interpretation of Scripture is the Scripture itself: and therefore, when there is a question about the true and full sense of any Scripture (which is not manifold, but one[29]), it must be searched and known by other places that speak more clearly.

---

expressions (its contexts), and its distinctive function within that field of expressions. Poythress understands these as perspectivally related, so it is possible (as in my discussion above) to understand all meaning as application, or as sense, or as import. Thus, my treatment simplifies that of Poythress. Of the categories *sense, import,* and *application,* I think the latter is the most "practical," the easiest for most readers to follow.

29. In this parenthesis, the confession repudiates the "fourfold sense" of the medieval interpreters. These interpreters (and some in the early church) thought that most Bible passages contain a literal sense, an allegorical sense, a tropological (moral-ethical) sense, and an anagogical sense (anticipating heaven and the last days). Often

Scripture interprets Scripture; *Scriptura ipsius interpres*. As believers live in the Word of God, they come to see how the later parts presuppose earlier parts and how the earlier anticipate the later. They see how the Scriptures are bound together in a common worldview, a common symbolic structure, a common ethic, a common history, a common gospel of salvation. One consequence of the fact that God has inspired the Scriptures is that they are consistent with one another, that they tell a common story, though they are written by many human authors over many centuries. So each part illumines other parts. As we live in God's Word, cultural differences make less difference. The unity of Scripture makes more.[30]

5. Many times in this book I have argued that the ultimate identification of the word of God is supernatural. This was true for Abraham; as we saw in chapter 1, he knew that God was talking to him because God himself gave him the assurance that God was talking. This was true when God led the church to recognize his canon (chapter 25). So I have often noted through this book that our confidence in the word of God in any form is given by God himself. We will see in the next chapter that God, in the person of the Holy Spirit, also gives us grace to understand what God is saying to us. The Spirit illumines the Word and enables us to interpret.

So the difficulties of interpretation do not stand in the way of God's communicating his personal words to his people. We do not understand everything in Scripture,[31] but we understand much, by God's grace. And what we understand becomes the foundation of our lives, our only comfort in life and death.[32]

Key Terms
Autograph
Autographic text
Apographa
Inscriptional curse
Textual criticism
Translation
Edition
Teaching

---

those who distinguished these senses took little care to relate their interpretations to the original biblical contexts, and their nonliteral interpretations were often arbitrary. Actually, however, they weren't always, or entirely, wrong. It is often appropriate, of course, to understand texts literally. But it can also be helpful to draw parallels to apparently unrelated matters (allegory, as Paul in Galatians 4:21–31), to indicate ethical applications (*tropological*, as often in the NT; see 1 Cor. 10:6–12), and to draw trajectories (*anagogical*—typology, prophecy) to the future.

While we're looking at WCF 1.9, we should also note the confession's emphasis that each passage has one, not many, meanings. This parenthetical observation is, I think, also a rejection of the "fourfold sense" type of interpretation. It does not imply that the meaning of a passage is never complex. One look at the elaborate accounts of the Ten Commandments in the WLC makes it clear that the writers of the confession often found very expansive levels of meaning in Scripture.

30. Compare my discussion in chapter 24 of *DWG* about the unity of Scripture.
31. See chapter 26, on the clarity of Scripture.
32. Alluding to HC 1.

Preaching
Theology
General office
Special office
Sacrament
Signs
Seals
Confession
Creed
Tradition
Human reception of Word
Objective revelation
Subjective revelation
Subjective revelation received in faith
Belief
Obedience
Participation
Interpretation
Hermeneutics
Meaning
Fourfold sense
Scriptura ipsius interpres

Study Questions

1. Why does Frame not put downward arrows between the items of his second list of revelatory events?

2. Is it biblical to limit inerrancy to the autographic text of Scripture? Discuss.

3. If only the autograph is fully God's Word, why do the NT writers quote the OT in copies, translations, versions?

4. "Limiting inerrancy to the autographic text is an apologetic dodge." Explain the complaint and respond.

5. Does the limitation of inerrancy to the autographic text make inerrancy a dead letter? Explain the question and respond.

6. Why did God allow the autographs to be lost?

7. Why did God not give us perfect copies?

8. How could God have allowed even the smallest loss of his precious Word?

9. Distinguish "good tradition" from "bad tradition."

10. Is there any reason for thinking that a translation can convey the autographic text of Scripture?

11. Do you believe that preaching is "central" to Christian worship? In what sense? Argue your case from Scripture.

12. Can sacraments convey the content of Scripture? How? Explain.

13. Discuss various uses of confessions and creeds in the church. Discuss which are useful, which are necessary.

14. Does revelation exist apart from human reception in faith? Discuss.

15. How is it possible for people in our time to rightly interpret the Bible, given that it was written in a culture very different from ours?

Memory Verses

Deut. 4:2: You shall not add to the word that I command you, nor take from it, that you may keep the commandments of the LORD your God that I command you.

Deut. 6:4–5: Hear, O Israel: The LORD our God, the LORD is one. You shall love the LORD your God with all your heart and with all your soul and with all your might.

Rom. 10:9–10: If you confess with your mouth that Jesus is Lord and believe in your heart that God raised him from the dead, you will be saved. For with the heart one believes and is justified, and with the mouth one confesses and is saved.

1 Cor. 11:26: For as often as you eat this bread and drink the cup, you proclaim the Lord's death until he comes.

Resources for Further Study

Bahnsen, Greg. "The Inerrancy of the Autographa." In *Inerrancy*, edited by Norman Geisler, 156–59. Grand Rapids: Zondervan, 1979.

Hall, David, ed. *The Practice of Confessional Subscription*. Lanham, MD: University Press of America, 1995.

Poythress, Vern S. *God-Centered Biblical Interpretation*. Phillipsburg, NJ: P&R Publishing, 1999.

FROM THE TEXT TO OUR HEARTS

IN THIS CHAPTER, I will focus on the personal dimension of God's revelation. We saw in chapter 24 that revelation comes to us by events, words, and persons. See fig. 28.1.

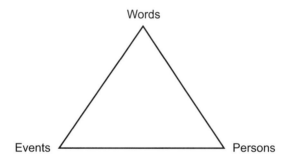

Fig. 28.1. Forms of Divine Revelation

Most of our attention so far has been given to revelation in words. But God's ultimate goal in revelation is not to produce a message on paper or other inanimate media, but to bring that message into human minds and hearts. To make that happen, God himself enters the stream of revelation and brings his Word to us. So revelation involves persons at two levels: the divine persons who reveal, and the human persons who receive the revelation. We must understand this interpersonal interaction if we are to know how to be assured of the truth of God's Word, and how we can become God's obedient servants.

Assurance

It may seem that we have been on a long, strenuous journey through the steps listed in chapter 27: copying, textual criticism, translation, editions, teaching, preaching, sacraments, confessions, creeds, traditions, human reception, interpretation, and understanding. It may seem that we can barely perceive the autographic text through the fog. And it may seem that with every step we lose assurance. For at every step, errors enter the picture. Can we be sure that our Bible is based on accurate copies, a proper textual tradition, sound teaching, interpretation, and so on?

But believers understand that reading the Bible is not like this. It's not like a slog through a jungle in which we have to hack away at thousands of pieces of underbrush before we reach our destination. Rather, it is very much like listening to our Father talking to us. As in Abraham's case, we hear in Scripture a personal word from God.

If the problems of text, translation, and such things are so difficult that we can never identify the voice of God, then, of course, our faith is an illusion. Faith in Scripture is precisely hearing the voice of God, believing, obeying, and participating in his words (chapter 27). Abraham is the primary model of Christian faith in the NT (Rom. 4:1–25; cf. John 8:56; Gal. 3:6–29; Heb. 6:13–20; 11:8–22; James 2:21–23). "He believed the LORD, and [God] counted it to him as righteousness" (Gen. 15:6) is quoted three times in the NT (Rom. 4:3; Gal. 3:6; James 2:23). We, too, are to believe Christ, and our faith in the promise of his free grace is the instrument of our salvation.

It will not do to say that revelation is something nonpropositional, perhaps an occasional mystical experience. That is not the kind of revelation that Abraham heard. God gave him commands, and an intelligible promise. Our own salvation is grounded in that promise. Without it, there is no hope.

In 1 Corinthians 15, Paul expresses amazement that some in the church have come to deny that the dead are raised. He replies:

> Now if Christ is proclaimed as raised from the dead, how can some of you say that there is no resurrection of the dead? But if there is no resurrection of the dead, then not even Christ has been raised. And if Christ has not been raised, then our preaching is in vain and your faith is in vain. We are even found to be misrepresenting God, because we testified about God that he raised Christ, whom he did not raise if it is true that the dead are not raised. For if the dead are not raised, not even Christ has been raised. And if Christ has not been raised, your faith is futile and you are still in your sins. Then those also who have fallen asleep in Christ have perished. If in Christ we have hope in this life only, we are of all people most to be pitied. (1 Cor. 15:12–19)

If there is no resurrection for human beings, then not even Christ has been raised. We know that Christ has been raised, so certainly there is a resurrection for all believers. But how are the Corinthians to be sure that Jesus was actually raised from the dead? The answer is that they have learned this in a personal word from God:

> Now I would remind you, brothers, of the gospel I preached to you, which you received, in which you stand, and by which you are being saved, if you hold fast to the word I preached to you—unless you believed in vain.
>
> For I delivered to you as of first importance what I also received: that Christ died for our sins in accordance with the Scriptures, that he was buried, that he was raised on the third day in accordance with the Scriptures, and that he appeared to Cephas,

then to the twelve. Then he appeared to more than five hundred brothers at one time, most of whom are still alive, though some have fallen asleep. Then he appeared to James, then to all the apostles. Last of all, as to one untimely born, he appeared also to me. For I am the least of the apostles, unworthy to be called an apostle, because I persecuted the church of God. But by the grace of God I am what I am, and his grace toward me was not in vain. On the contrary, I worked harder than any of them, though it was not I, but the grace of God that is with me. Whether then it was I or they, so we preach and so you believed.

Now if Christ is proclaimed as raised from the dead, how can some of you say that there is no resurrection of the dead? (1 Cor. 15:1–12)

Now, apologists often quote this passage as a list of evidences for the resurrection, and it certainly is that. Paul lists resurrection appearances to apostles, even one appearance to five hundred brothers at once, some of whom are still alive and therefore, we should assume, capable of testifying. But the Corinthians, most of them, had not personally witnessed the resurrection. Nor had they individually cross-examined the witnesses. For them, the knowledge of the resurrection comes from another source, namely, the preaching of Paul (1 Cor. 15:1–3, 11–12). Paul's primary argument is that the resurrection of Christ was part of the apostolic preaching, the preaching that God used to plant the church. To doubt that is to doubt the whole gospel. To reject the resurrection is to reject Paul's preaching as "vain" (v. 14) and faith itself as vain. And if our faith is futile, we are yet in our sins (v. 17).

Paul's preaching was like the promise to Abraham: a personal word from God. Our faith, too, is based on this personal word. If we have no personal word, our faith is futile, and we are yet in our sins. And if we cannot identify God's Word (despite the history of textual and interpretative problems), then we have no hope. Christianity is a sham.

But we have seen that God intends to speak personal words to his people. He acknowledges no barriers that can keep him from communicating with us successfully. And believers throughout the centuries have been assured that God's Word is true. They have found that Word to be trustworthy enough to build their lives upon it, to trust it as their only comfort in life or death, to believe and obey it no matter what the unbelieving world may say.

How is such assurance possible? For one thing, it is not at all difficult for God. Abraham's case was also problematic. Humanly speaking, it is hard to understand why he would accept God's word. His reason and emotions must have questioned the notion that he should leave his home to dwell in a new and strange land (Gen. 12:1). Even more, his conscience must have rebelled against the idea that God would want him to sacrifice his beloved son, the son of the covenant (22:2). Any of us would have been inclined to say that the voice asking him to do such things could not have been the voice of God. But God somehow managed to identify himself. Abraham was assured that this was the word of God. It was the highest assurance, because it came from God himself.

Similarly, God gets through to believers today. The unbelieving world, the academic establishment, and our own rebellious inclinations pose a thousand reasons why we should not accept Scripture as humble servants. The problems of text, interpretation, and theology often seem insuperable. But many still believe, and their number increases. It is hard to account for this. But it is God at work.

Subjectively, it works like this. When someone believes God's Word with true faith, he or she does not accept it through autonomous reasoning, through the consensus of scholars, or through an independent examination of evidences. We do not believe God because we have subjected God to our tests and the tests of others. Rather, God's Word is the foundation of our thought.[1] God's Word is the ultimate criterion of truth and right. It is the judge of what reasoning is valid and sound. The ultimate test of a scholar is whether his work agrees with Scripture. And Scripture determines what evidences are to be believed.

It is God himself who enables us to accept his Word as our foundation, our presupposition.

To say this is not to deny that Scripture presents problems to us. Often, it is not easy to know what Scripture is saying, or to answer the objections that arise in our hearts. So there is much in the Bible of which we do *not* have assurance, even when we seek to trust God's Word as our presupposition.

But the Christian life is a journey, a movement from faith to more faith (with, to be sure, ups and downs along the way). This is a journey both toward better understanding and toward overcoming our unbelief (Mark 9:24). The latter process is called *sanctification*. The former process is also related to sanctification: our level of understanding is related to our level of trust and obedience.[2] But our lack of understanding is also related to our finitude, our inability to resolve all the questions that the phenomena of Scripture pose to us.

Yet every believer begins with certainty. When we trust in Christ, we "know" that we have eternal life (1 John 5:13), and we "know" that he hears our prayers (v. 15).[3] As I mentioned earlier, if we have faith at all, we *know* that Christ has been raised from the dead. It is our fundamental confession that Jesus is the Christ, the son of the living God (Matt. 16:16; cf. John 6:69). Such facts become our presuppositions, the foundations of knowledge.

These presuppositions are the ultimate criteria of truth for a Christian. All other ideas must be consistent with them. They form the foundation on which all our other knowledge is to be built. When someone raises an objection that conflicts with one of these presuppositional beliefs, we know that objection is false, whether or not we can otherwise refute it.

---

1. It should be obvious to those who know about such things that I am not asserting *foundationalism* in the sense that it is usually criticized today. For some observations on the subject, see *DKG*, 128–29, 386–87. I do not believe that all human knowledge should be deduced from Scripture, as Descartes tried to deduce all human knowledge from his foundational argument. But I do maintain that all human knowledge must be reconcilable with Scripture.

2. See *DKG*, 40–49.

3. I am describing here the faith of normal adults. God is able to make special provision for those who are unable to understand propositional content. See WCF 10.3.

But there are things in the Bible that we do not understand well enough to affirm with this kind of assurance. My former colleague Richard Pratt uses a diagram that he calls the *cone of certainty* to illustrate this problem. It is simply a cone with the narrow end at the top and the broader end on the bottom. At the narrow end of the cone are those beliefs that we are sure of: say, the existence of God, the deity of Christ, his resurrection, salvation by grace through faith, and so on. At the bottom of the cone, there are matters in Scripture of which we are very unsure: Where did Cain get his wife (Gen. 4:17)? Why did Jephthah keep the vow to make his daughter an offering (Judg. 11:29–40)? Why was it such a serious crime for somebody to gather sticks on the Sabbath (Num. 15:32–36)? At the bottom of my cone is God's reason for bringing evil into the world, and the timing of the millennium. We may have views about such matters, but we are not always sure of them.

In between the bottom and the top are matters about which we may have opinions, but we would not normally claim that they are absolutely certain. For me, these would include the mode and subjects of baptism, the frequency of the Lord's Supper, the biblical pattern for church government, and the nature of Jesus' ignorance (Matt. 26:39).

As we grow as believers, there is movement through the cone. Some things of which we were once very certain become uncertain. Other things of which we have been uncertain become certain. But the overall progression, I think, is toward greater certainty. Scripture values certainty, and therefore our sanctification moves toward that goal, as part of the holiness that God seeks in us.

The Bible often tells us that Christians can, should, and do know God and the truths of revelation (Matt. 9:6; 11:27; 13:11; John 7:17; 8:32; 10:4–5; 14:17; 17:3; many other passages). Such passages present this knowledge not as something tentative, but as a firm basis for life and hope.

Scripture uses the language of certainty more sparingly, but that is also present. Luke wants his correspondent Theophilus to know the "certainty" (*asphaleia*) of the things he has been taught (Luke 1:4) and the "proofs" (*tekmeria*) by which Jesus showed himself alive after his death (Acts 1:3). The centurion at the cross says, "Certainly [*ontos*] this man was innocent!" (Luke 23:47).

The letter to the Hebrews says that God made a promise to Abraham, swearing by himself, for there was no one greater (Heb. 6:13). So God both made a promise and confirmed it with an oath, "two unchangeable things, in which it is impossible for God to lie" (v. 18). This is "a sure and steadfast anchor of the soul" (v. 19). Similarly, Paul (2 Tim. 3:16–17) and Peter (2 Peter 1:19–21) speak of Scripture as God's own words, which provide sure guidance in a world where false teaching abounds. God's special revelation is certain, and we ought to be certain about it.

On the other hand, the Bible presents doubt largely negatively. It is a spiritual impediment, an obstacle to doing God's work (Matt. 14:31; 21:21; 28:17; Acts 10:20; 11:12; Rom. 14:23; 1 Tim. 2:8 KJV; James 1:6). In Matthew 14:31 and Romans 14:23, it is the opposite of faith and therefore a sin. Of course, this sin, like other sins, might remain with us through our earthly life. But we should not be complacent about it. Just as the ideal for the Christian life is perfect holiness, the ideal for the Christian mind is absolute certainty about God's revelation.

We should not conclude that doubt is always sinful. Matthew 14:31 and Romans 14:23 (and indeed the others I have listed) speak of doubt in the face of clear special revelation. To doubt what God has clearly spoken to us is wrong. But in other situations, it is not wrong to doubt. In many cases, in fact, it is wrong for us to claim knowledge, much less certainty. Indeed, often the best course is to admit our ignorance (Deut. 29:29; Rom. 11:33–36). Paul is not wrong to express uncertainty about the number of people he baptized (1 Cor. 1:16). Indeed, James tells us, we are always ignorant of the future to some extent, and we ought not to pretend that we know more about it than we do (James 4:13–16). Job's friends were wrong to think they knew the reasons for his torment, and Job himself had to be humbled as God reminded him of his ignorance (Job 38–42).

So Christian epistemologist Esther Meek points out that the process of knowing through our earthly lives is a quest: following clues, noticing patterns, making commitments, respecting honest doubt. In much of life, she says, confidence, not certainty, should be our goal.[4]

I agree. But in regard to our knowledge of God's Word, certainty should be our goal. We should not be complacent with doubt, but we should use all the abilities God has given us to advance in knowledge of his Word. Besides following clues, noticing patterns, and the like, we should employ our spiritual resources: prayer, sacrament, teaching. In all these, God comes through to us. That is to say, as we obey the revelation of which we are certain, God grants us certainty about other things.

So the process I described in the previous chapter—copying, textual criticism, translations, and so on—is not a journey toward more and more uncertainty and confusion. To be sure, we encounter errors at each step of the human assimilation of God's Word. But each step also represents progress toward greater understanding. At each step, errors enter in, but errors are also corrected. By faith we expect that the overall trajectory of our assurance is upward. With each step, we grow in grace, knowledge, confidence, and certainty.

To speak of this journey toward certainty is to speak of the workings of the Holy Spirit, to whom we must now turn.[5]

Person-Revelation: The Divine Witness

We are now going to move on to the third group of media, *person-revelation*. I spent a very long time on word-revelation, because that is the greatest emphasis of Scripture, and because it is in that area that most controversy and confusion has arisen.

But person-revelation is also important, and vitally necessary for the process of divine-human communication. It is also necessary to our proper understanding and

---

4. Esther Meek, *Longing to Know: The Philosophy of Knowledge for Ordinary People* (Grand Rapids: Brazos Press, 2003). See also her more recent work, *Loving to Know: Covenant Epistemology* (Eugene, OR: Cascade Books, 2011).

5. The present section may be usefully compared to my article "Certainty," available at http://www.frame-poythress.org.

use of word-revelation. You may wish to review this threefold understanding as I presented it in chapter 23.

God reveals himself in events, words, and persons. That triad reflects the lordship attributes—control, authority, and presence—though each of the media conveys to us all the lordship attributes. Event-revelation, for example, especially demonstrates God's powerful control. But it also carries the full authority of God, and God himself is personally present in it. See fig. 28.2.

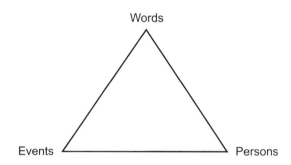

Fig. 28.2. Forms of Divine Revelation

Persons are an important means of divine communication. For one thing, God, the One who reveals himself, is personal rather than impersonal (chapter 2). Indeed, as we saw in chapter 23, God's word, his communication, is identical with himself. So revelation includes manifestation of divine persons, angelic persons,[6] and human persons in the image of God.

Another consideration: If meaning is application, at least from one perspective (chapters 1, 27), then we cannot understand language without understanding how its speakers apply it. Language is part of life. To understand language, we must see what people *do* with it, how it is *used*. So in understanding the word of God, it is important to learn how God intends that word to be used. That means, first, that we should understand how God himself makes use of his word. And second, we need to see examples of how fellow human beings use God's word—wrongly and rightly. So persons, as they speak, hear, and act out the word of God, are an important subject of our study.

In this section, we will consider the role of the three persons of the Trinity as person-revelation, with special emphasis on the witness of the Holy Spirit. In the next, we will look at human persons as God's image.

As we saw in chapter 23, the word is God, both as his divine attribute and as the second person of the Trinity. So wherever the word is, God is. God accompanies his

---

6. I will not consider angelic persons here, mainly because of my lack of insight into their role as revelation. Generally, they are messengers of God, as their names *malak* and *angelos* suggest. But how does the *person* of the angel reveal God? I have nothing much to offer on that subject. For some reflection on the role of angels in the Christian life, however, see *DCL*, 253–57, and chapter 33 of this book.

word to bring it to pass. So the word is never an impersonal object or force. It is God himself drawing near to us (recall Deut. 30:11–14; Rom. 10:6–9). As we hear or read the Word, God speaks it to us. In the previous chapter, we considered the chief difficulty of Bible interpretation, namely, the distance between the time and culture of the writers and of ourselves. The ultimate answer to that difficulty is that in an important sense, the Word of Scripture is always contemporary. God speaks it in our hearing, our time, our culture. This fact does not take away our responsibility to interpret Scripture in the context in which it was first given. But it does eliminate the possibility that the historical gap might make the Word inaccessible to us.

Let us consider now some forms of divine person-revelation.

Theophany

In theophany, God appears in the form of something created, often as an angel or man. The "angel of the Lord" appears as an angel, but at some point in the context identifies himself as God, as in Genesis 16:7–14; 21:17–21. In Genesis 32:22–32, Jacob wrestles with "a man" (v. 24) who turns out to be God (v. 30). Similarly, the "men" who met with Abraham in Genesis 18:1–33 are related in a mysterious way to "the Lord."

Most often the theophany takes the form of a glory-cloud,[7] in which God is surrounded by heavenly beings and the light of his glory. This is the cloud and pillar of fire by which God led Israel through the wilderness. In that cloud is God himself (Ex. 16:6–10). Here revelation has a strongly visual aspect. Although God is invisible, he voluntarily takes on visible forms that impress people with his terrifying power and magnificent glory.

But Jesus Christ is also a theophany. When Philip asked him, "Show us the Father," Jesus replied:

> Have I been with you so long, and you still do not know me, Philip? Whoever has seen me has seen the Father. How can you say, "Show us the Father"? (John 14:9)

Of course, Jesus is more than a theophany, for he is not only a visible revelation of the Father; he actually became a man. But that manhood is itself a profound revelation of God, since man himself is God's image, and Jesus was unfallen man, the most perfect of men. Against the docetists, who thought that Jesus only seemed to have a human body, John says:

> That which was from the beginning, which we have heard, which we have seen with our eyes, which we looked upon and have touched with our hands, concerning the word of life—the life was made manifest, and we have seen it, and testify to it and proclaim to you the eternal life, which was with the Father and was made manifest to us—that which we have seen and heard we proclaim also to you, so that you too may have fellowship with us; and indeed our fellowship is with the Father and with his Son Jesus Christ. (1 John 1:1–3)

---

7. See Meredith G. Kline, *Images of the Spirit* (Grand Rapids: Baker, 1980). See also *DG*, 585–87, 592–95.

Note the excited, eloquent sensory language about the disciples' knowledge of Jesus.

Theophany is also connected in Scripture with the Holy Spirit, the third person of the Trinity. Kline believes that the hovering of the Spirit over creation in Genesis 1:2 is the theophanic glory-cloud. So he regularly calls this theophany the *glory-Spirit*.

Christ, the Mediator of All Revelation

We have considered Jesus Christ in his divine identity with the Word of God (chapter 23) and, as man, the chief theophany of God. We have also looked at him as the chief speaker of God's authoritative word (chapter 24), and as the divine voice incarnate.

Here we will note that Christ speaks through all forms of revelation. This statement follows from the fact that he and the Father are both involved in all of God's works in the world. He does everything the Father does (John 5:19).

Like the Father, then, he is Creator (John 1:1–3; Col. 1:15–16; Heb. 1:2–3) and the Author of providence (Col. 1:17; Heb. 1:3). So natural revelation, the revelation of God through creation, is a revelation of Christ. It is not only God who speaks to us in creation; it is specifically Jesus.

He is also the Redeemer, who, not only in his own atoning death and resurrection, but also in all the events preparatory to these, accomplishes salvation for his people. So he is the chief theme of the Scriptures (Luke 24:25–27; John 5:45–47; 1 Cor. 10:4).

He is also the chief Prophet, who interprets these events (John 3:34–36; 6:63; 7:16; 8:28; 12:47–49; 17:8). His Father sent him into the world to utter the word of God, giving him the Spirit without measure (3:34). So his words are of utmost importance to the believer, as Peter understood when he said, "Lord, to whom shall we go? You have the words of eternal life" (6:68). So the words of the apostles, whom Jesus commissions to pass his words on to others, are also of utmost importance to us.

We will see later that human example is an important form of revelation, for as I said, it is important to see how exemplary persons use the word of God. God's revelation comes to us in both word and deed. Jesus is the chief example, as we see in Matthew 11:29; 16:24; John 13:35; 1 Corinthians 11:1; Philippians 2:5–11; 1 Peter 2:21; 1 John 3:16.

God, Word of God, theophany, divine voice, Creator, Provider, Redeemer, Prophet, example. Jesus is all of these, and, in all these ways, Jesus is the Mediator of all revelation. And Jesus' use of the word of God shows us how we should use it.

The Work of the Holy Spirit

As with Jesus the Son of God, the Spirit does everything that God does. He, too, is active in creation and providence (Gen. 1:2; Ps. 104:30). He gives life, both physical and spiritual (Job 33:4; Ps. 104:30; John 3:5–8; 6:63; Rom. 8:11). Through him we are washed, sanctified, and justified (1 Cor. 6:11). So God's word is a word about the works of the Spirit, as it is about the works of Christ and the Father.

The Spirit is also the Teacher of the church, the Spirit of the prophets and apostles (Num. 11:25; Matt. 10:20; 1 John 2:27). In Hebrews 10:15–17, the writer quotes words ascribed to God in Jeremiah 31:33 and ascribes them to the Spirit. The prophets speak their word by the authority of the Spirit (Gen. 41:38; Num. 24:2; 1 Sam. 10:6; Isa. 61:1; Luke 1:17; 1 Peter 1:11). So do Jesus and the apostles (Matt. 10:20; Luke 4:14; John 3:34; 14:16–17; 15:26; 16:13; Acts 2:4; 1 Cor. 2:4; 12:3). So the Spirit is the One who *inspires* the words of people, making those words identical with the word of God (see chapter 23). And he inspires the written Word as well. In 2 Timothy 3:16, as we have seen, all Scripture is God-breathed. The *breathed* in that expression refers to the work of the Spirit. Both Hebrew and Greek terms for *Spirit* refer to "breath" or "wind." The Spirit is God's breath. By him, God breathes out his words. So the Spirit is the Author of the Bible.

Not only does the Spirit *inspire* the Bible, he also *illumines* it to its readers. Scripture teaches that apart from God's grace, it is impossible for us to appropriate God's Word for our salvation. As with natural revelation in Romans 1, our sinful inclination is to suppress the truth, to exchange it for a lie. So Paul says that when the Jews read the law of Moses without Christ, "a veil lies over their hearts" (2 Cor. 3:15). In such darkness, we need God's light to see his Word properly. John Murray defines illumination as "regeneration on its noetic side."[8] The Spirit gives new birth (John 3:5), and that new life includes change in our noetic faculties, our ways of gaining knowledge (Col. 3:10). So he enables us to understand the Scriptures (Ps. 119:18; 1 Cor. 2:12–15; Eph. 1:17–19). Without him, we cannot gain spiritual knowledge from the Bible.[9]

John Murray believes that we should make a further distinction in the Spirit's work. He says:

> The question may properly be raised, however, whether or not the notion of illumination is fully adequate as an interpretation of the nature of the [Spirit's] testimony. On the view that it consists merely in illumination, the testimony, most strictly considered, resides entirely in the Scripture itself and not at all in the ever-present activity of the Spirit. And the question is, may we not properly regard the present work of the Spirit as not only imparting to us an understanding to perceive the evidence inhering in the Scripture but also as imparting what is of the nature of positive testimony?[10]

Murray answers yes, and finds that positive testimony in the "power and demonstration" of which Paul speaks in 1 Thessalonians 1:5:

> Our gospel came to you not only in word, but also in power and in the Holy Spirit and with full conviction. You know what kind of men we proved to be among you for your sake.

Compare 1 Corinthians 2:4–5:

8. John Murray, "The Attestation of Scripture," in *The Infallible Word*, ed. Ned Stonehouse and Paul Woolley (Philadelphia: Presbyterian and Reformed, 1946), 51.

9. Scripture never suggests that the Spirit's illumination *makes* the Bible into the Word of God, as many modern theologians have suggested. Even less does it suggest that the Spirit causes a momentary or transitory union between the Scripture and God's word, so that Scripture "becomes" God's Word from time to time. The Bible is objectively God's Word. The work of the Spirit is to make us understand and apply it.

10. Murray, "The Attestation of Scripture," 51.

My speech and my message were not in plausible words of wisdom, but in demonstration of the Spirit and of power, that your faith might not rest in the wisdom of men but in the power of God.

This demonstration and power leads to firm conviction. Paul's hearers accepted his message as the Word of God (1 Thess. 2:13). This "demonstration" (*apodeixis*) does not convey truth content in addition to that of Scripture itself. Rather, it persuades us to embrace the content of the Word itself. Cf. 1 John 2:20–27.

Frequently through our discussion of the word of God I have argued that our identification of God's word is supernatural. Only in this way could Abraham have been sure that God was talking to him, despite his natural resistance to the commands he heard. Only in this way could God's people identify the divine voice (chapter 24). Only in this way, in the final analysis, can God's people identify true prophets and distinguish them from false (chapter 24). The same is true of the church's recognition of the canon (chapter 25), the right interpretation of Scripture (chapter 27), and our final assurance of the truth (this chapter, previous section). The work of the Holy Spirit in illumination and demonstration is the supernatural factor that enables us to hear the words of Scripture as God's personal words to us. Here the author of the text opens the text to us.[11]

The *indwelling* of the Spirit is also revelatory. We are the temple of the Spirit (1 Cor. 3:16), and the Spirit dwells in us. The Spirit's intimate presence motivates our holiness, the only kind of character appropriate in the Spirit's temple. So Paul admonishes:

> But I say, walk by the Spirit, and you will not gratify the desires of the flesh. For the desires of the flesh are against the Spirit, and the desires of the Spirit are against the flesh, for these are opposed to each other, to keep you from doing the things you want to do. But if you are led by the Spirit, you are not under the law. Now the works of the flesh are evident: sexual immorality, impurity, sensuality, idolatry, sorcery, enmity, strife, jealousy, fits of anger, rivalries, dissensions, divisions, envy, drunkenness, orgies, and things like these. I warn you, as I warned you before, that those who do such things will not inherit the kingdom of God. But the fruit of the Spirit is love, joy, peace, patience, kindness, goodness, faithfulness, gentleness, self-control; against such things there is no law. And those who belong to Christ Jesus have crucified the flesh with its passions and desires.
>
> If we live by the Spirit, let us also walk by the Spirit. (Gal. 5:16–24)

So the Spirit not only inspires, illumines, and demonstrates the Word. He also takes residence in our lives as a person. And when we recognize the promptings of the Spirit, the kind of life he urges upon us, we seek to live in that way, to encourage the growth of his fruits in our lives.

For these reasons, the Spirit and the Word, God's breath and speech, are always together (Gen. 1:2; Ps. 33:6; Isa. 34:16; 59:21; John 6:63; 16:13; Acts 2:1–4; 1 Thess.

---

11. And in this case the author, and only the author, has the absolute right to explain his writing to us, contrary to some postmodern literary theory.

1:5; 2 Tim. 3:16; 2 Peter 1:21).[12] The Spirit inspires, illumines, and demonstrates the content of God's Word, and his indwelling presence motivates us to obey that Word.

So in the long trail of events that we have considered from the initial copying of the text to our present-day reception of Scripture, God himself walks with us. He never leaves us alone. He continues to speak his personal words to us through the biblical text. Hearing and learning Scripture are not impersonal, academic tasks. They are a person-to-person interaction with God as he teaches us his personal words.

Epistemology and the Spirit's Witness

In the previous section, I suggested a basis for our assurance of the truth of God's Word. That discussion concluded with a general reference to God's own witness. In this chapter, we have seen that that divine witness is especially connected with the testimony of the Holy Spirit. At this point I will try to show the relation between the Spirit's witness and the witness of Scripture itself that we discussed earlier. Many questions have been raised, for example, as to how the witness of the Spirit relates to evidence and arguments for Scripture's authority.

In *DKG*[13] I argued that human knowledge is triperspectival. It is an application of God's revealed norms for thought (normative) to the facts of God's creation (situational) by a person qualified to make such applications (existential). How, then, do we know that Scripture is the Word of God? By its self-witness (normative), as I described it earlier in this chapter, by facts and evidences (situational), and by the Spirit's working subjectively in our hearts (existential), enabling us to see the Bible's claims and the evidences in their proper light. See fig. 28.3.

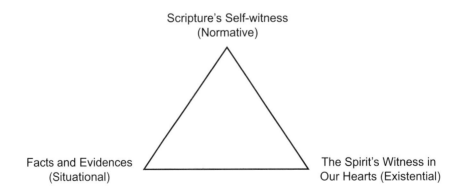

Fig. 28.3. Our Knowledge That Scripture Is God's Word

---

12. When Paul refers to counterfeit revelation in 2 Thessalonians 2:2, interestingly, he refers to a counterfeit spirit, as well as a counterfeit word.

13. See especially the section in *DKG* on epistemological justification, 104–64.

When we ask why someone (S) believes a proposition (p), there are several possible answers. One type of answer sets forth the *causes* of this belief. They may be psychological (e.g., "S believes it because he is delusional"), sociological (e.g., "S believes it because he was raised in a community where everyone believes it"), or of some other kind. Another type of answer sets forth the *reasons* for the belief ("S believes p because he thinks that p is rationally necessary"; or "S believes p because of items of evidence a, b, c"). The distinction between causes and reasons is often important. Thinkers such as Marx, Feuerbach, and Freud argued that religious belief is illegitimate because of its *cause* (for Marx, economic; for Feuerbach, projection; for Freud, wish-fulfillment). I reject these views of the origin of religious faith. But even if they are true, or one of them is true, the causes of a belief never disprove the reasons for it. Frank might believe that the world is round because he has a psychological preference for circles. That preference could be described as a cause of his belief. But the existence of that cause does not disprove his belief that the world is round. Nor does it disprove the reasons he might offer for holding that belief. Applied to the religious case: even if Christians are motivated to believe in God by, say, wish-fulfillment, that doesn't prove God doesn't exist, nor does it disprove any reasons we may give for believing in God.

That last paragraph might sound as though causes of beliefs are irrelevant and don't play any role in epistemology. That is not the case. Reasons for beliefs are important, but causes are as well. Unless something causes me to believe something, I won't believe it.[14]

In general, the internal testimony of the Spirit is a cause of faith, rather than a reason. That is to say, if someone asks my reasons for believing Scripture to be God's Word, I should not refer to the witness of the Spirit. I should say, rather, that I believe because the evidences available to me (situational), interpreted according to the laws of thought (logic, but ultimately God's revelation), yield that conclusion. The Holy Spirit's witness (existential[15]) is not a reason for faith, but a cause of faith.[16] He is the One who opens my eyes to see the evidence in the proper light, and to evaluate it by God's laws of thought. He *makes* me believe. Because of him, I cannot help believing.

I hope this discussion clarifies some debates about the relation of the Holy Spirit's witness to evidence and arguments. Consider this passage from WCF 1.5:

14. I am not taking account here of the issue of free will. If we are free in a libertarian sense (chapters 14, 35), then the cause of my belief may be a libertarian free choice to believe, but that is still a cause. So libertarianism does not eliminate causality at this level. I do, however, reject the libertarian theory, as I indicate in chapter 8 of *DG* and in chapter 35 of this volume.

15. But note distinctions in the following footnote.

16. We should not conclude that the existential perspective in general deals with causes rather than reasons. The existential perspective includes the other two perspectives. A mind that is renewed by the Spirit (existential) is one that will accept true evidences (situational) interpreted by the true laws of thought (normative). Such a mind draws its conclusions on the basis of what it subjectively prefers. But what it subjectively prefers is God's objective truth and God's laws of thought. So the existential perspective describes a way of reasoning as well as causes of that reasoning. Within this perspective, the Holy Spirit's witness is the chief cause. And since the Spirit enables us to choose proper evidence and true laws of thought, the Spirit's witness is relevant to the other two perspectives as well.

> We may be moved and induced by the testimony of the church to an high and reverent esteem of the Holy Scripture. And the heavenliness of the matter, the efficacy of the doctrine, the majesty of the style, the consent of all the parts, the scope of the whole (which is, to give all glory to God), the full discovery it makes of the only way of man's salvation, the many other incomparable excellencies, and the entire perfection thereof, are arguments whereby it doth abundantly evidence itself to be the Word of God: yet notwithstanding, our full persuasion and assurance of the infallible truth and divine authority thereof, is from the inward work of the Holy Spirit bearing witness by and with the Word in our hearts.

This statement begins by listing various evidences, reasons why we should accept Scripture as God's Word. The confession regards these evidences as substantial: they "abundantly evidence" the divine character of Scripture. This sentence does not quite say that these evidences warrant certainty that Scripture is God's Word, nor does it quite deny that.

But then it mentions the inward work of the Spirit as the basis for "our full persuasion and assurance of the infallible truth and divine authority" of Scripture. "Full" seems to be something more than "abundant evidence." The impression left is that the evidences take us maybe 90 percent of the way to full assurance, but we need the work of the Spirit to reach 100 percent assurance. The evidences give us partial persuasion, but the Spirit gives us full persuasion.

In my view, this statement (which is similar to many other statements in Reformed theological literature) needs refinement. First, the evidences in Scripture of its own divine authority are not merely probable. They are certain. They are not 90 percent cogent, but 100 percent cogent. I showed earlier in this chapter that Scripture adequately attests itself as God's Word. When Scripture is read according to scriptural presuppositions,[17] it provides certain evidence that it is God's Word.

Further, the work of the Spirit is not to add 10 percent to the probability of the argument, as if we could go 90 percent of the way without the Spirit, but we needed the inner work of the Spirit to go the rest of the way. Rather, without the Spirit's illuminating and demonstrating the truth of Scripture, we cannot even go 1 percent of the way. If the Spirit does not regenerate and guide us, we are blind to the truth; we suppress it (Rom. 1:18). We may know it well enough to use it for our own purposes, as the Pharisees in the Gospels, but we will not be able to use any piece of Scripture as God intended.

So the Spirit does not present more evidence or argument to us. His role is not to add another piece of evidence, or another argument to the case for faith. Nor does he miraculously turn uncertain evidence into certain evidence. Rather, he witnesses to the evidence for the truth that is objectively present in Scripture. He witnesses to what is certainly true. His role is to *cause* faith. His role is to take away our blindness so that

---

17. Again, I acknowledge a kind of circularity here. See my defenses of this circularity in chapter 1 and *DKG*, 130–33.

we can rightly see Scripture's self-attestation and be convinced by it. He enables us to see the evidence for what it is: God's clear and certain revelation of himself. He makes us accept Scripture's self-attestation.[18]

So the work of the Spirit is the cause of faith; the self-witness of Scripture is the reason for faith. We need both to be assured of the truth of Scripture. It is in this way that God comes with his personal words to attest them to our minds and hearts.[19]

The Spirit and the Sufficiency of Scripture

If we see the Spirit's work in this way, we will not find a tension between the work of the Spirit and the sufficiency of Scripture. The sufficiency of Scripture, as I indicated in chapter 26, means that Scripture contains all the divine words that we will ever need for any area of life. Sufficiency in this sense, however, does not deny that the work of the Spirit is also necessary. Indeed, the Spirit's work is indispensable if we are to properly understand Scripture and make use of it.

Nor does the continuing work of the Spirit mean that the canon is still open. Following the completion of Jesus' work, the Spirit is no longer inspiring books to be added to the Bible (see chapter 25).

Nevertheless, the Spirit continues to illumine the Word of God in all its forms, copies, texts, and editions, in preaching, teaching, theology, confession, and so on.

When we pray for our pastor, that he will preach a good sermon, we are praying that the Spirit will influence his speech. We pray that the Spirit will take away from the pastor any words that mislead or detract from the gospel, and that the Spirit will give him instead words that edify. Often God answers such prayers affirmatively. And when he does so, the Spirit does a verbal work, purifying our pastor's words. This is not inspiration. But it is something *like* inspiration. The Spirit is taking away the errors that the pastor may intend to make, and he is replacing those errors with sound, edifying, biblical teaching. The sermon will not be fully identical with God's own speech, as were the sermons of Isaiah and Paul. There may be errors in it. But in that sermon, the Word of God will be on our pastor's lips. And insofar as the biblical Word is on his lips, it is as authoritative as it was on the pages of Scripture itself (recall chapter 27).

This is a distinctively Reformed view, but it gives us some talking points to use with our brothers and sisters from the charismatic tradition. When they speak of "continuing revelation," they do not generally want to say that such revelation has the same status

18. Some may ask the relationship between Scripture's self-attestation and evidences external to Scripture. On this, see *DKG*, 104–64. Scripture itself testifies that the whole world speaks of God (Ps. 19:1; Rom. 1:18–20) and thus constitutes evidence of his reality. The firmness of God's control over the world testifies to the truth of his spoken word: note the relationships between Psalm 19:1–6 and verses 7–11, and between Psalm 147:1–18 and verses 19–20. So Scripture warrants the use of extrabiblical evidence. But that evidence must be used as Scripture requires, not offered as a rival to Scripture's self-witness. In this way, extrabiblical evidence becomes part of Scripture's self-authentication. It is evidence that Scripture itself authorizes.

19. For more discussion of the testimony of the Spirit, compared with the views of modern theologians Barth and Berkouwer, see my article "The Spirit and the Scriptures," Appendix Q of *DWG*.

as Scripture. But it is often hard for them to define just how this revelation is different from Scripture. Sometimes (not always) they seem to be describing "continuing prophecy" as something very much like what Reformed people call "Spirit-filled preaching," as I have described that concept above. It is something *like* inspired words, but also *unlike* the revelation given to Isaiah and Paul. We can be thankful that although the canon is closed, the Spirit continues to influence the words of believers, particularly the preaching and teaching of the Word of God.[20]

Human Beings as Revelation

Finite persons are also a means of God's revelation. We are made in the image of God (Gen. 1:26–27), meaning that everything we were created to be reflects God in some way.[21] Our bodies, minds, personalities reflect God, both individually and corporately.[22] That image continues after the fall, contrary to the position of some theological traditions (Gen. 5:1; 9:6; 1 Cor. 11:7; James 3:9). Sin does counteract the knowledge, righteousness, and holiness of the image (Eph. 4:24; Col. 3:10), but it does not entirely erase the image of God. Even sin, in one sense, images God, for sin is basically an attempt to *be* God, to replace God on the throne.[23]

When a person comes to trust Jesus as Savior and Lord, the distortions of sin begin to fade, and the believer images God in a deeper sense. So Scripture says that by grace we are "renewed in knowledge after the image of [our] creator" (Col. 3:10; cf. Eph. 4:24).

So we are created as images of God's nature, and in salvation God re-creates us as images, revelations, of his grace. People ought to be able to see the nature of the gospel by seeing how it changes us. We ought not only to obey God, but to be examples to others of such obedience (1 Thess. 1:7).

Imitation of other persons is an important means of learning in general, and specifically an important means of learning the Word of God. As I indicated in the previous chapter, understanding the Word is applying it, and there is no better way to learn the application of the Word than by seeing it lived out by others who understand it well. So God himself is the norm for our life, as he says, "Be holy, for I am holy" (Lev. 11:44; 1 Peter 1:15–16; cf. Matt. 5:48).[24] And as God and man, Jesus is an example to us in the way he lived his life, as are all the lives of people who follow him.

20. For more important talking points in the discussion over continuing revelation, see Vern S. Poythress, "Modern Spiritual Gifts as Analogous to Apostolic Gifts: Affirming Extraordinary Works of the Spirit within Cessationist Theology," *JETS* 39, 1 (1996): 71–101. Also available at http://www.frame-poythress.org.

21. I would add that each of us reflects all of God in some way. How can different persons each reflect "all of God"? By reflecting him from different perspectives!

22. For longer discussions of man in the image of God, see *SBL*, 85–99, and *DCL*, 318–23, 623–30, as well as chapter 34 of this volume.

23. The way in which sin images God is analogous to a mirror image: it reflects every aspect of him, but is lacking in two ways: (1) it reverses the reality of God, and (2) it is all image, no substance.

24. See the discussion of God as norm in *DCL*, chap. 9.

The *imitatio Christi* is a major theme of the NT. We are to be like Jesus.[25] We do that by obeying his teaching, but also by watching how he interacts with people in his earthly ministry.[26] We should copy not only what Jesus says, but the way he says it. Yet the most profound form of imitation is the imitation of Jesus' atonement.

We might think that we can imitate Jesus in many ways, but not in his atoning love. After all, none of us can bring about the salvation of others by giving our lives. But remarkably, in the NT, it is the atonement that is the main point of comparison between the love of Christ and the love of the Christian. The love of God that we are to imitate is most fully displayed in the atonement (John 3:16; 15:13; Rom. 5:8; 8:39 [in context], Eph. 2:4–5; 2 Thess. 2:16; 1 John 3:16; Rev. 1:5; cf. Mark 10:45; Phil. 2:1–11; 1 Peter 2:18–25). We are to love one another, specifically as Jesus first loved us, by dying for our sins (John 13:34–35; 1 John 4:9–11).

God's love to us in the atonement is beyond measure (Eph. 3:18–19), in the depth of Jesus' suffering, including his estrangement from his Father, in the greatness of the blessing he bought for us, and also in our total lack of fitness for this blessing. As recipients of God's grace, we are supremely unattractive to him. We are the tax collectors and sinners (Matt. 9:9–13), the "poor and crippled and blind and lame" (Luke 14:21), those who were "still sinners" (Rom. 5:8) when Jesus came to die for us.

Truly, no sacrifice of ours can atone for the sins of someone else. But these passages make abundantly clear that our obligation is nothing less than to lay down our lives for one another, as Jesus did for us.[27]

In a lesser and derivative sense, we can also find examples for imitation in godly people described in Scripture. The apostles, particularly, call on believers to imitate them (as they imitate Christ).

The apostles place great weight on themselves as person-revelation. We can see this in the passages where they express their desire to visit the churches personally, rather than merely to write letters to them. In other passages, they commend the personal visits of other church leaders and look forward to visits from those leaders. These passages are sometimes described as looking forward to the *apostolic parousia*, analogous somewhat to the return of Christ. See in this regard Rom. 1:8–17; 15:22–29; 1 Cor. 4:14–21; 5:1–5; 2 Cor. 7:5–16; 12:14; 13:10; Gal. 4:12–20; Eph. 6:21–22; Col. 4:7–9; 1 Tim. 3:14–15; 2 Tim. 4:6–18; Titus 3:12–14; Heb. 13:23; 2 John 12; 3 John 13–14. In 2 John 12, the apostle says that he would prefer to visit the "elect lady" personally, rather than with "paper and ink," so that "our joy may be complete." Other references to apostolic parousia are more threatening, as those in 1 Corinthians.

---

25. The liberal tradition often tried to reduce the atoning work of Christ to "moral influence." Evangelicals were perfectly right to reject this conception. Jesus' atonement was also a sacrifice, expiation, and propitiation. Nevertheless, Scripture does present Christ over and over again as someone we should imitate.

26. Earlier in this chapter, I spoke of the centrality of Christ in revelation, summarizing that idea by referring to him as God, Word of God, theophany, divine voice, Creator, Provider, Redeemer, Prophet, example. Here I further expound the latter category.

27. See examples of moral heroism in *DCL*, chap. 12.

There is evidently something about a personal visit that goes beyond what can be achieved in a letter. Certainly mutual expressions of love are more meaningful when presented face to face. The exercise of apostolic authority, too, is easier accomplished in the flesh. Paul does exercise discipline against a sinner in the Corinthian church, in 1 Corinthians 5:3, by letter. But he has to remind the church that "though absent in body, I am present in spirit." Another important element of the apostolic presence, however, is that then the church is better able to observe the apostle's life, the way he puts the Word into practice. In 2 Timothy 3:10–11, Paul commends his own lifestyle to Timothy as a model for Timothy's own ministry:

> You, however, have followed my teaching, my conduct, my aim in life, my faith, my patience, my love, my steadfastness, my persecutions and sufferings that happened to me at Antioch, at Iconium, and at Lystra—which persecutions I endured; yet from them all the Lord rescued me.

So he calls the Corinthians to "be imitators of me, as I am of Christ" (1 Cor. 11:1; cf. 1 Cor. 4:16; Phil. 3:17; 4:9; 1 Thess. 1:6; 2 Thess. 3:9). Paul's character is a revelation of Paul's gospel. It shows how Jesus' people should live. Paul is not perfect. But he is a mature believer, who has endured much suffering for Christ, and we should study his life as well as his doctrine.

But person-revelation continues beyond the generation of the apostles. A major qualification of leaders in the church is that they are to be examples of the Lord's saving work (1 Tim. 4:12; Titus 2:7; 1 Peter 5:3). An overseer

> must be above reproach, the husband of one wife, sober-minded, self-controlled, respectable, hospitable, able to teach, not a drunkard, not violent but gentle, not quarrelsome, not a lover of money. He must manage his own household well, with all dignity keeping his children submissive, for if someone does not know how to manage his own household, how will he care for God's church? He must not be a recent convert, or he may become puffed up with conceit and fall into the condemnation of the devil. Moreover, he must be well thought of by outsiders, so that he may not fall into disgrace, into a snare of the devil. (1 Tim. 3:2–7; cf. Titus 1:5–9)

Similarly for deacons (1 Tim. 3:8–13) and women teachers (Titus 2:2–5).

Learning by imitation is an important means of sanctification, a vital means of appropriating the Word of God. We should imitate God, Jesus, the apostles, and other exemplary characters in Scripture. Scripture often refers to such exemplary people (see Rom. 4:16–25; 1 Cor. 10:1–12; Heb. 6:11–12; 11:1–12:2; 13:7; James 5:17–18). For this reason I oppose the notion that preaching should merely expound the redemptive narrative of Scripture and should never appeal to biblical characters as examples. In expounding past revelation, the Bible itself appeals to such examples, and we are not preaching the Word as we should if we omit such references.

And we should ourselves seek to be examples that can be imitated by our fellow believers. Human life, redeemed and matured, is a profound form of revelation. We and others need to have it in order to rightly apply God's Word.

Writing on the Heart

Person-revelation manifests God's lordship attribute of covenant presence (chapter 2). In person-revelation, God himself comes into our midst and makes human persons into media of his revelation, as we have seen. But the most intimate way in which God's revelation is present with us is his saving revelation on the hearts of his people.

The Name of the Lord

There may be some anticipation of this idea in the many passages that speak of God's placing his *name* on his people, identifying himself with them. In the ancient Near East, names had significance. Today, we often give children names mainly for their sound or a family connection. But in Bible times, a person's name reflected events surrounding his birth, his parents' hopes for him, or some other meaning. The name always said something about the person.

In some passages, God gives new names to people to signify their place in his redemptive plan (Gen. 17:5; 32:28). The redemptive promise is a promise of a new name (Isa. 62:2; Rev. 2:17). Further, God knows his people by name (Isa. 43:1) (i.e., intimately and completely), and he calls on them by name (45:3–4) to serve his purposes.

In Scripture, "name of the Lord" is used both for various terms such as *Yahweh, elohim,* and *'adon* that apply to him, and for God's whole revelation of himself.[28] So God's name is a virtual synonym for his *word*. God vindicates his name, for it represents his reputation (1 Sam. 12:22), as we refer to a man's "good name" (Prov. 22:1). As with *word* (chapters 8–11), God's name is God himself.

As we sing praise to God, we sing praise to his name (Pss. 7:17; 9:2; 18:49; many other passages); we give the glory due to his name (29:2); we exalt the name (34:3) and fear it (61:5). God's name is an object of worship. Since in Scripture God alone is the proper object of worship, this language equates the name and the Lord himself.

Similarly, the name of God defends us (Ps. 20:1) and saves us (54:1). We trust in the name for deliverance (33:21). God's name endures forever (72:17; 135:13). It "reaches to the ends of the earth" (48:10). It is holy and awesome (111:9). God saves us by his name (54:1). He guides us "for his name's sake" (23:3). In Isaiah 30:27, it is the "name of the Lord" itself that comes to bring judgment on the nations and blessings on his people. So God's name has divine attributes and performs divine acts. In short, Scripture says about the name of God virtually everything it says about God.[29]

---

28. For a longer discussion of God's name and names, see *DG*, 21–35, 343–61. See also my treatment of the third commandment in *DCL*, 487–97. Much of the material in the following paragraphs is taken from *DG*.

29. Compare the discussion of the word of God as God himself, chapter 23 of this volume.

So when God chooses to make his "name" dwell in a place (Deut. 12:5, 11, 21; 14:23–24; 1 Kings 8:29; 9:3; 2 Kings 23:27), that place becomes a location of his special presence. To say that God's name dwells in that place is to say that God himself dwells there. God's name is his *glory*: When Moses asks to see his glory, he expounds his name (Ex. 33:18–19). (Note also parallels between the name and the glory in Psalm 102:15 and Isaiah 59:19.) To say that God's "name" is in an angel is to say that the angel has the authority of God (Ex. 23:21).

It is not surprising, then, that the third commandment of the Decalogue tells us not to misuse God's name. We should speak the name of God with the reverence that we should have in his personal presence.

One of the most remarkable proofs of the deity of Christ, then, is that the NT uses his name just as the OT used the name of Yahweh. When the Jewish rulers ask Peter and John "by what power or by what name" they healed a crippled man, Peter replies, "By the name of Jesus Christ of Nazareth" (Acts 4:10). He concludes, "There is salvation in no one else, for there is no other name under heaven given among men by which we must be saved" (v. 12; cf. v. 17). In 5:41, we read that the apostles "left the presence of the council, rejoicing that they were counted worthy to suffer dishonor for the name." Cf. 9:21; 22:16. We see that *name* can be used as a substitute for *Jesus*, as it substitutes for *Yahweh* in the OT, and that the name of Jesus has the same powers as the name of Yahweh. In Isaiah 45:23, Yahweh says, "To me every knee shall bow, every tongue shall swear allegiance." In Romans 14:11, Paul applies this passage to God (*theos*); but in Philippians 2:10–11, he applies it to Christ:

> That at the name of Jesus every knee should bow, in heaven and on earth and under the earth, and every tongue confess that Jesus Christ is Lord to the glory of God the Father.

In Romans 10:13, Paul quotes Joel 2:32, "Everyone who calls on the name of the Lord will be saved." Joel spoke of the name of Yahweh; Paul speaks specifically of the name of Jesus. In Genesis 4:26, the family of Seth begins to "call upon the name of the LORD," an indication of the beginnings of corporate worship. In 1 Corinthians 1:2, Paul describes the Christian church as "those who in every place call upon the name of our Lord Jesus Christ." We call on the name of Christ for salvation and to praise him. We pray for healing "in the name of the Lord" (James 5:14, certainly again a reference to Jesus).

According to Matthew 28:19, we are to baptize "in the name of the Father and of the Son and of the Holy Spirit." One name, threefold. *Son* is on the same level as *Father*. Baptism is initiation to discipleship, and it places upon us the name that brings together Father, Son, and Spirit.

The reference to baptism indicates that we also, as well as the Father and the Son, are bearers of the holy name of God. In our case, the name is not ours by nature; it does not make us objects of worship. Rather, God's name dwells in us as it dwelled in the tabernacle. God places his name upon us, as he placed his name in the tabernacle and in the Holy Land (Deut. 12:5). In the Aaronic benediction of Numbers 6:24–26, the priests, says Yahweh, will "put my name upon the people of Israel, and I will bless them" (v. 27). Certainly the Trinitarian apostolic benediction of 2 Corinthians 13:14 has the same significance. So God's people "bear" his name (Jer. 14:9 NIV; cf. Isa. 43:7) and on this basis pray to God for their deliverance (Jer. 14:21). We are temples of God's Spirit and thus bearers of his name.[30]

Once he has chosen a people for himself, he will not forsake them, for the sake of his own name, which he has identified with theirs (1 Sam. 12:22). In Amos 9:11–12, the Lord promises:

> "In that day I will raise up
>   the booth of David that is fallen
> and repair its breaches,
>   and raise up its ruins
>   and rebuild it as in the days of old,
> that they may possess the remnant of Edom
>   and all the nations who are called by my name,"
>   declares the LORD who does this.

God's word to Amos says that not only Israel is called by God's name, but other nations as well, speaking (see the quotation in Acts 15:17–18) of the outreach of the gospel of Christ to all the nations of the world. New believers are to be baptized into that one "name of the Father and of the Son and of the Holy Spirit" (Matt. 28:19). God's new name will be on the "foreheads" of the people of God in the last day (Rev. 22:4).

In a still broader sense, all creation bears the name of the Lord. As we saw earlier,[31] God's covenant lordship is over all the earth. He has made the world to be his temple, and of course his name must dwell in his temple. I believe that Jesus implies the presence of God's name in creation in Matthew 5:33–37 (cf. 23:16–22), his exposition of the third commandment. There he addresses those who tried to avoid the force of oaths by not using particular names of God. Rather than swearing by Yahweh or by God, they would swear by heaven, earth, Jerusalem, or even their own heads. Jesus' answer is that heaven, earth, Jerusalem—yes, and our heads—are subject to God's sovereignty, so that to invoke anything in creation is to invoke God himself. If we swear, "May the heavens collapse if I fail to do this," only God can bring about that collapse or prevent it. If I swear, "May my hair turn white if I am lying," only God can enforce that oath. So when we swear by created things, we are implicitly swearing by God himself, by his own name. That means that everything in creation is a dwelling place for God's name, a place of God's presence.

My application of this rich vein of biblical theology is that God sets his own name, a revelation of himself, indeed his own presence, upon every believer. He places upon

---

30. Cf. Rev. 3:12; 14:1; 22:4.
31. See especially the discussion of God's universal covenant in chapter 4.

us a seal that says we belong to him and he belongs to us. That is a word of God that defines who he is and who we are in relation to him. It says that our deepest nature is to be his covenant servants. We can be intelligibly described only as God's people, and as the people in whom he himself has chosen to dwell. We are, by our very nature, God's people, and therefore we are revelations of him.

Some of God's people, to be sure, rebel against him. But they, too, reveal God, even in their rebellion, as I indicated earlier. These people are members of God's covenant, but they receive the curses of the covenant rather than the blessings. Even in their case, their deepest nature is to be covenant servants of God—but in their case, rebellious servants.[32]

Heart-Revelation

Another expression in Scripture that shows the deep penetration of God's revelation into our being is the writing of God's word upon our heart. The heart is the inner core of a person, the basic direction of his life (for good or ill), the person as God sees him. The heart is what we really are, when all our masks are off. Jesus taught:

> The good person out of the good treasure of his heart produces good, and the evil person out of his evil treasure produces evil, for out of the abundance of the heart his mouth speaks. (Luke 6:45)

When God revealed his law to Israel, he intended it to reside not only on tablets of stone, but also in the people's hearts (Deut. 6:6). That means that it was to govern their deepest thoughts and motives, to control all their actions, in all areas of life. They were to live a life surrounded, saturated, by his words:

> You shall teach them diligently to your children, and shall talk of them when you sit in your house, and when you walk by the way, and when you lie down, and when you rise. You shall bind them as a sign on your hand, and they shall be as frontlets between your eyes. You shall write them on the doorposts of your house and on your gates. (Deut. 6:7–9; cf. Rev. 22:4)

God's word was to be everywhere. The people were to know it so well that it would direct their decisions even when they had no time to think about it. They were to be a people for whom obeying God's word was "second nature."

So the psalmist says, "I have stored up your word in my heart, that I might not sin against you" (Ps. 119:11). And the wisdom teacher tells his pupil, "Let not steadfast love and faithfulness forsake you; bind them around your neck; write them on the tablet of your heart" (Prov. 3:3; cf. 7:1–3). The righteous man is one who has the word in his

---

32. Here, of course, I am using *servants* to describe the covenant status of the rebels, not their heart-allegiance, which I will discuss in the following pages. In terms of chapter 11, these people are historically elect, not eternally elect. These two types of election are vastly different, though Scripture describes them in similar terms.

heart (Ps. 37:31). In Psalm 40:7–8, the redeemed man who delights to do God's will has God's word in his heart.[33]

Not all Israelites had God's word in their hearts. But some did. God says through Isaiah:

> Listen to me, you who know righteousness,
>   the people in whose heart is my law;
> fear not the reproach of man,
>   nor be dismayed at their revilings. (Isa. 51:7)

These people are the remnant, the believers within Israel, as opposed to those who rejected God. But God looks forward to a time when all his people will have a new heart and a new spirit (Ezek. 11:19; 18:31). Their new heart will be a gift of God's sheer grace (Jer. 24:7; Ezek. 36:26; 37:23). The gift of a new heart is part of a new covenant that God will make with his people:

> Behold, the days are coming, declares the LORD, when I will make a new covenant with the house of Israel and the house of Judah, not like the covenant that I made with their fathers on the day when I took them by the hand to bring them out of the land of Egypt, my covenant that they broke, though I was their husband, declares the LORD. But this is the covenant that I will make with the house of Israel after those days, declares the LORD: I will put my law within them, and I will write it on their hearts. And I will be their God, and they shall be my people. And no longer shall each one teach his neighbor and each his brother, saying, "Know the LORD," for they shall all know me, from the least of them to the greatest, declares the LORD. For I will forgive their iniquity, and I will remember their sin no more. (Jer. 31:31–34)

In this covenant, God will write his word not on stone tablets, but on the hearts of his people. Those hearts will be the covenant document (chapter 4). They will all know God, and he will forgive their sins. God himself will be their Teacher (cf. John 6:45; 1 Thess. 4:9; 1 John 2:27).

The writer to the Hebrews says that the new covenant was established by the new priesthood of Jesus, rendering the Mosaic covenant obsolete (Heb. 8:1–13). Through Christ, God has written his word on the hearts of his people. The people of God in the OT, the righteous remnant, were saved not by their works, but by looking forward to the promise of God to redeem his people through Christ. And those who had the word written on their hearts back then (as Pss. 37:31; 40:7–8) were righteous because of Christ, just as "Abraham believed God, and it was counted to him as righteousness" (Rom. 4:3, quoting Gen. 15:6). By anticipation, the old covenant saints were members of the new covenant, though it was yet to be sealed by the shedding of Jesus' blood.

---

33. The writer of Hebrews quotes this passage at 10:5–7 in his letter as applying to Christ. He doesn't refer to the writing of the word on his heart, doubtless because that was obvious in the case of Jesus, whose deepest inclination was to do the Father's will.

So we who believe in Christ have the word of God written on our hearts. Though we often fail, our deepest inclinations are to follow Jesus and to obey his Father. Paul is even able to say of the Corinthian church:

> You yourselves are our letter of recommendation, written on our hearts, to be known and read by all. And you show that you are a letter from Christ delivered by us, written not with ink but with the Spirit of the living God, not on tablets of stone but on tablets of human hearts. (2 Cor. 3:2–3)

The church at Corinth had many problems; Paul rebukes the Corinthians about many things. But God knew their hearts, and Paul knew also that their hearts were with Jesus. So they serve as person-revelation. They themselves are a letter recommending the ministry of Paul.

We have seen through this book that revelation begins in God's own heart, and that it typically follows a very indirect process between his speech and our hearts. In nature and Scripture, his word is objective. But the destination of revelation is deeply subjective. For the ultimate purpose of God's word is to communicate with his creatures, and that purpose is incomplete until the word resides within his hearers. So Scripture speaks of revelation in both objective terms and subjective terms. In these chapters on the word of God, I have focused on the objective. God's word exists in creation and in Scripture, regardless of what anyone thinks of that. But Scripture also speaks of revelation as something subjective.

In Isaiah 53:1, God through Isaiah asks the rhetorical question, "Who has believed what he has heard from us? And to whom has the arm of the LORD been revealed?" By the parallelism of these two questions, we can tell that here God's arm (his power) has been revealed only to those who have believed. This verse does not speak of a revelation given to everyone as an objective datum, but as a revelation given to those who have heard and believed the prophecy.

Similarly, Jesus, in Matthew 11:27, says:

> All things have been handed over to me by my Father, and no one knows the Son except the Father, and no one knows the Father except the Son and anyone to whom the Son chooses to reveal him.

"Reveal" here refers neither to natural or general revelation nor to the biblical canon. It is rather an event in the heart of the recipient. Jesus does not merely make the knowledge of the Father available objectively in case we might like to consider it. Rather, he gives us actual *knowledge* of the Father, as a gift.

A similar use of "revelation" appears in Ephesians 1:17, where Paul prays

> that the God of our Lord Jesus Christ, the Father of glory, may give you a spirit of wisdom and of revelation in the knowledge of him.

This "revelation" is not additional natural revelation. Nor is Paul asking that God will give to the Ephesians some new books to be included in the canon. Rather, he is praying that in all the objective revelation that God has given, the Spirit will actually reveal God so that the Ephesian Christians will subjectively know God better.

For other references to such subjective revelation, see the following: John 3:3; Rom. 1:17; 2 Cor. 4:6; Gal. 1:15–16; Phil. 3:15; 1 John 2:27.

Our hearts, then, are the destination of God's revelation. In us, the process of communication reaches its terminus. In our hearts we receive God's personal words to us in such a profound way that they become the foundation of all our thinking and living. We look forward to the consummation of this knowledge in the last day, when God will tear away from us our sinful inclinations to disobey and devalue this wonderful word. God has accompanied his word through all the vicissitudes of history, the problems of Scripture, and the spiritual battles of our lives,[34] so that we might receive it with joy. And he will continue to accompany it until he receives us into glory.

General, Special, and Existential Revelation

The structure of revelation as I have presented it here suggests the value of rethinking the traditional distinction between general and special revelation. In fact, as we have seen, there are many forms of revelation, and there is some peril in trying to group them under general categories. But some may want to know why I have chosen the distinction event/word/persons over the traditional general/special ordering.

The distinction between general and special revelation has always been a bit unclear. General revelation has usually been understood as follows:

1. Revelation by events (nature, history), rather than words.
2. Revelation given to all mankind.
3. Revelation that does not present the way of salvation.

Special revelation is:

1. Revelation by word.
2. Revelation not given to all mankind, but to people chosen by God to hear it.
3. Revelation about salvation.

This leads to trivial questions, such as the status of secular writings—Charles Dickens's novels, for example. They are words, and they are revelation (since everything is God's revelation in one sense or another). But since they are verbal, they don't seem to fit

---

34. After writing this sentence, I noticed that it contained a covenantal triad.

under the category of general revelation, and since they do not present God's plan of salvation, they don't fit under the category of special revelation either.

And I have given reasons in this book not to distinguish sharply between *matters of salvation* and other matters. See earlier discussions of the inerrancy, clarity, comprehensiveness, and sufficiency of Scripture. At least we ought to revise the third qualification of special revelation to read "revelation about salvation and other matters."

More seriously, some have asked whether there was special revelation in Eden, before the fall of our first parents. We are inclined to say yes, because God spoke to them verbally. But that speech was not about salvation, because it was not until later that Adam and Eve needed salvation. Some have called these divine words *preredemptive special revelation*, emphasizing the first characteristic of special revelation. Others have denied that there is any such thing, because of the third qualification. But it also seems quite awkward to fit this revelation under the *general* category.

This discussion, I think, like many other theological discussions, takes extrabiblical theological concepts too seriously. The terms *general* and *special revelation* are not found in Scripture. They are an attempt by theologians to summarize some of the variety in the ways in which God communicates with us. If they create problems, we should not be embarrassed about redefining them or abandoning them. Generally, it would have been better, I think, for theology to distinguish events, words, and persons, as I have here, and then to make further distinctions within these categories.

If we wish to maintain the old *general/special* terminology, I would suggest that we reconstruct it as follows:

- General: Revelation in all objects of human knowledge (situational).
- Special: Revelation in word, setting forth God's standards for human life (normative).[35]

Then I would add:

- Existential: God's revelation in our person, by which we appropriate the other forms of revelation. This kind of revelation is mentioned in Scripture at Isaiah 53:1; Matthew 11:27; Ephesians 1:17; etc.

These three forms are perspectival, in that you cannot have one without having the others. See fig. 28.4.

---

35. This would include, of course, both *law* and *gospel*, however those are defined. For my thoughts, see *DCL*, 182–92. My point here is that special revelation should be defined as those "spectacles" (Calvin) that God has given us, to enable us to rightly understand and use general revelation.

Fig. 28.4. Forms of Revelation

Key Terms
Presupposition
Foundationalism
Cone of certainty
Person-revelation
Theophany
Glory-cloud
Illumination
Power and demonstration
Indwelling
Causes of belief
Reasons for belief
Self-attestation of Scripture
Image of God
Imitatio Christi
Apostolic parousia
Name of the Lord
General revelation
Special revelation
Existential revelation

Study Questions
1. "And if we cannot identify God's Word (despite the history of textual and interpretative problems), then we have no hope. Christianity is a sham." State this problem in your own words. Seek to resolve it.
2. "But many still believe, and their number increases [despite the problems of texts, translations, etc.]. It is hard to account for this. But it is God at work." Explain; evaluate. What does God do to deal with this difficulty?
3. "Yet every believer begins with certainty." What certainty? Explain; evaluate.

4. Should we seek to eliminate all doubt? Make distinctions, citing Scripture texts.

5. "If meaning is application, at least from one perspective, then we cannot understand language without understanding how its speakers apply it." Explain. How does this bear on the subject of the importance of person-revelation?

6. "In the previous chapter, we considered the chief difficulty of Bible interpretation, namely, the distance between the time and culture of the writers and of ourselves. The ultimate answer to that difficulty is that in an important sense the Word of Scripture is always contemporary." In what sense? Explain.

7. "Here we will note that Christ speaks through all forms of revelation." How? Expound this theme, citing Scripture texts.

8. John Murray says that illumination is "regeneration on its noetic side." Explain. How does he believe that God supplements illumination?

9. Describe the relation between Scripture's self-witness, evidences of its truth, and the Holy Spirit's testimony.

10. "In general, the internal testimony of the Spirit is a cause of faith, rather than a reason." Explain; evaluate.

11. "Further, the work of the Spirit is not to add 10 percent to the probability of the argument, as if we could go 90 percent of the way without the Spirit, but we needed the inner work of the Spirit to go the rest of the way. Rather, without the Spirit's illuminating and demonstrating the truth of Scripture, we cannot even go 1 percent of the way." Explain.

12. How can Scripture be sufficient, if we need the Holy Spirit as well for our knowledge of God?

13. Does the Holy Spirit, in his illuminating work, give us "continuing revelation"? Explain; comment.

14. In what way are human beings revelation? How does that relate to (a) our fallen nature and (b) our redemption in Christ?

15. Why do the apostles sometimes say that they would prefer to present their teaching personally rather than by letter?

16. "Learning by imitation is an important means of sanctification, a vital means of appropriating the Word of God." Give biblical examples. How does this principle bear on the question whether sermons should present Bible characters as examples?

17. What does it mean for us to bear the name of the Lord? Discuss.

18. Cite and expound some NT texts describing revelation as a communication of God to the heart.

19. Why does Frame think it helpful to introduce the concept of *existential revelation*? Evaluate.

Memory Verses

Gen. 15:6: [Abram] believed the LORD, and [God] counted it to him as righteousness.

Jer. 31:33–34: But this is the covenant that I will make with the house of Israel after those days, declares the Lord: I will put my law within them, and I will write it on their hearts. And I will be their God, and they shall be my people. And no longer shall each one teach his neighbor and each his brother, saying, "Know the Lord," for they shall all know me, from the least of them to the greatest, declares the Lord. For I will forgive their iniquity, and I will remember their sin no more.

Matt. 11:27: All things have been handed over to me by my Father, and no one knows the Son except the Father, and no one knows the Father except the Son and anyone to whom the Son chooses to reveal him.

1 Cor. 15:1–4: Now I would remind you, brothers, of the gospel I preached to you, which you received, in which you stand, and by which you are being saved, if you hold fast to the word I preached to you—unless you believed in vain.

For I delivered to you as of first importance what I also received: that Christ died for our sins in accordance with the Scriptures, that he was buried, [and] that he was raised on the third day in accordance with the Scriptures.

2 Cor. 3:2–3: You yourselves are our letter of recommendation, written on our hearts, to be known and read by all. And you show that you are a letter from Christ delivered by us, written not with ink but with the Spirit of the living God, not on tablets of stone but on tablets of human hearts.

1 Thess. 1:5: Our gospel came to you not only in word, but also in power and in the Holy Spirit and with full conviction. You know what kind of men we proved to be among you for your sake.

Resources for Further Study

Frame, John M. "The Spirit and the Scriptures." Appendix Q of *DWG*.

Kline, Meredith G. *Images of the Spirit*. Grand Rapids: Baker, 1980. On theophany.

Meek, Esther. *Longing to Know: The Philosophy of Knowledge for Ordinary People*. Grand Rapids: Brazos Press, 2003. See also her more recent work, *Loving to Know: Covenant Epistemology*. Eugene, OR: Cascade Books, 2011.

Murray, John. "The Attestation of Scripture." In *The Infallible Word*, edited by Ned Stonehouse and Paul Woolley, 40–52. Philadelphia: Presbyterian and Reformed, 1946.

Poythress, Vern S. "Modern Spiritual Gifts as Analogous to Apostolic Gifts: Affirming Extraordinary Works of the Spirit within Cessationist Theology." *JETS* 39, 1 (1996): 71–101. Also available at http://www.frame-poythress.org.

PART 5

THE DOCTRINE OF THE KNOWLEDGE OF GOD

CHAPTER 29

GOD AND OUR KNOWLEDGE

JOHN CALVIN BEGAN his *Institutes* not, as I have, with a discussion of God himself, nor (as has become common) with a doctrine of Scripture, but with a discussion of human *knowledge* of God. In the famous first page of his book, Calvin points out that the knowledge of God and the knowledge of ourselves are interconnected, so that we cannot know ourselves without knowing God, or vice versa.[1] Since Calvin, Reformed theology has often emphasized the *knowledge of God* as an important subject of theology.[2]

Calvin's emphasis on the knowledge of God correlates with the later Reformed interest in the nature of theology, also with the doctrines of revelation and Scripture. It has also renewed the discussion between theology and philosophical epistemology found already in Augustine, Aquinas, and other pre-Reformation thinkers. Reformed thinkers such as Beza, Turretin, Mastricht, Edwards, Kuyper, Bavinck, Van Til, and Gordon Clark carried on this discussion, often comparing and contrasting biblical/Reformed epistemology with non-Christian philosophical schools.

In this volume, I have placed the doctrine of the knowledge of God in this location,[3] so that I may draw on our previous discussions of God (the foundation of our knowledge, its *principium essendi*) and the word of God (God's communication with us, the fundamental basis of our knowledge, its *principium cognoscendi*). In part 3, I set forth God as the foundation of everything. So in part 4 I emphasized that to know anything rightly, we must submit our thinking to God's word, particularly the Word in Scripture as the covenant constitution of God's people. In part 5, I will examine the knowledge that results either from submission to the word of God or from rebellion against it.[4]

---

1. *Institutes*, 1.1.1.

2. One important more recent example is Abraham Kuyper's *Encyclopedia*, partly translated into English as *Principles of Sacred Theology* (Grand Rapids: Eerdmans, 1965).

3. But compare the opening chapter in this volume.

4. Even in part 4, especially toward the end, these epistemological subjects inevitably came up. For as I indicated there, the word of God exists not only in nature and Scripture, but also in writing on our own hearts

I will consider our knowledge of God and also our knowledge of the world and of ourselves as God's creations.[5]

So the content of these chapters is relevant to any human attempt to know, whether in theology, philosophy, the arts, the sciences, or ordinary life. Scripture tells us that everything we do is to be done to the glory of God (1 Cor. 10:31). We Christians often fail to consider how to apply that commandment to our thinking, specifically to our attempts to gain knowledge. It is tempting to think that this passage is limited to our narrowly religious and ethical life. But in fact, it is about every part of life ("whatever you do"), including the intellectual. So there is a distinctly biblical doctrine of knowledge, just as there are distinctly biblical doctrines of God, sin, and redemption.[6] Consider all the passages of Scripture that deal with God's knowledge (chapter 15), his word (chapters 23–28), Christ as containing "all the treasures of wisdom and knowledge" (Col. 2:3), human wisdom and foolishness (e.g., in Proverbs), the wisdom of the world, and the wisdom of God (e.g., 1 Cor. 1–3). Surely no Christian can discuss epistemology without taking account of the teachings of the word of God.

God's Knowledge and Man's

In chapter 15, I discussed God's knowledge, expounding especially the nature of his omniscience. God knows everything, every fact, every person, every event. He not only knows every state of affairs; he knows each one from every possible perspective. He not only knows the number of books in my study, but also knows how those books appear from the perspective of a fly on the wall. And even if there were no fly, he knows how my study would look from the perspective of a *possible* fly. So he knows how anything looks, feels, sounds, tastes, smells, from any point in his vast universe, from any standpoint of any knower. Truly God's knowledge is "too wonderful" for us to imagine (Ps. 139:6).

God has a perfect knowledge of himself. Human beings have hidden depths within them that they themselves can scarcely fathom. So Paul says, "I do not understand my own actions. For I do not do what I want, but I do the very thing I hate" (Rom. 7:15). But there are no thoughts, plans, inclinations, or motives in God that he is unaware of. He knows himself perfectly.

(chapter 28). When God's revelation is written on our hearts through the testimony of the Holy Spirit, we come to *know* it. Review also the section on "Assurance" in that chapter and the subsection "Epistemology and the Spirit's Witness." The goal of revelation is knowledge.

5. I should note that as part 3 was a rewritten and abridged version of *DG* and part 4 of *DWG*, so part 5 will be based on *DKG*. But here the abridgment and rewriting of the original book will be more extensive than with the others. *DKG* was my first published book (1987), and I have had more years to rethink its ideas than in the case of *DG* and *DWG*. So my treatments of the same subjects here, I think, are in general more cogent, or at least more felicitously stated, than in *DKG*. Still, as in the other two cases, there are some parts of *DKG* not present in this rewriting that may be useful supplements to the present discussion.

6. For a contrary view, see Kelly James Clark, "Reformed Epistemology Apologetics," in *Five Views on Apologetics*, ed. Steven B. Cowan (Grand Rapids: Zondervan, 2000), 274–75, with my reply, 309–10. Note further discussion of the issue at 350–51, 370–71. I apologize to Clark for using "patronizing" language.

He perfectly knows both his nature and his actions. Among his actions, he knows both his eternal actions (such as the Father's eternal begetting of the Son, chapter 22), his eternal decrees for nature and history (chapter 11), and his actions as the immanent God within the world he has made (chapter 3). His knowledge of the created world includes what to us is past, present, and (contrary to open theism) future.

He has exhaustive knowledge of the creation because he first has exhaustive knowledge of himself.

Because of his exhaustive self-knowledge, he also has perfect knowledge of the creation. (1) He knows what is *possible* in the world because *possibility* means "possible for God." He knows what he can do, what he can foreordain, because he knows himself. (2) In a somewhat different sense of *possibility*, God knows what is possible in the world because he knows what he has eternally planned to take place in the world. Nothing can happen in the world that God hasn't planned to take place.

He knows what is *actual* in the world (1) because he knows what he has foreordained to take place at any time, and (2) because as he is present in the world, he is aware of what is happening in a way analogous to our own sense knowledge (Ps. 94:9–11).

God's knowledge is called *archetypal* knowledge in the theological literature. Our knowledge, which is an image of God's, is called *ectypal* knowledge. Here it is important for us to observe the Creator-creature distinction (chapter 3). See fig. 29.1.

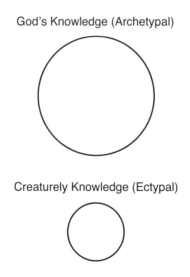

Fig. 29.1. Creator-Creature Distinction in Knowledge

Just as we should never confuse ourselves with God, so we should never confuse our knowledge with God's knowledge. Note especially the following differences between the two:

- God's knowledge is original, ours derivative from his.
- God's knowledge is exhaustive; ours is limited.
- God's knowledge serves as the ultimate criterion of truth and right; our knowledge must observe those standards.
- God never needs information or illumination from outside himself. We cannot know anything without the help of God and our experience of the world outside ourselves.
- God knows what he knows without process, simply by being what he is. His knowledge has sometimes been described as an *eternal intuition*. But our knowledge often requires hard efforts to accumulate facts and to figure out logical deductions.
- God's knowledge of the facts of creation precedes the existence of these facts. But the facts precede our knowledge of them.
- God's interpretation of the facts precedes the existence of the facts; our interpretation is a reinterpretation of God's prior interpretation. So the facts of our experience are not "brute" or uninterpreted facts, as if the human interpretation were the first. Rather, the facts are already interpreted before we come to know them. And God's interpretation is the normative interpretation that should govern ours.

To summarize: God's knowledge is divine, with all of God's attributes. Our knowledge is creaturely, with all the attributes of creatureliness. As God's image, human beings have a knowledge that reflects God's in many ways, but is by no means identical with it.

In the 1940s, there was a controversy between Gordon H. Clark and Cornelius Van Til. The debate is usually said to be about "the incomprehensibility of God," but is more accurately described as a debate over the relation between divine and human knowledge. Van Til said that there is no point of identity between any divine thought and any human thought; otherwise, we violate the Creator-creature distinction. Clark said that true human knowledge is identical to God's knowledge; otherwise, we are lost in skepticism. Clark assumed that any difference between God's thinking and man's was necessarily a difference in truth value. Van Til, rather, assumed that there were many differences between God's thought and ours that were simply differences between Creator and creature, not differences between truth and falsity.

Actually, Clark and Van Til were not as far apart as they (and their more militant disciples) seemed to think. Clark allowed that there were important differences between divine and human thought as to *mode*: that is, that God obtained and maintained his knowledge in ways very different from the ways in which we obtain and maintain ours. On the other hand, Van Til conceded Clark's main point: that God and man can know the same proposition (e.g., "the sky is blue") and that our belief in that proposition is true only when it agrees with God's.

To say that God and man can know the same proposition is not to violate the Creator-creature distinction. God knows the proposition with his divine knowledge, and man knows it with a human knowledge.[7]

Our Knowledge of God

We know God as *Lord*, for that is what he is (see chapters 2–3). As we saw in chapter 22, God's lordship is grounded in his Trinitarian existence. The Father determines the eternal divine plan (authority), the Son accomplishes that plan with his power (control), and the Spirit applies that plan to the hearts of people (presence). So we know him (1) as the One who has full *control* over us and over all things,[8] (2) as the One who speaks with ultimate *authority*,[9] and (3) as the One who is *present* to all his creatures.[10] Our knowledge, then, is the knowledge of servants. In much of our knowledge, we seek to "master" the things we know: to control them, define them, and/or invade their territory. In some cases and in some senses this is appropriate, since God has appointed human beings to be vassal kings over the created world (Gen. 1:28). But our knowledge of God must have a very different character. We cannot know God rightly without acknowledging his lordship over us.

So a necessary step in knowing God is to acknowledge the biblical worldview as I described it in chapters 2 and 3. I said in chapter 2:

> If God is in *control* of the world, then the world is under his control. If God is our supreme *authority*, then he has the right to tell us what to believe. And if he is *present* everywhere, our attempts to know the world ought to recognize that presence. The most important fact about anything in the world is its relationship to God's lordship.

And in chapter 3, I emphasized that there was an antithesis between the biblical worldview and any unbelieving worldview, using the diagram in fig. 29.2.

In the biblical understanding, God's *transcendence* over the world is his control and authority, his *immanence* in the world his covenantal presence. Non-Christian thought, too, often acknowledges some "transcendent reality." But on the non-Christian view, *transcendence* refers to a reality that is so far beyond us, so mysterious to us, that we cannot have certain knowledge about it. And for non-Christian thought, *immanence* means that supreme authority and power is vested in the world, not in something beyond the world. So biblical transcendence (1) contradicts nonbiblical immanence (4), and nonbiblical transcendence (3) contradicts biblical immanence (2). To know God rightly, we must view the world as Scripture does, not as non-Christian thought does.

---

7. For a more elaborate discussion of the Clark controversy, see *DKG*, 21–25, and, even more elaborate, *CVT*, 97–113.

8. Compare the discussion of *event-revelation* in chapter 24.

9. Compare the discussion of *word-revelation* in chapters 24–27.

10. Compare the discussion of *person-revelation* in chapter 28.

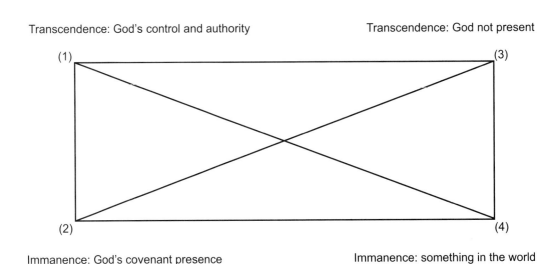

Fig. 29.2. Transcendence and Immanence: Rectangle of Opposition

Significantly, the nonbiblical worldview warrants human autonomous thought as its supreme authority for truth and right, the supreme criterion of knowledge. That is to say, on that basis human reason is the supreme authority. A biblical view of knowledge, however, repudiates the claim of autonomy in no uncertain terms and resolves to live by God's revelation, as I argued in part 4 of this book. As servants, we listen to Scripture to hear what he has to say to us. Then we believe and obey.

God's Knowability and Incomprehensibility

The incomprehensibility of God is a much-discussed theological topic. God is so much greater than we that the prospect of coming to know him can often seem daunting. How can we, with all our ignorance, weakness, and sin, come to know the Lord of the universe? And Scripture itself speaks of the discrepancy between God and our power to comprehend:

> For my thoughts are not your thoughts,
>   neither are your ways my ways, declares the LORD.
> For as the heavens are higher than the earth,
>   so are my ways higher than your ways
>   and my thoughts than your thoughts. (Isa. 55:8–9)

Oh, the depth of the riches and wisdom and knowledge of God! How unsearchable are his judgments and how inscrutable his ways!

"For who has known the mind of the Lord,
  or who has been his counselor?"
"Or who has given a gift to him
  that he might be repaid?"

For from him and through him and to him are all things. To him be glory forever.
Amen. (Rom. 11:33–36)

Cf. Judg. 13:18; Neh. 9:5; Pss. 139:6; 147:5; Isa. 9:6.

One reason God is incomprehensible is that he has chosen not to reveal to us everything about himself:

The secret things belong to the Lord our God, but the things that are revealed belong
to us and to our children forever, that we may do all the words of this law. (Deut. 29:29)

But God is incomprehensible not only in what is unrevealed, but also in his revelation.
For his revelation moves us to wonder. It never justifies a "now we know it" smugness.
Romans 11:33–36, quoted above, comes after many chapters of careful rational argument, setting forth the gospel in many dimensions and answering many questions.
But the conclusion of this argument does not move Paul to boast that he has set forth
a final account. Rather, it moves him to wonder and awe. It makes him all the more
aware of what we *don't* know of God's purposes. Yes, God has saved us from sin, by his
grace, through faith. But his reasons for stooping so low to redeem us still lie hidden
in the mists of his vast being.[11]

But Scripture never draws the inference that we cannot know God at all. On the
contrary:

And this is eternal life, that they know you the only true God, and Jesus Christ whom
you have sent. (John 17:3)

Knowing God, in one sense, is salvation itself (cf. Matt. 11:25–27). And every page of
Scripture describes or presupposes the knowledge of God by human beings. We know
God's character, his acts, his word, his judgments, his mercies.

So our analysis must do justice both to the reality of human knowledge of God and
to the limitations of that knowledge. God's *incomprehensibility* will refer to the limitations, as Scripture presents them, not to some general sense of mystery that we try to
articulate on our own.

---

11. I have found this illustration helpful. Consider your knowledge of God as a circle that begins small, but
increases as you get to know God better. But the larger the circle gets, the greater its circumference, its exposure
to what is outside. Similarly, the more we know God, the more we understand how little we know. The more we
know God, the more areas of mystery we encounter. And the more we know God, the less justification we have
for looking down in pride upon those who know a little less. (Thanks to Norman Shepherd for this illustration.
I take full responsibility for its formulation here.)

Understanding God's knowability and incomprehensibility proceeds best from the Creator-creature distinction as I have expounded it. God's incomprehensibility follows from his transcendence over us, and his knowability follows from his immanence. Isaiah 55:8–9 and Romans 11:33–36 (quoted above) say essentially that God is incomprehensible because he is God. In Isaiah 55, God's knowledge is above ours as the heavens are above the earth. The epistemological discrepancy has a metaphysical basis. In Romans 11:33–36, God's knowledge is "unsearchable" and "inscrutable" because it is so rich and deep. And he is the owner and Creator of all things (vv. 35–36). Our knowledge is different because we are different. We can't imagine what it would be like to own everything and to be the creators of everything we know. We cannot, in other words, know what it would be like to be Lord of all, and to know as Lord. We are essentially and irreparably servants, consigned to know as servants and only as servants.

So God is incomprehensible because he is Lord and we are his servants. But this does not mean that we cannot know him at all. His control and authority limit our knowledge, rendering it servant-knowledge. But God's covenant presence reveals God to us, so that we genuinely know him, as servants.

So knowing God is always in terms of the biblical worldview: positions 1 and 2 on the rectangular diagram. We do not believe that God is so far removed from us that he cannot be known (position 3) or that we can know him at all by autonomous reasoning (position 4). We believe, rather, that although we cannot know God as he knows himself, as ultimate controller and authority (1), we do know him as he has chosen to reveal himself to us, in a way appropriate to creatures (2).[12]

Some, including Calvin, have found it helpful to say that in revealing himself, God "accommodates" himself to us. That is, he does not speak to us in his own eternal Trinitarian language, but in ways that we can understand (recall chapters 23–24). God is like a loving parent who speaks "baby talk" to us, who "lisps" to us.[13] There is truth in this representation. But we should not infer from this illustration that God lies to us or speaks less than the truth.[14] A mother who speaks baby talk to a child does not intend to deceive him, but to convey truth in a way suited to the child's understanding.

Knowing God in Faith and in Unbelief

Epistemology (theory of knowledge) as a philosophical discipline has significant relationships to two other parts of philosophy: metaphysics/ontology (theory of being)

---

12. In *DKG*, 20–40, I discuss at great length some of the more specific limitations on our knowledge of God and a number of the ways in which our knowledge is like God's. Then I discuss several distinctions that I consider problematic, such as the question whether we know God's "essence" or whether we know "God in himself." *Essence* and *in himself* are philosophical terms, not biblical ones, and in my judgment they are not helpful ways to communicate the biblical teachings in these areas. There are ambiguities in these terms, and they are at best ill-suited to the dogmatic precision that many have demanded in theological statements.

13. *Institutes*, 1.13.1.

14. So I repudiate the statement of R. Scott Clark in *Recovering the Reformed Confession* (Phillipsburg, NJ: P&R Publishing, 2008), 130, that there is always "a certain degree of falsehood in human speech about God." This statement implies that there is falsehood in all speech and writing about God, including Scripture.

and ethics (theory of value). So far in this chapter, we have focused on the relationship of epistemology to ontology, its basis in the nature of God and of the creation. In this section, however, we will consider the relation of epistemology to ethics, that is, the relation of human knowledge to human obedience and disobedience to God. We will see that knowledge in obedience and knowledge in disobedience are very different from each other.

Knowledge in Obedience

As I indicated above, to know God is to know him as Lord. That is to say, it is a covenantal knowledge. As I indicated earlier, it is a knowledge about his control, authority, and presence. But knowing God in the highest sense is more than this. It is also a knowledge *under, subject to,* and *exposed to* his control, authority, and presence.

First, it is a knowledge *under God's control.* All our knowledge of God is based on revelation. When we come to know God, it is he who takes the initiative. He does not wait passively for us to discover him, but he makes himself known. In the postfall context, furthermore, his revelation is gracious. We do not deserve it, but God gives it as a favor to us, as part of his redemptive mercy (Ex. 33:12–13; 1 Chron. 28:6–9; Prov. 2:6; Isa. 33:5–6; Jer. 9:23–24; 31:33–4; Matt. 11:25–28; John 17:3; Eph. 4:13; Phil. 1:9; Col. 1:9–10; 3:10; 2 Tim. 2:25; 2 Peter 1:2–3; 2:20; 1 John 4:7). God's grace gives us *objective revelation,* revelation of objective truth, but also *subjective* or *existential revelation,* as we discussed it in chapters 27–28, the illumination or enlightenment of the Holy Spirit that opens our hearts, so that we acknowledge, understand, and rightly use his truth (2 Cor. 4:6; Eph. 1:18; Heb. 6:4; 10:32; cf. 1 Thess. 1:5). So the origin of our knowledge of God is God himself. It is Trinitarian: the Father knows all and reveals truth to us by the grace of his Son through the work of the Spirit in our hearts. Note how each person of the Trinity is involved in the knowing process: 1 Sam. 2:3; Ps. 73:11; Isa. 11:2; 28:9; 53:11; Matt. 11:25–27; Eph. 1:1; Col. 2:3. Thus it is all of God, all of grace. We know God because he has first known us as his children (cf. Ex. 22:12; 1 Cor. 8:1–3; Gal. 4:9).

Second, it is a knowledge *subject to God's authority.* In Scripture, knowledge is very closely linked with righteousness and holiness (cf. Eph. 4:24; Col. 3:10). These go together (1 Cor. 8:1–3; 1 John 4:7f.). So knowledge of God, in the fullest sense, is inevitably an *obedient* knowledge. Let me sketch five important relations between knowledge and obedience.

1. *Knowledge of God produces obedience* (John 17:26; 2 Peter 1:3, 5; 2:18–20). God's friends necessarily seek to obey him (John 14:15, 21; etc.), and the better they know him, the more obedient they become. Such a relation to God is inevitably a sanctifying experience; being near him transforms us, as in the biblical pictures of God's glory being transferred to his people, of his Spirit descending on them, and of their being conformed to his image.

2. Obedience to God leads to knowledge (John 7:17; Eph. 3:17–19; 2 Tim. 2:25–26; 1 John 3:16; cf. Ps. 111:10; Prov. 1:7; 15:33; Isa. 33:6).[15] This is the converse of the previous point; there is a "circular" relation between knowledge and obedience in Scripture. Neither is unilaterally prior to the other, either in time or in causality. They are inseparable, simultaneous. Each enriches the other (cf. 2 Peter 1:5f.). Some Reformed "intellectualists" (e.g., Gordon Clark applied this label to himself) have failed in my view to do justice to this circularity. Even in the writings of J. Gresham Machen, one often finds the slogan "life is built upon doctrine" used in such a way as to distort the fact that the opposite also holds true in some senses. It certainly is true that if you want to obey God more completely, you must get to know him; but it is also true that if you want to know God better, you must seek to obey him more perfectly.[16]

This emphasis does not contradict our earlier point that knowledge is by grace. Knowledge and obedience are given to us, simultaneously, by God on the basis of Jesus' sacrifice. Once they are given, God continues to give them in greater and greater fullness. But he uses means, and he uses our obedience as a means of giving us knowledge and vice versa.

The same is true when we seek to "know God's will for us." Romans 12:1–2 says that knowing God's will involves making your body a living sacrifice. Cf. Eph. 5:8; Phil. 1:10; Heb. 5:11–14.[17]

3. Obedience is knowledge, and knowledge is obedience. Very often in Scripture, *obedience* and *knowledge* are used as near-synonyms, either by being set in apposition to each other (e.g., Hos. 6:6) or by being used to define each other (e.g., Jer. 22:16). Occasionally, too, *knowledge* appears as one term in a general list of distinctly ethical categories (e.g., Hos. 4:1f.). Thus Scripture presents it as a form of obedience. Cf. also Jer. 31:31f.; John 8:55 (note context, esp. vv. 19, 32, 41); 1 Cor. 2:6 (cf. vv. 13–15; "mature" here is an ethical-religious quality); Eph. 4:13; Phil. 3:8–11; 2 Thess. 1:8f.; 2 Peter 1:5; 2:20f. In these passages, obedience is not merely a consequence of knowledge, but a constitutive aspect of it. Without obedience there is no knowledge, and vice versa.[18]

The point here is not that *obedience* and *knowledge* are synonymous terms, interchangeable in all contexts. They do differ. *Knowledge* designates the friendship between ourselves and God (see below), and *obedience* designates our activity within that relation-

---

15. The "fear of God" is that basic attitude of reverence and awe that inevitably carries with it a desire to do God's will.

16. The circle goes even further: knowledge originates in God's grace and leads to more grace (Ex. 33:13), which leads to more knowledge. In this case, however, there is a "unilateral" beginning. Grace originates knowledge, not vice versa.

17. These are important passages indicating the nature of divine guidance. See *DKG*, 154–55, for a discussion of them.

18. F. Gerald Downing, in his *Has Christianity a Revelation?* (London: SCM Press, 1964), virtually equates knowledge with obedience in such a way that he actually denies the existence of a revealed knowledge of God in the conceptual sense of *knowledge*. In my view, he presses his case much too far: see, for example, his exegesis of Philippians 3:8ff., which is somewhat bizarre. But he makes many useful suggestions, and the book is very helpful in combating our traditional picture of *knowledge* as something merely intellectual. (*Merely* can be such a helpful word in theology! If Downing had said that knowledge is not *merely* intellectual, he would have said something true and helpful.)

ship. But these two ideas are so inseparable from each other that often they can legitimately be used as synonyms, each describing the other from a particular perspective.

4. Thus, *obedience is the criterion of knowledge.* To determine whether someone knows God, we do not merely give him a written exam; we examine his life. Atheism in Scripture is a practical position, not merely a theoretical one: denying God is seen in the corruption of one's life (Pss. 10:4ff.; 14:1–7; 53). Similarly, the test of Christian faith or knowledge is a holy life (Matt. 7:21ff.; Luke 8:21; John 8:47; 14:15, 21, 23f.; 15:7, 10, 14; 17:6, 17; 1 John 2:3–5; 4:7; 5:2f.; 2 John 6f.; Rev. 12:17; 14:12). The ultimate reason for that is that God is the real, living, and true God, not an abstraction concerning whom we can only theorize, but he is profoundly involved with each of our lives. The very "I am" of Yahweh indicates his presence. As Francis Schaeffer said, he is "the God who is there." Thus, our involvement with him is a practical involvement, an involvement with him not only in our theoretical activity, but in all of life. To disobey is to be culpably ignorant of God's involvement in our lives. So disobedience involves ignorance and obedience involves knowledge.[19]

5. Therefore, it is clear that knowledge itself must be *sought in an obedient way.* There are commandments in Scripture that bear very directly on how we are to seek knowledge, that identify the differences between true and false knowledge. In this connection, we should meditate on 1 Corinthians 1–2; 3:18–23; 8:1–3; James 3:13–18. When we seek to know God obediently, we assume the fundamental point that Christian knowledge is a knowledge under authority, that our quest for knowledge is not autonomous, but subject to Scripture. And if this is true, it follows that the truth (and to some extent the content) of Scripture must be regarded as the most sure knowledge that we have. If this knowledge is to be the criterion for all other knowledge, if it is to govern our acceptance or rejection of other propositions, then there is no proposition that can call it into question. Thus, when we know God, we know him more certainly, more surely than we know anything else. When he speaks to us, our understanding of his Word must govern our understanding of everything else. Anything less than this is unacceptable to him.

This is a difficult point because, after all, our understanding of Scripture is fallible, and may sometimes need to be corrected. But those corrections may be made only on the basis of a deeper understanding of Scripture, not on the basis of some other kind of knowledge. In correcting our initial interpretations, we work on the basis of a biblical epistemology. As the Reformers said, Scripture is its own interpreter.[20]

It is at this point that we introduce ourselves to the term for which Van Til's apologetics is best known, the term *presupposition.* A presupposition is a belief that takes precedence over another and therefore serves as a criterion for another. An ultimate presupposition is a belief over which no other takes precedence.[21] For a Christian,

---

19. A number of ideas in this paragraph come from Norman Shepherd's lectures on the doctrine of God, which I attended in the late 1970s.

20. See the discussion of interpretation in chapter 27.

21. Some may feel that this definition of *presupposition* has too much of an intellectualistic ring. Of course, in this context we are concerned mainly with beliefs, propositions, and the like. But I would certainly want to stress that presuppositions are rooted in basic commitments of the heart. Whether we use the term *presupposition* as

the content of Scripture must serve as his ultimate presupposition. Our beliefs about Scripture may be corrected by other beliefs about Scripture, but, relative to the body of extrascriptural information we possess, those beliefs are presuppositional in character. This doctrine is merely the outworking of the lordship of God in the area of human thought. It merely applies the doctrine of scriptural infallibility to the realm of knowing.

Seen in this way, I really can't understand why any evangelical Christian could have a problem in accepting it. We are merely affirming that human knowledge is servant-knowledge—that in seeking to know anything, our first concern is to discover what our Lord thinks about it and to agree with his judgment, to think his thoughts after him. What alternative could there possibly be? Would anyone dare suggest that while we commit ourselves unreservedly to Christ, there is no place for such commitments in our intellectual work? The doctrine of presuppositions simply asserts the lordship of Christ over human thought.

As we continue to the third of the lordship attributes, we will now consider knowledge *exposed to God's presence.* We commonly distinguish between knowledge of facts ("knowing that . . ."), knowledge of skills ("knowing how . . ."), and knowledge of persons ("knowing whom").[22] These three are related, but they are not identical with one another. Knowing a person involves knowing facts about him (contrary to some "personalistic" theologians), but one can know facts about someone without knowing him, and vice versa. A political scientist may know many facts about the President of the United States without being able to say that he "knows" the President. The White House gardener may know far fewer facts and yet be able to say that he knows the President quite well.

All three kinds of knowledge are mentioned in Scripture, and all are important theologically. A believer must know certain facts about God—who he is, what he has done. Note the importance of the historical prologue within the covenant structure described in chapter 2: the Lord begins the covenant document by telling what he has done. The covenant begins in grace. Those who disparage the importance of factual knowledge in Christianity are in fact disparaging the message of grace (cf. Ps. 100:3; Rom. 3:19; 6:3; 1 John 2:3; 3:2—random examples of factual knowledge that is vital to the believer). Furthermore, a believer is one who learns new skills—how to obey God, how to pray, how to love—as well as skills in which believers differ from one another—preaching, evangelizing, diaconal service, and so forth (cf. Matt. 7:11; Col. 4:6; 1 Tim. 3:5). But (and perhaps most importantly) Christian knowledge is knowledge of a person. It is knowing God, Jesus Christ, and the Holy Spirit.[23]

---

defined above or whether we define it as "basic commitment" and find another term to employ in the narrowly epistemological context does not seem to me to be a very important problem.

22. Knowledge of things might be a fourth category. Often when we talk about knowing things (bananas, Switzerland, the price structure of the grain market), we are thinking about factual knowledge; other times, or perhaps always to an extent, we are thinking of an acquaintance somewhat analogous to the knowledge of persons. I don't think it would be edifying to try to sort out those questions now.

23. Although the three kinds of knowledge are distinct, each involves the others. You cannot know a person without knowing some facts about him and having some ability to relate meaningfully to him, and so forth. One can therefore describe Christian knowledge under one of three *perspectives*: as learning facts and mastering

Sometimes in the Scriptures, *knowing* a person refers mainly to knowing facts about him, but most often it means being involved with him either as a friend or as an enemy (cf. Gen. 29:5; Matt. 25:24; Acts 19:15; 1 Cor. 16:15; 1 Thess. 5:12). The common use of *know* to refer to sexual intercourse should also be noted at this point (e.g., Gen. 4:1). When Scripture speaks of God's "knowing" men, generally the reference is not to factual knowledge at all (since it goes without saying that God knows the facts). In such contexts, *knowing* generally means "loving," or "befriending" (note Ex. 33:12, 17; Ps. 1:5f.; Jer. 1:5; Nah. 1:7; Matt. 25:12; John 10:14, 27). This is frequently an important exegetical point, especially in Romans 8:29: the statement there that God "foreknew" certain persons cannot mean that he knew that they would believe; thus, it cannot teach that predestination is based on God's foresight of man's autonomous choices. Rather, the verse teaches that salvation originates in God's sovereign knowledge (i.e., love) of his elect. Hence, Scripture almost never speaks of God's "knowing" an unbeliever; the only examples I can find of that (John 2:25; 5:42) clearly refer to factual knowledge.

Man's knowledge of God, then, is very similar to God's knowledge of man. To know him is to be involved with him as a friend or as an enemy. For the believer, to know him is to love him, hence the strong emphasis on obedience (as we have seen) as a constitutive aspect of the knowledge of God. Here, however, we wish to focus on the fact that the God whom we know, whom we love, is of necessity present with us, and therefore our relationship with him is a truly personal one. The intimacy of love assumes the present reality of the beloved. We can love someone at a distance, but only if that person plays a significant continuing role in our thoughts, decisions, and emotions and is in that sense near to us. But if God controls all things and stands as the ultimate authority for all our decisions, then he confronts us at every moment: his power is manifest everywhere, and his Word makes a constant claim on our attention. He is the most unavoidable reality there is, and the most intimate, since his control and authority extend to the deepest recesses of the soul. Because of the very comprehensiveness of his control and authority, we may not think of God as far away. (Earthly controllers and authorities seem far away precisely because their authority and control are so limited.) Thus, God is not a mere controller or authority, but also an intimate acquaintance.

The covenantal language of Scripture brings out this intimacy. God speaks to Israel using the second-person singular, as if the whole nation were one person—God uses the language of "I and thou." He proclaims to his people blessings and curses, the mark of his continuing (priestly) presence. As the history of redemption progresses, the covenant relation is described in terms of marriage (Hosea; Eph. 5; etc.), sonship (John 1:12; Rom. 8:14–17; etc), and friendship (John 15:13–15).[24], [25]

---

the implications and uses of these facts, as developing skills in using facts in our relations with one another and with God, or as learning to know God, in which context we learn facts and skills.

24. Some writers find great "progress" being made here, from legal-covenantal categories to intimate-personal ones. I, however, see these latter metaphors as the natural outworking of that intimacy already involved in the covenantal relation. What more intimacy can anyone ask than that assumed in Deuteronomy 6:5? The idea that law is of necessity something cold and impersonal stems from modern humanistic thinking, not from Scripture.

25. Recall our earlier discussion of the family of God, chapter 6.

The sense of the believer's doing all things not only to the glory of God, but in God's presence (*coram deo*), has been a precious truth to Reformed people. Not only does God control and command, but in all our experience he is, ultimately, "the One with whom we have to do." Nothing can be further from the deterministic, impersonalistic, intellectualistic, unemotional brand of religion represented in the popular caricature of Calvinism.

In summary, *knowledge of God* essentially refers to a person's friendship (or enmity) with God. That friendship presupposes knowledge in other senses—knowledge of facts about God, knowledge of skills in righteous living, and so on. It therefore involves a covenantal response of the whole person to God in all areas of life, either in obedience or in disobedience. It involves, most focally, a knowledge of God's lordship—of his control, his authority, his present reality.

Knowledge in Disobedience

But what about the second alternative, knowledge in enmity? If *knowledge* in Scripture not only involves factual knowledge but also is (1) a gift of God's redemptive grace, (2) an obedient, covenantal response to God, and (3) a loving, personal involvement, then how can there be such a thing as knowledge in *disobedience*? Does not disobedience extinguish knowledge? But Scripture does say that in some sense rebellious people do know God:

> For the wrath of God is revealed from heaven against all ungodliness and unrighteousness of men, who by their unrighteousness suppress the truth. For what can be known about God is plain to them, because God has shown it to them. For his invisible attributes, namely, his eternal power and divine nature, have been clearly perceived, ever since the creation of the world, in the things that have been made. So they are without excuse. For although they knew God, they did not honor him as God or give thanks to him, but they became futile in their thinking, and their foolish hearts were darkened. Claiming to be wise, they became fools, and exchanged the glory of the immortal God for images resembling mortal man and birds and animals and creeping things.
>
> Therefore God gave them up in the lusts of their hearts to impurity, to the dishonoring of their bodies among themselves, because they exchanged the truth about God for a lie and worshiped and served the creature rather than the Creator, who is blessed forever! Amen.
>
> For this reason God gave them up to dishonorable passions. For their women exchanged natural relations for those that are contrary to nature; and the men likewise gave up natural relations with women and were consumed with passion for one another, men committing shameless acts with men and receiving in themselves the due penalty for their error.
>
> And since they did not see fit to acknowledge God, God gave them up to a debased mind to do what ought not to be done. They were filled with all manner of unrighteousness, evil, covetousness, malice. They are full of envy, murder, strife, deceit, maliciousness. They are gossips, slanderers, haters of God, insolent, haughty, boastful, inventors of evil, disobedient to parents, foolish, faithless, heartless, ruthless. Though they know God's decree that those who practice such things deserve to die, they not only do them but give approval to those who practice them. (Rom. 1:18–32)

This passage is the beginning of Paul's argument concluding that "all have sinned and fall short of the glory of God, and are justified by his grace as a gift, through the redemption that is in Christ Jesus" (Rom. 3:23–24). In Romans 1, he focuses on the disobedience of the Gentiles; in Romans 2, of the Jews. In chapter 3, he concludes that *all* are in the same category: sinners in need of grace. So the passage from Romans 1 that I have quoted, together with 2:1–3:22, pertains to *all* people, living at all places and times.[26]

So Romans 1:18–21 teaches clearly that all people know God. They know facts about God (vv. 18–20), indeed quite a lot of facts: they know God's eternal power and divine nature (v. 20), the way he wishes to be worshiped (vv. 21–25), and his standards for sexual and other morality (vv. 26–32). But their knowledge is not only a knowledge of facts. Verse 21 says that they "knew" God. This language indicates a personal relationship, similar to the believer's knowledge of God, but in context vastly different. We can say that if the believer's knowledge is a knowledge in friendship, the unbeliever's knowledge is a knowledge in enmity.

Any such relationship greatly colors the knowledge that one person has of another. The believer's knowledge of his Father and Lord necessitates obedience, as we saw in the previous section. The unbeliever's knowledge of God as an enemy necessitates rebellion and hatred. It also necessitates rejection of the very knowledge that the unbeliever has. According to Romans 1:18, unbelievers "by their unrighteousness suppress the truth." They "exchanged" the glory of God for images (v. 23) and "exchanged the truth . . . for a lie" (v. 25). Throughout the passage, this rejection of the truth and embracing of wickedness is their own responsibility ("without excuse," v. 20). But in the mysterious relation between divine sovereignty and human responsibility (see chapter 14), the passage also says that God "gave them up" to disobedience (vv. 24, 26, 28).

In any case, it is clear that according to Paul the pagans sin against their knowledge of God and therefore against their knowledge of the good. They really do know God, but in unbelief and disobedience. Earlier, however, I argued that Scripture often virtually defines the knowledge of God as a knowledge in obedience. How can it now ascribe knowledge of God to people who are identified by their disobedience?

This is a very difficult question to answer. We would be much more inclined to say that these rebels do *not* know God. Paul himself says that they have no understanding in 1 Corinthians 2:8 and 14,[27] and in 1 Corinthians 8:1–3 he denies that anyone who fails to love can

---

26. The aorists translated "knew," "honor," "give thanks," and "became futile" in verse 21 and beyond have led some readers to think Paul is talking about people living in a past time, not his own contemporaries. But that would imply that Paul is giving his contemporaries a pass from his solemn indictment. Note: (1) This passage, again, is part of an argument convicting *all* people of sin, all past, present, and future. So it presupposes that people in all times and places "know God." The aorists therefore do not designate a particular time of occurrence for the events they mention. (2) More generally, this passage is part of Paul's description to the Roman church of the gospel he proclaims (vv. 16–17). So clearly, the pagans he mentions in verses 18–32 are pagans to whom he preaches this gospel in his present labors. (3) Paul establishes his time reference at the beginning of the passage by a present active participle, *katechonton* in verse 18.

27. Compare the OT use of "understand" and "understanding" in passages such as Psalms 14:2; 32:9; 53:2; 82:5; Proverbs 12:11 KJV.

have knowledge. So the idea of someone who knows God, but does not love him, is very peculiar indeed. Yet we must try to understand it, because it is part of God's Word. Obviously, Scripture uses *knowledge* very differently when it says that unbelievers know God.

Part of the answer is found in God's common grace (chapter 12). God restrains sin, in part, by preventing his enemies from totally extinguishing their knowledge of God. But this is not the whole answer, because often the unbeliever's knowledge of God and God's truth actually equips him for greater sin. If he were able to entirely suppress the truth of God, his consciousness would be a total chaos, and he would not be able to make any meaningful decision, even a sinful one.

I don't think it is possible to describe the unbeliever's knowledge in a fully coherent way.[28] There is something paradoxical about the whole idea. We can better understand the context of the paradox if we consider Satan's knowledge of God. Scripture generally presents Satan as a knowledgeable being, one who knows more facts about God than most of us do. He understood the purpose of Jesus' coming so that he was able to launch a preemptive attack, before Jesus even began his preaching ministry (Matt. 4). Surely Satan understands that God is more powerful than he. Yet he nevertheless seeks nothing less than to overthrow God's lordship and to replace him on the throne. At some level, he must know that his defeat is sure, yet he perseveres in a warfare that he cannot hope to win. So in a being with vast knowledge and understanding of God, there is a streak of irrationality that renders him an utter fool.

Scripture presents unbelieving human beings as disciples of Satan, and as sharing his irrationality. They know God from the creation (Rom. 1), yet they somehow think they can prosper in lives that defy the Almighty.

Philosophically, the best description of this paradox can be found in Van Til's discussion of rationalism and irrationalism. The sinner is first a rationalist, in the sense that he tries to think autonomously. He believes that he can understand the world using his own mind as the ultimate standard of truth and right. But simultaneously he is an irrationalist. When he sees that his mind is, after all, not suited to serve as the ultimate standard of truth, when errors enter his thinking, he excuses himself by saying that the universe is not knowable after all. So his rationalism devolves into irrationalism. He affirms his reason without reason.

Van Til's illustration was the story in Genesis 3 of the fall of our first parents. God had told them clearly that they were not to take of a particular fruit. But for Eve, then Adam, God's word was not sufficient, despite their intimate knowledge of him in the garden. They

---

28. Cornelius Van Til, his disciples, and some others such as Gordon H. Clark labored hard to find ways to describe the differences between the believer's and the unbeliever's knowledge of God, in order to illumine what Van Til called the "antithesis" between believing and unbelieving thought. These writers were not always consistent in their formulations, and my general view is that on the whole these contrasts do not pass biblical muster. Van Til argued, for example, that the unbeliever *ought* to know God but doesn't (but how is that reconcilable with Romans 1:21?), that the unbeliever knows God "psychologically" but not "epistemologically" (I don't know what that means), and so on. I analyzed a number of these suggestions in *DKG*, 50–58, and in *CVT*, 187–238. But in the end, I think it's best to do what Van Til did not hesitate to do in other contexts: simply to state the paradox of unbelieving knowledge and to let the matter rest there. The fact is, as I indicate in the present discussion, unbelieving thought does *not* hold a consistent epistemology and cannot.

listened to Satan in the form of a talking snake and took Satan's side. From one standpoint, Eve was a rationalist, because she embraced autonomous thought, concluding that she herself was the ultimate standard of truth. On the other hand, she was an irrationalist, denying that there was any ultimate rationality to the universe to which she needed to conform. So she joined Satan in his irrational quest to replace God on the throne.

The history of non-Christian philosophy shows the same vacillation between rationalism and irrationalism. Some philosophers, such as Parmenides, promoted brilliant and bizarre speculations, following with a mad consistency what they took to be the dictates of their autonomous reason. Others, such as the Sophists, denied that there was any universal reason, arguing that what is true for me might not be true for you. Still others, such as Plato, Aristotle, and Kant, divided the universe in two, postulating one realm in which autonomous reason functioned successfully and another realm of which knowledge is impossible.[29]

The paradoxical relation between rationalism and irrationalism can be illustrated as I earlier illustrated the relations between transcendence and immanence (cf. chapter 3). See fig. 29.3.

Biblical   **Nonbiblical**

Reason limited by God's sovereignty   Irrationalism: no ultimate source of knowledge

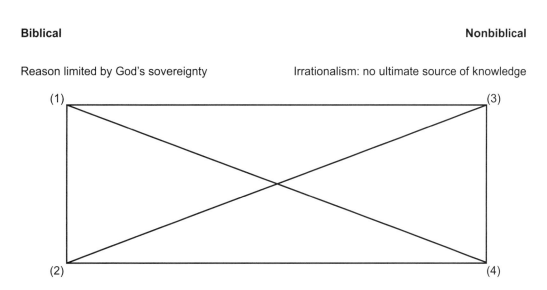

Reason competent to understand   Rationalism: human reason
the world via God's revelation   must function autonomously

Fig. 29.3. Rationalism and Irrationalism: Rectangle of Opposition

On this diagram, irrationalism is in corner 3 where I earlier placed nonbiblical transcendence. These are inseparable. When someone says that metaphysically the supreme

29. For more discussion of this paradox in Greek philosophy, see my "Greeks Bearing Gifts," in *Revolutions in Worldview*, ed. W. Andrew Hoffecker (Phillipsburg, NJ: P&R Publishing, 2007), 1–36.

being is so far from us that he cannot be known (unbiblical transcendence), there is an epistemological consequence: that we have no ultimate standard of truth. Similarly, when one affirms ontologically that the supreme being is identical with creation or something in it (immanence), that implies epistemologically (4) that human reason must function autonomously.

In one sense, 3 and 4 are inconsistent. One cannot logically say that there is no ultimate standard of truth and at the same time claim that human reason is the ultimate standard. But in another sense, 3 and 4 require each other. For as with Satan, and as with our first parents, autonomous reason (4) can be affirmed only irrationalistically (3). And irrational skepticism (3) can be defended only by appeal to autonomous reason (4).

Now, non-Christians typically reply that in fact the shoe is on the other foot. Christians, they say, are irrational because Christians surrender their reason to someone outside themselves (1). And they argue that Christians are rationalistic because they think absolute truth is available to them by revelation. We may well accept this disparaging language in an ironic way, which allows us to present the four assertions somewhat more clearly:

1. Christian irrationalism
2. Christian rationalism
3. Non-Christian irrationalism
4. Non-Christian rationalism

As with the ontological interpretation of the rectangle, the horizontal lines indicate similarities of terminology: that is, Christian (1) and non-Christian (3) irrationalism can be made to sound very similar, as can Christian (2) and non-Christian (4) rationalism. But the diagonal lines indicate substantive disagreement: for example, Christian irrationalism (1) directly contradicts non-Christian rationalism (4), and non-Christian irrationalism (3) directly contradicts Christian rationalism (2).

This schema does not remove the paradoxical character of non-Christian knowledge, but it helps us to see where the paradox lies, what its nature is, and how intractable it is apart from divine grace. And it helps us to see how non-Christians often utter truths (such as "the sky is blue") while being in a larger sense confused about *every* truth. It also helps us to see that it is impossible to predict (as Van Til sometimes imagined he could) how a non-Christian would likely respond to a presentation of the gospel or apologetic argument. A non-Christian may respond in faith (because the Spirit has planted faith in his heart), in intellectual agreement without faith (as with the Pharisees in the NT), in intellectual disagreement on irrationalist grounds, or in intellectual disagreement on rationalist grounds. In any case, as Paul says:

The natural person does not accept the things of the Spirit of God, for they are folly to him, and he is not able to understand them because they are spiritually discerned. (1 Cor. 2:14)

Key Terms

Principium essendi
Principium cognoscendi
Archetypal knowledge
Ectypal knowledge
Brute facts
Interpretations
Divine incomprehensibility
Divine knowability
Accommodation
Presupposition
Ultimate presupposition
Knowing facts
Knowing skills
Knowing persons
Coram deo
Knowledge of God
Christian irrationalism
Christian rationalism
Non-Christian irrationalism
Non-Christian rationalism

Study Questions

1. "So there is a distinctly biblical doctrine of knowledge, just as there are distinctly biblical doctrines of God, sin, and redemption." Explain; evaluate, citing Scripture.

2. Why are we sometimes tempted to think we can know ourselves without knowing God? The reverse?

3. Frame: God "not only knows every state of affairs; he knows each one from every possible perspective." Explain; evaluate; illustrate.

4. "God's interpretation of the facts precedes the existence of the facts; our interpretation is a reinterpretation of God's prior interpretation." Explain; evaluate.

5. "So the facts of our experience are not 'brute' or uninterpreted facts, as if the human interpretation were the first. Rather, the facts are already interpreted before we come to know them. And God's interpretation is the normative interpretation that should govern ours." Explain; evaluate.

6. State briefly the positions of Cornelius Van Til and Gordon H. Clark as to the relation of divine to human thought. Evaluate Frame's attempt to reconcile their positions.

7. Review from chapter 3 and this one the differences between biblical and unbiblical transcendence, and between biblical and unbiblical immanence.

8. "But God is incomprehensible not only in what is unrevealed, but also in his revelation." How does Romans 11:33–36 bear on this assertion? Show how the Shepherd-Frame illustration of the circle bears on the question.

9. "So God is incomprehensible because he is Lord and we are his servants." Formulate and discuss the implied relation between ontology and epistemology.

10. God "accommodates" his revelation to our finite minds, according to John Calvin. Does this fact imply that revelation is always partly false? Discuss.

11. Godly knowledge is "a knowledge *under, subject to,* and *exposed to* God's control, authority, and presence." Explain each part of this statement and evaluate.

12. "The Christian life is built upon Christian doctrine." Explain; evaluate. Describe the relationship(s) between knowledge and obedience found in Scripture.

13. Discuss the relationship between knowing facts, skills, and persons in our knowledge of God.

14. Frame: "I don't think it is possible to describe the unbeliever's knowledge in a fully coherent way." Explain; evaluate.

15. Explain the categories of rationalism and irrationalism, using Frame's rectangular diagram. Show the meaning of each line and point.

16. About his rectangular diagram, Frame says, "This schema does not remove the paradoxical character of non-Christian knowledge, but it helps us to see where the paradox lies, what its nature is, and how intractable it is apart from divine grace." Explain each statement and evaluate.

17. About the rectangular diagram, Frame says, "It also helps us to see that it is impossible to predict (as Van Til sometimes imagined he could) how a non-Christian would likely respond to a presentation of the gospel or apologetic argument." Explain; evaluate.

Memory Verses

Deut. 29:29: The secret things belong to the LORD our God, but the things that are revealed belong to us and to our children forever, that we may do all the words of this law.

John 17:3: And this is eternal life, that they know you the only true God, and Jesus Christ whom you have sent.

Rom. 1:20: For his invisible attributes, namely, his eternal power and divine nature, have been clearly perceived, ever since the creation of the world, in the things that have been made. So they are without excuse.

1 Cor. 2:14: The natural person does not accept the things of the Spirit of God, for they are folly to him, and he is not able to understand them because they are spiritually discerned.

1 Cor. 3:19: For the wisdom of this world is folly with God.

Col. 2:3: In [Christ] are hidden all the treasures of wisdom and knowledge.

Resources for Further Study

Frame, John M. *AGG.*

———. *DKG,* 11–61.

———. "Greeks Bearing Gifts." In *Revolutions in Worldview,* edited by W. Andrew Hoffecker, 1–36. Phillipsburg, NJ: P&R Publishing, 2007.

Van Til, Cornelius. *The Defense of the Faith,* edited by K. Scott Oliphint. Phillipsburg, NJ: P&R Publishing, 2008.

PERSPECTIVES ON HUMAN KNOWLEDGE

AS WE HAVE SEEN, when we know God, we come to understand everything in his creation in a new way. For the rest of part 5, I intend to explore the nature of our knowledge of the created world under the lordship of God.

Objects of Human Knowledge

An *object of knowledge* is anything that we know, or can know, or seek to know. This is a common enough phrase, but some are offended by the application of *object* to persons, or even God. They think that to speak this way involves "objectifying" people, treating people as things, and such like. In my use of the phrase, no such thing is implied. To say that someone or something is an object of knowledge is simply to say that he, she, or it is knowable. In this sense, persons are certainly objects of knowledge, because they are knowable. God, too, is knowable, as I indicated in the previous chapter. So persons and God, along with many impersonal realities, are objects of human knowledge. See fig. 30.1.

Fig. 30.1. Objects of Human Knowledge

For our purposes, it will be convenient to divide the created world into three objects of knowledge that are perspectivally related to one another and that correspond to our three lordship attributes. These are *self*, *world*, and *divine revelation*. I will argue that we cannot know one of these without knowing the other two, so that a complete knowledge of one is equivalent to a knowledge of all three. *Divine revelation* represents God's authority as the norm that determines the truth or falsity of what we claim to know. *World* is the situation into which God has placed us, the whole course of nature and history under his control. *Self* is the knowing subject, existing in personal intimacy with God as present to his covenant people. Let us consider these individually.

Divine Revelation

I discussed divine revelation in some detail in chapters 23–28. *Revelation* is a communication of knowledge. In theology, it is communication from God to man by means of the word of God, God's speech. So although *revelation* and *word of God* are not quite synonymous, they are often interchangeable. Here I will present revelation as the normative factor in human knowledge. Revelation represents God himself as he exerts his authority in the creation.

To know revelation is to know God, for it is to know what God has made known of himself. As we have seen (as, e.g., in chapters 2–3), God is both transcendent over the universe and immanent within it. Here we will understand revelation as God's representation of himself within the world he has made. The triad *revelation*, *world*, and *self* is in that respect equivalent to *God*, *world*, and *self*. That triad exhausts the possible objects of human knowledge. These objects are distinct from one another: God is not the world; the world is not the self; and so on. But *knowledge* of God is not separable from knowledge of the world or self. The *revelation* of God is not separable from his revelation in the world and in the self. So knowledge of the world is not separate from knowledge of God or the self, and so forth. Although these three objects are distinct from one another, one cannot know one of them without knowing the other two. I will explore some of those relationships in what follows.

As I indicated, revelation is the normative factor in human knowledge. It is important that we recognize the significance of norms in knowledge. Historically, students of epistemology have recognized the important distinction in knowledge between the *subject* (the one who knows or seeks knowledge) and the *object* (what the subject knows or seeks to know).[1] But the distinction between subject and object has sometimes been problematic. We often think that there is a clear distinction between the subject (our mind) and the object (something outside of us, beyond us, that we seek to know). But the philosopher Bishop George Berkeley (1685–1753) saw it differently. Berkeley was

---

1. In the previous paragraph, I distinguished God, world, and self as the three objects of human knowledge. In this paragraph, I distinguish the self as knower from the world as object. But of course, the self is an object of his own knowledge as well as subject of it. So the self functions both as a subject of all its knowledge and as an object of its knowledge (specifically its self-knowledge). I hope to clarify these statements in the remainder of this section.

an empiricist in the tradition of John Locke, who thought that knowledge was built up out of sense experience. Sense experience is preserved in memory and current mental data (what David Hume called "impressions and ideas"). But when we examine these mental data, Berkeley said, we find that we know only the content of our own mind, not data outside the mind. We may say, then, that for Berkeley the "external world" is indistinguishable from the mind, or, to put it epistemologically, the object is indistinguishable from the subject. For Berkeley, the only object of thought is thought itself; or, perhaps, there is no object of thought, only subject.

But Hume (1711–76) saw the situation in the opposite way. He, too, was an empiricist. But when he examined his sense experience, he saw trees, clouds, rocks, people— but not a "thinking subject." So Hume became skeptical over concepts such as *soul*, *spirit*, *mind*, *intellectual substance*, and the like. If we say that Berkeley dissolved the object of knowledge into the subject, Hume did the reverse: dissolved the subject into the object.

Later philosophers, such as Martin Heidegger, thought the whole subject-object distinction was a barrier to human understanding. In his view, it was necessary for us to somehow rise above that distinction. But he, like the mystics before him, was not able to clearly set forth what kind of knowledge he was talking about. What is knowledge, if it is not knowledge *of* something (an object) *by* someone (a subject)?

In my view, the way to solve this problem is not to try to transcend the subject-object distinction altogether but to recognize the existence of a third factor—a *norm*. The norm is the rule, standard, or criterion by which we determine truth. By the norm, we determine the truth apart from mere appearance. Put differently, by the norm we are able to distinguish the object of knowledge (what really is) from the subject (our thoughts and ideas). By the norm, we can test when our thoughts and ideas agree with the object of our study and when they differ. So it is the norm that enables us, contrary to Berkeley and Hume, to distinguish subject from object.

The supreme norm (rule, standard, criterion) of our knowledge is God's revelation. Where is that revelation to be found? Well, we saw in chapters 23–28 that in one sense everything is revelation. God himself is revelation, for God is his own word (chapter 23). God's word also comes to us through every event in the natural world, every prophetic or apostolic word, and all the books of Scripture (chapters 24–27), as well as in all persons, God's image (chapter 28). At the end of this discussion, I distinguished between general, special, and existential revelation, a distinction that covers everything there is, triperspectivally.

But what help is this? If everything is revelation, then everything is norm. When someone asks, "How may we distinguish the knowing subject from the object of its thought?" we must answer, "By everything." When someone asks, "Is our view of the universe illusion or reality?" we direct the person to answer the question by consulting everything. But how does one make use of *everything* to answer one specific question?

The answer isn't quite as unhelpful as it appears. For our errors are always at least in part the result of insufficient knowledge. So when we are confused about one question, it means that we need to ask another question. Theoretically, that can lead to another question, and still another, until we reach "everything." But in fact, the trail does not usually go forever. Sometimes it ends with an answer. But when we are beginning our quest, it is often hard to determine where the answer lies, so we often say, "It could be anywhere."

A more helpful limitation on our quest for normativity is to focus on the *Bible*. The Bible is not the whole of God's revelation, but it is a vitally important part of it.[2] As we saw in part 4, the Bible is God's covenant document, given to his people as their highest norm. God directs believers to hold to his written Word (2 Tim. 3:16–17; 2 Peter 1:19–21) against any human idea that would contradict it.

I said that we should *focus* on the Bible, however, not that we should look to the Bible exclusively. For our understanding of the Bible is dependent on our understanding of other forms of revelation. We often need to look at revelation outside of Scripture to understand Scripture. For example, we need to know the languages in which Scripture was written if we are to fully understand what Scripture says. But the Bible does not contain lessons in Hebrew or Greek grammar. We also need to learn facts about the history and culture of biblical times, beyond the references that Scripture itself supplies. And we need to understand our own culture, our own times, if we are rightly to *apply* the Bible to ourselves and to people today.[3] Further, we need to know ourselves if we are rightly to understand the Bible. We need to know our own level of intelligence and maturity (both physical and spiritual), lest we claim too much (or too little) for our interpretations of Scripture.

To *focus* on the Bible, then, is not to ignore revelation in the world and in the self. On the other hand, our interest in the world and the self should not rob Scripture of its unique function in our lives. Scripture is what we trust, even when other sources of knowledge say otherwise. How, then, should we understand the unique authority of Scripture over against all the other kinds of revelation that we rightly consult? I find the following formula helpful:

> When we have a settled view that Scripture teaches p, then we must believe p, over against any claim that p is false.

In this formula, a *settled view* is not a first impression or a slapdash interpretation; it is an interpretation of Scripture that we have thought through prayerfully, using what help may be available from other Bible texts and from scholars and pastors. P represents any proposition, such as "God is one being in three persons."

---

2. And as we will see, the Bible is not only part of revelation, but also an item in the world and an experience of our consciousness. It belongs to all three perspectives.

3. Scripture is clear that you cannot fully understand God's Word if you cannot apply it. See the discussion of interpretation in chapter 27. Scripture is given not merely to inform us about past events, but to guide our lives in the present (Rom. 15:4; 2 Tim. 3:15–17; 2 Peter 1:19–21). Jesus considers people to be ignorant of Scripture when they cannot see the applications of Scripture to the events of their own experience (Matt. 16:3; 22:29; Luke 24:25; John 5:39–40).

In that way, an understanding of revelation, focused in Scripture, enables us to distinguish truth from falsity and thus to distinguish object from subject. This does not mean that we can easily answer any question at all. But it gives us a framework wherein some certainties ("God created the world," "Jesus is the Son of God," "Christ died for our sins") form a foundation for other knowledge.[4]

The World

I use *world* to include everything that exists and every event that happens in nature or history. That includes God, for he exists in the world, immanently, as well as outside the world, transcendently. So just as revelation includes everything, the world includes everything. *Revelation* and *world*, therefore, are not separate from each other, but are the same reality viewed from two perspectives.[5] The world includes God's revelation, and it also includes ourselves.

To distinguish the perspectives, we may say that as revelation serves as the *norm* of human knowledge, so the world serves as its *object*. The world is what we seek to know, by means of the norm of revelation. So revelation and world serve distinct epistemological functions. But the world—that is, the facts—is normative, too, indicating the union between the two perspectives.

It is also worth pointing out that just as the Bible is an aspect of revelation, so it is an object in the world. As we look at the world around us, our situation, one of the things we find is a Book called the Bible. And just as we must deal with rocks, trees, planets, cities, other people, and other books, we must deal with the Bible. It would be wrong for us to think that the Bible is part of revelation but not part of the world—a norm of knowledge but not an object of knowledge. As I indicated earlier, the Bible itself is an object of our study, and as such we seek to relate it to other objects in the world. But when we do that rightly, we discover its uniqueness. It isn't *merely* an object; it is the object that illumines all other objects. Just as investigating our world leads us to human authority figures, such as a governor or president, so it leads us to recognize the chief authority of all authorities, the document of God's covenant with his people. Just as the Bible is the norm of norms, the norm that governs all other norms, so it is the object in the world that illumines all other objects.

Ourselves

We have seen that revelation and world each contain everything and therefore serve as perspectives on all reality. Can we say the same of ourselves? Do we in some sense contain everything? Is each of us a perspective on all reality?

---

4. On the nature of certainty, see the discussion of assurance in chapter 28 and my article "Certainty," at http://www.frame-poythress.org. On the term *foundation*, see the discussion of this subject later in this chapter.

5. Recall my earlier statement in this regard: God, world, and self are distinct from one another, but knowledge of each is not distinct from knowledge of the others. So God's *revelation* is identical with our means of knowing the world and ourselves.

Well, yes. Because, as Berkeley noted, we know everything by knowing ourselves. We know everything by knowing our sense perceptions, but also by knowing our reasoning, our memory, and our imagination. We even know God by knowing ourselves, for we are his image, and in him we live and move and have our being. So as I noted earlier, Calvin said that we cannot know God without knowing ourselves, and we cannot know ourselves without knowing God.

Our self-knowledge also includes knowledge of the world, for we cannot understand ourselves without understanding our environment, our situation. We learn much about ourselves when we learn about our heredity, our history, our education, our motives. Everything we know, we know by our own experience, broadly understood.[6]

In one sense, then, all knowledge is self-knowledge. It is knowledge of our own senses, our own memories, our own thought processes, our own emotional and spiritual inclinations, and our relationships with others.

And I should also mention that just as the Bible is part of God's revelation and an object in the world, so it is also an item of our experience. It is a subject of our memories, thoughts, meditations, reflections.

In a Berkeleyan mood, we might be tempted to think that we are trapped in our own subjectivity, unsure of the existence of anything beyond ourselves. But our very self-knowledge tells us otherwise. In our memories, experience, meditations, a host of clues indicate that we are not alone, not shut up in our heads. And the most vivid clue is the Bible within us, our Bible experience. For the Bible within *tells* us that we are not alone, that beyond the subject there is the object, and there is God. It tells us that there are others beyond ourselves, and that those make claims on us. And beyond ourselves there is the world, which God has called us to fill and subdue. So we cannot understand ourselves rightly without distinguishing ourselves (the subject) from the world (the object) and from God (the revelation). Solipsism, the view that only self exists, is not an alternative for us.

Epistemological Perspectives

As we have seen, the three objects of our knowledge are quite inseparable. To know one of them, we must know the others as well. We need God's revelation to understand the world, but we also need the world to understand God's revelation. We need God's revelation to understand ourselves, but the reverse is also true, as we have seen. We need the world to understand the self, for the world is our environment. And we need the self to understand the world. Something of ourselves enters into everything we know. One implication of this fact is that there is no such thing as a purely objective, unbiased knowledge. Everyone approaches knowledge with what I called *presuppositions* in the previous chapter. The goal in seeking knowledge is not to try to rid ourselves

---

6. That is, not just sense experience, as in philosophical empiricism, but also the experience of thinking, meditating, loving, hating, and so forth.

of all presuppositions, but to apply the right presuppositions, those of God's Word, to the data at hand.

Since revelation, world, and self are not separable, but incorporate one another, none functions as an isolated item of knowledge, but as a perspective on knowledge as a whole. At some times, we will focus on revelation (especially the Bible), but without neglecting the world and the self. Other times, we will focus on the world, in the context of revelation and the self, or on ourselves, without forgetting our environment of revelation and the world. The difference in these three views can be described as a difference of *focus*, *emphasis*, or *perspective*. In regard to these, I have found the following terminology helpful; see fig. 30.2.

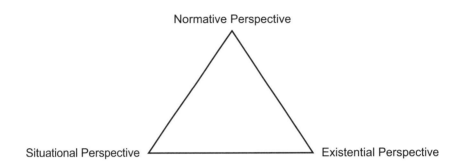

Fig. 30.2. Perspectives on Knowledge

- *The normative perspective* focuses on God's revelation (especially Scripture) in relation to the world and the self.
- *The situational perspective* focuses on the world in relation to God's revelation and to the self.
- *The existential perspective* focuses on oneself and one's own experience in the light of God's revelation and the world.

Foundations and Foundationalism

The following section is not essential to my argument, and readers without philosophical training and interests may skip over it without much loss. But some readers may at this point in the discussion wonder where I stand in the current discussion of *foundationalism.*

Historically, many philosophers have tried to build the edifice of human knowledge from the bottom up—starting with its most fundamental elements and proceeding from these to determine what we may legitimately claim to know. These elements were considered to be the foundation of knowledge. So thinkers in the rationalist tradition, such as Descartes and Spinoza, started with what they considered to be unassailable axioms and tried in logical or mathematical fashion to derive the whole of human knowledge from these. For empiricists, such as Locke, Berkeley, and Hume, the foundation was not to be found in logical axioms but in the primary data of sense experience. For Thomas Reid, the foundation was a set of commonsense observations. For Immanuel Kant, it was a set of synthetic, a priori judgments. For Georg Hegel, a dialectical method could guide us from the abstract idea of "Being" to an exhaustive knowledge of God and the world. In logical atomism (Russell and Wittgenstein), the foundation was (as in empiricism) sense-data, but sense-data referred to in elementary propositions, from which one could build up a picture of the world in a perfect language. In phenomenology, the foundation is the elementary data of consciousness, conceived as the primary reality, not as the representation of something else.

There have always been some thinkers who have been skeptical of these foundationalisms, but such skepticism has usually led them to despair of any possibility of objective knowledge. This was true of the Sophists and skeptics of ancient Greece. David Hume began as an empiricist foundationalist, but his analyses moved him again and again toward skepticism. Wittgenstein's *Tractatus* began as a precise attempt to develop a perfect language based on Russell's logic, but at the end of the book Wittgenstein confesses that in such a perfect language his own claims would be cognitively meaningless and it would be better to remain silent.

Without a means of gaining objective knowledge, these skeptical thinkers become, essentially, subjectivists. They have no way to gather knowledge except for the movements of ideas and feelings within their heads. Recent thought, such as that of the postmodern tradition, is skeptical about foundations, *nonfoundational* or *antifoundational*. They reject all claims to authority over our knowledge, all worldviews or *metanarratives*.

It may be illuminating to see these positions in terms of one of our triangular diagrams, shown in fig. 30.3.

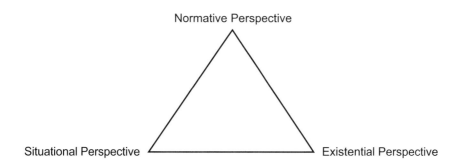

Fig. 30.3. Non-Christian Views of Knowledge

Rationalism seeks a *rule*, a *norm*, an axiom or set of axioms—such that by following it consistently, we may arrive at the truth. Empiricism seeks to explore the *world*, the *facts*, the *situation*. The subjectivist despairs of finding truth beyond himself and sees no alternative to searching his own head. Some philosophers, such as Plato, Aristotle,

Kant, and Hegel, have adopted various combinations of these motifs, but each motif brings its own weaknesses into the mix.[7]

What I have represented as a biblical epistemology is not rationalist, empiricist, or subjectivist, though it has some affinities with each. With the rationalists, Scripture recognizes our need for norms and rules governing knowledge. With the empiricists, Scripture recognizes the facts of God's creation as our object of knowledge. And with the subjectivists, Scripture recognizes that knowing is a mental process, something inward. But it refuses to isolate any of these three aspects of knowledge.

To isolate the norm, as in rationalism, gives you a rule for nothing. Isolating empirical facts gives you unordered, unstructured data. And isolating inward subjectivity keeps us from acknowledging any truth outside ourselves. Of course, individual rationalists, empiricists, and subjectivists are better than this at times, for God's common grace keeps them from utter chaos in their thinking (chapter 29). But the nature of their epistemology drives them toward skepticism.

The reason for this problem is that these philosophers try to operate without God. For God is the Author of the norms of knowledge, the Creator of the facts of the world, and the Creator of man's mind so that it is made to function in the world under the norm of God's revelation.[8] Under him, these three elements are consistent with one another, reinforce one another, and even, as we have seen, are in one sense one with one another.

Without God, there is no reason to think that what we consider norms of thought actually fit the facts and the workings of the human mind. So nontheistic epistemologists are often constrained to choose one of the three elements that will prevail when inconsistencies appear. Those who choose rational axioms are rationalists; those who choose empirical facts are empiricists; and those who choose human subjectivity are subjectivists. Those who try to combine these motifs in effect have no strategy for resolving conflicts except muddling through.

But a triperspectival biblical epistemology enables us to form a basically coherent understanding of the world by our own minds under God's revelation.

This epistemology is in the most obvious sense nonfoundationalist. That is, on this triperspectival approach one does not need to isolate a set of self-evident axioms or fundamental sense-data before one goes about knowing things. It is not necessary to try to derive all our knowledge from such foundational items. Rather, we can start anywhere; indeed, we start where we are, confident that all truth is God's truth. True facts, for example, will lead to true norms, and vice versa. Indeed, true facts *are* true norms, from a particular perspective, for God wants us to live according to all the truth he grants us. And of course, true norms are also factual. And our inner responses are factual and, rightly evaluated, normative.

---

7. In regard to the Greek philosophers, see my essay "Greeks Bearing Gifts," in *Revolutions in Worldview*, ed. W. Andrew Hoffecker (Phillipsburg, NJ: P&R Publishing, 2007), 1–36.

8. Many have remarked on how striking it is that man's mind and the universe are suited to each other, so that the mind is able to discover truth. Divine creation explains this amazing fit.

But of course, there is a sense in which revelation, our norm, particularly in the Bible, is the foundation of our knowledge. It is not that Scripture contains quasi-mathematical axioms from which all knowledge can be deduced, or that it records the most elementary facts of sense experience. Rather, Scripture is foundational in the sense I indicated earlier:

> When we have a settled view that Scripture teaches p, then we must believe p, over against any claim that p is false.

Applying this maxim throughout our quest for knowledge gives us a firm basis for finding truth, firm enough to describe it as a "foundation" of knowledge. But this is not the kind of foundationalism so regularly discussed and dismissed today.

Theories of Truth

In the philosophical tradition, there have been three main theories of truth—with, of course, many variations and combinations. The first has been called the *correspondence* theory. This is a fairly commonsense analysis: typically we think that we obtain knowledge by seeking a correspondence between our ideas and the real world. Our idea of snakes, for example, should somehow match the snakes that exist in the world. But there are several objections to this theory: (1) What is this "match," this "correspondence"? The early Wittgenstein thought that the idea (expressed in language) should be a kind of picture that resembled the idea. But he came to see at a later point that "anything can be a picture of anything given the right method of projection." (2) There will always be an important dissimilarity between any idea we have and any thing or fact in the world, namely, that our ideas are mental and the things are physical. Our ideas, that is, are never *identical* to the things we know. So correspondence must be something short of identity. But it is difficult to specify what such correspondence might be. (3) Idealists such as Berkeley and Hegel have argued that in one sense we can never get outside our own minds, in order to compare the content of the mind with something beyond itself. Rather, they said, we learn about the world only by observing our own perceptions of it, and perceptions are mental entities.

The idealists who questioned correspondence, especially on the third ground, proposed an alternative theory of truth: *coherence*. The coherence theory allows us to look at the mind exclusively, without trying to venture outside it. On this basis, truth is simply the most coherent set of ideas. Here coherence is mainly logical consistency, but it may include other criteria, such as aesthetic balance. The chief objection to the coherence theory is that it is possible for more than one system of ideas to be logically consistent, and for two logically consistent systems to be inconsistent with each other. In this case, we cannot choose between the two systems on the basis of logical consistency. But if some other kind of coherence is in view, such as aesthetic symmetry, it is hard to imagine how an objective conclusion can be reached.

A third alternative is the *pragmatic* theory of truth: roughly, the truth is what works. On this basis, the truth is what we can live by, what does not mislead us in the decisions of life. But often, in order to determine what ideas or concepts will work for us, we must look to see whether they correspond with facts and whether they fit together in a consistent system. So it seems as though the inadequacy of each theory sends us to consider the others.

On a Christian epistemology, the three theories can be understood triperspectivally; see fig. 30.4.

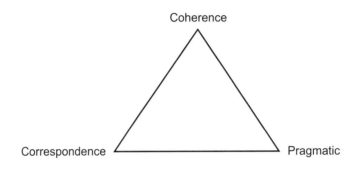

Fig. 30.4. Tests of Truth

Truth is ontologically the reality of God (including God the Son, John 14:6) and all he has made. Epistemologically, it is the content of his mind communicated in his word in all forms of his revelation. The three traditional theories do not tell us what truth is, but they specify ways in which we can test our own apprehension of the truth. Correspondence is the situational test, as we compare our ideas with God's creation. But of course, we cannot do that apart from God's revelation and the workings of our own minds. Coherence seeks truth by obtaining a consistent view of God's revelation, so I place it in the normative category. But of course, that coherence is a coherence within God's creation, for our benefit, so it embraces the other two perspectives. The pragmatic test is what we embrace in seeking to obey God's truth, to "walk in" it. God's Word is a lamp to our feet; it shows us how to meet the tests of each day. And what helps us to do that, and never misleads us, is God's truth. But to discover pragmatic truth, to discover how to live, we must attend to God's creation and God's norms. We must have pragmatic truth that accepts the world as God made it (correspondence) and that seeks consistency with God's Word.

Key Terms

Object of knowledge
Subject of knowledge
Norm of knowledge
Revelation

World
Self
Settled view
Focus
Presupposition
Normative perspective
Situational perspective
Existential perspective
Foundation
Foundationalism
Rationalism
Empiricism
Subjectivism
Postmodernism
Correspondence
Coherence
Pragmatic theory

Study Questions

1. Revelation is "God's representation of himself within the world he has made." Explain; evaluate.

2. "But the distinction between subject and object has sometimes been problematic." How? Address the problem, as you understand it, referring to the views of George Berkeley and David Hume. How does Frame deal with this difficulty?

3. "If everything is revelation, then everything is norm." Is this an adequate understanding of the norm of knowledge? How can we make the norm more specific, more useful?

4. "To *focus* on the Bible, then, is not to ignore revelation in the world and in the self." How do revelation in the world and in the self function when we are focusing on Scripture? Discuss.

5. "When we have a settled view that Scripture teaches p, then we must believe p, over against any claim that p is false." Explain; evaluate.

6. "Just as the Bible is an aspect of revelation, so it is an object in the world." Explain. Why is this important?

7. "Do we in some sense contain everything? Is each of us a perspective on all reality?" Give Frame's answer; explain; evaluate.

8. "In one sense, then, all knowledge is self-knowledge." Explain; evaluate.

9. "In a Berkeleyan mood, we might be tempted to think that we are trapped in our own subjectivity, unsure of the existence of anything beyond ourselves." How would you address this temptation?

10. Describe a secular school of epistemology, such as rationalism, empiricism, subjectivism, or postmodernism. What moves that school to take the positions it does? What is lacking in its approach?

11. "This epistemology is in the most obvious sense nonfoundationalist." Explain why. Is there any sense, then, in which Scripture serves as the *foundation* of Christian thought? Discuss.

12. Define the three traditional theories of truth. How should a Christian make use of these? Is it helpful to say that these are perspectival? Explain.

Memory Verses

John 14:6: Jesus said to him, "I am the way, and the truth, and the life. No one comes to the Father except through me."

Col. 2:3: In [Christ] are hidden all the treasures of wisdom and knowledge.

2 Tim. 3:15–17: From childhood you have been acquainted with the sacred writings, which are able to make you wise for salvation through faith in Christ Jesus. All Scripture is breathed out by God and profitable for teaching, for reproof, for correction, and for training in righteousness, that the man of God may be competent, equipped for every good work.

2 Peter 1:19–21: And we have something more sure, the prophetic word, to which you will do well to pay attention as to a lamp shining in a dark place, until the day dawns and the morning star rises in your hearts, knowing this first of all, that no prophecy of Scripture comes from someone's own interpretation. For no prophecy was ever produced by the will of man, but men spoke from God as they were carried along by the Holy Spirit.

Resources for Further Study

Frame, John M. "Certainty." Available at http://www.frame-poythress.org.

———. *DKG*, esp. 62–75, 109–22.

———. "Greeks Bearing Gifts." In *Revolutions in Worldview*, edited by W. Andrew Hoffecker, 1–36. Phillipsburg, NJ: P&R Publishing, 2007.

Wolterstorff, Nicholas. *Reason within the Bounds of Religion*. Grand Rapids: Eerdmans, 1984.

JUSTIFYING CLAIMS
TO KNOWLEDGE

A COMMON DEFINITION of *knowledge* in secular philosophy is "justified, true belief."[1] This definition is triperspectival, as shown in fig. 31.1.

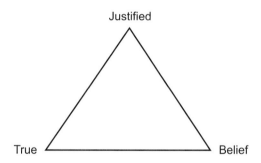

Fig. 31.1. Traditional Definition of Knowledge

On this definition, knowledge is a type of belief, belief that is true, and true belief that is justified. *Belief* represents the existential perspective, for it is something that exists in the mind, something subjective. But many of our beliefs do not constitute knowledge. To be knowledge, a belief must be *true.* That is, our belief must in some sense conform to fact. Truth, then, represents the situational perspective.

But something else is needed to convert our beliefs, even our true beliefs, into knowledge. If I believe that Jim Bailey lives in Atlanta, my belief may turn out to be true. But perhaps I have no adequate *reason* to think he lives there. I might be making that judgment on the basis of a dream, or palm-reading, or some biblical number game. In

---

1. It should be noted that this definition pertains to knowledge of propositions, not knowledge of skills, persons, or things, as I distinguished these kinds of knowledge in chapter 29.

such a case, I have a true belief, but I do not have *knowledge*. I cannot say that I *know* he lives in Atlanta. To have knowledge, on this common definition, I must have a good reason for holding this true belief. That is, my belief must be *justified*. Justification for belief[2] represents the normative perspective.

Now, not everybody accepts this traditional philosophical definition of knowledge. Edmund Gettier in 1963 published an article, "Is Justified True Belief Knowledge?"[3] He argued that there are counterexamples to the definition, that there are cases of justified true belief that we would not call knowledge. Since Gettier's article, the definition of knowledge as justified true belief has lost favor. Part of the problem, I think, has been uncertainty over the meaning of *justification* in such contexts.[4] I suggest that the concept does make sense as a reference to a normative perspective anchored in divine revelation.

Whether or not we regard justification as part of the definition of knowledge, it is an important epistemological concept. For among other things, epistemology teaches us how to reply when someone asks a reason for our belief, a justification. In 1 Peter 3:15, we are told to be ready "to make a defense to anyone who asks you for a reason for the hope that is in you." That "reason" is what I will be calling *justification* in this chapter.

Reasons play an important role in our knowledge of God, as well as our knowledge of God's world. Preaching and apologetics both aim to present people with reasons to believe and/or to behave in accord with God's Word. The Bible itself presents such reasons. Often it uses logical arguments, using language such as "because" and "therefore." We should present our bodies as living sacrifices to God *because* of the mercies of God (Rom. 12:1–2). We should seek the things that are above *because* we have been raised with Christ (Col. 3:1). In one sense, this is the point of the whole Bible: it gives us reasons to trust in Christ and to do his will.

Of course, people often find themselves believing or doing things without going through any reasoning process. Sometimes that is the result of thoughtlessness, intellectual laziness; sometimes it is a lack of intellectual capacity. But most of the time, it results from a kind of reasoning that is informal rather than formal. I don't usually utter a syllogism to myself before I enter a room. But if someone asks me, "Why did you go in there?" I can usually conjure up some kind of reason. That is to say, we can think and believe rationally without going through an explicit logical process. Or, as some writers have pointed out, it is possible to "have" a reason without being able to "give" a reason. Indeed, many people believe in God without being able to articulate a rational basis for doing so.

People were thinking and behaving rationally for many centuries before Aristotle taught us how to test our reasoning with syllogisms. Formal logic is merely a system

---

2. Please do not confuse the justification of beliefs with the justification of sinners by God's grace. The two are quite different.

3. *Analysis* 23 (1963): 121–23.

4. So Alvin Plantinga, in his *Warrant* trilogy—*Warrant: The Current Debate* (New York: Oxford University Press, 1993); *Warrant and Proper Function* (New York: Oxford University Press, 1993); *Warranted Christian Belief* (New York: Oxford University Press, 2000)—replaces *justification* with *warrant*, the latter term describing not our internal reasons for believing, but the external links between thought and reality.

for making our implicit reasoning explicit. But the business of "giving a justification" is more ancient and more primitive than the discipline of formal logic. It is the human activity that formal logic attempts to describe and evaluate.

In what follows I will distinguish three forms of justification, expressing the three perspectives that I have been exploring in this book. I will give to these the same names as I have given to the three perspectives described in the previous chapter. See fig. 31.2.

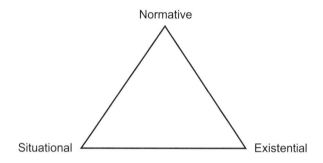

Fig. 31.2. Ways of Justifying Claims to Knowledge

In normative justification, we justify our belief by claiming that it accords with the norms for human thought. In situational justification, we justify our belief by showing that it is in accord with the facts. And in existential justification, we claim that our belief is the most profoundly satisfying of all the alternatives. Since these three forms of justification are perspectives, they are ultimately the same, and they ultimately lead to the same conclusions because God coordinates them with each other. In the discussions below, I will try to show how each incorporates each of the others.

These justifications are somewhat parallel to the non-Christian epistemologies I discussed in the previous chapter. Rationalism appears similar to a Christian normative justification. Empiricism resembles a Christian situational justification. And subjectivism looks somewhat like a Christian existential justification. But in Christian justification, God is central, and we acknowledge him as the One who brings unity to the whole triangle of knowledge. Therefore, the three Christian perspectives are not rivals, as the three similar non-Christian positions are. We can begin anywhere we like on the triangle, as long as we understand that other starting points are equally valid and that to do justice to any one perspective, we must eventually do justice to all three. I will try to clarify these relationships in what follows.

Normative Justification

In normative justification, I tell someone that I believe p[5] because believing p accords with the laws of human thought. When philosophers speak of *laws of thought*, they

5. P is a variable, standing for any proposition.

usually refer to the most fundamental propositions of logic, such as the law of identity,[6] the law of the excluded middle,[7] and the law of noncontradiction.[8] But for the Christian, the most fundamental law of thought is the same as the fundamental law of conduct,[9] namely, the Word of God.

As we saw in the previous chapter, the normative includes all of God's revelation, so in a sense everything is normative. But the Bible plays a special role within the normative perspective as the covenant document given by God to his people, by which all human thought and conduct is to be tested. To be sure, the Bible must be interpreted in the light of other forms of revelation, as they must be interpreted in the light of the Bible. But our settled convictions about what Scripture says take precedence over convictions derived from any other source.

As we have seen, we should therefore regard Scripture as our *presupposition*: our highest standard of truth and certainty.[10] This means admitting that in one sense we are biased. We are inclined to find Scripture reliable and to be suspicious of any view that contradicts Scripture. Some non-Christians will find this a damaging admission and will urge us to put away our bias and to be open-minded toward every alternative position. But on a biblical view, there is no such thing as unbiased human thought. Human thought is either biased against God, by repressing his revelation (Rom. 1), or biased in his favor (by the work of the Spirit, overcoming our sinful bias). Everyone has presuppositions, some false, some true. The first step in epistemological wisdom is to recognize that fact.

But in what way can we justify our own bias, our presupposition? How do we justify belief in the Bible as our presupposition? Strange as it may sound, by the Bible itself, as I sought to do in chapters 23–28. The Bible is our highest standard of truth, the ultimate criterion. But an ultimate criterion must justify itself. It would be contradictory to try to justify an ultimate by appealing to something supposedly higher.

But someone will now object: isn't this a circular argument? We prove Scripture on the basis of the presupposition of Scripture. We appeal to Scripture to prove Scripture.

But if this is a problem for Christian thought, it is equally a problem for non-Christian thought. All systems of thought are circular in a sense when they seek to defend their ultimate criterion of truth. If I challenge a rationalist for accepting human reason as his highest principle, he can defend his view in only one way: by appealing to reason. For him there is nothing higher than reason to which he may appeal in justifying reason. (If there were, he would not be a rationalist, but an advocate of that higher-than-reason standard.) Similarly, an empiricist must ultimately appeal to sense experience,[11] a sub-

---

6. Every proposition is identical to itself.

7. Every proposition is either true or false.

8. No proposition can be both true and false.

9. Thought is, of course, part of conduct, which is to say that epistemology is part of ethics.

10. Recall our discussion of assurance in chapter 28.

11. Empiricists rarely do this, if ever, because it's rather implausible to think that sense experience in itself could furnish grounds for believing in an epistemological philosophy. But that is one of the problems with empiricism. Our senses enable us to know objects, but our knowledge of standards, criteria, or norms requires some other basis.

jectivist to his subjectivity, a Hegelian to his dialectic, a Muslim to his Qur'an, and a mystic to his mystical experience.

A more difficult question, however, is this: how can such a circular argument *persuade* anyone? A good argument must have three qualities: validity, soundness, and persuasiveness. This is a perspectival triad; see fig. 31.3.

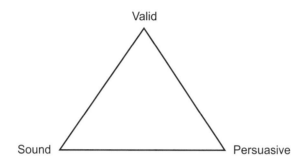

Fig. 31.3. Qualities of Good Arguments

Valid means that the logic of the argument is correct. *Sound* means that the premises of the argument are true, and that therefore the conclusion is true. But an argument can be both valid and sound and yet utterly unpersuasive. For example:

> What Scripture says is true.
> Scripture says that Scripture is infallible.
> Therefore, Scripture is infallible.

This argument is valid because the premises imply the conclusion. It is sound because (in my judgment) the premises are true and therefore the conclusion is true. But many would not find the argument persuasive because they would not consent to the premises.

Of course, persuasiveness is a subjective matter. What persuades one person will not necessarily persuade another. In that sense, apologetics is *person-variable*. But to make an argument more persuasive, it is often helpful to bring in additional arguments and evidence. I call that *broadening* an argument. All argument for an ultimate criterion is circular,[12] but there is a difference between a narrow circle and a broad circle. The argument for biblical infallibility that I formulated above is an example of a narrowly circular argument. We can broaden it by bringing in evidence for the premises. For example, I could use the discussion of chapters 23–28 to fortify the second premise. Some of that material would bear on the first premise, too. Or I could add evidence such as the following: (1) The biblical books were written close in time to the events

---

12. Notice that I did not say that "all argument is circular," but rather that "all argument *for an ultimate criterion* is circular." Most of the time it is fallacious to employ circular argument, but this one case is a necessary exception to that principle.

they describe, closer than any other ancient historical document. (2) First Corinthians 15 shows that the resurrection of Jesus was attested just a few years after it took place, showing that it is not a legend. (3) The story of Abraham in the OT adheres very closely to the customs of the ancient peoples it describes.

There is, however, a circularity even about points (1)–(3), because each depends on something in the Bible. And as I present this evidence as a Christian, I present it according to biblical standards of reasoning and historiography. So in one sense, my broader argument (and it could be still broader) is every bit as circular as the narrowly circular argument with which we began.

But the addition of more evidence and argument nevertheless improves the persuasiveness of the argument. Ultimately one will find the argument persuasive only through the grace of the Holy Spirit. But our responsibility is to present the truth as accurately as possible, as the Bible teaches it. And since the Bible presents the truth persuasively, cogently, and winsomely, we, too, should present the truth as persuasively as we can.

As we expose the inquirer to more data, evidence, and argument, the inquirer will see that our conclusion is part of a whole way of thinking, a worldview that as a whole makes sense.

How should we deal with competing circularities? This problem arises when there is an argument between two parties that are both fully self-conscious about their biases. For example, consider an argument between a Christian who is epistemologically self-conscious and a Muslim who understands that at all times he must presuppose the truth of the Qur'an. It may seem as though such an argument cannot go anywhere. The Christian argues that Jesus is God, appealing to Scripture. The Muslim replies that that cannot be true because it is inconsistent with the Qur'an, which is the highest standard of truth. Then back and forth, yes and no, with no resolution.

This kind of argument is certainly frustrating. How much easier for the Christian to argue with a non-Christian who is *not* so epistemologically self-conscious! But the argument need not degenerate into a shouting match.

Consider this: the Scriptures and the Qur'an are different books. They don't just say, "I am the Word of God." Rather, they present different worldviews, different histories, different ethics, different ways of salvation. In an argument over competing circularities, the Christian should not confine himself to saying that he is right according to the Bible. Rather, he should expound what the Bible says, broadening the circle. He should present the gospel of Jesus Christ. And he should ask the Muslim to present his view of salvation. The argument should be about not just which book is supreme, but how we can be right with God. The Christian should present Christ and him crucified, and trust that this gospel can be as persuasive today as when Paul preached it in Corinth.

The Christian knows that the biblical story is true, and the non-Christian knows that, too, at some level of his thinking (Rom. 1:18–21). The Spirit is able to bless the proclamation of that story today. We must not lose confidence in that fact. Certainly we must not imagine that we can reason on a presupposition acceptable to a non-

Christian, on some kind of neutral ground, for then we would be telling a lie to the inquirer. And God doesn't bless lying even as a means of evangelism.

In this section, we have explored the normative perspective on justification. But it is clear that one cannot do this without taking the other perspectives into account. In presenting a normative (and therefore circular) argument for the truth of Christianity, I have had to broaden the circle to include evidences. But evidences, facts, are elements of the situational perspective. And I have had to consider the matter of persuasion. But persuasion, as I indicated, is subjective, something more obviously associated with the existential perspective. So the normative perspective, important as it is, includes the other two perspectives and therefore cannot be isolated from them.

The situational perspective is part of the normative, because one rule of knowledge is that it must be in accord with the facts. The existential is also part of the normative, because we have a right to certainty only when subjective doubt is substantially removed. Knowing is itself a subjective process, and as I will argue later, all aspects of human subjectivity (will, emotions, imagination, etc.) are involved in knowing.

Situational Justification

So our discussion of the other two perspectives will inevitably repeat points already made. I can therefore be more brief in expounding them. A situational justification for believing p says, "I believe p because p accords with the facts." When we use facts to persuade someone of the truth of a proposition, we call them *evidence*.

The most important thing about facts and evidence is that they are completely under God's control, by his decree, creation, and providence.[13] So all facts reveal God (chapter 24). They cannot exist as facts apart from God.

So understanding the facts of experience must be done in a way that is pleasing to God, governed by his Word. In that sense, situational justification observes the laws of the normative. It includes the normative within it, just as the normative includes the situational.

But given our submission to the biblical laws of thought, there can be no objection to the use of evidences and arguments to prove the truth of Scripture. Indeed, our fund of evidence is much greater than is often supposed. Christian apologists have often referred to being, causality, and purpose as grounds for believing in God. But beyond this, every fact of God's creation witnesses to him. For the very fact that we can speak intelligibly about being, cause, and purpose, and also about physical laws, mathematics, astronomy, geology, and personal relationships, presupposes the biblical worldview.[14]

The only theological limitation on factual argument is that the apologist must not claim neutrality, but must admit (when the issue comes up) that he cannot argue coherently without presupposing the teachings of Scripture.

13. See chapters 9–11.
14. For an argument that scientists "must" believe in God because scientific laws are the very attributes of God, see Vern S. Poythress, *Redeeming Science* (Wheaton, IL: Crossway, 2006), chap. 1.

Nor is there any reason why we cannot use extrabiblical facts to establish biblical truth, such as historical and archaeological information. I have argued (chapter 27) that even to understand the Bible thoroughly, we need to have an understanding of biblical languages, of logic, of ancient history and culture. But even then, we should reason within the limits of a biblical epistemology.[15]

Existential Justification

I have indicated that knowledge is a subjective process. God's knowledge is, of course, not a process at all, for he knows everything immediately, by his exhaustive knowledge of his own nature and plan.[16] But for human beings, coming to know things or people is a process that often takes time, with lots of twists and turns along the way. We follow our inclinations, achieve tentative conviction, are attacked by doubts, consider evidence, receive confirmation, and on and on.[17]

We considered earlier in this chapter the importance of *persuasion*, alongside validity and soundness, as a significant criterion of good argument. And we saw that persuasion is a subjective process. In one sense, persuasion is everything. For it is a perspective that embraces validity and soundness. A valid argument is an argument in which the logic is correct; and of course, we must be persuaded that the logic is correct. Same for soundness. And an argument should not persuade us unless it is valid and sound. So persuasion includes the other two qualities, and they each include persuasiveness.[18]

So knowledge does not exist without the subjective element of persuasion. In the traditional philosophical definition, persuasion represents the term *belief*, for we do not fully believe something unless we are persuaded of it. Some writers want to insist that knowledge is purely objective, that it has nothing to do with subjective feelings or inner qualities. But in knowledge there is an unavoidable subjective side.

I have sometimes described knowledge as a search for cognitive satisfaction, a satisfaction that I call *cognitive rest*.[19] Seeking knowledge, inquiry, is very much like other tasks. We perform various operations to achieve it: sense observations, rational inductions and deductions, consulting authority, research of various kinds. We hope that eventually these tasks will lead to something called knowledge. But how do we know when that happens? How do we know when we can end our inquiry and claim to have the knowledge we sought?

---

15. See *DKG*, 215–318.

16. God's knowledge is subjective, however. As we saw in chapter 15, God knows what he knows by knowing his own nature and eternal plan.

17. The best account of this process I know is Esther Meek's *Longing to Know: The Philosophy of Knowledge for Ordinary People* (Grand Rapids: Brazos Press, 2003). See also her more recent and more comprehensive *Loving to Know: Covenant Epistemology* (Eugene, OR: Cascade Books, 2011).

18. The only barrier to making this triad fully perspectival is the question whether validity includes soundness. We can say that it does, I think, only if we consider validity broadly: not merely as logical rules, but as laws of thought generally. And of course, one of the laws of thought is that you should draw inferences only from true premises. Soundness is often construed as implying logical validity.

19. See, e.g., *DKG*, 152–53.

Let's say that we are trying to decide whether p is true or not. During our inquiry, we may be pressed at times toward believing that p is true. But then we encounter contrary evidence that points the other way. We may vacillate through the twists and turns. One authority will incline us in one direction, another in the opposite direction. Perhaps at one point we are ready to commit ourselves to the truth of p, but then we become uneasy, and for a time we are unable to make up our minds. But it often happens that we are, at some point, able to make such a commitment. At that point, we say, we know.

How should we describe that moment when we say, "Now I know"? It has to be something like a feeling. It is not the discovery of a new piece of evidence, because we need to evaluate that evidence, that is, to decide how we feel about it. It is not the discovery of a logical argument, for we must always assess the persuasiveness of any argument. Rather, we say "I know" on the basis of a feeling—a feeling *about* the arguments, a feeling *about* the evidence.

A person can go back and forth on a question for years: say, the propriety of infant baptism. One day the paedobaptist argument sounds pretty good; the next day the anti-paedobaptist argument does. But maybe after weeks, months, or years of such indecision, something happens to tilt the mind decisively toward one alternative or the other. It might be a new argument, or a new piece of exegetical evidence. Or maybe not. It might also be that an old argument or an old piece of evidence takes on new life, becomes persuasive as it hadn't been before. We are *satisfied* in a way that we hadn't been before. It is like reaching a point in a task at which we can say, "It is finished; now I can rest." So I call this feeling of completion *cognitive rest*.

Of course, our cognitive rest is not always permanent. Sometimes we lose it, as when we encounter a new argument (or old one) that moves us again to vacillate. But to say "I know" is certainly, in part, to report a feeling of cognitive rest.

I am not saying that knowledge is completely subjective and that there are no objective elements in it. For the question remains as to when we *ought* to rest. Sometimes we leave part of the task undone, as when a child forgets to wash behind his ears. Cognitive rest should not be entered lightly, any more than a person should go to bed without completing his responsibilities for the day. Cognitive rest, that is, must be earned. We have a right to cognitive rest only when we have done the tasks that need to be done to resolve our inquiry. Often that will require researching the evidence, analyzing the logical arguments, and so on. That is to say, subjective cognitive rest ought to be based on an objective view of the truth. But to judge truth to be objective requires a subjective evaluation. So at every point in the process of knowing, objective and subjective factors interact.

Knowledge, Regeneration, and Sanctification

Theologically, when we talk about the cognitive rest, we are talking about noetic regeneration and sanctification, the internal testimony of the Holy Spirit (chapter 28; see also chapters 41, 43). The Spirit accompanies his Word to produce conviction (John

3:3ff.; 1 Cor. 2:4–5, 14; 1 Thess. 1:5; 1 John 2:20f., 27). Also, the "mind of Christ," his wisdom, is communicated to believers (Matt. 11:25ff.; Luke 24:45; 1 Cor. 1:24, 30; 2:16; Phil. 2:5; Col. 2:3). Completing the trinity, there are also passages that speak of God the Father as Teacher of his people (Matt. 16:17; 23:8ff.; John 6:45). The cognitive rest, then, in which one commits himself to Christianity comes by the grace of God, nothing less.

Cognitive rest is an element of salvation. Sin has kept us from true knowledge (Rom. 1; 8:7–8; 1 Cor. 2:14; Eph. 1:19–2:6; 4:17–19). The grace of God in Christ is sufficient to rescue us from this ignorance (Ezek. 36:25ff.; John 1:11ff.; 3:1–8; 6:44f., 65; 7:17; 11:40; Acts 16:14; 1 Cor. 8:1–4; 12:3; 2 Cor. 4:3–6; Eph. 1:17f.; 2:1–10; 3:18f.; Col. 3:10; 1 Thess. 1:9f.; 1 Tim. 1:5–11; 1 John 2:3–6, 9–11, 20–27; 4:2f., 8, 13–17; 5:2f., 20).

Regeneration does not, however, immediately convey to the believer a sense of cognitive rest about all matters pertaining to the faith. Our basic presuppositional commitment to Christ begins at regeneration, but other commitments develop more gradually—or at least it takes a while for us to become conscious of them. Thus, there is not only noetic regeneration; there is also noetic sanctification. There is a radical change at the beginning, gradual change after that.

Scripture teaches that this gradual change is inseparable from the overall process of sanctification: that is, assurance on cognitive matters is inseparable from growth in obedience and holiness. It is sometimes said by theologians that "the Christian life is founded upon Christian doctrine"; but it also works the other way: our ability to discern doctrinal (and other) truth depends on the overall maturity of our Christian lives. In that regard, see John 7:17; also a group of passages that make an interesting use of the term "proof," *dokimazein*.

1. In Romans 12:1f., Paul urges us, in view of God's mercies, to offer our bodies as living sacrifices, which entails nonconformity to the world and transformation into holiness. This is the process of ethical renewal, and it is by this process, Paul says, that we will be able to "prove" what the will of God is. This is the opposite from what we usually hear: generally the advice we hear is to learn the will of God, and then we will be able to become more holy. That advice is true enough. But it also works the other way: be transformed, and then your renewed mind will be able to discern God's will.

2. Ephesians 5:8 starkly describes our fallen condition: you once *were* darkness. But now we *are* light! This light is defined as ethical transformation in verse 9. It is in the process of that ethical transformation that we "prove" what pleases the Lord (v. 10).

3. In Philippians 1:9–10, Paul prays that the Philippians' love will abound more and more in knowledge and depth of insight. Again, ethical renewal is the source of deeper knowledge. Then, in verse 10, it is that deeper knowledge that helps us to "prove" what is most excellent (perhaps = what is most fitting or proper to do on a particular occasion), and that in turn leads to more purity and blamelessness. Again, note the circular relation between ethical sanctification and Christian understanding.

4. Hebrews 5:11–14 is a similar passage to these, but without the word *dokimazein*. The author is impatient to begin his teaching on Melchizedek, but he knows his audience is not ready for such deep instruction. They are "slow to learn," ready only for

"elementary" teaching. Their trouble is that they are babes, spiritually immature (v. 13), without "experience" of the word of righteousness. Maturity, in contrast, means that one's "faculties" have been "exercised by constant use to discern good and evil" (v. 14).[20] Notice, again, that theological maturity occurs together with ethical maturity. Ability to understand Melchizedek occurs as we learn to discern good and evil. And this ethical maturity does not occur primarily in the classroom, but in the heat of the Christian warfare. There is "exercise" (*gymnazein*), "use" (*hexis*). It is a training process: the more experience we have in making tough decisions in obedience to God, the better we will be able to do it in the future. The better we are able to make ethical decisions, the more equipped we will be to make theological decisions; the two are of a piece with each other.

So ability to come to cognitive rest concerning Christian teaching comes with sanctification, with growth in holiness. Many doctrinal misunderstandings in the church are doubtless due to this spiritual-ethical immaturity. We need to pay more attention to this fact when we get into theological disputes. Sometimes we throw arguments back and forth over and over again, desperately trying to convince each other. But often there is in one of the disputers—or both!—the kind of spiritual immaturity that prevents clear perception. We all know how it works in practice. Lacking sufficient love for one another, we seek to interpret the other person's views in the worst possible sense. We forget the tremendous importance of love—even as an epistemological concept (see 1 Cor. 8:1–3; 1 Tim. 1:5ff.; 1 John 2:4f.; 3:18f.; 4:7ff.). Lacking a sufficient humility, too, we overestimate the extent of our own knowledge. In such a case, with one or more immature debaters, it may be best not to seek immediate agreement in our controversy. Sometimes we need to back off a bit, for a while. We need to go off and spend some time—months or years, perhaps—in constructive work for the Lord, fighting the Christian warfare, exercising our moral faculties. Then we can come back later to the doctrinal question and address it again from a more mature vantage point. Do you see how theological problems may sometimes, in effect, have practical solutions?

How many seminarians, I often wonder, have the spiritual maturity to warrant the theological decisions they are asked to make in preparation for licensure and ordination? In this context, Paul's words take on fresh importance when he tells Timothy not to ordain a recent convert, "or he may become puffed up with conceit and fall into the condemnation of the devil" (1 Tim. 3:6).

Seeing Things in Biblical Patterns

This cognitive rest, this godly sense of satisfaction—can anything more be said about it? Many questions arise at this point, for these ideas are rather vague and mysterious. In particular, some might be worried about the consistency of these concepts with the sufficiency of Scripture. Is this "satisfaction" a new revelation of the Spirit? Is it an addition to the canon? Is it an additional norm? If not, then what is it?

---

20. These are my renderings of the Greek terms.

I strongly defend the Reformation doctrine of scriptural sufficiency (see chapter 26). But the Reformers saw no difficulty in affirming both the sufficiency of Scripture and the necessity of the Spirit's testimony. They made it clear (for even in their time there were misunderstandings in this area) that the Spirit's testimony was not a new revelation. Rather, the Spirit's work is to illumine and confirm the revelation already given. In Scripture, the Spirit's testimony is to Christ (John 14:26; 15:26; 16:8–10, 13ff.) and to the Word of God (1 Cor. 2:4; 1 Thess. 1:5). The Spirit witnesses that the Word is true—but the Word has already told us that!

Still, as we saw in chapters 27 and 28, Scripture is not reluctant to describe this work as a work of revelation (Matt. 11:25–27; Eph. 1:17). It is revelation in the sense that through the Spirit's ministry we are learning something of which we would otherwise be ignorant; we are learning the Word of God. Or, put differently, we are being "persuaded," "noetically regenerated and sanctified," "brought to cognitive rest." We are being given a "godly sense of satisfaction."

In all of this, the Spirit is helping us to *use*, to *apply* the Word. Obviously, he cannot assure us of the truth of Scripture unless he also teaches us the meaning of it; and the meaning, as we have seen, includes the applications. We can see this in 2 Samuel 11–12 where David sins against God by committing adultery with Bathsheba and sending her husband Uriah to his death. Here, David, the "man after God's own heart," seems trapped in a peculiar spiritual blindness. What has happened here? In one sense, he knows Scripture perfectly well; he meditates on God's law day and night. And he is not ignorant about the facts of the case. Yet he is not convicted of sin. But Nathan the prophet comes to him and speaks God's word. He does not immediately rebuke David directly. He tells a parable—a story that makes David angry at someone else. Then Nathan tells David, "You are the man." At that point, David repents of his sin.

What has David learned at this point? He already knew God's law, and he already knew the facts, in a sense. What he learned was an application—what the law said about *him*. Previously, he may have rationalized; we can imagine it: "Kings of the earth have a right to take whatever women they want, and the commander-in-chief has the right to decide who fights on the front line. Therefore, my relation with Bathsheba was not *really* adultery, and my order to Uriah was not *really* murder." We all know how that works; we've done it ourselves. But what the Spirit did, through Nathan, was to take that rationalization away.

Thus, David came to call his actions by their right names: sin, adultery, murder. He came to read his own life in terms of the biblical concepts. He came to see his "relationship" as *adultery* and his "executive order" as *murder*. He learned to *see as*.

Seeing as is an interesting concept, which a number of recent thinkers, notably Ludwig Wittgenstein, have explored. *Seeing as* is not the same as *seeing*. One person, looking at a certain picture, will see it as a duck, another as a rabbit. In one sense, they see the same lines on the paper. But they see different patterns, shapes, or *gestalts*. So it is with us when we seek to see our lives in the light of Scripture. One person will look at a sexual relationship as a "recreational dalliance"; another will see it as adultery.

Sometimes the matter becomes more complicated, when there seems to be more than one possible biblical interpretation of an event. Say that I feel anger. Is this the righteous anger that Jesus displayed with the money-changers in the temple, or is it the murderous anger that he forbids under all circumstances? Which biblical category does it fit under? See fig. 31.4.

Fig. 31.4. Seeing As: Duck-Rabbit

These questions are not obviously questions about facts or norms. One usually doesn't answer them simply by giving information or a command. Rather, what is needed is exhortation that helps us to see things in a different way. Therefore, artistry, nuance, plays a particular role here. Nathan did not simply repeat the law; he told a story. That story had the effect of shaking David out of his rationalization, helping him to see things in different patterns, to call things by their right names. We need to be more sensitive as to when such methods are appropriate in theology.

Much of the Spirit's work in our lives is of this nature—assuring us that Scripture applies to our lives in particular ways. The Spirit does not add to the canon, but his work is really a work of teaching, of revelation. Without that revelation, we could make no use of Scripture at all; it would be a dead letter to us.

Thus, in one sense the Spirit adds nothing; in another sense he adds everything. When we are asked to justify our Christian beliefs, we point not to the Spirit, but to the Word, for it is the Word that *states* the justification. But apart from the Spirit, we would have no knowledge of that justification. And it often becomes important, in justifying beliefs, to give evidence of our own spiritual maturity, so as to indicate our spiritual qualifications for making the statements we make.

A Corporate Existential Perspective

Most of the discussion above has been focused on the individual's knowledge of God through his private inwardness. I make no apology for that; God does care for each individual and relates to each of us individually. In some ways, all of us are different—with different heredity, life histories, natural and spiritual gifts, natural and spiritual weaknesses. God counts every hair, watches each sparrow fall; all the diversities of the creation are in his hand. He meets each individual's special needs with his saving grace. Scripture tells with love the stories of how God's love meets individuals. And it tells us that there is joy in heaven over one sinner who repents.

Yet it may be argued that the *emphasis* of Scripture is different. That emphasis is not on the salvation of individuals, but on the salvation of a *people*. Throughout history, God has been concerned with families, nations, indeed a world. His goal is not merely the perfection of individuals, but the perfection of the church, the body of Christ.

Ephesians is one of the notable portions of Scripture in this regard. It also has much to say concerning the knowledge of God. We have cited Ephesians 1:17ff.; 3:14–19; 5:8–21 in regard to the existential perspective. These texts show that knowledge of God is inseparable from the Spirit's revelatory and sanctifying witness. But the "knowledge" of Ephesians seems not to be primarily the knowledge that each of us has as an individual; rather, it is the knowledge that the church shares as a body. It is ascribed to "you" (plural). It is a knowledge "together with all the saints" (3:18 NIV). The end result of that knowledge is attaining

> to the unity of the faith and of the knowledge of the Son of God, to mature manhood, to the measure of the stature of the fullness of Christ . . . . We are to grow up in every way into him who is the head, into Christ, from whom the whole body, joined and held together by every joint with which it is equipped, when each part is working properly, makes the body grow so that it builds itself up in love. (Eph. 4:13, 15–16)

The "maturity" here is not the maturity of each individual, though that is implied, but the maturity of the corporate body as it grows up into Christ, its Head. It is best, then, to see the knowledge, also, as something shared by the whole body, though of course the knowledge of individuals is not irrelevant to that.

Thus, it appears that there is a kind of knowledge possessed by the church, as well as a knowledge possessed by individuals. Like the individual's knowledge, it may be seen from three perspectives: it is based on scriptural norms, on the realities of creation and redemption, and also on the work of Christ and the Spirit in corporately sanctifying the body (Eph. 4:4f.; 5:22–33).

The *sociology of knowledge* has much to say about the effect of group loyalties on belief-commitments. Much has been written in this area from Marxist or Freudian viewpoints and by such philosophers of science as Kuhn, Hanson, Polanyi. Our presuppositions and our views of the objects in the world are profoundly affected by our various interpersonal relationships—family, nationality, religion, political party or ideology, economic status, educational background, occupation, professional association, and so forth. Groups tend to develop "group minds," which, without determining the thinking of individuals within the groups, do influence it deeply.

We tend to be suspicious of "groupthink," and in most cases rightly so. There are important intellectual benefits in cultivating independence of thought. But it is impossible to escape entirely from our associations with others, and such total independence is not really desirable. The ideal thing (a prefall situation) would be for the whole human race to work as a team, seeking out all the mysteries of the creation together, trusting one another, collaborating peacefully on a great edifice of learning, each contributing his bit to a body of knowledge far larger than any individual could comprehend.

Something like that is what God intends for his church. He wants us to grow together toward a knowledge of him that is broader than any of us, which, marvelously, somehow matches that of its Head, Jesus Christ. Cf. again Eph. 4:15f.

And of course, the growth of corporate knowledge will enrich each individual. When the church reaches maturity, its individuals will "no longer be children" (4:14). Thus, it is wise for us to listen to the church when it speaks through its elder-teachers and its judicial discipline (Matt. 18). The church (and obviously the churches) is not infallible, but each church does have the authority to govern the teaching within its jurisdiction. Individuals in the churches need to cultivate a spirit of submission and humility, a recognition that in most cases the whole body of believers (especially the whole body throughout church history) knows more than any member does. If conscience forces me to go against the body, then I must take my stand—but even then, I should not be hasty. Even the conscience is not infallible; it must be trained to discern properly, in accordance with Scripture.

And of course, the church does more for us than merely to overrule our errors! Even if we never made errors, it would still be through the processes of discussing issues, loving one another (Eph. 4:16), bearing one another's burdens, fighting the Christian warfare together, that we come to fullness of knowledge. God has given each of us as a gift to the others (4:4–13).

Should this matter be discussed under the existential perspective, or under the situational? One could argue that the body of believers functions as one aspect of our situation that our knowledge must take account of. Well, since all the perspectives are interdependent, it doesn't much matter. The church also has a normative function—a derived authority from God, as we've seen. But Scripture seems to present corporate knowledge primarily as a kind of super-individual subjectivity that grows and develops as the individual does, to which the individual is related not primarily as subject to object, but as member to body. Thus, my subjectivity is part of the church's, and its subjectivity is the fullness of mine. A pain felt by the finger is fully experienced and understood only by the whole body.

Key Terms

Knowledge (philosophical definition)
Justification (in epistemology)
Formal logic
Informal logic
Laws of thought
Law of identity
Law of the excluded middle
Law of noncontradiction

Normative justification
Situational justification
Existential justification
Presupposition
Validity
Soundness
Persuasiveness
Circularity
Narrow circularity
Broad circularity
Person-variable
Cognitive rest
Dokimazein
Seeing as
Corporate existential perspective

Study Questions

1. Frame says that the traditional definition of knowledge is triperspectival. Show how the three perspectives illumine that definition. Evaluate.

2. Frame says that rational arguments pervade Scripture and preaching. Explain; evaluate.

3. "It is possible to 'have' a reason without being able to 'give' a reason." Explain; evaluate.

4. Frame says that the three perspectives of Christian epistemologies are parallel to non-Christian rationalism, empiricism, and subjectivism. Show how these are parallel and also how they are not parallel.

5. "It is circular to appeal to the Bible to defend the Bible as our presupposition." Reply to this objection.

6. How can a circular argument for Scripture's authority be persuasive? Or can it be?

7. Describe a debate between two people advocating competing circular arguments. How can either party ever be persuaded?

8. Frame says that "now I know" is, among other things, the expression of a feeling. Describe that feeling. Does this reference to feeling invalidate the objectivity of knowledge?

9. Have you had the experience of feeling cognitive rest after searching for an answer? Tell the story of how that happened.

10. What point is Frame seeking to make by invoking the *dokimazein* passages? Evaluate.

11. What point is Frame seeking to make by invoking the story of David and Nathan? Evaluate. Explain how the duck-rabbit illustration fits in.

12. Does Scripture teach the existence of a corporate existential perspective? Discuss.

Memory Verses

Rom. 12:1–2: I appeal to you therefore, brothers, by the mercies of God, to present your bodies as a living sacrifice, holy and acceptable to God, which is your spiritual worship. Do not be conformed to this world, but be transformed by the renewal of your mind, that by testing you may discern what is the will of God, what is good and acceptable and perfect.

Eph. 4:13–15: Until we all attain to the unity of the faith and of the knowledge of the Son of God, to mature manhood, to the measure of the stature of the fullness of Christ, so that we may no longer be children, tossed to and fro by the waves and carried about by every wind of doctrine, by human cunning, by craftiness in deceitful schemes. Rather, speaking the truth in love, we are to grow up in every way into him who is the head, into Christ.

Eph. 5:8–10: For at one time you were darkness, but now you are light in the Lord. Walk as children of light (for the fruit of light is found in all that is good and right and true), and try to discern what is pleasing to the Lord.

Phil. 1:9–10: And it is my prayer that your love may abound more and more, with knowledge and all discernment, so that you may approve what is excellent, and so be pure and blameless for the day of Christ.

Heb. 5:11–14: About this we have much to say, and it is hard to explain, since you have become dull of hearing. For though by this time you ought to be teachers, you need someone to teach you again the basic principles of the oracles of God. You need milk, not solid food, for everyone who lives on milk is unskilled in the word of righteousness, since he is a child. But solid food is for the mature, for those who have their powers of discernment trained by constant practice to distinguish good from evil.

Resources for Further Study

Frame, John M. *DKG*, 123–64.

Meek, Esther. *Longing to Know: The Philosophy of Knowledge for Ordinary People.* Grand Rapids: Brazos, 2003.

Plantinga, Alvin. *Warrant: The Current Debate.* New York: Oxford University Press, 1993.

———. *Warrant and Proper Function.* New York: Oxford University Press, 1993.

———. *Warranted Christian Belief.* New York: Oxford University Press, 2000.

Poythress, Vern S. *Redeeming Science.* Wheaton, IL: Crossway, 2006.

CHAPTER 32

RESOURCES FOR KNOWING

THIS CHAPTER SOMEWHAT AMPLIFIES the previous chapter's description of the existential perspective. We have seen that knowing is, existentially speaking, a journey with many twists and turns, as we seek cognitive rest. But of course, God has not left us alone in this journey. He has provided us with many resources, chiefly his Word, the facts of the creation, and the guidance of the Spirit.[1] But he has also provided us with resources in ourselves. We are his image, and so he has made us to know in a way analogous to his own knowledge. He has given us minds, wills, imaginations, and so on. And with redemption, he has remade these gifts in the image of Jesus.

The Personalism of the Knowledge of God[2]

The believer's knowledge is the expression and application of his deepest convictions, his presuppositions. The presuppositions that govern our thinking arise from many sources—reason, sensation, and emotion, to name a few. The most ultimate presuppositions are religious in nature. All our experience testifies to the truth of these presuppositions.

These presuppositions influence our reading of Scripture, by which, in turn, we seek to validate our presuppositions. That is called the *hermeneutical circle*. Circularity of that sort, as we saw earlier, is inevitable. Under the leading of the Spirit, however, it is not a vicious circle. Contact with God's Word purifies our presuppositions. Then, in turn, when we use our purified presuppositions to interpret Scripture, we come to a clearer understanding of Scripture. Without the Spirit's work, however, the circle can be regressive: bad presuppositions distorting the meaning of Scripture, that distorted

---

1. The references to the Word and creation show how the existential perspective includes the other two. Our journey is not a journey through chaos, but through a world that God has already made, that he governs, and that he has eternally interpreted.

2. In this chapter, I will often be referring to *theology* as a synonym for *knowledge of God*, for these reasons: (1) This equation has been made in various Reformed writings. (2) The original discussion that I reiterate here (*DKG*, 319–46) was specifically about theological method, and I want it to continue to have a specific focus on that subject. But the considerations here are certainly not limited to theology as an academic discipline.

meaning leading to even worse presuppositions, and so forth. Hence, we ought not to be surprised when we see apparently sincere and intellectually sophisticated "seekers after truth"—often among the cults (and often among the ranks of professional theological scholars!)—whose conclusions seem *incredibly* far from the truth. This is one way in which obedience and knowledge are closely linked (cf. chapter 28).

The knowledge of God is intensely personal in character. Since God cannot generally be seen, heard, or touched, this knowledge is not reached by the experimental methods of natural science. Ian Ramsey uses the illustration of a courtroom scene in which everything proceeds quite impersonally, persons being referred to by titles ("the Crown," "the accused," "the prosecution," "your honor"). To his amazement, the magistrate looks up and sees as "the accused" his long-lost wife. Suddenly the whole situation takes on a different tone. The new tone is not due to anything that can be seen or heard, but rather to a whole range of memories, past histories, affections, disappointments.[3] Now, this illustration would be misleading if it were taken (as perhaps it is by Ramsey) to illustrate the *whole* nature of Christian truth. Christianity is not just an aura of personal relationships that surrounds purely natural events. The resurrection, for example, was not merely a recollection by the disciples of Jesus' relationship with them before his death. It was a miracle in space and time; the risen Jesus could be seen and heard and touched. But the illustration does indicate something that is present in all theology, indeed in all our knowledge of God, even as we speak of the resurrection and other great historical events. For all Christian discourse confesses a personal relation to God—a covenant relation. The Jesus who was raised from the dead is "my Lord and my God" (John 20:28). He is the One with whom we, too, are raised (Col. 2:12f.; 3:1).

It is for this reason that we tend to feel uncomfortable with certain attempts at theological talk. It doesn't seem quite right, for example, to speak of the resurrection of Jesus' body as the "resuscitation of a corpse." Some liberal theologians point this out in defense of the view that Jesus was raised only "spiritually" while his corpse remained dead. "Of course," they say, "the resurrection of Jesus has nothing to do with the resuscitation of a corpse!" But the Christian's hesitation about the phrase "resuscitation of a corpse" is not because of any doubt in his heart about the literal truth of the resurrection. The reason, I think, is rather that the phrase "resuscitation of a corpse" is not covenant language. It is not the language of personal relationship, the language of love. It does not connote all the rich context of the biblical teaching.

Propositional language is important to theology. Theology conveys information about God. The arguments of Emil Brunner and others that propositional knowledge weakens the personal character of relationships are absurd. Gaining information about someone often deepens our relationship with him. Good language about God, however, is never *merely* propositional. It is simultaneously an expression of love and praise. Preachers as well as theologians need to keep this in mind, to avoid language

3. Ian Ramsey, *Religious Language* (New York: Macmillan, 1957), 20.

that encourages their people to speak of God in a kind of clinical jargon. It is not that such jargon is always wrong or sinful. But lack of balance here can lead people (and preachers) into bad habits of thought and life. Personalism is a means of edification. When we neglect it, we are not communicating the whole counsel of God.

I have known professors of theology who are so zealous to defend the scientific character of theology, its academic respectability, that they actually forbid the use of personal references in theological writing. That is, they forbid the author to refer to himself, or to someone else (except, of course, to the *ideas* of another); they conceive theology to be wholly a matter of ideas rather than of personalities. Now, of course there are dangers that such professors are rightly seeking to avoid. There is the danger, for example, of using ad hominem arguments. There is also the danger of writing out of personal vindictiveness rather than concentrating on the theological issues. But *issues* are not sharply separable from *personalities*. People's ideas are closely related to their reputations and to their character (as God's word is one with God himself). Personal references can scarcely be avoided in theology. Even the most academic theology is an expression of a person's heart-relation to God. But if a theology did avoid them, it would be a theology without a soul.

Personalism is also evident in the nature of theology and apologetics as *persuasion*, as we saw in the previous chapter. The purpose of these disciplines is not merely to construct valid and sound arguments, but to persuade people, to edify. And the goal is not merely to bring them to intellectual assent, but to help them to embrace the truth from the heart in love and joy, to motivate them to live out its implications in all areas of life. Thus, theology must be "personalistic" not only in expressing the personhood of the theologian, but also in addressing the full personhood of its hearer.

The Heart

The knowledge of God is a heart-knowledge (see Ex. 35:5; 1 Sam. 2:1; 2 Sam. 7:3; Pss. 4:4; 7:10; 15:2; Isa. 6:10; Matt. 5:8; 12:34; 22:37; Eph. 1:18; etc.). The heart is the "center" of the personality, the person himself in his most basic character. Scripture represents it as the source of thought, of volition, of attitude, of speech. It is also the seat of moral knowledge. First Samuel 24:5 says that David's conviction of sin was that his "heart" slew him, here using the term as we use the word *conscience*.

The fact that the heart is depraved, then, means that apart from grace we are in radical ignorance of the things of God (chapter 29). Only the grace of God, which restores us from the heart outward, can restore to us that knowledge of God that belongs to God's covenant servants—that knowledge that is correlative to obedience.

One implication of this fact is that the believer's knowledge of God is inseparable from godly character (cf. chapter 28). The same Spirit that gives the first in regeneration also gives the second. And the qualifications for the ministry of teaching (theology) in Scripture are predominantly moral qualifications (1 Tim. 3:1ff.; 1 Peter 5:1ff.). Thus, the quality of theological work is not only dependent on propositional knowledge or on skills in logic, history, linguistics, and so forth (which, of course, believers and unbelievers share to a large extent); it is also dependent on the theologian's character. We saw in chapter 29 how knowledge and obedience are linked in Scripture.

A second implication is that the knowledge of God is gained not just through one *faculty* or another, such as the intellect or the emotions. It is a knowledge of the heart, the whole person. The theologian knows by means of everything he is and all the abilities and capacities that have been given to him by God. Intellect, emotions, will, imagination, sensation, natural and spiritual gifts of skills—all contribute toward the knowledge of God. All knowledge of God enlists *all* our faculties, because it engages everything that we are.

To say that theological knowledge is a "whole-person" knowledge raises questions about the relations of unity to diversity in the human personality. Traditionally, theologians and philosophers have distinguished various faculties within the human mind: reason, will, emotion, imagination, perception, intuition, and others. These distinctions have given rise to questions about which faculty is "primary." Some have argued the *primacy of the intellect*, reasoning that emotion, imagination, and the like will lead us astray if they are not disciplined, corrected, evaluated by intellectual processes. Others have said that the will is primary, for even intellectual belief is something that is *chosen*. Others have postulated the primacy of feeling, since everything we believe or choose to do, we choose because in some sense we *feel* like choosing it. And so on, with the other faculties.

Well, the alert reader can doubtless predict what is coming now: I think there is truth in all these contentions—contentions that can be reconciled with one another to an extent if we see these various faculties in perspectival unity with one another. These faculties are a diversity of "angles" from which we can look at the various acts and experiences of the human mind. None of them ever exists or acts apart from the others, each is dependent on the others, and each includes the others. Let us look at them one by one, noting some of these close relationships among them.[4]

Reason[5]

The term *reason* has a long history in Western philosophy and has been used in a variety of ways. It can refer to logic, to those particular laws of logic called *laws of thought* or more particularly the *law of noncontradiction*. Some philosophers have used *reason* to denote a particular *method* of thinking (defined, of course, by their philosophical system) or even to refer to their philosophy in general. (One is tempted to think that for Hegel, *reason* is synonymous with Hegelianism.)

In this context (and most others), I think it is least misleading to define reason in two ways: first as an ability or capacity—the human capacity for forming judgments and inferences. So understood, reasoning is something that we do all the time, not only

---

4. In *DCL*, 361–82, I discuss this list of faculties again, from an ethical viewpoint, as "organs of ethical knowledge."

5. For more discussion of reason, particularly logic, see *DKG*, 242–301. In that discussion, I argue some points that I take for granted here.

when we are pursuing academic or theoretical disciplines. That is how *reason* is used in a *descriptive* sense. I will also use the term in a *normative* sense: that is, not to denote all judgments and inferences, but to denote *correct* judgments and inferences. In the first descriptive sense, an incorrect inference would be rational, for it is an exercise of reason as a human capacity. In the second sense, it would not be rational, for it would not measure up to the criteria of sound reasoning.

Having defined reason in these ways, we can see that talk of God, theology, ought to be rational. Theology *is* the forming of judgments and inferences based on God's Word (applications being both judgments and inferences), and therefore it is a form of reasoning (descriptive) in the nature of the case. Further, Scripture warrants the making of judgments and inferences (as in Rom. 12:1–2; Col. 3:1). Theology that makes sound judgments and draws sound conclusions from Scripture would be rational in the normative sense.

To say that theology ought to be rational, really, is no different from saying that it ought to be scriptural or that it ought to be true. As we saw in our discussion of logic, logic done properly adds nothing to its premises. Rather, it is a tool that helps us to see what is implicit in these premises, that is, what they really say. That, indeed, is what logic is intended to do. When a deductive process changes the meaning of a set of premises, it is thereby defective. A system of logic that leads to such change is to that extent an inadequate system. The goal of logic is simply to set forth the premises as they really are. Similarly, the goal of theological reasoning is simply to set forth Scripture as it really is (including, of course, its applications that constitute its meaning). So rationality in theology is nothing more or less than scripturality. It is not a separate set of norms to which theology must conform in addition to its conformity to Scripture.[6] Thus, theologians ought not to feel threatened by the demand for rationality. Of course, if rationality is defined not as scripturality, but as conformity to some theories of modern science, history, philosophy, and the like, then conflict is inevitable.

Therefore, when someone tells me that reason must be the judge of theological ideas, I can agree with him in a sense. My rational capacity is the capacity to make judgments; thus, to say that theological judgments must be rational (in the descriptive sense) is a tautology. In the normative sense, too, theology ought to be judged by reason, for that only means that inferences and judgments based on Scripture ought to be *sound* inferences and judgments, that is, really in conformity with Scripture. To speak of reason as a "judge," however, is rather strange. That may suggest to some (though not necessarily and not to all) that reason operates with some criteria independent of Scripture. Or such language may confuse my norm (Scripture) with one of my psychological capacities.

Must theology, then, conform to reason? Yes. But that means only that theology must conform with rigorous logic to its proper criterion, the inspired Scriptures.

---

6. And even if it were, for the Christian those norms would be subordinate to the ultimate norm, Scripture itself. Thus, any demonstration of the rationality of Scripture would still be circular.

Does reason have a primacy over our other faculties? Well, all our emotional inclinations, imaginative ideas, intuitions, experiences, and so on must conform to reason or they do not tell us the truth. But what does "conformity to reason" mean in this context? As we have seen, it means nothing more than "conformity to Scripture" or "conformity with truth." Thus, to say that these must conform to reason in order to tell the truth is really a tautology. It is like saying that you must be unmarried in order to be a bachelor. But we would not want to say that "being a bachelor" is a criterion or test of being unmarried. (The opposite would be equally plausible and equally implausible.) Thus, there is circularity here.

So the *primacy of reason* in the sense described above says very little. It does not even rule out a similar primacy for other faculties, even the emotions. Say that someone claims that he has come to know something through his emotions. If his claim is correct, then his emotions have led him into "conformity with truth." On the above definition, this is the same as "conformity to reason." Emotion, in other words, is a form of reason. If his claim is not correct, one may still call his emotions a form of reason, for they are one of the capacities by which he makes judgments and inferences, even though they are not in this case reliable. In this case, we may say that his emotions are reason in a descriptive sense, but not in a normative sense.

Indeed, it is possible that *reason* is only a name that we give to the inference- and judgment-making capacities of the other faculties. Or, perhaps, that it is a perspective on those other faculties, looking at them from the "angle" of their role in discovering truth. (We will see that when we look at them from that angle, we must look at their other roles as well; thus, reason would be a perspective on *everything* done by these faculties.)

In what follows, I will try to clarify the discussion above by showing these relationships from the other side, that is, from the side of the emotions, imagination, and the like. I will try to show the role of these faculties in forming judgments and also mention their other roles and the inseparability of the various roles from one another. If I am right in my perspectival model, these subsequent discussions will also in effect be discussions of reason, enlarging upon what I have said in this section.

Perception, Experience

Perception is associated with the sense organs, but it is not merely a synonym for *sensation*. *Sensation* refers to the operations of the sense organs, whether or not these operations yield knowledge. Perception, on the other hand, is a form of knowledge, the knowledge gained through the process of sensation. We say "I perceive X" when we see, hear, smell, taste, or feel X, that is, when the operations of the sense organs yield knowledge of X.

Experience is a broader category than *perception*. It is possible to have an experience of something (say, a prophet's experience of the divine word) without perceiving it through the sense organs; at least that possibility is arguable. With George Mavrodes, however, we may understand experience in a way parallel to our account of perception.[7] Mavrodes takes the X in "I experienced X" to refer not merely to a psychological state, but to an object existing independently of the experiencer. Thus, to say "I experienced X" is to claim that through my experience I have gained some knowledge of X.

Mavrodes also argues that experiencing X involves making some judgment about X.[8] The same is true of perceptual language (perceiving X, seeing X, hearing X, etc.). He adds:

> But . . . I do not know how to make more precise just how appropriate the judgment must be. It is fairly clear that a man may really see a wolf in the woods, though he takes it to be a dog. It seems, therefore, that the judgment need not be entirely correct. On the other hand, it also seems clear that a man may be in the presence of a wolf, in the sense that light reflected from the wolf stimulates his eye, etc., and yet make no judgment whatever, perhaps because he is preoccupied. In that case we would probably say that he failed to see the animal at all.[9]

Perceiving and experiencing, then, are not activities sharply different from reasoning. They are processes by which we reach judgments, even if those judgments are not always perfectly correct. Are they, like reason, means of *inference*? Of course, experiencing or perceiving something does not usually, if ever, involve going through a syllogism in the head. But if *reasoning* or *informal logic* is something that goes on in all of life, even when no conscious syllogizing takes place, then nothing prevents us from seeing experience or perception as a kind of inference. Data are presented to the senses. From that data, we infer the presence of objects or the existence of states of affairs.

Of course, as I have often said in this book, we have no access to uninterpreted data, the "brute facts." "I see the tree" presupposes sense experience, but also a lifetime of conceptual learning by which we learn to place certain kinds of sensations in this particular category. "My father was here last night" might have been verified in part by sense experience, yet one cannot tell by sensation alone that a certain man is one's father. That judgment presupposes some historical knowledge beyond any possible verification by the direct experience of the individual. What we see is greatly influenced by what we expect to see, and that expectation is influenced by a wide variety of factors.[10]

Reasoning, then, the capacity for making judgments and inferences, is present in all *experience* and *perception* as we have defined them. And since a logical syllogism must have premises, and premises are not usually, if ever, supplied by logic alone (chapter 31), its validity relies on knowledge gained from other sources, such as perception. In any

---

7. George Mavrodes, *Belief in God* (New York, Random House, 1970), 50ff.

8. Ibid., 52.

9. Ibid.

10. Compare the anomalous playing-card experiments described by Thomas Kuhn in *The Structure of Scientific Revolutions* (Chicago: University of Chicago Press, 1970).

case, the use of logic is inconceivable without any experience at all, for we must at least experience the existence of logical principles if we are to perform any logical operations.

Thus, reasoning involves experience and experience involves reasoning. Epistemological attempts to build up the fabric of human knowledge from "pure experience" (corresponding to "brute facts"), untainted by any use of reason (empiricism), or from reason alone apart from experience (rationalism) cannot succeed. Attempts to account for knowledge in either of these ways are generally attempts to find some "bedrock" of truth, an "ultimate starting point" (either experience or reason) apart from God's Word. But God will not allow this. His creation is perspectival; all creatures are equally ultimate. There is no bedrock except the divine Word.

Thus, when Scripture speaks about "hearing," "seeing," and "touching" the Word of life (1 John 1:1), it is not speaking of mere sensation, the mere workings of the sense organs apart from any rational thought. Such a concept of *sensation*, a philosophical abstraction, is not found in Scripture. To see, hear, or touch the risen Christ involves making a judgment about him, an inference; it involves reasoning.

On the other hand, the knowledge of God, according to Scripture, does not come from mere reasoning apart from sensation, either. The verse cited above and many others make this fact evident.[11] Perception, rightly understood, is a legitimate means of knowledge. God has given us our sense organs (Ex. 4:11; Ps. 94:9; Prov. 20:12), and he assures us in his Word that although perception is fallible (so, of course, is reason), it is a means of knowledge (Matt. 5:16; 6:26ff.; 9:36; 15:10; Luke 1:2; 24:36–43; John 20:27; Rom. 1:20; 10:14–17; 2 Peter 1:16–18; 1 John 4:14).

Living between the apostolic age and the parousia, we are no longer in a position to see the risen Christ with the physical eye. But perception still plays a major role in theology. We perceive the biblical text through the senses, similarly other texts that serve as tools of theology. And by the senses we perceive the ancient manuscripts and artifacts of ancient culture that help us to reconstruct the meaning of the text. And of course, experience also reveals the present situation to which our theology will be applying the text.

And there is also that experience by which we grow in Christian maturity—the experience of living the Christian life, meeting challenges, succeeding, failing, praying, finding answers to prayer, persevering when answers aren't given, struggling against sin, enduring hardship for Christ's sake. In many situations we live out those experiences described in Scripture; we experience what the Lord Jesus and his great saints experienced. Experience in this sense is important in showing us the meaning of Scripture. Less experienced saints can always look things up in commentaries, but a special kind of insight comes to those who have had long firsthand experience of the Christian warfare. (A young soldier may learn the rules, history, and techniques of warfare in the military academy, but there is much that he can learn only on the actual

---

11. On this point, see the discussion by Robert Reymond in *The Justification of Knowledge* (Nutley, NJ: Presbyterian and Reformed, 1976).

field of battle.) There is much, for example, in the Psalms that one cannot understand very well until he has undergone some of the same experiences as the psalmists and has understood the analogies between his experience and theirs.[12]

Christian teachers with this kind of experience have greater credibility, too, than those who have merely theorized about the gospel. A professor of mine once complained about a Sunday school program at his church, at which his five-year-old son sang with other children a happy chorus about being "more than conquerors" in Christ. The professor thought this was somewhat silly: the kids hadn't conquered anything much! Well, I disagreed somewhat. I thought, and still do, that if the children were "in Christ," they had through Christ already conquered everything, in one sense. But my professor was not entirely wrong. He rightly sensed that, sung by the children, those words lacked the kind of credibility that they would have on the lips of, say, the apostle Paul himself. Paul endured imprisonment, stoning, abandonment, treachery, loneliness, the "thorn in the flesh" for the sake of Christ. When a man like that is still able to say, "We are more than conquerors," his words carry a special kind of force. For him, the victory of Christ has been worked out in his life in a great many concrete ways. And that kind of life deserves and evokes a profound respect, giving his words a greater impact.

Emotion

Scripture doesn't discuss the emotions in any systematic way any more than it discusses the intellect. Yet Scripture has much to say about our emotions: our joys, sorrows, anxieties, fears, gladness. (Love, too, has a large emotional component, though it is best not to define it as an emotion.) Satan's temptation in the garden appealed to Eve's emotions (Gen. 3:6) (but also, importantly, to her intellectual pretensions, her desire to determine the truth autonomously: 3:1, 4–5). Yet disobedience to God led not to happy feelings, but to shame (3:7). Fallen man has a distinctively fallen complex of emotions: hatred of God, his Word, his creation, his people; love of the world, the flesh, the devil. But redemption brings principal restoration: love of God, hatred of evil.

Redemption doesn't make us more emotional (as some charismatics might suppose) or less so (as many Reformed would prefer), any more than it makes us more or less intellectual. What redemption does to the intellect is to consecrate that intellect to God, whether the IQ is high or low. Similarly, the important thing is not whether you are highly emotional or not; the important thing is that whatever emotional capacities you have should be placed in God's hands to be used according to his purposes.

Thus, intellect and emotion are simply two aspects of human nature that together are fallen and together are regenerated and sanctified. Nothing in Scripture suggests that either is superior to the other. Neither is more fallen than the other; neither is necessarily more sanctified than the other.

12. I remember this point from a lecture by pastor Albert N. Martin of Essex Falls, New Jersey.

Greek philosophy traditionally presented a different picture: the human problem is a sort of derangement of the faculties. Whereas the reason ought to be in control, unfortunately the emotions often rule. Salvation comes (through philosophy, of course!) when we learn to subordinate emotions to reason. That idea is, of course, very plausible. We all know of people who get "carried away" by their feelings and do very stupid things. Such people are often told, rightly, by Christian counselors not to "follow their feelings."

But the fall is not a derangement of faculties within man. It is rebellion of the whole person—intellect as much as emotions, perception, will. My problem is not something within me; it is me. I must take the responsibility, unless Jesus Christ takes that responsibility in my place.

Emotions and Decisions

It is true, of course, that people sometimes "follow their feelings" rather than thinking responsibly. But it is also the case that people sometimes follow rationalistic schemes that run contrary to what they know in their guts (feelings) to be true. God gives us multiple faculties to serve as checks and balances on one another. Sometimes reason saves us from emotional craziness, but emotions can also check the extravagant pretenses of reason.

Imagine someone of Reformed background attending a charismatic meeting. He has been told that there is nothing good in the charismatic movement, and he has thought it all through intellectually. He thinks he has some pretty good arguments. Yet while at the meeting, he finds himself clapping, shouting "Amen," rejoicing in the fellowship. Afterward comes time to give account! What should he do? Should he repent of having allowed his emotions to overrule his carefully wrought theory?

Well, he ought to think some more, obviously! Something is wrong somewhere, but it is not obvious *what* is wrong. Possibly his emotions led him into a false path. Or possibly his emotions were leading him, properly, to reconsider the overly harsh judgments of his theoretical analysis. He must reason, under the authority of Scripture. But that reason will have to take his newfound feelings into account. And he will not achieve complete cognitive rest until his intellect and emotions are somehow reconciled.

Another illustration: Writing book reviews is one of the more "intellectual" tasks that I perform. But it is interesting to see the role that emotions play even in that activity. I read, say, the first chapter of the book and find that I have a certain feeling about the book. I like it, or I don't like it, or I have some reaction in between these. I then try to think it through. Why do I have this feeling? My rational reflection might lead to a change in feeling, or it might enable me to defend and articulate the feeling. Still, the feeling plays a crucial role. I cannot imagine doing academic work at all without having some feelings of this sort. If I had no feelings about the book I was reviewing, I would simply set it aside. The feeling guides my reflection; my reflection refines my feelings. Those refined feelings provoke additional reflection, and so on. The goal is a satisfying analysis, that is, an analysis I feel good about, one with which I have cognitive rest, a peaceful relation between intellect and emotion. That relation seems to me to be involved in all knowledge.

Scripture itself sometimes places emotion in the role often given to intellect or will: "Delight yourself in the Lord, and he will give you the desires of your heart" (Ps. 37:4); "Godly grief produces a repentance that leads to salvation without regret" (2 Cor. 7:10). It is not always wrong to "follow your feelings."

Emotions and Knowledge

The discussion above suggests that emotions contribute to knowledge. When I experience joy, that joy is itself a datum that must be accounted for within the fabric of my knowledge. The joy does not just happen. It has a cause. It is a response of my mind and body to something or other. It might not be a proper response (any more than my reasoning and sensations always lead me to the truth). But it is a means by which truth reaches me. It is a means of knowledge.

We saw in chapter 31 the importance of cognitive rest in human knowledge. That cognitive rest is something mysterious, hard to describe. But it would not be wrong, I think, to describe it as a feeling: not a feeling like that of hot or cold, which can be physically quantified, which is in fact a form of sensation; but a feeling like joy or sadness, the happiness at the completion of a task, the acceptance of the intellectual status quo, the confidence with which we entertain our idea. In other words, cognitive rest is something very much like an emotion.

Therefore (though my good friend and colleague Jay Adams balks at the suggestion), it is not entirely wrong to substitute "I feel" for "I believe." Of course, when people say, "I feel that X is the case," they are often seeking to avoid responsibility to objective truth; that is Adams's point, and it is quite right. But one may use that language without so intending to flee responsibility. That language does, moreover, say something true about the nature of knowledge. Having a belief is, indeed, having a certain kind of feeling about a proposition. And when that feeling leads us rightly, that belief, that feeling, constitutes knowledge.

Emotion as a Perspective

Our previous discussions indicate that emotion is an important factor in knowing, one that interacts with reason in important ways. There is a mutual dependence between reason and emotion. But the considerations in the previous section suggest that emotion is more than a mere "factor" in knowledge; it is a perspective on knowledge as a whole. "Feeling that p is true" *is* "believing that p is true," viewing that belief from a certain perspective. And a right (i.e., justified and true) feeling is a right belief, that is, knowledge.

Reasoning and feeling, then, are coterminous. To reason is to experience certain feelings concerning propositions. To emote is to draw from the data of experience certain logical applications to our subjectivity (which subjectivity is itself a perspective on the whole of reality).

Reasoning, perceiving, feeling can be seen, respectively, as normative, situational, and existential perspectives on the human mind. We speak of reasoning when we want to focus on the mind's use of various principles and laws. We speak of perceiving when we want to focus on its access to the objective world. And we speak of feeling when we want to focus on the integrity of our subjectivity in the cognitive process. See fig. 32.1.

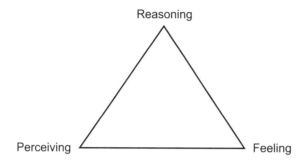

Fig. 32.1. Perspectives on the Human Mind

Emotion and Theology

Thus, emotion is unavoidably present in all theological work. It is important that we not stifle our emotional capacities by a model of theology that is too rigidly academic. We must be free in our theological work to make the proper emotional response to God's Word and to its applications. Otherwise, our theological knowledge itself will be in jeopardy.

The content of Scripture is not merely emotive, certainly. (The attempt by the logical positivists to classify all religious language as *emotive* seems rather silly today, even to those fairly sympathetic to the positivist movement.) But every part of it is emotive in the sense that every part is intended by God to generate a particular emotional response. He wants us to hate the evil, to rejoice in the good, to fear the threats, to embrace the promises.[13] That emotive content, as well as the conceptual content, must be applied to God's people. That, too, is the work of theology. If I read Romans 11:33–36 ("Oh, the depth of the riches and wisdom and knowledge of God! . . .") in a monotone, avoiding all trace of emotion, clearly I have not communicated the content of the verses very well, even if I have read every word perfectly. Similarly, if I expound those verses in a commentary or sermon, without somehow taking account of the depth of feeling there, I have obviously missed something enormously important. Systematic theology, too, must not ignore the emotive content of Scripture. This is not to say that theology must always be uttered, as it were, in an excited tone. But the theologian must *take account of* the Bible's emotive tone, as he would take account of any other biblical datum.

13. See WCF 16.2.

Romans 11:33–36, for instance, makes it plain that the incomprehensibility of God is an *exciting* doctrine. It is a significant theological question to ask what generates this excitement and what can be done to restore that excitement in our own time.[14]

Cultivating Godly Emotions

A theologian, therefore, ought to have godly emotions. He ought to be the sort of person who rejoices in what is good, who hates what is evil. He ought to be able to express and communicate that joy or hate infectiously.

To go into detail on how godly emotions are cultivated would take us afield. Some would argue that we cannot change our feelings per se; we can change feelings, they say, only by changing our behavior, our habits. I would reply that changing one's habits is important, but that presupposes growth in knowledge, Christian rationality, perception, imagination, will, and so on. Transformation of the emotions is part of the whole "package" of sanctification, transformation of the person as a whole. Growth in any one area can and will strengthen all the others.

In any case, it will not do to say that we "cannot" change how we feel. God demands change, and in one way or another, he will provide the means of change.

Imagination

Imagination has a rather bad reputation in some orthodox Christian circles. "Imagination" in the KJV OT generally refers to the inclinations of the rebellious heart (Gen. 6:5; 8:21; Deut. 29:19; 31:21; Jer. 3:17; 7:24; etc.—often in Jeremiah). That is not the normal meaning of the word in modern English, yet some of the stigma from the older usage still seems to attach to the word today among some Christians. I hope to rehabilitate the term somewhat.

Imagination refers to our ability to think about things that are not. We can think about the past, though the past is by definition no longer present. We can think of possible or probable futures, though the future cannot be perceived. Or we can imagine mere alternative states of affairs, whether or not they have existed or could exist in the present or future. Thus, our imaginations allow us to think of fantasy, of conditionals that are contrary to fact, of "what-if" scenarios.

Imagination therefore has much to do with creativity, with art. Many have sought to describe theology as a kind of science, but that model needs at least to be supplemented by others, such as "theology as art." Imagination has much to do with attempting to do things in a new or different way.

In some theological circles, creativity itself has a bad name—perhaps related in the minds of some to those "evil imaginations" of Jeremiah's prophecies, or perhaps merely offending conservative sensibilities. Some intelligent people, however, have also objected to the presence of creativity in theology, giving grounds: Charles Hodge said

---

14. Readers will have to judge whether the account of God's incomprehensibility in this volume (chapter 29) is suitably excited and/or exciting.

once that at Princeton Seminary ("Old" Princeton, of course) no new ideas had ever been advanced, and he hoped that none ever would be. Well, in a sense he was right. The work of theology is to proclaim the old ideas of Scripture and nothing else. But the work of theology is, indeed, to *proclaim* those old ideas to a new generation. This involves application, and that involves newness, since every new situation is somewhat different from its predecessors. This task involves interaction between Scripture and the subjectivities of human beings. But orchestrating that interaction requires art and creativity. Thus we are back to imagination. Imagination is indispensable to theology.

We have seen that theology requires attention to its technical terms, models, order of topics, style and form, central focus, applications to new audiences. In all these areas, imagination obviously provides important assistance. But imagination is also involved in *every* case of theological concept-formation. Consider my discussion of miracle (chapter 7) as an example. The English word *miracle* does not correspond precisely to any Hebrew or Greek term in the Bible. (That is, to a greater or lesser extent, the case with all English terms.) There are several Hebrew terms and three or four Greek terms that are translated "miracle," but these are also translated in other ways and can be used to denote events that from our point of view are not miraculous. Further, there are events described in Scripture that are miraculous on nearly everyone's view, but concerning which no distinctive miracle terms are used (e.g., 1 Kings 17:17–24). How, then, can we formulate a biblical concept of miracle?

If we cannot get our concept by studying the usage of miracle terms, perhaps we should try to study the miraculous events themselves as set forth in Scripture. But how do we know what events are miraculous until we already have a concept of miracle? It seems that we cannot look for an answer unless we already know it!

Well, that problem has philosophical ramifications that I will not try to deal with here. But practically, the only answer seems to be that we must formulate some concept of miracle *before* we systematically investigate the biblical text. Here is another form of the hermeneutical circle. We seek a biblical concept of miracle from the Bible's own narrations and explanations of actual miracles. But to decide which narratives and explanations are relevant to our study, we must begin by looking at those passages that *seem to us* to be talking about miracles. We must in one sense "begin with" our own idea of what miracle is.

Is such reasoning "autonomous"? Is it autonomous to determine theological concepts out of our own heads and use those to interpret Scripture? Well, not necessarily. Consider: (1) Even that initial concept of miracle that precedes serious Bible study is usually greatly influenced by Scripture. In Western culture, biblical miracles form a certain paradigm for the general concept of miracle. That is not to deny that Western thinkers often make serious errors in the definition of miracle, but they are usually at least in the right ballpark. (2) The initial concept, wherever it comes from, is just that—an initial concept. Our goal is, or should be, to refine it by continual interaction with Scripture. An initial concept should not be an ultimate presupposition. It should be quite tentative, open to the correction of Scripture—which, indeed, is our ultimate presupposition. (Many modern theologians make the mistake of using as ultimate presuppositions ideas that deserve to be only initial concepts.)

For example, we might use as our initial concept David Hume's view of miracle as a "violation of the laws of nature" and pick out as biblical examples only those narratives that seem to us to be violations of nature. But in the course of our study we would find that *natural law* is not a biblical concept, that events are never said to be miraculous by contrast with natural law, that the notion of a *violation* compromises the freedom of our sovereign God to do what he pleases in the world. Thus, our initial Humeanism must be revised in a more biblical direction. We will then use our "more biblical concept" to gain an even better understanding of the biblical teaching concerning miracle.

We can see, in any case, the importance of imagination. For the theologian must always set before himself, before he formally begins his study, one or more *possible* ways of answering his questions—possibilities that will guide his study of Scripture. In conceiving of possibilities, imagination is crucial.

It is therefore important that imagination be *godly*. That is, the imagination ought to be saturated in biblical teachings and thought patterns so that when an unanswered question is raised, the theologian will consider possibilities that are consistent with Scripture, those that are rendered likely by other biblical teachings.

Is imagination another epistemological perspective? Well, imagination is our faculty for knowing things that "are not": the past, the future, the possible as opposed to the actual, the impossible as opposed to the possible, the fantastic. In one sense, then, it does not embrace all human knowledge. Yet the point has often been made that humans know what is only by contrast with what is not. You cannot know that a book is on the table unless you know what it would mean for the book *not* to be on the table. And the reverse is also true. So positive knowledge involves negative knowledge and vice versa. And a perfect positive knowledge would include a positive negative knowledge.

Further, our concepts of possibility deeply influence our knowledge of actuality. Since Rudolf Bultmann does not believe that miracles are possible, he does not believe that any actually happened. Knowledge that something is the case presupposes a knowledge that it *might* be the case.

And as I said earlier, imagination is important in memory and anticipation—in knowing past and future. But how can we know the present if we cannot relate that present to the past and future? If we have no knowledge of what has been happening, how can we make any sense of what is happening now? And if we have no idea about the goal of events, where they are going, surely our knowledge of present events is at best highly defective. In fact, it is even difficult to conceive of the present merely as present. The moment we try to conceive of precisely what is "happening now," the events we are thinking about become past events. The present, as Augustine pointed out, can begin to look like an indivisible instant that cannot be characterized at all— for when we characterize it, it has become past. Perhaps, then, imagination, as our road to the past and the future, is also our only road to the present. Perhaps sensation, reason, emotion are only different forms of, perspectives on, imagination. Therefore, if imagination is not a perspective, at least it comes close. It is involved in every act of belief or knowledge.

There is a great need for imagination among theologians today. The crying need is for fresh applications to situations too long neglected, for translating the gospel into new forms. The artistic gift may be well employed in the theological profession.

Will

Will is our capacity to make choices, commitments, decisions. Philosophers have often debated whether intellect or will is "primary": do we make choices based on our knowledge, or does our knowledge arise from a choice to believe?

Well, as you might guess, I think there is truth in both assertions. Our choices do presuppose some knowledge—knowledge of the alternatives, knowledge of our own values, knowledge of data. On the other hand, all knowledge also presupposes choices: choices of how to interpret data, choices of values (criteria of truth and falsity, right and wrong), the choice whether to make a judgment or to suspend judgment, the choice to believe a proposition or its contradictory, the choice whether to acknowledge or to suppress our beliefs, the choice of how strongly we will believe, that is, how much that choice will influence our lives. Every belief, then, is an act of will, and every act of will is an expression, an application, of our knowledge (see John 7:17). Knowing and doing are one. (Recall the biblical equations of knowledge with obedience, chapter 28.)

Will is also involved in perception and emotion, which merely serves to underscore the point made above. It is involved in perception: we *choose* to pay attention to sensations or to ignore them. (Remember Mavrodes's example of the wolf in the woods.) We choose to interpret sensations in one way rather than another. (And remember: there is no sharp line between the interpretation of a sensation and the sensation itself—at least from our point of view.) Will is also involved in emotion. The same event will move different people in different ways. A thief will be joyful over a successful heist; his victims will be mournful. The emotional difference results from different choices made—differences in lifestyle, in values, in beliefs, in religious allegiance.

Will, then, is another perspective on knowledge in general and on reason, perception, and emotion as aspects of knowledge. Which perspective does it fall under? Well, it doesn't much matter, since each perspective includes the others. But I would be inclined to make it another aspect of the existential perspective alongside emotion. It could be argued that will is a function of an individual's strongest emotion: my choice is what I most feel like doing. (Advocates of libertarian freedom, such as H. D. Lewis and C. A. Campbell, would disagree, finding in will something radically mysterious, uncaused, distinct from all emotions.)

Habits, Skills

Habits are those choices that we are accustomed to making, those choices that we make "by force of habit," as we say, if not specifically moved to do otherwise. When those habits enable us to perform useful tasks, they are called skills.

Habits are important in our knowledge. Presuppositions are habits—values that we customarily bring to bear on questions of truth and right. We develop habits of reasoning in certain ways, of interpreting data in certain ways, of feeling certain ways, of imagining certain kinds of possibilities rather than others, of making certain kinds of choices. Thus, right or wrong choices in the past are reinforced by being repeated over and over. Godly decisions replicate themselves, leading to greater knowledge and sanctification (Rom. 12:1f.; Phil. 1:9f.; Heb. 5:11–14). Ungodly habits, on the contrary, lead to worse and worse error, worse and worse sin (Rom. 1). Habits are hard to break; breaking them usually requires pain. The theologian must be prepared to endure that pain if necessary, even if that may include retracting earlier positions and suffering academic disrespect.

Skills in knowledge are called *wisdom* in Scripture. These are the good epistemic habits by which we are able to understand the truth and to put that truth to work in life. Wisdom comes through Christ by means of his Word and Spirit. Godly wisdom is sharply different from the wisdom of the world (1 Cor. 1–2), for it is based on the Word of God, not man's autonomous thinking.

Wisdom, however, is the skill of "knowing how" rather than "knowing that." Both these kinds of knowing are important. A football quarterback must master his playbook (knowing that), but he must also be able to do the things required by the playbook (knowing how). Lacking either form of knowledge, he will not do his job properly.

At one level, it is possible to "know that" without "knowing how." The quarterback might memorize the playbook, but be unable to evade the oncoming tacklers. So someone might memorize the content of Scripture and the Reformed confessions, but be hopelessly weak in the face of temptation.

On the other hand, even "knowing that" requires skills—in our examples, academic skills, skills of memorizing. And "knowing how" presupposes "knowing that." A skillful quarterback is one who "knows that"—for example, that he must move in a certain direction to avoid the tackler—and who applies that knowledge to his life. Wisdom and propositional knowledge, therefore, are perspectivally related. Each is a help in remedying false concepts of the other.

Skills are important in theology as in all other disciplines: skills with languages, skills in exegesis, logic, communication, dealing with people's needs. Scripture also speaks much about wisdom as the skill of godly living (James 3:13ff.; cf. Proverbs, passim). Without godliness, wisdom is of no value. Here again, God's Word correlates knowledge with obedience.

Intuition

When we know something, but don't know *how* we know it, we are inclined to say that we know it "by intuition." Thus, intuition is a kind of "asylum of ignorance." But I prefer to look at it as an index of the mysteriousness of knowledge. Knowledge, like God himself and all his creations, is incomprehensible. We can gain some insight into it through his revelation. But we reach a place where our analysis ends, though all our questions are not answered. Hence another area in which knowledge requires faith.

Some specific mysteries: (1) The chain of justification cannot go on forever. If someone asks me why I believe Sacramento is the capital of California, I can point to a reference work. If he asks how I know that reference work is telling the truth, I can (perhaps!) refer to the credentials of the authors or the good reputation of the publisher. If he asks how I know those credentials or reputations, I might be able to cite further grounds, reasons, or arguments based on perception, reason, emotion, and so forth. But if I am asked how I know that my reason is leading me in the right direction, it is difficult to answer except circularly: by offering another rational argument. At some point we are forced into a corner where we say, "I just know." That is *intuition*. Ultimate presuppositions, in that sense, are known intuitively, although they are verified by circular arguments of various sorts. This is true not only of Christianity, but of all other systems of thought. The human mind is finite; it cannot present an infinitely long argument and give an exhaustive reason for anything. It must, at some point, begin with a faith commitment, whether in the true God or in an idol.

(2) Not only at the beginning of the chain of justification, but also at every point in the argument, we encounter God's mystery. Nothing physically forces us to draw logical conclusions. We draw them because, first, we find ourselves agreeing with them, and second, we sense a moral demand upon us to affirm them. At every point we make a choice—either in obedience to or in rebellion against those moral norms. What is our faculty for gaining knowledge of these imperatives? All the faculties are involved; it is the heart itself that makes the choice. But if anyone asks what it is that reveals to us the final decision that we ought to make, having integrated all the data from different sources, I suppose the answer would have to be "intuition." Our sense of when to stop investigating, our cognitive rest, as I said earlier, is like a feeling. But the term *intuition* may also be properly used for it, if we hesitate to sound emotionalistic!

Key Terms
Personalism
Hermeneutical circle
Faculty
Heart
Primacy of the intellect
Reason (two definitions)
Sensation
Perception
Experience
Imagination
Will
Habits
Skills
Wisdom
Intuition

Study Questions

1. Narrate Ian Ramsey's courtroom illustration. What point is he trying to make about theological language?
2. "The resurrection of Jesus has nothing to do with the resuscitation of a corpse!" Reply, making relevant distinctions.
3. Do you believe in the *primacy of the intellect*? Why or why not?
4. Frame proposes to look at all the faculties of the human mind as perspectives on the knowledge of the whole person. What sorts of views is he opposing in this argument? Explain; evaluate.
5. Should theology be rational? Discuss.
6. "To say that theology ought to be rational, really, is no different from saying that it ought to be scriptural or that it ought to be true." Explain; evaluate.
7. "Therefore, when someone tells me that reason must be the judge of theological ideas, I can agree with him in a sense." Explain; evaluate.
8. "Mavrodes also argues that experiencing X involves making some judgment about X." Explain; evaluate.
9. Describe the "more than conquerors" illustration. What point was the professor trying to make? What do you think about it? How does Frame make use of it?
10. Is it wrong to "follow your feelings"? Discuss, making proper distinctions.
11. Is it wrong to make use of our imagination in theology? Discuss.
12. Discuss the relation between intellect and will.
13. Discuss the role of habits in knowledge.
14. What is intuition, and what use does it have in theology?

Memory Verses

Ps. 9:1: I will give thanks to the Lord with my whole heart;
   I will recount all of your wonderful deeds.

Ps. 37:4: Delight yourself in the Lord,
   and he will give you the desires of your heart.

Ps. 94:9: He who planted the ear, does he not hear?
He who formed the eye, does he not see?

John 7:17: If anyone's will is to do God's will, he will know whether the teaching is from God or whether I am speaking on my own authority.

Rom. 11:33–36: Oh, the depth of the riches and wisdom and knowledge of God! How unsearchable are his judgments and how inscrutable his ways!

"For who has known the mind of the Lord,
  or who has been his counselor?"

"Or who has given a gift to him
  that he might be repaid?"

For from him and through him and to him are all things. To him be glory forever. Amen.

1 John 1:1–3: That which was from the beginning, which we have heard, which we have seen with our eyes, which we looked upon and have touched with our hands, concerning the word of life—the life was made manifest, and we have seen it, and testify to it and proclaim to you the eternal life, which was with the Father and was made manifest to us—that which we have seen and heard we proclaim also to you, so that you too may have fellowship with us; and indeed our fellowship is with the Father and with his Son Jesus Christ.

Resources for Further Study

Frame, John M. *DKG*, 167–346.

Mavrodes, George. *Belief in God*. New York, Random House, 1970.

Poythress, Vern S. *Logic: A God-Centered Approach to the Foundation of Western Thought.* Wheaton, IL: Crossway, 2013.

Ramsey, Ian. *Religious Language*. New York: Macmillan, 1957.

Reymond, Robert. *The Justification of Knowledge*. Nutley, NJ: Presbyterian and Reformed, 1976.

PART 6

THE DOCTRINE OF ANGELS AND DEMONS

CHAPTER 33

ANGELS AND DEMONS

IN PARTS 3–5 OF THIS VOLUME, we have been focusing on God the Creator. Part 3 dealt with his nature, actions, and Trinitarian being. In part 4 we considered his revelation of himself, and in part 5 the resulting human knowledge of him. Now in part 6 we turn to the created world, the lower circle in our Creator-creature diagram. In later parts, I will consider human beings as creatures and as sinners, and the history of salvation by which Christ brings to himself the people promised to him in the *pactum salutis* (chapters 4, 11). But for now we will briefly consider some nonhuman but intelligent members of creation, the angels and demons.

Nature and Work of Angels

Words translated "angel" occur 203 times in Scripture,[1] and similar beings appear under other names, such as "living creatures" (Ezek. 1:5ff.), "cherubim" (Gen. 3:24; Ex. 25:18ff.; many other references), "seraphim" (Isa. 6:2, 6), "sons of God" (Job 1:6; 2:1; 38:7), "sons of the mighty" (Pss. 29:1; 89:6 NASB), "spirits" (1 Kings 22:19ff.; Heb. 1:14), "holy ones" (Deut. 33:2–3; Ps. 89:5, 7), and "watchers" (Dan. 4:13, 17, 23). The "principalities and powers" (Rom. 8:38–39; Eph. 1:21; 3:10; 6:12; Col. 2:10) and "thrones" (Col. 1:16) are angelic beings. The "horses and chariots of fire" of 2 Kings 6:17 were evidently driven by angels.

Theologians and commentators have tried to analyze these names as different categories of angels, but speculation abounds in these discussions. Presumably the cherubim, for example, have particular qualifications for the job of guarding God's sanctuary; but it is not clear on what basis they were chosen for this task, whether by accomplishment or, somehow, by nature.

Two of them appear by name: Gabriel (Dan. 8:16; 9:21; Luke 1:19, 26) and Michael (Dan. 10:13, 21; 12:1; Jude 9; Rev. 12:7).

The angels are vast in number, as indicated by terms such as "hosts" (Luke 2:13), "camp" (Gen. 32:1–2), "legions" (Matt. 26:53), and "thousands" (Deut. 33:2; Ps. 68:17; Dan. 7:10; Jude 14; Rev. 5:11).

---

1. According to my computer search of the ESV.

These beings appear often in the biblical story, but Scripture never directly discusses their creation or nature. In most cases, angels are created beings (in Revelation 22:9, an angel refuses worship), but sometimes the term *angel* refers to a divine theophany, often called "the angel of the LORD" (chapter 20). Some writers have thought that Michael, identified to Daniel in Daniel 12:1 as "the great prince who has charge of your people," is a name of Christ. *Angel* also sometimes refers to human messengers, as likely in Revelation 2:1, 8, 12, etc. But I will focus on the uses of the term to refer to nonhuman intelligent beings.

Since the angels neither marry nor give in marriage (Matt. 22:30), it evidently follows that they do not reproduce and do not exist in families as we know them. Many theologians have deduced from this that when the angels fell they fell as individuals, not in a federal head, as human beings fell in Adam. So it is thought that angels do not exist as a common species, but that every individual angel is a species of his own.

Scripture is more explicit about the work of angels than about their nature. They are God's attendants, standing in his presence, worshiping God day and night (Job 38:7; Isa. 6; Pss. 103:20; 148:2; Rev. 5:11). The living creatures surround the Lord in the theophanic glory-cloud (chapter 18) (2 Sam. 22:11; Pss. 18:10; 80:1; 99:1; Isa. 37:16). They guard God's sanctuary against intrusion, first in Eden (Gen. 3:24), later by their symbolic presence in the tabernacle and temple (Ex. 25–26, 36–37; 1 Kings 6–8). The images of cherubim in the temple picture the presence of actual cherubim with the Lord himself (2 Kings 19:15).

In redemptive history, they serve as God's messengers to human beings. Both the Hebrew (*mal'ak*) and the Greek (*angelos*) terms for these beings designate them as bringers of the word of God. They appeared to Abraham (Gen. 18), Lot (chap. 19), and Jacob (28:12; 32:1). They announced the giving of the law (Acts 7:53; Gal. 3:19; Heb. 2:2) and the great events of salvation (Dan. 8:16; 9:21; 10:5–6; Matt. 1:20–21; Luke 1:11, 26; Rev. 18:21; 19:17; 22:6, 16). But they act as well as speak, participating in the redemptive drama. For example, they protected the prophet Elisha from the king of Syria:

> When the servant of the man of God rose early in the morning and went out, behold, an army with horses and chariots was all around the city. And the servant said, "Alas, my master! What shall we do?" He said, "Do not be afraid, for those who are with us are more than those who are with them." Then Elisha prayed and said, "O LORD, please open his eyes that he may see." So the LORD opened the eyes of the young man, and he saw, and behold, the mountain was full of horses and chariots of fire all around Elisha. (2 Kings 6:15–17)

Later, during the exile of the Jews, an angelic messenger to Daniel described to him some of the preternatural[2] conflict:

---

2. In theology, *preternatural* refers to creatures beyond the natural world and their deeds. *Supernatural* refers to God himself and his works.

The prince of the kingdom of Persia withstood me twenty-one days, but Michael, one of the chief princes, came to help me, for I was left there with the kings of Persia, and came to make you understand what is to happen to your people in the latter days. For the vision is for days yet to come. (Dan. 10:13–14)

Paul tells us that our own warfare is not

against flesh and blood, but against the rulers, against the authorities, against the cosmic powers over this present darkness, against the spiritual forces of evil in the heavenly places. (Eph. 6:12)

Herman Bavinck describes other parts of the "ordinary ministry of angels":

They rejoice over the conversion of a sinner (Luke 15:10), watch over believers (Ps. 32:7; 91:11), protect the little ones (Matt. 18:10),[3] are present in the church (1 Cor. 11:10; 1 Tim. 5:21), follow it on its journeys through history (Eph. 3:10), allow themselves to be taught by it (Eph. 3:10; 1 Peter 1:12), and carry believers into Abraham's bosom (Luke 16:22).[4]

Note especially their ministry in relation to Jesus (Matt. 4:11; 28:2–7; Luke 22:43; John 1:51; Acts 1:10) and to the apostles (Acts 5:19; 8:26; 12:7ff., 23; 27:23; Rev. 1:1). At Jesus' return, they will join again in the great events (Matt. 16:27; 25:31; Mark 8:38; Luke 9:26; 2 Thess. 1:7; Jude 14; Rev. 5:2; etc.). They will gather the elect (Matt. 24:31) and cast the ungodly into the fire (13:41, 49).

To summarize: the angels adore God and seek to carry out his purposes in the world, applying his lordship to their individual callings. Those callings may therefore be summarized in terms of the lordship attributes: See fig. 33.1.

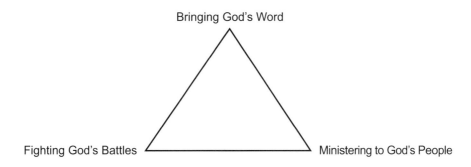

Fig. 33.1. Callings of Angels

3. Scripture doesn't teach specifically that every person, or even every child, has his own individual "guardian angel," nor does it deny this common view. But clearly, one function of the angels is to minister to believers and their children in various ways (Heb. 1:14).

4. *BRD*, 2:464. A number of the biblical points in this section are based on Bavinck's discussion.

Angels and Men

Angels are so great in number, and so powerful, that human beings are sometimes tempted to worship them. The apostle John fell down to worship at an angel's feet, but the angel rebuked him. So theologians have often pictured angels as a type of being above men, even a kind of midpoint between men and God. But Scripture teaches us a remarkable fact: what superiority angels possess over us is only temporary. Human beings, not angels, are in the image of God (Gen. 1:26–27). And the world to come belongs to men, not to angels:

> Now it was not to angels that God subjected the world to come, of which we are speaking. It has been testified somewhere,
>
> "What is man, that you are mindful of him,
>   or the son of man, that you care for him?
> You made him for a little while lower than the angels;
>   you have crowned him with glory and honor,
>   putting everything in subjection under his feet."
>
> Now in putting everything in subjection to him, he left nothing outside his control. At present, we do not yet see everything in subjection to him. But we see him who for a little while was made lower than the angels, namely Jesus, crowned with glory and honor because of the suffering of death, so that by the grace of God he might taste death for everyone. (Heb. 2:5–9)

As we are now, in a sense, lower than the angels, so Jesus was *for a little while* lower than the angels. But he accepted that humiliation so that, having defeated sin, he could rise above the angels and bring his people with him. So we are to be raised above the angels. In 1 Corinthians 6:3, Paul says (without explanation, as an incidental remark supporting a different point), "Do you not know that we are to judge angels?"

But since the future age in Christ has already begun, there is a sense in which we are already superior to the angels. Hebrews says, "Are they not all ministering spirits sent out to serve for the sake of those who are to inherit salvation?" (Heb. 1:14). They are more powerful than we, but they serve us.

Ephesians 3:10 and 1 Peter 1:12 present angels as witnesses, spectators, to the drama of human salvation. We have seen that they fight in the spiritual battles of that drama, but at some level they don't entirely understand it; they feel more like observers than participants. The main reason is that although they fight for the salvation of God's people, they don't experience salvation for themselves. The good angels don't need salvation, for they are unfallen. The angelic fall did not infect all the angels as the human fall infected all human beings. For the bad angels, there is no salvation, for Scripture never suggests that they are redeemed in any way analogous to human salvation. So I imagine that they are somewhat astounded that God would choose to save human weaklings rather than mighty angels. They look down, hoping to understand better, seeking to be taught. Amazingly, it is we, the church, who teach the angels. Paul preaches the gospel, so that "through the church the manifold wisdom of God might now be made known to the rulers and authorities in the heavenly places" (Eph. 3:10). Keep in mind that when we witness concerning Christ, there is an unseen audience: the angels.

Satan and Demons

The references to spiritual warfare imply that there are bad angels as well as good. And since everything God made was originally good, some angels must have defected from their good condition after the original creation. But since the tempter of Genesis 3 was a fallen angel, the angelic fall evidently preceded the fall of man.[5]

That tempter is later called "the dragon, that ancient serpent, who is the devil and Satan" (Rev. 20:2). He is evidently the chief of the fallen angels (cf. Matt. 12:24; 25:41), often called *devils* or *demons*. The fallen angels support Satan's activity in the world, which is always to fight against God's kingdom. Like the "prince of the kingdom of Persia" in Daniel 10:13 above, they take power over nations[6]—hence the names "principalities" and "powers" referring to them. They also take possession of individuals (Matt. 4:24; etc.).[7] Jesus calls Satan himself "the ruler of this world" (John 12:31; 14:30; 16:11).

We have seen that language is a central aspect of God's nature and in the ministry of the good angels as messengers of God. In chapter 34, we will see that it plays an analogous role in human nature as well. Similarly, Scripture regularly presents Satan in terms of his perverted speech. *Devil* means, etymologically, "slanderer" or "accuser" (as Rev. 12:10). Satan is "a liar and the father of lies" (John 8:44). In Genesis 3 he presents himself as a serpent, an animal that fascinates by his waving tongue until he bites. And more significantly, he tempts Eve (Gen. 3:1–7) and later Jesus (Matt. 4:1–11) precisely by his speech. In the latter case he even counterfeits the activity of the good angels, by quoting the Word of God.

As a liar, he counterfeits the appearance of good angels (2 Cor. 11:14), and his unholy trinity (the first beast, the second beast, and the false prophet of Revelation 13; 16:13) counterfeits the nature of God himself. So we can summarize his activity as mocking the lordship of God; see fig. 33.2.

---

5. Scripture does not narrate the fall of Satan and his angels, but Isaiah 14:3–21 and Ezekiel 28:2–19 deal with the defeat of the kings of Babylon and Tyre, respectively, using imagery suggesting analogies with the fall of Satan.

6. But the good angel, Michael, is the prince of Israel, according to Daniel 12:1.

7. I have no reason to think that demons no longer possess human beings. I do not believe that a demon can possess a believer in Christ, because the Holy Spirit indwells that person. Although believers do sin, Paul says that "sin will have no dominion over you" (Rom. 6:14), and a demonic possession would certainly be one form of the dominion of sin over a person. So although we are often tempted to sin by Satan and his followers, we always have, by God's grace, the power to say no to them (James 4:7; 1 Peter 5:8–9). Is it still possible for believers to cast out demons from other people in the name of Christ? I have no biblical reason to deny that this can happen today. But I do not have sufficient experience of such activity to comment further.

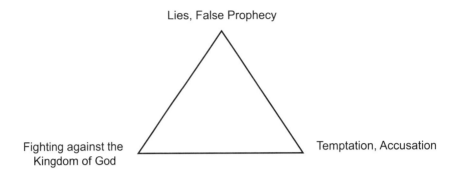

Fig. 33.2. Activities of Satan

But the work of Christ is more powerful. Through his cross and resurrection, Christ has defeated Satan. So although we need to be aware of Satan's devices (2 Cor. 2:11), we are able to say no to his temptations. James says:

> Submit yourselves therefore to God. Resist the devil, and he will flee from you. (James 4:7)

Peter presents the balance between wariness and confidence:

> Be sober-minded; be watchful. Your adversary the devil prowls around like a roaring lion, seeking someone to devour. Resist him, firm in your faith, knowing that the same kinds of suffering are being experienced by your brotherhood throughout the world. (1 Peter 5:8–9)

The destiny of Satan and his angels is unmistakable: the eternal lake of fire (Matt. 25:41; Rev. 20:9–10, 13–14).

C. S. Lewis said:

> There are two equal and opposite errors into which our race can fall about the devils. One is to disbelieve in their existence. The other is to believe, and to feel an excessive and unhealthy interest in them. They themselves are equally pleased by both errors and hail a materialist or a magician with the same delight.[8]

This is good advice. As often in the Christian life, there is a balance to be kept. Satan is defeated, but he is still doing harm. He has not yet been thrown into the lake of fire. But we can also look at him this way: he is still doing harm, but he is defeated.

Scripture presents Satan as a "crafty" being, who anticipates well the plans of God (as in Jesus' temptation, Matt. 4). Surely he knows that his rebellion against God is

---

8. C. S. Lewis, *The Screwtape Letters* (New York: HarperCollins, 1942; repr., San Francisco: HarperSanFrancisco, 2001), ix.

doomed. How can this creature imagine that he will succeed in replacing God on the throne? Despite Satan's intelligence, there is a deep irrationality in him. I indicated in chapter 29 that his irrationality is the source of human irrationality, the irrationality of those who know God and yet suppress the truth (Rom. 1:18–21).

Living with the Angels: A Sermon

The Bible presents angelic beings as beings "with whom we have to do," as one of the environments of the Christian life. It is hard for the modern Christian to know what to make of this. Believers in Bible times were deeply conscious of the presence of angels in their midst, as when Paul mentions that women should wear a head covering "because of the angels" (1 Cor. 11:10). Paul feels no need to explain this phrase. He assumes the Corinthians will understand what he means. But I recall my revered professor of theology, John Murray, shaking his head sadly after reading this passage and confessing that he had no idea what it meant. Nor can I offer insight. Modern Christians, including myself, have lost the vivid consciousness of angelic beings that NT believers took for granted. Some popular writers and television shows have recently explored claims to angelic activity in our time, but these seem like cultural curiosities without much intellectual or spiritual weight.

Part of the problem is that modern people have lost touch with the supernatural and preternatural. They have become skeptical of any world or any beings beyond those of our senses. Christians at least believe in God, but they have absorbed enough of the anti-supernaturalism of their culture that belief in angels seems foreign to them. It seems that belief in God is hard enough. Why add further difficulty by bringing angels into it? And if God is sovereign, what need do we have for preternatural beings? God is the One who judges and blesses us, sometimes in extraordinary ways. Why are angels important?

But Scripture itself mentions angels over three hundred times. This fact suggests that we need to take angels into account in the decisions of our lives. Being a modern person myself, I don't pretend to have gotten very deeply into the doctrine of angels, but I cautiously venture the following thoughts.

1. *The doctrine of angels rebukes the smallness and impersonalism of our cosmology.* Modern worldviews typically claim to have discovered a much larger universe than was known to the ancients and medievals. But they have a much smaller view of the universe of persons, having abandoned belief in God and in angels. According to Scripture, however, vast numbers of angels inhabit the world. So we need to develop a larger perspective. In 2 Kings 6, Elisha's servant was terrified by the armies of Syria surrounding their city. Elisha comforted him with a vision of angels:

> He said, "Do not be afraid, for those who are with us are more than those who are with them." Then Elisha prayed and said, "O Lord, please open his eyes that he may see." So the Lord opened the eyes of the young man, and he saw, and behold, the mountain was full of horses and chariots of fire all around Elisha. (2 Kings 6:16–17)

Mysterious warriors—even mysterious horses!—poised to bring victory to the prophet (in a most mysterious way, as the later verses indicate). Elisha's servant needed a larger cosmology, one allowing for more persons. He needed, further, to see that the physical conflict is only part of a larger spiritual conflict, a larger warfare, as we will discuss further below.

So the doctrine of angels makes our worldview even more personalistic. It reminds us not only that God is a personal God, but that many of the means he uses to bring about events in the world are also personal, rather than impersonal.[9] Scripture has little if anything to say about natural laws and forces, much to say about God's personal agents, both angels and men. Typically, God does not press buttons; he sends messengers. This is important, because impersonalism always detracts from our personal responsibility.

2. *The doctrine of angels shows us something of the dimensions of our ethical-spiritual warfare.* We see this in at least three ways:

(a) Angels participate in the kingdom warfare. Above and around us are good and evil angels, engaged in spiritual warfare. Satan and his hosts engage human beings in the battle by tempting them to sin. The good angels, however, are "ministering spirits sent out to serve for the sake of those who are to inherit salvation" (Heb. 1:14). The two armies fight each other, as well as fighting against and for us (Dan. 10:13, 21; Jude 9; Rev. 12:7).

So Scripture urges us not to underestimate the difficulty of the struggle, as if we could succeed with human resources alone (Eph. 6:10–20). If we were fighting human beings, physical weapons would prevail, though even in human warfare God's will is decisive. But we are fighting beings who are far more intelligent, strong, and numerous than we are, and who, to us, are exceedingly mysterious.

On the other hand, we should not overestimate the difficulty either, for there are angels fighting on our side (2 Kings 6:15–17), and the spiritual weapons of Ephesians 6 are sufficient.

It might seem uninteresting to conclude with the advice "don't underestimate" and "don't overestimate." But the main point here is that we should not base either our hopes or our fears on the empirical situation alone. News media and opinion-makers in our culture seem to think that the most important issues are political, followed closely by entertainment. But Scripture says otherwise. The really decisive issues of human life are ethical and spiritual. And it is the religious and ethical equipment God gives us that will prevail over the hosts of evil.

(b) Second, angels are witnesses to human salvation (Luke 12:8–9; 15:10; 1 Cor. 4:9; Eph. 3:10; 1 Tim. 3:16; 1 Peter 1:12; Rev. 14:10). Although (as above) angels participate in the redemptive drama, there is another sense in which they are spectators rather than participants. Redemption doesn't extend to them, for unfallen angels need no redemption, and fallen angels receive none (cf. Heb. 2:16). So although the angels contend

---

9. Compare my discussion in chapters 7–9.

for God's redemptive purposes, they do not have the experience of being redeemed themselves. Thus, Scripture sometimes pictures them as standing in amazement, looking in from the outside, as it were. Remarkably, they even *learn* the wisdom of God from observing the church (Eph. 3:10). It is our privilege to *teach* the angels by our words and life!

(c) Third, the doctrine of angels is a measure of the greatness of our salvation in Christ, for salvation lifts us above the angels. According to Hebrews 2:9, Jesus was made, for a little while, lower than the angels for the suffering of death. But in his resurrection he is again exalted above them. The passage implies that Jesus' brothers, the church, share that exaltation with him, fulfilling man's dominion over the earth (Gen. 1:28; Ps. 8). Although we do not yet see everything subject to man, we see this dominion in Jesus (Heb. 2:8). So the angels minister to us, not vice versa (1:14). The world to come is not theirs, but ours (2:5–8; cf. Paul's odd statement that we will judge angels, 1 Cor. 6:3). It belongs to man, God's image, not the angels.

Scripture applies these facts by indicating that angel-worship is not only a sin, but also a delusion, from which Christ has set us free (Col. 2:18–19; Rev. 19:10; 22:8–9). Further, because of redemption, the prince of the evil angels, Satan himself, is a defeated foe. We may resist him, and he will flee (James 4:7; 1 Peter 5:8–9).

Key Terms
Angel
Cherubim
Seraphim
Angel of the Lord
Preternatural
Supernatural
Devil
Demon
Satan

Study Questions
1. Summarize the activity of the angels under a triperspectival formula.
2. Same for Satan and the demons.
3. Describe the spiritual warfare as presented in 2 Kings 6; Daniel 10; and Ephesians 6.
4. Are human beings higher than the angels, or lower? Make appropriate distinctions.
5. What do the angels learn from human Christian believers? How should that affect our decisions?
6. Summarize "the centrality of language" in God, the good angels, the evil angels, and human beings.
7. Should we fear the devil? Give counsel to someone who is troubled about him.

8. Is Satan rational or irrational? Discuss.

9. "The doctrine of angels rebukes the smallness and impersonalism of our cosmology." Explain; evaluate.

10. "The doctrine of angels shows us something of the dimensions of our ethical-spiritual warfare. We see this in at least three ways." Enumerate those three ways and discuss.

Memory Verses

2 Kings 6:16–17: [Elisha] said, "Do not be afraid, for those who are with us are more than those who are with them." Then Elisha prayed and said, "O LORD, please open his eyes that he may see." So the LORD opened the eyes of the young man, and he saw, and behold, the mountain was full of horses and chariots of fire all around Elisha.

Eph. 6:12: For we do not wrestle against flesh and blood, but against the rulers, against the authorities, against the cosmic powers over this present darkness, against the spiritual forces of evil in the heavenly places.

Heb. 1:14: Are they not all ministering spirits sent out to serve for the sake of those who are to inherit salvation?

Heb. 2:9: But we see him who for a little while was made lower than the angels, namely Jesus, crowned with glory and honor because of the suffering of death, so that by the grace of God he might taste death for everyone.

James 4:7: Submit yourselves therefore to God. Resist the devil, and he will flee from you.

1 Peter 5:8–9: Be sober-minded; be watchful. Your adversary the devil prowls around like a roaring lion, seeking someone to devour. Resist him, firm in your faith, knowing that the same kinds of suffering are being experienced by your brotherhood throughout the world.

Resources for Further Study

Bavinck, Herman. *BRD*, 2:443–72.

Lewis, C. S. *The Screwtape Letters*. New York: HarperCollins, 1942. Repr., San Francisco: HarperSanFrancisco, 2001.

PART 7

THE DOCTRINE OF MAN

CHAPTER 34

MAN IN THE IMAGE OF GOD

IN PART 7, WE WILL LOOK AT ourselves and the historical beginning of the great biblical story of redemption.[1]

Genesis 1 teaches that after God brought the world into existence from nothing (chapter 10), he populated the heavens and the earth in six days. On the first day, he made light and separated it from the darkness. On day 2, he made the sky and separated the waters above from those below. On the third day, he made plants. On the fourth day, he gathered the light into heavenly bodies: sun, moon, and stars. On day 5, he filled the waters with aquatic life and the skies with winged creatures. On the sixth day, he populated the land with "livestock and creeping things and beasts" (Gen. 1:24). All the creatures were to reproduce "according to their kinds" (vv. 21, 24, 25). And "God saw that it was good" (v. 25).

But then something even more remarkable happens:

> Then God said, "Let us make man in our image, after our likeness. And let them have dominion over the fish of the sea and over the birds of the heavens and over the livestock and over all the earth and over every creeping thing that creeps on the earth."
>
> So God created man in his own image,
>   in the image of God he created him;
>   male and female he created them.
>
> And God blessed them. And God said to them, "Be fruitful and multiply and fill the earth and subdue it and have dominion over the fish of the sea and over the birds

---

1. As I have generally done in the rest of this book, I will use the term *man* generically in my discussion, referring to both men and women. Similarly with generic pronouns *he, his,* and so on. I choose this terminology not intending at all to demean women, though some will take it that way given today's politically correct usage. (See later in this chapter the subsection "Male and Female.") To summarize my reasons: (1) This usage is acceptable grammatically in English and in the original languages of Scripture. (2) Alternative locutions, such as *humankind* and *he/she,* are awkward. (3) This usage reflects the biblical pattern in which men represent women in the family and in the church. (4) Genesis 5:2 tells us that when God created man "male and female," he blessed them and "named them Man" (*Adam*). So at this point I am simply following God's example.

of the heavens and over every living thing that moves on the earth." And God said, "Behold, I have given you every plant yielding seed that is on the face of all the earth, and every tree with seed in its fruit. You shall have them for food. And to every beast of the earth and to every bird of the heavens and to everything that creeps on the earth, everything that has the breath of life, I have given every green plant for food." And it was so. And God saw everything that he had made, and behold, it was very good. And there was evening and there was morning, the sixth day. (Gen. 1:26–31)

This passage emphasizes the uniqueness of man in many ways. The first is what John Murray called the "unique engagement of God's counsel."[2] Murray says:

> The formula is not that of simple fiat as in the case of light (Gen. 1:3). Nor is it that of command in reference to existing entities—"let the earth bring forth tender herb" (Gen. 1:11); "let the waters swarm swarm[3] of living creature" (Gen. 1:20); "let the earth bring forth living creature" (Gen. 1:24). The terms "let us make"[4] indicate that there is unique engagement of divine thought and counsel, and bespeak the fact that something correspondingly unique is about to take place.[5]

The Image of God

The second indication of man's uniqueness in the passage is that he is made, God says, "in our image, after our likeness." The animals are made "according to their kinds," that is, according to a pattern prescribed by God. But man is made after the pattern of God himself. Murray comments:

> But the exemplar itself was not something willed to be; it is that which belongs to God himself intrinsically. Intelligent response to this datum of revelation is one of amazement, and we exclaim, "What is man, that thou art mindful of him!" (Ps. 8:4). Man's origin is not only the unique subject of God's counsel; man is from the outset the recipient of unique endowment and dignity.[6]

Theologians, however, have long puzzled over what exactly the image of God consists of. Some have referred it to man's unique intellectual power, others to the soul as distinct from the body, others to man's relationship to God. Karl Barth found a parallel between "image" and "male and female" and so argued that the image consists in sexual differentiation, and therefore, more broadly, social relationships. Others have thought

2. *MCW*, 2:4.
3. Here the editor comments, "Here and elsewhere John Murray employed his own translation to bring out the precise force of the original."
4. On the use of plurals in God's resolution here, see my brief comment in chapter 20. It more likely refers to the "heavenly council" than to the Trinity as such, but like other OT passages it presents God not as a solitary monad, but as a dynamic society. The OT presents these social pictures of God without explanation or embarrassment. That is relevant to the doctrine of the Trinity.
5. *MCW*, 2:4.
6. Ibid., 2:5.

the image consists in man's dominion over the rest of creation (Gen. 1:26, 28) because that is a mirror of God's lordship. Still others, with NT justification, have identified the image with ethical qualities such as knowledge, righteousness, and holiness (Eph. 4:24; Col. 3:10). Some have sought a Christological interpretation of the image, since the NT presents Christ as the image in a preeminent sense (2 Cor. 4:4; Col. 1:15; Heb. 1:3) and the image in which we are to be renewed (Rom. 8:29; 1 Cor. 15:49; 2 Cor. 3:18).

There is truth in all these representations. But there are so many of them that it is important for us to try to understand the conceptual patterns that bring them together.

"In our image" and "after our likeness" are more or less synonymous, using the Hebrew terms *tselem* and *demuth*, respectively. The passage makes no reference to nuanced differences between these terms, but pairs them to magnify the greatness of this particular creative act.[7] The writer evidently expects readers to understand these concepts without definition. It is worth reminding ourselves that "images" were common in the ancient world. Images were simply statues or pictures, intended to represent someone, often a god or a king. In the second commandment, God forbids worship of images. Yet there is an image of the true God—ourselves.[8]

The Hebrew terms themselves refer to a similarity[9] between God and man, but the nature of that similarity must be obtained from other passages. So if we are to speak of this image as more than an isolated title, our theological task is to determine the most theologically significant similarities between God and man, similarities that lift man above the other creatures. Those similarities will explain the use of "image" in this passage by showing that man's relationship to the rest of creation is analogous to God's relationship to the whole creation. But of course, man's relationship to the creation cannot be exactly the same as God's, because man himself is only a creature. The analogy between God and ourselves will always have disanalogy with it. So we are looking for qualities in man that constitute finite replicas of God's infinite qualities.

In Genesis 1:26, what immediately follows the references to image and likeness is God's appointment to man to "have dominion over" the rest of creation. This is also God's first command to men (v. 28) after he blesses them. This is surely an important datum for us to consider in interpreting the image language.

In this book, I have discussed the doctrine of God (part 3) as an exposition of God's lordship. His nature and attributes are what qualify him to be Lord of everything he makes, and they are, indeed, what his lordship looks like from the vantage point of his covenant servants. What Genesis 1:26–28 says is that God

---

7. Although theologians have sometimes drawn distinctions between "image" and "likeness," I believe that the terms both refer to the same thing: our resemblance to God. See *MCW*, 2:34, where Murray argues that the second term is "explanatory or definitive rather than supplementary" to the first.

8. In *DCL*, 460–61, I argue that the second commandment upholds the dignity of man as well as God, by making man God's only true image.

9. A number of writers have said that "image" denotes representation as well as resemblance. In idolatry, the image represents the god it images and the idolater worships it as a representation of his god. I do not disagree with this argument, but I believe that representation is based on resemblance. So resemblance is the main fact about images, and representation is based on that.

has made man like himself to equip him for his task as lord, a lord subordinate to God's ultimate lordship.

So the image of God consists of those qualities that equip man to be lord of the world, under God.[10] What can these qualities be, but analogies of God's own lordship attributes? As we consider these, I will also draw parallels between the three lordship attributes and the three anointed offices of Scripture: king, prophet, and priest. God, particularly Christ the Anointed One, is the original bearer of these offices. Man bears analogous offices in relation to the lower creation, and as redemptive history progresses, God appoints some individuals to be kings, prophets, and priests over his people. See fig. 34.1.

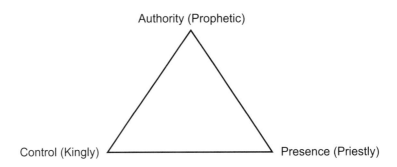

Fig. 34.1. Human Lordship and Offices

Control (Kingly Office)

In Genesis 1:26, the image of God equips man to exercise great power: "And let them have dominion over the fish of the sea and over the birds of the heavens and over the livestock and over all the earth and over every creeping thing that creeps on the earth." In verse 28, God says that to have dominion over the earth, man will have to "subdue" it (*kabash*, "make subservient"). This dominion extends to everything God made in the fourth through sixth days of creation. In verses 29–30, God gives his work of the third day, the plant kingdom, to be food for man. It is interesting that God does not place the work of the first day (light and darkness) and that of the second day (heaven and the waters) under man's power. In Scripture, "light" is closely connected with God himself. He *is* light according to 1 John 1:5, and in him is no darkness at all. He alone is the One who brings light to the world—not only physical light, but also light as a figure of salvation:

> For God, who said, "Let light shine out of darkness," has shone in our hearts to give the light of the knowledge of the glory of God in the face of Jesus Christ. (2 Cor. 4:6; cf. Eph. 5:8, 13–14; 1 Thess. 5:5; 1 Peter 2:9; Rev. 21:23–24; 22:5)

10. In part 2, I discussed three perspectival ways of understanding the Bible's story: God's covenants, his kingdom, and his family. These suggest that man's vassal lordship is at the same time a vassal kingship and a vassal fatherhood. In my discussion I will focus on man's lordship. But of course, that discussion can be broadened to fit the other two models, and later in this chapter I will attempt to do that.

As a metaphor for salvation, light comes from God alone and therefore serves as an image of the gracious character of redemption.

As for the work of the second day, God also keeps that to himself. Heaven is his own dwelling place, the location of his archetypal tabernacle, "the true tent that the Lord set up, not man" (Heb. 8:2). And God also maintains control of the waters of the second day, both those under and those above the expanse of heaven (Gen. 1:7). When he brings judgment on the ancient human world, Scripture says, "the fountains of the great deep burst forth, and the windows of the heavens were opened" (7:11). Here God removes the separations between waters that he erected on the second day of creation. Human beings have no power to deter the waters or the judgment. As with the light, God is sovereign in his disposition of the waters. After the judgment of Genesis 7, God still retains the power of sending or withholding rain. In an agricultural society, rain is a continually pressing need. Man cannot produce it for himself. He must keep coming to God for it (1 Kings 8:35–36). When God sends rain, it is a blessing, a mercy (Lev. 26:4; Deut. 11:11; 28:12; 2 Sam. 23:4; Ps. 147:8). When God withholds it, it is a judgment (Deut. 11:17; 28:24; 1 Kings 17:1ff.).

So man's dominion does not extend to the work of God's first two creative days. But the fact that he subdues and rules the creations of the last four is immensely significant. Man is not omnipotent as God is (chapter 16), but he is able to accomplish amazing things by his physical strength, intellectual acuity, and linguistic ability (see next section), abilities that no animal can match.

Man's responsibility to fill and subdue the earth is sometimes called the *cultural mandate*.[11] That language brings out the fact that man's task is one of turning the earth into a habitat for man, one suited to the needs and purposes of man. This task involves not only the cultivation of crops for food, but also the arts, sciences, and literature, by which human life becomes more than mere subsistence. And at the deepest level, man's labor has the goal of bringing praise and glory[12] to God. So he is to structure his life and culture according to God's standards.

Theologians have asked whether the image of God pertains to man's body or only to his soul. I will discuss the soul-body distinction at a later point. But it should already be evident that the image of God does pertain to the body. Man's physical strength is a major aspect of his power to subdue the earth and take dominion of it. Some have objected that the human body cannot be God's image because God is incorporeal. But God's incorporeality does not mean that he can never take physical form, only

11. For an extended discussion of this mandate and a comparison between it and the Great Commission of Matthew 28:18–20, see *DCL*, 307–11, and chapter 47 of the present volume. I disagree with the theory of Meredith Kline and others that the cultural mandate is canceled after the fall. Kline, *Kingdom Prologue* (Eugene, OR: Wipf and Stock, 2006), 156. I argue the point in my *The Escondido Theology* (Lakeland, FL: Whitefield Media, 2011), 215–18.

12. "Image" and "glory" are closely related, as in 1 Corinthians 11:7: "For a man ought not to cover his head [in praying or prophesying], since he is the image and glory of God, but woman is the glory of man." God's glory (chapter 18) is the visible light shining from his presence. Human glory reflects that, images it. Our good works broadcast that glory to others (Matt. 5:16). So WSC 1 says that man's chief end is "to glorify God, and to enjoy him forever." Cf. 1 Cor. 10:31: "whatever you do, do all to the glory of God." See also *DCL*, chap. 17.

that he is sovereign in his choice of whether or not to take a physical form; and if he chooses to take one, he is sovereign in choosing the form he takes (chapter 18).[13] He is superphysical—more than physical, not less. Further, whether or not he chooses to take a physical form, he is able to do everything that we can do with our bodies, and far more. Psalm 94:9 asks, "He who planted the ear, does he not hear? He who formed the eye, does he not see?" Human beings hear with their physical ears and see with physical eyes. God, however, is master of the processes of hearing and seeing. He does without physical organs what we do with them, and far more.

So man serves as a king over God's creation. But he is a king under God, responsible to worship and obey God, the King of kings.

Authority (Prophetic Office)

I mentioned above that man is to build his culture according to God's standards. Thus, he brings God's word, God's language, to his fellow men and to the world.

In chapter 23, I argued that God's language, his word, is one with himself, an attribute essential to his nature. God is a *speaking* God. In chapter 33, I referred to the work of the angels, bringing God's word to human beings, and to the devils as those who distort and pervert God's speech. Language is also fundamental to human nature in the image of God. In Genesis 1, man's first experience is linguistic: hearing God's words (Gen. 1:28–31). In Genesis 2:18–20, when God first gives Adam a specific task under the general mandate to take dominion of the earth, he gives him a linguistic task: that of naming the animals. This task is not simply attaching a sound to an object. It is rather the scientific task of understanding the nature of each animal, for the overall purpose is to determine whether any of these can be Adam's "helper" (2:18). The "names" that Adam gave the animals, therefore, were a system of sounds declaring the nature of each creature.[14] Adam's research determines that there is no helper for him in the animal kingdom, so God makes him a partner by special creation (2:21–25).

13. Meredith G. Kline, in *Images of the Spirit* (Grand Rapids: Baker, 1980), argues that "image" is primarily a real physical resemblance. Addressing the question how man can have a physical resemblance to God, Kline argues that the "Spirit of God" who hovered over the waters in Genesis 1:2 was actually a theophany, the divine glory-cloud that I mentioned in chapter 18. I think myself that the Spirit mentioned in verse 2 is too distant to be the referent of "image" in 1:26–28. But it would not be unscriptural to say that our bodies bear a physical resemblance to God's theophany, because of course they bear resemblance to the incarnate Christ. The human form is an accurate revelation of God, as accurate a picture as God can give us of himself using finite materials. For the perfect image of God, Christ, is a man.

I mention also that although Kline takes a different approach from mine in a number of ways, his conception of the aspects of the image is similar to mine. On verse 27, he distinguishes the "formal-physical" aspect, the "official-functional" aspect, and the "ethical dimension." I would distinguish these as representing man's control, authority, and presence, respectively, though Kline's correlations with the anointed offices are a bit different from mine. I correlate authority with the prophetic office, while Kline correlates it with the kingly. But the nature of perspectives is such that they interpenetrate. I'm sure Kline would agree that a true king must have both physical power and legitimate authority, and the same is true of priests and prophets. The distinctions that both Kline and I make are distinctions of emphasis.

14. Typically, names in Scripture are not mere sounds, selected for their attractiveness. Instead, a name is a meaningful sound, intended to say something about the person or object receiving it. *Abram*, for example,

Emphasizing further the centrality of language in human life, James 3:1–12, building on many of the proverbs, tells us that if a man can control his tongue, he can control his whole body. In Genesis 11:1–9, God judges the builders of the Tower of Babel by confusing their language. He says:

> Behold, they are one people, and they have all one language, and this is only the beginning of what they will do. And nothing that they propose to do will now be impossible for them. (Gen. 11:6)

Language is such a powerful capacity that a common language allows sin to run rampant. God determines that it must be checked. So sins of the tongue take prominence in biblical lists of sins, such as Romans 3:10–18. Scripture abounds in admonitions to speak for edification (Eph. 4:29), rather than speaking lies, blasphemies, and foolishness (1 Cor. 14:3, 12, 17, 26). Jesus says, "I tell you, on the day of judgment people will give account for every careless word they speak, for by your words you will be justified, and by your words you will be condemned" (Matt. 12:36–37). Redemption is often presented as a cleansing of the lips (Isa. 6:5–7) or of language (Ps. 12; Zeph. 3:9–13). Pentecost partially reverses the curse of Babel, so that the message of grace can be heard in the languages of all people (Acts 2).

So Adam's cultural task can be seen from a linguistic perspective: the work of developing a language analogous to the word of God himself, building throughout the world a culture in conformity with it. This is the root of the concept of prophecy that we looked at in chapter 24. As God first spoke words to him, Adam is to speak those and similar words to his family and to impose upon the earth cultural institutions that observe God's standards and bring glory to him. To the extent he does that, he speaks with God's authority.

What divine standards or norms were known to Adam before the fall? Of course, God told him to name the animals and to abstain from the forbidden fruit, but these commands were for a specific time and place. God also gave Adam and Eve broader ordinances, which rule human beings in all ages and places. Theologians have often called these *creation ordinances*: laws and institutions given to Adam and Eve before the fall, analogous to the laws of later covenants. John Murray lists among them "the procreation of offspring, the replenishing of the earth, subduing of the same, dominion over the creatures, labour, the weekly Sabbath, and marriage."[15] I have advocated two additions to this list: worship and respect for human life,[16] making the point also that

> the creation ordinances, like other biblical laws, have a threefold, indeed a triperspectival focus: on God (worship, Sabbath), on the natural world (replenishing, subduing, and dominating the earth), and on man himself (marriage, procreation, labor).[17]

---

means "high father," and his later name, *Abraham*, means "father of a multitude," reflecting God's covenant promise to him (Gen. 17:4–8).

15. John Murray, *Principles of Conduct* (Grand Rapids: Eerdmans, 1957), 27.

16. *DCL*, 202–3.

17. Ibid., 203.

According to the cultural mandate, man is to develop a culture through the whole earth that observes these creation ordinances, teaching them through his gift of speech, and through a life consistent with those words. Such speech is a necessary element of the "image of God." It makes man to be like God in an important way, and it lifts man above the other creatures so that he may have dominion over them. His physical might gives him de facto rule over the world, but it is the divine speech that makes his rule de jure. Power is might and authority right. By setting forth and observing God's norms, man shows himself to be the legitimate ruler of the world. His prophetic office and work legitimize his kingly office and work.

Presence (Priestly Office)

But Adam is not to be an absentee king. He is not only to subdue the earth and have dominion over it, but also to "be fruitful and multiply and fill the earth" (Gen. 1:28; cf. 9:1). As God transcends the world by his control and authority, but becomes immanent in the world by his covenant presence, so Adam, God's vassal king and prophet, is to fill the world over which he rules. Since he is not omnipresent as God is, he can fill it only by marrying and having children. So the cultural mandate is a historical, gradual process in which man progressively blesses every part of the earth with his presence.

Since he constructs his culture according to God's words, he brings with him God's goodness. So when we read of God's restoring his image to fallen men in Christ, Scripture describes the image in ethical terms:

> But that is not the way you learned Christ!—assuming that you have heard about him and were taught in him, as the truth is in Jesus, to put off your old self, which belongs to your former manner of life and is corrupt through deceitful desires, and to be renewed in the spirit of your minds, and to put on the new self, created after the likeness of God in true righteousness and holiness. (Eph. 4:20–24)

> Do not lie to one another, seeing that you have put off the old self with its practices and have put on the new self, which is being renewed in knowledge after the image of its creator. (Col. 3:9–10)

Man blesses every place to which he comes, appreciating and enhancing the good. To an extent, that means, as I said, man's making the world a fit habitation for himself. But that does not mean exploiting the earth in a selfish way. God has made the world for his glory, but the glory of God is also what is best for the world itself. So man seeks to humanize his environment, but not in a way that trashes the beauty and integrity of the creation. Being made of dust, man has an affinity with the creation. Since he lives by the air, water, and fruit of the earth, he has an interest in rotating crops, resting the land, maintaining clean air and water.

And Adam is to do all of this to the glory of God, fulfilling God's own purpose in creating the world. He is to pray and worship God in every place, consecrating his labors and seeking God's continued blessing. So God called upon Adam not only to work, but also to rest in celebration of his own divine rest (Gen. 2:2–3; Ex. 20:11).

Such is Adam's priestly work. The ministry of a priest is to pray for others and lead them in worship, and thereby to bring God's blessing upon the people he serves. So Adam is a priest to his people, in whatever territory they are led to settle. His blessing upon them will also be a blessing upon the earth.

After the fall, to be sure, the priest must also make sacrifice for the sins of the people. But he is still the one through whom God draws near to his people. Jesus Christ, God's Great High Priest, is the One who comes nearest, taking human nature upon himself, living our life, dying the death we deserve (Heb. 2:10–18; 7:1–10:18).

Man as God's Son

Another pervasive biblical model of man's relationship to God is that of sonship. In Luke's genealogy, Adam is "the son of God" (Luke 3:38). Scripture sometimes describes angels (Job 1:6; 2:1; 38:7; Dan. 3:25[18]) and human kings (Gen. 6:2, 4)[19] as sons of God. Israel is God's son (Deut. 1:31; 8:5; Hos. 1:10). Jesus is the eternal Son, the Son who succeeds to his Father's throne (Matt. 14:33; 16:16; 27:54; and often elsewhere—see chapter 21). In and through Christ, believers are redeemed from sin to be sons of God (Rom. 8:14, 16, 19; Gal. 4:1–6; Phil. 2:15; Heb. 12:7; 1 John 3:1–2).

The content of sonship is very similar to that of image. The son resembles his father as the image resembles the thing it reflects. In the Hebrew idiom, to say that someone is "son of" something is to say that it has the same characteristics. In Mark 3:17, Jesus named his disciples James and John "Sons of Thunder," indicating perhaps their loud and violent spirit. *Barnabas* (Acts 4:36) means "son of encouragement," which suggests a nurturing, comforting character. So a son of God is someone who resembles God, who is like God. Of course, there are many ways of being like God. The similarity of angels to God,[20] though genuine, is not the same as the resemblance of human kings to him, or Israel, or NT saints, or Jesus.

We also saw that man's status as the image of God gives to him an authority subordinate to God. Sonship, too, entails royal qualities. Like kings, the sons of God have power, authority, and presence within their domains. So God describes the church as "a chosen race, a royal priesthood, a holy nation, a people for his own possession" (1 Peter 2:9, reflecting language used of Israel in Exodus 19:6).

In chapters 4–6, I summarized the biblical story as a story of God's covenants (chapter 4), the kingdom of God (5), and the family of God (6). We have seen through the figures of image and son that God made man to be his covenant servant, his vassal

18. Or is this being a preincarnate manifestation of God's eternal Son, Jesus?
19. The phrase in this passage is often thought to denote angels, but I think Meredith Kline's view that the phrase refers to human kings is more likely. See his "Divine Kingship and Genesis 6:1–4," *WTJ* 24, 2 (1962): 187–204.
20. Scripture does not describe angels as the image of God, indicating some difference between the metaphor of image and that of sonship.

king, and sons within his family. So the three biblical stories come together as the story of God's dealings with man, the highest of his creatures.

Male and Female[21]

It is certainly significant that right after Scripture describes God as creating man in his image, it adds: "male and female he created them" (Gen. 1:27). I don't agree with Karl Barth's view that our sexual differentiation is the meaning of "image,"[22] but certainly we should take some trouble to understand how sexual differentiation and image are related to each other.

In the previous section, I described the image under three perspectives, as control, authority, and presence, reflecting the lordship attributes of God. In none of these respects is there any difference between men and women. Both sexes image God's control, for he charges men and women together to have dominion over the earth (Gen. 1:28). Thus, they are both vassal kings under God, bearing his authority. They are both subject to God's authoritative ordinances, both charged with building culture according to those ordinances. And filling the earth with children, bringing the presence of human beings throughout the world, is obviously a joint responsibility of the sexes.

In the fall, as we will see in more detail later (chapter 36), both the man and the woman disobey God, and God brings curses, mingled with blessing, upon them equally (Gen. 3:14–19). It is significant that the curse applies somewhat differently to the man and the woman. The woman will have pain in childbearing; the man will have pain and toil as he works the ground. But both are cursed and equally fallen. Although Scripture mentions that the woman was first deceived (1 Tim. 2:14), it never suggests that women are more or less sinful than men. Christ's redemption, therefore, applies equally to both. Scripture never suggests that women are more or less sanctified than men by the grace of Christ.

Positively, Scripture teaches:

Both Men and Women Are Made in God's Image

Genesis 1:27 makes this point quite explicitly, and 2:20 NIV ("suitable helper") and 2:23 ("bone of my bones and flesh of my flesh") underscore the man and woman's unity of nature in contrast (2:19–20) to the relationship between man and animals. See also 5:1–2. James Hurley points out that "man" in 1:26 and 27 is a collective noun (*adam* = "mankind"). The plural membership is indicated by the phrase "male and female" in verse 27, and then to both male and female is given the task appropriate to

---

21. Portions of this section are taken from my article "Men and Women in the Image of God," in *Recovering Biblical Manhood and Womanhood*, ed. John Piper and Wayne Grudem (Wheaton, IL: Crossway, 1991), 225–32. Used by permission of Crossway Books, a ministry of Good News Publishers, Wheaton, Illinois 60187, http://www.crossway.com. In *DCL*, chap. 33, I abridged the article and supplemented it with discussions of the roles of men and women in the family, church, and workplace.

22. I argue against this view in the article "Men and Women" cited above.

those created in the image of God (v. 28).[23] This is the uniform teaching of Scripture. Re-creation in the image of Christ applies equally to all believers without distinction (Col. 3:9–11); in fact, that renewal, that sonship (Gal. 3:26), is given to believers so indiscriminately that in this respect "there is no male and female" (v. 28).

Men and Women Are Equally in the Image of God

Nothing in Genesis would lead anyone to suppose otherwise. But some have come to another conclusion based on Paul's statement in 1 Corinthians 11:7, "A man ought not to cover his head, since he is the image and glory of God, but woman is the glory of man." Why does Paul omit speaking of woman as "image of God," after he has applied that title to man? One might even suppose that Paul is here denying that woman is the image of God and is attributing to her a lesser image, that of man.

I agree with C. K. Barrett that "in this context Paul values the term image only as leading to the term glory."[24] The reference to "image" is incidental to Paul's purpose, and therefore not applied to woman; but it notifies his readers of the OT basis for saying that man is the *glory* of God, "glory" and "image" being roughly, but not entirely, synonymous. Paul's emphasis is on "glory," which focuses on the honor that one person brings to another. Man, he says, was made to honor God. Of course, woman was also made to honor God; but in addition, she is made for a second purpose, namely, to honor man. God made her specifically to be a helper for Adam (Gen. 2:18, 20; cf. Prov. 12:4; Eph. 5:25–29).[25] Man honors and glorifies God by uncovering his head, for covering the head connoted subservience to another creature.[26] Such subservience to men is especially inappropriate for a male prophet, whose whole function is to speak for God. Woman, however, must not only honor God, but also honor man. Indeed, she honors God when she honors the specific task of "helper" for which God made her. Unlike the man, then, she honors God best by displaying her subordination to her fellow creature.

So Paul's point in 1 Corinthians 11:7, then, is not that woman does not image God; it is rather that in addition to imaging God, she is also made to honor man, and that her appearance must be appropriate to that latter function. Nor is there any need to speak of her imaging God in some lesser sense than does man.

---

23. James B. Hurley, *Man and Woman in Biblical Perspective* (Leicester: Inter-Varsity Press, 1981), 172. He points out further that Genesis 1 is concerned about the creation of various types of reality, not with hierarchical differentiations within those types. Therefore, Genesis 1:27 grants the image to the whole human race, not to man as distinguished from woman.

24. C. K. Barrett, *A Commentary on the First Epistle of Paul to the Corinthians* (New York: Harper and Row, 1968), 252.

25. I agree with those who say that "helper" does not in itself connote any subordination. God is himself the helper of Israel (Ps. 30:10; etc.). It is, however, significant that Eve was made after Adam, for the specific purpose of helping him. That cannot be said of God's relationship to Israel. That fact, I believe, lies behind Paul's statements in 1 Corinthians 11:8–9 and 1 Timothy 2:13.

26. Leon Morris, *The First Epistle of Paul to the Corinthians* (Grand Rapids: Eerdmans, 1958), on 11:4. Also James B. Hurley, "Did Paul Require Veils or the Silence of Women?" *WTJ* 35, 2 (Winter 1973): 205.

Does her subordination itself detract from her capacity to image God? That is an important question for us to ask at this point. But the answer must surely be negative. Men, too, are always placed in relations of subordination to other people (Ex. 20:12; Rom. 13:1; Heb. 13:17),[27] but that fact does not prejudice their being the image of God.

Jesus himself became subordinate to his Father, even subordinate to human authority structures, in order to redeem us. Human authority, therefore, imaging Jesus, is to be a servant-authority (Matt. 20:20–28). A willingness to subordinate oneself to others for God's sake is, indeed, itself a component of the image, not a compromise of it.[28] Even submission to *unjust* authority shows a special likeness to Christ (1 Peter 2:12, 19–25; 3:14–18).[29] It is often by submitting to others that we best display the ethical components of the divine image. How better to demonstrate God's love, his long-suffering, his gentleness, his self-control, than by submitting to others?

Sexual Differentiation Itself Images God

As indicated earlier, I don't agree with Karl Barth that sexual differentiation *is* the image of God. But I do believe that our sexual qualities, like all other human qualities, image God. The point is not that God is male, female, or both. To say that our eyes image God, remember, is not to say that God has eyes; it is rather to say that our eyes picture something divine. Similarly, our sexuality pictures God's attributes and capacities:

1. Human sexuality mirrors God's creativity. By sexual capacities, we bring forth sons and daughters; God does the same by other means (John 1:12; Rom. 8:14ff.; Gal. 4:4ff.; Heb. 2:10; 1 John 3:1f.).

2. Love between husband and wife pictures God's love for his people (Ezek. 16; Hos. 1–3; Eph. 5:25–33), which begins with a love within the Trinity itself (John 17:26).

3. The covenant relationship between husband and wife (Prov. 2:17; Mal. 2:14) pictures the covenant relation between God and man.

4. Scripture describes God both in male and in female terms, though the overwhelming preponderance of imagery is male. The reason, I think, is basically that Scripture wants us to think of God as Lord, and lordship, in Scripture, always con-

---

27. Even kings are usually answerable to someone, and even "absolute" monarchs get toppled if they do not succeed in pleasing other powerful members of society.

28. Underscoring this point: the head-covering of the woman, by which she honors male authority, also establishes her as an honorable woman. Thus Paul is able to speak of that head-covering as a sign of (her own!) authority (1 Cor. 11:10). That head-covering gives her the moral authority to prophesy in God's name. See Morris, *First Corinthians*, on v. 10.

29. Noel Weeks chides the feminist movement for confusing worth with ruling power. See his *The Sufficiency of Scripture* (Edinburgh: Banner of Truth, 1988), 137. The reader might also usefully peruse Royce Gruenler's *The Trinity in the Gospel of John* (Grand Rapids: Baker, 1986), in which he explores the relations of "mutual deference" within the Trinity. I don't agree with some of his points, but there is much stimulus here. Cf. *DG*, 694–96.

notes authority.[30] Since in the biblical view women are subject to male authority in the home and the church, as we will see, there is some awkwardness in speaking of God in female terms. Our need today, in my opinion, is for a far greater appreciation of the lordship of God and of Christ. Therefore, in my view, the movement to use unisex or female language in referring to God is fundamentally wrongheaded from a biblical perspective.

5. Nevertheless, the very submission of the woman also images God. God the Lord is not too proud to be our "helper." Christ the Lord is not unwilling to be a servant. Godly women stand as models, often as rebukes, to all who would be leaders (Matt. 20:20–28).[31]

Men and Women Equally Represent God

I argued earlier that the primary meaning of *image* is resemblance rather than representation. But because of images' resemblance, they often do represent the things or persons they resemble. The distinction is between structure and function, between nature and task.

King Nebuchadnezzar set up an image of himself to represent him. When people worshiped the image, they were thereby expressing loyalty to the king (Dan. 3:1–6). Images were understood this way in the ancient world. Clearly, a similar notion is expressed in Genesis 1:28, for there God gives Adam the task of filling and subduing the earth.

These tasks are similar to what God himself does in the world. God wants to be known as Lord, which I have expounded in terms of control, authority, and presence. In Genesis 1:28, God gives to Adam a "dominion," a kind of lordship subordinate to God's own. Man (generic!) is the vassal king of the universe. Subduing the earth is to extend human control over the world. It also involves authority: God gives Adam the right to name the animals, which is in the ancient world an exercise of authority (Gen. 2:19–20; cf. 2:23; 3:20). Mankind is also to "fill" the earth, that is, to make his presence felt everywhere.

That this dominion mandate continues after the fall is clear from Genesis 9:1–3. Yet sin greatly hinders the accomplishment of God's purpose in the mandate, which was to fill the earth with, and put it under the control of, people who would glorify him. Thus, the NT puts emphasis on the Great Commission (Matt. 28:18–20), also a command about filling and subduing, but in this case by the saving gospel of Jesus Christ. Through the sovereign authority of Jesus (v. 18), the people of God are to extend their control, authority, and presence throughout the earth. We are

---

30. Scripture also, of course, emphasizes God's masculinity over against the polytheism and degradation of pagan goddess-worship. For more considerations on this question, see *DG*, 378–86.

31. For this reason I disagree with Hurley's statement that according to 1 Corinthians 11:7, "the woman is not called to image God or Christ *in the relation which she sustains to her husband*." *Man and Woman*, 173 (emphasis his). The imaging is not precise, but as we have seen, imaging never is. I think there are better ways to handle the problem of 1 Corinthians 11:7; see my earlier discussion.

God's "ambassadors, as though God were making his appeal through us" (2 Cor. 5:20 NIV; cf. Phil. 2:14–15).[32]

Hence, we have the biblical doctrines of sonship, adoption, and inheritance (John 1:12; Rom. 8:14–17; Gal. 3:26–29; Heb. 2:10; 1 John 3:1–3). In these respects, man and woman share equally. Scripture makes no sexual distinction. Indeed, Galatians 3:26 ("in Christ Jesus you are all sons of God, through faith") precedes by two verses the famous "there is no male and female." And as we have seen, "male and female" are equally given the original dominion mandate (Gen. 1:27–28).

Does this fact conflict with the authority of men over women in the home and in the church? I think not. Authority and subordination are not, in the abstract, inconsistent with each other. Someone may have authority over one sphere but not over another; or he may be an authority in one respect, subordinate in another. Men individually rule in some areas, but must be subject to those in authority over them. Jesus himself is both Lord and servant.

So human authority itself is always a servant-authority, an authority with responsibility for those under authority (as in Matt. 20:25–28; John 13:12–17; Eph. 5:22–6:9). So when Scripture speaks of the primacy of man over woman, it often coordinates that teaching with reflections on the mutual dependence of the sexes (as in 1 Cor. 7:3; 11:11–12).

Women certainly share in the authority given to Adam. Together with men, they are made to rule the earth (Gen. 1:27–28; 1 Cor. 3:21).

Individually, they are given authority in various spheres: mothers over children (Ex. 20:12), older women training the younger (Titus 2:4). In some cases, women manage a family business (Prov. 31:10–31). Women exercise authority over everyone as prophets of God (Judg. 4:4; Acts 2:17; 21:9; 1 Cor. 11:5, 10 ["symbol of authority"]). They are also under human authority, to be sure; but so are men.

Citing Matthew 8:9, Stephen B. Clark well observes that one's own authority, far from conflicting with submission to higher authority, often finds its source in such submission.[33] The prophets had authority because they stood under God's authoritative word. Kings, priests, and parents also have authority because God has ordained it. The apostles had authority because of their obedience to Jesus' commission. Recall my earlier note to the effect that the head-covering of the woman (1 Cor. 11:10), a sign of submission, is also a sign of her own authority as a prophet.

Summary

Women and men equally image God, even in their sexual differences, even in their differences with regard to authority and submission. The reason is that the image of God embraces everything that is human. Both men and women, therefore, resemble God and are called to represent him throughout the creation, exercising control,

---

32. For a fuller account of these mandates, see chapter 47.
33. Stephen B. Clark, *Man and Woman in Christ* (Ann Arbor: Servant Books, 1980), 171.

authority, and presence in his name. This doctrine is not at all inconsistent with the subordination of women to men in the home and in the church. All human beings are under authority, both divine and human. Their submission to authority, as well as their authority itself, images God.

Body, Soul, and Spirit

Traditionally, theologians have discussed the relation between man's body, soul, and spirit. "Dichotomists" have claimed that man consists of body and soul, "trichotomists" that he consists of body, soul, and spirit.

Scripture does not, however, address such questions, nor does it ever reflect specifically on the nature of spirit, soul, or body or the relations between them. Further, these are only three of the many terms that Scripture uses to refer to aspects of human nature. Vern Poythress says:

> We find words like *sarx* ("flesh"), *soma* ("body"), *psyche* ("soul"), *pneuma* ("spirit"), *nous* ("mind"), *kardia* ("heart"), *zoe* ("life"), *bios* ("life"), *suneidesis* ("conscience"), *sunesis* ("understanding"), *dianoia* ("understanding"), *splanchna* ("bowels"), *chros* ("skin"), not to mention verbs describing various bodily and mental actions and states.[34]

He adds:

> I have glossed each Greek word with a corresponding English word. But the correspondences are only approximate. A close examination shows that no one English word matches exactly the full range of meaning and connotative associations of a single Greek word. When we bring in classical Hebrew of the Old Testament, we deal with still a third language whose vocabulary has still different properties, matching neither Greek nor English exactly.[35]

So one might ask why theologians have been so preoccupied with three of these categories, spirit, soul, and body, and why they have tried to define them precisely granted the imprecise correlations between the English terms and those of the original languages.

A large part of the reason has been concerns about the intermediate state (what happens to us between our death and the final resurrection at Christ's return). Scripture teaches that when a person dies, though he lies in the grave, either he is also experiencing blessing in fellowship "with Christ" (Phil. 1:23) or he is "in torment" (Luke 16:23). Trying to understand this dual existence, many theologians have said that it is the "body" that lies in the grave, but the "soul" or "spirit" that has gone to heaven or hell. In other words, each of us consists of a material part and an immaterial part; and at death, the material part goes to the earth, but the immaterial part goes to the afterlife.

---

34. Vern S. Poythress, "Body and Soul: The Metaphysical Composition of the Human Individual" (unpublished notes), 2.

35. Ibid., 2–3.

This traditional view correlates with some biblical data, but more should be said. These expressions should be traced back to Genesis 2:7:

> Then the LORD God formed the man of dust from the ground and breathed into his nostrils the breath of life, and the man became a living creature.

Now, the "dust" describes the original state of our physical nature, our original "body." God's "breath" (*neshamah*) describes the process by which God turns the material being into a "living creature" (*nephesh hayyah*). *Nephesh* is often translated "soul," but in Genesis 2:7 *nephesh* is not a component of man, but the whole person, the man himself constituted by the divine inbreathing. God's inbreathing itself may be the root of the idea of a "spirit" in man, but (1) the usual word for *spirit* in Hebrew is *ruach*, not found in Genesis 2:7, and (2) the breath of Genesis 2:7 is divine breath, not human. The passage makes no mention of a human spirit corresponding to the divine inbreathing. So Genesis 2:7 does not list any elements of the human constitution. It merely says that God's creative act turned dust into a living person.

Still, given the description of man's creation in Genesis 2:7, it is not surprising that later texts should refer to man's body, his soul (the *life* of the body), and his spirit (focusing on the divine origin of his animate life). And it is not surprising that in texts that speak of human death, the body is what is placed in the grave, and soul and spirit refer to man's ongoing life:[36]

> And the dust returns to the earth as it was, and the spirit returns to God who gave it. (Eccl. 12:7)

> But you have come to Mount Zion and to the city of the living God, the heavenly Jerusalem, and to innumerable angels in festal gathering, and to the assembly of the firstborn who are enrolled in heaven, and to God, the judge of all, and to the spirits of the righteous made perfect. (Heb. 12:22–23)

> For as the body apart from the spirit is dead, so also faith apart from works is dead. (James 2:26)

> When he opened the fifth seal, I saw under the altar the souls of those who had been slain for the word of God and for the witness they had borne. (Rev. 6:9; cf. 20:4)

These references may be correlated with passages such as Matthew 27:50 and John 19:30 that refer to dying as "yielding" or "giving up" one's spirit. Note also Matthew 10:28:

> And do not fear those who kill the body but cannot kill the soul. Rather fear him who can destroy both soul and body in hell.

---

36. But in Luke 24:39, the risen Jesus emphasizes to his disciples that he is not *merely* a spirit, as if he were a bodiless ghost. Rather, his resurrection is physical, the raising of his body as well as his spirit: "For a spirit does not have flesh and bones as you see that I have."

The point here is not that a murderer can destroy one component of a person's being, but not another part. Rather: a human murderer can put someone's body in the grave, but cannot destroy him as a living person (a soul). But it is possible for someone to "lay down" or "save" his life/soul. Cf. Matt. 16:25; 20:28; Mark 3:4; Luke 6:9; John 10:11–15; 12:25; Acts 15:26; 1 John 3:16.

But there are also passages in Scripture that refer to body, soul, and spirit, as continuing aspects of our earthly existence. For example, in Matthew 26:41, Jesus tells his disciples:

> Watch and pray that you may not enter into temptation. The spirit indeed is willing, but the flesh is weak.

"Flesh" here is the body, undergoing weariness and moral weakness, susceptible to temptation. "Spirit" is our inclination, by grace, to obey God, no matter how weary and weak we may be. Elsewhere, "body," "soul," and "spirit" are brought together to comprehensively describe a person's moral or spiritual character:

> Since we have these promises, beloved, let us cleanse ourselves from every defilement of body and spirit, bringing holiness to completion in the fear of God. (2 Cor. 7:1)

> Now may the God of peace himself sanctify you completely, and may your whole spirit and soul and body be kept blameless at the coming of our Lord Jesus Christ. (1 Thess. 5:23; cf. 1 Cor. 7:34)

The idea here is not that these terms designate separate entities within us, so that, for example, the soul might be morally perfect while the spirit is still wicked, or that after we have perfected the soul we might then work on the body. Rather, in these passages Paul piles up terms to describe the character of the whole person.

So spirit, soul, and body should not be understood as metaphysical components of man, as distinct entities within us, battling for supremacy. Rather, each refers to the whole person from a particular perspective. What the body does is not distinct from, let alone in conflict with, what the soul and spirit do. When the disciples disobeyed Jesus and fell asleep as Jesus prayed in Gethsemane (Matt. 26:41, quoted above), it was not that their bodies sinned while their spirits remained pure. Rather, their spirits (i.e., the disciples themselves) sinned by failing to persevere through physical weakness. So each *person* fell asleep, and we can describe that action from physical, psychical, and spiritual perspectives.[37]

---

37. I'm not sure that it would be wise to line these three terms up with the general set of perspectival triangles employed in this book, especially since these are only three of a great number of terms that could be called *aspects of human nature*: consider those we cited in chapter 32, such as *heart, mind, understanding*, and *will*. If pressed, however, I would suggest that *spirit* is normative, referring to the God-ordained direction of human life; *body* is situational, focusing on our interactions with our environment; and *soul* is existential, the self as experiencing himself, the world, and God.

But if spirit, soul, and body are not separate metaphysical components of human nature, then how is it possible to say that a person's spirit or soul is in heaven while his body is in the grave? To say that a person's spirit or soul is in heaven is simply to say that he, the person, is there. And to say that his body is in the grave is to say that he, the person, is there.

It seems paradoxical to put it this way, but in Scripture it is not a material part of the person that lies in the grave; rather, it is the person. It is the person who returns to the dust (Gen. 3:19). While in the grave, Lazarus was Lazarus (John 11:43), Jesus was Jesus (Matt. 28:6). Jesus says, "An hour is coming when all who are in the tombs will hear his voice" (John 5:28). So the bodies in the tombs are people, not former parts of people that have been discarded.[38] It is not, then, a material part of the person who goes to the tomb; it is the person.

Similarly, Scripture never says that immaterial parts of us (our souls or spirits) go to heaven or hell. Rather, *we* go there. The other Lazarus, the one of Luke 16, went to Abraham's side, while the rich man who despised him in life went to Hades (v. 23). The rich man also "was buried" (v. 22). So the rich man had a dual existence. He was really in the tomb, and he was also, really, somewhere else, in torment. Lazarus also had a dual existence: he was in the grave, and he was with Abraham.

How can a person be two places at once? I don't know. But that's the way Scripture presents the matter. Of course, as I indicated earlier, Scripture typically uses *soul* and *spirit* to speak of people in their heavenly location and *body* (as Matt. 27:58–59) to designate the person in the grave. So there is nothing wrong with believers' using the same language. But they should not forget that it is the *person*, not some part of the person, who is in heaven or hell, and it is the *person* who is in the grave.

In God's time, however, this paradox will be removed. When Jesus returns, there will be a physical resurrection of both the righteous and the wicked. Paul says that then "the dead in Christ will rise first" (1 Thess. 4:16). (Notice: he does not say that their bodies will rise, but that *they* will rise.) So God will reconstitute the original unity of the person, the unity between the person in the grave and the person who is with Christ. Similarly, but of course differently, for the wicked.

The notion of *soul* and *body* as metaphysical components of human nature goes back to Greek philosophy. In Plato's thought, the body is material and emotional, the soul intellectual and immaterial. Plato (and especially his successors, such as the Neoplatonists and Gnostics) associated unreason and evil with matter and so presented the body-soul dichotomy as a conflict within each of us. We fare better, he thought, when the immaterial/intellectual prevails over the material. Hence his view of the *primacy of the intellect* that I discussed in chapter 32. Descartes, in the seventeenth century, also saw the soul as purely immaterial and the body as purely material, and this dichotomy led to the *mind-body problem* in early modern thought: how can an immaterial mind affect a material body?[39]

---

38. John Murray said in his class lectures, "The corpse is the person as respects his body." On that principle he urged us to treat the dead body with dignity and care.

39. Descartes's answer: the mind can after all affect the body, but just a tiny bit, in the pineal gland. But to admit that is to admit that the mind has just a little bit of physical power, which is inconsistent with Descartes's

Given this history, it is not surprising that Christian thinkers sometimes confused Plato's and Descartes's ideas with those of Scripture. But the Bible never says that the soul is entirely immaterial or that the body is purely material. Nor does it say that the soul must gain control of the body. Rather, in Scripture *soul* and *body* equally describe the whole person. Both, therefore, are equally fallen, both equally in need of redemption.

Dichotomy and Trichotomy

If we reject the idea that the terms *spirit, soul,* and *body* designate metaphysical components of the human person, then we can avoid taking sides on two theological controversies: dichotomy-trichotomy and creationism-traducianism. Let us consider these in order.

I referred very briefly to dichotomy and trichotomy at the beginning of the previous section. Dichotomists have claimed that man consists of body and soul, trichotomists that he consists of body, soul, and spirit. Trichotomists say that the body is our material existence, soul is our intellect, will, and emotions, and spirit is our God-consciousness. On the trichotomist view, the spirit is dead or dormant in the sinner. Redemption restores it to life and primacy over our other faculties.

There are passages in which such terms as *spirit, soul,* and *body* are set alongside one another (as Rom. 8:10; 1 Cor. 2:14–3:4; 1 Thess. 5:23; Heb. 4:12). But often the biblical writers multiply such terms so as to describe the completeness and fullness of human nature. These passages do not make precise distinctions between these terms—certainly not precise enough to define metaphysical components of human existence. Scripture typically uses "spirit" and "soul" interchangeably.[40]

More seriously, the trichotomist view that sin shuts down the spirit and that redemption reawakens it is without biblical basis. Further, it contradicts the biblical emphasis that the whole person is fallen into sin (e.g., Gen. 6:5) and needs the deliverance of Christ. Redemption is not a rearrangement of human faculties, putting one of them on top of the others. Plato imagined something like this, but it is not a biblical view. Rather, redemption turns the whole person, including all aspects of his personality, from hating God to loving him. Salvation, as Cornelius Van Til used to say, is ethical, not metaphysical.

Creationism and Traducianism

Similarly, we can deal with the traditional controversy over the "origin of the soul" rather quickly, since we have rejected the idea of *soul* as a self-contained metaphysical component of human nature. Wayne Grudem formulates the issue thus:

> *Creationism* is the view that God creates a new soul for each person and sends it to the person's body sometime between conception and birth. *Traducianism,* on the other

---

fundamental principles. This inconsistency of Descartes has become a common philosophical joke. A Cartesian mind that can move the body just a little is like a woman who is "a little bit pregnant."

40. For a very thorough exegetical analysis, see *GST,* 472–82.

hand, holds that the soul as well as the body of a child are inherited from the baby's mother and father at the time of conception.[41]

Traducianism draws especially on the biblical texts that set forth the solidarity of the human race in Adam. Creationism emphasizes God's action in the giving of children (Ps. 127:3), particularly his knitting a baby together in his mother's womb (139:13). Cf. Isa. 42:5; Zech. 12:1; Heb. 12:9.

Now, in Scripture, the sovereignty of God generally works together with secondary causes within the creation. God makes the crops grow, but he usually accomplishes this through the hard work of the farmer. We will explore further the relation between divine sovereignty and human responsibility in the following chapter. But as we bring together the various biblical texts on human conception and gestation, it is clear that both divine sovereignty and human/natural causes are at work. Like nearly every other event in the world (creation itself and redemptive grace are exceptions), human children are both a gift of God and the result of their parents' actions.

As we have seen, the soul is not a separable part of a person. It is rather the person himself, seen from a particular aspect. So there is no particular period in time when the body exists without a soul, nor any point in time when a soul is added to a soulless body. The soul exists from conception, for it is an aspect of the total person, who exists from conception.[42]

The Creation of Adam and Eve

At the beginning of this chapter, I noted the strong emphasis of Genesis 1–2 on the distinctiveness of man over against the rest of creation. Man's creation was the result of a "unique engagement of God's counsel,"[43] and his nature, the image of God, was also unique among the creatures. That nature is correlative to man's distinctive task, to fill and subdue the earth. Underscoring man's uniqueness, too, was "God's procedure in the formation of man."[44]

In Genesis 2:7, we are told:

> Then the LORD God formed the man of dust from the ground and breathed into his nostrils the breath of life, and the man became a living creature.

The "dust" is inanimate matter from the earth. In this respect, man's formation is similar to that of animals, for God also forms them from the ground, according to Genesis 2:19. But unlike the animals, the existence of man does not result from God's commands to the earth itself, as in 1:24 ("Let the earth bring forth living creatures

---

41. Ibid., 484. As with the question of dichotomy and trichotomy, Grudem's exegetical analysis is thorough and helpful.

42. It is therefore wrongheaded to address the question of abortion by trying to figure out when the soul enters the body, as if it would then be permissible to abort the child during its time of soullessness. The child is a person from his conception. See my discussion of abortion in *DCL*, 717–32.

43. *MCW*, 2:4.

44. Ibid., 2:5.

according to their kinds"). Adam becomes a living creature not by the earth's bringing him forth, but by a second distinct act of God: God's breathing into his nostrils the breath of life. No other creature is the result of this inbreathing.

The two events described in Genesis 2:7 are often called *formation* and *impartation*.

Scripture does not describe this inbreathing except by stating its result: by it, man became a living creature.[45] So the picture of this verse is not that God chose some creature already living—an animal—and made him man; rather, he chose dead matter and gave life to it, and by that life the dust became man, with all of man's distinctiveness as God's image. Genesis 2:7, taken literally, describes an event quite incompatible with the theory of evolution, even theistic evolution.

That is even more obviously the case in Genesis 2:21–22, which describes the creation of woman:

> So the Lord God caused a deep sleep to fall upon the man, and while he slept took one of his ribs and closed up its place with flesh. And the rib that the Lord God had taken from the man he made into a woman and brought her to the man.

Again, this creation is a supernatural event, with no parallels in the animal kingdom. Indeed, it was the lack of any suitable helper for Adam in the animal kingdom that made the creation of woman necessary (Gen. 2:18–20).

So the biblical description of the creation of Adam and Eve reinforces the emphasis of Genesis 1–2 on the uniqueness of man as God's image and vassal king.[46]

The Historicity of Adam and Eve

Scripture, in a number of ways, affirms the historicity of Adam and Eve, beyond asserting their existence in Genesis 1–5. Later references to them in Scripture always presuppose that they are historical figures. In 1 Chronicles 1:1, Adam is first in a genealogy leading to King David. In Luke 3:38, he is the last man in a backward genealogy leading from Jesus to God. If Adam were a legendary figure, it would have been inappropriate to include his name in a genealogy, counterproductive to the purpose of such a passage.

In Romans 5:14, Paul says that "death reigned from Adam to Moses, even over those whose sinning was not like the transgression of Adam, who was a type of the one who was to come." This verse refutes the claim of Barth and others that Adam is "everyman," that we all sin as he did. Paul says that *not* everyone sins as Adam did, that there was something unique about Adam's sin.

---

45. The KJV says "living soul." But we saw earlier in this chapter that the word in Genesis 1:27 translated "soul" in the KJV is not a portion of man, but man himself as a living being.

46. Murray mentions some other features of the early chapters of Genesis that corroborate the emphasis on man's uniqueness: (1) the sacredness of human life (Gen. 4:10–15; 9:5–6), in contrast with the killing of animals for clothing and sacrifice (3:21; 4:4); (2) the commands and special probation given to Adam but not to any lesser creature (2:15–17); (3) the NT parallel between Adam, in whom we die, and Christ, in whom we are made alive (1 Cor. 15:45–47). No animal lives or dies on the basis of his covenant relationship to another being.

In the context of this verse, Romans 5:12–21, Paul sets forth at length the unique significance of Adam's sin, which I will explore in chapter 36. Paul's main point is to draw a parallel[47] between the work of Adam, who plunged the race into sin, and Jesus, who redeemed us from the sin of Adam. In 1 Corinthians 15:22 he again mentions Adam as the one through whom we die, parallel to Christ, in whom we live. Both Adam and Christ, as we will see, acted as covenant heads of their people, so that their actions are imputed to their people. If the story of Adam is unbelievable, is not the story of Christ unbelievable for the same reasons? And if the sin of Adam never occurred, what can it mean to say as Paul does that Christ saved us from that particular sin and from its consequences?

In 1 Timothy 2:13–14, Paul gives directions concerning the relationships of men to women in the church, basing these instructions on the relations of Adam and Eve.[48] His argument is not that these relationships should reflect or imitate the relations of Adam and Eve. Such an argument would be compatible with a view that these are fictional characters, as someone might say, "Be courageous, like Frodo." But Paul doesn't tell the church to be *like* Adam and Eve, though he often urges believers to imitate God-given models. Nor does he tell them to be *unlike* Adam and Eve. Rather, he says that the church should impose certain restrictions on women *because* (*gar*) Adam was first formed and Eve was first deceived. The implication is that if the story of Genesis 1–3 is fictional, the reason for Paul's command carries no weight.

Similarly, Jesus, in Matthew 19:4–6, replies to the Pharisees' question about divorce by saying:

> Have you not read that he who created them from the beginning made them male and female, and said, "Therefore a man shall leave his father and his mother and hold fast to his wife, and the two shall become one flesh"? So they are no longer two but one flesh. What therefore God has joined together, let not man separate.

Here, Jesus says that man and wife are one flesh because God declared them to be so in Genesis 2:24. Husbands and wives today are one flesh *because* God declared them to be so in the time of Adam and Eve. This argument would have no force if the Genesis narrative were fictional.

Today the claims of evolutionary theory present a special challenge to the historicity of Adam. I addressed the subject of evolution briefly in chapter 10, and here as there I will protest my lack of expertise in any matter dealing with science. But we have seen in this chapter that a literal reading of Genesis 1–2 cannot be reconciled with an evolutionary account of man's origin. And I have shown above that there are broader theological reasons for affirming the historical existence of Adam and Eve as our first parents, as opposed to evolutionary hypothesis.

---

47. Actually, he is mostly concerned with a *non*parallel: what Christ did was far greater than what Adam did (Rom. 5:15–19).

48. For my analysis of the application of this passage, see *DCL*, 635–47.

Recently, however, there has emerged another level of conflict between evolution and the Genesis record, this time from the sequencing of the human genome. Richard Ostling summarizes the problem:

> Over the past decade, researchers have attempted to use the genetic diversity within modern humans to estimate primordial population sizes. According to a consensus drawn from three independent avenues of research, [Dennis Venema] states, the history of human ancestry involved a population "bottleneck" around 150,000 years ago—and from this tiny group of hominids came everyone living today. But the size of the group was far larger than a lonely couple: it consisted of several thousand individuals at minimum, say the geneticists. Had humanity begun with only two individuals, without millions of years for development, says an ASA paper, it would have required God's miraculous intervention to increase the genetic diversity to what is observable today. A BioLogos paper by Venema and Falk declares it more flatly: The human population, they say, "was definitely never as small as two . . . . Our species diverged as a population. The data are absolutely clear on that."[49]

It's discouraging to read comments such as this from professing Christians who don't even consider the Word of God as part of the "data." It is true, however, that when we encounter an apparent conflict between Scripture and a scientific consensus, we should reconsider our *interpretation* of Scripture as well as the meaning and truth of the scientific theory.

As to the interpretation of Scripture, we should consider the possibility that Adam and Eve, though historical figures, were not literally the first parents of all present-day human beings. C. John Collins considers the suggestion[50] that Adam and Eve may not have been the first human beings, but rather "king and queen" of a tribe. In this case, the passages referring to their special creation (Gen. 2:7, 21–22) would likely (though not necessarily) be intended figuratively, representing God's investiture of this couple with special qualities (the image of God[51]) and a special vassal kingship, including the covenant headship of Adam over the existing human race. Covenant headship in Scripture does not necessarily presuppose biological parenthood: the relation of Christ to his people is adoptive. And such a hypothesis would more adequately explain some

49. Richard Ostling, "The Search for the Historical Adam," *Christianity Today*, June 26, 2011, 22–27. This discussion was provoked by a series of articles in American Scientific Affiliation, *Perspectives on Science and the Christian Faith* 62, 3 (September 2010). See also Karl W. Giberson and Francis S. Collins, *The Language of Science and Faith* (Downers Grove, IL: InterVarsity Press, 2011); C. John Collins, *Did Adam and Eve Really Exist?* (Wheaton, IL: Crossway, 2011). Collins defends the historicity of Adam and Eve while trying to account for the genetic evidence. The other authors deny the traditional doctrine of Adam's historical existence, believing that the authority of the Bible is only for "faith," not for science. But see my discussion of the comprehensiveness and sufficiency of Scripture in chapter 26 of this volume. See also Vern S. Poythress, "Adam vs. Claims from Genetics," *WTJ* 75, 1 (2013): 65–82.

50. Collins, *Did Adam and Eve Really Exist?*

51. By solidarity with Adam, the image would be given to the rest of the existing human race, as Christian believers are renewed in the image of Christ.

perplexing data of the Genesis history: (1) Cain's fear in Genesis 4:14 that someone might kill him to avenge his murder of Abel; (2) Cain's obtaining a wife in 4:17; (3) Cain's founding a city in 4:17 and the rapid development of culture, agriculture, and technology thereafter. These data are not impossible to explain if we assume (as theologians have traditionally done) that Adam and Eve had many, many sons and daughters in addition to Cain, Abel, and Seth. But the supposition of a tribe or community contemporary with Adam and Eve makes the history somewhat easier to understand.

On such an interpretation we would also have to take figuratively the statement in Genesis 3:20 that Eve "was the mother of all living." Of course, in Scripture, "father" and "mother" do not always refer to biological parentage.[52] Scripture sometimes refers to kings and other authority figures as fathers and mothers, and certainly adoptive parents have the right to these titles. So it is not inconceivable that Genesis 3:20 refers to Eve as the mother of the human nation, given that status and title by God's covenant investiture.

But the development of such interpretative hypotheses is in its infancy, and certainly no such interpretation should be made normative in the church.

On the other hand, we must also consider the possibility that the scientific consensus in favor of an original human race of thousands is wrong. Science constantly changes, and there is no place for the cocksureness with which some have insisted on this consensus view. The genetic arguments, like all other scientific judgments about the past, are based on models, and the assumptions governing these models can be and are being questioned. It is interesting to note that the consensus among evolutionary scientists is that the numbers of original humans have actually decreased—from millions to thousands. And if it is true that 150,000 years ago[53] there were, say, 10,000 modern humans on the earth, that is a remarkable fact. Evolutionary scientists have generally thought that common characteristics imply common ancestry. Why should they not seek a genealogy of human characteristics earlier than the 10,000 that would account for the 10,000? If the 10,000 sprang out of nowhere, their genesis begins to sound much like special creation. But if their genesis had a backstory, a backstory presumably different from the usual process of genetic transmission, couldn't that backstory lead to a single couple?

In any case, it does not seem to me that the hypothesis under consideration calls into question the special creation of Adam and Eve in God's image, their distinctive lordship over creation, or the historicity of the fall.

Key Terms

Image
Likeness
Helper
Naming the animals
Creation ordinances

---

52. See *DCL*, 583–90.

53. Of course, on a "young-earth" view, this estimate would be rejected at the outset, together with a wide range of other models and hypotheses used to reach such a number of years.

Cultural mandate
Son
Body
Soul
Spirit
Intermediate state
Mind-body problem
Dichotomy
Trichotomy
Creationism
Traducianism
Formation
Impartation

Study Questions

1. List some of the ways in which man is unique among all the creatures of God. How and why are these important?

2. "So the image of God consists of those qualities that equip man to be lord of the world, under God. What can these qualities be, but analogies of God's own lordship attributes?" Explain; evaluate.

3. "So man's dominion does not extend to the work of God's first two creative days. But the fact that he subdues and rules the creations of the last four is immensely significant." Explain; evaluate.

4. Explain Frame's parallel between the offices of prophet, priest, and king and the three lordship attributes.

5. Discuss "the centrality of language in human life," citing Scripture.

6. Discuss the power of human language according to Genesis 11:6 and James 3:1–12.

7. What does it mean to describe human beings as "sons" of God?

8. "Sexual differentiation itself images God." Explain; evaluate.

9. Given the many terms in Scripture designating aspects of man, why has so much attention been given to *body, soul,* and *spirit*?

10. "It seems paradoxical to put it this way, but in Scripture it is not a material part of the person that lies in the grave; rather, it is the person." Explain; evaluate.

11. Discuss the biblical cases for dichotomy and trichotomy. What is your conclusion? Why?

12. Same for creationism and traducianism.

13. Frame says that Genesis 2:7 and 2:21–22 literally exclude theistic evolution. Explain why. How is it the case that "the biblical description of the creation of Adam and Eve reinforces the emphasis of Genesis 1–2 on the uniqueness of man as God's image and vassal king"?

14. Is it important to believe that Adam and Eve were historical persons? Cite some biblical considerations.
15. Describe the problem for the historicity of the Genesis account recently raised by the sequencing of the human genome. Suggest a response to that problem.

Memory Verses

Gen. 1:26–27: Then God said, "Let us make man in our image, after our likeness. And let them have dominion over the fish of the sea and over the birds of the heavens and over the livestock and over all the earth and over every creeping thing that creeps on the earth."

So God created man in his own image,
in the image of God he created him;
male and female he created them.

Gen. 2:7: Then the Lord God formed the man of dust from the ground and breathed into his nostrils the breath of life, and the man became a living creature.

Matt. 12:36–37: I tell you, on the day of judgment people will give account for every careless word they speak, for by your words you will be justified, and by your words you will be condemned.

Eph. 4:20–24: But that is not the way you learned Christ!—assuming that you have heard about him and were taught in him, as the truth is in Jesus, to put off your old self, which belongs to your former manner of life and is corrupt through deceitful desires, and to be renewed in the spirit of your minds, and to put on the new self, created after the likeness of God in true righteousness and holiness.

Col. 3:9–10: Do not lie to one another, seeing that you have put off the old self with its practices and have put on the new self, which is being renewed in knowledge after the image of its creator.

Resources for Further Study

Collins, C. John. *Did Adam and Eve Really Exist?* Wheaton, IL: Crossway, 2011.

Hurley, James B. *Man and Woman in Biblical Perspective*. Leicester: Inter-Varsity Press, 1981.

Kline, Meredith G. *Images of the Spirit*. Grand Rapids: Baker, 1980.

Murray, John. *MCW*, 2:3–46.

Ostling, Richard. "The Search for the Historical Adam." *Christianity Today*, June 26, 2011, 22–27.

Poythress, Vern S. "Adam vs. Claims from Genetics," *WTJ* 75, 1 (2013): 65–82.

CHAPTER 35

HUMAN RESPONSIBILITY AND FREEDOM

THE DOCTRINE THAT GOD CONTROLS all things, including our own decisions, typically raises for us the question: "How, then, can we be responsible for our actions?" This question has been one of the major preoccupations of theologians. I discussed God's control of all things in chapter 8 (cf. chapters 2, 9, 11) as an aspect of his covenant lordship. Now we will consider what kind of human responsibility and freedom are possible in a universe exhaustively controlled by God.

The term *responsibility* is not found often in English translations of Scripture, so if we are to use the term, we need to link it to some biblical concepts and teachings. Let us distinguish first between two concepts of responsibility: (1) *accountability* to a higher authority, our being subject to the evaluation of someone else; and (2) *liability* for the consequences of our actions. We will consider these in turn.[1]

Responsibility as Accountability

In Scripture, human beings are clearly responsible in the first sense, because they are accountable to God as the supreme evaluator of human conduct. Human responsibility in this sense, therefore, is a consequence of God's lordship attribute of authority. God has made us according to his plan and for his purpose. That purpose is to glorify him, to please him. The fundamental standard of human conduct is that we should reflect God's own nature. As he has made us in his image (Gen. 1:27–28), so we should behave in a way that images him: "Be holy," he says, "for I the LORD your God am holy" (Lev. 19:1; cf. 11:44; Matt. 5:48; 1 Peter 1:15–16).

God reveals the nature of holiness by his Word. It is that Word that definitively reveals human obligations and therefore what we would call human responsibilities.

---

1. There is a third sense of some theological-ethical importance, the sense in which *responsible* indicates a quality of character, as in "Joe is a responsible businessman." Here *responsibility = integrity* or *honesty*. I will not be discussing that concept here. For those interested, the three senses form a triad: *accountability* is normative, *liability* situational, and *integrity* existential.

Human *responsibility* (accountability) means that human beings are subject to God's evaluation and therefore are under obligation to obey God's commands and to observe his standards. It presupposes that God is the Judge, the supreme evaluator, of our conduct, whether for covenant blessing or curse.

To ask the question, then, of the "relation between divine sovereignty and human responsibility" in this sense is initially to ask about the relationship between two lordship attributes, God's control and his authority. But at the end of this chapter we will also see the need to consider the third lordship attribute, covenant presence, to gain a fuller perspective.

Now, although theologians take great interest in the "problem" of divine sovereignty and human responsibility, this question is not one of the main concerns of the biblical writers, although they are aware of it. Just as it is plain to them that God controls everything, so it is plain to them that he is the supreme authority. Therefore, to the biblical writers, we are responsible, answerable to God, for our attitudes, thoughts, words, and actions. Everything we think and do, indeed everything we are, brings God's commendation or condemnation. Even actions such as eating and drinking, which we might consider to be ethically neutral or *adiaphora*,[2] must be done to God's glory (1 Cor. 10:31). *Whatever* we do should be done thankfully, in Jesus' name (Col. 3:17), with all our heart (v. 23). *Everything* that does not come from faith is sin (Rom. 14:23). Practically every page of Scripture displays God's sovereign evaluations of human attitudes, thoughts, words, and deeds.

Indeed, we are even responsible for our moral nature. Comparing bad trees to bad people, Jesus says that the bad trees will bring forth bad fruit and will thereby be cut down and thrown into the fire (Matt. 7:15–20; cf. Luke 6:43–45). Paul teaches that because of Adam's sin, his descendants were made sinners (Rom. 5:19), and that natural sinfulness, with which we are born, leads to our condemnation (vv. 15–18) if God does not bless us with saving grace. We are responsible for what we are. We did not individually make ourselves evil by nature, but we are responsible for that evil anyway.[3] Our inheritance from Adam is not the result of our individual choice, but we must bear the guilt of it, as we will see in the next chapter.

And we are responsible to seek salvation. We must make a decision to serve the Lord (Josh. 24:15–24). We must receive Christ (John 1:12) and believe in him (3:16; 6:40); we must repent, believe, and be baptized (Acts 2:38). As we have seen, God chooses us before we choose him; his choice brings ours about. But we must choose nevertheless; and if we do not make the right choice, we will not be saved.

So we are responsible for everything we do and are. On the whole, the biblical writers see no problem in affirming together both total divine sovereignty and complete human responsibility. In Romans 9, Paul does cite an imaginary objector who questions the justice of God (v. 14) and says, "Why does he still find fault? For who can resist his will?" (v. 19). But Paul replies:

2. But see my critique of the *adiaphora* concept in DCL, 168–70.

3. Therefore, the view that we are responsible only for what we freely choose at this point *diminishes* the biblical understanding of human responsibility.

> But who are you, O man, to answer back to God? Will what is molded say to its molder, "Why have you made me like this?" Has the potter no right over the clay, to make out of the same lump one vessel for honorable use and another for dishonorable use? (Rom. 9:20–21)

Earlier, Paul quoted Exodus 33:19: God will have mercy on whom he will have mercy.[4] But such debates in Scripture are rare. For the most part, the Bible sets forth God's involvement in everything, and alongside affirms the responsibility of all moral agents, without suggesting the existence of any sort of difficulty arising from this conjunction.

It is significant that Scripture often affirms divine sovereignty and human responsibility together in the same passage. As we saw in chapters 8 and 14, Genesis 50:20 rebukes the wicked intent of Joseph's brothers, but also reveals the good intention of God in bringing about Joseph's ministry in Egypt. We also discussed Isaiah 10:5–15, in which God uses the Assyrian king as his tool to punish Israel; nevertheless, the Assyrian is wicked, and he must take responsibility: "When the Lord has finished all his work on Mount Zion and on Jerusalem, he will punish the speech of the arrogant heart of the king of Assyria and the boastful look in his eyes" (v. 12).

Note the parallel in Proverbs:

> The Lord has made everything for its purpose,
>   even the wicked for the day of trouble.
> Everyone who is arrogant in heart is an abomination to the Lord;
>   be assured, he will not go unpunished. (Prov. 16:4–5)

God raises up the wicked for the day of disaster, but the wicked are nonetheless responsible; they will not go unpunished.

In 1 Kings 8:58, Solomon prays that God will "incline our hearts to him, to walk in all his ways and to keep his commandments, his statutes, and his rules, which he commanded our fathers." Three verses later, he exhorts Israel, "Let your heart therefore be wholly true to the Lord our God, walking in his statutes and keeping his commandments, as at this day" (v. 61; cf. Jer. 29:10–14).

Jesus also shows us both sides of the matter: "All that the Father gives me will come to me, and whoever comes to me I will never cast out" (John 6:37).

Note also the balance between John 1:12 and verse 13:

> But to all who did receive him, who believed in his name, he gave the right to become children of God, who were born, not of blood nor of the will of the flesh nor of the will of man, but of God.

It is God who gives new birth, but those who are born of God accept the responsibility to receive Christ and believe in his name.

---

4. See discussion of this and other texts in *AGG*, 149–90, and in chapter 14 of this book.

Scripture curses the wicked men who betrayed and crucified Jesus, but it also traces these events to the decree of God (Luke 22:22; Acts 2:23; 4:27–28).

The evangelistic work of the early church is the work of God, but it is also the product of human preaching. Acts 13:48, as we saw earlier, mentions that "as many as were appointed to eternal life believed," but 14:1b attributes faith to the preaching of Paul and Barnabas: They "spoke in such a way that a great number of both Jews and Greeks believed."[5] In Romans 9, Paul attributes the unbelief of Israel to God's sovereign working; but in chapter 10, he attributes it to Israel's unwillingness to respond to the preaching of the gospel (vv. 14–21, esp. v. 21). Paul does not hesitate, indeed, to say that it is his responsibility "that I might win more of them" (1 Cor. 9:19; cf. vv. 20–22) and even that "I have become all things to all people, that by all means I might save some" (v. 22b). As post-Reformation Christians, we tend to be uncomfortable with such language. We want to say, "No; it's God who saves, not human preachers." But elsewhere Paul asks, "How are they to hear without someone preaching?" (Rom. 10:14). Human preachers must seek nothing less than the salvation of the lost, recognizing all the time that no one will be saved unless God works through him.[6]

Throughout Paul's missionary labors, God's sovereignty governs what happens, but Paul gives himself to the most rigorous exertions (2 Cor. 4:7–12; 11:23–33). In Acts 27, during Paul's journey to Rome as a prisoner, he prophesies danger to the ship (v. 10). During the storm, he says on God's authority (v. 24) that no one on the ship will die (cf. v. 34). But when sailors try to escape the ship in a lifeboat, Paul says that "unless these men stay in the ship, you cannot be saved" (v. 31). So God has determined that all will live, yet the sailors must take responsibility for this deliverance.

The Christian life is the work of God in us, but it is also our effort to withstand temptation, to obey the Lord: "work out your own salvation with fear and trembling, for it is God who works in you, both to will and to work for his good pleasure" (Phil. 2:12b–13). In this passage, Paul not only brings the two emphases together, but shows their relation. We work *because* God works in us.

---

5. In our contemporary discussions of church growth, we must remember that although evangelism is God's work, it is still important to ask what human means will be most "effective." God works through the effective preaching of his Word. In 1 Corinthians 9, Paul enumerates many of the decisions that he has made as a missionary to make his preaching more effective. He does not hesitate to say that through these exertions he "wins" people to Christ (vv. 19–21) or even that through his efforts he "saves" some (v. 22). Many Calvinists would be embarrassed to use this language, which seems at first glance to detract from God's sovereignty in salvation. But since this language is in the Bible, this embarrassment will have to be traced to hyper-Calvinism, rather than genuine Calvinism. We should never argue, for example, that since God is the One who persuades men of the truth, we should never seek in our preaching to persuade. Or that since God is the One who reaches the heart, we should never seek in our ministry to reach the hearts of people.

6. I have, again, heard Calvinists say that our goal in preaching should be only to spread the Word, not to bring conversion, since that is God's work. The result is often a kind of preaching that covers biblical content, but unbiblically fails to plead with sinners to repent and believe. Let us be clear on this point: the goal of evangelistic preaching is conversion. And the goal of all preaching is a heart-response of repentance and faith. Hyper-Calvinism actually dishonors God's sovereignty, because it suggests (1) that vigorous, goal-directed human effort negates God's sovereign grace, and (2) that such vigorous effort cannot be God's chosen means of bringing people to salvation. God's sovereign purpose is a purpose to save people through the witness of other people.

Often, the NT presents the Christian life in terms of an indicative and an imperative. The indicative emphasizes the sovereign work of God, the imperative our obligation, our responsibility. For example, in Colossians 3:1–3, we read:

> If then you have been raised with Christ, seek the things that are above, where Christ is, seated at the right hand of God. Set your minds on things that are above, not on things that are on earth. For you have died, and your life is hidden with Christ in God.

"You have been raised" is the indicative, "set your minds on things that are above" the imperative. God raised us; we could not have raised ourselves. But Paul expects us to make a decision to give priority in our hearts and minds to the affairs of God. The Christian life is a wonderful gift of God, but it is also a spiritual battle that warrants great exertions.[7] As in Philippians 2:12–13, the sovereign gift of God motivates our exertions. Never in Scripture is there any hint that God's sovereignty should encourage passivity or sloth.

The book of Revelation shows over and over the wrath of God poured out upon Satan and his hosts. Satan is responsible for what he does. Nevertheless, God is on the throne. He anticipates what Satan does and limits it according to his plan.

Why do the biblical writers find it so natural to bring these themes together, a conjunction that seems so paradoxical to modern readers? Why does Paul in Philippians 2:12–13 actually appeal to God's sovereign working to motivate our responsibility? Here are some suggestions as to why this linkage makes sense in the context of a biblical worldview:

1. As we saw in chapter 2, God's sovereignty involves not only his control over everything, but also his authority, his evaluation of everything. He is the supreme standard, the source of all value. Control and evaluation are two aspects of lordship, mutually implicatory. It is therefore not at all surprising that they be conjoined in biblical passages. By his control, God foreordains our actions; by his authority, he evaluates them.[8] Because of that authority, we are answerable to him, responsible. Far from being inconsistent with God's lordship, therefore, our responsibility is based on it.

2. God's promises of success motivate believers to act in accord with those promises. Abstractly, of course, it is possible to imagine someone responding to such a promise by relaxing, waiting passively for God to do it all. Two opposite responses, therefore, to the certainty of God's promises are abstractly possible. But action to further God's goals is not an irrational response to revelation, and it is eminently rational when we consider that our obedience is not only commanded, but also a tool in God's hands by which he accomplishes his purpose. It is those who obey God's commandments who will receive his rewards.

---

7. Note Paul's language in 1 Corinthians 9:24–27, also the warfare motif, as in Ephesians 6:10–20. The Christian is to be active as he lives for Jesus. The Christian life is not a passive "letting go and letting God."

8. Even before God created man, he performed sovereign, creative acts and then evaluated them by calling them good (Gen. 1:1–31).

3. It is when we are most aware of God's providential control over us that we are also most aware of the necessity to live responsibly before him. When we are overwhelmed by his grace and love (or, obviously, by his wrath and judgment), we are powerfully impressed with our need to repent and believe. When we are amazed at God's work within us, then we are motivated to work out our own salvation. Note that in Philippians 2:12–13, we work out our salvation with "fear and trembling." "Fear and trembling" in Scripture is worship, the typical response of a human being to the presence of God. It is that presence of God with us and in us that motivates us to take responsibility. In the presence of the great King, we dare not refuse his commands.[9]

4. Without God's control over the universe, there could be no human responsibility. We live in a theistic universe, one governed by a person, not by impersonal forces and objects. Since God has planned, made, and governed all of nature and history, he has evaluated every event of history according to his perfect standards. If God did not exist, however, there would be no moral standards. Matter, motion, time, and space alone do not impose obligations.[10] And if God did not control everything that happens, then he would not be the ultimate interpreter, the ultimate valuer, of everything. The value of some things would then be independent of God, which is to say that they would have no value. Our responsibility, then, would be confused by two or more sources of value, possibly by two or more equally ultimate standards. Or we would be morally responsible in some areas of life, but not in others. But in Scripture there is one standard; we are to do everything to God's glory.

5. Scripture is therefore not nearly as concerned as we are to promote our self-esteem. We would like to believe that the meaning and significance of our lives depends on what we do for ourselves, without any outside influences or constraints. In Scripture, however, the goal of human life is to glorify God. Our dignity is to be found not in what we do, but in what God has done for us and in us. Our meaning and significance are to be found in the fact that God has created us in his image and redeemed us by the blood of his Son. The biblical writers, therefore, are not horrified, as modern writers tend to be, by the thought that we may be under the control of another. If the other is God, and he has made us for his glory, then we could not possibly ask for a more meaningful existence.

Responsibility as Liability

According to the concept of responsibility set forth above, we are responsible for everything that we are, think, say, or do. But we sometimes use the term *responsibility* in a somewhat different way, in the second sense noted at the beginning of this chapter, namely, to indicate our *liability* for a state of affairs. In the first sense of *responsibility*, we are always responsible and totally responsible. There is no distinction of degree,

9. This consideration shows the relevance of the third lordship attribute, covenant presence, to the questions that we are considering.

10. Compare the argument for God's existence in *AGG*, 93–118, and my debate with Paul Kurtz, "Without a Supreme Being, Everything Is Permitted," *Free Inquiry* 16, 2 (Spring 1996): 4–7.

no distinction between being *more* or *less* responsible. But in the second sense, there is a difference in degree. If Bill and Joe share a plate of cookies, each is *partly* responsible for the emptiness of the plate. Responsibility in the sense of liability has to do with the *results* of our actions. But the results of our actions are never entirely the results of our own decisions. Events in the world have multiple causes, and of course, none of us causes anything by his free decision alone. So courts must often ascertain the "degree" of liability for a crime or injury, and that judgment amounts to assigning partial *responsibility*. Responsibility in this second sense determines the degree of guilt that one bears as the result of wrongdoing, and the nature of the punishment.

In what follows, I will be thinking of responsibility in the second sense. We should not, however, forget the first sense. For it is important that in that sense we are exhaustively responsible for everything in our lives.

Responsibility and Ability

So far, I have analyzed human responsibility without mentioning freedom. Many have claimed, however, that freedom, defined in one way or another, is a condition of human responsibility, so that we are responsible (that is, in the sense of liability) only for what we do freely. We will have to investigate that claim at this point in our reflection.

Certainly there are cases in which that claim is credible. We might initially be appalled that eleven-year-old Billy covered the school door with graffiti. But when we learn that he did it unwillingly, under the threat of bodily harm by eighteen-year-old Mike, we tend to be far more sympathetic to Billy and, of course, indignant toward Mike. We say that Billy should not be held responsible because he did what he did under duress. His act was not a "free" act. He "could not have done otherwise."

Now, Billy was fully responsible, in the sense that he was accountable to God for everything he did. But none of us would say that Billy is responsible in the sense of being liable for the damage done to the door. So we can see how freedom and responsibility (in the second sense) are linked to ability. In judging someone's action, we should take into consideration whether he was *able* to act in a different way. So ability, to some extent, limits responsibility.

We often find this principle to be helpful in our judgments of other people. We may believe that, generally speaking, all Christians should attend church (Heb. 10:25). But if Aunt Martha is bedridden, we understand; she cannot help missing the service. Her inability removes her responsibility in this particular case.

Is this a biblical principle? Yes, up to a point. In Scripture, certain *kinds* of inability do limit responsibility *in some degree*. The case laws of the Pentateuch often take account of ability differences in prescribing penalties for lawbreaking. For instance, the law treats manslaughter differently from intentional killing, in Exodus 21:12–14. One who kills intentionally is "able to do otherwise," because the chief factor in the murder is his own willful decision. Manslaughter is more the product of accident—or, to put it theistically, as God himself does through Moses, "God let him fall into his hand" (v. 13). Manslaughter is less avoidable, less under the control of a human will, less a free act. Significantly, however, a manslayer does not get off scot-free. There is a punishment (described in more detail in Numbers 35:10–34). Scripture evidently presumes some degree of negligence in what we usually call "accidental killing." We have an obligation to guard against such accidents. When they happen, we must be prepared to accept liability.

If a thief breaks into the house of an Israelite by night, the homeowner has the right to defend himself and his household. If he kills the intruder, "there shall be no bloodguilt for him" (Ex. 22:2). But if he kills such an intruder after sunrise, he is guilty. Evidently the law presumes that in the dark of night the homeowner is less able to summon help or to determine proportionate means of defense. His inability limits his responsibility. I assume that judges in Israel would have recognized intermediate cases between the dead-of-night case and the sunrise case. What if burglars break in during the day, but the homeowner cannot speak and therefore cannot summon help? What if he lives alone, far from his neighbors, and confronts three strong men who seek his life? The judges would, in these cases, have to determine the penalty partly by deciding what alternatives were available to him, to what extent he was able to act otherwise.

Ignorance is a form of inability, and it does limit responsibility in some cases. Exodus 21:28–32 presents cases dealing with bulls that gore people to death. If a bull had the habit of attacking people, and the owner had been warned but did not confine the animal, he was punished severely. But if he had no such warning, "the owner of the ox shall not be liable" (v. 28).

Jesus teaches that

> that servant who knew his master's will but did not get ready or act according to his will, will receive a severe beating. But the one who did not know, and did what deserved a beating, will receive a light beating. Everyone to whom much was given, of him much will be required, and from him to whom they entrusted much, they will demand the more. (Luke 12:47–48)

Again, ignorance limits responsibility but in this case does not eliminate it. Why must the ignorant servant be punished "with few blows"? In typical cases, this kind of ignorance amounts to negligence. Servants normally have a responsibility to find out what the master expects of them. So ignorance itself can be a punishable offense. But it is also a mitigating circumstance in judgments about more serious offenses.

Jesus' teaching in Luke 12:47–48 is a parable in which the master is God. Paul also teaches that human ignorance of God's reality and his demands is culpable because it is willful:

> For although they knew God, they did not honor him as God or give thanks to him, but they became futile in their thinking, and their foolish hearts were darkened. Claiming to be wise, they became fools, and exchanged the glory of the immortal God for images resembling mortal man and birds and animals and creeping things. (Rom. 1:21–23)

These unbelievers received a clear revelation of God's nature and power (Rom. 1:18–20) and of his will (v. 32), but they repressed that knowledge, exchanging it for a lie (v. 25), and thus became ignorant. The result is that though they continue to know God, by virtue of his clear revelation, they now do not know God because of their own willful suppression of it (1 Cor. 1:21).[11]

Leviticus 4:13–26 deals with "unintentional" sins of the whole community and of community leaders, prescribing sacrifices. Verse 13 indicates that even though their sin is unintentional, they must make atonement. Verse 22 speaks similarly about a leader's sin. Here there is an objective guilt that must be atoned for by the shedding of blood. Why is the community responsible for evils of which it was ignorant? Scripture emphasizes that we think and act not only as individuals, but also as families and fellow citizens. What we do affects one another, and we do have responsibility for one another. When Adam sinned, his descendants inherited his guilt, as we will see. Fathers after Adam do not communicate guilt to their children in the same way. We do not die for the sins of our parents (Ezek. 18:1–32), but for our own sin. The sins of parents, however, do tend to influence children to sin, and in that way the sins of parents can lead to the condemnation of their children.[12] Similarly (and this principle is important in our time), a society that condones and even encourages sin must answer to God for sins committed in its midst, even sins of which it was largely ignorant.

Ability, therefore (of which knowledge is one kind), does limit responsibility in some cases, but usually it does not completely absolve.

It is also the case that an increase in ability often brings an increase in responsibility. Isaiah 5:1–7 presents God's grace to Israel in the image of a man planting a vineyard, doing everything he could to make it produce fruit, but harvesting only bad grapes. God gave Israel more than he gave to the other nations, but she betrayed him. From those to whom much is given, much will be demanded (Luke 12:48). So Israel's unique revelation and her experience of God's deliverance and providence increase the severity of her judgment. Compare Amos 3:2:

> You only have I known
>   of all the families of the earth;
> therefore I will punish you
>   for all your iniquities.

The miracles of Jesus increase the responsibility of the disbelieving cities (Matt. 11:20–24). If Sodom's people had seen the miracles that Jesus wrought in Chorazin and Bethsaida,

11. For more discussion of the unbeliever's knowledge and ignorance of God, see *DKG*, 49–61; *CVT*, 187–213.

12. I take this to be the meaning of Exodus 20:5, where God says, "I the LORD your God am a jealous God, visiting the iniquity of the fathers on the children to the third and fourth generation of those who hate me." Note that the third and the fourth generations are not innocent children being punished for the sins of ungodly parents. Rather, they are themselves "generation[s] of those who hate me."

they would have repented. So it will be worse for Chorazin and Bethsaida. And we should hear Jesus weeping over Jerusalem:

> O Jerusalem, Jerusalem, the city that kills the prophets and stones those who are sent to it! How often would I have gathered your children together as a hen gathers her brood under her wings, and you would not! See, your house is left to you desolate. For I tell you, you will not see me again, until you say, "Blessed is he who comes in the name of the Lord." (Matt. 23:37–39; cf. Luke 19:41–44)

Jesus has given special love to Jerusalem, only to be rejected. Few cities could boast that the Son of God himself called them to repentance. But that advantage increases the judgment upon them.

We have seen in various ways how ability is proportionate to responsibility. But in Scripture, inability rarely eliminates all guilt. Exodus 21:28 and 22:2 are two cases in which inability removes civil punishment. But in most cases inabilities do not completely absolve, because in the situation they are balanced with abilities. Ignorance is a disability, but it is often willful, and so avoidable. It is a disability, but we often have the ability to avoid it.

In our relationship with God, particularly, we are never disabled in such a way as to be innocent before him. Our inabilities are combined with abilities, so that we are convicted as willful sinners. Everything we do, apart from divine grace, is sinful in that sense. Therefore, even in the second sense of *responsible*, we are totally responsible before the ultimate Judge of liability. We can see now that the distinction between the two senses breaks down when we are speaking of God's final judgment. God judges all our actions by his perfect standard and finds them wanting. He knows what consequences are truly the results of our actions, and he declares us liable for those results. So when we stand before God, accountability and liability coincide. We distinguish them only on the human level, for human judges are not always able to assess liability precisely.[13]

Returning to our discussion of liability, there are some kinds of inability that do not mitigate it at all. One is our inability to avoid events that are divinely foreordained. As we saw in chapter 8, everything happens according to God's plan. Many events are predicted by God's prophets and so in one sense are inevitable. Human sins, too, are often specifically foreordained. Sometimes, indeed, as we have seen, Scripture describes God specifically as "hardening" people, making them more sinful. When God brings about sin, that sin is in one sense unavoidable.

The Assyrian warriors in Isaiah 10:5–11 cannot avoid being God's tool of judgment. Nevertheless, they are fully responsible, and they themselves are under God's judgment (vv. 15–19). Jesus predicted in advance that Judas would betray him, and several

---

13. So the triad I mentioned in footnote 1—*accountability, liability, integrity*—form a *perspectival* triad. To have one of these qualities is to have them all. Of course, to view these terms perspectivally, we must recognize that *integrity* can be integrity in righteousness or in sin.

texts include this betrayal under the decree of God (Luke 22:22; Acts 2:23; 4:27–28). But Judas is fully responsible.

Certainly there were some senses in which Judas could have avoided his sinful act. He was physically able to do otherwise, mentally able to understand his action and to judge moral and religious significance. He may well have known its consequences.[14] He did not act in ignorance. Nor was he forced to betray Jesus. He did what he wanted to do. So as biblical law assesses guilt, Judas was guilty. He was able to do otherwise. His condemnation was appropriate. But in a higher and mysterious sense, his action was not avoidable because he could not overcome the divine decree.

Another kind of inability that does not limit responsibility is *moral* inability. This disability, of course, also pertains to Judas. Indeed, it pertains to all of us. As we saw earlier, through the sin of Adam, we are "made sinners" (Rom. 5:19). We are by nature hostile to God (3:9–18).

> The mind of sinful man is death, but the mind controlled by the Spirit is life and peace; the sinful mind is hostile to God. It does not submit to God's law, nor can it do so. Those controlled by the sinful nature cannot please God. (Rom. 8:6–8 NIV)

Note the "can" and the "cannot."[15] Not only do we sin, but we cannot do otherwise. Does this moral inability mitigate our responsibility? Imagine Adolf Hitler, say, standing before God's throne and saying, "I couldn't help the evil things I did. I was morally unable to do good. I was such a rotten person that I couldn't help sinning." An earthly judge would not take such a defense seriously. Would God accept it?

Certainly not. "The wages of sin is death" (Rom. 6:23). Apart from grace, we are all afflicted with moral inability. And apart from grace, we will all die in our sins. An evil nature aggravates guilt rather than mitigates it. It marks us out as worthless pottery, fit only for destruction (9:21–22).

So the question "does ability limit responsibility?" does not admit of a simple answer. Ability limits responsibility in one sense of *responsibility*, in some cases, in various degrees, and for various reasons. Some inabilities are self-imposed, willful, and therefore themselves culpable. Only rarely does inability completely exonerate. Moral inability and our inability to frustrate God's purpose don't mitigate guilt at all.

Excursus on Ability

This section will be something of a parenthesis to the overall argument of this chapter, but it might help some readers to gain more clarity on the meanings of *ability*, *possibility*, *can*, and kindred expressions. These terms are important not only for the discussion of human freedom, but also in many other theological questions, such as the nature of God's omnipotence (what *can* God do?), miracles (what sorts of events

---

14. If such knowledge seems unlikely, the reader should consider Satan, who evidently knows perfectly well the futility of his project, yet irrationally perseveres in rebellion against God.

15. Cf. Matt. 7:18; John 8:43; 1 Cor. 2:14.

can happen?), total depravity and common grace (what *can* man do apart from saving grace?), regeneration-sanctification (what *can* believers do as the result of grace that unbelievers *cannot*?), Christology (was Jesus *able* to sin?), and prophecy (were Jesus' bones break*able*, granted the prophecy that they would not be broken?).

Let's say that the Rev. Welty is an excellent preacher. We ask him, "Can you preach for us on Sunday?" No, he answers. He has other commitments. Now, *can* he preach for us on Sunday, or can't he? Well, he *can* in the sense that he is well qualified and competent. He *can't* in the sense that he has insurmountable conflicts in his schedule.

When he is too ill to speak in public, we might say of him either that he *can* preach or that he *can't*. The *can* pertains to his general competence and qualifications, the *can't* to his current (we hope temporary) physical state. Both statements are true, despite the apparent contradiction, because they refer to two different kinds of ability.

When Welty was fourteen years old, did he have the ability to preach? We might well say that he did, in the sense that he had the potential to become a preacher. He had the qualities that, with training, godliness, and divine grace, could produce fine sermons. (We can imagine his pastor saying to him, "Young man, you have the ability to be a preacher.") But of course, there are more obvious senses in which fourteen-year-old boys, no matter how great their potential, are generally not "able" to preach.

I conclude that the concept of ability is complex. There are different kinds of abilities. We sometimes say to someone, "Either you can or you can't." But it's not that simple. Often one can in some respects, but can't in others.

Can always envisages a particular act or event (what someone can do) and some circumstance that might prevent that act or event. (From this point on, I will call these circumstances *preventers*.) When we say that Welty *can* preach, the event is preaching; the preventers would normally be lack of qualifications or training. When he is ill and we say that he *can't* preach, we envisage a different set of preventers: medical deficiencies rather than deficiencies of basic competence. He is homiletically able, medically unable.

Were Jesus' bones breakable? Was it possible that Jesus' bones could be broken? (The *able* in *breakable* and the *ible* in *possible* are related to the term *ability*. We are asking whether anyone or anything was *able* to break Jesus' legs.) Well, yes, in the sense that Jesus' bones had the same material composition as other human bones and therefore did not have the kind of physical strength to withstand certain kinds of blows. On the other hand, John declares that God intended to prevent the breaking of Jesus' bones to fulfill prophecy (John 19:36). So there is also a sense in which Jesus' bones *could not* be broken. Breaking them was *impossible*. Again, different preventers yield different kinds of ability or possibility. The breaking of Jesus' bones was physically possible, but impossible by virtue of God's decree.[16]

---

16. Compare John Calvin's discussion in *Concerning the Eternal Predestination of God* (London: James Clarke and Co., 1961), 170.

So the concept of possibility is also complex. We are inclined to say that every event is either possible or impossible. But we can see that some events (such as the breaking of Jesus' bones) are both possible and impossible in different respects.

Philosophers have therefore distinguished different kinds of possibility, according to the different kinds of preventers:

Logical possibility refers to the mere absence of inconsistency. In logical possibility, inconsistency[17] is the only preventer at issue. "2 + 2 = 5" is logically impossible because it creates an inconsistency with the rest of our mathematical system, a system that generates the proposition "2 + 2 is *not* 5." Similarly, "the Padres beat Pittsburgh and they did not beat Pittsburgh," referring to the same game, and using "beat" in the same sense twice, presents a logical impossibility. On the other hand, odd as it might seem, it is logically possible for Welty to read the book of Isaiah in thirty seconds, because the proposition that he did this is not logically contradictory. Normally we would not say that Welty "can" do this, but in the logical sense it is possible.

Physical possibility refers to the laws of physics. Events are physically possible if not prevented by the laws of physics. Miracles are sometimes said to be impossible in this sense, but see my discussion on that subject in chapter 7. We also sometimes use *physical possibility* to refer to the capabilities of our bodies. It is not physically possible for one man to lift a 10,000-pound weight, even though it is logically possible.

Economic possibility: someone might say that he cannot run for president, even though he is well qualified, because he cannot raise the money he would need. Running for president, of course, is not logically contradictory, and it does not violate the laws of physics or the capability of an average healthy body. But for many today, it is economically impossible.

Political possibility: We are often told that it would be good to pass some law, but that it is *politically impossible*, meaning that the votes aren't there and minds cannot be changed.

One can think of many other kinds of possibilities and abilities: legal, medical, musical, and so on. In the previous section, we referred to moral ability and to the human ability to frustrate God's plan, which we might call *metaphysical ability*.[18] Plainly, an act or event can be possible in one sense, but not in other senses. Jesus' bones were physically breakable, but they could not be broken in violation of God's intention. We could, but won't, take the time to sort out Welty's various abilities and disabilities in the previous illustrations.

Could Jesus sin? Perhaps the best short answer is that, yes, he was physically and mentally capable of sinning, but no, he was morally incapable, since he was perfectly

---

17. Of course, I am talking about *logical* inconsistency here. That there are other types introduces a kind of circularity into this discussion. But I can't take time to discuss that issue, and I think my overall point is clear enough.

18. In my view, of course, no creature has that ability.

holy. Could he struggle with temptation? He could struggle against physical obstacles; why not against mental and spiritual ones as well? As a man, and therefore as a divine-human person, he could struggle mentally with Satan's proposals, growing in his understanding of their nature and consequences, maturing in his ability to relate these to the will of his Father (Luke 2:40, 52). He understood, surely, how evil tempts a man, what pleasures, however fleeting, are to be found in sin. Yet he saw all of these in their true perspective and rejected them.

Can unregenerate people believe in Jesus apart from grace? Again: they are physically and mentally able, but morally unable. We should not, like some Calvinists, neglect the senses in which the unregenerate are *able*, for their abilities are relevant to their responsibility.[19] As we have seen, God gave to the people of Israel extraordinary resources of knowledge and experience, so that in important senses they *could* have obeyed God. The fact that they chose not to, despite these abilities, increases their responsibility.

In distinguishing different kinds of human abilities, however, there is some danger of drawing too-sharp lines between human faculties. Distinguishing between moral, mental, and physical ability is useful, as we have seen, but in doing so we may forget the extent to which these abilities are mutually dependent. Moral rebellion against God leads to foolishness and stupidity, as I have emphasized in *DKG*.[20] It can also lead to physical sickness (Ps. 32:3–4; 1 Cor. 11:30; James 5:14–16). If a person hates God, his mind and body will not do the things God approves.

God sees each of us, therefore, not as a loose collection of faculties and abilities, but as a whole person, acting from the heart (the integral center of human existence), a heart consecrated to sin or to righteousness. The distinctions that I have drawn above (like my earlier distinction between accountability and liability) are not of ultimate significance. From God's ultimate, transcendent point of view, they may not exist at all. But we do not have God's exhaustive knowledge of every human heart, and of that heart's connections with every other aspect of a person. So Scripture, speaking in human terms, honoring our finite perspective, urges us to inform sinners not only of the senses in which they are unable to believe, but also of the ways in which they are able.

19. In my view, it is not wise in an evangelistic meeting to tell non-Christians, without qualification, that they "cannot" come to Christ. I am not saying that it is wrong to mention their moral and spiritual inability, but when the evangelist brings it up, the moral and spiritual nature of that inability should be spelled out. He should also emphasize that in important respects the unbeliever *can* come to faith. In most cases he has the physical and mental prerequisites. No one keeps him from Christ by force. If he doesn't come, he has only himself to blame.

And we must not forget that at any time during an evangelistic witness (or, for that matter, at any other time as well), God might intervene to *give* the ability to respond. So when the evangelist says that the inquirer "cannot" respond, he might be denying the grace of God at work in his very ministry. To tell unbelievers that they "cannot" come could be, therefore, ironically, a denial of God's sovereignty. And as my correspondent Steve Hays writes, "It's precisely because the evangelist has no direct control over conversion that he shouldn't take it upon himself to assume the responsibility of screening prospective converts, as if he's otherwise at risk of overruling God's work in conversion."

20. See also the perspectival analysis of human faculties (reason, will, emotions, imagination, and the like) in *DKG*, 328–46, and here in chapter 32.

Freedom

Freedom refers to various kinds of abilities ("freedom to") and the lack of certain inabilities ("freedom from"), inabilities that I have been calling *preventers*. Now, we have spoken of logical, physical, political, legal, economic, and metaphysical *abilities* and *possibilities*. When we speak about the abilities of persons, or what is possible for a person to do, we can also describe these abilities as different kinds of *freedoms*. Of course, linguistically it is awkward to use *freedom* in some of these connections. We normally don't speak of *logical freedom*, for example, because it is impossible (logically, of course) even to conceive of someone's having the ability to perform logically inconsistent actions.

Several kinds of freedom are particularly important in discussions of human responsibility:

1. *Moral* freedom—the freedom to do good. As we have seen, Scripture teaches that Adam's fall took away our moral freedom so that apart from grace we "cannot" please God. Christ sets us free from this bondage:

> Jesus answered them, "Truly, truly, I say to you, everyone who commits sin is a slave to sin. The slave does not remain in the house forever; the son remains forever. So if the Son sets you free, you will be free indeed." (John 8:34–36; cf. Rom. 6:15–23; 2 Cor. 3:17)

Moral freedom is the most important kind of freedom mentioned in Scripture, the freedom from sin given to us by the redemptive work of Christ. But it is not a condition of moral responsibility. Those who are bound in slavery to sin are morally responsible, no more or less so than those who are free in Christ.[21]

2. *Compatibilist* freedom—the freedom to do what you want to do. Jesus says in Luke 6:45:

> The good person out of the good treasure of his heart produces good, and the evil person out of his evil treasure produces evil, for out of the abundance of the heart his mouth speaks.

Cf. Matt. 7:15–20; 12:33–35.

We act and speak, then, according to our character. We follow the deepest desires of our hearts. To my knowledge, Scripture never refers to this moral consistency as a kind of *freedom*, but the concept of heart-act consistency is important in Scripture, and theologians and philosophers have often referred to it as *freedom*. In everyday life, we

---

21. In footnote 1, I mentioned a third sense of *responsibility*, namely, *moral integrity*. In that sense, *responsible* is an honorific term, as in "Jeff is such a responsible person." In that usage, not only is Jeff subject to moral evaluation, but he receives high marks in that evaluation. On that usage, only good people are responsible. But we are here using the term differently, so that the term means only that people are subject to moral evaluation. In that sense, all people are *responsible*, whether or not they take their responsibilities seriously.

regularly think of freedom as doing what we want to do. When we don't do what we want, either we are acting irrationally or we are being forced to act against our will by someone or something outside ourselves.

This kind of freedom is sometimes called *compatibilism*, because it is compatible with determinism. Determinism is the view that every event (including human actions) has a sufficient cause other than itself. Compatibilist freedom means that even if every act we perform is caused by something outside ourselves (such as natural causes or God), we can still be free, for we can still act according to our character and desires.

There are some ambiguities in this concept, because there are different levels of human desires. Consider Billy again, who is forced by Mike, the older boy, to cover the school door with graffiti. Is Billy doing what he desires? In one sense, obviously no. Mike is forcing him to do what he doesn't want to do. But given Mike's threat, Billy is faced with two undesirable alternatives: defacing the door and undergoing bodily harm. Between those alternatives, he chooses the one he desires most. So in one sense he acts according to his strongest desire, and in another sense he does not. We must distinguish here between Billy's overall preferences and his immediate concerns and note that for a moment the two contradict each other. If we define compatibilist freedom in terms of Billy's overall preferences, then his act was not free. If we define it in terms of his immediate desires, then it was. But for purposes of judging Billy's responsibility, we would normally say that his action was not free.

On the compatibilist view, we can say, therefore, that in one sense we always act according to our strongest desire and in another sense we do not. We always act according to our strongest desire in the here and now, according to our strongest desire in a concrete situation. We would like to act always according to our broader preferences, but we do not always do that. So in a compatibilist concept of freedom, we are always free to follow our most concrete desires, not always free to carry out our more general desires.

Is compatibilist freedom a condition of moral responsibility? Yes, with the same qualifications we noted earlier in Scripture's use of the principle *ability limits responsibility*. The difference between murder and manslaughter, for example, is one of intention. In manslaughter, the perpetrator does not desire to take life. He does, in fact, take life, but that action does not reflect his desire. Or to put it as we usually do, he does not have a motive for murder. He does not make a free choice (compatibilist) to kill, and therefore he should not be penalized as a murderer. He made other free choices, which a court might judge to amount to negligence, and he should be penalized for those.

We have also seen in Scripture how ignorance limits responsibility to some extent. Part of the reason is that ignorance limits our freedom in a situation. We do what we would not want to do if we had greater knowledge. On the other hand, ignorance can be willful, as we have seen. We can *desire* ignorance over knowledge. So suppressing the truth can be a free act. Civil judges assume this freedom when they use the slogan "ignorance of the law is no excuse." That freedom is also relevant to God's judgment.

But as I indicated earlier, ability to overcome God's decree is not a condition of moral responsibility. Alleged "freedom to overcome God's decree" is not compatibilist, but libertarian (see below), and therefore not relevant to responsibility.

We also saw earlier that moral inability does not remove moral responsibility. Our study of compatibilist freedom can help us to see part of the reason why. *Moral inability* is simply the character of unregenerate human beings. They are free in the compatibilist sense: to do what they desire to do, though their desires are evil. Moral inability does not in the least mitigate compatibilist freedom, so it does not mitigate responsibility.

3. *Libertarianism.* But the concept of freedom most often discussed in connection with moral responsibility is libertarianism. R. K. McGregor Wright defines this view as follows:

> The belief that the human will has an inherent power to choose with equal ease between alternatives. This is commonly called "the power of contrary choice" or "the liberty of indifference." This belief does not claim that there are no influences that might affect the will, but it does insist that normally the will can overcome these factors and choose in spite of them. Ultimately, the will is free from any necessary causation. In other words, it is autonomous from outside determination.[22]

Libertarianism is sometimes called *incompatibilism* because it is not compatible with determinism. Thus, it is a clear alternative to compatibilism. Libertarians are particularly concerned to emphasize that our choices are not determined in advance by God. On their view, God may be the First Cause of the universe in general, but in the sphere of human decision, we are the first causes of our actions. We have a godlike independence when we make free choices.

Further, as Wright's definition implies, in libertarianism our decisions must also be independent of ourselves in a certain sense, paradoxical as that may sound. On the libertarian view, our character as currently established may influence our decisions, as may our desires of the moment. But we always have the freedom to choose contrary to our character, our desires, even our strongest desires ("strongest" both in the sense of long-term goals and of immediate preferences).

This position assumes that there is a part of human nature, which we might call the *will*, that is independent of every other aspect of our being, and that can therefore make a decision contrary to every motivation.

Libertarians maintain that only if we have this kind of radical freedom can we be held responsible for our actions. Their principle is simple enough: if our decisions are caused by anything or anyone (including our own desires), they are not properly our decisions, and we cannot be held responsible for them. To be responsible, we must be "able to do otherwise." And if our actions are caused by anything other than our free will, we are not able to do otherwise, and we are therefore not responsible.

22. R. K. McGregor Wright, *No Place for Sovereignty* (Downers Grove, IL: InterVarsity Press, 1996), 43–44.

Critique of Libertarianism

Libertarianism has a long history in Christian theology. Most of the church fathers held more or less this position until Augustine, during the Pelagian controversy, called it into question.[23] Since then, there has been a contest between the Augustinian and Pelagian conceptions of freedom, resulting sometimes in various unstable mixtures of the two. Both Martin Luther[24] and John Calvin[25] maintained an Augustinian compatibilism, but the Socinians, and later the Arminians, offered vigorous defenses of libertarianism. Today the libertarian view prevails in much of evangelical Christianity and among Christian philosophers.[26] Theologically, it is defended by traditional Arminians,[27] open theists,[28] process thinkers,[29] and many others. Few theologians oppose it, except for self-conscious Calvinists, and even thinkers in the Reformed tradition sometimes gravitate toward libertarianism[30] or speak unclearly on the subject.[31]

But libertarianism is subject to very severe criticisms:

1. Scripture does not teach it in any explicit way. No biblical passage can be construed to mean that the human will is independent of God's plan and of the rest of human personality. Libertarians generally don't even try to establish their position by direct exegesis (as, for example, I tried above to establish a biblical view of human ability and compatibilist freedom). Rather, they attempt to deduce it from other biblical concepts, such as human responsibility itself, and the divine commands, exhortations, and plead-

23. Those Calvinists who place great weight on antiquity and tradition will have to concede, therefore, that the oldest extracanonical traditions do not favor their position.

24. Martin Luther, *The Bondage of the Will* (London: James Clarke and Co., 1957).

25. See many writings of Calvin, especially the treatise *Concerning the Eternal Predestination of God.* The classic Calvinist refutation of libertarianism is Jonathan Edwards, *Freedom of the Will* (New Haven, CT: Yale University Press, 1973).

26. Many Christian philosophers believe that libertarian freedom is essential to an adequate answer to the problem of evil. Alvin Plantinga's argument has been especially influential in this connection. See his *God, Freedom, and Evil* (Grand Rapids: Eerdmans, 1974).

27. The most cogent and complete Arminian argument, in my view, is Jack Cottrell's *What the Bible Says about God the Ruler* (Joplin, MO: College Press, 1984). See also the other two books in his trilogy on the Doctrine of God.

28. Clark Pinnock et al., *The Openness of God* (Downers Grove, IL: InterVarsity Press, 1994).

29. For example, John B. Cobb and David Ray Griffin, *Process Theology: An Introductory Exposition* (Philadelphia: Westminster Press, 1976).

30. See, for example, Alvin Plantinga's influential *God, Freedom, and Evil.*

31. See, for example, Benjamin Wirt Farley, *The Providence of God* (Grand Rapids: Baker, 1988), and my review in *WTJ* 51, 2 (1989): 397–400. Richard Muller, in his "Grace, Election, and Contingent Choice: Arminius's Gambit and the Reformed Response," in *The Grace of God, The Bondage of the Will*, ed. Thomas R. Schreiner and Bruce A. Ware (Grand Rapids: Baker, 1995), 2:270, says, "It was never the Reformed view that the moral acts of human beings were predetermined, any more than it was ever the Reformed view that the fall of Adam was willed by God to the exclusion of Adam's free choice to sin." I agree that Reformed theology recognizes Adam's choice as free, but only in a compatibilist sense. Contrary to Muller, Reformed theologians did teach that God ordained the fall (or else whence the debate between supralapsarians and infralapsarians as to the *place* of the fall among God's decrees?) and therefore ordained at least one human moral decision. And Scripture mentions many more human moral decisions ordained by God, as we have seen in chapter 8. In fairness to Muller, he does recommend a compatibilist formulation on the top of 269. But compatibilist freedom does not exclude, as he suggests it does, divine predetermination of moral acts.

ings[32] that indicate human responsibility. But in this attempt, they accept a rather large burden of proof that their arguments do not bear. Libertarianism is a rather technical philosophical notion, making various assumptions about causality, the relation of will to action, the relation of will to character and desire, and the limitation of God's sovereignty. It is a huge order to try to derive all these technical concepts from the biblical view of human responsibility, and I will try to show below that libertarians' attempts to do so have been far from successful. If, however, they fail to bear this burden of proof, then we must abandon either libertarianism or *sola Scriptura*.

2. Scripture never grounds human responsibility (in the sense of accountability) in libertarian freedom—or, for that matter, any other kind of freedom. We are responsible because God has made us, God owns us, and God has a right to evaluate our conduct. God's authority is, therefore, according to Scripture, the necessary and sufficient ground of human responsibility. Sometimes our ability or inability is relevant to God's judgment, and therefore to our responsibility in the sense of liability, as we have seen. But Scripture never suggests that libertarian freedom has any relevance at all, even to liability.

3. Nor does Scripture indicate that God places any positive value on libertarian freedom (even granting that it exists). That is a significant point, because the free-will defense against the problem of evil (see chapter 14) argues that God places such a high value on independent human free choice that he gave it to creatures even at the risk that they would bring evil into the world. One would imagine, then, that Scripture would abound with statements by God to the effect that causeless free actions by creatures are terribly important to him, that they bring him glory. But Scripture never suggests that God honors causeless choice in any way or even recognizes its existence.

4. Scripture never judges anyone's conduct by reference to his libertarian freedom. Scripture never declares someone innocent because his conduct was not free in the libertarian sense, nor does it ever warrant a judgment of guilt by pointing to the libertarian freedom of the individual. We have seen that Scripture sometimes refers implicitly to freedom or ability in the compatibilist sense. But it never refers to freedom in a demonstrably incompatibilist sense.

5. In civil courts we never assume that libertarian freedom is a condition of moral responsibility. Consider Hubert, a bank robber. If guilt presupposed libertarian freedom, then in order to show that Hubert is guilty, the prosecutor would have to show that his decision to rob a bank was without any cause. But what evidence could a prosecutor bring forth to show that? Proving a negative is always difficult, and it would clearly be impossible to show that Hubert's inner decision was completely independent of any divine decree, natural cause, character, or motive. Similarly for any other criminal or civil prosecution. Libertarianism would make it impossible to prove the guilt of anybody at all.

---

32. I showed in chapter 16 how God can command and plead with sinners even though he has foreordained their actions. Essentially the answer is to distinguish between God's decrees and God's precepts.

6. Indeed, law courts normally assume the opposite of libertarianism, namely, that the conduct of criminals arises from motives. Therefore, courts often spend much time discussing whether a defendant had an adequate motive to commit the crime. If Hubert's action *could* be shown (contrary to point 2 above) to be causeless, independent of motives, then he would likely be judged insane and therefore *not* responsible, rather than guilty. Indeed, if Hubert's action is completely independent of his character, desires, and motives, one can well ask in what sense this action is really Hubert's.[33] And if it is not Hubert's action, how can he be held responsible for it? We can see, then, that rather than being the foundation of moral responsibility, libertarianism destroys moral responsibility.[34]

7. Indeed, Scripture contradicts the proposition that only uncaused decisions are morally responsible. As we saw in chapter 8, God in Scripture often brings about the free actions, even sinful actions, of human beings, without in the least diminishing their responsibility. In the present chapter, we have seen how God's sovereign control of human actions and man's responsibility for the same actions often appear together in the same passage.

8. Scripture also denies that we have the independence demanded by libertarian theory. We are not independent of God, for God controls human free actions. Nor can we choose to act independently of our own character and desire. Recall our earlier references to Matthew 7:15–20 and Luke 6:43–45. The good tree brings forth good fruit, the evil tree evil. If one's heart is right, his actions will be right; otherwise, no.

9. Libertarianism, therefore, violates the biblical teaching concerning the unity of human personality in the heart. Scripture teaches that the heart, and therefore our decisions, is wicked because of the fall, but the work of Christ and the regenerating power of the Spirit cleanse the heart so that our actions can be good. We are fallen and renewed as whole persons. This integrity of human personality is not possible in a libertarian construction, for in that view the will must always be independent of the heart, the character, and all our faculties.

10. If libertarian freedom is necessary to moral responsibility, then evidently God is not morally responsible, for he is not free to act against his holy character. Nor are the glorified saints in heaven. If the glorified saints do have libertarian freedom, then,

---

33. One libertarian reply is that the *will* is Hubert's, and so the action is his. But what is meant by *will* here? Does Hubert's will have a character? Does it have preferences or desires? If so, then we are back to actions controlled by one's nature, which libertarianism rejects. Does it have no character at all? Then how is it any different from a mere force that acts at random and is quite separate from anything in Hubert? On that supposition, how can it be *Hubert's* will?

34. Calvinists and other antilibertarians often make this point in colorful ways. James Henley Thornwell says, "As well might a weather-cock be held responsible for its lawless motions as a being whose arbitrary, uncontrollable will is his only law." *Collected Writings of James Henley Thornwell*, vol. 2 (Edinburgh: Banner of Truth, 1974), 180. R. E. Hobart, arguing a secular form of determinism, says, "In proportion as [a person's action] is undetermined, it is just as if his legs should suddenly spring up and carry him off where he did not prefer to go." "Free Will as Involving Determinism and Inconceivable without It," *Mind* 43 (January 1934): 7.

as Origen speculated, they could fall again into sin. The implication would be that the redemption accomplished by Jesus is insufficient to deal with sin, for it is not sufficient to deal with the inherent waywardness of human free will.

11. Libertarianism is essentially a highly abstract generalization of the principle *ability limits responsibility*. Libertarians say that if our decision is afflicted by *any* kind of inability *at all*, it is not truly free and responsible. We saw earlier that there is some truth in the principle *ability limits responsibility*, but I emphasized then that this principle is not always valid, that we are always afflicted by some kinds of inability, and that the principle must therefore be used with great caution. Libertarianism throws caution to the winds.

12. Libertarianism is inconsistent not only with God's foreordination of all things, but even with his knowledge of future events. If God knew in 1930[35] that I would wear a green shirt on July 21, 1998, then I am not free to avoid wearing such a shirt on that date. Now, libertarians make the point that God can know such future events without causing them. But if in 1930 God knows the events of 1998, on what basis does he know them? The Calvinist answer is that he knows them because he knows his own plan. But how, on an Arminian basis, does God *know* my free act 68 years in advance? Is it that my decision is governed by a deterministic chain of finite causes and effects? Is there some force or person *other* than God that renders future events certain, a being whom God passively observes? (That is a scary possibility, hardly consistent with monotheism.) None of these answers, nor any other I can think of, is consistent with libertarianism. For this reason, the open theists,[36] like the Socinian opponents of Calvin, have taken the step of denying what is so important to traditional Arminianism: God's exhaustive foreknowledge. But that step is a drastic one, as we saw in our discussion of God's knowledge (chapter 15). It seems to me that they would have been wiser to reject libertarianism, rather than to drastically reconstruct their theology to make it consistent with libertarianism.

13. As with open theists Pinnock and Rice, libertarians tend to make their view of free will a nonnegotiable, central truth, with which all other theological statements must be made consistent. Libertarian freedom then takes on a kind of paradigmatic or presuppositional status. But as we have seen, libertarianism is unscriptural. It would be bad enough merely to *assert* libertarianism contrary to the Bible. But making it a central truth or governing perspective is very dangerous indeed. An incidental error can be corrected without much trouble. But when such an error becomes a major principle, a grid through which all other doctrinal statements are filtered, then a theological system is in grave danger of shipwreck.

---

35. This is, of course, a manner of speaking. I will argue later that God's knowledge is timeless in a sense. But if God knows timelessly that I will wear a green shirt on July 21, 1998, then even in 1930 it was true to say that he knew I would wear a green shirt on July 21, 1998.

36. Clark Pinnock, Richard Rice, and others. See the reference to their book *The Openness of God* in footnote 28 and my critique of open theism in chapter 15.

14. Philosophical defenses of libertarianism often appeal to intuition as the ground of belief in free will:[37] anytime we are faced with a choice, we *feel* that we could choose either way, even against our strongest desire.[38] We are sometimes conscious, they say, of *combating* our strongest desires. But whatever one may say generally about the appeal to intuition,[39] intuition can never be the ground of a universal negative. That is to say, intuition cannot reveal to anyone that his decisions have no cause. We never have anything that might be called "a feeling of lack of causation."

Nor can intuition reveal to us that all our actions *do* have an outside cause. If all our actions were determined by an agency outside ourselves, we could not identify that causation by any intuition or feeling, for we would have no way of comparing a feeling of causation with a feeling of noncausation. We can identify influences that sometimes prevail over us and sometimes don't, forces that we sometimes but not always resist successfully. But we cannot identify forces that constantly and irresistibly determine our thoughts and behavior. So intuition never reveals to us whether or not we are determined by causes outside ourselves.[40]

15. If libertarianism is true, then God has somehow limited his sovereignty so that he does not bring all things to pass. But Scripture contains no hint that God has limited his sovereignty in any degree. God is the Lord, from Genesis 1 to Revelation 22. He is always completely sovereign. He does whatever pleases him (Ps. 115:3). He works in all things according to the counsel of his will (Eph. 1:11). Further, God's very nature is to be sovereign. Sovereignty is his name, the very meaning of the name *Yahweh* in terms of both control and authority. If God limited his sovereignty, he would become something less than Lord of all, something less than God. And if God became something less than God, he would destroy himself. If God becomes less than God, God no longer exists. We can see that the consequences of libertarianism are serious indeed.

Creaturely Otherness, Integrity, and Significance

We have seen that according to Scripture, human beings are fully responsible for their actions, responsible to do everything to the glory of God. Responsibility is based on the fact that the Lord is our supreme authority, our supreme evaluator. In the course of God's evaluation, he sometimes, in various ways, takes our ability—our freedom—into account. In many cases, but not all, more ability means higher divine

37. See, for example, C. A. Campbell, "The Psychology of Effort of Will," *Proceedings of the Aristotelian Society* 40 (1939–40): 49–74.

38. There is much argument in the literature over whether we can ever choose against our "strongest desire." See my earlier comments on this question. Further, it seems to me that some confusion exists here as to the different ways in which a desire can be *strong*. If *strength* refers to an emotional power, then it is plausible to argue that however strong the desire is, we can always choose against it. But if *strength* refers to motivational effectiveness, then of course the strongest desire is that which actually motivates, and it is nonsense to talk about choosing contrary to one's strongest desire.

39. See *DKG*, 345–46, for my account.

40. Thanks to Steve Hays for this observation. He also points out that the libertarian appeal to intuition ignores the role of the subconscious in motivating our thoughts and behavior.

expectations; less ability means lower ones. But some abilities (moral ability, meta-physical ability) are not relevant at all to moral evaluation. In the previous section, I rejected the claim of libertarianism that its abstract, generalized view of free will is essential to responsibility.

But the discussion so far leaves some important questions unanswered. We have so far concluded that human actions are completely under God's control. We are responsible for them, simply because God has the right to evaluate them and to judge us for them. This conclusion is highly distasteful to many, especially to those attracted to libertarianism. They sense that this view dishonors man, reduces human significance. They think that on a compatibilist view of freedom, human beings are mere "robots," treated as things rather than as persons. Even worse, the view that I am presenting sounds to libertarians as though God judges and punishes man for things that God himself is actually responsible for.

The first thing to be said is that we cannot distort the Bible's teaching in order to make it more palatable to people today. Even if there were no more to be said, even if there were no reply to these libertarian objections, we could not accept a nonbiblical view as the price of answering those objections. It would be better to leave the questions unanswered. For the time being, at least, these questions would define a realm of mystery. But our God is so great, his thoughts above our thoughts; how could there *not* be unresolved mysteries in our attempts to chart his ways?

The concern of Scripture is, above all, to glorify God. Sometimes glorifying God humbles man, and those who believe Scripture must be willing to accept that consequence. We covet for ourselves ever more dignity, more honor, more status, and we resist accepting a lower place. But Scripture assaults our pride and honors the humble. Scripture compares us, after all, not to robots, but to a potter's clay.

What if it turns out that we are robots, after all? Clay fashioned into marvelous robots, rather than being left as mere clay? Should we complain to God about that? Or should we rather feel honored, that our bodies and minds are fashioned so completely to fulfill our assigned roles in God's great drama? Some creatures are born as rabbits, some as cockroaches, some as bacteria. By comparison, would it not be a privilege to be born as an intelligent robot?

Indeed, what remarkable robots we would be! Capable of love and intimacy with God, assigned to rule over all the creatures. Is it not a wonderful blessing of grace that, when we sinned in Adam, God did not simply discard us, as a potter might very well do with his clay, and as a robot-operator might well do with his machine, but sent his only Son to die for us? Risen with him to new life, believers enjoy unimaginably wonderful fellowship with him forever.

As we meditate on these dignities and blessings, the image of the robot becomes less and less appropriate, not because God's control over us appears less complete, but because one doesn't treat robots with such love and honor.

Some writers seem to think that the lack of "real" (that is, libertarian) freedom would invalidate all the other blessings of this life. But is that really the case? Libertarian freedom, as we have seen, amounts to the arbitrary activity of a meaningless "will." Would we really give up all the blessings of this life in order to gain experiences of random activity?

But even if we set aside the objections of libertarians, we are left with some uneasiness and many unanswered questions. Why does God lavish such attention and love upon creatures over whom he has complete control? With the psalmist, we wonder:

> What is man, that you are mindful of him,
>   and the son of man that you care for him? (Ps. 8:4)

The psalmist's question comes precisely out of meditation on God's majesty and sovereignty. God "ordain[s] praise" from the lips of children to silence his enemies (Ps. 8:2 NIV). Why should such a God, who can simply ordain praise to himself anytime he wants, even from stones (Luke 19:40), give to man the lavish care and high authority described in the later verses?

It is evident that God's relationship to his creatures, even though it involves complete "control," is far more than what we usually think of as control. And it is more, too, than is normally connoted in the term *authority*. So far in this chapter, we have focused on the first two lordship attributes. Now we must see how the third might help us.

Covenant presence means that God cares for his world. He does not set it in motion and leave it to run on its own. He remains with and in the world, to control it, to evaluate it, to bless and to judge. He is the potter and the world is his clay—but it is not *mere* clay. The potter-clay analogy is a good image of God's prerogatives over us, and indeed it is literally true that we are made of dust (Gen. 2:7). But other biblical images and metaphors, such as the "image of God" in which man is made (1:27–28), indicate that we are very special dust. And the dust itself, the material creation, is, as we have seen, itself the object of God's wise providence.

Why should the world matter to God? Why is it significant and important to him? Some have argued that it can have no meaning if God has complete control over it. Scripture, rather, says that the world is meaningful and significant *because* it is God's creature and the subject of God's providence. But what is its significance, apart from the significance of God himself?

At this point, we need to consider in more detail the relation between Creator and creature. First, as we have seen, it is wrong to say that because God is present, the world is God and God is the world. Covenant presence is quite inconsistent with pantheism. For covenant presence presupposes that God and the world are different from each other. It distinguishes the world from the God who is present in and with it. For he is present as the Sovereign Lord, as the controller and authority. So the world is significant not because it is divine. It is, rather, to God a "significant other."

God's decrees foreordain, and his creative act brings into actuality, beings other than God. Creation marks the beginning, therefore, of nondivine "otherness." Now, of course, otherness does exist eternally within the triune divine nature. But creation is the beginning of something new: a *nondivine* otherness, a *creaturely* otherness. Creatures are the work of God, fully planned by God, dependent on him, and under his control. But they are not God, not extensions of God's nature.

Creaturely otherness is linked to a number of Christian mysteries and controversies. One is the doctrine of *creation out of nothing* (chapter 10), the divine act that brings the creaturely other into being. How can anything come out of nothing? And granted that God has the power to create, how can the creation be anything other than God, since prior to creation only God exists?

There is also some mystery about the *integrity* of creaturely otherness. By *integrity*, I mean the ability of things to exist and function on their own terms, to be distinct from other objects, to play their own distinct roles in history. The integrity of creatures is not simply the integrity of God's nature, although creatures are certainly dependent on God (*contingent*) for their existence and function. God's own integrity certainly sustains the existence and functions of creatures. But since God has ordained creatures to be different from him, he has given them natures and functions different from his own. When a man dies, for example, God does not die. The man dies because that is his peculiar, individual destiny. Each item in creation has its own role to play in God's wise plan. Its role is different in some way from the roles of other created things, and certainly different from God's own role.

Therefore, if the words *independence* and *autonomy* were not so often attached to unbiblical notions such as libertarianism, it might be possible to use them to describe the integrity of creaturely otherness. The human life you live has its own significance, granted by God to be sure, but different from God's own significance and in that sense *independent* of it. Of course, that life is also *dependent* on God's plan for history and his providential rule. Once God formulates his plan and creates the world, created individuals have stable historical roles distinct from God himself and sometimes even opposed to him. And once God grants creatures these roles, he will not take them away, for to do so would violate his own plan.

If God has ordained that Bill will live to be eighty years old, he will not change his mind and take Bill's life at sixty. God's plan is eternal, unchangeable. It is consistent with itself. Just as God keeps his promises, he also sees to it that his decree will be fulfilled.[41] But that means that Bill has the power to live until age eighty and that not even God can change that, for not even God can violate his own decree.

Does God, then, limit his sovereignty? Yes and no. No, because this creaturely integrity is itself part of God's decree. At no point does God relinquish control over his world.

But I stress again that God's decree is not irrational or inconsistent with itself. In that sense, as Reformed theologians have always said, God cannot do simply anything. He cannot do something that contradicts his nature. And he cannot include one thing

---

41. Compare our distinction between God's decretive and preceptive wills in chapter 16. In general, God's decrees represent his control, his precepts his authority.

in his plan that contradicts another. In that sense, God is limited by the consistency of his own plan.

And that limitation has something to do with the nature of creaturely otherness. For God to be consistent with himself, he must also be consistent with Bill. God knows that according to his plan Bill will die at eighty. That is a fact about God's plan; it is also a fact that God foreknows about Bill. All other things that God ordains for Bill must be consistent with this reality.

We can picture God planning the universe as a man puts together a jigsaw puzzle. The individual pieces must fit with one another and with the whole. The shape of one piece determines what piece may fit next to it. The analogy is imperfect, of course, because God is not faced, as puzzle-players are, with pieces made by somebody else. He makes all the pieces, and he fully controls each part as well as the whole. But he does plan the universe both as a whole and in its individual parts.[42] So because he is a wise God, like the puzzle-player, God must fit the pieces together in a consistent, meaningful, and rational way.[43]

One can say, then, that God's plan is limited by what he knows about Bill. He foreordains according to his foreknowledge.[44] But it would be equally true to say that in this case one part of God's plan is simply furnishing a logical limit to another part of it.

Arminians say that God's foreordination is based on his foreknowledge. The Calvinist need not deny that this is the case. But he should go on, then, and point out to the Arminian that that foreknowledge itself is in turn based on foreordination!

There is in God's mind a reciprocity between foreknowledge and foreordination. Neither is simply "prior" to the other. Both are eternal. And logically, God's knowledge is based on what he foreordains. But his foreordination is not an ignorant foreordination. He does not foreordain at random a set of circumstances and then look upon those circumstances with surprise. His plan is a wise plan, a plan formulated according to knowledge.[45]

42. Recall, for example, that individual believers are chosen in Christ before the foundation of the world (Eph. 1:4).

43. In our discussion of God's omnipotence (chapter 16), we discussed how God is, and is not, limited by logic and by his own nature. In general, God cannot do anything that contradicts who he is. He cannot, therefore, be other than wise, and therefore logical. But his logic is not necessarily identical with that of any human logical system.

44. Note how the WCF describes God's providence (5.1): "God, the great Creator of all things doth uphold, direct, dispose, and govern all creatures, actions, and things . . . by his most wise and holy providence, *according to his infallible foreknowledge*, and the free and immutable counsel of his own will" (emphasis mine). Here *foreknowledge*, I think, refers to God's prescience, his knowledge of the future, rather than (as sometimes in Scripture and Calvinist theology) God's eternal decree of salvation, for it is joined to the word *infallible* and followed by a statement of the eternal decree. So God's governance of the world is both by his eternal decree and by his infallible foreknowledge.

45. I am always suspicious of the idea of priorities within the mind of God. God's mind is eternal and simple. It is not a process in which one thought leads to another, nor is it a contest in which ideas strive to supplant one another. Everything in God's mind takes everything else into consideration. So his foreordination and his knowledge are eternally in perfect accord. There is no process by which the one produces the other or gets reconciled

Here we may reflect a bit on the concept of God's *middle knowledge* as it has developed in the history of theology.[46] Middle knowledge (chapter 15) is God's knowledge of what takes place under various conditions. His *necessary knowledge* is of everything possible, his *free knowledge* of everything actual. Middle knowledge is of things hypothetical and their results. To Molina, who first formulated the concept, middle knowledge is based not on God's nature or plan, but on his perceptions of the independent (in the bad sense!) behavior of possible creatures in possible circumstances. Molina held, in other words, to a radical libertarianism. Reformed theology, of course, denies this. But Reformed theology does not deny that God has a knowledge of matters hypothetical. He knows what will happen "if David goes to Keilah" and "if David does not go to Keilah."[47]

So God knows that if Bill is fatally shot at sixty, he cannot live to be eighty. Therefore, God prevents, as part of his eternal plan, the possibility of Bill's being fatally shot at sixty. God's will is formulated according to knowledge, including his foreknowledge concerning creatures, but his knowledge is also dependent on the decisions of his will.

My point is that God does not limit his sovereignty, but his eternal plan does take creaturely integrity into account. God does not want to make creatures who have no integrity. Thus, he makes beings who are fitted to carry out their distinctive purposes, and the other elements in God's plan respect those distinctive purposes.

While this position is clearly Reformed rather than Arminian, it does provide us with some talking points in discussions with our Arminian brothers and sisters. When they argue on behalf of free will and limited divine sovereignty, they may be erroneously groping for a genuinely scriptural point, namely, the reality of creaturely otherness and its integrity.

Indeed, we can tell the Arminian that God does take human nature into account when he formulates his eternal plan for us. But that is only one perspective! The other perspective is that God's knowledge of our nature is itself dependent on his plan to make us in a particular way. God's will is based on his knowledge, and his knowledge is based on his will. Ultimately all the attributes, including knowledge and will, are identical in the divine simplicity. But each attribute is a perspective on his nature and plan. The problem with the Arminian, then, is not so much in what he affirms, but in what he denies. And his problem may also be described as monoperspectivalism, insistence on looking at the problem from only one perspective.[48]

---

to the other. Of course, God's settled purpose does contain priorities in the sense that it establishes certain events as more important than others, some as instrumental to others, and so on.

46. For a thorough discussion of middle knowledge, see chapter 15. In that chapter, I give reasons for rejecting the concept as used by Molina, Suarez, Arminius, and such modern writers as William L. Craig and Alvin Plantinga.

47. See 1 Samuel 23:9–13, where God reveals to David what the men of Keilah will do to him if he stays there. So he leaves Keilah, and of course what God revealed to David does not take place. The passage indicates God's knowledge of what will happen in any hypothetical situation, even those that never take place. For more on the subject of middle knowledge, see the discussion of God's omniscience in chapter 15.

48. I might add that such monoperspectivalism is also a problem in hyper-Calvinism, from the opposite side.

Another way to understand what I am saying is to take into account the third lordship attribute, God's covenant presence. God not only controls us, and speaks to us with authority. He also grants to us covenantally a role to play in his great plan. In one sense, we are tools in his hand to accomplish his vast purpose for the universe. But in another sense, the universe is his tool for accomplishing his purpose in each of us. His vast power controls us, but he always acts in full knowledge of who we are, and in profound commitment to accomplish his individual purpose for each of us. Everything that happens furthers that commitment. Therefore, Paul can say:

> And we know that for those who love God all things work together for good, for those who are called according to his purpose. (Rom. 8:28)

Paul here speaks of believers, but we recall that God raises up even the wicked for the day of disaster.

In this sense, we can say reverently that human beings (more precisely, God's knowledge of each of us before creation) influence God's eternal plan.[49] God's sovereign plan includes a covenant commitment to every creature, to fulfill the role of that creature. That should also be, I think, a central element in our view of human freedom, responsibility, and significance. To feel free is to feel that one has a significant role to play in the world; and that is true of all of us. To feel responsible is to affirm for ourselves the purpose for which God has made us. To feel significant is to recognize that God has given each of us an important role in history, and that he has arranged everything else in the universe to be consistent with that role.

Divine and Human Creativity

We are important not only because we are different from God and in covenant with him, but also because we are his image (chapter 34). Much about the divine image is mysterious, because God himself is mysterious. But among other things, there does seem to be something in us analogous to God's *creativity*, and that is relevant to our freedom and significance.[50]

When God creates, he chooses to actualize one world among many possible worlds, as contemporary modal logicians like to put it. He chooses one possible world and rejects others. Human choice, also, is an activity of affirming one alternative and rejecting others. This aspect of choice, I think, has much to do with our intuition or feeling of freedom. Perhaps, indeed, it deserves to be called a fourth sense of *freedom*, in addition

---

49. Reformed theology has acknowledged this kind of divine-human relationship, for example, in the doctrine of *accommodation*. This doctrine says that God reveals himself in a form suited to creaturely understanding. In Scripture, for example, he uses human language, generally understandable to people with ordinary intelligence. Remember that revelation itself is the execution of a divine decree. God decrees to reveal himself in a way that is consistent with the nature of the creatures he has decreed to make. For other examples, see the storyteller model later in this chapter.

50. I am indebted (with thanks) to Vern Poythress for many of the thoughts in this section.

to moral agency, compatibilism, and libertarianism. I am inclined, however, to see it as an aspect of compatibilism: we act according to our desires, and our desires move us to choose some possibilities over others.

It is an interesting philosophical question to ask the ontological status of rejected possibilities. They are not simply nothing, for they are objects of knowledge. As we saw in the previous section, God *knows* what will happen if David remains in Keilah. God knows not only facts, but hypothetical situations, the outcome of contrary-to-fact conditionals.[51] But in the most obvious sense, these possibilities are not "real" either.

However we respond to that question, we should note that human beings, too, steer their lives through a thicket of possibilities, choosing again and again what direction to take, what possibility to actualize, what possibility to leave to the side. There are, I think, analogies to such choices in the animal kingdom, but the uniqueness of human rationality, power, and community gives our choices a complexity and significance far beyond the decisions of any animal.

God holds us responsible for these choices not only because of his lordship attribute of authority, but also because he is imaged in our power of choice. In that power, he has given us a wonderful gift: wonderful not because of any connection with libertarian freedom, but because it is truly Godlike. This gift speaks not of our independence from divine causation, but of our participation in God's creativity. For our choices among possible alternatives image the choices that God himself has made in eternity, and they serve as the means by which God actualizes and rejects possibilities in history.

This is another reason why we "feel" free. We often feel that we face real alternatives, that in some sense we "can" choose any of them. So for still another reason, the robot metaphor is inappropriate.

Models of Divine and Human Agency

I have argued that God is completely in control of the world and that man is nevertheless fully responsible for his own actions. I have also tried to shed some light on the mystery of how this can be so, and of how God and man can both play significant roles in the course of nature and history. But that discussion has been complicated. Are there any useful pictures or illustrations that will assist our thinking in these areas? Let us consider some proposals:[52]

1. *Pilot and Copilot*: The pilot and copilot both play roles in bringing the plane to its destination. But this is not a good picture of divine and human agency. Because when the copilot is flying the plane, the pilot is not doing so. Only one of them is directing the plane at any time. But in Scripture, God's control and man's action are both involved in bringing about the same historical results: recall God's action and the action of Joseph's brothers in sending Joseph to Egypt.

---

51. So the philosophical literature sometimes speaks of "counterfactuals of freedom."

52. Thanks here also to Vern Poythress for suggesting a discussion along these lines and for many of the ideas of this section. I take full responsibility, of course!

2. *Teacher and Classroom*: A good schoolteacher is in control of his class, but he does not necessarily cause every action of every student. He is in control, in that he has set boundaries that he has the power to enforce. But the students make their decisions independent of him, within those boundaries. In this picture, of course, the teacher represents God, and the students represent the creation, especially God's rational creatures. This model is favorable to a libertarian view of freedom, and it attempts to reconcile libertarianism with a significant form of divine sovereignty.

Certainly in Scripture God does set boundaries. Sometimes, as with the king of Assyria in Isaiah 10, or with the devil himself in the book of Job, God permits his creatures to do certain evil things, but sets limits. God, however, is different from even the best human teacher, in that he has the power to control every thought, word, and deed of those under his lordship. So when the king of Assyria invades Israel, God could have prevented that action, but he explicitly chose not to. So when God "permits" creatures to do things contrary to his will, it is because he intends for them to do those things.[53] That is the same as if he had explicitly brought those things to pass. So the teacher-classroom model is misleading as a picture of divine sovereignty and human freedom.

3. *Primary and Secondary Cause*: We are accustomed to thinking of nature as a sequence of causes and effects, in which cause A brings about effect B, which in turn serves as the cause of effect C, and so on. We may picture these relationships on a billiard table: the motion of one ball causes the motion of a second, and of a third, and so on. We sometimes describe A as the *primary* or *remote* cause of C, and B as the *secondary* or *proximate* cause of C.

This model has been common in Reformed thought. Calvin defended God against the charge of being the author of sin by pointing out that God was not the proximate, but only the remote, cause of human sin.[54] Many other Reformed thinkers have followed suit.[55] But I find it unpersuasive to defend God's goodness merely by saying that his involvement with sin is indirect.[56] In legal contexts, we hold a gang leader guilty for the crimes that he orders his subordinates to commit, even though the leader does not personally commit them; we may recall the infamous case of Charles Manson in this connection. This principle is scriptural. As we have seen, the owner of a bull is responsible for the damage his bull causes, even though the owner did not do the damage himself (Ex. 21:28–36).

Further, as we saw in our discussion of providence, God's involvement with creation is in some senses always direct (chapter 9). For not even the smallest motion of the

---

53. How can God intend for people to do wicked things? That is the problem of evil, the subject of chapter 14.

54. Calvin, *Concerning the Eternal Predestination of God*.

55. See, for examples, Cornelius Van Til, *The Defense of the Faith*, ed. K. Scott Oliphint (Phillipsburg, NJ: P&R Publishing, 2008), 242–47; Gordon H. Clark, *Religion, Reason, and Revelation* (Philadelphia: Presbyterian and Reformed, 1961), 238–40.

56. James, of course, tells us that God never *tempts* or *entices* us to sin (James 1:13–15); his Word always prompts us toward holiness and righteousness. But that is a different issue. Again, I refer the reader to the discussion of God's decretive and preceptive wills (see chapter 16). Preceptively, God commends only goodness; decretively, he sometimes ordains evil. See, again, the discussion of the problem of evil in chapter 14.

smallest object can occur without his government, preservation, and concurrence. He operates in and with the secondary causes, as well as by them.

The model is not wrong in saying that God often works through secondary causes. It is wrong, however, in suggesting that God does not also work directly, in and with his creation. Insofar as it does, it compromises with the nonbiblical concept of transcendence that we mention in chapter 3 and often through the book.

4. *The Commander and His Troops*: This model brings out the fact that God exercises his control particularly through his *word*, illustrating the unity of his control with his authority. He performs all his works by speaking: creation, providence, judgment, redemption. He makes the world by speaking (Gen. 1:3; Ps. 33:6), directs nature by his speech (Pss. 147:15–20; 148:7–8), judges us by his law, saves us by his gospel, draws us into his fellowship by his effectual calling. Jesus heals the centurion's servant by *commanding* the disease to leave him, just as the centurion commands his troops and they obey (Luke 7:1–10).

This model focuses on the lordship attribute of authority, as the previous one focused on the lordship attribute of control. This one emphasizes the personal character of God's causality. God is much less like a billiard ball in motion than he is like a general—even better, a father, who accomplishes his purposes by that very personal means of speaking.

The model does need to be generalized, however, to include forms of the word of God other than commands. God also accomplishes his purposes (in Scripture, for example) by promising, by expressing love, by sharing with us the poetry of his own heart.

5. *Author and Characters in a Story*: No analogy is a perfect description of the Creator-creature relationship, because that relationship is unique. But I do believe that the author-character model conveys significant insight. The author has complete control over his characters. But as I indicated in my discussion of creaturely otherness, the author seeks to make the characters and events fit together in a coherent and artistic way. Once he conceives of a character, that character "takes on a life of its own," as we say, and the author takes responsibility to shape the events of the story in light of the integrity of the character. And of course, the reverse is also true: he shapes the character to fit with complete integrity into the story.

In a well-wrought story, there is a causal nexus *within* the world that the author creates. Events can be explained not only by the author's intention, but also by the structure of "secondary causes" within the world of the story. When events can be explained only by the author's intention, we often use terms such as *deus ex machina*. Not always, but often, the intrusion of arbitrary elements not explainable from within the world of the story is the mark of an unskilled writer.

In Shakespeare's play, Macbeth kills King Duncan for his own reasons, using resources available to him.[57] Duncan's death can be described entirely by causes and effects within the world of the play. But the author, William Shakespeare, is the ultimate cause of everything. Furthermore, although Duncan's death can be explained by causes within

---

57. I have adapted the Shakespeare-Macbeth illustration from *GST*, 321–22.

the drama, the author is not just a "primary cause" who sets in motion a chain of causes and effects that unfold without his further involvement. Rather, he writes every detail of the narrative and dialogue; as author, he is involved in everything that happens. So there are two complete causal chains. Every event in Macbeth has two causes, two sets of necessary and sufficient conditions: the causes within the novel itself, and the intentions of Shakespeare.

The reason why every event in *Macbeth* can have two complete causes without irrationality is that the two sets of causes are on different levels. In a sense, Shakespeare and his character Macbeth live in two different worlds. Shakespeare could, of course, have written into the play a part for a character representing himself. He could have entered the drama from his side. But Macbeth cannot ascend from his position in the drama and become an author on the same level as Shakespeare.

The two worlds, then, are sufficiently distinct that the two causal chains play different roles. Perhaps it is misleading to call them both *causal*, though we can certainly understand why it is natural to do so.

On this analogy, we can see one reason why Macbeth is responsible for his actions, even though Shakespeare in one sense "made him" kill Duncan. In his world, on his level, Macbeth is the necessary and sufficient cause of Duncan's death. He is fully to blame.

So Macbeth is responsible within the plane of the story—*horizontally*, we might say. But is he also responsible vertically? Is he responsible to Shakespeare as we are responsible to God? Well, here the analogy bogs down a bit, but some things can be said: (a) Macbeth the character has not received revelation of Shakespeare's existence, nor is he held responsible for a covenant relationship with Shakespeare, as we are for our relationship with God. But an author other than Shakespeare might take on an even more godlike role: enter the drama to reveal his own standards to the characters, provoke them in some way to respond to this revelation, and then judge their responses. So vertical responsibility is possible within the authorial model. (b) Shakespeare was likely a theist, and in the play he created a world in which characters are responsible to God, not to himself. But Shakespeare is also an authority in Macbeth's world, for he sets up the standards by which Macbeth's actions will be evaluated. Shakespeare is not a modern nihilist; the world of his plays is a world in which traditional (mainly biblical) moral standards prevail. Indeed, Shakespeare is his judge, for Shakespeare invents the plot that brings Macbeth's downfall, since Shakespeare judges that downfall appropriate to Macbeth's actions. So in an important sense, Macbeth is responsible to Shakespeare.

We can see how various elements of this analogy reflect God's relationship to us: (a) God's creativity, (b) his fitting of characters to plot and vice versa, (c) the two complete causal structures, (d) God's complete control, (e) his involvement in every detail of the story, (f) the two distinct levels of reality, (g) the asymmetry by which God has the power in himself to become man, but we don't have power to become God, and (h) creaturely responsibility to other creatures and to God.

The relation between the author and his characters is analogous to the third lordship attribute: covenant presence. The author is always present in the drama, arranging the whole drama to fit the characters and the characters to fit the drama. He blesses and judges, using his own standards of evaluation. He is committed to the world that he has made. His characters take on lives of their own, lives of creaturely otherness. He does not treat them as robots, even though he has complete control over them. Rather, he interacts with them as person to persons, treating them as responsible individuals with whom he enjoys a certain communion.[58] In the sense I mentioned earlier, even though God has complete control over nature and history, his creatures do influence his plan. So between God and his creatures there is a certain give-and-take, as is characteristic of personal relationships.

The analogy is imperfect, chiefly in that the characters of a novel are fictitious, but the creatures of God are real.[59] God's creative achievement is therefore far greater than that of any human writer. Nevertheless, the parallels are worth our meditation.

Our model suggests exciting ways of looking at the course of nature and history. As with any story, human history is plagued by terrible difficulties that seem impossible to remedy. The fall brings a radical change in the human character. We have no resources for dealing with it. But God surprises us with the most amazing and wonderful deliverance: life from the death of his Son. This is not a deus ex machina, for Jesus is perfectly human as well as perfectly divine. As man, he must endure all the temptations, sorrows, and miseries of the fallen world. But he rises glorious from the dead to rule all the nations and to bring his purposes to pass. We continue to live amid sorrows that are, from the standpoint of our own resources, impenetrable. But we look forward to great surprises, as God comes to humble the proud and exalt the lowly in his grand resolution of the story.

Jesus also emerges from the broader historical process in the most wonderful way. For many centuries, God has prepared Israel for the coming of Christ, through prophecies, types, shadows, and redemptive events. When he arrives, he frustrates their existing messianic expectations. But with a deeper understanding of Scripture (see Luke 24:25–32), we perceive a profound organic unity between the OT Scriptures and Jesus' life, death, and resurrection. There is tension, but a deeper unity between the Lord and his historical environment. Thus, Scripture bears the mark of a great drama: tension, surprise, and shock, but nevertheless with a profound sense of inevitability.

As literature alone, this story would be fascinating. What is all the more wonderful is that it is real. And as we read on excitedly through a high-quality novel to delight in the author's creative resolutions of tensions, far more we may look at the trials of this

---

58. Dorothy Sayers is said to have fallen in love with her fictional detective, Lord Peter Wimsey. When Ayn Rand was asked whom she most admired, she cited several heroes from her novels. Writing a novel is often a give-and-take between author and characters, similar to relations among persons. Indeed, a novelist is much like a mother, in whom the characters gestate, are born, nurtured, matured, until they come to behave like real human beings.

59. Also, human authors are limited by their finite intellect and imagination, by the constraints of time, by the need to write according to socially approved genres, and so on. God's creation transcends these limitations.

life in the confident expectation that God will resolve the tensions in a way that will delight. Thus, we are encouraged to look toward God's complete victory over sin as the final solution of the problem of evil.

In chapter 14, we explored in other ways how this model may aid our consideration of the problem of evil. The model is not the final statement on the relationship between God and ourselves, but I do believe it draws our attention to genuine biblical emphases and encourages biblical ways of thinking.

Key Terms

Responsibility
Accountability
Liability
Integrity
Preventers
Ability
Moral inability
Determinism
Freedom
Moral freedom
Compatibilist freedom
Libertarian freedom
Incompatibilist freedom
Creaturely otherness
Integrity of creaturely otherness
Middle knowledge
Pilot and copilot
Teacher and classroom
Primary and secondary cause
Remote cause
Commander and troops
Author and character

Study Questions

1. Distinguish between responsibility as accountability and responsibility as liability. Why is this distinction important?

2. "To ask the question, then, of the 'relation between divine sovereignty and human responsibility' in this sense is initially to ask about the relationship between two lordship attributes, God's control and his authority." Explain; evaluate.

3. Show how responsibility, liability, and integrity line up with Frame's three perspectives.

4. "Indeed, we are even responsible for our moral nature." Explain; evaluate.

5. Cite some texts that refer to both divine sovereignty and human responsibility. Does the context of these texts indicate any tension between these two principles?

6. Does God's sovereignty ever imply that we should respond to him passively? Support your answer with examples.

7. Does ability ever limit our responsibility in the sense of liability? Give examples.

8. Does God's sovereign control over our actions ever constitute an excuse for sin? Discuss.

9. "Moral inability does not in the least mitigate compatibilist freedom, so it does not mitigate responsibility." Explain; evaluate.

10. Of Frame's criticisms of libertarianism, which do you think is most cogent? Discuss why. Are any of them worthless? Discuss why.

11. Would it be terrible if human beings were robots, programmed by God? Explain; evaluate. Is that a good way to describe our relation to God's sovereignty? Why or why not?

12. "Therefore, if the words *independence* and *autonomy* were not so often attached to unbiblical notions such as libertarianism, it might be possible to use them to describe the integrity of creaturely otherness." Explain; evaluate.

13. "There is in God's mind a reciprocity between foreknowledge and foreordination. Neither is simply 'prior' to the other." Explain; evaluate. Is this an Arminian position? Why or why not? How is this question related to God's middle knowledge?

14. Describe and evaluate the five models that Frame lists of divine-human interaction. Can you think of a better model?

Memory Verses

Matt. 23:37–39: O Jerusalem, Jerusalem, the city that kills the prophets and stones those who are sent to it! How often would I have gathered your children together as a hen gathers her brood under her wings, and you would not! See, your house is left to you desolate. For I tell you, you will not see me again, until you say, "Blessed is he who comes in the name of the Lord."

John 6:37: All that the Father gives me will come to me, and whoever comes to me I will never cast out.

Rom. 9:20–21: But who are you, O man, to answer back to God? Will what is molded say to its molder, "Why have you made me like this?" Has the potter no right over the clay, to make out of the same lump one vessel for honorable use and another for dishonorable use?

Phil. 2:12–13: Work out your own salvation with fear and trembling, for it is God who works in you, both to will and to work for his good pleasure.

Resources for Further Study

Calvin, John. *Concerning the Eternal Predestination of God.* London: James Clarke and Co., 1961.

Edwards, Jonathan. *Freedom of the Will.* New Haven: Yale University Press, 1973.

Frame, John M. *NOG.*

Frame, John M., and Paul Kurtz. "Without a Supreme Being, Everything Is Permitted." *Free Inquiry* 16, 2 (Spring 1996): 4–7.

Luther, Martin. *The Bondage of the Will.* London: James Clarke and Co., 1957.

CHAPTER 36

SIN

IN THE TWO PRECEDING CHAPTERS, I have focused on the metaphysical-ontological side of man's being. Man is made in the image of God, as God's vassal king over the earth, free and responsible. Now we must look at his ethical nature: made as a good creature of God, but fallen into sin.

Man's Original Goodness

Following each stage of creation in Genesis 1, God gives a positive evaluation of what he has made: it is good (vv. 4, 10, 12, 18, 21, 25, 31). The last of these verses includes the entire, finished creation, including man. *Good* is the broadest possible term of approval. There are, of course, various kinds of *goodness*. There is teleological goodness, that is, usefulness for some purpose, as when we speak of a "good hammer" or a "good tomato." There is aesthetic goodness, which in turn can refer to beauty, or aesthetic technique, or any number of other factors in a work of art. There is also moral goodness, applied to persons who have obeyed God's commands and therefore deserve God's blessing.[1] Scripture applies the vocabulary of moral goodness to persons, acts, and attitudes.[2] A hammer may be teleologically good, but it does not obey God's moral law so as to merit God's blessing, so it cannot be described as morally good. Moral goodness is a personal quality, applying only to humans, angels, and God himself.

When God declared the creation good, he meant *good* in every sense appropriate to every creature. The earth, plants, and animals were useful, fascinating, and beautiful. Each was formed and acted perfectly according to its God-given purpose. Adam and Eve were good in these senses, but also ethically good. Their actions, thoughts, words, and deeds pleased God. Otherwise, God would not have declared them good. And their very nature pleased him. They were good people, good servants of God. They bore God's image without distortion.

---

1. Of course, following the fall, none of us is good, as we will see (Isa. 64:6; Rom. 3:23). We can become good only by union with Christ and the work of the Spirit in our hearts.

2. I have discussed this distinction at greater length in *DCL*, 14–15.

So we must reject the notion that God created us in a morally neutral state, so that we could achieve goodness by our own decisions. God gave to Adam and Eve a *created character*. Scripture does not teach, contrary to much Arminian theology, that moral goodness and sin are always the result of conscious choice. Even before the fall, it is God who determines the moral character of his creatures. To say this, of course, is to raise again the problem of the relation of divine sovereignty and human responsibility. How can man be good if his moral character is created into him? Of course, the same problem arises with man's responsibility for sin and for that goodness in him that comes through redemptive grace. I know of no final answer to this mystery, but I would respond to it as I did in the previous chapter.

Another mystery also greets us at this point. If God conferred on Adam a morally good character, how did he become a sinner? Again, I know of no satisfying answer to this problem. But we should take pains to avoid speculative answers that the Scriptures do not warrant. As with the problem of evil that we discussed in chapter 14, many have sought to make Adam's transition from righteousness to sin more acceptable to reason, by invoking various philosophical concepts. The most common is the concept of libertarian freedom that I discussed in the previous chapter and in chapter 14. The argument is that God created Adam good, but free in the libertarian sense. And libertarian freedom has no constraint. It is not constrained by a person's character or by God's decree. But Scripture teaches that character does indeed constrain our decisions. Jesus says:

> The good person out of the good treasure of his heart produces good, and the evil person out of his evil treasure produces evil, for out of the abundance of the heart his mouth speaks. (Luke 6:45)

And as we saw in chapter 8, God himself controls the free decisions of man. That fact, along with the other arguments I offered in chapter 35, eliminates the possibility of libertarian free choice.

Others have tried to mitigate Scripture's confession of Adam's goodness, to find in Adam's original nature at least a small seed that would one day grow into full-blown sin. Roman Catholic theology, for example, distinguishes two elements in man's original constitution: (1) *Status naturae purae*, man's creation as soul and body, with "natural gifts," everything that makes him human. This is also called man *in puris naturalibus*. Now, the difference between soul and body leads to *pugna concupiscentiae*, the tendency (or, in some writers, the actuality) of a conflict between the desires of the body and the limits of reason. This tendency is not itself sinful, but it can lead to sin and therefore shows the need for additional divine gifts to maintain man's integrity. (2) *Dona superaddita*, "higher divine gifts," sometimes called *original righteousness*, by which body and soul are kept in harmony, the desires of the body in subjection to the dictates of reason. The highest of these gifts is *sanctity*,

> whereby man was made a partaker of the divine nature, elevated to a higher order of existence, endowed with what is above the essence of any created nature, adopted

into the position occupied by the only-begotten Son, and given the capacity for the beatific vision.[3]

In the fall, man loses the *dona superaddita* and reverts back to the *status naturae purae*.

So in Roman Catholic thought, the distinction between nature and grace extends back before the fall. The distinction between nature and grace is at the heart of Roman Catholic theology. At the beginning of his *ST*, Thomas Aquinas distinguishes between natural reason and faith and claims that the former can function without divine revelation, but the latter cannot. Similarly the distinction between church and state: the state governs man's natural life, the church man's life under grace.[4]

The fall itself, on the Roman Catholic view, is the result of man's free will (libertarian, evidently) to act against God's command. So clearly, the threefold scheme does nothing to make the first sin understandable. The *pugna concupiscentiae* is not itself sinful. It does not constrain man to sin. Only his free choice could have done that. So the Roman Catholic analysis is based on libertarian freedom. The two-layer analysis of the human condition, though it seems designed to rationalize man's sin to some extent, does not help at all.

Further:

1. As we saw in chapter 34, Scripture does not distinguish man's soul and body as metaphysical, separable components of his being. And certainly it does not present these as opposed to each other, as in Greek philosophy and in Roman Catholic theology.

2. On the Roman view, the desires of the body, seen in themselves, are often irrational, or else they could not be in conflict with reason. If so, then even in his original condition man was not *good* in a comprehensive sense. Further, he could not have been good in a specifically moral sense, because irrational desires seek ends that are contrary to God's glory.

3. The Roman distinction between nature and grace is not biblical. It claims that there is a part of man, nature, made to function apart from God (cf. Aquinas's "natural reason") and another part that brings us into a proper relation to God. What Scripture teaches is that no part of man, indeed no part of creation, can function apart from God's eternal decree, his law, and his covenantal presence.

4. The language quoted above about the result of the *dona superaddita* comes close to saying that man under grace can transcend the Creator-creature distinction. It is true that 2 Peter 1:4 speaks of our partaking of the divine nature.[5] But in context, Peter is talking about God's promises by which we have escaped the corruptions of sinful desire. This language is not metaphysical (transcending our finitude) but ethical (imaging God as we were created to do).

5. In discussing man's created character, it is important to distinguish metaphysics from ethics. In Scripture, the plight of human beings is not finitude (metaphysical) but

---

3. *MCW*, 2:43. In this discussion, I have followed John Murray's analysis at a number of points.

4. It is this distinction, in my view, that underlies the Lutheran conception of the "two kingdoms," which has also influenced Reformed theology. See my *The Escondido Theology* (Lakeland, FL: Whitefield Media, 2011).

5. This passage frequently comes up in Roman Catholic writings and in Eastern Orthodoxy's defense of its notion of *theopoiesis*, "deification." Cornelius Van Til used to say, jokingly, that this was the only Roman Catholic verse in the Bible. For my understanding of it, see chapter 45.

sin (ethical). Our need is not to rise to a higher ontological level by becoming divine or getting rid of our bodies,[6] but to be reconciled to God for our disobedience to him. If sin is a metaphysical defect, then it is just part of being human, and we will have to cope with it throughout our human existence. In that case, the only way to overcome sin is to become something other than human. But if sin is ethical, as Scripture teaches, then it is an estrangement with another person, and the remedy is personal reconciliation. Since God is willing to be reconciled to us through Christ, we have hope.

6. As we will see, the state of man after the fall is nothing like the Roman Catholic description of the *status naturae purae*. It is rather a state in which man is actually sinful, in all aspects of his being.

So it is best for us to stick to what Scripture says about man's original condition, even though that teaching fails to solve to our satisfaction the mystery of how sin entered the world. Adam and Eve were purely and simply good. Like the rest of creation, there was no defect in them, nothing that could have been criticized. They were the image of God, they performed their functions well, and they were holy in thought, word, and deed. So WLC 17 says that Adam and Eve at their creation had "the law of God written in their hearts, and power to fulfil it, and dominion over the creatures; yet subject to fall."

"Subject to fall" is the mystery that I have been speaking of. The Westminster Standards wisely refrain from trying to spell out what it was in Adam and Eve that made the fall possible.

The Nature of Sin

Scripture defines human righteousness in three ways that reflect God's lordship attributes. See fig. 36.1.

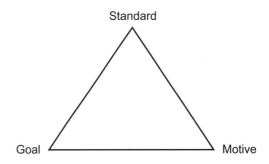

Fig. 36.1. Criteria for Good Works

A good or righteous deed is one that (1) obeys the proper standard, God's law (James 4:11; 1 John 3:4), (2) seeks the proper goal, God's glory (1 Cor. 10:31) and the success

---

6. In Gnosticism, Neoplatonism, and religions such as Buddhism, salvation is metaphysical—a method of escaping our earthly existence.

of his kingdom (Matt. 6:33), and (3) is motivated by true faith (Rom. 14:23) and love (1 Cor. 13:1–3).[7] WCF 16.7 uses these perspectives to illumine the difference between the good works of believers and those of the unregenerate:

> Works done by unregenerate men, although for the matter of them they may be things which God commands; and of good use both to themselves and others: yet, because they proceed not from a heart purified by faith; nor are done in a right manner, according to the Word; nor to a right end, the glory of God, they are therefore sinful, and cannot please God, or make a man meet to receive grace from God: and yet, their neglect of them is more sinful and displeasing unto God.

If this is the case, then the best definition of sin will accommodate this threefold defectiveness in unregenerate behavior: a false standard (normative), a false goal (situational), and a false motive (existential). The Westminster catechisms, when they present their actual definitions of sin, focus on the normative: disobedience to God's law. WLC 24: "Sin is any want of conformity unto, or transgression of, any law of God, given as a rule to the reasonable creature." WSC 14: "Sin is any want of conformity unto, or transgression of, the law of God." The normative perspective, of course, embraces the other two. To adopt the wrong ethical goal is certainly opposed to God's law, as is acting from the wrong motive. But the situational and existential perspectives remind us that ethical behavior is not just a response to commands, but commitment to a historical program (the kingdom of God, magnifying his glory) and a personal relationship (our faith in and love for Christ).[8] A complete, triperspectival definition of sin might be as shown in fig. 36.2.

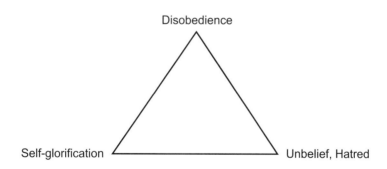

Fig. 36.2. Definition of Sin

The normative definition of sin ("sin is lawlessness," 1 John 3:4) is often prominent in Scripture, especially because the first sin was disobedience to a specific divine com-

---

7. I have discussed this triad at great length in *DCL* as an analysis of biblical ethics.
8. I discuss this ethical triad at length in *DCL*, chaps. 9–21.

mand. That needs to be emphasized today especially, when even the church seems to have a distaste for keeping authoritative commands. All of Scripture calls us to obey God. Indeed, all of Scripture functions as command, because it is the Word of God. Whether we are reading the books of law, the books of history, the Psalms, or the Epistles, the text of Scripture comes to us with the force of a divine command: to believe, do, assimilate, and appreciate everything we hear. And for believers, obeying the law is not necessarily a burden, let alone the "threat" and "terror" of Lutheran theology, but a delight (Pss. 1:2; 119:16, 24, 97).[9] There is no biblical justification for the mistaken equation between obedience and *legalism*[10] that one often hears today. Nor should we encourage believers to worry that trying to obey God will lead them toward justification by works. We are saved entirely by God's grace, but grace saves us "for good works" (Eph. 2:8–10). God gives grace, and we seek to obey. This is the relationship between divine sovereignty and human responsibility that we explored in chapter 35. As Paul says:

> The saying is trustworthy, and I want you to insist on these things, so that those who have believed in God may be careful to devote themselves to good works. These things are excellent and profitable for people. (Titus 3:8)

But our life in covenant with God is not only a life of obeying commands. As the situational perspective indicates, it is a journey toward God's kingdom, seeking to bring glory to him. And the existential perspective indicates that it is a relationship of faith and love, walking with our precious Savior.

Our triperspectival understanding of sin helps us to understand that sin is a condition of the human heart and therefore affects all areas of our lives. Jesus says:

> Either make the tree good and its fruit good, or make the tree bad and its fruit bad, for the tree is known by its fruit. You brood of vipers! How can you speak good, when you are evil? For out of the abundance of the heart the mouth speaks. The good person out of his good treasure brings forth good, and the evil person out of his evil treasure brings forth evil. (Matt. 12:33–35; cf. Gen. 6:5–6; 8:21; Ps. 14:1; Jer. 17:9)

The fall, therefore, did not begin with Eve's eating the fruit, but with her inner *intention* to eat the fruit. As Jesus repeatedly emphasizes in the Sermon on the Mount, God's commandments are not merely about externals. The sixth commandment forbids not only murder, but the anger that leads to murder (Matt. 5:21–26). The seventh commandment forbids not only adultery, but also lust (Matt. 5:27–30).

So sin is a radical disruption in the core of our being. In sin, we turn from God's good commandments, his kingdom and glory, faith, and love. It embraces rebellious

---

9. The delight of keeping the law pervades Psalm 119, the longest chapter in the Bible.

10. A *legalist* is someone who puts law in the role that Scripture assigns to grace. The word should not be used to describe a believer whose "delight is in the law of the Lord" (Ps. 1:2).

disobedience, the kingdom of Satan, and evil attitudes (hatred, immorality, strife, jealousy, anger, envy, and so on).[11]

Thus, sin is *irrational*. Why would anyone turn from the beauty and joy of covenant life with God and embrace its opposite? Or why would anyone think he could succeed in opposing God's omnipotent power? Satan is the example. Evidently he thought he could replace God on the throne. Although we generally consider Satan to be knowledgeable and intelligent, and although many opponents of God seem wise to the world and to themselves, they are guilty of the worst imaginable stupidity. They haven't a ghost of a chance to defeat God. Yet sinners embrace sin with reckless enthusiasm. This is the root of its noetic effects.

It might seem that since all sin is of the heart, every sin is equally heinous. But Scripture does indicate that some sins are worse than others. They are the same in that any and every sin merits eternal judgment (Gen. 2:17; Deut. 27:26; Ezek. 18:4; 33:8; Rom. 5:16; 6:23; Gal. 3:10; James 2:10–11). But some have more harmful consequences than others in this life, and so they offend God more deeply. Scripture distinguishes "greater" from "lesser" sins (Ezek. 8:6, 13ff.; Matt. 5:19; 23:23; John 19:11). The law of Moses distinguishes between "unintentional" sins (Lev. 4:2, 13, 22; 5:17) and sins committed with a "high hand" (Num. 15:27–30). In the NT, Paul tells us that some sins should lead to excommunication (1 Cor. 6), but others need not (Rom. 14:1–4). James indicates that those who teach "will be judged with greater strictness" (James 3:1). So a sin committed by a teacher could be more serious than the same sin committed by someone who is not a teacher.

One sin is "unpardonable" (Matt. 12:31–32; Heb. 6:4–6; 10:26–27; 1 John 5:16–17). It is difficult to know exactly what this sin is, but the contexts give us some guidance as to its general character. Wayne Grudem's definition seems appropriate: "malicious, wilful rejection and slander against the Holy Spirit's work attesting to Christ, and attributing that work to Satan."[12] This definition helps us to see that the unpardonable sin is not an isolated thought or comment, but a settled pattern of thought and behavior, an irreparable hardening of the heart against Christ. Clearly, those who are sorry for their sin and conscience-stricken have not committed the unpardonable sin.[13]

The Origin of Sin

I indicated above that in the Bible, sin is not an aspect of man's created nature. It is not simply part of what we are. It is rather the disruption of a personal relationship. And like all personal estrangements, it began in a series of events. The origin of sin is historical, an event that the church has called the *fall of man*.

Sin began in the angelic realm before it infected man (see chapter 33). Then, after God created man, a serpent approached the woman. Scripture identifies the serpent

---

11. See, e.g., Gal. 5:19–21.

12. *GST*, 508.

13. I will not consider in this chapter the argument in Roman Catholic and Barthian theology that sin is a form of nonbeing, a privation. I have discussed that subject in chapter 14 in connection with the problem of evil.

with Satan, the leader of the angelic rebellion (Rev. 12:9, 14–15; 20:2). The Genesis narrative describes their conversation:

> He said to the woman, "Did God actually say, 'You shall not eat of any tree in the garden'?" And the woman said to the serpent, "We may eat of the fruit of the trees in the garden, but God said, 'You shall not eat of the fruit of the tree that is in the midst of the garden, neither shall you touch it, lest you die.'" But the serpent said to the woman, "You will not surely die. For God knows that when you eat of it your eyes will be opened, and you will be like God, knowing good and evil." So when the woman saw that the tree was good for food, and that it was a delight to the eyes, and that the tree was to be desired to make one wise, she took of its fruit and ate, and she also gave some to her husband who was with her, and he ate. Then the eyes of both were opened, and they knew that they were naked. And they sewed fig leaves together and made themselves loincloths.
>
>   And they heard the sound of the LORD God walking in the garden in the cool of the day, and the man and his wife hid themselves from the presence of the LORD God among the trees of the garden. But the LORD God called to the man and said to him, "Where are you?" And he said, "I heard the sound of you in the garden, and I was afraid, because I was naked, and I hid myself." He said, "Who told you that you were naked? Have you eaten of the tree of which I commanded you not to eat?" The man said, "The woman whom you gave to be with me, she gave me fruit of the tree, and I ate." Then the LORD God said to the woman, "What is this that you have done?" The woman said, "The serpent deceived me, and I ate." (Gen. 3:1–13)

Satan begins by questioning God's word. Such questioning is arguably the root of all sin (see chapters 23–28). After Eve replies that, yes, God has spoken, and after she corrects Satan's implied misrepresentation of God's word, Satan directly contradicts what God has said: "You will not surely die." He implies that God is withholding a blessing that Eve really ought to have. Then Eve turns from consideration of God's word and begins to think autonomously. She follows her senses, noting the genuinely good qualities of the forbidden fruit. Then she mistakenly reasons that these good qualities are sufficient justification for eating the fruit in disobedience to God. She eats, and gives some to her husband. Though Adam was evidently present during this conversation, he does not exercise godly leadership over his wife, but follows her in following Satan. When God confronts them, Eve blames the serpent and Adam blames Eve. Ultimately he blames God, who gave Eve to be his wife, "the woman whom you gave to be with me" (Gen. 3:12).

   So sin is the disruption of a personal relationship, and it brings further disruption. Indeed, it is an attempt to overturn the order of creation. In God's order, he is the ultimate authority. Adam is a subordinate authority, to whom Eve is to be submissive (Eph. 5:22). Together, Adam and Eve are to have dominion over the animals. But in the story of the fall, the woman submits to an animal, the man submits to his wife, and both of them claim to be judges of God's behavior.

Many have questioned the historicity of the fall, but it is important for us to maintain that it actually happened. In chapter 34, I defended the historicity of Adam and Eve as persons, based on the NT references to them, especially the parallel between Adam and Christ. Of course, many of those references pertain to the fall. "As in Adam all die, so also in Christ shall all be made alive" (1 Cor. 15:22). As we die in sin because of the one sin of the one man Adam, we live by the one act of the one man Jesus Christ (Rom. 5:12–21).

There are two possibilities: either sin is a component of human nature (as some have said, "Adam is everyman") or it began after God had already established human nature, in a historical event. The first possibility leaves us without hope. For we can never escape our nature, and if sin is part of that nature, we can never escape sin or its consequences. But if sin came into the world through a historical event, it is possible for other events to reverse the first.

God's Response to the Fall

Almost immediately after the first sin comes the beginning of the history of redemption. God conducts an inquiry of the serpent, the woman, and the man to prepare the terms of his verdict. Having conducted his inquiry, he pronounces sentence:

The LORD God said to the serpent,

"Because you have done this,
      cursed are you above all livestock
      and above all beasts of the field;
on your belly you shall go,
      and dust you shall eat
      all the days of your life.
I will put enmity between you and the woman,
      and between your offspring and her offspring;
he shall bruise your head,
      and you shall bruise his heel."

To the woman he said,

"I will surely multiply your pain in childbearing;
      in pain you shall bring forth children.
Your desire shall be for your husband,
      and he shall rule over you."

And to Adam he said,

"Because you have listened to the voice of your wife
      and have eaten of the tree

of which I commanded you,
   'You shall not eat of it,'
cursed is the ground because of you;
   in pain you shall eat of it all the days of your life;
thorns and thistles it shall bring forth for you;
   and you shall eat the plants of the field.
By the sweat of your face
   you shall eat bread,
till you return to the ground,
   for out of it you were taken;
for you are dust,
   and to dust you shall return."

The man called his wife's name Eve, because she was the mother of all living. And the Lord God made for Adam and for his wife garments of skins and clothed them.
   Then the Lord God said, "Behold, the man has become like one of us in knowing good and evil. Now, lest he reach out his hand and take also of the tree of life and eat, and live forever—" therefore the Lord God sent him out from the garden of Eden to work the ground from which he was taken. (Gen. 3:14–23)

As we would expect, God pronounces curses on the three defendants. But surprisingly, these curses are mixed with blessings. Among the curses on the Satan-serpent, there is the promise of enmity between his offspring and man's. This is a blessing for man, because it implies that man will not be a passive servant of Satan; he will fight back. Further, one of man's offspring will deal to Satan a deadly blow, crushing his head, though in the process Satan will bruise his heel. The church has regarded this as the first messianic promise, to be fulfilled in Jesus Christ, whose atoning death was the bruise on the heel by which Satan's head was crushed.

   God curses the woman with pain in childbearing. The blessing, however, is that there will indeed be childbearing. The threat "in the day that you eat of it you shall surely die" (Gen. 2:17) is not to be carried out fully or immediately.[14] God is giving time for redemption. And the woman's childbearing is the very means of redemption. Her offspring will crush the head of Satan. God also curses the man in the work of farming: the ground will bear thorns and thistles until the man dies physically. But there is blessing there, too, for man's work, like the woman's childbearing, is to be successful. He will supply food to his family so that their childbearing can continue. So, as in the cultural mandate (1:28), man is to subdue the earth (through labor) and to fill the earth (through childbearing).

---

14. Scripture describes various kinds of death: physical (Gen. 3:19), spiritual (Eph. 2:1), and eternal (Rev. 2:11; 20:6, 14; 21:8). These are all the result of sin, so clearly the fall unleashed death in all its forms. God would have had the right after the fall to bring all forms of death on man simultaneously. But his intention was to apply the death penalty through a history rather than through a single event, just as his intention to redeem was to take a long time. Of course, the very delay in the fulfillment of the death penalty is due to grace. As Peter says (2 Peter 3:9), God delays the final judgment so that all the elect may be brought to repentance.

Adam might have named his wife "death," because her decision brought death into the world.[15] But instead Adam called her Eve, "life-giver." Adam believes God's promise that she will bring forth living children and that one of those will bring redemption from death altogether. Similarly, when Eve bears Cain in Genesis 4:1, she says, "I have gotten a man with the help of the Lord." So both Adam and Eve express faith in God's promise. On this basis, we may be confident of their salvation.

But there is another curse. God expels Adam and Eve from the garden and forbids them to return. They are sent away from the temple, the area of God's most intimate presence, and they must make their way as pilgrims. To these pilgrims, God's cultural mandate still applies: they are to fill the earth and subdue it (cf. Gen. 9:1–7).[16]

But in their exile, they take with them faith in God's promise of salvation. They instruct their sons in the need for sacrifice, though one of them fails to bring a proper offering (Gen. 4:1–7). And in the time of their third son, Seth, and his son Enosh, there is a worshiping community: "At that time people began to call upon the name of the Lord" (Gen. 4:26).

The Effects of the Fall

Despite these evidences of God's grace and human faith, sin does not end with the fall of Adam and Eve. After the fall their children, indeed all later generations of human beings, commit sin. Cain murders his brother Abel (Gen. 4:1–16), and several generations later Lamech boasts of murder and vengeance (4:23–24). Eventually sin becomes so prevalent and deep that God destroys the world by a flood (chaps. 6–9). But the flood does not wash away sin from the earth. God says, "I will never again curse the ground because of man, for the intention of man's heart is evil from his youth" (8:21). And many generations later, Paul, referring to the whole human race, said that "none is righteous, no, not one" (Rom. 3:10).

The effects of the fall on the human race can be summarized in our familiar three-fold way as shown in fig. 36.3.

15. Clearly, there was no human death before the fall. But Bible students sometimes ask whether there could have been death in the animal kingdom before the fall of man. Scripture does not explicitly discuss this subject, though the frequent biblical connection between death and sin in general might lead one to say that even nonhuman death came after the fall. On the other hand, we know that Adam ate fruit from the garden before the fall, and eating plants does kill living cells.

16. The reason for their expulsion: "lest he reach out his hand and take also of the tree of life and eat, and live forever." This is connected with the fact that "the man has become like one of us in knowing good and evil" (Gen. 3:22). I don't entirely understand this, but I look at it this way. Adam and Eve have come to know good and evil in a new way. They had known these concepts before as possible alternatives, but now they know them from practical experience. Specifically, they now know the *pleasure* of disobedience. And although that disobedience leads eventually to curse, and they have survived the curse with promises of blessing, disobedience is still a temptation. Just as Adam and Eve have illegitimately taken the fruit of one forbidden tree, so they might very well take the fruit of the other tree, the Tree of Life, without God's permission. If they do that, God says, they will live forever, but they will have stolen that life, taken it by their own effort rather than receiving it by God's grace. So their eternal life will be a life under curse. God's intention is to give them eternal life his own way, not through their grasping but through his grace, in the cross of Jesus.

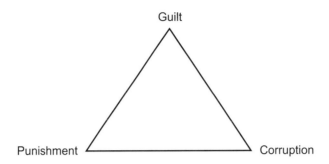

Fig. 36.3. Effects of the Fall

Guilt is the normative perspective, our liability for breaking God's command. Scripture teaches that all human beings except Jesus are guilty of Adam's sin. *Punishment,* the situational perspective, is the curse that comes upon the creation and upon ourselves because of the first sin. The Westminster Standards speak of this as "misery."[17] *Corruption,* the existential perspective, is our continuing sinfulness, including our sinful heart, and our resulting delight in sin.

Guilt

Scripture teaches that we are all guilty of Adam's sin. Not just that we are punished for it (for without guilt, punishment is unjust), but that we are actually guilty of it.[18] It is hard for modern people to accept that a person can be guilty of someone else's sin, even the sin of an ancestor. But first we must be clear that Scripture actually teaches this doctrine.

It is sometimes called *original sin*, but I will avoid that phrase because of its ambiguity. Sometimes *original sin* refers to Adam's first sin, sometimes to our guilt in him, sometimes to our present sinful condition. Wayne Grudem has suggested the term "inherited sin," and I will follow him in using it.[19]

Scripture teaches the doctrine of inherited sin most clearly in Romans 5:12–19 and 1 Corinthians 15:21–22. We should have the former passage open before us:

> Therefore, just as sin came into the world through one man, and death through sin, and so death spread to all men because all sinned—for sin indeed was in the world before the law was given, but sin is not counted where there is no law. Yet death reigned from Adam to Moses, even over those whose sinning was not like the transgression of Adam, who was a type of the one who was to come.
>
> But the free gift is not like the trespass. For if many died through one man's trespass, much more have the grace of God and the free gift by the grace of that one

17. WCF 6.6; WLC 23; WSC 17, 19.

18. In technical theological language, we are liable both to guilt (*reatus culpa*) and to punishment (*reatus poena*). God *imputes* the sin of Adam to us.

19. *GST,* 494n8.

man Jesus Christ abounded for many. And the free gift is not like the result of that one man's sin. For the judgment following one trespass brought condemnation, but the free gift following many trespasses brought justification. For if, because of one man's trespass, death reigned through that one man, much more will those who receive the abundance of grace and the free gift of righteousness reign in life through the one man Jesus Christ.

Therefore, as one trespass led to condemnation for all men, so one act of righteousness leads to justification and life for all men. For as by the one man's disobedience the many were made sinners, so by the one man's obedience the many will be made righteous.[20]

Consistently with the rest of the passage, the "all sinned" in verse 12 must refer to the sin of all human beings in Adam. We should be reminded by this phrase that, strictly speaking, we do not bear the guilt of *someone else's* sin. For the sin of Adam was in some sense *our own* sin, and therefore God is right to judge us for it. How is it fair for God to give us ownership of Adam's sin? I will attempt to deal with this question below.

In verses 13–14, Paul says that sin was in the world before God gave his law to Moses.[21] People in that time could not have been judged sinners by a law that would be given only in the future. So on what basis were they judged to be sinners and condemned to death? Because of their solidarity with Adam. In verse 14, Paul does point out that their sin "was not like the transgression of Adam." That is, the pre-Mosaic peoples did not sin in the garden by eating forbidden fruit as Adam did. But they sinned *in* Adam and are judged in him.

Verse 15 makes this point explicit: Many (everybody) died through one man's trespass. In verse 16, then, we are condemned for the sin of the one man. In verse 17, death came through the one man. In verse 18, Adam's one trespass "led to condemnation for all men." Verse 19 says that through Adam's disobedience "the many were made sinners." Note that in verses 18 and 19 it is not just that Adam's sin led to our punishment, but that it led to our sinful status before God, our guilt. So in 1 Corinthians 15:21–22, Paul can say:

For as by a man came death, by a man has come also the resurrection of the dead. For as in Adam all die, so also in Christ shall all be made alive.

Now we must face the objection: is this fair? Consider the following:

1. We never have the right to charge God with unfairness, even when he has chosen not to provide us with a justification for his actions. I discussed this principle in chapter 14.

20. I follow largely John Murray's exegesis of this passage, from his *The Imputation of Adam's Sin* (Grand Rapids: Eerdmans, 1959), which I consider definitive.

21. People did, of course, have access to God's moral law in creation (Rom. 1), and most likely, they had access to the creation ordinances by some kind of tradition. But in Paul's letter, the law of Moses is a major subject of discussion. Paul wants to tell his Jewish readers that the basis of human sin is broader than the law of Moses. Both Jews and Gentiles are guilty of sin, whether or not they have had access to the law of Moses.

2. Whether or not we are implicated in Adam's sin, we are certainly guilty of many sins that are indisputably our own. So to charge God with unfairness in the teaching of Romans 5:12–19 is either a mere theoretical exercise or an attempt to justify ourselves. But given our actual sins, that desire is futile.

3. Most likely, if we had been in Adam's place, we would have sinned as he did. He had advantages that we do not have today: a good character, a perfect, uncursed environment, a very open relationship with God. He had all the food and water he wanted. There was only one source of temptation: a clear, identifiable, external being. If he did not resist the tempter under those conditions, it is unlikely that any of us could have done any better. Indeed, it is a measure of the righteousness of Christ that he resisted Satan in a world cursed by sin, in a wilderness, having fasted for forty days, and, later, facing death on the cross. So we should be thankful that God determined to judge the human race on the basis of a representative rather than judging each of us individually.

4. Human life always has a corporate dimension. Inevitably, what one person does has consequences for others. We don't exist as isolated individuals, but we are dependent on one another. We live in families, for example, and parents have an enormous influence on their children, to such an extent that God visits "the iniquity of the fathers on the children" (Ex. 20:5). Parents influence their children so as to pass on to them their own moral character, as well as their physical characteristics. Similarly, nations often suffer for the sins of their rulers. And the same is true in other spheres of authority: church, business, education. Adam, of course, did not have to deal with such preexisting influences. He, and only he, was a true "individual." He could make his ethical decisions without their being skewed by family or society. This is another reason why it was best for Adam, and only Adam, to be judged as an individual, and us as represented by him.

5. If we object to God's act of condemning us in Adam, we should equally object to his justifying us in Christ. In Romans 5:12–19 and 1 Corinthians 15:21–22, these two relationships are parallel. We should, then, reject Christ's sacrifice and accept the task of trying to save ourselves as individuals. But that task is doomed from the start. Scripture gives us no hope that we can save ourselves. We cannot atone for our past sins, nor can we force ourselves to stop sinning, apart from divine grace (Eph. 2:8–9).

Punishment

In Genesis 3, we saw that God pronounced punishments on the serpent, Eve, and Adam. Those punishments continue with us. The serpent still travels on his belly. Enmity between man and Satan continues and defines the major conflict of subsequent human history. Woman still experiences pain in childbearing, and man pain and toil in his labor. All of this leads to death (Gen. 3:19), and *death* describes the punishment as a whole. All of human life is in the shadow of impending death, and the other ills of this life foreshadow it.[22] So Ezekiel says that "the soul who sins shall die" (Ezek.

---

22. Many existentialist philosophers are far from the gospel of Christ, but they do express eloquently what Martin Heidegger called "being toward death" and Jean-Paul Sartre our constant confrontation with "nothingness."

18:4), and Paul says that "the wages of sin is death" (Rom. 6:23). And in the passage we looked at earlier, Paul says that "death spread to all men because all sinned" (Rom. 5:12). Ultimately that death will be an eternal separation from God if God's grace does not avert it.

The punishment on Adam had implications for the rest of creation: "cursed is the ground because of you" (Gen. 3:17). Now the ground, which so easily provided fruit for Adam and Eve in the garden, resists Adam's attempts to feed himself and his family. Paul comments further:

> For the creation waits with eager longing for the revealing of the sons of God. For the creation was subjected to futility, not willingly, but because of him who subjected it, in hope that the creation itself will be set free from its bondage to corruption and obtain the freedom of the glory of the children of God. For we know that the whole creation has been groaning together in the pains of childbirth until now. (Rom. 8:19–22)

Here creation itself experiences effects of man's fall. God appointed mankind to rule the creation, and here as elsewhere the ruler's sins rebound upon his kingdom. So symbolically at least (but who knows the full extent of what these symbols refer to?), the creation itself longs, groans, for the consummation of redemption. So the return of Christ will be not only the completion of redemption for man, but also "the time for restoring all . . . things" (Acts 3:21). Jesus' redemption applies to the entire universe, not only to mankind. He is the One by whom, through whom, and for whom all things were made (Col. 1:16).

> For in him all the fullness of God was pleased to dwell, and through him to reconcile to himself all things, whether on earth or in heaven, making peace by the blood of his cross. (Col. 1:19–20)

This is sometimes called *cosmic redemption*. The point is not that the stars and planets have sinned and need atonement as human beings do. But rather, the sin of human beings has led to a twisting of the whole universe that only redemption of human sin can set right.

This cosmic disruption is an index of the seriousness of human sin. Sin affects us all. But not only us—also the entire creation. To confess the guilt of Adam's sin is to confess our responsibility for the evil in the natural world. Natural evil is the result of moral evil. Natural disasters are among God's means of punishing sin and reminding us of our need of redemption. When the tower of Siloam fell, killing eighteen people, Jesus asked:

> Do you think that they were worse offenders than all the others who lived in Jerusalem? No, I tell you; but unless you repent, you will all likewise perish. (Luke 13:4–5)

Corruption

The third consequence of the first sin is its impact on the moral character of Adam's descendants. Adam's sin begets more sin: the sin of Cain, who murdered his brother; the sin of Lamech, who boasted of his murder and vengeance; and all the other sins we commit every day. Neither the punishments discussed above nor our striving to be better can keep us from sinning.

In what follows, I will gather biblical descriptions of our sin. In this section, I will be considering our sinful nature and actions apart from the influences of God's grace. These passages describe what we are apart from Christ. There is some danger in this procedure, because the Bible's descriptions of sin apart from grace are terrible. Taken in themselves, they destroy hope. But the Bible does encourage us to take these evaluations in themselves, in order to take away the hope that we can save ourselves. We need to see sin at its worst in order to appreciate best what Christ has done for us. Afterward, we must quickly turn to Christ, for the Bible's depiction of sin is for that purpose: to move us to turn to Christ to deliver us from ourselves.

This continuing sin is, first of all, a heart condition. We have seen (chapter 32) that the heart is the "center" of our being, the inner disposition that governs all our thoughts, words, and deeds (Matt. 12:34–35; 15:8, 18–19). Of that heart, God says through Jeremiah, "The heart is deceitful above all things, and desperately sick; who can understand it?" (Jer. 17:9). To speak of corruption at the level of the heart is to speak of a "sinful nature," a moral "deadness":

> And you were dead in the trespasses and sins in which you once walked, following the course of this world, following the prince of the power of the air, the spirit that is now at work in the sons of disobedience—among whom we all once lived in the passions of our flesh, carrying out the desires of the body and the mind, and were by nature children of wrath, like the rest of mankind. (Eph. 2:1–3; cf. 4:18)

As a dead man cannot get up and walk around, so a morally dead person cannot do works pleasing to God. Another biblical figure is bondage: we are *slaves* to sin (John 8:34).

The sinful nature is not something we acquired during our lifetime. It is ours from birth, even from conception. David says, "Behold, I was brought forth in iniquity, and in sin did my mother conceive me" (Ps. 51:5; cf. Gen. 8:21; Ps. 58:3). So we cannot prevent it any more than we can do away with it in our own strength.

Therefore, *all* of us, except Jesus, are sinners. "All" have sinned (Rom. 3:23; cf. 1 Kings 8:46; Pss. 14:3; 143:2; Prov. 20:9; 1 John 1:8–10). In Romans, Paul develops the argument that all Gentiles have sinned and are therefore under God's wrath (chap. 1), and then that the Jews are just as bad (2:1–3:8). He concludes:

> What then? Are we Jews any better off? No, not at all. For we have already charged that all, both Jews and Greeks, are under sin, as it is written:

"None is righteous, no, not one;
    no one understands;
    no one seeks for God.
All have turned aside; together they have become worthless;
    no one does good,
    not even one."
"Their throat is an open grave;
    they use their tongues to deceive."
"The venom of asps is under their lips."
    "Their mouth is full of curses and bitterness."
"Their feet are swift to shed blood;
    in their paths are ruin and misery,
and the way of peace they have not known."
    "There is no fear of God before their eyes."

Now we know that whatever the law says it speaks to those who are under the law, so that every mouth may be stopped, and the whole world may be held accountable to God. For by works of the law no human being will be justified in his sight, since through the law comes knowledge of sin. (Rom. 3:9–20)

So all human beings, except Jesus, are sinful from birth, and from the heart. We now face the question: *how* sinful are we? The expressions of Romans 3, above, are very severe, not to mention Ephesians 2:1–3. Even more so is this verse:

The LORD saw that the wickedness of man was great in the earth, and that every intention of the thoughts of his heart was only evil continually. (Gen. 6:5)

This is an extraordinary passage. The "every," the "only," and the "continually" are extreme expressions that leave no room for mitigation. We do, of course, have to recognize that this divine judgment came at one of the darkest points in human history. Human wickedness had reached an extreme level, so that God counts man worthy of destruction by flood, saving only Noah and his family. But God's judgment of man's moral condition is virtually the same after the flood: "the intention of man's heart is evil from his youth" (Gen. 8:21). The flood demonstrated that man's sin cannot be washed away by water.

So we should conclude that sinful man cannot do anything good in God's sight. Consider these passages:

We have all become like one who is unclean,
    and all our righteous deeds are like a polluted garment.
We all fade like a leaf,
    and our iniquities, like the wind, take us away. (Isa. 64:6)

For I know that nothing good dwells in me, that is, in my flesh. For I have the desire to do what is right, but not the ability to carry it out. (Rom. 7:18)

> To the pure, all things are pure, but to the defiled and unbelieving, nothing is pure; but both their minds and their consciences are defiled. (Titus 1:15)

And we should remind ourselves of what we discussed in chapter 29, that sinful man cannot even *understand* the things of God:

> The natural person does not accept the things of the Spirit of God, for they are folly to him, and he is not able to understand them because they are spiritually discerned. (1 Cor. 2:14)

These passages present the sin of the human race in extreme terms. There is nothing here to give us any hope that we can achieve anything good, let alone save ourselves from sin. Sin pervades our existence.

But is it really true that there is "no good in us"? We see many people around us who have no interest in God, but who appear to be kind, gentle, generous, indeed to be better people than many who trust in Christ. This is sometimes called *the problem of the virtuous pagan*. There are several ways of responding to it.

1. In an earlier section, "The Nature of Sin," I defined moral goodness in a threefold way, developing thoughts from WCF 16.7. A morally good work is one that is in accord with the right standard (God's law), seeking the right goal (God's glory), motivated by love and faith. Similarly, a sinful act is one that lacks one or more of these aspects. Now, one cannot perfectly follow the right standard without having the right goal and the right motive; indeed, each of these presupposes the other two. But unbelievers sometimes *appear* to manifest one or more of these criteria. One may do things that externally conform to God's law (e.g., giving to the poor) without a biblical goal or motive. But the threefold criterion shows how painfully difficult it is for anyone to perform a good work, and how precarious it is to claim that anyone is good, whether ourselves or others.

2. Another way to put this same point is that it is possible to perform an act that is good for society, at least at a surface level, without being good in the triperspectival way just noted. Some people contribute much to the well-being of society—by helping the poor, by becoming great artists, musicians, authors, and public servants, and in other ways—without a heart to serve God. This is often called *civic righteousness* in the theological literature. We might be inclined to call this righteousness *teleological goodness* rather than *moral goodness*, to use a distinction made early in this chapter. Such people are "good for" their communities. But it is also possible to speak of their actions as a partial moral goodness. Such social benefactors are depraved, according to Scripture, but since we don't know the hearts of others it is difficult to know, or to show, in what ways they fail to measure up to God's standards. In any case, partial moral goodness is not enough to please God.

3. Although Scripture says that evil attaches to our deepest dispositions and to everything we think, say, or do, it does not teach that man is "as evil as he can be." We

saw earlier that the Bible recognizes various degrees of sin. Any degree, of course, is sufficient to bring condemnation. But the fact that there are different degrees is one fact that lies behind our perception that some people are good apart from grace.

4. In chapter 12 I discussed God's common grace, the benefits that God gives to those who are his enemies (as Matt. 5:45). Among those benefits is the restraint of sin. God does prevent people from being as bad as they can be. He prevents the men of Babel from doing all the wickedness that was in their hearts (Gen. 11:6–8). He keeps King Abimelech from sexual sin with Abraham's wife Sarah (20:6). Indeed, he restricts even the evil of Satan himself (Job 1:12; 2:6). Scripture even speaks of unregenerate people doing good (2 Kings 10:29–31; 12:2; Luke 6:33).

So Scripture's extreme language about the sinfulness of human beings must be qualified by these considerations. Still, this extreme language is to be taken seriously. We are truly *dead* in sin; even our best deeds are filthy rags; there is none righteous, no, not one. The deadness pertains to every aspect of life.

Calvinists often describe the extent of sin as *total depravity*. That phrase catches the thrust of passages such as Genesis 6:5. But it can easily be misunderstood to suggest that man is "as bad as he can be." I think the essence of Scripture's teaching is better and best expressed in the words of Romans 8:8: "Those who are in the flesh cannot please God." That is what is crucial. No matter how good a person may be by common grace, no matter how high is his degree of relative goodness, no matter how much he contributes to the well-being of society, no matter how little the degree of his sin or the extent of God's common grace to him, he will always fail in this respect: he cannot please God. Those who are in the flesh, as Paul says, apart from God's saving grace, cannot do anything that deserves God's blessing.

Seizing on that *cannot*, other Calvinists prefer the phrase *total inability* to the phrase *total depravity*. We cannot please God, and therefore we cannot save ourselves from his wrath. Jesus says, "No one can come to me unless the Father who sent me draws him. And I will raise him up on the last day" (John 6:44). We cannot come to God out of our own strength or resources. We have no hope but grace, no hope but in Christ.

Temptation and Sin

Temptation exists when one person tries to influence another to sin. Thus, it is typically the work of Satan, never the work of God. Other people sometimes tempt us as well, and indeed we are tempted by our own lusts. James summarizes:

> Let no one say when he is tempted, "I am being tempted by God," for God cannot be tempted with evil, and he himself tempts no one. But each person is tempted when he is lured and enticed by his own desire. Then desire when it has conceived gives birth to sin, and sin when it is fully grown brings forth death. (James 1:13–15)

So temptation "gives birth to" sin, but it is not itself sin. Jesus was tempted, but never committed sin:

> For we do not have a high priest who is unable to sympathize with our weaknesses, but one who in every respect has been tempted as we are, yet without sin. (Heb. 4:15)

One particularly instructive example of Jesus' temptations occurred when he was driven out into the wilderness after his baptism, but before his earthly ministry (Matt. 4; Luke 4). These passages record (in slightly different order) three temptations from Satan: (1) to turn stones into bread, (2) to throw himself down from the temple, testing God's promise of angelic protection, and (3) to worship Satan in order to gain all the kingdoms of the world. In terms of our three perspectives, temptation 1 is existential, satisfying a personal need, 2 is situational, controlling the forces of nature, and 3 is normative, the choice of a false lord.

We can be thankful that Jesus rejected these temptations. He refuted Satan's false applications of Scripture with right uses of it, turning Satan away by the sword of the Spirit. But these are the same temptations that we continue to face each day. Satan continually seeks to make us embrace his lordship in place of God's, to make us seek control over the world in God's place and for our own glory, and to make us place our own needs and feelings above all else. So for many centuries, the church has summarized temptation by the triad *the world*, *the flesh*, and *the devil*, representing temptations 2, 1, and 3, respectively; see fig. 36.4.

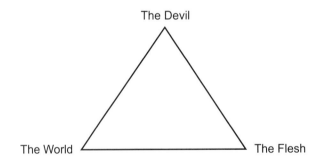

Fig. 36.4. Sources of Temptation

Biblically, however, *world* embraces *flesh* in 1 John 2:16: "For all that is in the world— the desires of the flesh and the desires of the eyes and pride in possessions—is not from the Father but is from the world." To say that *world* is a *perspective* is to say, among other things, that it embraces the other perspectives. And note the threefold structure of this verse. Desires of the flesh are existential—satisfaction of one's feelings. Desires of the eyes are desires for what I see around me—situational. Pride of possessions ("pride of life," KJV) is normative—the desire to live for self rather than for God.

Compare also the temptations of Eve in Genesis 3:6: "So when the woman saw that the tree was good for food, and that it was a delight to the eyes, and that the tree was to be desired to make one wise, she took of its fruit and ate, and she also gave some to her husband who was with her, and he ate." Parallel with 1 John 2:16, I see these as existential, situational, and normative, respectively.

Are Believers Totally Depraved?

I have discussed earlier in this chapter, under "Corruption," the doctrine of *total depravity*. This phrase expresses the extent and depth of the corruption of fallen man. But the title of this section suggests a further question: should you and I, as believers in Jesus Christ, think of ourselves as "totally depraved"? This is a somewhat difficult question. Some Christians have a habit of thinking very negatively of themselves, even though they have received God's grace in Christ, and some passages of Scripture and of the Reformed confessional documents seem to justify this negative self-appraisal. But on the whole, I think we should come to a negative answer to the titular question: we are indeed unworthy, but we are no longer totally depraved. God's grace in us prevails over sin. In discussing this issue, I will focus more closely on the formulations of the Westminster Standards.

The Westminster Confession and catechisms do not use the phrase *total depravity*. But they speak of sin in these terms:

> By this sin they fell from their original righteousness and communion, with God, and so became dead in sin, and wholly defiled in all the parts and faculties of soul and body.[23]

> From this original corruption, whereby we are utterly indisposed, disabled, and made opposite to all good, and wholly inclined to all evil, do proceed all actual transgressions.[24]

> Wherein consisteth the sinfulness of that estate whereinto man fell?

> The sinfulness of that estate whereinto man fell, consisteth in the guilt of Adam's first sin, the want of that righteousness wherein he was created, and the corruption of his nature, whereby he is utterly indisposed, disabled, and made opposite unto all that is spiritually good, and wholly inclined to all evil, and that continually; which is commonly called original sin, and from which do proceed all actual transgressions.[25]

These statements describe sin in very dark terms indeed. Many Calvinists, however, after stating the doctrine in confessional terms, are quick to qualify it as I did earlier in this chapter: total depravity, they say, is not "absolute" depravity. Absolute depravity is the condition of the devil himself, the condition of someone who is "as bad as he can be." The distinction between *total* and *absolute* is that the former does not mean that

23. WCF 6.2.
24. Ibid., 6.4.
25. WLC 25.

man is as bad as he can be, but only that all our thoughts, words, and deeds are affected by sin. In my view, however, the confession's and catechism's statements quoted above seem to describe absolute rather than total depravity, given this distinction.

On these formulations, it is hard to make any room for common grace, the possibility of unredeemed human beings' doing good. Nevertheless, the confession in chapter 16, "Of Good Works," does present some qualifications to its doctrine of depravity:

> Works done by unregenerate men, although for the matter of them they may be things which God commands; and of good use both to themselves and others: yet, because they proceed not from an heart purified by faith; nor are done in a right manner, according to the Word; nor to a right end, the glory of God, they are therefore sinful and cannot please God, or make a man meet to receive grace from God: and yet, their neglect of them is more sinful and displeasing unto God.[26]

The Westminster divines believed that some sins were worse than others.[27] So that although unregenerate people cannot perform good works, they can perform some works that are less bad than others. Those appear to be good, and they may be called "good" because of that appearance. They externally conform to Scripture, and (in comparison with works that are even worse) they bring benefit to society. But they are not pleasing to God.

Some have suggested that we put the emphasis there. That is, we should speak not of total depravity, but of total inability—inability to please God. That is Paul's summary of the matter in Romans 8:7–8:

> For the mind that is set on the flesh is hostile to God, for it does not submit to God's law; indeed, it cannot. Those who are in the flesh cannot please God.

Total inability has a moral basis. Inability is grounded in depravity. So it is important to ground total inability in total depravity. Unregenerate human beings are not capable of doing anything genuinely good. Though they are able to do works that are less bad than others, they are never able to do anything that pleases God.

But what of the regenerate? The confession says:

> This corruption of nature, during this life, does remain in those that are regenerated; and although it be, through Christ, pardoned, and mortified; yet both itself, and all the motions thereof, are truly and properly sin.[28]

It might seem at first glance that there is no subjective change in the regenerate believer, for the "corruption of nature" remains and remains "truly and properly sin." But notice

26. WCF 16.7.
27. WLC 150.
28. WCF 6.5.

that through Christ, the believer's sin is not only "pardoned" but "mortified"—that is, put to death. How can sin be mortified while our "truly sinful" corruption continues? That is not clear in this particular confessional statement.

But again, we must take account of the fact that on the Westminster view some sins are worse than others. There are degrees of sinfulness in the unregenerate, as we have seen in WLC 150. And we should assume that there are also degrees of sinfulness in the regenerate as well. WCF chapter 16 says this about regenerate good works:

> We cannot by our best works merit pardon of sin, or eternal life at the hand of God, by reason of the great disproportion that is between them and the glory to come; and the infinite distance that is between us and God, whom, by them, we can neither profit, nor satisfy for the debt of our former sins, but when we have done all we can, we have done but our duty, and are unprofitable servants: and because, as they are good, they proceed from his Spirit, and as they are wrought by us, they are defiled, and mixed with so much weakness and imperfection, that they cannot endure the severity of God's judgment.[29]

> Notwithstanding, the persons of believers being accepted through Christ, their good works also are accepted in him; not as though they were in this life wholly unblamable and unreproveable in God's sight; but that he, looking upon them in his Son, is pleased to accept and reward that which is sincere, although accompanied with many weaknesses and imperfections.[30]

On the confession's view, regenerate good works are so mixed with sin that they "cannot endure the severity of God's judgment." None of our good works is perfectly good. This is true even though we do perform works that "proceed from [the] Spirit," and of course, the Spirit never does anything wicked. But the Spirit enables us to do good only to a certain degree. He has not chosen to enable us to do works that can endure God's judgment.

Why, then, should these works be called good at all? We learned in WCF 16.7 that the "good works" done by the unregenerate may be very impressive in some respects, but cannot please God, since they are not done with a proper motive, standard, and goal. But are regenerate good works any better? Are any of them done from a proper motive, standard, or goal? Based on 16.5–6, the answer would have to be no. They are "defiled," "mixed with . . . weakness and imperfection," neither "unblamable" nor "unreproveable." So why, then, does the confession call them good works?

It seems to indicate two reasons to call them good. One is that these works are partly the work of God's Spirit: "as they are good, they proceed from [the] Spirit, and as they are wrought by us, they are defiled." So, insofar as these works are good, they are the work of God. Insofar as they are human, they are not good. This

29. Ibid., 16.5.
30. Ibid., 16.6.

seems to imply that we, as human beings, are not changed by regeneration. What we do as human beings is still totally depraved, no better than the unregenerate. But we may call the works of regenerate people "good" because God does good in and through them.

There is another reason, too, why we may describe works of the regenerate as good. That is indicated in WCF 16.6. Now, we know that in justification God imputes to the believer the righteousness of Christ, so that we are righteous in him. The righteousness of justification pertains to our legal standing, not our personal holiness. The righteousness of justification is our standing before God's law. Christ has taken our guilt that we may receive his righteousness. But in 16.6 it almost seems as though a second imputation takes place, in the sphere of sanctification. God looks upon our defiled, imperfect works "in his Son."

In justification, God looks at the whole sinful person in his Son, and because the Son has borne that person's sins, God accepts that person as legally righteous. Now in sanctification, says the confession, God also accepts our works as righteous for the sake of Christ, not because our works merit that verdict in themselves. As in the sphere of justification, then, it can be said that our goodness is in Christ, not in ourselves.

This teaching does not encourage us to expect much of ourselves or other believers by way of practical goodness. The question "Can I as a believer do anything good?" receives a negative answer, or at most an ambiguous one.

But the discussion of sanctification in chapter 13 introduces more positive notes:

> They, who are once effectually called, and regenerated, having a new heart, and a new spirit created in them, are further sanctified, really and personally, through the virtue of Christ's death and resurrection, by his Word and Spirit dwelling in them: the dominion of the whole body of sin is destroyed, and the several lusts thereof are more and more weakened and mortified; and they more and more quickened and strengthened in all saving graces, to the practice of true holiness, without which no man shall see the Lord.[31]

In WCF 13.2 we do read again of our moral disability:

> This sanctification is throughout, in the whole man; yet imperfect in this life, there abiding still some remnants of corruption in every part; whence arises a continual and irreconcilable war, the flesh lusting against the Spirit, and the Spirit against the flesh.

But in this chapter the triumph of grace is unmistakable:

> In which war, although the remaining corruption, for a time, may much prevail; yet, through the continual supply of strength from the sanctifying Spirit of Christ, the

---

31. Ibid., 13.1.

regenerate part does overcome; and so, the saints grow in grace, perfecting holiness in the fear of God.[32]

Is it possible to reconcile these confessional statements with one another? How can it be said that we are "perfecting holiness in the fear of God" (just above) while WLC 25 ascribes to the believer

corruption of his nature, whereby he is utterly indisposed, disabled, and made opposite unto all that is spiritually good, and wholly inclined to all evil, and that continually.

The key, I think, is to note that the confession's language of depravity pertains not to the believer as such, but to the "corruption of nature" in the believer (WCF 6.5), a corruption that is overcome by God's grace. The confession never compromises in its negative description of the corruption: "both itself, and all the motions thereof, are truly and properly sin." That corruption remains in the believer. But in the believer, the corruption is not the whole story. In 13.1 quoted above, "the dominion of the whole body of sin is destroyed." The expression "body of sin" comes from Romans 6:6:

We know that our old self was crucified with him in order that the body of sin might be brought to nothing, so that we would no longer be enslaved to sin.

The corruption itself is as bad as ever, "truly and properly sin," but it is made weak by God's grace. The result is that although some corruption remains (WCF 13.3), we are no longer enslaved to sin. We have victories in the spiritual battle (13.1). The result is that "the regenerate part does overcome," and we "grow in grace, perfecting holiness in the fear of God" (13.3).

The confession, then, makes these assertions:

1. Because of the fall of man in Adam, human beings have "original corruption, whereby we are utterly indisposed, disabled, and made opposite to all good, and wholly inclined to all evil" (WCF 6.4).
2. From that corruption comes all our individual, actual transgressions (6.4).
3. Unregenerate people do nothing good. They do things that appear to be good, but are really evil, because they lack the proper goal, standard, and motive (16.7).
4. The regenerate retain their original corruption, and what it is and what it does are both properly sin (6.5).
5. Our best works cannot justify ourselves before God (16.5).
6. Yet God rewards our good works for the sake of Christ, though they are imperfect (16.6).

32. Ibid., 13.3.

7. But besides this, God also creates in his elect a new heart and spirit, enabling us to "practice . . . true holiness" (13.1), even "perfecting holiness in the fear of God" (13.3).
8. Indeed, "through the continual supply of strength from the sanctifying Spirit of Christ, the regenerate part does overcome" (13.3).

The final word about the believer, then, is not *corruption*, but *overcoming*. As Paul says, "For sin will have no dominion over you, since you are not under law but under grace" (Rom. 6:14). The corruption of sin remains until death, but it grows weaker and weaker, through the continual strength from the sanctifying Spirit of Christ. Scripture promises victory in Jesus.

Given that pattern of biblical teaching, summarized in the confession,[33] I do not think it is helpful to speak of believers as "totally depraved." Depravity is what the confession calls "corruption," the sinful disposition that comes through Adam. But that corruption does not enslave the believer. The believer can say no to sin. He can "resist" the devil (1 Peter 5:8–9), and resist him successfully. And Scripture over and over again exhorts him to do that.

The biblical citations that I have presented here and will present in chapters 41 and 43 indicate to me that, although Scripture does teach that believers sin and continue to need forgiveness, its emphasis is on Jesus' victory over sin, and our victory in him. When Scripture exhorts us to obey, it never describes us as hopeless or desperate sinners who cannot accomplish anything good. If we are concerned about our continuing corruption and want to deal with it, God has shown us how to do that. He has given us means of grace: the Word of God, the sacraments, and prayer. Scripture *commands* us to make use of these, and it never suggests that our corruption makes that impossible. So victory over corruption is found through obedience to God's commands.

Our continuing corruption, therefore, does not invalidate our attempts to obey God. On the contrary, for those who enjoy the saving grace of God, obedience is the way to receive his blessings.

I think, therefore, that it is unbiblical to describe believers as "totally depraved." In Scripture, the corruption of sin is a terrible thing. But through Christ we have victory over it.

I also hesitate to pray some of the traditional "prayers of confession," in which we say things such as "there is no health in us." That simply is not true, given Jesus' work of redemption. Jesus has made us to be his saints, his servants, his sons and daughters. We are the "righteous man" of the Psalms. We have the "fruit of the Spirit": love, joy, peace, patience, and so on (Gal. 5:22–23). Paul says that "those who belong to Christ Jesus have crucified the flesh with its passions and desires" (v. 24). We are "not in the flesh but in the Spirit" (Rom. 8:9).

---

33. The confession has more passages emphasizing our continuing sinfulness than emphasizing our overcoming sin through the Spirit. That in my judgment is unfortunate. Although I subscribe to the confession's teaching in both areas, I would like to see revisions here. The generally negative cast of the confession's formulations tends to discourage believers from actively waging the spiritual warfare.

"Dead in . . . trespasses and sins" (Eph. 2:1) is in the past tense. Paul describes our present in verse 10: "For we are his workmanship, created in Christ Jesus for good works, which God prepared beforehand, that we should walk in them." So in 4:1–2 Paul calls on our obedience: "walk in a manner worthy of the calling to which you have been called, with all humility and gentleness, with patience, bearing with one another in love." Paul here has no foreboding that our remaining corruption will make it impossible for us to obey God. Rather, he believes that we have been changed, so that obedience is now second nature.

Key Terms

Teleological goodness
Moral goodness
Status naturae purae
In puris naturalibus
Pugna concupiscentiae
Dona superaddita
Goal
Motive
Standard
Legalist
Guilt
Punishment
Corruption
Cosmic redemption
Death
Curse
Total depravity
Total inability
Temptation
World
Flesh
Devil

Study Questions

1. "So we must reject the notion that God created us in a morally neutral state, so that we could achieve goodness by our own decisions." Explain; evaluate. What are some dangers in this view?

2. Frame discusses two "mysteries" in the story of Adam and the fall. Identify these; explain what is mysterious about them. Can you shed any light on them that might suggest solutions?

3. Describe the distinctions in Roman Catholic theology within man's original created nature. Evaluate.

4. Describe triperspectivally the biblical criteria for morally good works. How is each of these distorted in sinful deeds?

5. How is it best to define sin? Why?

6. "Sin is *irrational*." Explain; evaluate.

7. "The fall, therefore, did not begin with Eve's eating the fruit, but with her inner *intention* to eat the fruit." Explain; evaluate.

8. Is every sin equally heinous? Why or why not? What are the most heinous ones, in your view?

9. What is the unpardonable sin? Why is it unpardonable?

10. "So sin is the disruption of a personal relationship, and it brings further disruption. Indeed, it is an attempt to overturn the order of creation." Explain; evaluate.

11. Is it important to believe that the fall really took place in history? Why or why not?

12. "As we would expect, God pronounces curses on the three defendants. But surprisingly, these curses are mixed with blessings." Set forth that narrative and explain.

13. Expound the teaching of Romans 5:12–19 as to our involvement in the guilt of Adam's sin.

14. Is it fair for God to impute to us the guilt of Adam's sin? Why or why not?

15. Describe the punishment that we bear for Adam's sin. How is this related to *cosmic redemption*?

16. How sinful are we? Discuss the biblical basis for saying that we are *totally depraved*. Should that phrase be qualified in any way?

17. Formulate and respond to *the problem of the virtuous pagan*.

18. "Temptation 'gives birth to' sin, but it is not itself sin." Explain; evaluate.

19. Describe Frame's understanding of the triperspectival nature of temptation. Evaluate.

20. Are believers totally depraved? Summarize and evaluate Frame's argument.

Memory Verses

Gen. 6:5: The LORD saw that the wickedness of man was great in the earth, and that every intention of the thoughts of his heart was only evil continually.

Luke 6:45: The good person out of the good treasure of his heart produces good, and the evil person out of his evil treasure produces evil, for out of the abundance of the heart his mouth speaks.

Rom. 8:19–22: For the creation waits with eager longing for the revealing of the sons of God. For the creation was subjected to futility, not willingly, but because of him who subjected it, in hope that the creation itself will be set free from its bondage to corruption and obtain the freedom of the glory of the children of God. For we know that the whole creation has been groaning together in the pains of childbirth until now.

1 Cor. 2:14: The natural person does not accept the things of the Spirit of God, for they are folly to him, and he is not able to understand them because they are spiritually discerned.

Eph. 2:1–3: And you were dead in the trespasses and sins in which you once walked, following the course of this world, following the prince of the power of the air, the spirit that is now at work in the sons of disobedience—among whom we all once lived in the passions of our flesh, carrying out the desires of the body and the mind, and were by nature children of wrath, like the rest of mankind.

Col. 1:19–20: For in him all the fullness of God was pleased to dwell, and through him to reconcile to himself all things, whether on earth or in heaven, making peace by the blood of his cross.

Titus 3:8: The saying is trustworthy, and I want you to insist on these things, so that those who have believed in God may be careful to devote themselves to good works. These things are excellent and profitable for people.

Resources for Further Study

Murray, John. *The Imputation of Adam's Sin*. Grand Rapids: Eerdmans, 1959.

Plantinga, Cornelius. *Not the Way It's Supposed to Be: A Breviary of Sin*. Grand Rapids: Eerdmans, 1995.

PART 8

THE DOCTRINE OF CHRIST

CHAPTER 37

THE PERSON OF CHRIST

IN PART 8, WE WILL DISCUSS "the only Redeemer of God's elect,"[1] the Lord Jesus Christ. Chapter 36 indicated the condemnation we face because of sin. Now we will begin to explore God's plan to bring blessing in place of condemnation, through his Son. We saw in the previous chapter that even the curses that God set forth in Genesis 3 were mixed with blessings, including the first promise of a Redeemer, who would crush the serpent's head.[2] In this chapter we will discuss who the Redeemer is, and in the next we will discuss what he has done, following the traditional theological pattern of "the person and work of Christ."

Christ-Centeredness

In 1 Corinthians 2:2, Paul reminds the Corinthian church that when he first preached among them, he "decided to know nothing among you except Jesus Christ and him crucified." So Christians of all times and places have professed that Christ himself is the center of our preaching, our gospel, and our theology. "Christianity is Christ."[3] This phrase is a way of saying that what is most important about Christian faith is not a set of doctrines or laws or practices or liturgies, but a person. To be a Christian is to have a personal relationship to Jesus Christ, in which he is our Lord and Savior.

In chapter 3, I discussed the importance of the fact that in Scripture, God is personal as well as absolute. The combination of absoluteness and personality is unique to biblical religion. I emphasized that fact in our discussions of the doctrine of God. It bears reassertion in the doctrine of Christ. He is our Lord, Savior, Redeemer, King, Friend, Shepherd, Leader, Teacher. Our first allegiance is not to a set of eternal truths, as in Buddhism or Platonism, but to a person who lived in history to save us and who lives eternally as our heavenly High Priest (Heb. 2:17–18; 5:1–10).[4]

---

1. WSC 21.

2. See also chapters 4–6, in which I provide three overviews of the biblical story of redemption, focused on covenants (4), kingdom (5), and family (6).

3. This phrase is common among us, but its modern use comes from a book of this title by W. H. Griffith Thomas (London: Longmans, Green and Co., 1916).

4. It is also important to remember, as I stressed in chapter 36, that we, too, are persons. That is, redemption is ethical, not metaphysical. In saving us, God does not treat us as mere finite objects, to be rescued from

But the personhood of our Lord does not mean that we can be indifferent to doctrines about him or to the content of his teaching. It is important, first, that we identify the true, biblical Christ as opposed to false christs (Matt. 24:24). So Paul not only mentions Christ in 1 Corinthians 2:2, but identifies him as "him crucified." The crucifixion distinguishes Jesus from all the pseudo-messiahs who tried to gain prominence by political conflict.[5] Rather than brandish the sword against his enemies, Jesus went to Jerusalem to die. And the weakness of Jesus in his crucifixion sets Paul free from having to use "lofty speech or wisdom" (v. 1) in his preaching. God can use the weak to shame the strong, so he can use a man who speaks "in weakness and in fear and much trembling" (v. 3) to create a "demonstration of the Spirit and of power, that your faith might not rest in the wisdom of men but in the power of God" (vv. 4–5).

But even Jesus' crucifixion and its saving power (the atonement), which we will discuss more fully in the next chapter, does not exhaust the meaning of Christ. Although in 1 Corinthians 2:2 Paul seems to limit his speech to Jesus Christ himself and his crucifixion, he elsewhere discusses many other things related to Christ. In 1 Corinthians 15, it is the resurrection that takes center stage, and Paul says that without faith in the resurrection "we are of all people most to be pitied" (v. 19). In verses 3–11 he mentions "as of first importance" (v. 3) not only Jesus' death for our sins, but also his burial and resurrection (v. 4), his appearances to many after his resurrection, including an appearance to Paul himself, and Paul's subsequent preaching mission (vv. 5–11).

So we should not take "Christ and him crucified" in a reductive sense, as if our preaching and teaching must be confined to the person of Christ and the atonement. Indeed, Paul in 1 Corinthians and his other writings, as well as his sermons in Acts, discusses many other subjects: factionalism (1 Cor. 1:10–17; 3:1–23), wisdom (1:18–26), the nature of the apostleship (4:1–21), sexual immorality (5:1–13; 6:12–20), lawsuits (6:1–11), marriage (7:1–29), food offered to idols (8:1–11:1), worship (11:1–34; 14:1–40), spiritual gifts (12:1–31), love (13:1–13), our own resurrection (15:1–58), collections for the saints (16:1–4), Paul's personal plans (16:5–21). "Christ and him crucified" is not a boundary, but a center. Though Paul speaks of many things, in the end it all traces back to Christ.

For that is the way God has made the world. In Christ "all things hold together" (Col. 1:17). Without Christ, nothing could be the way it is. But as the world really is, all its affairs, all its objects and forces, trace back to Christ their Creator and Governor. Although Christ entered history at a particular time and place, he governs all times and places. His person and his work apply to every circumstance in nature and history. The story of Christ is a distinct set of events that has limitless applications.

So to be "Christ-centered" is not to speak only of Christ, ignoring all the effects and applications of his work. Christ-centered preaching is not preaching that limits itself to the events of the history of redemption and eschews the applications of his work to

---

our finitude. Rather, he treats us as persons who need to be reconciled to him. So our relationship with Christ is personal through and through.

5. And it distinguishes him also, significantly, from (1) the immaterial Gnostic Christ who was incapable of crucifixion, and (2) the Muslim Isa (Qur'an, sura 4 [An-Nisa] ayat 157–58) who ascended to heaven without dying.

marriage, suffering, anxiety, wealth, and poverty. Neither Jesus nor Paul restricted the gospel in that way, and we should not do so either. Christ is a great light that shines into every corner of human life, because he is Lord of all.

And it is possible to look at our message even more broadly. Cornelius Van Til wrote:

> Again, there is much in the Scriptures about Christ. After the entrance of sin into the world, Christ is the only way through whom God can be known. He is not only the one through whom we can <u>more fully</u> than otherwise know the Father; it is through him <u>alone</u> that we can come to the Father. Furthermore, Christ is God, so that when we know him we know God. In spite of all this it should always be remembered that Christ's work is a means to an end. Even if we think of the fact that Christ is the second person of the Trinity, we ought still to remember that it is the full Godhead with whom we ultimately have to do and about whom, in the last analysis, we wish to know. Hence, theology is primarily God centered rather than Christ centered.[6]

That last sentence is a bit jarring after we have considered Paul's "Christ and him crucified." Perhaps it would be better to say that theology is Christ-centered, but expansively rather than reductively. To use terms more common today, Christ and his works, Christ and the areas of his relevance, are a centered set, not a bounded set. For Van Til, by the way, even *God-centeredness* is something very broad. Speaking of the subject matter of theology, he says:

> It is the God of the Scriptures about whom we wish to obtain knowledge.
> It does not follow from this that it is about God <u>alone</u> that we wish to obtain knowledge. It only means that it is <u>primarily</u> of God that we speak. We wish to know all that God wishes us to know about anything. The Bible has much to say about the universe. But it is the business of science and philosophy to deal with this revelation. Indirectly even science and philosophy should be theological. The Scriptures are also full of information about our salvation and about many other things that concern us. But it will not do to say on this account that man is the center of theology. All that the Scriptures say about man, and particularly all that they say about man's salvation, is after all for the glory of God. Our theology should be God centered because our life should be God centered.[7]

So a theology text like this one certainly ought to be God-centered, and also Christ-centered in the nonreductive sense that we have described.

On the other hand, it means rather less than the Christ-centeredness of Karl Barth, for whom the answer to every theological question seems to be "Jesus Christ."[8]

6. Cornelius Van Til, *An Introduction to Systematic Theology* (Nutley, NJ: Presbyterian and Reformed, 1974), 1–2 (underscores in original).

7. Ibid., 1, immediately preceding the previous quotation.

8. I recall that when my wife and I had devotions with our children in their early years, we would ask them questions about Bible stories, and they quickly learned that the most common answer to every question was "God." So that was the answer they gave to questions that they hadn't understood or hadn't paid attention

Here I exaggerate, of course. But it is remarkable that for Barth revelation is Christ, redemptive history is somehow identical to Christ (*Geschichte*), there is to be no distinction between the person and work of Christ, and so on. Paul Althaus described Barth as a "Christomonist," a label universally rejected by Barth and Barth scholars, but certainly not unworthy of discussion.[9] Certainly Scripture is the story of Christ, and the blessings of salvation are all blessings "in" Christ, as we will see. But Scripture distinguishes between Christ and his people, and it speaks of many other things that are distinct from Christ, even opposed to him.[10]

But I have tried to make this volume Christocentric in the sense that all the theological themes illuminate and are illuminated by Christ. My intention has been to write this book as a distinctly Christian systematic theology, a book that could not have been written by a Jew, Muslim, or secularist. So when we considered the doctrine of God, I sought to emphasize that in Scripture all the acts of God are also acts of Christ, that all of God's attributes are also attributes of Christ, that Christ is the second person of the divine Trinity. In part 4, I emphasized that Christ is the living Word of God and that that fact does not obscure but validates the concrete words that he brings to us as Prophet. Christ is also the central theme of Scripture and therefore of the church's preaching and sacraments. We also noted that to know God rightly, we must know Jesus his Son, that Christ is the fullness of the image of God in which God created us, and that sin is a condition from which only Christ can set us free. The summaries of the biblical story in chapters 4–6 present Christ as Lord of God's covenants, the King whose kingdom comes, and the Kinsman-Redeemer who reconciles us to the Father.

So we have already learned much about Christ, and we should be prepared to take up here the topics traditionally reserved for "Christology proper."[11]

---

to. That was fine for questions such as "Who made the world?" and "Who made the doggies and kitties?" and "Who made the lions and tigers?" But their answer didn't work for such questions as "Where was Jesus born?" or "Who did Jesus feed with the loaves and fishes?" For what it is worth, I will state that I am not "equating," as we say, Barth's sophisticated theology with my sons' childish mistakes.

9. See especially Richard R. Niebuhr's critique of Barth in *Resurrection and Historical Reason* (New York: Scribner's, 1957). He argues that it is difficult to accommodate all the things that Barth says are "in Christ" unless we understand Christ as an ontological category, the equivalent of "reality."

10. The ideas that all creation is "in Christ" for Barth, that we are not to "take unbelief seriously," and that redemption is something that takes place within Christ himself lead to a doctrine of universal salvation alien to Scripture.

11. What I have just said will explain what might seem to some to be a lopsided structure of this book. Some of my correspondents have noticed that the chapters on Christology are rather short compared to other systematic theologies. One would think that a truly Christian and Christ-centered theology would be more voluminous in the sections dealing most explicitly with the Lord of our salvation. But as I have indicated above, I have tried to show how *every* topic of this book centers on Christ. The introductory discussion of lordship deals in a focal way with the lordship of Christ. The summaries of biblical narrative in chapters 4–6 show Christ as the central figure of biblical history. In the following chapters, 7–11, we learn that Christ performs the acts of the Lord. In 12–19, he bears all the divine attributes. Chapter 21 is a thorough discussion of his deity, and 20–22 set forth in detail his place in the Trinity. In 23–28, he is the Word of God. In 29–32, to know him is the knowledge of eternal life. In 33, he is the angel of the Lord. In 34, he is the consummate image of God. In 36, I show that human sin is such that only Christ can deliver us from it. In 39–45, we will learn of Christ's work in our hearts through the Spirit; in

The Deity of Christ

I discussed the deity of Christ in some detail in chapter 21, in our discussion of the Trinity. As I indicated there, one of the assertions made by the doctrine of the Trinity is that all the persons are fully God, equally worthy of worship. So it was important to show that the second person of the Trinity, even in his incarnate life, is fully God.

To review: the most important datum is that Jesus is Lord, *kyrios*. "Jesus is Lord" summarizes the proclamation of the NT, according to Acts 10:36; Romans 10:9; 1 Corinthians 12:3; and Philippians 2:11. *Kyrios* represents the name *Yahweh* of the OT. It is the "I AM" of Exodus 3:14, the name Jesus claims in John 8:58. It says not only that Jesus is God, but that Jesus, as Yahweh, is the head of the covenant between God and man.

The present book, like my other books, is an exposition of the lordship of God. That lordship pertains to Jesus as much as to God the Father and the Holy Spirit. To say that "Jesus is Lord" is to say that he is everything that God is.

In chapter 21, we also discussed other titles of Jesus that indicate his divinity: Son of God, Christ-Messiah, God, Fullness of Deity, Son of Man, Word of God, Image of God, Savior, Holy One, Alpha and Omega. Further, I tried to indicate there as in earlier chapters that all the necessary and defining attributes of God pertain also to Jesus, as well as the biblical images and names of God. And Jesus performs all the actions distinctive to God: creation, providence, miracle, and redemption.

Especially significant is the phenomenon with which I introduced chapter 21, that the biblical writers take Jesus' deity for granted: that is, when discussing other subjects they use language that presumes or presupposes Jesus' deity, not apologizing, not feeling as though this language needed to be defended. The evidence, therefore, is that among the Christians of the NT period, the deity of Christ was entirely uncontroversial.[12] Although the early Christians battled among themselves over a number of issues (including Jesus' true humanity, as we will see!), there is no evidence that any of them denied the deity of Christ.

In that chapter I also looked in more detail at several passages especially relevant to the deity of Christ. One of these was Philippians 2:5–11, in which Paul says that Jesus, though being "in the form [*morphe*] of God," became a man. I followed Vincent in understanding *morphe* to refer to the "essential qualities" of God. So this passage strongly indicates the deity of Christ. But some have argued that the "emptying" (*kenosis*) of verse 7 (NASB) means that when Jesus became man he divested himself of some, or all, divine attributes. This view has become known as the *kenosis theory*. But if Jesus, in his incarnation, divested himself of any essential divine attributes (*morphe*), as on this view, then during his incarnation (which continues without end!) he was and is not God at all. For God is not God without his essential attributes. But the idea that Jesus

---

46–49, the church as his body; in 50–51, his coming in judgment; in 52, the meaning of a Christ-centered life. So apart from the formal discussion of Christology, I believe I have included a substantial Christological emphasis.

12. Second- and third-century writers, including Irenaeus and Origen, refer to various groups designated as "Ebionites," Judaizing Christians who regarded Jesus primarily as a human prophet and rejected some of the church's supernatural assertions about him. Accounts of these groups differ.

was not God when he was in the flesh contradicts a vast amount of biblical data, as we have seen. The nature of the *kenosis* of Philippians 2:7 can be understood perfectly well as the self-humbling of God's servant, expressed for example in the servant songs of Isaiah, which lie behind the language of verse 8.[13] That is, of course, Paul's point in the larger context. Jesus' self-humbling is an example for the believers in Philippi, to serve one another rather than themselves. This is an ethical point, not a metaphysical one. Paul is telling them to behave differently, not to divest their metaphysical status (finite humanity) to become something else.

The Humanity of Christ

I mentioned above that although there was no controversy in the early church about Jesus' deity, there was some controversy about his true manhood. That is an additional tribute to his deity: some people were so impressed by his divine nature that they could scarcely believe that he was human! Still, the NT sharply rebukes those who denied Jesus' humanity:

> By this you know the Spirit of God: every spirit that confesses that Jesus Christ has come in the flesh is from God, and every spirit that does not confess Jesus is not from God. This is the spirit of the antichrist, which you heard was coming and now is in the world already. (1 John 4:2–3; cf. 2 John 7)

What could have led someone to hold the view that John opposes? These people were later called *docetists*, from *dokeo*, meaning "to seem." They believed that Jesus only *seemed* to have a human body, but was actually a purely immaterial, "spiritual" being.[14] This view has much in common with the Platonic traditions of Greek philosophy, in which man is a spiritual being who once dwelt in the realm of the eternal Forms, but who has somehow fallen into the prison-house of a material body. Matter, on this view, is an impediment to the life of the spirit, and a man must seek to rise above physical existence by contemplating his recollections of the Forms. Ultimately, matter is the source of evil.

Sometime around the first two centuries A.D., a movement called *Gnosticism* arose that invested this metaphysic with religious trappings. The Gnostics claimed to have a secret knowledge by which human beings could ascend beyond their bodies to higher realms with the help of aeons, or semidivine emanations of the supreme being. Different Gnostic sects offered different religious methods of climbing the metaphysical ladder back to unity with the supreme being. Evidently the docetists were Gnostics, or influenced by Gnosticism.

But biblical religion could not abide the idea that matter was an impediment to spiritual life, or the source of evil. In Scripture, God created Adam to be good, though he

---

13. See, e.g., Robert B. Strimple, "Philippians 2:5–11 in Recent Studies: Some Exegetical Conclusions," *WTJ* 41, 2 (Spring 1979): 247–68.

14. We should, however, question the equation between immaterial and spiritual. See the discussion of *soul* and *spirit* in chapter 34.

made him from the dust of the ground. Before the fall, Adam and Eve were material beings, but sinless. Redeemed, in the new heavens and new earth, we will have material resurrection bodies, but without sin (1 Cor. 15:35–58). There is nothing wrong with man's material component. The first sin was not a metaphysical defect in the human constitution, but a personal act of willful disobedience. What we need to be rescued from is not our physical nature, our metaphysical finitude, but our personal estrangement from God. Indeed, it is sin even to seek the identity with God that the Gnostics promoted. Creatures should never seek to become God. To be renewed is to be satisfied with our finite humanity and to acknowledge the lordship of our Creator God.

So Jesus came in the flesh, to be a true man, as Adam was a true man. Like Adam and Adam's descendants, Jesus lived in a body that was made of dust, part of the creation. In that body he lived, ate, drank, suffered, died, and was buried. In that body he was raised from the dead. (That his body was absent from the tomb was the first indication that he had risen.) Jesus displayed himself physically, wounds and all, before the disciples after his resurrection (John 20:26–29). In his ascension, Jesus' body "was lifted up, and a cloud took him out of their sight" (Acts 1:9). Two angels then announced to the disciples that Jesus would return "in the same way as you saw him go into heaven" (v. 11), that is, physically. When he returns, he will return "with the clouds, and every eye will see him" (Rev. 1:7).

The Incarnation

When Jesus became man, he underwent a major change. John Murray says:

> It is on the premises of his eternal identity as God, his eternal subsistence as the only-begotten Son, his creative activity at the beginning, and his continued activity in sustaining all created reality, that we can conceive the fact and meaning of the incarnation. The doctrine of the incarnation is vitiated if it is conceived of as the beginning to be of the person of Christ. The incarnation means that he who never began to be in his specific identity as Son of God, *began* to be what he eternally was not.
>
> The thought of incarnation is stupendous, for it means the conjunction in one person of all that belongs to Godhead and all that belongs to manhood.[15]

But even more stupendous is the thought that Jesus took on manhood in a sinful world. Murray continues:

> It would have been humiliation for the Son of God to have become man under the most ideal conditions, humiliation because of the discrepancy between God and his creation, between the majesty of the Creator on the one hand, and the humble status of the most dignified creature on the other. But it was not such an incarnation that took place. The Son of God was sent and came into this world of sin, misery, and death. These describe the situation into which he came. Paul draws our attention to

---

15. *MCW*, 2:132–33.

this by the use of a formula that is on the verge of peril—"in the likeness of sinful flesh" (Rom. 8:3). He could have used other expressions—"made of the seed of David according to the flesh" (Rom. 1:3), "made of a woman" (Gal. 4:4), "made in the likeness of men" (Phil. 2:7), "manifested in flesh" (1 Tim. 3:16). But, instead, in this case he uses a formula that staggers us by its uniqueness. When he uses the term "likeness" he does not mean to suggest any unreality to the flesh of Christ (cf. Rom. 1:3). He employs the word to obviate any thought of sinfulness. . . . Thereby is enunciated the great truth that the Son of God was sent in that very nature which in every other instance is sinful.[16]

Why did he take on manhood in a fallen world? To save us from our sins:

> For even the Son of Man came not to be served but to serve, and to give his life as a ransom for "many" (Mark 10:45).

> But when the fullness of time had come, God sent forth his Son, born of woman, born under the law, to redeem those who were under the law, so that we might receive adoption as sons. (Gal. 4:4–5)

Why was it *necessary* for him to become flesh?

> Since therefore the children share in flesh and blood, he himself likewise partook of the same things, that through death he might destroy the one who has the power of death, that is, the devil, and deliver all those who through fear of death were subject to lifelong slavery. For surely it is not angels that he helps, but he helps the offspring of Abraham. Therefore he had to be made like his brothers in every respect, so that he might become a merciful and faithful high priest in the service of God, to make propitiation for the sins of the people. For because he himself has suffered when tempted, he is able to help those who are being tempted. (Heb. 2:14–18)

A priest is a mediator between God and man. His work is to bring sacrifice to God on behalf of men. As we will see, Jesus' sacrifice, fulfilling all sacrifices, was the sacrifice of his own perfect flesh, bearing the death that we all deserved. For that work, it was necessary (*ophelen*, Heb. 2:17) for him to be human, to be like his brothers in every respect, except for sin (4:15).[17] And the writer to the Hebrews continues by saying that Jesus' human nature enables him to help us when we suffer through temptation, for he, too, was tempted (2:18; 4:15). A particularly important aspect of this priestly help is Jesus' intercession with the Father (Rom. 8:34; Heb.

---

16. Ibid., 2:133.

17. It was not necessary for God the Father or Son to redeem sinful human beings. Redemption, like creation itself, resulted from a free decision of God; that is to say, it was grace, not something that human beings deserved. But once God had made the decision to redeem his people, there was only one way it could have been done. There had to be a substitutionary sacrifice, and only the Son was sufficient. And to become a sacrifice, he had to become man.

7:25). I will have more to say about Jesus' priestly work later in this chapter and in the following one.

Jesus' humanity is also necessary for him to be our example:

> For to this you have been called, because Christ also suffered for you, leaving you an example, so that you might follow in his steps. (1 Peter 2:21)

Jesus himself and the NT writers regularly present the Christian life as an imitation of Jesus and an imitation of God in sending Jesus:

> A new commandment I give to you, that you love one another: just as I have loved you, you also are to love one another. (John 13:34; cf. 15:12; Eph. 5:2; 1 John 4:10–11)

> Have this mind among yourselves, which is yours in Christ Jesus, who, though he was in the form of God, did not count equality with God a thing to be grasped, but made himself nothing, taking the form of a servant, being born in the likeness of men. And being found in human form, he humbled himself by becoming obedient to the point of death, even death on a cross. (Phil. 2:5–8)

In the NT, Christ the example is not isolated from Christ the Priest. In the verses quoted above, the particular point at which we are to imitate Christ is in his sacrifice for us. The point, of course, is not that any of us can atone for another's sin, but that the attitude, the "mind," that led Christ to lay down his life for us should lead us to be prepared to lay down our lives for one another:

> By this we know love, that he laid down his life for us, and we ought to lay down our lives for the brothers. (1 John 3:16)

Some liberal theologians rejected the idea that Jesus made himself a blood sacrifice for us, but they attempted to substitute for that the idea that Jesus serves as our example. But that is wrong. The imitation of Christ in the NT is rooted in his blood sacrifice for us. And as we will see in our consideration of the atonement, Jesus' death is not fit to be an example to us unless it is a blood sacrifice.

Jesus' Virginal Conception[18]

We often speak of the *virgin birth* as the great miracle by which Jesus came into the world. Actually, Jesus' birth was a natural and normal birth. But his *conception* in the womb of the virgin Mary was supernatural, the work of the Holy Spirit without a human father (Matt. 1:20; Luke 1:34–35).

---

18. I have discussed this doctrine at greater length in my "Virgin Birth of Jesus," in *Evangelical Dictionary of Theology*, ed. Walter A. Elwell (Grand Rapids: Baker, 1984), 1143–46. This article deals with some of the criticisms of the doctrine based on philosophy and biblical criticism. Also available at http://www.frame-poythress.org.

The virginal conception of Jesus is theologically important in a number of ways.

1. It is a sign to Israel that momentous redemptive events are to come. In the history of redemption, miraculous births typically signify major developments: for example, the births of Isaac, Samson, Samuel, and John the Baptist. In these cases, God graciously opens the wombs of women who had been unable to have children. But a virgin birth is a far greater sign than these, and indicates that something far greater is to take place. When the angel of the Lord announces to Joseph the birth of Jesus, he quotes Isaiah 7:14:

> Behold, the virgin shall conceive and bear a son,
>   and they shall call his name "Immanuel"

(which means, God with us). (Matt. 1:23)

Biblical scholars have debated the meaning of *almah*, the word translated "virgin" in the Isaiah text, but Matthew's Greek uses the word *parthenos*, which in this context certainly means "virgin." The miraculous birth of Isaiah 7:14 was God's sign to unbelieving King Ahaz that the kings he dreaded would soon be defeated. Typical of his use of OT prophecy, Matthew sees the birth of Jesus as the fulfillment (Matt. 1:22) of Isaiah 7:14: a parallel but greater sign of a greater event.

2. The virginal conception guards both the deity and the humanity of Christ. It is miraculous, indicating that the child is God. But conception and birth are (except in the cases of Adam and Eve) the origin of all human beings. It was necessary that Jesus should be conceived and born as we are, just as it was necessary that he be tempted as we are (Heb. 4:15). So the virginal conception is not only God's entrance into the world, but God's taking to himself a human nature by becoming the son of a woman.[19]

3. The virginal conception and birth signals to us that salvation is by the grace of God, without human effort. God takes the entire initiative, and Mary is passive:

> And Mary said, "Behold, I am the servant of the Lord; let it be to me according to your word." (Luke 1:38)

The gospel of John, which does not specifically mention the birth of Jesus, may be alluding to the virgin birth when it describes believers,

> who were born, not of blood nor of the will of the flesh nor of the will of man, but of God. (John 1:13)

Aner, translated "man" in the ESV, is sometimes translated "husband," so this verse, whether or not the author was conscious of it, draws a close parallel between the birth of Jesus and the new birth of believers.

---

19. That he is the son of a woman, rather than of two human parents, recalls the original messianic promise given after the fall, that the offspring of the woman would bruise the head of the serpent (Gen. 3:15; cf. also Gal. 4:4).

4. It is sometimes said that the virgin birth preserves Jesus from the contamination of the sin of Adam.[20] But although Adam's sin comes upon everyone born of natural generation, it is not proved that inherited sin comes *by means of* natural generation. To say that it does presupposes a traducianist view of the origin of the soul (see chapter 34). If the soul (i.e., the human life) is entirely an inheritance from the person's parents, then sin is an inheritance from them as well. But if, as on the creationist view, each human life is a special creation of God, then sin is by a divine imputation to each individual. On a creationist view, then, Jesus can be genuinely the son of Mary, without God's imputing to him the sin of Adam. On a traducianist view, there evidently had to be a supernatural action of God to exempt Jesus from inherited sin. But that accords with the supernatural character of the whole event.

On either a creationist or traducianist account, however, it is God's decision, not the absence of a human father, that exempted Jesus from inherited sin. Scripture tells us specifically that it was the Spirit's involvement that made the child to be holy (Luke 1:35). So the doctrine of the virgin birth should not be used to suggest that sin is transmitted through the male lineage rather than one's female ancestry.

The virgin birth, therefore, is relevant to original sin in that it shows in Jesus both a continuity and a discontinuity with Adam and his descendants. But the mysteriousness of the event should discourage easy deductions from either his divine or his human nature.

The Hypostatic Union

The phrase *hypostatic union* refers to the combination of Jesus' two natures in one person (Gk. *hypostasis*). The phrase does not occur in Scripture, but the church formulated this concept in order to better understand how one person can be both divine and human. The Council of Chalcedon, A.D. 451, formulated the doctrine as follows:[21]

> Therefore, following the holy fathers, we all with one accord teach men to acknowledge one and the same Son, our Lord Jesus Christ, at once complete in Godhead and complete in manhood, truly God and truly man, consisting also of a reasonable soul and body; of one substance with the Father as regards his Godhead, and at the same time of one substance with us as regards his manhood; like us in all respects, apart from sin; as regards his Godhead, begotten of the Father before the ages, but yet as regards his manhood begotten, for us men and for our salvation, of Mary the Virgin, the God-bearer;[22] one and the same Christ, Son, Lord, Only-begotten, recognized in two natures, without confusion, without change, without division, without separa-

---

20. See the discussion of inherited sin in chapter 36.

21. I omit some introductory material.

22. "God-bearer" is *theotokos*, sometimes translated "mother of God." This phrase is somewhat jarring to Protestants, but it is perfectly orthodox. The Nestorian party thought Mary should be considered the mother of Christ, but not the mother of God. To them, she was the mother only of Jesus' human nature, not his divine nature. But the Council of Chalcedon denied that Jesus' person could be divided in this way. She was the mother of Jesus, the divine-human person, and therefore of both natures.

tion; the distinction of natures being in no way annulled by the union, but rather the characteristics of each nature being preserved and coming together to form one person and subsistence, not as parted or separated into two persons, but one and the same Son and Only-begotten God the Word, Lord Jesus Christ; even as the prophets from earliest times spoke of him, and our Lord Jesus Christ himself taught us, and the creed of the fathers has handed down to us.

Almost all branches of the church accepted this Chalcedonian Declaration. Some exceptions were the "old oriental" churches, namely, the Egyptian Coptic Orthodox, Ethiopian Orthodox, Eritrean Orthodox, Syriac Orthodox, Malankara Orthodox Syrian (India), and Armenian Apostolic.[23]

Like the Nicene Creed, which opposed the heresies of Sabellianism and Arianism (see chapter 22), the Chalcedonian Declaration opposed heresies at two extremes of the debate: Monophysitism,[24] or Eutychianism,[25] maintained that Jesus had only one nature. Nestorianism[26] taught that Jesus' deity and humanity were so divided that he was in effect two persons living in one body.[27] Against the Monophysites, the council affirmed that Jesus had two distinct natures, divine and human. Against the Nestorians, it affirmed that these two natures were indivisible and belonged to one person, the Lord Jesus Christ. The four famous adverbs, "without confusion [*asugchutos*], without change [*atreptos*], without division [*adiaretos*], without separation [*achoristos*]," address these issues, the first two emphasizing the distinctness of the two natures, the second two emphasizing their inseparability and therefore the unity of Jesus' person.

23. Since the word *orthodox* appears in most of these names, I should add by way of clarification that the better-known Orthodox churches, the Greek and the Russian, did embrace the Chalcedonian Declaration.

24. From the Greek *monos physis*, "one nature."

25. After the monk Eutyches, who held that the whole body of Jesus came from heaven.

26. Many historians believe that Nestorius, supposedly the leader of this party, did not hold the position ascribed to that party.

27. The council also discussed the position of Apollinaris, who died around 390, some decades before the council. Apollinaris believed that Christ was fully human, except for his "rational soul." In Christ, the divine *logos* replaced that soul. The Declaration rejects Apollinaris's position, saying that Christ did in fact have a "reasonable soul." At a later time, there was also a controversy over the "Monotholete" view, namely, that Jesus had a complete human nature except for his will, which was only the will of the Father. Certainly the idea that Jesus had two wills was counterintuitive. But the one-will view, too, did not prevail. Luke 22:42 distinguishes between Jesus' human will and the Father's divine will. So it was impossible to compromise by ascribing to Jesus only a partial human nature.

Indeed, the saying became common that "what is not assumed is not redeemed." It was necessary for Jesus to assume all aspects of human nature, if every aspect of human nature was to be saved (Heb. 2:17). This saying suggests the ancient view that Christ saves us by somehow taking our humanity up into deity, a process sometimes described by the term *deification* (*theopoiesis*). Eastern Orthodox theologians use this language today, basing it on 2 Peter 1:4. They insist that they don't mean to confuse or mitigate the Creator-creature distinction. But in my judgment, (1) this language creates confusion, and (2) it suggests that we are saved primarily by Jesus' incarnation rather than by his atonement. Scripture, rather, points to the atonement as the great exchange in which Jesus took on our sins and we received his righteousness. As we saw earlier, Paul's summary of his teaching is "Christ and him crucified."

This language reverses the language used in the doctrine of the Trinity. That doctrine affirms three persons with one nature;[28] Chalcedonian Christology affirms one person with two natures. A *nature* (*physis*) is a group of attributes; a *person* is a being who bears those attributes. So Chalcedon teaches that the one person Jesus Christ bears divine attributes and also human attributes. His divine attributes include all those I discussed in chapters 12–19. Jesus, like God the Father and the Holy Spirit, is perfect love, righteousness, holiness, omniscient, omnipotent, eternal, immense, self-contained. His human attributes are all those I discussed in chapters 34 and 35: God's image, offices of Prophet, Priest, and King, the intellectual, physical, and moral qualifications for these offices, responsible, free.

As we saw in chapter 36, man is also sinful. But sin is not an essential component of human nature. God made man good, but he became a sinner by violating God's command. In Jesus, the human race marks a new beginning. He is the "last Adam" (1 Cor. 15:45) and the "second man" (v. 47). As such, he is conceived and born without sin, as we indicated earlier. And the NT writers affirm the sinlessness of his life:

> For we do not have a high priest who is unable to sympathize with our weaknesses, but one who in every respect has been tempted as we are, yet without sin. (Heb. 4:15; cf. John 8:46; 14:30; Heb. 7:26; 1 John 3:5)

It is amazing that people who knew Jesus intimately through the years of his ministry would affirm his sinlessness. No other human being could sustain such a claim.

His sinlessness, like the other aspects of his humanity, is essential to his saving work. As a sacrifice, he had to be pure, unblemished, a spotless lamb. If he himself had committed sins, he would have died for those, for his own sins. But only a sinless life could qualify him to be a sacrifice for others.

Living with Two Natures

Such are Jesus' two natures: full deity (all the attributes of God) and full humanity, except for sin. But it is perplexing as to how deity and humanity, so understood, can exist in the same person. The Eutychians or Monophysites were wrong to deny that Jesus had two distinct natures. But their position is understandable. For people who encountered Jesus saw one person, not two. All the biblical references to him are in the singular, not the plural. So Chalcedon spoke of him as "one person and subsistence."

But how can one person be both divine and human, infinite and finite, invisible and visible, eternal and temporal, omnipotent and suffering,[29] omniscient and limited

---

28. Of course, the Niceno-Constantinopolitan doctrine of the Trinity states not only that God has one nature (*physis*), but also that he is one substance (*ousia*, *substantia*). He is not just a group of attributes; he is a substantive being.

29. On the possibility of divine suffering, see chapter 16. In some senses, I believe that suffering is not excluded from God's own experience. He cannot suffer in the sense of experiencing loss of any aspect of his eternal nature. But he can and does experience feelings of pain, grief, and affliction. It is certainly mysterious to us *how*

in knowledge? Trying to imagine the psychology, the feeling or experience, of such a person is baffling.

The general pattern, I think, is that while on earth in the "state of humiliation," Jesus often limited his specifically divine attributes. For as we have seen, the specific purpose of the incarnation was that God should live our life and feel our sufferings, in order to be a perfect substitutionary sacrifice for our sins. Consider this incident following Jesus' arrest:

> And behold, one of those who were with Jesus stretched out his hand and drew his sword and struck the servant of the high priest and cut off his ear. Then Jesus said to him, "Put your sword back into its place. For all who take the sword will perish by the sword. Do you think that I cannot appeal to my Father, and he will at once send me more than twelve legions of angels? But how then should the Scriptures be fulfilled, that it must be so?" (Matt. 26:51–54)

Jesus had proved on many occasions that he had access to the Father's power. So he performed healings and other miracles. But the Father had not sent him to accomplish salvation with a display of power. The cross beckoned, and that was a call to weakness. However one distinguishes between the Father's power and Jesus' own omnipotence, Jesus certainly limited the use of his might in order to exercise that power that is made perfect in weakness (2 Cor. 12:9).

The same must be said for Jesus' knowledge. To the question of the time of his return and the final judgment, Jesus says:

> But concerning that day and hour no one knows, not even the angels of heaven, nor the Son, but the Father only. (Matt. 24:36)

It is hard to imagine how one with divine knowledge at his disposal could be ignorant of the day and hour of his own return in glory. But I would understand this as strictly analogous to Jesus' intentional limits on his power. Knowledge, of course, is also power, and here Jesus limits his power to know. As in Matthew 26:51–54 Jesus limited himself to the power in weakness that the Father had set at his disposal, so in 24:36 he limits himself to the limited knowledge by which the Father expected him to live during the time of his humiliation.

Communication of Attributes

Problems of this sort have led the church to discuss the *communication of attributes* (*koinonia idiomaton, communicatio idiomatum*). This is the question of how Jesus' unique hypostatic union affects his being, individual natures, and particular attributes. For example: we have said that Jesus has a human and a divine attribute of knowledge. But

---

he can experience such suffering. But Scripture is clear that he does and that this experience is not contrary to the divine nature.

how remarkable it is that a person should have two distinct faculties of knowledge! How difficult that is for us to conceive! So we ask: how does his divine knowledge affect his human knowledge, or vice versa? Jesus has human knowledge; but it would seem that his human knowledge cannot be ordinary human knowledge, since it exists alongside a divine knowledge. Do they just sit alongside each other like two unconnected blocks of wood? Or does each enrich the other somehow, or detract from it? It is hard to imagine how a man's knowledge can remain within the bounds of human knowledge, when he can always resort to divine knowledge to assist him. But when he does resort to his divine knowledge, how can his human knowledge remain truly human?

For another example, given that Jesus is all-powerful, how does that affect, say, his desire for food? Can that be a fully human desire, when we consider that he could always have satisfied it by drawing on his divine powers?

The broader question: do Jesus' divine attributes *communicate* with his human attributes and/or vice versa? Do they enter transactions with one another? What kind? And what of the relationships between each group of attributes and Jesus' *person*?

The danger here is that poor answers to such questions can lead back to the heresies that generated the Christological controversy that led to Chalcedon. Either one nature becomes isolated from the other (as was the charge against Nestorianism) or the two natures are blended into one (the charge against Monophysitism). To refer back to the language of Chalcedon, it is important that the two natures are not confused or changed into each other (the danger of Monophysitism) or divided or separated from each other (the danger of Nestorianism).

WCF 8.7 addresses this issue as follows:

> Christ, in the work of mediation, acts according to both natures, by each nature doing that which is proper to itself; yet, by reason of the unity of the person, that which is proper to one nature is sometimes in Scripture attributed to the person denominated by the other nature.

Here the confession distinguishes between two classes of actions, each "proper to" one nature or the other. Presumably, miraculous healings are proper to his divine nature, hungering and pain to his human nature. But we should remember that natures as such do not do anything. A nature is a collection of attributes. Attributes don't act—only the things or persons that possess those attributes act. So it was not Jesus' divine nature that wrought miraculous healings. It was the *person* of Jesus, Jesus himself. Jesus healed people miraculously because of his divine nature. Similarly, it was not Jesus' human nature that hungered and suffered pain. Rather, it was Jesus himself: the person, not his nature. We should never say that "Jesus' human nature did this or that," or "Jesus' divine nature did thus and so." Jesus himself was the actor, the One who performed the great works that brought us salvation.

So Jesus himself performed miracles, and Jesus himself suffered and hungered. He was able to do the former because of his divine nature, and the latter because of his human nature. But in both cases, it was Jesus, not his attributes or nature, who did these things. Therefore, it is important to say that Jesus is one person, not two. That is the answer to the Nestorian error.

But is there a sense in which the two natures affect each other? Is Jesus' human knowledge changed by its proximity to his divine knowledge? Two principles are important: (1) Even in the person of Jesus, the Creator-creature distinction must be preserved. In chapter 3 I emphasized the importance of this distinction: God is not the world, and the world is not God. Now, in Jesus, the Creator and the creature are in intimate proximity, more intimate than anywhere else on earth. Yet even in him, divinity and humanity are distinct. Jesus' divine nature is Creator, his human nature creature. For this reason Chalcedon insists that the two natures cannot be changed or confused.

(2) The second principle is that as the two natures cannot be changed or confused, neither can they be divided or separated. They constitute one person and only one. They reside intimately together, in the closest imaginable fellowship. Our fellowship with God is interrupted by our sinful inclinations. That was never the case for Jesus except on the cross. Was Jesus' human nature affected by his divine nature? Of course. If you or I were living in uninterrupted fellowship with God, as were Adam and Eve in the garden, every moment of our experience would be dominated by God. We would constantly be seeking to please him. So did Jesus. His humanity was a perfectly faithful humanity, unlike any other human life since the fall.

Was Jesus' divinity affected by his perfect humanity? The word *affected* here is probably not appropriate. We should not leave the impression that a human action or a group of human actions wrought changes in God. But Scripture speaks often of God's being "pleased" by faithful human persons, behavior, and attitudes. We may say, certainly, that Jesus' human nature constantly pleased God as God was present within him.

So the presence of Jesus' two natures in one person implies a rich, dynamic fellowship between Jesus and the Father. But the dynamism is not ontological, as if God were becoming confused with man, or vice versa.

Lutherans have often insisted that Jesus' human nature, because of its proximity to his divine nature, has become "ubiquitous," or omnipresent. So Jesus' humanity, because of its proximity to his divinity, has acquired a divine attribute: omnipresence. This notion reflects the Lutheran view that Jesus' physical body is always present in the sacrament.[30] Calvinists reject this notion, prompting the following dialogue:

> Calvinists: The Lutheran view violates the Creator-creature distinction in teaching that Jesus' physical body has the divine attribute of omnipresence.

---

30. Lutherans typically insist that the doctrine of ubiquity was not developed to fit their sacramental theology. But unquestionably the two do fit together.

Lutherans: The Calvinist view of the *communicatio idiomatum* sets the two natures of Christ alongside each other as inert blocks of wood, with no real interaction between them.

Calvinists: The *communicatio* is not primarily about how one nature affects the other, but about how each nature, and both natures, affects the *person* of Christ. In this case, Christ's *person* is certainly omnipresent because of his divine nature. That is, *he* is omnipresent. But it would be wrong to say that Jesus' *human nature* is omnipresent because of his divine nature.

Christ the Image of God

In chapter 34, I expounded the biblical teaching that man is the image of God. Here it is important to consider that Scripture presents Jesus as the image of God par excellence. We would expect this because of his perfect humanity. But Scripture speaks of him as the image even apart from the incarnation, in his eternal nature as the divine Son:

In their case the god of this world has blinded the minds of the unbelievers, to keep them from seeing the light of the gospel of the glory of Christ, who is the image of God. (2 Cor. 4:4)

He is the image of the invisible God, the firstborn of all creation. (Col. 1:15)[31]

He is the radiance of the glory of God and the exact imprint of his nature, and he upholds the universe by the word of his power. After making purification for sins, he sat down at the right hand of the Majesty on high. (Heb. 1:3).[32]

Even apart from his humanity, the Son is the perfect reflection of his Father and therefore the Father's perfect representative. This is essentially the same relationship expressed in a different figure in John 1, where the Father is the speaker, the Son the Word he speaks.

So it can be said truly that he who has seen the Son has seen the Father (John 14:9). Jesus is the supreme theophany of God. So although we are discussing Jesus as God's image three chapters later than our discussion of man in general as God's image, it is clear that Jesus is the prototype, we the ectype. For man, even unfallen Adam, to be in the image of God is for him to be like Jesus. So when we are redeemed from sin and come to image God in a renewed way, Scripture speaks of our being renewed specifically in the image of Christ.

For those whom he foreknew he also predestined to be conformed to the image of his Son, in order that he might be the firstborn among many brothers. (Rom. 8:29)

31. For a discussion of the phrase "firstborn of all creation," see *DG*, 684–85.

32. In these two verses, different Greek terms are found: *eikon* in Colossians 1:15, *character* in Hebrews 1:3. But though different terms are used, they are both terms that recall the language from Genesis 1 about the "image of God."

In chapter 34, I argued that the clearest way of describing the image of God in which Adam was created is to set forth the nature of his lordship over the earth. The image of God in Genesis 1:28 is what equips Adam to be lord of the earth, as God himself is the Lord of all. So the image in which God made Adam is a reflection at a finite level of God's lordship attributes: control, authority, and presence. Those attributes also constitute the image of God ascribed to Christ. See fig. 37.1.

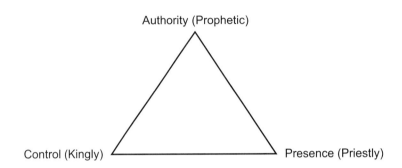

Fig. 37.1. The Three Offices of Christ

I will expound these briefly here, but in the next chapter I will expand on them because they are the best description I know of the *work* of Christ.

Control (Kingly Office)

Because Jesus is both God and man, his lordship attributes function as descriptions both of his deity and of his human messiahship. So they have meaning both as ontological categories (descriptions of his fundamental nature) and as historical categories (descriptions of the roles he plays in his Father's historical drama). It is, of course, appropriate that One who is ontologically the Word of God should be God's spokesman in history. Similarly, it is appropriate that the One who is God's eternal Son should be born in such a way that "the child to be born will be called holy—the Son of God" (Luke 1:35), and that he should be "declared to be the Son of God in power according to the Spirit of holiness by his resurrection from the dead" (Rom. 1:4).

Similarly, his title *King* refers both to who he is ontologically, the Ruler of all things, and to what he becomes historically, as he accomplishes his redemptive work. His control over all the objects and forces of the creation exists throughout the gospel accounts, attested by his miracles. He is also King from birth, as the Magi attest when they come seeking the "king of the Jews" (Matt. 2:2). His control over all things, based on his ontological sonship, qualifies him for his historical roles as King of the Jews and then as "King of kings and Lord of lords" (Rev. 19:16). In that historical role he receives recognition as King at the historical junctures representing the completion of his redemptive acts: resurrection (Rom. 1:4) and final judgment (Rev. 19:16). For a fuller account of the redemptive-historical course of Jesus' kingship, see chapter 5.

So in the gospel narrative, Jesus becomes (historically) what he is (ontologically). In the former sense, he becomes King; in the latter sense he is always King. Those two meanings of kingship produce some perplexities for Bible students, but to distinguish them dissolves, I think, the source of difficulty.

Authority (Prophetic Office)

As we have seen (chapters 23–24), Jesus is the eternal Word of God, the One who perfectly expresses the Father's will in thought, word, and deed. So he is the prototype of the prophet, the Prophet par excellence. So all his words spoken to human beings are words of God himself, bearing all the power, authority, and presence of God's own lordship.

Thus, Jesus presents God's commands as the true criteria of human obedience, and God's promises as the only means of salvation to those who have broken God's law. As with his kingly control, the nature of his deity determines the outworking of his prophetic authority in history. Ontologically, his authority governs all things. Historically, some take exception to it. But in the history of redemption, we will see the drama unfold in which all creatures bend the knee to that authority, happily or begrudgingly.

So as with his control, there is one level (the ontological) in which Jesus' authority is forever established, and another level (the historical) in which his authority is established through a temporal process.

Presence (Priestly Office)

We saw that out of the rich mutual indwelling of the persons of the Trinity (chapter 22), God dwells in and with all that he has made. Creation itself establishes an intimate relation between God and his world, for there is nothing in between Creator and creature that might separate the two. In providence, God governs the world not only from above, but from below as well, by entering concurrently into every event no matter how minor. Similarly, when God determines to redeem sinful human beings, he does it from up close. As the holy God, he is separate from sinners (Heb. 7:26). But as our Redeemer, he draws us into the circle of his holiness (chapter 13), the result being not that he is defiled but that we become holy, his holy people.

As with the other lordship attributes, God's presence is both ontological and historical. As I have said, creation and providence already bring God together with his creatures. But God's lordship in itself does not guarantee that he will redeem sinners. That he does this is his free choice, what Scripture calls *grace*. So God's nearness to us has two aspects: (1) ontological, by creation and providence, and (2) historical, by grace. Grace comes through a historical, dramatic process. So it has a different form in the time of Moses from the form it has in the time of Jesus' incarnation and in our own time. Through Moses, God displayed his grace through animal sacrifices; through Jesus, he displayed it in his own Son, the Lamb of God.

In that sense, Jesus is the Great High Priest of God. The priest makes offering to God for the sins of the people, and he intercedes to God for them. Jesus as Priest offers the greatest sacrifice, his own body, and he now lives forever to make intercession for his redeemed people (Heb. 2:17–18; chaps. 5–10).

Jesus' three offices, therefore, are natural applications of his three lordship attributes, his unchangeable nature worked out in the historical process. So Jesus is the image of God in its highest form. In the next chapter, we will see what Jesus accomplishes for us in each of these three offices.

Key Terms

Christ-centeredness (reductive sense)
Christomonism
Kenosis
Ebionites
Docetists
Gnostics
Incarnation (Murray's definition)
Virginal conception
Hypostasis
Hypostatic union
Chalcedon
Mother of God
Eutychian
Monophysite
Nestorian
Apollinarian
Nature
Person
Communication of attributes
Ubiquitous
King
Prophet
Priest

Study Questions

1. Who is the only Redeemer of God's elect? Present the catechism's answer.
2. Van Til: "Theology is primarily God centered rather than Christ centered." What does this mean? Do you agree? Why or why not?
3. Why does Frame find fault with Karl Barth's form of Christ-centeredness?

4. Summarize the biblical argument for the deity of Christ. Evaluate the *kenosis theory*.

5. Why were some in the early church reluctant to confess Jesus' true humanity? Where were they coming from? How did the NT writers reply to them?

6. What does it mean to say that Christ came "in the likeness of sinful flesh"? Why is that important?

7. Why was it *necessary* for the Son of God to become man? Explain.

8. What is the importance of Jesus' *virginal conception*? Why does Frame prefer that phrase to the phrase *virgin birth*?

9. Summarize the meanings and importance of the four famous adverbs in the Chalcedon formula.

10. Frame: "The general pattern, I think, is that while on earth in the 'state of humiliation,' Jesus often limited his specifically divine attributes." Give examples. How does this apply to Jesus' expressed ignorance of the time of his return?

11. Quote WCF 8.7 and explain.

12. "We should never say that 'Jesus' human nature did this or that,' or 'Jesus' divine nature did thus and so.'" Why does Frame say this? Evaluate.

13. "Jesus' two natures should never be divided or separated." What does this imply for Jesus' personal relation to God?

14. Formulate and discuss the debate between Calvinists and Lutherans about the *communicatio idiomatum*.

15. Expound Jesus as the image of God by way of the lordship attributes.

16. Frame argues that in each of his lordship attributes, there is an ontological constancy and a historical process. Explain; evaluate.

Memory Verses

Mark 10:45: For even the Son of Man came not to be served but to serve, and to give his life as a ransom for many.

1 Cor. 2:2: For I decided to know nothing among you except Jesus Christ and him crucified.

Gal. 4:4–5: But when the fullness of time had come, God sent forth his Son, born of woman, born under the law, to redeem those who were under the law, so that we might receive adoption as sons.

Col. 1:15: He is the image of the invisible God, the firstborn of all creation.

Heb. 2:14: Since therefore the children share in flesh and blood, he himself likewise partook of the same things, that through death he might destroy the one who has the power of death, that is, the devil.

1 John 4:2–3: By this you know the Spirit of God: every spirit that confesses that Jesus Christ has come in the flesh is from God, and every spirit that does not confess Jesus is not from God. This is the spirit of the antichrist, which you heard was coming and now is in the world already.

Resources for Further Study

Frame, John M. "Virgin Birth of Jesus." In *Evangelical Dictionary of Theology*, edited by Walter A. Elwell, 1143–46. Grand Rapids: Baker, 1984. This article deals with some of the criticisms of the doctrine based on philosophy and biblical criticism. Also available at http://www.frame-poythress.org.

Murray, John. *MCW*, 2:132–33.

Strimple, Robert B. "Philippians 2:5–11 in Recent Studies: Some Exegetical Conclusions." *WTJ* 41, 2 (Spring 1979): 247–68.

Van Til, Cornelius. *An Introduction to Systematic Theology*. Nutley, NJ: Presbyterian and Reformed, 1974.

CHAPTER 38

THE WORK OF CHRIST

IN THE PREVIOUS CHAPTER, we asked who Jesus is. In this chapter, we will ask what he has done, following the traditional distinction between Jesus' *person* and *work*. In this chapter, I will look at the work of Christ from three perspectives: normatively through his execution of his offices, situationally through his states of humiliation and exaltation, and existentially through his union with his people and ours with him. See fig. 38.1.

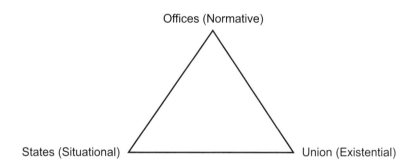

Fig. 38.1. Perspectives on the Work of Christ

Jesus' Offices

As we saw in the previous chapter, the Son of God became incarnate for a distinct purpose: to save his people from their sins (Mark 10:45; Gal. 4:4–5; Heb. 2:14–18). Everything in Scripture about the person of Christ has this work in view. As I indicated in chapter 37, Jesus did not become incarnate for incarnation's sake, as if the incarnation were itself sufficient to save his people. Our plight is not that we are finite, that we are not-God; and the remedy for our plight is not some new metaphysical connection to God. Rather, our plight is ethical: We have sinned, and therefore we are in a state of personal estrangement from our Creator. Jesus' incarnation was a means of bringing about reconciliation between ourselves and God.

So Scripture's description of Jesus's nature coheres perfectly with its description of his work. Since Jesus is perfect God, redemption is certain and permanent. Since he is perfect man, he is able to perform as God's image, his Father's perfect likeness as Lord of all. He displays those lordship attributes that Adam bore at his creation: his control, authority, and presence. And Jesus is able to apply those qualities to meet our need of redemption, executing the offices of King, Prophet, and Priest.

These offices help us to understand Jesus' redemptive work. As Prophet, he brings us the true word of God. As Priest, he brings sacrifice (ultimately the sacrifice is himself) and makes intercession. And as King, he rules all things in his mighty power. Let us consider each of these in turn.

Prophet

First, Jesus is the greatest of the prophets, indeed more than a prophet. As we saw in chapter 24, a prophet is one who has the very word of God on his lips. Deuteronomy 18:15–22 and Jeremiah 1:9–10, as well as other passages, show that the prophet's words are God's words, and so they are just as authoritative as the divine voice uttered from heaven.

But Jesus is more than a prophet. He is the very Word of God himself. John 1:1 reads, "In the beginning was the Word, and the Word was with God, and the Word was God." And we see from verse 14 that that Word was Jesus.

So when Jesus begins his teaching ministry, people are amazed at the authority with which he speaks, not at all like the Scribes and Pharisees (Matt. 7:28–29). He declares God's Word truly (John 1:18; 15:15), cutting through all the distortions and compromises of the Jewish traditions.

Further, he teaches that his word is to be the foundation of all of life (Matt. 7:21–27). Peter recognizes this when he says, "Lord, to whom shall we go? You have the words of eternal life" (John 6:68). It is the word of his grace that builds us up (Acts 20:32). And Jesus' word will judge us all in the last day (John 12:48).

Jesus did not speak his word only during his earthly ministry. The whole OT is his Word, "for the testimony of Jesus is the spirit of prophecy" (Rev. 19:10). He taught his disciples that everything in the Law, the Prophets, and the Writings of the OT was about him. So the whole Bible is not only the Word of God, but the Word of Jesus as well. He is both the Author and the chief theme of Scripture. It is his gospel, his promise, and by that Word we are saved.

Following his resurrection, Jesus spoke with two disciples who were confused about the meaning of Jesus' death:

> And he said to them, "O foolish ones, and slow of heart to believe all that the prophets have spoken! Was it not necessary that the Christ should suffer these things and enter into his glory?" And beginning with Moses and all the Prophets, he interpreted to them in all the Scriptures the things concerning himself. (Luke 24:25–27)

When we see Scripture as a testimony to Christ, every part of it takes on new significance. It is his Book. So he is in one sense the only Prophet. He determines the meaning of every prophecy.

Priest

Second, Jesus is our Great High Priest. We can summarize the duties of a priest in two categories: sacrifice and intercession.

Jesus' sacrifice is what we usually think of first when we think of the *work* of Christ. The theological name for that sacrifice is *atonement*. That word comes from an Old English expression referring to reconciliation, bringing people to oneness, at-one-ment. Certainly reconciliation is part of the meaning of atonement. But there is much more as well.

Jesus' atoning sacrifice fulfills the OT sacrifices of bulls, goats, lambs, doves, flour, wine, and oil. In the OT, God used those sacrifices to teach the people what Jesus was later going to do. So we can learn from those sacrifices about the meaning of Jesus' atonement.

First, the sacrificial animal had to be perfect, spotless, without blemish (Ex. 12:5; 29:1; Lev. 1:3; etc.). The Israelite was not to bring an offering to God that was cheap or worthless. He had to bring something really valuable, something perfect, something that he would otherwise treasure for himself. Similarly, Jesus offered himself as the sinless Lamb of God. As we saw in chapters 21 and 37, Jesus committed no sin. Neither his friends nor his enemies were able to find any fault in him. He loved as no one had ever loved (John 15:3–4; 1 John 3:16). Even the demons recognized him as the Holy One of God (Luke 1:35; 4:34; Acts 3:14; 7:52). So the OT language of "spotless" sacrifice and sacrifice "without blemish" applies to Jesus' sacrifice in Hebrews 9:14 and 1 Peter 1:19. Significantly, the same language is used of those who receive the atonement of Jesus' sacrifice:

> Husbands, love your wives, as Christ loved the church and gave himself up for her, that he might sanctify her, having cleansed her by the washing of water with the word, so that he might present the church to himself in splendor, without spot or wrinkle or any such thing, that she might be holy and without blemish. (Eph. 5:25–27)

> I charge you in the presence of God, who gives life to all things, and of Christ Jesus, who in his testimony before Pontius Pilate made the good confession, to keep the commandment unstained and free from reproach until the appearing of our Lord Jesus Christ. (1 Tim. 6:13–14)

> But according to his promise we are waiting for new heavens and a new earth in which righteousness dwells.
> Therefore, beloved, since you are waiting for these, be diligent to be found by him without spot or blemish, and at peace. (2 Peter 3:13–14)

These passages do not imply that every follower of Christ now shares his sinless perfection. But such perfection is our destiny and our present goal. And there is a sense in which God sees us even now as bearing the perfection of Christ.

Theologians call Jesus' perfect life his *active obedience*. When we believe in Christ, God counts us as righteous in Christ. That is to say, God *imputes* to us the active obedience of Christ, so he sees us, regards us, counts us, declares us as righteous and holy, as Jesus is. Paul tells us in 2 Corinthians 5:21 that "for our sake he made him to be sin who knew no sin, so that in him we might become the righteousness of God." God imputes our sin to Christ and his righteousness to us. God judges our sin in Christ, and he regards us as righteous in Christ. That is sometimes called *double imputation*: our sin to Christ, his righteousness to us. So God not only forgives our sins; he gives to us the very righteousness of Christ. So not only are we acquitted, but we are positively good.[1]

Jesus' death on the cross is called his *passive obedience*. The word *passive* may not be the best, because in English the term is usually contrasted with *active*. But Jesus is very active in sacrificing himself. He is the Priest who offers the sacrifice. He lays down his life, and he says in John 10:18:

> No one takes it from me, but I lay it down of my own accord. I have authority to lay it down, and I have authority to take it up again. This charge I have received from my Father.

But the word *passive* is related to the Greek and Latin terms for *suffering*, so we can accept the term *passive obedience* simply as referring to his suffering and death.

Jesus' passive obedience is an atoning sacrifice. That sacrifice accomplishes a number of things. First, *expiation*. This means that Jesus bore our sins, took them on himself, and therefore did away with them (Isa. 53:6, 12; John 1:29; Heb. 9:28; 1 Peter 2:24). As we saw earlier in 2 Corinthians 5:21, he was "made sin" for us. He became our *substitute*. As such, he took the full penalty that we owed God, the penalty of death (Ezek. 18:4; Rom. 6:23). By expiation, Jesus wiped our slate clean. We have nothing to fear from God. God forgives our sins fully and completely, taking them as far from us as the east is from the west.

---

1. There is some controversy over this assertion today in American Presbyterian theology. Norman Shepherd has questioned it, for example, in his "Justification by Works in Reformed Theology," in *Backbone of the Bible*, ed. P. Andrew Sandlin (Nacodoches, TX: Covenant Media Press, 2004), 103–20. Despite my great respect for Shepherd, I cannot accept his argument, though I think his position (contrary to some) is certainly within the bounds of Reformed orthodoxy. There are legitimate questions about whether the NT uses specific language of imputation in regard to Christ's active righteousness. But however those questions come out, the imputation of Christ's righteousness to us is certainly *implicit* in the imputation of our sin to him, which Shepherd accepts. If our sin is placed on Christ, so that we are thenceforth *in Christ* (as the NT pervasively emphasizes), then we are righteous for his sake. God holds nothing more against us. People not charged with sin are righteous people. There is no such thing as ethical neutrality. Every human act or attitude, every human person, is either righteous or unrighteous. In Christ, then, we are not ethically neutral, but positively righteous and therefore fit for heaven. But we are righteous only in Christ, not in ourselves. That point is obviously biblical, and it seems to me that it is equivalent to a doctrine of imputed active righteousness.

Second, *propitiation*. This means that he bore the wrath and anger of God that was due to sin (Rom. 3:25; Heb. 2:17; 1 John 2:2; 4:10). In some mysterious way, he was even estranged from his Father on the cross, as the Father regarded him bearing our sins. "My God, my God, why have you forsaken me?" he cried, quoting Psalm 22 (Matt. 27:46). Some scholars have tried to eliminate the theme of *propitiation* from the Bible, trying to make it a synonym for *expiation*.[2] These scholars don't like the idea of God's being angry with people because of sin. But that attempt has failed. Our God cares about right and wrong. "God is a righteous judge, and a God who feels indignation every day," Psalm 7:11 tells us. God is angry with the wicked, and Jesus on the cross turned God's anger away from his people. See my discussion of the wrath of God in chapter 13 of this book.

We should not forget, however, that God's anger against the wicked coexists with his love for his elect, indeed even for the wicked elect. God sent his Son because he loved the sinful world (John 3:16). All of us were "dead in . . . trespasses and sins" (Eph. 2:1), but before we had committed any sin, God loved us in Christ (1:4). It is certainly mysterious how God can hate and love the same people at the same time, but that is the testimony of Scripture (chapter 13).

Third, the atonement is *reconciliation*, as the English word implies. Since we are now righteous in God's sight (expiation), and he is no longer angry with us (propitiation), we are reconciled, no longer enemies (2 Cor. 5:18–19). Again, some scholars have tried to soften this idea, by saying that the atonement purges our enmity against God, not God's against us. They think, again, that God has no enmity toward sinners. But that is biblically wrong. Scores of Scripture verses speak of God's anger with the wicked. In sin, man is the enemy of God and vice versa. Christ brings us together, so that believers will live together with God in blessed fellowship forever and ever. We anticipate that fellowship in the Lord's Supper, in which we have table fellowship with God.

Finally, the atonement is *redemption*. *Redemption* means literally "buying back" something. In the OT, when someone sold his property, or even got so far into debt that he sold himself into slavery, a relative could buy back the property, or buy the man's freedom. This relative is often called the *kinsman-redeemer*, and Leviticus 25 describes him. In the book of Ruth, Boaz redeems Ruth and her mother-in-law from poverty by marrying her. In Mark 10:45, Jesus says that he has come to give his life "as a ransom for many," buying us back as God's lost property. His sacrifice on the cross was an act of great value, and it purchased for him a people of his own possession. So we belong to God, both by creation and by redemption.

Those four terms summarize what the atonement is, according to Scripture. But I should also warn against some false ways of looking at the atonement. Some theologians have not liked the idea of Jesus' dying in our place, so they have tried to make the atonement an easier concept. First, some, such as the third-century writer Origen,

---

2. Especially influential in this regard was C. H. Dodd. See his *The Bible and the Greeks* (London: Hodder and Stoughton, 1935).

have picked up on the ransom passage in Mark 10:45, and have suggested that Jesus paid the ransom to Satan. That idea has no biblical basis. Satan has no rights over us. It is to God alone that Jesus pays our ransom.

Second, some, such as the medieval thinker Abelard, together with many modern liberals, have argued that the atonement is not a sacrifice, but only a moral example. On this view, Jesus dies on the cross to show us how to behave. This position does have some biblical basis: 1 Peter 2:21 says, "For to this you have been called, because Christ also suffered for you, leaving you an example, so that you might follow in his steps." The atonement is an example to us. The question is whether the atonement is *only* an example. If it is only an example, then, as Roger Nicole has pointed out,[3] it is a very poor example. For if Jesus died merely to encourage us to do the same thing, he is encouraging suicide, something that Scripture never honors. But if Jesus laid down his life to bring life to others, then there is something here that we can imitate. We should be cautious at this point: in one sense, we can never do what Jesus did. He took away the punishment of our sins; I cannot do that for anyone else. Yet his self-sacrifice is an excellent model for us, in that it tells us to give ourselves in love for the benefit of others. First John 3:16 says, "By this we know love, that he laid down his life for us, and we ought to lay down our lives for the brothers."

The third wrong view of the atonement is the governmental view of Grotius, Charles Finney, and others. It teaches that God forgives our sins without any need of sacrifice. But to impress us of the seriousness and solemnity of God's law, God put his Son to death. This view is unbiblical in a number of ways. First, Scripture teaches that sacrifice is required to receive God's forgiveness: without the shedding of blood, there is no forgiveness of sins (Heb. 9:22). As we have seen, the wages of sin is death (Rom. 6:23; cf. Ezek. 18:4). Second, on this view, God demonstrates the severity of his law by putting to death an innocent man. But unless Jesus is a substitute for us, his death is a demonstration of injustice, not justice.

For Whom Did Christ Die?

Many theologians have devoted a lot of attention to the question: for whom did Christ die? There are basically two views on the subject. One view, called *unlimited atonement*, says that Christ died for every human being. The other view, called *limited atonement*, *definite atonement*, or *particular redemption*, says that Christ died only for the elect, only for those who in God's plan will be ultimately saved.

The unlimited view seems fairly obvious from a number of Scriptures that say that Christ died for "the world" (John 1:29; 3:16; 6:51; 2 Cor. 5:19; 1 John 2:2), "for all" (1 Cor. 15:22; 2 Cor. 5:15; 1 Tim. 2:6; Heb. 2:9), or even, apparently, for people who ultimately reject him, as in 2 Peter 2:1, where Peter speaks of some who are "even denying the Master who bought them, bringing upon themselves swift destruction." This sounds

---

3. In a public lecture at Reformed Theological Seminary, spring 2004.

very much as though Jesus died on the cross to buy, to redeem, some people who nevertheless will be lost in the end.

In Hebrews 10:29, we read, "How much worse punishment, do you think, will be deserved by the one who has spurned the Son of God, and has profaned the blood of the covenant by which he was sanctified, and has outraged the Spirit of grace?" Again, it sounds as though some people are sanctified, made holy, by the blood of Christ, who nevertheless spurn and profane that blood, and receive eternal punishment.

But although this view sounds obvious from the verses I have quoted, there are some real problems with it. If the atonement is unlimited, universal, then it would seem to bring salvation to everybody. For, as we have seen, the atonement is a substitutionary sacrifice. Jesus' atonement takes our sins away, bringing us full forgiveness. So if the atonement is universal, it guarantees salvation for everybody. But we know from Scripture, indeed from 2 Peter 2:1 and Hebrews 10:29, which I just quoted, that not everyone in the world is saved. Some people spurn Jesus' blood. They trample it down. So they receive swift destruction.

If you believe in a universal atonement, therefore, you must hold a weaker view of what the atonement is. It must be something less than a substitutionary sacrifice that brings full forgiveness. What could that be? Some theologians have suggested that the atonement does not actually save anybody, but it takes away the barrier of original sin, so that we are now free to choose Christ or reject him. So the atonement does not actually save; it only makes salvation possible for those who freely decide to come to faith. In the end, it is our free decision that saves us; the atonement only prepares the way, so that we can make a free decision. And in this context, *free decision* refers to the idea of libertarian freedom that I rejected in chapter 35.

The trouble is, however, that Scripture never hints at any such meaning for the atonement. In Scripture, the atonement does not merely make salvation possible. The atonement actually saves. It is not merely a prelude to our free decision. It brings to us all the benefits of God's forgiveness, and eternal life. Those who say that the atonement has an unlimited extent believe that it has a limited efficacy, a limited power to save. Those who believe the atonement is limited to the elect, however, believe that it has an unlimited efficacy. So everyone believes in some kind of limitation. Either the atonement is limited in its extent or it is limited in its efficacy. I think the Bible teaches that it is limited in its extent, unlimited in its efficacy.

Therefore, mainly because I believe that Scripture teaches the efficacy of the atonement, I hold to the view that the atonement is limited in its extent. It doesn't save everybody, but it fully saves everybody that it does save. The fundamental point here is not the limited extent of the atonement, though that is a biblical teaching. The fundamental point is the *efficacy* of the atonement.

Let's, then, look at the *particular redemption* view, namely, that Christ died only for the elect, his people, those whom God chose to save before the foundation of the world. On this view, the atonement does not just make salvation possible; it actually saves. Many biblical texts indicate that the atonement is limited to Jesus' own people. In John

10:11 and 15, Jesus says that he lays down his life for his sheep; but in the context, not everybody is one of Jesus' sheep.

Further, as we've seen, many texts about the atonement indicate that it fully saves. Romans 8:32–39 says:

> He who did not spare his own Son but gave him up for us all, how will he not also with him graciously give us all things? Who shall bring any charge against God's elect? It is God who justifies. Who is to condemn? Christ Jesus is the one who died—more than that, who was raised—who is at the right hand of God, who indeed is interceding for us. Who shall separate us from the love of Christ? Shall tribulation, or distress, or persecution, or famine, or nakedness, or danger, or sword? As it is written,
>
> "For your sake we are being killed all the day long;
>   we are regarded as sheep to be slaughtered."
>
> No, in all these things we are more than conquerors through him who loved us. For I am sure that neither death nor life, nor angels nor rulers, nor things present nor things to come, nor powers, nor height nor depth, nor anything else in all creation, will be able to separate us from the love of God in Christ Jesus our Lord.

You see, Paul says that God gave his Son for "us all." The consequence is salvation in the fullest sense, a salvation that can never be lost or taken away. If Christ died for you, no one can ever bring a charge against you before God, not even Satan. If Christ died for you, nothing can separate you from the love of Christ.

There are, to be sure, passages that say that Christ died for the "world." Some of these passages emphasize the cosmic dimension of Jesus' work, as in John 3:16. In Colossians 1:20, Paul says that Jesus in his atonement intends "through him to reconcile to himself all things, whether on earth or in heaven, making peace by the blood of his cross." Other passages use "world" in an ethical sense, as when 1 John 2:15 says, "Do not love the world or the things in the world. If anyone loves the world, the love of the Father is not in him." That may have been in the mind of John the Baptist when he said in John 1:29, "Behold, the Lamb of God, who takes away the sin of the world!"

And there are passages that say that Christ died for "all." But the extent of the word *all* is notoriously flexible. Mark 1:5 says that "all" Judea and Jerusalem went out to hear John the Baptist. But clearly, we should not take that "all" literally. In some of the "all" texts, it is plain that the writer is referring to "all Christians" or "all the elect."

Note 1 Corinthians 15:22: "For as in Adam all die, so also in Christ shall all be made alive." Taken literally, this means that everybody will be saved. But it does not mean that. Rather, what it means is that everyone who dies, dies in Adam; and everyone who lives, lives in Christ.

Consider 2 Corinthians 5:15: "and he died for all, that those who live might no longer live for themselves but for him who for their sake died and was raised." Here it says that Jesus died for all. But it also says that the "all" receive new hearts so that they no longer live to themselves, but for Christ. Even in this "all" text, the atonement is efficacious: when Christ dies for someone, that person is fully saved. He receives a new heart and a new life. Clearly, not everyone in the world receives a new heart and a new life. So not everyone in the world is included under that term "all."

In still other "all" texts, the reference may be to what we call "ethnic" universalism, namely, that Jesus died for people of all nations, tongues, races, and tribes. That may be the meaning in 1 Timothy 2:6, which mentions the nations in the first two verses of the chapter. But I prefer to take this verse as meaning that the death of Christ warrants a free offer of the gospel to everybody, for he is the *only* Savior. That point is clearer in 1 John 2:2, for example, where the writer says that Jesus "is the propitiation for our sins, and not for ours only but also for the sins of the whole world." His point is that Jesus is the *only* Savior. There is none other in the whole wide world. So that if anyone, anywhere, say, in Thailand or Sri Lanka, is seeking a propitiation with God, he will find no other except in the blood of Jesus.

What about the texts, such as Hebrews 10:29 and 2 Peter 2:1, that describe some people as denying the Lord who bought them, in some sense? I take these texts to describe members of the visible church, who have confessed Christ at their baptism. These have claimed that Jesus died for them. On the basis of that profession, they have entered a solemn covenant relationship with God and with the church, a relationship made solemn by the blood of Christ. But now they blaspheme the blood of Christ. They were never united to Christ in a saving way. But having professed Christ, they are subject to the curses of the covenant, as covenant-breakers.[4]

Intercession

I said earlier that the two main duties of the priest were sacrifice and intercession. We have spent far more time on the first, mainly because the ideas are harder to understand and much more controversial. But intercession is just as important, and the truth of Jesus' intercession is just as precious.

Hebrews 4:15 tells us, "For we do not have a high priest who is unable to sympathize with our weaknesses, but one who in every respect has been tempted as we are, yet without sin." Hebrews 7:25 tells us, also speaking of Jesus' priesthood, "Consequently, he is able to save to the uttermost those who draw near to God through him, since he always lives to make intercession for them." Romans 8:34 is also an important verse: "Who is to condemn? Christ Jesus is the one who died—more than that, who was raised—who is at the right hand of God, who indeed is interceding for us."

You see from the Hebrews verses that Jesus' humanity is important here. His human nature enables him to sympathize or empathize, to feel our feelings, to actually suffer our sufferings. He has also undergone all our temptations. So among all the members of the Trinity, he is able to be a Priest: to make sacrifice, and also to intercede.

---

4. Compare our discussion of covenants in chapter 4. All covenants have an external side and an internal side. It is possible to be a member of the covenant in good standing, based on keeping external conditions, without a transformed heart.

What is the resurrected Christ doing—right now? He is interceding at the Father's right hand. Even now, he is thinking of us, bringing our needs to the Father's attention. Of course, Scripture also speaks of the Holy Spirit's interceding (Rom. 8:26–27). The two persons act in unity to bring the believer's needs before God's great throne of grace. The Father willingly hears the intercession of his Son and his Spirit. The bottom line is that we can be sure that the Father will withhold no good thing from us. The whole Trinity is on our side. God is of one mind on our behalf, and if God be for us, who can be against us?

King

Jesus is not only Prophet and Priest. He is also King of kings and Lord of lords. *King* is very closely related to *Lord* in the Bible, and we have seen in chapter 21 that Jesus is *Lord*, the head of the covenant, Yahweh the Lord himself.[5]

We see his kingship over the whole earth in his great works of power. Again, everything God the Father does, the Son does as well. That includes creation (John 1:3; Col. 1:16), providence (Col. 1:17; Heb. 1:3), miracle (John 10:37–38).

More specifically, Jesus is of the royal family of David: Great David's greater son; both David's son and David's Lord (Matt. 22:42; Ps. 110). Although he was always King, he demonstrated his kingship especially in his resurrection. Paul tells us that Jesus "was declared to be the Son of God in power according to the Spirit of holiness by his resurrection from the dead, Jesus Christ our Lord" (Rom. 1:4).

In connection with Jesus' priesthood, we focused especially on his atoning death. In connection with his kingship, we focus on his resurrection. The resurrection, like the atonement, is part of our salvation from sin. It is Jesus' great triumph over death and sin: death could not hold him. It is also the Father's witness that Jesus' claims are true and that his atonement accomplished its purpose. And consider this as well: Romans 6:4 tells us that when Jesus died, we died with him—to sin. And when he rose from the dead, we rose with him—to new life. Somehow, when Jesus rose from the dead, we were there. The basis of our new life is Jesus' resurrection. So Paul says in Colossians 3:1–3:

> If then you have been raised with Christ, seek the things that are above, where Christ is, seated at the right hand of God. Set your minds on things that are above, not on things that are on earth. For you have died, and your life is hidden with Christ in God.

I don't know exactly what that means, but at least it is this: Christ's glorious resurrection life is now ours in some sense. This is the beginning of the new life that we will enjoy fully when Jesus also raises our bodies on the last day.[6]

---

5. Chapter 4 also presents Jesus as Lord of the covenant and chapter 5 as the coming King. See also my summary discussions in chapter 37.

6. Richard B. Gaffin has done important study in the relation of Jesus' resurrection to our union with him as the second Adam. So Jesus' resurrection has important relevance to our justification, adoption, sanctification,

So Paul tells us that the resurrection of Christ is the very basis of our faith (1 Cor. 15). If Jesus is not raised from the dead, we are still dead in our sins; we are of all people the most miserable (v. 19).

The risen Christ has all authority and power throughout the created universe (Matt. 28:18–20). When he returns, every eye will see him and bow before him as the rightful King over all the earth (1 Thess. 4:16–17; Rev. 1:7). On that day, his royal word will judge all the living and the dead (John 12:48). So he is the object of all our worship and praise (John 5:23; Rev. 5:12).

Never forget that the gospel is good news about the coming of a King. This is plain in Isaiah, where the prophet gives us important background for understanding *gospel*: "How beautiful upon the mountains are the feet of him who brings good news, who publishes peace, who brings good news of happiness, who publishes salvation, who says to Zion, 'Your God reigns'" (Isa. 52:7). In Isaiah 61:1–2, which Jesus quoted in the synagogue at Capernaum, we hear a similar gospel:

> The Spirit of the Lord God is upon me,
>   because the Lord has anointed me
> to bring good news to the poor;
>   he has sent me to bind up the brokenhearted,
> to proclaim liberty to the captives,
>   and the opening of the prison to those who are bound;
> to proclaim the year of the Lord's favor,
>   and the day of vengeance of our God.

Isaiah goes on to mention other things. But here, too, the gospel is about the coming of the Anointed One, the Messiah, the King, and all the things the King will do: bind up the brokenhearted, set captives free (who but a king can do that?), and proclaim both God's favor and his vengeance.

At the beginning of their ministries, both John the Baptist and Jesus proclaimed as gospel, "Repent, for the kingdom of heaven is at hand" (Matt. 3:2; 4:17). Again, the gospel is the coming of a great King. The gospel is not just about us. It's not limited to justification by faith. It is focused on God and his coming. It is in fact political in its force. To the Romans, the *gospel* or *good news* was that a new emperor had come into power. They proclaimed *Kyrios Caesar*, "Caesar is Lord." The Christians proclaimed *Kyrios Iesous*, "Jesus is Lord." You can understand why the Roman rulers became nervous. Of course, they misunderstood to some degree what kind of King Jesus was. But they were not wrong to feel threatened. King Jesus claims sovereignty over them. (Think of Psalm 2, where God calls the rulers of the world to kiss the anointed Son.)

Never forget that Jesus is Lord and King of all, and will not accept any lesser position. He demands that we do all things to his glory, everything in accord with his will. His

---

and glorification. Compare my discussion of union with Christ later in this chapter. See Gaffin, *Resurrection and Redemption: A Study in Paul's Soteriology* (Phillipsburg, NJ: P&R Publishing, 1987).

gospel contains law, we may say. But service to this King is wonderful freedom. To trust this King is to trust a Priest who gives us full forgiveness from God and constant intercession. And to trust this King is to trust a Prophet whose word is completely true and trustworthy.

The States of Christ

In this chapter so far, we have considered the work of Christ in terms of his offices of Prophet, Priest, and King. Jesus saves his people from sin by exercising these offices and the powers inherent in them. Although all the lordship perspectives are implicit in these offices, I summarize them as different forms of authority, and therefore as representing the normative perspective.

It is also common in the theological tradition, however, to look at the work of Christ from a more narrative perspective, from a temporal-historical view. I look at that as the situational perspective on the work of Christ. Paul himself presents this view in Philippians 2:5–11:

> Have this mind among yourselves, which is yours in Christ Jesus, who, though he was in the form of God, did not count equality with God a thing to be grasped, but made himself nothing, taking the form of a servant, being born in the likeness of men. And being found in human form, he humbled himself by becoming obedient to the point of death, even death on a cross. Therefore God has highly exalted him and bestowed on him the name that is above every name, so that at the name of Jesus every knee should bow, in heaven and on earth and under the earth, and every tongue confess that Jesus Christ is Lord, to the glory of God the Father.

This passage moves from descent to ascent, from humiliation to exaltation. So the WLC distinguishes Jesus' "estate [or *state*] of humiliation" and his "estate of exaltation." It expounds the state of humiliation as follows:

Q. 46. What was the estate of Christ's humiliation?

A. The estate of Christ's humiliation was that low condition, wherein he for our sakes, emptying himself of his glory, took upon him the form of a servant, in his conception and birth, life, death, and after his death, until his resurrection (Phil. 2:6–8; Luke 1:31; 2 Cor. 8:9; Acts 2:24).

Q. 47. How did Christ humble himself in his conception and birth?

A. Christ humbled himself in his conception and birth, in that, being from all eternity the Son of God, in the bosom of the Father, he was pleased in the fulness of time to become the son of man,[7] made of a woman of low estate, and to be

---

7. Given the glory associated with the *Son of Man* title in Scripture, it may not have been best to include it as an aspect of Jesus' humiliation. Evidently the divines thought that the very fact of Jesus' becoming man was a humiliation for him. Certainly it was, given that the incarnation took place after the fall, so that the incarnation

born of her; with divers circumstances of more than ordinary abasement (John 1:14, 18; Gal. 4:4; Luke 2:7).

Q. 48. How did Christ humble himself in his life?

A. Christ humbled himself in his life, by subjecting himself to the law (Gal. 4:4), which he perfectly fulfilled (Matt. 5:17; Rom. 5:19); and by conflicting with the indignities of the world (Ps. 22:6; Heb. 12:2–3), temptations of Satan (Matt. 4:1–12), and infirmities in his flesh, whether common to the nature of man, or particularly accompanying that his low condition (Heb. 2:17–18; 4:15; Isa. 52:13–14).

Q. 49. How did Christ humble himself in his death?

A. Christ humbled himself in his death, in that having been betrayed by Judas (Matt. 27:4), forsaken by his disciples (Matt. 26:56), scorned and rejected by the world (Isa. 53:2–3), condemned by Pilate, and tormented by his persecutors (Matt. 27:26–50; John 19:34); having also conflicted with the terrors of death, and the powers of darkness, felt and borne the weight of God's wrath (Luke 22:44; Matt. 27:46), he laid down his life an offering for sin (Isa. 53:10), enduring the painful, shameful, and cursed death of the cross (Phil. 2:8; Heb. 12:2; Gal. 3:13).

Q. 50. Wherein consisted Christ's humiliation after his death?

A. Christ's humiliation after his death consisted in his being buried (1 Cor. 15:3) and continuing in the state of the dead, and under the power of death till the third day (Ps. 16:10; Acts 2:24–27, 31; Rom. 6:9; Matt. 12:40); which hath been otherwise expressed in these words, *He descended into hell.*

It is an edifying devotional exercise to trace Jesus' humiliation through each of these individual steps, to gain a sense of how great were the sufferings he endured for our sakes. But this journey should also govern our own growth in grace, for Paul in Philippians 2 wants us to let the mind of Christ be in us—the same mind, the same attitude, that led him to the lowest reaches of the earth for our sakes.

The "descent into hell" is found in the Apostles' Creed and has been recited by Christians in worship for centuries. But there has been no consensus in the church as to what it means, and many theories have been proposed. My own view, suggested to me in a chapel talk by my colleague Charles E. Hill,[8] is that by his sacrifice for sin Jesus brought the OT saints from the realm of the dead (Hades, Sheol) to a place of triumphant fellowship with God. The writer to the Hebrews says that the faithful people of the OT did not receive the city that God promised to them (Heb. 11:39–40) until the time that they could share it with believers of the new covenant. But following Jesus' atonement and resurrection,

---

was "in the likeness of sinful flesh" (Rom. 8:3). But apart from sin, there is no dishonor in being a man; and the "son of man" of Daniel 7 is certainly an exalted figure, rather than a humiliated one.

8. I take, however, full responsibility for the formulation.

we come to a "festal gathering," a worship assembly in heaven including the OT saints (Heb. 12:22).

The catechism then traces the "estate of Christ's exaltation":

Q. 51. What was the estate of Christ's exaltation?

A. The estate of Christ's exaltation comprehendeth his resurrection (1 Cor. 15:4), ascension (Mark 16:19), sitting at the right hand of the Father (Eph. 1:20), and his coming again to judge the world (Acts 1:11).

Q. 52. How was Christ exalted in his resurrection?

A. Christ was exalted in his resurrection, in that, not having seen corruption in death (of which it was not possible for him to be held) (Acts 2:24, 27), and having the very same body in which he suffered, with the essential properties thereof (Luke 24:39) (but without mortality, and other common infirmities belonging to this life), really united to his soul (Rom. 6:9; Rev. 1:18), he rose again from the dead the third day by his own power (John 10:18); whereby he declared himself to be the Son of God (Rom. 1:4), to have satisfied divine justice (Rom. 8:34), to have vanquished death, and him that had the power of it (Heb. 2:14), and to be Lord of quick and dead (Rom. 14:9): all which he did as a public person (1 Cor. 15:21–22), the head of his church (Eph. 1:20, 22–23; Col. 1:18), for their justification (Rom. 4:25), quickening in grace (Eph. 2:1, 5–6; Col. 2:12), support against enemies (1 Cor. 15:25–27), and to assure them of their resurrection from the dead at the last day (1 Cor. 15:20).

Q. 53. How was Christ exalted in his ascension?

A. Christ was exalted in his ascension, in that having after his resurrection often appeared unto and conversed with his apostles, speaking to them of the things pertaining to the kingdom of God (Acts 1:2–3), and giving them commission to preach the gospel to all nations (Matt. 28:19–20), forty days after his resurrection, he, in our nature, and as our head (Heb. 6:20), triumphing over enemies (Eph. 4:8), visibly went up into the highest heavens, there to receive gifts for men (Acts 1:9–11; Eph. 4:10; Ps. 68:18), to raise up our affections thither (Col. 3:1–2), and to prepare a place for us (John 16:3), where he himself is, and shall continue till his second coming at the end of the world (Acts 3:21).

Q. 54. How is Christ exalted in his sitting at the right hand of God?

A. Christ is exalted in his sitting at the right hand of God, in that as God-man he is advanced to the highest favour with God the Father (Phil. 2:9), with all fulness of joy (Acts 2:28; Ps. 16:11), glory (John 17:5), and power over all things in heaven and earth (Eph. 1:22; 1 Peter 3:22); and does gather and defend his church, and subdue their enemies; furnisheth his ministers and people with gifts and graces (Eph. 4:10–12; Ps. 110), and maketh intercession for them (Rom. 8:34).

Q. 55. How doth Christ make intercession?

A. Christ maketh intercession, by his appearing in our nature continually before the Father in heaven (Heb. 9:12, 24), in the merit of his obedience and sacrifice on earth (Heb. 1:3), declaring his will to have it applied to all believers (John 3:16; 17:9, 20, 24); answering all accusations against them (Rom. 8:33–34), and procuring for them quiet of conscience, notwithstanding daily failings (Rom. 5:1–2; 1 John 2:1–2), access with boldness to the throne of grace (Heb. 4:16), and acceptance of their persons (Eph. 1:6) and services (1 Peter 2:5).

Q. 56. How is Christ to be exalted in his coming again to judge the world?

A. Christ is to be exalted in his coming again to judge the world, in that he, who was unjustly judged and condemned by wicked men (Acts 3:14–15), shall come again at the last day in great power (Matt. 24:30), and in the full manifestation of his own glory, and of his Father's, with all his holy angels (Luke 9:26; Matt. 25:31), with a shout, with the voice of the archangel, and with the trumpet of God (1 Thess. 4:16), to judge the world in righteousness (Acts 17:31).

In the context of Philippians 2, it is remarkable that Paul mentions Christ's exaltation in a context focusing on our need to humble ourselves. Evidently Paul is saying that if we follow Christ in humbling ourselves, God will exalt us as he exalted Jesus. Not that we will ever be on the same level of Jesus: every tongue will confess the lordship of Jesus, not of ourselves (v. 11). But one of the great blessings of following Jesus is that as he is exalted, his followers are also exalted:

> For everyone who exalts himself will be humbled, and he who humbles himself will be exalted. (Luke 14:11; cf. 18:14)

> Humble yourselves, therefore, under the mighty hand of God so that at the proper time he may exalt you. (1 Peter 5:6)

In his exaltation as well as in his humiliation, he is one with us, and we with him.

Union with Christ

That last comment suggests a significant transition to this next topic. For we are inclined to ask: if we are one with Christ in his humiliation and exaltation, how far does this unity extend? Indeed, union with Christ is in Scripture the most general way of characterizing Jesus' work of salvation. Jesus saves us by uniting us to himself.

The intimacy of this language justifies the use of this topic as an "existential perspective" on the work of Christ. For in this aspect of his work he is, in a distinct sense, "God with us," Immanuel. As in chapters 2–4, we find here the fulfillment of the covenant: "I will be your God, and you shall be my people" (Jer. 7:23).

So union with Christ is an exceedingly broad topic. We will see that it underlies all the works of God in our lives: election, calling, regeneration, faith, justification, adoption, sanctification, perseverance, and glorification. All of these blessings are "in Christ." To study union with Christ is to explore all of these particular blessings, and therefore the vast range of meaning in that little word *in*.

Scripture traces union of the believer with Christ into eternity past:

> Blessed be the God and Father of our Lord Jesus Christ, who has blessed us in Christ with every spiritual blessing in the heavenly places, even as he chose us in him before the foundation of the world, that we should be holy and blameless before him. (Eph. 1:3–4a)

This is the relationship that we discussed in chapter 4 as the eternal covenant of redemption, or *pactum salutis*. In this covenant, before anything was made, the Father gave to the Son a people who would be "holy and blameless before him." The holiness and blamelessness of this people, however, is problematic from the start. Rather, even before creation the Father and the Son knew that these people would fall into sin, and their redemption would require nothing less than the death of the Son of God. So the fact that these people are holy and blameless is a huge tribute to the grace of God (Eph. 1:6). But the success of this divine effort is never questionable. Even before redemption, even before creation, these people are chosen in Christ. The outcome of redemption is known in advance.

In a sense, then, Jesus' people are in Christ *before* they are actually redeemed. They are in Christ before they are humbled with him in his humiliation and exalted with him in his exaltation. This is to say that union with Christ, being "in" Christ, is the most general thing that can be said about us as his people. These phrases cover all the blessings of salvation from eternity past to eternity future. We are in Christ before we are baptized, before we are regenerate, in fact while we are still "dead in . . . trespasses and sins" (Eph. 2:1).

Yet in a narrower sense, we are not in Christ unless we are justified before God, for otherwise we would still be under God's condemnation, and Paul says in Romans 8:1 that there is "no condemnation for those who are in Christ Jesus." What of those who are elect, but not yet justified by faith? They are "in Christ" by the covenant of redemption, but yet outside of Christ so far as justification is concerned.[9]

So the phrases "union with Christ" and being "in Christ" have a wide range of meaning. A person can be in Christ in one sense, outside of him in another. Union with Christ is not a single condition, constant through history. It is rather a series of conditions, anchored by union with Christ in the sense of eternal election. Below I will consider the more prominent biblical senses of union with Christ.

---

9. In chapters 12 and 13, I indicated that it is possible for God to love and hate the same person in different respects. So God is genuinely wrathful toward those who are dead in trespasses and sins. But some of these are also elect in Christ, and God loves them for his sake.

Election

Above, I said that Ephesians 1:4 states the origin of our union with Christ. God *chose* us "in him" before the foundation of the world. The passage begins with the Father's intention to bless us in Christ "with every spiritual blessing in the heavenly places" (v. 3). The Father's first step toward bestowing these blessings is to choose us "in him." The goal of this union is "that we should be holy and blameless before him." But that goal is eons away. In Ephesians 1:4, the setting is God's own eternity, and the people have yet to be created. Before the foundation of the world, the people exist only as God's ideas. But even as God's ideas, they are objects of his love. They are not, of course, *mere* ideas. God has already planned to create them and to give them lives within history. And even though they will spend part of their life spans in rebellion against God, spiritual death, they are surrounded by God's love. They are predestined to be holy and blameless because they are "in Christ," and so God will certainly love them forever. Cf. 2 Tim. 1:9:

> [God] saved us and called us to a holy calling, not because of our works but because of his own purpose and grace, which he gave us in Christ Jesus before the ages began.

Why are we chosen "in Christ," rather than merely "chosen"? In Ephesians 1:3–4, Christ is the One who secures our holiness and blamelessness. He guarantees that far in advance of our historical existence. So even in the ideal existence of God's eternity, there is nothing that can separate us from the love of God in Jesus Christ.

Adoption

The Ephesians passage continues:

> In love he predestined us for adoption as sons through Jesus Christ, according to the purpose of his will, to the praise of his glorious grace, with which he has blessed us in the Beloved. (Eph. 1:4b–6)

Election in Christ leads not only to our holiness and blamelessness, but even to our adoption as God's sons and daughters. To be a son of God is not only to be like him, to image him, but also to have a position of privilege, entitling us to an inheritance:

> In him we have obtained an inheritance, having been predestined according to the purpose of him who works all things according to the counsel of his will, so that we who were the first to hope in Christ might be to the praise of his glory. In him you also, when you heard the word of truth, the gospel of your salvation, and believed in him, were sealed with the promised Holy Spirit, who is the guarantee of our inheritance until we acquire possession of it, to the praise of his glory. (Eph. 1:11–14)

Redemption

In Ephesians 1, verses 3–6 and 11–14 describe God's dealings with us in eternity. But verses 7–10, though also alluding to God's eternal plan, focus on Christ's redemption in history:

> In him we have redemption through his blood, the forgiveness of our trespasses, according to the riches of his grace, which he lavished upon us, in all wisdom and insight making known to us the mystery of his will, according to his purpose, which he set forth in Christ as a plan for the fullness of time, to unite all things in him, things in heaven and things on earth.

God's eternal plan to unite all things in Christ (v. 10) is revealed to us in history (v. 9) when God forgave our sins on the basis of Jesus' shed blood (vv. 7–8). So God's eternal intentions for us come through historical events, through the crucifixion of Christ. On the basis of his blood atonement, we receive forgiveness of sins. Not only is redemption on the basis of his work, but it is "in him." That is, God's forgiveness of our sins arises out of that relationship that began in eternity past and continues into human history. And it is through that redemptive forgiveness that we gain an understanding of the eternal mystery (vv. 8–10).

Paul teaches in Romans not only the general fact that we are redeemed in Christ, but that when Christ died we died in him, and when he rose from the dead we rose with him:

> Do you not know that all of us who have been baptized into Christ Jesus were baptized into his death? We were buried therefore with him by baptism into death, in order that, just as Christ was raised from the dead by the glory of the Father, we too might walk in newness of life. (Rom. 6:3–4)

Similarly, Peter says that our regeneration to new life comes from Jesus' resurrection (1 Peter 1:3–4). Jesus' death for sin is our death to sin, and his resurrection from the dead is our resurrection to newness of life:

> [God,] even when we were dead in our trespasses, made us alive together with Christ—by grace you have been saved—and raised us up with him and seated us with him in the heavenly places in Christ Jesus. (Eph. 2:5–6)

Paul says that just as Abraham believed God and it was counted to him for righteousness, so our faith

> will be counted to us who believe in him who raised from the dead Jesus our Lord, who was delivered up for our trespasses and raised for our justification. (Rom. 4:24–25)

So our justification, God's verdict that our sins will not be counted against us, is "in Christ," through his death and resurrection.

Similarly our sanctification, by which God makes us holy:

> To [the saints] God chose to make known how great among the Gentiles are the riches of the glory of this mystery, which is Christ in you, the hope of glory. Him we proclaim, warning everyone and teaching everyone with all wisdom, that we may present everyone mature in Christ. (Col. 1:27–28)

Christ in us, ourselves spiritually mature in Christ.

> Therefore, as you received Christ Jesus the Lord, so walk in him, rooted and built up in him and established in the faith, just as you were taught, abounding in thanksgiving. (Col. 2:6–7)

To be godly is to walk in Christ, rooted and built up in him, indeed created in Christ Jesus for good works:

> For we are his workmanship, created in Christ Jesus for good works, which God prepared beforehand, that we should walk in them. (Eph. 2:10)

So the Christian life is a life in Christ: he in us and we in him. As Jesus looks toward the cross with his disciples in the gospel of John, he promises that after he is raised, he will come to them and impart to them a rich fellowship with himself, analogous to the relationship that he enjoys with the Father: "In that day you will know that I am in my Father, and you in me, and I in you" (John 14:20). So in the familiar passage Jesus says:

> I am the true vine, and my Father is the vinedresser. Every branch in me that does not bear fruit he takes away, and every branch that does bear fruit he prunes, that it may bear more fruit. Already you are clean because of the word that I have spoken to you. Abide in me, and I in you. As the branch cannot bear fruit by itself, unless it abides in the vine, neither can you, unless you abide in me. I am the vine; you are the branches. Whoever abides in me and I in him, he it is that bears much fruit, for apart from me you can do nothing. If anyone does not abide in me he is thrown away like a branch and withers; and the branches are gathered, thrown into the fire, and burned. If you abide in me, and my words abide in you, ask whatever you wish, and it will be done for you. By this my Father is glorified, that you bear much fruit and so prove to be my disciples. As the Father has loved me, so have I loved you. Abide in my love. (John 15:1–9)

Key Terms
Person of Christ
Work of Christ
Offices
States
Union with Christ

Metaphysical
Ethical
Prophet
Priest
Sacrifice
Intercession
Atonement
King
Active obedience
Passive obedience
Imputes
Double imputation
Expiation
Substitute
Propitiation
Reconciliation
Redemption
Kinsman-redeemer
Ransom
Governmental theory
Unlimited atonement
Limited atonement
Efficacy of the atonement
Ethnic universalism
State of humiliation
State of exaltation
Descent into hell

Study Questions

1. Explain Frame's triperspectival model for the work of Christ.

2. Explain what it means to say that our plight is ethical, not metaphysical. Why is this important?

3. Show how the offices of Prophet, Priest, and King are related to the elements of the image of God.

4. In the OT, a sacrifice must be without fault. How does this help us to understand the work of Christ?

5. Describe the "double imputation" between Christ and ourselves. Why is it important that his active righteousness be imputed to us?

6. "We should not forget, however, that God's anger against the wicked coexists with his love for his elect." Does this mean that God can hate and love some of the same people at the same time? Explain; deal with the problem.

7. Some scholars have said that the atonement purges our enmity against God, not God's against us. Explain and reply.

8. Discuss and evaluate these views of the atonement: (a) ransom to Satan, (b) moral example, (c) governmental.

9. For whom did Christ die? Present arguments for both unlimited and limited atonement and defend your own view.

10. Does 1 John 2:2 teach unlimited atonement? Explain.

11. How is Jesus' humanity important to his intercession?

12. "The resurrection, like the atonement, is part of our salvation from sin." In what way? Explain.

13. "Never forget that the gospel is good news about the coming of a King." Explain, giving references. Why is this important?

14. Describe Jesus' states of humiliation and exaltation.

15. How does Paul apply the doctrine of the humiliation and exaltation of Christ to the church of Philippi?

16. When does the union of the believer with Christ begin? Explain the importance of this.

17. Show the relation of union with Christ to election, adoption, redemption.

Memory Verses

Luke 24:25–27: And he said to them, "O foolish ones, and slow of heart to believe all that the prophets have spoken! Was it not necessary that the Christ should suffer these things and enter into his glory?" And beginning with Moses and all the Prophets, he interpreted to them in all the Scriptures the things concerning himself.

John 15:1–9: I am the true vine, and my Father is the vinedresser. Every branch in me that does not bear fruit he takes away, and every branch that does bear fruit he prunes, that it may bear more fruit. Already you are clean because of the word that I have spoken to you. Abide in me, and I in you. As the branch cannot bear fruit by itself, unless it abides in the vine, neither can you, unless you abide in me. I am the vine; you are the branches. Whoever abides in me and I in him, he it is that bears much fruit, for apart from me you can do nothing. If anyone does not abide in me he is thrown away like a branch and withers; and the branches are gathered, thrown into the fire, and burned. If you abide in me, and my words abide in you, ask whatever you wish, and it will be done for you. By this my Father is glorified, that you bear much fruit and so prove to be my disciples. As the Father has loved me, so have I loved you. Abide in my love.

2 Cor. 5:15: And he died for all, that those who live might no longer live for themselves but for him who for their sake died and was raised.

2 Cor. 5:21: For our sake he made him to be sin who knew no sin, so that in him we might become the righteousness of God.

Eph. 1:3–6: Blessed be the God and Father of our Lord Jesus Christ, who has blessed us in Christ with every spiritual blessing in the heavenly places, even as he chose us in him before the foundation of the world, that we should be holy and blameless before him. In love he predestined us for adoption as sons through Jesus Christ, according to the purpose of his will, to the praise of his glorious grace, with which he has blessed us in the Beloved.

Phil. 2:5–11: Have this mind among yourselves, which is yours in Christ Jesus, who, though he was in the form of God, did not count equality with God a thing to be grasped, but made himself nothing, taking the form of a servant, being born in the likeness of men. And being found in human form, he humbled himself by becoming obedient to the point of death, even death on a cross. Therefore God has highly exalted him and bestowed on him the name that is above every name, so that at the name of Jesus every knee should bow, in heaven and on earth and under the earth, and every tongue confess that Jesus Christ is Lord, to the glory of God the Father.

Col. 3:1–3: If then you have been raised with Christ, seek the things that are above, where Christ is, seated at the right hand of God. Set your minds on things that are above, not on things that are on earth. For you have died, and your life is hidden with Christ in God.

1 Tim. 6:13–14: I charge you in the presence of God, who gives life to all things, and of Christ Jesus, who in his testimony before Pontius Pilate made the good confession, to keep the commandment unstained and free from reproach until the appearing of our Lord Jesus Christ.

Heb. 4:15: For we do not have a high priest who is unable to sympathize with our weaknesses, but one who in every respect has been tempted as we are, yet without sin.

Resources for Further Study

Gaffin, Richard B. *Resurrection and Redemption: A Study in Paul's Soteriology.* Phillipsburg, NJ: P&R Publishing, 1987.

Letham, Robert. *Union with Christ in Scripture, History, and Theology.* Phillipsburg, NJ: P&R Publishing, 2011.

Murray, John. *Redemption Accomplished and Applied.* Grand Rapids: Eerdmans, 1955.

PART 9

THE DOCTRINE OF THE HOLY SPIRIT

CHAPTER 39

THE HOLY SPIRIT

THIS SYSTEMATIC THEOLOGY follows more or less the traditional Trinitarian plan of organization, though I have interspersed other subjects between the main discussions of the Trinitarian persons. The main Trinitarian pattern can be traced through part 3, "The Doctrine of God," part 8, "The Doctrine of Christ," and now part 9, "The Doctrine of the Holy Spirit."

As I have indicated, the general distinction between the three persons in the works of creation and redemption is that the Father plans, the Son accomplishes, and the Spirit applies. So orthodox theologians typically place the *ordo salutis*, or the application of redemption, under the discussion of the Holy Spirit. At points this decision leads to inaccuracies. Effectual calling, as we will see, though it is an element of the traditional *ordo salutis*, is better described as a work of the Father than of the Spirit. The same is true of justification. These are reasons to rethink the traditional *ordo salutis* and the order of topics that normally accompanies it. But I will not attempt to come up with a better organizational structure in this volume.

In this chapter, however, I will discuss the Holy Spirit in a more direct way, before passing on to the events associated with him in the application of redemption. As we considered the person and work of Christ, we will, in this chapter, consider in general terms the person and work of the Holy Spirit.

Who Is the Spirit?

First, as I indicated in chapter 21, the Spirit is God, like the Father and the Son. He stands alongside them as an object of worship. We baptize people in the threefold divine name, which includes the Spirit (Matt. 28:19). And the apostolic blessing, too, places the threefold name of God on the people: Father, Son, and Holy Spirit (2 Cor. 13:14).

We also saw that biblical writers coordinate the Spirit with the Father and Son when they write about the source of spiritual blessing. See how Paul in Ephesians 2:21–22 coordinates the three persons. He speaks of Christ, "in whom the whole structure, being joined together, grows into a holy temple in the Lord. In him you also are being built together into a dwelling place for God by the Spirit." Cf. also Rom. 15:19; Eph. 4:4–6; Phil. 3:3; Rev. 1:4–5; 2:7.

We noted also how NT writers often quote OT texts that contain the name of God and replace that name with the name of Jesus. The same is true of the Holy Spirit. In Jeremiah 31:33–34, the Lord is the speaker. But when the author of Hebrews quotes this text in Hebrews 10:15–17, the speaker is the Holy Spirit. Note also Leviticus 16 and Hebrews 9:8.

The Spirit is called "God" in Acts 5:4. He bears divine attributes of eternity (Heb. 9:14), omniscience (Isa. 40:13; 1 Cor. 2:10–11), wisdom (Isa. 11:2), omnipresence (Ps. 139:7–10; Acts 1:8), and incomprehensibility (Isa. 40:13). He is called *holy* nearly a hundred times. Clearly, his holiness is not a merely creaturely holiness. He is perfectly holy by his very nature, the very definition of holiness for us. His holiness is a divine holiness, a divine attribute.

And just as Jesus performs all the acts of God, all the things that God alone can do, so does the Spirit: creation (Gen. 1:2; Ps. 104:30), judgment (John 16:8–11), giving of life (both physical and spiritual) (Job 33:4; Ps. 104:30; John 3:5–8; 6:63; Rom. 8:11). Like the Father and the Son, he participates in our salvation. Through him we are washed, sanctified, and justified (1 Cor. 6:11). And he is the Teacher of the church (Num. 11:25; Matt. 10:20; 2 Tim. 3:16; 1 John 2:27).

So the Spirit is God. He is equal to the Father and the Son, worthy of honor equal to theirs.

The next thing to keep in mind is that the Spirit is a divine *person*, not an impersonal force. This is obvious to most of us as we read the Bible, but some cultists have actually wanted to deny that the Spirit is personal. They believe that the Spirit is an *it*, not a *he*: a kind of force or power from God, but not a person.

But in my judgment, the Bible is very clear on this. It's true that the Greek word for "Spirit," *pneuma*, is neuter (the OT *ruach* is feminine), but the NT writers regularly use masculine pronouns to refer to the Spirit. He is "he," which emphasizes his personality (John 14:17, 26; 16:14; 1 Cor. 12:11).

He is, to be sure, the power of God (Acts 1:8), which might suggest an impersonal force. But he is also God's *wisdom* (Isa. 11:2; Acts 6:10; 1 Cor. 2:4), and wisdom cannot be impersonal. The Spirit also has a mind (Rom. 8:27), and he speaks. He speaks in the first person (Acts 10:19–20; 13:2) and performs personal actions such as creating, judging, and so on.

The fact that the Spirit is coordinate with the Father and Son in passages such as Matthew 28:19; 2 Corinthians 13:14; Ephesians 2:21–22; and elsewhere, the divine attributes ascribed to him, and the divine acts he performs make it plain that the Spirit is a person, together with the Father and the Son.

What Does the Spirit Do?

For the rest of the chapter, then, let's think about what the Spirit does, his work. I've already mentioned that he is involved in all the works of God, for he is God. As we've seen, Scripture often presents him as the *power* of God exerted in the world. This power is the *control* of God, the first of the lordship attributes. He is the Creator and the Provider, as we have seen. He also empowers and strengthens angels (Ezek. 1:12, 20) and human beings. Remember how the Spirit fell upon Samson, and he tore a lion in pieces (Judg. 13:25; 14:6)? Remember how later the Spirit came upon him and he killed thirty Philistines all by himself (Judg. 14:19; cf. 15:14)? Well, then you have a way of understanding how the Spirit in the NT empowers preaching. In 1 Corinthians 2:4, Paul says that "my speech and my message were not in plausible words of wisdom, but in demonstration of the Spirit and of power." Cf. Luke 4:14; Acts 2:1–4; Rom. 15:19; 1 Thess. 1:5. When you present the gospel to others, think of Samson tearing that lion in pieces. The same Spirit is present in you.

As the Spirit speaks the word powerfully, he also speaks it *authoritatively*: Prophets speak their word by the authority of the Spirit (Gen. 41:38; Num. 24:2; 1 Sam. 10:6; Isa. 61:1; Luke 1:17; 1 Peter 1:11). So do Jesus and the apostles (Matt. 10:20; Luke 4:14; John 3:34; 14:16–17; 15:26; 16:13; Acts 2:4; 1 Cor. 2:4; 12:3). So the Spirit gives wisdom: both in the sense of practical skills, such as Bezalel and Oholiab had to build the tabernacle (Ex. 28:3; 31:3; Deut. 34:9), and in the sense of ethical understanding (James 3:13–18). As we will see, the Spirit's authority also comes with the gifts that he gives to the church (1 Cor. 12:1–11).

Power, authority, and now the third lordship attribute: presence. The Spirit is God's presence on earth. David asks, "Where shall I go from your Spirit?" (Ps. 139:7). It is the Spirit who dwells in Christians as his temple (1 Cor. 3:16; Gal. 4:6; 5:16–26; 1 Peter 1:2), so that we worship God "in spirit" (John 4:24).

In chapter 18, I discussed God's *spirituality*. Scripture associates this attribute of God with the Holy Spirit. Particularly when God makes himself visible to human beings, he often takes on a form that Meredith Kline calls the "glory-cloud," which is identified in turn with the Spirit.

The Spirit is God's control, authority, and presence in the world. That is to say, he is the Lord. As Jesus is Prophet, Priest, and King, the Spirit is God's authoritative word, his abiding and mediating presence, and his powerful control over all things.

The Spirit in the Lives of Believers

Now let's focus in on ourselves more narrowly and ask what the Spirit does in the lives of believers. Well, there are a great many things that the Spirit does for us and in us. We will here look through a long list of things, and every item on that list could be treated at much greater length. To make a long story short, the Spirit does everything for us that we need in our life with God.

The atoning work of Jesus occurred in the past, objectively, definitively. And the Spirit continues to work today, often in our own subjectivity. Now, this is not to separate the work of the Spirit from the work of Christ. The Spirit is the Spirit of Christ. Christ is in him and he in Christ. As we said earlier, everything that any person of the Trinity does, he does along with the other two. But the main emphasis of the Bible in the Spirit's work is that he gives us what we need for our present, continuing walk with God.

Indeed, he did the same for Jesus, during Jesus' earthly ministry. Remember how the Spirit descended on him like a dove at his baptism (Matt. 3:16). The Spirit filled him with power for preaching and for working miracles. Cf. Isa. 11:2–3; 42:1; 61:1; Luke 4:1, 14, 18; John 1:32; 3:34. Well, if Jesus needed the Spirit's ministry to him, we certainly need the Spirit as well. He is the One who equips us to serve God (Num. 27:18; Deut. 34:9; Judg. 3:10), to preach (Acts 1:8; Rom. 15:19; 1 Cor. 2:4), to pray effectively (Rom. 8:26; Eph. 2:18). He regenerates us (John 3:5), gives us the new birth. He sanctifies us (Rom. 8:4, 15–16; 1 Cor. 6:11; 2 Thess. 2:13; Titus 3:5; 1 Peter 1:2), makes us holy in thought and deed, putting to death the sins of the body (Rom. 7:6; 8:13; Phil. 1:19). He is grieved when we sin (Eph. 4:30).

The Bible puts a special emphasis on the work of the Spirit to create unity and peace in the body (2 Cor. 13:14; Gal. 5:18–20; Eph. 2:18; 4:3; Phil. 2:1–2; Col. 3:14). He is the One, after all, who enables us to cry, "Abba! Father!" (Rom. 8:15; Gal. 4:6), and thereby establishes the church as God's sons and daughters together in a family.

And of course, the Spirit is the great Teacher of the church. The writers of Scripture, both Testaments, were inspired by the Holy Spirit to write God's truth (2 Tim. 3:16; 2 Peter 1:21). The prophets and apostles spoke God's truth because the Spirit came upon them and enabled them to do it (Matt. 22:43; John 14:26; 15:26; 16:13; Acts 1:16). And the Spirit comes not only upon speakers and authors, but also upon hearers and readers. The Spirit illumines us, enabling us to understand the Scriptures (Ps. 119:18; 1 Cor. 2:12–15; Eph. 1:17–19) and persuading us that the Word is true (1 Thess. 1:5).

Baptism in the Spirit

How do people receive the Spirit? First, the Spirit regenerates, gives us a new birth, which we'll talk more about in chapter 41. In the new birth, the Spirit is like the wind, which goes anywhere it wants (John 3:8). So in the first instance, it is not we who receive the Spirit, but it is the Spirit who receives us.

This initial regeneration is sometimes called in Scripture the "baptism in the Holy Spirit." Paul describes it this way in 1 Corinthians 12:13: "For in one Spirit we were all baptized into one body—Jews or Greeks, slaves or free—and all were made to drink of one Spirit." Cf. Matt. 3:11; John 1:33; Acts 1:5; 11:16. You see that the baptism of the Spirit includes *all* believers. In fact, the baptism of the Spirit is what makes us one body. Without that baptism, we are not part of the body of Christ. So everyone in the body has been baptized in the Spirit.

Some people think that the baptism of the Spirit is an experience that comes after conversion. But 1 Corinthians 12:13 and other texts show that that is not so. Everybody who is converted, everyone who is a Christian, is baptized in the Spirit. There are not two groups in the church, one baptized in the Spirit and the other not. If that were true, it would be a basis for *disunity*, rather than, as Paul says, a basis for unity.

Nor is this a repeated experience. It happens at regeneration, at the new birth. And as we will see, the new birth happens only once.

In the baptism of the Spirit, the Spirit comes on us with power to serve Jesus as his covenant people. He unites us to all the other people in his body, so that together with them we may do God's work in the world.

Filling of the Spirit

Now, although the baptism of the Spirit occurs only once, there are other experiences of the Spirit that occur repeatedly. Ephesians 5:18 says, "And do not get drunk with wine, for that is debauchery, but be filled with the Spirit." Paul addresses this command to Christians, and so to people who are already baptized in the Spirit. The filling is something more. We see it also in passages such as Acts 4:31, where the disciples are filled with the Spirit and go on to "speak the word of God with boldness." The filling of the Spirit gives fresh power for ministry.

Here, too, the Spirit is sovereign. But interestingly, Ephesians 5:18 is a command addressed to us: we are to "be filled with the Spirit." There is both divine sovereignty and human responsibility here. It is hard to imagine what we can do to fill ourselves with the Spirit. It would be easier to think that since the Spirit is sovereign, we can only wait passively for him to decide whether to fill us. But according to this verse, our decisions have something to do with his filling. Evidently our behavior has some bearing on the degree and frequency with which we are filled with the Spirit. In the context of Ephesians 5:18: if you are a drunkard, don't expect the Spirit to fill you. You have filled yourself with drink, abusing a good creation of God, and in doing so you have said that you don't want the Spirit to fill you. Conversely, I would think, those who fill their hearts with Scripture and prayer open themselves to a greater fullness of the Spirit.

Fruit of the Spirit

I should also mention the *fruit* of the Spirit, described in Galatians 5:22–23: "But the fruit of the Spirit is love, joy, peace, patience, kindness, goodness, faithfulness, gentleness, self-control; against such things there is no law." The picture of a "filling" of the Spirit is the picture of a discrete event, repeated on a number of occasions. The picture of the "fruit" of the Spirit is the picture of a slow process that is always going on. The Spirit not only grabs us at various moments, but also works inside us moment by moment, changing us to conform to the image of Christ. This is the doctrine of sanctification, which we will discuss in chapter 43.

Gifts of the Spirit

Now, besides the baptism of the Spirit, the filling of the Spirit, and the fruit of the Spirit, there are also *gifts* of the Spirit, according to Scripture (Rom. 12:3–8; 1 Cor. 7:7; 12:4–11, 27–31; Eph. 4:7–16; 1 Peter 4:11). Wayne Grudem defines a spiritual gift as "any ability that is empowered by the Holy Spirit and used in any ministry of the church."[1] He points out that some of these are related to our natural abilities, such as teaching,

---

1. *GST*, 1016.

showing mercy, and administration. Others are more "supernatural," such as tongues, prophecy, healing, distinguishing spirits.

The biblical lists of gifts are not exhaustive. Notice that they differ from passage to passage. Any divinely given ability that edifies the church should be considered a spiritual gift. I wouldn't hesitate to say that the ability to sing in worship is a spiritual gift. Or the ability to cook meals for church gatherings or mercy ministry. Or the ability to manage finances for the church body.

Now, if you are a believer in Christ, God has given you one or more gifts that the church needs for its ministry. If you are a pastor or other church leader, one of your chief responsibilities is to help your people to identify their spiritual gifts, and then to stir up those gifts so that they can flourish in the body.

How do you discover your spiritual gifts? Pray that God will make them evident to you. Then test out your abilities in different areas until you find out in what ways you can make the best contribution. Ask other believers to help you. Their perspective will add much to your own.

Miracles

Now, there have been many controversies about spiritual gifts, and we must look at them here. In our own time, the main controversies have to do with the more "miraculous" gifts, such as prophecy, tongues, and healing. I say "more miraculous," because I don't believe we can draw a sharp line between miraculous and nonmiraculous events. Recall our discussion on that subject in chapter 7.

Does God give miraculous gifts to the church today? We should recall that miracles are actually fairly rare in biblical history. Hundreds of years pass by in the history of the Bible without any reference to miracles. Evidently God did not intend to make miracles a regular part of his people's lives.

Miracles do appear at *special* times, when God is doing some great deed of mercy and/or judgment. We read of many miracles in the time of Moses, in the time of Elisha and Elijah, and in the earthly ministries of Jesus and the apostles. In the time of the apostles, the miracles had a special connection with the apostles' witness to Jesus. They are called "signs of a true apostle" in 2 Corinthians 12:12. In that text, Paul appeals to his miracles to show that he was a true apostle. His argument wouldn't be very strong if *everyone* worked miracles. Rather, he implies that miracles are a special gift given to the apostles, to identify them as God's messengers all around the world where they preached Christ. Hebrews 2:4 also shows God using signs and wonders (miracles) to bear witness to the message of the apostles.

So it looks as though the more miraculous kinds of gifts were given mainly to apostles in the NT period, and to prophets such as Moses, Elijah, and Elisha in the OT. But the point is probably not that they were the only ones in the world who could work miracles. Rather, the Lord enabled the prophets and apostles to work many, many miracles, to show everyone that God had appointed them.

For us, at any rate, the point is that we should not *expect* God to work miracles for us. They are not a regular part of the Christian life. They may happen, certainly, at

God's pleasure, and we should be thankful when they do. Indeed, as I indicated in chapters 7–9, there is a sense in which even God's general providence is miraculous. But we must not demand miracles, or be angry at God when he chooses not to work them for us. Even Paul could not work miracles all the time, for the Lord refused Paul's prayer for his own healing (2 Cor. 12:7–9).

Prophecy

But what about that special kind of miracle called *prophecy*? In prophecy, as we saw in chapter 24, God enables a human being to speak God's very word (Deut. 18:18–22). Does God still inspire prophets today?

Wayne Grudem believes that the people called prophets in the NT were rather different from those called prophets in the OT.[2] In the OT, the prophets spoke God's very word, and so what they said was absolutely true, reliable, infallible, and inerrant. But in the NT, according to Grudem, the gift of prophecy was a lesser gift. It was simply the ability to put a message from God into human but fallible words. In other words, in the NT, God revealed his thoughts to the prophets, but their actual words were not identical with his.

Grudem believes that there are today no prophets in the OT sense, but there are prophets in the NT sense. He recognizes that if there were prophets in the OT sense in the church today, then they would be adding to Scripture. Scripture would not then be sufficient, since there would be other words of God of the same authority. But Grudem does believe that there are prophets in the NT sense in the church today. Since their words are fallible, those words don't challenge the sufficiency of Scripture.

I am not convinced of Grudem's thesis. If it is true, then there may well be in the church today prophets in the NT sense. But I think it is not, and therefore there are no prophets, defined biblically, in the church today. There is nobody in the church today who can give us a message of the same authority as Scripture. So as I indicated in chapter 26, *only* Scripture serves as our ultimate authority. We live by Scripture *alone*, **sola** *Scriptura*.

Of course, the word *prophecy* can be used more loosely. People sometimes speak of preaching as prophecy, since it conveys the teaching of Scripture, and since it often receives special power from the Holy Spirit. People sometimes refer to the church as having the offices of prophet, as well as priest and king. Nothing I've said in this chapter should keep us from using the term *prophet* in that general way. All I want to emphasize is that there are in the church today no prophets who have the authority described in Deuteronomy 18.

Nor do I want to say that God cannot reveal himself in unusual, surprising ways. I've heard of believers dreaming of some great disaster coming, in time to warn others to avoid a real disaster. Could that be of God? Certainly. He is sovereign over our dreams and subconscious, just as he is sovereign over the workings of our eyes, ears, and noses.

---

2. Ibid., 1050–55. Important texts in this discussion are Acts 21:4, 10–11; 1 Corinthians 14:29–38; 1 Thessalonians 5:19–21.

Every event in some way reveals him, as we saw in chapter 8. All I am saying is that the only place we can go to find supremely authoritative *words* of God is the Bible.

Tongues

Now, what about tongues? Grudem says that "speaking in tongues is prayer or praise spoken in syllables not understood by the speaker."[3] In Acts 2, Jews from many nations, who spoke many languages, were gathered in Jerusalem for the feast of Pentecost, and they heard Peter's sermon in their own languages. Certainly this was a great miracle, given by God. Elsewhere, the NT speaks of the gift of tongues as a gift used in worship, both public and private. Apparently, people were praying or teaching in languages that they themselves did not know, and that other people listening did not know. It is hard for us to imagine the purpose of this, but apparently it had some devotional value (1 Cor. 14:14). Evidently, in many cases at least, God himself spoke to the people through the unknown language.

When someone used a tongue in public worship, there would often be an interpreter present, who would tell the congregation what the first speaker meant. Since God was speaking through the tongue-speaker, the interpretation of that tongue was also God's speech. So the interpretation of the tongue was equivalent to prophecy. Indeed, since it was a God-given interpretation of a God-given message, it was equivalent to prophecy in the OT sense. Both in the unknown tongue and in the interpreted tongue, the message was the very word of God.

Now, in 1 Corinthians 14, Paul is very concerned that the worship of the church not only honor God, but also edify the people. It's not enough in worship to speak to God; we must also teach one another, encourage one another (Heb. 10:25), edify one another, lead one another toward spiritual growth. Someone who speaks in tongues, Paul says, communes with God, but he does not edify the congregation, unless there is an interpretation. So, Paul says, Christians should not speak in tongues in worship unless someone present has the gift of interpretation, unless someone is able to translate the tongue-speech into a known language.

By the way, it is obvious from 1 Corinthians 14 (and from 12:30) that not every Christian spoke in tongues. Some people think that every genuine Christian speaks in tongues, or at least everyone who is baptized in the Spirit. But as we have seen, every Christian is baptized in the Spirit, and not every Christian speaks in tongues.

Does God give the gift of tongues today, or are tongues, like prophecy, a temporary gift that God gave to the church, not needed now that we have a completed Bible? Well, since interpreted tongues are the same as prophecy, our previous argument implies that there are no interpreted tongues today. Therefore, 1 Corinthians 14 would tell us that we should not practice the use of tongues in public worship services.

Paul does not, however, condemn the use of tongues in private devotions. Indeed, he says, in 1 Corinthians 14:2, "For one who speaks in a tongue speaks not to men but to God; for no one understands him, but he utters mysteries in the Spirit." Does God

---

3. Ibid., 1070.

still give this ability to some Christians, to speak to him privately in an unknown language? It is hard to imagine why God would give such a remarkable gift to be used only privately. The general teaching of Scripture about the gifts of the Spirit is that they are not for our private use, but are to be used for the whole body. Still, there may be something about the private use of tongues that might enable a person to minister to others more effectively. It's also hard to imagine why God would withdraw from the church the gifts of prophecy and interpretation, leaving intact the gift of the private use of tongues. Nevertheless, I think it is best to leave that question open for now.

Healings

In the NT, God gave miraculous healings as a witness to Jesus and the apostles (Matt. 9:18; Mark 6:13; Luke 4:40; Acts 28:8). Jesus could heal at his mere word, or by using materials such as mud and saliva. He was Lord over all the forces of nature, and he could reverse the curse on the ground at will.

The apostles also healed the sick frequently, but with them the healing was not automatic. In Mark 9:28, the disciples are not able to cast a demon out of a boy, and Jesus teaches that this kind of exorcism requires prayer. Paul, too, was unable to heal at one point, namely, to heal himself from what he calls a "thorn" (2 Cor. 12:7). He pleaded with God three times about this (v. 8), but God replied, "My grace is sufficient for you, for my power is made perfect in weakness" (v. 9; cf. 2 Tim. 4:20). We note also that all the apostles died, in God's time. They were not able, through the gift of healing, to prevent death forever. The death rate continued as something less than one per person.[4]

We also read in the Psalms (as 119:67, 71) and elsewhere that God uses affliction, certainly including sickness and injury, for his good purposes.

Does the gift of miraculous healing exist today? I would say that God gave special ability to heal to the apostles and to some others during the apostolic age (1 Cor. 12:9). Though that ability was limited, it was sufficient to bear witness to the watching world that the new Christian sect had the blessing of God. Like other miraculous gifts, this ability was not given to all Christians, nor was it given throughout the period of biblical history. Rather, it was given for a special purpose in a special time. So we should not expect to find people with this gift of healing in the church today. But this is not to say that God will never, ever, give that gift to anybody. We just don't know the purposes of God well enough to make such a generalization.

It is certain, however, that the church does have *some* access to divine healing. There may be no people today with the NT gift of healing. But we certainly do continue to have access to God's throne by prayer. And the NT encourages us to pray for healing. James 5:14–15 says, "Is anyone among you sick? Let him call for the elders of the church, and let them pray over him, anointing him with oil in the name of the Lord. And the prayer of faith will save the one who is sick, and the Lord will raise him up. And if he has committed sins, he will be forgiven." Here we read not only about prayer

---

4. Evidently, Enoch and Elijah did not experience death.

for healing, but about such prayer as a special ministry of the church. The passage is difficult in some ways, for there is a connection here between healing and forgiveness that is hard to understand. I take it that the passage promises that when a person is sick because of some sin, he may confess that sin to the elders of the church and that their prayer of faith, with the anointing of oil, will raise him up.

Certainly, though, even when there is no clear connection between sickness and sin, we have the privilege of bringing that up before our heavenly Father. As with the apostles, such prayer is limited; there is nothing automatic about it. God may say no for any number of reasons, among them the reason he gave to Paul in 2 Corinthians 12:9. But the power of prayer has not been lessened since the time of the apostles. We are to come boldly before the throne of grace, confident that in God's way and in his time, we will receive his mercy (Heb. 4:16).

Key Terms

Baptism in the Spirit
Filling of the Spirit
Fruit of the Spirit
Gifts of the Spirit
Miraculous gifts
Signs of an apostle
Prophecy
Tongues
Healings

Study Questions

1. Summarize the biblical evidence for the deity of the Holy Spirit.
2. Is the Holy Spirit in Scripture a person, or an impersonal force? Defend your answer.
3. Show how the Spirit embodies God's lordship attributes.
4. "And of course, the Spirit is the great Teacher of the church." Explain; elaborate.
5. When are believers baptized in the Spirit? At conversion or after? Present biblical considerations.
6. Paul commands believers to be filled with the Spirit. How is that possible? What can we do to bring about the Spirit's filling?
7. How is the fruit of the Spirit different from the filling of the Spirit?
8. What are some of the gifts of the Spirit? How are they related to our natural abilities? How can we determine what gifts we have?
9. Does God give miraculous gifts to the church today?
10. Does prophecy continue today? Discuss Wayne Grudem's thesis in this connection.
11. Do tongues continue today? If so, are there any differences between their use in the NT period and the uses they should have today?

12. Does the gift of miraculous healing continue in the church today? Discuss any differences between the use of this gift now and its use in the NT period.

Memory Verses

Rom. 12:6–8: Having gifts that differ according to the grace given to us, let us use them: if prophecy, in proportion to our faith; if service, in our serving; the one who teaches, in his teaching; the one who exhorts, in his exhortation; the one who contributes, in generosity; the one who leads, with zeal; the one who does acts of mercy, with cheerfulness.

1 Cor. 12:12–13: For just as the body is one and has many members, and all the members of the body, though many, are one body, so it is with Christ. For in one Spirit we were all baptized into one body—Jews or Greeks, slaves or free—and all were made to drink of one Spirit.

2 Cor. 12:7–9: So to keep me from becoming conceited because of the surpassing greatness of the revelations, a thorn was given me in the flesh, a messenger of Satan to harass me, to keep me from becoming conceited. Three times I pleaded with the Lord about this, that it should leave me. But he said to me, "My grace is sufficient for you, for my power is made perfect in weakness." Therefore I will boast all the more gladly of my weaknesses, so that the power of Christ may rest upon me.

2 Cor. 12:12: The signs of a true apostle were performed among you with utmost patience, with signs and wonders and mighty works.

Heb. 2:3–4: How shall we escape if we neglect such a great salvation? It was declared at first by the Lord, and it was attested to us by those who heard, while God also bore witness by signs and wonders and various miracles and by gifts of the Holy Spirit distributed according to his will.

James 5:14–15: Is anyone among you sick? Let him call for the elders of the church, and let them pray over him, anointing him with oil in the name of the Lord. And the prayer of faith will save the one who is sick, and the Lord will raise him up. And if he has committed sins, he will be forgiven.

Resources for Further Study

Ferguson, Sinclair. *The Holy Spirit.* Downers Grove, IL: InterVarsity Press, 1997.

Grudem, Wayne. *GST.*

Owen, John. *The Holy Spirit.* Peabody, MA: Christian Heritage Publishers, 2005.

Poythress, Vern S. *What Are Spiritual Gifts?* Phillipsburg, NJ: P&R Publishing, 2010.

CHAPTER 40

CALLING

IN THIS AND FOLLOWING CHAPTERS, we will explore a series of divine blessings flowing to us from the atoning work of Christ, dealing with sin in our lives, and preparing us for eternal fellowship with God. The Spirit is the most prominent source of these blessings, so it is appropriate that these chapters fall under the general description of the "Doctrine of the Holy Spirit." But we will see that all three persons of the Trinity are involved in these transformations of our lives.

The list of these blessings is fairly traditional among theologians: calling, regeneration, conversion (faith, repentance), justification, adoption, sanctification, perseverance, and glorification. As we have seen, these blessings are sometimes described as the *application of redemption*. In the application of redemption, the work of Jesus brings the blessings of salvation to individuals. John Murray titled one of his books *Redemption Accomplished and Applied*,[1] a phrase that well expresses the distinction in view. Redemption was accomplished at the cross, once for all. But the blessings of redemption must then be applied to each individual believer. So Jesus died for the sins of each of his people, but God calls each of us to Christ, regenerates us, converts us, and so on. Although the atoning work of Christ is complete, God has much to do in and for each one of us.

To emphasize the individual at this point is not to deny the importance of the church as the body of Christ. God intends that the blessings of the atonement will come to us together with other Christians, each believer enriching the whole body with the gifts and fruits of the Spirit. But salvation is irreducibly individual in one sense: the salvation of another believer will not save me. Each of us is accountable to God for his own works, and for his own relationship to Christ (Ezek. 18:4; Rom. 14:12). Salvation is both individual and corporate, not merely one or the other. I will focus on individual salvation in this and following chapters. Later (in chapters 46–49), we will look more closely at the church.

This distinction between accomplishment and application suggests a way of summarizing the course of our salvation in Christ in accord with our triperspectival understanding. Salvation begins in God's eternal decree, the *pactum salutis* (normative perspective), is

1. Grand Rapids: Eerdmans, 1955.

accomplished through Jesus' atonement in history (situational perspective), and is applied by the Spirit to each of us (existential perspective). Note that this distinction is based on the different roles played in redemption by the Father, Son, and Holy Spirit. You can also see these three stages in a passage such as Ephesians 1. There, Paul speaks of election in verse 4:

> He chose us in him before the foundation of the world, that we should be holy and blameless before him.

Then in verse 7 he speaks of the atonement:

> In him we have redemption through his blood, the forgiveness of our trespasses, according to the riches of his grace.

And in verse 13 he speaks of the events of our experience that brought us to trust in Christ:

> In him you also, when you heard the word of truth, the gospel of your salvation, and believed in him, were sealed with the promised Holy Spirit.

These three verses provide three complementary answers to the question "when were you saved?" We may answer: (1) before the foundation of the world, (2) on the cross of Calvary, and (3) when we came to believe in Christ.[2] In terms of our triperspectival approach, this analysis yields the picture shown in fig. 40.1.

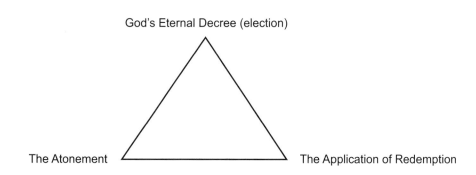

Fig. 40.1. Aspects of Salvation

The *Ordo Salutis*

As we have seen, theologians have a propensity to summarize biblical teaching in ordered lists. In chapter 11, we discussed the order of the decrees, supposedly a summary

---

2. And of course, there is also the important sense in which we "are being saved" through our earthly life (1 Cor. 1:18) and "will be saved" (Matt. 24:13) when Jesus returns.

of the order of God's thoughts in his eternal plan for creation. In the supralapsarian version of the list, the first item was God's *pactum salutis*, the covenant between Father and Son to secure blessing for an elect, creatable people. Then followed the decrees to create, to permit the fall, to send Christ to atone for sin, and so on. Infralapsarians proposed a rival order, and there were still others. Rather than taking for granted the legitimacy of this project and criticizing individual proposals, I called into question whether Scripture authorizes us to chart the contents of God's mind in this sort of way.

Many theologians have also gathered the blessings of the application of redemption into an ordered list, called the *ordo salutis*, or "order of salvation." But there are problems with this order similar to the problems in the order of the decrees. One is that neither order is mentioned in Scripture. Another is that Scripture itself does not show any interest in arranging these events in an ordered list.

The idea of an *ordo salutis* is sometimes based on Romans 8:29–30:

> For those whom he foreknew he also predestined to be conformed to the image of his Son, in order that he might be the firstborn among many brothers. And those whom he predestined he also called, and those whom he called he also justified, and those whom he justified he also glorified.

We are tempted here to put all these divine acts into an ordered list: foreknowledge, predestination, calling, justification, glorification. Paul's placing of calling, justification, and glorification agrees with the order of these in the traditional theological list. But Paul's list does not include some items on the traditional *ordo* (regeneration, conversion, adoption, sanctification, perseverance), and it adds the events of foreknowledge and predestination, which are not usually included in the *ordo* by the theological systems.

More important, the actual text of this passage does not emphasize whatever aspects of order there may be in the list. All the passage says is that God has given these five blessings to the same people. These are the people who are "called" (Rom. 8:28), for whom "all things work together for good." Paul assures them that if they are called by God, they will certainly experience all the other blessings mentioned in the passage. Paul does not encourage the called ones to meditate on the order in which these blessings come.

Further, if the believer were to meditate on the order in which God's blessings come to him, what kind of order would he have in mind? As I indicated in the discussion of the order of the decrees (chapter 11), there are different kinds of order, such as temporal, causal, and conditional, pedagogical.[3] And as with the order of the decrees, no one kind of order determines the traditional list. Note:

---

3. People sometimes talk about *logical order* in this connection, but it is not clear what they mean by the term. Logical order occurs in syllogisms, where a major premise precedes a minor premise, the premises precede a conclusion, and one conclusion must be proved before another one. But nobody construes the *ordo salutis* as a collection of syllogisms, and it is not clear what else *logical order* might mean in this context, unless it is a synonym for *pedagogical order*.

1. Calling comes before regeneration both temporally and causally.
2. Regeneration comes before faith causally, but many theologians regard them as simultaneous.
3. Faith is prior to justification, but neither causally nor temporally. Most theologians describe the relation as "instrumental." But instrumental priority is relevant only to these two items of the list.
4. Justification precedes adoption and sanctification, but neither causally nor temporally. Perhaps it is best to say that justification provides the legal-forensic basis for adoption and sanctification; but the *legal-forensic* category is useful only here on the list.
5. There is no obvious reason why adoption should precede sanctification, or vice versa.

So in my view, the "order" of the *ordo salutis* does not reflect an objective arrangement in God's redemptive provisions. There are various kinds of order throughout the list, as I indicated above, but no general kind of order that runs through the list as a whole.

Nevertheless, I do think the *ordo* has value as a *pedagogical* device. It is edifying for a teacher to lead students through the traditional list, explaining the meanings of the terms and the various relationships linking the items in the series. Theologians need to give more, not less, attention to pedagogy, and the *ordo* is a pedagogical device that is effective and that emerges from the theological tradition itself.

Perspectives on the Application of Redemption

My discussion of the application will follow the traditional *ordo* in a general way. But I think there is another way of looking at these blessings that is more helpful to us in seeing their relation. No reader of this book should be surprised to hear that this approach is triperspectival.

In chapter 36, I described triperspectivally the major effects of the fall; see fig. 40.2.

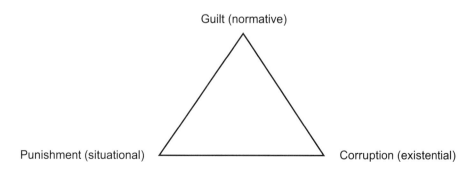

Fig. 40.2. Effects of the Fall

Guilt is our legal status, implying that we have violated God's law, so I characterize it as the normative perspective. Punishment is the consequence of guilt in which God has set the course of nature and history against sinful man. It is a change in our natural environment that brings pain, suffering, and frustration, the situational aspect of our fallen condition. Corruption is the continuing sin in ourselves, and its effects within us, the existential perspective.

Now, the application of redemption deals with these three aspects of sin; see fig. 40.3.

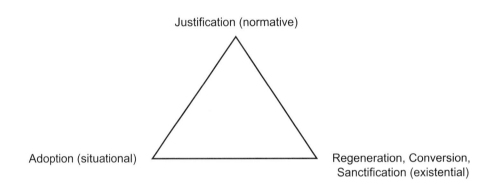

Fig. 40.3. Three Aspects of Redemption

In justification, God deals with our guilt and accounts us righteous for the sake of Christ. In adoption, God provides us with a new environment, a new family. He makes us heirs of Christ and with him lords of creation. In regeneration, conversion, and sanctification, God deals with us inwardly, giving us new hearts. As we grow in grace, we gain more and more the ability to say no to sin.

An important clarification: By placing these blessings on a triperspectival diagram, I am not claiming that they are ultimately identical. Protestant theology has always insisted with good reason, for example, that justification should never be confused with sanctification, nor vice versa. This is, indeed, an important aspect of the conflict between Protestant and Roman Catholic doctrines of justification, which I will discuss when we come to consider that subject. Nevertheless, I do want to insist that none of these blessings functions properly without the others. It is impossible to imagine someone who is regenerate and sanctified in the biblical sense, but not justified. Or one who is an adopted son of God, but who is neither justified nor regenerate. And it is impossible to imagine that anyone can be justified who is not converted. That is to say, since we are justified by faith alone, we cannot be justified unless the Spirit has wrought faith in our hearts, and faith comes by regeneration.

So just as sin is a derangement of our legal standing, our relation to our environment, and our inner life, so redemption deals thoroughly with all these aspects of life to bring us toward a comprehensively righteous life.

I have not placed *effectual calling* on the diagram. It does not belong to one perspective or another. Rather, it serves as our entrance to all the blessings from all the perspectives.

Effectual Calling

The term *call* in Scripture has several meanings that I will explore later in this chapter. But the most predominant meaning in Scripture and the most important for the application of redemption is what theologians call *effectual calling*. John Murray defines it thus:

> Calling is the efficacious summons on the part of God the Father, in accordance with and in pursuance of his eternal purpose in Christ Jesus, addressed to sinners dead in trespasses and sins, a call that ushers them into fellowship with Christ and into the possession of the salvation of which he is the embodiment; a call immutable in its character by reason of the purpose from which it proceeds and the bond it effects.[4]

Romans 8:28–30, quoted earlier, is one of the most important passages on the subject. It indicates that "those who are called" have a very special status in God's eyes, and that call confers on them all the blessings of Jesus' work. See also Rom. 1:6–7; 11:29; 1 Cor. 1:2, 9, 24, 26; 7:18; Gal. 1:15; 2 Thess. 2:13–14; 2 Tim. 1:9; Heb. 3:1–2; 1 Peter 2:9; 5:10; 2 Peter 1:10. Calling in this sense is a sovereign act of God and "does not derive its definition from any activity on our part, such as faith or repentance or conversion."[5] We cannot resist it.

Effectual calling helps us to deal with a paradox: Many people in the world are elect but nevertheless "dead in the trespasses and sins" (Eph. 2:1). Although they are chosen in Christ before the foundation of the world, they live as unbelievers, without any faith in Christ. This paradox is due to the historical character of redemption. God has sovereignly determined that election is the first step, not the final step, in the story of each believer's life with Jesus. Subsequent to election, God leads each of his people through a process by which they become more intimately attached to Christ. Effectual calling is the first step in that historical process.

Effectual calling summons us into all the blessings of salvation: the kingdom (1 Thess. 2:12), holiness (Rom. 1:7; 1 Cor. 1:2; 1 Thess. 4:7; 5:23–24), peace (1 Cor. 7:15), freedom (Gal. 5:13), hope (Eph. 1:18; 4:4), light (1 Peter 2:9), patient endurance (1 Peter 2:20–21), God's kingdom of glory (1 Thess. 2:12), eternal life (2 Thess. 2:14; 1 Tim. 6:12; Heb. 9:15; 1 Peter 5:10; Rev. 19:9). So this calling is "high" (Phil. 3:14 KJV), "holy" (2 Tim. 1:9), and "heavenly" (Heb. 3:1). Ultimately it calls us into fellowship with Christ (1 Cor. 1:9), for it is in Christ that we have all the blessings of salvation. So in the life of the believer, God acts first, before we offer him any response, but his act calls forth from us a godly response.

---

4. *MCW*, 2:165.
5. Ibid., 2:162.

So not only does God call us into blessing; he also calls us into obligation. Peter exhorts:

> Therefore, brothers, be all the more diligent to make your calling and election sure, for if you practice these qualities you will never fall. (2 Peter 1:10)

The "qualities" are listed in verses 3–9: faith, virtue, knowledge, self-control, steadfastness, godliness, brotherly affection, love. Calling is a gracious act of God, but it inevitably produces good works in the believer, works that demonstrate that one is in fact called.

Note that in the application of redemption, each step intensifies our union with Christ (see chapter 38). We are "in Christ" by virtue of our eternal election (Eph. 1:3), but by effectual calling we enter the "fellowship" of Christ (1 Cor. 1:9). The application of redemption draws us more and more deeply into Christ, who is the source of all its blessings. The difference between one who is uncalled and one who is called is a difference between night and day, death and life. But from another perspective it is a difference between one union with Christ and another deeper union.

The author of effectual calling is God the Father[6] (Rom. 8:30; 1 Cor. 1:9; Gal. 1:15; Eph. 1:17–18). Murray says:

> To use the terms used by our Lord, [the Father] donates men to his own Son in the effectual operations of his grace (John 6:37).[7]

Though the Spirit is dominant in biblical descriptions of the application of redemption, it is worth reminding ourselves that in all the works of salvation, the persons of the Trinity are all active. We will see that the Father is also the One who justifies, adopts, and sanctifies us. It is good to know that the Father who devised the eternal covenant of redemption (*pactum salutis*) remains involved in the outworkings of this covenant. As we are drawn into fellowship with Christ through the Spirit, we become sons of his Father.

Applications of God's Call

As I mentioned earlier, the term *call* in Scripture does not always refer to effectual calling as such. Biblical writers also use the term for more specific calls of God. For as God calls us into fellowship with Christ, he also calls us to play particular roles in that fellowship. It is helpful to think of these as John Murray does,[8] as "applications" of the call of God, rather than as separate callings. For in these additional callings, God is

---

6. WSC 31, to the contrary, describes it as "the work of God's Spirit." The Westminster Standards, however, appear to conflate *effectual calling* with what we now call *regeneration*. (They do not discuss regeneration as a distinct topic.) Of course it is the Spirit (John 3) who is the principal Author of regeneration. I believe that it is best to distinguish calling and regeneration as, for example, John Murray does in *MCW*, 2:161–201.

7. Ibid., 2:163.

8. Ibid., 2:161.

setting forth what roles we are to play in the fellowship of Christ. He specifies where we are to be located in the fellowship of the Lord Jesus Christ.

So Scripture speaks of calling to church office:

> Paul, a servant of Christ Jesus, [is] called to be an apostle, set apart for the gospel of God. (Rom. 1:1; cf. 1 Cor. 1:1)

The term is also used for the *gospel call*, the invitation to all people to put their faith in Christ. In this sense, God (usually through preaching) calls some people who are not finally saved, as well as some who are. Effectual calling, we recall, cannot be resisted, but the gospel call can be and often is. Thus, "many are called, but few are chosen" (Matt. 22:14). We recall the tone of pleading in the voice of wisdom in Proverbs 8:4–5:

> To you, O men, I call,
>   and my cry is to the children of man.
> O simple ones, learn prudence;
>   O fools, learn sense.

Theologians have also used the biblical terminology of calling to refer to *vocation*, the specific relationships and responsibilities in which God has placed us, such as marriage, singleness, or a profession. They have sometimes invoked 1 Corinthians 7:20–24 as referring to vocation in this sense:

> Each one should remain in the condition in which he was called. Were you a slave when called? Do not be concerned about it. (But if you can gain your freedom, avail yourself of the opportunity.) For he who was called in the Lord as a slave is a freedman of the Lord. Likewise he who was free when called is a slave of Christ. You were bought with a price; do not become slaves of men. So, brothers, in whatever condition each was called, there let him remain with God.

On this reading, slavery and freedom (and in context marriage and singleness) would be callings of God. Yet I am inclined to take "called" in this passage to refer to effectual calling. So Paul is saying to these people who face unique hardship to remain in the walk of life where they were when God called them into fellowship with Christ.[9]

Of course, the difference in the two readings is not great. Our current walk of life (singleness, marriage, farming, carpentry) is given to us in God's providence, and in some cases, like the situation of 1 Corinthians 7, it is normative; it is the walk of life in which we should stay. And if we should not equate *calling* with *vocation*, certainly it's not wrong to find reference to vocation in Paul's references to one's walk of life.

---

9. The point is not that we should never change jobs. It appears that the Corinthians were going through a particularly difficult period that Paul calls "the present distress" (1 Cor. 7:26). Given the difficulties of making big changes in one's life during such a trial, Paul urges the single people not to marry, married people not to seek divorce, and other people not to change jobs.

So it is not surprising that Martin Luther and others have interpreted one's profession as a calling of God. Certainly there is an analogy between God's effectual calling and God's providential work of bringing someone into a particular profession.[10]

Key Terms

Accomplishment of redemption
Application of redemption
Ordo salutis
Temporal order
Causal order
Logical order
Pedagogical order
Effectual calling
Gospel call
Vocation

Study Questions

1. Describe and evaluate Frame's triperspectival understanding of the blessings that Paul enumerates in Ephesians 1:4, 7, and 13.

2. When were you saved? Discuss.

3. What does Romans 8:29–30 teach about the existence of an *ordo salutis*? Do you believe that *ordo salutis* is a useful concept? Explain.

4. Describe Frame's comparison between the perspectives on the fall's effects and the perspectives on redemption's effects. Evaluate.

5. "Calling in this sense is a sovereign act of God and does not derive its definition from any activity on our part, such as faith or repentance or conversion." Explain; evaluate.

6. How is it possible to be elect in Christ and at the same time to be dead in trespasses and sins? What does that paradox reveal about God's plan for realizing the *pactum salutis*?

7. List some of the blessings into which effectual calling brings us. List some of the obligations.

8. "The difference between one who is uncalled and one who is called is a difference between night and day, death and life. But from another perspective it is a difference between one union with Christ and another deeper union." Explain; evaluate.

9. Which person of the Trinity is particularly the Author of effectual calling? Is that important? In what way? Can you reconcile your view with the WSC?

10. What is the relation of other divine "calls" to effectual calling? Is there any value in calling these "applications" of effectual calling? Discuss.

---

10. Compare my discussion of the vocational will of God in chapter 16.

11. "Effectual calling, we recall, cannot be resisted, but the gospel call can be and often is." Explain; evaluate.

12. Are marriage and work-professions callings of God? Discuss.

Memory Verses

Rom. 8:28–30: And we know that for those who love God all things work together for good, for those who are called according to his purpose. For those whom he foreknew he also predestined to be conformed to the image of his Son, in order that he might be the firstborn among many brothers. And those whom he predestined he also called, and those whom he called he also justified, and those whom he justified he also glorified.

1 Cor. 15:1–4: Now I would remind you, brothers, of the gospel I preached to you, which you received, in which you stand, and by which you are being saved, if you hold fast to the word I preached to you—unless you believed in vain.

For I delivered to you as of first importance what I also received: that Christ died for our sins in accordance with the Scriptures, that he was buried, [and] that he was raised on the third day in accordance with the Scriptures.

Eph. 1:4: He chose us in him before the foundation of the world, that we should be holy and blameless before him.

Eph. 1:7: In him we have redemption through his blood, the forgiveness of our trespasses, according to the riches of his grace.

Eph. 1:13: In him you also, when you heard the word of truth, the gospel of your salvation, and believed in him, were sealed with the promised Holy Spirit.

2 Peter 1:10: Therefore, brothers, be all the more diligent to make your calling and election sure, for if you practice these qualities you will never fall.

Resources for Further Study

Murray, John. *MCW*, 2:161–66.

———. *Redemption Accomplished and Applied.* Grand Rapids: Eerdmans, 1955.

CHAPTER 41

REGENERATION AND CONVERSION— SUBJECTIVE SALVATION

THE TERMS *OBJECTIVE* AND *SUBJECTIVE* are frequently used in discussions of the *ordo salutis*, the application of redemption. In one sense all these blessings are subjective, because they are given to each individual believer and they have major implications for our individual spiritual lives. But it is confusing to describe, particularly, justification and adoption as *subjective*. An important aspect of justification and adoption is that they convey to us a new status: as righteous (justification) and as sons and daughters (adoption). These are not matters of degree; they do not describe our inner feelings or dispositions. So theologians generally describe them as objective, not subjective.

Other blessings in the *ordo salutis* are inward, subjective, including regeneration, conversion, and sanctification. In one sense, however, these blessings are also objective. Those who are regenerate really are regenerate, objectively so; and those who are unregenerate really are unregenerate. Same for conversion and sanctification, although the latter admits of degrees.

So all the blessings of the application of redemption are objective in the sense that they are real blessings, not dependent on our interpretations or feelings. All are subjective in the sense that they all bring about major changes in our individual lives. And some (regeneration, conversion, sanctification) are subjective in a further sense: they change us within. They change the heart of the believer. These are the blessings that, in the previous chapter, I aligned with the existential perspective.

Some writers have claimed that the gospel is entirely objective and not at all subjective in this second sense. It is true that in some biblical passages the term *gospel* refers to objective events in the sense of things that happen outside us rather than inside us. In 1 Corinthians 15, for example, Paul expounds his "gospel" (v. 1) by referring to Jesus' death for us according to the Scriptures (v. 3), his burial, resurrection, and post-resurrection appearances (vv. 4–9). But it is clear in this passage as in many

944

others that these objective events have huge subjective consequences. In verse 10 of 1 Corinthians 15, Paul says:

> But by the grace of God I am what I am, and his grace toward me was not in vain. On the contrary, I worked harder than any of them, though it was not I, but the grace of God that is with me.

Objectively, Christ appeared to Paul; but when he appeared, he wrought great changes in Paul's mind and heart, creating within him a new disposition to work hard in the preaching of the gospel that he had once opposed. Indeed, throughout the NT, the gospel brings about profound subjective change. Not only did Christ die and rise again, but when he died, his people died to sin, and when he rose, we rose with him to new life (Rom. 6:4; cf. Col. 3:12–14). It is "Christ in you" who is our hope of glory (Col. 1:27; cf. Rom. 8:10). The doctrine of union with Christ (chapter 38) is not only about ourselves in Christ, but also about Christ in us (2 Cor. 13:5; Gal. 4:19).

So the gospel not only narrates the objective events of the history of redemption. It says that these events happened *for us* ("for our sins in accordance with the Scriptures," 1 Cor. 15:3) and promises that those who believe will experience the inward blessings of those events. Indeed, *gospel* is even broader than that. The gospel announces the coming of the kingdom of God, God's victory over sin and all its effects in the creation (Matt. 3:1–2; 4:17; Acts 8:12; 20:25; 28:31).

Regeneration

In the previous chapter, we considered effectual calling, the first event of the application of redemption, or *ordo salutis*. Now we come to the second event, namely, regeneration, or the new birth. When God calls us into fellowship with Christ, he gives us a new life, a new heart. Regeneration is the first effect of effectual calling. And regeneration is the first item on the list that occurs inside of us. It is a subjective blessing, in the second sense of *subjective* noted above.

The presupposition of Scripture is that apart from God's grace, we are spiritually dead (Eph. 2:1–3), as we saw in chapter 36. This means that in and of ourselves, we can do nothing to please God. So just as conception and birth bring new physical life, so the work of regeneration brings new spiritual life. Through the new birth, we gain new desire and new ability to serve God. So my definition of regeneration is this: a sovereign act of God, beginning a new spiritual life in us.

Regeneration in the Old Testament

The most familiar references to regeneration are in the NT, but we can expect that since man's need is the same in both Testaments, the OT teaches the same thing, from its own perspective. When Jesus teaches Nicodemus about the new birth in John 3, he expresses amazement that Nicodemus, "the teacher of Israel," does not understand his teaching (v. 10). And indeed the OT does speak of the new birth in a number of ways.

As I indicated in chapter 4, God's covenants commanded his people to write the law on their hearts (Deut. 6:6; 11:18; 32:46). It is the heart, the core of man himself, that is "deceitful" and "desperately sick" (Jer. 17:9), so in redemption God must change the heart. In another figure, God calls the people to "circumcise" their hearts (Deut. 10:16; 30:6). The people cannot, of course, accomplish this change through their own strength. God, rather, promises grace to them (Jer. 24:7; 31:33; 32:39; Ezek. 11:19; 36:25–27). Note also the prophecies of abundant, sufficient grace for God's people when the Messiah comes (Isa. 32:15; 34:16; 44:3; 59:21; etc.). God seeks regeneration among the people as a whole, and to secure that result he deals graciously with individuals:

> For thus says the One who is high and lifted up,
>   who inhabits eternity, whose name is Holy:
> "I dwell in the high and holy place,
>   and also with him who is of a contrite and lowly spirit,
> to revive the spirit of the lowly,
>   and to revive the heart of the contrite." (Isa. 57:15)

So Paul rightly describes the nature of OT Judaism when he says:

> For no one is a Jew who is merely one outwardly, nor is circumcision outward and phys-ical. But a Jew is one inwardly, and circumcision is a matter of the heart, by the Spirit, not by the letter. His praise is not from man but from God. (Rom. 2:28–29; cf. 9:6–8)

God's intention for the Israelites was that they should be a regenerate people, inwardly righteous, circumcised of heart, the law written on their hearts. As I indicated in chap-ter 4, the new covenant in Christ (Jer. 31:31–34) applied to elect Israelites retroactively. In terms of that covenant, God himself indeed wrote his law on their hearts, circumcised their hearts, and created in them new spiritual life.

The teaching of Jesus, similarly, flows from the understanding that man's righ-teousness does not suffice to please God:

> For I tell you, unless your righteousness exceeds that of the scribes and Pharisees, you will never enter the kingdom of heaven. (Matt. 5:20)

Unless God himself does a work of grace in a man, he can do only evil (Matt. 12:33–35; cf. 19:16–26; John 6:63–65).

The Johannine Teaching

The familiar NT language of new birth comes from the writings of John. In John 3, Jesus tells Nicodemus that unless a man is born again,[1] he cannot see the

---

1. Or "born from above." The Greek *anothen* can be taken either way, and exegetes have made huge efforts to establish each conclusion. See, for example, *MCW*, 2:174–79. I don't think much of theological importance hinges

kingdom of God (v. 3) or enter the kingdom of God (v. 5). John Murray distinguishes these:

> "To see" may express the idea of intelligent understanding, cognition, appreciation, not mere observation in the sense of being spectator; and "entering into" means actual entrance into the kingdom as members in the realm of life and privilege.[2]

This passage, then, reinforces the frequent emphasis of this book (especially chapters 28–32) that our knowledge of God is part of redemption. The intellect, with the rest of our faculties, must be redeemed from the distortions of sin. In Paul's language, our new self is "being renewed in knowledge after the image of its creator" (Col. 3:10). The new birth turns back the repression of the truth that Paul describes in Romans 1:18. And of course, the new birth is also a qualification for entering the kingdom (see chapter 5), enlisting on God's side in the cosmic battle.

In John 3:4, Nicodemus literalizes Jesus' saying, exposing his failure to understand.

> Jesus answered, "Truly, truly, I say to you, unless one is born of water and the Spirit, he cannot enter the kingdom of God." (John 3:5)

Much has been written about the phrase "water and the Spirit." Since "Spirit" obviously refers to the Holy Spirit, the discussion has focused on "water." Many have thought that this term is an allusion to Christian baptism, and it is possible that Jesus provides an advance reference to that here, as he may provide an advance reference to the Lord's Supper in John 6:25–65. But the Christian sacraments did not exist as such in the setting of these passages. So we must ask the likely meaning of "water" to Nicodemus himself in his context. We do not have to look far to answer this question, since the OT was replete with the use of water as a redemptive symbol. Note the symbolism of water as purification from sin and defilement in the following: Ex. 30:18–21; Ps. 51:2f.; Isa. 1:16; Jer. 33:8; Ezek. 36:25; Zech. 13:1. Jewish proselyte baptism cannot be excluded from this reference, nor the early baptizing of John and Jesus. Pharisees like Nicodemus resisted the notion that they needed to be purified of sin (cf. Luke 7:30), but God frequently used water to teach his people their need for cleansing, and the new birth is a definitive cleansing from sin.[3]

With the reference to the Spirit, we may distinguish in the new birth a negative and a positive aspect: negatively purification from sin, and positively creation of new life through the Spirit. Compare the coordination of these aspects in Ezekiel 36:25–26:

---

on the controversy. The remarkable thing about the passage is the reference to *birth*. The one interpretation indicates its temporal relation to ordinary birth, the other the figurative location of its source.

2. Ibid., 2:179. Much of the following discussion is indebted to John Murray's treatment, though I take full responsibility for the formulation here.

3. Compare the pride of Naaman, the Syrian commander, who resisted (but eventually accepted) Elisha's command to wash in the Jordan to be cured of his leprosy (2 Kings 5:11–14).

> I will sprinkle clean water on you, and you shall be clean from all your uncleannesses, and from all your idols I will cleanse you. And I will give you a new heart, and a new spirit I will put within you. And I will remove the heart of stone from your flesh and give you a heart of flesh.

Cf. Ps. 51:2, 7, 10; Titus 3:5.

John 3:6 expands the imagery of birth: "That which is born of the flesh is flesh, and that which is born of the Spirit is spirit." "Flesh" here has a negative moral connotation, as elsewhere in the NT. So the old birth, from sinful parents, gives rise to a sinful child. Ordinary birth does not deal with sin. But birth by the Spirit creates children with the qualities of the Spirit, children with a new life.

John 3:7–8 emphasizes the mysteriousness of the event:

> Do not marvel that I said to you, "You must be born again." The wind blows where it wishes, and you hear its sound, but you do not know where it comes from or where it goes. So it is with everyone who is born of the Spirit.

How do you know whether someone is born again? It's not a visible event. Jesus says that the regenerating work of the Spirit is like the blowing of the wind: you don't see it; you don't know where it comes from or where it goes. But as with the wind, you can see the results, though you cannot be *infallibly* sure that regeneration has taken place. Faith and good works are the effects of regeneration, and these show that we have been born of God. In his first letter, John speaks about being born of God and its results:

> If you know that he is righteous, you may be sure that everyone who practices righteousness has been born of him. (1 John 2:29)

That new birth is like a seed that God plants in believers that grows into a holy life that resists temptation:

> No one born of God makes a practice of sinning, for God's seed abides in him, and he cannot keep on sinning because he has been born of God. (1 John 3:9)

Love is evidence that a person is born of God:

> Beloved, let us love one another, for love is from God, and whoever loves has been born of God and knows God. (1 John 4:7)

Faith in Christ is also evidence of the new birth (1 John 5:1).

Similarly with all the fruits of the Spirit in Galatians 5:22–23:

But the fruit of the Spirit is love, joy, peace, patience, kindness, goodness, faithfulness, gentleness, self-control; against such things there is no law.

When people's lives are changed from disobedience to obedience to God, we can know, though not infallibly, that the Spirit has been at work, giving new birth.

Those who are born of God will surely overcome the world (1 John 5:4). The new birth protects the believer against sin and the devil (5:18).

Paul on Regeneration

Paul's writings also teach that God acts to bring new spiritual life in his people. As we have seen, Paul also recognizes that sin makes us totally unable to please God through our works (Rom. 3:10–18; 6:23; 8:8). Only God's grace in Christ is able to produce good works in us (Eph. 2:8–10).

Paul uses the language of "new creation" (2 Cor. 5:17; Gal. 6:15; Eph. 2:10; cf. James 1:18) or the theme of giving life (Gal. 3:21), as well as the term "regeneration" itself (Titus 3:5), to describe God's way of bringing new spiritual life. We also find the idea of resurrection in passages such as Romans 6, which speak of us as dying and rising with Christ: we die with him unto sin, and we are raised with him unto righteousness. As effectual calling calls us into union with Christ, so regeneration is our union with him in his resurrection life. So new birth, new creation, life from the dead are alternative ways of speaking of the ways in which God gives us new life.

All these expressions emphasize God's sovereignty. New birth is obviously an act of God (note Ezek. 36:26–27; John 3:8). You didn't give birth to yourself; you didn't have anything to do with your own birth. Others gave birth to you. Your birth was a gift of grace. So your new birth was a gift of God, in this case God the Holy Spirit. (As effectual calling is an act of the Father, so regeneration is an act of the Holy Spirit, as Scripture usually represents it.)

Similarly with *new creation*. Creation is "out of nothing," as we saw in chapter 10. Before creation, there was nothing. Nothing can't produce anything. Reality all comes by the creative act of God. Same with *resurrection*. Before resurrection, there is death. Death can't produce life. Only God can. So in the new birth we are passive.

Since regeneration enables us to see the kingdom of God and to stop repressing the truth that he has revealed, it comes before our faith, bringing it about. People sometimes say, "Believe in Jesus, and you will be born again." This expression is biblically inaccurate. It's true that believing in Jesus is the path to blessing. But the new birth is the cause of faith, rather than the other way around. Again, you can't give birth to yourself, even by faith. Rather, God gives new birth to you and enables you to have faith. It's always God's sovereignty, isn't it?

A Second Meaning of Regeneration

Like effectual calling, regeneration usually occurs when we hear the gospel. First Peter 1:23 reads, "You have been born again, not of perishable seed but of imperishable, through the living and abiding word of God" (cf. v. 25). The Spirit's great power to give us new birth typically comes through the power of the Word of God. James 1:18 says, "Of his own will he brought us forth [that's the idea of regeneration] by the word of truth, that we should be a kind of firstfruits of his creatures."

There is, however, a distinction between regeneration as it appears in these two passages and the more common descriptions of regeneration that we have considered in the NT. In 1 Peter 1:23 and James 1:18, it would naturally seem that our new birth comes through a faithful appropriation of the Word of God, while in John 3 and other passages, regeneration clearly precedes and causes any such faithful hearing of God's Word. We should remember (what Nicodemus did not originally understand) that regeneration is a metaphor of spiritual renewal. As a metaphor, it can be applied to several phases of the redeemed life. In the main Johannine and Pauline passages, regeneration is the absolute beginning of new life, coming before anything we do to grow in Christ. But in these verses of Peter and James, regeneration is a broader concept indicating the process of spiritual growth through the Word of God.

This ambiguity of two senses of regeneration shows a weakness in the concept of an *ordo salutis*. Regeneration is "prior to faith" in John 3, but in 1 Peter 1:23 and James 1:18 it is subsequent to faith, or possibly a way of describing the activity of faith as it appropriates God's revelation.

Regenerate Infants

Regeneration in the Johannine and Pauline senses, then, is "prior to faith" and does not presuppose any intellectual deliberation on the part of the person. In that respect, it is different from regeneration in 1 Peter 1:23 and James 1:18. It is a divine act, causally and temporally prior to any human thought or act. So there is no reason to suppose that this blessing is given only to adults or to people of a certain level of intellectual maturity.

It is in this context that we should understand the leaping "for joy" of the unborn John the Baptist when his mother met Mary the mother of Jesus (Luke 1:41, 44). This passage does not describe a typical random movement of an unborn baby. Rather, it imputes to that baby a significant motive in making that movement: he leaped for joy. And one who rejoices in the coming of the Messiah, *because of* the coming of the Messiah, is certainly regenerate.

Nothing can stop God from bringing an infant to newness of life. Scripture doesn't tell us how regeneration affects such a child's experience, feelings, and understanding. Certainly we should not assume that regeneration immediately gives the child the intellectual ability to confess creedal doctrine. For him, then, regeneration is prior to any kind of profession of faith. But if that child has the new life of Christ within him, then he has what John Murray used to call a new "dispositional complex." That child will have the inclination (despite remaining sin) to love righteousness and hate wickedness. And he will tend to appropriate God's revelation in nature and Scripture without wickedly resisting it and working against it. And when he comes of age, he will have an inner disposition to receive with joy the teaching of the Word and to profess his faith in it.

Thus, we can understand more clearly this statement of WCF 10.3:

> Elect infants, dying in infancy, are regenerated, and saved by Christ, through the Spirit, who worketh when, and where, and how he pleaseth: so also are all other elect persons who are incapable of being outwardly called by the ministry of the Word.

The confession does not specify who these "other elect persons" might be. I assume the divines had in mind people lacking in intellectual competence or with defective sense organs. But it is interesting to consider how wide this provision may in fact extend, and I will return to this subject later in the chapter.

Faith

Regeneration confers on the elect person a desire to live a holy and righteous life. We saw that this new disposition embraces all the fruit of the Holy Spirit, such as it is described in Galatians 5:22–23, and it includes all the Christian virtues. Among those virtues, three of the most prominent in the NT are faith, hope, and love (1 Cor. 13:13; Eph. 4:1–5; 1 Thess. 1:3; cf. Rom. 5:2; Gal. 5:5; Eph. 1:15; 3:17; 6:23; Col. 1:4, 23; 1 Thess. 5:8; 1 Tim. 1:14; 6:11–12; 2 Tim. 1:13; Titus 3:15; Philem. 5; James 2:5; 1 Peter 1:21). But even though "the greatest of these is love" (1 Cor. 13:13), Paul gives to faith a special distinction within the *ordo salutis*: faith is the means by which we receive the grace of God. As we will see, Paul teaches that we are justified by faith, and by faith alone.

Faith and repentance together are often called *conversion*. Faith and repentance are gifts of God, but they are nevertheless also something we do. We choose to believe, or not to believe, to repent or not to repent. In this respect, faith and repentance differ from those elements of the *ordo salutis* that we have already considered: effectual calling and regeneration.

Let's look first at faith. As you study the Bible, notice that *faith* and *belief* are closely related. Usually the English translations use "faith" for the Greek noun *pistis*, and "believe" for the Greek verb *pisteuo*. So *believe* is the verb form of *faith*, and *faith* is the noun form of *believe*.

In this chapter, we will focus on saving faith, faith in Christ as Savior and Lord. There are, of course, other kinds of faith—faith in our friends, faith in the regularity of nature, and so on—which are similar to and different from saving faith in different ways. It is useful to know that all our actions in the world, and all our knowledge of the world, involve some kind of faith. When you get out of bed in the morning, you believe, you have faith, that the floor will be beneath your feet and will stay there. This is sometimes called *general faith*. But we will instead be talking in this chapter about a specifically biblical, theological concept: *special faith* or *saving faith*.

Definition of Saving Faith

Theologians have traditionally analyzed faith according to three elements: knowledge, belief, and trust. *Knowledge* in this context is simply a knowledge of God's revelation, either special or general (Rom. 1:32; 10:14). It is a knowledge *about* God, not a personal knowledge, or friendship, with God. Nor is it a knowledge that the revelation is true. Rather, it's simply a knowledge of what the revelation says.

Now, it is good to emphasize that faith is based on knowledge. Some people think faith is a leap in the dark, or believing something without any evidence. But it is a knowledge of the Word, and the Word provides evidence of its truth. Faith does sometimes call us to go against the evidence of our senses, as Abraham did, according to Romans 4:19–21:

> He did not weaken in faith when he considered his own body, which was as good as dead (since he was about a hundred years old), or when he considered the barrenness of Sarah's womb. No distrust made him waver concerning the promise of God, but he grew strong in his faith as he gave glory to God, fully convinced that God was able to do what he had promised.

Cf. 2 Cor. 5:5. So far as Abraham's senses were concerned, God's promise seemed to go against the evidence. God had promised a son, but both Abraham and Sarah were too old to have children. But remember that the best evidence is the word of God itself. Abraham knew that if God *told* him that he would have a child, he could rely on that. So in the most important sense, Abraham's faith was based on evidence, the highest evidence. Or as we are saying at this point, it is based on knowledge. Compare my argument in chapters 23–28.

The second element of faith in the traditional analysis is *belief* (John 3:2; Acts 26:27). That is, faith is not only knowing what God's revelation says. It is also believing that that revelation is true. This is sometimes called *assent*. Theologians have been known to say that assent is not important; in other words, it doesn't matter what you believe in your head, as long as you love God in your heart. That idea is not biblical. Scripturally, assent is necessary for true faith. Hebrews 11:6 says, "And without faith it is impossible to please him, for whoever would draw near to God must believe that he exists and that he rewards those who seek him."

But is assent *sufficient* for true faith? James 2:19 says that the devils believe that God is one, and they tremble. It is possible to assent to some of the truths of the Bible and not be saved. But is it possible to assent to *all* the truths of the Bible and to be lost? Hard question to answer. I suspect that Satan believes in all the truths of the Bible in some sense, yet he is not saved.

I think it depends somewhat on the strength of assent. That is, if you assent to the truths of Scripture, not feebly or forgetfully, but in a way that determines your behavior, thoughts, and feelings, then it seems to me that you have all that is needed for true faith. But then your faith is better described not merely as assent, but according to the third component of faith, *trust*. Trust *includes* knowledge and assent. But it is a richer concept. Satan believes quite a lot of God's revelation, maybe all of it. But he doesn't allow his knowledge of God's Word to govern his thoughts, actions, and behavior. If he did, he would plead for God's mercy and ask forgiveness. But he doesn't do that. In other words, he doesn't *trust* in God.

Trust (the Latin word is *fiducia*) is trust in Christ as Savior and Lord. We trust him as Savior to save us from sin and to give us eternal life (John 3:16). Many Scripture verses present this trust in other terms, such as receiving Christ (John 1:12), coming to him (Matt. 11:28–30; John 6:37; 7:37), drawing near to God through him (Heb. 7:25). Notice that the primary meaning of this is not believing that I am saved, but believing in Jesus, trusting him for salvation. Not only believing *that*, but believing *in*. This is what the devils can never do. They can believe abstractly that Jesus is the Savior of his people, but they cannot trust him for salvation.

The second element of trust is subjection to Christ as Lord, a willingness to obey. As James 2:14–26 says, faith must be living faith, obedient faith, faith that works, or else it is dead. "Jesus is Lord" (Rom. 10:9–10; 1 Cor. 12:3; Phil. 2:11; cf. John 20:28) is, as we've seen, the most fundamental confession of the NT people of God. And it is to be not only a confession of the mouth, but a commitment that directs all of life.

So true saving faith involves knowledge, belief, and trust in Christ. I should warn you, however, that Scripture sometimes speaks about believing, about faith, in lesser senses. For example, in John 8:31, Jesus begins a dialogue with some Jews who, says John, "believed in him." But their responses to him indicate anything but true faith. By verse 44 he tells them, "You are of your father the devil." These Jews are like the devils who give assent to certain Christian teachings, but in the end set themselves against the kingdom of God.

The triad *knowledge*, *belief*, and *trust* can be illustrated as a perspectival triangle; see fig. 41.1.

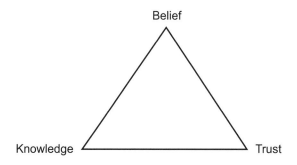

Fig. 41.1. Aspects of Saving Faith

Here I put *knowledge* as the situational perspective because in the traditional understanding, knowledge is simply the data that we are acquainted with. *Belief* is normative because it involves commitment to a right understanding of that data. And of course, *trust* is existential, since it grasps the heart.

Saving Faith Is a Gift of God

So much for the definition of saving faith. Now let's look at some more biblical teachings *about* faith. First, saving faith is a gift of God. Ephesians 2:8–9 says, "For by grace you have been saved through faith. And this is not your own doing; it is the gift of God, not a result of works, so that no one may boast" (cf. Phil. 1:29). In John 6:44, Jesus says that nobody can believe in him unless the Father draws him. No one, indeed, has any spiritual understanding without God's grace (Matt. 11:25–27; John 3:3; 1 Cor. 2:14; 1 John 5:20). Apart from grace, we repress the truth of God (Rom. 1:18, 21, 23, 25). So in Scripture, when people believe in Christ, they do it because God appointed them to eternal life (Acts 13:48) or because he opens their hearts, as with Lydia in Acts 16:14. We have seen that the gospel is a word of God that has power to save. That power works to make people believe, and it comes from God himself (1 Cor. 2:4–5, 12–16; 1 Thess. 1:5; 2 Thess. 2:14).

Faith and Good Works

Next, saving faith and good works are closely related. Paul does emphasize that we are saved by faith and not by the works of the law (Gal. 2:16). Salvation, in other words, comes through trusting Jesus, not by trying to earn your salvation through good works. But since saving faith is living, not dead (James 2:14–26), some works will be present. They don't earn you anything, but they always accompany true faith. Paul, who contrasts faith and works, understood that faith works by love (Gal. 5:6). And those who love Jesus keep his commandments (John 14:15, 21; 15:10; Titus 3:8). So works are an evidence of faith.[4]

The Role of Faith in Salvation

Now, we say that we are "saved by faith" or "justified by faith." What does that mean? Faith, after all, is something we do. We are the ones who believe, not God. But isn't salvation entirely of God? Isn't it entirely by God's grace? Or is faith the one thing *we* do, in order to merit God's forgiveness?

Certainly not. It's important to be precise about this, to see what faith does and what it doesn't do for us. First, it is not the *ground* of our salvation. The ground is what entitles us to eternal life. The sacrifice of Christ is the only ground of our salvation. His righteousness, not ours, entitles us to fellowship with God. Nothing we do is good enough to gain God's forgiveness and fellowship. Not even our faith is worthy of him.

Nor is our faith the *cause* of our salvation, for the same reason.[5] The *cause* is the power that brings us into relation with Christ. But as we've seen, this power does not

---

4. In chapter 4, I argued that God's covenants often include gracious blessings, but they always call on man to respond with a living and active faith.

5. Aristotle spoke of four senses of *cause*. Here we consider the *efficient cause*, the cause that makes the effect take place.

come from ourselves; it comes from the power of the Spirit, making us believe the Word and trust in Christ. We cannot do anything to save ourselves, to bring about our own salvation.

So what is the role of faith? Theologians struggle for words here, but Reformed theology has settled on the word *instrument*. By this we mean to say that faith, even though imperfect and unworthy, is the means (instrument = means) by which we reach out and receive God's grace. Some have compared it to an empty hand, reaching out to be filled. As the hymn "Rock of Ages" puts it, "nothing in my hand I bring; simply to thy cross I cling."

But rather than tying yourself in knots trying to understand these technical expressions, it's better to just remember that faith is trust. Jesus has died for you; that's your only hope, the only means by which you can be saved. Your faith is simply trust in him. Your trust is not going to earn you anything, but it connects you with Christ, who has earned everything for you.

Faith in the Christian Life

We've been speaking so far mainly of faith at the beginning of the Christian life. That's quite important: faith as that first moment of trust in Christ that brings us into eternal fellowship with God. But faith doesn't stop after that first moment. It persists throughout the Christian life and is important in our day-to-day relationship with God. Paul says that faith, hope, and love "abide"; they remain throughout life (1 Cor. 13:13).

We see in Hebrews 11 how the great saints of the OT acted again and again "by faith." In this passage and elsewhere, there is a contrast between faith and sight (cf. 2 Cor. 5:7). Don't take this the wrong way. Walking by faith is not walking in the dark. The heroes of faith in Hebrews 11 had a good understanding of where they were going. God's word had promised them the blessings of the covenant, and they knew they could trust those promises. As we have seen, faith is based on knowledge. But it's the knowledge of God's word, not the knowledge of the eyes. God told Abraham that he would have a son, but that didn't *appear* possible, since Abraham and Sarah were far too old. Yet he believed anyway (Rom. 4:19–21). His faith was based on knowledge of God's promise. But until Isaac was born, he didn't see the fulfillment of the promise. Similarly the saints of Hebrews 11: they didn't see the city that God had promised his people. They didn't see the fulfillment. But they continued believing, because they knew that God's promise was sure—more sure, even, than the evidence of their eyes.

So the Lord calls all believers to walk by faith. As Paul says, "the life I now live in the flesh I live by faith in the Son of God, who loved me and gave himself for me" (Gal. 2:20).

Faith, Hope, and Love

As we have seen, NT writers frequently combine *faith* with two other virtues, *hope* and *love* (1 Cor. 13:13; Eph. 4:1–5; 1 Thess. 1:3; cf. Rom. 5:2; Gal. 5:5; Eph. 1:15; 3:17; 6:23; Col. 1:4, 23; 1 Thess. 5:8; 1 Tim. 1:14; 6:11–12; 2 Tim. 1:13; Titus 3:15; Philem. 5; James

2:5; 1 Peter 1:21). Hope is not something radically different from faith, but it is a kind of faith: faith directed toward the future fulfillment of the promises of God. Since it is based on God's promises, it is not something tentative, uncertain, the way in which we usually use the word *hope* in modern life. Rather, it is firm and certain. The words *faith* and *hope* differ only in that *hope* has more of a futuristic emphasis. Or we can think of it in terms of the lordship attributes: faith is directed toward God's authority, because it focuses on the Word. Hope focuses on God's control, which will bring his words to pass in the future. But of course, you can't have faith without hope, or hope without faith.

The third and highest of the three central virtues is love. Love focuses on the third lordship attribute, God's personal presence. We can think of love as faith and hope dwelling in the heart to produce the deepest personal commitment. Love is a commitment of the whole person. God calls us to love the Lord with all our heart, soul, mind, and strength, and our neighbor as ourselves. See fig. 41.2.

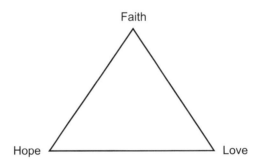

Fig. 41.2. The Three Chief Christian Virtues

So love is commitment, loyalty, or allegiance. In marriage, when we pledge our love, we at the same time pledge an exclusive loyalty to that person over against all others. Covenant love to God is the same. It is exclusive. We are to worship God alone, not in competition with other gods, or with our money, ambition, pride, or anything else.

But love is also *action*. It is doing something to show your loyalty. In marriage, if you love your wife, you will take out the trash and such like. With Jesus, if you love him, you will keep his commandments. And third, love is *affection*. When you love someone, you have *feelings* of love. You rejoice in your wife's presence, her beauty, all that she is. That's true in marriage, and it's also true with God. As John Piper has often told us,[6] God wants us to delight in him, to desire him, to find him sweet and lovely.

So love is allegiance, action, and affection. I line these up as normative, situational, and existential, respectively. See fig. 41.3.

6. John Piper, *Desiring God* (Sisters, OR: Multnomah Publishers, 1986, 2003).

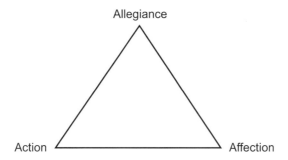

Fig. 41.3. Three Aspects of Love

The Necessity of Faith

Now, many today don't think that we must have faith in Jesus in order to be saved. Some of these are *pluralists*, who think that one can be saved through any number of religions. Others are *universalists*, who believe that everybody will be saved, whether or not he believes in Jesus. Others believe that some people who never hear of Jesus will be saved because they *would have* believed if they had had a chance. We might say that these believe in the salvation of all *potential believers*.

But Scripture is clear that nobody is saved apart from Jesus Christ. He is "the way, and the truth, and the life," so that he can say, "No one comes to the Father except through me" (John 14:6). Peter said, "And there is salvation in no one else, for there is no other name under heaven given among men by which we must be saved" (Acts 4:12; cf. John 1:12; 3:16, 18, 36). On the last day, everyone in heaven will confess that he was saved by Jesus Christ and him alone. He is the *exclusive* Lord and the *exclusive* Savior.

Does this mean that no one can be saved unless he makes a verbal confession of Christ in this life? Well, that is a different question, and it is more difficult. Reformed Christians believe, for example, that children who die in the womb, or before being able to talk, may nevertheless be saved by God's grace. As we saw earlier in this chapter, WCF 10.3 says this:

> Elect infants, dying in infancy, are regenerated, and saved by Christ, through the Spirit, who worketh when, and where, and how he pleaseth: so also are all other elect persons who are incapable of being outwardly called by the ministry of the Word.

Is this statement biblical? I believe so. Luke 1:15 says that John the Baptist would be "filled with the Holy Spirit, even from his mother's womb," and in verse 41, John, then in his mother's womb, leaped for joy in the presence of Mary the mother of Jesus. I believe also that in Luke 18:15, when Jesus laid his hands on the infants, he meant to place God's name on them and identify them with the kingdom of God.

If God saves children who are too young to make a public profession of faith, says the confession, he may save others, too, who are unable for some other reason to make a confession. We can't be dogmatic about what classes of people fall into that category. We naturally think about people who are handicapped so as to be unable to think or speak normally.

But it is certain that however wide the divine net might be, it never reaches outside the grace of Christ. When the Spirit regenerates a person, that person will eventually come to faith in Christ. And if and when he is able to profess faith in Christ, he will do so. The confession's statement should not encourage anybody to think that he can be saved without trusting in Christ. "There is no other name under heaven given among men by which we must be saved," said Peter in Acts 4:12.

So Christ alone is the name by which we may be saved. It is vitally important to proclaim the name of Christ throughout the world, so that people of all nations may believe in him.

Repentance

In the theological tradition, both repentance and faith are part of conversion. Salvation comes through faith, but also through repentance. That may sound strange, since we are accustomed to thinking of faith *alone* as the instrument of salvation. Where does repentance fit in?

Wayne Grudem defines repentance as "a heartfelt sorrow for sin, a renouncing of it, and a sincere commitment to forsake it and walk in obedience to Christ."[7] As with faith, this definition has three elements. First, as faith is based on knowledge, so repentance is based on an understanding that we have sinned and our sins are hateful to God. So the first element of repentance is *sorrow*. In Scripture, there is a difference between godly sorrow and worldly sorrow (2 Cor. 7:9–10; Heb. 12:17). Worldly sorrow is like the sorrow of Judas, who had no hope. Godly sorrow recognizes how terrible I must look to God and confesses that honestly. But it is hopeful. It recognizes sin in its true light, because it knows that God is able and ready to forgive.

Then, just as faith involves assent, belief, so repentance involves *renunciation*. In assent, I say that I believe, I agree with what God says. So renunciation goes beyond sorrow. It is agreeing with God's evaluation of my sin.

And finally, repentance is actually *turning* away from sin, just as faith is turning to Christ. As faith makes a personal commitment to Christ, repentance makes a personal commitment against sin. See fig. 41.4.

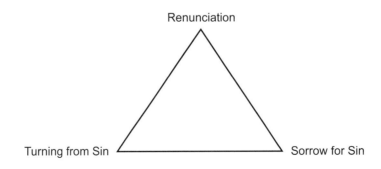

Fig. 41.4. Three Aspects of Repentance

7. *GST*, 713.

You can see, then, that repentance and faith are inseparable. They are two sides of a coin. You cannot turn from sin without turning to Christ, or vice versa. Turning from sin points you in the direction of Christ. You don't need to turn twice, only once. So faith and repentance are the same thing, viewed positively and negatively. Neither exists before the other, and neither exists without the other. The two are simultaneous and perspectival.

This means, in turn, that you cannot accept Christ as Savior without accepting him as Lord. Jesus says that if we love him, we must keep his commandments (John 14:15; many other texts cited earlier). To receive Jesus as Lord is to make a commitment to keeping his commandments. This is to say that to trust Jesus for forgiveness is to repent of sin. So it is unbiblical to say as some people do that you can accept Christ as Savior without accepting him as Lord. The Bible teaches what is called *lordship salvation*. To be saved, we call upon the Lord (Rom. 10:13); Paul has said in verse 9, "If you confess with your mouth that Jesus is Lord and believe in your heart that God raised him from the dead, you will be saved." So our salvation begins with the confession "Jesus is Lord."

Some have said that lordship salvation means that you must be sinlessly perfect, obedient to the Lord, from the first moment of your Christian life. That is not the case. It does mean that from the beginning of our life with God, we must be *committed* to Jesus' lordship (Rom. 10:9–10; 1 Cor. 12:3; Phil. 2:11).

Repentance and Salvation

Does this mean that repentance, as well as faith, is necessary for salvation? In a word, yes. But it's not as though there were two different things that are necessary. *Faith* and *repentance* are two names for the same heart-attitude. The gospel of the NT includes a demand for repentance, as many texts indicate. "Repent, for the kingdom of heaven is at hand" (Matt. 3:2; 4:17; cf. Mark 1:15; Luke 24:46–47; Acts 2:37–38; 3:19; 5:31; 17:30; 20:21; 2 Cor. 7:10; Heb. 6:1). To believe the gospel is to repent. WCF 15.3 also teaches that repentance is necessary for salvation:

> Although repentance is not to be rested in, as any satisfaction for sin, or any cause of the pardon thereof, which is the act of God's free grace in Christ; yet it is of such necessity to all sinners, that none may expect pardon without it.

This is the same thing the confession says about faith. Repentance is not the ground or cause of salvation. It does not make satisfaction for our sins; only Jesus does. It does not cause us to receive pardon; only God's grace does. But it is necessary for us, so much so that we will not receive pardon without it. Scripture cannot imagine anyone believing in Christ who wants at the same time to cling to his sin.

Repentance and the Christian Life

I said earlier that the Christian life does not just begin with faith, but continues by faith. It is a life of faith. Similarly, the Christian life is a life of repentance. When Jesus saves us, we do not instantly become sinlessly perfect, and indeed we will not become perfect until the consummation. Jesus teaches us to pray, "Forgive us our debts, as we also have forgiven our debtors" (Matt. 6:12; cf. 2 Cor. 7:10). Jesus tells those he loves to "be zealous and repent" (Rev. 3:19).

When Jesus washed the disciples' feet, Peter resisted at first, but then asked Jesus to wash everything: his head, his whole body. Jesus replied that "the one who has bathed does not need to wash, except for his feet, but is completely clean" (John 13:10). By his death for us, Jesus has cleansed us completely from sin. But as one's feet accumulate dust on the paths of Palestine, so we accumulate sin in the Christian life, and we need to ask God's forgiveness on a regular basis. This sin does not affect our eternal salvation. You needn't worry that if you die with sin you haven't repented of, you will go to hell. But if you love Jesus, your daily sin will grieve you, as it grieves him, and you will run to him, saying that you are sorry, you renounce it, and you intend to act differently. And of course, Scripture also says that when you sin against another human being, you should also go to him, express your sorrow, renounce your sin, and promise to do better (Matt. 5:23–26; 18:15–20). You may also need to make restitution, to make up for the wrong that you did to the other person.

The other person might or might not forgive you. But God will. We have his promise that "if we confess our sins, he is faithful and just to forgive us our sins and to cleanse us from all unrighteousness" (1 John 1:9). He is faithful, and also just. He is just to forgive our daily sins, because Jesus has borne the penalty for *all* our sin, past, present, and future.

We need more Christians who will lead lives of repentance. For repentance always challenges pride. If you're coming to God daily to confess to him how much you have sinned, you will find it hard to pretend that you are holier than everybody else. You'll find it hard to put on airs, to pose as the perfect Christian. When others accuse you of sin, you won't immediately jump to defend yourself, as if of course you could never do wrong and any accusation must spring from a misunderstanding. Rather, when someone accuses you of sin, you'll respond by thinking there is a high probability that the accusation is true, and you won't be embarrassed to say, "Oh, yes, I did do that, and I am terribly sorry. Will you forgive me?" If we are able to humble ourselves before God, we will be humble before men as well. And the church will be far better off if there are more of us like that.

Key Terms

Objective salvation
Subjective salvation
Regeneration
New creation
Dispositional complex
Faith

Conversion
Belief
Saving faith
Knowledge (in faith)
Belief (in faith)
Trust (in faith)
Ground (of salvation)
Cause (of salvation)
Instrument (of salvation)
Hope
Love
Allegiance
Action
Affection
Pluralism
Universalism
Repentance
Sorrow
Renunciation
Turning

Study Questions

1. Distinguish various meanings of *objective* and *subjective* in understanding the blessings of the application of redemption.

2. Summarize the teaching of the OT that bears on regeneration.

3. Explain from John 3 in what ways the new birth deals with sin in our lives.

4. What is meant by "born of water" in John 3:5?

5. Frame says that the phrase "born of water and the Spirit" in John 3:5 distinguishes "in the new birth a negative and a positive aspect." What are these? Are these aspects distinguished elsewhere in Scripture? Evaluate.

6. How do you know when someone is born again? Or can you know? Discuss.

7. How does Paul describe the new birth? Why are these terms appropriate?

8. "Believe in Jesus, and you will be born again." Is this exhortation biblically legitimate? Why or why not?

9. What is meant by the regeneration language in 1 Peter 1:23 and James 1:18? How does this concept differ from that in John 3?

10. Is it possible for infants to be regenerate? Present biblical evidence.

11. Expound the traditional definition of faith in terms of knowledge, belief, and trust. Explain Frame's triperspectival interpretation of it.

12. "Saving faith is a gift of God." Show biblical evidence.

13. What is the relation between faith and good works? Support your answer from Scripture.

14. Describe the relation of saving faith to salvation, defining the terminology used.

15. What does it mean to lead a life of faith?

16. Why are faith, hope, and love linked to one another in the NT? Expound the meaning of love.

17. Can someone be saved without faith in Christ? Give biblical grounds for your answer.

18. Can one have faith without repentance? Can one be saved without repentance? Discuss.

19. Describe a life of repentance.

Memory Verses

Isa. 57:15: For thus says the One who is high and lifted up,
   who inhabits eternity, whose name is Holy:
"I dwell in the high and holy place,
   and also with him who is of a contrite and lowly spirit,
to revive the spirit of the lowly,
   and to revive the heart of the contrite."

John 3:1–8: Now there was a man of the Pharisees named Nicodemus, a ruler of the Jews. This man came to Jesus by night and said to him, "Rabbi, we know that you are a teacher come from God, for no one can do these signs that you do unless God is with him." Jesus answered him, "Truly, truly, I say to you, unless one is born again he cannot see the kingdom of God." Nicodemus said to him, "How can a man be born when he is old? Can he enter a second time into his mother's womb and be born?" Jesus answered, "Truly, truly, I say to you, unless one is born of water and the Spirit, he cannot enter the kingdom of God. That which is born of the flesh is flesh, and that which is born of the Spirit is spirit. Do not marvel that I said to you, 'You must be born again.' The wind blows where it wishes, and you hear its sound, but you do not know where it comes from or where it goes. So it is with everyone who is born of the Spirit."

Acts 4:12: And there is salvation in no one else, for there is no other name under heaven given among men by which we must be saved.

Rom. 2:28–29: For no one is a Jew who is merely one outwardly, nor is circumcision outward and physical. But a Jew is one inwardly, and circumcision is a matter of the heart, by the Spirit, not by the letter. His praise is not from man but from God.

1 Cor. 15:10: But by the grace of God I am what I am, and his grace toward me was not in vain. On the contrary, I worked harder than any of them, though it was not I, but the grace of God that is with me.

Col. 1:27: To [the saints] God chose to make known how great among the Gentiles are the riches of the glory of this mystery, which is Christ in you, the hope of glory.

Resources for Further Study

Miller, C. John. *Repentance: A Daring Call to Real Surrender.* Fort Washington, PA: Christian Literature Crusade, 2009.

Murray, John. *MCW,* 2:167–201.

Piper, John. *Desiring God.* Sisters, OR: Multnomah Publishers, 1986, 2003.

CHAPTER 42

JUSTIFICATION AND ADOPTION

IN OUR STUDY OF THE APPLICATION of redemption (*ordo salutis*), we have so far discussed effectual calling, regeneration, faith, and repentance. In this chapter we will look at justification and adoption, and in subsequent chapters sanctification, perseverance, and glorification.

In chapter 36, I pointed out three effects of sin, effects that reflect our oft-cited triperspectival analysis; see fig. 42.1.

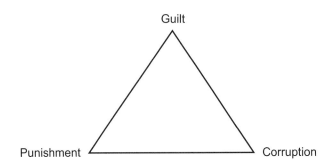

Fig. 42.1. Three Effects of Sin

Our redemption in Christ deals with all these effects of sin, and Scripture distinguishes the blessings of salvation in each of these areas: justification deals with our guilt, adoption with our punishment, and subjective salvation (regeneration, conversion, sanctification) with our corruption; see fig. 42.2.

Later in this chapter, I will address some aspects of this diagram that might occasion confusion. (1) It might appear that in this diagram justification and subjective salvation are ultimately identical, a Roman Catholic position. This is not my view, and I will indicate why. (2) It is not obvious why *adoption* should replace *punishment* in the previous diagram. I will try to clarify how adoption and punishment are related.

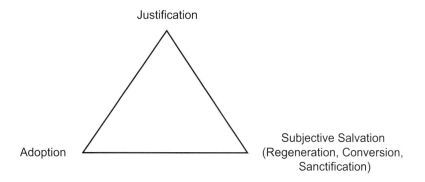

Fig. 42.2. Blessings of Salvation

Righteousness

There are three chief forms of moral predication: goodness, righteousness, and holiness. We discussed these as divine attributes in chapters 12 and 13. In the application of redemption, God restores to sinners these moral qualities, though he does not separate us entirely from sin until death or the final judgment. These qualities can be diagrammed perspectivally; see fig. 42.3.

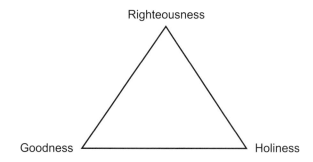

Fig. 42.3. Three Forms of Moral Predication

Good is the most general term of commendation. Applied to God, as we saw, it refers mostly to benevolence—providing benefits to others. *Righteous* comes from the legal vocabulary. To say that God is righteous is to say that his works accord with his standards of truth. (But we should not forget the redemptive use of the term, in which God saves his people by his righteous deeds; here *good* and *righteous* overlap.) *Holy* deals with God's transcendent otherness, but also with his drawing people into fellowship with him.

So *goodness* corresponds to adoption: bringing sinners into an inheritance instead of the punishment due to them. *Righteous* pertains to justification, and *holiness*, obviously, to subjective salvation, particularly sanctification.

Here I will focus first on righteousness and justification. In line with the definition of righteousness above, God's righteousness is connected with his judgment. Only God is perfectly suited to judge our lives, because only he is perfectly righteous. But of course, we are fallen and sinful, and so we can expect from God's righteousness only condemnation.

But as we saw, Scripture presents God's righteousness not only as a standard of judgment, but also as a means of salvation. God's "righteous deeds" are his acts to redeem his people from oppressors. What this means is that when God makes a gracious commitment to a covenant people, he is right to take their side. It is hard to understand in the OT context why God's righteousness sometimes condemns Israel and sometimes supports and rescues Israel. God repeatedly tells his people that he will surely condemn their sins, yet he also holds out hope that he will fulfill the promises of salvation made to Adam, Abraham, and David. Only in Christ does the mystery find resolution. He endures God's righteous condemnation, so that his people may be righteous for his sake. That is the essence of justification.

The Nature of Justification

Now let us focus on the doctrine of justification. Note the definition from WLC 70:

> Justification is an act of God's free grace unto sinners, in which he pardoneth all their sins, accepteth and accounteth their persons righteous in his sight; not for any thing wrought in them, or done by them, but only for the perfect obedience and full satisfaction of Christ, by God imputed to them, and received by faith alone.

A Legal Declaration

The language here is *forensic*, that is, the language of a law court. In that court God is the Judge, and we are on trial for our sins—both the sin of Adam and the sins that we have committed in this life. The wages of sin is death, so clearly we deserve to die. But Jesus has taken that death penalty in our place. So the divine Judge turns to us and pronounces us not guilty. Indeed, he even goes beyond that, as a secular judge would never do, and says that we are positively righteous because of Christ. That is our justification.

It is important to distinguish between justification and sanctification, though Roman Catholic theology makes them overlap. In justification, God *declares* us righteous; in sanctification, he *makes* us righteous. Justification is forensic. It is about our legal status, not our inner character. For the important thing is that in justification God justifies the *ungodly*, those who by their inner character are wicked. Contrary to Roman Catholicism, God does not justify us because he likes our inner character, even because he likes what he himself has done within us (our "infused" righteousness). He justifies us only because of Christ.

In Scripture, many passages indicate the forensic nature of justification. In Deuteronomy 25:1, judges in Israel are to justify the righteous and condemn the wicked.

Clearly, this means that judges are to *declare* the innocence of the righteous and the wickedness of the wicked. It cannot mean that the judges are to *make* people righteous or wicked. In Luke 7:29, we read that some people "declared God just," literally, "justified God" (as in the KJV), because of Jesus' words. Clearly, that cannot mean that the people *made* God just. "Declared God just" is the correct translation.

In Romans 4:5, God "justifies the ungodly" apart from works. Since it is apart from works, *justify* cannot mean "to make righteous," only "to declare righteous." In Romans 8:33–34 and other passages, the word *justify* is the opposite of *condemn*. But *condemn* means "to declare someone guilty," not "to make the person guilty." Thus, it makes sense to take *justify* to mean "*declare* righteous."

This is the consistent meaning of *justify* throughout Paul's writings, when he is talking about the justification of sinners unto salvation (see Rom. 3:20, 26, 28; 5:1; 8:30; 10:4, 10; Gal. 2:15; 3:24).

A Constitutive Declaration

Someone might object that a *mere* declaration is not enough. Obviously, if a judge were to declare a defendant not guilty, when he was really guilty, that would not be just. We saw earlier the admonition to judges in Deuteronomy 25:1: a judge is to justify those who are really righteous and condemn those who are really wicked. Some have objected that the Protestant doctrine of justification violates this principle: God looks at wicked people and falsely declares them to be righteous.

But this is to forget the work of Christ. Because Christ died in our place, God's declaration is true. It is not a legal fiction or a false judgment. Jesus really did pay the complete penalty for sin. So in him we really are innocent and righteous, because he is innocent and righteous. So John Murray[1] argued that justification is not a *mere* declaration, but a declaration that "constitutes" a new legal status, a "constitutive declaration," as he put it. He took the phrase "made righteous" in Romans 5:19 to mean "constituted righteous."

That is fine, but the word *constitute* might confuse some people; it's very close to the word *make*. But we're not talking about making righteous here in the sense of sanctification. Even when we talk about God's *constituting* us righteous, we're still in the legal, or forensic, sphere. To "constitute righteous" means that God is constituting a new *legal* status for us. So remember that this constitutive declaration is still forensic, still in the legal, courtroom sphere. It is not the same thing as sanctification. It does not renew us from within. It rather provides us a new legal position: righteous in Christ.

The elements of this declaration, of justification, are the forgiveness of sins and the imputation of Christ's righteousness to us. Because of Christ, God takes our sins away from us, so that they may never again rise to condemn us (Pss. 103:3; 130:4; Rom. 4:6–8; 8:1, 33–34; Eph. 1:7; 4:32; 1 John 1:9). God removes our transgressions "as far as the east is from the west," as Psalm 103:12 puts it.

---

1. *MCW*, 2:213–15.

He also imputes Christ's righteousness (Isa. 61:10; Rom. 3:21–22; 4:3; 5:19; 1 Cor. 1:30; 2 Cor. 5:21). This means not only that he removes our sins, but that he positively adds to us the perfect righteousness of Christ. So our legal status is not just not-guilty, not neutral, but righteous. If you think of your legal status numerically, sin had plunged you deep into negative numbers. God's forgiveness brought you back up to zero. But the righteousness of Christ took you far above zero in the eyes of God.

Here is what is often called a *double imputation*.[2] God imputes our sins to Christ and imputes his righteousness to us. This follows from the doctrine we discussed in chapter 38, that the atonement is a substitutionary sacrifice. Christ receives the punishment for our sins, and we receive the blessings of his righteousness. This is also an implication of our union with Christ (also discussed in chapter 38): we become the righteousness of God "in him."

Writers[3] have often objected to the idea of imputation, arguing that guilt and righteousness are not the sorts of things that can be transferred from one person to another, even by God. How this can happen is certainly a mystery. It could never happen in any human court, that the guilt or innocence of one defendant could be transferred to another. But marvelously, this is precisely what happens in God's economy. It is clearly the teaching of Scripture, and in Scripture it is an aspect of our union with Christ. Romans 5:12–21[4] makes it clear that God imputed Adam's sin to all his descendants, parallel to his grace in imputing the righteousness of Christ to his people. Verse 19 reads:

> For as by the one man's disobedience the many were made sinners, so by the one man's obedience the many will be made righteous.[5]

To reject the idea of divine imputation is to confuse the whole biblical account of sin and salvation. Illustrations and parallels in other areas of human life can help us better to understand and appreciate this doctrine. See chapter 36 for some considerations that clarify God's imputation of Adam's sin. But none of the illustrations or parallels is perfect. In the end, our justification is mysterious, even miraculous. We must be ready to see God as Lord of the moral universe as well as the physical.

The Ground of Justification

The *ground* of justification is the basis on which we are justified. It answers the question: why should God declare me to be just? The answer is, simply: Christ. In his work on the cross, his people are united to him, and God sees us as righteous in him. Although we often say that justification is "by faith," faith is not the ground of

---

2. In the overall biblical doctrine there are, of course, three imputations: of Adam's sin to us (Rom. 5:1–12; cf. chapter 36), of our sins to Christ, and of Christ's righteousness to us.

3. Such as N. T. Wright, whose general position I will consider later in this chapter.

4. Review the exposition of this passage in chapter 36.

5. The two instances of "made" represent the Greek *kathistemi*, which Murray understands to mean "constitute." It is not the term generally translated "impute," but in context it clearly amounts to what we have called a constitutive declaration, God's imputation of a new legal standing.

justification. It has another role that I will mention below. God does not declare us righteous because of our faith. Our faith is always impure, imperfect. Only Christ is perfect, and perfectly righteous.

Theologians have often distinguished between Christ's active and passive obedience (cf. chapter 38). His passive obedience is his suffering and death for us. His active obedience is his perfect life. So often when theologians talk about justification, they say that Christ's passive obedience brings us the forgiveness of sins; his active obedience is the basis for God's declaring us positively righteous. For God imputes Christ's righteousness to us, making us righteous in him.

There is some controversy in Protestant circles now about the imputation to us of Christ's active obedience, even among writers who accept the imputation of his passive obedience, his death. We do not have space to enter this controversy in detail. But it seems obvious to me that (1) God declares us righteous "in him," that is, by union with Christ (2 Cor. 5:21). Jesus expresses his righteous character in all that he does, both in his perfect life and in his atoning death. It is that righteous character, that sinlessness, that is ours by our union with him, not merely its passive expression. (2) Jesus' perfect life is a necessary aspect of his atonement. In the OT, sacrificial animals had to be "without blemish" (Ex. 12:5). The NT often speaks of Jesus as a lamb. As a sacrifice he, too, had to be without blemish, and in a man that implies sinlessness. First Peter 1:19 speaks of Jesus as "a lamb without blemish or spot." Cf. Heb. 9:14. Since Jesus' atonement is substitutionary, God imputes to us the sinlessness of Jesus' life as a whole. (3) Our union with Christ is a union both in his death and in his resurrection. When Jesus died for us, we died to sin; when he rose from the dead, we rose with him to new life (Rom. 6:1–14). The resurrection life of Christ is (among many other things) a continuation and fulfillment of the sinless life that he lived on earth.

The Instrument of Justification

I have said that although justification is "by faith alone," faith is not the ground of justification; only Christ is that. What role, then, is played by faith? Faith is what *receives* the grace of God in Christ. So theologians have described its role as *instrumental*. Faith claims no merit for itself; it makes no claim to deserve the gift of God's righteousness. It confesses that only Christ can save, and only his righteousness can justify.

This is the main difference between Protestant and Roman Catholic views of justification. For Roman Catholicism, justification is primarily God's making us righteous, not declaring us righteous. It is not a consistently forensic concept, but overlaps sanctification. So on the Roman view, God makes us righteous within and declares us to be righteous on the basis of this "infused righteousness." That infused righteousness, which includes both faith and works, merits eternal life. This means, then, that salvation is based partly on our works. The consequence, then, is that we cannot be assured of our salvation in this life, because we are never sure whether our works have been sufficient.

This kind of anxiety over salvation led to the Protestant Reformation. Martin Luther, first of the Protestant Reformers, while he was a priest in the Roman Catholic Church, was in agony over whether he had enough good works to stand before God's throne on the judgment day. When he read Romans 1:16–17, he wondered how the righteousness of God could be *gospel*, "good news." Paul says there that the gospel, the good news, reveals the righteousness of God. But how, Luther asked, can that be good news, since God's righteousness is precisely what condemns us?

But as he thought some more about this passage, it occurred to him that the "righteousness" here is not the righteousness that condemns, but the righteousness that God offers to us in Christ as a free gift. Understood that way, the righteousness of God really is good news. For by counting us righteous in Christ, God forgives our sins and brings us irrevocably into fellowship with him.

One more important point: Justification is by faith apart from works. We touched on this in chapter 41 when we discussed saving faith, but the point cannot be left out of the discussion of justification here. Even though saving faith is a faith that works, Paul regularly contrasts faith with works in justification. Justification is by faith apart from works, apart from works of the law, without works (Rom. 3:27–28; 4:5–6; 9:32; Gal. 2:16; 3:2, 5; Eph. 2:8–9).

How can Paul draw such a contrast, when faith and works elsewhere appear inseparable? We saw in James 2 that faith without works is dead. Paul says the same thing in Galatians 5:6, where he speaks of faith working through love. Indeed, justification is by a living faith, not a dead faith, a faith that works, rather than a mere profession. But faith does not justify because of its connection with works. It justifies because its nature is to trust, in this case to trust the grace of God in Christ. That trust motivates us to please God and therefore to do good works. Since God has saved from sin, this is the only appropriate response. Yet salvation is not through the works, but through the trust that motivates them. The point is that salvation is a free gift (Eph. 2:8). We cannot work for it, but only *trust* the One who gives it. Faith is central because faith is *trust*. But of course, after we receive that gift, it is important for us to show our gratefulness by our actions, and that is what we want to do.

James 2:24, which even speaks of justification by works, tells us that a faith without works is not saving faith, not true faith. So works are evidence of a true, saving faith.

Justification and Sanctification

Since justification is by faith apart from works, it is distinct from sanctification, which, as we will see in the following chapter, is the development of good works in the believer. That fact raises a problem with my triangular diagram of justification, adoption, and sanctification,[6] and I must address that problem to prevent misunderstandings.

In some of my triangular diagrams, each corner embraces the others. For example, in fig. 42.4 (expounded in chapter 2)—

6. In what follows, I will abbreviate *subjective salvation* by the term *sanctification*.

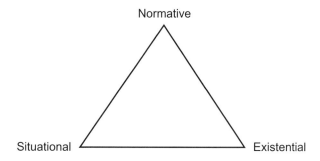

Fig. 42.4. Three Perspectives on Knowledge

—the normative includes the situational and existential, and they include it. So ultimately the three perspectives are identical. But in the triad *justification, adoption, sanctification*, it seems not to be the case that each corner includes the other two. Indeed, it would seem that to take it that way would be to invite doctrinal errors. In Protestant theology (which I affirm), for example, sanctification is not identical with justification, nor is adoption. Indeed, there are grave dangers in confusing justification with sanctification, dangers that I will describe later in this chapter.

Why, then, does this triad differ from some of the others I have presented? The key point is that in dealing with these triangles, it is important to note what the whole triangle represents. In the triad *normative, situational, existential*, the whole triangle represents all of reality. So each corner of it also deals with all of reality, and each is ultimately identical with the others. But in the triad *justification, adoption, sanctification*, the whole triangle does not deal with all of reality. Rather, just as the triad *guilt, punishment, corruption* dealt with the effects of sin, so the present triad *justification, adoption, sanctification* deals with the effects of redemption. Guilt, punishment, and corruption are parts, aspects, of the devastation wrought by sin. Similarly, justification, adoption, and sanctification are aspects of the renewal accomplished by our redemption in union with Christ.

Now, this triad indicates a very close union among its three aspects. Everyone united to Christ by faith is justified, adopted, and sanctified. So there is nobody who is justified but not adopted, or adopted but not sanctified. Justification is not the same thing as sanctification. But justification without sanctification is unthinkable. A justified person will certainly be sanctified in some ways and in some degree. In that sense, sanctification is the inevitable context of justification.

The best language, perhaps, is that justification, adoption, and subjective salvation are "inseparable." They are not synonymous, nor is one the ground of the other. But they are never found apart, and each proves the presence of the others. The point is this: that the redeemed man is justified, adopted, and sanctified. Together, these three qualities describe the blessedness of the believer.

We often say in theology that you cannot understand a concept unless you understand its context. Adoption and sanctification serve as a context for justification, just as the tune of a hymn serves as a context for its words. Although the words are distinct from the tune, even to the extent that the tune could appear with different words and the words with a different tune, you cannot sing a particular hymn unless you express the two together. So it is not meaningful to say that someone is justified in a biblical sense if he is not in other respects a believer (justification is by faith), that is, if he is not adopted and sanctified.

The triangular diagram means, therefore, in this case that justification, adoption, and sanctification form a total context for one another. And in that sense, to use a metaphor that I have used in other cases, each "embraces" the other two. True justification is a justification *with* adoption and sanctification, not without them. And the whole triangle represents the blessings of the saved person.

This is the main point of James 2:14–26:

> What good is it, my brothers, if someone says he has faith but does not have works? Can that faith save him? If a brother or sister is poorly clothed and lacking in daily food, and one of you says to them, "Go in peace, be warmed and filled," without giving them the things needed for the body, what good is that? So also faith by itself, if it does not have works, is dead.
>
> But someone will say, "You have faith and I have works." Show me your faith apart from your works, and I will show you my faith by my works. You believe that God is one; you do well. Even the demons believe—and shudder! Do you want to be shown, you foolish person, that faith apart from works is useless? Was not Abraham our father justified by works when he offered up his son Isaac on the altar? You see that faith was active along with his works, and faith was completed by his works; and the Scripture was fulfilled that says, "Abraham believed God, and it was counted to him as righteousness"—and he was called a friend of God. You see that a person is justified by works and not by faith alone. And in the same way was not also Rahab the prostitute justified by works when she received the messengers and sent them out by another way? For as the body apart from the spirit is dead, so also faith apart from works is dead.

Although James says that Abraham was "justified by works" (v. 21) when he offered his son on the altar, he is not contradicting Paul, who says that we are justified apart from works (Rom. 3:28). James says that a faith that justifies is a living, working faith, not a dead faith (vv. 17, 26). Works are what *show* (v. 18) that faith is genuine.

Recent Controversy over Justification

The New Perspective on Paul

Several NT scholars, including Krister Stendahl, E. P. Sanders, James D. G. Dunn, and N. T. Wright, have developed what has become known as the *New Perspective on Paul*. Although this viewpoint has more complications than I can discuss here, it is important that we consider its bearing on justification. The main contention of the

New Perspective is that when he speaks of justification Paul is not primarily interested in how a sinner can get right with God, but rather in the conditions for belonging to God's covenant community. On this view, Paul is primarily a champion of Gentile membership in the kingdom of God through Christ. Paul is not criticizing his fellow Jews because of their attempts to save themselves by their works, as Luther thought. Rather, he is criticizing them for being exclusive, for rejecting religious fellowship with Gentiles. These Jews expected the Gentiles to become Jews, through circumcision and the Jewish law, before they could be accepted as followers of Christ. On this basis, to be "justified" is to be a member of the covenant community in good standing. As covenant membership, justification is not by works of the law (i.e., circumcision and the Jewish boundary markers) but by faith. So justification is not primarily "soterio-logical," but "ecclesiastical."

I disagree with this view.[7] (1) The Greek lexicons do not define *dikaiosune, righteousness*, as "membership in a group," even as "membership in a covenant community." On the contrary, righteousness has to do with one's standing before God as Judge. (2) Romans 1–5, the main context of Paul's chief discussion of justification, is precisely an account of how human beings (both Gentiles and Jews) have sinned against God and the means of their forgiveness. Only through Christ does God declare sinners to be righteous, and that declaration is their justification. In Romans 1:18–32, Paul shows how deeply the Gentiles have fallen into sin. In 2:1–3:8, he indicates that the same is true of the Jews, regardless of their boasts of moral superiority. His conclusion is in 3:10–20: "None is righteous, no, not one." But God's grace astonishes:

> But now the righteousness of God has been manifested apart from the law, although the Law and the Prophets bear witness to it—the righteousness of God through faith in Jesus Christ for all who believe. For there is no distinction: for all have sinned and fall short of the glory of God, and are justified by his grace as a gift, through the redemption that is in Christ Jesus, whom God put forward as a propitiation by his blood, to be received by faith. This was to show God's righteousness, because in his divine forbearance he had passed over former sins. It was to show his righteousness at the present time, so that he might be just and the justifier of the one who has faith in Jesus. (Rom. 3:21–26)

The New Perspective scholars are right to emphasize Paul's concern with the unity between Jews and Gentiles in the church of Jesus Christ. But not everything in Paul's writing can be assimilated to that theme. I believe that the New Perspective fails to deal adequately with a number of Pauline passages, such as Romans 4:4–5; 11:6; Ephesians 2:8–10; Philippians 3:9, which make it plain that Paul rejects not only legal barriers between Jew and Gentile, but also all attempts of people to save themselves by

---

7. The following discussion draws heavily on Charles E. Hill's excellent article "N. T. Wright on Justification," *Third Millennium Magazine Online* 3, 22 (May 28–June 2, 2001), available at http://www.thirdmill.org/files /english/html/nt/NT.h.Hill.Wright.html. I take full responsibility for the formulation here.

their works. For Paul, justification is not a person's covenant membership. It is God's declaration that the person is righteous for the sake of Jesus Christ. Therefore, it is God's imputation to us of Christ's righteousness.[8]

Norman Shepherd

Norman Shepherd[9] taught systematic theology at Westminster Theological Seminary (Philadelphia) from 1963 to 1981, and after that served two pastorates in the Christian Reformed Church. After his retirement in 1998, he wrote two books[10] and several articles that touch on the doctrine of justification. Both his earlier and later writings on this subject have aroused considerable controversy in Presbyterian and Reformed circles. This controversy concerns the following emphases in his work:

1. He believes, on the basis of James 2:14–26, that saving faith, that is, justifying faith, is a faith that works. In this connection, he sometimes said that works are "necessary" to justification. This choice of words, I think, was not wise. Some thought Shepherd was saying that works are the efficient (or meritorious) cause of justification. This is not what he meant to say, and the word *necessary* does not need to be taken that way. Indeed, as we will see, Shepherd denies that merit has anything to do with our salvation. His assertion, rather, was based on simple logic: (a) Without faith, no justification, since justification is by faith. (b) Without works, no faith. (c) Therefore, without works, no justification. The term *necessary* here refers simply to this logical relation, not to efficient or meritorious causality. Shepherd is saying that a living faith is a *necessary condition* of justification, not its ground, efficient cause, or meritorious wage. Shepherd's choice of words may not have been the best, but his idea is quite commonplace in Reformed theology: it's faith alone that saves, but the faith that saves is never alone.

2. He denies that merit (either that of Jesus or of the believer) plays any role in salvation. This belief is controversial, because we are familiar with the formula "salvation is by Jesus' merit, not ours." *Merit*, as Shepherd understands it, is a means of earning reward. Jesus earned salvation for his people by the merits of his life, and therefore we need not try to earn our way, to seek merit of our own. But Shepherd questions this formula. He does not believe that God assigned human beings the task of earning anything. Rather, God forbade Adam from eating a particular fruit. Abstaining from the fruit was not a job by which Adam could earn a reward; rather, it was simple obedience. Similarly, when Jesus became man, his charge from the Father was not to do a certain number of good works to earn favor, but simply to obey. I agree with Shepherd that salvation in the Bible is not a matter of earning anything, not a quasi-commercial transaction.[11] But if we define *merit* simply as "just deserts," it may play a

8. Wright is critical of the very idea of imputed righteousness, as I indicated earlier in the chapter.

9. Full disclosure: Shepherd was my senior colleague when I taught at Westminster/Philadelphia from 1968–80. He has been a good friend to me ever since. But as the reader will see, I do not agree with all of his views.

10. Norman Shepherd, *The Call of Grace: How the Covenant Illuminates Salvation and Evangelism* (Phillipsburg, NJ: P&R Publishing, 2000); *The Way of Righteousness* (La Grange, CA: Kerygma Press, 2009).

11. I've discussed that issue in chapter 4 of this book.

role. Certainly Jesus *deserved* the honor he gained through his cross and resurrection. That honor was rightly his. And the honor that believers receive "in" Christ is rightly theirs,[12] because it is rightly his.

3. Shepherd also came to deny that Jesus' "active" obedience is imputed to the believer in justification.[13] In his view, we are justified only by his death and resurrection, not by his righteous incarnate life. Shepherd regards the imputation of Christ's active obedience as an addition to Scripture and as an incentive to merit-based soteriology (point 2 above). On this matter I disagree. As I explained in chapter 38, I believe that we are saved "in" Christ, and therefore by union with his righteous character, displayed in all his works. That character is constituted by everything in his nature and all his works, including his *active righteousness*. Compare my treatment of this question earlier in this chapter in the section "The Ground of Justification."

Shepherd's critics, in my view, responded more to the *sound* of what he said than to the actual content of his assertions. In points 1 and 2, Shepherd questioned certain standard ways in which Protestants have traditionally presented the doctrine of justification. But I think these two assertions of Shepherd reflected remarkable insight into the teaching of Scripture. In point 3 I think he was simply wrong, but not wrong to such an extent as to question any fundamentals of the Reformed system of doctrine. The Reformed confessions have not been unanimous on this issue. Shepherd appeals to the earlier confessions, those of the sixteenth century. So neither position should be made a test of Reformed orthodoxy.

Adoption

Now let us consider the doctrine of adoption. WLC 74 defines it thus:

> Adoption is an act of the free grace of God, in and for his only Son Jesus Christ, whereby all those that are justified are received into the number of his children, have his name put upon them, the Spirit of his Son given to them, are under his fatherly care and dispensations, admitted to all the liberties and privileges of the sons of God, made heirs of all the promises, and fellow heirs with Christ in glory.

In adoption, God places us in his family. So this doctrine fulfills the theme of the family of God that pervades Scripture. I summarized this theme in chapter 6, noting the biblical emphasis on the redeemed as God's royal family under his fatherhood.

It may be asked why in my triangular diagrams at the beginning of the chapter *adoption* serves as the remedy for *punishment*. Recall that in our discussion of sin in chapter 36, *punishment* refers initially to woman's pain in childbearing (Gen. 3:16) and

---

12. This statement is implicit in the biblical teaching we considered earlier, that justification "constitutes" our legal standing before God as righteous.

13. See Norman Shepherd, "The Imputation of Active Obedience," in *A Faith That Is Never Alone*, ed. P. Andrew Sandlin (La Grange, CA: Kerygma Press, 2007), 249–78. He argues his view both from Scripture and from the earlier generation of Reformed theologians and confessions.

man's toil in securing food (Gen. 3:17–19). But of course, these curses represent all the pain and suffering of human life, culminating in physical death (v. 19; cf. 2:17). What this entails is that the creation, man's "situation," resists his efforts to fulfill the cultural mandate of Genesis 1:28.

Now, the blessing of adoption, our inheritance, places the believer into a new situation.[14] What this means ultimately is a new family. Believers become sons and daughters of God, not of Satan. And that new family relation to God implies a new relation to the entire creation. The creation, says Paul, looks forward to being "set free from its bondage to corruption" and thus obtaining "the freedom of the glory of the children of God" (Rom. 8:21). The creation's "groaning" for this fulfillment (v. 22) parallels our inward groaning as "we wait eagerly for adoption as sons" (v. 23).

Of course, the believer's adoption exists from the beginning of his regenerate life. But as with many of God's other blessings, there is in adoption an *already* and a *not yet*. Although we are already sons and daughters of God, we await a higher fulfillment of our adoption. And that fulfillment is what the creation also awaits. So adoption should be understood in the context of the transformation of man's environment and thus the reversal of his punishment as the work of Christ overcomes all the forces of death on the earth.

So adoption meets our need for a new family. The Bible teaches that because of sin we are children of the devil (John 8:41–44; cf. Eph. 2:2–3; 5:6). By faith, Jesus gives us authority to become sons (and daughters) of God (John 1:12; Rom. 8:14–17; Gal. 3:23–26; 4:28, 31; 1 Peter 3:6; 1 John 3:1–2). In Christ, God loves us so much that we become his people, his nation, his family (1 John 3:1). So Jesus taught his disciples to pray, "Our Father in heaven" (Matt. 6:9). And he also taught them to speak intimately with God, using the Aramaic term *Abba*, a child's name for his father, like our word *Daddy* (Mark 14:36; Rom. 8:15; Gal. 4:4–7). We would not dare speak to God with such familiarity, except that Jesus has given us permission.

Jesus himself is *the* Son of God, as we saw in chapter 21. He has a unique sonship, a relation to God that we cannot attain. To say that he is the Son is to designate his position in the Holy Trinity. So his sonship is higher than ours, and it is the source of ours, for only those who receive Christ (John 1:12) gain the authority to be sons of God. In John 20:17, Jesus distinguishes his sonship from ours when he says to Mary, "Do not cling to me, for I have not yet ascended to the Father; but go to my brothers and say to them, 'I am ascending to my Father and your Father, to my God and your God.'" Jesus never describes God as "our" Father in a way that equalizes the relationship between Jesus' sonship and ours. Nevertheless, we are sons of God because God

---

14. Alert readers might note that in chapters 4–6 I put *family of God* as the existential perspective, contrasted with *God's covenants* (normative) and *kingdom of God* (situational). So why should family be existential in chapter 6, but situational here? Well, the beauty of perspectives is that each perspective is integrated with the others, and that each plays different roles in different contexts. *Family*, like *covenant* and *kingdom*, has normative and situational aspects as well as existential. Family is our situation, and it is also our subjective comfort. In chapter 6 I made use of its existential aspects, and here I focus on its situational aspects.

sees us in Christ, in his beloved Son. So we share the blessings that the Father gives to his unique Son, Jesus.

The Holy Spirit is also important to our adoption. He witnesses in our hearts that we are the sons of God (Rom. 8:15–16).

Our sonship is both present and future. We are God's sons here and now (1 John 3:2), but the creation awaits the full manifestation of that sonship (Rom. 8:23). We have grasped only the beginning of what it means to be a son or daughter of God.

Like saving faith and justification, adoption is demonstrated by good works. It is through our good works that we glorify our Father in heaven (Matt. 5:16; cf. Phil. 2:15; 1 John 3:10).

Adoption relates us not only to God, but also to one another. We are sons and daughters of God, and therefore brothers and sisters of one another. Even Jesus is our brother, according to Hebrews 2:17. We are to love our brothers and sisters as Jesus loved us.

Relation of Adoption to Other Doctrines

Regeneration

We may have questions about the relation of adoption to regeneration, for they both refer to family. Regeneration is about birth, and in the Bible birth happens in a family. Adoption, too, tells how we enter God's family. But the two doctrines are not the same. Regeneration describes natural descent, while adoption describes admission to a family that we were *not* born into. So we have two different metaphors here, each making a somewhat different point. Regeneration tells us that our spiritual life comes from God. Adoption emphasizes that God admits us into a family that we did not originally belong to. Both metaphors are biblical, though at first glance they might seem to point in opposite directions.

The two doctrines also differ in this way: in regeneration, God grants new life; in adoption, God grants new privileges, a new inheritance.

Faith

Adoption, like justification, is through faith (John 1:12; Gal. 3:23–26). We are not entitled to the privileges of sonship by our efforts, but we receive them as a gift, reaching out with the empty hands of faith.

Justification

Justification gives us a new legal standing. Adoption gives us the additional privileges of inheritance. So adoption carries us beyond justification. Justification is amazing and wonderful, but adoption is the apex, the high point, in our relationship with God. So the doctrine of adoption deserves far more emphasis in our preaching and theological work than it has usually received.

Privileges of Adoption

Let us, then, consider the privileges of adoption. These can be summed up in the word *inheritance*. First, there is sonship itself, as distinguished from slavery (Gal. 4:7).

We are not merely slaves in God's household, though we are slaves, servants, from one point of view. We are bound to serve the Lord. But we are not *mere* slaves. We are sons of God.

Sonship also describes a kind of maturity in our relation to God. Even a son, when he is a child, is very much like a slave, for he knows very little and must be taught, often through harsh discipline. Paul describes in that way the old covenant of the Jewish people under Moses. It was a time when they were sons, but children. Jesus' coming brings us to maturity and freedom.

Mature sonship gives us new freedom and confidence in prayer (Matt. 6:9). The Jews of the old covenant also prayed to God, but they feared coming into the most intimate sphere of God's presence, and indeed they were barred from it by temple curtains and many regulations. But when Christ died, the veil of the temple was torn in two. Now there is no barrier between ourselves and the greatest intimacy with God that a human being can enjoy. Now we enter boldly into the Most Holy Place, praising our Father and asking him for what we need. We can count on his compassion and care. Just as a father shows compassion to his children, so the Lord shows compassion to those who fear him (Ps. 103:13; Matt. 6:32).

There is still discipline in our family. The writer to the Hebrews says that any father chastens his children (Heb. 12:5–10). He adds that our father's discipline is one proof that we are real sons and daughters, not illegitimate children.

And just as adoption gives us a new vertical relationship to God, it also gives us new horizontal relationships to one another, to the brothers and sisters in the family (1 Tim. 5:1–2).

Among other things, our brothers and sisters are God's gifts to us, and we receive God's gifts to build them up. That includes the great gift of the Holy Spirit himself, and the gifts that the Spirit gives to each of us (Matt. 7:11; Luke 11:13; Rom. 8:14).

Adoption also gives us a forward-looking vision. In this world, we look forward to the privilege of suffering with Jesus, which according to Paul is part of our sonship (Rom. 8:17). But then, of course, comes the fullness of privilege, the final inheritance (Gal. 4:7; 1 Peter 1:4), the privilege of reigning with Christ over the entire world (Rev. 2:26–27; 3:21). All things are ours, Paul tells us in 1 Corinthians 3:21. We will judge angels (1 Cor. 6:3). That fullness of inheritance is so great that Paul in Romans 8:23 refers to it as another adoption, one that we await in the future. That shouldn't surprise you. The NT teaches often that salvation is complete in Christ, yet the full unfolding of it is yet to come. That is sometimes called the "paradox of the *already* and the *not yet.*" Jesus' atonement has taken away the guilt of our sin, but it is now taking away the power of sin, and one day it will take away the very presence of sin. So our salvation is *already*, but *not yet*. Justification is ours already, but one day we will be pronounced righteous before the Father's throne. So there is a past justification and a future justification. Similarly for adoption. When we believe in Christ, we become members of his family. But the fullness of our privileges as sons and daughters remains for the future. Adoption, too, is past and future.

Christian believers are usually not highly regarded in this world. But our ultimate destiny is a life of such great dignity and authority that we can hardly imagine it now. So even the creation groans, awaiting the manifestation of the sons of God: that's you and me. In Romans 8, Paul says this about our adoption past and future, with some references also to justification:

> For the creation waits with eager longing for the revealing of the sons of God. For the creation was subjected to futility, not willingly, but because of him who subjected it, in hope that the creation itself will be set free from its bondage to corruption and obtain the freedom of the glory of the children of God. For we know that the whole creation has been groaning together in the pains of childbirth until now. And not only the creation, but we ourselves, who have the firstfruits of the Spirit, groan inwardly as we wait eagerly for adoption as sons, the redemption of our bodies. For in this hope we were saved. Now hope that is seen is not hope. For who hopes for what he sees? But if we hope for what we do not see, we wait for it with patience.
>
> Likewise the Spirit helps us in our weakness. For we do not know what to pray for as we ought, but the Spirit himself intercedes for us with groanings too deep for words. And he who searches hearts knows what is the mind of the Spirit, because the Spirit intercedes for the saints according to the will of God. And we know that for those who love God all things work together for good, for those who are called according to his purpose. For those whom he foreknew he also predestined to be conformed to the image of his Son, in order that he might be the firstborn among many brothers. And those whom he predestined he also called, and those whom he called he also justified, and those whom he justified he also glorified.
>
> What then shall we say to these things? If God is for us, who can be against us? He who did not spare his own Son but gave him up for us all, how will he not also with him graciously give us all things? Who shall bring any charge against God's elect? It is God who justifies. Who is to condemn? Christ Jesus is the one who died—more than that, who was raised—who is at the right hand of God, who indeed is interceding for us. Who shall separate us from the love of Christ? Shall tribulation, or distress, or persecution, or famine, or nakedness, or danger, or sword? As it is written,
>
> "For your sake we are being killed all the day long;
>   we are regarded as sheep to be slaughtered."
>
> No, in all these things we are more than conquerors through him who loved us. For I am sure that neither death nor life, nor angels nor rulers, nor things present nor things to come, nor powers, nor height nor depth, nor anything else in all creation, will be able to separate us from the love of God in Christ Jesus our Lord. (Rom. 8:19–39)

That's the way our God treats his sons and daughters.

Adoption is really a wonderful teaching of God's Word. Again, I think it gets neglected in our preaching and teaching. We tend to focus on justification because of the importance of that doctrine in the Reformation, and on sanctification because it describes the progress of salvation in our hearts in a practical way, day by day. But adoption, belonging to God's family, is the height of our privilege as God's people, and the beginning of our heavenly reward. It is the foundation of all our relationships with God and one another. God's name is our family name, the name by which we will be known through all eternity.

Key Terms

Righteousness
Justification
Forensic
Constitutive declaration
Imputation
Double imputation
Ground
Instrument
Active obedience
Passive obedience
Infused righteousness
New Perspective on Paul
Norman Shepherd
Adoption
Inheritance

Study Questions

1. Review the nature of God's righteousness. Why does Frame find the relationship between its two aspects mysterious? How does Christ's work address that mystery?
2. Explain Frame's triangular diagram of justification, adoption, and subjective salvation. Show how it corresponds to the triangle representing the effects of sin.
3. Why is it important to distinguish between justification and sanctification?
4. Does *justify* in Scripture mean "declare righteous" or "make righteous"? Cite references.
5. Is justification a *mere* declaration? What problems might arise in such a view? What more is needed?
6. "So our legal status is not just not-guilty, not neutral, but righteous." Why is this important?
7. Does God impute to us Christ's active obedience, or only his passive obedience? Explain the question and answer it from Scripture.

8. Describe Martin Luther's anxiety over Romans 1:17 and his solution to it.

9. How can Paul draw a sharp contrast between faith and works in salvation, though elsewhere he presents them as inseparable?

10. Do Paul and James disagree over the relation of faith and works? Explain.

11. Does Frame's triangular diagram imply that justification and sanctification are ultimately identical? Why or why not?

12. Describe and evaluate the view of justification among the advocates of the New Perspective on Paul.

13. Describe and evaluate Norman Shepherd's view of justification.

14. Frame's diagrams suggest that adoption is a remedy for the punishment of sin. Explain; evaluate.

15. Compare Jesus' sonship to ours.

16. "Our sonship is both present and future." Explain both aspects.

17. Compare and contrast adoption and regeneration.

18. "Adoption carries us beyond justification." How? Explain.

19. Enumerate the privileges of sonship and describe them.

Memory Verses

Ps. 103:11–12: For as high as the heavens are above the earth,
   so great is his steadfast love toward those who fear him;
as far as the east is from the west,
   so far does he remove our transgressions from us.

Rom. 3:21–22: But now the righteousness of God has been manifested apart from the law, although the Law and the Prophets bear witness to it—the righteousness of God through faith in Jesus Christ for all who believe.

Rom. 8:1: There is therefore now no condemnation for those who are in Christ Jesus.

Rom. 8:14–17: For all who are led by the Spirit of God are sons of God. For you did not receive the spirit of slavery to fall back into fear, but you have received the Spirit of adoption as sons, by whom we cry, "Abba! Father!" The Spirit himself bears witness with our spirit that we are children of God, and if children, then heirs—heirs of God and fellow heirs with Christ, provided we suffer with him in order that we may also be glorified with him.

Rom. 8:19: For the creation waits with eager longing for the revealing of the sons of God.

2 Cor. 5:21: For our sake he made him to be sin who knew no sin, so that in him we might become the righteousness of God.

Eph. 2:8–9: For by grace you have been saved through faith. And this is not your own doing; it is the gift of God, not a result of works, so that no one may boast.

James 2:26: For as the body apart from the spirit is dead, so also faith apart from works is dead.

1 John 3:1: See what kind of love the Father has given to us, that we should be called children of God; and so we are.

Resources for Further Study

Milton, Michael. *What Is the Doctrine of Adoption?* Phillipsburg, NJ: P&R Publishing, 2012.

Murray, John. *MCW*, 2:202–74.

Oliphint, K. Scott, ed. *Justified in Christ.* Fearn, Ross-shire, UK: Christian Focus, 2007. Essays on the recent controversy about justification. It also includes as an appendix John Murray's important exegesis of Romans 5:12–21, *The Imputation of Adam's Sin.*

CHAPTER 43

SANCTIFICATION

AS WE HAVE SEEN, GOD *DECLARES* believers to be righteous in Christ (justification) and welcomes them into his own family (adoption). But he also works within believers to *make* them holy. We spent some time insisting that justification is not God's *making* us righteous, but *declaring* us righteous as a legal status. But we should never forget that God also *makes* his people righteous and holy, and that this work of God forms a necessary context for justification and adoption. Faith without works is dead.

God's work to make us holy is called *sanctification*. This discussion brings us back to the sphere of subjective salvation, which we discussed in chapter 41 under the topics of regeneration and conversion. We then employed the following diagram, which will be useful to review at this point; see fig. 43.1.

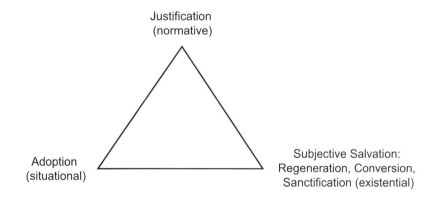

Fig. 43.1. Aspects of Salvation

We should never fall into the temptation of disparaging the subjective work of God. Although the ground of our salvation is objective, outside us, what theologians have sometimes called an *alien righteousness*, this objective work of Christ has profound

983

effects within us. And as we have seen, justification and adoption do not exist apart from regeneration, conversion, and sanctification. Justification is "by" faith, and faith is part of subjective salvation. So the justification of the individual, although its ground is external to the believer, depends on the work of the Spirit within the believer, enabling him to embrace the salvation of Christ.

Holiness

To sanctify is to make holy. Holiness, of course, includes righteousness. But the concept of sanctification focuses on the concept of holiness, which we explored in chapter 13 as a divine attribute.

God's holiness is his capacity and right to arouse our reverent awe and wonder. Think of what it would be like to meet God directly. When Moses met God in Exodus 3:5–6, God told him to remove his shoes, for the place of this meeting was holy ground. Cf. Ex. 19:12–13, 23. When God came to be there, the very space around him became sacred, holy. When Isaiah met God, the seraphim (angels) flew around, crying, "Holy, holy, holy is the Lord of hosts; the whole earth is full of his glory!" (Isa. 6:3). God's holiness is his radical difference—literally, separation—from human beings, which arouses our amazement. It puts us in contact with a being vastly different from anyone or anything in the universe.

God is different and separate from us because he is our Creator, because of his lordship, his attributes of control, authority, presence. After the fall, he is also separate from us in another way: he is perfectly righteous and good, but we are wicked and sinful. So when God met with Isaiah, the result was not only Isaiah's amazement at God's greatness, but also Isaiah's profound conviction of sin. "Woe is me!" he cried, "for I am lost; for I am a man of unclean lips, and I dwell in the midst of a people of unclean lips; for my eyes have seen the King, the Lord of hosts!" (Isa. 6:5). Isaiah knew that God was pure and would judge all wickedness. He knew he had no right to stand in the presence of such intense purity. He may well have expected to be destroyed then and there.

But God showed kindness to Isaiah. One of the angels took a live coal from the temple altar and placed it on Isaiah's lips, symbolically taking away Isaiah's sin, in anticipation of the work of Christ (Isa. 6:6–7). God deals with all believers after that pattern. Amazingly, God promises that we will be holy, even as he is holy (Lev. 19:2; 1 Peter 1:15–16).

Remarkably, then, God's attribute of holiness, which creates such a distance between God and human beings, also joins us to him in the most intimate fellowship. God makes us holy, which means that he associates us with his holiness. He brings us into his holy ground. So we become his holy people, his saints. As we compare justification and sanctification, it is instructive to recall the similar duality in God's righteousness that we noted in the previous chapter. Both righteousness and holiness as attributes of God are frightening. Both separate us from God. But both of these are also ways in which God draws near to his people and redeems them.

As we have seen, God comes to us in his covenant presence, and he takes us to be his people, saying, "I will be your God, and you shall be my people" (Jer. 7:23). In the case of Israel, that meant that the people were a *holy* people, a people separate from all the other nations of the world (Ex. 19:6). For the children of Israel, holiness was both a fact and a norm, both a reality and a command. They were in fact the holy people of God, distinct from all the nations. But God also commanded them to *be* holy (Lev. 20:7). God made them holy, but they were to make themselves holy. Here divine sovereignty and human responsibility come together.[1] This is not true in justification. God does not command us to be justified, for justification is entirely his work, not ours. But he does command us to be sanctified, to be holy, for sanctification is both a work of God and a work of the believer.

The same language can be found in the NT. God has made us his holy people (1 Peter 2:9), his saints (Rom. 1:7; 1 Cor. 1:2). But he also commands us to be holy as he is holy (1 Peter 1:15–16; cf. Rom. 6:19; 2 Cor. 7:1; 1 Thess. 4:7).

Definition of Sanctification

As we begin our discussion of sanctification, consider the definition in the WLC:

Q. 75. What is sanctification?

A. Sanctification is a work of God's grace, whereby they whom God hath, before the foundation of the world, chosen to be holy, are in time, through the powerful operation of his Spirit applying the death and resurrection of Christ unto them, renewed in their whole man after the image of God; having the seeds of repentance unto life, and all other saving graces, put into their hearts, and those graces so stirred up, increased, and strengthened, as that they more and more die unto sin, and rise unto newness of life.

Note one difference at the outset between this definition and the catechism definitions of justification and adoption that I have quoted in previous chapters. The catechism describes justification and adoption each as an "act" of God's free grace. It describes sanctification, however, as a "work" of God's grace. I think the distinction is this: an act is instantaneous, a single divine intervention that is never repeated. A work, however, is an ongoing activity of God, a process. The suggestion is that God does not continually justify us or adopt us, but he does continually work within us to sanctify us.

This distinction describes well the biblical emphasis. We should remember, however, that all three of these divine activities play continuing roles in the history of redemption. Abraham, for example, was justified by faith apart from works, according to Romans 4:1–8. Paul here refers to Genesis 15:6. But James tells us that Abraham was also justified at a later time, when he obeyed God's commandment to sacrifice his son (James

---

1. Compare my discussion of divine sovereignty and human responsibility in chapter 35.

2:21–23). God justifies us upon initial faith, but he continues to declare righteous our acts of obedience through life.

Similarly, our adoption is once and once for all. But Paul mentions a future adoption for which we wait, along with all creation (Rom. 8:23). There is an *already* and a *not yet* to our adoption. We belong to God's family, but our experience in that family continues to grow, and at one future point it will seem that we are adopted all over again.

So although the catechism presents sanctification as a continuing process, we find in Scripture that it, too, has an instantaneous beginning as well as a continuous development.

Definitive Sanctification

The instantaneous beginning of sanctification is called *definitive sanctification*, contrasted with the ongoing process of *progressive sanctification*.[2] The first is a single act of God that happens at a single point in time. The second is a continuing work of God with which he calls us to cooperate. This distinction reflects the fact we have noted, that for the believer holiness is both a fact and a command. Let us first look at definitive sanctification.

Definitive sanctification is a once-for-all event, simultaneous with effectual calling and regeneration, that transfers us from the sphere of sin to the sphere of God's holiness, from the kingdom of Satan to the kingdom of God (Heb. 9:13–14; 10:10; 13:12). It is at this point that each of us joins the people of God. This is analogous to God's bringing Israel out of all the surrounding nations to be his holy people. It is at this point that we enter his very presence and find his welcoming smile, rather than his condemnation. So the NT says that all Christians are saints, that is, holy (Acts 20:32; Rom. 1:7; 1 Cor. 1:2; 6:11). Sainthood does not belong to just a few special Christians, as on the Roman Catholic view. It belongs to all believers.

Definitive sanctification is based on the fact that we belong to Christ. We have also said that about justification and adoption. These are all aspects of our union with Christ. Remember from our discussion of effectual calling that God calls us into union with Christ. Paul expresses this often by the phrase "in Christ." We are justified in Christ, adopted in Christ, sanctified in Christ. We are set apart from all other people, holy, because we are in Christ. So in him we have been sanctified, past tense.

So Paul is able to say that when Christ died, we died with him. When he died for sin, we died to sin. So definitive sanctification involves a clean break with sin (Rom. 6:11; Gal. 2:20; Col. 3:3). And as we have died to sin in Christ, we are raised to new life in his resurrection. This does not mean that believers are sinlessly perfect. John tells us plainly that if we say that we do not sin, we deceive ourselves (1 John 1:8, 10). But in Christ, God breaks our bondage, our slavery to sin (Rom. 6:14–23), so that it has no more dominion over us (Rom. 8:13). So now we can say no to Satan's temptations. Definitive sanctification (overlapping regeneration, of course) has given

---

2. In recent years, this distinction has been developed especially by John Murray. See his *MCW*, 2:277–317.

us a new basic reorientation of the mind, will, and affections, so that we have a new desire to do God's will.

Progressive Sanctification

But sanctification is not only that initial reorientation. It is also our gradual growth in holiness and righteousness, our progress in God's way, the way of good works. This is what we usually think of when we hear the word *sanctification*.

Definitive sanctification is a break with our sinful past. But as we've seen, it does not make us sinlessly perfect. We are not perfectly free from sin until our death or the last judgment (Phil. 3:12; 1 John 1:8, 10). As with other aspects of salvation, sanctification displays the tension of the *already* and the *not yet*. We are already saved through the finished work of Christ, but we must wait for the fulfillment of our salvation at the return of Jesus on the last day.

Some have thought that 1 John 3:6 teaches sinless perfection, but it does not. That belief might arise from the KJV translation, which reads, "Whosoever abideth in him sinneth not: whosoever sinneth hath not seen him, neither known him." But this verse teaches only that believers will not sin *continually*, that is, they will not carry on a sinful lifestyle. The ESV translation reads, "No one who abides in him keeps on sinning; no one who keeps on sinning has either seen him or known him," and that is a better rendering of the Greek original.[3] John knows that we sin daily, as he writes in 1 John 1:8 and 10, and Jesus tells us in the Lord's Prayer to ask forgiveness for our sins (Matt. 6:12; cf. 1 Kings 8:46; Prov. 20:9; Eccl. 7:20).

But we should not be complacent about the presence of sin in our lives. Rather, there is a battle to be fought, with God's help (1 Cor. 9:24–27).

So sanctification is not only a past event, but also an ongoing process. It begins in regeneration, and we can think of sanctification as the outworking of the new life given in regeneration. In that ongoing process, God works in us (1 Thess. 5:23; Heb. 13:20–21), but he also calls us to work out our salvation (Phil. 2:12–13). It is all of God, for all things are of God. Sanctification is a work of the Holy Spirit (Gal. 5:16–18, 22–23; 2 Thess. 2:13; 1 Peter 1:2) on the basis of Christ, who is our sanctification (1 Cor. 1:30). Notice again how the elements of the *ordo salutis* are aspects of our union with Christ.

The good works and attitudes that arise through sanctification are called "fruit of the Spirit" in Galatians 5:22–23. So as we see ourselves growing in grace, we should thank and praise God. It is by his grace that we are able to grow at all.

Nevertheless, we should not wait passively for God to sanctify us. Some have taught that the way to holiness is to "let go and let God."[4] But that idea is not biblical. In the first place, we don't need to "let God," for God is sovereign and does not need to wait for us to let go before he can work. And we should not let go, for God

---

3. John Murray, however, understands 1 John 3:6 differently, in ibid., 282–83. He believes that John is speaking of a particular sin, the sin of disbelieving that Christ is come in the flesh (1 John 4:2).

4. This was the slogan of the Keswick Victorious Life teaching. See Andrew D. Naselli, *Let Go and Let God? A Survey & Analysis of Keswick Theology* (Bellingham, WA: Logos Bible Software, 2010), for analysis and critique.

commands us to fight in the spiritual battle. So the paradox: "work out your own salvation with fear and trembling, for it is God who works in you, both to will and to work for his good pleasure" (Phil. 2:12b–13). God does it all, but he does it (as he often does, as I emphasized in chapters 1, 7, and 35) by the use of human effort. Cf. 2 Peter 1:5–11.

Just as God told the children of Israel in Exodus 19 that they were already his holy people, but also commanded them to be holy as he is holy in Leviticus 19, so in defini-tive sanctification he tells us that we *are* his holy people, and then he commands us in progressive sanctification to *become* holy as he is holy.

So, as in many other contexts, divine sovereignty and human responsibility are not opposed. The former works through the latter (as well as sometimes work-ing above and beyond it). The latter always depends on the former. But our role in sanctification is never passive. Our work is to fight, to run the race, to pursue holiness.

We should beware of slogans that disparage one side or the other of this tension. "Sanctification by grace alone" minimizes our responsibility, while "synergistic sanctification" misses the sense in which *all* our progress in holiness is by God's grace.

I have noted a tendency among some Christians to find some inconsistency between moral effort and justification by grace through faith. Some seem to think that "try-ing" to obey God, pursuing holiness, and so on are incompatible with trust in the finished work of Christ. One hears testimony such as "keeping this command [e.g., to love my neighbor] was something I could never do, so I took the biblical com-mand as an occasion for repentance and for turning to the cross for forgiveness." It is certainly true that we need God's grace to love one another or to keep any divine command. But God does not give his commands in Scripture merely as occasions for repentance, or even as occasions to turn to the cross. He gives his commands for us to obey.[5]

So Scripture commands us to yield our lives to God (Rom. 6:19; Phil. 3:13–14; Col. 3:10; Heb. 12:1), to strive for holiness (Rom. 8:13; 2 Cor. 7:1; 1 Thess. 4:3; Heb. 12:14; 1 Peter 1:15; 2 Peter 1:5; 1 John 3:3), to don the whole armor of God (Eph. 6:10–20) in order to fight against Satan and his angels, to put to death our sinful dispositions (Rom. 8:13; Col. 3:5). We can win this battle, not by the sword, but by truth, righteousness, the gospel, faith, salvation. Our only offensive weapons are the Word of God and prayer. This may seem a puny arsenal to the rulers of this world, but God tells us that it has more power than any of those rulers. People sometimes say mockingly, "Well, we can always try prayer." But God's weapons are more powerful than anything in the mockers' arsenal. A gun will subdue a man, but only the sword of God's Word, wielded in prayer, will subdue Satan.

---

5. Compare my discussion of these issues in my article "Simple Obedience," in *Selected Shorter Writings of John Frame* (Phillipsburg, NJ: P&R Publishing, 2013).

Means of Sanctification

Scripture describes the spiritual battle, the walk of faith, in many ways. To summarize, I will (of course) suggest three general categories of resources that God has provided to us; see fig. 43.2.

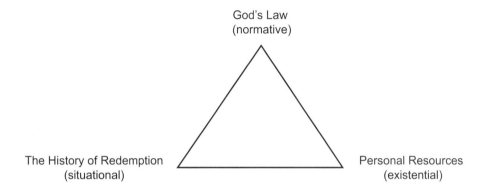

Fig. 43.2. Resources for the Walk of Faith

God's Law

First, God has provided us with a norm or standard to tell us what is right and what is wrong. His moral revelation is part of natural or general revelation (Rom. 1:18–32), but as we saw in chapter 24, fallen human beings suppress the truth in creation until they receive God's grace in Christ. When they come to believe, they are able to look at natural revelation through the "spectacles" of Scripture, and Scripture becomes their sufficient norm. Scripture is sufficient (chapter 26) in that it contains all the divine words that we need to do anything to the glory of God.

So when Scripture motivates us to pursue holiness, it often calls us to be obedient to God's commands—commands that for us are located in Scripture itself. As Joshua prepared to take possession of the Land of Promise, God said to him:

> Only be strong and very courageous, being careful to do according to all the law that Moses my servant commanded you. Do not turn from it to the right hand or to the left, that you may have good success wherever you go. This Book of the Law shall not depart from your mouth, but you shall meditate on it day and night, so that you may be careful to do according to all that is written in it. For then you will make your way prosperous, and then you will have good success. Have I not commanded you? Be strong and courageous. Do not be frightened, and do not be dismayed, for the Lord your God is with you wherever you go. (Josh. 1:7–9)

Jesus, too, urged his disciples and all people to obey the Law and the Prophets (Matt. 7:12; 19:18–19). Paul reminds us that God has redeemed us so that the law might be fulfilled in us:

> For God has done what the law, weakened by the flesh, could not do. By sending his own Son in the likeness of sinful flesh and for sin, he condemned sin in the flesh, in order that the righteous requirement of the law might be fulfilled in us, who walk not according to the flesh but according to the Spirit. (Rom. 8:3–4)

In these passages, the law of God serves as the standard of what we should do in order to glorify God. And therefore it also provides a motivation for us to do what is right. When we learn that God has commanded something, that fact should move us to act on it (as in Josh. 1:7–9). Further, although we are not entirely free from sin, we know that through Christ God has given us the ability to obey the law (Rom. 8:4). God's law, therefore, comes to us with the promise of a better way to live.

I am here advocating what has been called, especially in Reformed and Lutheran circles, the *third use of the law*. The first use is the use of the law to order civil society. The second is the use of the law to drive people to Christ. (In some accounts, the first and second are reversed.) The third use is the use of the law as a guide to believers. Some Lutherans rejected the third use because they thought that in Scripture the law serves only as "terror" and "threat."[6] But the prevailing view among Lutherans is that the third use is legitimate if it guides us by terrorizing us: making our sins vivid to drive us back to Christ again and again. The Reformed generally deny the premise that the law can serve only as terror and threat, though the Lutheran view is gaining some advocates in Reformed circles.

But there are some in both Lutheran and Reformed circles who hesitate to refer to the law in their quest for holiness, suspecting that considering the law will compromise their dependence on God's grace. This suspicion is wrong. Paul tells us, "So the law is holy, and the commandment is holy and righteous and good" (Rom. 7:12). And it is a good thing for believers to meditate on the law:

> Blessed is the man
> who walks not in the counsel of the wicked
> nor stands in the way of sinners
>   nor sits in the seat of scoffers;
> but his delight is in the law of the LORD,
>   and on his law he meditates day and night. (Ps. 1:1–2)

The History of Redemption

The second way in which Scripture helps us in the quest for sanctification is by reminding us of what God has done for our salvation. The Ten Commandments in Exodus 20 begin by reminding Israel:

---

6. Lutherans distinguish sharply between law and gospel. The former instills terror of judgment without any indication of grace. It is all bad news and no good news. The gospel is opposite: a free promise of salvation through grace, without any threat. I do not agree with this construction, as I have argued in *DCL*, 182–92.

I am the LORD your God, who brought you out of the land of Egypt, out of the house of slavery. (Ex. 20:1)

The passage then continues by setting forth God's commands. But the motivation for keeping the commands is God's great deliverance of Israel from slavery in Egypt. So throughout Scripture God motivates his people to holiness by reminding us of what he has done to save us.

Most dramatic in this connection is Romans 6. Here, Paul has expounded the doctrine that we are saved entirely by grace apart from works. But that raises the question: "Are we to continue in sin that grace may abound?" (Rom. 6:1). Paul replies:

By no means! How can we who died to sin still live in it? Do you not know that all of us who have been baptized into Christ Jesus were baptized into his death? We were buried therefore with him by baptism into death, in order that, just as Christ was raised from the dead by the glory of the Father, we too might walk in newness of life. (Rom. 6:2–4)

He goes on to emphasize that before we came to know Christ, we were slaves to sin (Rom. 6:6). When we died to sin in Christ, that bondage was broken. Our deepest desire is no longer to sin; rather, we are "obedient from the heart" (v. 17) and therefore "slaves to righteousness leading to sanctification" (v. 19).

So if we continue to sin, we are violating our very heart; we are doing what we most hate. It is not impossible for us to do precisely that, of course, as Paul indicates in Romans 7. But a sinful existence will create an intolerable tension between the believer's actions and his deepest desire. So we should consciously adopt the stance of those who are dead to sin and free from it:

So you also must consider yourselves dead to sin and alive to God in Christ Jesus.

Let not sin therefore reign in your mortal body, to make you obey its passions. Do not present your members to sin as instruments for unrighteousness, but present yourselves to God as those who have been brought from death to life, and your members to God as instruments for righteousness. For sin will have no dominion over you, since you are not under law but under grace. (Rom. 6:11–14)

Paul makes the same point more concisely in Colossians 3:1–4:

If then you have been raised with Christ, seek the things that are above, where Christ is, seated at the right hand of God. Set your minds on things that are above, not on things that are on earth. For you have died, and your life is hidden with Christ in God. When Christ who is your life appears, then you also will appear with him in glory.

In these passages, Paul applies our union with Christ to our sanctification. Again, the blessing of salvation is our relationship to Christ himself.

Our Personal Resources

But Scripture doesn't call us to restrict our meditation to events in the past. God has redeemed us in the past, but the repercussions of those past events continue to have great effects today, as I have already noted. We have died to sin and been raised to new life, but those events have changed our hearts, so that today our dispositions are entirely different. We have already experienced the first stages of what I have called *subjective soteriology*: regeneration, conversion, and now sanctification.

So it is not wrong to consider sanctification from a subjective, inward perspective. I have already mentioned the change of heart brought about by Christ (Rom. 6:17). That inner change is correlative to the indwelling of the Holy Spirit in the believer. The Spirit dominates the redeemed life. Believers walk "not according to the flesh but according to the Spirit" (Rom. 8:4).

The Spirit is sovereign, and as we have seen, he works mysteriously. He is not under our control. Yet the believer is able to make a conscious decision to follow the Spirit's leading. So Paul commands, "Walk by the Spirit, and you will not gratify the desires of the flesh" (Gal. 5:16). Again we note the subtle interaction between divine sovereignty and human responsibility.

The Spirit bears "fruit": new traits of character that replace the "works of the flesh":

> But the fruit of the Spirit is love, joy, peace, patience, kindness, goodness, faithfulness, gentleness, self-control; against such things there is no law. And those who belong to Christ Jesus have crucified the flesh with its passions and desires.
> If we live by the Spirit, let us also walk by the Spirit. (Gal. 5:22–25)

Although the Spirit's work is invisible and mysterious, therefore, we know in what direction he is moving, and we know how to follow him. Cultivating such fruit is what it means to walk in the Spirit. Cf. Rom. 8:1–17.

And it is important to recognize that our personal resources are not only individual. As I will emphasize in chapters 46–49, God brings individuals into a body of believers, the church. They, too, are resources for our sanctification. Not only the officers of the church, the elders and deacons, but all believers have the power and the responsibility to build one another up in the grace of Christ (Heb. 10:24–25). God gives to each member gifts for the edification of the church as a whole (Rom. 12; 1 Cor. 12; Col. 3:16). And it is in the church primarily that we encounter the means of grace: the Word, sacraments, and prayer.

We serve as resources to one another, not only by teaching and preaching, but also by living as examples. Scripture puts much emphasis on the example of Christ (as John 13:15; 1 Peter 2:21) and the examples of characters in the biblical narrative (positive: Heb. 11; James 5:10; negative: Heb. 4:11).[7] Leaders of the church are to be examples of sanctification to one another (1 Tim. 3; 4:12).

---

7. Hence I resist the too-prevalent notion that sermons should never use biblical characters as moral or spiritual examples.

Spiritual Exercises and Simple Obedience

Much of the current evangelical discussion of sanctification concerns proposed methods and techniques designed to help believers fight the spiritual warfare. That warfare is often difficult, and just as we are tempted by schemes for quick weight loss, so we are often led to enroll in methods that promise rapid progress in sanctification.

I have already referred to the "let go and let God" slogan of the Keswick Victorious Life teaching and have criticized it as unbiblical. This doctrine is a form of what theologians have called *quietism*, the view that in sanctification our proper role is entirely passive. A similar approach may be found in the Formula of Concord, the Lutheran confessional standard, wherein truly good works are never motivated by any command, threat, or reward, but are produced spontaneously by the Spirit within.[8] This is perhaps the root of Lutheran theologian Gerhard Forde's view that "sanctification is thus simply *the art of getting used to justification*."[9] A number of Reformed writers have taken similar positions, thinking that an active pursuit of holiness is somehow inconsistent with justification by faith alone.

But as we have seen, Scripture opposes the notion that sanctification is passive, or even that it is simply an outworking of justification. As I indicated in the previous chapter, Protestant theology warns us against confusing justification and sanctification. Certainly God's free justification is a significant motivation for ethical obedience, for it means that we do not need to earn God's love in Christ. But the biblical writers never tell their readers simply to count on their justification as a way of evading the spiritual warfare.

I think part of the confusion is this: God has certainly accepted believers once and for all in Christ. They belong to him as his sons and daughters and can never be cast out. But there is another level of divine approval, arising from his fatherly discipline. The book of Hebrews emphasizes it:

> And have you forgotten the exhortation that addresses you as sons?
>
> "My son, do not regard lightly the discipline of the Lord,
>   nor be weary when reproved by him.
> For the Lord disciplines the one he loves,
>   and chastises every son whom he receives."
>
> It is for discipline that you have to endure. God is treating you as sons. For what son is there whom his father does not discipline? If you are left without discipline, in which all have participated, then you are illegitimate children and not sons. Besides this, we have had earthly fathers who disciplined us and we respected them. Shall we not much more be subject to the Father of spirits and live? For they disciplined us for a

---

8. Epitome of the Formula of Concord 6.5. See my *DKG*, 189–91, for further discussion.

9. Gerhard Forde, "The Lutheran View," in *Christian Spirituality*, ed. Donald L. Alexander (Downers Grove, IL: InterVarsity Press, 1988), 13 (emphasis his).

short time as it seemed best to them, but he disciplines us for our good, that we may share his holiness. For the moment all discipline seems painful rather than pleasant, but later it yields the peaceful fruit of righteousness to those who have been trained by it. (Heb. 12:5–11)

We do not need to fear God's final judgment, but we should fear his fatherly displeasure.[10] Hebrews and other books of the NT speak against our complacency and passivity, urging us to spiritual exertions:

Therefore lift your drooping hands and strengthen your weak knees, and make straight paths for your feet, so that what is lame may not be put out of joint but rather be healed. Strive for peace with everyone, and for the holiness without which no one will see the Lord. (Heb. 12:12–14)

Do you not know that in a race all the runners run, but only one receives the prize? So run that you may obtain it. Every athlete exercises self-control in all things. They do it to receive a perishable wreath, but we an imperishable. So I do not run aimlessly; I do not box as one beating the air. But I discipline my body and keep it under control, lest after preaching to others I myself should be disqualified. (1 Cor. 9:24–27)

Although God is fully pleased with the sacrifice of Jesus on our behalf, still the NT calls us to "please God" (Rom. 8:8; Gal. 1:10; 1 Thess. 4:1; 2 Tim. 2:4; Heb. 11:6). Since we have been saved by God's grace alone, we cannot be indifferent to his pleasure.[11]

Certainly it is a good spiritual exercise to remind ourselves of our justification, or of the cross; certainly it is good to "preach the gospel to ourselves" and to repent of our idolatries (to mention some other approaches). But none of these exercises replaces the act of obedience itself. In the end, God expects us to obey his commands.

The end of the matter; all has been heard. Fear God and keep his commandments, for this is the whole duty of man. (Eccl. 12:13)[12]

10. It is also important (especially for the writer to the Hebrews) to keep in mind that some who are formally members of the church may not have true faith. It is possible that people who at one time are members of the church in good standing will at a later point apostatize. The warning passages of Hebrews and other NT books serve to urge us both to seek our Father's pleasure and to examine ourselves as to whether we are in fact believers. Self-examination, of course, should not become a morbid introspection, wallowing in our memories of past sins. Rather, it should be a simple inquiry whether we are on the Lord's side. For more discussion of this, see the following chapter on the assurance of salvation.

11. I have actually heard Christians say that it is wrong to try to please God because trying to do that is self-righteousness. Their argument is that God is already pleased with us for the sake of Christ, and we cannot please him further. But Scripture often urges us to please God, to seek his approval: Ps. 69:31; Prov. 16:7; Isa. 56:4; 1 Cor. 7:32; Gal. 1:10; 1 Thess. 2:15; 4:1; 2 Tim. 2:4; Heb. 11:6.

12. In a number of places, Scripture summarizes the law, as here: Matt. 7:12; 22:40; Rom. 13:8; 1 Cor. 13; Col. 3:14. Love, particularly, fulfills the law, and Jesus defines that as keeping his commandments (John 13:34–35; 14:15; etc.). Our whole duty toward God is obedience, motivated by love.

In the end, it's a matter of simple obedience.

Key Terms
Holiness
Sanctification
Definitive sanctification
Progressive sanctification
Three uses of the law
Indwelling of the Spirit
Fruit of the Spirit
Keswick Victorious Life
Fatherly discipline

Study Questions
1. Frame says that our justification depends in some way on our inner subjective change. Explain; evaluate.
2. How are holiness and righteousness different? In what very significant way are they alike?
3. Why does the catechism say that justification and adoption are "acts" of God's grace, while sanctification is a "work" of God's grace? Explain; evaluate.
4. Distinguish definitive and progressive sanctification, citing Scripture.
5. Given that we are not sinlessly perfect, what is the nature of the change wrought by sanctification?
6. Define and evaluate: "sanctification by grace alone"; "synergistic sanctification."
7. Outline and discuss the relation of God's sovereignty to human responsibility in sanctification.
8. Why do some Christians hesitate to refer to the law in their pursuit of holiness? Evaluate their view. What role should the law play in the believer's sanctification?
9. How does the teaching of Romans 6 bear on our sanctification?
10. How can Paul command us to walk in the Spirit, given that the Spirit is sovereign and invisible?
11. Describe our individual and corporate resources for living godly lives.
12. Is sanctification a matter of "getting used to justification"? Argue pro or con.
13. Is it wrong to try to please God? Why might someone say this? Evaluate.

Memory Verses
Josh. 1:7–9: Only be strong and very courageous, being careful to do according to all the law that Moses my servant commanded you. Do not turn from it to the right hand or to the left, that you may have good success wherever you go. This Book

of the Law shall not depart from your mouth, but you shall meditate on it day and night, so that you may be careful to do according to all that is written in it. For then you will make your way prosperous, and then you will have good success. Have I not commanded you? Be strong and courageous. Do not be frightened, and do not be dismayed, for the LORD your God is with you wherever you go.

Ps. 1:1–2: Blessed is the man
who walks not in the counsel of the wicked,
nor stands in the way of sinners,
    nor sits in the seat of scoffers;
but his delight is in the law of the LORD,
    and on his law he meditates day and night.

Eccl. 12:13: The end of the matter; all has been heard. Fear God and keep his commandments, for this is the whole duty of man.

John 14:15: If you love me, you will keep my commandments.

Rom. 6:1–4: Are we to continue in sin that grace may abound? By no means! How can we who died to sin still live in it? Do you not know that all of us who have been baptized into Christ Jesus were baptized into his death? We were buried therefore with him by baptism into death, in order that, just as Christ was raised from the dead by the glory of the Father, we too might walk in newness of life.

Rom. 8:3–4: For God has done what the law, weakened by the flesh, could not do. By sending his own Son in the likeness of sinful flesh and for sin, he condemned sin in the flesh, in order that the righteous requirement of the law might be fulfilled in us, who walk not according to the flesh but according to the Spirit.

1 Cor. 9:24–27: Do you not know that in a race all the runners run, but only one receives the prize? So run that you may obtain it. Every athlete exercises self-control in all things. They do it to receive a perishable wreath, but we an imperishable. So I do not run aimlessly; I do not box as one beating the air. But I discipline my body and keep it under control, lest after preaching to others I myself should be disqualified.

Gal. 5:22–25: But the fruit of the Spirit is love, joy, peace, patience, kindness, goodness, faithfulness, gentleness, self-control; against such things there is no law. And those who belong to Christ Jesus have crucified the flesh with its passions and desires.
    If we live by the Spirit, let us also walk by the Spirit.

Phil. 2:12–13: Therefore, my beloved, as you have always obeyed, so now, not only as in my presence but much more in my absence, work out your own salvation with fear and trembling, for it is God who works in you, both to will and to work for his good pleasure.

Col. 3:1–4: If then you have been raised with Christ, seek the things that are above, where Christ is, seated at the right hand of God. Set your minds on things that are above, not on things that are on earth. For you have died, and your life is hidden with Christ in God. When Christ who is your life appears, then you also will appear with him in glory.

1 Peter 1:15–16: But as he who called you is holy, you also be holy in all your conduct, since it is written, "You shall be holy, for I am holy."

Resources for Further Study

Alexander, Donald L., ed. *Christian Spirituality: Five Views of Sanctification.* Downers Grove, IL: InterVarsity Press, 1988.

Marshall, Walter. *The Gospel Mystery of Sanctification.* Lafayette, IN: Sovereign Grace Publishers, 2001.

Murray, John. *MCW*, 2:277–317.

CHAPTER 44

PERSEVERANCE AND ASSURANCE

IN OUR CONSIDERATION of the application of redemption (*ordo salutis*), we have considered effectual calling and regeneration, the beginning of our experience of salvation in space and time. Effectual calling is God's act to bring us into fellowship with Christ, and regeneration describes the change that God works in us to become like Christ. Faith and repentance, sometimes together called *conversion*, describe our regenerate response to God's calling, as we turn to Christ as Lord and Savior (faith) and turn away from sin (repentance). Then comes the triad *justification*, *adoption*, and *sanctification*. In justification, God gives us a new legal standing before him. In adoption, he brings us into the family of God as his sons and daughters. In sanctification, he makes us saints, holy people, working out our regenerate nature to renew us in the image of Jesus.

In this chapter, we will consider *perseverance*, the doctrine that this new life continues to the end, indeed to eternity, and in the next *glorification*, which refers to the consummation of human nature in God's image. That consummation begins with effectual calling and continues through eternity. In this chapter, we will also discuss the problem of *assurance*: how do we know that we belong to Christ? Scripture says that those who belong to Christ persevere to the end, but how can we be sure of belonging to that number?

Perseverance

Let us first consider the doctrine of the *perseverance of the saints*, sometimes called the doctrine of *eternal security*. I use these two phrases as synonyms, though as we will see, they do carry somewhat different nuances with different people. Perseverance simply means that those who are truly regenerate, in saving union with Christ, can't lose their salvation. As WCF 17.1 puts it:

> They, whom God hath accepted in his Beloved, effectually called, and sanctified by his Spirit, can neither totally nor finally fall away from the state of grace, but shall certainly persevere therein to the end, and be eternally saved.

In Matthew 10:21–22, Jesus describes a period of persecution for the church. He says:

> Brother will deliver brother over to death, and the father his child, and children will rise against parents and have them put to death, and you will be hated by all for my name's sake. But the one who endures to the end will be saved.

As we will see, people do fall away under temptation, trial, and persecution. Salvation is for those who endure, who persevere. But Scripture teaches that everyone who is effectually called, regenerated, converted, justified, adopted, and sanctified by God will surely persevere to the end.

We can see that this is true from a number of statements in Scripture. In John 6:39–40, Jesus says:

> And this is the will of him who sent me, that I should lose nothing of all that he has given me, but raise it up on the last day. For this is the will of my Father, that everyone who looks on the Son and believes in him should have eternal life, and I will raise him up on the last day.

So everyone who believes in Jesus—not hypocritically, but who sincerely believes— will have eternal life. Jesus will raise him up on the last day. So if you have believed in Jesus now, you cannot lose your salvation. Be confident that Jesus will raise you up on the last day.

Notice also John 10:27–29:

> My sheep hear my voice, and I know them, and they follow me. I give them eternal life, and they will never perish, and no one will snatch them out of my hand. My Father, who has given them to me, is greater than all, and no one is able to snatch them out of the Father's hand.

Nobody can snatch a believer out of God's hand.

These verses speak of eternal life in the future for those who believe today. But other passages put the point even more strongly: we have eternal life here and now, not only in the future: "Whoever believes in the Son *has* eternal life; whoever does not obey the Son shall not see life, but the wrath of God remains on him" (John 3:36); "Truly, truly, I say to you, whoever hears my word and believes him who sent me *has* eternal life. He does not come into judgment, but has passed from death to life" (John 5:24); "I write these things to you who believe in the name of the Son of God that you may know that you have eternal life" (1 John 5:13).

So Paul is able to say that there is *now* no condemnation for those in Christ Jesus (Rom. 8:1). When we believe in Jesus, our sins are immediately forgiven, past, present, and future. At that point, every barrier is removed to eternal fellowship with God. So we will certainly persevere.

But remember that our salvation goes back even before the beginning of our faith, into eternity past. Salvation begins in election. This is an even more ultimate reason why we will persevere. In chapter 11, I quoted Romans 8 at some length. Note there how the apostle Paul connects election and perseverance.

Paul sees a golden chain: from God's foreknowledge and predestination in eternity past, to calling and justification, to glorification. Those who are predestined to be conformed to the image of Christ cannot fail to be glorified. So we hear the language of perseverance. No one can accuse us; no one can separate us from the love of Christ. When Paul writes about death, life, angels, rulers, the present and future, powers, height, depth, he knows what he is talking about. Many times he was beaten, left for dead, shipwrecked, persecuted. But he knows that nothing can separate him from Christ, because he has been predestined, called, and justified. You see how the doctrine of perseverance adds something important to the doctrine of assurance?

We should also note what Paul calls the "seal" of the Holy Spirit in Ephesians 1:13–14:

> In him you also, when you heard the word of truth, the gospel of your salvation, and believed in him, were sealed with the promised Holy Spirit, who is the guarantee of our inheritance until we acquire possession of it, to the praise of his glory.

We receive the Holy Spirit at the beginning of our regenerate lives, and anyone who has the Holy Spirit has a guarantee of final perseverance.

All of this is to say, simply, that God completes the work he begins (Phil. 1:6). He guards every believer to the end. "By God's power [we] are being guarded through faith for a salvation ready to be revealed in the last time" (1 Peter 1:5).

Now, with all this biblical evidence before us, how can anybody doubt the doctrine of perseverance? Well, there is one major problem in this. That is that people sometimes do turn away from Christ after professing him. You probably know people who have fallen away, after seeming like faithful Christians for years. And such defections, called *apostasy*, occurred during the NT period as well. There were false professions, people who said "Lord, Lord" to Christ, but were "workers of lawlessness" (Matt. 7:21–23). There were false brothers (2 Cor. 11:15, 26; Gal. 2:4), false branches on the Vine of Christ (John 15:1–2, 6), wolves in sheep's clothing (Matt. 7:15). There was, as in Jesus' parable, seed sown on rocky soil, which sprang up and looked healthy for a time, but eventually withered away (Mark 4:5–6, 16–17).

It can be difficult to tell whether a professing believer is true or false. Listen to Hebrews 6:4–8:

> For it is impossible, in the case of those who have once been enlightened, who have tasted the heavenly gift, and have shared in the Holy Spirit, and have tasted the goodness of the word of God and the powers of the age to come, and then have fallen away, to restore them again to repentance, since they are crucifying once again the Son of God to their own harm and holding him up to contempt. For land that has drunk the rain that often falls on it, and produces a crop useful to those for whose

sake it is cultivated, receives a blessing from God. But if it bears thorns and thistles, it is worthless and near to being cursed, and its end is to be burned.

This writer is speaking about false believers. But he describes them much as one might describe a true believer: repentant, enlightened, tasting the heavenly gift (possibly some supernatural gift—tongues, prophecy, healing), sharing the Spirit, tasting the goodness of the Word and the powers of the age to come (again, probably referring to miraculous events). So there are some Christians who believe that this passage describes true believers, and that these true believers do not persevere, but fall away. That position, in my view, however, contradicts that great number of Bible texts we discussed earlier.

Can we regard the people in this passage as false believers? I think we can. Think of Judas Iscariot, chosen by Jesus to be one of the twelve disciples. By joining Jesus' band of followers, he turned away from the sinful world, a kind of repentance. Doubtless he received the baptism of repentance for the forgiveness of sins, either from Jesus or from John. He was enlightened by hearing Jesus' teaching. He tasted the heavenly gift as he watched Jesus heal and prophesy.[1] He shared the Spirit, at least as much as King Saul did when he prophesied, and people asked, "Is Saul also among the prophets?" (1 Sam. 10:11). Judas also tasted the good word of Christ and Jesus' miraculous powers, the powers of the age to come, the powers of the coming kingdom. Judas himself preached Christ and worked miracles in his name (Matt. 10:1–42). But he proved to be reprobate, unbelieving. He betrayed Jesus, who said of him that it would have been better if he had not been born. Externally, he seemed to be a believer, and indeed, he had many advantages that believers have, hearing Jesus' words and watching his miracles.

Perhaps even more to the focus of the letter to the Hebrews: OT Israel was much like this—enlightened in comparison with the other nations, experiencing all sorts of heavenly gifts, powers, and words. But many of the Israelites were wicked and turned against God.

Hebrews 10:26–31 also speaks of apostasy. Here, the writer says that the apostate "has spurned the Son of God, and has profaned the blood of the covenant by which he was sanctified, and has outraged the Spirit of grace." The most difficult point here is the clause that says the apostates were once sanctified by the blood of Christ. How can that be said of someone who falls short of final salvation?

Well, the language of sanctification means a setting apart. It can refer to moral cleansing, as we saw in the doctrine of sanctification in the previous chapter. But it can also refer to other kinds of setting apart. God said that Israel was his holy people because he had set it apart from all the nations of the world; yet Israel was not always sanctified in the sense of being obedient to God. In 1 Corinthians 7:14, Paul says that children of believers are holy, even though they may not be old enough to perform good works. I believe that those in Hebrews 10 are people who became part of God's

---

1. God does temporarily give gifts of the Spirit to people who are not finally saved. Review here our discussion of common grace in chapter 12.

holy people, separated from all others. As Israel was set apart by sacrifices, those in Hebrews 10 were set apart by the blood of Christ, which separates the visible church from everyone else in the world. But God did not change their hearts, and they came to despise the blood of Christ, as Judas Iscariot certainly did.[2]

So people can have all these blessings without being saved, and so without the ability to persevere. The apostates of Hebrews 6 did not have regenerate hearts or true faith. So in Hebrews 6:9, the writer says, "Yet in your case, beloved, we feel sure of better things—things that belong to salvation." The writer believes that his readers have regenerate hearts and true faith, and so they are saved and will be saved in the end. He knows that the apostates he has spoken of do not have gifts of God sufficient for salvation.

In our own time, this passage applies to many who make a minimal commitment to Christ. How many nominal church members there are in our time! How many have "come forward" at an evangelistic meeting, or even receive baptism and join a church, only to lose interest shortly afterward. And there are some today like Judas, or like the Pharisees, who even get very active in the Lord's work, who may become pillars of the church over a period of years, whose hearts are not right with God, who have never experienced the regenerating power of the Holy Spirit.

Some people have taught that anyone who makes a minimal commitment to Christianity—for example, by coming forward, professing faith, being baptized—will certainly be saved in the end, even if the person then renounces Christ and lives a sinful life. That, of course, is not biblical teaching. In Scripture, those who persevere are those who are regenerate by God's Spirit and who grow in grace. We cannot read the hearts of people, so we sometimes fail to discern that growth, or the lack of it. But God sees, and in the end it's God who will judge.

The view that those who make a minimal commitment will certainly be saved is sometimes called *eternal security*, though not everyone who uses this phrase teaches this error. Perseverance is not guaranteed to everyone who professes faith, only to those who really trust Christ. Indeed, some who make initial professions of faith get involved in such serious sins that they should be cast out of the church, excommunicated (1 Cor. 5). Excommunication means that someone whom the church originally considered to be a believer will no longer be considered as such.

But this teaching is not intended to frighten believers into morbid self-examination. Christians sometimes experience periods of doubt over whether they have "truly believed." But Hebrews 6 and 10 are not about immature believers who are trying to serve Christ but who struggle with sins in their lives. The apostates of Hebrews 6 and 10 were wolves in sheep's clothing. Their profession was playacting. You remember how the disciples trusted Judas with the treasury, and he used it for his personal wants. He put on a show of caring for the poor, when all he cared about was himself. The Hebrews 6 apostates never confessed their sins and trusted Jesus for forgiveness.

---

2. In terms of our discussion in chapter 11, these were historically elect, but not eternally elect.

To those who are not playacting, but have faith, even as a grain of mustard seed, God promises to preserve them to the very end, and into all eternity. If you are concerned about your faithfulness and devotion to Christ, your concern is a mark of true faith. Wolves in sheep's clothing are not concerned about such things.

Assurance of Salvation

We have seen that those who are truly elect, called, regenerate, and believing are saved from sin through the work of Christ and can never lose their salvation. This doctrine is intended to be a great comfort to Christians. But for many, this is where the trouble begins, for they question whether indeed they are truly elect, called, regenerate, and believing. How can somebody know, beyond tentative guessing, that he himself belongs to Christ?

Assurance naturally follows the discussion of justification, adoption, and sanctification, and our perseverance in these blessings. For our assurance is based on the reality of these three divine blessings in our lives.

WCF 18.1–2 tells us this about assurance:

> Although hypocrites and other unregenerate men may vainly deceive themselves with false hopes and carnal presumptions of being in the favor of God, and estate of salvation (which hope of theirs shall perish): yet such as truly believe in the Lord Jesus, and love him in sincerity, endeavoring to walk in all good conscience before him, may, in this life, be certainly assured that they are in the state of grace, and may rejoice in the hope of the glory of God, which hope shall never make them ashamed.
>
> This certainty is not a bare conjectural and probable persuasion grounded upon a fallible hope; but an infallible assurance of faith founded upon the divine truth of the promises of salvation, the inward evidence of those graces unto which these promises are made, the testimony of the Spirit of adoption witnessing with our spirits that we are the children of God, which Spirit is the earnest of our inheritance, whereby we are sealed to the day of redemption.

First, let us note that God intends for us to have assurance. He calls us to draw near to him "in full assurance of faith" (Heb. 10:22). Scripture says that we *know* God, not merely that we hope or suppose that he exists. God's promises are absolutely sure, for they are based on his own oath, which cannot lie (Heb. 6:13, 18). This is "a sure and steadfast anchor of the soul" (v. 19). Similarly, Paul (2 Tim. 3:16–17) and Peter (2 Peter 1:19–21) speak of Scripture as God's own words, which provide sure guidance in a world where false teaching abounds. God's special revelation is certain, and we ought to be certain about it. The apostle John writes to believers "that you may know that you have eternal life" (1 John 5:13).

On the other hand, the Bible presents doubt largely negatively. It is a spiritual impediment, an obstacle to doing God's work (Matt. 14:31; 21:21; 28:17; Acts 10:20 KJV; 11:12 KJV; Rom. 14:23; 1 Tim. 2:8 KJV; James 1:6). In Matthew 14:31 and Romans 14:23, it is the opposite of faith and therefore a sin. Of course, this sin, like other sins, might remain with us through our earthly life. But we should not be complacent about it. Just as the ideal for the Christian life is perfect holiness, the ideal for the Christian mind is absolute certainty about God's revelation.[3]

We should not conclude, however, that doubt is *always* sinful. Matthew 14:31 and Romans 14:23 (and indeed the others I have listed) speak of doubt in the face of clear special revelation. To doubt what God has clearly spoken to us is wrong. But in other situations, it is not wrong to doubt. In many cases, in fact, it is wrong for us to claim knowledge, much less certainty. Indeed, often the best course is to admit our ignorance (Deut. 29:29; Rom. 11:33–36). Paul is not wrong to express uncertainty about the number of people he baptized (1 Cor. 1:16). Indeed, James tells us, we are always ignorant of the future to some extent, and we should not pretend that we know more about it than we do (James 4:13–16). Job's friends were wrong to think they knew the reasons for his torment, and Job himself had to be humbled as God reminded him of his ignorance (Job 38–42).

But as to our salvation, God wants us to *know* that we know him (1 John 5:13). In the Roman Catholic view, you cannot be fully assured of your salvation because salvation is partly based on works, and your works can always pull you down. But in Protestant theology, as in Scripture, salvation is the work of God. Nobody can destroy it, not even the believer's sins. Those who are justified by faith in Christ have the right to believe that they belong to God forever.

Grounds of Assurance

But *how* can we be assured that we are saved? We generally hold that only the Bible teaches absolutely certain truths. But your name is not in the Bible, nor is mine. So on what basis can we have what the confession calls the "infallible" assurance that our faith is true and that we belong to God?

The confession lists three realities that our infallible assurance is founded on. These correspond to justification, sanctification, and adoption, respectively—putting these in a different order from the order in which we studied them. First, the confession speaks of "the divine truth of the promises of salvation." Clearly, God promises eternal life to all who receive Christ (John 1:12; 3:15–18, 36; 5:24; 6:35, 40, 47; etc.). His promises are absolutely infallible. How can we doubt them? To be sure, the promises don't explicitly contain my name or yours. But they contain our names *implicitly*; that is, they *apply* to us.

Let me give you a similar example: When the eighth commandment says, "Thou shalt not steal," it doesn't mention my name. It doesn't say that *John Frame* should not steal. Does that mean that I am free to take your wallet? Well, of course not. Because "Thou shalt not steal" means *"Everybody* should not steal," or *"Nobody* should steal." That includes John Frame. So although my name is not in the text explicitly, the text

---

3. Compare the discussion of our assurance of the truth of Scripture in chapter 28 and of the certainty of knowledge in chapters 29–32.

applies to me, which is to say that my name is there *implicitly*. Same with the promises of salvation. God promises salvation to *everybody* who believes. If you believe, then, that promise is yours. God promises to save *you*. And that promise is infallible, certain. You dare not doubt it.

Justification comes from faith, from trusting God's promise, just as Abraham did, when he believed what God said, even when God's promise seemed impossible. If you believe God's promise, you are justified, and you also have a right to assurance. Believing God's promise is the instrument of justification, as I put it in chapter 42, the essence of justifying faith (Rom. 4:3, 20–21; Gal. 3:7–9). And continuing in faith brings assurance (Col. 1:23; Heb. 3:14; 6:12). This does not mean, of course, that anyone who raises his hand at an evangelistic meeting is saved. People sometimes do that hypocritically. Faith is an inward reality. But if it is there, you have a right to be assured. If you can honestly say, "I am trusting Jesus for my salvation, not my own works, not my family, not my church, but Jesus," then you can say without doubt that you are saved. And as we saw earlier in this chapter, you cannot lose that salvation.

The second basis of assurance that the confession mentions is "the inward evidence of those graces unto which these promises are made." This ground corresponds to the doctrine of sanctification. When we introspect in this way, we are asking whether the Lord is indeed sanctifying us.

Now, under the first basis of assurance, I mentioned God's promises. God's promises include a promise of new life, of regeneration and sanctification. God has promised to make his people holy (1 Peter 1:15–16; 2 Peter 1:4). So as we observe what God is doing within us, as we observe our own progress in sanctification, we "make [our] calling and election sure," as Peter says (2 Peter 1:10–11).

Now, I know that self-examination can be a discouraging business. When we look at ourselves, we see continuing sin, as well as the effects of grace. So we wonder how we can ever gain assurance by self-examination. Many say that we should not look at ourselves, but that we should look beyond ourselves, outward, at the work of Christ, at his word of promise. It is important to remember that the object of our faith is Christ, not faith itself.

That was what we advised under the first ground of assurance, and certainly we should not look inward without looking outward at the same time. But it is important not only to look at God's promises, but to see how God is fulfilling those promises within us. The continuing presence of sin should not discourage us, because God does not promise to make us sinlessly perfect in this life. But he does promise growth in grace, growth in holiness. When we see that, it increases our confidence that God's promises apply to us. And if we don't see that, it is a danger signal. In that case, we should seriously ask ourselves whether we have understood the promises of God. If we see ourselves dominated by sinful patterns, we should ask whether we have really trusted Christ as *Lord* and Savior.

The third ground of assurance, corresponding to the doctrine of adoption, is "the testimony of the Spirit of adoption witnessing with our spirits that we are the children of God." This confessional statement comes right out of Romans 8:16–17. This is to say that in the end, our assurance is supernatural. Note in Romans 8 that it is not only the witness of our own spirit, but something over and above that, a witness of God's Spirit *with* our spirit, that we are the children of God. Our scrutiny of God's promises and our own sanctification, in the end, is fallible. We make mistakes in our judgments. But the Spirit never makes a mistake. So he persuades us that what we observe in God's Word and in our own lives is really true, really evidence of grace.

In chapter 28, I spoke of the Spirit's work in illuminating God's Word to us. I called that work *existential revelation.* His work in giving us assurance is no different from that. He is not whispering in our ears some new truths that are not found in the Bible. Rather, he is helping us to understand the promises of God in the Bible, to believe those promises, and to see that they apply to us.

Note the triadic structure of these three aspects of assurance, corresponding to justification, sanctification, and adoption, and therefore to God's authority, presence, and control. This suggests that these three grounds of assurance are not independent of one another, but that they work together, that each requires the others. And that is indeed the way we should look at it. The Spirit's witness enables us to be sure of the promises of God and the fruits of our sanctification. The promises of the Word are the promises of the Spirit, who inspired the Word, and he continues to speak through the Word. Our sanctification helps us better to appreciate and apply the promises of God to ourselves. See fig. 44.1.

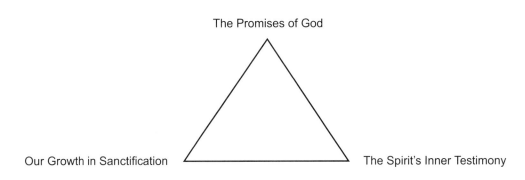

Fig. 44.1. Means of Assurance

Given these powerful resources, how can a Christian ever lack assurance? Yet we sometimes do seem to fluctuate between assurance and doubt. The Reformed confessions look at this problem from two perspectives. HC 21 says that assurance is of the essence of faith: you can't really have faith without having assurance. And that is true in a way. If you believe in Jesus, as I said earlier, you cannot doubt that his promises are true. And if you believe in him, you cannot doubt that those promises apply to you, because they apply to everyone who believes.

But the WCF differs somewhat from the HC. It says (18.3–4), "This infallible assurance doth not so belong to the essence of faith, but that a true believer may wait long, and conflict with many difficulties, before he be partaker of it," and then:

> True believers may have the assurance of their salvation divers ways shaken, diminished, and intermitted; as, by negligence in preserving of it, by falling into some special sin which woundeth the conscience and grieveth the Spirit; by some sudden or vehement temptation, by God's withdrawing the light of his countenance, and suffering even such as fear him to walk in darkness and to have no light: yet are they never so utterly destitute of that seed of God, and life of faith, that love of Christ and the brethren, that sincerity of heart, and conscience of duty, out of which, by the operation of the Spirit, this assurance may, in due time, be revived; and by the which, in the meantime, they are supported from utter despair.

Note the difference from the HC: the Westminster statement says that assurance does not *so* belong to the essence of faith as to preclude periods of doubt. The bigger picture is that if we believe in Christ, we have assurance in our heart; but that assurance can be weakened by sin of various kinds, so that our psychological feeling of assurance has its ups and downs. Assurance is logically implied in faith, but notoriously we miss logical implications. Sin sometimes weakens our confidence that our faith is genuine. But God has given us adequate resources to return to a state of full assurance. He has given us his promises, his sanctifying work, and the Spirit's testimony. We have a right to assurance if we believe God's promises. When we are in doubt, we should keep coming back to those resources, and to the means of grace, which we will discuss in chapter 48: the Word, Christian fellowship, and prayer.

Key Terms
Perseverance
Eternal security
Apostasy
Assurance of salvation
Promises of salvation
Fruits of sanctification
Inner testimony of the Spirit

Study Questions
1. Do those who believe in Christ necessarily persevere to the end? Cite biblical texts to defend your answer.
2. What is the major problem with the doctrine of assurance? Cite biblical references.
3. Can Hebrews 6:4–8 refer to false believers? Analyze clause by clause. Can you relate this passage to any historical examples?
4. Same for Hebrews 10:26–31.

5. Frame says about the apostasy texts, "But this teaching is not intended to frighten believers into morbid self-examination." Why not?

6. "God wants us to *know* that we know him." How do we know that?

7. Enumerate the grounds of assurance mentioned in the WCF. Does Scripture warrant these? How?

8. Show how the three grounds of salvation can be diagrammed as a Frame-triangle.

9. Since we continue to sin in many ways, how can self-examination contribute to assurance?

10. Why is the Spirit's witness to our sonship so important?

11. Describe the difference between the HC and the WCF as to the nature of assurance. Are these reconcilable? How? Or why not?

Memory Verses

John 5:24: Truly, truly, I say to you, whoever hears my word and believes him who sent me has eternal life. He does not come into judgment, but has passed from death to life.

John 6:39–40: And this is the will of him who sent me, that I should lose nothing of all that he has given me, but raise it up on the last day. For this is the will of my Father, that everyone who looks on the Son and believes in him should have eternal life, and I will raise him up on the last day.

John 10:27–29: My sheep hear my voice, and I know them, and they follow me. I give them eternal life, and they will never perish, and no one will snatch them out of my hand. My Father, who has given them to me, is greater than all, and no one is able to snatch them out of the Father's hand.

Eph. 1:13–14: In him you also, when you heard the word of truth, the gospel of your salvation, and believed in him, were sealed with the promised Holy Spirit, who is the guarantee of our inheritance until we acquire possession of it, to the praise of his glory.

1 John 5:13: I write these things to you who believe in the name of the Son of God that you may know that you have eternal life.

Resources for Further Study

Frame, John M. *DKG*.

———. *DWG*, 297–327, 615–40.

CHAPTER 45

GLORIFICATION

SINCE BELIEVERS PERSEVERE to the end, their inevitable final blessing is glory. So we discuss glorification, appropriately, at the end of the *ordo salutis*. But there is also a sense in which glorification occurs here and now, as we will see.

First, let's review what we know about the glory of God. Glory is God's visible presence among people. Glory is an adornment: a woman's hair is her crowning glory (1 Cor. 11:15). Woman is the glory of man (11:7). God always has the adornment of a great light, light that people often see when they meet God. God's glory was in the cloud that led Israel through the wilderness (Ex. 16:6–10). It shone on Mount Sinai (24:16), and then it came and dwelled in the midst of Israel, in the tabernacle, and later in the temple (29:43; 40:34). This indwelling presence of God was called the *shekinah*, the Hebrew word meaning "settle down, abide, dwell." So in the glory, God dwelled as Lord among his people. You remember God's lordship attribute of covenantal presence. His glory is a form of that presence. In the NT, Jesus is God tabernacling with his people (John 1:14). He is our *shekinah*.

Now, God wants human beings to glorify him. "Whether you eat or drink, or whatever you do," says Paul in 1 Corinthians 10:31, "do all to the glory of God." Cf. Matt. 5:16. That sounds as though we are to increase God's glory by what we do. But is that possible? Isn't God's glory infinite? How can we add anything to the glory of God?

Well, that is mysterious. Cornelius Van Til called it the "full-bucket problem." We can put it this way: given the vast importance of God, how can human actions have any importance at all? But as we have seen, God's greatness doesn't exclude a subordinate greatness for human beings. God's sovereignty doesn't exclude human responsibility.

It is hard to understand literally what it means for us to glorify God, but on the level of the metaphor, we can think of it this way: We are God's image, and so he wants us to reflect back the glory shining out of him. When that reflected glory shines from us, back to him, we become more like God: both God and we have glory shining out of us. And God receives more light because we reflect it back to him. So we can be said to glorify God.

1009

Returning to a more literal description of this process: remember that *glory* refers to all of God's perfections, such as his love, grace, goodness. For us to glorify God is to be holy as he is holy, good as he is good, loving as he is loving. To glorify God is to image him. Remember that the image of God is both a fact and a norm. It is a fact, what we are, how God made us. But it is also a norm, a duty, a responsibility. God wants us to be like him, for he says, "Be holy, for I am holy" (Lev. 11:44–45).

And glory is also one of the blessings of salvation, the *ordo salutis*. For God not only asks us to glorify him, but ordains that we will. Hard as it is to imagine that we will reflect God's glory and thereby glorify him, Scripture says that it will happen to everyone who is joined to Christ by faith.

Present Glorification

As with many other doctrines in the *ordo salutis*, this one has a present and a future aspect. Let's look first at our present glorification. Psalm 8 speaks of God's creation of human beings in glorious terms. The writer to the Hebrews quotes Psalm 8 in Hebrews 2:7–8 as follows: "You made him for a little while lower than the angels; you have crowned him with glory and honor, putting everything in subjection under his feet." In one sense, that is true of all human beings. God has made us in his image and to have dominion over the whole earth. So we are like God, and we play a divine role. As God has dominion over the whole creation, so Adam was to take dominion of all the earth in God's name.

But as we know, Adam failed to take dominion as God commanded. He sought to glorify himself rather than his Creator. So redemption must restore to us the glory that we forfeited by sin. Jesus glorified his disciples. In John 17:22, he prayed to his Father, "The glory that you have given me I have given to them, that they may be one even as we are one." In 2 Corinthians 3:18, Paul says, "And we all, with unveiled face, beholding the glory of the Lord, are being transformed into the same image from one degree of glory to another. For this comes from the Lord who is the Spirit." In John 17:22, glorification is in the past. In 2 Corinthians 3:18, it is in the present. Cf. 1 Peter 1:8; 2 Peter 1:3.

This is one way in which the Bible talks about the benefits of salvation, as a great light reflected from God, more and more reflected back to him. Scripture also uses this image of glory in regard to the ministry of the gospel. Paul's ministry glorifies the church (Eph. 3:10), and the church glorifies him in return (1 Thess. 2:20). So the ministry of the new covenant exceeds the glory of the old (2 Cor. 3:9).

Through that ministry of the gospel, we even now partake of that glory that will be revealed: "So I exhort the elders among you, as a fellow elder and a witness of the sufferings of Christ, as well as a partaker in the glory that is going to be revealed" (1 Peter 5:1).

Future Glorification

But most biblical references to glorification place it in the future. Like most of God's other blessings, there is a beginning in this life and a consummation at the end, an *already* and a *not yet*, as the theologians say. Present glorification is usually presented as a moral conformity to God's will. Future glorification is often the glorification of the *body*. Note the large number of passages on this subject (Rom. 8:11, 18–19, 22–23; 1 Cor. 15:42–44; 2 Cor. 4:17; Phil. 3:21). Scripture is not ashamed of the human body, as some philosophers and religions have been. It recognizes that the human body is weak, weary, and sick because of the fall. But it also recognizes that because of Christ, our bodies, not just our souls, will be raised in glory—never again to experience suffering, sickness, or death. The resurrection body will be imperishable, without corruption, powerful. It will be spiritual—not in the sense of being immaterial, for it will be quite material. It will be spiritual, rather, in being fully dominated by the Spirit of God, like Jesus (1 John 3:2).

More generally, our glorification will be a consummation of human nature in God's image, humanity as God intended for it to be (Rom. 2:10; 5:2; 9:23; 1 Cor. 2:7; Eph. 1:18; Col. 1:27; 2 Thess. 2:14; 2 Tim. 2:10; Heb. 2:10; 1 Peter 1:7; 5:10). We cannot now imagine how wonderful it will be, how wonderful we will be, and, indeed, how wonderful even those we consider lowliest will be in their glorified bodies.

He rewards us with a crown of glory (1 Peter 5:4). That image might be cause for pride as we look forward to it. But look at how Peter deals with this promise (1 Peter 5:1–4):

> So I exhort the elders among you, as a fellow elder and a witness of the sufferings of Christ, as well as a partaker in the glory that is going to be revealed: shepherd the flock of God that is among you, exercising oversight, not under compulsion, but willingly, as God would have you; not for shameful gain, but eagerly; not domineering over those in your charge, but being examples to the flock. And when the chief Shepherd appears, you will receive the unfading crown of glory.

For Peter, the coming glory should motivate elders to be examples to the people in their churches. They should not seek their own gain, or to dominate their brothers and sisters, but to serve them, as Jesus taught in Matthew 20. We can humbly serve one another in this life, knowing that our crown will come with Jesus. This is the time for us to be willing to suffer, knowing that the glory is coming later (Rom. 8:18–39; 1 Peter 1:11).

But there is a glory even now, as we've seen: the glory of serving Jesus and one another, the glory of being willing to suffer for his sake.

Partaking in the Divine Nature

The biblical doctrine of glorification, I think, has been the main motivation for some theologians (especially the tradition from Irenaeus and Eastern Orthodoxy today) to speak of our sanctification in terms of *theosis*, or "deification." One text of Scripture especially has led many to this formulation:

> His divine power has granted to us all things that pertain to life and godliness, through the knowledge of him who called us to his own glory and excellence, by which he has granted to us his precious and very great promises, so that through them you may become partakers of the divine nature, having escaped

from the corruption that is in the world because of sinful desire. For this very reason, make every effort to supplement your faith with virtue, and virtue with knowledge, and knowledge with self-control, and self-control with steadfastness, and steadfastness with godliness, and godliness with brotherly affection, and brotherly affection with love. For if these qualities are yours and are increasing, they keep you from being ineffective or unfruitful in the knowledge of our Lord Jesus Christ. For whoever lacks these qualities is so nearsighted that he is blind, having forgotten that he was cleansed from his former sins. Therefore, brothers, be all the more diligent to make your calling and election sure, for if you practice these qualities you will never fall. For in this way there will be richly provided for you an entrance into the eternal kingdom of our Lord and Savior Jesus Christ. (2 Peter 1:3–11)

Note especially verse 4, "that . . . you may become partakers of the divine nature." That sounds to some as if it compromises the Creator-creature distinction on which I have placed much weight in this book (see especially chapter 3). Most people who speak in terms of deification say that they are not at all violating this distinction. But they do want to draw metaphysical conclusions from the passage, saying, for example, that we cannot become God, but we can possess divine "energies." This terminology is quite obscure and, in my mind, somewhat dangerous.

The passage itself is not at all metaphysical, but ethical. Recall my argument in chapter 36 that, contrary to Roman Catholic doctrine, sin is not a metaphysical derangement of human faculties but personal rebellion—ethical disobedience against God. Similarly, in 2 Peter 1:3–11 the writer's interest is not man's metaphysical nature, but the ethical qualities fulfilling God's promises to us, by which we can "make [our] calling and election sure" (v. 10).

The reference to the divine nature in verse 4 should therefore be seen as God's ethical attributes, reflected in us as we are renewed in the image of Christ. It is in that way that we can "partake" of the divine nature. We share it as we reflect God's glory and do the things he does.

Glory with God and with Christ

The WSC famously says in its first question and answer that "man's chief end is to glorify God, and to enjoy him forever." So although our glorification comes at the end of the *ordo salutis*, we must not think of the goal of our life as merely to glorify ourselves, even if that glory comes from the reflection of God's glory. As John Murray says:

When we think of the glory of God as the chief end in the goal of sanctification, we must appreciate the extent to which God will be glorified in the glorification of his people. . . . This great truth, that the glorification of the saints has not only as its chief end the glory of God, but is really constituted by the exhibition and vindication of the glory of God, is illustrated by the word of the apostle when he says that "we rejoice in hope of the glory of God" (Rom. 5:2). There is good reason for believing that "the glory of God" refers to God's own glory (possessive genitive; cf. John 11:4; Rom. 1:23; 15:7 . . .), and not to the glory that comes from God and is bestowed upon us (cf. Rom. 2:7, 10; 8:18, 21; 9:23b . . .). So when Paul says, "We rejoice in hope of the glory of God," he represents the eschatological finale of the believer's hope as hope of the manifestation of God's own glory (cf. 1 Thess. 2:12; 1 Peter 5:10). This is simply to say that the theocentric interest of the believer is paramount in the hope which constitutes the completion of the redemptive process.[1]

Murray continues by saying that our glorification in the NT is specifically a glorification with Christ himself (Rom. 8:17, 29–30). Christ is glorified as the "firstborn among many brothers" (8:29), and Murray adds:

> We thus see how, in the final realization of the goal of sanctification, there is exemplified and vindicated to the fullest extent, an extent that staggers our thought by reason of its stupendous reality, the truth inscribed upon the whole process of redemption, from its inception in the electing grace of the Father (cf. Eph. 1:4; Rom. 8:29) to its consummation in the adoption (cf. Rom. 8:23; Eph. 1:5), that Christ in all his offices as Redeemer is never to be conceived of apart from the church, and the church is not to be conceived of apart from Christ. There is correlativity in election, there is correlativity in redemption once for all accomplished, there is correlativity in the mediatorial ministry which Christ continues to exercise at the right hand of the Father, and there is correlativity in the consummation, when Christ will come the second time without sin for those who look for him unto salvation. This is the goal of sanctification; this is the hope it enshrines, and thereby its demands upon us are invested with sanctions of surpassing glory.[2]

There is, then, more to be said about glorification in our later discussions of heaven (chapter 50) and of the return of Christ (chapter 51).

Key Terms
Glory of God
Shekinah
Full-bucket problem
Already and *not yet*
Crown of glory
Theosis
Deification
Energies

Study Questions

1. *MCW*, 2:314–15.
2. Ibid., 2:316–17.

1. "Jesus is our *shekinah*." Explain; evaluate.
2. If God is all-glorious, what can it mean for us to glorify him?
3. Relate *glory* and *image*.
4. Is glorification only a future hope, or is it a blessing for our lives today? Explain.
5. Does glorification pertain to the *body*? Explain how, or why not.
6. Is it possible for human beings to "partake in the divine nature"? How? Or why not? Explain how 2 Peter 1:3–11 bears on this question.
7. Discuss the relationship between our glorification and the glorification of God himself, and specifically of Jesus Christ.

Memory Verses

Rom. 5:2: Through him we have also obtained access by faith into this grace in which we stand, and we rejoice in hope of the glory of God.

1 Cor. 10:31: Whether you eat or drink, or whatever you do, do all to the glory of God.

2 Cor. 3:18: And we all, with unveiled face, beholding the glory of the Lord, are being transformed into the same image from one degree of glory to another.

1 Peter 5:1–4: So I exhort the elders among you, as a fellow elder and a witness of the sufferings of Christ, as well as a partaker in the glory that is going to be revealed: shepherd the flock of God that is among you, exercising oversight, not under compulsion, but willingly, as God would have you; not for shameful gain, but eagerly; not domineering over those in your charge, but being examples to the flock. And when the chief Shepherd appears, you will receive the unfading crown of glory.

2 Peter 1:3–4: His divine power has granted to us all things that pertain to life and godliness, through the knowledge of him who called us to his own glory and excellence, by which he has granted to us his precious and very great promises, so that through them you may become partakers of the divine nature, having escaped from the corruption that is in the world because of sinful desire.

Resources for Further Study

Frame, John M. *DCL*, 298–313 (on man's "chief end").

Murray, John. *MCW*, 2:305–17.

PART 10

THE DOCTRINE OF THE CHURCH

CHAPTER 46

THE CHURCH

IN OUR STUDY OF THE *ORDO SALUTIS*, we considered mainly the salvation of individuals. Election, calling, regeneration, and so on are events that happen to each individual. But in the Bible, salvation is more than that. In Acts 20:28, Paul tells the Ephesian elders, "Pay careful attention to yourselves and to all the flock, in which the Holy Spirit has made you overseers, to care for the church of God, which he obtained with his own blood." Jesus died for the *church*, obtaining it for himself with his own blood. Jesus did not just die for individuals; he died for a *people*, a *body*, a *bride*, consisting of many people, united in the bonds of a larger whole.[1]

So throughout the Bible, we read of God's bringing to himself not only individuals, but also families: the families of Noah, Abraham, Isaac, and Jacob. Eventually Jacob's family becomes a nation, and God calls that nation to be his holy people. In the NT, that nation is the church of Jesus Christ.

Old Testament Background

As a community of people worshiping God, the church goes back to the garden of Eden. After the fall, Cain and Abel brought sacrifices to the Lord, so then, too, there was the existence of a worshiping community. Seth, the third son of Adam and Eve, had a son named Enosh. And Scripture tells us that "at that time [the time of Seth and Enosh] people began to call upon the name of the LORD" (Gen. 4:26).

So there has always been a community of people on the earth worshiping the true God. But something special happened when God led Israel out of Egypt to meet with him on Mount Sinai (Ex. 19–20). As the people camped around the mountain, they did not see the form of the Lord, but the mountain was full of his presence. There were thunders, lightnings, trumpet blasts, a thick cloud, smoke; the mountain itself trembled. The people had to wash themselves, to be ceremonially clean in God's presence. Then

---

1. We should also emphasize, however, the other side. Jesus died for individuals, not only for a corporate group, as I have indicated in my discussion of the application of redemption. Sometimes writers become so upset with "American individualism" that they do injustice to the indubitably individual aspects of biblical salvation.

God spoke words to them. This was the only time in history that the whole people of God had been assembled in one place to hear words directly from God's own mouth.

These words were the covenant that I described in chapter 4. In that covenant, God gives his name, Yahweh, the Lord, and then declares his previous mercies to Israel: he has brought them out of the land of Egypt, the house of slavery. Then he sets forth the Ten Commandments, the fundamental law of the covenant. When the people hear these words, they are terribly afraid. They do not want to hear God speak to them anymore. They ask Moses to speak to God in their place: "You speak to us, and we will listen, but do not let God speak to us, lest we die" (Ex. 20:19).

In Deuteronomy, written sometime afterward, this wonderful and terrible meeting between God and Israel is called "the day of the assembly" (Deut. 9:10; 10:4; 18:16; cf. 4:10). The word *assembly* is *qahal* in Hebrew, sometimes translated "congregation." In an important sense, this is the beginning of the church. It was on this day that the nation of Israel became, by covenant, God's holy nation, distinguished from all the other nations of the world. God has redeemed the Israelites from Egypt; they are his treasured possession among all peoples (Ex. 19:4–5). They are a kingdom of priests and a holy nation (v. 6). Their constitution is the covenant-treaty called the Ten Commandments.

We hear these titles of Israel, *kingdom of priests* and *holy nation*, again in the NT, in 1 Peter 2:9, where the apostle says, "You are a chosen race, a royal priesthood, a holy nation, a people for his own possession." So the NT church, like OT Israel, is God's own special people, the continuation of Israel. Significantly, the Greek translation of Deuteronomy uses the term *ecclesia*, "church," to represent the "gathering" of the people into God's presence. Israel was the church of the old covenant; the NT church is the Israel of the new covenant, what Paul calls "the Israel of God" in Galatians 6:16.

Now, some Christians, called dispensationalists, believe that Israel and the church are two distinct peoples of God, given different sets of promises. I believe Scripture teaches, on the contrary, that God's people are one body, the same in the OT and NT. Israel and the new covenant church differ in some important ways. God gave Israel title to the geographical area of Canaan and dwelled there in the temple, a replica of heaven itself. The NT church, on the contrary, is sent to all parts of the world, and its temple is found in believers' own bodies. But there is only one salvation, only one set of promises, all of which are fulfilled in Jesus Christ. We can see that by the fact that the NT church bears the same titles that God gave to Israel in Exodus 19:5–6. In Romans 11:11–24, Paul speaks of the people of God as one olive tree. Some branches, unbelieving Jews, are broken off, and believing Gentiles are grafted in. But there is one tree, not two.

Paul also teaches that there is to be no dividing wall in the church between Jews and Gentiles (Eph. 2:11–22; 3:6; cf. Acts 10; 11:1–18). Gentiles do not need to become Jews in order to be saved (Gal. 3:29). They do not need circumcision. Rather, they are Abraham's children by faith, the Israel of God (Gal. 6:16), part of one body in Christ (Rom. 12:13). There is one family.

So the OT belongs to the Christian church. Jesus is the theme of the OT (Luke 24:13–35). OT saints such as Abraham are examples of the same faith that the NT speaks of (Rom. 4; Heb. 11), and they stand as witnesses to the life of faith. It is even the case that OT prophecies about Israel are fulfilled in the church. In Joel 2:28–32, the prophet says that God will pour out his Spirit on Israel. In Acts 2:17–21, Peter says that God has fulfilled this prophecy by sending his Spirit to bring the first large number of converts into the Christian church. Similarly, compare Amos 9:11–12 with Acts 15:16–17, and Jeremiah 31:31–34 with Hebrews 8:8–12. Here and elsewhere, Scripture applies OT promises to the NT church.

The Nature of the Church

I would now like to look systematically at the nature of the church, then the government of the church. In the next chapter, we will consider the church's task, and in chapters 48–49, the means of grace and the sacraments. Remember that when we discussed Christ (chapters 37–38) and the Spirit (chapter 39), I presented first their persons, then their work. We will do the same with the church.

What is the church? Essentially the church is the people of God in all ages. Notice that the church is people, not buildings, although it is right that the people have buildings in which to meet. In one church I have attended, the worship leader typically welcomes the people at the beginning of the service and thanks them for "bringing the church into this room." That greeting epitomizes the biblical emphasis.

The church is not, however, just any people. It is the people in covenant with God, through Jesus Christ. In one sense, the church is the elect, those joined to Christ in eternity past and through eternity future. In another sense, it is the people who sincerely or insincerely have identified themselves with God's people by profession and baptism. Don't forget the discussion of the previous chapter, that the visible church contains both elect and nonelect. The nonelect are covenant-breakers, not covenant-keepers, but they, too, are in the covenant. They are branches in the Vine of Christ that one day will be broken off.

Visible and Invisible

That leads us to the distinction between the visible and the invisible church. This language is from tradition, not the Bible (as in WCF 25.1–2). But it does give us language to express the presence of both believers and unbelievers in the church. We should not take this to mean that there are two churches. *Visible* and *invisible* are just two different ways of looking at the same church, two perspectives. The invisible church is, to use Wayne Grudem's definition, "the church as God sees it."[2] God knows for sure who is truly joined to Christ by faith, for he can see people's hearts. We cannot, for the heart is invisible to us.

2. *GST*, 855.

The visible church is the church as man sees it, though of course God sees the visible as well as the invisible. The visible church consists of all who credibly *profess* faith in Christ, with their children (more on the children later). When someone applies for church membership, usually some church leaders examine the person to see whether he understands the gospel and trusts Jesus as Lord and Savior. If the person is living in some sin that flagrantly contradicts the gospel, such as worshiping idols in his home or living in a homosexual relationship, the leaders should decline to admit the person to church membership. But as we know, many sins are hard for us to evaluate: greed, resentment, bitterness, and so on. People with such sins usually find it easy to hide from human scrutiny. The elders should determine, as best they can, not whether the person is sinlessly perfect, for none of us is, but whether the person has made a sincere commitment to Christ. But they cannot see a person's heart. So visible churches will include some unbelievers, even some nonelect.

Are those unbelievers "in" the church? In one sense, no, for they are not united to Christ in a saving way. Recall Paul's statement:

> For no one is a Jew who is merely one outwardly, nor is circumcision outward and physical. But a Jew is one inwardly, and circumcision is a matter of the heart, by the Spirit, not by the letter. His praise is not from man but from God. (Rom. 2:28–29; cf. 9:6–7)

So we may say that they are not part of the *invisible* church. But in another sense, yes, they are in the church, because they have taken vows. They have become part of the covenant relation with God. God will hold them accountable, even those who take the vows fraudulently. They are members of the covenant, but covenant-breakers, not covenant-keepers. Unless they repent and trust Christ, they will receive the curses of the covenant rather than its blessings.

Local, Regional, Universal

Another important distinction concerns the geographical extent of the church. The word *church* in the NT refers to local, regional, and universal bodies. Locally, the early Christians met mostly in homes, in house churches (Rom. 16:5; 1 Cor. 16:19; Col. 4:15).

Regionally, there was the city church, such as the church of Rome, of Corinth (1 Cor. 1:2), and of Antioch. We know that the church of Jerusalem, for example, had three thousand members following the events of Acts 2, and later even more thousands were added. But it is unlikely that those thousands worshiped together in the same place. So the city church is divided into house churches. Yet there is a unity in the city church, even a common government, as indicated in Philippians 1:1.

Then there is the universal church, the whole body of believers throughout the world (Matt. 16:18; Acts 15:22; 1 Cor. 12:28; Eph. 1:22). On at least one occasion, in Acts 15, the leaders met in Jerusalem to make decisions binding on the entire church throughout the world.

Images

Another way to get an idea of the nature of the church is to look at the images of the church in Scripture. We have already looked often at the idea of covenant, from which we learn that the church is the *covenant people of God*. In the covenant, God is Lord and we are servants. On this, see especially chapters 2–4.

And also at the beginning of this book, we have looked at two other master metaphors that govern the flow of the biblical story: the *kingdom* of God (chapter 5) and the *family* of God (chapter 6).

The kingdom is not identical with the church. Recall Geerhardus Vos's definition of the kingdom quoted in chapter 5:

> To [Jesus] the kingdom exists there, where not merely God is supreme, for that is true at all times and under all circumstances, but where God supernaturally carries through his supremacy against all opposing powers and brings men to the willing recognition of the same.[3]

So the kingdom is God's historical program, bringing all areas of life on earth subject to Christ, as I indicated in chapter 5.

Another important image that we have already looked at is the family of God (chapter 6). This figure stresses the intimacy of life in the church. We saw in our study of the doctrine of adoption (chapter 42) that God is our Father, and the members of the church are our brothers and sisters. Jesus is our older brother (Heb. 2:11–12).

But there is even greater intimacy in the metaphor of the church as the *bride* of Christ, a wonderful picture, which we see in both Testaments. In the OT, Israel is the unfaithful wife of the Lord. In the NT, the church is the bride, who will be presented spotless to Jesus at the marriage supper of the Lamb (Rev. 21:2, 9; cf. Isa. 61:10; 62:5; Ezek. 16; Hos. 1–3; John 3:29; Eph. 5:22–33).

And there is also the figure of the *body* of Christ. This metaphor stresses the unity of the church with Christ, and the unity of each Christian with all the others. One part of our physical body is dependent on the others, so every member of the body of Christ, each believer, depends on the others, and the others depend on him. So we should work together, as the arms, legs, and head work together in a rightly functioning physical body. We are one body in Christ (Rom. 12:5; 1 Cor. 12:12), the body of Christ (1 Cor. 10:16), and therefore all the gifts God gives to each of these he wants us to use for the benefit of the whole body. In a somewhat different use of the image, Christ is the head, distinguished from the rest of the body (Eph. 5:23; Col. 1:18; 2:19). This image encourages us to be subject to him, to accept his direction.

Then there is the *temple* metaphor. We are corporately the temple of the living God (1 Cor. 3:16–17; Eph. 2:21–22; 1 Peter 2:5). We are all living stones, held together by Jesus the chief cornerstone (1 Peter 2:4–8). Scripture also speaks of each individual

---

3. Geerhardus Vos, *The Teaching of Jesus concerning the Kingdom of God and the Church* (Grand Rapids: Eerdmans, 1958), 50.

Christian as a temple of the Holy Spirit (1 Cor. 6:19; Rev. 3:12), who should not allow that temple to be defiled by sin. In a related figure, believers are priests (1 Peter 2:5, 9; Rev. 1:6; 5:10; 20:6), serving under Jesus the High Priest (Heb. 7–8). This is the doctrine of the priesthood of all believers.

The church is also the *branches of the Vine*, which is Christ (John 15:5). It is the olive tree, from which some branches have been broken off and others grafted in (Rom. 11:17–24). It is God's field (1 Cor. 3:6–9), and it is the harvest brought forth from that field (Matt. 13:1–9; John 4:35).

Attributes

We should also look at the traditional *attributes* of the church. In the Nicene Creed, we confess to believing in "one holy catholic and apostolic" church. The Roman Catholic Church interprets these adjectives in a somewhat self-serving way, emphasizing its oneness against the many churches of Protestantism; its holiness as seen in its Masses and ceremonies; its catholicity, for it is the Roman *Catholic* Church; and its apostolicity, for it claims to have a priesthood in direct succession from the apostles, by the laying on of hands from generation to generation.

But the Nicene Creed was written centuries before the Catholic-Protestant division, so we should not assume that these adjectives were written with future Roman polemics in mind. We should rather ask what these words mean in the context of a biblical doctrine of the church.

First, the church is *one*. Paul teaches that it is one body in Christ, with one Lord, one faith, one baptism. But Jesus prayed for the unity of the church in John 17. Both Paul and Jesus, indeed, anticipated disunity as a problem in the church. They knew that disunity was something that we should pray about and try to eliminate. So, as with some other concepts that we've discussed in this book, the unity of the church is both a fact and a norm. God has made it one, but he commands us to seek oneness.

The unity of the church is spiritual, but also organizational. Jesus (John 17) and Paul do not distinguish between spiritual and organizational. They call us to seek unity in all these respects: to agree with one another, to love one another, to serve one another, and to glorify one another, as Jesus says in John 17:4 that he glorified the Father. The unity of the church is also organizational, for Jesus founded one church, not many denominations. He founded a church to be ruled by apostles (Eph. 2:20), elders (1 Tim. 3:1–7), and deacons (1 Tim. 3:8–13), and his Word tells us to "obey your leaders" (Heb. 13:17). When there are disputes within the church, Jesus gives us in Matthew 18 directions for resolving them. But he never gives us the option of leaving one church and starting another. That is what has happened in the history of denominationalism. I believe that denominationalism is an offense against God and that it has weakened the church's witness. The rise of denominations is caused by sin, either sin of those who left the original church or sin of those who forced them to leave—or, most likely, both. For more on that, look at my book *ER*.

Second, the church is *holy*. As I indicated in chapter 43 on sanctification, we are God's "saints," his "holy people." Paul regularly addresses the churches as the "saints." This does not imply that every member of the visible church is elect, or that any of them are sinlessly perfect. But we are God's people. He has bought us to be his, to be associated with him as his servants, sons, and daughters. Since God is holy, anyone associated with him in those ways is also holy. We are the temple of the Spirit. Those who persecute Christians persecute the Lord (Acts 9:4).

Third, the church is *catholic*. That word simply means "universal," though the Roman church has tried to steal it from the rest of us. This means that the church does not belong only to one nation or race. In the OT period, the church was closely associated with one nation, Israel. But in the NT, the church is scattered throughout the nations, fulfilling God's promise to Abraham that in him all the nations of the earth would be blessed.

Finally, the church is *apostolic*. This does not mean, as Roman Catholics think, that every elder must be in a historical succession going back to the apostles. The NT knows of no such succession, nor does it suggest that the office of the apostle continues in the church. It does tell us, however, that the early Christians "devoted themselves to the apostles' teaching and the fellowship, to the breaking of bread and the prayers" (Acts 2:42). The church must always be in fellowship with the apostles, believing the apostles' teaching, following the apostles' example (1 Cor. 11:1).

Marks

Another tradition seeks to describe the church by certain *marks*. A mark of the church distinguishes the true church from everything else that is not the church, especially from false churches, churches that only pretend to be churches of Jesus Christ. This discussion arose especially during the Reformation period, when the church became very divided and questions arose as to which churches were true churches and which were not.

The Reformers generally acknowledged three marks: the true preaching of the Word, the right administration of the sacraments, and church discipline. The first two of these marks come from Acts 2:42, which I quoted earlier. Acts 2:42 doesn't say that these are marks of the church, but certainly as we look at the NT teaching as a whole, it would be hard to conceive of any genuine church without these. Discipline was the third mark, for it seemed that the first two marks were in jeopardy unless there was sufficient discipline to guard the true preaching of the Word and the right administration of the sacraments.

I think these marks are important, but it is not always easy to apply them. Protestants differ, for example, as to whether baptism should be given to covenant children. Should Baptists therefore judge that Presbyterians do not rightly administer the sacraments and that therefore their churches are not true churches? Or vice versa? Most Protestant denominations have not taken the principle this far, but how far should it be taken? As for the true preaching of the Word: how much must I disagree with the preaching in a church before I consider it a false church? These questions are difficult. So we should not pretend that these criteria easily solve the problems of distinguishing true churches from false.

And we should also ask: are these the *only* marks of the church? Scripture does not say that any of the previous three are marks, but it does say that love is a mark. Jesus said, "By this all people will know that you are my disciples, if you have love for one another" (John 13:35). Strange that love has been ignored in the discussion of marks. Perhaps if love, and not only true doctrine, had been recognized as a mark, the church would have been less characterized by theological battling.

A good case could also be made for worship as a mark. The church gets its very name from the worshiping community gathered around Mount Sinai. If it is not a body that gathers to praise God, it certainly is not the church. And worship is certainly more than the sacraments, as we will see. Worship, like the other marks, clearly distinguishes the true church from false churches, for false churches do not worship God in spirit and truth (John 4:24).

And what of the Great Commission (Matt. 28:19–20)? As we will see, this is the central task of the church, to evangelize and nurture. How can the church possibly be the church if it is not doing this? And who else does this except the church? So I think a good biblical case can be made for worship (normative perspective), love (existential perspective), and the Great Commission (situational perspective) as marks of the church. The Great Commission, of course, includes the preaching of the Word, and worship includes the sacraments. Discipline is a form of love. So my triad of marks is broader than the older triad and includes them. And it seems to me important that we recognize these marks in their broader form. See fig. 46.1.

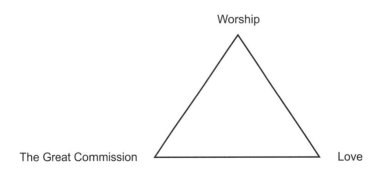

Fig. 46.1. Church Government

Church Government

Finally, a summary discussion of church government. Jesus gave certain powers to the church. He did not give the church the right to use physical force to accomplish its tasks. As theologians say, he did not give the church the power of the sword (John

18:36; 2 Cor. 10:4). Only the civil government has that power. But he did give to the church the sword of the Spirit, the Word of God (Eph. 6:17). No matter how much people despise that Word, it is the most powerful force on the face of the earth (Rom. 1:16). Jesus also gave to the church "the keys of the kingdom of heaven" (Matt. 16:19; cf. 18:17–18). That is, the church has the authority to say who belongs to the covenant and who does not. It has the power to admit people to the fellowship and to cast them out.

We usually refer to the power of the keys as the power of church discipline. Scripture takes discipline in the church very seriously. In 1 Corinthians 5, the apostle Paul says five times that a church member guilty of serious sin should be cast out of the church, excommunicated. We rarely hear of excommunication today, except in the Roman Catholic Church. People usually think that excommunication is an ancient, outmoded practice, and very cruel. If the church represents the love of Christ, people ask, how can it ever throw anybody out?

But discipline is biblical. It can be more or less serious, from excommunication at one extreme, to admonition or rebuke for lesser sins. But every church ought to practice it. There are at least three purposes of discipline. The first is to restore a sinning believer (Matt. 18:15; 1 Cor. 5:5; Gal. 6:1; 1 Tim. 1:20; James 5:20). That is, discipline aims not merely to punish, but to turn the offender away from his sins, to repentance. It's for *his* sake. So church discipline is not a cruel thing, but a loving thing. Second, discipline exists to deter such sins by others, to instruct the congregation as to what is and is not acceptable (1 Cor. 5:2, 6–7; 1 Tim. 5:20; Heb. 12:15). Third, discipline exists to protect the honor of Christ and his church (Rom. 2:24; 1 Cor. 6:6; Eph. 5:27). When churches ignore sin, the world despises them, and the reputation of Jesus Christ himself is dragged through the mud. Instructing, honoring Christ before the world, and helping the offender: normative, situational, existential. See fig. 46.2.

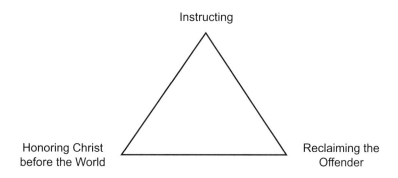

Fig. 46.2. Purposes of Discipline

Discipline takes several forms. The first is teaching. The church must make clear what behavior is acceptable to God. And it must present the gospel in such a way as to motivate obedience. Remember that people aren't motivated by denunciations and scolding nearly as well as they are motivated by the love of Jesus for them and the joy of living a godly life.

Matthew 18:15–20 lists the steps of discipline in cases in which the teaching of the church has not had its desired effect. If someone sins against you, sometimes you should ignore it, for love covers a multitude of sins (Prov. 10:12; 1 Peter 4:8). But sometimes you can't. So Matthew 18:15 tells you to go to the person who has sinned against you. Don't gossip, but go. If that doesn't lead to reconciliation, go again and take a witness or two with you (v. 16). If that doesn't work, go to the church, the ruling body (v. 17). The leaders are authorized to make a decision whether the person is guilty or innocent and, if guilty, whether the person should be admonished, rebuked, removed from office, or excommunicated.

Scripture also tells us that when we hear that someone else has something against us, we should go to him and seek reconciliation (Matt. 5:23–26). So the responsibility of seeking reconciliation does not lie exclusively with the person who accuses or the person who is accused. Both have a biblical obligation to reconcile. Ideally, they should meet each other on the way to visiting each other.

Not all sins should be the subject of formal discipline. Indeed, we sin so often that most of them cannot be. Romans 14 talks about some disagreements in the church that are not to be resolved by formal discipline, but rather by Christians of different views living together in love. The sins to be disciplined formally are sins against individual brothers in the church, as in Matthew 18, and the outward, scandalous sins like the man who was sleeping with his father's wife in 1 Corinthians 5.

Now a bit about the formal structure of church government. Jesus himself, of course, is King of the church, the ultimate Head. Under him, there were three kinds of officers in the NT church. The highest office was the apostle, those who had seen the risen Christ and were appointed by him to be the official witnesses to his resurrection. Scripture doesn't suggest that that office continues past the original generation of apostles. Certainly, as time passed, it would eventually have been impossible to find people who had seen the risen Christ and who had been appointed by him as official witnesses.

The next office has various names in the NT (Acts 14:23; 20:17; 1 Tim. 3:1–7; 5:17; Titus 1:6–9; 1 Peter 5:2–5). I believe that the words *elder, overseer, pastor,* and *bishop* are interchangeable titles of the same office. This is the ruling office. It is the elder who is charged with setting and administering the rules of the church, subject to the Word of God. Among the elders, some are official teachers, those who "labor in preaching and teaching" (1 Tim. 5:17).

Then there are the deacons (1 Tim. 3:8–13). Little is said about their role in the church, but traditionally they have been associated with the seven men in Acts 6 who were appointed to the ministry of mercy. They are not called *deacons* in Acts 6, but the qualifications for deacons are described extensively in 1 Timothy 3:8–13. Those qualifications are largely spiritual and moral, and they are identical to those of elders, with the exception that elders are required to be "able to teach" (v. 2) and deacons are not.

These three offices fit in with our threefold analysis that we've discussed in previous chapters. The apostle is normative, for his teaching governs all the teaching in the church for all generations. The elder is situational, the one who applies the apostles' teaching to all the situations and problems of each church. The deacon is existential, the one who ministers Jesus' love to those in need. See fig. 46.3.

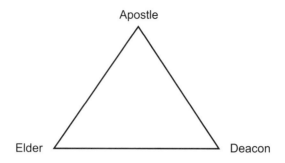

Fig. 46.3. Officers of the Church

There have been three main theories of how these offices are to function: episcopalian, presbyterian, and congregational. In the episcopal system found in the Roman Catholic Church, the Church of England, the worldwide Anglican communion, and the various other churches called *Episcopal*, the churches in a region are under the authority of one man, called a bishop. (The word *episcopal* comes from the Greek word for *bishop*.) The bishop has power to consecrate and appoint other officers, following the model of the apostles in Acts 14:23 and Titus in Titus 1:5.

In the presbyterian system, common in churches called *Reformed* as well as *Presbyterian*, there is a plurality of elders in every church. (*Presbyterian* comes from the Greek word for *elder*.) These are elected by the people. The elders meet as the ruling body of each particular church, and the elders of a region meet together as a broader court, dealing with the ministry of the whole area. Usually once a year, all the elders of the denomination, or a representative group of them, meet as a General Assembly, or Synod, to resolve questions of importance to the whole church, as did the apostles and other leaders in Acts 15.

In the congregational or independent system, found often in Baptist churches as well as Congregational and independent churches, there is no church government beyond the individual congregation. The local governing body may be called *elders* or *deacons*, or there may be both elders and deacons. There may be voluntary organizations of churches, involving meetings of elders similar to a presbytery. Those organizations may give advice and mutual assistance, but they have no authority to compel a local congregation to do as they wish.

In my judgment, Scripture doesn't teach us clearly that one of these is right, or what other alternatives there may be. Evidently there was some flexibility of government in the NT period, with Titus acting as an episcopal bishop (Titus 1:5) and Timothy being gifted by God through the hands of a number of elders (1 Tim. 4:14). But I personally believe that the presbyterian system offers the best balance of authority and freedom. Episcopal churches face the dangers implicit in one-man rule, and congregational churches give the local church no court of appeal when things go wrong locally. The presbyterian system avoids those dangers. In presbyterianism, leadership is always multiple, avoiding one-man rule, and churches are connected with other churches so that broader assemblies of churches can adjudicate appeals from local bodies. Since Scripture speaks of the church as regional and universal as well as local, these assemblies are biblically appropriate.

I have sometimes thought that these three forms of government reflect concerns that parallel my three perspectives: episcopal government reflects desire for a clear standard of authority; presbyterian government offers a system of different authorities adapted to the various situations that the church faces; and congregational government provides the greatest intimacy between the rulers and the ruled (existential). So the following model is possible; see fig. 46.4.[4]

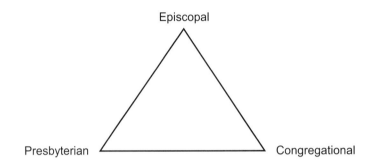

Fig. 46.4. Forms of Church Government

The moral of this illustration is not that a church must choose between, say, authority and intimacy, but rather that whatever government it adopts, it should seek to achieve all three of these values. It also suggests that since these values are all genuinely biblical, each of the three kinds of churches should seek to become more like the others.

But the well-being of the church has more to do with the work of the Spirit than with its form of government. That should seem obvious, but it is a point that we need to keep making. No form of government has shown itself adequate in itself to keep churches on track doctrinally and practically. So we need to be much in prayer for our churches, that its leaders especially will have a double portion of the Spirit—the Spirit's wisdom, grace, and peace.

Key Terms
Day of the assembly
Qahal

4. But here is another possibility: The episcopal bishop can act quickly in response to situations; the presbyterian system is deeply analogous to a system of legal authority. On this understanding, the episcopal system would be more situational and the presbyterian more normative.

Ecclesia
Dispensationalists
Church
Visible church
Invisible church
Local church
Regional church
Universal church
Covenant people of God
Kingdom of God
Family of God
Body of Christ
Temple of God
Bride of Christ
Branches of the Vine
Attributes of the church
Unity
Spiritual unity
Organizational unity
Denomination
Holiness
Catholicity
Apostolicity
Marks of the church
Preaching of the Word
Administration of the sacraments
Church discipline
Worship
The Great Commission
Love
Excommunication
Apostle
Elder
Bishop
Overseer
Pastor
Deacon

Study Questions

1. Frame says that Jesus died for the church, not just for individuals. Explain; evaluate, using biblical references.
2. When did the church begin? Show from Scripture.

3. Describe the continuities and discontinuities between Israel and the NT church. Does dispensationalism do justice to these?

4. Frame cites a worship leader who thanks the congregation for "bringing the church into this room." What is the point of that? Evaluate.

5. What should church leaders require of someone who asks to become a member of their congregation?

6. Are there unbelievers in the church? Make necessary distinctions.

7. Frame distinguishes local, regional, and universal churches. How does this distinction bear upon church government?

8. How is the church related to the kingdom of God? The family of God?

9. What do we learn about the church from the metaphors used in Scripture to describe it? Consider covenant people of God, kingdom of God, family of God, bride of Christ, body of Christ, temple of God, branches of the Vine.

10. What can we learn of the church from its traditional attributes (*one, holy, catholic, apostolic*)?

11. Is the unity of the church organizational, or only "spiritual"? How does your answer affect your evaluation of denominationalism?

12. What are the traditional marks of the church? What can we learn from them about the church? Should there be other marks? Discuss.

13. What are the purposes of excommunication? Relate these to the lordship perspectives.

14. Expound the steps outlined in Matthew 18:15–18 for dealing with a believer who has offended you. Should every sin in the church be the subject of formal discipline?

15. If I think someone has sinned against me, which of us should begin the process of reconciliation, him or me? Explain and defend your answer.

16. Describe the offices of the church, under Christ, mentioned in Scripture.

17. Do you believe in episcopal, presbyterian, or congregational church government? Some other? Explain and defend your answer.

18. "But the well-being of the church has more to do with the work of the Spirit than with its form of government." Why? In what practical ways does the Spirit enter into the government of the church?

Memory Verses

Matt. 28:19–20: Go therefore and make disciples of all nations, baptizing them in the name of the Father and of the Son and of the Holy Spirit, teaching them to observe all that I have commanded you. And behold, I am with you always, to the end of the age.

John 13:35: By this all people will know that you are my disciples, if you have love for one another.

John 15:5: I am the vine; you are the branches. Whoever abides in me and I in him, he it is that bears much fruit, for apart from me you can do nothing.

Acts 2:42: And [the Christians] devoted themselves to the apostles' teaching and the fellowship, to the breaking of bread and the prayers.

Rom. 2:28–29: For no one is a Jew who is merely one outwardly, nor is circumcision outward and physical. But a Jew is one inwardly, and circumcision is a matter of the heart, by the Spirit, not by the letter. His praise is not from man but from God.

Rom. 12:4–5: For as in one body we have many members, and the members do not all have the same function, so we, though many, are one body in Christ, and individually members one of another.

1 Peter 2:9: But you are a chosen race, a royal priesthood, a holy nation, a people for his own possession, that you may proclaim the excellencies of him who called you out of darkness into his marvelous light.

Resources for Further Study

Bannerman, James. *The Church of Christ.* 2 vols. Vestavia, AL: Solid Ground Christian Books, 2009.

Clowney, Edmund P. *The Church.* Downers Grove, IL: InterVarsity Press, 1995.

Frame, John M. *ER.*

Poythress, Vern S. *Understanding Dispensationalists.* Phillipsburg, NJ: P&R Publishing, 1993. Also available at http://www.frame-poythress.org.

CHAPTER 47

THE TASK OF THE CHURCH

IN THE PREVIOUS CHAPTER, we talked about the nature of the church. In this one, we will discuss its task: first what the church is; then what the church does. It is actually hard, however, to separate these two things, just as it is difficult to separate the nature and attributes of God, the person and work of Christ, or the person and work of the Holy Spirit. If a church isn't doing what it's supposed to do, we may well question whether it is a church. So I argued in the previous chapter that carrying out the Great Commission is one of the marks of the church. On the other hand, if a so-called church does not fit the biblical definition of what a church is (the people of God, the body of Christ, and so on), it surely cannot carry out the task that God has assigned to the church. So the nature and task of the church are very closely related; you can't have the one without the other.

I don't agree, however, with theologians who say that the task of the church *is* its nature. When people say that, they usually intend to emphasize the ministries of the church and de-emphasize qualities such as body of Christ and bride of Christ. Sometimes they put this by saying that the church is "service, not status." But Scripture teaches that God has given both status and tasks to the church. We saw that this was the case with the individual Christian. God gives us the status of being his sons and daughters. But he also calls us to serve him, and to serve one another. Certainly the same is true of the church as a corporate body.

When we think of the task of the church, we think of the dynamic pictures in Scripture about the kingdom of God coming into the world, overwhelming God's enemies, and filling the earth with God's glory. So we should ask first how the church is related to the kingdom, and what role the church plays in the coming of the kingdom of God.

The Church and the Kingdom

In chapter 38, in connection with the kingly office of Christ, I emphasized that the *gospel*, the "good news," is originally the message about the coming of the kingdom of God. Recall from that discussion that Isaiah 52:7; 61:1–2; Matthew 3:2; and 4:17 all present the gospel as the news that a King is coming. Compare also the previous discussion of the kingdom of God in chapter 5. The gospel, then, is the report of the coming of the kingdom—that is, the coming of the King to make things right. Incidentally, there is no dichotomy here between gospel and law. The coming of the King means that he will enforce his law in the world, that he will bring righteousness. That is the gospel, the good news. It is important for us to distinguish between salvation by grace and salvation by works. But I don't think Scripture justifies a sharp distinction between law and gospel.

Now, what is the kingdom? To recall a definition that I have quoted before, Geerhardus Vos put it this way: "To him [Jesus] the kingdom exists there, where not merely God is supreme, for that is true at all times and under all circumstances, but where God supernaturally carries through his supremacy against all opposing powers and brings men to the willing recognition of the same."[1] *Kingdom of God* is not merely a synonym for *God's sovereignty*. Rather, it is a specific historical program. God is always sovereign, always King in a general way. But since the fall, he must, as King, put down opposition and bring human beings to acknowledge his kingship. The kingdom of God in the NT is that historical program, the series of events by which God drives his kingship home to sinful human beings. And of course, he does this by sending his Son as a sacrifice for sin and raising him up in victory over Satan and all the forces of evil. But even after the resurrection of Christ, the kingdom will make further advances, as the people of God spread all over the earth, presenting the gospel to subdue men's hearts to the rule of the King.

Where does the church fit into this kingdom program? The church consists of those who have been conquered by God's saving power, who are now enlisted in the warfare of God's kingdom against the kingdom of Satan. Those who do not voluntarily give allegiance to God's kingdom will be conquered by God's judgment and, eventually, destroyed by his power.

The church, then, is, to maintain the military metaphor, the headquarters of the kingdom of God, the base from which God's dominion extends and expands.

God's Mandates for the Church

So the church is a dynamic body, in action. It is through the church that God's kingdom comes to all the ends of the earth. The church is not the church unless it is in action, that is, in other words, unless it is in mission.

But what is our mission? If we are an army, what are our marching orders? Essentially, our task is to keep all of God's commandments. But two of these stand out as fundamental. The first is called the *cultural mandate*, the second the *Great Commission*. The cultural mandate is found in Genesis 1:28, after the story of Adam's and Eve's creation. "And God blessed them. And God said to them, 'Be fruitful and multiply and fill the earth and subdue it and have dominion over the fish of the sea and over

---

1. Geerhardus Vos, *The Teaching of Jesus concerning the Kingdom of God and the Church* (Grand Rapids: Eerdmans, 1958), 50.

the birds of the heavens and over every living thing that moves on the earth.'" This is especially important because God addresses it to the entire human race, which at the time consists of only two people. This is the task of the whole human race.

It has three parts. The first is the divine *blessing*. The cultural mandate is not a burdensome rule, but an expression of God's goodwill to us. But there is an element of command in the blessing. Given the other elements of the mandate, God calls us to spread his blessing throughout the earth.

The second and third parts are commands. One is to have children, grandchildren, and so on, so as to *fill* the entire earth with people. Of course, those people would glorify God. The cultural mandate does not anticipate the fall. So Adam and Eve would fill the earth with people who were eager to do the will of God, and who would therefore live in God's presence, under his blessing.

The second command is to *subdue* the earth, to have "dominion" over it. This means to bring out the potential of everything in the earth so that it will be of service to human beings as they bring glory to God. It doesn't mean to "exploit" the earth. Some secular environmentalists blame the cultural mandate for pollution, for they think *subdue* means "to exploit," to take anything in creation for our selfish gain. But of course, subduing includes preserving, nurturing, as we see, for example, in Genesis 2:15. Human beings cannot live on God's earth if it is utterly polluted. So God expected them as part of their stewardship to keep that from happening. See fig. 47.1.

Fig. 47.1. Aspects of Divine Covenants

So we have three elements: a divine blessing, a commandment to fill, and a commandment to subdue. I think of the first as normative, the second as existential, the third as situational. God's blessing comes first, so his command sets our direction. Filling the earth is the personal, existential commandment, and subduing it focuses on what we do in and with our environment.

These three elements recur over and over again in the Bible. In every covenant that God makes, with Noah, Abraham, Moses, David, and Jesus, there are these three elements: a divine blessing, a seed, and a land. God blesses his people by giving them descendants to live in a land, subduing that land to bring glory to God.

Then comes the second major divine mandate, the Great Commission, Matthew 28:18–20. After his resurrection, Jesus tells his disciples:

> All authority in heaven and on earth has been given to me. Go therefore and make disciples of all nations, baptizing them in the name of the Father and of the Son and of the Holy Spirit, teaching them to observe all that I have commanded you. And behold, I am with you always, to the end of the age.

People sometimes argue whether the Great Commission or the cultural mandate is more fundamental. But I believe they are essentially the same. The Great Commission is the application of the cultural mandate to a fallen human race. As I said, the cultural mandate does not anticipate the fall. But what happens after the fall? People still try to subdue the earth. In Genesis 4, we find the development of civilization among the descendants of wicked Cain. But they are not filling and subduing the earth to God's glory. So the result is wars, pollution, sickness, and so on. If human beings are to fulfill the cultural mandate, their hearts must be subdued to God, before the earth can be subdued to them. That's what the Great Commission does. It brings about a transformation of people, so that they can go and fill the earth, subduing it to the glory of God.

So the Great Commission has the same three elements. Just as God blessed his people after his great work of creation, so the Lord Jesus blesses his people after the new creation, his resurrection from the dead. All authority is his, and he will be with his people to the end. That "I will be with you," remember, is the heart of the covenant. So the first element here, as in Genesis, is blessing. See fig. 47.2.

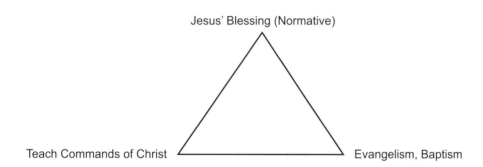

Fig. 47.2. Perspectives on the Great Commission

The second element is filling the earth with disciples. That means baptism in the name of the Trinity. The sword of the Spirit, the Word of God, brings fallen human beings under the lordship of Christ. So the Word, the preaching, is to be evangelistic. It is to bring conversions. But beyond that, the Word is to teach these new Christians to obey all the commands of Christ. So as in the cultural mandate, we have both filling and subduing. The preaching of the Word fills the whole world with disciples and subdues their hearts to obey God's commands. This teaching qualifies them to subdue the earth, to have dominion over it, to the glory of God.

The OT church also had a missional focus. Through the covenant made with Abraham, God intended to bless all the nations (Gen. 12:3). Often in the OT we read of people from other nations coming to worship the God of Israel. This has sometimes been called a *centripetal* concept of missions. But in the NT, God reverses this motion. Now God's people go to the other nations to bring them the gospel, a *centrifugal* view of missions.

The task of the church, then, is to carry out the Great Commission. When it does this, it will also be enabling people to carry out the cultural mandate. But the Great Commission must be the focus of everything the church does. Indeed, it must be the focus of the life of every believer. All that we do must be done so that the world may be filled with believers and that these believers may be subdued to obey all of God's commands.

What is the goal of your life today? Paul says that he became all things to all men so that "by all means I might save some" (1 Cor. 9:22). Of course, only God can save, but Paul (unlike some Calvinists today) did not hesitate to acknowledge his own role in the salvation of people. There is both divine sovereignty and human responsibility in the work of bringing the gospel to the world. It has pleased God to save men through human preaching and teaching. So a chapter later, Paul says, "I try to please everyone in everything I do, not seeking my own advantage, but that of many, that they may be saved" (10:33). Notice: that's the goal of *everything* he does with his life, to bring salvation to people. Now, you might say, "Well, Paul was an apostle, so of course he is primarily concerned with the salvation of men. I'm not an apostle, not even a preacher, so I don't need to have the same goal as Paul." But Paul follows that sentence with this one in 1 Corinthians 11:1: "Be imitators of me, as I am of Christ." Paul says that the whole Corinthian church should have the same goal as he does. He wants them, too, to have as their supreme goal in life bringing salvation to other people.

In Philippians 3 also, Paul speaks of his pattern of self-denial, counting everything as garbage that he might gain Christ. Of course, he is referring to his ministry of bringing the gospel to the Gentiles. In this, he is willing to give everything up to do the will of Christ, and in verse 17 he tells the Christians to "join in imitating me." Note also Jesus' words in Matthew 6:33: "But seek first the kingdom of God and his righteousness, and all these things will be added to you." This, too, is a statement of the supreme goal of the believer's life. And here our ultimate concern is to further the kingdom of God, that program of redemption by which God establishes his kingship on earth as it is in heaven.

So our goal should be the advance of the kingdom of God, against all opposing powers, bringing man to a willing recognition of it, either through conversion or through judgment. Our goal should be that of Paul, bringing the gospel to people.

Now, that doesn't mean that all of us have to quit our jobs and be full-time personal evangelists. Some of us should be. Some should be missionaries and pastors. Others are differently gifted by God, and they should be geared toward *supporting* the advance of the gospel, paying to send people into the harvest fields. Someone has said that we must all be either radical goers or radical senders; the only alternative is disobedience.[2]

And our churches should have that goal as well. It's nice for churches to hold bake sales and take kids to the beach. Those sorts of activities promote fellowship in the body, and that is good. But the overall goal has to be mission. Everything we do in the church has to be planned with the gospel as the center. If you have a bake sale, invite non-Christians to bake and to come. If you take kids to the beach, teach your kids how to witness to other surfers and swimmers, and invite non-Christians to come along. This concept is sometimes called the *missional church*, in which missions and evangelism are not just activities of the church, or departments of the church, but the very heart of the church, in which everything is focused on the advance of the gospel.

Specific Tasks

More specifically, what goes on in the missional church? Basically three things (there's that number again!): worship, nurture, and witness. Each of these finds its justification in the Great Commission.

Worship is acknowledging the greatness of our covenant Lord. This is the goal of mission. Why do we want to save people? Ultimately the answer is this: so that they will glorify God, so that they will worship him. Jesus says that throughout history, God has been seeking worshipers (John 4:23). That's what missions is: God's seeking of worshipers. See fig. 47.3.

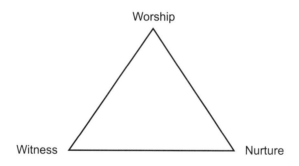

Fig. 47.3. Tasks of the Church

The Bible speaks of worship in broad and narrow senses. The narrow sense is public, corporate worship, what the Jews did in the temple, and what Christians do in their weekly gathering to celebrate the resurrection. The broad sense is the sense of Romans 12:1–2: "I appeal to you therefore, brothers, by the mercies of God, to present your bodies as a living sacrifice, holy and acceptable to God, which is your spiritual

2. I wish I could remember the source of these words, because I would like to express my gratefulness for them.

worship. Do not be conformed to this world, but be transformed by the renewal of your mind, that by testing you may discern what is the will of God, what is good and acceptable and perfect." Notice here the language of sacrifice, holiness, worship. But the worship here is not the weekly worship of the Lord's Day. Rather, it is a worship that we perform all the time, as we seek to live godly lives. When we glorify God, it is a living sacrifice; it is true worship.

In regard to worship in the narrow sense, OT worship was primarily a worship of sacrifice. The sacrifices of animals, grain, oil, and wine pictured Christ's sacrifice, taught the people the ways of God, and brought God and the believer together for fellowship. NT worship, I think, is rather different, since our sacrifice for sin is complete in Christ. NT worship moves from the seventh day to the first day and, appropriately, is essentially a celebration of the resurrection.

Three principles are especially important in the biblical teaching about worship: First, worship must be biblical. Jesus upbraided the Pharisees for following their own traditions rather than the Word of God (Isa. 29:13; Matt. 15:8–9). Worship is for God's pleasure, not our own, and so everything we do in worship must have a biblical basis. In Reformed theology, that idea is sometimes called the *regulative principle*. See fig. 47.4.

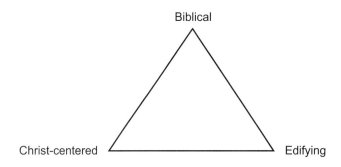

Fig. 47.4. Criteria for Biblical Worship

Second, worship should be God-centered and therefore Christ-centered. Look at the Psalms, how they constantly dwell on God's nature and actions. In the NT celebration of the resurrection, of course the theme is: "Worthy is the Lamb who was slain, to receive power and wealth and wisdom and might and honor and glory and blessing!" (Rev. 5:12). That does not mean, of course, that we should never think about ourselves in worship. In Psalm 18, the first-person pronouns *I, me,* and *my* are found around seventy times. But Psalm 18 is a profoundly God-centered psalm. The psalmist is aware of his own needs, but he knows that God is his only hope. He is aware of himself as someone who trusts only in God's mercy.

So, third, worship is edifying (Heb. 10:24–25). This is not opposed to God-centeredness, for God wants people, like the writer of Psalm 18, to grow through worship and thus to be blessed. First Corinthians 14 is the only extended treatment in the Bible of post-resurrection Christian worship, and the whole emphasis of the chapter is on edification. Paul tells the Corinthians that they should not speak in tongues in worship without interpretation, because speaking in unintelligible language does not *edify*. It doesn't help anybody. For that reason, the Protestant Reformers declared that worship should no longer be in Latin, but in the vernacular languages of the people: German, French, English, and so on. I believe that we need today to take some pains to make our worship clear, understandable to people in our communities. Our language and music should communicate to the mind and the heart. In my judgment, this principle encourages contemporary worship expressions, both contemporary language and contemporary music.

The second specific task of the missional church is nurture, or edification. See how easily this task follows from the first! Nurture is preaching, teaching, counseling, pastoral care, ministries of mercy. Because sin continues in the lives of the regenerate, the church needs to bring us again and again to repentance. It needs to turn us away from pride and self-satisfaction, so that we will be humbled, so that we will turn again and again to the all-sufficiency of Christ.

This is not only the work of the clergy. It is the work of all of us. Paul asks those who are "spiritual" (that is, all of us, regenerated by the Spirit) to restore people who have fallen into sin (Gal. 6:1). We should do it in a spirit of gentleness and guard ourselves, lest we also be tempted. When you correct a brother or sister, don't do it from a high horse. Correct as one sinner talking to another, in the love of Christ.

So the NT abounds in one-anothering texts (John 13:34–35; Rom. 12:10; 13:8; 15:5; 16:16; 1 Cor. 12:25; Gal. 5:13; Eph. 4:2, 32; 5:21; Col. 3:13, 16; 1 Thess. 3:12; 4:9, 18; 5:11; Heb. 3:13; 10:24–25; James 5:16; 1 Peter 1:22; 3:8; 1 John 3:11, 23; 4:7, 11). We are to love one another, forgive one another, pray for one another, edify one another, and so on. That's the work of everyone in the church.

How is nurture a missional activity? For one thing, unbelievers should notice how much we love one another. This is a wonderful testimony to the watching world. Second, when an unbeliever becomes a Christian, he will immediately need a lot of help from his new brothers and sisters to get started in the Christian life. As in the Great Commission, after baptism comes teaching.

Finally, the third task of the church is evangelism itself: witness to the world. Because of the Great Commission, the unbeliever must be in view in everything the church does. That's true even in worship. Worship, in the narrow sense, is mainly for believers. But in 1 Corinthians 14:20–26, Paul talks about an unbeliever who visits the worship service. He tells the worshipers that their service should be clear enough, edifying enough, so that "he is convicted by all, he is called to account by all, the secrets of his heart are disclosed, and so, falling on his face, he will worship God and declare that God is really among you" (vv. 24–25).[3]

---

3. Many writers criticize churches that "gear worship toward unbelievers." But as this passage says, worship services should be planned in the expectation that some unbelievers will attend. Today, inviting non-Christian neighbors to church is a good way of beginning an evangelistic witness.

As we've seen, Paul's goal is to "save some" (1 Cor. 9:22), and all the NT statements of the goal of the Christian life focus on redemption, on bringing unbelievers into the kingdom.

So all the work of the church is missional.[4] Worship, nurture, and witness. In terms of our threefold scheme of organization, I would say that worship is normative, nurture existential, and witness situational. But always remember that each perspective includes the other two.

Ministries of the Church

Now let us look at the ministries of the church that God has given us to carry out the Great Commission. These are the ministry of the Word, the ministry of rule, and the ministry of mercy. See fig. 47.5.

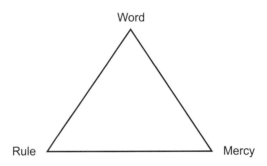

Fig. 47.5. Ministries of the Church

When we discussed church government, we saw that there were three offices in the church: apostle, elder, and deacon. The apostolic office does not continue today, but we still have elders and deacons. The deacons are primarily concerned with the ministry of mercy. The elders carry on ministries of both teaching and rule, some emphasizing the one, some the other. So Paul says, in 1 Timothy 5:17, "Let the elders who rule well be considered worthy of double honor, especially those who labor in preaching and teaching." Note that the work of every elder is to rule, but some are also to labor in preaching and teaching. So in many churches there is a distinction between the teaching elder and the ruling elder.

The teaching elder focuses on the ministry of the Word. Note the qualifications of elders in 1 Timothy 3:2–7 and Titus 1:6–9, and Paul's charge to Timothy in 2 Timothy

---

4. Some recent critics of the missional concept of the church have claimed that it is "legalistic" and that it strains the resources of church people, forcing them to exert themselves in all sorts of evangelistic and charitable activities. Of course, I cannot vouch for how the concept might have been misused in particular instances. And I agree with the critics that there should be a place in the church for believers who are less energetic, who "lead a peaceful and quiet life, godly and dignified in every way" (1 Tim. 2:2). But of course, this depends on the gifts of the Spirit and the opportunities given by God's providence. The church needs to understand the wide differences of gifts. Yet every believer needs to remember that he is part of an army.

4:2. Remarkably, there are no educational requirements for this office. Churches today tend to focus on educational requirements, but these cannot be found in Scripture, though there are certainly aspects of the work of teaching for which education can be valuable. Rather, the requirements are spiritual and moral. An elder is first of all to be a good example to others in the church. A godly life is the body language of sound teaching. A godly life teaches people how sound doctrine should be put into practice. And where godliness is absent, teaching is unpersuasive, even meaningless.

One controversy today is whether the church should ever choose women as elders. Certainly in Scripture men and women are equally valuable in God's sight, equally fallen, equally redeemed by Christ (Gen. 1:27).[5] Paul, who is sometimes accused of male chauvinism, goes out of his way in a number of passages to underscore the equality of women to men in the church (1 Cor. 7:2–4; 11:11–12). Women did pray and prophesy in the church, even, evidently, during public worship services (11:5). But the NT does not assume that men and women are exactly the same, any more than rich and poor, Jew and Greek, are exactly the same. Obviously, a rich person should be expected to give more to the church than a poor person. A Jew would usually be more appropriate than a Greek to teach an Aramaic-speaking congregation. So there are some activities that are more appropriate for men than for women, and vice versa. The husband is the head of the family, the authority over his wife and children. Similarly, I believe, the NT teaches that the teaching and ruling offices in the church, that is, the eldership, are limited to men. I'll mention a couple of passages on this subject that have been much discussed. My interpretations may not seem obvious, and I can't get into details of my reasons for taking them this way, but I think that in the end these are the best ways of taking them.

In 1 Corinthians 14:34–35, Paul teaches that when the elders of the church meet to judge whether a prophecy is authentic, the women should not participate in this judgment. In 1 Timothy 2:11–15, Paul says that women should not participate in the official teaching of the church, nor should they exercise church authority over men. I take it, from these passages, that women should not be elected to the office of elder. I do not think these passages prohibit women from speaking in worship under the elders' authority: remember that in 1 Corinthians 11 women prayed and prophesied in public worship. And I do not think anything in Scripture prohibits women from being deacons.[6]

It's important to distinguish in Scripture between what is called the *general office* and the *special office*. In the case of teaching, there is a sense in which all Christians are called to teach. In Colossians 3:16, we all teach and admonish one another when we sing worship songs. So we all hold the general office of teacher. This includes

---

5. See my discussion in chapter 34.

6. I recommend Robert B. Strimple's argument in favor of women deacons, "Women Deacons? Focusing the Issue," available at http://opc.org/GA/women_in_office.html#APPENDIX. This is an appendix to a committee report to the 55th General Assembly of the Orthodox Presbyterian Church (1988). It is also available in the Minutes of that denomination.

women. Priscilla as well as her husband Aquila taught Apollos the Word of God more accurately than he had known it before (Acts 18:26). According to Titus 2, older women are to teach younger women. In Hebrews 5:12, the writer tells his audience that they should all, by the present stage of their Christian lives, be teachers. That is the general office.

But there is also the special office. When we talk about the office of the teaching elder, we are talking about the special office. That is an office that doesn't belong to every Christian. That office has special qualifications. People must be elected or appointed to it by the laying on of hands. That office, I believe, is limited to men—and, of course, not to all men, but to men specially qualified. How does special-office teaching differ from general-office teaching? Chiefly in that special-office teachers are approved and set apart to speak in the name of the church. But this distinction does not prohibit general-office teachers (including women) from addressing the church when the elders of the church think it wise.

You see, though, how important is the ministry of the Word of God. The Word is the sword of the Spirit. It is our means of nurture and evangelism. So it is important that the church guard the truth of its preaching and teaching through discipline. And it's important that the church be active in preaching the Word—locally and through-out the world. This is essential to the church's mission. Faith comes by hearing and hearing by the word of Christ (Rom. 10:17).

Not all elders are engaged in that special-office teaching, but they do have gifts of rule, a gift referred to in Romans 12:8. The church needs administrators, and the teaching elder is not necessarily the best administrator. So again, many churches have what are called *ruling elders*, distinguished from *teaching elders*.

And then there is the church's ministry of mercy. This is so important to the church's mission. The OT made many provisions for poor Israelites: no-interest loans, gleaning, open harvesting in the sabbatical years, and so on. But Israel often lacked compassion for those fallen on hard times, and God sent prophets to rebuke them. Jesus spoke much about the compassionate use of wealth, and he ministered to many more poor than rich. In the early church, Christians even sold their property to help one another (Acts 4:34–37), and they collected money from all the churches to help Jerusalem believers who were in need. When the church sent Paul and Barnabas to preach the gospel in faraway lands, they gave Paul one admonition: to remember the poor—which, Paul says, he was eager to do in any case.

So the church established a special office of people to administer the church's work of mercy. Seven were appointed for this purpose in Acts 6. Later, those assigned this responsibility were called *deacons*. The qualifications of a deacon in 1 Timothy 3:8–13 are the same as for an elder, except that an elder, not a deacon, must be "able to teach" (v. 2).

The ministry of mercy is also part of the church's mission. When we show love to the poor, both inside and outside the church, we show the love of Christ in a wonderfully eloquent way. When we ignore people's needs, that places a stigma on the work of the gospel.

There are some who maintain that the church should offer diaconal help only to its own members, not to people outside it, least of all to non-Christians. I believe, however, that the church as well as the individual believer should follow Paul's rule:

> So then, as we have opportunity, let us do good to everyone, and especially to those who are of the household of faith. (Gal. 6:10)

The church, as we saw earlier, is our extended family. We have a particular responsibility (stated emphatically in 1 Timothy 5:8) to care for members of our natural families. Since the church is the family of God, we have a special responsibility to our needy brothers and sisters in Christ. But as we are faithful in these relationships, Paul gives us reason to think that we will have some funds left over—to help people who are needy outside the household of faith. The story of the Good Samaritan (Luke 10:25–37) is an illustration: when the Samaritan finds a person lying on the road half-dead, he makes no judgment about the victim's religion, but simply gives assistance. We, too, should be available to help others who cross our paths without regard to their church membership.[7]

Teaching, ruling, and showing mercy fit together well. In terms that we have used throughout the book, these are normative, situational, and existential, respectively. The teacher sets forth God's authoritative commands. The ruler applies these to situations requiring administration. And the deacon brings the love of Christ into people's lives. Each of these fails if the other two are not present. All three are essential to the church's mission.

So we should see that everything the church does is, or ought to be, a fulfillment of the Great Commission. We are to go and teach all nations, baptizing them and teaching them everything the Lord taught us. When we do that, the Lord assures us that he will be with us always, even to the end of the age.

Key Terms

Kingdom of God
Gospel
Cultural mandate
Great Commission
Missional church
Centripetal concept of missions
Centrifugal concept of missions
Worship
Worship in the broad sense

---

7. This is, of course, different from the notion that Christians are required to relieve all the suffering in the world. I do believe that if we were more faithful we could make a significant difference in world hunger. But Scripture realizes that we are finite, limited to what we have, and able to help only some, especially those whom God brings directly into our lives.

Worship in the narrow sense
Nurture
Witness
Regulative principle
Ministry of the Word
Ministry of rule
Ministry of mercy
Elder
Deacon
General office
Special office

Study Questions

1. "There is no dichotomy between gospel and law." Explain, relating this statement to the coming of the kingdom.

2. Where does the church fit into the kingdom program?

3. Describe the three elements of the cultural mandate.

4. Same with the Great Commission. How is it related to the cultural mandate?

5. "There is both divine sovereignty and human responsibility in the work of bringing the gospel to the world." Explain; evaluate.

6. Should every Christian be an evangelist? Discuss.

7. Formulate the overall goals of the believer's life.

8. "Everything we do in the church has to be planned with the gospel as the center." How would your own church be different if it followed this principle?

9. Show how missions and worship are related to each other.

10. Frame distinguishes two concepts of worship in Scripture. What is the biblical basis of this distinction? Evaluate.

11. How is worship in the new covenant different from worship under the old? Discuss the consequences of this.

12. Frame says, "Three principles are especially important in the biblical teaching about worship." Identify these and discuss their biblical basis.

13. Discuss the work of the whole congregation in nurturing one another.

14. How is nurture a missional activity?

15. "Churches today tend to focus on educational requirements [for pastors and elders], but these cannot be found in Scripture, though there are certainly aspects of the work of teaching for which education can be valuable." Explain; evaluate. What requirements does your own church have for officers? Evaluate those in the light of Scripture.

16. Should the church ever choose women as elders? Why or why not? Are there other ways in which women may use teaching gifts in the ministry of the church?

17. How does general-office teaching differ from special-office teaching?

18. Should the church's ministry of mercy be limited to church members? To believers? Why or why not?

19. "So we should see that everything the church does is, or ought to be, a fulfillment of the Great Commission." Explain; evaluate.

Memory Verses

Gen. 1:28: And God blessed them. And God said to them, "Be fruitful and multiply and fill the earth and subdue it and have dominion over the fish of the sea and over the birds of the heavens and over every living thing that moves on the earth."

Gen. 12:3: I will bless those who bless you, and him who dishonors you I will curse, and in you all the families of the earth shall be blessed.

Matt. 6:33: But seek first the kingdom of God and his righteousness, and all these things will be added to you.

Matt. 28:18–20: And Jesus came and said to them, "All authority in heaven and on earth has been given to me. Go therefore and make disciples of all nations, baptizing them in the name of the Father and of the Son and of the Holy Spirit, teaching them to observe all that I have commanded you. And behold, I am with you always, to the end of the age."

John 4:23: But the hour is coming, and is now here, when the true worshipers will worship the Father in spirit and truth, for the Father is seeking such people to worship him.

Rom. 12:1–2: I appeal to you therefore, brothers, by the mercies of God, to present your bodies as a living sacrifice, holy and acceptable to God, which is your spiritual worship. Do not be conformed to this world, but be transformed by the renewal of your mind, that by testing you may discern what is the will of God, what is good and acceptable and perfect.

1 Cor. 10:33: I try to please everyone in everything I do, not seeking my own advantage, but that of many, that they may be saved.

1 Cor. 14:24: But if all prophesy, and an unbeliever or outsider enters, he is convicted by all, he is called to account by all, the secrets of his heart are disclosed, and so, falling on his face, he will worship God and declare that God is really among you.

1 Cor. 14:26b: Let all things be done for building up.

1 Cor. 14:34–35: The women should keep silent in the churches. For they are not permitted to speak, but should be in submission, as the Law also says. If there is anything they desire to learn, let them ask their husbands at home. For it is shameful for a woman to speak in church.

1 Tim. 2:11–12: Let a woman learn quietly with all submissiveness. I do not permit a woman to teach or to exercise authority over a man; rather, she is to remain quiet.

Resources for Further Study

Belcher, Jim. *Deep Church*. Downers Grove, IL: InterVarsity Press, 2009.

Keller, Timothy. *Center Church*. Grand Rapids: Zondervan, 2012.

Recall suggestions of previous chapter.

CHAPTER 48

THE MEANS OF GRACE

WE'VE BEEN TALKING ABOUT the nature of the church, chapter 46, and the task of the church, chapter 47. Now, we should remember that God's sovereignty and human responsibility work together to accomplish his purposes in the world. Under "The Task of the Church," we focused on human responsibility, the things that *we* do to further the gospel. Of course, I also emphasized that in doing these things, we rely on the resources that God has given us. But we need now to look at those more carefully. In this chapter, the question is: how does God equip us for the task of the church? What does God do for us so that we can carry out the mission that he has given us, the Great Commission?

These divine resources are sometimes called the *means of grace*. Some Christians prefer not to use that phrase. Let's not live or die over terminology. But we should agree that there are certain channels by which God gives spiritual power to his church. And for now, let's just agree to call these the *means of grace*.

The Idea of a Means of Grace

First, let's examine what a means of grace is. We all know what *grace* is: God's unmerited favor, indeed, his unmerited favor where we deserve wrath. Without God's grace, we are lost. Yet we need God's grace not only at the beginning of the Christian life, but throughout. So naturally, we ask: where can we go to find God's continuing grace to us? Where do we go to get the resources for sanctification, for continuing spiritual growth? The short answer is that there are three places: the Word, fellowship, and prayer.

Except for the second, we can find those resources either privately or publicly. The second, of course, fellowship, is by definition public. But we can receive the Word either by individual Bible study or through the public preaching and teaching of the church. And we can pray, of course, either privately or publicly. But in our private use of the means of grace, we come to God as members of the church, that is, as members of the body of Christ. Apart from Christ, our Bible study and prayer will not help us. Indeed, we need other members of the church to help us to understand the Bible, and to teach us how to pray. So in an important sense, even the private means of grace are within the church.

Let's think a bit more about that triad, *the Word, fellowship,* and *prayer.* I hope you've already seen that it ties in with other threefold distinctions I've made in this book. The Word is normative, fellowship is situational (interacting with fellow believers in our environment), and prayer is existential (interacting with God in the depths of our hearts). Some might wonder why I haven't mentioned worship, and especially the sacraments. But I think these and other means fit as subdivisions of one of my three headings. Sacraments, I believe, are forms of church fellowship, and I will discuss them specifically in chapter 49. Worship is an overarching category that includes all three. See fig. 48.1.

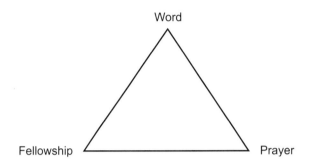

Fig. 48.1. Means of Grace

It is not common in Reformed theology to regard fellowship as a means of grace. But it clearly is. Remember all the passages I listed in chapter 47 on *one-anothering?* Those make it plain that our spiritual health depends on one another: both what other believers do for us and what we do for them. The larger concept that includes all those one-anotherings is the concept of fellowship. More on that in a little bit.

The Word

First let's think about the Word of God as a means of grace. Recall our basic teaching on the word in chapters 23–28. It is God's powerful, authoritative self-expression. So it is the power of God unto salvation (Rom. 1:16). People come to Christ through the Word not just by reading it, but by hearing it in preaching and teaching (10:17). Most people, historically, have not come to Christ just by sitting at home and reading the Bible, though some have. Far more have come to Christ through another person's preaching, teaching, witnessing, answering questions (1 Cor. 1:21). Most people in the ancient world, of course, were not able to read at all. So it became especially important that believers reach out and *tell* them what God's Word says. Thus, communication of the Word comes by mission. It is a corporate enterprise, not just an individual experience. It is a means of grace brought through the church.[1]

---

1. This fact does not imply that the Word is in any sense subordinate to the church. The church communicates the Word, and the church is under the authority of the Word.

Of course, God is also involved in the communication of the Word. God never leaves his church alone. He comes with the church to reach and save the lost. So, as we've seen, the Holy Spirit accompanies the Word, enabling people to receive it, "not only in word, but also in power and in the Holy Spirit and with full conviction" (1 Thess. 1:5).

Because the Spirit accompanies the Word in saving power, it is a *living* and *active* Word (Heb. 4:12). So when more and more people come to faith, Scripture speaks of the *Word* increasing (Acts 6:7; 13:49).

But as I said earlier, the Word is active not only in our initial salvation, but throughout our lives, in our sanctification as well. Psalm 19:7–9 says:

> The law of the Lord is perfect,
>   reviving the soul;
> the testimony of the Lord is sure,
>   making wise the simple;
> the precepts of the Lord are right,
>   rejoicing the heart;
> the commandment of the Lord is pure,
>   enlightening the eyes;
> the fear of the Lord is clean,
>   enduring forever;
> the rules of the Lord are true,
>   and righteous altogether.

Many Scripture passages (such as Ps. 119:105; Matt. 4:4; Acts 20:32; Rom. 15:4; 2 Tim. 3:16; Heb. 4:12–13; 2 Peter 1:19) tell us that God's Word changes us, sanctifies us, drives us to repentance for sin, incites us to love of God and one another. It's so important, therefore, to read the Word, to study it, indeed to meditate in it:

> Blessed is the man
> who walks not in the counsel of the wicked,
> nor stands in the way of sinners,
>   nor sits in the seat of scoffers;
> but his delight is in the law of the Lord,
>   and on his law he meditates day and night.
>
> He is like a tree
>   planted by streams of water
> that yields its fruit in its season,
>   and its leaf does not wither.
> In all that he does, he prospers. (Ps. 1:1–3)

The word for "meditate" there refers literally to an animal chewing its cud, over and over again. That's what we need to do, less literally, of course. (Don't chew the pages of your Bible.) We need to run the Bible passages through our minds over and over again, until we take it to heart. Look at the blessing of doing this: "He is like a tree planted by streams of water that yields its fruit in its season, and its leaf does not wither. In all that he does, he prospers" (Ps. 1:3). This is the way to fruitfulness and prosperity in the Lord—meditating in his Word.

Fellowship

The second means of grace is fellowship with God and other believers. We usually think of fellowship as parties and dinners, but in the NT it is much more. The Greek word for *fellowship* is *koinonia*, which comes from the adjective *koinos*, "common." Fellowship is a commonness; it is sharing something with someone else. In the NT, it sometimes means sharing goods. In 2 Corinthians 8:4 and Philippians 1:5, it refers to giving gifts to help needy fellow Christians. In that sense, the early church had a truly radical fellowship. In Acts 4:32, we read:

> Now the full number of those who believed were of one heart and soul, and no one said that any of the things that belonged to him was his own, but they had everything in common.

They shared their hearts, they shared their souls, and they shared their property. Some of the Christians sold property and gave the proceeds to the apostles for the needs of fellow Christians. That is a kind of fellowship that we rarely see in the church today, but it is simply an expression of the love Jesus taught us. He told us to love one another as he loved us. That means being ready to lay down your life for another Christian.

Koinonia in the NT also refers to a religious sharing, a religious commonness (1 Cor. 1:9; 10:20; 2 Cor. 6:14; Gal. 2:9; 1 John 1:3). To have fellowship is to worship together. Together with God, with Jesus, with other believers in the Lord. Finally, fellowship is a heartfelt sense of brotherhood, of closeness, of belonging to one family in the Lord (Phil. 2:1).

So fellowship refers to all the kinds of one-anothering discussed in chapter 47: loving one another, encouraging one another, and so on. So let's look at some specific forms of fellowship:

As I mentioned earlier, *worship* is one of the meanings of fellowship in the NT. Fellowship is a religious commonness, a worshiping together. In worship, we fellowship with God. We come to be with him, and he comes to be with us (2 Chron. 5:13–14; Ps. 22:25; Rom. 15:9; 1 Cor. 14:25; James 4:8). But as we saw in chapter 47, worship is also a fellowship with other believers, in which God edifies us, builds us up. In worship, we often come to insights that we haven't been able to attain any other way. In Psalm 73, the writer says that he despaired in his heart because he saw the prosperity of the wicked and the oppression of the righteous, until (v. 17), he says, "I went into the sanctuary of God; then I discerned their end." It was in the sanctuary, in worship, that the psalmist became convinced that the prosperity of the wicked was temporary, that God would bring the wicked into his terrible judgments in his own time.

So one form of fellowship is worship, and we'll see in the next chapter how the sacraments are a special part of that.

Fellowship is also *giving*. I mentioned earlier the radical sharing of the church in Acts 4–5. This giving, as Paul says, is first a giving of oneself, then of one's wealth (2 Cor. 8:5). After all, if you have given yourself away to the Lord and to your brothers and sisters, it shouldn't be too much to give your wealth. This may sound masochistic, but the Lord is not Moloch. He doesn't call on us to destroy ourselves. When you give yourself away, you receive back all the rich blessings of the Lord. There is a reward; Paul says in 2 Corinthians 9:6–12:

> The point is this: whoever sows sparingly will also reap sparingly, and whoever sows bountifully will also reap bountifully. Each one must give as he has decided in his heart, not reluctantly or under compulsion, for God loves a cheerful giver. And God is able to make all grace abound to you, so that having all sufficiency in all things at all times, you may abound in every good work. As it is written,
>
> "He has distributed freely, he has given to the poor;
>   his righteousness endures forever."
>
> He who supplies seed to the sower and bread for food will supply and multiply your seed for sowing and increase the harvest of your righteousness. You will be enriched in every way to be generous in every way, which through us will produce thanksgiving to God. For the ministry of this service is not only supplying the needs of the saints but is also overflowing in many thanksgivings to God.

There's the language of the means of grace, in spades: "And God is able to make all grace abound to you, so that having all sufficiency in all things at all times, you may abound in every good work" (2 Cor. 9:8). Through giving we reap bountifully; we will experience hilarious joy; we will have plenty of seed, plenty of bread. And what we do will lead people to thank God. Giving is a source of the most wonderful blessings![2]

Scripture tells us, first, to give to our own families: "But if anyone does not provide for his relatives, and especially for members of his household, he has denied the faith and is worse than an unbeliever" (1 Tim. 5:8). Strong language there, some of the strongest condemnation in the whole NT.

Then, we should *do good* to all people, but especially to the "household of faith" (Gal. 6:10). The household of faith is the church, our extended family. So God has called us to take care of the poor members of the body of Christ. First John 3:17 says,

---

2. Cf. Mal. 3:10: "Bring the full tithe into the storehouse, that there may be food in my house. And thereby put me to the test, says the LORD of hosts, if I will not open the windows of heaven for you and pour down for you a blessing until there is no more need."

"But if anyone has the world's goods and sees his brother in need, yet closes his heart against him, how does God's love abide in him?" The love of Christ puts us in a special relationship with our poor brothers and sisters, so that God's love constrains, presses us to give them help (Gal. 2:10; James 2:16; 1 John 3:17).

But remember that in Galatians 6:10, Paul says to do good *especially* to those of the household of faith. It doesn't say *only*, but *especially*. This means that we have a biblical mandate to meet the needs of the poor outside the body of Christ. Galatians 6:10 does state a priority: family first. But it doesn't restrict us from doing good to others. Indeed, it encourages us: do good to *all* people.

Here we may cringe a bit. How can I, you might ask, who can barely afford to feed my kids, have a responsibility to help the poor of the whole world? Well, one example that Scripture gives us is the Good Samaritan parable (Luke 10:25–37). When the Samaritan sees a man dying by the side of the road, he does not pass by on the other side, as did the priest and the Levite. Nor does he ask questions about the victim's religious allegiance. He simply gives what help he can. The Bible doesn't ask us in an abstract way to divide our resources up among all the millions of people throughout the world who are in need. Rather, what Paul has in mind in Galatians 6:10 is being ready to help those whom God brings across our path. When we have resources that can be used to help someone, we should be generous; that's all.

But I suspect that if all of God's people tithed, that is, gave a tenth of their income to the work of the Lord, the church would be in a far better position to help the needy within the church and outside as well (see Mal. 3:8–10). And "offerings" in Scripture are something above and beyond the tithe. Let that be a word to the wise.

The word *fellowship* also applies to our relation to the Spirit (2 Cor. 13:14) and his gifts, as we saw in chapter 39. The work of evangelism is closely connected with that. Paul speaks of our fellowship with him in the gospel (Phil. 1:5). Scripture connects evangelism with the filling of the Spirit (Acts 2:4, 14–36; 4:8, 31; 9:17, 20; 13:9, 52).

Nurture is obviously part of our fellowship with one another. In Ephesians 4:29, Paul says that the talk that comes out of our mouths must always seek to build up one another. When a brother sins, we seek to reclaim him (Gal. 6:1; James 5:20). When someone is in need, we help. When someone is sick, we pray (James 5:14). The negative side, of course, is that when a brother will not repent after teaching and admonition, we must sometimes exercise formal discipline against him, even, as we've seen, to the point of excommunication. But even that is for his benefit (1 Cor. 5:5).

So we can understand fellowship as worship, sharing goods, and that intimacy with one another in the Spirit that nurtures and edifies. In terms of our threefold pattern, we can think of worship as normative, sharing goods as situational, and nurture as existential. See fig. 48.2.

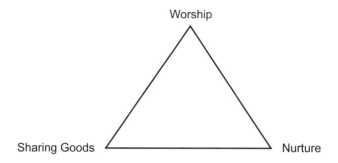

Fig. 48.2. Perspectives on Fellowship

Prayer

We have talked about the Word and fellowship as means of grace. The third category is prayer. Wayne Grudem defines prayer as personal communication with God, corporate or individual.[3] The aspects of prayer are (1) adoration, when we praise God for who he is and what he has done, (2) confession of sin, in which we humble ourselves before God, who sees our hearts as they really are, (3) thanksgiving, in which we acknowledge that everything we have comes from him, and without him we have no good thing, and (4) supplication, making requests for ourselves and for others. Over a period of time, our prayer should include all four elements (abbreviated by the acronym ACTS). But we will focus on supplication here, since most of the theological questions center on that.

Why should we pray? People often ask this question out of a concern for the sovereignty of God. If God is in control of everything, then what difference can our prayers make? God already knows and has planned what he will do; we can't change his eternal plan. So why should we bother to pray? See fig. 48.3.

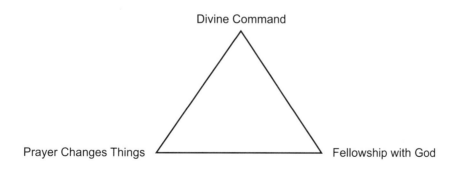

Fig. 48.3. Reasons to Pray

3. *GST*, 376.

First, the normative reason: because God commands it in Scripture. First Thessalonians 5:17 says, succinctly, "Pray without ceasing," and this is one of many biblical commands to pray. Even if we don't understand how prayer and God's sovereignty work together, we should pray simply because our heavenly Father wants us to. But why does he want us to pray, if praying is not going to change his eternal plan?

That takes us to the second reason, which I have called the existential: prayer is a means of fellowship with our heavenly Father. We saw earlier the importance of fellowship, and prayer is a form of fellowship as well. In Luke 11:9–13, Jesus says that prayer is like a child's going to his earthly father. Cf. Matt. 6:9. The child wants something, and the father is eager to give. But the father does not give until the child asks. Any of us who are parents understand the dynamic here. We want to give good things to our children, but even more, we want a good relationship with them. Our heavenly Father wants the same. He does not want to be a kind of machine that dispenses goods, but to really be our Father, a real person. We saw early in the book how important it is that God is a person, not an impersonal or abstract being. How good it is to be able to talk to the Ruler of the universe. How good that he delights to have this conversation!

But there's a third reason as well. If our prayers could not change anything, then the relationship would be rather hollow. If a child had no hope that his father could change anything on his behalf, he would not be motivated to ask. So there is also what I call a situational motive for prayer, and that is that prayer changes things. Or to put it more theologically, God ordains prayer as a means to change history. There are things that happen because of prayer, and things that do not happen because of no prayer. In 2 Chronicles 7:14, God says that if his people will humble themselves and pray, then he will forgive their sin and heal their land. In Luke 11:9–10, Jesus says that he who seeks, finds. And James 4:2 says that if we don't have things we need, it is because we do not ask. Prayer really does work.

Now, of course, prayer doesn't change the eternal plan of God. But within that eternal plan are many plans for means and ends. God ordains that crops will grow, but not without water and sun. He ordains that people will be saved, but (ordinarily) not without the teaching of the Word. And he ordains that we will have everything we truly need, but not without prayer. God's eternal plan has determined that many things will be achieved by prayer, and many things will not be achieved without prayer.

But since prayer is a personal relationship with God, it does not operate mechanically or automatically. We know that prayer sometimes disappoints, and that, too, is part of the relationship. When we pray, we ought to trust that God, like a loving father, is much wiser than we are, and that in the end he does what he knows is best. There is mystery here, as we can well understand. How many four-year-olds understand why their fathers do and do not choose to honor their requests?

But the Bible does give us some amount of insight on the question of why some prayers are better than others. Wayne Grudem, whose theology has been very helpful to me in this chapter, says that good prayer, effective prayer, prayer that honors God and that God honors, typically occurs in several "spheres."[4] That is, good prayer is *in* Jesus' name, *in* the Spirit, *according to* his will, and so on. Figuratively speaking, these are the locations of prayer. Let's look at these briefly.

Good prayer, first of all, is in Jesus' name. "Jesus' name" is not a mechanical expression that we tag on to the end of a prayer. Sometimes that's a good thing to do. Other times, it's a mere form, perhaps a magical expression intended to make the prayer more powerful or to impress other people of how pious we are. But whether you use that formula or not, the important thing is that our prayer really be in Jesus' name. That means recognizing that he is our only Mediator with God (1 Tim. 2:5), our one and only High Priest (Heb. 4:14–15). So he is the only person who can give us access to the Father. We come through him because he has made the final sacrifice. When he died, the veil of the temple was torn in two, so the Lord opened wide our access to him (Heb. 10:22). So the NT tells us not to be timid and scared, afraid that God will destroy us if we come too close. That actually was the situation in the OT. But he wants us, rather, to be bold in coming before God, bold in prayer, asking big things.

As the High Priest, Jesus is also our intercessor. He is the One who brings our prayers to the Father.

So when you pray, come with Jesus' authorization. Tell God, either orally or by your attitude of heart, that you are coming only because of Jesus. Jesus has said: "In that day you will ask nothing of me. Truly, truly, I say to you, whatever you ask of the Father in my name, he will give it to you. Until now you have asked nothing in my name. Ask, and you will receive, that your joy may be full" (John 16:23–24; cf. Eph. 5:20).

So we pray in Jesus' name. We also pray in the Holy Spirit (Rom. 8:26–27). The Spirit dwells in our hearts and knows our inmost thoughts. He bears witness to us that we are, in fact, children of God by faith in Christ. When we don't know what to pray for, he brings his own prayers to the Father, out of his own infinite wisdom. Sometimes a loved one is terribly ill, and we don't know whether to pray for healing or for God to take the person home. We call on God to act according to his love and wisdom. Within us, the Spirit is praying the prayer that needs to be offered.

Good prayer is according to God's will: "And this is the confidence that we have toward him, that if we ask anything according to his will he hears us. And if we know that he hears us in whatever we ask, we know that we have the requests that we have asked of him" (1 John 5:14–15; cf. Matt. 6:10). So we should not pray anything contrary to the Scriptures. Usually we do not know God's decretive will, his eternal plan. So I may pray for God to heal a friend, not knowing whether that is what God ultimately wants to do. That's all right, if in my heart I pray at the same time, "Lord, your will be done."

Scripture also tells us to pray in faith (Matt. 21:22; Mark 11:24; James 1:6). These passages refer not only to saving faith in Christ, but also to faith that we will receive

---

4. Ibid., 382–91.

what we have prayed for. This principle follows from the last. If prayer is in God's will, then of course he will grant it. If we *believe* that our prayer is in God's will, then we must *believe* that he will grant it. Of course, we may be wrong, in the previous step and therefore in this one. And of course if, along with our prayer for what we want, we pray in our hearts, "Thy will be done," then we know that our prayer will always be answered.

Scripture also presents obedience as a condition of answered prayer, or perhaps as another "sphere" of prayer. "If I had cherished iniquity in my heart, the Lord would not have listened" (Ps. 66:18); "Beloved, if our heart does not condemn us, we have confidence before God; and whatever we ask we receive from him, because we keep his commandments and do what pleases him" (1 John 3:21–22; cf. Prov. 15:8, 29; 28:9; 1 Peter 3:7, 12). Now, these verses don't teach that we must be sinlessly perfect for God to answer our prayers. None of us is sinlessly perfect, but God answers the prayers of many of us. Yet sin does sometimes stand in the way. If we are complacent about sin, "cherish[ing] iniquity," as the psalmist says, we had better repent before we do any other business with God. So confession of sin is a vitally important part of prayer (Matt. 6:12; James 5:16; 1 John 1:9).

And when we pray, God wants us not only to request forgiveness for ourselves, but also to grant forgiveness to those who have sinned against us (Matt. 6:14–15; Mark 11:25). Lack of forgiveness can hinder our petitions to the Lord.

Scripture also describes various attitudes appropriate to prayer. Humility is one (Matt. 6:5; Luke 18:11–13). How inappropriate it is for us to be proud of ourselves when we are standing before almighty God. His greatness should show us how small we are, how trivial our abilities and accomplishments. He should make us aware that everything we are and everything we've accomplished comes from him.

The Pharisee in Jesus' parable is a good example of pride before God. But notice: he put his pride in the form of thanks. Formally, at least, he acknowledged that all his virtues came from God: "I thank *you* that I am not like other men." But the pride just billowed from his heart: "God, I thank you that I am not like other men, extortioners, unjust, adulterers, or even like this tax collector. I fast twice a week; I give tithes of all that I get" (Luke 18:11–12). Standing before God, like the tax collector in the parable, we should recognize that we have nothing to boast of: "Nothing in my hand I bring; simply to thy cross I cling."[5] That's one reason that confession of sin is so important. Nobody can be proud if he really understands how much he has sinned against God, and what a great price God paid to bring forgiveness.

Persistence is another virtue in prayer (Gen. 32:26; Deut. 9:25–26; Mark 14:39; Luke 6:12; 2 Cor. 12:8; Col. 4:2; 1 Thess. 5:17). If God doesn't answer, you should ask again whether your prayer is in the will of God. But if you still believe it is, keep going. God may have his reasons for postponing the answer that he still intends to give. And wait for his answer (Pss. 27:14; 38:15; 130:5–6).

---

5. This is a line from the hymn "Rock of Ages," by Augustus Toplady.

Earnestness is a quality we see in the prayers of many of God's people in Scripture. See how passionate they are in prayer, how urgent: "O Lord, hear; O Lord, forgive. O Lord, pay attention and act. Delay not, for your own sake, O my God, because your city and your people are called by your name" (Dan. 9:19; cf. Heb. 5:7). People sometimes ask why we need to be passionate in prayer. Does God need to be urged? Does God respond more readily to emotional appeals than nonemotional ones? Well, think what you will, but remember that our relation to God is personal. He is our Father, not a favor-dispensing machine. Our emotions, our repetitions show our persistence; they show that our hope is only in God. And sometimes the nature of our requests is such that they are falsified by an unemotional approach to God.

After all this, what happens when God doesn't answer our prayers, or doesn't answer them right away? He may indeed be planning to answer, but other things have to happen first. Think of how many years God's people prayed for God to redeem them from Egypt. Think how many years they prayed for the coming of the Messiah. Think how many years we have been praying for his return: "Even so, come, Lord Jesus" (Rev. 22:20 KJV). But God chose the right time to send Moses, and to send Jesus—"the fullness of time," Paul says in Galatians 4:4. And his answers will always come—at the *right* time.

Our sin may be another reason why God has not answered (James 1:6–8; 4:3). We may not be in the right sphere when we pray for something. Or, as mentioned earlier, we may be complacent with some area of our lives that violates God's standards.

But there is still a third reason for unanswered prayer, and that is God's sovereign purposes. As I said earlier, we don't know God's secret decree, and so again, when we pray we should always say under our breath or in our hearts if not openly, "Thy will be done." Jesus qualified his prayer that way in the garden before his crucifixion (Luke 22:42). Surely we, too, must qualify our prayers that way. The apostle Paul prayed to God three times that God would remove the impediment that Paul called his "thorn in the flesh." But God said no: "My grace is sufficient for you, for my power is made perfect in weakness" (2 Cor. 12:9). Paul could not have known all the ways in which his thorn in the flesh would magnify God's power. But God did, and he did what was best for Paul's ministry, which was also what was best for Paul.

So prayer is a means of God's grace to us, both individual prayer and public prayer. Public prayer in worship brings all the members of the body together in agreement. In Matthew 18:19, Jesus says, "Again I say to you, if two of you agree on earth about anything they ask, it will be done for them by my Father in heaven." So when two, three, or more agree in prayer, as in public worship, their prayers have a special power. We see in the NT how the prayer meeting of Acts 4 led to a powerful witness for the gospel: "And when they had prayed, the place in which they were gathered together was shaken, and they were all filled with the Holy Spirit and continued to speak the word of God with boldness" (Acts 4:31). Corporate prayer is a fellowship with the Holy Spirit, something we do in him (Eph. 6:18; Jude 20). In the sphere of the Spirit, we draw upon his power, his love, and his wisdom as he intercedes for us.

Key Terms

Means of grace
The Word (as means of grace)
Fellowship (as means of grace)
Prayer (as means of grace)
Humility
Persistence
Earnestness

Study Questions

1. "It is not common in Reformed theology to regard fellowship as a means of grace. But it clearly is." Explain; evaluate.
2. "So fellowship refers to all the kinds of one-anothering discussed in chapter 47." List some of these and discuss, using Bible references.
3. "*Worship* is one of the meanings of fellowship in the NT." How is worship a form of fellowship? Explain; evaluate.
4. "How can I, you might ask, who can barely afford to feed my kids, have a responsibility to help the poor of the whole world?"
5. Why pray, if God is sovereign?
6. Discuss the reasons for "unanswered prayer."
7. What does it mean to pray in Jesus' name? to pray in faith? to pray according to God's will?
8. List some attributes appropriate to prayer.

Memory Verses

Ps. 1:1–3: Blessed is the man
  who walks not in the counsel of the wicked,
nor stands in the way of sinners,
  nor sits in the seat of scoffers;
but his delight is in the law of the LORD,
  and on his law he meditates day and night.

He is like a tree
  planted by streams of water
that yields its fruit in its season,
  and its leaf does not wither.
In all that he does, he prospers.

Ps. 73:17: I went into the sanctuary of God;
  then I discerned their end.

Acts 4:32: Now the full number of those who believed were of one heart and soul, and no one said that any of the things that belonged to him was his own, but they had everything in common.

2 Cor. 9:8: And God is able to make all grace abound to you, so that having all sufficiency in all things at all times, you may abound in every good work.

Gal. 6:10: So then, as we have opportunity, let us do good to everyone, and especially to those who are of the household of faith.

Eph. 4:29: Let no corrupting talk come out of your mouths, but only such as is good for building up, as fits the occasion, that it may give grace to those who hear.

1 Tim. 5:8: But if anyone does not provide for his relatives, and especially for members of his household, he has denied the faith and is worse than an unbeliever.

1 John 3:17: But if anyone has the world's goods and sees his brother in need, yet closes his heart against him, how does God's love abide in him?

Resources for Further Study

Bennett, Arthur G., ed. *The Valley of Vision: A Collection of Puritan Prayers and Devotions.* Edinburgh: Banner of Truth, 1975.

Chappell, Bryan. *Praying Backwards: Transform Your Prayer Life by Beginning in Jesus' Name.* Grand Rapids: Baker, 2005.

Miller, Paul. *A Praying Life.* Colorado Springs: NavPress, 2009.

CHAPTER 49

THE SACRAMENTS

AMONG THE MEANS OF GRACE discussed in the previous chapter, I omitted the sacraments, baptism and the Lord's Supper, with their OT counterparts, circumcision and Passover. They are certainly the most theologically controversial of all the means of grace and therefore require special treatment.

Scripture has much to say about baptism and the Lord's Supper, but it never groups these two, or the four I listed earlier, into a larger category called *sacrament*. One wonders whether the theological world would have been more peaceful if the church had never developed the concept of sacrament. Nevertheless, there do appear to be significant similarities between these institutions that make it useful to discuss them together. Here is the WCF's definition of sacrament, a definition that certainly pertains to both baptism and the Lord's Supper:

> Sacraments are holy signs and seals of the covenant of grace, immediately instituted by God, to represent Christ, and his benefits; and to confirm our interest in him: as also, to put a visible difference between those that belong unto the church, and the rest of the world; and solemnly to engage them to the service of God in Christ, according to his Word. (WCF 27.1)

Gathering these ideas together, we can see (unsurprisingly) three main aspects of a sacrament: they are signs, divine actions, and means of divine presence, which I assign to the categories normative, situational, and existential, respectively. See fig. 49.1.

First, normatively, the sacraments are signs. That is, they are authoritative divine communications, revelations to us. They symbolize the gospel and teach us authoritatively what the gospel is. They teach us not by words, but by pictures, by actions. In baptism, not only do we hear about our cleansing, but we see and feel it, depicted dramatically. In the Supper, not only do we hear about Jesus' death for us, but we see his body given for us, and we taste, smell, and touch it. As the Reformers used to say, the sacraments are visible words. They supplement the

Word of God by divinely authorized dramatic images. So the fullness of divine teaching is by Word *and* sacrament.

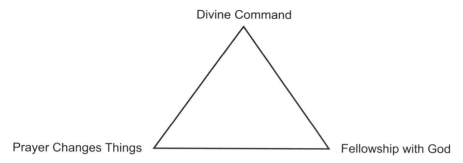

Fig. 49.1. Aspects of the Sacraments

Second, situationally, the sacraments are God's actions on our behalf. The sacrament is not just our doing something in God's presence; it is his doing something for us. He is really there, acting. For one thing, the sacraments are not only signs, but *seals*. When we talk about a seal here, we are talking about something like the government seal on your birth certificate, which makes it official that you are a citizen of the country, with all rights and privileges appertaining. Baptism and the Lord's Supper are seals of God's covenant of grace with us in Christ, as Abraham's circumcision was a seal of his righteousness of faith (Rom. 4:11). As seals, the sacraments confirm and guarantee the covenant promises. In this respect, as I said earlier, they are visible words. As the word of God guarantees the promises of God, so do the sacraments.

Therefore, as the confession says, they separate us from the world, locating us in the people of God.

Third, existentially, the sacraments are locations of God's presence. That is implicit in what I have already said. If God is *doing* something for us in and through the sacrament, then he is, of course, present, and that itself is a wonderful blessing. So Paul speaks of the Supper as a *communion* of the body and blood of Christ (1 Cor. 10:16). The word translated "communion" in the KJV, "participation" in the ESV, is *koinonia*, "fellowship," the word that we discussed in the previous chapter. I indicated there that the sacraments fell under the category of fellowship, and here we see that.

In his intimate presence, God helps us to grow in faith. Roman Catholics understand this process as something automatic. It happens *ex opere operato*, that is, from the very act of participating in the sacrament. But Scripture teaches that, no, our growth comes through the presence of Christ by his Spirit dealing with us personally.[1] So the efficacy of the sacrament is by faith alone.

---

1. Recall my frequent emphasis in this book on the importance of personality in God and of personal relationships between him and us.

Baptism

Let us think more specifically, first about baptism and then about the Supper. Note the confessional definition of baptism:

> Baptism is a sacrament of the New Testament, ordained by Jesus Christ, not only for the solemn admission of the party baptized into the visible church; but also, to be unto him a sign and seal of the covenant of grace, of his ingrafting into Christ, of regeneration, of remission of sins, and of his giving up unto God, through Jesus Christ, to walk in the newness of life. Which sacrament is, by Christ's own appointment, to be continued in his church until the end of the world. (WCF 28.1)

In this statement, we see that baptism is, first, the rite of entrance into the visible church. As a person takes an oath of citizenship to become an American citizen, so we undergo baptism to become members of the Christian church. It is baptism that gives us the right to be recognized as Christians, unless or until we are excommunicated. Thus, it gives us the right to be part of the great work that God is doing through his church.

As an administration of the covenant, baptism is a sign and seal, as we indicated earlier. As a sign, it represents cleansing, repentance, and union with Christ. See fig. 49.2.

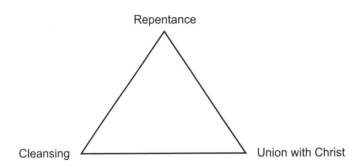

Fig. 49.2. Symbolism of Baptism

Cleansing (Lev. 8:5–6; 14:8–9, 15–16), like the OT ceremonial washings, is a requirement for entering God's presence. In this case, it symbolizes cleansing from sin. Not everybody who is baptized is cleansed or forgiven from sin. But that's what baptism symbolizes, pictures. Baptism, as a sacrament, pictures the gospel, and the gospel is about the forgiveness of sins. Scripture does not say, as some do, that baptism is the new birth, or that our forgiveness comes through baptism. But it *pictures* forgiveness, so that people who are baptized as well as those who witness the ceremony will know what the gospel says, that God offers cleansing, forgiveness in Christ.

Second, baptism represents repentance, as in the early ministry of John (Matt. 3:6, 11). For we must recognize that we are in need of God's cleansing, that we are sinners.

When an adult is baptized, he confesses his own sin, turns from it, and asks God's forgiveness. In churches where infants are baptized, the parents make this confession on behalf of their children. In the diagram above, I have placed repentance as the normative perspective, because it represents the demand of God's law on us.

Third, baptism symbolizes union with Christ. It is "into the name of" the Trinity (Matt. 28:19 ASV). To be baptized into the name of someone is to belong to that person. Cf. 1 Cor. 1:13, 15; 10:2. In Romans 6:3–6 (cf. 1 Cor. 12:13; Gal. 3:27–28; Col. 2:11–12), Paul says that we have been baptized with Christ in his death and resurrection, dying with him to sin and rising with him to new life. So Paul many, many times speaks of Christians as being "in Christ." This is the doctrine of union with Christ that we considered in chapter 38. We are also baptized into the Spirit, as we discussed in chapter 39 (Matt. 3:11; 1 Cor. 12:13).

We have been talking of baptism as a sign. It is also a seal, God's confirmation that we belong to the covenant. Again, baptism is a name-giving ceremony (Matt. 28:19), placing the name of God on us, as the high priest placed the name of God on Israel in Numbers 6:24–27. On the basis of that seal, we are admitted into the visible church. Again, baptism does not give us eternal salvation. As I indicated in our discussion of assurance in chapter 44, baptized people do sometimes betray the Lord. When they do that, they receive the curses of the covenant rather than the blessings. But baptism does entitle the baptized person to all the blessings of fellowship with God in the church and with God's people.

So I must disagree with the position ascribed to the early Swiss Reformer Ulrich Zwingli, that baptism is a *mere* symbol, a *mere* sign. Also, we must take issue with the Roman Catholic notion that baptism is the new birth, or any other idea of baptismal regeneration.

The Mode of Baptism

Now, having put this off as long as possible, we need to think about the two major controversies concerning baptism, one about the mode and one about the subjects. The question of mode is whether one method of baptism, such as immersion, is the only legitimate means of baptism, and the question of subjects is whether baptism may be administered to infants. Let me say first that godly people disagree on these matters, even within the Reformed tradition. I would be tempted to describe these as minor issues, except that they are relevant to the important question of who is and is not a member of the church. For some churches will exclude anybody from membership if the person has not been immersed, or has not been baptized as an adult upon profession of faith. That makes this issue more important than one would judge from reading the Scriptures. Actually, the Scriptures say very little explicitly about the mode of baptism or about whether the sacrament requires an adult confession of faith.

But let's look first at the question of mode. There are some who believe that immersion alone has biblical warrant. They argue (1) that the Greek word *baptize* means "to immerse," (2) that John chose a place for his ministry, Aenon, where there was "much water" (John 3:23 KJV), which suggests immersion, (3) that Matthew 3:16 speaks of Jesus' coming up out of water, which also suggests immersion. And the strongest argument, I think, for this position is (4) that immersion is better suited than, say, sprinkling to fit the apostle's use of baptism to symbolize our death and resurrection with Christ (Rom. 6:2–6; Col. 2:11–12).

But (1) there are others who reply that the Greek word *baptize* does not necessarily mean "immerse." In Luke 11:38, for example, it refers to people's washing before dinner, which was almost certainly not by immersion. (2) They say that John needed "much water" at Aenon not necessarily to immerse people, but simply to have enough water to baptize everybody who came. (3) They note that the phrases "going down into the water" and "coming up out of the water" do not necessarily refer to immersion, for people may have come into the stream and *then* received baptism by sprinkling or pouring. Indeed, some locations of baptism make immersion unlikely (Acts 9:11, 18; 10:25, 47; 16:32–33), and there are no unmistakable examples of immersion in the NT.

Further, there is some biblical evidence for sprinkling and pouring as modes of baptism. In Hebrews 9:10, the "sprinklings" of the OT law (9:13, 19, 21) are called "baptisms." Christians are said to be "sprinkled" with Jesus' blood in Hebrews 10:22; 12:24; 1 Peter 1:2. Passages such as Acts 2:17 and others (Acts 2:33; Rom. 5:5) present baptism in the Spirit as a "pouring." The Spirit "comes upon" us (Acts 1:8), or "falls upon" us (10:44).

My own conclusion is inconclusive. I think that immersion, sprinkling, and pouring are all legitimate means of baptism and that none should be excluded.

Infant Baptism

The second controversy over baptism is whether the rite should ever be administered to infant children. People who say that it should be are called *paedobaptists*, which means "child baptizers." People who say that infants are excluded from baptism are called *baptists*, or *antipaedobaptists*. But the real point the baptists want to make is that baptism should be given only to people who are able to make a profession of faith in Christ, and that is impossible for infants. So it has been common lately to call them *credobaptists*, those who baptize on the basis of a credo or profession.

Now, the question is difficult because, like the mode question, the Bible does not discuss it explicitly. There is no command in the NT either to baptize infants or not to baptize them. Baptists say that since there is no command to baptize infants, we shouldn't do it. Paedobaptists say that the total biblical evidence requires us to baptize the children of believers, unless there is a NT command forbidding it. Since there is no such command, we must baptize the children of believers. So it is a question of the burden of proof. Baptists say the burden of proof is on those who would argue infant baptism. Since explicit proof is lacking, we shouldn't do it. Paedobaptists say the reverse: the burden of proof is on those who would forbid infant baptism. Since that proof is lacking, we must do it.

But let's look at the specific arguments. The baptist argues, first, that there is no NT command to baptize the children of believers. Second, he says that in the NT baptism is always linked to professions of faith—and of course, there are many examples of that connection (Acts 2:41; 8:12; 10:44–48; 16:14–15, 32–33).

The Reformed paedobaptist holds a different view. I use the phrase *Reformed paedobaptist* not because I believe that credobaptists are not Reformed; indeed, many of them are. Rather, I use the term to distinguish the Reformed argument for infant baptism from the Roman Catholic argument and that of other groups that are not part of the Reformed tradition. So I will not argue that we should baptize infants in order to get them into heaven, or in order to give them new birth.

Rather, the argument is like this: in the OT, circumcision was the rite of entrance into Israel, as baptism is now the rite of entrance into the visible church. Clearly, God commanded the Israelites to circumcise their male children, on the eighth day of their lives. The rite of circumcision sealed the promises of God to the people as baptism seals those promises to Christian believers. Paul says in Romans 4:11 that Abraham "received the sign of circumcision as a seal of the righteousness that he had by faith while he was still uncircumcised." A seal of the righteousness of faith—the same thing that baptism seals for us today. So any argument against the appropriateness of baptism to infants would also apply to infant circumcision. It is true that infants cannot profess their faith and thus appropriate the righteousness of faith, but neither could infants do this in the time of Abraham.

It is clear that in both Testaments, God's covenant is for us and for our children (Gen. 26:3–4; 28:13–14; Deut. 29:9–13; Josh. 5:2–9). In the OT, the words of the covenant were read to Israelites of all ages (Josh. 8:35; 2 Chron. 20:13; Joel 2:15–16). The flood (1 Peter 3:20–21) and the exodus through the Red Sea (1 Cor. 10:1–2), which are used in the NT as pictures of baptism, sprinkled equally people of all ages.

In the NT, Jesus pronounced the blessing of God on infants (Luke 18:15–17). Jesus wasn't just showing affection for the babies. Blessing is a very serious matter in Scripture. In blessing, God places his name on his people, as the high priest did in Numbers 6:27. In blessing the children, Jesus put his name on them. Significantly, baptism in the NT is baptism into the name of Jesus (Acts 2:38; 8:12, 16; 10:48; 19:5; cf. 22:16).

Further, in Acts 2:39, Peter proclaims that the promise of the new covenant is "for you and for your children." That is OT covenantal language. To a first-century Jew, this language would indicate that just as God included Abraham's children in covenant with him, so God includes the children of believers in the new covenant.

We should also notice that baptisms in the NT after Jesus' resurrection tend to be baptisms of households (Acts 11:14; 16:15, 31–34; 1 Cor. 1:16), just as in the OT God brought households to himself. Most likely there were children in these households. But even if there were not, the principle is that God is gathering families, not just individuals, into his kingdom. As families come into the kingdom, children come, too, represented by their parents, as in the OT.

The baptist reply to this argument is that the new covenant is very different from the old—the old based on physical birth, family, and nation, the new based on spiritual realities such as faith. But it is hard to find that sort of distinction in the Bible itself.

Abraham circumcised his sons as a seal of the righteousness of faith. God's covenant with him was as spiritual as his covenant with us in Christ. Paul says in Romans 4:16:

> That is why it depends on faith, in order that the promise may rest on grace and be guaranteed to all his offspring—not only to the adherent of the law but also to the one who shares the faith of Abraham, who is the father of us all.

God's covenant with Abraham was fully spiritual. Yet his children were part of that covenant, as on the paedobaptist view our children are part of our covenant relation to Christ.

Note also that in 1 Corinthians 7:14, children, even in a marriage in which only one parent is a believer, are holy, that is, they belong to God. And in his letters, Paul addresses children, along with adults, as saints, holy people. Cf. Eph. 1:1 with 6:1. So we should conclude that children of believers are members of the covenant of grace and so ought to be baptized. I don't believe that Christians should break fellowship over this issue. Indeed, I wish there were a way that believers holding different positions on this matter could belong to the same church. But that doesn't seem to be a widely held position in the evangelical church today.

The Lord's Supper

We must now turn to the Lord's Supper. If baptism is the sacrament of initiation, given only once, the Lord's Supper is the sacrament of continuing fellowship with God, to be received over and over again.

WCF 29.1 defines it as follows:

> Our Lord Jesus, in the night wherein he was betrayed, instituted the sacrament of his body and blood, called the Lord's Supper, to be observed in his church, unto the end of the world, for the perpetual remembrance of the sacrifice of himself in his death; the sealing all benefits thereof unto true believers, their spiritual nourishment and growth in him, their further engagement in and to all duties which they owe unto him; and, to be a bond and pledge of their communion with him, and with each other, as members of his mystical body.

Like baptism, this ordinance is instituted by Christ for us to observe perpetually until the last day. It has past, present, and future references: we look to the past as we remember his death, to the present as we receive nourishment, and to the future as we anticipate his coming, remembering "the Lord's death until he comes" (1 Cor. 11:26; cf. Rev. 19:9). Our present nourishment comes by feeding on Christ (1 Cor. 10:16–18; cf. John 6:53–58), and by a closer relationship with others in the body (1 Cor. 11:18–22; notice the confession's reference to "communion with him, and with each other, as members of his mystical body"). So the Lord's Supper is a means of grace, a way in which God equips us to better serve him.

One major theological controversy concerns the presence of Christ in the Supper. The Roman Catholic view is called *transubstantiation*. That means that after the priest consecrates the bread and the wine, they actually *become* the physical body and blood of Christ, though they still *appear* to be bread and wine. So the Supper is a continual sacrifice of Christ's body and blood. But Scripture never suggests anything like this. When Jesus said to his disciples, "This is my body," he cannot have meant that the bread and wine on the table were his literal body, for his literal body was *behind* the table, not on it. Rather, what he plainly meant was that the bread and wine *represent* his body and blood. It's like a professor pointing to a map and saying, "This is France." He doesn't mean that the map is literally France, but that the picture represents France.[2]

The most serious error in this view, however, is that it represents the Lord's Supper as a continuing sacrifice. Scripture is clear that there is no continuing sacrifice and cannot be. Jesus' atonement is final and complete. There is no other sacrifice for sins. It needs no continuation, repetition, or supplementation.

The Lutheran view is midway between the Roman Catholic and the Reformed. Lutherans teach that in the sacrament Jesus' physical body is "in, with, and under" the bread and the wine. That is, the elements are still bread and wine, but Jesus' body and blood are there, too. They do deny the Roman Catholic idea of the sacrament as a continuing sacrifice, and that is good. But I do think their emphasis on a literal physical presence of Christ dilutes the biblical emphasis on receiving Christ by faith alone.

The view attributed to Ulrich Zwingli, the early Swiss Reformer, is that the sacrament is *only* a sign, only a memorial. The mainstream Swiss Reformers, following John Calvin, believe, however, that the Supper is not a mere memorial, but a means of grace. Calvin said that when we take the Supper, Christ is present in the Spirit. So we "participate" in his body and blood, as Paul says in 1 Corinthians 10:16–18. We "feed" on him, as Jesus teaches in John 6:53–58. These benefits come by faith alone. The physical body of Christ is in heaven, not on earth. I think this mainstream Reformed view is best: it incorporates more of the riches of Scripture than the others, and it avoids superstitions that are not based on Scripture.

Table Fellowship with God

But I'd rather not end on a controversial note. I think it's unfortunate that these wonderful sacraments have become so much a source of battles in the church. It seems sometimes that they are more a cause for warfare than a blessing to God's people. So as we close, let's just think of the richness of the blessings that God has given us in the Lord's Supper.

In our church, we have the Lord's Supper every Sunday, and I am usually asked to lead it once a month. So every month I have to come up with a new devotional message

2. Further, the doctrine of transubstantiation teaches that the Supper involves a metaphysical miracle, in which the appearances of bread and wine remain, but the essence of the elements is transformed into something else. The notion of one reality that exists with all the appearances of a different reality is philosophically problematic and in any case is never suggested in Scripture.

focusing on the Lord's Supper. I worried about this at first, because the sacraments are not a specialty of mine, and I wondered how I could possibly come up with twelve communion messages per year. But as I studied the Scriptures, God showed me how rich was the background and symbolism of the Lord's Supper. We usually say that the Supper symbolizes Jesus' death for us, and it certainly does. But there is much more that comes with this.

In Scripture, even in the OT, table fellowship with God is an important element of the covenant blessing. When two people are at odds with each other, they need to be reconciled. Reconciliation can, of course, be rather superficial. But when it is deep and profound, when it is complete reconciliation, not only do you become friends again with your former enemy, but you have him to dinner. That was often the case in the ancient Near East (see Gen. 31:51–54; 2 Sam. 9:7–13; 19:28; 1 Kings 2:7).

Now, the fall has made us enemies of God. God provided food for Adam and Eve before the fall (Gen. 1:29), but they abused that privilege by taking the one fruit that he kept from them. But through Christ he seeks reconciliation with us. And that reconciliation is so deep, so complete, that he invites us to share meals with him. So after the great flood, God provides food for Noah and his family, inviting them to eat the flesh of animals as well as the fruits of the garden (Gen. 9:3). When God redeemed the children of Israel from Egypt, he gave them a sacramental meal, the Passover, as a memorial of their salvation and their covenant with God (Ex. 12). When the Israelites met with God around Mount Sinai on the "day of the assembly" (Deut. 9:10), God made a covenant with them as his people and called the seventy elders up to the mountain to eat and drink with him (Ex. 24:9–11). For all the people, God provided manna, supernatural food, for them to eat on their long journey to the Promised Land (Ex. 16:1–35; cf. Ps. 78:19–20).

And the tabernacle offerings were offerings of food. Bread and flagons of wine were kept on a table in the tabernacle and again in the temple (Ex. 25:30; 37:16; Lev. 24:5–9). This food ("the bread of the Presence," Num. 4:7) is an offering to the Lord (Lev. 24:7), and it represents a covenant relation between God and Israel (Lev. 24:8). The animal sacrifices, the whole burnt offering, the sin offering, and the guilt offering focused on the idea of atonement. Another of the tabernacle offerings, the peace offering, reckons on that atonement's already being completed. It focuses on the reconciliation between God and the Israelite following atonement. The peace offering was a meal, of which part was burned up for God, part eaten by the priests, and part eaten by the worshipers, celebrating reconciliation (Lev. 7:11–18; 19:5–8; Deut. 27:7).

So a first-century Jew would not have been surprised to hear that the Lord's Supper was the new covenant in Jesus' blood (Luke 22:20; 1 Cor. 11:25). Whenever we take the Supper, as when Israel took the Passover and the other meals, we renew the covenant relationship between God and ourselves.

Further, meals with God also provide continuing nourishment and fellowship with him. Think of how David in Psalm 23:5 speaks of God's preparing a table for him in the midst of his enemies. Think of how God's personified wisdom, in Proverbs 9:1–6, invites the young man into her home for a meal. Think of Jesus, who twice miraculously fed great multitudes (Matt. 14:13–21; 15:32–38). Think of how Jesus, after his resurrection, invited his disciples to eat and drink with him (Luke 24:30; John 21:9–14; Acts 10:41). This all anticipates the great meal in heaven, the messianic banquet, the wedding supper of the Lamb, in which we celebrate the consummation of redemption (Luke 13:29; 14:15–24; 22:30; Rev. 19:9). So as we eat and drink now, we look forward to his coming, when we will eat and drink with consummate joy (1 Cor. 11:26).

The Experience of the Lord's Supper

So when we take the Lord's Supper, we should reflect on the past, the present, and the future. We should remember Christ in his death, thanking him for his complete salvation. The Supper is called a thanksgiving (Matt. 26:27; Luke 22:17, 19; 1 Cor. 11:24), hence the word *eucharist*.

In the present, we know that we can gain spiritual nourishment only from Christ (John 6:35–59; 1 Cor. 10:16). By eating and drinking, we participate in his body and blood, and we sense a greater union with him. Calvin, who emphasized that Christ is not physically present in the Supper but lives physically in heaven, thought that the Supper was not so much Christ's coming to be with us as our being caught up to heaven to be with him, as we join him in the heavenly places.

And then as we eat and drink, we look forward to the greater banquet to come (1 Cor. 11:26). We eat only little bits of bread and drink little cups of wine, for we know that our fellowship with Christ in this life cannot begin to compare with the glory that awaits us in him.

Key Terms

Sacrament
Signs
Divine actions
Means of divine presence
Visible words
Seals
Communion
Ex opere operato
Baptism
Zwingli's view of baptism
Mode of baptism
Immersion
Sprinkling
Paedobaptist
Reformed paedobaptist
Antipaedobaptist
Credobaptist

Household baptisms
Lord's Supper
Transubstantiation
Memorial
Table fellowship with God
Eucharist

Study Questions

1. "As the Reformers used to say, the sacraments are visible words." Explain.

2. "The sacraments are not only signs, but *seals*." Explain. How do they "separate us from the world"?

3. "So the efficacy of the sacrament is by faith alone." Explain why it is important to say this.

4. "Baptism is, first, the rite of entrance into the visible church." Explain, noting the consequences of this fact.

5. Discuss the meaning of the symbolism of baptism. How is baptism related to union with Christ?

6. "Baptism is a name-giving ceremony." Explain.

7. What biblical arguments are given for immersion as the exclusive mode of baptism? How can these arguments be countered? Is there any biblical evidence for sprinkling or pouring as a mode of baptism?

8. Determining the subjects of baptism is "a question of the burden of proof." Explain.

9. Present an argument for Reformed paedobaptism, referring to Scripture texts.

10. What was the significance of Jesus' blessing children in Luke 18:15–17? How is that relevant to the discussion of infant baptism?

11. Baptists say that "the new covenant is very different from the old—the old based on physical birth, family, and nation, the new based on spiritual realities such as faith." Reply.

12. How does 1 Corinthians 7:14 bear upon baptism?

13. Frame says, "Indeed, I wish there were a way that believers holding different positions on [infant baptism] could belong to the same church." Explain; evaluate. Why would it be difficult to practice this suggestion?

14. Frame says that the Lord's Supper has "past, present, and future references." What are these?

15. Respond to the Roman Catholic doctrine of transubstantiation.

16. Respond to the Lutheran view of Christ's presence in the Lord's Supper.

17. Respond to Ulrich Zwingli's view of the presence of Christ in the Lord's Supper.

18. Expound and evaluate John Calvin's view of Christ's presence in the Lord's Supper.

19. Expound the biblical theme of "table fellowship with God."

20. How can we have table fellowship with Christ, considering that he lives in heaven? Give Calvin's answer and evaluate.

Memory Verses

Ps. 23:5–6: You prepare a table before me
   in the presence of my enemies;
you anoint my head with oil;
   my cup overflows.
Surely goodness and mercy shall follow me
   all the days of my life,
and I shall dwell in the house of the LORD
   forever.

Matt. 28:19: Go therefore and make disciples of all nations, baptizing them in the name of the Father and of the Son and of the Holy Spirit.

Luke 18:15–17: Now they were bringing even infants to him that he might touch them. And when the disciples saw it, they rebuked them. But Jesus called them to him, saying, "Let the children come to me, and do not hinder them, for to such belongs the kingdom of God. Truly, I say to you, whoever does not receive the kingdom of God like a child shall not enter it."

Acts 2:39: For the promise is for you and for your children and for all who are far off, everyone whom the Lord our God calls to himself.

Rom. 6:3–5: Do you not know that all of us who have been baptized into Christ Jesus were baptized into his death? We were buried therefore with him by baptism into death, in order that, just as Christ was raised from the dead by the glory of the Father, we too might walk in newness of life.
   For if we have been united with him in a death like his, we shall certainly be united with him in a resurrection like his.

1 Cor. 7:14: For the unbelieving husband is made holy because of his wife, and the unbelieving wife is made holy because of her husband. Otherwise your children would be unclean, but as it is, they are holy.

1 Cor. 11:23–26: For I received from the Lord what I also delivered to you, that the Lord Jesus on the night when he was betrayed took bread, and when he had given thanks, he broke it, and said, "This is my body which is for you. Do this in remembrance of me." In the same way also he took the cup, after supper, saying, "This cup is the new covenant in my blood. Do this, as often as you drink it, in remembrance of me." For as often as you eat this bread and drink the cup, you proclaim the Lord's death until he comes.

Col. 2:11–12: In him also you were circumcised with a circumcision made without hands, by putting off the body of the flesh, by the circumcision of Christ, having been buried with him in baptism, in which you were also raised with him through faith in the powerful working of God, who raised him from the dead.

Resources for Further Study

Adams, Jay. *The Meaning and Mode of Baptism*. Phillipsburg, NJ: P&R Publishing, 1992.

Armstrong, John H., ed. *Understanding Four Views of the Lord's Supper*. Grand Rapids: Zondervan, 2007.

Chaney, James M. *William the Baptist*. Charleston: CreateSpace, 2009.

Murray, John. *Christian Baptism*. Phillipsburg, NJ: P&R Publishing, 1992.

PART 11

THE DOCTRINE OF
THE LAST THINGS

CHAPTER 50

HEAVEN AND HELL

AT THE END OF THE PREVIOUS CHAPTER, I indicated how the Lord's Supper points us to the future, toward the great marriage supper of the Lamb. So it is appropriate that in these last few chapters we move to the subject of eschatology, or the "last things." Eschatology deals with the end of things. It includes personal eschatology, what happens to each individual after death, and also historical eschatology, the return of Christ to judge the world. Here I will be talking mainly about individual eschatology. In chapter 51, I will discuss the return of Christ and the eternal new heavens and new earth.

What happens to us after death? Well, we go on living! Both the righteous and the wicked continue to exist consciously. There are two phases to our life after death. Theologians call the first the intermediate state and the second the eternal state. We'll look at these in order.

The Intermediate State

First, the intermediate state. This is an interval of time in which the dead await the final judgment and the resurrection of the body. During this time, the experience of the righteous is very different from the experience of the wicked. We look first at the experience of believers in Christ, those who are righteous by faith in him.

The Bible is clear in teaching that after death believers go immediately to be with Christ. Since Christ is at the Father's right hand, and the Father's dwelling place is often called *heaven* in Scripture, we can say that when believers die, they go to heaven. But the name of the place is less important than the persons who are there: the Father and the Son, and doubtless the Holy Spirit as well. Paul says in Philippians 1:23 that he desired to die and be with Christ, more than to live. In 2 Corinthians 5:8, he says, "Yes, we are of good courage, and we would rather be away from the body and at home with the Lord." We recall that when he was on the cross, our Lord said to the repentant thief, "Truly, I say to you, today you will be with me in Paradise" (Luke 23:43; cf. 2 Cor. 5:8; Heb. 12:23; Rev. 6:9–11; 7:9–10).

The word *heaven* has various meanings in Scripture. It can refer to the sky, to everything above the earth. But the predominant theological meaning is that it is a place where God dwells. It is a real place, in space and time. God, of course, is immaterial, and so is not limited to any place, not even to heaven (1 Kings 8:27). But God does choose places to manifest himself in intense ways, such as Mount Sinai, the tabernacle, and the temple. When those manifestations are visible, we call them *theophanies*.

Heaven seems to be the place where God manifests his presence in the most intense way. According to Hebrews 8:1–2:

> We have such a high priest, one who is seated at the right hand of the throne of the Majesty in heaven, a minister in the holy places, in the true tent that the Lord set up, not man.

The writer understands this true tent or tabernacle, this heavenly tabernacle, to be the model of which the earthly tabernacle is only an image, a picture (Heb. 8:5). So the sacrifices of the earthly tabernacle are only images, pictures, of the sacrifice of Jesus, and the earthly priests are only images of the Great High Priest, Jesus, who ministers in the heavenly tabernacle.

Jesus has gone into heaven, Peter tells us (1 Peter 3:22), and has sat down at God's right hand. That the Priest has sat down means that his atoning work is finished. That he sits at the right hand of God's throne means that he reigns as King. But he has said that he goes to prepare a place for us (John 14:2). He wants us to be there, too, with him.

This was also true of OT believers. We read of Enoch (Gen. 5:24) and Elijah (2 Kings 2:11; cf. Matt. 17:3) that they did not die, but went immediately into God's presence. It is unlikely that those who did die were any different. Cf. Pss. 16:10–11; 17:15; 23:6; Matt. 22:32. Elijah later appeared with Moses, who did die, and Jesus on the Mount of Transfiguration. Clearly, both Moses and Elijah continued to live in God's presence, a life without end. Indeed, Jesus tells a story in the OT context about a man, Lazarus, who dies and goes to "Abraham's bosom" (Luke 16:22–23 kjv). His rich oppressor dies and finds himself in a place of torment.

There are two alternatives to the doctrine that believers go immediately into God's presence at death, both in my view unbiblical. One is the Roman Catholic doctrine of purgatory, the other the sectarian doctrine of soul sleep.

Roman Catholics believe that although some especially great saints go directly to heaven when they die, most of us won't be good enough for heaven. So we need to undergo some purging (hence the name *purgatory*) before we enter heaven. That purging includes suffering. The Bible, however, says nothing about a place called *purgatory*, or a time of suffering for believers between death and heaven. A text in the apocryphal book of 2 Maccabees (12:42–45) suggests some such thing, but Protestants have agreed that this book is not part of the Word of God. More important, the doctrine of purgatory conflicts with the biblical teaching that Jesus has dealt with the sins of believers once for all, that our suffering and good works can add nothing to the atoning work of Christ.

The other erroneous teaching about the intermediate state is the doctrine of soul sleep, held by Seventh-day Adventists and some other groups. This is the view that the dead person is unconscious until the final judgment. According to these groups, just as the body lies dormant until the return of Christ, so the soul, or the consciousness of the person, is oblivious until the final resurrection.

It is true that Scripture uses sleep as a metaphor for death (Matt. 9:24; 27:52; John 11:11). All cultures are hesitant to speak of death directly, so we today say that someone has "passed away." But Scripture is very explicit in distinguishing sleep from death. In John 11:11–14, Jesus says that his friend Lazarus has "fallen asleep." But when the disciples misunderstand and question him further, he tells them plainly, "Lazarus has died." Sleep is enough like death to be used as a metaphor for death, but the Bible clearly does not regard the two as the same.

Some OT passages suggest that those who die are unconscious. Psalm 115:17 says, "The dead do not praise the Lord, nor do any who go down into silence." Cf. 6:5. This is a description of the dead body as it lies in the grave. But interestingly, the following verse gives a fuller picture: "But we will bless the Lord from this time forth and forevermore." The Psalms reflect a period of revelation in which God had not made known many details about life after death. But they do affirm it, as we have seen.

The OT teaches that after death, people go to a place called *Sheol*, a shadowy abode awaiting the coming of Christ. As we saw in chapter 38, there is biblical evidence that after his death, Jesus took the inhabitants of Sheol with him to the very presence of God. This is the best interpretation of Jesus' "descent into hell" as described in the Apostles' Creed.

In any case, Scripture does not teach soul sleep, and of course soul sleep is contrary to the teaching of the passages we saw earlier, which affirm that at death the believer goes directly to be with the Lord.

What is the intermediate state like for believers? That's hard to answer in detail, for Scripture says little about it. The important thing is that in that state we are with the Lord and the Lord is with us—Immanuel, God with us. This is not the final state. Though we are with the Lord, there is still much for us to look forward to.

And contrary to the way we usually think, the saints in the intermediate state are not perfectly happy and satisfied. They long for the completion of God's plan. Notice Revelation 6:10–11, which says of the martyrs:

> They cried out with a loud voice, "O Sovereign Lord, holy and true, how long before you will judge and avenge our blood on those who dwell on the earth?" Then they were each given a white robe and told to rest a little longer, until the number of their fellow servants and their brothers should be complete, who were to be killed as they themselves had been.

In this cry there is a longing, a holy dissatisfaction. The glorified saints are perfected. Their cry is not a sinful one, but like Jesus in the garden they agonize over the course of the divine will. But God assures them that he will accomplish all his will. He is sovereign, so that he knows some others are destined to die for the testimony of Jesus, and he will not bring vengeance until their number is complete.

Are the saints in heaven immaterial, or somehow material? We tend to think they are disembodied, immaterial, because, of course, their material bodies are in the grave. But especially given the biblical understanding of human beings as physical as well as spiritual (chapter 34), it is hard to conceive of human beings' living in a disembodied state. Certainly, if they do, that is as imperfection, not as perfection. We tend to think of disembodiment as a pleasurable kind of existence; our bodies often seem to weigh us down. But in Scripture the body is a good thing. What we look forward to, according to Scripture, is the resurrection of the body, not a disembodied life. And I don't think Scripture rules out the possibility that God will give us some temporary embodiment in the intermediate state. Some have taken 1 Corinthians 5:1–10 to teach that the tent of the body will be replaced in heaven by heavenly clothing (described in the metaphor of a house or dwelling).

Where are the wicked in the intermediate state? In torment, awaiting judgment. Jesus' story of the rich man and Lazarus is not just a story, as I understand it. It pictures Jesus' own view of what the afterlife is really like. The poor man is in Abraham's bosom. The rich man is in torment, receiving no mercy. No one can cross from the one place to the other.

This fact tells us that although the final judgment remains future, our eternal destinies are set at death. After death, no one can change from righteousness to wickedness, nor can any wicked person repent of sin and be accepted by God.

The Eternal State

Now let's move on to consider what the Bible teaches about the eternal state. When Jesus returns to earth, he will bring all his saints with him (1 Thess. 3:13; Jude 14). Their bodies will rise from the ground, and believers living on earth will be caught up to meet the Lord in the air (1 Thess. 4:16–17). This rising up to meet Christ in the air is called the *rapture*, and though there is a lot of debate among theologians as to when it happens, there can be no doubt that it will take place.

After that comes God's final judgment (Matt. 10:15; 11:22, 24; Acts 17:30–31; Rev. 20:11–15). It is a judgment of both the righteous and the wicked. Those who do not believe in Christ will be judged according to their works (Rom. 2:5–8; Rev. 20:12–13). Note how thorough the judgment is: every work, indeed every thought, will receive God's judgment (Eccl. 12:14; Matt. 12:36). All secrets will be made known (Luke 12:2–3), and God will judge them (Rom. 2:16). Of course, nobody's works, words, or thoughts are perfectly acceptable to God. So God's judgment on those outside of Christ is invariably negative, and the punishment is death, in this case eternal death, eternal punishment, eternal separation from God.

The final judgment includes believers also. Paul says, "For we must all appear before the judgment seat of Christ, so that each one may receive what is due for what he has done in the body, whether good or evil" (2 Cor. 5:10; cf. Matt. 25:31–46; Rom. 14:10, 12). Of course, because of Christ, we have no fear of eternal condemnation. For his sake, our sins are forgiven, so, as Paul says in Romans 8:1, there is no condemnation to those who are in Christ Jesus. Indeed, Jesus says in John 5:24 that those who believe in him, even here in this world, already *have* everlasting life. That life will not be taken away from us at the final judgment. Rather, God will affirm that life that Jesus has bought for us with his own blood.

This event will be a great event for all of us. And it will be tremendously important also for the physical cosmos. We saw earlier how the creation now groans and travails in pain until the manifestation of the children of God (Rom. 8:19–22). At the return of Christ, the travail is over, and the creation gives birth to something new.

Scripture speaks of this new reality as a new heavens and new earth (2 Peter 3:13; Rev. 21:1). "Heaven and earth" is a Hebrew way of referring to everything there is, the universe. So we can say that God makes a new universe. It is a physical reality, appropriate to our resurrected bodies (Rom. 8:19–21). Remember, the consummation of human existence doesn't take us above and beyond the physical. Rather, as with Jesus' resurrection body, our existence in the new heavens and earth will be physical. There will be eating and drinking (Luke 22:18; Rev. 19:9; 22:1; 22:2) and travel through a city, with streets (Rev. 21:10–11, 21–26). Doubtless much of the description of the New Jerusalem in Revelation is symbolic, but it does describe some heightened, consummate form of physical existence.

I do expect that, like Jesus' body, our resurrection bodies might have powers that they do not now have. Jesus was able to come through closed doors, for example. The resurrection body will be imperishable, powerful, and spiritual. Paul says, "So is it with the resurrection of the dead. What is sown is perishable; what is raised is imperishable. It is sown in dishonor; it is raised in glory. It is sown in weakness; it is raised in power. It is sown a natural body; it is raised a spiritual body. If there is a natural body, there is also a spiritual body" (1 Cor. 15:42–44). *Spiritual* means directed by the Spirit, empowered by the Spirit.

Evidently there will be no sexual activity in the new creation. Jesus says that in the age to come, there will be no marrying or giving in marriage (Matt. 22:30). Our earthly families will be transcended by the worldwide family of God. But doubtless the new creation is not a time of lesser intimacy, but greater: intimacy with God and with other members of his body. I have no doubt that we will share our gifts with one another to a degree unheard of today. We will no longer be suspicious or fearful or envious of one another, so we will share openly what we are, what we think, what we are able to do. I don't know exactly what will replace sexual pleasure, but I know that our intimacy with God and one another will be something greater and better than anything we know and enjoy on this earth—as everything will be.

Much of our time will be spent in worship, as the book of Revelation suggests. Hence the frequent picture in cartoons of glorified saints playing harps. But remember that worship in Scripture is both narrow and broad. Narrowly, it includes specific times for gathering to praise God; broadly, worship is making our bodies living sacrifices, which is our spiritual worship (Rom. 12:1–2). There will be lots of things to do in the new creation. New things to learn, to make, to do.

But whether we are gathered around the throne to sing of God, or whether we are exploring the far reaches of the new creation, the most significant fact will be that God is there in consummate fullness (Rev. 21:3–4; 22:3–4). There is no temple in the new city, for the Lord Almighty and the Lamb are themselves the temple (21:22). That is, we will always be in direct contact with God, wherever we are.

Now, as our existence in this new creation is physical, so it is also temporal. Only God is above time. Human beings are temporal creatures, in time, and will always be. A physical body implies a spatiotemporal existence. People sometimes interpret Revelation 10:6 ("there should be time no longer" in the KJV) to mean that our future existence is above or beyond time, but I think more modern translations are more accurate to render the verse "there would be no more delay," that is, no more delay before the fulfillment of God's mystery (v. 7). In the new creation, as now, one event will follow another in time (Rev. 21:24–26; 22:2).

So our existence in the new heavens and new earth will be spatial and temporal. We do not become divine. But we will be *with* God in a consummate way. Remember that the heart of the covenant is the word, "I will be your God, and you shall be my people." In Revelation 21:3 and 7, God repeats that word, with a consummated meaning. He is now "with us" in a greater way than ever before. He is fully Immanuel, God with us. This is the great hope of the psalmist in Psalms 16:11; 27:4; 73:25–26. That is the reality of the new creation:

> And I heard a loud voice from the throne saying, "Behold, the dwelling place of God is with man. He will dwell with them, and they will be his people, and God himself will be with them as their God. He will wipe away every tear from their eyes, and death shall be no more, neither shall there be mourning, nor crying, nor pain anymore, for the former things have passed away." (Rev. 21:3–4)

> No longer will there be anything accursed, but the throne of God and of the Lamb will be in it, and his servants will worship him. They will see his face, and his name will be on their foreheads. (Rev. 22:3–4)

Eternal Blessing of Believers (Heaven)

The most important blessing of believers in the eternal state is the presence of God himself. For all eternity, we live with Jesus, seeing God face to face. Sin is the great barrier to our intimacy with God, and in the eternal state we are forever separated not only from the guilt of sin, but also from its power and presence in our lives. There is joy in his presence. We are all invited to the marriage supper of the Lamb (Rev. 19:9). There are feasting and good times.

Another blessing, or perhaps another way in which Scripture describes our consummate blessing, is *inheritance* (Matt. 25:34; Acts 26:18; Eph. 1:11, 14, 18; Col. 1:12; 3:24; Heb. 9:15; 1 Peter 1:4; Rev. 21:7). I mentioned under the doctrine of adoption, chapter 42, that being God's son or daughter means receiving an inheritance.

What is the inheritance? Well, chiefly it is God himself! We keep coming back to that. God was the inheritance of Israel (Ps. 16:5), as she was his. But we can be more specific. One thing that God gives as an inheritance to his people is authority (Rev. 20:4; 22:5). We are to reign with Christ. That includes judging angels (1 Cor. 6:3), judging Israel (Matt. 19:28; Luke 22:30), ruling cities (Luke 19:11–27). God gave to Adam and Eve authority to have dominion over the earth. Now the saints of Christ receive the authority that Adam forfeited by his sin.

It is not always clear how literally we should take these promises, but there is no doubt that there is a reward to those who belong to Jesus. Some philosophers, such as Immanuel Kant, have thought that to do good for the sake of a reward is wrong, immoral. They have thought that we really ought to do our duty for duty's sake, without any thought of reward. But that's not scriptural. Over and over again, Scripture motivates our good works with promises of reward. There is, of course, the promise of eternal life itself to everyone who believes (John 3:16; Rom. 2:7). And that eternal life is a life of happiness, inheritance, possession, as we have seen. If we serve Christ faithfully, we will receive a reward (1 Cor. 3:14). Paul says in Colossians 3:23–24, "Whatever you do, work heartily, as for the Lord and not for men, knowing that from the Lord you will receive the inheritance as your reward. You are serving the Lord Christ."

It also appears that there are *degrees* of reward. In the parable of the minas or the pounds (Luke 19:11–27), the master gave greater degrees of authority to those servants who had served him most faithfully. Cf. 1 Cor. 3:12–15. We might imagine that this unequal division would cause unhappiness or jealousy among those who are redeemed, but of course that will not happen. The first thing to remember about the eternal state of the redeemed is that there will be no sin, and that includes no jealousy, no envy, no coveting. If a friend of yours gets a greater reward than you do, you will be happy for him, and you will declare that God's allocation is completely just.

Eternal Punishment of Unbelievers (Hell)

Now I must, with some reluctance, look at the other side of the eternal state: the eternal punishment of the wicked, those who are outside of Christ. I am reluctant because it is always unpleasant to think about, or talk about, eternal punishment. If I were free to invent my own religion, I can assure you that eternal punishment would not be part of it. But I must talk about it now, because I am not free to invent my own religion; I must teach only what the Bible teaches, and the Bible certainly has a lot to say about eternal punishment. Indeed, of all the teachers mentioned in the Bible, Jesus himself has the most to say about eternal punishment, and he put considerable emphasis on it. It is no small detail in his view of human destiny.

First, it is clear from many passages that those who do not believe in Christ stand condemned. John 3:18 says, "Whoever believes in him is not condemned, but whoever does not believe is condemned already, because he has not believed in the name of the only Son of God." And John 3:36: "Whoever believes in the Son has eternal life; whoever does not obey the Son shall not see life, but the wrath of God remains on him."

The wrath of God is something terrible. When God led Israel across the Red Sea on dry land, he destroyed the Egyptian army. Exodus 15:6–7 says, "Your right hand, O Lord, glorious in power, your right hand, O Lord, shatters the enemy. In the greatness of your majesty you overthrow your adversaries; you send out your fury [that's God's wrath, his anger]; it consumes them like stubble." The OT contains many terrifying, graphic descriptions of what happens when God's wrath "waxes hot."

Now, of course, the OT descriptions of God's wrath mainly concern what happens in this life. But many wicked people do not receive full punishment for their wickedness in this life. Indeed, how can anyone who has violated God's law pay for his sins in this life, in a finite period of time? We know as believers that we could never pay out of our own resources the debt we owe to God. Nothing but the death of the Son of God would suffice. Then what remains for people who have refused Christ, who want no part of his ultimate sacrifice? Hebrews 10:26–27 says, "For if we go on sinning deliberately after receiving the knowledge of the truth, there no longer remains a sacrifice for sins, but a fearful expectation of judgment, and a fury of fire that will consume the adversaries." If we turn from Christ and prefer to sin, all we have to look forward to is God's furious judgment.

That judgment occurs after this life is done, but it is based on deeds done during this life, here on earth: "It is appointed for man to die once, and after that comes judgment" (Heb. 9:27). So there is no second chance. Those who die as unbelievers rest under this terrible judgment of God.

The punishment is everlasting. At the final judgment, the sheep, Jesus' people, receive eternal life, while the goats, the wicked, go into eternal punishment (Matt. 25:41, 46). "And the smoke of their torment goes up forever and ever, and they have no rest, day or night, these worshipers of the beast and its image, and whoever receives the mark of its name" (Rev. 14:11; cf. Mark 9:43, 48; Luke 16:22–24, 28; Rev. 19:3; 20:10).

Some people have tried to say that although the smoke and fire continue forever, the torment of the lost has an end, because eventually they are burned up. This position is called annihilationism: that the wicked are not punished forever, but at some point are simply put out of existence. But Scripture suggests the opposite, that not only does the fire continue forever, but the torment of the wicked continues forever as well (Rev. 14:11; 20:10). There is language in Scripture that says the wicked will be destroyed. But that does not necessarily mean annihilation. In 1 Corinthians 5:5, Paul urges the church to excommunicate a sinner "for the destruction of the flesh." That doesn't mean that the sinner will be annihilated, only that he will turn from his wicked ways. Of course, in hell, nobody will turn from his wicked ways, so the destruction, the punishment, continues without end.

I do believe there will be degrees of punishment in hell, just as there are degrees of reward for believers. In Matthew 11:22, Jesus says, "It will be more bearable on the day of judgment for Tyre and Sidon than for" Chorazin and Bethsaida. In Luke 20:47, he says that the scribes will receive "greater condemnation" than some others. In Luke 12:47–48, Jesus says that servants who sin ignorantly will receive lighter beatings than those who sin with greater knowledge. The chief variable appears to be knowledge. Those who sin against greater knowledge will be subject to the greatest condemnation. That's a message that we theologians especially need to hear.

Nevertheless, even a relatively lighter beating from God, lasting through eternity, is a terrible thing to contemplate. No one should try by some exegetical or theological trick to mitigate the harshness of this doctrine. That harshness is the whole point. To be separate from God, from his inheritance, from his people, and to be under his wrath forever is terrible to contemplate.

We are reluctant to talk about hell today. We would like to motivate people to embrace Jesus out of love, not fear. Certainly it is not wrong to focus on the love of Christ. Scripture itself does not always bring up hell in an evangelistic context. But sometimes it does. Sometimes it uses threats rather than loving entreaties. When people reported to Jesus some awful tragedies, he said to them, "Unless you repent, you will all likewise perish" (Luke 13:3, 5). Some people won't respond to love, at least not to love alone.

Is it unfair for God to punish people eternally? It might seem that way. How can one sin lead to an eternity of misery? But remember that, as with Adam's first sin, each sin is an affront to the dignity of the eternal God, a violation of his perfect righteousness, a betrayal of his perfect love. Calculations of this sort go beyond our powers, but it shouldn't surprise us to have God tell us that such sins are infinitely offensive and merit an eternal penalty. It is up to him to determine penalties, and we know from Scripture that his decisions are perfectly just.

We might not see the justice of it now. But that is the problem of evil, which we looked at in chapter 14. When we are gathered around the throne, singing God's praises in the eternal state, we will not be raising objections to God's justice, but we will be praising it without reservation: "Great and amazing are your deeds, O Lord God the Almighty! Just and true are your ways, O King of the nations! Who will not fear, O Lord, and glorify your name? For you alone are holy. All nations will come and worship you, for your righteous acts have been revealed" (Rev. 15:3–4).

Key Terms

Last things
Eschatology
Personal eschatology
Historical eschatology
Intermediate state
Heaven

Theophanies
True tabernacle
Purgatory
Soul sleep
Sheol
Rapture
Eternal state
Final judgment
New heavens and new earth
Inheritance
Hell
Annihilationism

Study Questions

1. Does Scripture teach that believers go to heaven when they die? Cite some Bible references in this connection.
2. What is the "true tabernacle"? What does Scripture teach us about it?
3. What is purgatory? Does Scripture teach that it exists? Discuss.
4. Same for soul sleep.
5. "And contrary to the way we usually think, the saints in the intermediate state are not perfectly happy and satisfied." Explain; evaluate.
6. Are the saints in heaven immaterial, or somehow material? Discuss.
7. Where are the wicked in the intermediate state? Discuss.
8. Describe the events surrounding the return of Christ and the final judgment.
9. Will we worship in heaven? Describe that worship.
10. "So our existence in the new heavens and new earth will be spatial and temporal." Explain. Why is this important?
11. Describe in general terms the nature of the blessings for believers in the new heavens and new earth.
12. Should we do our duty for duty's sake, without hope of reward? Why or why not?
13. Are there degrees of reward? Discuss.
14. Evaluate annihilationism.
15. Are there degrees of punishment in hell?
16. Should we preach hellfire? Why or why not?
17. Is eternal punishment just? Pose the difficulty and respond.

Memory Verses

2 Cor. 5:8: Yes, we are of good courage, and we would rather be away from the body and at home with the Lord.

Phil. 1:23–24: I am hard pressed between the two. My desire is to depart and be with Christ, for that is far better. But to remain in the flesh is more necessary on your account.

1 Thess. 4:16–17: For the Lord himself will descend from heaven with a cry of command, with the voice of an archangel, and with the sound of the trumpet of God. And the dead in Christ will rise first. Then we who are alive, who are left, will be caught up together with them in the clouds to meet the Lord in the air, and so we will always be with the Lord.

Heb. 8:1–2: Now the point in what we are saying is this: we have such a high priest, one who is seated at the right hand of the throne of the Majesty in heaven, a minister in the holy places, in the true tent that the Lord set up, not man.

Rev. 6:10–11: They cried out with a loud voice, "O Sovereign Lord, holy and true, how long before you will judge and avenge our blood on those who dwell on the earth?" Then they were each given a white robe and told to rest a little longer, until the number of their fellow servants and their brothers should be complete, who were to be killed as they themselves had been.

Rev. 14:11: And the smoke of their torment goes up forever and ever, and they have no rest, day or night, these worshipers of the beast and its image, and whoever receives the mark of its name.

Rev. 21:1: Then I saw a new heaven and a new earth, for the first heaven and the first earth had passed away, and the sea was no more.

Rev. 21:3–4: And I heard a loud voice from the throne saying, "Behold, the dwelling place of God is with man. He will dwell with them, and they will be his people, and God himself will be with them as their God. He will wipe away every tear from their eyes, and death shall be no more, neither shall there be mourning, nor crying, nor pain anymore, for the former things have passed away."

Resources for Further Study

Alcorn, Randy. *Heaven*. Carol Stream, IL: Tyndale House, 2004.

Crockett, William, ed. *Four Views on Hell*. Grand Rapids: Zondervan, 1992.

Morgan, Christopher, and Robert Peterson, eds. *Hell under Fire*. Grand Rapids: Zondervan, 2004.

Peterson, Robert. *Hell on Trial*. Phillipsburg, NJ: P&R Publishing, 1995.

CHAPTER 51

THE EVENTS OF THE LAST DAYS

IN THE PREVIOUS CHAPTER, we looked at the Bible's teachings about individual eschatology, what happens to each of us when we die. In this chapter, we will consider the great events of future world history, those events surrounding the return of Jesus.

The chief event is, of course, the return of Christ, or his second coming. In this discussion, theologians have often focused on the relation of Jesus' return to the *millennium*, the thousand-year period mentioned in Revelation 20. In my judgment, this is somewhat unfortunate. Scripture specifically mentions the millennium only in Revelation 20. And when it speaks about the return of Christ, it is more interested in the impact of that hope upon our lives today than in the scheduling of the events. Nevertheless, since this discussion has been a frequent topic of theological debate, we will have to spend some time on it here.

Revelation 20:1–8 reads:

> Then I saw an angel coming down from heaven, holding in his hand the key to the bottomless pit and a great chain. And he seized the dragon, that ancient serpent, who is the devil and Satan, and bound him for a thousand years, and threw him into the pit, and shut it and sealed it over him, so that he might not deceive the nations any longer, until the thousand years were ended. After that he must be released for a little while.
>
> Then I saw thrones, and seated on them were those to whom the authority to judge was committed. Also I saw the souls of those who had been beheaded for the testimony of Jesus and for the word of God, and those who had not worshiped the beast or its image and had not received its mark on their foreheads or their hands. They came to life and reigned with Christ for a thousand years. The rest of the dead did not come to life until the thousand years were ended. This is the first resurrection. Blessed and holy is the one who shares in the first resurrection! Over such the second death has no power, but they will be priests of God and of Christ, and they will reign with him for a thousand years.
>
> And when the thousand years are ended, Satan will be released from his prison and will come out to deceive the nations that are at the four corners of the earth, Gog and Magog, to gather them for battle; their number is like the sand of the sea.

Theologians differ, first, on whether or not the thousand years represents a literal period of time. Since the numbers in Revelation are highly symbolic, it is unlikely that the author expects us to take the number as a literal thousand years. "Thousand" in Scripture is proverbial for a very long time. See Psalm 50:10, where the Lord says, "For every beast of the forest is mine, the cattle on a thousand hills." Psalm 84:10 reads, "For a day in your courts is better than a thousand elsewhere." And Psalm 90:4: "For a thousand years in your sight are but as yesterday when it is past, or as a watch in the night."

The discussion has focused, second, on whether the return of Christ precedes, follows, or divides this period. Premillennialism teaches that Christ will return *before* the millennium. Postmillennialism means that Christ will return *after* the millennium. Amillennialists believe that there will be no literal millennium. *A* is a negative prefix in Greek, so the word means "no millennium." But that is not to say that amillennialists deny the authority of Revelation 20. Rather, they interpret the thousand years there as the period of time between the resurrection of Jesus and his return. I will also discuss a position called *preterism*, which states that in some respects at least, the return of Christ has already happened. *Preterism* means "past," so a preterist believes that some of the passages referring to the return of Christ have been fulfilled in the past.

Amillennialism

First, let's look at the amillennial position. We'll abbreviate the term to *amil*, and similarly the others. The amil believes that the millennium is now, the whole period from Jesus' ascension to his return. He emphasizes that the resurrection and ascension of Jesus ushered in a new era of world history. Jesus has now achieved a great victory over Satan, sin, and death. And although we don't see all the effects of that victory now, it is certainly real. It is, perhaps, hard for us to imagine that right now Satan is "bound" (Rev. 20:2), sealed in a bottomless pit (v. 3), but it certainly is the case that his power is weakened. The amil says that Satan no longer deceives the nations (v. 3) as he did before the coming of Christ. Before Jesus came, believers in the true God existed mainly in Israel. The other nations were deceived by Satan into worshiping idols. But after the resurrection, the Christian church received power to reach people of all nations with the message of the gospel. And God will continue to empower this mission until the last day, until there are believers from every kingdom, tongue, tribe, and nation.

The amil, however, emphasizes that this period is also a period of suffering and persecution for the church. God's triumph at this time is spiritual, not material. We should not expect to have wealth or possessions. We should not expect to dominate the cultures in which we live—in politics, the arts, education, and so on. God will take from those cultures those he chooses to save. But culture itself will not be redeemed. Indeed, some amils believe that the cultures of the world will get worse and worse until Jesus returns.

Amils affirm that toward the end of this era Satan will be released briefly, as Revelation 20:3 indicates (also vv. 7–8). He will then deceive the nations again, presumably achieving some measure of his old power. But he will be frustrated and defeated by the return of Christ and the judgment that will result in his final destruction.

Amils hesitate to draw up timetables of the events preceding Jesus' return, beyond what we have already described. They do confess that when Jesus returns, there will be a general resurrection, a resurrection of both the righteous and the wicked, both believers and unbelievers. All people, then, will be gathered for the final judgment, and they will pass from what we earlier called the intermediate state into the eternal state. That eternal state is the new heavens and new earth, in which dwell righteousness.

The "first resurrection" of Revelation 20:5 is, on the amil view, what we called in the previous chapter the *intermediate state*. In that state, martyrs and other deceased believers reign with Christ through the thousand years, that is, the present age. The second resurrection is the physical resurrection of all the dead preceding the final judgment. Similarly, the first death is the physical death of human beings; the second death is the condemnation of the wicked, a death that believers do not experience.

Postmillennialism

Now let's look at the postmillennial view. Most recent postmils agree with the amils that the millennium is now, the period from Jesus' ascension to his return. Some postmils, however, especially in the older literature, have said that the millennium is a portion of that period, toward the end of it, before the return of Christ. The postmil agrees that this is the time in which the gospel is preached throughout the world. He agrees with the amil as to the meaning of Satan's binding and Satan's brief release before Jesus' return. He also agrees with the amil on the general course of events in the end times: Jesus comes, then the general physical resurrection of the righteous and the wicked, then the final judgment, then the new heavens and new earth.

So, someone will ask, how does the postmil differ from the amil? Well, although the postmil agrees with the amil that our age is a time of persecution for the church, he also thinks that during this time Christians will come to have more and more influence in the general culture. Believers will indeed gain wealth, influence, and even dominance.

Premillennialism

Now let us look at premillennialism. There are two forms of premillennialism, one of which is usually called *classical* or *historic*, and the other of which is called *dispensational*. Both these views believe that the millennium is yet future, and that it begins after the Lord returns to earth.

Let us consider first the classical form of premillennialism. This is a very ancient view that goes back to some of the earliest church fathers. They taught that at the end of the present age, Jesus will come and raise believers to be with him. Then he will reign upon the earth for a thousand years, or some other long period of time. During this time (and not until then), Satan is bound in the bottomless pit. At the end of this time, God will release Satan, and at his instigation some on earth will rebel against

Jesus (Rev. 20:3, 7–8). But the Lord will put down the revolt and raise all the dead for final judgment. Then comes the new heavens and new earth.

The dispensational form of premillennialism is more recent (nineteenth century) and more complicated. The key to understanding the dispensational view is the idea that Jesus actually returns twice, making three times altogether that Jesus comes to earth. His first coming was, of course, his conception in the womb of Mary two thousand years ago. At his second coming, at the end of this age, he comes secretly and raptures believers to be with him. The rapture is described in 1 Thessalonians 4:16–17, where Paul says:

> For the Lord himself will descend from heaven with a cry of command, with the voice of an archangel, and with the sound of the trumpet of God. And the dead in Christ will rise first. Then we who are alive, who are left, will be caught up together with them in the clouds to meet the Lord in the air, and so we will always be with the Lord.

The rapture is the Lord's taking his people to be with him in the air. All Christians believe in the rapture. What is unique to the dispensational view is that in that view the rapture is invisible and secret. This is the picture presented in the *Left Behind*[1] novels and movies: believers mysteriously disappear from offices, streets, airplanes, and so forth, and nobody knows where they are.[2]

Then, according to the dispensational premil, comes a seven-year period of satanic dominance, which gets much worse in the last three and a half years. (These figures come from Daniel 7:25; 9:27; 12:7; Rev. 12:14.) The seven-year period is called the *great tribulation*. Most dispensationalists believe that Jesus' secret coming to rapture his saints takes place *before* the great tribulation. So their view of Jesus' return is not only premillennial, but also pretribulational—*pretrib*, as we say. Some dispensationalists, however, hold that the rapture is midtribulational (that is, three and a half years into the tribulation, before the worst part of it) or posttribulational. On the majority pretribulational view, of course, believers do not have to endure the great tribulation at all. Jesus rescues them from it.

After the tribulation, Jesus returns again—his second second coming, or his third coming. In the earlier secret coming, Jesus comes *for* his saints; in the visible third coming, he comes *with* his saints. This coming is public and visible. He then reigns on earth for a thousand years, which may or may not be a literal number. This is the millennium described in Revelation 20:1–6. At the end of this time, there will be another apostasy, a period in which Satan is loosed. Then comes the final judgment, and the new heavens and new earth.

1. Tim LaHaye and Jerry Jenkins, *Left Behind* (Carol Stream, IL: Tyndale House, 1996), and many sequel volumes.
2. I'm trying to avoid editorializing in this section, but given the shout and the trumpet of 1 Thessalonians 4:16, the rapture does not seem to be very secret.

For the dispensational premil, the millennium is a time in which God fulfills promises that he has specifically made to the Jews. In the dispensational view, there are two distinct people of God: the Jews and the church of Christ (which contains both Jews and Gentiles). God has promised that the Jews will rule in an expanded land of Palestine, and that will literally take place in the millennium. Nondispensationalists believe that the promise of land to Israel is fulfilled in the promise to all Christian believers of a new heavens and new earth. For the nondispensationalist, there is only one people of God: that olive tree of Romans 11, from which some branches have been removed (unbelieving Jews) and others (believing Gentiles) have been grafted in.

Arguments for Amillennialism

I have described for you the chief millennial views. Let us now consider the arguments that are offered for each. First, amillennialism. The idea that Satan is bound during the present age is, perhaps, a little hard to swallow at first. At first glance at least, the view expressed in Hal Lindsey's book title *Satan Is Alive and Well on Planet Earth*[3] seems more likely. But we should always ask whether the biblical writers saw things in the same perspective. Remarkably, Jesus, even in his earthly ministry, reports that he saw Satan fall from heaven (Luke 10:18). The binding of Satan, to the early church, probably did not mean that Satan has no power at all, but that he can no longer prevent the Great Commission from happening. The Great Commission mandate, the worldwide mission of the church, is the most important event of our present age. The important thing, to the early Christians, is that people from all nations are being saved, despite Satan's best efforts. Revelation 20:3 gives us precisely that interpretation. Satan is not yet deprived of all his power, but he is no longer able to deceive the nations.

Over against premillennialism, Scripture never suggests that there is more than one coming of Christ in the future, preceding one general resurrection (Dan. 12:2; John 5:28–29; Acts 24:15). The return of Christ, the resurrection of the dead, and the final judgment all occur together (Matt. 24:29–31).

And it certainly is the case, as the amil says, that the age in which we live, even though it is a time when the nations come to Christ, is also an age of persecution, lawlessness, and evil (Matt. 24:21–30; 2 Tim. 3:1–5, 12–13; 4:3–4).

Arguments for Postmillennialism

But the postmil replies that in this age the kingdom of God is going to be triumphant. Not all at once. It is a gradual thing, certainly. But in time it will fill the earth (Matt. 13:31–33). The Great Commission will be entirely successful. Further, it will triumph over all opposition to God's purposes. Postmils understand in this way the great number of Bible passages that speak of God's victory over all his opponents (Pss. 22:27; 37:9–11; 46:8–10; 47:1–3; 66:4; 72:8–11; 86:9; 138:4–5; 149:5–9; Isa. 9:2–7; 11:1–10; 32:15–17; 40:4–11; 42:1–12; 49:1–26; 56:3–8; 60:1–22; 61:1–11; 62:1–12; 65:1–25; 66:1–24; cf.

---

3. Grand Rapids: Zondervan, 1972.

1 John 5:4). Amils and premils will protest that these refer to the new heavens and the new earth, but it's hard to avoid the impression that God's people, even his OT people, looked forward to this kind of victory before the final judgment.

Further, it is not as easy as premils and amils think to distinguish spiritual from cultural success. When people embrace the spiritual benefits of the gospel, it changes their lives comprehensively. It gives them new values and a new power to emulate God's holiness. God charges them to bring that new holiness into every sphere of life: "whether you eat or drink, or whatever you do, do all to the glory of God" (1 Cor. 10:31). So Christians throughout history have indeed transformed many spheres of human life: science, the arts, politics, education, the care of the poor and sick. This is almost inevitable: regenerate people renew the institutions and practices of the world. Of course, this process has its ups and downs. On the whole, the gospel had more cultural influence in America three hundred years ago than it does today. But that is because there is a smaller proportion today of people who profess Christ as Savior and Lord.

We see this process in Scripture. Joseph, Esther, and Daniel lived in pagan countries, but they were faithful to the true God. Their faithfulness led them into conflict with the values of the society around them. Nevertheless, God blessed their faithfulness, and that faithfulness brought benefit to the unbelieving societies of which they were part.

In the early centuries of the church, believers patiently endured much persecution for the sake of Christ. But the blood of the martyrs was the seed of the church, and it grew despite all that Satan could do. By the fourth century, the Roman Empire was officially Christian. We may disagree as to whether Constantine's conversion did more harm than good for the church. But we cannot doubt that it gave the church a great deal of cultural power, which lasted through the medieval period and later.

Arguments for Premillennialism

But there is also a case to be made for premillennialism. For one thing, the evidence from the church fathers, one or two generations removed from the apostles, is impressive. Further, some Bible passages describe a reign of God on the earth that doesn't seem to fit either the present age or the eternal state. God reigns visibly on earth, and yet there is continuing sin and rebellion. In Isaiah 65:18–20, we read:

> But be glad and rejoice forever
>   in that which I create;
> for behold, I create Jerusalem to be a joy,
>   and her people to be a gladness.
> I will rejoice in Jerusalem
>   and be glad in my people;
> no more shall be heard in it the sound of weeping
>   and the cry of distress.

No more shall there be in it
    an infant who lives but a few days,
    or an old man who does not fill out his days,
for the young man shall die a hundred years old,
    and the sinner a hundred years old shall be accursed.

This seems to be a prophecy of the last days, in which God reigns on earth. It might seem at first hearing to be a description of the eternal state, the new heavens and new earth. But in this image, God has not finally done away with sin and death (similarly Ps. 72:8–14; Isa. 11:6–11; Zech. 14:5–17; Rev. 2:26–27). Further, the most natural reading of Revelation 20 is that it describes future events, rather than past ones. The binding of Satan is not normally something that we would associate with the age in which we live, even granting the possibility of that meaning. Further, the idea of saints' coming to life is certainly compatible with a future resurrection, and although there is a sense in which we reign with Christ now, and a stronger sense in which the glorified saints and martyrs reign with Christ now, Luke 19:17 does present this as a reward for believers in the last days.

Preterism

Now, there is another approach to the biblical teaching about the last days, which is rather different from any of the positions that I have described above. That is preterism, which says that many, or all, of the prophecies of Jesus' coming were fulfilled by God's judgment on Jerusalem in A.D. 70. That means that there was a coming of Jesus that is past from our point of view. The word *preterism* comes from a word that means "past."

The arguments for preterism largely hinge on the passages that speak of the *nearness* of Jesus' coming from a first-century perspective. In Luke 21, for example, where Jesus speaks extensively of the end times, he says in verses 31–32, "So also, when you see these things taking place, you know that the kingdom of God is near. Truly, I say to you, this generation will not pass away until all has taken place." That suggests that the fulfillment of Jesus' prophecies is going to be near, perhaps thirty or forty years hence, not thousands of years in the future.

Others counter that passages such as Luke 21 and Matthew 24 speak not just of the destruction of Jerusalem, but of a cosmic destruction—the end of the world. But that language can be figurative. It is used in other prophecies describing war, such as Isaiah 34:1–4 and verses 9–10. And when Jesus speaks in Matthew 24:3 of "the end of the world" (KJV), preterists say that he is speaking of the end of the world of the Jews—of their temple, holy land, and covenant with God.

Now, with regard to the prophecies of the *nearness* of the last days, there are other possible explanations. The most common one is that the kingdom of God came in power when Jesus rose from the dead, ascended into heaven, and sent the Spirit upon the church. That would explain Jesus' statement in Matthew 16:28, for example, "Truly, I say to you, there are some standing here who will not taste death until they see the Son of Man coming in his kingdom." But another explanation of that statement might be found in the first verses of the following chapter: that the disciples witnessed Jesus' glorification on the Mount of Transfiguration. At least, it is not necessary to explain the nearness of the kingdom by making it refer to the events of A.D. 70.

As for the use of language suggesting cosmic destruction and the end of the world, while that language can be used figuratively in Scripture, the figurative interpretation is not necessary.

Preterism may turn out to be right with regard to some predicted events. Certainly the Olivet Discourse in Matthew 24 and Mark 13 is at least partly about the fall of Jerusalem. But there are a number of predicted events that clearly did *not* take place in A.D. 70. Among those are the resurrection of the righteous and the wicked, the final judgment, the visible appearing of Jesus to every eye, the visible dwelling of God with men in the new heavens and new earth, and the removal of all sin and sorrow from this world.

It is also significant that the early church fathers of the generation following the apostles never speak of a return of Christ that occurred in A.D. 70. If this were the momentous event that preterists make it out to be, one would think that the fathers would have made that one of the main themes of their writings. But in fact, they don't even mention it.

Now, some extreme preterists (sometimes called *full preterists*) say that there is no coming of Christ that is future to us; we have no return of Christ to look forward to. On their view, *all* the prophecies of Jesus' return were fulfilled in A.D. 70. I believe this view is quite wrong, even heretical. Scripture quite clearly teaches that Jesus will come to judge all the living and the dead. That has not happened yet. Every branch of the Christian church has maintained that truth and has found it to be a blessed hope, as in Titus 2:13. Extreme preterism takes away that hope.

The *Already* and the *Not Yet*

In all this talk of the return of Christ and the millennium, we have missed one of the most fundamental biblical emphases. That is that we ourselves live in the "last days." Hebrews 1:2 says, "In these last days he [God] has spoken to us by his Son, whom he appointed the heir of all things, through whom also he created the world." The "last days" in this passage is the period following Jesus' resurrection and ascension. The term "last days" is used in similar ways in Acts 2:17; 2 Timothy 3:1; and 2 Peter 3:3. As the amils, postmils, and preterists emphasize, there is a sense in which the kingdom of God *has* come.[4] It was established by Christ's atonement, and we have all entered it (Col. 1:13). Yet in another sense the kingdom remains future, as we pray in the Lord's Prayer, "Thy kingdom come"

4. Premils sometimes admit that the kingdom has come "in one sense."

(Matt. 6:10 KJV). So the kingdom is here, but yet to come. The last days are here, but yet to come. The fulfillment of history has occurred *already*, in Christ, but is also *not yet*, for there is more to come. This is the tension that theologians refer to as the *already* and the *not yet*.

So in his atonement, Jesus destroyed the power of sin, yet sin will cling to us until his return. He has destroyed Satan in principle, but this victory will not be consummated until the Lord's return. Oscar Cullmann compares this to the distinction between D-Day and V-Day in World War II. On D-Day, allied troops entered France, in principle dooming the Third Reich. But it took many months of bitter fighting before the Nazis surrendered on V-Day, "Victory Day." The cross was like D-Day, and Jesus' return will be like V-Day. We live between the times, always in the tension of the *already* and the *not yet*; and during that time, there are many battles to be fought.

Postmils, amils, and preterists emphasize the *already*, premils the *not yet*. A balanced eschatology will recognize the importance of both. Recall the longer discussion of the *already* and the *not yet* in chapter 5, with the diagram in fig. 51.1.

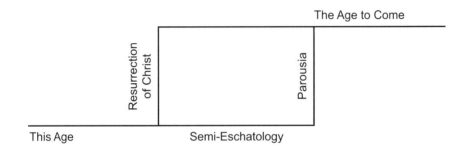

Fig. 51.1. The Two Ages

Eschatology and the Christian Life

This discussion suggests that biblical eschatology has important practical consequences. I confess my disappointment that so much teaching about the last days is focused on the order of events. I suppose I'm more of a postmil than anything else, but I honestly don't believe that the Bible is perfectly clear on the order of events. In my view, when Scripture tells us about the return of Christ, it doesn't give us this information so that we can put it on a chart and watch the events as they pass by. That would be catering to our intellectual pride, among other things. Why, then, does Scripture have so much to say about the last days? So that we can reorder our lives in the light of Jesus' coming.

So far as I can see, every Bible passage about the return of Christ is written for a practical purpose—not to help us to develop a theory of history, but to motivate our obedience. These doctrines motivate our obedience in several ways.

First, the coming of Christ should *reorder our priorities*. In 2 Peter 3:11–12, the apostle says:

> Since all these things are thus to be dissolved, what sort of people ought you to be in lives of holiness and godliness, waiting for and hastening the coming of the day of God, because of which the heavens will be set on fire and dissolved, and the heavenly bodies will melt as they burn!

Cf. 1 Cor. 7:26. Since God is going to destroy the present earth and replace it with a new heavens and a new earth, what sort of people should we be? The implicit answer: not people who care a lot about material things, or the pleasures of this life, but people who are passionate about the kingdom of God, which will remain for all eternity. That's not to say that there is something evil about material things, only that we should be using them for God's purposes, not just our own.

Second, if we are *eager* for Christ to return, we should be purifying ourselves (2 Peter 3:11–12). Every Christian not only should believe in the return of Christ, but should be *eager* for it to come. At the end of the book of Revelation, the church prays, "Even so, come, Lord Jesus" (Rev. 22:20 кjv). But if we are really so eager for Jesus to return, so eager for the new heavens and new earth, we should be seeking to be as pure as we will one day be in God's presence. First John 3:2–3 says:

> Beloved, we are God's children now, and what we will be has not yet appeared; but we know that when he appears we shall be like him, because we shall see him as he is. And everyone who thus hopes in him purifies himself as he is pure.

Another ethical implication of the return of Christ is its *encouragement*. It shows us that our labors for him today are not in vain. Paul says in 1 Corinthians 15:58, "Therefore, my beloved brothers, be steadfast, immovable, always abounding in the work of the Lord, knowing that in the Lord your labor is not in vain." That's a great comfort in the midst of difficulty. The things of this world are going to be burned up, but our labor for the Lord will bear fruit for eternity.

Fourth, our very ignorance of the time of Jesus' return has ethical implications. For that ignorance implies that *we must be ready at any time* for his return (Matt. 24:44; 1 Thess. 5:1–10; 1 Peter 1:7; 2 Peter 3:14). When he comes, we want him to find us busy in our callings, in the work of the Great Commission.

Finally, when Jesus comes, we will receive a *reward*, and we should look forward to that reward in our labors here. That reward should motivate us to good works here and now. In chapter 50, I mentioned that biblical emphasis on rewards, and many Scripture texts emphasize this: Matt. 5:12, 46; 6:1–4; 10:41–42; Rom. 14:10; 1 Cor. 3:8–15; 9:17–18, 25; 2 Cor. 5:10; Eph. 6:7–8; Col. 3:23–25; 2 Tim. 4:8; James 1:12; 1 Peter 5:4; 2 John 8; Rev. 11:18. Again, God doesn't expect us to do our duty merely for duty's sake, but to do our duty with full understanding that our Father will reward his children, not only in this life (Mark 10:29–30), but in eternity as well.

From the biblical emphasis, I conclude that the main reason that God speaks so much in Scripture about the return of Jesus is that this doctrine purifies the hearts of his people. May he use it to purify you and me, as we continue on our journey to glory.

Key Terms

Millennium
Premillennialism
Amillennialism
Postmillennialism
Preterism
First resurrection
Second resurrection
First death
Second death
Classical premillennialism
Dispensationalism
Rapture
Great tribulation
Pretribulationism
Midtribulationism
Posttribulationism
Full preterism
Already and *not yet*

Study Questions

1. Describe amillennialism and the biblical arguments for it. Evaluate these.
2. Same with postmillennialism.
3. Same with classical premillennialism.
4. Same with dispensational premillennialism.
5. Same with preterism.
6. How does postmillennialism differ from amillennialism? Which position is more biblical?
7. "For the dispensational premil, the millennium is a time in which God fulfills promises that he has specifically made to the Jews." Does Scripture describe such a time? Evaluate.
8. Frame: "Further, it is not as easy as premils and amils think to distinguish spiritual from cultural success." Explain; evaluate.

9. Premillennialists say that during the millennium Christ will rule on earth, but sin will not be finally judged. Is there biblical basis for this idea? Evaluate.

10. How do you explain Jesus' statements about the *nearness* of the last days?

11. Respond to full preterism.

12. In what sense is the kingdom present today, according to the NT? Describe Oscar Cullmann's D-Day illustration.

13. How do the Bible's eschatological predictions influence our attempts today to serve Christ?

Memory Verses

Matt. 5:11–12: Blessed are you when others revile you and persecute you and utter all kinds of evil against you falsely on my account. Rejoice and be glad, for your reward is great in heaven, for so they persecuted the prophets who were before you.

Matt. 24:44: Therefore you also must be ready, for the Son of Man is coming at an hour you do not expect.

1 Cor. 15:58: Therefore, my beloved brothers, be steadfast, immovable, always abounding in the work of the Lord, knowing that in the Lord your labor is not in vain.

1 Thess. 4:16–17: For the Lord himself will descend from heaven with a cry of command, with the voice of an archangel, and with the sound of the trumpet of God. And the dead in Christ will rise first. Then we who are alive, who are left, will be caught up together with them in the clouds to meet the Lord in the air, and so we will always be with the Lord.

2 Peter 3:11–12: Since all these things are thus to be dissolved, what sort of people ought you to be in lives of holiness and godliness, waiting for and hastening the coming of the day of God, because of which the heavens will be set on fire and dissolved, and the heavenly bodies will melt as they burn!

1 John 3:2–3: Beloved, we are God's children now, and what we will be has not yet appeared; but we know that when he appears we shall be like him, because we shall see him as he is. And everyone who thus hopes in him purifies himself as he is pure.

Resources for Further Study

Clouse, Robert, ed. *The Meaning of the Millennium: Four Views*. Downers Grove, IL: IVP Academic, 1977.

Gundry, Stanley, ed. *Three Views of the Millennium and Beyond*. Grand Rapids: Zondervan, 1999.

Hoekema, Anthony. *The Bible and the Future*. Grand Rapids: Eerdmans, 1994.

PART 12

THE DOCTRINE OF
THE CHRISTIAN LIFE

CHAPTER 52

HOW THEN SHALL WE LIVE?

PEOPLE HAVE SOMETIMES THOUGHT that ethics and theology are very different disciplines. But many great theology books, such as John Calvin's *Institutes* and Charles Hodge's *Systematic Theology*, together with church catechisms such as the HC, the WLC, and the WSC, contain expositions of the Ten Commandments. When you think about it, you can see that ethics is certainly part of theology. For one thing, texts such as 2 Timothy 3:16–17 teach clearly that the purpose of the Bible is to produce good works:

> All Scripture is breathed out by God and profitable for teaching, for reproof, for correction, and for training in righteousness, that the man of God may be competent, equipped for every good work.

Redemption itself, the main theme of the Bible, is important not for its own sake, but so that the redeemed might glorify God in their actions:

> For by grace you have been saved through faith. And this is not your own doing; it is the gift of God, not a result of works, so that no one may boast. For we are his workmanship, created in Christ Jesus for good works, which God prepared beforehand, that we should walk in them. (Eph. 2:8–10)

We are not saved by works, but we are certainly saved *for* works.

Furthermore, all theology *is* ethics. Throughout this book, we have been studying what we *ought* to believe. That *ought* is an ethical *ought*. Certainly, if it is this important to know what we ought to believe, it is equally important to know what we ought to do. Indeed, doing is a wider category than believing. Belief is one of the things we do. So perhaps we should consider ethics to be a broader discipline of which theology is a part. But I prefer to look at them as equally extensive, for as I argued in chapter 1, theology is the application of the Word of God, by persons, to all areas of life. That definition certainly includes ethics as well as theology. I define ethics, therefore, as "theology, viewed as a means of determining what human persons, acts, and attitudes receive God's blessing."[1]

---

1. Much of the following material is taken from chapter 3 of my *DCL*.

Lordship and Ethics

So ethics, like theology, is based on God's lordship, in several ways:

How God Governs Our Ethical Life

God governs our ethical life in three ways. First, by his control, God plans and rules nature and history so that certain human acts are conducive to his glory and others are not.

Second, by his authority, he speaks to us clearly, telling us what norms govern our behavior.

Third, by his covenant presence, he commits himself to be with us in our ethical walk, blessing our obedience, punishing our disobedience. But his presence also provides us with two important means of ethical guidance: (1) Because he is present with us, he is able to serve as a moral example. "You shall be holy, for I the LORD your God am holy" (Lev. 19:2; cf. Matt. 5:48). (2) He, and he alone, is able to provide, for sinners, the power to do good, to set us free from the power of sin (John 8:34–36). See fig. 52.1.

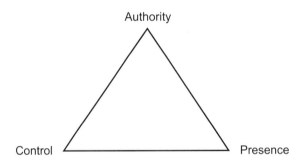

Fig. 52.1. God's Lordship Attributes

Necessary and Sufficient Criteria of Good Works

What is a good work? Reformed theologians have addressed this question in response to the *problem of the virtuous pagan*. Reformed theology teaches that human beings by nature are *totally depraved* (chapter 36). This means not that they are as bad as they can be, but that it is impossible for them to please God in any of their thoughts, words, or deeds (Rom. 8:8). So apart from grace, none of us can do anything good in the sight of God. Yet all around us we see non-Christians who seem, at least, to be doing good works: they love their families, work hard at their jobs, contribute to the needs of the poor, show kindness to their neighbors. It seems that these pagans are virtuous by normal measures.

Reformed theology, however, questions these normal measures. It acknowledges that unbelievers often contribute to the betterment of society. These contributions are called *civic righteousness* and come from God's common grace, which restrains their sin. Their civic righteousness does not please God, however, because it is altogether devoid of three characteristics:

> Works done by unregenerate men, although for the matter of them they may be things which God commands; and of good use both to themselves and others: yet, because they proceed not from an heart purified by faith; nor are done in a right manner, according to the Word; nor to a right end, the glory of God, they are therefore sinful, and cannot please God, or make a man meet to receive grace from God: and yet, their neglect of them is more sinful and displeasing unto God. (WCF 16.7)

Note the three necessary ingredients: (1) a heart purified by faith, (2) obedience to God's Word, and (3) the right end, the glory of God.

The first is a plainly biblical emphasis. The confession cites Hebrews 11:4 and some other texts. Romans 14:23b also comes to mind: "For whatever does not proceed from faith is sin." In Jesus' arguments with the Pharisees, too, it is evident that our righteousness must not be merely external (see esp. Matt. 23:25–26). In describing the necessity of an internal motive of good works, Scripture refers not only to faith, but especially to love, as in 1 Corinthians 13:1–3 and many other passages. We learn from these passages that love is not only necessary for good works, but also sufficient: that is, if our act is motivated by a true love of God and neighbor, we have fulfilled the law (Matt. 22:40; Rom. 13:8; Gal. 5:14).

The second element of good works, according to the confession, is obedience to God's Word, to his law. Note the references in the previous section to the importance of obeying God's Word. Certainly, obedience to God's Word is a necessary condition of good works, for disobedience to God's law is the very definition of sin (1 John 3:4). It is also a sufficient condition: for if we have obeyed God perfectly, we have done everything necessary to be good in his sight. Of course, among God's commands are his command to love (see the paragraph above) and to seek his glory (see the next paragraph).

The third element is the right end, the glory of God. Ethical literature has often discussed the *summum bonum*, or "highest good," for human beings. What is it that we are trying to achieve in our ethical actions? Many secular writers have said that this goal is pleasure or human happiness. But Scripture says that in everything we do, we should be seeking the glory of God (1 Cor. 10:31). Certainly, any act must glorify God if it is to be good, so seeking God's glory is a necessary condition of good works. And if the act does glorify God, then it is good; so it is a sufficient condition.[2]

So there are three necessary and sufficient conditions of good works: right motive, right standard, and right goal.[3] Right motive corresponds to the lordship attribute of

---

2. There is a sense, of course, in which even wicked acts bring glory to God, for God uses the wickedness of people to bring about his good purposes (Rom. 8:28). But the wicked person does not *intend* to glorify God by his actions. So 1 Corinthians 10:31 speaks of intent as well as action. Cf. Matt. 6:33.

3. Cornelius Van Til, in his *Christian-Theistic Ethics* (Philadelphia: Den Dulk Foundation, 1971), was the first to think through the significance of this confessional triad for ethical methodology. I gratefully acknowledge

covenant presence: for it is God's Spirit dwelling in us who places faith and love in our hearts. Right standard corresponds, obviously, to God's lordship attribute of authority. And right goal corresponds to the lordship attribute of control, for it is God's creation and providence that determines what acts will and will not lead to God's glory. God determines the consequences of our actions, and he determines which actions lead to our *summum bonum*. See fig. 52.2.

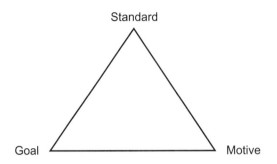

Fig. 52.2. Biblical Reasons to Do Good Works

Biblical Reasons to Do Good Works

The History of Redemption

Scripture uses basically three means to encourage believers to do good works. First, it appeals to the history of redemption. This is the chief motivation in the Decalogue itself: God has redeemed the Israelites from slavery in Egypt; therefore, they should obey.

In the NT, the writers often urge us to do good works because of what Christ did to redeem us. Jesus himself urges that the disciples "love one another: just as I have loved you, you also are to love one another" (John 13:34). Jesus' love, ultimately displayed on the cross, commands our response of love to one another. Another well-known appeal is found in Colossians 3:1–3:

> If then you have been raised with Christ, seek the things that are above, where Christ is, seated at the right hand of God. Set your minds on things that are above, not on things that are on earth. For you have died, and your life is hidden with Christ in God.

When Christ died, we died to sin; when he rose, we rose to righteousness. We are one with Christ in his death and resurrection. So those historic facts have moral implications. We should live in accord with the new life, given to us by God's grace when we rose with Christ. See also Rom. 6:1–23; 13:11–12; 1 Cor. 6:20; 10:11; 15:58; Eph. 4:1–5, 25, 32; 5:25–33; Phil. 2:1–11; Heb. 12:1–28; 1 Peter 2:1–3; 4:1–6.

---

his influence on my formulation here. In fact, Van Til's discussion was the seed thought behind all the triads in this book, and in my four-volume Theology of Lordship series.

So the HC emphasizes that our good works come from *gratitude*. They are not attempts to gain God's favor, but rather grateful responses to the favor that he has already shown to us.[4]

But our focus on the history of redemption is not limited to the past. It is also an anticipation of what God will do for us in the future. God's promises of future blessing also motivate us to obey him. Jesus commands us, "Seek first the kingdom of God and his righteousness, and all these things will be added to you" (Matt. 6:33).[5]

This motivation emphasizes God's control, for history is the sphere of God's control, the outworking of his eternal plan.

The Authority of God's Commands

Scripture also motivates our good works by calling attention to God's commands. Jesus said that he did not come to abrogate the law, but to fulfill it, so

> whoever relaxes one of the least of these commandments and teaches others to do the same will be called least in the kingdom of heaven, but whoever does them and teaches them will be called great in the kingdom of heaven. (Matt. 5:19)

So in their preaching, Jesus and the apostles often appeal to the commandments of the law, and to their own commandments (as in Josh. 1:8–9; Matt. 7:12; 12:5; 19:18–19; 22:36–40; 23:23; Luke 10:26; John 8:17; 13:34–35; 14:15, 21; Rom. 8:4; 12:19; 13:8–10; 1 Cor. 5:13; 9:8–9; 14:34, 37; 2 Cor. 8:15; 9:9; Gal. 4:21–22; Eph. 4:20–24; 6:1–3; 1 Thess. 4:1; 2 Tim. 3:16–17; Titus 2:1; James 1:22–25; 2:8–13; 1 Peter 1:16; 1 John 2:3–5; 3:24; 5:2).

God's commandment is sufficient to place an obligation upon us. We should need no other incentive. But God gives us other motivations as well, because we are fallen, and because he loves us as his redeemed children.

This motivation reflects God's lordship attribute of authority. We should obey him simply because he has the right to absolute obedience.

The Presence of the Spirit

Third, Scripture calls us to a godly life, based on the activity of the Spirit within us. This motivation is based on God's lordship attribute of presence. Paul says:

> But I say, walk by the Spirit, and you will not gratify the desires of the flesh. For the desires of the flesh are against the Spirit, and the desires of the Spirit are against the flesh, for these are opposed to each other, to keep you from doing the things you want to do. (Gal. 5:16–17)

---

4. This motivation is not what John Piper calls the "debtors' ethic," in which we do good works in a vain attempt to pay God back for our redemption. We can, of course, never do that, and we should not try to do it. See John Piper, *The Purifying Power of Living by Faith in Future Grace* (Sisters, OR: Multnomah Publishers, 1995), and the summary discussion on pages 33–38 of his *Brothers, We Are Not Professionals* (Nashville: Broadman and Holman, 2002). But gratefulness, nonetheless, is the only legitimate response to the grace that God has given us in Christ.

5. This is what Piper calls "future grace" in the works cited in the previous note.

God has placed his Spirit within us, to give us new life, and therefore new ethical inclinations. There is still conflict among our impulses, but we have the resources to follow the desires of the Spirit, rather than those of the flesh. So Paul appeals to the inner change that God has worked in us by regeneration and sanctification. In Ephesians 5:8–11, he puts it this way:

> At one time you were darkness, but now you are light in the Lord. Walk as children of light (for the fruit of light is found in all that is good and right and true), and try to discern what is pleasing to the Lord. Take no part in the unfruitful works of darkness, but instead expose them.

In the following verses, Paul continues to expound on the ethical results of this transformation. Cf. also Rom. 8:1–17; Gal. 5:22–26.

So Scripture motivates us to do good works by the history of redemption, the commandments of God, and the work of the Spirit within us, corresponding to God's lordship attributes of control, authority, and presence, respectively. See fig. 52.3.

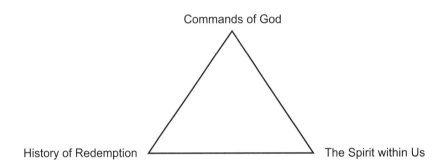

Fig. 52.3. Biblical Motivations for Good Works

Types of Christian Ethics

These three motivations have led Christian thinkers to develop three main types of Christian ethics: command ethics, narrative ethics, and virtue ethics. Command ethics emphasizes the authority of God's moral law. Narrative ethics emphasizes the history of redemption. It teaches ethics by telling the story of salvation. Virtue ethics discusses the inner character of the regenerate person, focusing on virtues listed in passages such as Romans 5:1–5; Galatians 5:22–23; Colossians 3:12–17.

Sometimes a writer will pit these types of ethics against one another, designating one as superior to the others. I don't see any biblical justification for that kind of argument. As we saw, Scripture uses all these methods to motivate righteous behavior. And it is hard to see how any of these could function without the others. It is God's commands that define the virtues and enable us to evaluate the behavior of characters in the narrative. It is the narrative that shows us how God saves us from sin and enables us to keep his law from the heart. And the virtues define what the redeemed person looks like when he obeys God from the heart. See fig. 52.4.

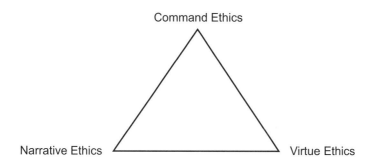

Fig. 52.4. Three Types of Christian Ethics

What Really Matters

We can see the same triadic structure in the actual content of biblical ethics. Let us first note sayings of the apostle Paul that intend to show the highest priorities of the Christian life. In these passages, he is opposing Judaizers, who think that one must be circumcised to enter the kingdom of God. He replies that neither circumcision nor uncircumcision is important, but rather the following:

> For neither circumcision counts for anything nor uncircumcision, but keeping the commandments of God. (1 Cor. 7:19)

> For in Christ Jesus neither circumcision nor uncircumcision counts for anything, but only faith working through love. (Gal. 5:6)

> For neither circumcision counts for anything, nor uncircumcision, but a new creation. (Gal. 6:15)

As in our previous discussion, there is a reference in 1 Corinthians 7:19 to keeping the commandments of God. It corresponds to God's lordship attribute of authority. "Faith working through love" in Galatians 5:6 is the work of the Spirit within us, and refers to God's covenant presence. "New creation" in Galatians 6:15 is the great redemptive-historical change brought about by Jesus' death and resurrection, the powerful work of God's sovereign control over history.[6] See fig. 52.5.

---

6. Thanks to my colleague Prof. Reggie Kidd for bringing these texts to my attention.

Fig. 52.5. What Is Most Important

Factors in Ethical Judgment

Now imagine that you are a pastor or counselor, and someone comes to your office with an ethical problem. Basically, you will need to discuss three things: the situation, the Word of God, and the inquirer himself. See fig. 52.6.

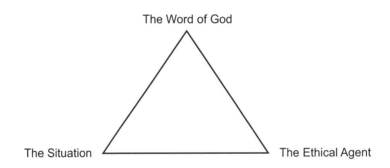

Fig. 52.6. Factors in Ethical Judgment

Normally, we ask first about the situation: "What's your problem? What brings you to see me?" This question is ultimately about God's lordship attribute of control, for God is the One who brings situations about.

Then we ask, "What does God's Word say about the problem?" This discussion invokes God's lordship attribute of authority.

Third, we focus on the inquirer, asking how he needs to change in order to apply God's solution to the problem. At this point, we are thinking especially about God's presence within the individual. If the person is a non-Christian, then obviously he needs to be born again by God's Spirit before he can apply the Word of God to his life. If the person is a believer, he may need to grow in certain ways before he will be able to deal with the issue before him.

We note in such conversations that each of these subjects influences the other two. We may start with a "presentation problem": "My wife is angry all the time." But as we move to a focus on God's Word, gaining a better understanding of Scripture, we may gain a better understanding of the problem as well. For example, Scripture tells us to remove the log from our own eye before trying to get the speck out of another's eye (Matt. 7:3). So the inquirer may come to see that his wife is angry because he has provoked her. So the problem now is not only in her, but in him as well. Reflection on God's Word has changed our understanding of the problem.

But this new understanding of the problem pushes us to look at more and different Scripture texts than we considered in the beginning. As we understand the problem better, we understand better how Scripture relates to it. Scripture and the situation illumine one another.

Then when we move to the third question and ask the inquirer to look within, he may see even more things in himself that have provoked his wife's anger. So the problem, the Word, and the inquirer have all illumined one another. Evidently you cannot understand your problem, or yourself, adequately until you have seen it through what John Calvin called the "spectacles of Scripture." And you can't understand the problem until you see yourself as a part of it.

And you can't understand God's Word rightly until you can use it, until you see how it applies to this situation and that. This is a more difficult point, but I think it is important. If someone says that he understands "you shall not steal," but has no idea to what situations that commandment applies (such as embezzling, cheating on taxes, shoplifting), then he hasn't really understood the biblical command. Understanding Scripture, understanding its meaning, is *applying* it to situations. A person who understands the Bible is a person who is able to use the Bible to answer his questions, to guide his life. As I argued in chapter 6, theology is application.

Perspectives on the Discipline of Ethics

In general, then, ethical judgment always involves the application of a *norm* to a *situation* by a *person*. These three factors can also be seen as overall perspectives on the study of ethics, just as in chapters 1–6 I argued that theology may be seen from three perspectives; see fig. 52.7.

1. *The Situational Perspective.* In this perspective, we examine situations, problems. This study focuses on God's actions in creation and providence that have made the situations what they are, hence God's lordship attribute of control. The situational perspective asks, "What are the best means of accomplishing God's purposes?" That is, how can we take the present situation and change it so that more of God's purposes are achieved?

God's ultimate purpose is his own glory (1 Cor. 10:31). But God has more specific goals as well: the filling and subduing of the earth (Gen. 1:28); the evangelization and nurture of people of all nations (Matt. 28:19–20); the success of his kingdom (6:33).

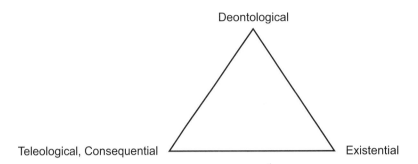

Fig. 52.7. Perspectives on the Study of Ethics

The situational perspective explores the consequences of our actions. Under the situational perspective, we ask, "If we do X, will that enhance the glory of God and his blessing on his people?" So we seek the best means to the ends that please God. So we might describe ethics from this perspective as a Christian *teleological*, or *consequential*, ethic.

2. *The Normative Perspective.* Under the normative perspective, we focus on Scripture more directly. Our purpose is to determine our duty, our ethical norm, our obligation. So we bring our problem to the Bible and ask, "What does Scripture say about this situation?" At this point we invoke God's lordship attribute of authority. Since we are focusing on duties and obligations, we might call this perspective a Christian *deontological* ethic.

3. *The Existential Perspective.* The existential perspective focuses on the ethical agent, the person or persons who are trying to find out what to do. Under this perspective, the ethical question becomes: "How must I change if I am to do God's will?" Here the focus is inward, examining our heart-relation to God. It deals with our regeneration, our sanctification, our inner character. These are all the product of God's lordship-presence within us. We may call this reasoning a Christian *existential* ethic.

Interdependence of the Perspectives

Now, we saw that knowledge of our situation, norm, and self are interdependent. You can't understand the situation fully until you know what Scripture says about it, and until you understand your own role in the situation. You can't understand yourself fully apart from Scripture, or apart from the situation that is your environment. And you can't understand Scripture unless you can apply it to situations and to yourself.

So the situational perspective includes the other two. When we understand the situation rightly, we see that Scripture and the self are elements of that situation, facts to be taken account of. So we can't rightly assess the situation unless we assess the other two factors.

Similarly the normative perspective: to understand Scripture is to understand its applications to the situation and the self.

And the existential perspective: as we ask questions about our inner life, we find that the situation and God's revelation are both elements of our personal experience, apart from which we cannot make sense of ourselves.

So each perspective necessitates consideration of the others. Each includes the others. You can picture the content of ethics as a triangle; see fig. 52.8.

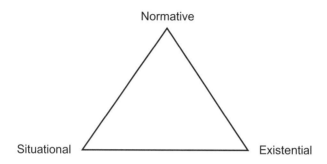

Fig. 52.8. Perspectives on the Content of Ethics

Now, you can study the ethical triangle beginning at any of the three corners. But as you advance through the triangle, you will eventually meet up with the other corners. That is to say, if you start to study the situation, you will eventually find yourself studying the norm and the ethical agent. Same with the other corners.

That's why I describe these approaches as *perspectives*. I don't think of them as "parts" of ethics, as though you could divide the triangle into three distinct parts and then do one part first, another second, and another third. No, you can't really study the situation without the norm, and so on.

So the triangle represents the whole subject matter of ethics, and the corners represent different entrances to that subject matter, different emphases, different initial questions. But the goal is always to cover the whole triangle with regard to any ethical question.

In the end, then, the three perspectives coincide. A true understanding of the situation will not contradict a true understanding of the Word or the self. And a true understanding of each will include true understandings of the others.

But if the three are ultimately identical, why do we need three? Why not just one? The reason has to do with our finitude and sin. God knows all truth simultaneously, from every possible perspective. He knows what the whole universe looks like to the eye of the snail on my window ledge. But you and I are finite, not omniscient. We can see only a portion of reality at a time. That is to say, we can see the world from only one perspective at a time. For that reason, it is good for us to move from one perspective to another. Just as the blind man had to move from the elephant's leg, to its trunk, to its torso, to its head and tail in order to get an adequate picture of the elephant, so we need to move from one perspective to another to get a full understanding of God's world.

And we are sinners in Adam. According to Romans 1, that means that we have a tendency to suppress the truth, to exchange the truth for a lie, to try to push God out of our knowledge. Salvation turns us in a different direction, so that we are able to seek the truth. But the continued presence of sin in our minds and hearts means that we need to keep checking up on ourselves, and multiplying perspectives is one helpful way to do that.

In ethics, the three perspectives I have mentioned are especially helpful. The three perspectives serve as checks and balances on one another. The normative perspective can correct mistakes in my understanding of the situational. But the opposite is also true: my understanding of the norm can be improved when I better understand the situation to which the norm is to be applied. Same, *mutatis mutandis*, for the existential perspective.

Multiperspectivalism is not relativism. I am not saying that any viewpoint is a legitimate perspective. There is in ethics and in other disciplines an absolute right and wrong. The procedure I have outlined above is a means for us to discover that absolute right and wrong.

Scripture itself is absolutely right: inspired, infallible, inerrant. But we are fallible in our study of Scripture. To understand it rightly, we need information outside the Bible, including knowledge of Hebrew and Greek grammar, knowledge of ancient history, and an understanding of those contemporary questions that people pose to Scripture.

The Ethical Life

So far, we have discussed methodology, the means by which Christians make ethical decisions. But we should also think a bit about the actual content of biblical ethics. That is, what does the Bible teach about God's commands, our ethical situation, and the human being as an ethical agent?

We have already discussed many ethical implications of the Bible's theology. In chapters 23–28, we considered the authority of Scripture, God's ultimate norm for all of human life. In chapter 34, I argued that the image of God is both a fact and a norm, and therefore our fundamental responsibility is to image God, to be like him (Lev. 19:2; Matt. 5:48). This means especially to be like Christ, to love one another as he loved us (John 13:34–35).

In chapters 36–45, I discussed sin and redemption. In ourselves, we cannot obey God. But because he has sent his Son to die for us and rise again, we, too, have died to sin and have been raised with him to newness of life (Rom. 6; Col. 3:1–3). So we are able to say no to sin and to serve God, though imperfectly in this life.

Through Christ, too, the kingdom of God has come, is coming, and will come (chapter 5). It is our job to "seek first the kingdom of God and his righteousness" (Matt. 6:33) here on earth.

In chapter 41, I emphasized that the Christian life is especially one of faith and repentance. It is believing God's promises and acting on them, and turning more and more from sin, anticipating the glory to come. In chapters 46–49, I stressed that the Christian life is a life shared with others in the body of Christ. In chapter 47, especially, I emphasized the centrality of God's mandates: the cultural mandate and the Great

Commission. In chapter 51, I stressed that biblical eschatology, the doctrine of the last days, is a purifying doctrine. We seek to be obedient when Christ comes, and we look forward to his rewards. So Christian ethics is oriented toward the past (our creation in God's image and Jesus' work of redemption), the present (seeking the kingdom of God in the present), and the future (looking forward to Jesus' return and the consummation of righteousness in the new heavens and new earth).

The Lord's Commands

But I should also briefly summarize what God commands us to do. For this purpose, the Ten Commandments (Ex. 20:1–17; Deut. 5:1–21) (sometimes called the Decalogue) are especially useful. These commands are part of the document of the covenant that God made with Israel under Moses,[7] and other passages of Scripture refer to them. Jesus' Sermon on the Mount (Matt. 5–7) is largely an exposition of the deeper meanings of these commandments. In Matthew 19:17–21, Jesus tells a rich young man the essence of his obligation to God, using commandments from the Decalogue. See also Rom. 13:8–10; James 2:10–11.

As Jesus says (Matt. 22:36–40), the greatest commandments are those to love God with all our heart (Deut. 6:4–5) and our neighbor as ourselves (Lev. 19:18). These sum up the Law and the Prophets, emphasizing the frequent theme of the NT that love fulfills the law (Rom. 13:8, 10; Col. 3:14). So the Decalogue speaks of loving God (commandments 1–4) and loving our neighbors (commandments 5–10).

We love God by worshiping him alone and renouncing all other gods and lords (first commandment), by worshiping him as he desires and not according to our own idolatrous devices (second), by using his name only with a full understanding of its holiness (third), and by acknowledging the Sabbath as a day to rest and worship him, not to carry on our own business (fourth).

We love our neighbors by honoring our parents and all others in authority over us (fifth),[8] by revering human life as sacred in God's sight (sixth), by respecting the marriage bed (seventh), the property of others (eighth), and the truth (ninth), and by guarding our hearts against desires that lead to breaking other commandments (tenth).

Key Terms

Ethics
Necessary criteria of good works
Sufficient criteria of good works
Problem of the virtuous pagan

---

7. See chapters 2–4 and 25 for an analysis of the literary structure of this covenant document and its importance as the written Word of the Lord, the fundamental constitution of the people of God.

8. I follow the Westminster catechisms in saying that although the fifth commandment refers specifically only to parents, its principles extend to all other relations of loyalty, love, and authority, such as the church (our extended family, according to Scripture) and the state. The catechisms similarly read the other commandments as containing principles that extend beyond the literal.

Total depravity
Civic righteousness
Summum bonum
Motive
Standard
Goal
Debtors' ethic
Command ethics
Narrative ethics
Virtue ethics
Deontological
Teleological
Consequential
Existential
Multiperspectivalism

Study Questions

1. "All theology *is* ethics." Explain; evaluate.
2. How does God govern our ethical life? State and evaluate Frame's triperspectival answer.
3. What are the "necessary and sufficient criteria of good works"? Explain the answer of the WCF and discuss.
4. List the most typical biblical reasons for doing good works. Discuss.
5. "Our good works come from *gratitude*." Explain and evaluate this statement of the HC.
6. Paul tells believers to "keep in step with the Spirit" (Gal. 5:25 NIV). How can we do that, when the Spirit's work is invisible?
7. What are the "things that really matter" in the Christian life? Why does Paul single these out?
8. What are the "factors in ethical judgment"? Explain; evaluate. How are these interrelated?
9. "In general, then, ethical judgment always involves the application of a *norm* to a *situation* by a *person*." Explain; evaluate.
10. Explain and evaluate the three types of ethics distinguished by Frame.
11. How are the three perspectives "interdependent"?
12. Summarize the Ten Commandments.

Memory Verses

Matt. 5:19: Therefore whoever relaxes one of the least of these commandments and teaches others to do the same will be called least in the kingdom of heaven, but whoever does them and teaches them will be called great in the kingdom of heaven.

Matt. 6:33: But seek first the kingdom of God and his righteousness, and all these things will be added to you.

1 Cor. 7:19: For neither circumcision counts for anything nor uncircumcision, but keeping the commandments of God.

Gal. 5:6: For in Christ Jesus neither circumcision nor uncircumcision counts for anything, but only faith working through love.

Gal. 5:16–17: But I say, walk by the Spirit, and you will not gratify the desires of the flesh. For the desires of the flesh are against the Spirit, and the desires of the Spirit are against the flesh, for these are opposed to each other, to keep you from doing the things you want to do.

Gal. 6:15: For neither circumcision counts for anything, nor uncircumcision, but a new creation.

Eph. 2:8–10: For by grace you have been saved through faith. And this is not your own doing; it is the gift of God, not a result of works, so that no one may boast. For we are his workmanship, created in Christ Jesus for good works, which God prepared beforehand, that we should walk in them.

Eph. 5:8–11: At one time you were darkness, but now you are light in the Lord. Walk as children of light (for the fruit of light is found in all that is good and right and true), and try to discern what is pleasing to the Lord. Take no part in the unfruitful works of darkness, but instead expose them.

Col. 3:1–3: If then you have been raised with Christ, seek the things that are above, where Christ is, seated at the right hand of God. Set your minds on things that are above, not on things that are on earth. For you have died, and your life is hidden with Christ in God.

2 Tim. 3:16–17: All Scripture is breathed out by God and profitable for teaching, for reproof, for correction, and for training in righteousness, that the man of God may be competent, equipped for every good work.

Resources for Further Study

Davis, John Jefferson. *Evangelical Ethics*. Phillipsburg, NJ: P&R Publishing, 2004.

Frame, John M. *DCL*.

———. *Medical Ethics*. Phillipsburg, NJ: Presbyterian and Reformed, 1988.

Murray, John. *Principles of Conduct*. Grand Rapids: Eerdmans, 1957.

APPENDIX A: TRIADS

IN THIS LIST OF THE TRIADS that were presented in the preceding chapters, I will mention the normative first, then the situational, then the existential.

Chapter	Subject	Normative	Situational	Existential
1	Theology	Scripture	areas of life	persons
2	Divine lordship attributes	authority	control	presence
	Covenant	stipulations	historical prologue	sanctions
	Theological perspectives	normative	situational	existential
	Elements of knowledge	norms	facts	subjectivity
3	Tripersonality	Father	Son	Spirit
4	Narratives of Scripture	the Lord's covenants	the kingdom of God	the family of God
	Elements of covenants	divine word (blessing)	land	seed
	Covenants for all God's people	eternal covenant of redemption	universal covenant	new covenant
5	Two ages	not yet	already	overlap
6	Members of God's people	covenant-servants	kingdom-subjects	family-sons and daughters

Chapter	Subject	Normative	Situational	Existential
7	Biblical teaching about God	authoritative descriptions	divine acts	triune inner life
	God's acts	decrees	miracle-providence-creation	redemption
	Miracles	signs	powers	wonders
8	Providence	signs	powers	wonders
9	Providence	revelation	government-preservation	concurrence
10	Creation	by his word	God's control at the beginning	intimate directness
11	Decrees	interpret all	control all	elect people to enjoy God
12	Attribute groups	knowledge	power	love
	Lordship attributes	authority	control	presence
13	God's righteousness	standards	deeds	character
14	Defenses against the problem of evil	God sets the standards	greater good	new heart
15	Philosophical definition of knowledge	justified	true	belief
	Objects of knowledge	propositions	skills	persons
	God's knowledge	as his authority	as his control	as his presence
16	Aspects of God's will	preceptive	decretive	wisdom
17	God's lordship of time	knowledge	power	presence

Chapter	Subject	Normative	Situational	Existential
18	God's lordship of space	knowledge	power	presence
	Spirit	as authority	as power	as presence
19	God's aseity	self-attesting	self-existing	self-justifying
20	God's oneness	as authority	as control	as presence
21	Blessings (2 Cor. 13:14)	love	grace	fellowship
22	The Trinity	Father	Son	Spirit
	Physical science	particle	field	wave
	Linguistics	contrast	distribution	variation
	Divine speech	informational	productive	expressive
	Aspects of the Trinitarian persons	classificational	instantiational	associational
	Trinity	God's authority	God's control	God's presence
23	The word of God	God's authority	God's power	God's presence
	The linguistic model of the Trinity	the speaker	the word	the breath
	Virtues of the word	law	wisdom	love
24	Media	words	events	persons
26	Scripture	God's authority	God's control	God's presence
	Clarity of Scripture presupposes	God's authority	God's control	God's presence
	Scripture	necessity	comprehensiveness	sufficiency
	Scripture and life	all Scripture (*tota Scriptura*)	for all of life (*tota vita*)	only Scripture (*sola Scriptura*)

Chapter	Subject	Normative	Situational	Existential
	Sacraments	signs	actions of God	locations of God's presence
27	Reception of the Word	belief	obedience	participation
	Meaning	sense	import	application
	Knowledge	norms	facts	persons
28	Assurance of Scripture truth	Scripture's self-witness	facts and evidence	the Spirit's witness
	Revelation	special	general	existential
29	Knowledge	subject to God's authority	under God's control	exposed to God's presence
	Factors in knowledge	norm	object	subject
	Factors in Christian knowledge	God's revelation	the world	the self
30	Epistemological perspectives	normative	situational	existential
	Non-Christian epistemology	rationalism	empiricism	subjectivism
	Theories of truth	coherence	correspondence	pragmatic
	Secular definition of knowledge	justified	true	belief
31	Forms of justification	normative	situational	existential
	A good argument	valid	sound	persuasive
	Faculties of knowledge	intellect	will	emotions
32	Capacities of the mind	reasoning	perceiving	feeling

Chapter	Subject	Normative	Situational	Existential
33	Work of angels	bringing God's word	fighting God's battles	ministering to God's people
	Activity of Satan and his demons	lying prophecy	fighting against the kingdom of God	temptation and accusation of believers
34	Man's offices	prophet	king	priest
	Foci of the creation ordinances	God	the natural world	man himself
	Adam	image	king	son
	Perspectives on human existence	spirit	body	soul
35	Responsibility	accountability	liability	integrity
36	Conditions of good works	standard	goal	motive
	Nature of sin	disobedience	self-glorification	hatred
	Effects of the fall	guilt	punishment	corruption
	Sources of temptation	the devil	the world	the flesh
	Sinful desires (1 John 2:16)	of the pride of life	of the eyes	of the flesh
	Eve's temptations (Gen. 3:6)	desirable to make one wise	delight to the eyes	good for food
37	Christ as the image of God	Prophet	King	Priest
38	The work of Christ	offices	states	union
	The offices of Christ	Prophet	King	Priest

Chapter	Subject	Normative	Situational	Existential
40	Aspects of salvation	God's eternal decree	the atonement	the application of redemption
	Redemption from three aspects of sin	justification	adoption	regeneration-conversion-sanctification
41	Elements of saving faith	belief	knowledge	trust
	The theological virtues	faith	hope	love
	The nature of love	allegiance	action	affection
	The nature of repentance	renunciation	turning from sin	sorrow for sin
42	Elements of the application of redemption	justification	adoption	subjective salvation
	Forms of moral predication	righteous	good	holy
43	Means of sanctification	God's law	the history of redemption	personal resources
44	Factors in our assurance of salvation	the promises of God	growth in sanctification	the Spirit's inner testimony
46	Marks of the church	worship	the Great Commission	love
	Purposes of discipline	instructing	honoring Christ	reclaiming the offender
	Officers	apostle	elder	deacon
	Forms of church government	episcopal	presbyterian	congregational
	Forms of church government (variation)	presbyterian	episcopal	congregational

Chapter	Subject	Normative	Situational	Existential
47	Aspects of the cultural mandate	God's blessing	subduing the earth	filling the earth
	Aspects of the Great Commission	teaching the commands of Christ	evangelism and baptism	Jesus' blessing
	Specific tasks of the church	worship	witness	nurture
	Goals for worship	biblical	Christ-centered	edifying
	Ministries of the church	Word	rule	mercy
48	Means of grace	Word	fellowship	prayer
	Fellowship	worship	sharing goods	nurture
	Why pray?	God commands it	prayer changes things	fellowship with God
49	Aspects of a sacrament	signs	divine actions	means of God's presence
	Symbolism of baptism	repentance	cleansing	union with Christ

Chapter	Subject	Normative	Situational	Existential
52	How God governs our ethical lives	authority	control	presence
	Necessary and sufficient criteria of good works	the standard of God's Word	the goal of the glory of God	the motive of love and faith
	Biblical reasons to do good works	the command of God	the history of redemption	the presence of the Spirit within
	Types of Christian ethics	command	narrative	virtue
	What really matters	keeping God's commands	a new creation	faith working through love
	Factors in ethical judgment	the Word	the situation	the ethical agent
	Perspectives on the discipline of ethics	deontological	teleological	existential

APPENDIX B: GLOSSARY

I WROTE UP THIS GLOSSARY for inclusion in my festschrift, *Speaking the Truth in Love*.[1] It is not a standard theological dictionary, but a dictionary of my peculiar technical terms and their definitions. The more traditional theological terms (with traditional definitions) appear in the present book when I discuss the corresponding doctrines. It is easy enough to find them, with the help of the Key Terms list at the end of each chapter. So I have not included the more standard theological definitions here. But I thought some readers might want help with my idiosyncratic terminology, and might want to know other writings of mine where these terms are more fully explained.

One of the fun things about being a theologian (or any other kind of academic) is that you get to invent new words and sometimes attach new meanings to old ones. I try not to do this too often, but over the years I have done some of it. In the Glossary below, I do not, for the most part, define standard theological terms (such as *holiness* and *justification*). These definitions can be obtained from standard theologies, theological dictionaries, and online sources. But I include terms that I have invented, or that I have attached unusual definitions to, or that have a special prominence in my writings (even though the definitions may be standard). I here use the same topical headings as in my Bibliography in *Speaking the Truth*, but I omit the topics in which there are no distinctive terms to be defined.

I include references to places in my books and articles where I discuss these concepts. For this purpose, I use these abbreviations:

AGG   *Apologetics to the Glory of God*

CWM   *Contemporary Worship Music: A Biblical Defense*

DCL   *The Doctrine of the Christian Life*

---

1. John J. Hughes, ed., *Speaking the Truth in Love: The Theology of John M. Frame* (Phillipsburg, NJ: P&R Publishing, 2009).

DG	*The Doctrine of God*
DKG	*The Doctrine of the Knowledge of God*
DWG	*The Doctrine of the Word of God*
ER	*Evangelical Reunion: Denominations and the One Body of Christ*
IRF	"Introduction to the Reformed Faith"
NOG	*No Other God*
PP	"A Primer on Perspectivalism"
PWG	*Perspectives on the Word of God*
SBL	*Salvation Belongs to the Lord*
WST	*Worship in Spirit and Truth*

Often, words or forms of words that are defined elsewhere in this Glossary are in bold. For more key terms, with references to my writings, see the study guides for my books, included in my *Collected Works* CD and DVD sets.

Introductory: Lordship and Perspectivalism

authority. God's right to demand unqualified obedience from his creatures. A **lordship attribute.** *DKG*, 15–18; *DG*, 80–93; *PP*.

control. God's power over the world, a **lordship attribute.** *DKG*, 15–18; *DG*, 36–79; *PP*.

covenant. Relation between the Lord and his servants. In divine-human covenants, God as covenant Lord selects a certain people from among all the nations of the earth to be his own. He rules over them by his law, in terms of which all who obey are blessed and all who disobey are cursed. But there is grace as well as law. God's grace establishes the covenant, and, since all men are sinners, it's only by grace that God sends any covenant blessing. God's creation and government of the world is analogous to covenant: he rules all things as the Lord. *DKG*, 12–13; *DG*, 21–35; *PP*.

covenant solidarity. See **presence.**

existential perspective. Dealing with a subject, emphasizing its character as a part of human experience, an aspect of human subjectivity. Derived from the **lordship attribute** of **presence,** for God is present to our innermost heart and mind. *DKG*, 62–75; *DCL*, 33–37, 131–382; *PP*; *PWG*, 50–56.

lordship. God's relation to his **covenant** people, involving his **control** and **authority** over them and his **presence** with them. Analogously, God's relationship to the whole creation. *DG*, 21–35; *PP*.

lordship attributes. Qualities that appear prominently in biblical descriptions of God's **lordship**: his **control, authority,** and **presence.** *DKG*, 15–18; *DG*, 36–115; *DCL*, 19–37; *PP*.

multiperspectival. Of or relating to an account of something that considers more than one **perspective.** *PP.*

normative perspective. Dealing with a subject, emphasizing its character as divine revelation. Derived from the **lordship attribute** of divine **authority.** *DKG,* 62–75; *DCL,* 33–37, 131–238; *PP*; *PWG,* 50–56.

perspective. A view or study of an object from a particular angle. When a tree is viewed from the north, the south, the east, and the west, these views constitute four perspectives. *DKG,* 73–75; *PP.*

presence. Also termed **covenant solidarity.** God's taking a people from among the other peoples to be his own exclusive possession. He commits himself to being with them ("Immanuel, God with us"), to be their God and for them to be his people. Often his presence is literal, as in the burning bush, the tabernacle, the temple, the person of Jesus (John 1:14), and the bodies of believers. A **lordship attribute.** *DKG,* 15–18; *DG,* 94–102.

situational perspective. Dealing with a subject, emphasizing its character as a fact of nature, history, or both. Derived from the **lordship attribute** of **control,** for God's control governs all the facts of nature and history. *DKG,* 62–75; *DCL,* 33–37, 239–313; *PP*; *PWG,* 50–56.

triperspectival. Of or relating to considering a subject from three perspectives connected with the **lordship attributes: normative, situational,** and **existential.** *PP.*

Theology

1. Nature, Method of Theology

application. *Teaching* in the NT sense; using the content of Scripture to answer human questions, meet human needs, and promote spiritual health. See **theology.** *DKG,* 81.

biblical theology. Theology that seeks to apply the Bible, seen as a history of redemption. *DKG,* 207–12.

exegetical theology. Theology that seeks to apply particular passages of Scripture (of any length, including the whole Bible). *DKG,* 206–7.

historical theology. A study of the church's **theology** through history, **applying** the Word of God to the church's past for the sake of the church's present edification. *DKG,* 310.

practical theology. Part of **systematic theology** that applies what Scripture says about communicating the gospel. *DKG,* 214.

progress in theology. Application of Scripture to more and more situations as the church encounters them. *DKG,* 307.

Reformed theology. A tradition of **theology** that emphasizes evangelical distinctives, the sovereignty of God, and the comprehensive covenant **lordship** of Jesus Christ. *IRF*.

systematic theology. **Theology** that seeks to apply the Bible as a whole. *DKG*, 212–14.

theology. The application of the Word of God, by persons, to all areas of life. *DKG*, 81.

traditionalism. Coming to theological conclusions on the basis of human tradition, without sufficient biblical grounding. See essay "Traditionalism," Appendix P of *DWG*.

triangulation. Coming to theological conclusions by comparing historical or contemporary views without direct reference to Scripture. Often it proceeds by comparing view A on this side and view B on that side, and formulating view C, perceived to preserve the good, but not the bad, of both extremes. See essay "Traditionalism," Appendix P of *DWG*.

2. Doctrine of the Word of God, Scripture

I do not provide as many references in this part of the Glossary. I use these terms in my lectures in the course Scripture and God, included in my *Collected Works*, set 1. I also deal with these terms in my *DWG*. *PWG* and a few of my articles address some of these concepts as well.

authority of the Word. The right of God's Word to be obeyed and believed without question. Corresponds to the **lordship attribute** of **authority**. *PWG*, 12–13.

bibliolatry. Giving the devotion to the Bible that is appropriate to give only to God himself.

clarity of Scripture. The view that Scripture is clear enough so that the plan of God's salvation can be understood by all persons through the use of ordinary means of grace (teaching, sacraments, prayer).

covenant document. The suzerainty treaty that served in Hittite culture as a binding attestation of the lord's words governing the covenant relationship. Parallel to God's covenant words to his people.

divine voice. God's speech without human or written mediation, as when God spoke to Israel at Mount Sinai. *PWG*, 23–24.

event-media. Events of nature and history that bring God's word to us. Corresponds to God's **lordship attribute** of **control**. Sometimes called *general* or *natural revelation*. *PWG*, 21–22.

existential revelation. Revelation through our own nature as the image of God, and as God's writing on our heart, creating in us an obedient disposition. Correlative to the traditional concepts of general and special revelation. Roughly equivalent to the traditional concept of illumination, or the internal testimony of the Spirit.

free speech of God. Speech not essential to God's being, but expressed by his decision to speak; his speech about creatures and to them. Cf. **necessary speech of God.** *DG*, 236, 474.

general sufficiency of Scripture. The view that at all times in redemptive history, Scripture has been **sufficient** for God's people. Cf. **particular sufficiency.**

God's word through prophets and apostles. God's speech through mediation of human speakers and writers. Has the same power and authority as the **divine voice.** *PWG*, 24.

inerrancy. Truth in the sense of correspondence to fact. To say that Scripture is inerrant is to say that everything it asserts is true. It makes good on its claims.

infallibility. A stronger term than **inerrancy.** *Inerrant* means that there are no errors; *infallible* means that there *can be* no errors, that errors are impossible. I reject looser or weaker definitions of *infallible*.

inspiration. An act of God creating identity between a divine word and a human word.

linguistic model of the Trinity. The view that the Father is the speaker, the Son is his speech, and the Spirit is the breath that carries his speech to its destination.

media of the Word. Means that God uses to bring his Word to us. *PWG*, 19–35.

necessary speech of God. That speech that is essential to God's being God; the eternal communication between the persons of the Trinity. Cf. **free speech of God.** *DG*, 236, 474.

necessity of Scripture. The view that without Scripture, we have no adequate basis for faith in Christ.

particular sufficiency of Scripture. The doctrine that, following the completion of the canon, we should not expect any more divine additions to Scripture or any revelation of the same level as Scripture. Cf. **general sufficiency.**

person-media. God's word's coming to us through divine and human persons: theophany, Christ, the Spirit, prophets and apostles, church leaders, other believers, all people in the image of God. *PWG*, 30–32.

power of the Word. The capacity of the Word, through the Holy Spirit, to accomplish God's purposes in the world and in persons. Corresponds to the **lordship attribute** of **control.** *PWG*, 10–12.

precision. Stating the truth without any approximation. Scripture is true, but not always precise.

propositions. Assertions claiming to state facts. There are propositions in Scripture, but there are other kinds of language there as well. *PWG*, 11–12.

self-authenticating; self-attesting. The principle that since God's Word is the highest authority for us, it cannot be validated by anything higher than itself. So the ultimate source of Scripture's authority is its own word, validated to our hearts and minds by the Holy Spirit.

sufficiency of Scripture. The view that Scripture contains all the divine words necessary for us to please God in any area of life.

suzerainty treaty. See **covenant document.**

word as God's address. God's word speaking authoritatively to rational agents. Synonym for God's *preceptive will*. Corresponds to God's **lordship attribute** of **authority.**

word as God's decree. God's word governing all that comes to pass. Synonym for God's *decretive will* or *decree*. Corresponds to the **lordship attribute** of **control.**

word as God's presence. God's word conveying God to creatures. Corresponds to the **lordship attribute** of **presence.** *PWG,* 13–16.

word as God's self-expression. The word as God's dwelling place, so that to encounter the word is to encounter him, and vice versa. Corresponds to the **lordship attribute** of **presence.**

word-media. God's word's coming to us through human words, by God directly, by the prophets and apostles, and by their writings. *PWG,* 22–23.

word of God. God's powerful, meaningful self-expression. Note correlation with the three **lordship attributes.** *DG,* 471; *PWG,* 9–16.

written Word of God. God's Word in written form. It has the same power and authority as other forms of the word. *PWG,* 24–29.

3. Doctrine of God

attributes of authority. Divine attributes that emphasize God's constant or static character, his eternal truth: righteousness, justice, truth, aseity, simplicity, essence. Cf. the **lordship attributes** of **control, authority,** and **presence.** *DG,* 398–99.

attributes of control. Divine attributes that emphasize God's dynamic or active character: goodness, love, speech, will, power, etc. Cf. the **lordship attributes** of **control, authority,** and **presence.** *DG,* 398–99.

attributes of goodness. Divine attributes pertaining to God's moral nature: goodness, love, grace, justice, righteousness, holiness, joy. *DG,* 398, 402–68.

attributes of knowledge. Divine attributes pertaining to God's intellectual capacity: speech, incomprehensibility, truth, knowledge, wisdom, mind, knowability. *DG,* 399, 469–512.

attributes of power. Divine attributes pertaining to God's transcendence and exaltation over other things: eternity, immensity, incorporeality, will, power, existence, aseity, essence, glory, spirituality, omnipresence. *DG,* 399, 513–616.

attributes of presence. Divine attributes that emphasize God's presence to himself and to the world: integrity, involvement, blessedness, joy, beauty, perfection, holiness, knowledge, glory, spirituality, omnipresence. Cf. the **lordship attributes** of **control, authority,** and **presence.** *DG*, 398–99.

author-character model. The best illustration I know of the relation between divine sovereignty and human responsibility. Like a playwright, God controls everything that happens in the "drama" of nature and history. But as in a good play, the events of the drama also have an explanation within the world of the play itself. So, as with God's relation to the world, each event of the play has two causes: divine and creaturely. *DG*, 156–59.

covenant preservation. An aspect of providence whereby God shows his love to his covenant people by rescuing them from danger and providing for their earthly needs. *DG*, 282–84.

creaturely otherness. God's making of creatures to be genuinely different from himself, so that their acts are not his, although he foreordains them, and his acts are not ours. This is one source of our sense of freedom and independence. *DG*, 146.

essential invisibility. God's not being limited to any particular visible form, but being able to use any visible form in revealing himself. *DG*, 590.

eternal election. God's eternal choice of a people to enjoy the full blessing of fellowship with him forever. *DG*, 325–30.

eternal preservation. An aspect of providence, the fulfillment of **covenant preservation** and of all of God's promises to his people.

God in himself. An ambiguous expression that can mean (1) God as he exists apart from us, or (2) God as he is revealed to us, and therefore as he really and truly is. We cannot know God in himself in sense 1, but we can in sense 2.

historical election. God's choosing people and nations in history for specific tasks related to redemptive history. *DG*, 317–25, 329–30.

"I am he" or "ani hu" passages. Passages using these phrases or similar ones, in which God or Jesus identifies himself as the "I AM" of Exodus 3:14. Deut. 32:39; Isa. 41:4; 43:10, etc.; John 8:24, 28; 9:9; 18:5–6, 8. *DG*, 22n41.

immanence (biblical). The **lordship attribute** of **covenant presence.** *DG*, 103–6.

immanence (nonbiblical). God's being so near to us that he cannot be distinguished from finite persons and objects. Thus, when he draws near, he becomes a creature, or the creatures become God. In this sense, modern theologians sometimes say that God is "wholly revealed." *DG*, 107–14.

incomprehensibility of God. The doctrine that although we can genuinely know God, we cannot know him exhaustively or know him as he knows himself. *DG*, 200–207.

metaphysical preservation. An aspect of providence whereby God preserves the metaphysical existence of the world, so that it is constantly dependent on him, although it has no specific tendency to fall into nonbeing. *DG*, 278–79.

miracle. An extraordinary demonstration of God's covenant lordship. *DG*, 258.

monogenes. A Greek term that I translate in the older way, "only-begotten," rather than (as do modern translators) "unique." *DG*, 659n21, 710–11n53.

open theism. The view that God does not know the future exhaustively, because he cannot know in advance the free choices of rational agents. *DG*, 485–86, and my smaller book *NOG*.

preservation. An aspect of divine providence. I subdivide this into **metaphysical, redemptive-historical, covenantal,** and **eternal preservation.** *DG*, 274–88.

redemptive-historical preservation. As an aspect of providence, God's preservation of the world from his own judgment of sin until redemption is complete. *DG*, 279–82.

semi-cessationist. The view that **miracles** in a broad sense continue, and that spectacular miracles may occur, but that we should not expect them as a normal part of the Christian life. I also call this view *semi-continuationist*. *DG*, 264–65.

transcendence (biblical). God's exaltation as King, involving the **lordship attributes** of **control** and **authority.** *DG*, 103–6.

transcendence (nonbiblical). God's being so far from us that we cannot know him or truly speak of him. In this sense, modern theologians sometimes say that God is "wholly other" or "wholly hidden." *DG*, 107–14.

vocation; God's will of wisdom. God's knowledge of what choices will be best for individuals; his will that we make the wisest choices, by prayerfully applying Scripture to our circumstances. Adds a third concept to the traditional ones of God's *decretive* and *preceptive* wills. *DG*, 539–42.

Apologetics
1. Apologetic Method and Epistemology

apologetics. (1) The application of Scripture to unbelief (including the unbelief remaining in the Christian). *DKG*, 86–87. (2) The study of how to give to inquirers a reason for the hope that is in us (1 Peter 3:15). *AGG*, 1.

apologetics as defense. Giving answers to objections, "defending and confirming the gospel" (Phil. 1:7 NIV). *AGG*, 2, 149–90.

apologetics as offense. Attacking the foolishness of unbelieving thought (Ps. 14:1; 1 Cor. 1:18–2:16). *AGG*, 2, 191–202.

apologetics as proof. Presenting a rational basis for faith; demonstrating Christianity to be true. *AGG*, 2, 57–148.

argument by presupposition. Showing that Christianity is the necessary presupposition of meaning and rationality, and that the denial of Christianity destroys all meaning and rationality. Synonym for **transcendental argument.** *AGG,* 69–75.

autonomy. The claim that one is competent to serve as the final criterion of truth and right.

broad circularity. A **circular** argument enriched by evidence. For example: "Scripture is true because evidences X, Y, and Z imply its truth," when X, Y, and Z themselves are warranted by Scripture. *DKG,* 131.

circularity. An argument in which the conclusion **justifies** itself. All arguments seeking to prove the existence of an ultimate or final authority are circular in this sense. *DKG,* 130.

cognitive rest. A godly sense of satisfaction, which is the goal of **existential justification.** *DKG,* 152–53.

competing circularities. Arguments in which each party appeals to an authority that he considers to be self-attesting. *DKG,* 132–33.

epistemology. Theory of knowledge. One of the major divisions of **philosophy,** along with **metaphysics** and **value theory.**

existential justification. Justifying a belief according to the **existential perspective,** by showing that it brings true subjective satisfaction. *DKG,* 108, 149–62.

fact. What is the case. Inseparable from **interpretation.** *DKG,* 71.

faculties of the mind. Intellect, will, emotions, imagination, perception, intuition, etc., all perspectives on the heart, for human beings know and experience the world as whole persons. *DKG,* 319–46.

interpretation. A person's understanding of what the facts are. Inseparable from **fact.** *DKG,* 71.

irrationalism. The view that human reason has no reliable access to truth. *DKG,* 60–61.

justification (in epistemology). An account of why someone should believe a proposition to be true. *DKG,* 104–6.

knowledge of God. A relationship of friendship or enmity with God, involving a covenantal response of the whole person to God's **lordship,** in obedience or disobedience. *DKG,* 48.

metaphysics. Theory of being, dealing with the general structure of the world. One of the major divisions of **philosophy,** along with **epistemology** and **value theory.**

narrow circularity. A **circular** argument that directly asserts the self-justification of a conclusion without additional premises: for example, "God exists because God exists." *DKG,* 130–31.

neutrality. An attempt to reason without any religious **presupposition.**

normative justification. Justifying a belief from the **normative perspective,** by showing that it conforms to the norms of thought. *DKG,* 108, 123–39.

ontology. In my work, a synonym for **metaphysics.**

person-variable. Of or relating to the fact that a particular person's response to an apologetic argument may differ from that of another person. Because an argument that will **persuade** one person will not necessary **persuade** another, arguments should be formulated with a particular audience in mind. *AGG,* 64, 67–68, 89–90.

persuasion. Convincing a person that your belief is true (as a goal of apologetics). An apologetic argument, therefore, should be valid (employing right logic), sound (incorporating true premises), and persuasive. Persuasion is the **existential perspective** of apologetic argument. Synonym for **cognitive rest.** *AGG,* 60–64; *DKG,* 119, 131, 355–58.

philosophy. An attempt to understand the world in its broadest, most general features; the exposition and defense of a **worldview.** Its constituents are **metaphysics, epistemology,** and **value theory.** A subdivision of **theology.** *DKG,* 85–86.

presupposition. A belief that takes precedence over another and therefore serves as a criterion for determining the truth of another. An *ultimate* presupposition takes precedence over all other beliefs. The ultimate presupposition is the basic commitment of the heart. *DKG,* 45, 125–26.

presuppositionalism of the heart. A basic commitment of the heart to bring all reasoning under the **lordship** of Christ. In my judgment, it is impossible to distinguish presuppositional from traditional apologetics merely by the form of their arguments, claims to certainty or probability, etc. *AGG,* 85–88.

rationalism. (1) The view that human reason is the final judge of truth and falsity, right and wrong. (2) The philosophical position that human reason is to be trusted above human sense experience. *DKG,* 60–61.

rationalist-irrationalist dialectic. The view that would-be autonomous thought is **rationalistic** in that it believes itself to be the final judge of truth and right; but that it is **irrationalistic** in that it believes the universe has no intrinsic order beyond the human person himself. So autonomous thought vacillates from optimistic to pessimistic views of reason, and back again. *DKG,* 360–63; *AGG,* 193–202.

situational justification. Justifying a belief from the **situational perspective,** by showing that it is in accord with the **facts.** *DKG,* 108, 140–49.

transcendental argument. Arguing that something is a condition of meaning or rationality. Synonym for **argument by presupposition.** *AGG,* 69–75.

value theory. Chiefly ethics and aesthetics. One of the major divisions of **philosophy,** along with **metaphysics** and **epistemology.**

worldview. General understanding of the universe. The biblical worldview is unique in its view of (1) the Supreme Being as absolute personality, (2) the **lordship** of God, and (3) the Creator-creature distinction.

2. Cornelius Van Til

To my knowledge, I have not developed any distinctive terminology in my writing about Van Til. But Van Til himself developed a great deal of distinctive terminology in expounding his own position. A few years ago, I formulated "A Van Til Glossary," providing my own definitions of Van Til's distinctive terms. In my writings about Van Til (and about other subjects), I use these definitions. His technical terms are also my technical terms. So I reproduce the Glossary below. As in the original version, I refer both to my own *CVT* and to Greg Bahnsen, *Van Til's Apologetic: Readings and Analysis* (Phillipsburg, NJ: P&R Publishing, 1998). In the Glossary below, *Frame* refers to the former, *Bahnsen* to the latter, and *VT* to Van Til.

absolute personality. VT's basic characterization of God. Unlike any non-Christian view, the biblical God is both absolute (*a se*, self-existent, self-sufficient, self-contained) and personal (thinking, speaking, acting, loving, judging). See Frame, 51ff.

ad hominem argument. Argument that exposes deficiencies in the arguer rather than deficiencies in the proposition under discussion—thus, a logical fallacy. But ad hominem argument is often appropriate. See Bahnsen, 116ff., 468, 492; Frame, 153.

all-conditioner. VT's characterization of God in "Why I Believe in God" (see Bahnsen, 121–43). God is the One who ultimately influences all reality, including our own thinking and reasoning about him.

analogy; analogical reasoning. (1) (Aquinas) Thinking in language that is neither literally true (univocal) nor unrelated to the subject matter (equivocal), but that bears a genuine resemblance to that subject matter. (2) (VT) Thinking in subjection to God's revelation and therefore thinking God's thoughts after him.

antithesis. The opposition between Christian and non-Christian thought. See Frame, 187ff.

apologetics. That branch of theology that gives reasons for our hope. VT saw it as involving proof, defense, and offense.

a priori knowledge. Knowledge acquired prior to experience, used to interpret and evaluate experience. Contrasted with *a posteriori knowledge*, knowledge arising out of experience. See Bahnsen, 107n177.

authority of the expert. The principle that submission to the knowledge of someone better informed, rather than absolute submission to God, is the best way to truth. To VT, this is the only kind of authority that the unbeliever will accept.

autonomy. The attempt to live apart from any law external to the self. To VT, this is the paradigm attitude of unbelief. See Bahnsen, 109n.

blockhouse methodology. An apologetic approach that begins with beliefs supposedly held in common between believers and unbelievers, and then tries to supplement that common ground with additional truth. VT finds this methodology in Aquinas's distinction between natural reason and faith, and in other forms of "traditional apologetics." See Bahnsen, 64, 535f., 708f.

borrowed capital. The truth known and acknowledged by the unbeliever. He has no right to believe or assert truth based on his own presuppositions, but only on Christian ones. So his assertions of truth are based on borrowed capital.

brute fact. (1) (in VT) Fact that is uninterpreted (by God, man, or both) and therefore the basis of all interpretation. (2) Objective fact; fact not dependent on what man thinks about it.

certainty. (1) Assurance of one's beliefs. Also termed *certitude*. (2) The impossibility of a proposition's being false. VT emphasized that Christian truth is certain and should be presented as a certainty, not a mere **probability.**

chance. The condition of events' occurring without cause or reason. See Bahnsen, 728.

circular argument. (1) Argument in which the conclusion of an argument is one of its premises. (2) Argument assuming something that would ordinarily not be assumed by someone who didn't believe the conclusion. See Bahnsen, 518ff.; Frame, 299ff.

common ground. That which believer and unbeliever have in common, making it possible for them to engage in apologetic discussion. See **point of contact.** VT sometimes denied that Christians and non-Christians had any beliefs in common. But his actual view was that they *would* not have such common beliefs if each were fully consistent with his presuppositions. See Bahnsen 276, 420–24, 730.

common notions. Beliefs that Christians and non-Christians have in common. VT sometimes denied that there were any of these. But see **common ground.**

contingency. (1) Dependence on something else for origin or continued being; the opposite of necessity. (2) **Chance.**

correlative. Mutually dependent. For VT, the unbeliever holds that God and the world are correlative.

creatively constructive. What unbelieving thought attempts to be on VT's view. It attempts to be the original standard of all truth, as opposed to Christian thought, which is "receptively reconstructive" (= **analogical** in the second sense).

deductivism. (1) Trying to deduce the whole of theology from one "master concept." (2) Drawing deductions from one biblical concept that are incompatible with other biblical concepts. See Frame, 166.

determinism. (1) The view that every event in the world has a cause. (2) The view that every event in the world has a *finite* cause. VT might be considered a determinist in sense 1, but not in sense 2. Determinisms of both kinds, however, often presuppose *impersonal* causation as ultimate. In that sense, VT rejected determinism and pointed out that it is equivalent to **chance.**

eminence. Way of knowing God by reasoning that he must possess the best qualities of creatures in infinite degree. One of Aquinas's three means of knowing God, the others being causality and **negation.** Van Til believes that this method, if not governed by Scripture, yields a finite God, only somewhat larger than creatures.

epistemology. Theory of knowledge.

ethics. Theory of behavior.

evidence. (1) The facts used in an argument to establish a conclusion. (2) Statements of such facts. See Frame, 177ff.

fact. A state of affairs in the real world, governed by law.

fideism. Belief that God is known by faith and not by reason. VT is sometimes accused of fideism, but he repudiated it frequently. See Bahnsen, 77–82.

full-bucket difficulty. God is all-glorious, and no glory can be added to him; yet he calls on creatures to glorify him. VT said, therefore, that glorifying God was like trying to add water to a full bucket.

implication. (1) The act of drawing a conclusion from a premise or premises. (2) The conclusion derived from the premises. (3) In idealist philosophy, a method of thinking that employs logic with an understanding of the psychological workings of the mind in its situational context. VT sometimes speaks of his approach as a "method of implication" in the third sense, something more than mere deduction or induction, but including both of them. See Bahnsen, 172–73.

incomprehensibility of God. (1) Our inability to know God exhaustively. (2) The lack of identity between any human thought and any divine thought. Sense 1 is the more common meaning in theology; sense 2 was the subject of the VT-Clark controversy.

indirect argument. Synonym for **reductio.**

irrationalism. Belief that human reason is inadequate to discover truth. VT believes that unbelievers are both irrationalistic and rationalistic at the same time. See Bahnsen, 717ff.; Frame, 231ff.

limiting concept. Concept of something (such as an actual infinity of objects) that doesn't exist (or cannot be proved to exist), but that can serve a useful purpose in thought. Also termed *supplementative concept.* Kant believed that the concepts of God, freedom, and immortality were limiting concepts. On his view, we should live "as if" these existed. VT holds that some theological concepts (e.g., the idea that sin can destroy the work of God) are not literally true, but can be affirmed on a similar "as if" basis. See Frame, 165–69.

metaphysics; ontology. (1) A general view of the world, a world-and-life view. (2) The fundamental realities that exist.

monism. Belief that reality is all of one kind; hence, denial of the Creator-creature distinction.

negation; remotion; via negativa. Way of knowing God by ascribing to him the opposite of creaturely qualities that are perceived as limits. One of Aquinas's three means of knowing God, the others being **eminence** and causality. In VT's view, when this method is used apart from Scripture, it yields a god who is a "pure blank," a mere negation of finite reality.

neutrality. Trying to think or live without making a religious commitment or ultimate **presupposition.** In VT's view, this is impossible. Attempting it presupposes a commitment against the true God.

noetic effects of sin. The effects of sin on human thought, reasoning, knowledge. In VT, the sinner knows God, but represses that knowledge (Rom. 1).

objective knowledge; truth. Knowledge or truth whose truth does not depend on what man thinks.

one-and-many problem. Knowledge involves uniting particulars into universal categories. But if every particular is exhaustively described by universal categories, then it is no longer particular. But if some particularities cannot be described by universal categories, then they can't be known, or they have no nature. The same problem can be described in terms of the relation of logic to fact, and of that of subject to object. See Bahnsen, 706; Frame, 63ff.

point of contact. A belief held in common between two people that enables them to reason toward further agreement. In VT, particularly the point of contact between believer and unbeliever. See **common ground.** For VT it is found not in a common **worldview,** but in the true knowledge of God that the believer has, and the unbeliever also has but suppresses. See Bahnsen, 105n.

predication. Attaching a predicate to a subject; hence, making an assertion. VT says that only the Christian **worldview** makes predication possible.

presupposition. (1) A belief that precedes other beliefs. (2) A belief that governs other beliefs. (3) Ultimate presupposition: the belief that governs all other beliefs, or the most fundamental commitment of the heart.

probability. The degree to which a proposition approaches certainty. VT believed that Christianity was certain, not merely probable, and that for an apologist to claim mere probability is to deny the clarity of God's revelation.

proof. An argument that establishes the truth of a conclusion. VT believed that there was "absolutely certain proof" of Christian theism by way of his transcendental argument. See Bahnsen, 78–82.

qualitative-quantitative difference. In the Clark controversy, the difference in views of God's **incomprehensibility.** Clark denied holding a "merely quantitative" view (that God knows more propositions than we), because he held that God knows the world by a different *mode* from man. VT found Clark's view of the difference to be insufficient, but he refused to state precisely the difference he referred to as "qualitative."

rationalism. (1) Belief that human reason (seen as the whole apparatus of human thought, including sensation and memory) is the ultimate arbiter of truth and falsity. (2) Belief that human reason (as opposed to sense experience) is the road to knowledge. VT believes that all unbelievers are rationalistic in the first sense—and also **irrationalistic.**

reductio ad absurdum. A form of argument in which, rather than directly proving a conclusion, the arguer reduces the contrary conclusion to an absurdity. Hence, it is also called *indirect argument* or *argument from the impossibility of the contrary.* VT believed that all transcendental arguments must take this form. Frame disagrees.

self-attestation; self-authentication. In any system of thought, that the ultimate authority justifies itself. For VT, that ultimate authority is God, especially when speaking in Scripture. See Bahnsen, 209–19, 715.

sense of deity, divinity. Calvin's way of describing the knowledge that the unbeliever has but suppresses. Also termed *sensus deitatis, divinitatis, semen religionis.*

starting point. In VT, synonym for **presupposition.** Therefore, it doesn't necessarily refer to a beginning point in time, but rather to a belief that governs other beliefs.

suaviter in modo, fortiter in re. Gentle in manner, strong in substance. VT's description of an ideal apologetic presentation. See Bahnsen, 441.

supplementation. In apologetics, presenting Christian truth as something merely additional to what the non-Christian believes already. See **blockhouse methodology.**

system. One's attempt to express his **worldview** in a coherent set of thoughts.

that and what. In VT, criticism of some apologists for trying to prove *that* God is, without considering *what* he is. In Frame, emphasis that one can never prove God's entire nature in one argument, so the *what* is a matter of degree. We cannot actually mention everything. But an apologetic argument must be consistent with everything the Bible says about God. See **unit.** See also Bahnsen, 217, 708.

transcendental argument. An argument that seeks to show the necessary conditions for the possibility of rational thought or meaningful discourse. VT believed this was the only kind of argument appropriate to a Christian apologetic, since the biblical God is the Author of all meaning and rationality.

unit, whole (defending Christianity as a). Defending the particular elements of Christianity with an awareness of the connection of each element with the overall system of truth; not proving everything at once, although VT sometimes seems almost to demand that proof from apologists he criticizes. See Bahnsen, 26, 103n, 511.

univocal. (1) (Aquinas) Language that describes its object literally. (2) (VT) Thinking **autonomously** rather than **analogously,** as if one were divine.

worldview. A philosophy, particularly a metaphysic; a way of understanding reality that governs all thought and life. Also termed *world-and-life view.*

3. Existence of God

My versions of the traditional arguments have a **transcendental** twist.

cosmological argument. The argument that if we try to discuss "cause" without God, our reasoning degenerates into **rationalism, irrationalism,** or both. *AGG,* 109–14.

epistemological argument. The argument that human reasoning is futile without moral standards, and that those standards in turn presuppose God. See **moral argument.** *AGG,* 102–4.

moral argument. The argument that all meaning and reasoning presupposes moral principles. But moral principles in turn presuppose God as **absolute personality.** *AGG,* 93–102.

ontological argument. The argument that a definition of God (a being with all perfections) implies his existence. Works only as a **presuppositional** argument that assumes a distinctively biblical concept of perfection.

teleological argument. The argument that one cannot even speak of "purpose" or "design" apart from moral values (see **moral argument**), which in turn presuppose God. *AGG,* 105–9.

4. The Problem of Evil

This is the question of how evil can exist if God is all-good, all-powerful, and all-wise. I reject a number of traditional defenses and accept three (there's that number again).

God-is-his-own-standard defense. The defense that because of who God is, human beings have no right to bring accusations against him (Job 38–42; Rom. 9:14–15, 19–21). I sometimes call this the "shut-up" defense, as in the gag line " 'Shut up,' he explained." This is the **normative perspective.** *AGG,* 171–78.

greater-good defense. The defense that God promises us that he will bring good out of evil (Rom. 8:28). This is the **situational perspective.** *AGG,* 179–87.

new-heart defense. The defense that regeneration and our eventual glorification change our values and presuppositions so that we lose the inclination to charge God with wrongdoing. This is the **existential perspective.** *AGG,* 187–90.

The Church

1. Unity

biblical presbyterianism. Government by multiple elders in each congregation, with church courts at various regional levels to deal with matters that cannot be resolved in the local congregation. In its biblical form, these courts encompass the wisdom of *all* the churches in a region, not just the Presbyterian ones. *ER*, 29–31.

breadwinners (ecclesiastical). My metaphor for those who are called to focus on evangelism and missions. Cf. **homemakers.** *DCL*, 230.

courtship metaphor. The view that church-union discussions between denominations are like courtship: trying to determine whether a union would be advantageous for both parties. Opposed to **reconciliation metaphor.** *ER*, 142–44.

denomination. A faction of the church, out of fellowship with other factions, holding to some "distinctives" of doctrine, practice, worship, ethnicity, style, history, social class, etc.

denominationalism. Attempts to justify and maintain the separate existence of denominations.

homemakers (ecclesiastical). My metaphor for those who are called to focus on the church's internal condition (orthodox doctrine, proper procedures). Cf. **breadwinners.** *DCL*, 230.

marks of the church. Traditionally, the true preaching of the Word, the right administration of the sacraments, and church discipline. I would add love (John 13:34–35), the Great Commission (Matt. 28:19–20), and true worship (John 4:24). *ER*, 132–41; *SBL*, 241–42.

one true church. The church as it existed during the apostolic period: one in spirit, fellowship, doctrine, and government. *ER*, 38–40.

post-denominational view of the church. The view that we should not take biblical promises concerning the gifts of the Spirit, divine preservation of the church, etc., to apply to **denominations.** God has promised that the gates of hell will not prevail against the church (Matt. 16:18). He has not made the same promise to any denomination, for the NT does not mention denominations. *ER*, 41–44.

reconciliation metaphor. My view that a union between two denominations should be thought of not as a kind of **courtship,** but as reconciliation following an illegitimate divorce. *ER*, 142–44.

reunion. The restoration of the original unity of the church, breaking down current denominational divisions.

tolerance. Willingness to live within the church with those who hold different views on some matters, without seeking to impede their ministries or exercise church discipline. Paul urges toleration between meat-eaters and vegetarians in Romans 14, for example. The church should not expect uniformity in all doctrinal and practical matters. *ER*, 84–104.

2. Worship, Preaching

celebration of the resurrection. The main purpose of NT worship after the resurrection and ascension of Jesus. Not emphasized in *WST*, but I emphasize it today.

dialogue model. Worship arranged into (1) speeches of God to us and (2) our response to him. In my judgment this structure can be valuable, but Scripture doesn't require it, and it can confuse the fact that in one sense God is always speaking to us and we are always responding to him. It can also lead to rigid role distinctions (e.g., the preacher alone being permitted to speak as an individual, because he alone speaks for God) that are not biblically justified. *WST*, 69–71.

horizontal focus in worship. Seeking in worship to edify one another (1 Cor. 14; Heb. 10:24–25). *WST*, 7–8; *CWM*, 17–20, 90–97.

redemptive-historical preaching. Preaching that focuses on the historical narrative of Scripture, culminating in the atonement and resurrection of Christ. In some circles, this kind of preaching avoids reference to Bible characters as moral examples and even avoids ethical applications of texts. In my opinion, the focus on redemptive history is often edifying but not biblically required. The avoidance of moral content is, in my view, a distortion of biblical preaching, and such preaching is a distortion of Scripture. *DCL*, 290–97.

reenactment of redemption. An order of worship in which the congregation confesses its sins, receives absolution, and then receives instruction. This is legitimate, but it may confuse the fact that the congregation assembles as people already redeemed by Christ. *WST*, 68–69.

regulative principle of worship. The principle that everything we do in worship must be prescribed in Scripture, either as an explicit requirement or as an application of an explicit requirement. *WST*, 37–43, *DCL*, 464–86.

vertical focus in worship. Seeking above all to please God in worship. *WST*, 4–5, 7–8.

worship. Acknowledging the greatness of our covenant Lord. *WST*, 1.

worship in the broad sense. All of life carried on to God's glory; presenting our bodies as living sacrifices (Rom. 12:1). *WST*, 9–10, 29–30.

worship in the narrow sense. Special occasions at which we explicitly, publicly or privately, acknowledge the greatness of God. *WST*, 9–10, 30–35.

Ethics

aisthesis. Our capacity for moral perception; our ability to see resemblances between our experiences and biblical descriptions of good and evil. *DCL*, 356–59.

broad meaning (of the commandments). The application of each commandment by which it can be seen as a perspective of all of life. *DCL*, 399.

ceremonial laws. (1) Laws pertaining to the ceremonies of religious worship. (2) Laws that are given for a limited time or place, rescinded upon their fulfillment by a greater reality. *DCL*, 213–17.

change in symbolic weight. The view that the change of day of the Sabbath from the seventh day to the first was mainly symbolic: looking backward to a completed redemption, rather than forward to a redemption to come. But that is a change of emphasis, not of absolute meaning. *DCL*, 567–68.

choice between two evils. Choice between two alternatives, each of which will bring some harm: for example, a surgeon's choosing between whether to operate (and bring some pain) and not to operate (and leave someone to die). *DCL*, 230–34.

choice between two wrongs. Choice between alternatives that are both sinful. Also termed **tragic moral choice.** I deny that these exist. *DCL*, 230–34.

Christian "irrationalism." The renunciation of rational autonomy. *DCL*, 43–45.

Christian "rationalism." The belief that divine revelation gives us access to truth. *DCL*, 43–45.

Christian teleological ethic. An ethic focused on the **situational perspective,** examining the environment in which we make ethical decisions, especially the means necessary to reach the goal of the glory of God. *DCL*, 240.

command ethics. A value system that emphasizes objective moral norms. *DCL*, 31.

covenant document. The written text setting forth the terms of a covenant. *DCL*, 20–21.

currently normative. The condition of biblical laws' governing our conduct today, rather than being restricted to a past time. *DCL*, 200.

Decalogical hermeneutics. The rules for interpreting and applying the Ten Commandments. *DCL*, 390–95.

deontological principle. The principle that a good deed is a response to duty, even at the price of self-sacrifice. Divine duties are necessary and universal. They take precedence over any other consideration. Corresponds to the **lordship attribute** of **authority.** *DCL*, 49–51.

doctrine of carefulness. The doctrine that God not only forbids murder, but requires us to take special precautions against the possibility of human life being destroyed. *DCL*, 688–90, 724–25.

dokimazein. "Proof," in Romans 12:1–2 and elsewhere; knowledge that comes through the process of ethical discipline. *DCL*, 355.

duck-rabbit. Picture that can be seen either as a duck or as a rabbit, used as an illustration of the importance of comparing the patterns of our experience to those of Scripture. *DCL*, 356–59.

dying. A condition in which medical help is unable to restore circulation, respiration, and brain activity. *DCL*, 732–36.

emotions. Human feelings, inclinations, dispositions. *DCL*, 370–82.

envy. Being upset or angry at the prosperity of someone else. *DCL*, 845–46.

epistemological truth. True knowledge of facts. *DCL*, 352.

ethical analogies. Resemblances between our experiences and the biblical descriptions of good and evil. *DCL*, 356–59.

ethical conservatism. Seeking answers to ethical problems that are as rigorous/demanding as possible. *DCL*, 6–7.

ethical liberalism. Seeking answers to ethical problems that maximize liberty and minimize legalistic restrictions. *DCL*, 6–7.

ethical truth. Good behavior, as walking in God's statutes. *DCL*, 352.

ethics. Theology when viewed as a means of determining which human persons, acts, and attitudes receive God's blessing or curse. *DCL*, 10–11.

ethics based on fate. A religiously oriented value system with an impersonal, necessitarian causality and empiricist epistemology. Has a situational emphasis. *DCL*, 57–63.

ethics based on self-realization. A monistic, pantheistic value system that stresses self-discipline and personal emancipation. *DCL*, 63–66.

ethics de facto. What standards we actually have, whether right or wrong. *DCL*, 12.

ethics de jure. What moral standards we ought to have. *DCL*, 12.

existential ethics. A value system holding that a good deed is a deed that is true to you. A form of self-realization. *DCL*, 72–90.

existential principle. The principle that a good deed comes from a good motive. Corresponds to the **lordship attribute** of **presence.** *DCL*, 50–51.

existential priorities. Priorities among divine commands arising from individual callings: for example, some may be called to pray much longer than others. *DCL*, 227–30.

experience (in ethics). Ethical knowledge gained from the senses and from continual wrestling with good and evil. *DCL*, 364–66.

fate. A synonym for **chance**; whatever happens. *DCL*, 57–63.

freedom in society. In the Christian view, freedom that implies limited government. In the non-Christian view, freedom that leads to moral anarchy. *DCL*, 48–49.

general office. Authority given to all believers to teach, rule, and show mercy. *DCL*, 639.

glorifying God. Reflecting God's glory in our being and behavior. *DCL*, 302–3.

heart. The center of human existence; the whole person as God sees him. The good or evil nature, which motivates all action. *DCL*, 362.

honor. In the fifth commandment, reverence, submission, and financial support owed to a superior. *DCL*, 576–77.

immanence (biblical view). God's truly revealing himself in word and deed. *DCL*, 41–43.

immanence (nonbiblical view). God's being indistinguishable from the world. *DCL*, 41–43.

individual vs. corporate obligations. The view that individual obligations must be carried out by an individual, by himself. Corporate obligations must be carried out by a group, with individuals playing various roles. *DCL*, 229.

inwardness. The condition of God's law being internalized. Outward conformity is necessary, but insufficient. *DCL*, 325.

justice (general and specific meanings). In general, what is morally right, in the sense of fairness or equity. With special reference to the system of justice, in the fair administration of the law. *DCL*, 18.

kingdom of God. God's acts in history to establish his rule on earth, by defeating his enemies and bringing all people to a conscious awareness of his sovereignty. *DCL*, 278.

less explicitly religious ethics. Sometimes called *secular ethics*, though these approaches have presuppositions not unlike religious ones. *DCL*, 55–57.

literally normative. The condition of biblical laws' current application being literal rather than merely symbolic. *DCL*, 200.

lust. Desire to break God's law in sexual matters. *DCL*, 766–68.

metaethics. A second-order discipline, a theological reflection on the nature of right and wrong, ethical methods, and ethical presuppositions. *DCL*, 11–12.

metaphysical truth. The absolute as contrasted with the relative; what is ultimate, eternal, complete, permanent, substantial. *DCL*, 352.

moral heroism. Actions that display love in extreme ways: for example, the widow who gave all she had to the Lord. *DCL*, 196–200.

morality (Frame). My view that *morality* and *ethics* are synonymous terms that can refer to the description of human customs as well as the (**normative**) evaluation of those customs (i.e., as right or wrong). *DCL*, 12.

moral syllogism. A syllogism in which the major premise sets forth a moral principle, the second premise sets forth a situation to which that principle needs to be applied, and the conclusion states the application of the principle to the situation. *DCL*, 166–68.

motive. An inner disposition that governs ethical action. *DCL*, 324–25.

narrative ethic. Learning our ethical responsibilities by hearing stories; trying to understand how these stories should affect our lives. *DCL*, 31.

naturalistic fallacy. Inferring what ought to be from what is. *DCL*, 59–63.

natural-law ethics. Ethics based on natural revelation, usually thought to be knowable to man through reason and conscience alone, apart from Scripture. *DCL*, 242–50.

non-Christian irrationalism. Skepticism. *DCL*, 43–45.

non-Christian rationalism. Grounding human reason in some mundane authority. *DCL*, 43–45.

normative priorities. Priorities among divine commands specified explicitly in Scripture itself. *DCL*, 225–26.

paradox of ethical decision. The paradox that when our conscience is misinformed we ought nevertheless to follow it, because it defines for us what is good. *DCL*, 363–64.

patterns. Structures of human experience reflecting those of biblical teaching, so that we are able to call things in our experience by their biblical names. *DCL*, 356–59.

permission. A good action that is not prescribed or proscribed. *DCL*, 17–18.

problem of the virtuous pagan. How can unbelievers do good works, granting that people are totally depraved apart from grace? *DCL*, 27–29.

propositional truth. Epistemological truth formulated in statements. *DCL*, 352.

punishment. The legitimate response of authority to someone's wrongdoing. *DCL*, 694–95.

rational autonomy. Reason, apart from tradition or revelation, as the final standard of knowledge. *DCL*, 43–45.

redemptive-historical invisibility. According to Deuteronomy 4:15–19, God's choice at Mount Sinai to reveal himself to Israel without a visible form. At other times in redemptive history, he chooses to reveal himself visibly. *DCL*, 456–60.

redemptive history. (1) The historical events by which God prepares for and achieves human redemption from sin. (2) The written accounts of these events in Scripture. *DCL*, 271–97.

right. (1) Conformity to norms, laws, standards. (2) Deserved privilege; legal/ethical permission to have or do something. *DCL*, 15–16.

seeing as. Seeing the events of our experience as examples of biblical categories. *DCL*, 356–58.

situational perspective (in ethics). The perspective that focuses on the object of knowledge. Answers the question: "What are the best means to accomplish God's purpose?" *DCL*, 33.

situational priorities. Priorities among divine commands arising from situational factors: for example, the legitimacy of David's men's eating the consecrated bread when they were hungry. *DCL*, 226–27.

sound doctrine. Doctrine not merely as a set of theological propositions, but as an active process of learning that leads to spiritual health. *DCL*, 9.

subjects of ethical predication. Persons, acts, and attitudes. These are the only things that Scripture regards as ethically good or bad, right or wrong. *DCL*, 11.

teleological ethics. The view that the ethical value of an action is measured by the extent to which it maximizes happiness and minimizes unhappiness. *DCL*, 91–100.

teleological principle. The principle that a good deed maximizes the happiness of living creatures. A good deed does good. Corresponds to the **lordship attribute** of **control.** *DCL*, 49–51.

theonomy. The view that the civil laws of Israel (along with the penalties for crimes given in those laws) continue to bind present-day civil governments. *DCL*, 217–24.

tragic moral choice. The notion that in some situations we have no choice but to sin, as a result of the lack of nonsinful alternatives. Also termed **choice between two wrongs.** *DCL*, 23–34.

transcendence (biblical view). God's being sovereign in his right and might. *DCL*, 41–42.

transcendence (nonbiblical view). God's being unknowable. *DCL*, 41–42.

two-age structure. The view that the old age, "this age" in the NT, is the period of the reign of sin; the new age is the coming of the kingdom of God, which began with Jesus' incarnation, atonement, resurrection, and ascension. Until Jesus returns, the two ages overlap. *DCL*, 276–79.

value. A quality of worth or merit. *DCL*, 13.

virtue. Ground of praise for something or someone. Subdivided into moral virtues such as love, fidelity, integrity; elements of good character and nonmoral virtues such as efficiency, skill, talent. *DCL*, 14.

virtue ethic. An ethic that focuses on the virtues, describing them and employing them as motivations for ethical behavior. *DCL*, 31.

works of mercy. Works done on the Sabbath to heal or meet other important human needs. Part of the fundamental meaning of the Sabbath. *DCL*, 550–52.

works of necessity. Works that must be done on the Sabbath to keep human life on an even keel. *DCL*, 547–50.

Culture

borrowed capital. Van Til's view of how unbelieving culture borrows elements of Christian theism in order to maintain stability. *DCL*, 880.

Christ, the transformer of culture. H. Richard Niebuhr's term for the common Reformed view that Christ has given his people a mission to transform every area of human life to reflect God's glory. *DCL*, 874–75.

Christ above culture. H. Richard Niebuhr's term for the view of medieval scholasticism, in which there is a synthesis between Christianity and culture, and redemption is a supplement to nature. *DCL*, 868–70.

Christ against culture. H. Richard Niebuhr's term for the view that places Christ and culture in antithesis to one another. *DCL*, 864–67.

Christ and culture in paradox. H. Richard Niebuhr's term for the Lutheran "two-kingdom" view, in which God rules the church by his law and and gospel, and rules the state by natural law only. *DCL*, 870–73.

Christian culturalists. Those who believe that every Christian is responsible to be knowledgeable about cultural movements. *DCL*, 894.

Christ of culture. H. Richard Niebuhr's term for the view that Christ affirms all that is good and right in culture. *DCL*, 867–68.

common grace. Nonsaving grace, which leads to many good things even in fallen culture. *DCL*, 860–61.

"culchah." Refinement, education, good taste as found among the elite. *DCL*, 857.

cultural mirror. Harvie Conn's description of film as an indicator of cultural trends. *DCL*, 897.

culture. What God makes through us, as opposed to creation, which is what God makes by himself. *DCL*, 864.

dualism. Another term for **Christ and culture in paradox.**

egalitarianism. Belief that everyone is morally equal. Stems from disbelief in God as a person who makes choices among people. *DCL*, 899.

folk culture. Ken Myers's term for culture that is less sophisticated and urban than **high culture,** but that provides meaning in traditional societies and has virtues of "honesty, integrity, commitment to tradition, and perseverance in the face of opposition." *DCL*, 883.

genetic fallacy. A cousin to the **naturalistic fallacy,** which argues that something is good because it comes from a good source, or bad because it comes from a bad source. Often found in literature dealing with Christians' use of elements of culture. *DCL*, 908.

high culture. Ken Myers's term for what has been considered the noblest kind of culture, which in his view can provide a transcendent perspective. *DCL*, 882–83.

intelligible communication. Paul's main concern about worship in 1 Corinthians 14, to which churches today need to give more attention. *DCL*, 905.

language of worship. The verbal and musical vocabulary understood by a particular body of Christians, in which they clearly hear the gospel and are motivated to praise and testify. *DCL*, 905.

line of despair. In Francis Schaeffer's analysis, the historical point (occurring at different times in different areas of culture) at which hope was lost for the attainment of objective truth. *DCL*, 880.

modern culture. Culture as transformed by the Enlightenment and the Industrial Revolution. Emphasizes rational scientific method, physical reality, individuality, written communication, a view of history moving toward utopia. *DCL*, 884–85.

optimistic humanism. Os Guinness's term for nonbelievers who persist in affirming the meaningfulness of life, while rejecting God, who is the only basis for such meaning. *DCL*, 880.

pessimistic humanism. Os Guinness's term for nonbelievers who honestly recognize that without God there can be no meaning, and who therefore embrace meaninglessness. *DCL*, 880–81.

popular culture. Ken Myers's term for the lowest cultural denominator, encouraged by the Industrial Revolution and the increasing amount of leisure in society. Disposable entertainment, with none of the virtues of **high culture** and **folk culture.** *DCL*, 883.

postmodern culture. Development since the mid-twentieth century, calling into question the assurances of **modern culture.** Combines elements of the modern with some of those of the premodern: both mythology and science, etc. *DCL*, 884–85.

power of communication. In my view, an important element in judging the quality of art and communication, more so than generally understood. *DCL*, 892–93.

premodern culture. Culture as it existed before the modern period, which persists in some parts of the world. Emphasizes spiritual reality, community, oral communication, a cyclical view of history. *DCL*, 884–85.

special grace. God's redemption of sinners, which also impacts society and culture. *DCL*, 860.

synthesis. Another name for **Christ above culture.**

world. (1) The whole creation of God. (2) Everything opposed to God under Satan's dominion. Not identical to **culture;** rather, the bad part of culture. *DCL*, 865–67.

BIBLIOGRAPHY

Adams, Jay. *The Meaning and Mode of Baptism*. Phillipsburg, NJ: P&R Publishing, 1992.

Alcorn, Randy. *Heaven*. Carol Stream, IL: Tyndale House, 2004.

Alexander, Donald L., ed. *Christian Spirituality: Five Views of Sanctification*. Downers Grove, IL: InterVarsity Press, 1988.

The American Heritage College Dictionary. 3rd ed. Boston and New York: Houghton Mifflin, 2000.

American Scientific Affiliation. *Perspectives on Science & Christian Faith* 62, 3 (September 2010).

Ames, William. *The Marrow of Theology*. Grand Rapids: Baker, 1997.

Anderson, James. *Paradox in Christian Theology*. Eugene, OR: Wipf and Stock, 2007.

Anselm. *Cur Deus Homo*.

Aquinas, Thomas. *Summa contra Gentiles*.

———. *Summa Theologiae*.

Armstrong, John H., ed. *The Coming Evangelical Crisis*. Chicago: Moody Press, 1996.

———, ed. *Understanding Four Views of the Lord's Supper*. Grand Rapids: Zondervan, 2007.

Arndt, William F., and F. Wilbur Gingrich. *A Greek-English Lexicon of the New Testament and Other Early Christian Literature*. Chicago: University of Chicago Press, 1957.

Athanasius. *De Decretis*.

———. *Discourse II against the Arians*.

Athenagoras. *Plea on Behalf of Christians*.

Auer, Johann. *Die Entwicklung der Gnadenlehre in der Hochscholastik*. Vol. 1. *Das Wesen der Gnade*. Freiburg: Herder, 1942.

Augustine. *The City of God*.

———. *Confessions*.

———. *On the Trinity*.

Bahnsen, Greg. "The Inerrancy of the Autographa." In *Inerrancy*, edited by Norman Geisler, 156–59. Grand Rapids: Zondervan, 1979.

———. *Van Til's Apologetic: Readings and Analysis*. Phillipsburg, NJ: P&R Publishing, 1998.

Baker's Dictionary of Theology. Grand Rapids: Baker, 1960.

Bannerman, James. *The Church of Christ*. 2 vols. Vestavia, AL: Solid Ground Christian Books, 2009.

Barr, James. *Biblical Words for Time*. Naperville, IL: Alec R. Allenson, 1969.

———. *The Semantics of Biblical Language*. London and Oxford: Oxford University Press, 1961.

Barrett, C. K. *A Commentary on the First Epistle of Paul to the Corinthians*. New York: Harper and Row, 1968.

Barth, Karl. *Church Dogmatics*. 4 vols. Edinburgh: T. and T. Clark, 1936–62.

———. *Evangelical Theology: An Introduction*. Grand Rapids: Eerdmans, 1963.

Bauckham, Richard. "In Defence of *The Crucified God*." In *The Power and Weakness of God*, edited by Nigel M. de S. Cameron, 93–99. Edinburgh: Rutherford House Books, 1990.

Bavinck, Herman. *The Doctrine of God*. Grand Rapids: Baker, 1951.

———. *Reformed Dogmatics*. 4 vols. Grand Rapids: Baker, 2003–8.

Beisner, E. Calvin. *Evangelical Heathenism*. Moscow, ID: Canon Press, 1996.

Belcher, Jim. *Deep Church*. Downers Grove, IL: InterVarsity Press, 2009.

Bennett, Arthur G., ed. *The Valley of Vision: A Collection of Puritan Prayers and Devotions*. Edinburgh: Banner of Truth, 1975.

Berkhof, Louis. *Systematic Theology*. London: Banner of Truth, 1941.

Berkouwer, G. C. *Divine Election*. Grand Rapids: Eerdmans, 1960.

———. *The Providence of God*. Grand Rapids: Eerdmans, 1952.

———. *The Triumph of Grace in the Theology of Karl Barth*. Grand Rapids: Eerdmans, 1956.

Bilezikian, Gilbert. *Beyond Sex Roles*. Grand Rapids: Baker, 1985.

———. "Hermeneutical Bungee-Jumping: Subordination in the Godhead." *JETS* 40, 1 (1997): 57–68.

Blocher, Henri. *In the Beginning*. Downers Grove, IL: InterVarsity Press, 1984.

Boethius. *A Treatise against Eutychus and Nestorius*.

Boettner, Loraine. *The Reformed Doctrine of Predestination*. Grand Rapids: Eerdmans, 1957.

The Book of Church Order. 6th ed. N.p.: Office of the Stated Clerk of the General Assembly of the Presbyterian Church in America, 2012.

Bray, Gerald. *The Doctrine of God*. Downers Grove, IL: InterVarsity Press, 1993.

Brown, David. "Trinitarian Personhood and Individuality." In *Trinity, Incarnation, and Atonement*, edited by Ronald J. Feenstra and Cornelius Plantinga. Notre Dame, IN: University of Notre Dame Press, 1989.

Bruce, F. F. *The Gospel of John*. Grand Rapids: Eerdmans, 1984.

Brunner, Emil. *Truth as Encounter*. Philadelphia: Westminster Press, 1964.

Calvin, John. *Commentary on 2 Timothy*, ad loc.

———. *Concerning the Eternal Predestination of God*. London: James Clarke and Co., 1961.

———. *Institutes of the Christian Religion*. Edited by John T. McNeill. Translated by Ford Lewis Battles. 2 vols. Philadelphia: Westminster Press, 1960.

Cameron, Nigel M. de S., ed. *The Power and Weakness of God*. Edinburgh: Rutherford House Books, 1990.

Campbell, C. A. "The Psychology of Effort of Will." *Proceedings of the Aristotelian Society* 40 (1939–40): 49–74.

Carson, Donald A. *Divine Sovereignty and Human Responsibility*. Atlanta: John Knox Press, 1981.

Chaney, James M. *William the Baptist*. Charleston: CreateSpace, 2009.

Chappell, Bryan. *Praying Backwards: Transform Your Prayer Life by Beginning in Jesus' Name*. Grand Rapids: Baker, 2005.

Clark, Gordon H. "Attributes, The Divine." In *Baker's Dictionary of Theology*, 78–79. Grand Rapids: Baker, 1960.

———. *The Johannine Logos*. Nutley, NJ: Presbyterian and Reformed, 1972.

———. *Predestination in the Old Testament*. Phillipsburg, NJ: Presbyterian and Reformed, 1978.

———. *Religion, Reason, and Revelation*. Philadelphia: Presbyterian and Reformed, 1961.

———. *The Trinity*. Jefferson, MD: Trinity Foundation, 1985.

Clark, Kelly James. "Reformed Epistemology Apologetics." In *Five Views on Apologetics*, edited by Steven B. Cowan, 265–312. Grand Rapids: Zondervan, 2000.

Clark, R. Scott. *Recovering the Reformed Confession*. Phillipsburg, NJ: P&R Publishing, 2008.

Clark, Stephen B. *Man and Woman in Christ*. Ann Arbor: Servant Books, 1980.

Clouse, Robert, ed. *The Meaning of the Millennium: Four Views*. Downers Grove, IL: IVP Academic, 1977.

Clowney, Edmund P. *Called to the Ministry*. Philadelphia: Westminster Theological Seminary, 1964.

———. *The Church*. Downers Grove, IL: InterVarsity Press, 1995.

Cobb, John B., and David Ray Griffin. *Process Theology: An Introductory Exposition*. Philadelphia: Westminster Press, 1976.

Coles, Elisha. *A Practical Discourse on God's Sovereignty*. 17th c. Repr., Marshallton, DE: National Foundation for Christian Education, 1968.

Collins, C. John. *Did Adam and Eve Really Exist?* Wheaton, IL: Crossway, 2011.

———. "How Old Is the Earth?" *Presbuteron* 20 (1994): 109–30.

———. "Reading Genesis 1:1–2:3 as an Act of Communication." In *Did God Create in Six Days?*, edited by Joseph Pipa Jr. and David Hall, 131–51. Oak Ridge, TN: Covenant Foundation, 1999.

Cottrell, Jack. *What the Bible Says about God the Redeemer.* Joplin, MO: College Press, 1987.

———. *What the Bible Says about God the Ruler.* Joplin, MO: College Press, 1984.

Cowan, Steven B., ed. *Five Views on Apologetics.* Grand Rapids: Zondervan, 2000.

Craig, William Lane. *The Only Wise God.* Grand Rapids: Baker, 1987.

Creel, Richard. *Divine Impassibility.* Cambridge: Cambridge University Press, 1986.

Crockett, William, ed. *Four Views on Hell.* Grand Rapids: Zondervan, 1992.

Cullmann, Oscar. *Christ and Time.* Philadelphia: Westminster Press, 1950.

Dabney, Robert Lewis. *Lectures in Systematic Theology.* Grand Rapids: Zondervan, 1972.

Dahms, John V. "The Johannine Use of *Monogenes* Reconsidered." *New Testament Studies* 29 (1983): 222–32.

———. "The Subordination of the Son." *JETS* 37, 3 (September 1994): 351–64.

Dana, H. E., and Julius R. Mantey. *A Manual Grammar of the Greek New Testament.* New York: Macmillan, 1955.

Davis, John Jefferson. *Evangelical Ethics.* Phillipsburg, NJ: P&R Publishing, 2004.

Deane, S. N., ed. *St. Anselm Basic Writings.* La Salle, IL: Open Court, 1974.

Dodd, C. H. *The Apostolic Preaching and Its Developments.* London: Hodder and Stoughton, 1936.

———. *The Bible and the Greeks.* London: Hodder and Stoughton, 1935.

———. *The Epistle of St. Paul to the Romans.* New York: Harper, 1932.

———. "New Testament Translation Problems II." *Bible Translator* 28 (January 1977): 101–4.

Downing, F. Gerald. *Has Christianity a Revelation?* London: SCM Press, 1964.

Edwards, Jonathan. *Freedom of the Will.* New Haven, CT: Yale University Press, 1973.

Edwards, Paul, ed. *The Encyclopedia of Philosophy.* Vol. 3. New York: Macmillan and The Free Press, 1967.

Elwell, Walter A., ed. *Evangelical Dictionary of Theology.* Grand Rapids: Baker, 1984.

Erickson, Millard. *God the Father Almighty.* Grand Rapids: Baker, 1998.

Farley, Benjamin Wirt. *The Providence of God.* Grand Rapids: Baker, 1988.

Feenstra, Ronald J., and Cornelius Plantinga, eds. *Trinity, Incarnation, and Atonement.* Notre Dame, IN: University of Notre Dame Press, 1989.

Ferguson, Sinclair. *A Heart for God*. Colorado Springs: NavPress, 1985.

———. *The Holy Spirit*. Downers Grove, IL: InterVarsity Press, 1997.

Foh, Susan. *Women and the Word of God*. Phillipsburg, NJ: Presbyterian and Reformed, 1979.

Forde, Gerhard. "The Lutheran View." In *Christian Spirituality: Five Views of Sanctification*, edited by Donald L. Alexander, 13–46. Downers Grove, IL: InterVarsity Press, 1988.

Fortman, Edmund J. *The Triune God*. Grand Rapids: Baker, 1972.

Frame, John M. *Apologetics to the Glory of God*. Phillipsburg, NJ: P&R Publishing, 1994.

———. "Certainty." Available at http://www.frame-poythress.org.

———. "Christianity and Contemporary Epistemology." *WTJ* 52, 1 (1990): 131–41.

———. *Contemporary Worship Music: A Biblical Defense*. Phillipsburg, NJ: P&R Publishing, 1997.

———. *Cornelius Van Til: An Analysis of His Thought*. Phillipsburg, NJ: P&R Publishing, 1995.

———. *The Doctrine of the Christian Life*. Phillipsburg, NJ: P&R Publishing, 2008.

———. *The Doctrine of God*. Phillipsburg, NJ: P&R Publishing, 2002.

———. *The Doctrine of the Knowledge of God*. Phillipsburg, NJ: P&R Publishing, 1987.

———. *The Doctrine of the Word of God*. Phillipsburg, NJ: P&R Publishing, 2010.

———. *The Escondido Theology*. Lakeland, FL: Whitefield Media, 2011.

———. *Evangelical Reunion: Denominations and the One Body of Christ*. Grand Rapids: Baker, 1991. Available at http://www.frame-poythress.org; http://www.evangelicalreunion.org.

———. "Greeks Bearing Gifts." In *Revolutions in Worldview*, edited by W. Andrew Hoffecker, 1–36. Phillipsburg, NJ: P&R Publishing, 2007.

———. "Introduction to the Reformed Faith." Available at http://www.frame-poythress.org.

———. *Medical Ethics*. Phillipsburg, NJ: Presbyterian and Reformed, 1988.

———. "Men and Women in the Image of God." In *Recovering Biblical Manhood and Womanhood*, edited by John Piper and Wayne Grudem, 225–32. Wheaton, IL: Crossway, 1991.

———. *No Other God*. Phillipsburg, NJ: P&R Publishing, 2001.

———. *Perspectives on the Word of God*. Eugene, OR: Wipf and Stock, 2000.

———. "A Primer on Perspectivalism." Available at http://www.frame-poythress.org.

———. "Proposal for a New Seminary." Available at http://www.frame-poythress.org.

———. Review of *A Biblical Case for Natural Law*, by David VanDrunen. Available at http://www.frame-poythress.org.

———. Review of *Calvinism and the Amyraut Heresy*, by Brian Armstrong. *WTJ* 34, 2 (May 1972): 186–92.

———. Review of *Evil Revisited*, by David Ray Griffin. *CTJ* 27, 2 (November 1992): 435–38.

———. Review of *The Providence of God*, by Benjamin Wirt Farley. *WTJ* 51, 2 (1989): 397–400.

———. *Salvation Belongs to the Lord: An Introduction to Systematic Theology*. Phillipsburg, NJ: P&R Publishing, 2006.

———. *Selected Shorter Writings of John Frame*. Phillipsburg, NJ: P&R Publishing, 2013.

———. "Virgin Birth of Jesus." In *Evangelical Dictionary of Theology*, edited by Walter A. Elwell, 1143–46. Grand Rapids: Baker, 1984. Available at http://www.frame-poythress .org.

———. "Walking Together." Available at http://www.frame-poythress.org.

Frame, John M., and Paul Kurtz. "Without a Supreme Being, Everything Is Permitted." *Free Inquiry* 16, 2 (Spring 1996): 4–7.

France, R. T. *The Living God*. London: Inter-Varsity Press, 1970.

Futato, Mark D. "Because It Had Rained." *WTJ* 60, 1 (1998): 1–21.

Gaffin, Richard B. *Perspectives on Pentecost*. Phillipsburg, NJ: Presbyterian and Reformed, 1979.

———. *Resurrection and Redemption: A Study in Paul's Soteriology*. Phillipsburg, NJ: P&R Publishing, 1987.

Geisler, Norman, ed. *Inerrancy*. Grand Rapids: Zondervan, 1979.

Geisler, Norman, and Thomas Howe. *When Critics Ask*. Wheaton, IL: Victor Books, 1992.

Gerstner, John H. *The Rational Biblical Theology of Jonathan Edwards*. Orlando, FL: Ligonier Ministries, 1992.

Gettier, Edmund. "Is Justified True Belief Knowledge?" *Analysis* 23 (1963): 121–23.

Giberson, Karl W., and Francis S. Collins. *The Language of Science and Faith*. Downers Grove, IL: InterVarsity Press, 2011.

Gilkey, Langdon. *Maker of Heaven and Earth*. Garden City, NY: Doubleday, 1959.

Gilson, Étienne. *The Philosophy of St. Thomas Aquinas*. Translated by Edward Bullough. New York: Arno Press, 1979.

———. *The Spirit of Medieval Philosophy*. New York: Charles Scribner's Sons, 1940.

Grenz, Stanley. *Theology for the Community of God*. Nashville: Broadman and Holman, 1994.

Grenz, Stanley, and Roger Olson. *Twentieth-Century Theology: God and the World in a Transitional Age.* Downers Grove, IL: InterVarsity Press, 1992.

Griffin, David Ray. *Evil Revisited.* Albany, NY: State University of New York Press, 1991.

———. *God, Power, and Evil.* Philadelphia: Westminster, 1976.

Grudem, Wayne. "The Meaning of *Kephale.*" App. 1 in *Recovering Biblical Manhood and Womanhood,* edited by John Piper and Wayne Grudem. Wheaton, IL: Crossway, 1991.

———. *Systematic Theology.* Grand Rapids: Zondervan, 1994.

Gruenler, Royce. *The Trinity in the Gospel of John.* Grand Rapids: Baker, 1986.

Gundry, Stanley, ed. *Three Views of the Millennium and Beyond.* Grand Rapids: Zondervan, 1999.

Gunton, Colin. *The Promise of Trinitarian Theology.* Edinburgh: T. and T. Clark, 1991.

Gutierrez, Gustavo. *A Theology of Liberation.* Maryknoll, NY: Orbis, 1973.

Hall, David, ed. *The Practice of Confessional Subscription.* Lanham, MD: University Press of America, 1995.

Harris, Murray J. *Jesus as God.* Grand Rapids: Baker, 1992.

Hart, Darryl. *A Secular Faith.* Chicago: Ivan R. Dee, 2006.

Helm, Paul. *Eternal God: A Study of God without Time.* Oxford: Clarendon Press, 1988.

———. *The Providence of God.* Leicester: Inter-Varsity Press, 1993.

Hendriksen, William. *A Commentary on the Epistles to Timothy and Titus.* London: Banner of Truth, 1960.

Henry, Carl F. H. *God, Revelation and Authority.* 6 vols. Waco, TX: Word Books, 1976–83.

———. *Remaking the Modern Mind.* Grand Rapids: Eerdmans, 1948.

Heppe, Heinrich. *Reformed Dogmatics.* Grand Rapids: Baker, 1950, 1978.

Hick, John. *Evil and the God of Love.* London: Collins, 1966.

Hilary of Poitiers. *On the Trinity.*

Hill, Charles E. "N. T. Wright on Justification." *Third Millennium Magazine Online* 3, 22 (May 28–June 2, 2001). Available at http://www.thirdmill.org/files/english/html/nt/NT.h.Hill.Wright.html.

———. *Who Chose the Gospels? Probing the Great Gospel Conspiracy.* London: Oxford University Press, 2012.

Hill, Edmund. *The Mystery of the Trinity.* London: Chapman, 1985.

Hill, William. *The Three-Personed God.* Washington, DC: Catholic University of America Press, 1982.

Hobart, R. E. "Free Will as Involving Determinism and Inconceivable without It." *Mind* 43 (January 1934): 1–27.

Hodge, A. A. *Outlines of Theology*. 1879. Repr., Grand Rapids: Zondervan, 1972.

Hodge, Charles. *Systematic Theology*. 3 vols. Grand Rapids: Eerdmans, 1952.

Hodges, Zane C. *Absolutely Free! A Biblical Reply to Lordship Salvation*. Grand Rapids: Zondervan, 1989.

Hodgson, Leonard. *The Doctrine of the Trinity*. New York: Scribner, 1944, 1963.

Hoekema, Anthony. *The Bible and the Future*. Grand Rapids: Eerdmans, 1994.

Hoffecker, W. Andrew, ed. *Revolutions in Worldview*. Phillipsburg, NJ: P&R Publishing, 2007.

Hooper, Walter, ed. *Christian Reflections*. Grand Rapids: Eerdmans, 1967.

Hughes, John J., ed. *Speaking the Truth in Love: The Theology of John M. Frame*. Phillipsburg, NJ: P&R Publishing, 2009.

Hume, David. *An Inquiry concerning Human Understanding*. New York: Liberal Arts Press, 1955.

Hurley, James B. "Did Paul Require Veils or the Silence of Women?" *WTJ* 35, 2 (Winter 1973): 190–220.

———. *Man and Woman in Biblical Perspective*. Leicester: Inter-Varsity Press, 1981; Grand Rapids: Zondervan, 1981.

Irenaeus, *Against Heresies*.

Irons, Lee. "The Eternal Generation of the Son." Available at http://members.aol.com /ironslee/private/Monogenes.htm.

Jewett, Paul K. *God, Creation, and Revelation*. Grand Rapids: Eerdmans, 1991.

Johnson, Elizabeth. *She Who Is*. New York: Crossroad Publishing, 1996.

Johnson, Phillip. *Darwin on Trial*. Downers Grove, IL: InterVarsity Press, 1993.

———. *Reason in the Balance*. Downers Grove, IL: InterVarsity Press, 1995.

Jones, Peter. *One or Two: Seeing a World of Difference*. Escondido, CA: Main Entry Editions, 2010.

———. *Spirit Wars: Pagan Revival in Christian America*. Escondido, CA: Main Entry Editions, 1997.

Jordan, James B. *Creation in Six Days*. Moscow, ID: Canon Press, 1999.

———. "Creation with the Appearance of Age." *Open Book* 45 (April 1999): 2.

Jüngel, Eberhard. *God as the Mystery of the World*. Grand Rapids: Eerdmans, 1983.

Kaiser, Christopher. *The Doctrine of God*. Westchester, IL: Crossway, 1982.

Keller, Timothy. *Center Church*. Grand Rapids: Zondervan, 2012.

Kelly, J. N. D. *Early Christian Creeds*. London: Longman, 1972.

Kennedy, D. James. *Truths That Transform*. Old Tappan, NJ: Fleming H. Revell, 1974.

Kenny, Anthony. *The God of the Philosophers*. Oxford: Clarendon Press, 1979.

Kitamori, Kayoh. *Theology of the Pain of God*. Richmond, VA: John Knox Press, 1965.

Kline, Meredith G. "Because It Had Not Rained." *WTJ* 20, 2 (1957–58): 146–57.

———. "Divine Kingship and Genesis 6:1–4." *WTJ* 24, 2 (1962): 187–204.

———. *Images of the Spirit*. Grand Rapids: Baker, 1980.

———. *Kingdom Prologue*. Eugene, OR: Wipf and Stock, 2006.

———. "Space and Time in the Genesis Cosmogony." *Perspectives on Science and Christian Faith* 48 (1996): 2–15.

———. *The Structure of Biblical Authority*. Grand Rapids: Eerdmans, 1972; rev. 1975.

Kline, Meredith M. "The Holy Spirit as Covenant Witness." Th.M. diss., Westminster Theological Seminary, 1972.

Knoppers, Gary. "Ancient Near Eastern Royal Grants and the Davidic Covenant: A Parallel?" *Journal of the American Oriental Society* 116, 4 (October–December 1996): 670–97.

Kovach, Stephen D., and Peter R. Schemm Jr. "A Defense of the Eternal Subordination of the Son." *JETS* 42, 3 (September 1999): 461–76.

Kruger, Michael. *Canon Revisited: Establishing the Origins and Authority of the NT Books*. Wheaton, IL: Crossway, 2012.

Kuhn, Thomas. *The Structure of Scientific Revolutions*. Chicago: University of Chicago Press, 1970.

Kuiper, Herman. *Calvin on Common Grace*. Netherlands and Grand Rapids: Oosterbaan and Le Cointre, Goes, and Smitter Book Co., 1928.

Kushner, Harold. *When Bad Things Happen to Good People*. New York: Schocken, 1981.

Kuyper, Abraham. *De Gemeene Gratie*. 3 vols. Kampen: Kok, 1945.

———. *Principles of Sacred Theology*. Grand Rapids: Eerdmans, 1965.

———. *You Can Do Greater Things than Christ: Demons, Miracles, Healing and Science*. Translated by Jan H. Boer. Jos, Nigeria: Institute for Church and Society, 1991.

LaHaye, Tim, and Jerry Jenkins. *Left Behind*. Carol Stream, IL: Tyndale House, 1996.

Leibniz, G. W. *Theodicy*. New Haven, CT: Yale University Press, 1952.

Leith, John. *Creeds of the Churches*. Richmond, VA: John Knox Press, 1973.

Letham, Robert. *Union with Christ in Scripture, History, and Theology*. Phillipsburg, NJ: P&R Publishing, 2011.

Lewis, C. S. *The Four Loves*. London: Geoffrey Bles, 1960.

———. *A Grief Observed*. New York: HarperOne, 2001.

———. *Miracles*. New York: Macmillan, 1947.

———. "Modern Theology and Biblical Criticism." In *Christian Reflections*, edited by Walter Hooper, 152–66. Grand Rapids: Eerdmans, 1967.

———. *The Problem of Pain*. New York: HarperOne, 2001.

———. *The Screwtape Letters*. New York: HarperCollins, 1942. Repr., San Francisco: HarperSanFrancisco, 2001.

Lindars, Barnabas, Stephen S. Smalley, and C. F. D. Moule, eds. *Christ and Spirit in the New Testament*. Cambridge: Cambridge University Press, 1973.

Lindsey, Hal. *Satan Is Alive and Well on Planet Earth*. Grand Rapids: Zondervan, 1972.

Luther, Martin. *The Bondage of the Will*. London: James Clarke and Co., 1957.

MacArthur, John. *The Gospel according to Jesus*. Grand Rapids: Zondervan, 1988.

Machen, J. Gresham. *Machen's Notes on Galatians*. Nutley, NJ: Presbyterian and Reformed, 1972.

———. *What Is Christianity? and Other Addresses*. Grand Rapids: Eerdmans, 1951.

Macleod, Donald. *Behold Your God*. 2nd ed. Fearn, Ross-shire, UK: Christian Focus, 1995.

Marshall, I. Howard. *The Origins of New Testament Christology*. Downers Grove, IL: InterVarsity Press, 1976.

———. "Universal Grace and Atonement in the Pastoral Epistles." In *The Grace of God and the Will of Man*, edited by Clark Pinnock, 51–69. Grand Rapids: Zondervan, 1989.

Marshall, Walter. *The Gospel Mystery of Sanctification*. Lafayette, IN: Sovereign Grace Publishers, 2001.

Mavrodes, George. *Belief in God*. New York: Random House, 1970.

McGaughy, Lane C. *Toward a Descriptive Analysis of EINAI as a Linking Verb in New Testament Greek*. Society of Biblical Literature Dissertation Series 6. Missoula, MT: Society of Biblical Literature for the Linguistics Seminar, 1972.

Meek, Esther. *Longing to Know: The Philosophy of Knowledge for Ordinary People*. Grand Rapids: Brazos Press, 2003.

———. *Loving to Know: Covenant Epistemology*. Eugene, OR: Cascade Books, 2011.

Metzger, Bruce. "The Punctuation of Rom. 9:5." In *Christ and Spirit in the New Testament*, edited by Barnabas Lindars, Stephen S. Smalley, and C. F. D. Moule, 95–112. Cambridge: Cambridge University Press, 1973.

Miller, C. John. *Repentance: A Daring Call to Real Surrender*. Fort Washington, PA: Christian Literature Crusade, 2009.

Miller, John. *Is God a Trinity?* Hazelwood, MO: Word Aflame Press, 1975.

Miller, Paul. *A Praying Life*. Colorado Springs: NavPress, 2009.

Milton, Michael. *What Is the Doctrine of Adoption?* Phillipsburg, NJ: P&R Publishing, 2012.

Moltmann, Jürgen. *The Crucified God*. London: SCM Press, 1974. Repr., San Francisco: HarperSanFrancisco, 1990.

———. *The Experiment Hope*. Philadelphia: Fortress, 1975.

———. *Theology of Hope*. New York: Harper and Row, 1967.

———. *The Trinity and the Kingdom*. San Francisco: HarperCollins, 1981, 1991.

Morgan, Christopher, and Robert Peterson, eds. *Hell under Fire*. Grand Rapids: Zondervan, 2004.

Morris, Leon. *The Cross in the New Testament*. Grand Rapids: Eerdmans, 1965.

———. *The First Epistle of Paul to the Corinthians*. Grand Rapids: Eerdmans, 1958.

Mueller, J. Theodore. *Christian Dogmatics*. St. Louis: Concordia, 1934, 1955.

Muller, Richard. "Grace, Election, and Contingent Choice: Arminius's Gambit and the Reformed Response." In *The Grace of God, The Bondage of the Will*, edited by Thomas R. Schreiner and Bruce A. Ware, 2:251–78. Grand Rapids: Baker, 1995.

Murray, John. "The Attestation of Scripture." In *The Infallible Word*, edited by Ned Stonehouse and Paul Woolley, 40–52. Grand Rapids: Eerdmans, 1946.

———. *Christian Baptism*. Phillipsburg, NJ: P&R Publishing, 1992.

———. *Collected Writings of John Murray*. 4 vols. Edinburgh: Banner of Truth, 1976–82.

———. *The Covenant of Grace*. London: Tyndale Press, 1950.

———. *The Imputation of Adam's Sin*. Grand Rapids: Eerdmans, 1959.

———. *Principles of Conduct*. Grand Rapids: Eerdmans, 1957.

———. *Redemption Accomplished and Applied*. Grand Rapids: Eerdmans, 1955.

Nash, Ronald. *Faith and Reason*. Grand Rapids: Zondervan, 1988.

Naselli, Andrew D. *Let Go and Let God? A Survey & Analysis of Keswick Theology*. Bellingham, WA: Logos Bible Software, 2010.

New Spirit Filled Life Bible. Nashville: Thomas Nelson, 2002.

Niebuhr, Richard R. *Resurrection and Historical Reason*. New York: Scribner's, 1957.

Nygren, Anders. *Agape and Eros*. Translated by Philip Watson. London: SPCK, 1953.

Oliphint, K. Scott, ed. *Justified in Christ*. Fearn, Ross-shire, UK: Christian Focus, 2007.

Orlebeke, Clifton, and Lewis Smedes. *God and the Good*. Grand Rapids: Eerdmans, 1975.

Orr, James. *Revelation and Inspiration*. New York: Scribner's, 1910. Repr., Grand Rapids: Baker, 1969.

Orthodox Presbyterian Church. General Assembly Committee Report on Women in Office. Minutes of the General Assembly, 1987–88.

Ostling, Richard. "The Search for the Historical Adam." *Christianity Today*, June 26, 2011, 22–27.

Owen, H. P. "God, Concepts of." In *The Encyclopedia of Philosophy*, edited by Paul Edwards, 3:344–48. New York: Macmillan and The Free Press, 1967.

Owen, John. *The Holy Spirit*. Peabody, MA: Christian Heritage Publishers, 2005.

Pannenberg, Wolfhart. *The Idea of God and Human Freedom*. Philadelphia: Westminster Press, 1973.

———. *Systematic Theology*. Vol. 1. Grand Rapids: Eerdmans, 1988, 1991.

Peterson, Robert. *Hell on Trial*. Phillipsburg, NJ: P&R Publishing, 1995.

Petty, James C. *Step by Step*. Phillipsburg, NJ: P&R Publishing, 1999.

Pike, Kenneth. *Language in Relation to a Unified Theory of the Structure of Human Behavior*. The Hague and Paris: Mouton, 1967.

———. *Linguistic Concepts: An Introduction to Tagmemics*. Lincoln: University of Nebraska Press, 1982.

Pinnock, Clark, ed. *The Grace of God and the Will of Man*. Grand Rapids: Zondervan, 1989.

———. "Systematic Theology." In *The Openness of God*, edited by Clark Pinnock et al., 107–9. Downers Grove, IL: InterVarsity Press, 1994.

Pinnock, Clark, et al. *The Openness of God*. Downers Grove, IL: InterVarsity Press, 1994.

Pipa, Joseph, Jr., and David Hall. *Did God Create in Six Days?* Oak Ridge, TN: Covenant Foundation, 1999.

Piper, John. *Brothers, We Are Not Professionals*. Nashville: Broadman and Holman, 2002.

———. *Desiring God*. Sisters, OR: Multnomah Publishers, 1986, 2003.

———. *The Purifying Power of Living by Faith in Future Grace*. Sisters, OR: Multnomah Publishers, 1995.

Piper, John, and Wayne Grudem, eds. *Recovering Biblical Manhood and Womanhood*. Wheaton, IL: Crossway, 1991.

Piper, John, Justin Taylor, and Paul K. Helseth. *Beyond the Bounds: Open Theism and the Undermining of Biblical Christianity*. Wheaton, IL: Crossway, 2003.

Plantinga, Alvin. *Does God Have a Nature?* Milwaukee: Marquette University Press, 1980.

———. *God, Freedom, and Evil*. Grand Rapids: Eerdmans, 1974.

———. *God and Other Minds*. Ithaca, NY: Cornell University Press, 1967.

———. *The Nature of Necessity*. Oxford: Clarendon Press, 1974.

———. *Warrant: The Current Debate*. New York: Oxford University Press, 1993.

———. *Warrant and Proper Function*. New York: Oxford University Press, 1993.

———. *Warranted Christian Belief*. New York: Oxford University Press, 2000.

Plantinga, Cornelius. *Not the Way It's Supposed to Be: A Breviary of Sin*. Grand Rapids: Eerdmans, 1995.

———. "The Perfect Family." *Christianity Today*, March 4, 1988, 24–27.

———. "Social Trinity and Tritheism." In *Trinity, Incarnation, and Atonement*, edited by Ronald J. Feenstra and Cornelius Plantinga, 21–47. Notre Dame, IN: University of Notre Dame Press, 1989.

———. "The Threeness/Oneness Problem of the Trinity." *CTJ* 23, 1 (April 1988): 38–52.

Pollock, John. *Contemporary Theories of Knowledge*. Totowa, NJ: Rowman and Littlefield, 1986.

Poythress, Vern S. "Adam vs. Claims from Genetics." *WTJ* 75, 1 (2013): 65–82.

———. "Body and Soul: The Metaphysical Composition of the Human Individual." Unpublished notes.

———. "The Church as a Family: Why Male Leadership in the Family Requires Male Leadership in the Church as Well." In *Recovering Biblical Manhood and Womanhood*, edited by John Piper and Wayne Grudem, 237–50. Wheaton, IL: Crossway, 1991. Available at http://www.frame-poythress.org.

———. "A Framework for Discourse Analysis." *Semiotica* 38, 3/4 (1982): 277–98.

———. *God-Centered Biblical Interpretation*. Phillipsburg, NJ: P&R Publishing, 1999.

———. *Logic: A God-Centered Approach to the Foundation of Western Thought*. Wheaton, IL: Crossway, 2013.

———. "Modern Spiritual Gifts as Analogous to Apostolic Gifts: Affirming Extraordinary Works of the Spirit within Cessationist Theology." *JETS* 39, 1 (1996): 71–101. Available at http://www.frame-poythress.org.

———. *Redeeming Science*. Wheaton, IL: Crossway, 2006.

———. "Reforming Ontology and Logic in the Light of the Trinity." *WTJ* 57, 1 (1995): 187–219.

———. *The Shadow of Christ in the Law of Moses*. Brentwood, TN: Wolgemuth and Hyatt, 1991. Available at http://www.frame-poythress.org.

———. *Understanding Dispensationalists*. Phillipsburg, NJ: P&R Publishing, 1993. Available at http://www.frame-poythress.org.

———. *What Are Spiritual Gifts?* Phillipsburg, NJ: P&R Publishing, 2010. Available at http://www.frame-poythress.org.

Poythress, Vern S., and Wayne Grudem. *The Gender-Neutral Bible Controversy*. Nashville: Broadman and Holman, 2000.

Pratt, Richard. "Historical Contingencies and Biblical Predictions." Available at http://reformedperspectives.org/newfiles/ric_pratt/TH.Pratt.Historical_Contingencies.html.

———. "Prophecy and Historical Contingency." Available at http://www.thirdmill.org.

———. "Reformed Theology Is Covenant Theology." Available at http://old.thirdmill .org/newfiles/ric_pratt/ric_pratt.RTiscovenant.html.

Rahner, Karl. *The Trinity*. New York: Seabury Press, 1974.

Rahner, Karl, et al., eds. *Sacramentum Mundi: An Encyclopedia of Theology*. New York: Herder and Herder, 1970.

Ramsey, Ian. *Religious Language*. New York: Macmillan, 1957.

Reymond, Robert. *Jesus, Divine Messiah*. Phillipsburg, NJ: Presbyterian and Reformed, 1990.

———. *The Justification of Knowledge*. Nutley, NJ: Presbyterian and Reformed, 1976.

———. *A New Systematic Theology of the Christian Faith*. Nashville: Thomas Nelson, 1998.

Rice, Richard. "Biblical Support for a New Perspective." In *The Openness of God*, edited by Clark Pinnock et al., 50–53. Downers Grove, IL: InterVarsity Press, 1994.

———. *God's Foreknowledge and Man's Free Will*. Minneapolis: Bethany House, 1985.

Ridderbos, Herman N. *The Coming of the Kingdom*. Vineland, ON: Paideia Press, 1979.

Ridderbos, N. H. *Is There a Conflict between Genesis 1 and Natural Science?* Grand Rapids: Eerdmans, 1957.

Robbins, John. *Cornelius Van Til: The Man and the Myth*. Jefferson, MD: Trinity Foundation, 1986.

Sailhamer, John. *Introduction to Old Testament Theology: A Canonical Approach*. Grand Rapids: Zondervan, 1995.

Sandlin, P. Andrew, ed. *Backbone of the Bible*. Nacodoches, TX: Covenant Media Press, 2004.

———, ed. *A Faith That Is Never Alone*. La Grange, CA: Kerygma Press, 2007.

———. *Wrongly Dividing the Word: Overcoming the Law-Gospel Distinction*. Mount Hermon, CA: Center for Cultural Leadership, 2010.

Schleiermacher, Friedrich. *The Christian Faith*. 2 vols. New York: Harper, 1963.

Schlette, Heinz R. "Monotheism." In *Sacramentum Mundi: An Encyclopedia of Theology*, edited by Karl Rahner et al., 979–81. New York: Herder and Herder, 1970.

Schreiner, Thomas R., and Bruce A. Ware, eds. *The Grace of God, The Bondage of the Will*. Vol. 2. Grand Rapids: Baker, 1995.

Shepherd, Norman. *The Call of Grace: How the Covenant Illuminates Salvation and Evangelism*. Phillipsburg, NJ: P&R Publishing, 2000.

———. "The Imputation of Active Obedience." In *A Faith That Is Never Alone*, edited by P. Andrew Sandlin, 249–78. La Grange, CA: Kerygma Press, 2007.

———. "Justification by Works in Reformed Theology." In *Backbone of the Bible*, edited by P. Andrew Sandlin, 103–20. Nacodoches, TX: Covenant Media Press, 2004.

———. *The Way of Righteousness*. La Grange, CA: Kerygma Press, 2009.

Silva, Moisés. *Biblical Words and Their Meaning*. Grand Rapids: Zondervan, 1983.

Smith, Ralph A. *Paradox and Truth*. Tokyo: Covenant Worldview Institute, 2000.

Stewart, H. F., and E. K. Rand, eds. and trans. *Boethius: The Theological Treatises*. Cambridge, MA: Harvard University Press, 1926.

Stonehouse, Ned, and Paul Woolley, eds. *The Infallible Word*. Grand Rapids: Eerdmans, 1946; Philadelphia: Presbyterian and Reformed, 1946.

Strimple, Robert B. *The Modern Search for the Real Jesus*. Phillipsburg, NJ: P&R Publishing, 1995.

———. "Philippians 2:5–11 in Recent Studies: Some Exegetical Conclusions." *WTJ* 41, 2 (Spring 1979): 247–68.

———. "What Does God Know?" In *The Coming Evangelical Crisis*, edited by John H. Armstrong, 139–54. Chicago: Moody Press, 1996.

———. "Women Deacons? Focusing the Issue." 1988. Available at http://opc.org/GA/women_in_office.html#APPENDIX.

Swinburne, Richard. *The Coherence of Theism*. Oxford: Clarendon Press, 1977.

Tada, Joni Eareckson, and Stephen Estes. *When God Weeps*. Grand Rapids: Zondervan, 1997.

Thielicke, Helmut. *The Evangelical Faith*. Vol. 2. Grand Rapids: Eerdmans, 1977.

Thomas, W. H. Griffith. *Christianity Is Christ*. London: Longmans, Green and Co., 1916.

Thornwell, James Henley. *The Collected Writings of James Henley Thornwell*. Vol. 2. Edinburgh: Banner of Truth, 1974.

Tillich, Paul. *Systematic Theology*. 3 vols. Chicago: University of Chicago Press, 1951–63.

Toon, Peter. *Our Triune God*. Wheaton, IL: Victor Books, 1996.

Turner, Nigel. *Grammatical Insights into the New Testament*. Edinburgh: T. and T. Clark, 1977.

Turretin, Francis. *Institutes of Elenctic Theology*. Vol. 1. Phillipsburg, NJ: P&R Publishing, 1992.

Urban, Linwood, and Douglas N. Walton. *The Power of God*. New York: Oxford University Press, 1978.

Ursinus, Zacharias. *Commentary on the Heidelberg Catechism*. Cincinnati: T. P. Bucher, 1851.

VanDrunen, David. *A Biblical Case for Natural Law*. Grand Rapids: Acton Institute, 2006.

Van Til, Cornelius. *Christianity and Barthianism*. Philadelphia: Presbyterian and Reformed, 1962.

———. *Christian-Theistic Ethics*. Philadelphia: Den Dulk Foundation, 1971.

———. *The Defense of the Faith*. Edited by K. Scott Oliphint. Phillipsburg, NJ: P&R Publishing, 2008.

———. *An Introduction to Systematic Theology*. Nutley, NJ: Presbyterian and Reformed, 1974.

———. *The New Modernism*. Philadelphia: Presbyterian and Reformed, 1946. Repr., Nutley, NJ: Presbyterian and Reformed, 1973.

Van Till, Howard. Review of *Evolution and Creation*, edited by Ernan McMullin. *Faith and Philosophy* 5, 1 (January 1988): 104–11.

Vincent, M. R. *The International Critical Commentary: A Critical and Exegetical Commentary on the Epistles to the Philippians and to Philemon*. New York: Scribner, 1897.

Vos, Geerhardus. *The Pauline Eschatology*. Phillipsburg, NJ: Presbyterian and Reformed, 1986.

———. *The Teaching of Jesus concerning the Kingdom of God and the Church*. Grand Rapids: Eerdmans, 1958.

Warfield, B. B. *Biblical and Theological Studies*. Philadelphia: Presbyterian and Reformed, 1952.

———. *Biblical Doctrines*. Grand Rapids: Baker, 1981. Repr., Edinburgh: Banner of Truth, 1988.

———. *The Inspiration and Authority of the Bible*. Grand Rapids: Baker, 1948, 1960.

———. *The Lord of Glory*. New York: American Tract Society, 1907. Repr., Grand Rapids: Baker, 1974.

———. *Miracles: Yesterday and Today, True and False*. Grand Rapids: Eerdmans, 1965.

———. *The Person and Work of Christ*. Philadelphia: Presbyterian and Reformed, 1950.

———. *Selected Shorter Writings of Benjamin B. Warfield*. Vol. 2. Nutley, NJ: Presbyterian and Reformed, 1973.

Weber, Otto. *Foundations of Dogmatics*. 2 vols. Grand Rapids: Eerdmans, 1981, 1983.

Weeks, Noel. *The Sufficiency of Scripture*. Edinburgh: Banner of Truth, 1988.

Weinandy, Thomas G. *Does God Suffer?* Notre Dame, IN: University of Notre Dame Press, 2000.

Wells, David. *The Person of Christ*. Westchester, IL: Crossway, 1984.

Westminster Theological Seminary Faculty. "Westminster Theological Seminary and the Days of Creation." Philadelphia: June 1, 1998.

Wilson, Douglas. *Knowledge, Foreknowledge, and the Gospel*. Moscow, ID: Canon Press, 1997.

Wiseman, P. J. *Ancient Records and the Structure of Genesis*. Nashville: Thomas Nelson, 1985.

Wittgenstein, Ludwig. *Philosophical Investigations*. New York: Macmillan, 1968.

Wolterstorff, Nicholas. "God Everlasting." In *God and the Good*, edited by Clifton Orlebeke and Lewis Smedes, 181–203. Grand Rapids: Eerdmans, 1975.

———. *Reason within the Bounds of Religion*. Grand Rapids: Eerdmans, 1984.

Wright, N. T. *The Last Word*. San Francisco: Harper, 2005.

Wright, R. K. McGregor. *No Place for Sovereignty*. Downers Grove, IL: InterVarsity Press, 1996.

Yi, Mil Am. *Women and the Church: A Biblical Perspective*. Columbus, GA: Brentwood Christian Press, 1990.

Young, Davis A. *Creation and the Flood*. Grand Rapids: Baker, 1977.

Young, Edward J. *Studies in Genesis One*. Philadelphia: Presbyterian and Reformed, 1964.

Zanchius, Jerome. *Observations on the Divine Attributes*. In *Absolute Predestination*. Marshallton, DE: National Foundation for Christian Education, n.d.

INDEX OF SCRIPTURE

15:8—1056
15:11—308
15:29—388, 404, 1056
15:33—166n46, 328, 706
16:1—156
16:4—162, 187
16:4–5—811
16:5—162n31, 271
16:7—994n11
16:9—144, 156
16:16—328, 329
17:15—271
17:16—329
18:17—196
19:21—144, 156
20:4—266
20:9—860, 987
20:12—755
21:1—156
21:2—308
21:30—37, 144, 336
21:31—149
22:1—683
24:2—308
24:12—308
26:16—266
26:27—261, 281
28:9—1056
28:10—261
29:6—261
31:10–31—796

Ecclesiastes
7:14—158n24
7:20—987
12:1—434
12:7—798
12:13—328, 994, 996
12:14—1078

Song of Solomon
8:6—268

Isaiah
1:1–17—211
1:4—278, 337
1:9—212
1:16—947
1:17—264–65
1:18—211
1:19–20—211
1:24—337
1:25—211

1:26–28—212
2:10—452
2:19—452
2:21—452
5:1–7—817
5:16—40, 51
5:19—278
6—161, 772
6:1—39, 131, 393
6:1–5—92
6:1–10—452
6:1–13—391n9
6:2—771
6:3—233, 277, 278, 281, 437, 984
6:5—131, 278, 393, 453, 984
6:5–7—789
6:6—771
6:6–7—984
6:9–10—159, 166, 222, 472
6:10—750
7:14—30, 42, 461, 886
8:13—452
8:14—452
9:2–7—1090
9:6—253, 459–60, 461, 474, 703
9:6–7—78, 312
9:7—253
10—838
10:5–11—160, 818
10:5–12—149
10:5–15—811
10:6—160
10:12—811
10:15–19—818
10:20—278
10:20–34—212
10:21—212
11:1–3a—212
11:1–4—401
11:1–9—312
11:1–10—1090
11:2—111, 328, 401, 472, 477, 705, 924
11:2–3—926
11:3b-5—213, 264
11:6–11—1092
11:9—213
11:11–12:6—212
11:12–16—213

12:1–6—213
12:6—278
13:8—110
13:9—312
14:3–21—775n5
14:24—208, 372
14:24–25—149
14:24–27—143, 337–38
14:26–27—150
14:27—171
16:6—434
17:7—278
19:13—28
19:20—470
19:23–25—73
21:3—110
24:5—62
24:21—62
26:3—254
26:17—110
28:9—705
29:10—161
29:13—1038
29:14b—329
29:15—309
29:15–16.—308
29:16—145
30:18—349
30:27—435, 683
31:2—144
31:3—399
32:15—946
32:15–17—1090
33:5–6—705
33:6—166n46, 706
33:14—275, 276n23
33:22—437
34:1–4—1092
34:9–10—1092
34:16—675, 946
35:5—130
37:4—321n38
37:16—425, 772
37:20—16
37:26—149, 208
38:1–5—370
40—412
40–49—311
40:1–41:20—23
40:3—451, 453
40:4—264
40:4–11—1090
40:6–7—472

40:9—94
40:10—452
40:12—307
40:12–14—307
40:13—170, 452, 472, 924
40:13–14—307
40:18–20—36
40:19–20—409
40:21—185, 195, 363, 376
40:25–26—36
40:26—309
40:26–31—192
40:27—309
40:28—309
41:2—377
41:4—16n5, 21, 185, 195, 363, 376, 377, 455
41:7—409
41:8-7—212
41:8–9—210
41:8–20—213
41:21—91
41:21–23—311
41:21–24—36
41:21–29—23
41:26—363
41:27—94
42:1—401, 926
42:1–12—1090
42:5—802
42:5–6—190
42:6—217
42:8—269
42:8–9—426
42:9—311
42:10—370
42:14–15—109, 110
42:21—261
43:1—683
43:1–7—190, 213
43:2–7—177
43:3—436
43:6–7—186–87, 187n7
43:7—685
43:8–13—23
43:9–12—311
43:10—16n5, 214
43:10–12—73
43:10–13—455
43:11—436, 450, 470, 512
43:11–12—25, 36, 51
43:11–13—21, 36, 151
43:12—214, 376

INDEX OF SUBJECTS AND NAMES